CARIBBEAN
GUIDE

BE A TRAVELER - NOT A TOURIST!

OPEN ROAD TRAVEL GUIDES SHOW YOU
HOW TO BE A TRAVELER – NOT A TOURIST!

Whether you're going abroad or planning a trip in the United States, take Open Road along on your journey. Our books have been praised by **Travel & Leisure, The Los Angeles Times, Newsday, Booklist, US News & World Report, Endless Vacation, American Bookseller, Coast to Coast,** *and many other magazines and newspapers!*

Don't just see the world – experience it with Open Road!

ABOUT THE AUTHOR

Janet Groene and her husband Gordon changed directions while in their young 30s, leaving behind Gordon's career as a professional pilot in Illinois. They sold everything, loaded Janet's typewriter and Gordon's cameras aboard a small sloop, and lived happily ever after cruising in the Bahamas and the Caribbean.

Now based in Florida, they travel worldwide and have written more than a dozen books and thousands of newspaper and magazine features. They won the NMMA Director's Award for boating journalism and Janet is a recipient of the Distinguished Achievement in RV Journalism Award.

BE A TRAVELER, NOT A TOURIST - WITH OPEN ROAD TRAVEL GUIDES!

Open Road Publishing has guide books to exciting, fun destinations on four continents. As veteran travelers, our goal is to bring you the best travel guides available anywhere!

No small task, but here's what we offer:

• All Open Road travel guides are written by authors with a distinct, opinionated point of view – not some sterile committee or team of writers. Our authors are experts in the areas covered and are polished writers.

• Our guides are geared to people who want to make their own travel choices. We'll show you how to discover the real destination – not just see some place from a tour bus window.

• We're strong on the basics, but we also provide terrific choices for those looking to get off the beaten path and *experience* the country or city – not just *see* it or pass through it.

• We give you the best, but we also tell you about the worst and what to avoid. Nobody should waste their time and money on their hard-earned vacation because of bad or inadequate travel advice.

• Our guides assume nothing. We tell you everything you need to know to have the trip of a lifetime – presented in a fun, literate, no-nonsense style.

• And, above all, we welcome your input, ideas, and suggestions to help us put out the best travel guides possible.

CARIBBEAN GUIDE

BE A TRAVELER - NOT A TOURIST!

Janet Groene
with Gordon Groene

OPEN ROAD PUBLISHING

1st Edition

To Robert Irving Hawkins, my baby brother and first travel buddy, with thanks for the memories as well as the macros.

Front cover and bottom back cover photo by Donald Nausbaum, Carib Photo, Toronto, Canada; top back cover photo courtesy of Windstar Cruises & Harvey Lloyd.

The authors have made every effort to be as accurate as possible, but neither they nor the publisher assume responsibility for the services provided by any business listed in this guide; for any errors or omissions; or any loss, damage, or disruptions in your travels for any reason.

TABLE OF CONTENTS

CONTENTS

CONTENTS

THE BRITISH WINDWARDS

CONTENTS

CONTENTS

CONTENTS

THE FRENCH WEST INDIES

33. GUADELOUPE   551

34. MARTINIQUE   578

35. ST. BARTS   608

CONTENTS

CONTENTS

SIDEBARS

1. INTRODUCTION

Christopher Columbus must have felt more than mere relief at making landfall in the West Indies. He had to feel the same, spellbinding enchantment we did when we sailed our small sloop for the first time into waters where we could see bottom through clear crystal seas thirty and forty feet deep. Except for the Dry Tortugas west of Key West, there are no waters like them in the United States. It isn't uncommon in Bonaire for visibility to be 100 feet or more.

In later years we were to see the islands time and again from airplanes large and small. We cruise them in cockleshells and aboard ocean liners. We trudge their rain forests and rutted roads. We luxuriate in the best hotels and delight in funky guest houses. We lurk on beaches that are alive with families and fun seekers, and we like even better to find a lonely stretch of sand with no footsteps but our own. We salute the islands for the sophistication of the dining in even the smallest settlements, yet we are happy with a breakfast of sliced mangoes and a lunch of rice and beans. Most of all, we love the people of the islands whose bloods have blended to create a unique beauty in many skin colors.

We have seen many islands surge ahead in tourism and then fall into public disfavor after a messy revolution, a devastating hurricane, civil unrest, or a high-profile crime against tourists. Always they have bounced back, buoyed by locals' loyalty to their homelands and by unending streams of investor dollars from newcomers convinced they had found Shangri-La.

A few islands are rich in resources such as agriculture, forestry, or mining, but as these reserves dwindle, governments know that their one unfailing resource is the Caribbean's sun and seas; their one renewable cash crop is tourism. Many islands, especially those with a memory of slavery, still have far to go in creating a mentality in which service is not equated with servitude. You may still find the occasional surly waiter, sulking storekeeper, or rude bureaucrat. Yet in most cases the Caribbean peoples' natural hospitality shines proudly through.

Say hello to the new, tourist-savvy Caribbean!

2. EXCITING CARIBBEAN!
- OVERVIEW

The **Caribbean Sea** is ringed with a diadem of islands that starts with Cuba, which is only 90 miles off Florida, and spirals southwards through Haiti and the Dominican Republic, the Virgin Islands, the Leewards and Windwards, and Trinidad. Below Cuba are Jamaica and the Caymans; afloat in the Caribbean north of Venezuela are the Dutch Leeward Islands of Aruba, Bonaire, and Curacao as well as some resort islands owned by Venezuela.

If you are confused about what to call them, you're not alone. Even longtime Caribbean visitors have their own favorite ways of calling, categorizing, and collating the islands. All of them are the **West Indies**, called that because Columbus thought he had found India, not a new world. They are also the **Antilles**, called the Lesser Antilles from Puerto Rico south to Trinidad and the Greater Antilles from Cuba to Puerto Rico.

Some of the islands often lumped with the Caribbean, such as Bermuda and the Bahamas, aren't even in the Caribbean Sea. And others that are on the Caribbean off Central America – the Bay Islands of Honduras, for example – are rarely listed in Caribbean guidebooks. They're handled separately in Open Road's *Honduras & Bay Islands Guide*, as are the Cayes off Belize in our *Belize Guide*. The tiara of islands that curves south from Puerto Rico towards Venezuela starts with the Leeward Islands and ends with the Windward Islands.

To make things even more confusing, they are also grouped according to political loyalties such as the British Virgin Islands, the British Windwards, the French West Indies, or the Dutch Windwards in the Leewards. In short, you're always safe in referring to the islands in this book as the West Indies, the Caribbean, or the Antilles.

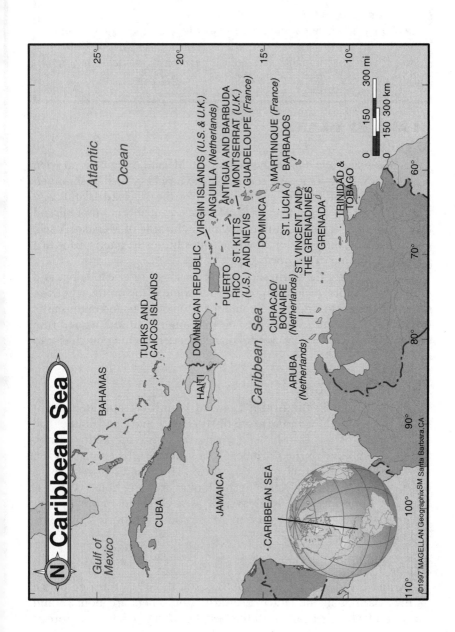

ABOUT CURRENCIES

Throughout this book, rates are given in U.S. dollars because most Caribbean hotels, restaurants, merchants and even governments think, quote, and price in dollar terms. Sometimes both local or U.S. currency are accepted but rarely must all transactions be done in local funds. When that is the case, we give prices in the appropriate currencies.

ISLAND BY ISLAND

Anguilla

A 35-square-mile dot on the map off St. Martin, **Anguilla** is an eden of dunes, low-lying scrub, and scrunchy sand beaches edged by shimmering blue-green waters. The northernmost of the Leeward Islands and reached by air from San Juan or St. Martin, it probably has more grand luxe resorts per square foot than any place this side of Monaco. A self-governing British possession, it attracts mostly North Americans with a growing following of Europeans.

Come here for the warm sun, superb beaches, upscale lodgings and dining, watersports including good diving, some of the prettiest postage stamps in the world, and friendly staff made up of locals and enthusiastic expatriots. The word *limin'*, which means hanging out with a good rum drink, was invented for this restful place. There is nothing much else to do.

Antigua & Barbuda

These islands in the British Leeward Islands are an independent nation south of St. Martin and north of Montserrat and Guadeloupe. The headquarters of the British fleet during the roistering 18th century, **Antigua** is still one of the Caribbean's best harbors. Its annual regatta attracts yachties from all over the world. The island's prizes are its beaches, diving, and a selection of small, ultra-exclusive hotels (Princess Margaret honeymooned here) as well as a choice of more modest lodgings. Come not just for the sun and sea but for historic sightseeing and nature watching.

Aruba

Aruba is independent now, but it's still thought of as one of the "A.B.C." islands in the Dutch Leewards (the others are Bonaire and Curacao). Its beaches rank with the best, but don't look for rain forests and lush foliage here. Instead, the island offers gardens of giant boulders, bold coastal scenery pocked with wind-sculpted watapana trees, forests of cactus, and measured growth that has limited the building of hotels. Barely off the coast of Venezuela, Aruba is at the far edge of the Caribbean two hours from Miami.

Barbados

Look at a map and you'll see that **Barbados** lies east of the chain of islands in what might technically be called the Atlantic Ocean, not the Caribbean Sea. It was colonized early by English and to this day remains more British than almost any other Caribbean island, even though it has been independent since 1966. Come to Barbados for a friendly welcome, unfailing sunshine, warm seas that brim against pretty beaches, fishing and golf, and a sense of off-the-beaten-path getaway.

Bonaire

Bonaire has two standout attractions, its underwater world for divers and snorkelers and its bird life, especially its brilliant flamingoes. One of the Dutch Leeward "A.B.C." islands, Bonaire remains aloof from the development that has consumed much of its sister islands. Still, it is reachable nonstop from North America once or twice a week and it spreads a selection of things to do and see, plus a variety of accommodations ranging from exclusive resorts to unpretentious inns for the scuba crowd. Sightseeing centers on nature and a few historic haunts; activities focus on the water, especially the scuba diving.

British Virgin Islands

They're only a brief boat ride from American shores. They're tiny and unspoiled. Yet they are British, lending a sense of "foreign" travel to a vacation out of North America. So closely tangled with the U.S. Virgin Islands that boaters tire of clearing in and out of the two countries, they are known as the **B.V.I.** to loyal visitors who come back year after year. **Tortola** is the chief settlement but travelers can also sample the sun-bleached beaches and limpid seas of **Virgin Gorda**, **Jost Van Dyke**, and some thirty other rocks and islets plus the worlds-end island of **Anegada**. It lies north of the B.V.I. in the boundless Atlantic, creating a resting place for seabirds and world-weary humans.

Cayman Islands

A British crown colony that lies south of Cuba, the **Caymans** are made up of Grand Cayman, Cayman Brac, and Little Cayman, a trio that is rich in reefs and clear seas favored by divers wheelers and dealers looking for less-than-strict banking laws. The land is flat and fairly featureless, but without mass or mountains to create storm clouds, it is almost always sunny and dry. Tourism is important to the Caymans, which are a popular cruise ship stop, but it is not the only game in town. Come here for the sunshine, grainy sand beaches, unrivaled scuba diving and snorkeling, upscale accommodations and dining, and prim but friendly English ambiance. Shopping and sightseeing won't occupy much of your time.

Cuba

The largest of the Caribbean islands and one of the most beautiful and varied, **Cuba** is on its way back to becoming the tourism top dog of the tropics. Its Veradero Resort is the largest in the Caribbean. Tourism is a $1 billion-per-year industry, yet because the island is so big, tourism hardly makes a wave. That's good news for travelers in search of unspoiled shores that aren't yet overrun by group tours, conventioneers, and cruise ship passengers. Because it's awkward for Americans to travel to Cuba, Cuba has been addressed only briefly in this book.

Curacao

The third of the Netherlands Antilles "A.B.C." islands, **Curacao** is the political, cultural, and population center of the Dutch islands. Air service comes direct from Miami, making it an easy flight to a faraway island that lies only 35 miles off the coast of Venezuela. An international oil refining center, it is a hub of commerce that attracts traders from all over the world as well as leisure travelers who flee to such stellar resorts as the Sonesta Beach Hotel & Casino on Piscadera Bay. Hurricanes are rare in this pocket of the Caribbean, so come to enjoy the constant temperatures, see-through seas, quaint Dutch architecture, and shopping for Delft and Gouda.

Dominica

Found in the British Windward Islands between Guadeloupe and Martinique, **Dominica** is a beguiling blend of its Spanish, French, and British ancestry. Exceedingly hilly, its massifs rising to almost 5,000 feet, it is so rugged that the development of roads has been painfully slow. The Carib community, one of the few pockets of aborigines that remain in the Caribbean, still produces basketry in motifs that pre-date European discovery. The nature watching, hiking, and diving here are unbeatable and accommodations can be found in modest hotels at modest prices.

The Dominican Republic

Known familiarly as the **D.R.**, which is a good practice to avoid confusion with the island of Dominica, **The Dominican Republic** shares the island of Hispaniola with Haiti. Both lushly beautiful and blessed with mountains and beaches, both are plagued with poverty, overpopulation, and politics that drive tourists away.

Yet the D.R. has a good and growing tourism industry thanks to prices that are still stuck in the 1970s. Visitors like the sense of "insider" discovery here because tourists are few yet the climate, terrain and sightseeing are superior. Add to this the vivacious Latin culture, golf, outdoor sports, casino gambling, music and nightlife, bargain shopping, and nonstop flights from the United States, and the D.R. looks better every year.

Grenada

Lying at the tail end of the Windward Island chain, south of the Grenadines and north of Trinidad, **Grenada** and her sister islands **Carriacou** and **Petite Martinique** form an independent nation known for its exports of nutmeg and its byproduct, the spice called mace. Grenada has pioneered its own route into modern tourism after taking a detour in the late 1970s to flirt with dictatorship and secret police. That ended when troops from the United States and other islands landed on Grenada to restore order. Still today, Americans are often thanked for their role in what is called the "intervention."

Although early development was done under British or French rule, modern progress has been made by Grenadians themselves. Proud of their homeland and eager to welcome outsiders, they are among the most genuine, pleasant hosts in the islands.

Guadeloupe, Ile des Saintes, & Marie Galante

A "department" of France, granted full privileges of French citizenship, residents of the **French West Indies** bask in the trade winds of the northern Windward Islands below Antigua and north of Dominica. Direct flights are rare, so tourism here depends on the French and French Canadians, on visitors who prefer longer vacations that justify the long trip to get here, and on cruise ships that send shoppers ashore in search of good buys on French perfume. North Americans will feel welcome here but not entirely at home unless they speak French.

Haiti

Haiti isn't a hospitable place for tourism at this time, but a wondrous country it can be with its beaches and forested mountains. See the chapter on Haiti for the United States State Department's advisory at press time. You can get the latest advisories on the Internet.

THE OTHER CARIBBEAN

In producing this book, we are well aware that the Caribbean Sea is bounded not just by the islands we cover here but by miles of Central American coastline and the north coast of Venezuela. We don't cover them because Open Road Publishing offers separate, detailed guides to Costa Rica, Belize, Honduras & The Bay Islands, Guatemala, and Central America.

Jamaica

When it's good, it's very, very good, but when **Jamaica** goes through one of its periodic snits, it loses tourists for a generation. Nevertheless, we love this brash island with its many distinct tourism neighborhoods. Crime is a problem, but we simply take the same precautions we would at home. In our latest visits we have dealt with kind and capable people and with a sophisticated new breed of tourism professionals.

The island is large enough to offer a new vacation experience with each visit: the celebrity resorts of the northeast coast, the family-friendly resorts of the northwest, and romantic getaways in all-inclusive resorts that accept only (heterosexual) couples. Choose a mountain hideaway, a sun-baked beach house, an old English-style hotel in a minor town, or a suite in a four-star Kingston hotel equipped with everything a business traveler could ask for.

Martinique

Midway down the Windward chain between Dominica and St. Lucia, **Martinique** is French to the core and its citizens have all the rights of Parisians and Nicoise. Unfortunately, its attitudes can also be snooty to those who don't speak *la belle Francais*. Tourists here are more likely to be day-trippers off cruise ships and gaggles of young French vacationers in scanty attire. The island is pricier than, say, Jamaica or Puerto Rico, but it offers everything you could want in a Caribbean vacation – beaches, sunshine, clear seas, outdoor sports, casino gambling, and that ooh-la-la French food.

Montserrat

A tiny volcanic cone in the Lesser Antilles below Nevis, the British crown colony of **Montserrat** remains in the daily news because of its active volcano, on which you can get daily reports on the Internet. Despite the hardships and displacement endured by some of the locals, tourism is sure to make a comeback when the emergency is over. It's an exciting time to be here to enjoy some of the world's best hiking and nature watching, scuba diving, deep sea fishing, and agreeable hosts who appreciate your visit.

Nevis & St. Kitts

Nestled in the Caribbean Sea just below St. Martin, these once-English islands are now an independent federation. Once farmed for sugar, the islands have turned to tourism and are tending it lovingly. Visitors are housed in attractive, historic, unique places, some woefully expensive and others pittance priced, but none of them the kind of "factory" hotel that brings in merrymakers by the jumbo jet-load. Come here for the old-English ambiance, historic sites, good beaches, and nature watching.

Puerto Rico

As colorful as a serape and as warm as a freshly baked tortilla, **Puerto Rico** offers American can-do and convenience, gregarious Latin gaiety, and the kinds of beaches and clear waters for which the Caribbean is richly famed. An airline hub that hosts dozens of nonstop flights each day from North America and Europe, San Juan is the logical place for the kind of four- or five-day getaway so popular in two-career families.

Stay in the mountains in a rustic parador or take a suite in a four-star resort patronized by celebrities from around the world. For dining, golf, watersports, a romantic getaway or a family holiday, it's hard to beat America's "shining star," found just east of Cuba and west of the U.S. Virgin Islands.

Statia & Saba

Two of the "S" islands of the Dutch West Indies, **St. Eustatius**, called **Statia**, and **Saba** are thimble-size islands south of St. Martin and north of St. Kitts and Nevis. They're only a few square miles each, yet history assigned them important roles that left them with enough legends and old forts to fascinate tourists.

Saba, the tip of a volcanic cone, is distinguished by having no beaches at all unless you count one small handkerchief of sand. Its residents are mostly white; its views breathtaking. Statia, an important trading center in the 17th and 18 centuries, is also not known for fabulous beaches. There are some, but they are mostly black, volcanic sand. Come instead for the surfing, snorkeling, scuba diving, excellent history hunting, wildlife watching, and friendly, efficient Dutch hosts.

St. Barts

St. Barthélemy, never called anything but St. Barts or St. Barths, is a sweet Norman village plunked down in a wintergreen sea and surrounded by sugar beaches. It doesn't even show on most maps, but on a large-scale Caribbean map look for it just off St. Martin. It's as rich as Grand Cayman and as French as Martinique, yet its capital, Gustavia, was named for a Swedish king.

A hangout for jetsetters wealthy with old money, and with newly rich Hollywood stars, it is somewhat more English-friendly than some of the other French islands – perhaps because it is costlier and attracts fewer young French people traveling on cheap packages. Come here for the food, bargains in French perfumes, watersports including good windsurfing, and upscale lodgings.

St. Lucia

Hotels, condos, and sailing fleets have mushroomed on **St. Lucia**, which lies between Martinique and St. Vincent, but the population seems to keep mushrooming even faster – vendors have become too aggressive for our taste. Yet there is much to love about St. Lucia: its magnificent peaks and rain forests, its undersea gardens and wrecks for diving, a good selection of resorts including all-inclusives, awesome birdwatching, good beaches, and enough old stones to satisfy history buffs. Its duty-free shopping center is convenient for cruisers, whose purchases are delivered to cabins before the ship sails.

St. Martin/Sint Maarten

The best and worst of the Caribbean can be found in this hyphenated island, which is half Dutch and half French. On the plus side, it offers a full menu of resorts and its dining is legendary. Access is among the best in the Caribbean because nonstop flights arrive daily from both North America and Europe. On the minus side is its mega-developed resort area near the airport, a concrete jungle of shops, hotel rooms, restaurants, and noisy night clubs. We like downtown Philipsburg for city life, shopping, Dutch hospitality, and a fine little Dutch museum.

The French side is best known for its nude beaches and for rows of restaurants, each better than the one before. Both sides offer a wide range of accommodations in all price ranges. French and Dutch are the official languages, but English seems to be the preferred tongue. If you want to stay on a French island, this one is more accommodating to non-Francophones than most.

St. Vincent & The Grenadines

Without question one of the finest sailing areas in the world, the **Grenadines** are administered by **St. Vincent**, and there is the rub. As former liveaboards, we have avidly followed the tales of two murders involving visiting yachties and what appears to be government corruption and cover-up. As reported in *Cruising World* magazine, some sources recommend avoiding the area completely; others suggest staying away only from Cumberland Bay. Chris Doyle, author of cruising guides to the Windwards and Leewards, argues that hundreds of boats stay safely in the Grenadines, and these two murders are the first violence against sailors in 20 years.

Still, we're concerned that the government seems to have sanctioned the reported shakedowns. The latest travel advisories are available from the U.S. State Department, *Tel. 202/647-5225*, or online at *http://www.travel.state.gov*.

Trinidad & Tobago

Variety and diversity make Caribbean travel a new adventure with each trip, and **Trinidad** tops the list when it comes to exotic, offbeat cultures. It is the birthplace of the steel drum and the limbo. It's a whirlpool of cultures that doesn't stop with African and European. After slavery was abolished, coulees were brought in from the Orient. East Indians came to work in the oil industry, Venezuelans drifted in from the nearby mainland, and Amerindians survive from before European discovery. Yet they all live in relative harmony. Trinidad is the commercial center, throbbing with industry and intensive agriculture. Tourists compete with business travelers for hotel space and everyone pays a whopping 15 per cent government hotel tax plus service charges of 10 per cent or more. During Carnival everyone pays higher tariffs plus the 25 per cent add-ons. For touring, stick to a commercial operator or drive the North Coast Road to Maracas Beach, the island's best.

The island of **Tobago** is really the nation's playground, a 27-mile-long paradise said to be the home of Robinson Crusoe. During its heyday before the sugar market collapsed in the 1880s, it was one of the Caribbean's richest plantations. Come here for the historic relics, resorts ranging from budget to regal, golf, and fabulous watersports.

U.S. Virgin Islands

St. Thomas and **St. John** are just east of Puerto Rico and can be seen from there on a clear day. Sister islands, they are polar opposites. St. John is mostly national park land, focusing on eco-tourism and the outdoors. St. Thomas too has picturebook bays and beaches, but its cash registers jingle and its streets stream with cruise ship passengers and day-trippers in search of "duty-free" bargains. To find the "real" St. Thomas means getting out of Charlotte Amalie and into country lodgings that range from charming inns to the plush Ritz-Carlton.

The third of the American islands, **St. Croix**, is in a world of its own well away from the other U.S. and British Virgin Islands. Its scuba diving and underwater national park are alone worth the trip, but the island also has historic plantations, picturesque settlements at Frederiksted and Christiansted, and great beaches and resorts, all under the U.S. flag.

EXPECT A LITTLE CHAOS!

In each section of this book we've described what to expect after you land on the island, but be prepared financially, psychologically, and physically for more hassle, higher heat and humidity, and more expense than you expect. Often, Caribbean hosts dismiss the post-airport part of the trip breezily with, "No problem. Just grab a taxi at the airport and we're only 30 miles away." The truth is that the cab will probably not be air conditioned. The day is hot and clammy compared to the climate you just left and, even though you dressed for the tropics, you're still wearing too much. By the time you settle into the broiling cab and drive 30 miles over goat tracks with the windows open, you are hot, dusty, thirsty, and thoroughly bummed.

To get to the most remote resorts will require even more: a ride in a rattletrap of a bus or small airplane, and perhaps a ferry ride during which you and your luggage get drenched. Even at the most expensive resorts where airport transfers are included, we have fried in nearly-new vehicles whose air conditioners were as dead as their shock absorbers. Vehicles age quickly on small islands. If you rent a car, be prepared for bad roads with few aids to navigation, and for a long squawk list of things that don't work. Public transportation is almost unknown; where it exists, it's often better suited to the crates of chickens that are your fellow travelers than to tourists in their newest resort duds.

Because of the high costs of buying, operating, and maintaining anything mechanical in the islands, transfers will cost far more than you think they should. Have plenty of change on hand for tips; your bags will be grabbed away from you even if they are small and have to be carried only a few feet. As you arrive at the airport in a cab, they'll be whisked out of the trunk and handed to a porter even before you can get out of the car. It's contrived but, in the poorer islands, we never mind handing over the money to men who try so hard to earn it.

Take sturdy, waterproof luggage that can stand up to rough handling, rain, and sea spray. We once stood inside a terminal in Mayaguez during a torrential tropical rain, looking out at our bags sitting in a puddle in the downpour. Covered luggage carts as seen on the mainland are rare here. Even traveling with all carry-ons isn't the answer. They're not allowed aboard small commuter planes, and will be taken from you and crammed into the cargo hold with the rest of the luggage. On some commuter flights, the limit is as little as 25 pounds. When the planes are full, luggage is brought on the next flight.

Be prepared for the worst. Hope for the best. Once you arrive in paradise, you'll know that it was all worthwhile.

3. SUGGESTED ITINERARIES

This is a book about islands, so itineraries will be governed by airlines and ferry schedules unless you take a cruise or charter a boat. Cruise ship ports of call provide only a short look at a small patch of each island, but you'll have enough of a taste of each to help decide which ones you want to return to for longer stays. Don't make too quick a judgment, however. Cruisers who hate St. Thomas or Montego Bay find when they fly in that the "real" island isn't at all the border-town frenzy they saw at the pier.

Aboard a charter boat, you can see strings of islets and cays in a week. In two weeks you can voyage through a briar patch of islands, stopping at some on the way out and the rest during your return sail. Even if you sail no more than a few miles each day, you'll see dozens of coves, villages, good snorkeling reefs, and shoreside attractions.

IF YOU HAVE THREE TO FOUR DAYS

When all you need is a quick trip to re-charge your batteries in the Caribbean sun, minimize travel time by choosing an island that has the fastest, most direct service from your home city. This will vary according to where you live, the season, and whether charters are available in addition to scheduled airlines. Some islands have direct flights only once or twice a week, so careful planning is essential when you are making a quick trip.

Islands that have nonstop flights from the United States and Canada include Antigua, Bonaire, Barbados, Curacao, the Dominican Republic, Dominica, Grand Cayman, Grenada, Jamaica (Kingston and Montego Bay), Martinique, Puerto Rico, Saba, St. Martin, St, Croix, St. Thomas, and Trinidad.

Among our suggested itineraries are:

• Fly into **San Juan** and check into one of the beach hotels within an hour of the airport, which gives you a choice of prices from the regal Hyatt in Dorado and the Westin Rio Mar to smaller hotels and guest houses in metropolitan San Juan itself. In the resorts, spend days in a hammock,

walking the beach barefoot, sailing a small boat, or playing golf or tennis. If you stay in the city, walk Old San Juan and spend your time in museums and great restaurants.
  • Fly to **St. Thomas** or **St. Croix**, where a drive of less than 30 minutes from the airport brings you to a hotel, resort, condo, or guest house. Just as in San Juan, you won't waste time in lines for customs, immigration, and currency exchange. Bring your golf clubs or a suitcase filled with good reading, and let the sun shine in.
  • Fly into **Montego Bay, Jamaica**, where a driver will take you six miles to the Half Moon Club. It's known by international jet setters for its privacy and impeccable service. An immaculate beach is strewn with Sunfish, their sails set and ready for your hand at the helm. If you take the Platinum Plan, you won't open your wallet during your entire stay. Everything from drinks to dinner, airport transfers to entertainment, is laid on. Or check out one of the less expensive, all- inclusive resorts such as Jack Tar or Sandals. Then forget everything else but the feasting and romance.
  • Fly to **Barbados** to find a bit of Britain in the tropical sun. If price is no object, check into Cobblers Cove or Royal Pavilion for a woosome vacation in the lap of luxury. The slightly formal ambiance, afternoon teas, and international guest list lend a fetching, foreign flair to your stay here. Even though you've been away only a few days, you'll be as refreshed as if you went abroad for a month. Leave the children at home and don't come in September or October when many resorts close.
  • Fly to friendly **Grenada** during peak periods, when planes arrive nonstop from JFK in New York. (At other times, direct flights are available with one stop but without a plane change). The drive to the resorts along famous Grand Anse Beach is only about 20 minutes, with some hotels just 3-5 minutes from the airport. Within two minutes of checking into the Spice Island Inn you can be in the ocean and in less time than that you can be soaking in your own private double whirlpool. Play tennis, tone up in the fitness center, or just claim a hammock on the beach and read until it's time to fly home.

IF YOU HAVE A WEEK
  • Fly into **Anguilla** via St. Martin or San Juan and settle into a luxury resort. The island has them by the handsful: Cap Juluca, Malliouhana, and the exotic, Morroccan-look Sonesta Beach Resort. Take a day voyage to Sombrero Island, which was mined for phosphate until late in the 1890s. Today only caretakers live here, seeing the supply boat twice a month. Unless you're here for Carnival (the Friday before the first Monday in August) there isn't much to tempt you to leave your hammock or beach

chair. Dive, snorkel, work out, or play tennis if you must, but Anguilla is the place to take great, delicious doses of indolence. You'll love every minute of it.

• Book a scuba diving package to **Carriacou**, **Little Cayman Island**, or **Bonaire**, and alternate diving with beachcombing, local exploring, reading, and shopping. If you're not a certified diver, you can get certified on this vacation. Or just take a "resort" course or an introductory course to see if scuba is for you.

• Fly to **Curacao** and take the ten-minute ride to the Sonesta Beach Hotel and Casino. If the glamorous hotel, grounds, beach, casino, and tennis courts aren't enough to keep you wowed for the week, take a barbecue and snorkel voyage to Port Marie and a day sail aboard the tall ship *Insulinde*. Shop the picturesque Floating Market where boats from Venezuela sell fruits and vegetables. Dine in the hotel's sumptuous Portofino, saving one night for Rijsttafel Indonesia in suburban Salinja and another for dinner at the hilltop Fort Nassau, a 200-year-old fort that is now a restaurant with a heart-stopping view.

IF YOU HAVE TWO OR MORE WEEKS

• Book a charter boat with The Moorings out of **Tortola** for a week, starting and ending your vacation with a couple of days ashore at the company's own Mariner Inn. By the time you board the boat you'll be rested and will have provisions rounded up. Under sail you can seek out lonely beaches and seaside bars patronized by yachties from all over the world. Build the ultimate sand castle. Snorkel over pristine reefs. Have a rum swizzle on deck in a quiet anchorage, and hope to see the green flash.

After your cruise when you return to the inn, you'll be grateful for long showers, restaurant meals, and the company of other returning sailors to swap tales with. Explore the rain forest on Mount Sage, drive to beaches you didn't get to by boat, ride horseback on Cane Garden Bay, and shop the quaint boutiques of Road Town. The Moorings also has fleets based in St. Martin, St. Lucia, and Grenada. Try them all.

• Fly into **St. Thomas** and then catch the ferry to **St. John** to camp Virgin Islands National Park. Spend days hiking and snorkeling the underwater trail, cooking on a camp stove, and enrolling in ranger-led nature programs. Then reward yourself with a few days in an air conditioned hotel on St. Thomas before flying home.

• Give a week and take a week. As a volunteer in a poor area of **Jamaica**, you'll be fed and billeted simply while you work with children, re-roof a school, do a nature survey, or in some other way make a lasting contribution through Global Volunteers, *Tel. 800/487-1074*. Before or after the week you give away, pamper yourself with a stay at swank

Strawberry Hill in the Blue Mountains outside Kingston. It's a ride of less than 10 minutes by helicopter or an hour by car into an aerie more than 3,000 feet above the sea. Relax in the gardens surrounded by birdsong, take a spa treatment, ride a mountain bike, hike the famous Blue Mountains, and tour a coffee plantation.

• Fly into **St. Martin** and stay near the airport at the charming guest house Mary's Boon. When you have a yen to explore afield, hop an airplane to **Statia, Saba**, or **St. Barts**. Then drive to the French side of St. Martin and check into fabulously expensive La Samanna for celebrity watching, French meals, sailing, and boutique shopping.

• Make **Martinique** your headquarters for total immersion in things French. Explore this exotic, historic island then take overnight or day trips to **Guadeloupe, Marie Galante, Iles des Saintes, La Desirade, St. Martin**, and **St. Barts**.

• Fly to **Puerto Rico**, rent a car, and stay a night or two at each parador, or government guest house. Built in scenic areas and points of interest such as beaches, mountains, forests or hot springs, these accommodations aren't fancy but they have the basics. All have wholesome, delicious, native food. By the end of two weeks, you will have savored a Puerto Rico that few visitors see.

• Headquarter in **Antigua** at Curtain Bluff or Jumby Bay, allowing plenty of time for seeking out beaches, playing golf, day sailing and scuba diving. See the historic highlights, forts, and the interpretation center for the ancient dockyard, the only one of its kind in the islands. From Antigua, take a 15-minute flight to **Barbuda** and rent a jeep for the day so you can see the frigate bird sanctuary. Make a day trip to **Monserrat** where the volcano will be smoldering if not spewing. Antigua is a good airline hub where you can also connect to Nevis, St. Kitts, Barbados, and Caracas.

4. LAND & PEOPLE

LAND & SEA

The lands and seas of the Caribbean make up one of the most geologically interesting places on planet Earth. Much of the Caribbean Sea is on the continental shelf with great expanses of clear, shallow waters where small boats can cruise for days without losing a view of the bottom 50 or 60 feet below. Yet vast trenches plunge to ocean depths of 29,000 feet and more near Puerto Rico and Grand Cayman.

Much of the land is volcanic, rising to peaks that are, in some cases such as Saba, the entire island. The total land area of the islands is only about 90,000 square miles, half the land mass of the United Kingdom, yet only a handful of cities have a population of more than 100,000 people.

Of the land mass, about half is flatlands and the other half is hills and mountains. Some islands such as Anguilla and the Caymans are flat as a flapjack. Others have cloud-cloaked mountains rising as high as 10,000 feet. Dominica is so hilly that it has hardly a handkerchief-size patch of flat ground. Saba rises so steeply from the sea that it has no beaches.

Most islands, however, are a combination of mountains and plains, rimmed with sandy beaches and surrounded by coral reefs. Around them, waters shoal so gradually that the white sand bottom shines through, creating a neon luminescence in the turquoise waters.

The plates of the earth continue to shift, resulting in the occasional earthquake in this region. In one at Port Royal, Jamaica, in the 17th century, an entire community slid into the sea. Restless volcanoes still spring to life. Soufrière on Montserrat is active as this is written. The eruption of Mont Pele on Martinique in 1902 destroyed an entire community. Soufriere on St. Vincent blew in 1979; Guadeloupe had volcanic eruptions in 1956 and 1976.

Today these violent historic incidents are merely tourist attractions. You can hike around lakes that have collected in volcanic cones, climb giant boulders once spewn up by massive volcanoes, and snorkel over 18th century warehouses that sank into harbors when the earth cracked open.

Caves have been formed by underwater rivers on Puerto Rico; blowholes have been carved into cliffs by crashing waves on Cayman Brac. On Statia, a perfect volcanic cone is a hiking favorite known as The Quill. On St. Lucia, steaming fumaroles can still be seen. In the Caymans, an area called Hell is a wasteland of pitted, black, lifeless lava.

The beaches alone are a geology lesson. All of them are formed by nature's grindstone, the sea, which pulverizes volcanic rock to make black sand beaches, or grinds limestone or chalk to create lighter-colored sands. Regularly they are rearranged as storms suck away all the sand from some shores and deposit it somewhere else. New islets are formed, sometimes to be swept away in the next storm. Others grow, rooted with mangroves whose roots capture more sand, and become real islands.

Geology has also played a role in the animal life found in the Caribbean, where species often evolved independently for centuries. Trinidad's unique fauna population includes many South American natives such as anteaters, boa constrictors, and howling monkeys. The caiman, a Central American crocodile, gives one island group its name. A cheerful tree frog called coqui, found only on Puerto Rico, is the island's symbol. Dominica, so hilly that development has been difficult, hosts dozens of species that are found on no other islands.

Where mongoose were introduced to control native snakes, they bred in the wild and themselves became problem. Non-native monkeys brought in by settlers escaped into the wild and formed large populations in some rain forests. Creatures such as whales and turtles, hunted almost to extinction, are making a comeback.

The larger islands of Jamaica, Cuba, Hispaniola, and Puerto Rico offer the largest variety of vegetation, ranging from savannah to tropical scrub. Woodlands include mangrove swamps, dry forests, and jungles euphemistically called rain forests. Cuba's Isle of Pines takes its name from a coniferous forest of a kind of pine tree found commonly in North and Central America.

Crops native to the Americas thrive in the islands. They include tobacco, ackee, mango, avocado, cacao and sisal. Crops introduced by settlers, all of them still important, include sugar cane, coffee, bananas, coconut, rice, cotton, pineapple, nutmeg, citrus, and many produce crops ranging from cabbage to tomatoes.

THE PEOPLE

Except for a few islands, the Caribbean is overwhelmingly black and mulatto, with a sprinkling of Amerindian, Asian, and East Indian blood, resulting in a handsome new race. Their official languages may still be Dutch, Spanish, or French, but various patois are still spoken in their

DON'T CALL THEM NATIVES

You are always safe in saying West Indian or Islander, but the word native is offensive to many people in the Caribbean. We have also encountered situations where locals were offended by the terms "boy" and "guy."

People who live in...	Are called...
Carriacou	(Slang) Kayaks
Jamaica	(Slang) Jamdowns
St. Croix	Crucians or Cruzans
St. Kitts	Kittitians
St. Lucia	Lucians
Trinidad	(Slang) Trinis
Trinidad-Tobago	(Slang) Trinibagonians

homes and English is the lingua franca of business and leisure throughout the Caribbean.

Most islanders are Christians, often with an undercurrent of African Voodoo, Obeah, Santeria, or Shango (also spelled Xango). Roman Catholic and major Protestant churches are found on almost every island. In Trinidad, which had the greatest influx of Indian immigrants a century ago, a large portion of the populace is Hindu and the faith is spreading northward as Indians take over more of the islands' retailing. Judaism has made an important contribution in the Caribbean since the 16th century and it remains a tiny but vital force there today.

Rastafarianism, which hails the late Ethiopian emperor Haile Selassie as its messiah, took root in Jamaica and has some adherents in other islands. Its members are usually recognized by their beehive "dreadlock" hair, usually covered in a black, red, gold, and green cap indicating traditional Rasta colors.

For all their shades of color and belief, the peoples of the Caribbean have much in common. Except for the French- and Spanish-speaking islands, the West Indian accent has minor variations but it shares a softness, lilt, and range of octaves that is captivating. A question in a man's deep voice can start in a basso profundo and lift at the end to soprano range. A woman's silvery laugh can turn harsh and scolding. A balladeer's voice can turn to gravel or velvet.

If you have an ear for language, you'll find yourself falling into its rhythms and convoluted sentence structure. For example, Jamaicans say, "No care how teacher cross, school bound fo' gi' recess," a saying that means roughly that every cloud has a silver lining.

ISLANDSPEAK: A PRONUNCIATION GUIDE

You're usually safe in pronouncing words according to their original language, such as San WHAHN (San Juan) and Cordi-YER-ah (Cordillera) in Puerto Rico, or La day-sidder-AHD (La Désiderade), the island off French Guadeloupe. However, in islands that have changed many times among French, British, and Dutch rulers, and are now visited mostly by North Americans, there is no guessing how far they have departed, if at all, from the original tongue.

Gros Islet on St. Lucia has become Grossly, yet the Spanish pronunciation of Anguilla, An-GWEE-ya, has lost out to the more English An-GWILL-a. Just ask, and a friendly local will be glad to set you straight.

- *Anguilla: an-GWILL-a*
- *Antigua: an-TEEG-ah (not ant-TEEG-gwa)*
- *Bequia: BECK-kwee*
- *Bonaire: BAHN-air*
- *Conch: conk*
- *Curacao: cure-a-sow; locals may say coor-sow or coor-soo*
- *Dominica: dahm-a-NEEK-ah (not doh-MIN-ica)*
- *El Yunque: el JUNK-cay*
- *Grand: in Grand Cayman it rhymes with band; down-island where the French lingered longer, it is usually GRAHND Anse, GRAHNd Terre, GRAHnd Etang.*
- *Grenada: gren-NAY-dah. Gren-NAH-da is in Spain*
- *Guadaloupe: gwah-da-loop*
- *Cay: pronounced key.*
- *Kralendijk: crahl-in-dike*
- *Leewards: LOOrds*
- *Mustique: moo-STEEK*
- *Nevis: NEEvis*

Ocho Rios: most visitors and locals say ocho REE-ohs, but some locals say ocho RYE-ohs

- *St. Lucia: saint LOU-sha*
- *Tobago: Toe BAY go*

Culturally, the Caribbean is on a fast track that began with the realization that its own unique cultures need to be cherished and preserved. Dance groups, art galleries, theater and musicals celebrate ancient African, French, English, and Spanish forms. New forms, such as reggae and salsa, have been exported around the world.

Modern arts are welcomed in the islands. San Juan is as sophisticated as any other American city when it comes to symphony, opera, theater, and the internationally famous Casals Festival. Literary forms known as *digenisme* in Haiti and *negrismo* in Cuba were born in the islands and developed in Paris. Haitian art is collected worldwide; Old San Juan has become the Greenwich Village of the tropics; Jamaica has some of the most sophisticated photographers in the hemisphere.

Even on small islands, the culture seeker stumbles on enormously talented locals such as sculptor Cheddie Richardson on Anguilla, primitive painter Canute Caliste on Carriacou, and fabric designer Alice Bagshaw on St. Lucia. St. Barts is the scene of a film festival featuring Caribbean films for five days each year.

MUSIC OF THE CARIBBEAN

The words pound and punish, puzzling tourists who have no idea what they mean. Music forms called dubbing, reggae, calypso, salsa, plena, and bomba are as familiar in the Caribbean as rockabilly, heavy metal, and leadbelly are to North American ears.

The music and dance of the Caribbean have a language all their own, a patois born in the gavottes and quadrilles of ancient Europe, tempered in torrid Africa, and spun into unique, New World rhythms and harmonies. Early Spanish explorers told of graceful dances performed by Arawak slaves who, with the warlike Caribs, had populated the Caribbean before the first European explorers arrived. Their traditions were added to those of British, Dutch, French, Spanish, and Danish settlers.

Most compelling of all were the contributions of African slaves, who soon outnumbered the combined total of whites and Amerindians, and whose dances and drumbeats were a lifeline of familiarity to captives in a strange land. Even in manacles, they sang and danced. Some say that the languid movements of the merengue are based on the limping gait of a slave wearing a ball and chain.

Unfortunately, islanders love and live their music so fully that it's impossible to escape it. Taxi drivers never turn off their radios and tapes. Airplanes and ships are often met by strolling musicians. Raucous radio sounds rise on the winds to serenade hilltop hotels. Calypso singers stop by diners' tables to improvise outrageous rhymes that are made up on the spot. In Spanish islands, your table is serenaded by mariachis. Trinidad invented the steel drum, now the national instrument of the entire Caribbean.

When anyone turns on a boom box or brings out a guitar in the villages, a spontaneous "jump-up" erupts. It's called a rub-up on some islands and a bram on others. In Jamaica, a "jump alleluia" is a celebration dance and a "dinki minie" goes on for nine nights. On Sunday mornings, joyous Gospel music rings out from open-air churches in every island hamlet. On the anniversary of a death in Carriacou, the dead person is honored with a rousing Big Drum ceremony.

As you travel the Caribbean and sort out its great diversity of cultures, the differences in music become clearer. Reggae, which evolved from forms called ska and mento, began in Jamaica in the 1920s and '30s when Jamaican cane cutters were sent to Cuba to help with the sugar harvest and Cubans came to Jamaica to return the favor. They sang together, adding a Latin tinge to mento street songs. Radio programs bouncing in from Miami and Memphis added American boogie, blues, and jazz to the mix. Bluesy songs with a mento rhythm formed a short-lived movement called rock steady, which grew into reggae.

Puerto Rico's music has a strong Latin air. Trinidad gave us calypso. In Jamaica, musical instruments called abengs are made from cow horn. Goombay, the Bantu word for rhythm, was born in the Bahamas as African tribal rhythms mated with British colonial patterns. The melody is usually played on a piano, guitar or saxophone accompanied by bongos, maracas, or "click sticks." Traditionally performed only by males, it's passed down from father to son.

Goombay in turn has become Junkanoo (sometimes spelled Jonkanoo or Jonkunnu), a word used to describe festivals in some islands but now also used to describe the music itself. In Puerto Rico, ballads of 18th and 19th century Spain were performed on native Caribbean instruments used by pre-Columbian Taino Indians. Today part of the Puerto Rican sound are the six-stringed Spanish classical guitar as well as the 10-string cuatro, tambours made from hollowed-out trees, and guiros made from hollow gourds.

To the trained ear, each form is unique but to newcomers there is a quaint and compelling sameness. Common to almost all Caribbean music is a pattern of call and response and the hypnotic repetition of the same phrase dozens and even hundreds of times. In music, it's called *ostinato,* from a root word meaning obstinate. In addition to their own music, the people of the Caribbean embrace the finest music and dance from throughout the world. The annual Casals Festival held each June in Puerto Rico and named for immortal cellist Pablo Casals, attracts an international who's who of classical music artists. Traditional Puerto Rican folkloric music is kept alive by groups including the Compania Musical Perla del Sur, which performs locally and overseas.

The Island Center amphitheater on St. Croix and the Reichold Center of the Performing Arts on St. Thomas host programs ranging from ballet to opera, folk dance, to folk rock. The Cayman National Theatre Company presents classics as well as Broadway and West Indian musicals.

On Aruba, the Tumba Contest for musicians is a highlight of Carnival, which goes on from mid-January to Ash Wednesday. Most major islands host at least one major jazz festival yearly. Many islands, especially those with casinos such as Puerto Rico and Aruba, have glittering cabaret shows blaring the brightest new show tunes from New York and London.

Most tourist hotels have lounges offering a variety of music from mellow piano bar and easy listening to floor shows and disco as well as combos playing rousing rhumbas and merengues for dancing. Adventurous travelers also like to sample local nightlife, which is often found at its best in tiny, thatch-roofed bars or right on the streets.

Every Wednesday evening in Ocho Rios, Coyaba River Garden and Museum offers a Moonshine Festival of Jamaica food and Jonkanoo dance troupes. In Montego Bay, a street party closes Gloucester Avenue every Monday from 7pm to midnight for a street party with live reggae and calypso.

On St. Lucia, the little village of Gros Islet comes alive with street dancing after dark each Friday. When a cruise ship is docked at Frederiksted on St. Croix, the entire harbor throngs with music and dancing.

The Caribbean has a music all its own born of sunshine and pounding surf, a bonding of many peoples of all colors and backgrounds, and a welcome as wide as the sea itself. Listen. Then let it carry your feet away.

For a list of upcoming Caribbean music events, write the **Caribbean Tourism Organization**, *20 East 46th Street, New York NY 10017, Tel. 212/ 682-0435.*

THE CARIBBEAN'S JEWISH HISTORY

Jewish settlers came early to the islands and added yet another golden thread to a tapestry of African, European, and Asian immigrants. Jews, most of them fleeing persecution starting with the Spanish Inquisition and continuing through the Nazi years, began settling in the islands with the earliest Europeans, some directly from Europe and others from other refuges such as Brazil. From here they brought sugar cane, the first to be introduced into the islands. For centuries, other Jews came to the islands from Israel, bringing their expertise in irrigation. Many others were merchants or ship chandlers.

The ceremonial bath in Nevis is thought to be the oldest mikva (ritual bath) in the oldest synagogue in the Caribbean. According to documents found in Holland, a synagogue existed on Nevis before 1688; the oldest date in the Jewish cemetery there is 1658. Archaeological research began in 1996 at the synagogue site in downtown Charlestown and visitors are welcome.

A synagogue on Curacao, once thought to be the oldest in the Caribbean and still the oldest one in continuous service, dates to 1732. Graves in the Beth Haim Cemetery on the island date to 1668. Barbados also had a synagogue early in British colonial days. Statia, which was active during the American Revolution, has a synagogue dating to the 1700s, as well as a Jewish cemetery. Its Jews were expelled by the British during the American Revolution because of their loyalty to the United States.

Many of them settled in St. Thomas, where a Jewish congregation was founded in 1796. Tombstones in the island's Jewish cemetery date as early as 1792. The present synagogue was used in recent years by a congregation of Palestinian Arabs until their mosque could be built – one more example of the mellow melting pot that is the Caribbean.

Alexander Hamilton, who was Secretary of the Treasury under George Washington, was born on Nevis to a Jewish mother. Impressionist painter Camille Pissarro was born to Marrano Jewish parents in St. Thomas. The story is told in Irving Stone's novel Depths of Glory. Victor Borge fled the Holocaust in Europe to settle on St. Croix. Other famous Jews from the islands have included Judah Benjamin, secretary of state for the Confederacy, and U.S. Senator David Yulee.

5. A SHORT HISTORY

For thousands of years before European settlement, the Caribbean islands were roamed by canoes carrying peoples who came to be known as **Caribs** and **Arawaks**. Although other tribal names such as Ciboney, Caiqueto, and Taino crop up, the people who met Christopher Columbus were primarily the warlike, cannibalistic Caribs and the peaceful, agrarian Arawaks.

Tragically, most Amerindian tribes disappeared within a few decades. Many were taken as slaves; others caught European diseases such as measles and pox because they had no natural immunity. They died in droves from disease, hunger, oppression, and massacre. Only a few pockets of Caribs remain.

Modern history is considered to have begun on October 12, 1492, when Christopher Columbus landed on an island that the aborigines knew as Guanahani and the Spanish called San Salvador in what we now call The Bahamas.

Between then and 1504, Columbus made four trans-Atlantic voyages, discovering and claiming island after island for Spain. By 1504 he had found Trinidad, the coast of South America, and the Central American coast, which he still called the **Indies** because he thought he had found a route to Asia.

The first maps, however, began appearing in 1507 with the name America after a Florentine explorer, Amerigo Vespucci, who had discovered the Amazon River. It wasn't until 1513 that Florida, which he thought was another island, was sighted by Juan Ponce de Leon. His ornate tomb is now a tourist attraction in San Juan Cathedral.

Almost from the beginning, powerful struggles and intrigues marked Caribbean history. The 38 men left in the Dominican Republic in 1492, supplied only with what they could salvage from the wreckage of the *Santa Maria*, disappeared by the time the next vessels arrived. Spain worked quickly to fortify its holdings, founding settlements in Hispaniola in 1496, Puerto Rico in 1508, and Cuba in 1515.

The Caribbean yielded some gold, which was quickly pounced upon by the conquerors and their queen back in Seville, but by 1521 greater riches were discovered in Mexico and the islands were left to chart their own riches the hard way, by planting sugar and raising cattle.

By 1536, all Europe wanted a piece of the action. The seas were aboil with mighty warships belonging to nations, pirates, and privateers. The Dutch plundered Santiago de Cuba in 1554; Havana fell in 1555; Santo Domingo surrendered in 1586. The British won San Juan in 1595 and the Dutch captured the Spanish silver fleet off Cuba in 1628.

Only part of the battle was fought in the Caribbean. The fortunes of many islands rose and fell according to European treaties resulting from wars thousands of miles from the Caribbean. Some islands changed hands 20 times or more. Meanwhile in the islands, wars were fought on land and sea among Europeans and between Europeans and the few surviving Caribs.

The total land area of all the islands is less than that of England and Scotland, but each harbor was a precious resource and every arable acre of land an economic battleground. The Dutch took Curacao in 1634; the French moved into Martinique in 1635; the British took Jamaica from the Spanish twenty years later. By 1665, France had half of Hispaniola, calling it Haiti. Battles roared on, almost always in favor of the British, whose fleet based in Antigua ruled the seas.

The plot thickened during the American revolution, when Statia became a transfer point for arms to the rebels led by General George Washington. When American independence was declared in 1776, the Dutch guns of Statia were the first to fire a salute to the Stars and Stripes. A century later, during the American Civil War, the islands would again become havens for smugglers and blockade runners sympathetic to the Confederacy.

In addition to the battles sanctioned by European monarchs, honest settlers had to endure raids by pirates such as Henry Morgan, who operated out of Nassau, and Edward Teach, known as Blackbeard, whose hideaway at Port Royal, Jamaica, was destroyed in an earthquake of Biblical proportions. Two French pirates headquartered in little Saba. Dutchman Piet Heyn is said to have taken $5 million in booty back to Holland.

It is clear why the motto of The Bahamas is Latin for "Expel pirates; restore commerce." The islands were a no-man's land, worked by slaves who were being brought in at the rate of as many as 75,000 persons a year and exploited by anyone who had ships and cannons.

THE END OF SLAVERY

The first major slave rebellion came in 1801, when blacks led by Toussaint Louverture rebelled against the Spanish and set up a free society. Haiti declared itself independent in 1804 under the emperorship of former slave Jean-Jacques Dessalines. By 1834, slaves in all the British islands were free; freedom in the Dutch islands came soon after.

With the introduction of sugar beets into European agriculture, the continent's sweet tooth no longer had to be satisfied by Caribbean plantations. Without slaves to work them, many lands weren't replanted. Experiments in cotton, pineapple, and other crops were tried, often ending in disaster after a blight, a drought, or a market collapse.

Suddenly the Caribbean was hardly worth fighting over.

After the Treaty of Paris ended the Spanish-American War, Cuba and Puerto Rico were ceded to the United States, which also bought the Danish Virgin Islands to protect the Americas against the Germans in World War I. Even as late as 1983, when Cuba's building of a major landing field on Grenada was halted by American intervention, the strategic value of the lands and harbors of the Caribbean was realized. Today the same coves that sheltered pirates long ago are transfer points for illegal drugs. The French have a saying: the more things change, the more they stay the same.

INDEPENDENCE & TOURISM

Although Cuba became independent as early as 1901, independence fever began hitting the islands in earnest in the 1960s. Jamaica and Trinidad and Tobago became independent states within the British Commonwealth in 1962. Barbados followed in 1966, then Antigua, Barbuda, Redonda, Anguilla, St. Kitts and Nevis, St. Lucia, St. Vincent, and Dominica. Some fine-tuning has occurred, such as the withdrawal of Anguilla from the St. Kitts federation, but the islands have continued a steady course towards increasing self-reliance.

An exception is the French possessions, which are *départements* of France. Citizens of French islands have all the rights and privileges of French men and women born in Burgundy or Provence.

Although American troops have been used to restore order in Haiti, the Dominican Republic, and Grenada, it is really the American dollar that affects the islands most. Dollars circulate almost everywhere, and are even the black market currency of choice in Cuba. Some islands tie their local currencies to the US dollar; in most islands there is no reason ever to use local coinage at all. Only in a few islands is it necessary, or even advisable, to use other currencies.

Although tourism is crucial to most island economies, many have parlayed it into a double play in which people invest in a local condo or sailboat, rent it out for fun and profit, and pocket the tax savings. Banks of Grand Cayman, Jamaica, Nassau, and Tortola thrive on overseas accounts attracted by secrecy laws. Almost every island has dozens of foreign-owned properties, most of them for rent by the week or month. Where is history leading the Caribbean? Our guess is that tourism will continue to get bigger and better in the islands, including Cuba. With insightful and early recognition of the islands' fragile environment, eco-tourism is becoming an important alternative. Taking a lesson from Florida, where living reefs have been almost completely destroyed, conch populations decimated, and fisheries endangered, the Caribbean has clamped a lid on anchoring, pollution, high-rise development, and other ills. With luck, the wrecking ball of Progress will come slowly and with great care.

STEPPING STONES OF HISTORY

1492-1504 Columbus' four voyages to the New World.

1496 Columbus' brother Bartolomé Colon founds Santo Domingo; the first written description of the tobacco plant reaches Europe.

1504 Columbus returns from his last voyage; Isabella of Castille dies.

1521 San Juan is founded; its walls will be completed by 1630; Hernando Cortez destroys the Aztec state and claims Mexico.

1523 The first Christian church in the Americas, San Jose Church, is built in Puerto Rico by the Dominican order; the first marine insurance policies are issued in Florence.

1580 Sir Francis Drake returns from a circumnavigation of the globe; Dutch painter Franz Hals is born; coffee is introduced to Italy. In England, the hit tune of the day is *Greensleeves*.

1593 Bermuda is discovered; Shakespeare debuts *The Taming of the Shrew*; Izaak Walton is born.

1595 Britons Sir Francis Drake and Sir John Hawkins take San Juan; Hawkins dies. The Dutch begin to colonize Indonesia; Sir Walter Raleigh reaches a point 300 miles up the Orinoco River.

1596 Sir Francis Drake dies; the first water closets come into use; tomatoes are introduced to England and soon make their way to the New World.

1605 Fort George is built on a hill 1,100 feet above Port of Spain, Trinidad; Barbados is claimed as an English colony; 120 colonists land in Virginia; Rembrandt van Rijn is born.

1621 The 12-year truce between Holland and Spain ends and war renews; Britain begins colonizing the Canadian Maritimes.

1623 Velázquez is made court painter to King Philip 1V; Oliver Cromwell banishes a shipload of Irish Catholics to St. Kitts but they soon leave to form a colony on Montserrat.

1625 Sir William Courteen leads a group of settlers to Barbados; Ben Jonson's comedy *The Staple of News* plays London.

1628 A band of Englishmen seize Nevis; construction of a new harbor at Le Havre and the building of the Taj Mahal begin.

1629 The Colony of Massachusetts is founded; a war between England and France ends with the Peace of Susa; English and French unite on St. Kitts against the bloodthirsty Caribs.

1634 The Dutch capture Curacao; Covent Garden opens in London.

1639 English settlers come to St. Lucia and are murdered by the Caribs; the first printing press in the Americas is set up in Cambridge, Massachusetts.

1646 England takes The Bahamas; the first lime trees are planted in London.

1650 Holland and England reach an accord about their turf in the New World; Harvard College is founded.

1693 Kingston, Jamaica is founded after the destruction of Port Royal the previous year; Scarlatti's opera *Teodora* opens.

1728 James Cook, who would later introduce breadfruit to the Caribbean, is born; Spain stops its 14-month siege of the English at Gibralter.

1732 Mikve Israel Synagogue is built in Curacao, an outstanding example of Dutch colonial architecture; Benjamin Franklin begins publishing *Poor Richard's Almanac.*

1763 The Seven Years War ends, with Britain gaining much territory including Grenada; a Chamber of Commerce is established in New York.

1779 The French take St. Vincent and Grenada; Captain James Cook dies.

1780 Fort Josephine is built by the French in the Iles Des Saintes. Charleston, South Carolina surrenders to the British. The fountain pen, circular saw, and Spanish dance Bolero are invented.

1784 Nelson's Dockyard is built in English Harbour, Antigua, under the leadership of 25-year-old Horatio Nelson, who would be married on Nevis in 1787.

1791 Slaves revolt on Santo Domingo; the first guillotine is set up in Paris; gaslights appear in England.

1793 Rum production in Trinidad is 500,000 gallons. The cotton gin is invented. Sir Alexander Mackenzie crosses Canada from coast to coast.

1795 Black and Red Caribs unite against the English in St. Vincent, slaughtering and pillaging. When reinforcements arrive in June 1796, the English prevail and send more than 5,000 blacks to Honduras.

1796 Napoleon marries Josephine de Beauharnais, who was born in the West Indies; Spain declares war on England.

1797 Spain captures some bronze cannon from the British and melts them down to cast a statue of Ponce de Leon, which tourists can now see on San Jose Plaza.

1805 The French sack and burn Roseau, Dominica. They agree to leave the island on payment of 12,000 Pounds Sterling.

1808 importation of slaves from Africa is outlawed in the United States.

1834 Britain frees its Caribbean slaves and in gratitude slaves on Montserrat donate two silver chalices to St. Anthony's Church. Abraham Lincoln wins his first election and becomes an assemblyman in Illinois.

1841 The Grand Hotel opens in Charlotte Amalie; English travel agent Thomas Cook books his first trip.

1843 The slave population of Cuba is estimated at 436,000. The first telegraph line is installed between Washington and Baltimore; Wagner's opera *Flying Dutchman* debuts in Dresden.

1844-1930 The Dominican Republic has 56 revolutions.

1848 France frees its Caribbean slaves; serfdom is outlawed in Austria; Wisconsin becomes a state.

1845 Moravians build a church on Antigua for freed slaves; Texas and Florida become states; the hydraulic crane is patented.

1863 Holland frees its Caribbean slaves; the American Civil War rages; construction of the London subway is begun.

1887 Paul Gauguin lives in the French West Indies, while in England the first Sherlock Holmes story is published.

1888 A floating bridge is laid across Willemstad Harbor, Curacao; some travelers become seasick while crossing it.

1902 Mont Pelé erupts in Martinique, obliterating the city of St. Pierre, killing more than 29,000 people. A bitter, six-month coal strike grips the United States. Paul Gauguin paints *Raiders by the Sea*.

1917 Kaiser Wilhelm has his eyes on the Panama Canal. To protect American interests, the United States buys the Virgin Islands from Denmark for $300 an acre, or $25 million. The United States and Cuba declare war on Germany; John F. Kennedy is born.

1929 World markets collapse, bringing increased suffering to the Caribbean; Kodak introduces 16mm film. In Chicago, a gangland hit becomes known as the St. Valentine's Day Massacre.

1930 Rafael Trujillo seizes power in the Dominican Republic and reigns as dictator until his assassination in 1961.

1943 Although it was known as early as 1880 that Jamaica had rich reserves of bauxite, its export begins only now with a shipment to Canada.

1957 Francois Duvalier consolidates his power in Haiti; after his death in 1971, his son continues to rule.

1960 Cuba expropriates holdings of American companies.

1965 An uprising in the Dominican Republic brings intervention from the United States.

1967 Antigua, Barbuda, Redonda, Anguilla, St. Kitts, Nevis, St. Lucia, St. Vincent, and Dominica form the West Indies Associated States; in Puerto Rico, voters choose to remain associated with the United States.

1972 Cuba joins the Eastern Bloc's Conecom (their common market association).

1973 The Caribbean Common Market, or Caricom, is formed.

1980 The pro-American Labor Party defeats the Cuba-leaning People's National Party in elections in Jamaica.

1981 Bob Marley, whose reggae music galvanized Jamaica and spread worldwide, dies.

1983 American and Caribbean troops land on Grenada to restore order after a coup d'etat that followed four years of leftist rule.

1989 Hurricane Hugo devastates St. Croix

1996 The first Ritz-Carlton opens in the islands at St. Thomas; a second opens in 1997 on Puerto Rico.

1997-1998 Recognizing the increasing popularity of the islands for foreigners' weddings , the islands one by one liberalize their marriage rules to allow easier, quicker licensing and documentation.

6. PLANNING YOUR TRIP

BEFORE YOU GO

WHEN TO GO

Weather doesn't vary much in the Caribbean winter and summer but when it does hit the news, it makes headlines. After your first visit to the islands, where you'll see buildings that have stood for hundreds of years, you'll have a better perspective. Yes, hurricanes can cause horrendous destruction, as we have seen on television. But they are also so infrequent in any given spot that they are barely worth considering when planning a vacation.

We once met the elderly caretaker of a half-ruined mansion on a remote island. Hungry to hear the history of this mysterious place, we pressed for dates but she said gently, "I can't read, you know." It was obvious that she couldn't relate to the events of the outside world. The best she could do for a time reference was The Storm. Births, deaths, and the building of the mansion were all before or after The Storm.

Researching it later, we deduced that she was probably talking about the hurricane of 1936. Obviously, it had been decades since a hurricane had touched her life. Although some islands get the occasional one-two punch for a couple of years in a row, this woman's story is more typical. When it's bad, it's bad, but it's so rare in any one family that histories are written around it.

Generally, hurricane season starts June 1 and ends on November 1, a day that on some islands is celebrated as Hurricane Deliverance Day. Most storms hit in August and September; the season in general is hotter and rainier than November through May. Daytime highs at sea level range from the 80s or 90s by day to the low 60s by night, all year. Occasionally a very strong cold front from the United States will reach as far south as the west coast of Cuba, where the thermometer might plunge as low as 50 degrees for a few hours.

Only on mountainous islands is there substantial variation. On an 85-degree day on the beach, it can drop 10 degrees as you climb to 1,800 feet. At 3,000 feet it can be downright chilly. The highest mountains in the islands, those rising to 10,000 feet in the Dominican Republic, can be cold indeed. Always take a windbreaker when going to sea or hiking the hills; for serious climbing to higher altitudes, a lined jacket will be welcome. Some villas in the mountains of Jamaica have fireplaces. Even on Grenada, where the highest mountain is only 2,757 feet, it's wise to take a windbreaker when hiking high in Grand Etang.

Many islands have minor micro-climates that are unique. For example, it is said about Port Antonio in Jamaica that it "rains all the time" when in fact rains come quick and early, leaving the rest of the day sparkling clear and filled with dewy flowers. Generally, small and flat islands generate less rain; on mountainous islands, altitude and trade winds bring pockets of wet and dry.

Cuba's north coast and its hills get more rainfall than than the southeast area around Guantanamo, which may get only 20 inches of rain all year. The north coast of the Dominican Republic is more wet than most of the Caribbean. Afternoon humidity in Port au Prince is lower than is typical of the Caribbean because the wet trade winds dry as they blow across the mountains of the interior. Haiti's north coast is wetter than the south. Jamaica's south coast is exceptionally dry except during rain-dumping hurricanes.

The southern islands of the Netherlands Antilles, namely Aruba, Bonaire, and Curacao, share the desert-dry climate of the north coast of Venezuela. Even in the wet season on Curacao, a four-inch rainfall is a lot. The three islands plus Trinidad and Tobago are below the hurricane belt. However, hurricanes to the north seem to suck all the air out of these latitudes, leaving them still and stifling hot.

Puerto Rico's north coast has such an even rainfall that it has no real "wet" season. Trinidad, the southernmost of the islands, is one of a handful that has ever seen a temperature higher than 100 degrees. It has a well-defined wet season, June through November.

During hurricane season, June through October, the air is sultrier and breezes less constant. September and October can be obscenely still and sticky, and many restaurants and hotels – especially those that are not air conditioned – close at this time. These months are, however, among the best for scuba diving unless, of course, there's a big storm. Although hurricanes can be devastating, they give plenty of warning. The chances of one choosing the island where you're vacationing are surprisingly slim.

The Caribbean has become a year-round vacationland. The chief change in summer is the cost. Rates plunge and resorts add sweeteners such as free greens fees, airport transfers, meals, and much more.

ENTERTAINMENT GUIDES

*For years we have used the **Entertainment Guides** series of discount books that list hotels, restaurants, and attractions offering a discount of up to 50% to book buyers. Each volume comes with a credit card-like membership card, which must be used to get the deals mentioned.*

*Although the books are costly, they pay for themselves in just a few days at a hotel or resort. **Entertainment International™ Hotel & Travel Ultimate Savings Directory** sells for under $65 and lists lodgings throughout the world including a few islands in the Caribbean. Also available is **Entertainment Puerto Rico™**, which includes lodgings and restaurants in Puerto Rico and other islands. For information Tel. 800/ 445-4137 or write Entertainment Publications, Inc., 2125 Butterfield Road, Troy MI 48084.*

As in most discount deals, some restrictions apply. Hot dates are excluded; reservations may be available only a month or less before the trip; discounts vary. No matter how you slice it however, these books are a budget bonanza.

The company publishes dozens of discount books for cities, countries, and continents worldwide, so choose carefully to get the book that will serve you best at home as well as during your Caribbean travels. Note that they are not guidebooks, but are simply catalogs of discount coupons.

In each life some rain must fall, but I can't remember a day when we didn't see at least some sunshine. Here, even the liquid sunshine is warm and sweet.

BOOKING YOUR TRIP
Travelers with Special Needs

Groups that can help with special travel plans – from nudist resorts to packages for physically-challenged travelers – include:

AMERICAN ASSOCIATION FOR NUDE RECREATION, *1703 North Main Street, Kissimmee FL 34744, Tel. 800/TRY-NUDE, Fax 407/933-7577.*

CARIBBEAN ISLANDS TRAVEL SERVICE, *7145 Deer Valley Road, Highland MD 20777, Tel. 800/476-5849 or 301/854-2027,* offers full booking service including the best airfares to St. Martin. They specialize in the naturist resorts of Orient Beach but can also book other St. Martin accommodations.

BARE NECESSITIES, *1802 West 6th Street, Austin TX 78703, Tel. 512/ 499-0405, Fax 469-0179.* This travel agency specializes in clothing-optional tours, cruises, and resorts.

SOCIETY FOR THE ADVANCEMENT OF TRAVEL FOR THE HANDICAPPED, *347 Fifth Avenue, Suite 610, New York NY 10016, Tel. 212/447-0027, Fax 725-8253.*

Tour Packagers

Start with your home-town travel agent and local newspaper travel pages, where you'll find news of Caribbean packages that start at your nearest airport. Often, charters are organized once or twice a year from cities that don't usually have non-stop service to the Caribbean.

Countless packagers in North America and Europe offer Caribbean trips, usually focusing on some theme such as diving or adventure travel (see the Eco-Tourism chapter), senior travel, or general travel. They include:

AMERICAN AIRLINES, *Tel. 800/433-7300,* offers complete vacation packages. Ask for the international tour desk.

BACKROADS, 801 Cedar Street, Berkeley CA 94710, *Tel. 510/527-1555, Fax 527-1444; toll-free 800/GO-ACTIVE,* organizes walking, bicycling, hiking, and multi-sport adventure tours in the Caribbean for a few weeks in November and December. Featured are unspoiled islands known for their scenic beauty.

BRITISH WEST INDIAN AIRWAYS VACATIONS, *Tel. 800/780-5501,* offers packages that include airfares. Also included can be stops at more than one island.

GRAND CIRCLE TRAVEL, *347 Congress Street, Boston MA, Tel. 617/350-7500 or 800/248-3737,* is a highly regarded packager of escorted, upscale tours for active senior citizens.

INTERNATIONAL GAY TRAVEL ASSOCIATION, *Tel. 800/448-8550,* in the U.S. and Canada, is a membership organization that offers networking and travel packages for homosexuals and Lesbians.

SAGA INTERNATIONAL HOLIDAYS, *222 Berkeley Street, Boston MA, Tel. 800/343-0273,* specializes in packages for senior citizens aged 50 and older.

TFI TOURS INTERNATIONAL, *34 West 32nd Street, 12th Floor, New York NY 10001, Tel. 212/736-1140 or 800/745-8000,* offers discounted tours and upscale, escorted trips for senior citizens.

TRAVEL PROFESSIONALS LTD., *444 East 52nd Street, Suite 7F, New York NY 10022, Tel. 212/753-1133,* specializes in Caribbean packages including airfare, cruises, condos, villas, hotels, and tours. ASTA member Miriam Johnson, CTC, DS, can also offer low bulk airfares to Anguilla, St. Maarten, and most Caribbean gateways.

HOME EXCHANGE

Your house or vacation home anywhere in the world could be traded with someone who has a house or vacation villa in Anguilla, the Virgin Islands, Jamaica, St. Martin, Barbados, or the Dominican Republic. A two-year membership in the program costs $295. Call Home Exchange, Tel. 404/843-2779 or 800/750-0797.

Cancellations

Reservation and cancellation policies in most Caribbean hostelries are much tighter than in other areas. To confirm a reservation you may have to make a deposit weeks and even months in advance. The most popular accommodations in the most popular weeks are booked a year or more in advance. To get a refund, advance notice of four to eight weeks may be required and even then you may not get all of your money back. Before making reservations, ask about cancellation policies. It's always wise to buy trip cancellation insurance.

The USTOA

When you deal with a tour operator who is an active member of the **United States Tour Operators Association**, you are dealing with a professional who has been in business at least three years under the same ownership and/or management, participates in a Consumer Protection Plan with a $1 million nest egg, has presented at least 16 professional references, and carries $1 million in professional liability insurance. The group has 52 members representing more than 60 companies as well as 223 associated members (such as carriers and suppliers) and 330 allied members (such as public relations firms).

USTOA members who offer packages in the Caribbean include:

CENTRAL HOLIDAYS, *206 Central Avenue, Jersey City NJ 07307, Tel. 201/798-5777*

FRIENDLY HOLIDAYS, INC., *1983 Marcus Avenue, Lake Success NY 11042, Tel. 518/358-1320, Fax 358-1319*

FUNJET VACATIONS, *8907 North Port Washington Road, Milwaukee WI 53217, Tel. 414/351-3553 or 800/558-3050*

GOGO WORLDWIDE VACATIONS, *69 Spring Street, Ramsey NJ 07446, Tel. 201/934-3500, Fax 934-3764*

HOLLAND AMERICA LINE-WESTOURS, *300 Elliott Avenue West, Seattle WA 98119, Tel. 206/281-3535, Fax 281-7110, toll-free 800/637-5029*

KINGDOM TOURS, *22 South River Street, Plains PA 18705, Tel. 717/824-5800, Fax 824-5900*

LAKELAND TOURS, *2000 Holiday Drive, Charlottesville VA 22901, Tel. 804/982-8600, Fax 982-8690*
MLT VACATIONS, *5130 Highway 101, Minnetonka MN 53345, Tel. 612/672-3111, fax 474-9730; toll-free 800/328-0025*
MTU VACATIONS, *2211 Butterfield Road, Downers Grove IL 60515, Tel. 630/271-6000, Fax 271-6011*
NORTHWEST WORLD VACATIONS, *5130 Highway 101, Minnetonka MN 55345, Tel. 612/474-2540, Fax 474-9730*
PREFERRED HOLIDAYS, *1202 Southwest i41st Court, Fort Lauderdale FL 33315, Tel. 954/359-7000, Fax 359-0374*
TNT VACATIONS, *2 Charlesgate West, Boston MA 02215, Tel. 617/262-9200, Fax 638-3418*

For further information write or call USTOA at: *342 Madison Avenue, Suite 1522, New York NY 10173, Tel. 212/599-6599, Fax 599- 6744.*

ABOUT CLUB MEDS

Club Med is the mother of the all-inclusive concept, with properties throughout the world including the Caribbean. For information about membership, which entitles you to book at any of the resorts, Tel. 800/258-2633 or Fax 602/948-4562.

Travel Checklist
According to the National Tour Association, the following tips will assure a more carefree vacation:
• Verify that the travel agent or tour company is a member of a professional association such as the National Tour Association (NTA), United States Tour Operators Association (USTOA), or the American Society of Travel Agents (ASTA).
• Make sure the company offers a consumer protection plan.
• Carefully read the company's cancellation and refund policies.
• Use a credit card. If you pay cash, get a receipt. Get everything in writing.
• Verify that the tour company has errors and omissions, protectional liability insurance coverage.
• Ask for a reference from a client with whom you are familiar.
• Avoid high pressure sales with limited time to evaluate the offer.
• Beware of companies sending a courier for a check or requesting a direct bank deposit or certified check.
• Decline offers requiring a property sales presentation.
• Prior to payment, review written details of the trip.

• Request specific hotel and airline names. Terms such as "all major hotels" or "all major airlines" are a warning flag.
• If you are given a toll-free number, insist on getting the local number too. This establishes that the tour company has a central office. Never use 900 numbers.
• To report travel-related fraud, call the **National Fraud Information Center**, *Tel. 800/876-7060* or the **Federal Trade Commission**, *Tel. 202/326-2000* as well as your local and state consumer agencies.

GOING SOLO

Single supplements are the bane of solo travelers who see what appears to be an attractive rate and then find it is charged per person, based on two people sharing a room or ship cabin. If you want to have that room to yourself you may have to pay 20-100% more than the per-person fee.

In most cases, that's only reasonable. You think of yourself as using only half the towels and only one of the twin beds, but management sees you as occupying a room that must be cleaned, air conditioned, insured, and maintained.

Generally, the lowest single supplements are in all-inclusive resorts where meals, sports, and drinks are included. Rates are for two but hosts realize that you're eating and drinking only for one and they give you a price break. A few resorts and ships, and they will be included in individual listings in this book, have single accommodations with one bunk and no extra charges.

Often the single supplement is waived for special seasons or promotions. Still other resorts guarantee to match you with a same-sex roommate. You take your chances that you'll be able to get along with a stranger but, if a roommate can't be found, you get the room or cabin at the "double occupancy" rate. Many travelers think it's worth the gamble. If you prefer to find your own roommate, you can join a club such as **Travel Companion Exchange**, *Box 833, Amityville NY 11701*.

If you're going to share accommodations anyway, think big. The best buys in Caribbean accommodations are not doubles but triples and quads. A typical two-bedroom condo sleeps six, with two in each bedroom and two on a sofabed in the living room. Each twosome pays less than the cost of a double hotel room and you get a full kitchen to boot.

It can be crowded, but some ship cabins also sleep two or more extra people. Or, consider renting an entire villa or chartering a yacht. Per-person costs go down as numbers go up. Just arrange the deal so that others can't back out at the last minute, leaving you with a bill for a five-bedroom mansion.

GETTING TO THE CARIBBEAN

BY AIR

The airfare nightmare seems to get worse every year. Our personal rule is to call any airline at least three times. Invariably, we get three different stories so we take the best deal. If we are shopping between two or more airlines, we make several calls to each.

A few points:

• Caribbean old-timers travel only with carry-ons if at all possible. If you're on the same airline all the way to your destination, there's a chance that your luggage will get lost in Miami or San Juan. If you are on more than one line, which is usually required to reach the more remote islands, chances of loss increase.

• Put new luggage tags on every piece including carry-ons, with the address of your destination in the islands. On the return trip, use tags with your home address.

• Don't buy second-hand tickets or frequent flyer coupons that were issued in someone else's name. Tighter security means a great chance of having your ticket confiscated, leaving you stranded.

• Package tours are almost always a better buy than a la carte travel, but before signing up for air add-on call the airlines and compare. If you have frequent flyer points or are a senior citizen, you can probably do better.

U.S. Numbers for Airlines Operating in the Caribbean

Numbers for large carriers may vary in your city. Check your local phone directory or, to get a different toll-free number that applies in your area, *Tel. 800/555-1212.* Calls to Information are not free.

• **Aeroflot**, *Tel. 800/995-5555*
• **Aeromexico**, *Tel. 800/237-6639*
• **ALM**, *Tel. 800/327-7230*
• **Air Aruba**, *Tel. 305/551-2400 or 800/882-7822*
• **Air Anguilla**, *Tel. 264/497-2643*
• **Air Canada**, *Tel. 800/776-3000*
• **Air Caribbean** (Trinidad and Tobago), *Tel. 868/623-2500*
• **Air St. Barthélemy**, *Tel.590/87-73-46*
• **Air St. Thomas**, *Tel. 590/27-71-76*
• **Air France**, *Tel. 800/237-2747*
• **Air Jamaica**, *Tel. 800/523-5585* in the U.S. and Canada
• **Air Martinique**, *Tel. 784/458-4528*

- **Air Sunshine**, *Tel. 800/327-8900*
- **Airlines of Carriacou**, *Tel. 483/444-2898*
- **American Airlines**, *Tel. 800/433-7300*; in the USVI *Tel. 800/474- 4884*; in Puerto Rico, *Tel. 800/462-4757*; **American Eagle**, *Tel. 800/433-7300*
- **American Trans Air**, *Tel. 800/225-2995 or 800/382-5892*
- **APR International Air**, *Tel. 305/599-1299*
- **Avia Air**, *Tel.(599/7-30178*
- **British Airways**, *Tel. 800/247-9297*
- **British West Indian Airways** (BWIA), *Tel. 800/538-2942*
- **Canadian Airlines**, *Tel. 800/426-7000* in the U.S. and Puerto Rico; in Canada, *Tel. 800/235-9292.*
- **Cardinal Airlines**, *Tel. 767/449-0322; in Florida, (305) 238- 9040*
- **Carib Aviation**, *Tel. 869/465-3055*
- **Carnival Airlines**, *Tel. 800/437-2110*
- **Cayman Airways**, *Tel. 800/422-9626*
- **Cayman Airtours**, *Tel. 800/247-2966*
- **Continental Airlines**, *Tel. 800/231-0856*
- **Delta Airlines**, *Tel. 800/241-4141*
- **Gorda Aero Service**, *Tel. 284/495-2271*
- **Guyana Air**, *Tel. 599/9-613033*
- **Iberia Airlines**, *Tel. 800/772-4642*
- **Island Air** (Caymans), *Tel. 345/949-5152 or 800/922-9606*
- **LACSA**, *Tel. 800/225-2272*
- **Leeward Islands Air Transport** (LIAT), *Tel. 246/495-1187*
- **Lufthansa**, *Tel. 800/645-3880*
- **Mexicana Air Lines**, *Tel. 800/531-7921*
- **Midway Airlines**, *Tel. 800/446-4392*
- **Northwest Airlines**, *Tel. 800/447-4747*
- **Sunaire Express**, *Tel. 800/595-9501*
- **TWA**, *Tel. 800/221-2000*; in the USVI and Puerto Rico, *Tel. 800/892-8466*
- **Tyden Air** is the official Anguillan carrier, *Tel. 800/842- 0261*
- **TransGlobal Tours** (charter Minneapolis to the Dominican Republic), *Tel. 800/338-2160*
- **Tower Air**, *Tel. 800/452-5531*
- **Mustique Airways**, *Tel. 784/458-4380*
- **St. Vincent Grenadines Air** (SVG Air), *Tel. 784/456-5610*
- **United Air Lines**, *Tel. 800/241-6522*
- **USAirways**, *Tel. 800/428-4322*

Travel Insurance

Travel insurance plans are always recommended. What if you get sick and have already paid for an expensive cruise? What if your luggage is lost? What if you are injured and have to be air-lifted home from the Leewards? It's usually best to get trip cancellation and lost luggage insurance from your travel agency, packager, or cruise line. As with most travel purchases, there is no substitute for doing your homework.

First, know what coverage you already have through existing policies (homeowner, personal liability, and collision damage waiver). Confirm that this coverage applies in the Caribbean, not just in your home country.

Second, know what protection is automatically extended to you by the airline, resort, travel agency, or resort and what is required to be bought from the company that rents you the villa, car, or boat. Lastly, look into several policies to see what features make sense for you. If you travel often, year-round coverage is a better buy. Most travel policies are for trips of a few days or weeks. Policies range from a simple refund of your deposit in a medical emergency to such premium coverages such as the Love Boat Care Gold policy from Princess Cruises, which allows credit if you cancel even for a non-emergency reason. Available as add-ons to this policy are higher limits for lost baggage and medical coverage.

Medical insurance coverage is available from:

AIR-EVAC INTERNATIONAL, *28193 Skywest Drive, Hayward CA 94541, Tel. 510/293-5968. or 800/854-2569.*

HEALTH CARE ABROAD, *107 West Federal Street, Middleburg VA 22118.*

INTERNATIONAL ASSOCIATION FOR MEDICAL ASSISTANCE TO TRAVELERS, *417 Center Street, Lewiston NY 14902, or 40 Regal Road, Guelph, Ontario, Canada N1K 1B5,* provides its members a list of English-speaking doctors in other countries.

INTERNATIONAL SOS ASSISTANCE, *Box 11568, Philadelphia PA 19116, Tel. 215/244-1500 or 800/523-8930.*

INTERNATIONAL MEDICAL ASSISTANCE, *Tel. 800/679-2020, Fax 510/293-0458*

MEDIC ALERT, *Tel. 800/825-3785,* provides body-worn identification that reveals to health care workers your allergies or chronic health problem even if you can't speak for yourself. Also offered is a booklet "Hot Weather Survival Guide."

NEAR INC., *Box 1339, Calumet City IL 60409, Tel. 708/868-6700 or 800/654-6700.*

WORLD ACCESS, INC., *6600 West Broad Street, Richmond VA 23236, Tel. 804.673-1522 or 800/482-0016.*

TRAVEL PROTECTION PLAN, *P.O. Box 585627, Orlando FL 32858-5627,* charges a one-time, pre-paid fee of $295 to cover the shipment home of anyone who dies while away from home. Included are embalming, air freight, and the container any time, anywhere. Once signed on, you're covered for life and for anywhere you meet your end.

PASSPORTS & VISAS

Most (but not all) islands don't require a passport, and citizens of the United States don't need any papers to visit the U.S. Virgin Islands or Puerto Rico. Read individual chapters to see what is required. If you're going to stay longer than three weeks, get further information from the tourism information sources listed. Some islands require a visa for longer stays. Keep in mind too that we are talking about pleasure travel. If you want to get work in the islands, write ahead to see what is required to get a work permit.

Islands that do **not** require current passports include: Anguilla, Antigua, Aruba, Barbados, Bonaire, British Virgin Islands, Caymans, Curacao, Dominica, Dominica Republic, Guadeloupe, Grenada, Jamaica, Martinique, Montserrat, Saba, Statia, St. Kitts and Nevis, St. Lucia, St. Martin/St. Maarten, and St. Vincent and the Grenadines. A driver's license, however, is not enough. You must have photo ID and proof of citizenship, such as voter registration or a birth certificate. An expired passport not more than five years old qualifies as such ID.

A passport is needed for Trinidad and Tobago. British citizens need passports for all the islands. Rules for Canadians are usually the same as for Americans. Again, longer stays, residence, financial transfers, and working abroad are a different story.

CUSTOMS

Things have changed a lot since the days when some islands didn't even permit travelers to bring portable radios with them. The only time we've seen anyone have to open their luggage for island Customs is when the traveler dressed in a style that the official might have perceived as hippie.

Drug laws are severe, so don't bring any recreational drugs or look as though you're the kind of person who might use them. Rum is cheap, so there is no point in bringing in your limit of booze. If you're a smoker, bring your limit (usually 200) of cigarettes.

GETTING AROUND THE CARIBBEAN

Aviation has replaced the old mail boat as the means of getting around the islands, but ferries are still the most affordable way to go. And they are the only way to get to islands that have no air service. The most economical, reliable way to get to a remote destination by air is to book your ongoing flight with your primary carrier, which will do its best to get the most convenient times and connections.

Packages that include airfare, accommodations, and inter-island connections or side trips can be arranged through **American Airlines Vacations,** *Tel. 800/321-2121;* **British West Indian Airways (BWIA) Vacations,** *Tel. 800/247-9297;* **Delta's Dream Vacations,** *Tel. 800/872-7786;* **TWA Getaways,** *Tel. 800/GETAWAY;* and **United Airlines Vacations,** *Tel. 800/328-6877.* **LIAT,** *Tel. 246/495-1187* offers multi- island tickets. See individual chapters for information on getting between islands by ferry or air.

RENTAL CAR ALERT

If you are younger than 25 or older than age 65, check age limits before counting on renting a car. Some island car rental agencies have minimum or maximum age limits.

CRUISING THE CARIBBEAN

No waters on the planet are more inviting than the clear, cradling seas that surround the islands. Choose among dozens of ways to get out on these waters: liveaboard dive boats, bareboating (you're the driver), crewed charter yachts (with captain only, captain and cook, or captain, cook, and crew), and leviathan "love boats" sailed by almost every major cruise line in the world.

Cruise ships are best booked through travel agents, especially cruise-only agencies. They're found in every major city, so check your Yellow Pages. A time-proven travel agency that books only cruises is **Cruises, Inc.**, *5000 Campuswood Drive, East Syracuse NY 13057, Tel. 800/854-0500 or 315/463-9695.* The company is always abreast of the latest bargains, especially for early or last-minute booking. **Cruise Planners,** *Tel. 888/820-9197,* are also cruise specialists who can offer exciting deals. Good background reading on individual ships is provided by such books as *The World's Most Exciting Cruises* (Hippocrene) and the *Total Traveler by Ship* (Graphic Arts Center Publishing).

Among ships or lines that call at one or more Caribbean islands are:
Carnival Cruise Lines, *Tel. 800/327-7373,* has several ships that sail the Caribbean out of San Juan, Miami, and Fort Lauderdale.
Commodore Cruise Lines, *800/237-5361,* cruise older ships on seven- and 14-day Caribbean cruises that may also include stops in Mexico.

CostaRomantica and **CostaVictoria** offer seven-night luxury Caribbean cruises December through April. Ports of call include San Juan, St. Thomas, Nassau, Key West, Cozumel, Ocho Rios, and Grand Cayman. *Tel. 800/33-COSTA.*

Crystal Cruises, *Tel. 800/446-6620,* is a spacious, up-market line offering cruises with the finest service.

Cunard's *Sea Goddess 1,* carrying only 116 pampered guests, sails round-trip from St. Thomas to the British Virgin Islands, St. Barts, Antigua, and St. Martin, *Tel. 800/5-CUNARD.* One of the most luxurious ships in the world, *Sea Goddess* offers round-the-clock complimentary caviar and champagne in an atmosphere of an ultra-luxurious resort without canned activities, deck sports, assigned seating nor gratuities. Cunard also sails a variety of other ships in and out of the Caribbean.

Dolphin Cruise Line, *Tel. 800/992-4299,* has older ships that serve a price-appeal audience.

Holland America, *Tel. 800/426-0327,* is one of our favorite cruise lines because of its tipping-optional policy. Indonesian crew are so eager to please you may want to tip sometimes, but it's not like other cruise lines where you're told not just to tip but how much is expected. Enroll the children in Club HAL, which has a pod for ages 5-8, another for ages 9-12, and another for teens ages 13 to 17. They'll have their own playmates, supervisors, and play, joining you for lunch and dinner and for family events such as movies and shore excursions.

Norwegian Cruise Line, *Tel. 800/327-7030,* brings out the Viking in you. Handsome Nordic officers bring spit-and-polish to big, comfortable ships that have all the luxuries as well as superb cuisine that cruising is known for.

Princess Cruises, *Tel. 800/LOVE-BOAT,* the line that cruised the original Love Boat, offers seven- and ten-day Caribbean cruises aboard a half dozen luxurious ships. Ports of call include San Juan, St. Thomas, St. Croix, Sint Maarten, Guadeloupe, Dominica, Martinique, St. Lucia, Barbados, Grenada, Caracas, and Aruba.

Regal Empress, *Tel. 800/270-SAIL,* sails out of Sarasota on six-and seven-night Caribbean itineraries and a 10-night Panama Canal cruise that includes a stop in Grand Cayman. Small and comparatively hassle-free Port Manatee on Tampa Bay offers an alternative to Miami and Fort Lauderdale departures. The ship is small (only 453 cabins) and one of the older cruisers, which adds a burnished charm. It has all the usual razzmatazz such as Las Vegas-style shows, lounges, dancing, casino, children's programs, and gourmet dining. Caribbean ports of call include Grand Cayman and Montego Bay plus, depending on the length of your cruise, Columbia, Mexico, or Central American ports including the Panama Canal. Rates start at about $400 per person for an inside cabin and four-night cruise and range to about $2300 for a suite on a 10-night Panama Canal cruise. *Regal Princess* sails the Caribbean November through May.

Star Clippers (see Chapter 13, *BestPlaces to Stay*) are authentic clipper ships built in modern times, offering the silence of sail and the luxury of a fine yacht or small cruise liner, *Tel. 800/442-0551.*

Windjammer Barefoot Cruises, *Tel. 305/672-6453,* are barebones on the luxuries but laidback and youthful, with a heavy accent on fun and eco-tourism. Five classic sailing ships, the largest fleet of tall ships in the world, sail to more than 60 ports of call in the West Indies and Yucatan,

Windstar Cruises, *Tel. 800/258-7245,* offer the best of sailing and the best of cruise liner luxury in small ships that really sail (see Chapter 13, *BestPlaces to Stay*).

ABOUT CRUISE PRICES

Cruise ships offer a dozen or more cabin categories with hundreds of dollars difference in cost, but that isn't the end of the story. Everything else in the ship is the same for everyone: dining, attentive service, and use of all the ship's facilities. You have to decide if a more spacious cabin is worth the difference in an otherwise-classless society. For many people, it is.

Usually the largest, lightest, airiest cabins are those on top decks, which means the disadvantage of greater motion in rough seas, especially if the cabin is well forward or aft. It's here that you can get a suite with king-size bed and sitting area, big windows, and perhaps a private balcony, mini-bar, personal steward, and other perks.

At the bottom end of the rate scale are windowless, inside cabins deep in the hull. Small and furnished with narrow bunk beds, they aren't for the claustrophobic but in rough seas the lowest cabins amidships have the least motion. A good compromise is an outside cabin two or three decks from the top, as close to amidships as possible for the least movement. Incidentally, the most expensive and cheapest cabins go first. For either, book as early as possible.

In addition to the basic rate, customs and port charges can add up to $200 per week to the cost of a cruise. Most lines also make it crystal clear that tips are not only expected but should amount to $X per passenger per day for the cabin steward, $Y for waiters, and so on. If this sticks in your craw, sail a tips-optional line such as Holland America or Windstar.

Other extras include optional shore excursions plus tips for drivers and guides, bar drinks including soft drinks, and personal needs such as laundry, gambling, babysitting (children's programs are usually free but individual child care is not), beauty salon and spa services, and much more. It's easy to spend twice as much on a cruise as the cost of your initial fare. Ask about packages that include airfare and pre- or past-cruise accommodations and tours. They're almost always a better buy than deals you put together by yourself.

BOOKING YOUR CRUISE OR CHARTER

Finding the right cruise in the Caribbean requires plenty of advance planning, starting with knowing where to book a cruise. Travel agencies, especially those that specialize in cruises, are the best places to shop the vast and confusing Caribbean cruise market. However, travel agents rarely book charters, which are another market entirely. Your best bet is to get copies of *Yachting, Sail,* and *Cruising World* magazines, where crewed and bareboat charters are advertised. You'll see dozens of ads for owner-operated, crewed charters, charter brokers, as well as ads for large fleets, such as **The Moorings**, which can book the entire charter including airfare, pre- and post-charter overnights, and provisioning.

Unless you're an experienced charterer, don't deal directly with a boat owner or owner-crewed charter. In a one-on-one deal, you could arrive to find that the boat is dirty or mechanically suspect. Go through a charter broker who can give you a choice of boats and locales, who has personally seen the boat, and can give you the names of some recent clients. If you're going to spend a week or more alone with crew, personality matches are crucial. Generally, owner-crew are the most eager to please but, even here, there are a few weirdos in the business. If the boat is absentee-owned and managed, crew could range from rude to unqualified. Check it out thoroughly.

Two of the best charter outfits in the business, both with long track records, are **The Moorings**, *19345 U.S. 19 North, Clearwater FL 34624, Tel. 800/535-7289*; and **Nicholson Yacht Charters**, *78 Bolton Street, Cambridge MA 02140, Tel. 800/662-6066.* The Moorings has fleets in Tortola, St. Martin, Guadeloupe, Martinique, St. Lucia, and Grenada. Boats are available without crew, with captain only, or with captain and cook. Nicholson's is based in Antigua and has listings throughout the Caribbean. Either outfit can arrange a pre- or post-charter land stay.

LIVE-ABOARD YACHTING

Let's sort out the lingo of **chartering**, a verb that means both to hire the yacht and to allow your yacht to be hired. You can charter a live-aboard boat three ways:

Bareboat means with no crew. If you have sufficient credentials as a sailor to satisfy the fleet owners and their insurance company, you and your family or crew may take command and sail away. Navigation,

CRUISING SOLO

The best way for a solo traveler to see the Caribbean is aboard ship, but most cruise and charter lines charge a hefty single supplement. You'll save by finding a roommate to share a cabin, each paying half the double occupancy fee. The larger the ship, the more there is to keep you mingling with other passengers. During open seating on most ships, waiters steer you to a table as you enter, filling tables rather than allowing people to sit alone. (It saves work for them if they don't have people scattered all over the dining room.) You'll soon make friends and, if your roommie isn't as companionable as you had hoped, it hardly matters.

One of the best ways to find a fellow traveler is through Jens Jurgen's **Travel Companion Exchange**, *Box 833, Amityville NY 11701, Tel. 516/454-0880, Fax 454-0170. Your travel agent can also match you up with the occasional singles cruise (make sure it's in the age bracket you want). Senior citizens can also travel solo on singles excursions organized by* **Grand Circle Travel,** *347 Congress Street, Boston MA 02210, Tel. 800/221-2610 or 617/350-7500.*

provisioning and cooking, swabbing the decks, sailing, and all other responsibilities are yours.

Captained charters have a captain aboard to take charge of the boat's sailing, navigation, and maintenance. Cleaning and cooking are still your responsibility.

Crewed charters let you play the guest while others do all the chores and sailing. You can still decide on destinations and schedules, pending the captain's approval depending on safety factors, and the captain will be glad to teach you as much about sailing and piloting as you care to know.

THINGS TO KNOW BEFORE YOU GO

• Get recent, firsthand knowledge of the boat and its crew before you book it. Most owner-crews are liveaboards who take great pride in their boats and their hospitality. They charter part of the year to support their own sailing the rest of the year. Corporation-owned boats may or may not have this personal touch.

• If you're bareboating, take the provisioning package, at least for the first day or two. It's far easier than running all over the island to round up a grocery list of staples.

• Know exactly what is provided. Most crewed yachts provide all food and drink, and some provide airport transfers, but others do not provide alcohol. On a captained cruise, you will probably be asked to pay for the captain's food as well as your own

• Not all yachts are suitable for very young children, and some skippers do not accept them. Check ahead.

• If possible, get a pre-charter package including a night or two in a hotel before you move aboard, especially if you're bareboating. To reach the island, move aboard, get checked out, and set sail all in the same day is too much.

For further information:

BVI Charter Yacht Society, *P. O. Box 8309, Cruz Bay USVI 00831.* Fully crewed, luxury sailing craft sleep four to 20 for cruising the British and U.S. Virgin Islands.

The Moorings, *Tel. 800/437-7880* is a worldwide charter power-house, offering 15 crewed yachts and 165 bareboats out of Tortola alone.

Nicholson Yacht Charters, *78 Bolton Street, Cambridge MA 02140, Tel. 800/662-6066,* has been in Antigua since Horatio Nelson's day and knows the charter business well.

Yacht Promenade, *Tel. 800/526-5503,* offers six-night cruises for up to 12 passengers.

DIVE CRUISING

Princess Cruises in cooperation with the **Professional Association of Diving Instructors** (PADI) offers a cruise add-on scuba course in which a passenger can become fully certified for $299. The program includes an open water dive manual, workbook, dive log book with carrying case, class and video instruction, four supervised dives in the ship's pool, four supervised open water dives in port, and a written exam. Most of the cruise lines listed above offer scuba diving as an extra. **Windstar,** for one, has a divemaster on board.

ECO-TOUR SAILING

A 12-passenger luxury schooner that winters in the Caribbean, often with experts on board to conduct seminars on the environment is **Kathryn B.,** *Tel. 800/500-6077.* Rates are about $2,800 per person, double occupancy, per week. Itineraries vary each year.

ACCOMMODATIONS

Accommodations in the islands range from some of the world's most palatial hotels to seedy inns, but we've found that even the most humble hostels are usually clean and are furnished with at least the basics. In fact it's rather heartwarming when we see a small inn, struggling to accommodate its guests in the aftermath of a hurricane, doing the best they can with futons and plastic lawn chairs until full refurbishing can be done.

Hosts battle bugs constantly, and the sighting of the occasional roach shouldn't be taken as poor housekeeping. Indoors, we have rarely found bugs to be a problem even in open-air lodgings that have no glass nor screens in the windows. Many areas are surprisingly mosquito-free. The smart traveler always brings bug repellent just in case. Unfortunately for travelers who are on tight budgets, Hostelling International has not yet come to the Caribbean and tent camping/backpacking is limited, if it's allowed at all.

Almost every community has a guest house, usually with breakfast thrown in. It probably won't have a private bath, or even hot water at all, let alone a telephone, radio, or television. No matter how much you pay for a room, don't take it for granted that it will be air conditioned. Many travelers dislike AC even on the hottest days, but it's our opinion that you can always turn if off if you don't want it. The islands, except in the mountains, are hot and humid winter and summer. Invariably, innkeepers will look you straight in the eye and tell you that "we really don't need air conditioning here" even though you're both sweating like pigs. A good fan is a must; air conditioning is a plus even if only during the mid-day heat. The only other escape is to get into the water, which most visitors do anyway.

After hotels, the most common accommodation is in a privately-owned home, condo, apartment, or villa built by an overseas investor – usually American, Canadian, or British – as a tax shelter. Many are booked through word of mouth, with happy customers returning year after year, but don't book blindly. Unless the place is professionally managed, you could arrive to find things broken or uncleaned. It's best to get one that has full-time, on-site management. Many are part of a large resort with a restaurant, swimming pool, and other hotel-like features. You may not even know that you're staying in a time share or in a privately-owned villa.

Wheelchair access isn't always good in the Caribbean except in the U.S. islands, where the Americans with Disabilities Act is making some progress. On many islands, paving is almost non-existent, let alone sidewalks and good wheelchair ramps. Yet we've seen young paraplegics in agile chairs go everywhere if they're willing to accept a little help. It's willingly given everywhere – in and out of little airplanes, off and on dive boats, up and down steps, and in and out of hotels that cling to steep hillsides.

As you read these pages, you may be surprised at what constitutes Expensive, Moderate, and Budget in various islands. Among the highest priced are the U.S. and British Virgin Islands, Anguilla, Barbuda, St.

Barts, Antigua, Martinique, the Caymans, Barbados, and St. Martin on both the French and Dutch sides.

Among the cheapest are Dominica, the Dominican Republic, St. Vincent, Saba, Puerto Rico, and Trinidad. The more affordable islands are often the most family-friendly, although the best children's programs are often those at the priciest resorts. If all you want is an inexpensive place to stay with your family while you teach the children to snorkel, the Caribbean is just as affordable for you as for wealthy families. In Caribbean hotels, you can find everything but skiing and snowmobiling.

RATING THE RATES

Although we've listed hotels under Expensive, Moderate, and Budget, it wasn't always easy to make the call because all-inclusive resorts are just that. When comparing rates, you must take into consideration what you're getting for the price. Full American Plan (FAP) means three meals daily; MAP, which means Modified American Plan, provides breakfast and dinner. Many resorts offer FAP or MAP for an extra $50 or so per person per day. European Plan, or EP, means accommodations only.

The trend in the Caribbean has been to go well beyond FAP and MAP, with all-inclusive resorts offering all meals, sports, and entertainment. Many such resorts throw in unlimited bar drinks and wine with meals; others serve wine or beer with meals other drinks are charged for

*To get to the bottom line, factor in the cost of eating, drinking, tennis or golf, watersports rentals, scuba tank refills, spa services, airport transfers, tips or service charges, and hotel taxes. Look especially for two terms: **all-inclusive** and **package**. Either could mean a big difference in the final cost of a Caribbean holiday.*

*In an effort to leave happy surprises on the down side, **this book quotes winter rates**. In spring and fall, you might save 20-30% and in summer as much as 50% off high season rates. However, there's a trend in the Caribbean to offer more features in summer rather than to chop rates. The word "package" is solid gold in any season, but especially during the dog days. You may be able to get a week's vacation with all the bells and whistles for the cost of accommodations alone at the height of the season.*

Note that the definition of "low-season" can vary widely among islands, and among resorts on the same island. The only way to know for sure is to contact each resort individually. By delaying or advancing your trip just a few days, you can save hundreds of dollars.

Hotel Chains

Chains, alliances and groups that have Caribbean properties that can be booked through toll-free numbers in the U.S. and Canada include:

- **Best Western International**, *Tel.* *800/528-1234*
- **Club Med** (ask about memberships), *Tel.* *800/259-2633*
- **Crowne Plaza**, *Tel.* *800/327-3286*
- **Days Inn**, *Tel.* *800/325-2525*
- **Econo Lodge**, *Tel.* *800/446-6900*
- **Embassy Suites**, *Tel.* *800/362-2779*
- **Golden Tulip Hotels**, *Tel.* *800/344-1212*
- **Hilton Hotels**, *800/HILTONS*
- **Hyatt Hotels**, *Tel.* *800/228-9000*
- **Holiday Inn**, *Tel.* *800/HOLIDAY*
- **Leading Hotels of the World**, *Tel.* *800/223-6800*
- **Marriott Hotels**, *Tel.* *800/228-9290*
- **Meridien/Forte Hotels & Resorts**, *Tel.* *800/543-4300*
- **Mondotels, Inc.** , *Tel.* *800/847-4249*
- **Novotel**, *Tel.* *800/NOVOTEL*
- **Quality Inn**, *Tel.* *800/228-5151*
- **Radisson Hotels**, *800/333-3333*
- **Ramada Inns**, *Tel.* *800/2-RAMADA*
- **Ritz-Carlton**, *Tel.* *800/241-3333*
- **Rosewood Hotels & Resorts**, *Tel.* *800/854-2252*
- **Small Luxury Hotels of the World**, *Tel.* *800/525-4800*
- **Sofitel**, *Tel.* *800/221-4542*
- **Sonesta Hotels**, *Tel.* *800/766-3782*
- **Westin Resorts**, *Tel.* *800/WESTINS*
- **Wyndham Hotels**, *Tel.* *800/822-4200*

RECOMMENDED READING

Magazines

Caribbean Travel & Life, and *Spa Finder*, which are on newsstands, and *Affordable Caribbean*, P.O. Box 3000, Denville NJ 07834, which is available by mail.

A NOTE FROM THE U.S. STATE DEPARTMENT

*Request **Tips for Travelers to the Caribbean**, a booklet available for $1 from the Superintendent of Documents, U.S. Government Printing Office, Washington DC 20402. It was last revised in 1993, so can be taken only as a general advisory.*

Books

Books that are set in the Caribbean or have Caribbean flavor:

• *A Cruising Guide to the Caribbean* by William T. Stone and Anne M. Hays is published by Sheridan House, *145 Palisade Street, Dobbs Ferry NY 10522, Tel. 888/743-7425.* The book is invaluable as a guide to cruising the islands by boat, but it also makes fascinating armchair reading before and after any Caribbean visit whether by land, air, or sea. The book covers many of the islands in this guidebook as well as ports along the Latin American coast of the Caribbean. It's especially fun to read about spots, such as Barbuda, that landlubbers consider enchanted islands but to mariners are merely a hazard to navigation. The authors' personal anecdotes call for reading and re-reading over the years.

• *A Small Place* by Jamaica Kincaid
• *Caribbean* by James Michener
• *Caribbean Mystery* by Agatha Christie
• *The Comedians* by Graham Greene
• *Church and Des*, a book of short stories by Philip Wylie
• *The Deep* by Peter Benchley
• *Don't Stop the Carnival* by Herman Wouk
• *Far Tortuga* by Peter Matthiessen
• *Golden Rendezvous* by Alistair MacLean
• *Islands in the Stream* by Ernest Hemingway
• *Mosquito Coast* by Paul Theroux
• *Murder on the Atlantic* by Steve Allen.
• *Wide Sargasso Sea* by Jean Rhys Specialized guides:
• *Caribbean Hideaways* by Ian McKeown (Prentice Hall Travel) covers 100 romantic places for couples.
• *Caribbean Afoot* by M. Timothy O'Keefe (Menasha Ridge Press) is a walking and hiking guide to 29 islands.
• *Cockpit Companion* by Gordon & Janet Groene (Jones Publishing) is available for $15 post paid from R.V. Books, Box 248, DeLeon Springs FL 32130. The book, aimed at passengers in small aircraft, is a useful guide for the family that flies the Caribbean for fun and for those who fear flying in the small airplanes that are such a common part of Caribbean travel.
• *World Guide to Nude Beaches and Resorts* by Lee Baxandall
• *Out and About, Resorts and Warm-Weather Vacations*, a travel guide for homosexuals. (Hyperion)
• *Cruising Guide to the Leeward Islands* and *Cruising Guide to the Windward Islands* by Chris Doyle (Cruising Guide Publications, Box 1017, Dunedin FL 34697; available through yachting book stores or *Tel. 800/749-8151.)*

These guides are indispensable to boaters:

• *St. John Feet, Fins, and Four-Wheel Drive* by Pam Griffin (American Paradise Publishing, ISBN 0-9631060-7-4).

• *Yachtsman's Guide to the Virgin Islands and Puerto Rico* (Yachtsman's Guides Publications, Box 281, Atlantic Highlands NJ 07716, *Tel. 800/ 849-8151).*

7. BASIC INFORMATION

BANKING

Banks throughout the Caribbean keep abbreviated hours and, on the smallest islands, may be open only one or two days a week. On the plus side, currency exchanges, and sometimes full-service banks, are often open when flights arrive, even at odd hours. Banks almost always offer better exchange rates than hotels and shops, so they are the place to change money. Most have Automatic Teller Machines, which are found throughout the region, but, as with anything else in the islands, it's best not to bet the farm on finding a machine where it's supposed to be, and in working order.

Before leaving on your trip, check with your home bank to see if you need a different PIN in the islands. Your home bank may also be able to give you a list of ATM addresses in the island you'll be visiting.

BUSINESS HOURS

The **siesta** is a time-honored tradition in the Caribbean where "only mad dogs and Englishmen go out in the noonday sun." Only the largest stores stay open through the lunch hour. Most museums and other attractions will be closed for one or two hours in the middle of the day.

CARNIVAL!

Carnival (spelled Carnaval on some islands) in the Caribbean can take place any time of year.

Antigua's Carnival features stilt walkers known as the Moka Jumbies, who dance to calypso tunes. An ancient tradition that almost died out as its practitioners aged, the practice has been revived by the Museum of Antigua and Barbuda.

Barbados' 11-day De Congaline Carnival is held in late April and early May. It features the Caribbean's longest conga line. The island's largest party day is not during Carnival but during Crop Over Festival in August. Its biggest event is Kadooment Day, the first Monday in August.

Dominican Republic celebrates Carnival in February with costumes, food and merengue dancing in the streets of Santo Domingo, La Vega, and Santiago. .

Puerto Rico celebrates most of its carnivals just before Lent, but regional dates could vary.

St. Barts: celebrations here reach their peak on Mardi Gras and the Sunday and Monday preceding it. A curtain descends on Ash Wednesday as Lent begins but, inexplicably, it lifts on the third Thursday in Lent for another day of masquerades and tomfoolery. Celebrations include parades, dancing, and music on the main pier at Gustavia, and the burning of King Vaval.

St. Eustatius celebrates its Carnival from late July into early August. It begins with a morning jump-up and includes competitions, parades, calypso, and the burning of King Momo, the spirit of carnival.

St. Kitts & Nevis: Carnival runs Christmas Eve through New Year's Day.

St. Maarten: Carnival is held after Easter, usually incorporating the Queen's birthday. During the event, seven parades are held including the 4am Jouvert (pronounced jou-VAY) in which the Calypso Queen or King is crowned. In the Grand Carnival Parade, troupes walk four miles. Carnival also includes a Calypso competition, food booths selling West Indian staples such as johnny cake, and stages filled with soca, merengue, reggae, and calypso musicians. For this year's dates, call *Tel. 5995-22337.*

St. Martin holds its Carnival in February prior to Ash Wednesday.

St. Vincent and the Grenadines celebrate Carnival in early July with parades, costumes, shows, calypsos and parties everywhere.

Trinidad and Tobago party hearty in early February. "Mas" bands parade at sunup with pitchforks and pointed tails. Visitors are invited to join a mas camp, don a costume, and become a member of one of the parading bands.

Virgin Islands: Carnival is two days before Ash Wednesday, when it's celebrated with bambooshay, kill t'ing pappy and roas-a-time, all meaning "live it up". There's a carnival queen, prince and princess, calypso singers, street vendors, high hats, horse racing, food fairs, masquerades, parades and enough excess and insanity to last through Lent.

CREDIT CARDS

MasterCard and Visa cards are accepted in almost every tourist shop, hotel, and restaurant in the Caribbean. Discover has some acceptance, with American Express and Diners Club in a distant fourth place. Wherever possible, charge purchases rather than dealing in local currency because you'll get the optimum rate of exchange on the day the transaction occurred.

CURRENCY

In this book, unless otherwise noted all dollar prices are in U.S. dollars. On many islands it's possible to operate completely in U.S. dollars. Since something is lost with each exchange, and some Caribbean currencies are almost worthless outside their home island, it's best to avoid changing funds if possible. Still, it's fun to try using local currencies, and most airports have a collection box where valueless leftover currency can be deposited to a good cause.

If you plan to deal only in U.S. funds (where practical, possible, and legal) carry small denominations. Any change will probably be given you in local funds. In most cases, hard currency goes directly into a lock box and will not be surrendered to make change. In any case, U.S. coins aren't popular. Carry a lot of small bills.

ELECTRICITY

Electrical service and plugs vary throughout the Caribbean. Many hotels have built-in hair dryers and many have razor points that accommodate North American electric shavers (but don't use this plug for hair curlers or any other electric service). See individual chapters for island-by-island details. Some islands use 220-volt service and require converters and adapters.

EMERGENCIES

When you arrive in your hotel, review emergency procedures. They will include the usual things about what to do in case of fire, and may also include hurricane instructions. Power outages are a fact of life, so locate the candle(s) and matches that are usually provided. On some islands it's also wise to draw a half gallon or so of water to provide a rinse in case the water fails when you're soapy.

Keep in mind that the 911 system is *not* used in most of the islands.

BRING YOUR CAMERA

Some islanders object to being photographed on religious grounds, others are shy, some are surly, some will pose only for money, and nobody likes to be snapped in their work clothes with sweat streaming down their faces. Always ask before shooting a picture. A gesture that wins over all but the most camera shy is to use a Polaroid first. Ask families to form a group, take a picture, and give it to the parents or eldest child. Then ask if you can take pictures with your own camera to take home to your family. For us, it almost always works.

HEALTH CONCERNS

People from northern climes often picture the islands as hurricane-lashed sandspits inhabited mostly by boa constrictors, clouds of mosquitoes, and spiders the size of Siamese cats. The good news is that most of the islands are highly advanced in terms of safe drinking water, the availability of emergency medical care, and food sanitation. See individual chapters for specific warnings.

The Caribbean does have its pests, but its chief danger by far is Ol' Sol, the faithful sunshine that brings most of us here in the first place. Sunglasses are crucial, according to Dr. Wayne J. Riley of Baylor College of Medicine in Houston, "especially in ...equatorial sand beaches."

Bring with you a supply of high-SPF sunscreen, preferably a waterproof brand that won't come off with perspiration or swimming. Some of the worst sunburns are suffered by swimmers and snorkelers who don't realize they're getting burned right through the water. If you're especially sensitive to sunburn, bring a lightweight, long-sleeve, long-leg outfit such as pajamas to wear while snorkeling, and wear waterproof sunscreen too.

Mosquitoes can always be a problem in the tropics, and the World Health Organization now admits that they can't be eradicated. Travelers must bring their own spray-on protection; if you're staying in primitive surroundings, bring your own mosquito netting too. Various designs of drapings for beds or sleeping bags are available from **Magellan's**, *Box 5485, Santa Barbara CA 93150, Tel. 800/962-4943*. Request a free catalog.

Many people find "no-see-ums" to be far peskier than mosquitoes. They can fly through screens and are not deterred by all mosquito sprays. They can cause a watery blister that itches for weeks and scars for months. Some tourists, especially heavy drinkers, have had such severe reactions they had to be hospitalized.

Since different repellents work on different body chemistries, take two types in hopes that one of them will work on your skin against no-see-ums. Many people swear by Avon's Skin-So-Soft bath oil, but it doesn't work for everyone.

The same precautions that apply anywhere are also wise in the Caribbean. When in doubt about water, ask. Don't drink water in remote streams and waterfalls; giardia are found throughout the world. Wash or peel fruit before eating it just as you would at home; in the least developed areas where sanitation is at question, eat only cooked foods and drink only commercially bottled water.

Fish poisoning isn't unique to the islands, but one toxin that occurs here is not destroyed by cooking. It's **cigatuera**, sometimes found in fish that feed on reefs. It's rarely a problem in hotels and restaurants but could be a threat if you cook your own catch. Ask locals for guidance before eating barracuda, amberjack, or colorful reef fish.

Cigatuera is a neurotoxin that causes tingling in the mouth, fingers, and toes. Often an initial dose produces only mild symptoms, which get worse with each exposure. So locals, who could be made sicker than a newcomer who is getting cigatuera for the first time, are usually very savvy about what fish to catch and where to catch them.

In years of traipsing through the bush, we've never had an allergic reaction to vegetation. Fortunately we never tangled with the **manchineel tree**, found throughout the Caribbean, which is so poisonous that people have gone temporarily blind just by breathing smoke from a manchineel fire. The trees are not uncommon; ask a local to point one out so you'll always recognize them. Don't touch. Don't even stand under one in the rain. Drips could give you a nasty rash.

As long as you don't taste strange plants, and watch that you don't walk into thorns or cactus, it's likely you won't have severe reactions to plants.

Poisonous snakes are rare in the Caribbean, although Aruba's most remote scrub is home to the Colebra rattlesnake and the dreaded fer-de-lance is found in the warm coastal areas of some islands, including St. Lucia and Martinique. You can thank a creature that is even scarier and more slithery than snakes for the fact that snakes are so rare in the Caribbean. The mongoose was introduced generations ago on some islands, promptly wiped out most of the indigenous snakes, and multiplied in the wild until it became a pest too. Looking like a cross between a dachshund and an alley cat, it's startling more than harmful. Once you've seen one and realized it's not an oversize rat, you'll know what to expect.

This is a good place to point out that a Caribbean plantation doesn't always look like the neatly fenced farm or orchard that is familiar to people from Europe or North America. If you stumble onto a field of fruit or vegetables, don't assume that they are growing wild and are free for the taking. The plants probably belong to someone, perhaps a poor villager who walks miles to bring water to the family "farm." Don't pick anything. It's stealing. Worse, you could get a mouthful of dumb cane, which looks like sugar cane but is planted around the edges of a cane field to deter poachers. One taste and the mouth swells, hence the term "dumb" cane.

POST SERVICE
Mail Without Fail

Unless you'll be in the Caribbean for a length of time somewhere between a coon's age and a decade, forget having any mail sent there. If the message absolutely, positively must get through, use fax, e-mail, telephones, Federal Express, radio-telephone, or ham radio – anything but the mails. That said, I admit that I've never had any mail lost or stolen

HEALTH ADVISORIES

*Get the latest information from the **Centers for Disease Control**, Tel. 404/332-4559. It's a 24-hour hotline. Typhoid shots are recommended for remote areas of Haiti or Jamaica. Polio is endemic in Haiti and the Dominican Republic. Malaria is prevalent in Haiti and in nearby, rural Dominican areas; a deadly form of dengue fever is reported in Cuba. Sunburn is the most common health problem. Use sunscreen and wear a long-sleeve shirt, even while snorkeling in shallow water.*

For those of you planning repeated trips to the region (or anywhere else in the world), pick up a copy of Open Road's "CDC's Complete Guide to Healthy Travel," which presents the Centers for Disease Control's authoritative summaries for all international travel.

in the islands. Our postcards always reached their targets, usually a month or two after I'd reached home. I've had incoming mail delayed, misfiled, and returned to sender because a Mrs. Green had just checked out, but never lost. Here are a few wrinkles that can help.

If your schedule is really vague, use General Delivery, which is also called Poste Restante, especially in the French islands. When you call at the window to claim your mail, write your name in block letters, and hand it to the clerk to avoid confusion. With a name like Groene, which we pronounce GRAYnee, even the Dutch can't find us.

Just speaking your name is not enough, especially in islands where English is not the first language. The prudent clerk may also ask to see your passport or other identification, so take it to the post office with you. If you'll be staying long enough in one spot, ask your host(s) in advance how they recommend that mail be sent to you while there. It's essential that you know the mailing address that they recommend, then make sure that your friends and family don't cut corners. They must write out Commonwealth of Dominica, or whatever, plus the name of the island group such as British Virgin Islands rather than BVI.

If you'll be receiving packages or Federal Express, ask your host what address should be used for them. We once waited weeks for a package, not realizing that parcels go to a special customs post office and not to the General Post Office where we picked up our letters.

Some larger resorts and companies have addresses in the United States where mail can be sent using U.S. postage. It's then flown in daily by the company's own plane or shipping service. If you can tie in with one of these set-ups, getting mail is a breeze.

For Americans traveling to Puerto Rico or the U.S. Virgin Islands, things are simpler. Mail goes by an American zip code, and first class mail can be forwarded free, just as it is on the mainland.

RELIGIOUS SERVICES

The most "insider" thing you can do as a tourist in the Caribbean is to attend local worship services. Dress in your best and act responsibly even if you don't know what is going on. We'd suggest sticking to mainstream denominations, which are found on every island, rather than unusual cults and sects that might suspect that you are merely curious. In fact, some of the darker rites (voodoo, obeah, some Mormon sacraments) are not open to outsiders and it would be a gaffe to try to attend.

We can promise you a warm welcome in church, and a new dimension to the friendships you make on the island. Attending a tiny, open air Baptist church on one cay, we found ourselves the subject of a lengthy sermon, the gist of which was a prayerful request for our safety at sea. We've never felt so loved and honored.

SERVICE CHARGES

Instead of tipping, most hotels and restaurants automatically add 10-15 per cent to bills. Check your bill before leaving additional money under the plate. There's no point in tipping twice.

TAXES

Hotel taxes seem to be soaring in recent years at a pace that is hard for an annual guidebook to keep up with. When asking for rate information, always ask whether taxes and tips are included. If not, be sure you know how much they add because it's not uncommon for tax and service to add another 20-25 per cent to the room rate.

TIPS

Tips are always welcome but foreign coins are difficult for islanders to change. Use local currency or U.S. bills. Tipping for the taking of photographs hasn't caught on widely here and we're hoping you won't start a trend. Locals either allow you to take their picture or they don't.

TELEPHONES

Hotel phone charges for overseas calls are excessively high in most cases so, even though you can dial anywhere in the world from most room phones, ask the cost first. Pre-paid cards are used almost exclusively in the Caribbean; most pay phones accept nothing else. Before leaving home, check with your long distance carrier to get the access code you'll use

PHONE HOME

Through the **Cable & Wireless Caribbean Cellular** *(formerly Boatphone) you can place or answer calls from almost anywhere on your own cell telephone. In many areas, voice and fax mail can also be arranged. Before leaving home, make arrangements by calling 800/262-8366 U.S., 800/567-8366 Canada, and Tel. 268/480-2628 elsewhere.*

Islands served include Antigua & Barbuda, Jamaica, St. Kitts and Nevis, St. Lucia, St. Vincent & the Grenadines, the British Virgin Islands, Cayman Islands, Grenada, Martinique, Montserrat and St. Martin. If you pre-register with the company you can be given a local number in the islands to give to family and business associates before you leave home. You can also begin making calls immediately on your arrival on the island.

*There is no charge for pre-registering. You pay only a $5 daily activation charged on days when the phone is used. Calls made to emergency numbers are free. On any island served by Cable & Wireless, dial O and SND. On Jamaica, dial *O SND.*

while in the Caribbean. One bright spot: pay phones in Puerto Rico still work on a dime.

TIME ZONE

Most of the Caribbean covered in this book is on **Atlantic Time**, which is the same as **Eastern Daylight Savings Time**. When the East is on Standard Time, the island time is one hour later than New York time.

TROUBLE SPOTS

Caribbean-wide

Crime varies among islands but it is an increasing problem, not just in the theft of money and valuables but in the stealing of U.S. passports and I.D. (Keep two extra passport photos and a photocopy of your passport in a separate bag to facilitate replacement in case of theft.) Don't bring unnecessary credit cards or expensive jewelry and keep close tabs on electronics, laptops, cameras, and other items that are easily lifted and sold. Don't take valuables to the beach, not even to be locked in the trunk of the car.

Firearms are generally verboten in the islands, even if you arrive in your own airplane or boat. Penalties are swift and severe.

Driving on many islands is on the left. Unlike in the United Kingdom, where steering wheels are also on the left and serve as a constant reminder to drive on the left, the most common cars in the Caribbean were built for the North American market and have right-hand steering. Add to this the poor roads on most islands, and the absence of good maps and road signs, and driving injuries claim far too many visitors. Log some time as a passenger before attempting to solo.

Drowning is one of the leading causes of death for Americans visiting the Caribbean. Unwary tourists get in over their heads, literally, with watersports equipment that is not up to international safety standards or on surf-pounded beaches that have no warnings nor lifeguards. Sea conditions can change suddenly. Respect local advice.

Drug laws are strict in the islands, but they catch North American visitors unawares because of the lazy, laidback pace of life. If you are caught with even small amounts of marijuana, let alone cocaine or other illegal substances, you could get as much as 20 years in jail – beyond the reach of your home country or hometown attorney (who is not licensed to practice there). In many places there is no bail and, while you wait for trial, you could be held for months in a prison that doesn't meet even minimum U.S. standards. If you carry prescription medications, keep them in the original container labeled with the doctor's name, pharmacy, and contents.

Shopping can be a waste of money if you buy products that will be confiscated on your return. Don't rely on locals to tell you, or even to know, what items cannot be brought into the United States. They include any products made from sea turtles including cosmetics and turtle shell jewelry, fur from spotted cats, feathers and feather products, birds stuffed or alive, crocodile and cayman leather, and black coral. In fact, it's best to avoid buying any coral either in jewelry and au naturel, according to the U.S. Department of State.

Specific Problems

Cayman Islands – Persons wearing their hair in dreadlocks, or otherwise umkempt or unconventional may be barred from entry. It's up to the officiating immigration officer.

Cuba – Fidel's island is still pretty much off limits to American travelers, even those who enter through a third country such as Canada or Mexico. Those who can go are journalists, government officials on official business, persons visiting close relatives who live in Cuba, and full-time professionals engaged in academic research. Americans whose transactions are not authorized for one of the above reasons may not buy foods, including airline services or a meal in a restaurant in Cuba. (This is the U.S. State Department's way of saying that you shouldn't buy anything in Cuba including a meal, hotel room, or airline ticket.) Credit cards issued by U.S. firms are not valid in Cuba, nor are U.S. travelers checks regardless of where they were issued. If you're jailed for any offense, not matter how unwittingly committed, it's likely that you're beyond the help of the American government or its Swiss spokespersons. Those who carry dual American and Cuban citizenship can be subjected to even stricter obligations including service in the Cuban military. Street crime, warns the U.S. State Department, is a growing problem in Havana. Add to this a potential nuclear threat if the nuclear power plants being built there are put on line. According to the *Wall Street Journal,* January 21, 1997, the plants don't even meet minimal Russian standards for such plants.

Dominican Republic – U.S. passports and other documents are often stolen here. Beware of drug laws, which can land you in the pokey for 20 years. The peso is the only legal currency, yet at press time dollars were circulating freely. Don't trade on the black market. Although regular visitors boast that they trade on the black market "all the time," Americans have been arrested and fined for even small infractions. If you're traveling with children, they need separate passports.

WEDDINGS

Most islands welcome the increasingly popular trend among visitors to get married in paradise and they have streamlined the procedure as much as possible. Nevertheless, it's essential to allow plenty of time because all the paper work must be done during government business hours. Each island has its own holidays; government offices usually close earlier than other businesses. Start by rounding up all the paper work that will be required, including copies of any applicable divorce or death papers and parental consent for underage applicants. In islands where the official language is not English, you'll also have to provide translations of every document submitted.

Choose a hotel that has a full-time wedding planner, who can work miracles with the paper work as well as arranging flowers, a photographer, music, and the reception. Usually, residence in the islands of two or more business days is required before application can be made. If the wedding is to be performed by a clergyman, it will be helpful if your home clergyman coordinates with the island-based clergyman who will preside. This is especially important in Catholic rites.

Lastly, bring your wedding clothes in carry-on baggage. Murphy's Law requires that if luggage is to be lost, it will be the bags with the wedding gown, veil, tux, and all the matching shoes.

SOUR NOTES

Every vacation has its grace notes and its clams, those sour notes that can detract from an otherwise perfect vacation. Under individual chapters we've listed warnings but some generalities apply.

In most of the Caribbean be prepared for such things as:

Arrogant airlines *– American Air Lines and its subsidiary, American Eagle, "own" the Caribbean through its hub at Puerto Rico, so most ground support personnel (but not flight personnel) that we've encountered have a don't-give-a-damn attitude towards passengers and baggage. Food service is scanty if at all. If you have another airline choice from your home city, explore it. If you can avoid connections through Miami, especially on American Eagle, do so. Don't travel with a pet unless you can take it as carry-on luggage. Baggage handlers in the Caribbean are the roughest in the world.*

Bold birds *can turn outdoor dining into a swatting war. It's common for greckles or bananaquits to perch at your elbow, waiting for a chance to steal a morsel. And, as soon as you leave the table, they're on your plate. The more they're fed by tourists, the worse things become. At first, you think it's cute but just let one make a mess in your hair or your omelette and you're cured forever of sharing your table with poultry.*

Bloody sports *such as cockfights and bullfights are part of the Latin culture.*

Food attitudes *are different in the islands, where family loyalty and sharing are a way of life. Taking food is not a crime, so a cook may maneuver cleverly to minimize what you are fed and to maximize the leftovers that she, by common practice, takes home. If you are paying for food that is prepared by someone else in your lodgings or charter boat, take a close look at where your money goes.*

Island time *is a way of life in which nothing ever happens at the appointed hour. Except for official schedules such as closing time for government bureaus (which may close early, but never late) most things start many minutes later than the announced time. Nothing steams North Americans more than the feeling that locals are doing this just to get your dander up. It isn't you. It's the culture. Relax and enjoy it. Promptness is likely to be more reliable, but is not guaranteed, in the American and Dutch islands.*

Pushy vendors *are a problem in some islands. In most cases, beaches cannot be privately owned. To the vexation of hotel owners, local people come to tourist beaches to hawk trinkets, drinks, or dolls, and generally make pests of themselves. It can be colorful, but it can also be a pain in the neck. The basic rule is, don't touch. If you do, it is considered sufficient interest to keep bugging you until you buy.*

Starving animals *are heartbreaking to see, but they are a fact of life even in affluent islands. Skinny, starving dogs and cats roam the streets and beg around the edges of outdoor restaurants. By the bitter end of the dry season, known as "let go" season because desperate goats and cattle are let loose to find whatever grazing and water they can, these animals are reduced to skin and bones. At first, we tried to feed every stray we saw, especially the scrawny bitches that were nursing pups, but soon realized it was hopeless. Instead, we now send donations to local shelters and neutering clinics.*

WEIGHTS & MEASURES

Many speed limits and other road signs in the Caribbean are in kilometers and gasoline may be served in liters. Meat may be sold by the kilogram. A kilometer is .621 mile. A liter is 1.101 quarts; a British quart is 1.032 U.S. liquid quarts.

If you're math impaired, think of a kilometer as a bit more than a half mile, a liter as a generous quart, and a kilo as two pounds of ground round with one extra patty. If you're in a speed zone rated 50 kilometers per hour, don't go faster than 30 miles per hour.

8. SPORTS & RECREATION

The Caribbean has been one of the most sports-mad areas on earth since before European settlement. Ball courts used by the Arawaks and Caribs have been excavated and it's now known that games similar to those played by the Mayans were played here. The progress of South American Indians up the Caribbean chain could be traced by the ball fields because the game was played with a rubber-like ball made from chicle that could be harvested only on the South American mainland.

Puerto Ricans and Cubans are passionate baseball players, so North American ball fans will have no shortage of teams to cheer. Golf and tennis came to the islands with Scottish and British settlers. Today's sophisticated golf courses were designed by the biggest names such as Robert Trent Jones, Sr., Robert Trent Jones, Jr., and Pete Dye. Pétanque, which might be compared to boccie, is a favorite on the French islands.

Locals have their own favorite sports, and it's always fun for a visitor to see a spirited local game of soccer, rugby, or cricket. Most islands have large gyms, teams, and coaches for all the Olympic sports. See individual chapters for more coverage of the local sports scene.

BEACHES

About the only islands that do not attract travelers whose entire focus is the beach are Dominica and Saba. The best beaches, which have also attracted the most visitors and hotel building include **Cane Garden Bay** on Tortola, **Trunk Bay** on St. John, **Luquillo Beach** in Puerto Rico, **Seven Mile Beach** on Grand Cayman, **Shoal Bay** (or just about anywhere else) on Anguilla, **Palm Island** off Carriacou, **Scilly Cay** off Anguilla, **Negril Beach** in Jamaica, and **Grand Anse beach** on Grenada.

The Baths on Virgin Gorda are a spectacular spread of sand and cathedral-size boulders. Find your own favorite beach, and keep it secret. We did.

BICYCLING

Try **BACKROADS**, *Tel. 800/GO-ACTIVE,* for bicycle and mountain biking tours.

BIRDING

Birding tours worldwide are offered by **Field Guides Incorporated,** *Box 60723, Austin TX, Tel. 512/327-4953, Fax 327-9231; toll-free 800/728-4953.* Their Caribbean tours focus is on Trinidad and Tobago.

BOATING

There are more ways to get out on the Caribbean waters than can be mentioned here, but of special interest is **Club Nautico** *in Fajardo, Puerto Rico, Tel. 800/BOAT-RENT.* A worldwide membership organization, the Club rents powerboats to its members at a highly discounted price. Many travelers join by the year because it means a big savings on boat rentals at home and anywhere travels take them.

DIVING & SNORKELING

Even though there is a big difference between the training and equipment needed by scuba divers and mere snorkelers, both look for the clearest waters with the furthest visibility. Highlights include:

Bonaire has built most of its tourist business around diving, which is so good that many divers come back year after year. Night diving, which isn't always available elsewhere, is offered here.

Buck Island on **St. Croix** is a national park completely surrounded by waters filled with dive and snorkel sites. **Cane Bay** on St. Croix has spectacular drop-offs favored for wall diving.

Tobago has some of the best diving in the world because of the vast diversity of its marine life where major currents meet.

Curacao's underwater park is a paradise for divers and snorkelers. **St. John's Trunk Bay** is also a favorite with snorkelers, who can swim an underwater trail and follow the signs.

Grand Cayman, especially the area called **Stingray City,** offers awesome diving.. Reefs and wrecks are found at all levels.

The **Wreck of the Rhone** off **Salt Island** in the **Virgin Islands** is one of the most famous, photographed dives in the Caribbean.

Saba makes up in diving what it lacks in beaches. It is almost without equal as a dive destination.

FITNESS

For muscle building, slimming, toning, and other specialized workout vacations, try **Spa Finders,** *Tel. 212/924-6800 or 800/ALL-SPAS.*

GOLF

Among visitors, favorite golf resorts are:

Casa de Campo *in the Dominican Republic, Tel. 809/523-3333 or 800/877-3643,* has two 18-hole golf courses that are renowned for their diabolical difficulty. They're The Links and Teeth of the Dog.

El Conquistador, *San Juan, Puerto Rico, Tel. 787/863-1000 or 800/468-5228,* has an 18-hole championship golf course for the use of its guests.

Four Seasons Resort, *Nevis, Tel. 869/1111 or 800/332-3442,* is as challenging as it is varied and beautiful.

Half Moon Golf, Tennis, and Beach Club, *Montego Bay, Jamaica,* is a beautiful beach resort with an 18-hole golf course, *Tel. 876/953-2211 or 800/626-0592.*

Hyatt Dorado Beach, *Puerto Rico, Tel. 787/796-1234 or 800/233-1234,* is one of two resorts (the other is the **Hyatt Cerromar Beach**) that offer memorable golf to guests. Between the two resorts, which are side by side, you can play four courses.

Palmas del Mar, *near Humacao in Puerto Rico,* offers outstanding golf in an outstanding resort setting, *Tel. 787/852-6000 or 800/468-3331.*

Tryall Resort, *Montego Bay, Jamaica, Tel. 876/956-5660,* covers an old sugarcane plantation and is scenically placed where ocean breezes can play ball with your game.

Westin Rio Mar, *Puerto Rico, Tel. 800/WESTINS,* has two 18-hole championship golf courses in the shadow of El Yunque rain forest.

HIKING

According to outdoor writer M. Timothy O'Keefe, author of *Caribbean Afoot* (Menasha Ridge Press), the ten top hikes in the Caribbean are:

The Valley of Desolation and **Boiling Lake** *in Dominica,* a seven-hour round trip into what he calls a prehistoric setting.

La Soufrière Volcano *in Guadeloupe,* which he calls an "easy" climb.

Blue Mountain Peak, *Jamaica,* where hikers leave at 2 am to arrive in time to see the sunrise from the mountaintop.

Little Tobago, *Tobago,* is an easy hike on a small island that is a bird sanctuary.

Asa Wright Nature Preserve *in Trinidad* has pathways through what he calls an open-air aviary.

St. John, *U.S. Virgin Islands,* the entire island.

The Baths, *Virgin Gorda*. It's a tourist attraction, but hikers can walk the entire area beyond the crowds.

El Yunque, *Puerto Rico*. Again it's touristy, but once you get away from the bus stops there are miles of rain forest trails to explore.

Mount Qua Qua, *Grenada*.

Bloody River, *St. Kitts* is a brief walk into a canyon where you'll see about 100 Carib petroglyphs.

ABOUT GPS

*More and more tourists are relying on **Global Positioning Satellites**, long known to sailors and pilots as a navigation aid and now coming into land use in trucking fleets, auto travel, and even for hiking. GPS receivers, now available for about $200, fit in a shirt pocket. Taking their reading from three or more satellites, they can tell you exactly where you in relation to a known destination, such as your hotel or the place you parked your car at the airport.*

Until all maps and guidebooks are geo-coded to give the exact longitude and latitude of every hotel and point of interest, GPS won't replace street addresses. However, once you reach a spot, note your location, and program it into your receiver, you can always ask it how to get back there. It will point the right direction and tell you how far it is as the crow flies. And it's accurate to a matter of meters! If you'll be doing a lot of hiking and exploring on larger islands, you're ready for GPS.

HORSEBACK RIDING

Puerto Rico is especially well known for its paso fino horses. Many other islands also offer riding on mountain trails or beaches. Try **Excursions Extraordinaires**, *Tel. 800/678-2252.*

KAYAKING

Sea kayaking is catching on throughout the islands, so it's likely that your hotel has kayaks for rent or can arrange a kayak expedition for you. A company that can book your trip with major emphasis on kayaking is **Island Trails**, *Tel. 800/233-4366.*

SAILING

Most beach resorts have Sunfish and other small, non-motorized sailboats for guest use, often at no added cost. Fleets are also available at almost all of the all-inclusive resorts.

The two best places to get a bareboat are **The Moorings**, *Tel. 800/353-7289*, and **Nicholson Yacht Charters**, *Tel. 800/662-6066*. **Steve Colgate's Offshore Sailing School** in Tortola offers sailing instruction for future racers and cruisers, *Tel. 941/454-1700 or 800/221-4326*.

For crewed charters, contact the **Virgin Islands Charterboat League**, *Tel. 340/774-3944 or 800/524-2061*.

TENNIS

Virtually every large resort, including all the **Sandals** and **Club Meds** as well as most medium-size resorts in the Caribbean, offer tennis. See individual chapters for many more choices.

Biras Creek Estate *on Virgin Gorda* is the perfect hideaway for people who love tennis, sailing, the beach, and nature walks, *Tel. 340/494-3555 or 800/608-9661*.

Buccaneer Resort *on St. Croix* offers tennis on Laykold courts and a pro shop to non-guests as well as to guests, *Tel. 340/773-2100 or 800/255-3881*.

Grafton Beach Resort *on Tobago* has tennis courts and two air-conditioned square courts, *Tel. 868/639-0191, Fax 639-0030*.

Curtain Bluff *on Antigua* is one of the prettiest places in the world to play tennis, *Tel. 268/462-8400 or 800/672-5833*.

El Conquistador *in Puerto Rico* has a full-service tennis facility with a tennis pro, pro shop, clubhouse, and Har-Tru courts, *Tel. 787/863-1000 or 800/468-5228*.

Half Moon Golf, Tennis, and Beach Club, *Montego Bay, Jamaica,* is a wonderful place to stay as well as a superb tennis facility with a dozen courts, *Tel. 876/953-2211 or 800/626-0592*.

Hyatt Dorado Beach, *Puerto Rico, Tel. 787/796-1234 or 800/233-1234* is one of two resorts (the other is the Hyatt Cerromar Beach) that have plenty of tennis courts for day or night play.

Sandals, the all-inclusive resorts, offer a special tennis package *on Jamaica, Tel. 800/SANDALS*.

Spice Island Resort *on Grenada* has tennis play day or night in addition to a fabulous beach and the most luxurious luxury suites in the islands, *Tel. (473) 444-4258 or 800/223-9815*.

Wyndham Sugar Bay Resort *on St. Thomas* has a dozen Laykold courts, a stadium tennis court, a tennis pro, and plush resort facilities, *Tel. 340/777-7100 or 800/927-7100*.

WHITEWATER RAFTING

Book a rafting vacation with **Excursions Extraordinaires**, *Tel. 800/678-2252*.

WINDSURFING

Most beach resorts offer board sailers for guest use and, on good surfing beaches, concessions often offer board rentals. One company that specializes in vacation packages that center around windsurfing is **Sailboard Vacations**, *Tel. 800/252-1070.*

9. SHOPPING

Thanks to a growing network of international alliances such as NAFTA and the European Union, the words "duty free" are fast losing their magic around the world. Where once the traveler could save smartly in the Caribbean by buying duty-free French perfumes, English China, Irish crystal, and Scottish cashmeres, today's bargains lie only in the fact that you are paying full price minus whatever sales tax or VAT might have applied in your hometown.

For the canny shopper who buys on sale or at discounts, which are rarely seen in Caribbean duty-free shops, the savings can be unimpressive. Add to this the expense of shipping or the hassle of packing and carrying things home, plus the fact that the customs officer is waiting as you get off the plane, and the luster of old-fashioned Caribbean shopping fades.

It's still possible to buy everything from porcelain to silver and expensive watches, but today's tourist is taking a closer look at the works of a growing network of local artists, crafters, writers, chefs, sculptors, wood carvers, potters, ironmongers, goldsmiths, basket makers, photographers, publishers, ceramists, weavers, fabric designers, batik artists, knitters, lace makers and seamstresses. You can still shop for South American amethysts and South African diamonds, but you can also get unique gems, corals, and amber that are found only here.

Today's Caribbean shopper can walk past Chinese textiles and Italian leather goods to find exciting arrays of products made by local hands from local raw materials – many of them collectibles that will grow in value. Haitian paintings, for example, have soared in price and Jamaican art is not far behind. Every island has its artisans and artists, many of them gaining international attention.

On almost every island, locals have learned that it is more profitable to work with locally available products. Tropical flowers are turned into floral perfumes more compelling than any found in Paris. Locally-grown hot peppers end up in fiery sauces that travelers love to take home to their friends. Exotic fruits end up in jams and preserves, allowing visits to introduce seagrape or guava or nutmeg jelly to their friends at home.

Local sugar cane ends up not only in time-proven rums but in other alcoholic drinks enhanced by such tropic flavors as coconut, guavaberry, coffee, and spices. Hand-picked mountain coffees in Jamaica and Puerto Rico are world famous.

The Caribbean isn't always the "duty-free" shopping paradise that many travelers expect. If you're shopping for specific items, such as your Waterford pattern or a Kosta Boda vase, make note of hometown prices and compare them with what you find in the islands. According to travel shopping expert Suzy Gershman in *Travel Holiday* magazine, big savings in the Caribbean are rare. "In my experience, 10 to 20% discounts are the norm," she says. Often you can do better than that at home during a sale.

THE CONTRARIAN SHOPPER

Sorry, but we just can't rhapsodize as other guidebook writers do about the countless, look-alike, "duty-free" stores found throughout the Caribbean. How many expensive rings and watches can you wear? What's so good about French cosmetics and English woolens and Irish lace? Do you really need a $2,000 watch to tell time, and are you sure you couldn't get it at home at just as good a price?

When we travel, we look for the essence and heart of each destination. When we choose souvenirs, we hope to bring back only something that has meaning and lasting value, a souvenir that will always bring a destination alive for us again. We may buy a recording of local music, a bottle of perfume distilled from local flowers, a painting of a scene we loved, or a craft made by hands we personally grasped. It is this sort of shopping, tied to the land and its people, that we hope to bring you in these pages.

Island-grown spices turn up in liqueurs, cosmetics and soaps, preserves, jerk mixtures, and spice blends for everything from cakes to pot roast. Whole spices and native seashells are strung into necklaces. An ostrich farm on Curacao produces decorated ostrich eggs and ostrich leather. A turtle farm in the Caymans produces turtle meat and turtleshell products (which are forbidden entry to the United States). Local earths are turned into museum-quality pottery pieces. Shards of broken glass are fished from the sea after being tumbled into smooth-edged jewels, and are mounted to make brooches and earrings.

On almost every island, local palm fronds, straws, grasses and barks are made into basketry unique to that culture. Each island has its own laces too made from ages-old patterns passed from mother to daughter. Dominican cigars rival those from Cuba. Plantation-era antiques are sold in many island shops, and it's also possible to shop for new furniture made form native hardwoods.

The more you know about Caribbean cultures, the more fun it is to bring home souvenirs that capture some element of it: carnival masks, dolls in native costume, and santos, the carved saints so loved by Puerto Ricans. Great varieties of music come out of the Caribbean and now it has its own recording studios producing tapes and CDs. You can bring home the best in reggae, salsa, calypso, and steel drum, performed and recorded in the islands. And, if you want tee shirts, they are being printed in the Caribbean now too.

ABOUT WOOD CARVINGS

Throughout the Caribbean, woodcarvers ply their craft and offer it at prices that are, for the most part, hard to resist. Whether you're a serious collector or a novice, the biggest misstep is in buying a piece that is perfect in context but looks simply silly in your living room back in Manchester or Minneapolis. Most carvings are large, crude, and almost impossible to get into your luggage. They may also be (1) made in China or Africa, (2) made from green wood that will split when you get it back to the dry heat of your home, (3) full of worms – look for tiny holes – or (4) all of the above.

Another thing to check for is balance. If the piece is to be hung up or displayed on a flat surface, try it that way. It may sit or hang quite differently from the way it looks in the carver's hands in the village bazaar.

To get a serious sculpture as a serious investment, it's better to pay a little more to buy from a trusted gallery. When dealing with a native woodcarver, make sure you're talking the same currency. In the most remote areas where people deal almost exclusively in local currency, they are not quoting the price in dollars. Yet U.S. dollar prices are used almost exclusively in tourist areas and duty-free shops.

The Caribbean now has North American-style malls, some of them in special shopping centers built at quays where cruise ship passengers debark. By contrast you can also shop in scores of tiny shops sardined into centuries-old downtown buildings. Through the islands, entire new merchant classes have taken root, from the Indians and Pakistanis who operate so many of the shops, to ex-patriot painters and sculptors who came to the islands and never left. The fabulous Altos de Chavon artist colony in the Dominican Republic is one of the largest in the world.

To make the most of the Caribbean shopping trip, start before you leave home by finding out from your own country what you are allowed to bring back. Limits vary according to the island and according to the country of origin of goods you buy. For example, limits on local rums and liqueurs are usually more generous than allowances on French wines or Scotch whiskey. Locally-made goods can be brought into the United States almost without monetary limit, unlike trans-shipped luxury goods such as crystal and watches, on which duty must be paid on purchases after so-many dollars. Don't count on sales clerks in the islands to know these prohibitions and limits, or to tell you about them if they do know.

Write the **Superintendent of Documents**, *Mail Stop SSOP, Washington DC 20402-9328*, for information on the booklets *Tips for Travelers to the Caribbean* and *Know Before You Go*. Ask too about booklets covering other of your interests and concerns such as relocating to the islands, working abroad, travel health, and so on.

THE BEST ISLANDS FOR POWER SHOPPING

For Megabucks Shopping: if you're shopping for a really costly jewel, set of china, or watch, keep in mind that you can bring home more than twice as much in duty-free merchandise from the U.S. Virgin Islands than from other islands. From Puerto Rico, you can bring in unlimited merchandise tax free.

For Convenient Malls: the concentration of shops in downtown Charlotte Amalie, St. Thomas, makes for some of the Caribbean's most interesting browsing in old warehouses that have been selling goods for 400 years. Puerto Rico and the Caymans have well-stocked, modern, American-style malls. Quayside shopping in convenient centers is especially good at St. Lucia, St. Thomas, and the new (1999-2000) center at St. Martin. St. Croix also has a concentration of good downtown shopping at Christiansted.

For Bulk Shopping: if you are buying wholesale to stock your retail shops at home, shop the Tax-Free Zone on Curacao. Note that large quantities must be purchased; don't go here unless you buy by the case or containerload.

For Native Goods: shop Jamaica and Puerto Rico for art, Dominica for Carib baskets, the French islands for lace and embroideries, the Dominican Republic for amber, Bequia for model sailboats, St. Croix for Cruzan bracelets. Almost all the islands have local rums and liqueurs, and a number offer excellent coffee as well, particularly Jamaica, Puerto Rica, and the Dominican Republic.

For Imported Goods: Barbados is the place to buy products from England, Scotland, Wales, and Ireland. St. Thomas, St. Croix, and St. Martin have excellent selections of luxury goods from around the world. The Dutch islands have tempting arrays of goods from Holland. The French islands specialize in French perfumes at discount prices.

10. TAKING THE KIDS

West Indians love their children, and family is a strong and loving force here. Resorts that don't have children's programs can always find a capable babysitter for you. Those resorts that do cater to families with kids do it with a capital C.

At family-friendly places you can expect all the usual features such as a crib, children's pool, children's program, high chairs, and kiddy menu. Many resorts, especially on Jamaica, provide all these plus your own nanny or "Gal Friday" with each unit.

On the minus side, most nations outside the United States require its citizens to take responsibility for their actions. It's up to you to see that your children don't eat the eyes out of the handmade native doll, drown in the pool, swallow the landscaping, drink rum punch, or go crazy with a scooter or jetski. A lawsuit, if you could bring one at all, would probably be futile.

If your kids are old enough to be tempted by drugs, drill into them that foreign laws apply. At best you could all be thrown off the island after payment of a big fine. At worst, a young person could be thrown into a squalid jail beyond the help of Mom, Dad, or Uncle Sam. We saw a teenager pulled out of line for drug possession just as he was re-boarding a cruise ship at Montego Bay. You can bet that his family's vacation was ruined and his immediate future a nightmare.

CARIBBEAN WITH KIDS

If you're looking for a guide book catering to families, pick up a copy of Open Road's "Caribbean With Kids," by Paris Permenter and John Bigley, available in Spring 1998. The authors guide you to the best of the family-friendly resorts that are growing throughout the Caribbean.

It takes some planning to find the right resort for all children. Even those resorts that cater to children may not have programs for toddlers under the age of three or four, for children who are not potty trained, or for teenagers. Some resorts welcome children only in summer; some have separate sections for families so couples won't be disturbed. Exclusive **Caneel Bay**, for example, added a children's program after years of childlessness. Families are housed well away from cottages designed for couples, but many long-time Caneel Bay visitors still grouse about the policy.

Some children's programs operate all year; others are in session only during school holidays. Some resorts welcome children but don't want them in the dining room after 6:30 or 7pm. Do your homework and you'll have the time of your life.

KEEPING KIDS SAFE

The tropics hold few unique hazards for children. However, if your toddler is at the age when everything goes into its mouth, don't let it get hold of any plants, beads, seeds, sticks, or flowers. Even the beautiful oleander, a common landscaping shrub, can be poisonous when eaten. The manchineel tree, found on many tropical beaches, is so poisonous that rain dripping from its leaves can raise skin blisters.

As long as your child's shots are up to date, the Caribbean holds no special fears. Malaria and other tropical diseases are found only in the more remote areas of the most undeveloped island nations. Cuba is battling an epidemic of hemmorhagic dengue fever, which the government is trying to keep quiet.

Thankfully, rabies is virtually nonexistent, which is one reason why pet restrictions in the islands are so tight. It is, however, found on Trinidad, where bats are major rabies carriers. In any case, warn the children against befriending stray dogs and cats here and anywhere else. Hepatitis is no more common here than it is at home, but it is a worldwide health threat, so ask your pediatrician about protection for yourself and the children.

Mosquito and sandfly bites are a nuisance, easily evaded through the use of bug repellents. Teach children not to touch coral, sea urchins, or pretty jellyfish. They can sting. Wasps, scorpions, and spiders may be seen in the West Indies, just as they are almost everywhere, but aren't worth worrying about unless your child is subject to anaphylactic reactions. In years of tropic travel we have rarely seen them and have never been stung.

The tropics' chief threat is its greatest blessing: the sun. In fact, a tropical tree with red, peeling bark is known by natives as the Tourist Tree. Bring a good supply of a strong waterproof or water resistant sun block as well as light, coverup clothing and a hat with a brim. If the child is old enough to wear sun glasses, bring them too.

A bad burn can occur even on cloudy days. In a white boat on bright sea on a clear day, a burn takes only minutes. Apply the sun block before leaving your lodgings, and re-apply it according to manufacturer directions, especially if you're in and out of the water. According to *Travel Holiday* magazine, a sun block with the SPF of 15 blocks 96 per cent of the sun's burning rays and a 30SPF blocks 98.5 per cent. While a 45 SPF blocks less than three percent more than a 15, it lasts about three times as long.

Seasoned island visitors bring light cotton pajamas with long sleeves and trousers for snorkeling. In clear, shallow water, you may not feel the sun's heat but it can give a bad burn even underwater. Bring a big umbrella to shade tender young skin from sun and rain. Socks help protect bare feet from sun when swimming, and they cushion the fit of rented snorkel fins. Adopt the siesta habit, staying out of the sun at mid-day.

Take beach shoes (jellies, reef runners) for the whole family to protect feet against sharp coral, stones, and broken glass on the beach. Most resort beaches are sandy and clean, so you may not need the shoes after a first, exploratory swim.

Drink lots of water, avoiding sugary drinks, making sure that babies who can't talk also get frequent drinks. In the Indies' cooling breezes, perspiration is blown away and children can become dehydrated before you realize it.

Additional tips for traveling parents include:

• Don't board the airplane first even though people with children are invited to do so. Why confine restless kids any longer than necessary? Delta, for one, has stopped allowing parents with children to board first.

• Ask cabin attendants if any of the bathrooms have changing tables. Usually at least one does.

• Until the children are older, avoid islands that are reached by multiple transfers involving small airplanes, ferries, and other delays. For now, the big bird and direct flights are best. Remember that after your arrival you have to go through customs, immigration, and perhaps a long taxi ride on bad roads, usually in torrid heat.

• In the Caribbean, you can't count on wheels as you do at home. Strollers and wheeled luggage are no help where you must negotiate stairs, deep sand, and unpaved roads. Except for Puerto Rico and the U.S. Virgin Islands, where the Americans with Disabilities Act applies, wheelchair/stroller access is usually poor or unavailable. Consider getting a backpack to carry a small child. You'll need your own child safety seat for the airplane(s) and rental cars. Few rental agencies have them.

HOW TO HANDLE A JELLYFISH STING

For jellyfish stings, "Do not rub the wound," says Dr. Wayne J. Riley, director of the Travel Medicine Service at Baylor College of Medicine in Houston. Soak it in salt water, apply baking soda, and remove the animal's tentacles. For a man-o-war, use the same procedure but substitute vinegar for the baking soda. "In treating (these) wounds, do not use fresh water," says Dr. Riley. "The change in salt concentration will increase the toxin release."

Discomfort usually lasts only a few hours but if you have any reason to think a severe reaction is occurring, such as nausea or weakness, get professional help, urges Dr. Riley.

• Disposable hand wipes are lifesavers, but they're quickly gone. Instead, seal wet wash cloths in zippered plastic bags and use them to clean up sticky hands and faces. Each time you can get to a bathroom, they can be soaped and rinsed for unlimited re-use.

• Disposable diapers are available in all but the smallest island stores. Pack extra zip-top plastic bags for sealing up nasty diapers until they can be disposed up properly.

• A 36-inch inflatable swimming pool packs in less space than a rain coat, yet it blows up to provide hours of splashy fun for a toddler. If your lodgings have no baby pool, take your own.

• Take plenty of medicated baby powder for heat rash and, if the baby is susceptible, a good salve for diaper rash.

• Don't forget a plastic pail and shovel for building sand castles. The pail can serve as a catch-all for lots of small toys.

• Don't bring home seashells unless you know them to be empty and dry. Even an old shell may contain a hermit crab. Sealed in your luggage, the smell is indescribable.

BEST RESORTS FOR CHILDREN

Resorts that are especially recommended for children include the **Hyatts** that have Camp Hyatt, **Casa de Campo** in the Dominican Republic, **El Conquistador** or the **Westin Rio Mar** in Puerto Rico, **Chenay Bay Beach Resort** on St. Croix, **Sapphire Beach Resort & Marina** on St. Thomas, the **Sonestas** on Anguilla and Curacao, **Four Seasons** on Nevis, **Sandy Beach Hotel** on Barbados, and, on Jamaica, **Boscobel Beach**, **Franklyn D. Resort**, **Round Hill Hotel & Villas**, and **Holiday Inn SunSpree Resort**. See individual listings for many more kid-friendly resorts.

On the minus side are those resorts that have a supervised children's play center that is really more a place to warehouse children who would rather be out on the beach. When booking a family place that advertises a children's program, ask for more specifics about where the kids will play while you're on the golf course or tennis courts. Ask too about children's dining because many restaurants in the tropics don't open until 7pm, which is late for some children to eat.

THE PUERTO RICAN ADVANTAGE

In Puerto Rico, teenagers can learn Latin dances and conversational Spanish. Youngsters can learn to snorkel. Children of all ages can discover nature on their own level. Parents, grandparents, and children romp on beaches and in swimming pools. Children can stay happy in a supervised "camp" where they make crafts, play games, and hear stories. At most hotels, children under age 18 stay free in a room with two paying adults.

CONDADO PLAZA HOTEL & CASINO, *Tel. 800/468-8588*, has Camp Taino for children ages five to 12. The $25 fee includes lunch and camp fun from 10 a.m. to 4 p.m. The hotel also offers teenagers a video room, tennis courts, putting greens, and organized activities.

EL CONQUISTADOR RESORT & COUNTRY CLUB, *Tel. 800/468-5228* offers Camp Coqui for $38 per day including lunch. Age groups of three to nine and nine to 13 go on adventures to the resort's own Palomino Island, take nature hikes, learn crafts, and much more.

EL SAN JUAN HOTEL & CASINO, *Tel. 800/231-3320*, has a daily camp for ages five to 12 at a cost of $28 including lunch and gifts such as a disposable camera, tee shirt, and "sand dollars" for use in the game room.

HYATT RESORTS, *Tel. 800/233-1234* at Dorado Beach have bilingual, certified counselors who direct children's activities 9am to 4pm. The daily fee of $40 includes lunch and gifts such as a hat and, after the fourth visit, a Camp Hyatt backpack. Night camp is $28 per child.

WESTIN RIO MAR RESORT & COUNTRY CLUB, *Tel. 800/WESTIN-1*, has Camp Iguana where "kids are kings." The three-room camp center has an arts and crafts room, playroom, and a TV room that converts to a sleeping room for late night campers. For older children, the Westin offers sailing, tennis, and golf clinics for beginners through advanced. The price is $35 per day for 9am to 3pm including lunch and snacks. A half-day program from 9am to noon without lunch is $20.

WYNDHAM PALMAS DEL MAR RESORT, *Tel. 800/WYNDHAM*, provides a long list of children's groups, activities and discounts depending on the time of year. The Adventure Club plays daily 8:30am to 4:30pm with groupings for children ages four to 13. The rate of $95 weekly, $25 daily, and $15 per half day gets your child lunch, snacks, and a tee shirt.

11. ECO-TOURISM
& TRAVEL ALTERNATIVES

Environmental tourism is hot worldwide and the Caribbean has caught the fever for good reason. The islands have some of the world's most pristine beaches, most unspoiled waters, most virgin reefs, and ruins and rain forests that have yet to be fully explored. In few other regions of the earth can you find more a sense of ground-floor discovery.

Most islands have climbed aboard the eco-tourism bandwagon early, and often with such zeal that old-timers are surprised. Where lone travelers could once hike into the bush and set up camp, or cruising boats could drop anchor in remote coves where dinner could be speared, all sorts of new laws, permits, and prohibitions apply. Welcome to the new, environmentally-sensitive Caribbean. See individual chapters for the names of hiking guides, dive operators, and nature tours.

ECO-TOURISM

Agencies that can book your trip include:

BACKROADS, *801 Cedar Street, Berkeley CA 94710, Tel. 510/527-1555, fax 527-1444; toll-free 800/GO-ACTIVE* is a group that organizes walking, bicycling, hiking, and multi-sport adventure tours in the Caribbean for a few weeks in November and December. Featured are unspoiled islands known for their scenic beauty.

CARBONNA CARIBBEAN TOURS, *Box 3299. Longwood FL 32799,* offers nature tours, including dive tours, of Saba.

ECANTOS TOURS, *Tel. 800/272-7241,* offers trips to Puerto Rico's Mona Island where only 100 visitors are permitted at a time. A camping permit must be obtained, and all food, water and camping gear brought with you. All waste must be packed out. If you want to camp Mona Island on your own, a permit must be obtained from the Puerto Rico Department of Natural resources, *Tel. 809/724-3724.* Camp fees are $4 nightly for adults and $2 for children.

EXCURSIONS EXTRAORDINAIRES puts together packages involving mountain biking, horseback riding, water skiing, whitewater rafting, sailing and other activities in Tobago or and Margarita Island, *Tel. 800/678-2252*. The company can also design an entire package around board sailing.

ISLAND TRAILS, *P.O. Box 869, Springfield OR 97477, Tel. 800/233-4366, Fax 541/747-7781* offers hike-kayak, hike-bike, and hike-whale watching packages including island hoppers on Saba/Statia, Montserrat, and Dominica. Included are accommodations, guide, equipment, and most meals.

SENSE ADVENTURES, c/o Peter Bentley, Box 216, Kingston 7, Jamaica, *Tel. 876/927-2097* is your Jamaica connection. Guides, camping, and accommodations can be arranged in the Blue Mountains.

SWEAT EQUITY

Imagine spending your vacation working your socks off in Jamaica's Blue Mountains. You might paint a school, re-roof a children's home, catalog endangered butterflies, or sift through tons of dirt picking out pieces of Arawak pottery. It's possible through **Global Volunteers**, *375 East Little Canada Road, St. Paul MN 55117, Tel. 800/487-1074, Fax 612/482-0915*. You'll have the most satisfying time of your life and the cost of your hard-working "vacation" will be tax deductible.

SAILBOARDING

Book a sailboard vacation on Margarita Island, Bonaire, Cabrete, Barbados, or Aruba with **Sailboard Vacations**, *Tel. 800/252-1070*. Accommodations, instruction, and equipment are included.

SPA VACATIONS

With the explosion of interest in spas, healthful living, weight loss, muscle building, and other lifestyle-enhancing vacations has come a mushrooming of spa choices in the Caribbean. Some focus on total pampering with massage and therapy; others specialize in a lifestyle change such as heart attack rehabilitation or weight loss; still others accent a skill such as muscle building or toning. Your key to finding the right package is **SPA FINDERS**, *91 Fifth Avenue, New York NY 10003, Tel. 212/924-6800, Fax 924-7420, toll-free 800/ALL-SPAS*.

ECOTOUR SAILING

A 12-passenger luxury schooner that winters in the Caribbean, often with experts on board to conduct seminars on the environment is **Kathryn B.**, *Tel. 800/500-6077*. Rates are about $2,800 per person, double occupancy, per week. Itineraries vary each year.

12. FOOD & DRINK

Lucky the Caribbean traveler who gets into the neighborhoods to seek out small restaurants that are frequented by the islanders themselves. Foods here are made by cooks who learned island ways from their parents.

Stop at roadside stands, where sanitation standards are god-knows-what, to buy fresh fruit, homemade drinks such as mavi, an icy jelly nut, sizzling jerk fresh from the fire, fish tea, or goat water. In her book *Jamaican Cooking* (Macmillan), author Lucinda Scala Quinn tells of a Rastaman who cooks a big kettle of Peanut Porridge and ladles it out, with a topping of molasses, to passers-by on a Kingston street corner.

An entirely new language is to be learned here for every island group.

A CARIBBEAN FOOD DICTIONARY

Love 'em or hate 'em, the key to discovering different cultures is to try their foods, the more traditional the better. Take every opportunity to try them in restaurants, where they have been prepared by expert hands, and stop in the outback at roadside stands where a local person can tell you how to eat or prepare strange fruits and vegetables.

Here are some words that will help you in your search:

Accra: a fritter known in Jamaica as **stamp and go**, in Puerto Rico as **bacalaito**, in the French islands as **acrat de morue**, and in the Dutch islands as **cala**. The batter is made from ground beans and a meat or fish, usually salt cod.

Annato: a seed used as flavoring and coloring in Latin dishes.

Asopao: a Puerto Rican soupy stew usually made with rice plus chicken, pork or fish.

Ayacas are meat patties wrapped in leaves. They're found in the Dutch islands.

Bacalao is the Spanish word for salt cod, which persists as an island favorite centuries after refrigeration made it unnecessary to smother fish in salt as a preservative. It's found on many menus under its English or Spanish name.

Bakes: in Trinidad, baking powder biscuits that are fried.

Bananas, which are known as figs on some islands, come in so many shapes, colors, and sizes in the Caribbean that it's fun to try them all. Don't confuse them with plantains, which never soften and sweeten. They are cooked as a starch.

Bammy is a cassava bread usually sold by "bammy ladies" on the street and in native markets in Jamaica..

Blaff is named for the sound made when live fish are thrown into a big pot of spiced boiling water.

Boterkoek are Dutch butter cookies.

Boucan: another word for barbecue and the source for the word buccaneer.

Breadfruit: literally a staff of life in some islands, it's a starchy fruit that shows up on almost every dinner plate fried, baked, or boiled. It has little taste of its own.

Cachapas are corn pancakes served in the Dutch islands.

Calabaza: any of several varieties of squash, usually called pumpkin.

Calas are bean fritters.

Callaloo: the word refers to the green, which could be compared to spinach, and also to a soup made with the greens plus crabmeat.

Capsicum: another name for peppers, which are found in huge variety and abundance, from sweet to fiery, in Caribbean kitchens.

Carambola: a very tart citrus often called star fruit because of its shape. It's sliced thinly and used as a garnish, usually in drinks.

Cashew apple: the part of the cashew that produces the nut, this apple-size red fruit may be stewed or made into jelly.

Cassareep is a flavoring ingredient made by reducing grated cassava root.

Cassava, also called manioc, yuca, or mandioca. More familiar to us as tapioca, this starchy root can be poisonous if eaten raw. It's said that many of the native Arawaks and Caribs committed suicide by eating it to avoid being taken and enslaved by the Spanish.

Chayote is a pear-like vegetable that has little taste but adds a nice crispness to a salad. It can also be cooked and buttered like squash. In French islands it's called christophene and may be served stuffed. In other islands it's called chocho.

Cherimoya is a sweet, juicy fruit.

Cocido: stew in Spanish speaking areas.

Coconut is a basic staple, served in countless main dishes, drinks, and desserts. If you buy from a roadside stand, let the seller remove the husk and either crack it for eating or hole it for drinking. Coconut water is cool and refreshing but if the nut is too green its water can cause diarrhea in some people. Cold "jelly" nuts are sold along roadsides.

Conch: picture the seashell that sounds like the sea when you hold it to your ear. The delicate white meat from this shell is served in fritters, chowder, or "cracked," which means pounded, dipped in cracker crumbs, and fried. In conch salad, it's served raw and marinated in lime juice. It can be compared to breast of chicken. In French islands it's called lambi.

Coo-coo: a buttery cornbread or polenta studded with okra.

Court Bouillon: (pronounced coor bweeyon) in the French islands does not refer to a liquid as it does elsewhere, but to poached fish.

Crapaud: a large frog that tastes like chicken.

Dolphin, the food fish, does not refer to Flipper, the bottle-nose dolphin, but to a meaty, iridescent fish known in the Pacific as mahi-mahi and in the Spanish Caribbean as dorado.

Djon djon: small Haitian mushrooms.

Duckanoo, spelled many ways, is a steamed cornmeal pudding served as a sweet.

Dumb Bread: a dense, crusty, non-yeast bread popular in the Virgin Islands. It derives its name from Dum, which refers to an Indian way of baking bread.

Dumplings are a common starch accompaniment for a Caribbean meal. They can be made with flour or cornmeal, with or without leavening, and are cooked in boiling water, broth, or stew. In Jamaica, they're also called **fufu** or **spinners**.

Escabeche: Fish and sometimes poultry that is cooked, then pickled. In Jamaica it's called **escovitch**. Not to be confused with seviche, which is marinated raw fish.

Festival is a fritter made with flour and cornmeal, deep fried, and sold to go with fried fish. It is flavored with vanilla and allspice.

Frio-frio: means cold-cold and refers to a snow cone, a paper cone filled with crushed ice and dosed with a fruit-flavored syrup.

Fungi, also spelled **funchi** or **fungee**, is a creamy cornmeal pudding usually served as a starch course. In Barbados it's called **coo coo** and in Haiti, **tum-tum**.

Genep, spelled many ways, is a common dooryard fruit rarely served in restaurants or sold at road stands, but you may be offered some. It has a large seed and a sweet, gluey flesh. Pop it into your mouth and smoosh it around for a while, then spit out the seed.

Goat is as familiar to island tables as lamb is to North American menus. It looks and tastes much the same too. It may be called mutton or goat mutton. In Spanish islands it is called **cabrito**. **Goat Water** is actually a hearty soup.

Grizzadas are coconut tarts, sold at almost every market and served at every church bazaar.

Groundnuts is the old African name for peanuts, which are used here in main dish recipes.

Guava is a tartly astringent fruit, lumpy in appearance and loaded with Vitamin C. It appears in ice cream, tarts, and other sweets but especially in firm, sweet guava jelly that is served with cheese and crackers as a dessert. Guavaberry is a cranberry-size red or yellow fruit that grows on trees and is used to flavor liqueurs.

Jack fruit: also called **jaca** or **jaquier**, it looks like a huge breadfruit and has a terrible smell. Its flesh, however, is sweet and its seeds, like breadfruit seeds, can be roasted like chesnuts.

Johnny cake: a cornbread in the United States, Johnny cake in the islands is made with white flour and may be baked or deep fried. Its name derives from "journey" cake because it's a good travel staple.

Kachoiri is a fritter made with garbanzo flour and green onions.

Keshi yena is a favorite in the Dutch islands. It's Edam cheese stuffed with meat, chicken, or fish.

Land crab: anyone who has encountered one of these sci-fi night-mares on a dark beach immediately discards any romantic notions about making love on moonlit sands. The idea of eating these scavengers is even more repulsive, but in skilled hands they're a succulent sensation. The crabs are captured and put on a diet of clean corn for several days until they lose their gamey taste. Only then are they served in the shell, in chowders, and in other traditional crab recipes.

Langouste: also called **langosta** or **lobster**, the spiny lobster provides a chunk of sweet, rich meat in its tail, which is the only part that is eaten.

Loquat: also called Japanese plum in the United States, it's a small, sweet fruit the size of an apricot.

Mamey apple: a colorful favorite on fruit plates, this juicy red fruit is similar to mango.

Mango: a peachy, juicy, very sweet fruit that comes in many shapes, colors, and sizes. Press it with the thumb. When it yields gently, it's ready to peel and eat. Some people are allergic to the skin, so peel it with caution.

Manicou is opossum, which is popular in Grenada.

Mofongo: a Puerto Rican favorite made from boiled, mashed plan-tains. They have little taste of their own and are seasoned to the chef's whim.

Old sour: the juice of sour orange trees (you haven't tasted sour until you've tried wild oranges) is salted and allowed to age. It's a popular sauce, shaken over foods much as you'd use vinegar.

Papaya is a sweet, melon-like fruit ranging from deep orange to delicate yellow, often served for breakfast. Papaya, also called **pawpaw,**

lachosa, or **fruta bomba**, can be peeled, boiled, buttered, and served as a vegetable when it is unripe.

Pasteles: also called **ayucas**, it's a mixture of meat and some starch such as cornmeal plus raisins, almonds, and other flavorings and then steamed in a plantain leaf. In the Dutch islands, meat patties are called **pastechi**.

Patty: pronounced pahtty in Jamaica, and called **pastelitis**, **pastelillos**, or **pastechi**, these are meat pies, perfect for lunch on the go. Down-island, **rotis** are somewhat the same. Think of a Cornish pasty, an inexpensive and filling dish.

Peas: could refer to any number of beans, usually dried, such as kidney beans, habichuelas (red kidney beans), gandules (also called pigeon peas, goongoo, or gunga peas) or frijoles negros (black beans). Some form of peas/beans and rice is a staple dish in most islands. When referring to green peas, islanders usually say English peas.

Pepper Pot or pepperpot is one dish in Trinidad and another in Jamaica because of the different seasonings favored. In both cases, it's a soup or stew.

Picadillo is a Cuban classic that is a favorite in Miami and Key West as well as in Cuba itself. Made with ground beef, it's somewhat like sloppy joe with raisins and sliced, stuffed olives.

Pineapple: they're black on Antigua and on Nevis are giants that can weigh as much as eight pounds.

Pilau is also called **pilaf** or **pelau**, a rice dish that often includes meat, poultry, or fish. It may also be just rice and peas.

Plaintains look like bananas, but don't try to eat them raw. They're cooked as a starch or are thinly sliced, fried in oil, salted, and served as a snack. Boiled in a stew, they have only the faintest banana taste and tend to take on the flavor of whatever they are cooked with.

Rotis are dough wrapped around a mixture of meat and potatoes, often spiced with curry.

Rundown is pickled or salt fish cooked with coconut milk, usually served with boiled bananas.

Sanchoco is a Spanish stew, made differently in each stewpot but basically a blend of meat and vegetables.

Sapodilla have a short season, so be sure to try them if you have a chance. Furry green or brown skin peels away to reveal a sweet pulp that tastes like a very juicy pear. Also called **naseberry**.

Scotch bonnet is one of the hottest peppers under the sun.

Sea urchin: the spiny menace that you try to avoid when swimming or diving produces delicious, caviar-like eggs. Also called **sea eggs** or, in the French islands, **oursin**.

Shaddock: also called **pomelo**, is a pungent, grapefruit-like fruit named for the Captain Shaddock who first brought seeds to the islands from Polynesia. It's also called **pomelo**.

Sofrito: a sauce that is central to many Latin dishes. It's made with onions, garlics, spices, tomatoes, peppers, and a little ham.

Sopito: a rich chowder made with fish and coconut milk.

Soursop: a horrible looking fruit with a heavenly taste somewhat like kiwi.

Stamp and go refers to codfish fritters, especially in Jamaica.

Star apple has a short season and is tricky to harvest, so count yourself lucky if you get a chance to try one. Under its purple flesh is a jelly-like sweetness.

Sweet potato or **boniato** comes in many colors and may not look at all like the familiar sweet potato eaten in North America. One type of sweet potato is called **tannia**.

Taro is also called **dasheen**, **tannia**, **malanga**, or **elephant's ear**. It looks like a baking potato, has a bland taste, and is used as a starch or filler. Taro leaves are also called callaloo or elephant's ears. Fritters made from taro leaves and split-pea flour are known as **sahina**.

Tatou, or armadillo, is eaten in Grenada.

Totoes and **Bullas** are Jamaican sweets sold at bakeries and snack counters. They're made with flour, spices, and the familiar cookie ingredients.

Tripe Soup is a specialty in the Dutch islands.

Ugli fruit: sometimes seen now in North American supermarkets, this cross-bred fruit was developed in Jamaica by joining orange, grapefruit, and tangerine. It's ugly to look at, sweet and citrusy to eat. Jamaicans, whose language borrows from Cockney and Irish, pronounce it *whoogly*.

Yam: different botanically from what we call the sweet potato, this enormous tuber has a furry skin and starchy meat that may be white, orange, or red.

DRINKS OF THE CARIBBEAN

A wise mother once cautioned her children never to drink anything with an umbrella in it. Caribbean drinks tend to be sickly sweet and fruity, laced with rum, and capable of delivering a delayed knockout that catches newcomers unaware. At one all-inclusive resort where all drinks are on the house, we asked how they could afford to serve unlimited bar drinks. "It only takes one day," chuckled the manager. "Drinking drops off dramatically after that. If fact, some guests never drink again."

Rum punch, called *planteur* in the French islands, is every bartender's pride, and each has his or her own secret recipe. Most are largely a blend of sugary fruit juices. The more subtle, untouristy punches combine light and dark rum with a little lime juice and ice.

Every islander has a favorite rum, often tied in with loyalty to a local distillery or bottling plant, and they love it when tourists ask for their recommendations. Reputable bottlers put the country of origin on their labels, so you'll soon be able to make a wise choice. **Cruzan** comes from St. Croix, **Westerhall** from Grenada, **Gosling's** from Bermuda, **Bacardi** mostly from Puerto Rico. On Grand Cayman, which has no sugar cane, blended Jamaican rums under sold under the **Tortuga** label. **Pusser's Rum**, sold in its own bar in Tortola, was the official rum of the Royal Navy. Although some of the cheaper, no-name rums taste like kerosene, it's possible to get a superb rum for less than the cost of the Coke you mix it with.

Light rums are recommended for use in drinks where gin or vodka might be used, such as martinis. Medium dark rums are the color of bourbon or scotch and are good in almost any drink. Myers dark rum is in a class by itself ` – inky, acrid, and the finishing touch in most good rum punches.

RUM PUNCH RECIPE

The time-honored recipe for the perfect punch is easy to remember: One of sour, One of sweet, Three of strong, Four of weak.

The sour can be lemon or lime juice, the sweet is simple syrup (two cups sugar boiled with one cup water, then cooled), the strong is the rum, and the weak is water or fruit juice. Measured by the shot, cupful, or hogshead, the proportions are the same. Depending on the type of rum and juices you choose, you can create an exotic new punch with each try. Traditionally, it's served with a few specks of grated nutmeg.

Caribbean Drinks

Carib beer is brewed in St. Kitts and Trinidad, with each island claiming theirs the finest.

CSR is a clear, sugar cane-based liquor unique to St. Kitts and Nevis. Often mistaken for rum, it is really more like vodka with a faint hint of white rum. It's usually mixed with a grapefruit-flavored Caribbean soft drink called Ting.

Guavaberries are harvested in the islands and made into a liqueur best known in St. Maarten.

Matrimony is a Jamaican fruit drink made from oranges and star apples

Mauby: made from tree bark, spices, and sugar, this drink is non-alcoholic.

Mavi is a slightly fermented drink made from bark. It's sold along Puerto Rican roadsides.

Mistress Bliden: a specialty of Little Dix Bay on Virgin Gorda and served only during winter holidays, this potent liqueur is made from prickly pear cactus.

Purple Rain is a blend of vodka, blue Curacao, and fruit juices.

Shrob: more likely to be called shrub in English islands, this is a French island liqueur made from rum and bitter oranges.

Coffees of the Caribbean

The world's new love affair with coffee brings new awareness of the variety, quality, and subtle shadings of the coffees to be tasted in the Caribbean. Most notable among them is the small harvest of Puerto Rican coffee, so cherished that it is sent to the Vatican.

Probably the most famous and abundant of Caribbean coffees is Jamaica's **Blue Mountain** bean of the arabica family, which has more intense fragrance and taste and only one-third the caffeine of the South American robusta bean. Costs are higher because the plants are propagated and cultivated by a method that requires five years until the first cash crop. Climate must be just right – cool and moist in the high elevations of the Blue Mountains. The beans, actually cherries, must be hand picked one by one.

Legend says that the first coffee plants, which are native to Yemen and had been introduced into Europe, were sent to Martinique by France's Louis XV in 1723. Of the three plants, two died and the survivor ended up in Jamaica. Whatever the true story, Jamaica's governor brought seedlings in from Martinique in 1728 and encouraged coffee planting as an alternative to sugar, on which the island economy was totally dependent.

13. BEST PLACES TO STAY

These are my picks for the best places to stay throughout the Caribbean. Rates are for a double room in high season. Check with individual chapters for further information about these hotels in their island context.

ANGUILLA

SONESTA BEACH RESORT, *Rendezvous Bay West, Anguilla, British West Indies. Tel. 264/497-6999, Fax 264/497-6899. In the U.S. and Canada dial 800/SONESTA. It's three miles from the airport or an $18 cab ride for two. Rooms start at $290; ask about packages. Suites start at $410. The resort closes in September.*

Straight out of Arabian Nights, the former Casablanca Resort (the name remains in the resort's restaurant) is a picture postcard with a moon of satin sand beach, rustling palm trees, and a Moorish motif lavished with intricate mosaics, stained glass, arches, and fretwork as fine as any Arabian palace. The 100 rooms and suites are plushly appointed with marble baths, individual balconies that look out to sea towards St. Martin, ceiling fans, mini-bars, hair dryers, safes, and fabrics dyed in tropical hues. Luxury appointments in the spacious rooms include satellite television, in-room safes, and hair dryers. The resort has its own hair salon.

Dining is poolside at the Seabreeze, which specializes in tandoori grill, or more formally at the Casablanca with its fringe of lacey openwork allowing ocean breezes to steal through. In the nearby Casablanca bar you almost expect to find Bogie and Bergman, and Sam at the piano. Or, order from room service, which offers breakfast, lunch, and dinner until midnight. Afternoon tea is complimentary.

Children's dining is from 6pm to 7pm, and Sonesta's popular children's programs are available according to the season. Watersports equipment is provided for kayaking, snorkeling, or board sailing, or the hotel can arrange a dive, sail, island tour, baby sitter, or fishing trip. There's no charge for court time on the lighted plexiplane tennis courts or for using the Fitness Center or massive, beachfront pool.

For a large family or group, ask about a week in a four-suite villa complete with kitchen and living area. Each suite is privacy-protected by double doors and has its own en suite bath; villas have private pools and a privacy fence.

ANTIGUA

CURTAIN BLUFF, *P.O. Box 288, Antigua. Tel. 268/462-8400, Fax 268/462-8409, U.S. and Canada 888/289-9898 or 212/289-8888. The 63-room resort hotel is on Old Road, 35-minute taxi ride from the airport. Rates start at $655 double and $555 single including gourmet meals.*

Snowy cottages blend against the bluff like a nun's wimple, a sight as arresting as the first view of the Sydney Opera House. It is all part of a plan hatched by Howard Hulford who fell in love with Antigua as a young pilot and came back to stake his claim. Before building, he camped on the property until he knew every nuance of the breezes and night sounds. Today as resident owner, he is the hotel's most enthusiastic guest, inviting other guests to his home for cocktails at least once a week. Rooms are done in warm beiges and blues, with wicker furniture and straw mats on the floors under raised pine ceilings.

The list of perks brings new meaning to the term "all inclusive:" sailing, waterskiing, dive trips, snorkeling, tennis, swimming in the 75-foot-long pool, deep sea fishing, squash, a putting green and equipment, croquet, fitness facilities and aerobics classes plus three meals chosen from extensive menus, afternoon tea, cocktails and canapes, and entertainment every evening. Hulford will even stamp your postcards for mailing! Only vintage wines from his extensive cellar, beauty shop services, and airport transfers are extra. For late departures, a changing room is available.

Rooms have telephones, 110-volt current, and room and bar service at no extra charge. The dress code requires beach coverups at lunch and breakfast and jackets (but not ties) for gentlemen after 7pm, December 19 through April 14, except on Sunday and Wednesday. "No jeans, please," says Hulford, who prefers that guests wear a collared shirt and enclosed shoes in the evening.

BARBADOS

PEMBERTON PRINCESS HOTELS, *Side-by-side sister hotels are the Royal Pavilion, Porters, Parish of St. James. Tel. 246/422-4444, Fax 246/422-0118, U.S. 800/223-1818; Canada except Toronto, 800/268-7176; Toronto Tel. 416/964-6641; and Glitter Bay, Porters, Parish of St. James. Tel. 246/442-*

4111, Fax 246/422-1367. U.S. Tel. 800/223-1818; Canada except Toronto, 800/268-7176; Toronto Tel. 416/964-6641. Rates at the 83-room Royal Pavilion resort start at $445. Suites and penthouse suites with one, two, and three bedrooms are available. Beach House suites start at $480. Rates at this 75-unit Glitter Bay start at $565. Suites and villas that sleep up to six persons are available. Add $60 per person daily for breakfast and dinner. During some periods, children under age 12 can't be accommodated. During low season, children stay free in a parents' room.

Together, Glitter Bay and the Royal Pavilion are known as **Pemberton Princess Hotels** under management by Princess International (of Bermuda Princess fame).

At the **Royal Pavilion**, the more elegant and quiet of the two, drive up an avenue of royal palms to a grand sweep of greenery and blooms to what looks like a Mediterranean mansion. Moorish arches open onto endless sea views in this cool, three-story white building on a brown sugar beach lined with palm trees and flowering shrubs. All 72 junior suites have ocean views from a private balcony or patio, two twins or one king-size bed, clock radio, safe, telephone, air conditioning, hair dryer, and mini-bar with refrigerator. Next to the tennis courts, a three-bedroom villa makes a spacious home for three couples or a large family.

Play tennis on astroturf courts, swim in the pools and through the waterfall, or use any of the non-motorized watersports equipment at no added charge. Play golf at the Royal Westmoreland nearby or let the concierge book your scuba or deep-sea fishing trip. The air-conditioned fitness center has all the latest Life Cycle equipment, and a masseuse on call.

Dine in the two restaurants here or in the sister property, Glitter Bay, next door. Afternoon tea and the weekly manager's cocktail party are the best way to meet interesting people from all over the world, especially from England. Or, if you prefer a private hideaway, order from room service around the clock.

Sir Edward Cunard, the cruise ship magnate, chose the **Glitter Bay** site along the Platinum Coast to build his mansion, designing it after the family palazzo in Venice. In its day, the greathouse and its guest houses entertained the rich and famous of the international jet set. A new day dawned in 1981 when the home became an exclusive hotel. A Princess International property, as its sister hotel next door, the Royal Pavilion, this one rises four stories into the sunshine, with most rooms offering garden and pool views and some overlooking the ocean. Just footsteps from the sea, the Beach House has five suites that can be rented separately. Play tennis, swim in the pool, use any of the sailboats or snorkel gear, or go water skiing, all at no added charge. Golf, deep-sea fishing, and scuba diving can be arranged for a fee.

Use the fitness center, visit the beauty/barber shop, or shop in the boutiques. Dining is in Piperade, which has a weekly floor show, or in either of the two restaurants at the Royal Pavilion. Afternoon tea and a manager's weekly cocktail party are on the house; room service can be brought 24 hours a day.

GRAND BARBADOS BEACH RESORT, *Carlisle Bay, Parish of St. Michael. Tel. 246/426-0890, Fax 246/436-9823; U.S 800/742-4276. Rates at this 133-unit hotel start at $250. It's a mile from Bridgetown and ten from the airport.*

Active business and leisure travelers treasure this hotel for its closeness to town and the horse track, and its on-site windsurfing school, health club, diving, sailing and snorkeling. They're all complimentary.

Relax on one of the beach chairs lined up on a long pier built out over the clear, aquamarine water. Burrow into the sun-warmed beach sands, or soak in the whirlpool to lose the winter blues. Golf and horseback riding are nearby. The hotel has its own bars and two restaurants with nightly entertainment. Rooms have mini-bar, satellite television, air conditioning, radio, and telephone.

BARBUDA

K CLUB, *Barbuda, Antigua, West Indies. Tel. 268/460-0300, Fax 268/460-0305; in the U.S., Canada, Puerto Rico, and U.S. Virgin Islands, 800/223-6800. Rates at this 36-room, nine-suite resort start at $500 including all meals. From Antigua airport, take a 12-minute flight to Barbuda aboard the Club's own airplane and transfer to ground transportation for a 15-minute ride.*

Fashion designer Krizia owns and oversees this elegant European resort. Set in a 230-acre shorefront park, it is a community of white bungalows, each nestled in a privacy screen of greenery and facing an incredibly white sand beach. The cuisine is Mediterranean; the wine list comprehensive. Dress in your most chic resort wear; your fellow guests are likely to be pace-setters from the worlds of fashion, industry, and entertainment.

Swim in the sea or pool, water ski, snorkel, play tennis day or night, play the nine-hole golf course, or enjoy the cozy game room, video room, and library. Massage is available and deep sea fishing can be arranged.

CURACAO

SONESTA BEACH RESORT & CASINO, *Piscadera Bay, P.O. Box 6003, Curacao. Tel. 5999/736-8800, Fax 5999/462-7502. From the U.S. and Canada dial 800/SONESTA or 800/766-3782. Rates at the 248-room resort start at $255 for a double in high season plus a choice of optional meal plans.*

Visitors are often struck silent when they see the dramatic hotel entrance for the first time. A grand, butter-yellow greathouse design has been translated to the 20th century with massive white columns and wings that go on forever. A pool runs through the lobby, falling off the edge into nothingness while the eye falls on the big swimming pool below and, beyond it, endless sea.

Rich pastels and jewel tones are used in the white, light guest rooms. Each room has its own terrace or balcony, television with remote control, safe, iron and ironing board, and mini-bar as well as original art from the famous Sonesta collection. Turndown service and robes are available on request. If you like planned activities, be sure to ask about a schedule that includes a few choices each day: Papiamento lessons (the local *patois* language), a fitness walk along the Koredor, beach volleyball, or merengue classes.

Dine Italian style in Portofino or in the covered Palm Cafe outdoors. The Emerald Bar & Grill is a supper club with piano serenades and a special, late-night supper menu. Poolside, the Seabreeze serves frosty drinks, sandwiches, and grilled favorites. Play blackjack, roulette, craps, mini-baccarat or Caribbean stud poker in the Emerald Casino. Outside there's complimentary tennis, a sandy beach (wear beach shoes for the few rocky stretches), a swimming pool with swim-up bar, two big whirlpools, and a full list of watersports. The children's play area is on a grassy spot near the beach. If you want to play golf, the concierge can arrange it at the nine-hole Curacao Golf and Squash Club 15 minutes away. The Fitness Center offers aerobic and strength-building equipment, sauna, plunge pools, steam room, and massage.

Sonesta's popular Just Us Kids program plays Wednesday through Sunday from 10am to 4:30pm for children ages five to 12. For business travelers there's a full business center with computers, fax, copier, and secretarial services; the shopping arcade is a mini-mall of five shops. A car rental service is on property but the hotel also runs a free daily shuttle to Willemstad for duty-free shopping. In the lobby there's a full-service tour desk, but tours must be paid in cash or travelers checks. They can't be charged to your room or to a credit card.

DOMINICAN REPUBLIC

HOTEL V CENTENARIO INTER-CONTINENTAL SANTO DOMINGO, *Avenue George Washington 218, mailing address Box 2890, Santo Domingo. Tel. 809/221-0000, toll-free 800/327-0200. Rates at this 200-room, 29-suite hotel start at $230. It's a ride of about 25 minutes from the Santo Domingo airport.*

Your air conditioned room or suite overlooks the Caribbean from the heart of the capital's Malecón, the seaside boulevard that is the center of all things in the capital. Suites, which have balconies, include 20 sea-front suites, deluxe club suites, and a Presidential Penthouse suite the size of Rhode Island. The hotel is a skyscraper built with interesting angles so your room isn't cookie-cutter square. In a setting of sandy beiges and mellow melons, you'll live the big-city life with 24-hour room service, laundry and valet service, a casino, and a choice of restaurants and bars. Rooms have color cable television with 35 channels, marble bathroom with hair dryer, dual-line dial telephone, mini-bar, safe, radio, and a connection for your modem. The complex offers underground parking, a swimming pool with outdoor whirlpool, shops, a floodlit tennis court, air conditioned square courts, massage and workout facilities, and a paddle tennis court. The hotel has full conference facilities and secretarial service too, so it's an ideal choice for the business traveler as well for the pleasure traveler who prefers a full-service city hotel.

GRENADA

CALABASH HOTEL, *L'Anse aux Pines, mail address P.O. Box 382, St. George's. Tel. 473/444-4334, Fax 473/444-5050. Rates at this 30-suite hotel start at $350 including breakfast brought to your room and afternoon tea. Add $35 adults and $17.50 children for dinner. The hotel is on the south shore of the island, ten minutes or a $10 taxi ride from the airport.*

Lush lawns center a cluster of villas that turn their other face to the sea. The beach is baby powder dappled with the shade of coconut palms and sea grapes; the water clear as gin fizz. Rooms are a splendor of wicker and pastels, each with its own whirlpool or plunge pool in a very private garden. Mornings begin with breakfast served on your private balcony by your own maid. Work out in the gym, play tennis day or night, swim in the sea or pool, use the complimentary watersports equipment, shop the boutique, then dine in the hotel, home of one of the island's best restaurants. After dinner, go to the library to read or play snooker. The manager throws a cocktail party once a week; live music plays often at the pool bar, grounds, or beach bar. The resort is dressy, with shorts and jeans not acceptable at dinner. Golf is ten minutes away.

In high season, don't bring children under age 12 or, for the rest of the season, children under age 3. Children of all ages are welcome in summer but kids under age six should not be in the bar and restaurant after 6pm. Babysitters are available, and children can be served from room service.

SPICE ISLAND BEACH RESORT, *Grand Anse, mail address P.O. Box 6, St. George's, Grenada, West Indies. Tel. 473/444-4258. Rates at this 56-suite resort are $375 to $900 including breakfast and dinner. It's ten minutes or $10 from the airport.*

We thought we'd seen luxury suites before, but the Royal Private Pool Suites at this resort are beyond superlatives. Imagine opening a garden gate that enters your own, very private garden with a 16 x 12-foot swimming pool, sauna, exercise bicycle, patio with lounges and dining table, and flowering vines twining down varnished hardwood fences. Stepping into your suite you find a sitting area with television and full sound system, a bedroom richly hung with brocades and furnished in handmade mahogany pieces, and marble bath with double whirlpool and bidet.

Outside your door is one of Grenada's best beaches, thick with sugary dunes and awash in incandescent blue waters. Even the humblest suites here are grand, with double whirlpools sitting under big skylights, air conditioning, direct dial phone, clock radio, coffee maker, mini-bar, built-in hair dryer, private balcony or patio and spacious sitting area decorated with original Susan Mains paintings. Suites with private plunge pools are enclosed by a privacy fence.

Order breakfast from room service at no added charge. Dining is in the hotel's locally popular, open-air, beachfront restaurant where the chef melds local produce, spices, and seafood with continental presentations. Manager's cocktail parties, offered several times a month, feature full bar service and scrumptious canapes, not just the rum punch offered at some hotels' freebie parties.

Included are use of the air conditioned fitness center, tennis courts day or night, bicycles, watersports equipment, and greens fees at a nearby course. The hotel doesn't have a pool but guests who don't have private pool suites can use the one at the resort's sister property, Blue Horizons. Laundry, dry cleaning, babysitting, and tours can be arranged.

JAMAICA

TRIDENT VILLAS & HOTEL, *Route 4, Port Antonio, Jamaica, West Indies. Tel. 876/993-2602, Fax 876/993-2590, toll-free 800/237-3237. The 27-unit resort is about two miles from of the local airport, which is served by commuter planes. The drive from Kingston is about three hours. Rates start at $350 double; meal plans include MAP at $65 per person daily; all-inclusive plans are also available.*

Peacocks strut and preen for guests as they breakfast on the patio of one of Jamaica's most elegant resorts. The Levy family have been Jamaicans for generations, ever since a Jewish ancestor escaped to the Caribbean to avoid religious persecution in Europe. Consummate hosts and filled with pride in their island, they pamper ordinary guests as if they were all as rich and famous as the big-name elite of politics, show business, and fashion who vacation here. Some reserve the entire Castle, a movie set in itself with a grand dining room and massive chandelier, and suites with plantation furniture, Laura Ashley-look fabrics, and 1930s cathedral radios.

The beach is small, but some guests prefer rooms that overlook the stony shore with its pounding waves. There's always the big pool for swimming. Play tennis, hike the nature trails, have a massage, or play croquet. Get a book from the library, and go there to watch television if you must. Rooms have mini-bars, safes, room service, and air conditioning, but not TV.

Dining here is old-Jamaica elegance at its finest and most dressy. Breakfast and lunch are more relaxed but with the same impeccable service. If you're lucky enough to be here for one of the benefits or special events, you'll rub shoulders with Jamaica's social elite as well as name guests.

WYNDHAM KINGSTON HOTEL, *77 Knutsford Boulevard, Kingston 10, Jamaica. Tel. 876/926-5430, Fax 876/929-7439. U.S. and Canada toll-free 800/WYNDHAM.*

If you need a first class business hotel for all or part of your stay, the Wyndham is equal to the best anywhere. On the four Presidential Club floors, rooms have two-line phones with computer port access. The Business Centre is open 24 hours a day. Four Presidential Club floors have complimentary breakfast, cocktails, and hors d'oeuvres in a gracious Club Lounge with its own concierge. When we arrived late one night just as the lounge was about to close, the host stayed on to mix us drinks and to pass hot canapes so we could unwind before going down to dinner.

All rooms have direct dial phones, individual thermostatic control, satellite television with remote control, and a hair dryer and coffeemaker in each room. Every room has its own safe. This isn't the place to schmooz with other tourists. Your fellow guests are more likely to be international businesspeople, dressy and busy. It's a popular spot for locals to meet for a drink after work, and to hold meetings, weddings, and other special events. Still, there is plenty here for the leisure traveler who wants to stay in the heart of downtown Kingston: an Olympic-size swimming pool, health club, duty-free shopping, lighted tennis courts, and a gaming room with 50 slot machines.

The hotel's Jonkanoo Lounge is one of the city's most upscale nightspots, featuring live jazz. For more casual dining and drinking, try the pool bar where there's a poolside barbecue once a week. The Terrace Cafe serves informally breakfast through dinner; the Palm Court with its pasta bar is the hotel's destination restaurant, serving international cuisine.

PUERTO RICO

WESTIN RIO MAR BEACH RESORT & COUNTRY CLUB, *6000 Rio Mar Boulevard, Rio Grande PR 00745. Tel. 787/888-6200; U.S. and Canada 800/4-RIO-MAR OR 800/WESTIN-1. Rates start at this 600-room* *start at $325 double for a luxury room in winter. Suites are $550 to $2500. The hotel is 19 miles (one hour in most traffic conditions) east of Luis Munoz Marin International Airport, or about $65 by cab. Take Route 3 east to Rio Grande, then left on PR 968.*

This exclusive golf resort is built around an earlier country club development anchored by a Fazio-designed golf course. A Greg Norman-designed, 7,004-yard course opened in 1997. Sprawling across 481 acres framed by miles of beach on one side and El Yunque National Forest on the other, the property has largely been left au naturel with manicured lawns surrounded by swampy lagoons and tangled woodlands bangled with birdlife. Rooms are more cozy than cavernous, filled with comfortable furnishings in Mediterranean moods and colors accented with classic and modern pieces. Balconies look out over the beach or gardens. Even the tiniest balconies have a table and two chairs, just perfect for a breakfast serenaded by coquis.

Rooms have key-lock safe, hair dryer, lighted magnifying mirror, remote control cable television, clock radio, two telephones with voice mail, 24-hour room service, mini-bar with refrigerator, triple sheeting, and other appointments of an outstanding, deluxe hotel.

Dine in two signature restaurants, Palio for gourmet northern Italian and the Club Grille & Chop House for steaks overlooking the golf course. Cafe Carnaval and La Estancia feature Puerto Rican foods and Marbella has menu service and buffet. There's also a poolside restaurant with light meals and frosty drinks, and appetizers and drinks at the Players Bay in the casino. For tapas before dinner or cigars and brandy after, visit Bolero with its sensuous basketweave leather furniture. The Lobby Bar is the resort's nerve center, serving continental breakfast each morning, drinks all day, and entertainment nightly.

The casino opens at noon and buzzes until 2am on week nights, 4am on Friday and Saturday. Le Spa is one of the island's most sophisticated, offering a long menu of services and products. Workout facilities feature the latest machines; a daily activities schedule provides group aerobics as well as games and outings.

Put the children into the Kid's Club; let the teens play the video room; shop the 6,000 square feet of retail space; make an appointment in the beauty salon; use the guest laundry if you like. Car rental, a complete tour desk, and savvy concierge services are all in the front lobby.

All the features of a fine resort are here, but it's staff attitude that provides the final flourish in a winning combination of Puerto Rican warmth and Yanqui can-do.

PALMAS DEL MAR, *Kilometer 84.6 on Road #3, Route 906, Humacao; mailing address: Box 2020, Humacoa, Puerto Rico 00792-2020. Tel. 787/852-6000 or U.S. 800/725-6273. A 45-minute drive from the San Juan airport, the* *resort has 250 rooms and suites. Rates start at $138 nightly for a double room in low season and range to $710 nightly for a three- bedroom villa in high season. Ask about packages. Included in the resort are the Candelero Hotel and Palmas Inn, which are reserved through the telephone numbers above and the Wyndham Hotel & Villas Tel. 787/852-6000 or 800/468-3331.*

Developed in the 1960s by Charles Fraser, known for his ecologically-sensitive developments, the resort is a complete city with branch banks, churches, school, shops, casino, beauty services, restaurants, lounges, and permanent residents living in homes costing $225,000 to $1 million. Once registered, you can charge everything in "town" to your account.

Your domain includes a Gary Player-designed, 18-hole golf course said to have more scenic holes than any other course in the world, and a tennis center managed by Peter Burwash International. Snorkel right off the beach; take a horse from the Equestrian Center and cantor off through the surf. Scuba dive with the resort's own dive masters, the only on-site dive operation on the island.

Choose a spacious hotel room with a private balcony or a villa to house the entire family. Furnishings are tropical and bright; accessories are drawn from Puerto Rican folk art. The Adventure Club gives children, ages 3 to 13, the time of their lives while adults sun, read, or play golf or tennis. Every day finds a new list of planned activities.

Dine in your choice of a dozen restaurants. Use the workout facilities, scuba, go deep-sea fishing, sail, swim in pools galore, bicycle, and enjoy the camaraderie or keep to yourself. The grounds, graced with 3,000 coconut palms, cover 2,750 acres. If you like a big resort with all the bells and whistles and enough to do for weeks without having to traipse all over the island, this is the place.

U.S. VIRGIN ISLANDS

RITZ-CARLTON, *699 Great Bay, St. Thomas 00802. Tel. 340/241-3333, Fax 340/775-4444; toll-free 800/241-3333. U.S. and Canada 800/241-3333. High season rates start at $400 per room. Ask about packages. The 148-room, four-suite hotel is 30 minutes from the airport or about $10 per person by taxi. Airport transfer by limousine can be arranged by the hotel, which is found on the island's eastern tip.*

Surely the *ne plus ultra* of St. Thomas resorts and the first Ritz-Carlton in the Caribbean, this one has all the five-star features of other Ritz-Carltons around the globe. From the moment you're welcomed at the portico and ushered across gleaming marble floors to the check-in desk, the coddling from perkily-uniformed staff is complete. Built in the fashion of a grand palazzo, the property rims a fine beach and overlooks a brimming pool with an "infinity" edge that makes you think you're swimming on the horizon.

From the main building, which houses some guest rooms, the lobby, meeting rooms, and The Cafe for fine dining, buildings cluster around a salt pond nature preserve filled with waterfowl. Even from the farthest building, it's only a brief walk to the main building through meticulously groomed grounds and gardens. If you prefer to ride, a driver is only a phone call away. If you'd rather dine in your room, order room service around the clock. It's brought in wicker hampers and set up with starched linens, fresh flowers, shining silver, and Villeroy and Boch tableware.

Everything about the hotel spells quality, from upscale amenities to the waffle weave robes and slippers provided for guest use. Spacious rooms are done in bold royal blue and gold, accented with plaids and colorful prints on the walls. Rooms have hair dryer, iron, mini-bar with refrigerator, telephones in the bath, at bedside, and on the desk, and a private balcony or terrace. Some are roofed and others have a lattice covering, so specify sun or shade when you book the room.

Plan your days around swimming, the beach, sailing excursions aboard the resort's own catamaran, or the tennis courts. The fitness center offers cardio-vascular and advanced strength equipment, private trainers, and aerobics classes. Scuba, deep sea fishing, golf, picnic sails, and in-room massage can be arranged. The hotel has its own beauty salon, and shops selling designer clothing and accessories. We didn't see neckties, and jackets are not required, but this resort calls for your very best resort wear.

CRUISING

The two cruises below deserve to be placed in this chapter, since this is the Caribbean and the best places include these magnificent vessels! Rates are about $500 per person per day, but many special events, discounts, and promotions mean that you can usually pay less.

STAR CLIPPER, *4101 Salzedo Avenue, Coral Gables FL 33146, Tel. 305/442-1611, Fax 305/443-0666; toll-free 800/422-0551.*

"The noblest of all sailing vessels...these were our Gothic cathedrals," wrote historian Samuel Eliot Morison in describing the great clipper ships that once danced around the globe at speeds never before seen at sea. It was thought that their kind would never be seen again. Now clipper ships have entered a luxurious new era with two four-masted barkentines, *Star Clipper* and *Star Flyer*. Classic clippers in the tradition of the majestic clippers of old, the ships are designed from the keel up to house pampered passengers in enormous hulls once destined to hold cargoes of tea and crates of Chinese porcelain.

World trade was transformed with the introduction of spritely, seakindly clipper ships. Their names made history: *Cutty Sark, Flying*

Cloud, Sea Witch. Then suddenly, it was over. In 1869, the Suez Canal opened. Steamships replaced sail. A railroad crossed the United States. The splendor of sail was silenced. Until now.

The two new clippers bring all the romance of sail into a twentieth century cruise scene where haute cuisine, air conditioning, spacious cabins, and private baths are expected by even the saltiest of sailors. These ships have it all. Don't confuse them with the many old, wooden windjammers that offer no-frills cabins and shared baths. Swedish yachtsman Mikael Krafft has built authentic, all new clipper ships in a gamble that affluent travelers will pay "love boat" prices to live in luxury while tacking, heeling, luffing, and furling.

Don't worry about jargon. You don't have to know a spanker from a mizzen staysail to bask in all the breezy good fun of a Star Clipper cruise. However, the more you know about sailing, the more you'll be surprised and pleased. All the traditional touches abound: wooden belaying pins, bronze winches, teak decks, miles of brightwork, shrouds surrounded by baggywrinkle, and neat coils of line. Yet the ships also sport high-tech touches: roller furling, self-tailing winches, sparkling white sails in tough new synthetic sailcloths, satellite navigation, and a television in every cabin. Star Clipper has a modest diesel engine, but make no mistake. This sister sails.

Itineraries vary with each trip, but generally sail from St. Thomas to Montserrat through the U.S. and British Virgin Islands, Anguilla, St. Maarten, Saba, St. Barts, Statia, St. Kitts, Antigua, Nevis and Iles Des Saintes. Another itinerary sails between Tobago and Dominica, calling at Martinique, St. Lucia, St. Vincent and the Grenadines, and Barbados. In summer, at least one of the clippers sails a Mediterranean route. Passengers can also sail the transatlantic positioning cruise.

An international staff serves an international passenger list. Half the 200-odd guests aboard a typical clipper cruise are from Europe; many others are yachtsmen; a few are landlubbers in search of an offbeat vacation. Like cruise ships, *Star Clipper* and *Star Flyer* have a couple of swimming pools and plenty of deck chairs. Like charter boats, they carry a full watersports inventory of board sailers, SCUBA and snorkel gear, and inflatable runabouts. Sports operations are directed by professional, multilingual staff. Unlike the ocean-going leviathans, the clippers are able to nose into shallow bays and tie up at smaller docks.

There's a cozy library with fireplace, but that's about the end of the entertainment menu. Passengers are invited to heave halyards, spin the big mahogany wheel, or check charts if they like. There is a versatile singer-instrumentalist aboard to play for nightly Happy Hour, and an Amateur Night in which talented crew members and willing passengers put on a show. There's even gambling aboard, if you don't mind betting on crab races. This old pirate ship tradition has been revived aboard the clippers. Aside from that, nightlife consists of stargazing on deck before retiring to a bunk that jostles gently with the seas, heeled to port or starboard as the winds decree.

WINDSTAR CRUISES, *300 Elliott Avenue West, Seattle WA 98119. Tel. 206/281-3535. Book through your travel agent. Week-long Caribbean cruises start at about $2,000 per person per week including port charges.*

No cruising grounds in the world can compete with the Caribbean's clear waters, faithful trade winds, and a United Nations of islands only a few hours sail from each other. Aboard a Windstar ship, passengers have the best of all worlds: a ship that really sails, cabins as plush as a small hotel room, a different island each morning, and knockout cuisine that's included in one price. A Holland America Line company, Windstar is a slick, savvy operation that offers the best airfares, shore tours, entertainers, and special events thanks to its international network of hospitality professionals.

You'll join your ship in Barbados or St. Thomas depending on the itinerary. Ports of call include the Tobago Cays, Bequia, Barbados, Martinique, Grenada, St. Barts, Iles des Saintes, St. John in the U.S. Virgin Islands, and Tortola, Jost Van Dyke, and Virgin Gorda in the British Virgin Islands. Aruba, Curacao, and Bonaire are included in a 15-day Panama Canal itinerary.

A typical cabin has a queen-size bed that can be converted to two twins, a full-length hanging locker, big portholes, twin vanities, and a private bathroom with shower. Your cabin attendant makes the bed, tidies up, and fills your ice bucket while you're at breakfast. While you're a dinner, your attendant leaves fresh towels, turns down the bed and puts a treat on your pillow. Most activities and watersports, endless meals including beach barbecues, and entertainment are included. The only extras are shore excursions and drinks. These ships cruise the world, sailing the Caribbean only in winter. Plan your cruise as far in advance as possible, both to get the week you want and to take advantage of early booking discounts.

THE
ABC
ISLANDS

14. ARUBA

Because prevailing winds and currents made **Aruba** difficult to reach from its sister islands in the days when natives traveled by canoe, its cultural and economic ties were stronger with the peoples of the mainland. Still today, it continues to hew out its own history. It is no longer politically a part of the Dutch West Indies, but is a separate entity within the Kingdom of the Netherlands.

Even during the cruel, early days of the Conquistadores, Aruba had a different fate. Its Indians, like those of most of the other islands, had been rounded up for shipment to the mines of Hispaniola. Then gold was discovered on Aruba and its Indians, the Caiqueto tribe of the Arawak nation, were sent home. Because they formed the slave class, few Africans were landed here. As a result, Arawaks didn't begin integrating until later than on the other islands. The last pure-blood Arawak lived until 1862 – rather a miracle considering that most Arawak populations were wiped out before the end of the 1600s.

Even today, the tree called divi-divi in other islands is called by its ancient Arawak name, watapana, and Aruban housewives continue to sweep clean the yards around their homes. It's thought to be a holdover from ancient times, when the Indians cleared the area around their homes so they could immediately see any approaching snakes or bugs.

Arawak petroglyphs can still be seen in ancient caves. Although researchers don't know the significance of markings the Arawaks made on rocks, using dyes made from paintwood trees, the sketches can still be seen clearly on huge boulders at **Ayo** and at **Arikok National Park**.

The language of the people is **Papiamento** (spelled Papiamentu on Curacao), a mixture of Spanish, Dutch, Portuguese, English and French. Dutch is the language of schools and government, and we never met anyone who couldn't speak at least passable English. The language of island artists embraces Arawak motifs as well as patterns left by Dutch and Spanish settlers since as early as the 1500s.

ARUBA'S NATIONAL ANTHEM

One of the best ways to see the bouillabaisse of languages that make up **Papiamento** *is to read Aruba's national anthem and its translation. If you have ever studied a Romance language, this will sound familiar.*

Aruba patria aprecia = *Aruba beloved home*
Nos cuna venera = *our venerated cradle*
Chikito y simpel bopor ta = *though small and simple you may be*
Pero si respeta = *you are esteemed*

Since 1996, Aruba has been in a frenzy of building and improvements in an $800 million investment in tourism. Arikok National Park, bounded by Boca Prins, San Fuego and the coastline as far as Boca Keto, is being expanded to cover a full 25 per cent of the entire island. An interpretive center is being built and hiking and biking paths are being added and improved.

San Nicolas, the island's largest city with a population of 25,000, is the site of a large, unlovely Exxon refinery that now sits idle. It will probably never be rekindled, so the city is being revitalized as the home of the **Caribbean Cultural Center** and other tourism-friendly installations. A pedestrian walk called the **Civic Spine** will link together museums, the waterfront, sports center, and retail districts. The waterfront is being restored, with an eye to making it into an artist colony. Roads are being upgraded and bike trails added.

Because a fourth of the national budget goes to education, you'll find in Aruba one of the highest standards of living in the islands. Roads are good. Everything in hotel rooms works and is clean. Rental cars are air conditioned. Schedules and appointments are kept. Aruba is an island that can spoil you.

Climate

Unlike the mountainous islands with their rain forests, Aruba is flat and desert-like. Its lands are scattered with enormous boulders; its fields are filled with cactus and sere scrub. Rainfall is scant, so you don't find here the lush green of a St. Lucia, but that means more cloudless days for you to splay on the sands of the luscious beaches.

Temperatures can be torrid, averaging 82 degrees around the calendar, but the never-ending brisk, dry winds blow away the perspiration and the comfort index soars. Best of all, hurricanes are almost unknown this far south in the Caribbean.

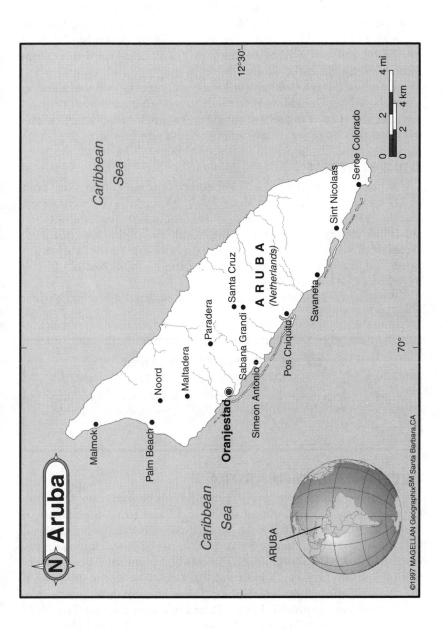

Aruba

N

Caribbean Sea

Caribbean Sea

Malmok

Palm Beach

Noord

Maltadera

Paradera

Santa Cruz

ARUBA
(Netherlands)

Sabana Grandi

Simeon Antonio

Oranjestad

Pos Chiquito

Savaneta

Sint Nicolaas

Seroe Colorado

12°30'

70°

0 · 2 · 4 mi
0 · 2 · 4 km

ARUBA

©1997 MAGELLAN GeographixSM Santa Barbara,CA

ARRIVALS & DEPARTURES

Aruba's **Queen Beatrix International Airport**, which can accommodate jumbo jets, is served by **ALM**, *Tel. 800/327-7230*; **American Airlines**, *Tel. 800/433-7300*; **Air Canada**, *Tel. 800/363-5440*; **Air Aruba**, *Tel. 800/88-ARUBA* and also by **KLM** and a number of air lines that fly here from Venezuela, Brazil, and Colombia.

Your best bet is to talk to your local travel agent because, in addition to regular service from Miami and San Juan and other gateways, the island has irregular charter flights from many other North American cities. The packages they offer are usually among the island's best buys.

ORIENTATION

Aruba is just off the coast of Venezuela, four hours from New York and two and a half hours from Miami by air. It's six miles wide at its widest and about 19.6 miles long, a total land area of about 70 square miles. Good roads link almost every corner of the island. The capital and chief city, **Oranjestad**, is best seen on foot. Most of the hotels are on the beaches just north and just south of the city, most of them on **Palm Beach**, which is edged by J.E. Irausquin Boulevard.

When a street address ends in "z/n," that means the site has no street number.

BIRDS OF THE ABC ISLANDS

*While you're in the bush, try to spot the **Trupial** high in a tree, feeding on sweet, date-like fruit. The bright, darting, little **Sugar Thief** will try to steal food from your table. The rare **Burrowing Owl** is found only on Aruba.*

GETTING AROUND ARUBA

Unmetered taxis meet every flight and charge a flat rate. From the airport to most hotels the cost is $8 to $12 and from most hotels to Oranjestad it's $3 to $6. It's best to confirm the rate with the driver ahead of time. If you need to phone a taxi, *Tel. 22116 or 21604*. Tipping isn't as common on the Dutch islands as it is elsewhere, but drivers can be very helpful and you may want to leave an extra dollar or let the driver keep the change. Touring by taxi costs about $35 an hour for up to four people.

Limousines are provided by **De Palm Limousine Service**, *Tel. 24440* in Aruba or *Tel. 800/766-6016* from the U.S.; or try **Tuxedo Limousine Service**, *Tel. 25800*.

Rental cars usually have a minimum age requirement of 21 to 25 and a maximum of 65 to 70. Driving is on the right; international road signs are easy to understand. If you want to reserve a car from the U.S. to be waiting when you arrive at the airport, call **Avis**, *Tel. 800/331-1084*; **Budget Rent-a-Car**, *Tel. 800/472-3325*; or **Hertz**, *Tel. 800/654-3001.* Major hotels also have car rentals, or rentals can be arranged locally from **Avis**, *Tel. 28787*; **Budget**, *Tel. 28600*; or **Hertz**, *Tel. 24545.* Motor bikes, which rent for about $40 a day, are available from **George's Scooter Rentals**, *Tel. 25975*, or **Nelson Motorcycle Rental**, *Tel. 66801.* Bicycles are available through most hotels.

Aruba has dependable bus service at sites marked **Bushalte** and from the downtown bus station on Zoutmanstraat. Stops are made at or near the hotels along "hotel row" and at points of interest throughout the island. Buses generally run from 6am to midnight and the fare from most hotels to town is about $1.75. Here's where it pays to have exact change, and in Aruba's currency – Dutch guilders.

WHERE TO STAY

Room rates are for a double room in high season. Room tax is 11 percent. When booking, ask if tax is included in the rate you are quoted. A service charge of 10-15 percent is added to food and beverage bills. Ask about packages, which often include taxes and service charges. Hotel tariffs in Aruba are quoted and paid in American dollars unless stated otherwise.

Expensive

AMERICANA ARUBA BEACH RESORT & CASINO, *J.E. Irausquin Boulevard 83. Tel. 2978/64500, Fax 63191, U.S. 800/866-6606. Rates at this 421-room resort start at $390 including meals, drinks, activities, entertainment, and airport transfers.*

Button your wallet pocket when you check into this high-rise hotel. You won't need a cent (except for gambling) while here. The rooms aren't as elegant as those of some newer hotels, but the price is extraordinary for all you get. Play the casino, take in a glittering revue, choose among three places to eat and even more to have a drink, use a sailboat or wind surfer, swim off the sandbox beach, or book a dive with the one-site watersports center. The big swimming pool has its own waterfall and whirlpools. Rooms, done in pearly blues and greens accented with the white or blond of bamboo and wicker, have satellite television, telephone, hair dryer and air conditioning. The hotel does a lot of group and conference business but it's family-friendly and the beach, with its backdrop of palm trees, is a showy white sand.

ARUBA MARRIOTT RESORT & STELLARIS CASINO, *L.G. Smith Boulevard. Tel. 2978/69000 or U.S. 800/223-6388. Rates at this 413-room resort start at $300. Meal plans are available. It's seven miles from the airport.*
A high-rise concrete hotel forms a "u" around a garden and pool that overlook fabulous Palm Beach and the turquoise shimmer beyond it. Enjoy the pool with its waterfall and swim-up bar, or stake your claim to a patch of sand. Do your daily constitutional in the up-to-the-minute health club, then arrange a sail or dive, play tennis, have a beauty treatment or massage, or play a round a golf. Air conditioned rooms are larger than most hotel rooms on Aruba. Each has a mini-bar refrigerator, television, telephone, safe and a balcony. Room service is available; babysitting can be arranged.

ARUBA SONESTA SUITES & CASINO AT SEAPORT VILLAGE, *L.G. Smith Boulevard 9. Tel. 2978/36000, Fax 25317; U.S. and Canada 800/ SONESTA. Rates at this 250-suite resort start at $260. Cab fare from the airport is about $10.*
Sonesta has a certain style that keeps the faithful following it around the world, so here's your chance to sample it in Aruba. This resort is just outside Oranjestad on its own island. Its 40 acres are a world alone with two marinas, six beaches, two restaurants, watersports, tennis courts, a nightclub lounge, more than 50 shops, and a swimming pool that suggests a swim immediately, even before you unpack. There's a salty feel about the place, which attracts yachties who split their time between the time-share section of the resort on shore, and their boats in the marina. The casino, which is one of the most ambitious on the island, whirrs and jingles around the clock.
Prime Rib Night is Sunday 6 to 9pm; Monday is Carnival Night; Tuesday is Pasta Night; Wednesday features a Chinese buffet and so on. Try the Fajita Frenzy on Saturday from 6-9pm.

BUCUTI BEACH RESORT, *L.G. Smith Boulevard 55. Tel. 2978/ 36141, Fax 25272, U.S. 800/223-1108. Rates at this 63-room Best Western resort start at $120 with a minimum stay of seven nights. It's a $10 taxi ride from the airport.*
Clustered along "hotel row" on famous Eagle Beach, like a rose among the thorns, is this small boutique hotel with the look of a Mediterranean villa. Spacious rooms have a balcony or terrace, micro-wave, coffer maker, hair dryer, mini-bar, and in-room movies.
Dozens of restaurants, bars, and casinos are within shouting distance, making this the perfect find for travelers who want a big beach and a smaller hotel. It's a sister resort of the Manchebo Beach Resort across the street.

DIVI ARUBA BEACH RESORT, *J.E. Irausquin Boulevard 45. Tel. 2978/23300, Fax 34002, U.S. 800/554-2008. Rates at this 203-room resort* *start at $340 all-inclusive or $125 for accommodations only. It's an $8 taxi ride from the airport.* Flowering shrubs and palms shroud one pool area to provide patches of shade and sunshine. Choose from a variety of plans including the best-buy inclusive plan that provides meals, drinks, airport transfers, and activities all for one price. Rooms are constantly being brought back from the brink of shabbiness, so ask for one that has had a recent re-do. Luxury rooms and a bridal suite with its own Jacuzzi are available if you want to splurge. Accommodations have a safe and mini-bar, television, telephone, and air conditioning. By day, swim in the pools, play tennis, sail, water ski, dive, or kayak.

At night, have a romantic dinner overlooking the beach and then play the night away in Alhambra Casino next door. The hotel has mountain bikes for rent, beauty and barber shop, a tennis court, a whirlpool, and a nonstop list of activities including nightly theme parties. Every Sunday noon to 4pm, live musicians serenade a poolside barbecue following by a pirate's seafood cookout and limbo show at 6:30pm. Children's programs are provided and kids stay and eat free on some packages.

HYATT REGENCY ARUBA RESORT & CASINO, *J.E. Irausquin Boulevard 85. Tel. 2978/61234, Fax 61682, U.S. 800/233-1234. Rates at the 360-room hotel start at $350. Up to two children under age 18 can stay free in their parents' room, or guests can book a second room for kids at 50% off. The hotel is two miles from Oranjestad and four miles from the airport.*

The sensuous sands of Palm Beach are the setting for one of the Indies' finest resorts. Play the 18-hole Tierra del Sol desert links championship golf course, noted for its ocean views from almost every hole. Dive with the hotel's own Red Sail Sports; enroll the children in Camp Hyatt; take a sunset cruise aboard one of the hotel's boats. The hotel has an enormous casino, lighted tennis courts, and six restaurants and lounges.

RADISSON ARUBA CARIBBEAN RESORT & CASINO, *J.E. Irausquin Boulevard 81, Palm Beach. Tel. 2978/66555, Fax 63260, U.S. and Canada 800/333-3333. Rates at this 372-room, 19- suite resort start at $235 double. Ask about packages. The hotel is 20 minutes from the airport and 15 minutes from Oranjestad.*

Aruba's Palm Beach is one of those shorelines that photographers seek out when they want to shoot the perfect beach: shiny palms pooling their shade between long expanses of sun-splashed sands, waters in iridescent blues, gently lapping wavelets. Enjoy the pool, tennis on lighted courts, massage therapy and the fitness center, boccie ball, volleyball, the shopping arcade, and a full range of watersports including water skiing and wave runners.

Dine on French cuisine in Bistro 81 or on Caribbean dishes served in Watapana to piano accompaniment. For quicker meals and snacks there are Breezes, the Sunset Grill, and Frozen Madness. At sunset there's the Carnival Dinner Show, followed by gaming into the wee hours in the casino. All accommodations have a private balcony or patio, air conditioning, remote control color television with movies, telephone, refrigerator, safe, and radio. Fabrics and woods are sunny yellows and creams, contrasting smartly with vivid blues and greens outdoors.

TAMARIJN ARUBA BEACH RESORT, *J.E. Irausquin Boulevard 41. Tel. 2978/24150 or 800/554-2008. Rates start at $170 per person per night including meals, drinks, airport transfers, and non-motorized watersports. It's ten minutes from the airport. Golf and honeymoon packages are available.*

Located on Aruba's Duif Beach is this popular all-inclusive where all rooms face the ocean and have telephone, air conditioning, and satellite television. Choose among five restaurants and four bars including the spectacular, two-story Coconuts with its water views. Free shuttles go to the Albambra Casino, which is two minutes away. Children under age 12 stay free, eat free from the children's menu, and have the time of their lives in special camp activities such as sand sculpture, carnival, tennis, shirt decorating, storytelling, and dancing.

WYNDHAM ARUBA BEACH RESORT & CASINO, *Palm Beach. Toll-free reservations Tel. 800/822-4200. Rates at this 444-unit hotel start at $275 plus taxes and a set scale of gratuities. The resort is west of Oranjestad.*

It's hard to choose between the enormous, 8,000 square-foot, free-form pool and the deep, blue sea. Aruba's Palm Beach is a legend among legends – wide, white, and fringed with palms that provide patches of shade. Ask about packages and the kids-free program.

Moderate

BUSHIRI BOUNTY BEACH RESORT, *L.G. Smith Boulevard #35, Aruba. Tel. 2978/25216; U.S. 800/462-6868; Puerto Rico and Canada, 800/438-2686. Rates at this 150-room resort start at $150 per person daily, all inclusive, with two people in a room. Children ages 2-11 pay $62.50. Round trip airport transfers and baggage handling are included.*

Not just for swinging singles, this all-inclusive vacation bonanza also welcomes couples, families, and honeymooners. One price pays for the works: meals, drinks at three bars and wine with meals, sports, entertainment, taxes and tips. Rooms, which overlook the beach or verdant grounds, are air conditioned and have satellite television and in-room safes. They're big and basic, with breezy balconies.

Choose from a buffet at breakfast and order from the menu at sit-down lunches and dinners. Check the children into Camp Bounty, then spend your days sunning, boating, working out in the fitness center, swimming in the ocean or pool, soaking in the three oversized Jacuzzis, playing tennis, and taking side trips to the casinos or other points of interest. After dinner al fresco at La Terrazza or at the Beach Grill, dance to compelling Caribbean rhythms. Babysitting is available at additional charge.

HOLIDAY INN ARUBA BEACH RESORT & CASINO, *Tel. 2978/ 63600, Fax 2978/65165, U.S. and Canada 800/HOLIDAY. Rates at this 600-room resort start at $190. Meal plans are available. Up to two children aged 19 and under stay free when sharing a room with parents and using existing beds. The resort is 20 minutes (a $14 ride) from the airport and 10 minutes from downtown Oranjestad.*

There are times in international travel when we long for the predictable comforts of a Holiday Inn, and this one fills the cup to overflowing with creature comforts, modest rates, a free-form swimming pool with waterfall, fitness center, and free membership for kids in the rollicking Little Rascals Club. All this comes with Aruba's famous Palm Beach and ceaseless sunshine. Eat light in the Seabreeze Bar and Grill, Boardwalk Cafe, or Scoops ice cream parlor, or dress up for more elegant dining in Miramar Restaurant, known for its candlelight dinners.

The hotel has a casino, big swimming pool with waterfall, a separate children's pool, a beauty salon, and a shiny new fitness center with its own cable television. Stay in one of three towers with views of the sea of countryside. Each room has individually controlled air conditioning, telephone, cable television with pay-per- view movies, clock radio, and safe. Rooms are decorated in splashy prints coordinated with soft solids in carpeting and sofas. Play tennis, dive with the PADI operation, windsurf, sail or snorkel.

LA CABANA BEACH RESORT & CASINO, *Box 4273, Oranjestad. Tel. 2978/79000, U.S. 800/835-7193 or 212/251-1710, Fax 251-1767. The resort is on the northwest shore of the island, six miles from the airport. Taxi fare is about $20. The hotel has 803 suites ranging from studios to three bedrooms, all with kitchenette. Rates range from $200 nightly for a studio to $655 for six people in a three-bedroom suite. For two meals daily add $42 per person; three meals are $53.*

This isn't your father's Caribbean. It's a slick, modern, Miami-style resort plus a casino on a canvas of white beach and clear turquoise waters. A complete community, the resort has its own drug store, boutiques, tour desk, planned activities including fun-packed children's programs for age groups up to teenagers, 24-hour laundry and valet, car rental, video arcade, and food market. Every floor has a coin laundry; each suite has a private balcony or terrace, whirlpool bath, hair dryer, fully-equipped kitchen with microwave and full-size refrigerator, satellite color television with remote control, direct dial telephone, and radio alarm clock. Because every suite has a queen-size sleep sofa, a studio or one-bedroom can sleep four; the three-bedroom units sleeps up to eight.

Dine in the Prawnbroker for seafood and salad bar, Spats for northern Italian, La Cabana Trading Company for aged beef, The Captain's Table for continental fare, or the Pool Grill for burgers and bikinis. Snack here, in the Yogurt and Espresso Shop or the Dunkin' Donuts. Drink at walk-up or swim-up pool bars or the Galley Bar. In the casino find 320 slot machines and 33 tables playing blackjack, stud poker, Baccarat, and craps at stakes catering to all pocketbooks plus extravagant shows in its Tropicana showroom.

The resort has a bunch of swimming pools, a great beach, squash, racquetball, tennis courts, saunas for men and women, fitness center with all the latest machines, watersports galore, massage, lighted tennis courts with pro, and access to the 18-hole Tierra del Sol championship golf course.

Budget

AMSTERDAM MANOR BEACH RESORT, *J.E . Irausquin Boulevard 252. Tel. 2978/ 71492, Fax 71463; U.S. 800/766-6016. Rates at this all-suite resort start at $140 for a studio with kitchen. One- and two-bedroom apartments are also available. The hotel is a $10 taxi ride from the airport.*

Another in the line of hotels that stand sentinel along beautiful Eagle Beach is this sunny yellow hotel with ochre roofs, reminiscent of the buildings lined up along Handelskaade on Curacao. Its location across the street from all the costlier hotels is ideal, giving you a wide choice of restaurants, beach bars, casinos, and entertainment. The resort has its own restaurant and bar, a big swimming pool, and a little market where you can provision for breakfast and lunch from your own kitchenette.

Rooms, which are done in deep tones and mellow pine furniture, are air conditioned and have television, telephone, and private balcony or patio. On the top floors, your high ceiling may end in a gable. Guests have the use of laundry machines. There's a playground for children, and babysitting can be arranged.

WHERE TO EAT

Tax and a service charge are usually added, so don't tip twice. If you do tip, figure a percentage of the price of the meal and beverage before the tax was added. Unless stated otherwise, these restaurants take major credit cards. An unusually high number take American Express, and Visa and MasterCard are always acceptable. Only a handful take Diner's Club. If it matters to you, ask.

Expensive

BRISAS DEL MAR, *Savaneta 222A. Tel. 47718. Hours are noon to 3pm and 6:30 to 11pm daily except Monday, when it's open only for dinner.*

Reservations are essential. Main dishes average $15. Savaneta is ten miles east of Oranjestad.

A homey little place that seats only 48, this locally popular bar and restaurant lives up to its name, which means sea breezes. The food is simple and straightforward: catches of the day, steak, chicken, a mountainous mixed seafood platter, or grilled lobster. The house specialty is keri-keri, shredded fish sauteed in vegetables and fresh herbs. If you want a sauce, ask for the Creole sauce but don't take too big a bite until you get an idea of how many hot peppers went into it. At lunch have the Aruban fish cakes or conch.

BUCCANEER, *Gasparito 11. Tel. 66172. Main dishes average $22. Hours are 6-11pm nightly except Sunday. Reservations are not accepted.*

Dine on succulent seafood while gazing at an underwater show at your table's private aquarium or in the main, 5,000-gallon tank. The closer you sit to it, the better the view but the noisier the table. Arrive early or late; waits are long at 8pm and, during peak hours, service can be slow. The room is piney and salty, a veritable pirate's den of atmosphere. Fresh fish is an obvious choice, served solo or in a surf-and-turf combo. If you're not a seafood lover, there's a good choice of European and American favorites such as filet mignon, chicken, turtle, or ribchen (smoked pork chops) with kraut and boiled potatoes. For dessert, have ice cream or the peach Melba.

CHALET SUISSE, *J.E. Irausquin Boulevard 246. Tel. 75054. Hours are daily except Sunday 6 to 10:30pm. Main dishes average $15. It's near La Cabana Suites. Reservations are suggested.*

Picture an Austrian ski lodge on the non-slopes of flat, hot, sandy Aruba, and a menu prepared for the hungry, après- ski crowd. The food is Swiss-continental with such choices as crisp duckling a la orange, beef Stroganoff, lobster bisque, breaded veal, and pastas. Fortunately the room is air conditioned, or visitors from colder climates couldn't get up much of a taste for food this warm and filling.

CHEZ MATHILDE, *Havenstraade 23. Tel. 34968. Main dish prices average $30. Reservations are urged. Hours vary seasonally, so call ahead. It's five minutes from the airport, near the Sonesta.*

Fine French cuisine is served in a century-old Aruban house filled with tables beautifully set for up to 100 diners and serenaded by soft piano music. Seafood is served Mediterranean style with West Indian contributions such as sea urchin, snapper, crab, lobster, and shrimp. Have the bouillabaisse, snapper *en papillote*, rack of lamb, a veal dish, or chicken cooked in wine. The wine list is international with an especially good choice of French vintages.

EL GAUCHO, *Wilhelminastraade 8. Tel. 23677. Hours vary, so call for reservations. The restaurant is closed Sundays. Main dishes average $20.*

If you like meat and potatoes, it's hard to beat a true Argentine steak house where no-nonsense chunks of cow are cooked exactly to the doneness you want. Ours could have been cut with a feather. Order a salad and the steak fries, and worry about dieting tomorrow. The setting is an old Aruban house; the decor is rugged and leathery, straight out of the pampas.

GASPARITO, *Gasparito 3. Tel. 67044. Main dishes average $25. It's open Monday through Saturday 6:30 to 11pm Reservations are urged.*

The walls of this 64-seat restaurant are covered with the works of local artists, so take your time to browse them because they are for sale. Dine on homestyle chicken fricassee, stewed conch, sopi de pisca (fish stew), stuffed Dutch cheese (keshi yena), or a meltingly tender filet served plain or with a buttery mushroom sauce. Grilled lobster can be served with drawn butter or with a piquant Creole sauce.

LA NUEVA MARINA PIRATA, *Spanish Lagoon. Tel. 27372. It's open daily except Tuesday 6 to 11 P.M. Reservations are suggested. Main dish prices average $20.*

Dine in a pirate's lair overlooking rocky shores. Aruban palates are pleased with the curries, soups, and West Indian sauces. Visitors can "go native" on local dishes or order simply cooked fresh fish and lobster.

LE PETIT CAFE, *Emmastrasse 1. Tel. 26577. Hours are 11am to 11pm daily except Sunday when it's closed for lunch. Main dishes average $20.*

You're in the heart of town, with its people-watching and surging crowds of shoppers, in an oasis filled with greenery. A hot stone is brought to the table with your choice of raw fish, chicken, or beef, plus plenty of vegetables, and you stir-fry everything to taste. It's great fun, healthful, and an absorbing dinnertime activity.

LA DOLCE VITA, *Caya G.F. Betico Croes 164. Tel. 25675. Main dishes average $18. Hours are daily except Wednesday 6 to 11pm.*

Enjoy the sweet life of an Italian doge while you feast in a picturesque cactus garden on homemade pastas enhanced by fabulous sauces. Have the veal Parmesan, which is splashed with a hint of Marsala wine, with a glass of a robust red and a side of linguini. House specialties include pasta tossed with spinach, ricotta and mozzarella cheese, or linguini in red or white clam sauce. The fish stew is made Mediterranean-Italian style. The fresh fish, broiled simply and served with a spritz of lemon, is sublime. Italian desserts including ices and tiramisu await at the end of the meal.

THE NEW OLD CUNUCU HOUSE, *Palm Beach 150. Tel. 61666. Hours are daily 6-11pm Main dish prices average $20.*

International and Aruban dishes are prepared in this "old country house" which was built as a cunucu (country) house in the 1920s. Have a drink first in the charming garden. Traditional Dutch West Indian specialties are celebrated: fish soup, grilled seafood, shrimp with coconut, or baked chicken, all accompanied by local vegetables and a starch such as pan bati or funchi. On weekend evenings, live music entertains diners. **THE OLD MILL,** *J.E. Irausquin Boulevard 330. Tel. 62060. Main dishes average $15. The restaurant, which is known as De Olde Molen in Dutch, is open daily except Sunday 6 to 11pm.*

It really is an old mill, a cherished local landmark within walking distance of many of the hotels on Palm Beach. The surprise is that the old mill is new to Aruba; it is an old Dutch mill that was taken apart, shipped here, and re-assembled to provide a tourist attraction. Dine on trustworthy, northern European stalwarts such as Dutch pea soup, chicken or veal Cordon Bleu, fish or shrimp in spicy tomato sauce, or a showy Chateaubriand for two.

PAPIAMENTO RESTAURANT, *Washington 61. Tel. 64544. It's open daily 6 to 11pm. Main dishes average $20. Reservations are suggested.*

Dine in the Ellis family's old stone plantation house, which is furnished in old-world style with brass chandeliers, local art works, and traditional Dutch West Indian touches. In the garden, dine romantically on a terrace surrounded by trees strung with fairy lights. A hot stone and a platter of raw food is brought to your table and cooked to your order. Healthful, quick, and low-fat, stone cooking is a passion on Aruba and these folks present it well. From the kitchen comes a large choice of chicken, meat and fish dishes including a combination plate and a clay pot seafood feast for two.

TWINKLEBONES, *in the Turbana Plaza, Noord 124. Tel. 69806. Hours are 4pm to midnight daily. Main dishes average $17.*

Prime rib reigns here in a setting of whimsy and entertainment. Cooks and servers burst into song, and may grab diners for a twirl around the tables.

Moderate
BOONOONOONOOS, *Wilhelminastraade 18A. Tel. 31888. Main dishes average $15. It's open daily 11:30am to 10:30pm except Sunday, when it's open only for dinner. Reservations are suggested.*

Let's start with pronunciation. Say boo-noo and keep adding noos until it sounds about right. It's Jamaican slang for making a big deal out of something. That big street name simply means Wilhelmina Street. When this regal mansion was a private home, the story goes, aloe extract was first created and exported to England where it became a popular burn ointment and stomach cure. Downtown in the shopping district, in a pleasant oasis decorated in ice cream colors, it offers the full range of West Indian foods from Jamaican jerk and Barbadian pepperpot to a classic pumpkin soup and curried chicken. If you're not adventurous, there's steak or sauteed fresh fish. Servers, who are jauntily clad in stripes, try their best to keep up, but waits can sometimes be long. If you're in a hurry, ask what's ready to go – probably one of the soups or curries. If not, order another rum punch or one of the deadly Dutch genevers (gins). **KOWLOON**, *Emmastrasse 11. Tel. 24950. Hours are 11am to 10pm daily. Plan to spend $15 to $18 for dinner.*

A visit to the Dutch islands wouldn't be complete without an Indonesian meal. Try one of the rice or noodle Indonesian dishes, or classic Cantonese, Mandarin, and Szechuan favorites. The room, which seats 75, is crisply modern with touches of red, black, and gold.

LA PALOMA, *Noord 39. Tel. 74611. Hours are 6 to 11pm daily except Tuesday. Main dishes average $16. Reservations are suggested.*

Found ten minutes north of Oranjestad, this locally popular restaurant also attracts crowds of tourists to its pleasant tables, which are arranged around the round bar. Dishes rarely vary, but they are dependable. Dare the he-man steaks if you can – the New York strip weighs 14 ounces and the filet is almost as big. Order the seafood platter or a more modest portion of fresh fish in Creole sauce, shrimp marinara, or lobster.

MI CUSHINA, *L.G. Smith Boulevard in the La Quinta Beach Resort about a mile from San Nicolas. Tel. 72222. Reservations are urged. It's open daily except Thursday, noon to 2pm and 6-10pm. Main dishes average $14.*

Typical West Indian specialties such as funchi (polenta) and stewed lamb with pan bati, the local pancake, have been standards in this restaurant for years, even before it was moved into this resort. Coffee bags hang from the ceiling, light fixtures are made of old wagon wheels, and there's even a small museum with family memorabilia and the story of the aloe industry. A specialty is a seafood cazuela, a thick and hearty fish stew.

SANDRA'S, *J.E. Irausquin Boulevard between the city and Eagle Beach. Tel. 71517. Hours are daily except Sunday, 5:30 to 10:30pm It's closed for a few weeks in early September. Main dish prices start at $13.*

Dine indoors in a pleasantly pastel, air conditioned dining room or outdoors on the veranda. This is pretty much a meat-and-potatoes place. If you're a dedicated carnivore, have the impressive combination platter of raw chicken, beef, pork and sausage that you cook on a hot stone at your table. It's served for two or more. Choices include a pleasing selection of pastas and sauces, including sauces made with fresh fish or lobster. There's also chicken and steak.

WATERFRONT CRAB HOUSE, *in the Seaport Marketplace on L.G. Smith Boulevard. Tel. 35858. Main dishes average $15. It's open every day for lunch and dinner. Reservations are suggested.*

Crabs are the specialty here, and they're offered in a world of ways: Alaskan king crab claws, stuffed crab, soft-shell crab. The menu has a

Mediterranean accent in its tomato-based sauces, fried squid, and linguini with clam sauce. Blackened fish and shrimp are flash-cooked over an open grill. Ask for the catch of the day, which could be snapper, tuna, swordfish, wahoo or whatever, and you can't go wrong. The setting is a popular shopping mall surrounded by a small green. Eat indoors under the murals or outdoors under the stars.

Budget

CHARLIE'S BAR & RESTAURANT, *Zeppenfeldstraat 56, San Nicolas. Tel. 45086. Dishes are in the $6 to $10 range. It's open for lunch, snacks, and dinner Monday through Saturday. The kitchen is open noon to 9:30pm, but the drinking may start earlier and go on later.*

Since the days when working folk gathered here after a day at the oil refinery, Charlie's has been a favorite neighborhood pub. It caught on with tourists and it looks as though it will be here throughout and after the re-invention of San Nicolas. Local artists, writers, and musicians hang out here with a motley mix of tourists and locals, many of them leaving behind a memento to add to the junkyard decor. The house specialties are peel-and-eat shrimp, calamari Creole, and the catch of the day.

GRAN SLAM, *De La Sallestraade 41A. Tel. 30399. It's open nightly 5:30 to 11pm. Main dishes average $5.50.*

An international selection of fast food can be found here at pleasant prices. Have a burger, roti, curry, salad or sandwich.

STEAMBOAT BUFFET & DELI, *J.E. Irausquin Boulevard 370. Tel. 66700. This 300-seat restaurant is open 7am to midnight. Plan to spend $11 to $15 for dinner; $8 to $10 for breakfast. Reservations aren't taken.*

Buffets are almost always a bargain, especially for hearty eaters. This one, with a bar that opens before lunch and serves until closing, is one of the most popular feedbags on the island. The paddlewheeler theme carries through the decor and the uniforms of the servers, adding a gala sense of fun to all-you-can-eat dining. Breakfast features a groaning board of fruits, juices, cold meats and cheeses, breads and omelets cooked to order. Lunch is mile-high deli sandwiches. At dinner there are plenty of hot and cold choices. Don't expect pheasant under glass. This is delicious, affordable dining with something for everyone in the family.

TIMING IS EVERYTHING

Sunset watching is a religion on Aruba as it is in most of the Caribbean, and people begin streaming to restaurants immediately afterward. Make reservations early. If you have none, go early or late or you may be turned away.

SEEING THE SIGHTS

Oranjestad still lives in the shadow of its days as a colonial capital, a powerful city filled with the homes of rich burghers, stalwart defenders, and wealthy merchants. You might start before the beginning by prowling exhibits that go back to Arawak times. The **Archaeological Museum**, which has some impressive pre-Columbian artifacts, is at Zoutmanstraat 1, *Tel. 28979.* It's open weekdays 8am to noon and 1:30 to 4:30pm.

Moving on to the fort, you'll tread stones that were laid in the late 1700s to defend against the troublesome British. The landmark **Willem 111 Tower** was added in 1868. In the **Historical Museum** at the fort, the city's history is portrayed with displays, furniture, photographs, and drawings. The fort and its museum are open weekdays 9am to noon and 1:30 to 4:30pm, *Tel. 26099.* Admission is $1.50.

While you're downtown visit the **Numismatic Museum** at Zuidstraat 27, *Tel. 28831.* Admission is free. Hours are weekends 7:30am to noon and 1-4:30pm. It wasn't until it went its own way in 1986 that Aruba began issuing its own stamps, which are becoming collectable. New issues can be subscribed in person or by mail at the **Philatelic Service**, Post Office, Oranjestad, Aruba, *Tel. 21900, Fax 27930.* Even if you're not a stamp collector, these beautiful little pieces of art make good souvenirs. Post-cards sent home emblazoned with them are real attention-getters.

Island tours are pleasant and affordable compared to groping your way around in a rental car, and we recommend taking one to see the highlights and to get oriented before you strike out alone. Operators include **Aruba Friendly Tours**, *Tel. 25800,* and **De Palm Tours**, *Tel. 24400.*

A stop at **Natural Bridge** is one of those tourism "must-sees" that sounds hokey but is an utter delight. Sit at the cafe that overlooks the clear turquoise waters and the tireless waves, and ponder the years that it took for this formation to be eaten into the shoreline.

Guides will also show you remnants of the old gold smelters, and the gardens of giant boulders off Route A4. It's a day-long delight to wander among them and photograph their changing sculpture as the sun moves. You'll want to come back.

Some locals come here often to spread a picnic lunch and ponder the enormity of it all. Climbing the boulders is only for the young and daring. The rocks lie just as some mysterious force hurled them there untold millennia ago. There are no safety aids.

A drive to **San Nicolas** on the south end of the island brings you to a boom town that began in the 1920s when the oil refinery was built. It fought off German attacks during World War II and thrived until refining was discontinued in the 1980s. Now the clean-up of this popular city and the creation of a showplace waterfront will probably do away with some of the seediest dives.

You'll want to climb **Hooiberg**, **or Haystack Hill**, just because it's here. It's no Everest, but the views from the top of this 540-foot cone are panoramic. Take Route A7 out of Oranjestad on the way towards Santa Cruz.

Although "guides" guard the entrances, admission to the **Guadirikiri**, **Fontein**, **Tunnel of Love**, and **Huliba** caves on the southeast coast is free. Explore soaring dunes at **Boca Prins** and continuing north on the east coast, the ruins of the gold smelter at Bushiribana. At the northern peak of the island, **California Dunes** and the photogenic **California Lighthouse** are a wild seascape of sand and bald rock. As you ride through the cunucu, or countryside, watch for the occasional divi-divi tree, its back bent to the wind. Returning to your hotel, you might detour inland to the village of **Noord**, where a church that dates to the 1600s has an altar that was hand-carved in Holland.

Touring aside, Aruba's chief treasures are her beaches, especially **Palm Beach** in the north or **Oranjestad** and **Eagle Beach** to the south. Both are lined now with hotels, but there is still room for your deck chair under the sun or under the occasional palm tree. Not only are the stark sands a creamy white, the sea encroaches so gradually that you can wade out for yards before finally sinking into the cool water as clear as a gin fizz.

NIGHTLIFE & ENTERTAINMENT
Discos & Cabarets
CHEERS CAFE BISTRO, *in the Port of Call Marketplace, L.G. Smith Boulevard 17, Tel. 30838. It's open until 3am.*

CHESTERFIELD NIGHT CLUB, *Zeppenfeldstreet 57, San Nicolas, Tel. 45109.*

CLUB VISAGE, *L .G . Smith Boulevard 152A, Tel. 22397.*

OASIS LOUNGE/ON THE ROCKS *,in the Aruba Palm Beach Resort & Casino, J.E. Irausquin Boulevard 79, Tel. 63900.*

A live band plays for listening and dancing here.

THE MUSIC HALL, *in the Aruba Hilton & Casino, J.E. Irausquin Boulevard 77, Tel. 64466.*

This is the place to catch a cabaret show.

Casinos
Casinos, which offer Las Vegas-style shows, dancing, dining, and gambling into the wee hours are:

ALHAMBRA CASINO AND ALLADIN THEATER, *J.E. Irausquin Boulevard 93, Tel. 35000.*

PALACE CASINO AND LAS PALMAS BALLROOM, *in the Americana Aruba Beach Resort, J.E. Irausquin Boulevard 83, Tel. 64500.*

CASABLANCA CASINO AND MUSIC HALL, *in the Aruba Hilton, J.E. Irausquin Boulevard 77, Tel. 64470.*

STELLARIS CASINO, *in the Aruba Marriott, L.G. Smith Boulevard.*

THE PALM CASINO AND OASIS, *Tel. 69000, in the Aruba Palm Beach Resort, J.E. Irausquin Boulevard 79.*

CRYSTAL CASINO AND DESIRES NIGHTCLUB, *in the Aruba Sonesta at Seaport Village, Tel. 35600.*

GRAND HOLIDAY CASINO AND PLAYERS LOUNGE, *in the Holiday Inn Aruba, J.E. Irausquin Boulevard 230, Tel. 63600.*

COPACABANA CASINO, *in the Hyatt Regency Resort, J.E. Irausquin Boulevard 85, Tel. 61234.*

The **TROPICANA SHOWROOM** in the La Cabana resort brings in such big-name performers as Tito Puente, Kenny G, and Gloria Estefan. *It's at J.E. Irausquin Boulevard 250, Tel. 79000.* Also, try the **CASINO MASQUERADE** *in the Radisson Aruba, J.E. Irausquin Boulevard 81, Tel. 66555.* In most casinos, slots open at 11am and table games at 1pm. Play goes on until early the next morning. People under age 18 are not permitted in casinos.

Live Music

DESIRES NIGHTCLUB, *in the Sonesta, Tel. 36000.*

BEST WESTERN, *Manchebo Beach, Tel. 23444.*

PELICAN TERRACE, *at the Divi Aruba, Tel. 23300.*

PLAYERS CLUB & LOUNGE, *at the Holiday Inn, Tel. 63600.*

TROPICANA SHOWROOM, *at the La Cabana, Tel. 79000.*

SUN CLUB, *in the Costa Linda Beach Resort, J.E. Irausquin Boulevard 59, Tel. 38000.*

For a last round, try the **NIGHT CAP**, *Sabana Liber 18, Noord, Tel. 70450.*

You don't have to find a designated driver when you go pub crawling with the **Aruba Bar Hopper Tour**. Aboard a wooden 1947 Ford bus, painted to beat the band, fun seekers can check out the island's favorite nightspots. The tour leaves Tuesday and Thursday at 6:30pm, returning at half past midnight. Ask your hotel host to book it for you.

SPORTS & RECREATION
Bowling

Tenpins, it is said, was invented by the Dutch, who are among the few West Indians who bowl. The **Eagle Bowling Palace** on Pos Abou z/n, *Tel.*

35038, has 12 computerized lanes. You can rent bowling shoes and a ball. It's open 10am to 2am.

Deep Sea Fishing
The name wahoo comes from the shout that goes out when some lucky angler lands one of these gamefish. Charter a fishing boat and guide by the half day or full day to fish for kingfish, bonito, barracuda, amberjack, yellowfin tuna, blue or white marlin, or sailfish.
Sportfish boats include:
• **Amira Darina,** *Tel. 34424*
• **Dorothy,** *Tel. 23375*
• **Driftwood,** *Tel. 24400*
• **G String,** *Tel. 26101*
• **Kenny's Toy,** *Tel. 25088*
• **La Tanga,** *Tel. 46825*
• **Macabi,** *Tel. 28834*
• **Mahi-Mahi,** *Tel. 36611*
• **Mar Indi,** *Tel. 23375*
• **Pegasaya,** *Tel. 78399*
• **Queeny,** *Tel. 78399*
• **Sea Doll,** *Tel. 24478*
• **Sweet Mary,** *Tel. 27985*
• **Wyvern II,** *Tel. 339190*

Diving
Scuba diving off Aruba is sensational. Dive on kaleidoscopic coral reefs to play peekaboo with brilliant fish. Take a wall dive, or explore wrecks including a sunken World War II freighter. In many areas, visibility is as much as 100 feet.
Dive operators include:
• **Adventure Divers,** *Tel. 43881*
• **Aruba Aqua Sports,** *Tel. 23380*
• **Aruba Pro Dive,** *Tel. 25520*
• **Aruba Scuba Center,** *Tel. 25216*
• **Charlie's Buddies S .E .A . Scuba,** *Tel. 34877*
• **Dax Divers,** *Tel. 36000*
• **De Palm Watersports,** *Tel. 24545*
• **Mermaid Sports Divers,** *Tel. 35546*
• **Pelican Watersports,** *Tel. 31228*
• **Red Sail Sports,** *Tel. 61603*
• **Scuba Aruba,** *Tel. 34142*

In a different sort of dive, ride the **Atlantis Submarine**, *Tel. 36090 or from the U.S. 800/253-0493*, to a depth of about 150 feet. The same company operates Atlantis submarines in Hawaii, St. Thomas, and the Caymans, but every site is different every day. Go as often as you can afford it. Your hair stays dry while you play a real life Sea Hunt among the reefs and whatever denizens drift by to look in the windows at you. Tours leave from the Seaport Village Marina every hour, and the entire excursion including the boat ride to and from the submarine takes about two hours. Cost is $70 for adults and $30 for children ages 4 to 14. Children under age 4 aren't accepted. Reservations are required.

TAKE A DIVE

*The sinking of the luxury liner **Titanic** has an interesting sequel in Aruba. Remember the **California**, the ship that received distress signals from the Titantic and did not respond? There was a logical explanation, but nobody listened and the Califoria's captain was almost tarred and feathered when the ship docked. The California, which was only 20 miles from the Titanic, would have been first on the scene had her radio operator been on duty all night. She never heard the SOS, but an angry public accused the captain of ignoring cries for help in his rush to make his own schedule. The disgrace followed him to his grave.*

The California lies off Aruba's northern shore in waters 30-45 feet deep. Advanced divers who can dare the strong currents and choppy seas of this area will find her surrounded by coral growths and clouds of colorful fish.

Golf

Robert Trent Jones, Jr. designed the 18-hole, par-71 golf course at **Tierra Del Sol**, *Tel. 60978*. The course has a restaurant, club house, locker rooms, and pro shop.

Horseback Riding

Be Lawrence of Arabia as you canter across the desert dunes and wend your way around the old gold mine. Horses are available from **Ponderosa Ranch** at Papya 30, *Tel. 25027*; **Ramcho Daimari**, *Tel. 60239*; **Ramcho Del Campo**, *Tel. 20290*; *and* **Rancho El Paso**, *Tel. 63310*.

Tennis

If your hotel doesn't offer tennis, play at the **Aruba Racquet Club**, Rooi Sano 21 in the Palm Beach area, *Tel. 60215*. A world class club, it has lighted courts, an exhibition court, pro shop, a swimming pool, aerobics classes, a fitness center, a bar and a restaurant. The club is open daily 8am to 9pm. Reservations are required.

Snorkeling

Waters around Aruba are so clear that you don't have to be a certified scuba diver to see much of the best coral and some of the wrecks. Arrange a snorkel trip with:

- **Aruba Marine Services**, *Tel. 39091*
- **De Palm Tours**, *Tel. 24545*
- **Mi Dushi**, *Tel. 23513*
- **Pelican Watersports**, *Tel. 31228*
- **Red Sail Sports**, *Tel. 61603*
- **Unique Sports of Aruba**, *Tel. 60096*
- **Wave Dancer**, *Tel. 25520*

Windsurfing

Shops that can supply windsurfing equipment and lessons, and usually other watersports too, include:

- **Divi Winds**, *Tel. 24150*
- **Happy Surfpool**, *Tel. 66288*
- **Pelican Watersports**, *Tel. 63600*
- **Red Sail Sports**, *Tel. 61603*
- **Roger's Windsurf Place**, *Tel. 61918*
- **Sailboard Vacation**, *Tel. 62527*
- **Unique Sports of Aruba**, *Tel. 63900*

Shopping

Frankly, we avoid look-like shops that sell luxury goods made somewhere other than the country we are visiting, although Oranjestad is a happy hunting ground for discounts on pricey imports. More meaningful local and Dutch souvenirs include Edam and Gouda cheeses, Delftware, oils and watercolors showing familiar Aruban scenes, and cosmetics made from the healing aloe plants that grow wild across the island.

The works of local artists and potters can be found at **Creative Hands**, Socotorolaan A, *Tel. 35665*. **Trudy's Pottery** is in the Sun Plaza, *Tel. 22744*. Also try **Just Local** at Casher 51 in Santa Cruz. Every Tuesday between 6:30 and 8:30pm, the **Bonbini Festival** includes showings by local artists at Fort Zoutman. Shopping in Oranjestat centers around Caya G.F. Betico Croes, where shop after shop spills over with luxury goods: Lalique, Waterford, Rolex, Gucci, Swatch, Cuban cigars, French perfumes, premium liquors, diamonds and gold. Cruise passengers swarm ashore looking for just the right gift for Aunt Mary or one more charm to add to a bracelet.

While Aruba isn't exactly duty free, there is no sales tax and the price you pay is what you see on the sticker. Unfortunately, goods are almost always displayed with the price tag hidden. To see it you must ask, or pick up the item, and by then you are halfway hooked. Incidently, pay what is asked unless you get a broad hint that the price might be somehow adjusted. Haggling is considered rude here. Credit cards and travelers checks are accepted in all tourist shops and malls.

Seasoned cruisers have seen it all, and pass up the time-worn "duty free" shops in favor of shops such as **Artensia Aruba**, L.G. Smith Boulevard 178, *Tel. 37494*. Sold here are hand-thrown pottery, embroideries, and other traditional crafts. Aruban handmades are also found at the **Artistic Boutique**, Caya G.F. Betico Croes 25, *Tel. 23142*. Also shop **Creative Hands**, Socotorolaan 5, *Tel. 35665* and **Art and Tradition Handcrafts**, Caya G. F. Betico Croes 30, *Tel. 22078*.

Award-winning American designer Agatha Brown has **Les Accessories** in the Seaport Village Mall where she sells more than 70 Florentine-made leather purse designs found nowhere else. She also imports designer clothing and sells a nice choice of inexpensive hand-woven swimming suit cover-ups from Venezuela. A trusted old name in local jewelry is **Gandleman's** at Caya G.F. Betico Croes 5A, *Tel. 34433*. **Little Switzerland** nearby is one of the ubiquitous chain found throughout the islands. The selections are predictable but the store can be trusted to ship home anything you don't want to carry. Know the prices you'd have to pay at home for Lladro or Baccarat, and compare what they cost here.

Aruba has shopping malls as modern and exciting as any in Dallas or Chicago. **Seaport Village Mall**, a five-minute walk from the cruise terminal, has some 135 upscale shops, boutiques, and kiosks selling everything under the sun. The last Saturday of every month, a street art gallery is set up downtown between the Protestant Church and The Cellar. Every Thursday, from 6:30pm to 8pm, the parking lot in front of Parliament becomes a street carnival where arts and crafts are sold.

EXCURSIONS & DAY TRIPS

Sign up for a day-long snorkel sail, which includes picnicking and drinks, with **Aruba Marine Services**, *Tel. 39290*; **Andante**, *Tel. 47718*; **Aruba Pirates Cruises**, *Tel. 24554*, **De Palm Tours**, *Tel. 24545*; **Mi Dushi**, *Tel. 25313*; **Pelican Watersports**, *Tel. 31228*; **Red Sail Sports**, *Tel. 64500*; **Tattoo**, *Tel. 23513*; **Tranquillo**, *Tel. 31228*; **Wave Dancer**, *Tel. 25520 or* **Windfeathers**, *Tel. 23513*.

Charter a sailing ship overnight or by the day with **Aruba Marine Services**, *Tel. 39190*; **Aruba Pirates Cruises**, *Tel. 24554*; **Discovery Tours**,

Tel. 75875; **Octopus Sailing Cruises,** *Tel. 33081;* **Vab E&B Yacht Charters,** *Tel. 37723;* and **Windfeather Charters,** *Tel. 65842.*

PRACTICAL INFORMATION

Area Code: from the U.S., dial 011-297 plus the number.

Cell phones: can be rented on presentation of a passport and deposit, *Tel. 20005.*

Currency: The Aruba florin, divided into 100 cents, is tied to the dollar at the rate of AF 1.77 to US$1. American dollars are accepted everywhere, but you probably won't get change in U.S. funds.

Current: electrical service is at 110 volts, 60 cycles, the same as in the United States.

Handicap access isn't always available here. Check ahead with individual carriers and hotels.

Hazards: the most remote of Aruba's eastern scrub is home to the poisonous Colebra snake. It's seen so rarely that it's considered good luck to find one. Don't hike the bush in thin tennis shoes or flip-flops. The thorns of the hubada tree are longer and sharper than roofing nails.

Hours: downtown shops generally open Monday through Saturday at 8am and close at 6pm, with a break of an hour or two at noon. Mall shops open at 10:30am and most stay open through the lunch hour. Hours are extended when cruise ships are in port. At the Alhambra Bazaar, shop until midnight. Banks open Monday through Friday at 8am to noon and 1:30 to 4pm. The bank at the airport is open Saturday 9am to 4pm and Sunday 9am to 1pm. Bank and government holidays include New Year's, January 25, Carnival Mondays, Good Friday, Easter Monday, March 18 (Flag Day) the Queen's Birthday (April 30), Labor Day in early May, Ascension Day, Christmas, and Second Christmas Day, December 26.

Immigration: citizens of the United States and Canada need a valid passport or a birth or naturalization certificate plus photo ID.

Medical matters: Aruba hotels all have doctors on call. For an air ambulance, *Tel. 29197.* A 24-hour emergency medical center is Centro Medico, Bernardstraat 75, San Nicolas, *Tel. 48833.* The center is open for non-emergency consultations Monday through Friday, 8am to noon and 3-5pm. Wheelchairs and other medical assists can be rented from Labco, *Tel. 26651.*

Movies: drive-in movies have all but disappeared from the United States, but there is one here at Balashi.

Pets aren't allowed at most hotels, but they can enter the island when accompanied by a valid rabies and health certificate issued by a licensed veterinarian.

Telephone: to call Aruba from North America, the area code is **2978**. A USA Direct phone is found in the departure halls of the airport and the cruise terminal. You can buy phone cards, pre-paid telephone cards that are available at most snack bars, gas stations, and sundries shops. Look for a sign advertising Setar cards.

Tourist information is available Monday through Friday, 9am to 5pm from a hot-line, *Tel. 39000*. After hours, the number is answered by machine. From North America, *Tel. 800/577-7916* for information about activities. In Aruba, call *Tel. 25353*. Tourist information bureaus are found at the airport and at L.G. Smith Boulevard 172, Eagle Beach, *Tel. 23777*. Write the Aruba Tourism Authority, 1000 Harbor Boulevard Ground Level, Weehawken NJ 07087, *Tel. 800/ TO-ARUBA* or *201/330-0800*.

Water: drinking water, which is distilled, is pure and safe. It's expensive to produce, so don't waste it.

15. BONAIRE

It's easy to lump Aruba, **Bonaire**, and Curacao together as the ABC islands but they're actually separate, stellar jewels in the Caribbean tiara. In common they are washed by clear azure waters and sweet, warm winds. They are inhabited by a friendly mix of European, African, and Indian bloodlines. Before the Spanish arrived they were peopled by Caiquetios, a clan of the Arawak nation.

Because the islands are Dutch they blend a languid, tropical pace with a no-nonsense efficiency rarely found in the *mañana* latitudes. And, thanks to the Dutch, you can get a great rijsttafel (a delicious rice meal, brought back to Holland from Indonesia).

Bonaire was discovered in 1499 by Amerigo Vespucci, who gave his name to North and South America. Spanish colonization began in 1527 and the Dutch took over in 1636. By 1639 it was a thriving colony with corn fields, salt production, and stock breeding. Slaves were brought in to work the salt pans but were freed in 1863, plunging the island into recession. Blacks and whites alike migrated to Aruba and Curacao to find work. It wasn't until the 1950s, when oil industry jobs became scarce on the other islands, that Bonaireans came home to their still-unexploited homeland.

Salt, panned now using modern, solar methods, remains an important industry – but tourism, buoyed by some of the best scuba diving in the world, has been the island's major cash crop since the first hotel opened in 1951. The island, 24 miles long and no wider than seven miles, is fairly flat, rising only to 784 feet at **Brandaris Hill** and is desert-dry. Don't ignore the countryside with its flowering cactus, beaches, and national park, but it is underwater where Bonaire's greatest riches are found.

Climate

Flat little Bonaire is a paradise for sun seekers, barely disturbed by low-pressure areas that develop north of these islands during hurricane season. Rain is infrequent.

ARRIVALS & DEPARTURES

Bonaire is served nonstop from North America or via Curacao or San Juan, by **ALM**, *Tel. 800/327-7230*, **American Airlines**, *Tel. 800/433-7300*, and **Air Aruba**, *Tel. 800/882-7822*. **Delta Air Lines**, *Tel. 800/221-1212*, and **United Air Lines**, *Tel. 800/241-6522*, offer connecting flights into Bonaire on **ALM**. See your local travel agent and watch local newspapers because charter flights are often organized from cities all over North America.

Flights are into **Flamingo Airport**, which is a taxi ride of $10 to $15 from most hotels.

ORIENTATION

Everything centers around the main city of **Kralendijk**, which is just north of the airport. If you arrive by ship, you'll be at the docks downtown, handy to the post office and shops. The main streets include Kaya Grandi, one street in from the waterfront, and the waterfront road, which is variously called Kaya Charles Hellmund, Kaya J.N.E. Craane, and Kaya Play Lechi. Almost every street downtown is one-way, so if you drive here, allow extra time for finding a way to get where you want to go.

Down the west side of the island, a road follows the water from Plaza Frans in the north to the southern tip at **Willemstoren lighthouse**. Orientation is easy as long as you have sight of the sea. Inland, it's fun to roam the hills and dirt roads where you'll get lost, meet people, and see the sights. Be sure to ask for the Tourist Map, which shows all the best beaches, dives, and watersports sites.

PAPIAMENTO

*The local patois, **Papiamento**, is a mixture of Spanish, Indian, English, Portuguese, Dutch, French, and African. "**Bonbini**" welcomes the visitor, who replies "**Me ta bon, danki**." It's the age-old version of "How are you?" "I'm fine, thank you." English is spoken almost everywhere; Dutch is the official language.*

GETTING AROUND BONAIRE

Roads are rough and the sun is strong, so resist your urge to zip around on a motor scooter. You may be able to manage without wheels at all, depending on your hotel package. If not, rental cars can be reserved from North America through **Budget Rent-a-Car**, *Tel. 800/472-3325;* **Avis**, *Tel. 800/331-1084; or* **Dollar Rent-a-Car**, *Tel. 421-6868*. Driving is on the right; your U.S. or Canadian driver's license is accepted.

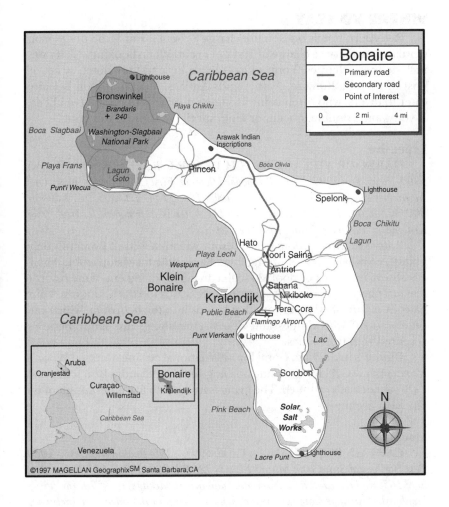

Bonaire
- Primary road
- Secondary road
- • Point of Interest

0   2 mi   4 mi

Caribbean Sea

• Lighthouse
Bronswinkel
Brandaris
+ 240
Boca Slagbaai   Washington-Slagbaai
National Park
Playa Chikitu
Playa Frans
Lagun
Goto
Punt'i Wecua
Rincon
Boca Olivia
Arawak Indian
Inscriptions

• Lighthouse
Spelonk
Boca Chikitu
Lagun
Hato
Playa Lechi
Westpunt
Klein
Bonaire
Noor'i Salina
Antriol
Sabana
Nikiboko
Tera Cora
Kralendijk
Public Beach
Flamingo Airport
Punt Vierkant • Lighthouse
Lac
Caribbean Sea
Sorobon
Aruba
Oranjestad
Bonaire
Kralendijk
Curaçao
Willemstad
Caribbean Sea
Pink Beach
Solar
Salt
Works
Venezuela
Lacre Punt • Lighthouse

N

©1997 MAGELLAN GeographixSM Santa Barbara,CA

Taxis have no meters, but rates are set and are no more than about $10 to $15 to almost any hotel on the island. Ask before you board. After 8 pm, you'll pay 25 per cent more than the standard rate and, between midnight and 6 am, a 50 per cent surcharge applies. Most drivers will be glad to quote you a flat rate for sightseeing by the hour.

WHERE TO STAY

Red Alert: hotels on Bonaire charge a room tax of $6.50 per person per day plus a service charge of 10-12 per cent. When booking, ask if rates include these charges. Your address while here will be: hotel, street or post office box, Bonaire, Netherlands Antilles. Most hotels on Bonaire cater to divers, who often come as same-sex groups that want twin beds. If you want a double, queen, or king, specify that when you book.

Expensive

HARBOUR VILLAGE BEACH RESORT, *Box 312, Kralendijk. Tel. 5997/7500, Fax 5997/7507. It is booked through First Class Resorts, N.A., One Alhambra Plaza, Suite 1150, Coral Gables FL 33134, Tel. 305/567-9509 or 800/424-0004. Rates start at $265. The hotel is a five-minute drive from Kralendijk and ten minutes from the airport.*

Rooms in this 72-room beach resort, which calls itself Bonaire's only luxury resort, are air conditioned and have cable television and kitchenette. Swim in the sea or pool, go scuba diving or sailing out of the resort's marina, play tennis, get a massage in the Spa, or shop the boutiques. Your balcony is furnished as a room that blends into the bedroom, which can be closed off with drapes and doors. Furnishings are sandy neutrals accented with fruit tones.

Dining is in the Kasa Coral for international cuisine, Captain Wook's Marina Bar & Grill for dockside noshing, and La Balandra Beach Bay and Grill for cocktails or lunch. The living is lively, with live entertainment on tap most evenings.

Moderate

CAPTAIN DON'S HABITAT, *Tel. 5997/8290. Booking address is 1080 Port Boulveard Suite 100, Miami FL 33132, Tel. 800/327-6709. Rooms start at $165 nightly and a seven-night, non-diver package is $570 including breakfast. Transfers from the airport, which is 10 minutes away, are included.*

Captain Don's bills itself as the Home of Diving Freedom, combining comfortable accommodations and island ambience with scuba and snorkel excursions. The 79 guest rooms are air conditioned. Kitchenettes, cottages, and villas are also available. When you're not exploring the underwater wonderland around Bonaire, relax in a chaise on the wood deck next to the big, blue pool. Take meals in Rum Runners; rent a mountain bike to roam the countryside. If you're not a certified diver, take the certification package. It requires at least four nights and costs $300.

CLUB NAUTICO BONAIRE, *Kaya Jan N.E. Cranne 24. Tel. 5997/ 5800, Fax 5997/5850. Rates start at $180 for a suite.*

Overlooking the waterfront on the promenade in Kralendijk is this yachting center where you're handy to everything the water offers: diving, deep sea fishing, snorkel trips, sailing, and water skiing including instructions. Swim in the big, free-form pool with its private sun deck, roam the city, or hang out with the boat crowd that congregates here. Luxury suites and penthouses are designed in a Dutch colonial theme; the complex has its own restaurant and bar, and plenty of others are within walking distance.

PLAZA RESORT BONAIRE, *Abraham Boulevard 80. Tel. 5997/2500, Fax 5997/2517; U.S. 800/766-6016. Rates at this 224-suite resort start at $125 for two in a junior suite. The resort is five minutes from Kralendijk or the airport. Ask about packages that include airport transfers, tax, and service charges.*

One- and two-bedroom villas are ideal for divers, lovers, beachcombers, and families. There's a complete watersports center to arrange dives and snorkel outings. Play tennis, squash, or basketball, jog, or join the exercise classes. All units overlook the beach or lagoon and have a full kitchen. Three restaurants, three bars, a mini-market and a car rental center are on site.

SAND DOLLAR CONDOMINIUM RESORT, *Kaya Gobernador Debrot 79. Tel. 5997/8738, Fax 5997/8760, U.S. 800/288-4773. Rates start at $170 for a studio apartment. Apartments with one, two or three bedrooms are available. Add $40 per person daily for breakfast and dinner, which is served in the popular Green Parrot Restaurant. The resort is three miles north of the airport and 1.5 miles north of Kralendijk.*

It's hard to beat the convenience and comfort of having your own apartment at condo prices in a resort that has a restaurant this good. Units are individually owned, so each one has a different decor but you can be sure it will be a typical rattan/wicker sort of thing accented with island colors. Every unit has cable television, full kitchen, and bath, a private terrace or patio with a view of the sea, and a convertible, queen-size sofa. Rooms are serviced by a maid daily.

The beach isn't much, but the dive operation is five-star PADI and there's a swimming pool. In season, a special program entertains kids ages five to 15.

SUNSET BEACH HOTEL, *Kaya Gobernador Debrot 75, mailing address Box 75, Karlendijk. Tel. 5997/8291, Fax 5997/4870, U.S. 800/344-4439 or, in the U.S. and Canada, Tel. 800/328-2288. Rates at this 142-room resort start at $140.*

The resort spreads over 12 acres including one of the island's best beaches. Dine in the beachside, grass-roof restaurant with its popular theme nights, swim in the freshwater pool, or play tennis day or night. Rooms have air conditioning, a refrigerator, safe, telephone, and cable television. The resort has been around for a while and its bathrooms are small by modern standards, but it's well kept and updated with lots of white tile, light rattan furniture, and tropical prints. Diving and snorkeling are good right off the beach, or book a dive trip with the on-site dive center

SOROBON BEACH RESORT, *Tel. 5997/8080, Fax 5997/5686, toll-free Tel. 800/253-6573. Rates start at $200. Located on Lac Bay, the resort is about four miles from the airport.*

This 30-room hotel won't be for everyone, but its claim to fame is a clothing optional beach and a starkly northern-European ambience that sweeps away clutter in favor of natural basics: good woods, comfortable furnishings, good views of the bay, good swimming on a good beach, sunning in your birthday suit, sailing, reading, and playing ping pong or volleyball. Its most popular water pastime is board sailing. The hotel has a restaurant, swimming pool, car rental, and tennis. If you're not a guest, don't blunder in for a curious look. If you're allowed to stay (and you won't be if you're here to ogle the nudity), you'll pay a fee to use the facilities. Studios, condos, and villas are available. Diving and bicycling can be arranged.

Budget

BLUE IGUANA, *Kaya Prinses Marie 6, Kralendijk. Tel. 5997/6855. Rates at this seven-room inn start at $50 for one and $65 for two including breakfast.*

Stay in the heart of town in a historic house with a pretty garden where breakfast is served. You'll share a bath and you're also welcome to use the kitchen. Stake out a hammock in the garden and read while your mate is out diving, or prowl the city's shops and restaurants. Your bedroom, furnished in antiques, has a ceiling fan but no air conditioning.

BRUCE BOWKER'S CARIB INN, *J.A. Abraham Boulevard, mailing address Box 68, Kralendijk. Tel. 5997/8819, Fax 5997/5295. Rates at this 16-unit inn start at $80 for a studio apartment that sleeps two. Apartments sleep four. It's one mile from the airport.*

Dive with the experts here or, if you need to be certified or upgraded to specialty diving, take lessons in a five-star PADI dive facility that has two dive boats, 60 tanks, two compressors, and 12 full sets of dive gear available to guests. Night dives are held on request, and Bruce takes trips to the east coast when weather allows. Rooms are air conditioned and have a kitchenette or full kitchen, except for two rooms that have only a refrigerator and electric kettle.

There's no restaurant on site, but a convenience store and restaurants are within walking distance. When you're not diving, lounge around the teardrop-shaped, freshwater swimming pool. Bowker is an American who lived his dream by coming to Bonaire and starting a shoestring dive operation that has grown to this inn, which is heavily booked with repeaters.

BUDDY BEACH AND DIVE RESORT, *Kaya Gobernador Debrot. Tel. 5997/5080, Fax 5997/8647, U.S. 800/359-0747. Rates at this 40-unit resort start at $85 for an apartment with twin beds, a sleeper sofa, and kitchenette. Apartments with up to three bedrooms are available. Ask about dive packages. The resort is a five-minute drive from the marina downtown and ten minutes from the airport.*

Diving is everything at this resort where two attractive, white, three-story buildings are filled with homey condos. Every unit has an ocean view, full cooking equipment including a microwave oven and dishwasher, air conditioning, and cable television.

Stock up at a small market five minutes away, and do your own cooking when you don't feel like dining in the hotel's restaurant. There are two bars in the resort, which operates two dive boats on daily schedules. Night dives and special guided dives to the east coast are available. Non-divers can stay in the resort to enjoy the two swimming pools or rent a car on site for island exploring.

WHERE TO EAT

Bonaire doesn't have any ultra-expensive restaurants, although even a budget restaurant can be a splurge when you order lobster and a couple of drinks.

Expensive

BEEFEATER GARDEN RESTAURANT & BAR, *Kaya Grandi 12. Tel. 77776. Hours are Monday to Friday from 10 am and weekends from 4 pm. Plan to spend $30-40 for dinner.*

You're dining in the heart of the city yet behind this traditional old Bonairean house is a large, lush country garden. Decorated with crafts and art work that are for sale, the Beefeater has steaks but it's also known for its native goat stew, Baka Stoba (beef stew), shrimp, curries, and a selection of vegetarian dishes. Live entertainers perform on Sunday.

BUDDYS REEF, *in Buddy Dive Resort on Kaya Gobernador Nicolaas Debrot between Kralendijk and Hato. Tel. 75080. Main dishes are priced $15 to $30. Call for reservations and hours.*

The most popular meal here with hungry divers is all the spareribs you can eat. Start with shrimp cocktail or escargot, then a green salad with fruit and cheese or bacon. Choose one of the six soups, fresh fish, or steak.

CROCCANTINO RESTAURANT & BAR, *Kaya Grandi 48. Tel. 75025. Hours are Monday to Friday noon to 2:30 and 6-11 pm. Light dishes and snacks are served between lunch and dinner. The bar stays open until the last guest leaves. Reservations are suggested.*

For years this has been the place for Italian classics but now the menu has expanded to include international dishes from Columbia, Venezuela, Indonesia, and Holland. The setting is an old house with a mosaic courtyard. Dine there or indoors in the air conditioning. Signature dishes are the penne with salmon and the Spaghetti Klein Bonaire, which has a seafood sauce. Complete the meal with a sweet, cappuccino, or espresso.

DEN LAMAN, *Kaya Gobernador Nicolaas Debrot 77. Tel. 78955. Main dishes are priced $15 to $30. Reservations are essential. Hours are 6-11 pm daily except for the second two weeks in September.*

Start with cocktails on the patio, then order the house specialty fish soup followed by the catch of the day in this popular seafood restaurant along "hotel" row north of Kralendijk. Or choose a live lobster from the tank and have it cooked to order. Save room for the homemade cheesecake.

MONA LISA BAR & RESTAURANT, *Kaya Grandi 15. Tel. 78718. It's open Monday through Friday for lunch and dinner; the bar stays open until 2 am. Reservations are suggested.*

The decor begins, unsurprisingly, with a copy of the Mona Lisa. The building is one of the island's oldest, centered with an old Dutch bar and decorated with original iron grillwork. International dishes range from Dutch and French to the popular Indonesian pork satay with peanut sauce. Order fresh fish or a steak, which are served with plenty of colorful vegetables.

OASIS BAR & GRILL, *Kaminada Sorobon 64, Lac Bay. Tel. 78198. Call for hours and reservations. Plan to spend $25 to $35 for dinner.*

This calls for a trip to the south end of the island for a meal that starts with a fruit punch and popcorn shrimp or a basket of yucca, plantain, and sweet potato chips served with black bean relish. Try the barbecued chicken with Caesar salad, grilled shrimp, a gargantuan burger topped with mushrooms, bacon and cheddar cheese, or a grilled ribeye steak. Tempting vegetarian specialties include a mammoth salad containing 12 fresh veggies. Dine outdoors overlooking Lac Bay, or indoors.

MI PORON BAR & RESTAURANT, *Kaya Caracas 1 near the church. Tel. 75199. Reservations aren't accepted. It's open Tuesday through Saturday noon to 2 pm and 6-10 pm and Sunday for dinner only.*

Locals love this hometown restaurant with its comfort foods and a quaint museum and shop, so waits can be long if you arrive during peak hours. Order fried fish, conch, or stewed goat in the airy courtyard of a restored house.

OTTELLO RESTAURANT & BAR, *Kaya Prinses Marie 4, near the Bonaire Twin Cinema. Tel. 74449. The bar is open 11 amto 2 pm. Lunch is served noon to 3 pm and dinner is 6-11 pm. Plan to spend $25 to $35 for dinner.*

Homemade pasta is the centerpiece for fabulous Italian meals. Have the lobster Siciliana, smoked fish pizza, or homemade minestrone. Let your server suggest a wine.

PLAYA LECHI RESTAURANT, *in the Sunset Beach Resort, Kaya Gobernador Nicolaas Debrot 75. Tel. 75300, extension 195. Reservations are advised for dinner. It's open 7am to 10:30pm.*

Relax in a beach hut where the buffet breakfasts are a good way to start the day and cocktails are served as the sun goes down. Happy Hour prices apply from 5:30-7 pm. The best time to be here is on Saturday when Bonairean Night features a buffet of local dishes and a steel band serenade, followed by a folkloric dance show. Be prepared to join in. On Monday a local band plays during happy hour and a duo entertains on Wednesday during dinner.

RENDEZ-VOUS, *Kaya L.D. Gerharts 3. Tel. 77261. It's open for lunch and dinner Monday through Saturday. Call for hours and reservations. Dinner costs $20 to $35.*

Comfort foods include the hearty soups and stews of old Holland, or have puff pastry stuffed with vegetables, fish, or meat. Fresh fish or juicy steaks are served with crusty bread, good Dutch butter, and plenty of vegetables or just order vegetables alone for a meatless meal. Dining is on a terrace under a ceiling filled with fairy lights.

Moderate

CHIBI CHIBI, *in the Divi Flamingo Beach Resort, J.A. Abraham Boulevard 40. Tel. 78285. It's open daily for dinner, which costs $15 to $25.*

Dine outdoors on a wood deck overlooking the beach. Try the Dutch stuffed cheese dish called keshi yena, or fresh fish. A house specialty is Fettucini Flamingo, a pasta with a rich, seafood sauce.

CHINA GARDEN, *Kaya Grandi 47. Tel. 78480. It's open daily except Tuesday for lunch and dinner. Main dishes average $11.*

Cantonese and Indonesian dishes, as well as steaks and American-style sandwiches are served in the heart of town in an old mansion that has been restored.

GREEN PARROT, *in the Sand Dollar Beach Club, Kaya Gobernador Nicolaas Debrot 79. Tel. 75454. Reservations are advised. Plan to spend $15-$35 for dinner. Hours are 8 am to 10 pm daily; Happy Hour specials are served 5-7 pm every day.*

This popular, out-island hangout sits over the water, inviting long evenings that start with a sundowner followed by fresh fish in a spicy Creole sauce, or steaks freshly sizzled on the charcoal grill and served with a loaf of onion rings. Or linger over a leisurely lunch anchored by the famous Green Parrot Giant Hamburger with a fruity margarita. Saturday nights feature a barbecue buffet and live music. If you're spending the day on the beach, order a carry-out picnic.

Budget

CHINA NOBO RESTAURANT & BAR, *Emerencianastraat 4. Tel. 78981. Open daily except Tuesday 11 am to 11 pm, it does not accept credit cards. Plan to spend $10 to $15 for dinner.*

Get a free egg roll with every main dish at this generous, air conditioned restaurant. Everyone's favorite Cantonese stir-fry dishes are on the menu, so mix and match to eat in or take out. Or, call for night deliveries.

SANDWICH FACTORY, *on Kaya Prinses Marie (one-way to the west) 1/2 block from Kaya Grandi (one-way to the south). Tel. 7369 is open every day from 7 a mto 8:30 pm. Lunch is from $5; dinner from $8. Credit cards aren't accepted.*

This American-style deli gets all of its meats and cheeses from the U.S. to assure the right tang to hoagies, mile-high sandwiches served on puffy rolls, steaks, and chicken. Meals are available eat in, take out, or delivered.

SUPER CORNER, *Kaya Simon Bolivar 21. Tel. 72112. Hours are Tuesday through Sunday 7 am to 11 pm and Monday 7 am to 3 pm. Eat for $10 or less. Reservations and credit cards aren't accepted.*

Stop in just for ice cream, a cold drink, or a snack, or fill up on heartier fare. Hamburgers or hot dogs with French fries are stalwarts here, but you can also try native favorites such as goat stew, meat or fish-filled pastries, fresh fish, fish soup, and Indonesian rice dishes, which are ready after 11:30 am.

SEEING THE SIGHTS

From its northern tip, which is a national park, to its southern tip, which is a flamingo sanctuary, Bonaire is a sightseeing bonanza. Sign on with **Bonaire Tours**, *Tel. 78778*, or **Baranka Tours**, *Tel. 22200*, for a guided tour, then strike out in your own car or scooter.

The entire northwest corner of the island, an area of 13,500 acres, is covered by **Washington-Slagbaai National Park**, *Tel. 78444*, open daily from 8am to 5pm, with no new tickets sold after 3 pm. Admission is $5 for adults, $1 for children under age 15, and it's worthwhile to spend an additional $5.50 for the guidebook.

The park was once a plantation. It was donated to the island with the provision that it never be developed. It's home to 189 species of birds that swoop among the cliffs and warble high in the cactus. Walk the beaches, valleys, and beaches of this quietly dramatic park. You won't see mountains and mahogany trees here, but observe closely and you'll find the desert's own smells and songs. The beaches and offshore dive sites are outstanding.

At the entrance to the park, a museum has historic exhibits so spend half an hour to get the feel of the place. In the **Bay of Shells**, you'll find fossils, but remember that this is a national park. Not even dead shells can be taken. Along Playa Cunhi, which was the harbor of the Washington Plantation that once covered these lands, look for lizards, coral, and darting fish in the shallows. Have a swim in Boca Slagbaai.

Arrive early for the best birding. Two routes are marked along rugged roads, so bring a picnic lunch and take your time for rubbernecking, photography, and snorkeling. Linger at **Bronswinkel Well**, where flocks of birds come for fresh water. Along the way you'll see the giant cactus that is one of the ABC islands' most photographable sights, plus lignum vitae trees, cliffs overlooking the ocean, and the occasional tomcat-size iguana.

PICTURE IMPERFECT

Bring plenty of film to the ABC islands, where film sells for $10 or more a roll – and don't leave it to be developed before asking the price. One recent tourist paid more than $40 for one-hour processing!

On a "Country Tour" with **Bonaire Sightseeing**, *Tel. 78778,* you'll see Indian inscriptions, **Goto Lake** with its brilliant flamingoes, stone huts that were homes for slaves who worked the salt flats, and some of the island's best lookouts. **Rincon**, in the northern part of the island, is its oldest settlement. It dates to the days of Spanish occupation, when newly-arrived slaves imprinted this settlement with a voodoo spell that lingers still on dark nights. Tour prices start at $25 per person; the all-day tour is $60 for adults and $30 for children.

Eco-tours with a Dutch biologist and dive instructor are from **Bonaire Nature Tours**, *Tel. 77714.* Her mini-bus holds no more than seven people for tours that last from 9am to 6pm.

In the city of **Kralendijk**, pronounced to rhyme with roll-in-dike but locally called Playa, there are some old churches and what is left of **Fort**

Oranje but, unless you want to shop and dine here, it's better to get away from the traffic and head out. From Kralindijk, drive south from the 500-foot-high radio tower, which is hard to miss. Stop at the public beach if you like, and continue on the shore road past miles of salt pans. Salt water is taken into the salt lake, then into ponds where it becomes increasingly briny. After it crystalizes it is cleaned, drained, and dried for several more months, then is loaded for shipping to the United States or other Caribbean islands.

You'll begin to see flamingoes from the road around the **Pekelmeer** (salt lake) but their breeding ground is a 135-acre sanctuary in the heart of the pans. The entire Caribbean flamingo population of some 40,000 birds headquarters here, building big nests two feet across and more than a foot high for the one egg that each mother lays. When you see the stone huts that were built in the mid-1800s to house slaves at Road Pan, stop and you'll be looking over the nesting area. The birds are easily spooked, so it's not permitted to enter the sanctuary.

At the island's southern tip at **Willemstoren**, see a lighthouse built in 1837. Pass pretty little Lac Bay with its piles of conch shells, then stop for a cold drink at **Nikiboka** on your way back to Kralendijk.

To make a northern swing, which takes about two hours, pass Sunset Beach Resort and Radio Nederland towards Rincon, stopping at **Gotomeer** to watch for more flamingoes. They are a sunset spectacle when they take off for Venezuela at sundown. At **Dos Pos**, which means Two Wells, you'll be in a greenbelt more lush than most of the rest of this sere island. Crest the next hill and stop to look down at the ancient village of **Rincon**, which has been inhabited since before the Conquistadores. Ask locally where to look for Arawak drawings, then climb to Seru Largu to look down on Kralendijk before you return there.

Offered by **Bonaire Tours**, *Tel. 78778 or 78300 ext. 212,* are five itineraries, all of them an ideal way to get your bearings before starting out on your own. Northern and southern island routes take two hours. The first visits the **1000 Steps** where divers walk down what seem like 1,000 steps to a dive site right offshore; Goto Lake with its flamingos; Indian inscriptions; and overlooks. The second goes to the salt flats with their mountains of white salt, pink flamingos, and clear, cloudless blue skies. In a three-hour tour, see a bit of both city and country. Four-and seven-hour itineraries focus on the national park.

NIGHTLIFE & ENTERTAINMENT

The dive hotels are always good places to gather at night for the latest scuttlebutt and shop talk on the underwater scene, which is the happening thing on Bonaire. Chances are, you won't have to leave your hotel for all the nightlife you want. Ask at your hotel desk for a guest pass to **E WOWO**, downtown at Kaya Grandi 38, *Tel. 78998*. It's a disco open to members only. The powwow starts at about 9 pm and goes on until all hours Wednesday through Sunday. Also popular downtown is **KAREL'S** on the waterfront, *Tel. 78434*. Local bands play on Friday and Saturday nights, and sometimes on other nights too. Look out over the moonlit sea or join in the conversation, which invariably has to do with boating or diving.

THE WHISKEY BAR & NIGHT CLUB, *Tel. 75300*, upstairs in the main building at the Sunset Beach Club, is a hangout fashioned with mirrored mosaics, marine murals, and a loud, laser-lit dance floor. You can also play darts or pool, drink at the bar, or snack on sandwiches or baked brie. Happy Hour offers discounts 11 pm to midnight and fun goes on until much later.

There's a casino at the **DIVI FLAMINGO BEACH RESORT** offering blackjack, roulette, poker, slot machines and other games 8 pm to 2 am. It's closed Sunday. Dress is very casual; admission is free.

SPORTS & RECREATION
Bicycling
Get a rental bike or book a bicycle tour with **Cycle Bonaire**, *Tel. 77558*. Tours can combine mountain biking with snorkeling and other exploring.

Boating
The **International Club Nautico** chain has a boat rental fleet on Bonaire, *Tel. 78500*. Members get a discounted rate, so if your home town has one, it may pay to join while you're here.

Ocean Breeze, *Tel. 75661*, a powerboat that is licensed for fishing or cruising, can take you on a half-day, all-day or overnight cruise to snorkel, sightsee, fish, or cruise other islands. Cruise the **Bonaire Marine Park** in a glass-bottom boat with **Bonaire Dream**, *Tel. 74514*.

Diving
More than 50 easily accessible dive sites are found around the island, which is a major scuba destination for divers from around the world. Snorkeling in shallow water, you're in a wonderland of blue tangs, foureye butterflyfish, queen angelfish, and lemon colored French grunts. A dozen resorts on the island offer free underwater slide shows, and encourage enlightened, environmentally sensitive snorkeling.

Snorkeling tours, equipment and instruction are available through:
• **Bonaire Caribbean Club**, *Tel. 5997/7901*
• **Bonbini Divers**, *Tel. 800/768-3484 or 5997/5425*

- **Buddy Dive Resort**, *Tel. 800/359-0749 or 5997/5080*
- **Captain Don's Habitat**, *Tel. 800/327-6709 or 5997/8290*
- **Dive Inn**, *Tel. 5997/8761*
- **Flamingo Beach Hotel**, *Tel. 5997/ 8285*
- **Harbour Village Beach Resort**, *Tel. 800/868- 7477 or 5997/7500*
- **Plaza Resort Bonaire**, *Tel. 800/766-6016 or 5997/2500*
- **Sand Dollar Condominium Resort**, *Tel. 800/288-4773 or 5997/8738*
- **Sunset Beach Dive Center**, *Tel. 800/328- 2288 or 5997/8330*

Bonaire's stunning underwater **Marine Park** has more than 80 dive sites, each marked with buoys or stones where divers can tie up, avoiding the reef damage than can be caused by anchoring. Entry to the park costs $10, a one-time fee that will be collected by your dive operator. It's illegal to take fish, coral or any other souvenir. The island has its own decompression chamber.

Scuba outfitters providing air, gear rental, instruction, dive boats, camcorder rental, and resort accommodations include:

BLUE DIVERS, *Kaya den Tera 1, Mainstreet Kralendijk, Tel. 5997/ 6860, Fax 5997/6865; U.S. 800/748-8733 or 601/353-7547, Fax 601/353-7559.*

BON BINI DIVERS, *Kaya Gobernador Debrot 90, Kralendijk, Tel. 5997/ 5425, Fax 5997/4425, U.S. 800/786-3483 or 800/327-8150.*

BLACK DRAGON SCUBA CENTER, *P.O. ox 200, Bonaire, Tel. 5997/ 5736, Fax 5997/8846, U.S. 800/526-2370.*

BRUCE BOWKER'S CARIB INN, *P.O. Box 68, Bonaire, Tel. 5997/ 8819, Fax 5997/5295, e-mail 75317,667@CompuServe.Com.*

BUDDY DIVE, *Kaya Gobernador Debrot, Kralendijk, Tel. 5997/5080, Fax 5997/8647; U.S. 800/786-DIVE or 800/359- 0747.*

CAPTAIN DON'S HABITAT, *P.O. Box 88, Bonaire, Tel. 5997/8290, Fax 5997/8420, U.S. 800/327-6709.*

DIVE INN BONAIRE, *P.O. Box 362, Bonaire, Tel. 5997/8761 or Fax 5997/8513*

GREAT ADVENTURES BONAIRE, *Kaya Gobernador Debrot 71, Tel. 5997/7500, Fax 5997/7507, U.S. 800/424-0004.*

JERRY SCHNABEL & SUZI SWUGERT'S PHOTO TOURS, *Kaya Utrecht 12, Bonaire, Tel. 5997/5390, Fax 5997/8060.*

PETER HUGHES DIVE BONAIRE, *J.A. Abraham Boulevard, Kralendijk, Tel. 5997/8285, Fax 5997/8238, U.S. 800/367-3484.*

SAND DOLLAR DIVE & PHOTO, *Kaya Gobernador Debrot 79, Tel. 5997/5252, Fax 599-7/8760; U.S. 800/288-4773.*

SUNSET BEACH DIVE CENTER, *P.O. Box 115 or 333, Kralendijk, Tel. and Fax 5997/8330, U.S. 800/328-2288.*

DIVING BONAIRE

More than 80 dive sites line the shores of Bonaire, which has more dive shops, operators, and divers per square inch than any other island we can think of. The island of Klein Bonaire acts like a barrier reef off **Kralendijk**, calming the seas. It's usual to have visibility of 100 feet. The north and east coasts, by contrast, is pounded by waves and is best enjoyed for its winds and dunes. Only a couple of dive sites are found in the southeast, just outside **Lac Bay**. Starting near **Willemstoren Lighthouse** on the south point, reefs and wrecks line the entire west coast, run a ring around Klein Bonaire and continue to the **Karpata** area, which is a reserve where no diving is allowed. Off the national park in the northwest, diving and snorkeling sites are found almost all the way to **Noordpunt** at the top of the island.

The best reefs are in the **lee of Klein Bonaire**, where the beach slopes gradually to 33 feet, followed by drop-offs to 100-200 feet. Included among the walk-in dive sites are **1,000 Steps** (not really 1,000) but it seems that many when you're wearing tanks and belts) and in **Nukove Doblet** in the northwest.

To reach **Alice in Wonderland**, a double reef separated by a sand channel and extending from Punt Vierkant south toward Salt Pier, take a boat. The reef system is filled with sea gardens, most marked by dive buoys. In one garden, Angel City, lies the wreck of the **Hilma Hooker**, which was busted for marijuana smuggling. When nobody showed up to claim her, the 80-foot cargo ship sank at her moorings.

Dives recommended for beginners and intermediate-level divers include **Bon Adventure**, a boat dive to 20-100 feet in a mild current to a site filled with soft corals and large tub sponges; and **Bon Bini Na Kas**, with light to moderate current in 20-100 feet to see sea fans, sponges, and soft corals that are home to French angel fish.

Experienced divers can try **Bloodlet**, a boat dive to 20-100 feet to see plate coral and, with luck, some turtles. **Oil Slick Leap** is a boat dive for intermediate and expert divers to see pencil coral, brain coral, and the angel fish that live among them. For elk horn coral, try **Wind Sock**, a dive that can be accessed from shore or by boat. It's in depths of 20 to 80 feet and is inhabited by rays and angelfish. The current is moderate. At **Light House Point**, intermediate and experienced divers will find brain coral, tube sponge, and parrot fish 30 to 100 feet down in currents that can be moderate to strong.

Any dive operator will tell you that the show is different every day even if you dive the same spot time and again. And, for a new look at a dive site you've seen a thousand times, go for a night dive. Night snorkeling is also catching on. Ask at your hotel or dive shop.

TOUCAN DIVING, *Abraham Boulevard 80, Kralendijk, Tel. 5997/ 2500, Fax 5997/7133, U.S. 800/766-6016.* To sail a 56-foot ketch with diving equipment try the *Sea Witch*, which carries up to four guests, *Tel. 75433.*

Fishing

Sportfish with **Captain Cornelius** aboard his 29-foot cabin cruiser, *Tel. 76500.* Stalk bonefish or go deep sea fishing with Captain Chris Morkis of **Piscatur Fishing**, *Tel. 78774.*

Fitness

For step aerobics, water aerobics, dancercize and body shaping, work out with **Bodywork**, Kaya Nikboko Noord 46, *Tel. 75446.* **Joe's Fitness Center**, in Les Galeries Shopping Mall, *Tel. 72842,* has equipment for working out, toning and body building, a health bar, and a boutique. The **Spa at Harbour Village**, *Tel. 77500,* offers complete workout facilities and equipment, steam rooms, saunas, and spa treatments including a Bonairean Salt Exfoliate treatment.

Horseback Riding

Kunuku Warahama Ranch, *Tel. 75558,* has been a part of the Bonaire farm scene since before tourism became trendy. Now it is a place to take riding lessons, rent a horse, let the children see the little zoo of exotic and farm animals, and have dinner or a show.

Kayaking

Book a kayak, bicycle tour, or snorkel outing with **Discover Bonaire**, *Tel. 75433,* or with **Jibe City Kayaking**, *Tel. 77363.*

Sailing

To sail a 56-foot ketch with diving equipment try the *Sea Witch*, which carries up to four guests, *Tel. 75433.* Sail and snorkel with *Woodwind*, a 37-foot trimaran, *Tel. 78285.* **Bonsail Charters** take sailing trips to the uninhabited islands off Venezuela, *Tel. 599/607159.* Take a dinner, snorkel, sightseeing, or sunset sail with the *Samur*, a Siamese junk, *Tel. 75433.*

Water Skiing

If your hotel does not offer water skiing, book with **Great Adventures Bonaire**, Harbour Village, *Tel. 77500.*

SHOPPING

Bonaire isn't a St. Thomas, but it does have upscale shops offering watches, gems, crystal, china, and other goods that travelers look for. For that very special Tag Heuer dive watch, shop **Littman Jewelers**, Kaya Grandi 35, *Tel. 78160*. At Kaya Grandi 5, **Island Fashions** is a bright pink and green building where you'll find wraps, swim suits, batik, and whimsical jewelry plus locally made pottery. Opposite the post office (which lies inland from Ro-Ro Pier) find **Fundashon Arte Boneriano**, which has coral jewelry, local art, handicrafts, and souvenirs. Littman also has a gift shop selling shirts, sandals and sea jewelry at the **Harborside Mall**, a downtown shopping center that is open daily except Sunday, when only the restaurants are open.

The **Bonaire Art Gallery**, Caya L.D. Gerbarts #10, *Tel. 71720*, has contemporary Caribbean art and jewelry. **Donzie** on the waterfront at Kaya Bonaire, across from Zeezicht, *Tel. 77642*, has original jewelry, Bonairean art, antiques, and secondhand clothing. For last-minute shopping at the airport, **Valerie's** has fine chocolates, tee shirts, and sundries.

You may encounter some closed stores on Sunday, and some shops close Tuesday afternoon.

EXCURSIONS & DAY TRIPS

Klein Bonaire, which lies off Kralendijk and is uninhabited, is part of a marine sanctuary that rims the island. It's surrounded by some of the world's best dive and snorkel sites. From the high-water mark to a depth of 200 feet, everything is protected against fishing, spearing, anchoring, or even touching. Nothing can be removed, not even dead shells and coral. Fish feeding should be done only under expert guidance. Go with a tour operator (see Diving under *Sports & Recreation* above) who knows the ropes.

Inter-island airlines (see *Arrivals & Departures*) can arrange a side trip to Curacao, Aruba, Trinidad, Tobago, or a number of sites along the South American coast.

PRACTICAL INFORMATION

Area Code: 5997

ATM: To find an ATM look for the following networks: ABN-AMRO, Caribbean Mercantile, Bankomatiko, and Geldautomaat. There's also an ATM at the airport.

Banking: generally, banks are open Monday through Friday 8 am to 4 pm. Bank holidays include New Year's Day, Carnival Monday, Good Friday, Easter Monday, the Queen's birthday (April 30), Labor Day on May 1, Ascension Day, Bonaire Day (on Bonaire) and Christmas.

Stores generally are open Monday through Saturday, 8 am to noon and 2 pm to 6 pm, but hours are extended when cruise ships are in.

Currency: U.S. dollars circulate freely. Local currency is the Netherlands Antilles florin or guilder at the rate of NAf 1.78 to U.S. $1.

Customs: Americans can take home, duty free, $600 worth of goods purchased here including one carton of cigarettes, and a fifth of liquor plus a second bottle of locally produced liquor. Check prices, though, because even after paying duty, some brands are an excellent buy. Unlimited gifts up to $25 can be mailed home as long as the recipient gets no more than one parcel a day. Local art, handicrafts, and jewelry items are duty free; get a certificate stating they were made here.

Driving & Gas: your home license will serve for driving, but not as proof of citizenship. Driving is on the right, North American style. Speedometers and road signs are in kilometers. Generally the speed limit is 35 kph in town and 60 kph in the open unless a lower speed is posted. Gas stations in Kralendijk are open Monday through Saturday 7am to 9pm, and Sunday 9amto 3:30 pm. Hours at other stations vary.

Electricity: 127/120 VAC at 50 cycles. North American appliances, except for clocks, will work just fine.

Emergencies: *Tel. 110* for police or fire, *Tel. 8900* for an ambulance, *Tel. 114* for the hospital. For Alcoholics Anonymous, *Tel. 8164*; Al-Anon *Tel. 4309*; Narc Non, *Tel. 5330 ext. 26 or after hours 5792.*

Government: The ABC islands are commonwealths of the Netherlands, with Aruba having independent status. American consular services are provided through Curacao.

Hazards: thorns that fall from the Hubada tree are as long, sharp, and hard as nails. Don't hike the bush wearing flip-flops; watch carefully where you step. The Colebra rattlesnake inhabits the remotest pockets of the outback. Beware of sudden showers that can turn hard dirt roads into mud traps.

Hours: Sunday shopping can be iffy and some shops close Tuesday afternoon. Generally, stores are open Monday through Saturday 8 am to noon and 2-6pm.

Holidays: bank and government holidays include Carnival in early spring, depending on the dates of Lent; Easter and Easter Monday; Ash Wednesday; Good Friday; April 30, Queen's Day; March 18, National Anthem and Flag Day; December 5, St. Nicholas Day; December 25, Christmas; December 26, Boxing Day; and New Year's Day.

Immigration: U.S. and Canadian residents need a return ticket plus proof of citizenship such as a voter registration, green card, passport that is not more than five years out of date, or a birth certificate. Photo ID is required.

Language: school sessions are taught in Dutch, and all students study English and at least one other language. The language spoken in homes is Papiamento. Everyone we met here spoke at least some English.

Mail address: to send mail to Bonaire, send it to the post office box number, city, Bonaire, Netherlands Antilles.

Pharmacies: call the Hospital Botika at *Tel. 78900*, Botika Bonaire at *Tel. 78905*, or Botika Korona at *Tel. 77552*.

Taxes: departure tax is $10 for international flights or $5.75 when leaving for another island. There is no tax for children aged two and under.

Telephone: To call Bonaire numbers while on the island, just dial the last four digits. From Bonaire, credit card dialing to the U.S. is available from Lansradio in town or at the airport.

Time zone: the ABCs are on Atlantic Standard Time, which is the same as Eastern Daylight Time, all year.

Tourist information: Bonaire Tourism information is available from Adams Unlimited, *10 Rockefeller Plaza, Suite 900, New York NY 10020, Tel. 212/956- 5911/5900, Fax 956-5913*, or *800/U-BONAIR*. A tourist information office on the island is located on Kaya Simon Bolivar 12, *Tel. 78322*.

16. CURACAO

It's easy to lump Aruba, Bonaire, and **Curacao** together as the ABC islands but they're actually separate, beautiful islands. In common they are washed by clear azure waters and sweet, warm winds. They are inhabited by a friendly mix of European, African, and Indian bloodlines. Before the Spanish arrived they were peopled by Caiquetios, a hunter-gatherer Arawak tribe that probably migrated from Venezuela about 2500 B.C.

Because the islands are Dutch they blend a languid, tropic pace with a no-nonsense efficiency rarely found in the manana latitudes. Things work with Teutonic efficiency. Most of the kitchens and hotel rooms we saw were immaculate. The roads are smooth and wide. Air conditioning works. Tap water, fresh from the distillery, is clear and safe. People are bright, proud, friendly, and they keep appointments on time.

Only 44 miles off the coast of Venezuela, Curacao is 61 kilometers long and 5-14 kilometers wide, with a population of about 150,000 people. Its only city is **Willemstad**, the capital. It is just 12 degrees north of the Equator, but dry winds temper the torrid sunshine.

The Spanish established a small colony here in the early 1500s but dubbed the island "useless" because it had no gold. Local Indians were put to work panning salt, felling timber, and tanning hides for shipment back to Spain. In 1634, the Spanish were routed by the Dutch, who realized that the goldmine in this "useless" island was really its large, deep harbor. For 400 years it has been one of the Caribbean's most important ports.

Despite English and French attempts at conquest, Curacao has been Dutch for almost 400 years. Today, the chief Spanish legacies are Catholicism, which is embraced by more than 80 per cent of the population, and the many Spanish words woven into **Papiamentu** (also spelled Papiamento), the local patois.

Almost from the beginning, Curacao has been a major trade center. Its climate and poor soil couldn't support large plantations, so slaves came here only to be processed for shipment to South America and other

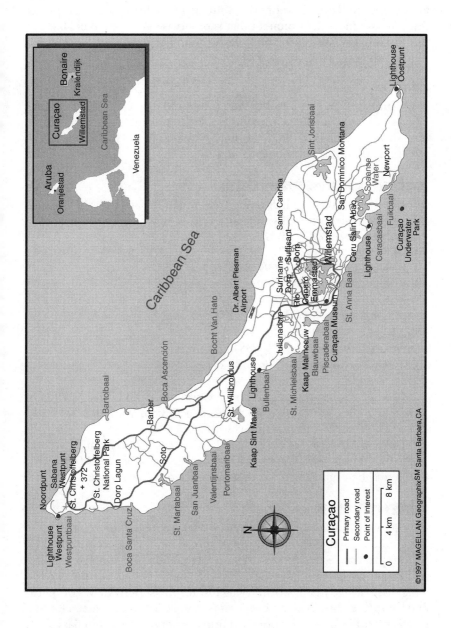

islands. After slavery was abolished in 1863, Curacao slumbered as a quiet crossroads of trade until the discovery of oil in Venezuela launched another boom. Today its refineries, with their telltale smell, are one of the few minuses in an environment that is otherwise an idyllic Bali Hai. For the very latest scoop on Curacao dining, nightlife, arts, sports and entertainment, check out *www.k-pasa.com*.

Climate

Temperatures rise into the 90s by day and are in the 70s at night. Winds are brisk and dry, providing a greater comfort factor at high temperatures than is found in the more humid islands. Hurricanes rarely affect this part of the Caribbean.

ARRIVALS & DEPARTURES

Less than two and a half hours from Miami by air, the ABC islands have modern airports and excellent service. Curacao is served by:
- **Air Aruba**, *Tel. 5999/868-3777*
- **ALM**, *Tel. 5999/869-5533*
- **American Airlines**, *Tel. 5999/868-5707*
- **Avianca**, *Tel. 5999/868-0122*
- **British Airways**, *Tel. 5999/461-7187*
- **BWIA**, *Tel. 5999/868-7835*
- **Servivensa**, *Tel. 5999/868-0500*
- **Surinam Airways**, *Tel. 5999/868-4360*
- **TAP Air Portugal**, *Tel. 5999/868-6241*

Charter flights are operated from Germany by **LTU**, *Tel. 0049-211-941-8029*, in Germany. Through a licensing agreement, **Delta**, *Tel. 800/241-6522*, offers connecting flights with **ALM**.

Guyana Airways, *Tel. 800/242-4210*, flies to Curacao from New York two to four days a week. Watch your local travel pages for news of charters, which may be organized from your city once or twice a year.

ORIENTATION

Picture Curacao as a bikini top with a round medallion at its middle. That's the capital **Willemstad**, which spreads in a ring around the big Schottegat that separates the city into **Otropanda**, the western section, and **Punda** to the east. By vehicle, it's an $8 taxi ride between the two via a high-rise bridge that is worth trying just for the superb view. For quick and free access, however, it's best simply to walk across the **Queen Emma floating bridge**. When the pontoon bridge opens to let a ship pass, free ferries immediately take over and continue shuttling the harbor until the bridge is closed again.

The waist of the island from the airport to Willemstad is covered with neat suburbs and modern shopping centers. A good divided highway called the Ring Road surrounds the city. The eastern end of the island is privately owned and visitors can stray only so far. The best sightseeing is in a loop to Westpunt (West Point) and back to the city.

Punda's trademark view is of **Handelskaade**, the "little Amsterdam" of tall buildings facing the bay. Its counterpart on the other side of the inlet in Otrobanda is **De Rouville Weg**. Both sides are a favorite with strollers and shoppers. The best tourist shopping is in the narrow streets and alleys of Punda in an area bounded by the Floating Market, Plaza Columbus Straat, and Breede Straat. As it goes east, Breede Straat becomes Pietermaai Weg, where the **Tourist Information Bureau** is found at number 19. Stop in for brochures and directions.

Pick up one of the very good AT&T/American Express road maps offered at the airport, car rental agencies, and concierge desks. The good news is that streets are well marked; the bad news is that streets change names for no reason and most street names are unpronounceable. Locals are friendly and helpful, but the Dutch street names, such as Schottegot weg (pronounced cough-gargle-vay-cough) or Schout Bij Nacht Doorman weg, are almost impossible to understand even if a helpful local is pointing a finger to it on your map.

Note: when you see a street address ending in z/n, it means there is no street number.

GETTING AROUND CURACAO

For only $15, hop on the town trolley for a one-hour tour of Willemstad. Offered on Monday and Wednesday and departing from Fort Amsterdam, the tours provide excellent orientation before you set out on your own. For day-trippers from cruise ships they are a superb shortcut to seeing all the highlights in the quickest time. Call *800/3-CURACAO* or, locally, *Tel. 628833.*

Curacao's bus service is frequent and reliable, with most routes served hourly in the city and every two hours to the countryside. Sunday service is more limited.

Simply stand at a *Bushalte* and wait for a large "konvoi." Major terminals are found at the post office in Punda and beside the underpass in Otrabanda. A bus schedule can be purchased for NAFl 1.45. Fare is NAFl 1 in town and NAFl 1.50 to outlying areas. Public transport is also offered by vans identified by BUS on their license plates. Many hotels operate free shuttles to town at least once a day.

Taxi stands are found at the airport, at major hotels, and in downtown Punda and Otrobanda. Fares are set at about $10 from the airport to town, $12-$15 to most hotels, and $8 from Otrobanda to Punda. Fares are based on up to four people, with surcharges for additional passengers, excess baggage, and service after 11pm. Sightseeing taxis can be hired for about $20 per hour. To call a cab, *Tel. 869-0747, 869- 0752, or 462-8686.*

Rental car agencies include **Avis**, *Tel. 868-1163;* **Budget**, *Tel. 868-3466;* **Car Rental 24 Hour**, *Tel. 868-9410;* **Dollar**, *869-0262;* **Hertz**, *Tel. 868-1182;* **Love Car Rental**, *Tel. 869- 0444;* and **National Interrent**, *Tel. 868-3489.* All have offices at the airport.

Bikes and motorcycles are available from **Easy Going**, *Tel. 869-5056;* **Motor Saloon Caribbean**, *Tel. 868-4400;* **Number One Cycle Rental**, *Tel. 868-7447* and **Koert's Motorcycle Rental**, *Tel. 737-7653.*

WHERE TO STAY

Government tax of seven per cent plus service charges of 10-15 per cent can add impressively to your hotel tab. In addition, a six per cent tax is levied on meals and on meal plans that may also have a built-in service charge. When booking, ask whether rates include tax and service charge; some do. Unless otherwise stated, these hotels take major credit cards, although credit cards often are not usable for some hotel services such as shops or tours.

Rates quoted are for a double room in high season. Ask about packages, especially dive packages. Almost every hotel offers excellent deals.

Expensive

CURACAO CARIBBEAN HOTEL & CASINO, *John F. Kennedy Boulevard. Tel. 800/223-9815 or 212/251-1800 in the U.S. or locally 462-5000. Rates at this 196-room resort start at $200. Fare from the airport is about $13.*

A casino adds pace and glamor to this resort near downtown Willemstad and the airport. Choose from a complete menu of watersports and dine and dance your way through the resort's three restaurants and two lounges. Swim off the beach or in the pool, or play tennis on the resort's own courts. At press time, the resort is holding its own but is awaiting new financing, so get current local knowledge before booking here.

KADUSHI CLIFFS RESORT, *Box 3673. Tel. 5999/864-0282 or from the U.S., 800/KADUSHI. Rates start at $295 for a two-bedroom, two-bath bungalow that sleeps four or six. The hotel is 30 minutes from town or the airport, near Westpunt at Playa Kalki Beach. By taxi the ride costs $37 by day and $46 after 11pm.*

Modern apartments with lofty ceilings, full kitchen, and sunny patio are the ideal choice for a family reunion. The hotel, which is a managed time share resort but also welcomes non-timeshare guests, has a picture postcard beach, a rustic restaurant featuring local foods at modest prices, planned activities, a big swimming pool, and an oceanview whirlpool.

PRINCESS BEACH RESORT & CASINO, *Dr. Martin Luther King Boulevard 8. Tel. 5999/736-7888, Fax 461-4131; U.S. and Canada 800/ HOLIDAY. The resort is two miles from downtown Willemstad and about a $10 taxi ride from the airport. Room rates start at $205.*

A Crowne Plaza resort, this winner is on a sugar beach next to the Seaquarium and in front of the National Underwater Park. Rooms have mini-bar, coffee maker, cable television with U.S. stations, safe, direct dialing, and dataport, making this a zesty leisure vacation for the businessperson who likes to stay in touch. Bring the children to enjoy the playground, kiddy pool, and play program, or come as a couple to enjoy Las Vegas-style gaming and entertainments, the shopping gallery, three restaurants, four bars, lighted tennis courts, two swimming pools, scuba diving, and snorkeling.

All of the 341 guest rooms and suites have a private terrace or balcony and air conditioning. Swim in the sea or two pools, play volleyball on the beach, work out in the fully-equipped gym, or play tennis day or night. The Peter Hughes Dive Center on property, a five-star PADI facility, can arrange your dives. Dine casually in the Floating Market or the Carousel Bar & Grill, or more formally in L'Orangerie. Bars are in the Floating Market, the lobby, and poolside. Supervised activities provide a custom vacation just for children ages two to twelve. If you want a meal plan, the hotel offers four choices: $6 for continental breakfast, $12 for American breakfast, $50 for breakfast plus lunch or dinner and $65 for three meals daily. All are per person, plus 12 per cent tax.

SONESTA BEACH RESORT & CASINO, *Piscadera Bay, P.O. Box 6003, Curacao. Tel. 5999/736-8800, Fax 5999/462-7502. From the U.S. and Canada dial 800/SONESTA or 800/766-3782. Rates at the 248-room resort start at $255 for a double in high season plus a choice of optional meal plans. It's about 15 minutes, or a $13 taxi ride, from the airport. Parking is free.*

Visitors are often struck silent when they see the dramatic entry for the first time. A grand, butter-yellow greathouse design has been translated to the 20th century with massive white columns and wings that go on forever. A pool runs through the lobby, falling off the edge into nothingness while the eye falls on the big swimming pool below and, beyond it, the endless sea.

Each room has its own terrace or balcony, television with remote control, safe, iron and ironing board, and mini-bar as well as original art from the famous Sonesta collection. Turndown service and robes are supplied on request. You can take Papiamento lessons, a fitness walk along the Koredor, beach volleyball, or merengue classes.

Dine Italian style in the air conditioned Portofino or more casually in the covered Palm Cafe outdoors. The Emerald Bar & Grill is an air conditioned supper club with piano serenades and a special, late-night supper menu. Poolside, the Seabreeze serves frosty drinks, sandwiches, and grilled favorites. Play blackjack, roulette, craps, mini-baccarat or Caribbean stud poker in the Emerald Casino.

Outdoors there's complimentary tennis, a sandy beach (wear beach shoes for the few rocky stretches), a swimming pool with swim-up bar, two big whirlpools, and a full list of watersports. If you want to play golf, the concierge can arrange it at the nine-hole Curacao Golf and Squash Club 15 minutes away. The Fitness Center offers aerobic and strength-building equipment, sauna, plunge pools, steam room, and massage.

Sonesta's popular Just Us Kids program plays Wednesday through Sunday from 10am to 4:30pm for children ages five to 12. For business travelers there's a full business center. A car rental service is on property but the hotel also runs a free daily shuttle to Willemstad for shopping and sightseeing.

Selected as one of my Best Places to Stay. See Chapter 13 for more details.

Moderate

AVILA BEACH HOTEL, *Penstraat 130, mailing address P.O. Box 791, Willemstad, Curacao, Netherlands Antilles. Tel. 5999/461-4377, Fax 461-1493. Rates at this 100-room hotel start at $108; suites in the new wing start at $260. Add $9.50 per person daily for breakfast or $50 for breakfast and dinner. Taxi fare from the airport is $13.*

The ambience is Dutch colonial, representative of the 18th century governor's mansion that is the core of this modern hotel. In the lobby, life-size ceramic dogs flank an ornately gilded 12-foot mirror; rattan chairs and an oriental rug create the look of an elegant living room. The hotel has two beaches, both sandy but with rocky stretches. Every room has a balcony or terrace and an ocean view; some have a kitchen; some have a whirlpool. Suites with one or two bedrooms are available. Play tennis day or night, dine in a choice of restaurants, and hang out every sunset at Blues, the island's favorite listening post. Rooms are air conditioned and have telephone and television. Beach towels and chairs are supplied free to hotel guests. Non-guests can swim for a fee. A free shuttle is run to downtown every day.

CLUB SERU CORAL, *Koraal Partier 10. Tel. 5999/767-8499, Fax 767-8256. Rates at this 89-room resort start at $91; apartments are priced $113 to $275. It's about 10 miles east of the airport in Santa Catharina.*

In a residential district handy to the sport club and drag strip, this is a reliable *pied-a-terre* if you have a car for exploring and shopping. Rooms are air conditioned and handicap accessible. The hotel has a restaurant, tennis courts, and swimming pool and is popular with European visitors who take longer holidays.

DIVE RESORT HABITAT, *Rif St. Marie. Tel. 5999/864-8800, Fax 864-8484; U.S. 800/327-6709. Located south of St. Willibrordus northwest of the capital, the resort is a $30 cab ride from the airport. Rates at the 82-room hotel start at $165.*

A five-star PADI resort, this is scuba diving at its best in or out of the water, with plenty for non-diving family members to do too. Air conditioned rooms have a small kitchen, cable television, and telephone. The hotel is on the beach and has a swimming pool, shops, planned activities, entertainment, a restaurant, and bar.

HOLIDAY BEACH HOTEL & CASINO, *P. Euwensweg 31, mailing address Box 2178, Curacao, Netherlands Antilles. Tel. 5999/462-5400. Rates at this 200-room hotel start at $135 plus tax and an energy surcharge of $3 daily. It's a $15 cab ride from the airport, which is five miles away. The town center is a mile away.*

Built as a Holiday Inn and now under new owners, this hotel is working hard at banishing a seediness that crept in over the past few years. Although we saw a few tatters and stains, they're offset by the vigorous pace of a refurbishing program. Spread on its own beach, it's also the home of a 24-hour Denny's restaurant and is near a 24-hour gas station. The hotel's own Tradewinds Restaurant on the beach serves local and international dishes from 7am to 11:30pm. The beach bar is a favorite with locals who gather here after work; the lounge indoors is air conditioned.

Rooms reflect typical Holiday Inn standards with two double beds, dresser with desk, a table with two wicker chairs, telephone, television, and private balcony or terrace. Swim in the Olympic-size pool or off the pearly beach, play tennis day or night (a small charge is made for lights) and let the children enjoy the playground. The casino is one of the island's zestiest, with all the usual games plus a 250-seat Bingo parlor. In the lobby there's a tour desk, car rental, and a drugstore. A free shuttle runs to the center of town.

HOTEL LIONS DIVE & MARINA, *Bapor Kibram. Tel. 5999/461-8100, Fax 461-8200. Rates at this 72-room hotel start at $125. It's a $16 cab ride from the airport and is located on the south shore just west of the Seaquarium.*

Divers can rough it easy in an airy room with two queen-size beds, television, telephone, patio or balcony, and air conditioning. One room is wheelchair accessible but most of the others involve climbing rough, outdoor stairs. The atmosphere breathes action; the clientele are young and active. Scuba dive, swim off the wide beach or in the pool, play tennis, have a massage, or use the workout equipment. Food and drink are lusty and moderately priced, always surrounded by a lively crowd discussing the day's dives. Rumours is one of the best nightspots on the island.

The hotel has a full-service dive operation offering everything from introductory diving to daily dive excursions to the island's best underwater sites.

OTROBANDA HOTEL & CASINO, *Breedestraat, Otrobanda, Willemstad. Tel. 5999/462-7400, Fax 462-7299. Rates at this 45-room hotel start at $115 including full American breakfast and parking.*

Stay in the heart of town, handy to shopping and sightseeing. Ask for a room overlooking the water and Handelskaade for a million-dollar view or, during Carnival, try to wangle a streetside room that will overlook the parade.

The hotel restaurant has the same, great harbor view as the harborside rooms and serves good steaks and native food. The elevator is snail paced and it doesn't go to the top floor, so don't book a fifth floor room if you have problems with stairs. Rooms are pretty ordinary but they're clean, efficient, and a perfect headquarters for business or vacation travel. All rooms have a queen-size bed, air conditioning, television, telephone, shower and bath. Room service is available and there's a swimming pool, guest laundry, shop, and casino. Car rental and tours can be arranged in the lobby. Suites and interconnecting rooms are available.

PLAZA HOTEL, *Plaza Pier. Tel. 5999/461-2500, Fax 461-6543. The hotel is 20 minutes from the airport, or $15 by taxi. Rates at this 254-room hotel start at $100 including full American breakfast.*

Town is a short walk away and the hotel has a pool so this is an ideal choice if you don't need to be on the beach. Beach privileges are extended by Seaquarium next door. The site is a historic waterfront and the hotel actually serves as one of the harbor entrance's lighthouses, so it's fun to watch the pounding waves and ship comings and goings from your balcony. Your room will have a safe, television, and air conditioning. Entering the lobby, you're struck by a look of luxury in marble, plush furnishings, and a waterfall. It's the ideal place to meet business contacts or friends. Kitchenette suites are available; room refrigerators are available on request. The hotel has a casino, restaurants, bars, room service, a swimming pool, and a free shuttle to the beach. It all adds up to a classy business or leisure address at moderate prices.

Budget

BUONA SERA INN, *Kaya Godett 104, Pietermaai. Tel. 5999/461-8286, Fax 465-8344. Rates at this 15-room hotel are $33 single, $47 double and $64 triple. It's a seven-minute walk from the center of Punda and ten minutes by car from the Salija Shopping Center or the free zone.*

A gracious old home welcomes a handful of guests to stay in clean, basic rooms with private bath and air conditioning. Television is available on request. The hotel has a lively bar with entertainment and a restaurant that serves international menus; its terrace overlooks the sea.

HOTEL & CASINO PORTO PASEO, *de Rouvilleweg 47, Otrobanda, Willemstad. Tel. 5999/462-7878. The rack rate is $95 including breakfast; ask about specials and packages.*

This gets our vote for one of the best values on the island for the business or leisure traveler who wants to stay in the heart of the city. Although it's within walking distance of almost everything downtown has to offer, the property winds through shaded pathways until you feel you're miles from anywhere. Deep in its interior is a courtyard centered with a pool and waterfall. Rooms and baths are tiny, but each has air conditioning, cable television, telephone, a small refrigerator and coffee maker.

The bar is a locally popular hangout and the restaurant, E Gai, offers some of the best Antillean fare in town. There's even a high-voltage casino in the hotel complex.

HOTEL CORAL CLIFF & CASINO, *St. Martha Bay. Tel. 5999/864-1588, Fax 864-1781. Rates at this 42-room hotel start at $70. It's a $30 cab ride from the airport.*

In the heart of dive country 30 minutes west of Willemstad, this is a perfect perch for beachcombers, divers, and visitors who want to power-hike the national park. Units are air conditioned, have cable television, and some are wheelchair accessible. Kitchenettes are available. The hotel has a restaurant, beach, swimming pool, and tennis courts as well as a small casino.

HOTEL HOLLAND, *F.D. Roosevelt 524. Tel. 5999/868-8044, Fax 868-8114. Rates at this 45-room hotel start at $79; suites at $117. It's a $6 taxi ride from the airport.*

This is budget beige living but it's clean and the hotel's bar is a happening place. Only a mile from the airport, the location is perfect for business travelers as well as vacationers who want to spend the day out on the island when they're not in the hotel swimming pool. The Cockpit Restaurant here is affordable and its traditional Antillean food is filling and good. Rooms have television with VCR, balcony, and a small refrigerator.

LANDHUIS CAS ABOU, *Cas Abou. Tel. 5999/864-9688, Fax 864-8599. Rates at this six- room inn start at $55. It's northwest of St. Willibrordus, a cab ride of about $30 from the airport.*

Combine the charm of an old landhouse with a country location near some of the island's best beaches and dive sites. Rooms are basic and are not air conditioned, but the restaurant is good and is moderately priced.

LANDHUIS DANIEL, *Weg n Westpunt. Tel. 5999/864-8400, Fax 864-9000. Rates at this 10-room guesthouse start at $57. Found halfway between Grote Berg and Tera Kora, it's a $25 taxi ride from the airport.*

The price is appealing, but even better is the chance to stay in a real landhouse, one dating to 1634 when it was built more as a traveler's rest than as a plantation house. Rooms aren't large but they have private baths and some are air conditioned (others have ceiling fans). Dine in the restaurant, play tennis, swim in the pool, or let the host arrange a watersports outing for you. The TV lounge with its games and books is a good place to meet fellow travelers.

TRUPIAL INN, *Groot Davelaanweg, Salinja. Tel. 5999/737-8200, Fax 737-1545. Rates at this 74-unit motel start at $70. From the airport or town, it's about 20 minutes.*

It looks like a cheesy, 1970s mom-and-pop motel but the location in the outskirts of Willemstad is handy to shopping centers and the free trade zone, and parking is ample. With an air conditioned suite including a kitchenette, it's an ideal home away from home. The motel has a small pool, tennis courts, solar hot water, and offers cable television and an AM-FM radio in each unit. Free shuttles run to town and the free zone.

ABOUT THE FREE ZONE

*Leisure travelers get excited about the **Free Zone** when they envision a duty-free Sam's Club, but it's only for commercial traders who buy by the gross, the ton, or the containerload. It's a major trading point for the Caribbean and the northern coast of South America.*

WHERE TO EAT

We have listed prices in guilders or dollars depending on how they are listed on menus. U.S. dollars are accepted everywhere. Unless otherwise stated, these restaurants accept major credit cards. A six per cent tax is charged on meals and a 10-12 per cent service charge is usually added in lieu of tipping.

Expensive

BISTRO DE CLOCHARD, *Riffort, Otrabanda. Tel. 462-5666. Plan to spend $50 to $60 per person for a four-course dinner. It's open Monday through Friday noon to 2pm and from 6:30 for dinner. On Saturday, only dinner is served and it's closed Sunday. The Terrace Bar is open from 5pm until closing. The Bistro is within walking distance of downtown hotels, and is on the Brionplein shuttle bus stop.*

Deep in the cool vaults of the 18th century Rif Fort, now opened up with picture windows, this gourmet Swiss and French restaurant serves you in a dungeon or cistern surrounded by delicious history. The decor is in red and black, accented with antiques and cream-colored stained glass lamp shades. Start with a cream soup, lobster ragout, or a smoked eel terrine with sour cream and herbs. Main courses include Norwegian salmon in potato crust, salmon roe in white wine, or a turkey filet stuffed with spinach and ham. Or, dine more simply on a Swiss cheese raclette with boiled potatoes. For dessert there are strawberries fresh from Holland. If you like, your aperitif or after-dinner coffee will be served on the harborside terrace.

CURNOSKY, *Caracasbaai weg, 20 minutes east of Punda. Tel. 747-1066. Plan to spend $40-50 per person. Call for hours and reservations, which are essential.*

Locals went wild for this new (1997) restaurant and visitors soon got the word about the view, the service, the French food prepared by Belgian chef Phillippe De Baere. Everything comes to the table looking like a lesson in food styling. Seafood bisque is garnished with sushi; lamb chops form a wreath around a volcano of vegetables; tropic fruits turn up in sorbets that are scooped onto a bed of fresh fruit. The menu changes often, so come for the view and what is sure to be a memorable meal.

DE TAVEERNE, *Landhuis Groot Davelaar near the Promenade Shopping Center, Salinja. Tel. 737-0669. Plan to spend about $50 per person for dinner. The air conditioned dining room is open weekdays for lunch and dinner and Saturday for dinner. It's closed Sunday. Call for reservations. Lighter fare is served outdoors on the Garden Terrace.*

The romance begins when you approach this towering red and white gingerbread house, one of the grand landhuizen (landhouses) of a bygone era. Start with a satiny lobster bisque or a salmon carpaccio in herb dressing, then have a seafood specialty such as salmon gratiné, lobster thermidor, or flour-dusted sole sautéed in butter. The juicy roast chicken or tender lamb chops can be ordered with a side dish of buttery polenta or one of the fragrant potato dishes. Order one of the desserts brandished with Curacao liqueur. After dinner, stroll the air conditioned art gallery upstairs, not just to see the works of talented local artists but to see more of this magnificent landhuis.

EMERALD GRILLE, *in the Sonesta Beach Resort, Piscadera Bay. Tel. 736- 8800, ext. 7921. Plan to spend $50 for dinner. The grille is open nightly for dinner, 6pm to 11pm Reservations are recommended. The bar, with seating available in the open air or in air conditioning, is open 4:30pm to 1am.*

All the best features of a great Chicago or New York steakhouse are found in this elegant dining room with its emerald-rimmed chargers, snowy linens, mahogany arm chairs, and Lenox china. Don't be misled by

ABOUT DRESS CODES

Curaçao is dressier than most Caribbean islands. Dutch businessmen often wear ties and even jackets. While ties and jackets are rarely required in restaurants (you are asked to wear a suit and tie to synagogue), all the restaurants in our Expensive category are dressy, which means wearing at least a shirt with sleeves and closed shoes rather than sandals. Shorts or Bermudas are verboten. When in doubt, dress up.

the looks of the Crocodile Dundee steak knives in the place settings. These steaks can be cut with a pussy willow, and the grilled fish flake at a touch. Everything is a la carte, allowing diners to customize the perfect meal.

Start with the Caesar salad for two or sliced beefsteak tomatoes followed by a hot or cold soup. To your steak or fish add the garlic-leek mashed potatoes, steak fries, baked potatoes, creamed spinach, sauteed mushrooms, or steamed asparagus. A vegetarian entree is made with grilled eggplant, tomato and goat cheese, with polenta and asparagus. Save room for the raspberry-robed chocolate cake finished with vanilla butter cream, or plan ahead by ordering a Grand Marnier soufflé when you order your entree. The restaurant is opposite the hotel's casino and shops, so make it an evening of gaming, feasting and shopping for that special diamond.

FORT NASSAU, *near Point Juliana. Tel. 461-3086. Reservations are essential for dinner seatings at 7pm and 9pm. It's also open for lunch on weekdays. Appetizers are priced NAFl 18.50 to 25.50; main dishes NAFl 36 to 48.50.*

Centuries slip away as you climb the stone stairs into an ancient, fairytale fort that has been transformed into an elegant aerie with a million-dollar view of the city below. Service is seamless as one course follows the next. Start with the unusual mustard soup, a creamy blend made with Dijon-style mustard and a crunchy sprinkling of pine nuts. Or try the classic French onion soup, garnished with croutons and Kernhem cheese, or a terrine of salmon and sunfish served with a teardrop of Iranian caviar.

Steaks are served with the Fort's famous "Paris" butter made with mustard, cognac, and port. Lamb chops fan out over a bed of beans; potato pie and stir-fry vegetables complete the plate. Choose fresh fish or lobster too, each sauced to perfection and accompanied by a panorama of vegetables. Exotic temptations include boneless wild pigeon served with broccoli and pine nut spread or steamed halibut with crayfish in lobster sauce with saffron potatoes. The desserts are eye-popping, ranging from a medley of light ices, fresh fruit, or apple tart to heartier chocolate and cream confections. If you're not a sweets eater, have one of the liquor-laced coffees from a list of unique specialties. Note that entering the restaurant and using the rest rooms involves steep steps.

L'ALOUETTE, *Orionweg 12, Salinja. Tel. 461-8222. Plan to spend $40 per person for dinner. It's open weekdays for lunch and dinner and Saturday for dinner only. Reservations are essential.*

This tiny jewel has only eight tables, so feel privileged to get a . reservation. The stark black and white of the color scheme is softened with stained glass, pastel walls, and lavish drapery adding up to a sophisticated, intimate dining room. Start with one of the cheese custard appetizers or the creamy langouste velouté, then dine on salmon in a very light herb and citrus sauce or one of the chef's inspired chicken dishes.

L'ORANGERIE, *in the Princess Beach Resort, Martin Luther King Boulevard 8. Tel. 465-5955. Reservations are strongly recommended. Dinner can cost $40-$50 but a fixed price menu is offered for about $30.*

Natural surroundings including wood walls and a marble floor provide an elegant setting for fine dining with the focus on good meats. Don't decide until you've heard the day's specials, which could include jumbo prawns in lobster sauce, a lean steak, or a catch of the day. Also in the hotel is the more casual Floating Market, with Theme Night meals in the moderate category. Call ahead to see what's cooking. It could be Latin Night, Carnival, Picnic Under the Stars, or a Sunday Splash, all with appropriate music, decor, and menu.

PORTOFINO, *in the Sonesta Beach Resort, Piscadera Bay. Tel. 736-8800, ext. 7920. Reservations are recommended. Dinner is served daily 6-11pm. Plan to spend $35-$40 per person.*

Sonesta's impeccable service shines in this elegant, bright, air conditioned room overlooking the beach and pool. Start with a beef or salmon carpaccio followed by a fragrant minestrone. Antipastos include a meat and vegetable plate substantial enough for a light meal, or try the portabello mushroom with roasted polenta. The tricolor salad is made with three greens; the Insalata Verde is rich with lettuces, sausage, and roasted walnuts.

The pastas include a vegetable lasagna, penne with fresh tomato and Parmigiana cheese, and a classic Tortellini Alfred. Or order a meat or fish entree from a list that includes filet of beef on a bed of sautéed spinach with roasted potatoes, grilled veal, oven-roasted salmon, or a mixture of shrimp and scallops with artichokes and mushrooms. Desserts are faithful to the Italian theme: tiramisu, mascarpone cheesecake, cannoli with chocolate and vanilla mousse, or a nougatine basket served with expresso Zabaglione.

WINE CELLAR, *Oosestraat/Concordiastraat, Punda. Tel. 461-2178 or 767-4909. Plan to spend $50 per person. It's open for lunch and dinner Tuesday through Friday and on Monday, Saturday and Sunday for dinner only. Reservations are strongly urged.*

The name tells you that this is one of the finest cellars in the city, offering a comprehensive wine list and fine cuisine in a setting reminiscent of an elegant Dutch home where eight tables are set for a family dinner. Owner-chef Nico Cornelisse, a former caterer to the Dutch royal family, is a master rotisseur of the Chaine des Rotisseurs, so you can expect fine food with meticulous attention to deft seasonings and flourishing presentation. Light choices include broiled fresh fish, but you can also feast on rabbit, venison, or goose as well as more conventional viands.

CURACAO CUISINE

When you order "half and half" it means half funchi (a creamy cornmeal pudding) and half rice. **Pan dushi** *is a sweet bread, usually offered for breakfast.* **Broodje,** *which means bread roll, is served with a variety of meats and cheeses and is usually listed on menus under "broodjes." An inexpensive lunch is* **uitsmijter,** *two fried eggs and cheese (or sometimes meat) on bread.* **Keshi yena,** *one of the national dishes of the Dutch islands, is stuffed cheese. Traditionally a whole Edam is baked with a filling of ground beef or chicken with spices, but it is also made with sliced cheese that forms a "crust" around the filling. It's found on most local menus.*

Water isn't served automatically with meals here so be sure to ask for it. If you drink a lot of water, which this climate invites, ask for a pitcher for the table. Waiters simply aren't tuned to Americans' insatiable thirst for ice water. Even in the best restaurants, we have trouble getting prompt refills for empty water glasses.

Moderate

BAY SIGHT TERRACE, *in the Hotel Otrobanda, Brion Plein. Tel. 462-7400. It's open daily breakfast through dinner. Main dishes are priced $13.75 to $22.*

The terrace here has the city's best view of Handelskaade, which lies across the water from this waterfront hotel. Dine on typical Netherlands Antilles treats such as pan-fried mula (a local fish) with Creole sauce, conch, chicken curry, shrimp in butter sauce, stewed goat, or keshi yena, the stuffed cheese that is one of the national dishes. Or, splurge on a

U.S.D.A. tenderloin or sirloin done to order. Vegetarian specials are always on the menu, as well as pastas and a choice of kiddy plates.

CLIFF HOUSE RESTAURANT, *in the Kadushi Cliffs Resort, Playa Kalki. Tel. 864-0282. Dine for $15 to $20. It's open breakfast through dinner.* To find this out-of-the-way, cliffside resort, take the road towards Westpunt and take the first right turn after seeing Jaanchi's on your left. At the T turn left and drive to the entry to Kadushi Cliffs. Meals here are a nice blend of traditional dishes, such as the fish soup, cactus soup, funchi roll or goat stew, and American standards such as a good bacon, lettuce, and tomato sandwich. The restaurant has great views and a wonderful thatched roof done by Venezuelan Indians.

COCKPIT, *in the Hotel Holland, F.D. Rooseveltweg 524. Tel. 868-8044. Open 7am to 10 p.m., the restaurant offers main courses for $20 and under. From the airport, it's a $6 taxi ride. Hours are 7am to 10pm daily.*

Because it's only a mile from the airport and has a view of some of the aviation action, this popular restaurant has an aeronautical theme. The food takes its richness from the Dutch (pea soup, smothered steak, melty cheese sauces) and its flavors from the West Indies. Try the curried chicken, shrimp in pasta, or goat stew with side dishes of vegetables and potatoes. Dine inside with the air conditioning or outside around the pool where you can see the airplanes better.

FORT WAAKZAAMHEID, *Seru Domi, Otrobanda. Tel. 462-3633. Reservations are suggested. Main dishes are priced $18 to $24, but the three-course fixed price meal is a bargain at under $20 if you can arrive before 7pm. The restaurant is open nightly except Tuesday for dinner.*

Because forts are built to overlook and protect harbors, this one has a superb sea view. Arrive just before sunset for a drink, then linger on to dine on steaks, seafood, and the salad bar.

HARD ROCK SOCIETY, *Keuken Plein 8, Punda. Tel. 465-6633. Lunch for under $20; dine for under $25. Hours are Monday through Thursday 9:30am to 1am; Friday and Saturday to 2am., Sunday 3:30pm to 1am.*

The atmosphere is switched-on rock with a menu designed to remind you of the Hard Rock Cafe chain with its thick burgers and supersize deli sandwiches. Dine outdoors under the trees or inside at the air conditioned bar. Nosh on nachos or satay, order a chowder or salad, or polish off grilled fish, ribs, or a steak. Choose a splurge dessert or one of the specialty coffees. Pool tables are upstairs.

LE JARDIN CAFE, *Pietermaai 16, across from the Tourist Bureau in Punda. Tel. 465-6091. Dine for under $30; lunch for under $25. Hours are Monday to Friday noon to 2pm and 6:30 to 11pm; until midnight on Saturday. It's closed Sunday. Happy Hour is 5-6:30pm.*

Two women have created a homelike living room in an 18th century merchant's townhouse. The bar basks under stained glass Coca-Cola shades; the dining room is serenaded by the soothing flow of water in a fountain created entirely from the Venezuelan pottery jugs and amphorae that are Curacao's current decorating rage. Tables are topped in pink linen and centered with a fresh rose wreathed in baby breath.

Menu choices range from simple soups, burgers, salads, and "broodji" sandwiches to inventive treats such as Double Fun Lamp Chops in tamarind, orange, and ginger sauce. Grilled frogs legs are served in garlic olive oil; sirloin steak is swimming in Roquefort sauce. Each week a new "Country Tour" menu is offered, featuring ethnic foods of a different nation. For dessert have one of the eight specialty coffees. If you can put together a group of 8-15 people, reserve the back room, which is right on the sea. It's ideal for a special occasion or small reception.

MARTHA KOOSJE CAFE RESTAURANT, *Martha Koosje 10. Tel. 864-8235. Find the restaurant at Martha Koosje at the narrowest part of the island, about 8 miles northwest of Willemstad on the road to Tera Kora. Dine for under $30. It's open daily except Monday.*

A 160-year-old goat ranch filled with antiques and surrounded by birdsong, this charming country restaurant is operated by Columbians Gibi and Maria Libier. Enjoy red snapper with coco rice, grilled tenderloin, a sea and turf combination known as Mary Tierra, or octopus vinaigrette; while you dine Gibi plays an organ serenade.

PISCES SEAFOOD RESTAURANT AND BAR, *Caracasbaaiweg 476. Tel. 767-2181. Plan to spend $40 for dinner. It's open daily from noon to midnight. Find it on the sea at the end of Caracasbaaiweg just off the fishermen's wharf near Fort Beekenburg, 20 minutes from downtown. Reservations are suggested.*

You can't go wrong with the catch of the day, so Curacaoans come here for the dradu, fresh tuna, wahoo, snapper, or shrimp, octopus, conch, or squid. A local icon is the seafood Zarzuela for two. If it's seafood, it is perfectly prepared in this unassuming, working class restaurant. Rice, vegetables, and fried green bananas complete the belly-busting meal.

RESTAURANT LAROUSSE, *Penstraat 5. Tel. 465-5481. Plan to spend $30- $40 for dinner. It's open nightly except Monday, 6pm to midnight.*

The scene is a quaintly cozy home built in the 1700s. Choose from a list of hot and cold hors d'oeuvres, then dine on shrimp or red snapper, or on tenderloin flown in fresh daily from Holland. It's pan-fried and served with fresh green pepper and cream sauce. For dessert have a parfait or mousse. Wine connoisseurs won't be disappointed in the chateaux represented on the wine carte here.

RYSTTAFEL INDONESIA, *Mercuriusstraat 13-15, Salinja. Tel. 461-2606. Reservations are recommended. A rijfstaffel with 16 dishes costs NAFl 38.50 per person; with 20 dishes, NAFl 42.50. Individual combinations are priced NAFL 26.50 to 37.50; a child's plate is NAFl 15.00.*

More than a memorable meal, a rijsttafel (rice table) is an experience. A parade of hot and cold dishes is placed on a heated lazy susan in the center of the table and a merry flurry begins as diners help themselves to snips of this and that to accompany mountains of fluffy white rice. The decor as straight out of old Jakarta (don't miss the puppet collection in the bar and the rickshaw out front). The air conditioning is a plus. Dishes can be fiery, so don't start until your water (which you have to request) or beer has been served. Selections include lots of chicken and beef dishes, vegetables in various sauces, boiled eggs in curry sauce, krupuk (shrimp chips) and the classic gado-gado salad with peanut dressing. A vegetarian rijsttafel is also available.

SEAVIEW, *in the Waterfront Arches. Tel. 767-5105. Open daily except Sunday for lunch and dinner and dinner only on Sunday, the restaurant does not require reservations. Plan to spend $25 for dinner.*

Snuggled into the thick walls of an old fort is this cozy eatery on the very edge of a pounding sea. It's worth seeing just for the site, but the food will make you glad you came: pastry-wrapped asparagus, shrimp dishes hot and cold, peppery octopus salad, hearty Antillean soups, and generous sandwiches.

TENTABOKA, *Schottegatweg Oost 185. Tel. 465-7678. Main dishes are priced NAFl 21-29. Call for hours and reservations. The restaurant is on the ring road, five minutes from Punda.*

Ask a local where to go for real Antillean food, and this name will always pop up. Try the fish patties, stewed conch, shrimp and snapper soup, cabbage stew with goat meat, keshi yena, or a funchi plate. For side dishes, choose among rice and beans, fried polenta with blackeye peas (tutu), or pumpkin fritters. More conventional choices include chicken cordon bleu or salmon in phyllo crust.

Budget
AWA DI PLAYA, *Piscadera Bay. Tel. 462-6939. Dine for under $10. It's open every day noon to 7:30pm.*

Little more than a shack, this is a favorite hangout for locals who use this popular beach. It's handy to the Koredo jogging track, the Trade Center, and the Sonesta. The menu is limited, but that is part of the fun. Have fried fish, a bowl of seafood chowder, and a cold beer or soda. Sunday fishermen's parties are local color at its best.

DE BRASSERIE, *in the Douglas Shopping Center, Salinja. Tel. 461-6899. Hours are 7:30am to 11pm. A three-course fixed price meal costs $20. Have breakfast or lunch for under $10.*

You'll feel you're among friends in this unpretentious hangout, which is popular with visitors from all over the world. Have a simple, bargain lunch of French onion soup and baguettes or linger over a specialty coffee at breakfast. For dinner, start with banana soup, then a funchi or stew, followed by the original Dutch apple pie.

CURACAO BOWLING CLUB, *Chuchubiweg 10. Tel. 737-9275. Open every day 4pm to 2am, it serves meals in the $8 to $12 range.*

This friendly, buzzing bowling alley with a bar, Indian food, and pool tables is a cross between an English pub and a North American sports bar. Come for an offbeat night out with the locals.

CRUISE CAFE WAAIKIKI, *on the wharf at Otrabanda on Rouvilleweg. Tel. 561-0364. Sandwiches and salads are priced NAFl 5.25 to 14.50. Hours are Monday through Saturday 10am to midnight.*

In the heart of the new cruise ship landing area is this breezy overlook where you can have a margarita or cappuccino and watch the world go by on land and sea. Lunch on a simple sandwich or salad. Brunch or snack on yogurt, a choice of five sorbets, or toast with ham or cheese. Happy Hour prices are in effect 5-6pm with free nibbles.

DENNY'S, *next to the Holiday Beach Hotel. Tel. 462-5232. It's open 24 hours a day. Main dishes are priced $6 to $8.*

Expect all the familiar Denny's touches including special menus for children and a discount for senior citizens, plus a Creole menu that gives visitors a chance to try funchi, stewed goat, stuffed cheese, and other local favorites at local prices.

E GAI, *Klipstraat 10, in the Hotel Porto Paseo, Otrabanda. Tel. 462-7878. Call for hours and reservations. Starters are priced NAFl 7.75 to 14.25; main dishes NAFl 18.25 to 34.50.*

Locals stream to this smash-hit restaurant, which is located in an old mansion just footsteps from the new cruise ship docks at Mattheywerf. Dine in the sunshine on the patio facing a brilliant mural depicting island life or inside under the paddle fans. The food is traditional "krioyo" or Creole, with a touch of Dutch. Start with the spicy patties or the banana soup, made with boiled green bananas and chunks of ham hock. For a main course have the beef, chicken, papaya, or goat stew, red snapper, a local fish called dradu served with cinnamon sauce, a curry, or one of the steaks. Meals are served with a choice of funchi, baked banana, and a vegetable or beans and rice. Desserts include a dynamite carrot cake, coconut ice cream, fresh fruit, caramel cream, or a vanilla liqueur cake.

JAANCHI'S, *Westpunt 15. Tel. 864-0126. Come for lunch until 6:30pm; later reservations might be arranged. It's 30 minutes from Willemstad on the road to Westpunt. Dine for less than $15.*

Partly it's the location that makes this a popular stop for individuals and tour buses that are sightseeing the west end of the island. Yet it's worth a special trip, if only to try iguana soup (order it in advance) and local specialties such as funchi with seafood fresh from the boats. The homespun, open-air ambience is Curacao country at its most natural. Jaanchi's also has three rooms for rent, starting at $30.

LANDHUIS PAPAYA, *on the road to Westpoint just before Grote Berg. Tel. 869-5850. The bar is open until 10pm; restaurant is open daily except Monday breakfast through dinner. Breakfast is priced from $2.25; a three-course tourist menu dinner is $14.95.*

This restored landhouse is a good choice for breakfast on the way to the national park and other pleasures of the western end of the island. The pancakes are always popular. For lunch and dinner there are sandwiches, soups, salads, barbecue, seafood and stews. Saturday dinner, 6pm to midnight, is Tropical Hot Salsa Night; on Sunday the barbecue is served with live music and dancing.

PALM CAFE *in the Sonesta Beach Resort, Piscadera Bay. Tel. 736-8800, ext. 7920. Reservations aren't required. Soups and sandwiches are priced $8 to $12.50; fish and steaks are $19-$21. Hours are 7am to 10pm.*

Dine on a budget in the lap of luxury at the island's most lavish resort. The tuna salad sandwich is served on a French roll with lettuce, tomato, and avocado; the grilled chicken sandwich comes with mango, hot pepper cheese, and salsa. Try the vegetarian yucca chili or pumpkin soup. The open-air restaurant overlooks the pool and sea. After eating, browse the shops or play one of the island's most glamorous casinos. The cafe is also renowned for its lavish breakfast buffets, which cost $10.50 for cold foods (including homemade breads and pastries) with juice and coffee or $15.50 for all you can eat from hot and cold tables including waffles, meats, and omelets made to order.

PIZZA HUT, *in Punda, Tel. 465-6767; on Jan Noorduynweg, Tel. 868-8278; and at Schottegatweg Oost 193, Tel. 461-3477. Call for hours. Dine for under $15.*

We all know about Pizza Huts, but these on Curacao serve native fare as well as the pizzas that the chain is famous for. Try a "panwich" on fresh pizza dough, the 10-layer, three-cheese lasagna, or an exquisite keshi yena (stuffed cheese) made with Gouda cheese. For dessert, have the whipped cream-topped chocolate mousse.

THE NATIONAL BEER

Amstel, Curacao's national beer, is said to be the only beer in the world made from distilled seawater. By appointment, tours of the distillery are offered, Tel. 461-6000.

PRONTO PIZZA, *Gomex Plaza, Punda. Tel. 465-6450. Eat for $5 to $8. Hours are 8am until 9pm daily except Sunday. Credit cards aren't accepted.*

Dine on the terrace of this popular downtown pizza place or have food delivered anywhere in the Punda area. Choose from pizzas, pastas, and salads tuned to North American taste buds.

RODEO RANCH SALOON AND STEAKHOUSE, *in the Seaquarium, off Martin Luther King Boulevard at Bapor Kibra. Tel. 461-5757. Have dinner for $20-$25 or lunch for $10 to $15. The bar opens at 5pm. Lunch is served daily noon to 2pm and dinner 6-11pm. Reservations are accepted.*

It's fun to experience the wild west, West Indian style. Sidle up to the chuckwagon for a U.S. prime steak, veal, chicken, ribs or roast pork loin with all the salad bar you can round up. For dessert order fresh fruit, chocolate mousse, or brownies. Dine inside with the air conditioning or seaside outdoors.

TEXAS STYLE APAPARIA, *Schottegatweg Oost 193A. Tel. 736- 8566. Dine for under $10. Credit cards are not accepted. Call for hours.*

This is Tex-Mex, Caribbean style featuring conch fajitas as well as the usual steak, chicken, or mixed fajitas. Try the nine-layer Cunchitos Supreme, Atomic Chicken Wings, or quesadillas, accompanied by one of the signature salads and washed down with beer or sangria. Texas Alaparia is found next to the Pizza Hut in Salinja, in Winkel Centrum Brievengat, and on Jan Joorduynweg, Santa Maria.

SEEING THE SIGHTS

Willemstad

By the early 1700s, the walled city of **Willemstad** was filled with more than 200 houses, so the town began spreading beyond the walls to Pietermaai, Otrobanda (literally other side), and Scharloo, which was filled with Italianate mansions built by the city's large community of Sephardic Jews. Now largely abandoned and in disrepair, this area is being restored to its former grandeur. Until it's revived, don't venture here alone at night without local advice.

Take a walking tour of old neighborhoods filled with a living museum of Dutch Colonial architecture. It's best not to venture into the narrow streets of the city by car but, if you do, parking is free at Brion Plaza in Otrobanda or in metered street spaces that take one guilder or one U.S. quarter. The best bet is the big, free Waaigat parking lot in Scharloo, a short walk from the center of **Punda**.

Starting a walk at the foot of the Emmabrug (Queen Emma Bridge), notice the Riffort that guards the harbor entrance, the **Otrobanda Hotel**, and the landing areas for cruise passengers, which are busy with shops and restaurants. Stroll the famous Handelskaade with its shops and cafes.

DRIVING TIPS

This is a desert island, so infrequent rains make for very slippery roads when a buildup of oils and dust mix with water. Before driving the dirt tracks that give drivers access to the northern coasts, check your tires and spare. Don't try these roads too soon after a rain because some roads flood or get muddy. If you're in an accident, don't move the car. Immediately call 114 for police help. If you're issued a "club" or other anti-theft device with a rental car, use it.

Signs are in kilometers; if your rental car is in miles, divide by half and add 10 per cent for a rough idea of kilometers. Where there are no other signs, traffic approaching from the right has the right-of-way.

Note the tall yellow Penha Building with its curlicues and wrap-around galleries. To seaward is **Fort Amsterdam**, which dates to the early 1600s.

In front of the fort, note the **Horn of Plenty Monument** commemorating the help given by the Netherlands Antilles to the embattled motherland during World War II. It remembers a poignant period in history when Holland was occupied by the Nazis and the Dutch islands in the Pacific were overrun by Japanese. Shipments of food and supplies from the West Indies made an essential contribution to Holland's recovery.

Tour the fort complex and **Fort Church Museum**, which offers tours in English and Dutch weekdays 9am to noon and 2-5pm, *Tel. 461-1139*. Admission is NAFl 3.00 adults and NAFl 1.50 children. Emerge on **Wilhelmina Plaza**, then look back at the wooden gingerbread on the back of Fort Amsterdam.

Near the Plaza you'll see the **Tele Museum** with its displays of antique communications equipment. Admission is free; hours are weekdays 9am to noon and 1:30-5pm. Now stop at the **Waterfort Arches** with their restaurants and shops built right into the old fort. Across the plaza, note a tall, steepled yellow and white building known as **The Temple**. Now waiting for restoration, it is a synagogue dating to the 1800s. Across from it, the Cinelandia Building is an old movie palace, one of the city's few Art Deco structures.

Along Petermaai, visit the **Tourist Bureau** to ask questions, pick up brochures, and have a look at the building itself, a restored architectural treasure that was once a private home. Then head back on Breedestraat towards the Queen Emma Bridge to the **Numismatic Museum**, housed in Punda's oldest standing building dating to 1693. It's open weekdays 9am to 5pm and Saturday 10am to 3pm, *Tel. 465-8010*. Collections include stamps, old post boxes, and ancient postal scales.

At **Gomezplein,** vendors can usually be seen displaying carvings from Haiti and the Dominican Republic. It's all right to haggle here, but in most island shops prices are fixed. Bargaining is considered bad form. Returning to the Queen Emma Bridge, note the **Heerenstreet,** the island's oldest commercial "merchant row." Its shops sell mostly clothing and electronics now but once it was Gentlemen's Row, a street of fine shops and haberdashers. As you stroll, don't forget to look up for architectural details and for dates near the peak of the facade of each building.

From Gomezplein, take Hanchi Snoa to the walled **Mikve'Israel-Emanuel Synagogue,** *Tel. 461-1067,* which can be toured Monday-Friday 9-11:45am and 2:30-5pm except on public and Jewish holidays. A small admission fee of about $2 is charged for upkeep. The synagogue's museum chronicles the history of a congregation that goes back to 1651. Visitors are also welcome to attend services. A suit and tie are required; kippot (skullcaps) are supplied. The oldest continuously operating synagogue in the western hemisphere, it is an architectural and historic gem as well as the seat of a vital, very active congregation.

Walking tours of Punda are offered Thursday afternoon and Tuesday morning. On Wednesday, walking tours of Otrobanda are offered by Mr. Jopi Hart, *Tel. 737-8718,* for information and reservations, which are essential.

Curacao Seaquarium, found just south of the Princess Beach Resort, *Tel. 461-6666,* is a sophisticated nature show in a controlled environment lagoon where visitors can get close to sea lions, sharks, turtles, stingrays, and toothy moray eels. A stationary semi-submarine provides an underwater platform for photographers. Plan to spend all day here. It's hard to tear yourself away from the nonstop nature show of sea creatures swimming in 46 tanks and in outdoor enclosures. Watch a feeding show. Take the glass-bottom boat tour to see the wreck of the steamship *SS Oranje Nassau,* which went down in 1906. Shop for souvenirs, have lunch in the restaurant, and swim off the sandy beach. The attraction is open daily 10am to 10pm. Admission is $30. In addition, divers can get into the water in an Animal Encounters attraction for $50. Snorkelers pay $30. Reserve your encounter 24 hours in advance.

New at press time and not yet fully furnished is the **Maritime Museum** on Maduro Plaza, *Tel. 767-6414, Fax 747-1740.* Its permanent and changing collections depict Curacao's long and rich maritime history. There's also a cafe and gift shop.

The **Curacao Ostrich and Game Farm** at Groot St. Joris West, *Tel. 560-4206,* is not very slick as a tourist attraction, nor does it have much to do with native fauna, but it's an interesting look at how ostriches live and breed. Admission is NAFl 12.50 adults and NAFl 7.50 for children, 8am to 5pm every day. After the tour you can buy a plain or decorated ostrich egg or choose from a few other souvenirs. Reservations are essential; call 12 hours in advance.

The **Curacao Museum** on V. Leeuwenhoestraat in western Otrobanda, about eight minutes from the cruise docks, *Tel. 462-3873*, houses works of local and foreign artists as well as a locomotive and antique furniture dating to the 17th and 18th centuries. It's open Monday through Friday 9am to noon and 2-3pm and Sunday 10am to 4pm. Admission is NAFl 4.00 adults and NAFl 2.00 children.

Insider Tip: although the **International Trade Center** is not in the spotlight unless a conference is being held, it is open daily and offers several boons to tourists including a bank, a full-service post office, and a triplex movie theater showing three first-run hits nightly. Find it at Piscadera Bay next to the **Sonesta Beach Resort.**

KIDS MEET KIDS

*Various people-to-people programs have been offered in the islands from time to time, but Curacao targets children in a charming **Kids Meet Kids** operation June through September. Children ages 8 through 14 go with local children on field trips to the aquarium, Indian sites in the countryside, sailing, or touring a big ship. Cost is $36 per child, which includes admissions and transportation from your hotel. Parents pay $10 if they want to go. This covers transportation but not admissions. The local number is Tel. 560-4007; from the U.S. or Canada Tel. 800/3-CURACAO.*

Around the Island

The **Hato Caves** on F.D. Rooseveltweg across from the Hotel Holland, *Tel. 868-0379*, are gaping caverns, cool and mysterious with their natural formations of stalactites and stalagmites. They're the only caves in the region with petroglyphs dating back at least 1,500 years; the caverns themselves were formed millions of years ago below sea level. As Curacao rose from the sea millennia ago, the caves emerged. Along the way you'll see the "little dinosaur" lizards living in the rocks and trees and, inside the caves, a colony of rare long-nose bats. Hours are daily 10am to 5pm with tours on the the hour. Admission is NAFl 10.75 for adults and NAFl 8.00 for children.

Near Ascencion, the **Country House Museum**, *Tel. 864-2742*, is a simple household from the mid-1800s. Admission is $1.50 adults and 50 cents for children. It's open daily 9am to 4pm and on the first Sunday of the month has live music with arts and crafts.

Christoffel National Park, *Tel. 864-0363*, covers much of the area between Westpunt and Barber, a 4,500-acre reserve topped by **Mount**

Christoffel. Compared to the lush drama of other islands' rain forests and soaring mountains, this one seems dry and colorless until you take a closer look at its skittering wildlife, sculpted divi-divi trees, a rare sabal palm, and two species of wild orchids. With luck, you may see a Curacao deer.

A 1,239-foot hiking path winds up to the top of the mountain. It's an easy climb by Jamaica or St. Lucia standards, but it's still a vigorous hike of about two hours. Or, drive the park's 20 miles of roads. Start at the visitor center, located in an 18th-century plantation house, and drive the Blue Route to the **Boca Grandi** caves and Indian paintings. Exploring the park you'll also find the ruins of **Zorgvliet Plantation**. The park is open daily 8am to 4pm and Sunday 6am to 3pm. Admission before 2pm is $9 for ages five and older and includes the visitor center and museum; after 2pm it is free. It's a 45-minute bus ride from Otrobanda, or take the road to Westpoint and, about five kilometers after the village of Barber, look for the sign to the park.

Flamingoes can usually be seen from the overlook near **Jan Kok**, where they spend the day feeding before flying home to their rookeries on Bonaire. Flamingoes are also seen at the **Curacao Botanical Garden and Zoo** on Chuchubiweag, *Tel. 737- 8500*. The zoo has a variety of animals plus playgrounds and refreshments. It's open daily 9am to 5:30pm.

Allow a day for a driving tour around the north end of the island, stopping at Shete Boka where the **Boka Tabla cave** is a spectacular explosion of ocean against eroding rock. A path takes you deep into a tumbled scattering of enormous boulders, where you can see the wide mouth of the cave entrance at the end of a long, black tunnel. Take care! It's very treacherous going, especially in wet spots that are mossy and slippery. Admission is NAFl 2.00 per carload. The area is threaded with hiking trails among the cliffs, and is well worth an entire day. Bring a picnic lunch.

The Greathouses of Curacao

Known as *Landhuizen* (pronounced lahhnd houzen), the plantation houses of Curacao are an architectural scrapbook of the 18th and 19th centuries. Many are open to the public as restaurants or inns; others are shown by appointment; some are privately owned and can be seen only from the road. This is just a partial listing; others are shown on maps but may not be open to the public.

LANDHUIS ASCENSION, located just north of San Pedro, dates to 1672. The first Sunday of each month it is open for music, handicrafts, and refreshments. *Tel. 864-1950*.

LANDHUIS BRIEVENGAT, north of Brievengat on the road to Playa Kanoa, once anchored a 1,200-acre cattle ranch. An antiques and crafts center, it is open for Happy Hour drinks and rijsttafel Wednesday and Friday. Live dance music plays Friday from 9pm. The house, which dates to the early 1700s, is open as a museum Monday through Friday 9:15am to 12:15pm and 3-6pm and at night as a nightspot. *Tel. 737-8344.*

LANDHUIS CHOBOLOBO in Salinja is the site of the Curacao Liqueur Distillery and it is open for tasting and tours Monday to Friday, 8am to noon and 1-5 pm. Admission is free. *Tel. 737-8459.*

LANDHUIS DANIEL, between Grote Berg and Tera Kora, dates to 1634 when it was built more as a travelers rest than as a plantation house. It's now a guest house with bar, restaurant, dive shop, and souvenir shop. It is open free except Monday and Tuesday, when it is closed to non-guests. *Tel. 864-8400.*

LANDHUIS FUIK, now a ruin, can be seen just past Fuik on the east end of the island.

LANDHUIS GROOT DAVELAAR, a red and white wedding cake, is now a fashionable restaurant behind the Promenade Shopping Center, Salinja. See De Taveerne under Restaurants.

LANDHUIS GROOT SANTA MARTHA, is now a care center for the handicapped, whose crafts are for sale here. Visitors are welcome Monday through Thursday 9am to noon and 1-3pm, Friday 9am to noon, and the first Sunday of the month, 9am to 1pm It's found just west of Soto. *Tel. 864-1559.*

LANDHUIS HABAAI in Otrabanda's old Jewish Quarter has a cobbled courtyard. Built in the 1600s, it is used only for special events and has no phone.

LANDHUIS JAN KOK, just east of St. Willibrordus, is open by appointment for tours Monday through Friday and on Sunday for pancakes and local foods. *Tel. 864- 8087.*

LANDHUIS KNIP, between Lagun and Westpunt, is a museum commemorating the massive slave uprising in 1795 that led eventually to emancipation. Once a prosperous farmhouse, it is partially furnished with period antiques. Its rooms and verandahs are often the scene of cultural events. Admission is NAFl 3.50 adults and NAFl 1 children. *Tel. 864- 0244.*

LANDHUIS ROOI CATOOTJE, is a private house used as a library for the collection of the Maduro family. To arrange a tour and to get directions, phone ahead. *Tel. 737-5119.*

LANDHUIS PAPAYA, found on the highway between Julianadorp and Grote Berg, was built as a country house for wealthy city dwellers. It's now an art gallery with local works for sale, a restaurant, guest house, and bar. Hours are Tuesday to Friday 9am to 10pm and weekends 10am to 10pm. On Sunday, enjoy barbecue and live music after 6pm. Admission is NAFl 2.50, which includes coffee or a soft drink. *Tel. 869-5850.*

LANDHUIS SAVONET, Christoffel Park, is still in private hands but some side buildings are open to the public. *Tel. 864-0363.*

NIGHTLIFE & ENTERTAINMENT

Night owls can always find action at the casinos, which are open 2pm to 4 or 5am. Note that almost every bar has Happy Hour with discounted drinks, free snacks, or both. Times vary.

HARD ROCK SOCIETY, Keuken Plein 8, Punda, *Tel. 465-6633,* is open nightly until 1am and Friday and Saturday until 2am. The music is hard rock; the crowd youngish; the food substantial and modestly priced. Upstairs you can play pool or get a tattoo. **RAFFLE'S GRAND CAFE** is a disco at Corrieweg 12, *Tel. 736-4399.* It's open Friday and Saturday 11am to 4am. The happening place for jazz is **THE BLUES** at the Avila Beach Club, Penstraat, *Tel. 461-4377* where Happy Hour is standing room only on the pier and in the bar. Live musicians raise the roof while patrons watch the sunset. Stay on for a light dinner, or come back after dinner for jazz and blues. It's closed Monday.

For pool, snooker, backgammon and other pub games, **ROYAL RED POOL LOUNGE & BAR** is also a restaurant at Caracasbaaiweg 55, *Tel. 461-5767.* It's open until 2am weekdays and Sunday, and 4am Friday and Saturday. **TIPSY CAFE**, Junostraat 16, is open until 3am weekdays and 4am on weekends. For an Indonesian evening of food and folkloric dancing the last Sunday of every month, check out the **TINASHI BAR** in the Landhuis Brievengat, *Tel. 737-8344.* **CLUB FACADE** Lindberghweg 32, *Tel. 461-4640,* has dancing and live entertainment.

INFINITY in Fort Nassau is the island's most romantic place to have a drink without blaring music. It overlooks the lights of town, *Tel. 461-3450.* Hours are Friday and Saturday 9pm to 2am. Dance through your sentence at **THE JAIL**, Keukenstraat 2-4-6, *Tel. 465-6810.* Call for hours and programs.

SPORTS & RECREATION

Beaches

Curacao's beaches range from cozy coves to long strands of white sand, all of them washed by waves of clear, turquoise water. Topless bathing is officially illegal, so be discreet. Actually, you'll see it almost everywhere. Stay away from the north coast, where undertows and surges are powerful, in favor of the more placid, sheltered southwest coast. All the beaches we've seen had at least some rocky areas. Bring aqua shoes in case they're needed.

Full-service beaches include:

Avila Beach Hotel has a small beach that is open to non-guests Monday through Friday, 7am to 6pm, for an admission charge of NAFl 5 adults and NAFl 2.50 children. A 15-minute walk from Punda, the hotel has a beach bar and restaurant and changing rooms. The beach around the Seaquarium is crowded and alive with bars, shops, watersports rental, and (sometimes topless) bathers. It's open daily 8:30am to 6pm, with the bar staying open later. Admission is NAFl 4.00.

East of town you'll find **Barbara Beach** with its shade trees and shallow waters and **Jan Thiel**, which has no sand but is a pretty wading beach. Both charge a small admission. West of town, pay a NAFl 5.00 admission at the **Coral Cliff Hotel** to use the beach any time sunrise to sunset. It's rocky and has little shade, but restrooms, showers, and a small bar are on the shore and the cliffside hotel above has a restaurant and children's play area. One section shelters the island's only nude beach.

Pay a small admission per carload to swim at **Kas Abou** west of town at the end of a dirt road between **St. Willibrordus** and **Soto**. Watch for the turn-off. Birding is good late in the day. Rentals offered here include beach chairs, paddle boats, and snorkel and dive equipment. **Vaersenbaai Beach** just west of St. Michael charges no admission except for divers. Sand is scanty and it's sometimes closed for private parties, but the cove is a picture, well worth a look.

Among the island's most popular beaches are two at **Kenepa** near **Landhuis Kenepa** just northwest of **Lagun**. Both are in secluded coves; between them is a cliffside lookout. Just west of town, **Boca St. Michael** has clear water, bobbing fishing smacks, and a dive platform but little sand. Come here to hike the salt marsh, watch bird life, eat in one of the seafood restaurants, and swim (wearing beach shoes).

A number of cove beaches are found off the main road between **Lagun** and **Westpunt**. All have clusters of anchored fishing smacks, restaurants nearby, snorkeling, and diving. One of the best beaches for sand is **Santa Cruz** between **Soto** and **Lagun**. A small snack bar and restrooms are open weekends.

Although they aren't recommended for women alone, remote beaches are found at **Playa Kanoa** on the northwest shore, **Port Marie** (admission) west of St. Willibrordus, and **San Juan** (admission), northwest of Kas Abou. Northwest of Sota, a cluster of cove beaches at **San Nicolas** (admission) is not easy to find and the access road is not good, but the swimming is lovely and, for divers, there's an underwater cave. The shore is more coral rubble than sand, so wear beach shoes.

Beaches most easily accessible by bus are the **Avila**, the **Princess**, **Marie Pompoen**, and **Seaquarium**. Take a van bus or the 6A bus from the depot at the Punda post office to Dominguito. Or, take the 8A bus to Boka Sami. To **Jeremi**, **Kenepa**, **Lagun** and **Santa Cruz**, take the 3C bus. The 9A (Westpunt) bus takes you to **Playa Forti** and **Playa Kiskado**.

Bicycling

Dutch Dream Adventure, *Tel. 465-3575*, offers bicycle tours, canoe safaris, mountain climbing, walks through the national park, and jeep safaris.

Bowling

Try the **Curacao Bowling Club**, Chuchubiweg 10A, *Tel. 737- 9275.*

Fishing

Charter with **Seascape**, *Tel. 462-5000.*

Diving

Curacao lists almost 70 dive sites from walls to wrecks, reefs to rocks. Among the unique dives are **The Valley**, **Lost Anchor**, one called **Alice in Wonderland**, and the depths surrounding an offshore desert island, **Klein Curacao**, with its pristine reefs and coral Mushroom Forest. All dives are in protected parks where anchoring is not allowed. Waters are usually calm and always warmly pleasant.

Dive operators include:
• **Habitat Curacao Dive Resort**, *Tel. 560-7263*
• **Big Blue Diving**, *Tel. 560-5454*
• **Coral Cliff Diving**, *Tel. 864-2822*
• **Diving School Wederfoort**, *Tel. 888-4414*
• **Dolphin Divers**, *Tel. 462-8304*
• **Underwater Curacao**, *Tel. 461- 8131*
• **Eden Rock Dive Center**, *Tel. 462-8878*
• **Toucan Diving**, *Tel. 461- 2500*
• **Atlantis Diving**, *Tel. 462-6200*
• **Ultimate Dive**, *Tel. 465-2571*

Fitness

If your hotel doesn't have workout facilities, contact the **Body Beach Sports Club**, *Tel. 465-7969*, or **Sundance Helth and Fitness Center**, *Tel. 462-7740.*

Golf & Squash

Contact the **Curacao Golf and Squash Club**, *Tel. 737-3590.*

Horseback Riding

Ride with **Ashari's Ranch**, *Tel. 560-8202* or **Ranch Alegre**, *Tel. 868-1181.*

Jogging

A 2.5-kilometer seaside jogging path called the **Koredo** is just west of town near the Sonesta Beach Resort. It's lighted for security and is a popular running spot pre-dawn to twilight.

Pool

Play pool at the **Royal Red Pool Lounge**, Caracasbaaiweg 55, *Tel. 461-5767.*

Sailing

Charter with **Sail Curacao** at Kimi Kalki Marina, Brakkeput Ariba 62, *Tel. 767- 6003.* Aboard the luxury power yacht *Kristel-Ann II*, take a day cruise to Klein Curacao for $65. Included are soft drinks, wine, beer, breakfast and a barbecue lunch. *Tel. 560-5450.*

Snorkeling

Book a boat and snorkel cruise with *Mermaid, Tel. 737-5416; Miss Ann, Tel. 767- 1579; Insulinde, Tel. 560-1340; Sail Curacao, Tel. 767-6003; Taber Tours, Tel. 737- 9539* or *Toucan II, Tel. 461-2500.*

Tennis

If your hotel doesn't have tennis courts, contact the **Santa Catarina Sports Club**, *Tel. 767-7028* or *767-7030;* also the **Curacao Sport Club**, *Tel. 737-9566.*

Watersports

To rent a water scooter or sailboard, contact **Top Watersports** at the Seaquarium Beach, *Tel. 461-5767.*

SHOPPING

When cruise ships are in, the streets of **Punda** and **Otrobanda** come alive with colorful vendors and festive flea markets. However, any day is a good day for snapping up some of the Caribbean's most meaningful finds: local art work, pottery, Dutch Delftware, wooden shoes, Curacao liqueur, brilliantly painted hanging planters made from old tires, carvings from Haiti, and worlds of trade goods from South America, which lies only 44 miles to the south.

The famous **Floating Market** sells mostly produce and fish for local consumption, but for tourists it's a good place to find spices and inexpensive terracotta planters. It's open Monday through Saturday, 5am to 6:30pm and Sunday 5am to 1pm. This is one of the few places where you might try bartering, but only with tact. In Curacao, prices are usually fixed and are non-negotiable.

Among the best souvenirs here are Dutch cheeses, sold in supermarkets for about half what North Americans usually pay for Edam and Gouda. Take home a five-pound ball of Edam for about $10 and a buttery wheel of Gouda for about $20. Shop supermarkets too for Indonesian spices and staples, wines and liqueurs including the famous Curacao, and the unique Dutch licorice. Unlike tourist stores, which price items in dollars, supermarkets trade in guilders, but with the touch of a cash register key will give you a total in dollars. Your change, however, will be paid in guilders.

Perhaps the most photographed building in Punda is **J.L. Penha & Sons** on the Handelskaade, a bright yellow and white birthday cake that has been a landmark since 1708. Sold here are perfumes, cosmetics, designer clothing, and Hummel figurines. Local ceramics and pottery, some by artists and others by handicapped citizens, are sold at **Arawak Craft Products** on Mattheywerf, *Tel. 462-7249*. From a balcony, potters can be observed at their work; another balcony houses fine arts and crafts. It's open Monday to Saturday 8:30am to 5pm and on Sundays when cruise ships are in port.

Just east of the post office, the **Old Market Place** is known locally as the Marché and is a good place to nosh on local specialties cooked over hot coals. At **Yaqui**, de Rouvilleweg 9A, Otrobanda, shop for pre-Columbian figurines, paintings on leather and bark, onyx, and other unusual primitives reflecting Mayan and Incan motifs. It's open Monday through Saturday, 10am to 6pm, *Tel. 462-7533*.

For a pleasant stop when you're riding around town, seek out **Caribbean Handcraft** at Kaya Kakina 8, Jan Thiel, *Tel. 767-1171*. At the end of Caracasbaaiweg, turn right onto Kaya Damasco, then right on Kaya Jan Thiel. At the top of the hill, turn right again at Kaya Kakina. You're rewarded for the climb with a view of Spanish Water, clean restrooms, cold drinks at reasonable prices, and a nice choice of handmade souvenirs. Last-minute shopping can be done at the airport for cheese, jewelry, Benetton, spirits, 18-karat gold and gems.

JUST SAY NO

Unlike Holland, where possession of small amounts of some drugs is tolerated, Curacao has very strict drug laws. Fines are enormous and jail sentences swift. Don't even think about bringing recreational drugs to the island.

EXCURSIONS & DAY TRIPS

Book an excursion to Bonaire or Klein Curacao with **Water World Boat-Trips**, *Tel. 465-6042 or 560-1490*; the sailing ship *Bounty, Tel. 560-1887; Miss Ann* **Boattrips**, *Tel. 767-1579*; or *Kristal-Ann II, Tel. 560-4558.*

Wild Curacao, *Tel. 561-0027*, offers an all-day trip to four caves, an underground spring, a field with 40 varieties of cactus, and beaches. The $50 price includes a barbecue lunch, pickup at your hotel, an air conditioned bus, fruit, and flashlights. Bus tours are offered by **ABC Tours**, *Tel. 767-5105*, **Blenchi Tours**, *Tel. 461-8660*; **Casper Tour**, *Tel. 465-3010*; **Curven Tours**, *Tel. 737-9806*; **Daltina Tours**, *Tel. 461-4888*; **Dornasol Tours**, *Tel. 868-2735*; **Kibra Hacha Tours**, *Tel. 560-6050* and **Taber Tours**, *Tel. 737-6713*. Even if you'll be exploring on your own, take a bus tour to get you oriented. Drivers supply jokes and narrative tidbits that make the tours well worthwhile.

Sail *Insulinde*, a 120-foot tall ship, to Bonaire for the weekend, leaving at noon Friday and returning Sunday at 5pm. For $115, you'll spend two nights on board in one of nine cabins and will have dinner Friday, breakfast Saturday and Sunday, and a buffet at anchor off Klein Curacao. If no cabin is available you can sleep in a hammock for $160. A six per cent sales tax applies to boat excursions. Bring your own beach towels. *Tel. 560-1340*. Or take a day sail to **Port Marie**, just up the scenic coast from Willemstad aboard *Insulinde* any Thursday 8:30am to 5:30pm. The fare of $55 includes morning coffee, tea and cookies, a barbecue and salad buffet, use of snorkel equipment, and fresh fruit during the sail home.

USING THE CURACAO PHONE BOOK

Look in the green pages for international dialing instructions and the white pages for the telephone and fax numbers of homes and businesses. Doctors are listed in the blue pages under their specialties, which are in Dutch, so it's difficult to navigate if you don't know the language. Yellow pages have indexes in English, Spanish, Dutch, and Papiementu.

PRACTICAL INFORMATION

Area Code: 5999

ATM: To find an ATM look for the following signs: ABN-AMRO, Caribbean Mercantile, Bankomatiko, and Geldautomaat. ATMs are found in major population centers and at the airport.

Banking: generally, banks are open Monday through Friday 8am to 4 p.m.

Consulate: U.S. Consulate General, St. Anna Boulevard 19, *Tel. 5999/461-3066.*

Currency: U.S. dollars circulate freely. Local currency is the Netherlands Antilles florin, commonly called the guilder, at the rate of NAfl 1.78 to US$1. The best exchange rates are often found at the casinos. It's possible to get by using only American dollars and credit cards, but vendors can rarely supply change in U.S. currency.

Customs: Americans can take home, duty free, $600 worth of goods purchased here including one carton of cigarettes and a fifth of liquor plus a second bottle of locally produced liquor. Check prices, though, because even after paying duty, some brands are an excellent buy. Unlimited gifts up to $25 can be mailed home as long as the recipient gets no more than one parcel a day. Local art, handicrafts, and jewelry items are duty free; get a certificate stating they were made here.

Driving & Gas: your home license will serve for driving, but not as proof of citizenship. Driving is on the right, North American style. Speedometers and road signs are in kilometers. Generally the speed limit is 35 kilometers per hour in town and 60 kph in the open unless a lower speed is posted. A 24-hour gas station is found near the airport opposite the 24-hour Denny's. Gasoline costs about NAFl 1.20 per liter.

Electricity is 127/120 VAC at 50 cycles. North American appliances, except for clocks, will work just fine.

Emergencies: dial 112 for an ambulance, 114 for police or fire and 461-7991 for 24-hour tourism security assistance.

Government: The island is a commonwealth of the Netherlands.

Hazards: thorns that fall from the hubada tree are as long, sharp, and hard as nails. Don't hike the bush wearing flip-flops or thin sneakers; watch carefully where you step. Fireworks are sold legally December 26-31. Beware of merrymakers.

Holidays include New Year's Day, Carnival Monday, March 18, Ash Wednesday, Good Friday, Easter Monday, the Queen's birthday (April 30), Labor Day on May 1, Ascension Day, and Christmas, December 24-26. Many Indian-owned stores close on January 26.

Hours: Sunday shopping can be iffy and some shops close Tuesday afternoon. Stores generally are open Monday through Saturday, 8am to noon and 2pm to 6pm but hours are extended when cruise ships are in.

Immigration: U.S. and Canadian residents need a return ticket plus proof of citizenship such as a voter registration, green card, passport that is not more than five years out of date, or a birth certificate. Photo ID is required.

Mail address: your address while in the islands will end in Curacao, Netherlands Antilles.

Medical matters: Curacao has the most modern hospital in the southern

Caribbean, Elizabeth Hospital, *Tel. 5999/462-4900*, with facilities for major surgery (except open heart surgery) and decompression. For minor complaints, over-the-counter medicines are found at pharmacies called *botikas*. Except for the lunch hour, noon to 2pm, most are open all day until 6pm and some stay open 24 hours on a rotating schedule. Ask at your hotel. English speaking doctors and dentists can be recommended by your hotel.

Taxes: departure tax is $12.50 for international flights or $5.75 for those leaving for another island. There is no tax for children aged two and under.

Time zone: Curacao is on Atlantic Standard Time, which is the same as Eastern Daylight Time, all year. In winter, there is a one-hour difference between Curacao and New York.

Tourist information: Write the Curacao Tourist Board, *475 Park Avenue South, New York NY 10016, Tel. 212/683-7660; Fax 683-9337 or Tel. toll-free 888/348-3287.* Visitor information offices are found at the airport and at Pietermaai 19, *Tel. 461-6000.* For 24-hour visitor assistance, *Tel. 461-7991.*

PARDON OUR FRENCH

Spellings for the same words vary greatly throughout the Caribbean, but nowhere more than in the Dutch islands, where citizens speak four and five languages. A map prepared for English speaking people might refer to the Handelskade, which in Dutch is Handelskaade. Things get even worse when the word derived from Amerindians, who had no written language. Every explorer simply wrote things down as he heard them: hamak, hammock, hummock. Some references are to the Caiqueto or Caiquetio Indians. When you find what appear to be inconsistencies in these pages, keep in mind that there are many right ways to spell many of the words in common use here.

THE
BRITISH
VIRGIN
ISLANDS

17. BRITISH VIRGIN ISLANDS

This tiny, 35-mile-long sprinkling of eden islands includes **Tortola,
Virgin Gorda, Anegada,** and **Jost Van Dyke,** all of them proudly flying the
Union Jack but otherwise much the same as their neighboring U.S. Virgin
Islands – small and easy to get around, rimmed with remarkable beaches
probing into hidden coves, and blessed with day-long sunshine.

Ports of entry are at Virgin Gorda, Jost Van Dyke, Anegada, Road
Town, Beef Island, and at the west end of Tortola. Communities are
found at **Great Harbour** on Jost Van Dyke; on Tortola at **Carrot Bay, Cane
Garden Bay, Road Town, Sea Cow Bay, and Long Swamp**; on Virgin
Gorda at **Spanish Town** and **North Sound**.

Most of the smaller islands are uninhabited but there are aloof, pricey
resorts on **Peter Island** and **Guana Island**, a resort on six-acre **Marina
Cay,** and a private mansion accommodating up to 24 guests on **Necker
Island**.

Columbus first noted the islands in 1493 and it wasn't long before
they, like the other islands of the Caribbean, were pawns in European
battles that pitted Dutch against Spanish and English against French.
Although the Dutch did settle here at Soper's Hole in the 17th century,
the islands were claimed by the British in 1672 and remain today a British
colony with its own, locally elected, government.

Climate

The strongest North American cold fronts may push this far south,
bringing stinging winds, but the climate in the BVI is a non-story except
during hurricane season when storms may occasionally spin up. Plan on
warm and sunny days and cool nights in the 60s.

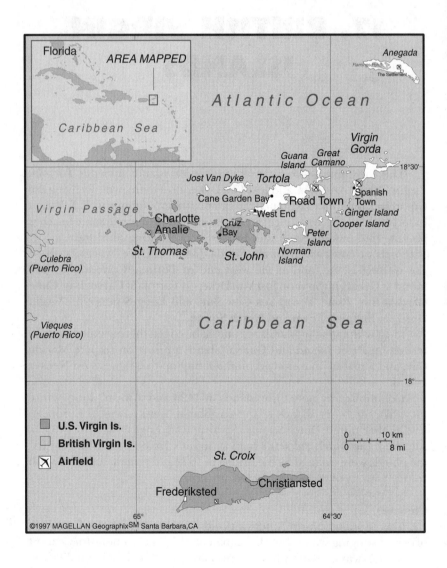

Florida

AREA MAPPED

Caribbean Sea

Atlantic Ocean

Anegada

Flamingo Pt.

The Settlement

Virgin Gorda

18°30'

Guana Island

Great Camano

Jost Van Dyke

Tortola

Spanish Town

Cane Garden Bay

Road Town

Virgin Passage

Charlotte Amalie

West End

Ginger Island

Cruz Bay

Cooper Island

St. Thomas

St. John

Peter Island

Norman Island

Culebra (Puerto Rico)

Vieques (Puerto Rico)

Caribbean Sea

18°

U.S. Virgin Is.

British Virgin Is.

Airfield

St. Croix

0   10 km
0   8 mi

Frederiksted

Christiansted

65°

64°30'

©1997 MAGELLAN GeographixSM Santa Barbara,CA

ARRIVALS & DEPARTURES

Plan your arrival as early in the day as possible, especially if your trip will involve road and ferry travel after you've landed at the airport and gone through the customs and immigration gristmill. Sometimes the post-flight part of the trip is the most arduous.

By Air

Beef Island/Tortola, the main airport for Tortola and all the BVI, is served daily from San Juan by **American Eagle**, *Tel. 800/433-7300*, **LIAT**, *Tel. 246/495-1187*, **Virgin Islands Airways**, *Tel. 284/495-1972*. **Air St. Thomas**, *Tel. 246/776-2722* flies to **Virgin Gorda** from San Juan, a route also served by **Virgin Islands Airways**, and **Carib Air**, *Tel. 284/495-5965*. Air St. Thomas and Carib Air fly between Virgin Gorda and St. Thomas. **Gorda Aero Services**, *Tel. 284/ 495-2271*, flies three days a week from Beef Island/Tortola to Anegada and Virgin Island Airways flies daily between Virgin Gorda and Beef Island/Tortola.

Inter-island service is available via **LIAT** daily from Beef Island to Antigua, St. Kitts, and Dominica. Virgin Islands Airways flies daily from Beef Island to St. Kitts. **LIAT** and **Winair** fly one or two days a week between Beef Island and St. Maarten. Charter flights are available through **Fly BVI**, *Tel. 800/1-FLY BVI (U.S.); 800/469-5955 (Canada) or 284/495-1747* elsewhere. Gorda Air Services and Air St. Thomas also offer planes for charter.

By Ferry

Ferries are an important mode of inter-island transportation, always cheaper than flying and sometimes quicker if you want to go downtown-to-downtown. Schedules vary according to the day of the week and can be affected by sea conditions, so it's crucial to verify your time of departure by telephone.

Ferry companies include:
- **Inter-Island Boat Services**, *Tel. 284/495-4166*, operates between West End and Cruz Bay.
- **Jost Van Dyke Ferry Service**, *Tel. 284/494-2997*, operates between West End and Jost Van Dyke on schedule or on charter.
- **Native Son, Inc.**, *Tel. 284/495-461*, runs between Road Town, West End, and downtown St. Thomas. There's also daily service from West End to St. John and Red Hook, St. Thomas.
- **North Sound Express**, *Tel. 284/495-2271*, operates between Beef Island and North Sound, Virgin Gorda, with a stop at The Valley with four-hour notice.
- **Peter Island Ferry**, *Tel. 284/494-2561*, links Road Town at the Peter Island Ferry dock to Peter Island Resort & Yacht Harbour.

• **Smith's Ferry Service**, *Tel. 284/495-4495 or 494-2355*, runs between Virgin Gorda and Road Town. Also from Road Town and West End to downtown St. Thomas.

• **Speedy's Fantasy/Speedy's Delight**, *Tel. 284/495-5240 or 5235*, operates between Virgin Gorda and Road Town.

ORIENTATION

It's easy to get your bearings on any island if you can just remember where you are in relation to the ferry dock (except for Anagada, where the airport is the center of interest). If you're not being met by your hotel host, you'll find plenty of friendly, eager drivers at the airports and docks. If you choose a rental car or mo-ped, a good map will be provided. A Tourist Board office is on the waterfront at Wickham's Cay, conveniently located between the ferry dock and the cruise ship dock.

GETTING AROUND THE BRITISH VIRGIN ISLANDS

Taxis meet all flights, and you can get a cab from the **Beef Island Airport** to Road Town for $5. The town itself can be walked from one end to the other in half an hour. A leisurely tour, hitting all the high points, takes two hours or less. Waterfront Drive, home of **Pusser's Company Store and Pub**, follows the east side of the bay, with a British Virgin Islands Tourist Office at its north end. Main Street and the settlement's shopping district plus the extravagant cruise ship shops are all packed into the **Wickham's Cay** area.

Don't assume automatically that you can't manage without a rental car. Rental and fuel costs are high; roads are not good; and you can probably find better uses for the $10 that they nick you for a driver's license. You can see a lot of these small islands on foot and by boat, then take a taxi or tour if you want to explore an island or try restaurants different from those at your resort.

The most popular rentals in the British Virgins are four-wheel-drive Jeeps ($35-$60 daily), with discounts for weekly rentals. Scooters, which rent for $30 a day or $170 a week are available on most islands. Insurance of $7-$10 may be additional. Collision damage waiver is optional, although a deposit of $500 or so may be required. Bicycles are available through rental agencies and many resorts. Most rental agencies pick up free at resorts or airports, but ask in advance to be sure about pick-up and drop-off requirements, which can be complicated if they involve meeting a ferry or private launch. Auto and scooter rental agencies include:

Anegada
• **Anegada Reef Hotel**, *Tel. 284/495-8002*
• **D.W. Jeep Rentals**, *Tel. 284/495-8018*

Tortola
- **Airways Car Rentals**, *Tel. 284/495-2161*
- **Alphonso Car Rentals**, *Tel. 284/494-3137*
- **Avis Rent-A-Car**, *Tel. 284/494-3322 or 494-2193*
- **Budget Rent-A-Car**, *Tel. 284/494-2639 or 494-2531*
- **Caribbean Car Rental**, *Tel. 284/494-2595*
- **Del's Jeep & Car Rental**, *Tel. 284/495-8018*
- **Denzil Clyne Car Rentals**, *Tel. 284/495-4900*
- **Hertz Car Rental**, *Tel. 284/495-5803*
- **International Car Rentals**, *Tel. 284/494-2516, Fax 494-4715*
- **National Car Rental**, *Tel. 284/494-3197*
- **Rencal Rent-A-Car**, *Tel. 284/495-4330, Fax 494-5085*

Virgin Gorda
- **Hertz Car Rental**, *Tel. 284/495-4405*
- **Honda Scooter Rentals**, *Tel. 284/495-5212*
- **L&S Jeep Rental**, *Tel. 284/495-5297, Fax 495-5342*
- **Mahogany Rentals**, *Tel. 284/495-5469, Fax 495-5072*
- **Speedy's Car Rental**, *Tel. 284/495-5235 or 495-5240*

WHERE TO STAY

Rates listed here do not include a seven per cent room tax and service charges, which are 10 to 15 per cent. Summer rates are usually 30-40 percent less than winter rates quoted here but some resorts add features and upgrades rather than lowering rates in the off season.

Private villas in the islands can be booked through **WIMCO**, *Tel. 800/932-3222 or 401/849-8012*. Maid service and staff are available. Guest houses, vacation houses and apartments are also available on arrangement with private owners. For a list call **BVI Tourism** in New York at *Tel. 800/835-8530*. All area codes are **284**.

Mail sent here should be posted to the address, island, then British Virgin Islands, fully spelled out. Many of the British islands hotels have mail drops in St. Thomas, where mail arrives quickly and at U.S. rates, in which case the address would end in VI, followed by the zip code. Ask.

ANEGADA
Moderate

ANEGADA REEF HOTEL, *Anegada. Tel. 284/495-8002, Fax 495-9362. Rates at this 12-room hotel, which is three miles west of the airport at Setting Point, start at $165 including three meals daily.*

So remote is the island that you're glad to find any place to lay your head, let alone a pleasant little hotel with its own restaurant and bar. In fact, the hotel is also where you can rent a car, find a taxi or bicycle, buy bait, tackle and ice, and have your air tanks refilled. Rooms are spacious and each has its own porch opening onto the beach. Be as private as you care to be, or let your host find you a deep sea fishing trip or a guide to take you out on the flats to hunt the elusive bonefish. There are just enough local characters, passing visitors, and yachties to justify the occasional barbecue or a festive evening with live music. Some rooms have telephones; all are air conditioned. Babysitting can be arranged.

Budget
OCEAN RANGE HOTEL, *in the settlement near the air strip, c/o General Delivery, Anegada. Tel. 284/485-8017 or radio VHF Channel 16. Rates start at $65 nightly.*
Ocean view rooms are plain vanilla, but you'll have a kitchenette and your own patio. Play Robinson Crusoe at bargain prices. Traveler's checks are accepted, but not credit cards.

GUANA ISLAND
GUANA ISLAND, *booking address 10 Timber Trail, Rye NY 10580, Tel. 914/967-6050. The island's number is 284/494-2334. Rates start at $675 for two including three meals daily, afternoon tea, wine with lunch and dinner, and use of tennis courts and watersports equipment. Groups can rent the entire island, which has 15 double rooms and a one-bedroom cottage. For $25 per person round trip you'll be met at Beef Island Airport and taken by taxi to the dock for the ten-minute cruise to the island. Cash and checks are accepted, but not credit cards.*
They call this the only Virgin island that still is, an 850-acre piece of paradise plunked down in the dazzling sea north of Tortola. "You guessed it, teams of decorators were not flown in from New York," say the caretakers in explaining the furniture, which isn't Chippendale but looks just fine in an island setting. Wicker and woods complement white walls with accents of fresh flowers. Louvered doors admit the tradewinds.
The island's White Bay Beach is a stunner but if you want another beach all to yourself, take a boat and a picnic to one of the other six beaches on the island. Nature lovers will want to tramp the outback looking for wildlife and sea birds. See if you can find the rock outcropping that is shaped like an iguana, giving the island its name. Meals make use of fresh tropical fruits, vegetables and seafood; dinner is all crystal and candlelight, catered to your whim.
If you rent the cottage, which goes for $925 to $1290 nightly depending on the season, take your meals in the dining terrace or have them brought in. It's a three-room hillside overlook with living room, kitchen, and bath, surrounded by decks and reached by walking a secluded trail past an ancient stone wall built by the Quakers who originally peopled the island.

JOST VAN DYKE

Expensive

SANDCASTLE LTD., *White Bay. Mail address Suite 2-1, Red Hook Plaza, USVI 00802. Tel. 284/690-1611 or 340/775-5262. Winter rates start at $235 with all meals. Take the 20-minute ferry ride from Tortola.*

Four beachfront villas are garlanded with greenery and bright blooms to form the ultimate beach getaway. Dinner is served by candlelight after you've had a sundowner at the beachfront honor bar. (You make the drinks and total the tab). Snorkel or windsurf, shop the boutique, and take barefoot walks on the beach.

Budget

RUDY'S MARINER INN, *Great Harbour, Jost Van Dyke. Tel. 284/495-9282. In the USVI, Tel. 340/775-3558. Rates start at $85 single, with all meals. The island is 20 minutes by boat from Tortola. No credit cards are accepted.*

Living is easy at this three-room inn with its own beach bar and a locally popular restaurant revered for its fish and conch specialties served with generous helpings of side dishes. Your room has kitchen and dining areas, so you can shop local markets and try Caribbean cookery on your own if you choose not to take the meal plan.

NECKER ISLAND

NECKER ISLAND, *mail address Box 1109, Virgin Gorda. U.S. and Canada Tel. 800/557-4255. Rates for the entire island start at $11,000 per day for up to seven guests; $16,000 daily for 20-24 guests. During some periods, you don't have to book the entire island. Rooms and suites are rented separately at $9,000 per couple per week.*

The rate doesn't seem so startling when you realize that you're renting an entire, private, 74-acre island owned by Virgin Group chairman Richard Branson. With it come a ten-bedroom villa and two private Balinese cottages. All meals and drinks, helicopter transfer from St. Thomas or Beef Island, and everything else needed to pursue a grandly hedonist, out-island lifestyle are included. Use the boats, wind surfers, jet skiis, books, music, a video library, games, an exercise room, swimming pool and tennis court, and let the staff of 22 cater to your every whim.

A tiny island rises out of a turquoise sea. It's rimmed with beige beaches and is topped by a mansion that looks out to sea from every direction. When you move in, you're lord and lady of the manor. There are no menus because you tell the cooks what and when you care to eat; no schedules unless you make them; no other guests unless you invite them. The island, in short, is yours to throw a house party, a reunion, a wedding, or just a vacation in paradise.

Interiors are airily raftered, rising to high ceilings that draw hot air from below, bringing fresh sea breezes through the windows. A 22-foot Brazilian table in the dining room seats everyone in elegance. The Bali influence turns up time and again in the hand-carved furniture, teak and stone surfaces, expanses of iron-hard Brazilian Ipé wood and Yorkstone floors, gauzy canopies over a four-poster bedstead, straw matting covering the rafters in some rooms, and wood balconies suspended over a view of the sea far below. When doors are flung open, it's easy to forget where indoors ends and outdoors begins. A waterfall spills into the swimming pool, fed by a desalinization plant that is run by diesel generators. Relax in the Jacuzzis, barbecue around the pool or at the beach, use the floodlit tennis courts, play snooker, or use the workout equipment.

PETER ISLAND

PETER ISLAND RESORT & YACHT HARBOR, *Box 211, Tortola, or 220 Lyon Street NW, Grand Rapids MI 49503. Tel. 800/346-4451; locally 284/495-2500. Rates at this 50-room, three-villa resort start at $415 nightly; a four-bedroom villa is $3950. The island is reached from Road Town by a 20-minute ride aboard the island's private boats, which make the trip nine times a day. Transfers are $25 per person. Guests are discouraged from bringing children under age eight.*

An AAA Four-Diamond resort, Peter Island is so exclusive that, as bareboaters anchored in its harbor, we were warned not to dry our tea towels on deck. The tony resort, which reopened for the 1998 season after closing for major revitalization, shares this island only with some wild goats, skittering lizards, and a concert of wild birds. Owned by Amway Corporation, whose soaps and shampoos are subtly provided as bath amenities, it can accommodate up to 50 guests. Snorkel, sail a 19-foot Squibb, swim off one of the five secluded beaches, or float in the freshwater pool surrounded by forests of brilliant hibiscus. Ride a bike into the hills or hike the nature trails to watch royal terns swoop among the trees. Then have a massage or work out in the fitness center. Dining is in your choice of two restaurants. The resort is dressy in season, so take jacket and tie for dinner.

Rooms have the little luxury touches expected in a four-diamond resort: built-in hair dryer, air conditioning plus ceiling fans and cross ventilation, clock radio, bathrobes, and mini-bar. Cool tile floors complement wicker and walnut furnishings; indoor gardens screen sunken bathtubs. Each room has its own lanai or balcony. Ask about packages, which include a scuba vacation and an ashore-afloat deal that combines a land stay with two nights on a crewed yacht. The resort has massage and spa services, tennis courts and lessons, nightly movies, a library, and a basketball hoop with half a court. Each week the manager throws a cocktail party and in season wine tastings are held weekly.

TORTOLA
Expensive
FORT RECOVERY ESTATES VILLAS, *Towers, West End, Tortola, mailing address Box 11156, St. Thomas VI 00801. Tel. 284/495-4036 or 800/ 367-8455. Drive east from the West End ferry dock, then follow the coast road to Fort Recovery. Rates start at $185 in season, with breakfast for a one-bedroom villa.*

Bring your family and settle into a villa with one, two, three, or four bedrooms. There's a manager on duty around the clock, a bar, restaurant, yoga and massages, and spectacular views of a half dozen islands across a crystal verdigris sea from your own private beach. The fort was built in the 17th century by the Dutch. Now it forms the core of this homey, British-style seaside community. Units are air conditioned and have fully-equipped kitchens, cable television, and daily maid service.

FRENCHMAN'S CAY, *Box 1054, West End, Tortola. Tel. 284/495-4844, Fax 495-4056, 800/235-4077. Winter rates start at $200. The resort is on Frenchman's Cay, a separate island across from the ferry docks at West End.*

Each of the nine villas in this breeze-cooled beach resort has a full kitchen, dining and sitting areas, and terrace. When you're not eating "in," try the resort's bar and The Clubhouse Restaurant, featuring Caribbean flavors with a continental flair. Swim in the pool, play tennis, or just roam the 12 secluded acres to bask in the tradewinds. To get out on the water, rent one of the hotel's kayaks, Sunfish, boogie boards, or board sailers, or just borrow snorkel gear and go exploring. Horseback riding, scuba lessons, tours, and day sails are cheerfully arranged.

LONG BAY BEACH RESORT & VILLAS, *mailing address: Island Destinations, 1890 Palmer Avenue, Suite 201, Larchmont NY 10538. Tel. 284/ 495-4252; in the U.S. and Canada, Tel. 800/729-9599; United Kingdom, Tel. 0800-898-379. Rates start at $185. From Road Town, go south and west on Waterfront Drive, then north on Zion Hill Road and west to Long Bay. If you arrive by ferry at West End, it's a ten-minute taxi ride. Meal plans are available. Children under age 12 can sleep free in a parent's room and pay a modest daily fee for a children's meal plan. Ask about packages.*

Hillside suites look out towards Jost Van Dyke over a strand of white sand that will be your private playground while you're here. Take a day sail on an 80-foot schooner, swim, and dine in the resort's highly-rated restaurant. Air conditioned rooms suites have high ceilings and a balcony that floats out over the tropical splendor, your own seascape. Designer prints are a dramatic black and white design, which is an effective foil for the sandy walls, tile, floors, and woody ceilings. Other rooms are done in sea greens and blues while still others are sunny ochres with accents of blue. Dine outdoors on linen-covered tables under the sun or stars, or indoors in the stony dining room with a greathouse look. The resort plays intensive tennis, and offers an attractive package for tennis players, but there's also plenty here for families, divers, beachcombers, and those who want to do nothing but veg out.

SUGAR MILL HOTEL, *Box 425, Road Town. Tel. 284/495-4355, Fax 495-4696; U.S. 800/462-8834; Canada 800/209-6874. Winter rates at this 21-unit hotel start at $175 single and $190 double. A two-bedroom villa is $585 nightly. Take the MAP meal plan at $50 per person. Children under age 10 are not accepted during high season. The hotel closes August and September. It is eight minutes from the West End ferry dock.*

Visitors flock to the famous restaurant here, so consider staying here among the ruins of a 17th century sugar plantation, eating all your meals at the acclaimed restaurant hosted by Jeff and Jinx Morgan. Breezy rooms with private terraces admit tropic breezes and look out over blue seas afloat with hazy mountains. Cool tile floors and filmy draperies are complemented by candy pastels or, in the deluxe villa, mellow golds and beiges. Some of the deluxe units have a bed or beds plus a queen-size sofabed, accommodating three or four. Standard rooms are poolside and have twin beds, refrigerator, and coffee maker. Deluxe units have kitchens. All are air conditioned.

Moderate

FORT BURT HOTEL, *Box 3380, Road Town. Tel. 284/494-2587, Fax 494-2002. Winter rates start at $110 double. Take Waterfront Drive south from Road Town to Fisher Estate.*

A 300-year-old fort in the hills outside Road Town has been restored to provide seven rooms and a suite overlooking Sir Francis Drake Channel. Swim in the fresh water pool or walk to the marina for sailing, fishing, and other watersports. Each room has an ocean view, air conditioning, and television. The hotel's bar is a good place to meet locals; the restaurant features continental and West Indian favorites. Child care can be arranged.

MOORINGS MARINER INN, *Box 139, Road Town. Tel. 284/494-2332, Fax 4949-2226; U.S. and Canada 800/535-7289. Winter doubles start at $165. On Wickham's Cay 2. Take Waterfront Drive northwest from Road Town.*

The Moorings charter yacht fleet is one of the most impressive in the world, and the inn was probably planned originally as a place for visiting yachtsmen to overnight before and after their cruises. Even if you're not a sailor, however, the yachtiness is part of the charm of the place. Every room has a galley, and provisioning is available in a well-stocked general store, so you can make your own meals when you don't feel like going out. The resort's dockside restaurant and bar are abuzz with sailing yarns shared by local liveaboards as well as fly-in charterers who are here for only a week or two.

NANNY CAY RESORT & MARINA. *Box 281, Road Town. Tel. 284/ 494-2512, Fax 494-0555, U.S. and Canada Tel. 800/74-CHARMS. Rates start at $150. Just three miles south of Road Town, the resort is 10 miles from the airport. Taxis are available, but ask about packages that include transfers. At press time, the hotel is in receivership and is being operated by fill-in staff, so get recent references before booking. The location is good and the resort is an evergreen, so we expect it to attract a buyer.*

Twenty five acres surrounded by sea are home to a 42-unit resort and a 200-slip marina. The combination is always a winning one in the BVI where liveaboards and charter sailors come ashore for evening grog with locals and guests. Your studio suite will be furnished in fading Caribbean colors and textures chosen for carefree living. You'll also have cable television, direct-dial telephone, kitchenette, and your own patio or balcony. Choose between the resort's two restaurants, Pegleg Landing or the poolside cafe, and two swimming pools. Tennis courts are lighted for night play, and use of the volleyball court is free. The hotel can arrange a car rental, snorkeling equipment, dive trips, and anything else in watersports including board sailing lessons. It has its own, full-service marina

PROSPECT REEF RESORT, *Box 104, Road Town. Tel. 284/494-3311, Fax 494-5595, U.S. 800/356-8937; Canada, 800/463-3608. Winter rates start at $147. Take Waterfront Drive south from Road Town through Fisher Estate.*

Spreading across a patch of waterfront overlooking Sir Francis Drake Channel and split by a tidal lagoon, this 131-unit resort has its own marina with sailing and diving trips, fresh and salt water swimming pools, tennis courts, an upscale restaurant, bars, shops, fitness center, and a pitch-and-putt golf course. All you need for a Caribbean getaway is right here just west of town. Take a studio or villa if you plan to do some of your own cooking; you can buy provisions at the resort. A courtesy bus runs to the beach and to town. In family seasons, there's a supervised program for children ages 5-12.

PUSSER'S MARINA CAY, *Box 626, Road Town. Tel. 284/494-2174, Fax 494-4775. Rates start at $150 with breakfast. This is a small, private island north of Beef Island and reached only by boat.*

Bring friends and have the whole island resort to yourself. It has four rooms and two villas, a beach, a marina, a restaurant, and a bar that attracts a lot of passing boaters.

SEBASTIAN'S ON THE BEACH, *Box 441 Tortola. Tel. 284/495-4212, Fax 495-4466; 800/336-4870. Rates at this 26-room hotel start at $110. From*

Road Town, go south and west on Waterfront Drive, pass Fort Recovery, and turn north (right) on Zion Hill Road, then left on Long Bay Road where the resort will be on ocean side.

Choose a beachfront or garden room in a secluded hotel shaded by forests of palm trees. Some units are air conditioned. All have ceiling fans and refrigerator, and there's a commissary where you can stock up on snacks and cold drinks. The beach is a sugary strand, overlooked by the Seaside Grille where you can get lobster, fresh seafood, homemade soup or steak. It's open for three meals, but you're also close to other resorts and restaurants.

TAMARIND COUNTRY CLUB HOTEL, *Box 509, East End, Tortola., Tel. 284/495-2477 or 800/313-5662. Rooms start at $115. Drive west from East End for just over a mile, then right on Josiah's Bay Road. From Road Town, it's 15 minutes via Belle Vue Road to Ridge Road, then left on Josiah's Bay Road.*

High above yet another of Tortola's legendary beaches, (it's a 15-minute walk to the beach) the hotel offers ten poolside rooms and ten, two-bedroom villas. Television and air conditioning are available on request. Locals once voted the hotel's restaurant tops on Tortola; there's also a poolside bar and lounge.

Budget

BVI AQUATIC HOTEL, *Box 605, Tortola. Tel. 284/495-4541 or 494-2114. Found just east of the West End ferry docks, this 14-room hotel has rooms with bath from $25 and one-bedroom flats from $350 a week. No credit cards.*

If you want a plain vanilla place to stay close to the watersports, this is a utilitarian *pied-a-terre* with its own bar.

CANE GARDEN BAY BEACH HOTEL, *284/495-4639, Fax 495-4820. Doubles start at $80 in winter, $45 in summer. From Road Town, take Joes Hill Road to Cane Garden Road. It's a 15-minute drive to the hotel.*

There's nothing fancy about this 24-room hotel but rooms do have telephones, air conditioning, and television, and the wind-sheltered beach is as wide and handsome as any found at pricier resorts. Available are snorkel gear, sail boards, fishing, and glass-bottom paddle boats. Meals at the hotel's restaurant feature star lobster, conch fritters, and other seafood; Rhymer's Beach Bar is a favorite hangout. Once you've arrived here you can manage without a car. If you choose to leave the hotel, several restaurants and bars with entertainment are within walking distance.

HOTEL CASTLE MARIA, *Box 206, Road Town. Tel. 284/494-2553 or 2515; Fax 494-2111. Winter rates at this 30-room hotel start at $90 double. Take Waterfront Drive south from the ferry dock and turn right on MacNamara Road.*

Stay snug in the heart of things (this is one of the closest hotels to Road Town) in a mansion-like setting surrounded by flowers and foliage.

Private balconies overlook the sea; the hotel has its own swimming pool. Some kitchenettes are available; rooms have television, telephone, air conditioning or room fan, and refrigerator. Local art is used throughout. The hotel's restaurant and bar are locally popular, but you can also walk to town or the ferry dock. Babysitting can be arranged.

JOLLY ROGER INN, *Box 437, Road Town. Tel. 284/495-4559, Fax 495-4184. Rooms at this 6-room inn, which is a few minutes walk west of the ferry dock in West End, start at $50.*

You're in the heart of a community with a dockside restaurant, bar, and shops. This modest hotel does have maid service and television, and watersports can be arranged, but don't count on using credit cards. It's a good budget choice if you have a rental car to get you to beaches and other adventures.

OLE WORKS INN, *Box 560, Tortola, located on Cane Garden Bay. Tel. 284/495-4837, Fax 495-9618. Doubles at this 18-room inn start at $80 in winter. From Road Town, take Joes Hill Road east to Cane Garden Bay Road, then south along the sea to the resort.*

Stay in a charming, 300-year-old sugar factory overlooking Cane Garden Bay. Your host, "Quito" Rhymer, offers air conditioned accommodations, each with refrigerator and oceanview balcony. Island music is played several nights a week in Beachfront Quito's Gazebo, which serves meals and exotic drinks, and Quito also has his own art gallery and gift shop.

VIRGIN GORDA

Expensive

BIRAS CREEK RESORT, *Box 54, Virgin Gorda, Tel. 284/494-3555, Fax 494-3557; U.S. and Canada 800/223-1108; United Kingdom 0800/894-057. Arrange with the hotel for airport transfer. You'll be met at the Virgin Gorda airport and taken to the launch that will deliver you to the resort. If you arrive at Beef Island, take the scheduled ferry or Biras' private launch. Rates start at $4500 per couple per week including meals.*

A small thimble of land is surrounded on all sides by the blue waters of the Atlantic, Caribbean, and Sir Francis Drake Channel. It's a secluded, 140-acre setting for nature trails for hiking and jogging, two lighted tennis courts, a private beach, and a beachside, freshwater pool. Bicycles are parked outside each of the 32 suites.

Unpack in a spacious suite done in happy Caribbean colors. Your room overlooks the real thing: a neon-hued sea, an incredibly white sand beach, and blue skies that are streaked with pink morning and evening. Each room has a sitting area, separate bedroom, ceiling fans, air conditioning, direct-dial telephone, and a secluded, open-air shower. Private patios are tiled in terra cotta. In addition, Grand Suites have oversize terraces and sunken bathtubs. The meeting room is also the home of a little museum. Ask to see it. Watersports and instruction are all included, so you can snorkel, sail, spurt around in a motorboat, or board sail. Ask about the land-sea package that includes five nights in the resort and two romantic nights in a fully-provisioned, captained yacht.

BITTER END YACHT CLUB & RESORT, *Box 46, Virgin Gorda. Tel. 284/494-2746, U.S. 312/944-5855 or 800/872-2392. Rates start at $390 including all meals. Airport transfers, which are included, involve a taxi ride then a launch.*

Many of the resorts in the Caribbean are as yachty as they are landlubberly, but this one is especially salty because you can sleep on a boat or in one of the rooms for about the same price. You'll still get maid service, meals in the Yacht Club and, if you want to anchor off for a night, provisions to tide you over. Sea and sails are part of the scene everywhere, whether you're overlooking them from your hilltop villa, trading tall tales with sailors in the bar, or actually sailing one of the big fleet of Sunfish, Lasers, JY15s, Rhodes 19s and J-24s. Introduction to Sailing is a popular course for resort guests.

Zone out on your private veranda overlooking the verdant grounds, or plug into a carnival of good times: island excursions to The Baths and Anegada, snorkeling in reef-sheltered coves, swimming at the pool or one of the resort's three beaches, or joining a group to study marine science. Killbrides Underwater Tours is based at the Club and can do a complete dive package from beginner to advanced, Ginger Island to the wreck of the *Rhone*. Dine in the Clubhouse Steak and Seafood Grille or the English Carvery, then dance under the stars at Almond Walk. Not all units here are air conditioned, so specify AC if it's important to you. Provision at The Emporium, which has staples as well as baked goods and takeout dishes.

LITTLE DIX BAY, *P.O. Box 70, Virgin Gorda, British Virgin Islands. U.S. mailing address, P.O. Box 720, Cruz Bay, St. John, VI 00831. Tel. 284/495-5555, Fax 495-5661, U.S. and Canada 800/928-3000. Rates in the 102 units start at $450 double in season. For $95 daily you can add three meals daily; add $75 for breakfast and lunch. Children's meal plans for ages five to twelve are $47.50 and $37.50. Children aged four and under eat free. Escorted transfers from Tortola International Airport are $50 adults, $25 children.*

Lying serenely behind a barrier reef, Little Dix Bay has a half-mile crescent of beach surrounded by 500 acres of forest, seagrape, tamarind, and palms. Founded in 1964 by Laurance Rockefeller, it is now a grand Rosewood resort far different from the somewhat shabby resort that met us on our first visit 20 years ago. With three employees for every guest, it assures a level of pampering that's impressive even in the service-savvy Caribbean.

From the moment you are met at the airport or ferry dock, you're in a world of seabreeze, sun, and luxury. Airy, spacious rooms are furnished with wicker and bamboo, soft pastels and brightly contrasting tropic bouquets. Most rooms are air conditioned but not all are, so specify air if you want it. All have telephones, balconies or terraces. Hike nearby **Gorda National Park** or the resort's own nature trails. Walking sticks are provided in each room, and they come in handy on Cow Hill, the Savannah Trail, or the Pond Bay Trail.

Sightsee by boat or Jeep, play tennis, or enjoy a full menu of watersports. The resort has its own 120-slip marina where boats are waiting to take you sailing, deep sea fishing, or sunset cruising. Ferries run regularly to a sister resort, Caneel Bay on St. John, where you can eat if you're on the Little Dix meal plan. Dining here is in the Pavilion overseen by Executive Chef Benoit Pepin, in the Sugar Mill with its tropical bistro look and wood oven-baked pizzas, or the nautically themed Beach Grill featuring seafood and sandwiches. After dinner, dance to live music on the Pavilion Terrace and walk home along paths lit by tiki torches and scented with frangipani. There's a children's program in season.

Moderate

DIAMOND BEACH CLUB, *Box 69, Virgin Gorda. Tel. 284/495-5452, Fax 495-5875; U.S. 800/871-3551; Canada 800/487-1839. Rates at this 14-room inn start at $170. Villas with up to four bedrooms are available. Located on the island's west shore, the resort is two miles north of the Virgin Gorda airport and also about two miles north of the dock where ferries arrive from Road Town.*

All patios in this clubby little resort view the ocean, where you can swim or snorkel over colorful reefs. Looming over its shoulder is Virgin Gorda Peak, surrounded by a national park where you can hike and birdwatch. Units have maid service and fully-equipped kitchens where you can cook supplies bought in the commissary. Ask about packages that include a Jeep.

DRAKE'S ANCHORAGE RESORT INN, *Box 2510, North Sound, Virgin Gorda. Tel. 284/894-2254 or 800/624-6651. The resort can accommodate up to 28 guests at rates starting at $350 including all meals. The resort is on Mosquito Island, a five-minute boat ride from the dock.*

Each of the comfortable units, which include rooms, suites, or a posh villa, has its own veranda overlooking the sea. There's nothing to do and nowhere to go on this idyllic hideaway. Swim off the beach, water ski, snorkel, board sail, fish, or ride a bicycle to explore the island's four beaches. Scuba diving here is so good that the Cousteau Society visits regularly. Dining in the breezy, tropics-inspired restaurant is to die for, especially if you like flopping-fresh seafood and succulent lobster served overlooking the water. Your fellow diners will include boaters who sail over and dock here to sample the fine fare. If you prefer a native dish or something continental with a French accent, you'll find them on the *carte du jour* as well. Dining late, you'll be served by candlelight.

GUAVABERRY SPRING BAY, *Box 20, Virgin Gorda. Tel. 284/495-7227, Fax 495-5283. Only a few minutes south of the airport and five minutes from The Valley, this 21-room resort offers rooms from $135 but no credit cards are accepted.*

Available by the day or week, this homey resort is fun to say. It's named for a local, cranberry-size fruit used in the making of liqueurs. Houses on stilts soar airily over a sea of boulders and bougainvillaea, catching sea breezes. Each unit has one or two bedrooms, kitchenette, and dining area. You can buy provisions at Yacht Harbour or in the little commissary that is operated here for guests. Horseback riding, diving, fishing, or island tours can be arranged by your hosts, or swim from the beach at nearby Spring Bay. These are the handiest lodgings to The Baths and the Copper Mine, close to Little Fort National Park, the airport, and the settlements of The Valley.

LEVERICK BAY RESORT, *Box 63, The Valley, Virgin Gorda. Tel. 284/495-7421, Fax 495-7367; U.S. 800/848-7081; Canada 800/463-9396. Rooms start at $119.*

Stay in an air conditioned hotel room (there are 16) or rent the two-bedroom condo at this popular spot on Leverick Bay, a jump-off spot for out islands and for those Virgin Gorda resorts that can't be reached by road. The hotel looks out over Blunder Bay and North Sound toward Mosquito and Prickly Pear islands. Pass your days diving, playing tennis, water skiing, swimming or snorkeling off the beach, shopping the resort's own boutiques, or getting a massage or facial. Buck's Food Market at the marina sells everything you need to provision a villa or boat for a day or a week, including wines and liquors.

Pubby and popular, Pusser's Beach Bar here is a hangout for transient yachties, locals, and resort guests alike. For dinner, have steak or a meat pie at Pusser's or try the dining room. After dinner, dance to local bands.

OLDE YARD INN, *Box 26, Virgin Gorda. Tel 284/495-5544, Fax 495-5986, U.S. 800/633-7411. Rates at this 14-room resort start at $130. A few minutes from the airport, the Inn is on the island's southeastern thumb just outside The Valley. Included in rates are transfers from the airport or ferry dock.*

What a find! Although there are only 14 rooms, the hotel has its own locally-popular bar and restaurant, health club, a gift shop, and entertainers three times a week. You're welcomed at check-in with a rum punch, and your vacation officially begins. Choose a book from the hotel's library and stake out a patch of shade on meticulously gardened grounds. Stroll into town, relax in the pool or whirlpool, rent a Jeep or a boat, go snorkeling or day sailing, then be at the library by 9am for the nightly movie. In the gourmet restaurant, you'll dine to classical music; the Sip and Dip poolside is the place for a snack in your swim suit. Rooms are air conditioned and each has its own patio overlooking gardens alight with hibiscus, bushy palms, and bougainvillaea.

MANGO BAY RESORT, *Box 26, Virgin Gorda. Tel. 284/495-5672, Fax 495-5674; U.S. 800/223-6510; Canada 800/424-5500. Rooms start at $129; villas are priced to $338. From the airport go north on North Sound Road, then left on Plum Tree Bay Road for less than a mile.*

Book a room or one of the eight deluxe villas, each with spacious living area, fully-equipped kitchen and large porch, all just a seashell's throw from the sandy beach. If you like, the hotel will find you a cook. The hotel has its own bar and Italian restaurant. Wind surfing and snorkel equipment are available.

Budget
OCEAN VIEW HOTEL, *Box 66, Virgin Gorda. Tel. 284/495-5230; U.S. 800/621-1270. Rooms start at $70 with a discount for stays of 14 days or more. Credit cards and personal checks aren't accepted.*

In the heart of bustling West End and less than a mile from the airport, this modest hotel has 12 rooms with cable television, telephone, and air conditioning. Meals are available in the hotels' restaurant, the Wheel House, which is well liked locally for its hearty West Indian fare.

WHERE TO EAT

The international gourmet has nothing to fear when dining in the BVI's sophisticated restaurants. Here you can find the finest French, Italian, and Asian cuisine as well as Continental-Caribbean foods that blend the best of old and new worlds. However, you'll miss a lot if you don't try such local specialties as roti (curry-filled bread), boil fish (fish in tomato sauce with garlic and onions), peas and rice (beans and rice) or patties (pastry filled with spicy beef, salt fish, or lobster).

Except for local fish and lobster, just about every mouthful has to be imported, but hosts do a good job at providing fresh vegetables and preparing dishes with a West Indian flavor. Unless stated otherwise, these restaurants accept major credit cards. It's not unusual in small islands to ask you to make reservations early in the day and to order at that time.

TORTOLA
Expensive
THE APPLE, *Little Apple Bay. Tel. 495-4437. Open only for dinner Tuesdays through Sundays in season. Main dishes average $20. Reservations are recommended.*

Just over the hill from Long Bay, Apple Bay is the surfer's beach, incredibly creamy and clear as waves boil ashore and keep the sands scrubbed clean. For a special dinner, seek out this quaint West Indian homestead framed in banyan trees. The food features local ingredients: whelk, soursop, conch, and fresh fish, all deftly seasoned and generously served by Liston Molyneaux, a Tortola native.

BRANDYWINE BAY RESTAURANT, *Brandywine Estate, three miles east of Road Town off the south shore road, Blackburn Highway. Tel. 495-2301. Reservations are requested. Main dishes start at $15.*

Revered for its Italian food, especially Florentine specialties, this country inn serves guests on a romantic garden patio surrounded by birdsong and greenery. Lobster ravioli is a specialty. You're hosted by Cele and David Pugliese, whose restaurant was voted "our favorite in the Caribbean" by *Bon Appetit* magazine.

THE CLOUD ROOM, *Ridge Road. Tel. 494-2821. Main dishes start at $24. You'll be picked up at your hotel. Reservations are essential. The restaurant is closed June through October and Sundays, and is open only for dinner.*

One of the most memorable dining experiences in the Caribbean, this hilltop aerie looks down on the twinkling lights of Road Town while you dine on succulent steaks, lamb kebobs, and fish fresh from local nets. When weather permits, which is almost always, the roof opens and you'll dine under the moon and stars.

FORT BURT RESTAURANT, *in the Fort Burt Hotel, Fisher Estate, just south of Road Town. Tel. 494-2587. Dinner will cost about $50 with appetizer and dessert but without wine. An English breakfast is available in the morning, and luncheon is served in the pub from noon to 2:30pm For dinner, reservations are essential.*

The ruins of an ancient Dutch fort are part of the scene at this hotel and restaurant overlooking Careening Cove, Road Reef, and Burt Point. Dine in a seabreeze-cooled outdoor dining area with a million dollar view. Seafood with a Caribbean overtone is the rule, resulting in great sauced filets or seafood curries but the Brits being the Brits, there's also great roast beef. Desserts are made here so they're always worth a try.

SKY WORLD, *Ridge Road. Tel. 494-3567. Dinner with wine costs $50 or more for a six-course feast; lunch is in the $20 range. Reservations are essential.*

The best game plan for a celebration evening is to arrive here an hour before sundown to watch the sky streak with color and the sun sink into the sea. From this hilltop perch you're looking down on what seems like all of Tortola and across to all the other islands. When it's time to get serious about dining, pace yourself for a parade of courses that starts with an inventive salad and ends with a selection of meltingly flaky pastries. Dinner is dressy; lunch is resort-casual.

SUGAR MILL, *in the Little Dix Bay resort. Tel. 945-5555. Take the private ferry from the Beef Island airport to the resort. Plan to spend $60 for dinner. Reservations are essential.*

Dine in one of the Caribbean's most posh resorts, long a Rockefeller holding and completely refurbished under new management by the Rosewood chain of luxury hotels. Lunch is a buffet under the high-roofed pavilion. Dinner by candlelight in the Sugar Mill features simply grilled lobster, fresh fish, and steaks with dashing presentations and garnishes. Have a drink in the lounge, where live music plays just about every night. The restaurant is not air conditioned.

SUGAR MILL RESTAURANT, *Apple Bay. Tel. 495-4355; U.S. 800/ 462-8834. Fixed-price lunches start at $25; dinners at $40. Daily specials offer appetizers in the $7-$8 range and main dishes at $18-$25. Reservations are a must. Drive west from Road Town on Waterfront Drive, pass Fort Recovery, then turn right over Zion Hill and, watching for signs, turn right at the T.*

Celebrities Tex and Jinx Morgan, columnists for *Bon Appetit* magazine and authors of several cookbooks, have owned this 300-year-old sugar mill since the 1980s, and their touch shows in the superb cuisine. The dining room is surrounded by original stone walls, now hung with Haitian art. The *Washington Post* called it "the island's best restaurant," but they were topped by *Business Week*, which called it "the best restaurant in the Caribbean." You might start, for example, with New Zealand Mussels in Dilled Cream or a terrine of smoked conch, followed by Tropical Game Hen in orange-curry butter or Fish with West Indian Creole Sauce.

Their signature dish is curry-banana soup, but everything here is freshly made according to whim, inspiration, and the best of what's available from the marketplace and the Morgans' own herb garden.

Moderate

CAPRICCIO DI MARE, *Waterfront Road, Road Town. Tel. 494-5369. It's open daily except Sunday. No credit cards or reservations are accepted. Plan to spend $6 for breakfast, $10 to $12 for lunch, and $20 to $30 for dinner.*

Settle into a pleasant Italian bistro setting and start with a Mango Bellini, a mixture of mango juice and sparkling asti spumante. Then have one of the pastas with a choice of tomato, seafood, cream, or vegetarian sauces. Choose one of the pizzas, a hot or cold sandwich, or just snack on cappuccino with a sweet.

MRS. SCATLIFFE'S RESTAURANT, *North Coast Road, between Cane Garden Bay and Apple Bay. Tel. 495-4556. Reservations are essential for dinner and are recommended for lunch. Prix fixe meals are in the $25 range. No credit cards are accepted.*

Mrs. Scatliffe and her family welcome you to their West Indies-style home where she cooks with locally raised goat and vegetables from her own garden. Dinner starts with a rum punch and proceeds through soup and salad followed by a meat such as curried goat, chicken, or a fish (for example, West Indian boil fish). The meal ends with dessert, usually featuring an exotic tropical fruit, like coconut or guava, followed by a lively musicale performed by Mom and the kids.

Budget

THE AMPLE HAMPER, *at Inner Harbour Marina next to the Captain's Table on Wickham's Cay. Pick up picnic makings at prices that start under $10. Hours vary seasonally.*

A popular gourmet provisioning spot for yachts, the Hamper has a full-service deli, imported English specialties, and sandwiches made to order. It's the place to put together an elegant picnic to take to the beach or boat.

HAPPY LION, *next to the Botanic Gardens, Road Town. Tel. 494-2574. The restaurant serves breakfast, lunch, and dinner in the $10-$15 price range.*

Part of a little apartment hotel, this simple eatery is the place to get the real thing – johnnycake, goat mutton, and boil fish, as well as steaks, burgers, and sandwiches.

FORT WINE GOURMET, *Main Street, Road Town. Tel. 494-3036. Eat for $10 to $12. Reservations aren't accepted. Call for hours.*

This popular spot is a combination deli and eatery where you can linger over an espresso or grab a bag of sandwiches and cold salads for a beach picnic. The pastries are flaky and good, and the deli salads and sandwiches get high marks.

MR. FRITZ'S ORIENTAL RESTAURANT & TAKE AWAY, *on Wickham's Cay. Tel. 494-5592. Dine for under $10.*

Barbara and Fritz keep the woks sizzling with Lobster Love Boat, Singapore chicken, and fiery Szechwan pork and beef. Try the Cantonese-style shrimp.

VIRGIN GORDA

Expensive

BATH AND TURTLE, *in the yacht harbor at Spanish Town. Tel. 495-5239. Reservations are important. Main dishes are priced $15 to $28. It's open every day 7am to midnight.*

The breakfast crowd comes in early and the drinking begins with elevenses when the blender starts whirring with fruity margaritas or coladas. For lunch, have a chili dog, pizza, burger, Reuben, salad or a bowl of the four-alarm chili. Dine indoors or in the courtyard on fish fingers, coconut shrimp, lobster, grilled filet mignon, or chicken. Live music plays at least twice a week, never with a cover charge.

BIRAS CREEK ESTATE, *North Sound. Tel. 494-3555. Plan to spend $50 for dinner and more if you order a vintage wine. The dining rooms are open daily for breakfast, lunch, and dinner. Call for early for reservations. You may be asked to make your dinner selection when you phone.*

A longtime guest liked the resort so much, he bought it and the well-liked restaurant that goes with it. The view is worth the trip. Ask for a table that looks down from the hilltop to the seas below. Fresh seafood and lobster are the top draw here, but the chef is also happy to sizzle a steak any way you want it. At lunch there's a nice choice of salads, burgers, sandwiches and light dishes, and sometimes there's a beach barbecue during the day. At dinner, start with a cocktail in the elegant lounge. The menu offers plenty of variety in meats and seafood, and the wine list is comprehensive.

BITTER END YACHT CLUB, *North Sound. Tel. 494-2746. Reservations are essential for dinner, so call early. Plan to spend $50 for dinner. It's open breakfast through dinner.*

The bareboat crowd comes ashore here for drinks and dinner but the breakfast buffet is also worth the trip. Everything from fresh fruit and yogurt to cooked-to-order pancakes and omelets is on the groaning board. At lunch, choose from a big buffet of cold meats, cheese, breads, and salads, or order a hamburger or grilled fish. Grilled lobster is the dinner specialty, served plain or with a Creole sauce. There's also a choice of chicken, steak, or chops.

DRAKE'S ANCHORAGE, *on the North Sound Beach. Tel. 494-2252. Reservations are essential because you'll be brought here by boat. When you book, have an idea of what you'll want to eat because they have to know before 3:30pm. Plan to spend $50 for dinner.*

The spot seems like the end of the world but somehow the chef manages to have a good selection of roasts on hand as well as the famous banana-crusted lobster or the signature chicken crepe. The restaurant and its bar, which is built of local rock, is part of a small resort.

TOP OF THE BATHS RESTAURANT, *350 yards up the trail from The Baths. Tel. 495-5497. Lunch is less than $10.*

Restaurant patrons are offered a dip in the pool here, so it's a wonderful place to cool off after scrambling around The Baths. Food has a continental touch, always with a fresh fish dish and luscious salads.

Budget

THE BATH AND TURTLE BAR & RESTAURANT, *Virgin Gorda Yacht Harbour, The Galley. Tel. 495-5239. Breakfast, lunch or dinner dishes start at $5.*

A sort of out-island Grand Central Station, this busy dock area is a great place to shop, nosh, and people watch. Try local patties and rotis, pasta salads, burgers, fresh fish, and pizza. Happy Hour specials are sold daily 4:30 to 5:30; live entertainment is offered on Wednesday and Sunday nights.

PUSSER'S LEVERICK BAY, *Tel. 495-7369. Breakfasts and lunches are under $10; dinner is in the $25 range. Reservations are suggested.*

Picturesque Leverick Bay, with its fleets of sailboats, is the scene of yet another Pusser's, this one serving steak, seafood, and pasta until 10pm. Lunch and pizza are served in the Beach Bar from 11:30am to 6pm. On Tuesdays there's all the barbecue you can eat and on Fridays all the Cajun shrimp you can eat. Live music is often scheduled, but call ahead if you want to be sure. The notorious Pusser's Painkillers here are offered in strengths one through four. Caveat emptor.

RESTAURANTS FOR MARINERS

Some of these restaurants can be reached only by private boat; others have docks where you can tie up free for dining or overnight for a fee; others can be reached by launch or ferry. The voyage is part of the fun, and many visitors make a day-long project out of it. Most can be reached on VHF **Channel 16.** *Always call ahead to see if they're open. Dinner reservations must be made early in the day.*

Pirate's Pub, Saba Rock is a swim-in grill serving specialty drinks and international cuisine. **The William Thornton** *is afloat off Norman's Cay;* **The Last Resort** *is on Bellamy Cay off Beef Island. On Anegada, which makes a good day trip, try the* **Anegada Reef Hotel, Del's,** *or* **Pomato Point.**

Cooper Island Beach Club is a restaurant and bar, and also offers beachfront cottages. Each has a kitchen, balcony, bathroom with open-air shower, and outdoor hammock, Tel. 800/542-4624.

On Jost Van Dyke look for **Harris' Place, Sidney's Peace and Love,** *Abe's Little Harbor, Club Paradise, Ali Baba's and Foxy's.*

SEEING THE SIGHTS
ANEGADA

Anegada is as remote as the end of the world, a limestone and coral atoll rimmed with talcum powder beaches where you can walk for hours without seeing another human being. At its highest point, the island is only 27 feet above sea level. It's the quintessential nature sanctuary and the government is committed to keeping it that way.

Roam to your heart's content to see wild goats, donkeys and cattle, to look for 20-pound rock iguana (they look fierce but are harmless) and a host of heron, osprey, and terns. With luck you'll see some flamingoes too.

JOST VAN DYKE

Jost (yost) Van Dyke is the island that time forgot. A handful of people live in West Indian wooden homes around Great Harbour. **Norman Island**, famed for its caves and a port of call for boaters, has a floating bar and restaurant off The Bight.

SALT ISLAND

This little island between Cooper Island and Peter Island has only two residents, and its only point of interest is its salt ponds. Once a thriving and even crucial industry in the Caribbean, harvesting salt from the sea goes on today as it did a century ago. The island is best known as the gravesite of the *Rhone*, which sank in 1867.

TORTOLA

Take off on your own in rental car or scooter if you want only to find a beach and spend the day there. However, if you want narrative and direction, hire a taxi by the day or take a safari tour with a knowledgeable guide. Island tours of Virgin Gorda aboard safari buses are offered by **Andy's Taxi and Jeep Rental**, *Tel. 284/495-5511* and **Mahogany Taxi Service**, *Tel. 495-5469*.

Sightseeing tours of Tortola are available from the **BVI Taxi Association**, *Tel. 494-2875*; **Nanny Cay Taxi Association**, *Tel. 494-0539*; **Scato's Bus Service**, *Tel. 494-2365;* **Style's Tour Operator**, *Tel. 494-2260;* **Travel Plan Tours**, *Tel. 494-2872;* **Turtle Dove Tax Stand**, *Tel. 494-6274;* and **Waterfront Taxi Stand**, *Tel. 494-3456*.

Nature's Secret Adventure Company, *Tel. 495-2722*, sets up nature programs, sailing or kayaking adventures, fishing, and villa rentals. Flightseeing tours are available from **Fly BVI Ltd**, *Tel. 495-1747*.

North of downtown Road Town on Station Avenue, J.R. O'Neal Botanic Gardens are a four-acre oasis filled with native and imported tropicals plus a lily pond, waterfall, and orchid house. Bird houses attract an array of tropical birds. The gardens are open Monday through Saturday 8am to 4 p.m., Tel. 494-4557. Admission is free. Shop your way down Main Street, pausing to look at the churches, 19th century post office, and the huge, shady ficus trees in Sir Olva George's Plaza.

The Virgin Islands Folk Museum is housed in an authentic West Indian house on Main Street. There's no phone but it's usually open in the middle of the day except Wednesday and Sunday. Admission is free. Of special interest are artifacts from the wreck of the *Rhone*, which you'll see during your visit if you're a diver, and bits of pre-Columbian pottery. Proceeding north on Main, take a picture of Cockroach Hall, built atop a huge boulder in the 1800s to serve as a doctor's dispensary. It's now a private business. Officially its name is Britannic Hall.

Next to it are two churches, the Anglican dating to 1746 and rebuilt in 1819, and the Methodist Church, which was rebuilt after a hurricane in 1924. Its congregation dates to 1789. Between them is Her Majesty's Prison, dating to the 1700s, where a cruel planter was hanged for killing a slave.

Climb Fort Hill, which is just below the roundabout at Port Purcell to see the remains of **Fort George**. It was built by the Royal Engineers in 1794 to stand sentinel against foreign powers, especially the French, and such pirates as Edward Teach, the dreaded Blackbeard. At the west end of Tortola at **Fort Recovery Villas**, you can see the well-preserved round tower that is thought to have been built by Dutch settlers in the mid-1600s.

Touring on your own, head east from Road Town, and you'll pass the ruins of **Fort Charlotte**. Now just a few walls, a cistern, and a powder magazine, it tops Harrigan's Hill. Continuing east you'll see a ruined church, which is all that remains of Kingstown, a community that was founded for free slaves in the 1830s. Along the road that runs from Ridge Road down to Brewer's Bay on Tortola's north shore, find **Mount Healthy** and a largely intact stone windmill, once part of a sugar plantation. It's the only such windmill on Tortola.

A ride 'round the island can take only three hours, but you'll want to spend days seeking out secluded beaches, trying restaurants, and hiking the hills. Don't rush it. Stop at the North Shore Shell Museum in Carrot Bay, the Callwood Rum Distillery, and Soper's Hole for shopping and to watch boats come and go.

Among the historic ruins to look for: Fort Burt, now a hotel, was started by the Dutch in the 17th century. The ruins of **Fort George** are on Fort Hill. Fort Recovery on the west end of Tortola dates, it is thought, to the first Dutch settlers in 1648. In Pleasant Valley, the ruins of the **William Thornton Estate** remain from the home of the designer of the United States Capitol. **The Dungeon**, actually a fort that has an underground cell, is halfway between Road Town and West End. It dates to 1794. Just east of Road Town, look for the ruins of The Church at Kingstown, once the center of a community of freed slaves.

VIRGIN GORDA

Just south of the Yacht Harbour, which is a beehive of sailing and sailors, **Little Fort National Park** is on the site of a Spanish fortress. Now a wildlife sanctuary, the 36-acre park still has remnants of the original fort and its powder magazine.

Between Little Fort and The Baths, **Spring Bay** is a smooth sand beach studded with enormous boulders, thrown up 70 million years ago by a volcanic eruption. They set the scene for your arrival at **The Baths**, where city-size boulders are flung about as if by angry gods. The scene changes constantly as the sun passes over and tides roll in and out, so it's a spot you can come back to time and again to explore, photograph, swim in, and commune with one of nature's great structures.

On Virgin Gorda's remote southwestern end, look for the ruins of the **Copper Mine**, which was worked by Cornishmen between 1838 and 1867. Remains of some of the buildings and works can still be seen (from a distance; they are not safe to explore). Also on the west coast is Nail Bay, where you can roam the ruins of an 18th century sugar mill made from brick, stone, and coral rock.

Fallen Jerusalem, a separate island off the south end of Virgin Gorda, can be reached only by boat and only on calm days. Its terrain is bold and dramatic, much like The Baths, a birdwatcher's mecca because of its many nesting sites.

NIGHTLIFE & ENTERTAINMENT

It's likely that your hotel or the closest bar will have live music and it will be listed in one of the free magazines such as *Limin' Times* that you can pick up around the islands. If you want to venture off property, the hottest licks are at:

THE BATH AND TURTLE BAR, *Yacht Harbour, The Valley, Virgin Gorda. Tel. 495-5239.*

Inexpensive dinner fare is available until 9:30, so stoke up on burgers, pizza, or native dishes then stay on for live music on Sunday and Wednesday nights.

BOMBA'S SURFSIDE SHACK, *Cappoon's Bay, near Cane Garden Bay. Tel. 495-4148 is Tortola's happenin' place, especially on Wednesdays, Fridays, and on nights when the moon is full.*

The decor is early beach bum and the sound system could wake the dead, but drinks are cheap, barbecue is plentiful, and the music is authentically Caribbean until midnight or later.

THE LAST RESORT, *Ballamy Cay, off Beef Island. Tel. 495-2520. Can be reached only by launch from Trellis Bay, which will be arranged for you when you make your (required) reservations. Dinner with wine and the show cost about $50, which can can charge to a major card.*

Tuck into an English buffet including roast beef, Yorkshire pudding, homemade soups and all the trimmings, followed by a hilarious, two-hour, one-man music and comedy show.

PUSSER'S LTD, *Marina Cay, reached by a causeway from Tortola's West End. Tel. 494-2467. It stays open until 2:30 a.m.*

This is the British Virgin Islands, which means pubs and pub grub, most notably at the yachty Pusser's where the Painkiller is not for the faint of heart (or liver). Made with the rum that was once the official grog of the Royal Navy, the drink makes great accompaniment for an evening of music listening, people watching, and good conversation until 2:30am. Pusser's serves a broad range of sandwiches, pizza, and a creditable shepherd's pie.

QUITO'S GAZEBO *at the Ole Works Inn, Cane Garden Bay. Tel. 495-4837.*

Native-born Quito Rymer switches on his microphone at 8:30pm on Tuesday, Thursday, Friday and Sunday, sits on a stool with his guitar, and lets loose with his own ballads as well as reggae classics and popular tunes.

SPORTS & RECREATION

Beaches

• **Tortola: Smugglers Cove** on the western tip of Tortola has good snorkeling and children love its name. Try **Long Bay** on the north shore for white sand, **Apple Bay** for surfing and hanging out at Bomba's, **Cane Garden Bay** for picture postcard views, **Brewer's Bay** for beach bars, camping and snorkeling, **Josiah's Bay** for its scenery, and **Elizabeth Bay** for sands with a fringe of palm trees.

• **Virgin Gorda: The Baths** is a spectacular arrangement of boulders and grottos, always changing but best in the morning before the hordes arrive; **Spring Bay** next to The Baths has good snorkeling and white sand; **Trunk Bay** can be reached over a path from Spring Bay or by boat; **Savannah Bay** is found just north of Yacht Harbour, and **Mahoe Bay** is a superb beach at **the Bago Bay Resort**.

• **Other Islands: Long Bay** on Beef Island has a quiet beach, but enter from behind the salt pond so you don't disturb nesting terns. **Loblobby Bay** on Anegada has a beach bar; **White Bay** on Jost Van Dyke and Sandy Cay just off the island are reached by boat. **Deadman's Bay** on Peter Island can be reached by boat or ferry; **Vixen Point** in North Sound has white sand and a refreshment stand.

Camping

Camping on a bare site, or on a campsite with beds provided is available at **Anegada Beach Campground**, *Tel. 284/495-9466;* **Brewers Bay Campground**, *Tel. 284/494-3473;* **Tula'site Bay Campground** *on Jost Van Dyke, Tel. 284/495-9566,* and **White Bay Campground** *on Jost Van Dyke, Tel. 284/495-9312.*

THE BVI'S BEST BEACHES

Some of these beaches can be reached by car, but others can be reached only by boat. Find them on the road map that comes with your rental car, or on the marine chart that comes with your rental boat. They include:

Anegada: *Loblobby Bay*

Jost Van Dyke: *White Bay*

Sandy Cay: *The entire island, which lies just southeast of Jost Van Dyke is rimmed with a picture postcard beach.*

Peter Island: *Deadman's Bay*

Mosquito Island: *South Bay*

Prickly Bear Island: *Vixen Point*

Tortola: *Smuggler's Cove (where you'll see the Lincoln used by Queen Elizabeth when she visited the BVI in the 1950s), Long Bay, Apple Bay, Cane Garden Bay with its 1.5 miles of sifted sand shaded by towering palms, Brewer's Bay, Elizabeth Bay, and Long Bay for jogging or swimming. On Beef Island is Trellis Bay, loved for its good surfing and shelling.*

Virgin Gorda: *The Baths, Spring Bay, Trunk Bay, Savannah Bay, and Mahoe Bay.*

Diving

Diving and snorkeling in the BVI can be rewarding almost anywhere you fall off a boat, but the islands' most famous dive is the wreck of the *Rhone*, now crusted with corals and bright with darting fish in all colors of the rainbow. The pride of the Royal Mail Steam Packet Company, she hit Salt Island during a hurricane in 1867, broke in two, and sank in 80 feet of water. Best known as the site of filming for *The Deep*, the wreck still has a complete foremast with crow's nest and an enormous propeller.

Dive operators include **Baskin in the City,** *Tel. 284/494-2858,* **Blue Water Divers,** *Tel. 494-2847,* **Trimarine Boat Company Ltd.,** *Tel. 494-2490 or 800/648-3393,* **Underwater Safaris,** *Tel. 494-3965 or 800/537-7032,* and **Caribbean Images Tours,** *Tel. 494-1147,* all on Tortola and **Dive BVI Ltd.,** *Tel. 495-5513 or 800/848-7078* and **Kilbride's Underwater Tours,** *Tel. 495-9639 or 800/932-4286,* both based on Virgin Gorda.

Specializing in underwater photography is **Rainbow Visions** on Tortola, *Tel. 284/484-2749.* Book this service through one of the dive companies above to get a custom video of your dive or to rent an underwater camera or camcorder.

If you rent a boat to go diving on your own, you'll need a mooring permit. Anchoring in most of the best diving spots is illegal because it could damage the coral. Frankly, it's best to go with one of the outfitters listed above. They know both the rules and the best scuba and snorkel sites, such as:

Alice in Wonderland is a deep dive at South Bay on Ginger Island, where walls slope downward 100 feet to huge, mushroom-shaped coral heads.

Anegada has one of the world's most notorious fringe reefs, a graveyard for at least 300 known wrecks. While the wrecks continue to break up, they form a home for worlds of brilliant fish.

Blonde Rock, found between Dead Chest and Salt Island, rises from 60 feet down to within 15 feet of the surface. Explore it to see ledges, tunnels, caves and overhangs alive with lobster and other sea creatures as well as a wonderland of gently waving fan coral.

Brewers Bay Pinnacle is a towering sea mountain abounding in sea life. Seas can be rough, so this is a dive to take when conditions are right.

The Caves on Norman Island are so well known that they can be swarming with people, so try to arrive early in the day to see the place that is thought to have been Robert Louis Stevenson's inspiration for *Treasure Island*. The caves make for exciting snorkeling over dark waters; Angelfish Reef nearby is a good place to see rays and angelfish.

The *Chikuzen* is a 246-foot Japanese refrigeration ship that was sunk here in 1981 to form an artificial reef. It is in 75 feet of water six miles north of Beef Island and it's home to a huge aquarium of fish large and small.

Dead Chest Island, which is where Blackbeard is said to have marooned 15 of his men with a bottle of rum and a sword, offers good snorkeling over bands of sand and coral. Great Dog and The Chimneys lie in the "dog" islands between Virgin Gorda and Tortola. Underwater canyons, some of them shallow enough for snorkelers and rookie divers, are dazzling sea gardens.

Painted Walls is a shallow drive off the south point of Dead Chest. Four long gullies are crusted with colored coral and sponge only 20-30 feet down.

Santa Monica Rock, a mile south of Norman Island on the outer edge of the islands, lies close enough to deep water that it's a place to see pelagic fish (fish that roam freely rather than living in one reef), spotted eagle rays, and perhaps a nurse shark. The rock rises from the sea floor 100 feet deep to within about 10 feet of the surface.

Wreck of the Rhone, now a marine park, is the BVI's most popular dive. Broken in half and quickly sunk by a storm in 1867, she lies scattered and crusted, her innards open to view while coral and fish swirl through old cargo holds, the engine, and the immense propeller.

Sailing & Boating

Sailing courses including liveaboard cruise courses are available from **Thomas Sailing**, *Tel. 284/494-0333* and **Offshore Sailing School**, *Tel. 800/221-4326 or 813/454-1700*. Board sailing rentals are available from **Boardsailing BVI**, *Tel. 495-2447 or 494-0422*.

Boating is best arranged through your hotel or condo host, who has rental boats or knows where to find them plus the best fishing guide, deep sea fishing charter, day sail, or sunset cruise. This is a crowded category that changes often as boats come and go.

Hiking

The most popular hiking trails in the British Virgin Islands are the path to Sage Mountain on Tortola and the walk to **Gorda Peak** on Virgin Gorda. Sage Mountain National Park is a vest pocket-size, 92-acre preserve that the serious hiker can cover in half a day. From Road Town, drive up Joe's Hill Road and keep climbing (4WD rental cars are popular here and this is why), watching for the small sign to Sage Mountain. The road ends at a small parking lot.

Take off on any of the three trails, which are connected, to enjoy moderately easy walking through bowers of elephant ears, cocoplum, and butter-yellow palicourea under a canopy of mahogany and manilkara trees and white cedars. In the open, find magnificent views of Jost Van Dyke across the sea to the northwest.

The islands' other popular trail is an easy walk in **The Baths National Park** on Virgin Gorda, where you'll find yourself surrounded by cathedral-size boulders catching a swirling sea. Go early in the day. By the time land-based visitors get up and passengers stream ashore from charter boats and cruise ships, The Baths can be too crowded. Another path from the same road leads lead off to **Devil's Bay National Park** on an easy, 15-minute walk through a cactus garden and a sand beach that is less crowded than The Baths.

The more rugged, half-hour hike to Gorda Peak, which is at 1,359 feet, is found off North Sound Road. Ask directions at the ferry dock. To stay on the right path, which leads to a small picnic area, follow the red blazes.

To climb to the 1,359-foot peak that tops **Virgin Gorda National Park**, drive the North Sound Road and look for a sign that points to stairs that climb up into the woods. You can make it to the observation tower in about 15 minutes.

Sportfishing

Offshore sportfishing or action-packed bonefishing on the flats can be arranged through the **Anegada Reef Hotel**, *Tel. 284/495-8002*. Out of

Tortola, the *Miss Robbie* is available for charter by the half day, day, or cruise for marlin fishing and other blue water sportfishing, *Tel. 494-3311.*

SHOPPING

TORTOLA

Crafts Alive in the heart of Road Town is a collection of West Indies-style booths selling dollars, straw work, crochet, pottery, and the inevitable tee-shirts. One of the shops, **BVI House of Craft**, claims that at least 75 per cent of its stock is produced locally including local bush teas, honey, and condiments. It's open daily, 9am to 5pm, but hours can vary seasonally.

Local artists show their work at the gallery at **Ole Works Inn** on Cane Garden Bay and at **Caribbean Fine Arts Ltd.** on Upper Main Street. The shop sells original art as well as antique maps, pottery, and primitives. For out-of-town newspapers and magazines try **Esmé's Shoppe** in Sir Olva George's Plaza behind the government complex on Wickham's Cay. It's open every day including holidays.

Samarkand on Main Street in Road Town has been here for 25 years selling handcrafted tropical jewelry including their own exclusive line of Tortola green jasper. They're open daily 9am to 5pm and Saturdays 9am to 1pm.; closed Sunday. Nearby, **Caribbean Handprints** sells locally silk-screened printed fabrics by the card. Also on Main Street, **Local Stuff** sells hand-painted local pottery and art work and enough chutneys, salsas, and preserves to make up any size gift basket. Island books and maps are at **Heritage Books and Arts** on Main Street.

For a large selection of island music, try **Bolo's** on DeCastro Road, Wickham's Cay. The shop can also repair leather and develop film, and it has a good selection of souvenirs and sundries. **The Shirt Shack** on Chalwell Street between Main and Waterfront has one of the island's best selections of tee shirts and also sells handicrafts. For handmade clothes made locally, try **Caribbean Handprints** on Main Street.

Pusser's Road Town Pub & Company Store on lower Waterfront Drive south of Wickham's Cay offers one-stop shopping for pizza, burgers, dinner pies, and all the popular Pusser's logo merchandise that captivates tourists. It's open daily, 9am to midnight, and accepts credit cards. **Sunny Caribbee Spice Company** on Main Street just below Chalwell is a company spice shop and gallery. Choose island seasonings and sauces to take home, then shop the gallery for locally crafted arts.

VIRGIN GORDA

Kaunda's Kysy Tropix, *Tel. 495-5636,* at the yacht harbor in The Valley is the place to get batteries, personal electronics, film, tapes, jewelry and perfumes. Kuanda will also pierce your ears.

Pusser's Company Store is another arm of the Pusser's empire, a holy name in British islands because Pusser's Rum is the official grog of the Royal Navy. In their store at Leverick Bay, find sports and travel clothing, famous Pusser's sports watches as well as Swiss chronographs, and smart, resorty accessories.

STAMP OF APPROVAL
You don't have to be a stamp collector to go ga-ga over the stamps of the Caribbean. Each island nation strives for the brightest and best stamps featuring brilliant reef fish, butterflies, flowers, birds, and other gifts of nature. I usually hand over a dollar or two and ask the post office clerk to make a selection for me. Since stamp prices start at a penny or two, both the clerk and customer have a wonderful time with this carte blanche approach. Try it and you'll go home with a hodgepodge of the prettiest and most flamboyant stamps to paste in your scrapbook or to give as gifts.

PRACTICAL INFORMATION
Area Code: 284
Alcoholics Anonymous meets regularly, *Tel. 494-4549 or 494-3125.*
ATM: the Chase Manhattan Bank in Road Town has a MasterCard/Cirrus ATM.
Banking: hours are generally 9am to 2:30pm on weekdays except Fridays, when they are also open 4:30pm to 6pm. A Chase Manhattan Bank with a 24-hour ATM machine is at Wickham's Cay, *Tel. 494-2662.* Hours are Monday through Thursday 8:30am to 3pm, Friday 8:30am to 4pm.
Currency: U.S. dollars accepted. American Express, VISA, Diners Club, and Mastercard are widely accepted.
Dress: it is offensive to locals when tourists appear in residential and commercial areas in bathing suits. No bare chests or midriffs, please.
Driving: a $10 temporary driver's license is required. Driving is on the left, with a maximum speed of 30 miles per hour on the open road and 10-15 miles per hour in settlements.
Drugs: stiff fines and jail sentences will be levied for possession or use of illegal drugs.
Emergencies: dial 999 for fire, police, or ambulance.
Government: British Virgin Islands are part of the United Kingdom. U.S. consular needs are provided from the U.S. Embassy in St. John's, Antigua, *Tel. 462-3505.*

Holidays: dates can vary but public holidays generally include Christmas, Boxing Day (December 26), New Year's Day, Commonwealth Day on March 11, Good Friday, Easter Monday, Whit Monday, the Sovereign's Birthday on June 8, Territory Day on July 1, August Festival in early August, St. Ursula's Day on October 21, and the Birthday of the Heir to the Throne, November 14. When making business appointments or counting on finding a bank open, ask about upcoming holidays.

Immigration: citizens of the U.S. and Canada need only a birth certificate, citizenship certificate, or voter registration; others need passports and visitors from some nations need a visa. For information contact the Chief Immigration Officer, Government of the British Virgin Islands, Road Town. Tortola, British Virgin Islands, *Tel. 284/494-3701*. Rastafarians and "hippies" are prohibited entry.

Medical care: can be found at the B&F Medical Complex, *Tel. 494-2196*, just off the cruise ship dock at Road Town. Open daily from 7am, it offers family doctors, specialists, x-ray, ultrasound, lab work and a pharmacy. Walk-ins are welcome. At the north end of Wickham's Cay at the traffic circle Medicure Pharmacy, *Tel. 494-6189 or 494-6468*, has prescriptions, a medical lab, x-ray and medical personnel on duty.

Permits: A Fishing Permit is required for fishing or the gathering of any marine organisms. A Conservation Permit is required for mooring in any National Parks Trust moorings. If you'll be cruising the British Virgin Islands in a boat rented here or elsewhere, there's a charge of 75 cents to $4 per person per day depending on the season.

Pets: require advance permission and planning, so write well in advance to the Chief Agricultural Officer, Road Town, Tortola, British Virgin Islands.

Taxes: you'll pay a departure tax of $8 each if leaving by air and $5 per person if departing by sea. Hotel tax is seven per cent. A small tax or fee is charged to cash each traveler's check.

Telephone: the area code for the BVI is **284**; to access AT&T on your cellular phone dial 872, then Send. For Boatphone cell service dial O and Send, and an operator will take your credit card information. Cable & Wireless offices at Virgin Gorda and Road Town handle long distance calling, faxes, telegrams and telexes and also sell prepaid phone cards, which are used through the islands.

Time: add one hour to Eastern Standard Time.

Tourist Information: British Virgin Islands Tourist Board, *370 Lexington Avenue, Suite 313, New York NY 10017, Tel. 212/696-0400*. Serving the west coast, British Virgin Islands Tourist Board, *1804 Union Street, Union Street, San Francisco CA 94123; Tel. 415/775-0344*. U.S. and Canada toll-free *800/835-8530*. In the United Kingdom, write the British Virgin Islands Tourist Board, *110 St. Martin's Lane, London*

WC2N 4DY, Tel. 071-240-4259, Fax 071-240-4270. For reservations for hotels, villas, yacht charters, scuba diving and car rentals, contact Virgin Islands Vacations, *111-40 178th Street, St. Albans NY 11422, Tel. 718/523-5038, Fax 523-5032.* To book a resort, airline or car rental, contact CHR Worldwide, *235 Kensington Avenue, Norwood NJ 07648, Tel. 800/633-3284 or 201/767-9393, Fax 201/767-5510.* In Road Town, a tourist office is found on Wickham's Cay between the ferry dock and the cruise ship dock.

Weddings: you must be in the territory for three days before applying for a marriage license, which must be done in Road Town. For all details, write well in advance to the Registrar's Office, *Post Office Box 418, Road Town, Tortola,* or *Tel. 284/494-3701, extensions 303 or 304, or Tel. 284/ 494-492.*

THE
BRITISH
LEEWARDS

18. ANGUILLA

At last **Anguilla** is blooming and booming as a tourist destination, but it's still so serene, crime-free, and undiscovered that travel writers have mixed feelings about publicizing it. It's the kind of eden you'll want to keep to yourself. Before European settlement, the island called Malliouhana was home to peaceful Arawaks, farmers, and fisherfolk who lived here as early as 2000 BC. Remnants of their tools have been found around the island, but early English settlers as well as any remaining Arawaks were driven out by a Carib attack in 1656.

English and French battled over the little island and its sugar wealth until the 19th century, when it became part of a Leeward Islands Administration of the British West Indies. Slavery ended, droughts brought famine, and most of the white planters fled, leaving the island to ex-slaves who eked out a subsistence from soil and sea.

The greater the hardships, the more doggedly determined Anguillans became. During one famine, the British tried to move the entire population to British Guyana, but found few takers. Those who stayed on were the forebears of the smart, hard working, proud and friendly Anguillans of today.

After centuries as a poor stepsister to the powerful St.Kitts-Nevis federation, Anguillians stormed the local bastille in 1967, took possession of a handful of battered blunderbusses, and booted out the tyrants. When word of the Revolution reached England, 300 British marines parachuted in. They secured a beachhead, stripped to the buff, and plunged into an inviting sea, satisfied that peace had returned to the island. Anguilla remains happily British to this day.

The northernmost of the Leeward Islands, 145 miles east of Puerto Rico and a mere six mile swim from St. Martin, Anguilla is three miles at its widest and about 16 miles long. Its population is under 10,000; its settlements few and scattered; its tourism pleasures at first elusive. When a small cruise ship tried it as a one-day stop, passengers wandered around dazedly, finding little to see or do.

Dropped at its airport at night, you see only a flat, featureless land where arid scrub grows out of solid rock except in the few areas where a scraping of soil produces fields of corn or peas. With the dawn, however, comes a view of the sea from almost any point on the island, a neon sea edged by flawless beaches of purest sand.

What Anguilla lacks in rain forests, mountains, shopping and high-rise hotels it more than makes up for in its incomparable beaches. The nice part about vacationing here is that you don't feel you should be out climbing mountains or photographing historic ruins. This is the place to kick back, read in a hammock on the beach, work on a tan, and rediscover yourself.

Climate

Anguilla's climate varies little winter and summer, with highs in the high 80s or low 90s and lows in the low 70s. Rainfall is scanty in winter. In summer, low pressure systems can bring days of clouds, frequent showers, and the occasional hurricane threat.

ARRIVALS & DEPARTURES

Anguilla's **Wallblake International Airport** is served by **Air Anguilla**, *Tel. 264/497-2643*, **American Eagle**, *Tel. 264/497-3131*, **LIAT Ltd.**, *Tel. 264/497-2238*, **Tyden Air**, *Tel. 264/497-2719 and* **Winair**, *Tel. 264/497-2748*. Service is from San Juan, St. Maarten, St. Kitts, and Antigua. Thanks to its new official air carrier, Tyden Air, little Anguilla is more accessible than ever before. At press time, schedules are being devised to coincide with arrivals from North America into St. Maarten for the flight to Anguilla.

Passengers arriving in St. Maarten from Europe can connect to Anguilla via Tauten's Euro Express service, which expedites passengers through immigration and baggage claim. Immediately after passing immigration in St. Maarten, find the Tyden Air counter on your right and turn in your baggage. You can fill out your immigration form now or on arrival in Anguilla. The flight will take about five minutes. If you connect from Europe, roundtrip fare will cost $85; roundtrip airfare for flights connecting from the U.S. and Canada are $75. On arriving in Anguilla you will collect your baggage, hand in an immigration form, and go through customs. Taxis await in front of the terminal.

Ferries run about every half hour from 8am to 10:45pm between Marigot, St. Martin, and Blowing Point, Anguilla. Schedules can change, so always check locally. To take the ferry to Anguilla from Marigot, write your name and passport number on the manifest at the pier as soon as you arrive there. Pay a $2 departure tax, make sure all your luggage is at hand,

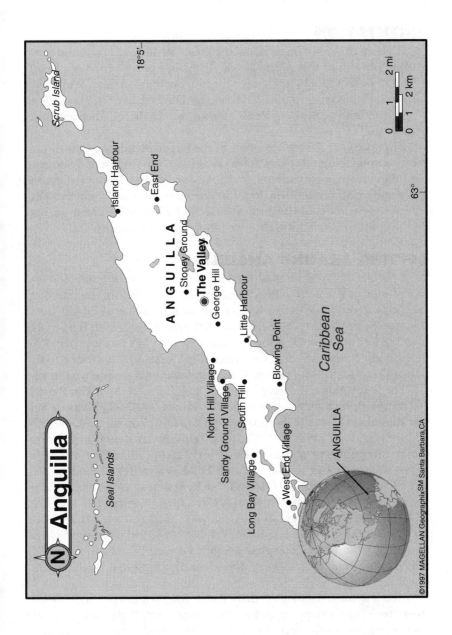

keep your passport handy, and board when an announcement is made. Fares are $10 by day and $12 evenings; E.C. dollars are accepted.

ORIENTATION

It's hard to get lost on an island this small. Road signs are almost non-existent but almost everything lies on the main east-west road or just off it. You're never more than a stone's throw from the shoreline. **Wallblake Airport** is in the center of the island. So is the chief settlement, **The Valley**.

Ferries land at **Blowing Point Harbor**, where there's another small settlement.

Trip Planning Note: while many of the larger islands are year-round vacation spots, Anguilla slows down considerably in August and September. Many resorts, restaurants, and shops are closed, to the delight of locals and island insiders who love this quiet time of year. If your favorite resort is open, this could be the best (and most affordable) time to go, but don't expect to find a wide choice of shops and restaurants.

GETTING AROUND ANGUILLA

Official taxi fares are published in the annual tourist guide, but it's always good practice to confirm them with the driver before you start out, especially if you have excess luggage or want to make an added stop. Because the airport is located mid-island, the rate to any resort is no more than $18 for two. From Blowing Point and the ferry, it's no more than $20 to any hotel. Each additional passenger pays $3. Island tours for up to six persons are $40 for one or two, with each additional person paying $5.

There's an **Avis** at Blowing Point, *Tel. 264/497-6221*. **Apex Car Rental** at The Quarter has jeeps, vans and cars, *Tel. 264/497-2642*. **Summer Set Car Rental** at George Hill offers free pickup and drop off, *Tel.264/497-5278* days and *Tel. 264/497-2298* nights. **Triple K Car Rental** is the **Hertz** outlet, offering jeeps and cars. *Tel.264/497-2934* days or *264/497-4233* nights. **Connor's Car Rental** in South Hill has a variety of models, *Tel. 264/497-6433, Fax 497-6541*. **Island Car Rental** next to the airport is at *Tel. 264/497-2723*. **High-Way Rent A Car Ltd**. on George Hill is at *Tel. 264/497-2183*. Bicycle rentals are from your hotel or from **Multiscenic Bicycle Rentals**, George Hill Road, *Tel. 264/497-5810*. Motorcycles can be rented from **C&C Enterprises**, Sandy Group, *Tel. 264/497-5196*. A fully computerized gas station is found on Blowing Point Road and it's open 7am to 11pm.

Keep to the left and don't drive faster than 30 miles per hour. Goats roam freely, often stopping traffic. Taxis meet every flight and ferry and some restaurants offer free shuttle from your hotel, so you can manage without a rental car. Many resorts also offer rental bicycles and motor bikes. Anguilla has no scheduled bus service, but a wave at a passing taxi or private car might get you a ride.

WHERE TO STAY

Rates are for a double room in high season; summer rates are greatly reduced but many hotels close in August and September. Add eight per cent government tax and a service charge of 10 per cent. All the hotels except Malliouhana accept major credit cards, but many of the villas and most of the inns and guesthouses do not.

Rates are quoted and paid in U.S. dollars; we have never seen any currency during our Anguilla stays. Always ask about packages.

Expensive

ANGUILLA GREAT HOUSE BEACH RESORT, *Rendezvous Bay, Anguilla, British West Indies. Tel. 264/497-6061, Fax 497-6019.*

Doubles at this 27-unit resort start at $440 all-inclusive, an uncommon concept on Anguillla. The resort is $18 by taxi from the airport. Build castles in the sunbaked white sand, swim in the clear waters, or plunge into the swimming pool. Included in the rates is a full menu of watersports including body boarding, snorkeling, sailing, kayaking, and fishing. Continental cuisine, which is included in the rate, is served in the Old Caribe Restaurant. Your room has a telephone, air conditioning, ceiling fan, and kitchenette. Furnishings are mahogany reproduction antiques, adding a rich complement to ice cream pastel fabrics. Television is available in the lounge.

CAP JULUCA, *Maundays Bay, Anguilla, British West Indies. Tel. 264/ 497-6666, Fax 6667; U.S. Tel. 800/323-0139. Rates at this 98-unit resort start at $625. It's an $18 taxi ride for two from the airport.*

From a distance, you think you're approaching the Little Town of Bethlehem as pictured in a child's hymn book. To see it in sunshine is dazzling; in moonlight it's surreal. Stunning domes and minarets rise behind a fringe of trees that face on one of the world's best beaches. Dining is in the elegant Pimms or in the more casual Chattertons. Play tennis or croquet, sail, snorkel, beachcomb, or swim in the sea or pool. Watersports and use of the well equipped fitness center are included. No room is more than 35 feet from the beach. Many of the marble bathrooms have couple-size bathtubs; most rooms have a private patio. Also furnished are a hair dryer and bathrobes.

Furnishings are exotically Moroccan; rooms are airy and spacious; the surrounding gardens a splendor of deep pink, snowy white, and buttery yellow. If the gazebo isn't being used by a wedding party, it's the perfect spot for sunset watching. Villas with three and five bedrooms have their own pools, each a little hideaway that would be heaven for a family reunion. Children are welcome.

CARIMAR BEACH CLUB, *Meads Bay, Anguilla, British West Indies. Tel. 264/497-6881, Fax 497-6071; U.S. 800/235-8667. Rates at this 23-unit club start at $300 for a one-bedroom apartment. Two-and three-bedroom units are available. The ride from the airport is $14 for two; it's $12 from the ferry.*

Although this is a club, not a hotel with a restaurant, it's next door to Blanchards Restaurant and not far from Malliouhana's celebration-priced dining. Spacious villas with living-dining room, full kitchen, bedrooms and bath have daily maid service. Each unit has a patio or balcony overlooking the beach, but there is no swimming pool. Watersports equipment, baby sitters, and a lounge with television are available.

CINNAMON REEF RESORT, *Little Harbour, Anguilla, British West Indies. Tel. 264/497-2727, Fax 497-3727, U.S. 800/346-7084 or 201/346-9095. Rates at this 22-suite resort start at $300 including continental breakfast. A meal plan is available. From the airport it's an $8 ride for two; from the pier it's $10. The resort closes in September and October.*

Stay on the sunny south coast of the island in a big, split-level suite on the beach or high on a breezy bluff. The stark white of the concrete construction is covered with bowers of bright flowers and relieved by artfully placed arches and openings. The hotel's Palm Court restaurant is enormously popular. Play tennis, swim in the freshwater pool, bubble in the hot tub, or use the workout facilities. Suites have a separate bedroom, private patio, telephone, television, and ceiling fan.

COVECASTLES, *Shoal Bay West, Anguilla, British West Indies. Tel. 264/497-6801, Fax 497-6051; U.S. 800/223-1108. Rates at this 12-unit hotel start at $595 for a cottage; villas start at $795. It's closed in September. Only American Express credit cards are accepted. Cab fare from the airport is $18.*

A stirring collection of uniquely designed white villas against blue sky, creamy surf and sapphire sea adds up to an architectural coup. You'll be assigned a personal housekeeper to take care of your suite's hand-embroidered linens and raw silk cushions while you read in a beachfront hammock, snorkel, play tennis, swim or sail. Secluded and sophisticated, the resort has a superb restaurant serving French-Caribbean fare.

FRANGIPANI BEACH CLUB, *Meads Bay, Anguilla, British West Indies. Tel. 264/497-6442, Fax 497-6440, U.S. 800/892-4564. Rates at this 15-unit resort start at $300; suites have up to three bedrooms; the penthouse suite is $1050. By cab it's $14 (two people) from the airport and $12 from the ferry dock.*

Classic elegance distinguishes a gaily red-roofed Mediterranean resort surrounded by towering palms and gorgeous gardens. The beach is one of Anguilla's finest, a bridal train of white sand edged with a meringue of wavelets pushed ashore by a translucent sea. The hotel's restaurant is locally popular for its French flair, fresh Caribbean ingredients, and heads-up service. Rooms, all of them different but unfailingly beguiling, have telephone, television, air conditioning and ceiling fan; some units have kitchen facilities. There's no swimming pool.

MALLIOUHANA, *Mead's Bay, Anguilla, British West Indies. Tel. 264/ 497-6111, Fax 497-6011; in the U.S. Tel. 800/835-0796. Credit cards aren't accepted. Rates at this 56-unit hotel start at $480. In season, a minimum stay of one week is required. It's a $12 cab ride for two from the airport, $10 from the ferry pier at Blowing Point. The resort closes in September.*

Take a villa on the cliff behind the pool or a room overlooking what seem like miles of unblemished sands and, beyond them, a sea that shades from baby blue to shimmering sapphire. One of the Caribbean's premier resorts, Malliouhana presents the best in comforts and cuisine. Its restaurant is a red hot ticket (reserve early) and its wine cellar one of the largest and most comprehensive in the Caribbean. Rooms are rich with tropical woods and cool tiles, set off by Haitian art. Wander the 25 acres among the flowers, pools, and fountains, or romance the days away in your secluded, hedge-hidden lodgings. Swim in the sea or pool; enjoy good satellite television reception in your room or in the lounge, sail or snorkel, work out in the fitness center, play tennis day or night, or have your hair done in the beauty salon.

Children are welcome and they'll love the big, imaginative playground. The plantings are so special that guests are offered a free garden tour of the resort with the resident horticulturist.

SONESTA BEACH RESORT, *Rendezvous Bay West, Anguilla, British West Indies. Tel. 264/497-6999, Fax 497-6899. In the U.S. and Canada dial 800/SONESTA. It's three miles from the airport or an $18 cab ride for two. Rooms start at $290; ask about packages. Suites start at $410. The resort closes in September.*

Straight out of Arabian Nights, this beachside paradise has a sprawl of satin sand beach, rustling palm trees, and a Moorish motif lavished with intricate mosaics, stained glass, arches, and fretwork as fine as any Arabian palace. The 100 rooms and suites are plushly appointed with marble baths, individual balconies that gaze across the sea to St. Martin, ceiling fans, mini-bars, hair dryers, safes, and fabrics dyed in tropical hues. Your extra-spacious room will have satellite television, a safe, and built-in hair dryer. The resort has its own beauty salon. Dine poolside at Seabreeze, which specializes in tandoori grill, or more formally at the Casablanca with its fringe of lacy openwork allowing ocean breezes to steal through. In the Casablanca bar you almost expect to find Bogie and Bergman, with Sam at the piano. Or, order from room service, which offers breakfast, lunch, and dinner until midnight. Afternoon tea is complimentary.

Children's dining is from 6pm to 7pm, and Sonesta's popular children's programs are available according to the season. Watersports equipment is provided for kayaking, snorkeling or board sailing, or the hotel can arrange a dive, sail, island tour, baby sitter, or fishing trip. There's no charge for court time on the lighted plexiplane tennis courts or for using the Fitness Center or massive, beachfront pool.

For a large family or group, ask about a week in a four-suite villa complete with kitchen and living area. Each suite is privacy-protected by double doors and has its own bath; villas have private pools and a privacy fence.

Selected as one of my Best Places to Stay. See Chapter 13 for more details.

Moderate

HARBOUR VILLAS, *Island Harbour, Anguilla, British West Indies. Tel. 264/497-4393, Fax 497-4096; U.S. and Canada, Tel. 206/822-0589, Fax 827-8907. Rates at this all-apartment complex start at $135 for a one-bedroom unit. A three-bedroom, three-bath apartment is $150 nightly. The hotel is a $17 taxi ride from the ferry or $13 from the airport.*

Overlook Scilly Cay and Island Harbour from the balcony of a villa with all the comforts of home including a full kitchen. Markets and restaurants are within walking distance and the talcum powder beach is just 100 yards from your front door. Some units have television; telephone with fax is available at the office. Laundry machines are available for guest use.

LA SIRENA, *Meads Bay, Anguilla, British West Indies. Tel. 264/497-6827, Fax 497-6829; U.S. 800/331-9358. In Canada, Tel. 800/223-9815. Rates at this 36-unit resort start at $245. Villas accommodate up to four; rates start at $330. From the airport, it's a $14 cab ride for two; from the pier it's $12. If you're driving, leave the airport on the main road to West End and watch for the turn-off to La Sirena on the right.*

Home of the renowned Top of the Palms Restaurant with its romantic dining and weekly folkloric musicals, La Sirena also offers dining in Coconuts, known for its pasta and quesadillas. The beach is only a four-minute walk away on an easy path through the garden, and the hotel supplies beach chairs and umbrellas there. In high season, drinks and sandwiches are also served at the beach. Swim in the big pool with the poolside bar or a smaller one among the villas. Rooms have telephone, television, stereo and/or VCR, hair dryer, air conditioning, and ceiling fan. Each villa has its own kitchen and parking space.

Accommodations could be compared to those at costlier resorts – airy and spacious – but because it's not smack on the beach, rates are lower than other beachside resorts of comparable quality.

MARINERS CLIFFSIDE, *Sandy Ground, Anguilla, British West Indies. Tel. 264/497-2671, Fax 497-2901, 800/848-7938. Rates at this 67-unit resort start at $220 for a double and $600 for a cottage. From the airport, it's an $8 taxi ride for two; from the ferry pier, $10.*

After a major renovation in 1997, this resort opened with a new name, new lobby building, and a new restaurant concept in the gala "Carnivals" with its costumes and montages of Anguillan life. Every week there's a live show. The resort is on the beach nestled against a cliff covered with pawpaw trees. It has a swimming pool, tennis, room phones, air conditioning, ceiling fans, kitchenettes in some units, and television.

PARADISE COVE, *The Cove, Anguilla, British West Indies. Tel. 264/497-6603, Fax 497-6927. Rates at this 14-villa complex start at $235 for a one-bedroom apartment and $320 for two bedrooms.*

You're getting the best of two worlds in the space and privacy of a one-bedroom apartment, plus resort features such as maid service and an on-site restaurant. Located 500 yards from Cove Bay beach and 300 yards from Rendezvous Bay West beach, and with a swimming pool too, the property features units with telephone, laundry, television, air conditioning, and full kitchens.

SHOAL BAY VILLAS, *Shoal Bay, Anguilla, British West Indies. Tel. 264/497-2051, Fax 3631; U.S. 800/223-9815. Rates at this 13-unit complex start at $235 for a studio apartment. Taxi fare from the airport is $18.*

The biggest selling point for these absentee-owned villas is that they are on Anguilla's busiest beach, the place to see and be seen. This isn't the place for you if you want a lonely beach all to yourself. Tourists flock to Shoal Bay for the powdery sands, patches of palm shade and sunshine, and groovy restaurants all in a row. The closest, Le Beach, is open breakfast through dinner. Each villa is privately owned so decor varies, but it's typical tropical with plenty of light pastels and ceiling fans for cooling. Do your own cooking in a complete kitchen. The complex has a freshwater swimming pool and units have maid service.

Budget

EASY CORNER COTTAGES, *South Hill, Anguilla, British West Indies. Tel. 264/497-6433, FAX 497-6410; U.S. 800/223-9815. Ten one-, two- and three-bedroom cottages start at $160. From the airport, cab fare is $8 for two.*

Although it's not on the beach, the shore is nearby and the cottages are handy to the airport. Rates include maid service, television, kitchen, porch, air conditioning in some units, and ceiling fans, making this a neat buy for the budget traveler. Yes, they take major credit cards, which most budget inns here do not. Don't bring children under age two.

FERRYBOAT INN, *Blowing Point, Anguilla, British West Indies. Tel. 264/497-6613, Fax 497-6713. Rates at this eight-unit inn start at $140 for a one-bedroom suite. Walk from the ferry or take a taxi from the airport for $8 for two. Credit cards are accepted.*

A Brit and his Anguillan wife operate this cozy inn, which is spread on green lawns bordering the beach. One of its best features is a fine Caribbean-continental restaurant known for its soups, a brandy-splashed lobster thermidor and killer rum punch. Units have telephone, television, maid service, complete kitchen, beach chairs, air conditioning and ceiling fan. Lodgings are basic, clean and handy for the thrifty traveler, and the adjoining restaurant is a plus.

Villas

Private villas can be booked through **Keene Enterprises**, *Box 28, The Valley, Anguilla, British West Indies, Tel. 264/497-2544, Fax 497-3544.* Packages including hotel or villa accommodations plus air fare can be booked through **Villa Vacations, Ltd.**, *212/753-1133, Fax 644-5959.*

WHERE TO EAT

Restaurants listed here take credit cards unless otherwise noted. Although it's not always advertised, it's not uncommon for restaurants on Anguilla to offer free shuttle service to and from your hotel. Most require reservations anyway, so ask when you call. Prices on Anguilla menus are listed in U.S. dollars. Although restaurants may be open for two or three meals, they commonly close for several hours between breakfast and lunch and again between lunch and dinner. Too, many close in August and September or maintain shortened hours. Call first.

Expensive

BARREL STAY, *Sandy Ground. Tel. 497-2831. Appetizers are $7 to $12, main dishes $19 to $35 and desserts $5 to $9. It's open daily for lunch and dinner. Reservations are advised.*

Dine on a seaside terrace on the famous fish soup, with its garnish, a red pepper mayonnaise with garlic. Appetizers include stuffed crab. Local lobster takes a starring role on the menu. Order your fish Vietnamese style, blackened, Portuguese style, meunière, almandine, or with a mustard seed sauce. Steaks are cut from U.S. Prime Black Angus beef. Wines tend to be French and pricey. The decor is, as the name suggests, all barrels, parts of barrels, cut-up barrels, and things that look like barrels.

CASABLANCA, *in the Sonesta Beach Resort, Rendezvous Bay, three miles from the airport. Tel. 497-6999. Dinner entrees are priced $19 to $31; appetizers $8 to $12; desserts $10. A two-course lunch will cost about $20. Reservations are recommended for dinner.*

Arrive early enough for a drink in the bar, where a grand piano serenades in the lounge. A sultan would feel at home on the overstuffed banquettes under original art works. While you wait for courses to arrive, nibble on delicately herbed focaccia served with a zesty eggplant and horseradish relish. Dine on pumpkin soup, pistachio crusted salmon, fresh fish in saffron vegetable broth, veal with braised spinach, local lobster, filet of beef done to perfection and served with garlic mashed potatoes, or beef sirloin smothered in crispy onions and Cabernet sauce. For vegetarians, there's grilled portabello mushroom with black pepper fettucini, artichokes, asparagus and herb cheese cake. A pungent pepperpot, rich with lobster, shrimp, mussels and scallops, is prepared for two. Save room for a sweet; the American pastry chef is exceptionally talented. Sonesta serves children all their favorites but only from 6pm to 7pm.

CYRIL'S FISH HOUSE, *call ahead for free shuttle service from your hotel. It's open daily for dinner. It's at Island Harbour. Tel. 497-4488. Plan to spend $40 for dinner.*

Dine in a seaside cabana on garlic crusted snapper with sour lemon mojo, wood grilled trigger fish with aoli and tomato coulis, or grilled dorado with red onion marmalade. The chef, Deon Thomas, is from Jamaica and his jerk chicken and pork are thought by many to be the best on the island. Live music plays on Monday, Wednesday, and Friday evenings.

HIBERNIA, *Island Harbour on the northeast shore. Tel. 497-4290. Reservations are essential. Plan to spend $50 for dinner and a drink.*

Tucked away in a fishing village is this remarkable find run by an owner-chef who travelled extensively to Vietnam, Laos, Burma, and Thailand, and completed a course in Thai cooking in Bangkok. His French-influenced Thai specialties are wrought with fresh island fish, vegetables and herbs, often incorporating great splashes of rum or a smoker to give the dish a touch of woodsmoke. Try the smoked fish du jour, Peking style chicken pancakes, basil crawfish casserole, or Oriental bouillabaisse.

KOAL KEEL, *east of The Valley heading towards Crocus Bay. Tel. 497-2930. Reservations are recommended. Plan to spend $50 or more per person for three courses and wine. Entrees are priced $22 to $35. Open daily, it serves lunch and dinner. Breakfast is available upstairs in the Petit Patissier, which is open 7am to 11pm daily for takeout baguettes and pastries.*

The setting is a Dutch planter's home built in the late 1700s. The name is a corruption of the island term "coal kiln," a special way of arranging green wood for the making of charcoal. From the outside it's a ramble of rock walls but the interior is aglow with quaint tables and warm hospitality that includes a complimentary rum tasting after dinner. With

24-hour notice, the centuries-old rock oven is fired up to create grapewood-smoked chicken ($55 for two). From an extensive menu, choose starters such as the island pea soup or curried pumpkin soup, lobster crepe, or escargots. Then choose from a long list of main dishes that includes pastas, grilled fish or spit-roasted lobster, stuffed Cornish game hen blazed with 151-proof Bacardi rum, or rack of lamb presented with polenta of pumpkin and garlic potatoes.

The presentation of your dinner is done by waiters who, all at once, whisk the tops off silver salvers with dash and a sense of whimsy. The wine cellar, built with separate cellars for whites and reds, is one of the Caribbean's largest and best-stocked, housing 20-30,000 bottles. Truly one of the Caribbean's important restaurants, this one is a must.

MALLIOUHANA, *Meads Bay. Tel. 497-6111. Open daily for lunch and dinner, this very expensive restaurant offers appetizers at $11 to $25, main courses for $27 to $34 and desserts for $11. Dinner reservations are essential.*

The hosting is Parisian, the setting a tropical paradise overlooking the sea, the cuisine French with fragrant drifts of fresh herbs. The conch chowder is faintly seasoned with fennel, the crayfish salad with vanilla, the grilled snapper with orange, the lobster ravioli with carrot. If you prefer meats or poultry there's always a good selection of lamb, chicken or steaks, all magnificently prepared and presented. The wine list is one of the most extensive in the tropics.

PALM COURT, *in Cinnamon Reef Resort, Little Harbour. Tel. 497-2770 or 2727. Reservations are advised. Open daily for lunch and dinner, serving main courses in the $25-$30 range.*

From the kitchen of Anguilla's chef of the year for three years running, try lobster with sweet potato pancakes, beignets of lobster with roasted eggplant, barbecued rabbit with coleslaw and apples, grilled rock grouper with cracked black pepper, and pumpkin cheesecake with pine nut and honey brittle. At lunch, order a mile-high lobster club sandwich with sweet potato fries or one of the piquant soups. True to its name, the eatery sits in a sweep of palms at the edge of the water overlooking distant St. Martin.

When Prince Philip came to Anguilla, this restaurant was chosen to host the state dinner in his honor.

PIMMS, *Cap Juluca Resort, Maundays Bay. Tel. 497-6666. Entrees are priced $25 to $35; reservations are required. It's open daily for dinner.*

Elegance reigns in the finest of restaurants in one of the island's finest resorts, which is also home to the more informal, eclectic Chattertons. Moorish motifs set the mood for Mediterranean dining. Anguillan lobster appears in many modes including ravioli, risotto, or freshly split and grilled. Start with a hot or cold soup or a salad of baby greens followed by bouillabaisse or grilled fish with an innovative sauce on a bed of lightly steamed vegetables. Desserts feature tropical fruits or a sinfully rich chocolate cake.

ROY'S PLACE, *Crocus Bay. Tel. 497-2470. Reservations are recommended. It's open daily for dinner with entrees priced at $15.50 to $32.50, less if you order one of the two-for-one specials served between 6 p.m and 7pm on Fridays.*

Come early for the beach, then for the sunsets and a cold English beer on tap in the pub. When you're ready to go in to dinner, relax in the open-air dining room while you dine on fresh island seafood including lobster and snapper, fish and chips, roast beef, ham steaks, and key lime pie. The roast beef brunch on Sundays is a belt-buster.

ZARA'S, *Upper Shoal Bay. Tel. 497-3229. Open daily for lunch and dinner, and breakfast by reservation, Zara's has appetizers for $6-$20 and main courses for $16 to $30. Reservations are recommended.*

Nestled in the poolside gardens of the Allamanda Beach Club, this Caribbean-Italian restaurant offers grilled chicken, steak and veal as well as lobster pasta with fresh herbs, or pasta in fresh tomato and basil sauce. Order the garlic crusted snapper or the combo featuring grilled fish, jumbo shrimp, lobster, golden calamari, and conch.

SCILLY CAY, *an island off Island Harbour, Tel. 497-5123. Stand on the pier and wave for the water taxi for the two-minute ride to the cay. Dinners, which are served 11am to 4pm, are $20 to $45. Call ahead; depending on where you're staying you may be able to charge the meal to your hotel. The cay is closed Mondays, Christmas, and for six weeks in September-October.*

Dress for the beach and live an island idyll for a day at Scilly Cay, a tiny island with good patches of beach. Eat on the sands in the sunshine or under a grass roof, or inside the bar where the crowd will include a nice mix of islanders, tourists, and showbiz greats who often arrive by helicopter. The outdoor barbecues produce a steady stream of grilled chicken and lobster, which are served with pasta salad, fruit and bread. Choose the vegetarian plate at $20, chicken for $25, lobster that is brought in fresh from the sea for $35, and a chicken-lobster combination for $45. Live music features Sprocka with his guitar and calypso on Wednesday and, on other days, scratch bands or a steel drum. If you play an instrument, bring it and join in. This is Robinson Crusoe living at its most relaxing, a must for the experience as well as the simple, hearty chow.

ANGUILLA'S NEW AREA CODE

At press time, Anguilla is in transition from the old area code, 809, to the new one, 264. If one doesn't work, try the other.

Moderate

ARLO'S RESTAURANT, *South Hill. Tel. 497-6810. Main dishes are priced $11 to $26, desserts $5 to $8. Reservations are suggested.*

Arlo's Parisian owner retains a strong Italian accent in long-popular menus but he's also added new interest in spinach, mushroom, or pepper-stuffed chicken with light lobster sauce and mashed potatoes or farfalle with fresh salmon in light dill sauce. Pizza is available to eat in or take out; Italian favorites include veal Milanese, pasta Carbonara or Bolognese, and seafood fettucini.

CARIB CAFE, *Long Bay next to Malliouhana. Tel. 497-6700. Closed Monday, the cafe is open only for dinner from 5:30pm. Reservations are recommended. Entrees are priced $12 to $20.*

Try authentic island standards such as stuffed christophene, pumpkin or pea soup, fish on a bed of lentils, banana crepes with papaya sauce, curry goat, or coconut soup.

LUCY'S HARBOUR VIEW, *Back Street, South Hill. Tel. 497-6253. Open daily except Sundays and late August to late October for lunch and dinner. Reservations are requested. Dinners are in the $30 range.*

From the oldest restaurant on the island, look over Road Bay beach from South Hill while you dine on Anguillan classics such as pumpkin soup, breadfruit pudding, grilled lobster, conch fritters, and curry goat, accompanied by fresh vegetables and pillowy bread. Once a private home, Lucy's still glows with homey informality and warm welcome. On Thursday evenings there's live music.

MANGO'S, *Barnes Bay. Tel. 497-6479. Open daily except Tuesday for lunch and dinner. Reservations are suggested. In season they're essential. Lunch is under $20; plan to spend $40-$50 for dinner with drinks.*

Simplicity is the key to an elegant meal based on fresh fish and produce, deft seasonings, and an eschewing of the heavy sauces and fats so often favored by chefs. Feast on meaty lobster cakes, jumbo shrimp in coconut and lemongrass, or red snapper subtly sensationalized with Mango's own blend of herbs.

CARNIVAL, *in Mariners Cliffside resort, Sandy Ground. Tel. 497-2671. Reservations are suggested. Entrees are $16 to $27. It's open daily for breakfast, lunch, and dinner.*

Located under the cliff overlooking Road Bay, this is the spot for Caribbean cookery in a decor inspired by carnavale. Dishes include jerk pork and chicken, bread pudding, sweet potato pudding and, on Thursday evenings, a West Indian buffet. Try such specialties as the seafood pancake, whole snapper, and goat cheese salad. On Fridays, Happy Hour from 6 to 7pm features drinks for half price.

THE OLD HOUSE, *George Hill Road. Tel. 497-2228. Main courses are priced $14 to $20. It's open daily for breakfast, lunch, dinner, and takeout.*

Fresh seafood is a standout here as it is on most Anguilla menus. There's also barbecue, charbroiled steak, chicken, curries, and tropical fruit drinks with or without alcohol. At breakfast, feast on pancakes or fresh eggs with hash browns. Luncheons feature hot and cold platters. **RIPPLES**, *Sandy Ground. Tel. 497-3380. Open noon to midnight daily except Thursday, when it's closed for lunch, Ripples offers appetizers at $5 to $8 and entrees for $12 to $25. Dinner specials are as little as $10. Make reservations as early as possible.*

A friendly international staff offers the island's most international menu: fish and chips, tacos and tostados, English cottage pie, American burgers, chicken Peking, Cajun snapper, and fresh Anguillan seafood including a lobster penne. The bar is a popular hangout after dinner. **RIVIERA**, *Sandy Ground. Tel. 497-2833. It's open for lunch and dinner daily with reservations recommended. Prices are in the $20-$30 range and a three-course $20 dinner is featured.*

Didier Van is a former world-roaming photographer who got this far and stayed. Thoroughly French, his beachside restaurant serves feasts fit for royalty in a gingerbread trimmed terrace walled on one side with flowers. Except for daring departures such as a tuna sashimi, the menu is faithfully French. Start with the Riviera Surprise cocktail then lose yourself in a meal of fish soup a la Provencale, followed by rosace de langouste and finished with mousse au chocolat and a Cuban cigar, all accompanied with a good French wine from Didier's "boutique" wine cellar. Live jazz plays on Saturday nights.

SEABREEZE, *in the Sonesta Beach Resort, Rendezvous Bay. Tel. 497-6999. Serving daily from 11am to 6pm at prices in the $7 to $12 range, this poolside/seaside resta*urant sometimes also stays open evenings for dinner at dinner prices. Enjoy Caribbean barbecue with live music under the stars. Call for dates of these events.

Drop in any day for lunch overlooking one of Anguilla's most pristine beaches. Start with a Sonesta Sea Mist (rum with Midori and fruit juice), then a burger or salad or one of the daily specials such as yellowfin tuna with Japanese horseradish or a grilled pizza made with fresh basil and tomato. The grilled vegetables with fontina cheese and rosemary pesto are a vegetarian delight.

SERENITY, *Upper Shoal Bay Beach. Tel. 497-3328. Appetizers are priced $5 to $23 and main courses $16 to $30. Call for hours.*

Come to spend the day at the beach if you like, then nurse a frozen daiquiri while soaking up the serenity of this light, airy room with its white columns. Dine on lightly cooked fresh snapper, salads, sandwiches, a steak, or grilled chicken breast with a medley of vegetables.

STRAW HAT, *Forest Bay, just south of the airport. Tel. 497-8300. Dinner is served nightly; reservations are recommended. Main dishes are priced $20 to $35.*

A bright band of energetic young American businesspeople whose families have long visited Anguilla are winning raves for their transformation of the former Smuggler's Grill. The straw hat theme is charmingly carried through with hats on the hatrack, the walls, and serving as bread baskets for freshly sliced baguettes brought from the island's patisserie. Open windows look out over the sea to St. Martin. The bouillabaisse is thick and flavorful, loaded with fresh lobster. Braised loin of pork is served with grilled vegetables. Fresh fish and lobster are always on the menu, offered with a selection of French, California, and Australian wines.

Budget

ARISTA, *South Hill Plaza on the West End road. Tel. 497-6506. Primarily a deli but with a small Oasis Cafe serving breakfast, lunch, and dinner, Arista's specials start at $6. It's open every day until 9pm, closing Sunday at 6pm. No credit cards.*

A mecca for picnickers and people who are staying in self-catering lodgings, Arista is a New York-style deli selling Boar's Head and DeParma products, more than 60 cheeses, fancy mustards, virgin olive oil, baby dills, bread sticks, and no end of ingredients needed for gourmet cooking. They'll make sandwiches and party platters to order, and can cater a meal for a family or a crowd.

DUNE PRESERVE, *Rendezvous Bay, no telephone nor credit cards. Find the turn-off to the south between Lower South Hill and Long Bay and follow the signs from the road. Or, if you have a boat, beach it below the dune. Soup and bread is $10; a chicken or fish platter is priced to $20.*

Taxis don't like to serve this end-of-the-world place, but it's ideal if you can walk in from the beach or drive in by rental car. The roads are long and rutted, so it's not recommended as a bicycle or motor bike trip. Windblown and beautiful in a funky, junky way, this series of decks clings to a high dune overlooking a beach that's perfect for walking or swimming. It's built from driftwood and parts of beached boats with seating willy-nilly all over the dune. Lunch on soup, a fruit plate or green salad, chicken or seafood salad, ribs or fish. At night and during the day on weekends there's live music sometimes starring reggae star Bankie Banx.

J&J's PIZZA, *South Hill. Tel. 497-3215. Takeout foods are under $10. Call for hours, which vary seasonally.*

Call ahead and order a pizza loaded with crab, pepperoni, ground beef, cheese, mushrooms, vegetables, lobster, and/or shrimp. Sweets and drinks can accompany your order. Then take it to the beach or back to your lodgings.

THE LANDING STRIP, *George Hill in the Clarita Mason Mall. Tel. 497-2268. Open daily, the restaurant serves lunch, dinner, and takeout. Items are priced $1 and up.*

Choose Chinese classics from a lengthy menu or go native with simple island dishes such as curry pork chops, conch egg rolls, Peking chicken, and always fresh fish in a variety of preparations. You'll sit on an air porch overlooking the landings and takeoffs at the airport.

PEPPERPOT, *The Valley, opposite the high school. Tel. 497-2328. Dishes are $5 to $10. It's open daily from 7am to 10pm.*

Anguillans eat here when they want authentically prepared salt fish, stewed chicken or pork, curried goat, and homemade soups. Try the roti, which are made with potato, meat and a touch of curry, all wrapped in a flour tortilla.

SHALACKS CAFE, *The Quarter, opposite Albert's Supermarket. Tel. 497-3272. Eat for $10 to $15. Hours vary seasonally.*

There's always a nice selection of home-style comfort foods at this cafeteria-style restaurant: baked chicken with mashed potatoes, barbecue ribs, pizza, patties, pork chops, peas and rice, macaroni and cheese, burgers, johnnycake, fries, and meatloaf just like Mom's. Call ahead for takeout or eat in.

SMITTY'S, *Island Harbor just west of the Shell station. Open daily from 11am until the last guest leaves, it does not take credit cards. Sandwiches start at $6; platters are priced $15 to $25.*

Sit indoors or on the beach under an umbrella while servers trot out huge platters of the island's best fried chicken and French fries. Conch, fresh fish, lobster and steaks are also offered in a laidback, good-times atmosphere with jukebox, big-screen cable sports broadcasts, and a jolly crowd who often take a break for beach volleyball. The exotic drinks, panoramic view, and superb beach make for a memorable day or evening. Longtime island fixture Smitty personally presides.

SEEING THE SIGHTS

The beaches are Anguilla's shining glory, and most tourists spend most of their time on them. Ancient forts and historic sites are in short supply and towering rain forests non-existent. Still, the island has some historic sites that make for a pleasant day's touring. As you drive around, look for the outdoor ovens that were once the chief cooking method here. Many of them remain, some still in use after 200 years. You'll also see natural salt ponds rich with bird life and manmade salt ponds remaining from a salt industry that flourished here from earliest settlement to the 1980s.

The **Lower Valley** is the oldest part of the settlement, with a variety of quaint old homes and the island's oldest church, **Ebenezer Methodist,** with arched Gothic windows. **Koal Keel** restaurant nearby began as a private home centuries ago. Stop in for a pastry at the upstairs Patissier or make a special evening of dining here. Across the way is a cluster of perfectly preserved private homes in quintessential Creole style. Your camera will love the colors.

At **Crocus Hill**, the remains of an old courthouse and dungeon can be seen. Near The Valley, you'll see **Wallblake House**, built in the 18th century next to **St. Gerard's Church**, a stately little church with openwork walls that let breezes blow through. Inside, it's aglow with wood benches and a magnificent wooden ceiling. In season, tours of the old house are sometimes offered; the church is open for services.

Colville Petty established his **Heritage Collection** as a labor of love and it shows. Rooms in his home are filled with caringly preserved artifacts from the Arawaks through the 1967 Revolution, all of them neatly labeled, displayed and organized. Find it at Pond Ground, East End, Monday through Saturday 10am to 5pm and Sundays by appointment, *Tel. 497-4067.* Admission is $5 adults and $2 children.

Tourists always end up eventually at **Sandy Ground** for one of the restaurants, which are easier to get to now that the wildly steep road has been improved. Don't leave without snooping around a charming old settlement with some fine old Caribbean houses lying two and three streets back from the beach. Just behind **Johnno's**, the white house is a typical Creole vernacular design. Driving east from Sandy Ground, **Mission House** on your right was originally a plantation house built in the early 19th century. **Bethel Methodist Church** at South Hill dates to 1878.

Rendezvous Bay, an especially dazzling beach known for its shelling, was once an Arawak settlement and has been dated to the late sixth century. Another fine old church is **St. Augustine Anglican** at East End village, built in 1890 and partially modernized in the 1980s.

NIGHTLIFE & ENTERTAINMENT

JOHNNO'S, an open shack on the beach at Sandy Ground, is the happening place on Anguilla. Admission is $5. Locals recommend an evening here for drinks and music, then a pre-dawn meal of kabob or barbecued chicken at **RAFE'S**, an open shack on the hill overlooking Sandy Ground. Sometimes it's open until after sunrise.

RED DRAGON DISCO on South Hill, The Valley, *Tel. 497-2687,* has special events including dances on Fridays for the over-30 crowd. It's open Saturdays from midnight on, offering live music twice a month, air conditioning indoors and dancing outdoors on a deck under the stars. Call for schedules and opening times. A cover charge is paid. **CAP JULUCA** resort also has disco dancing nightly.

FOLKLORIC THEATER

Every Thursday night, a dinner show at La Sirena Hotel at Meads Bay features poolside barbecue and an evening of West Indian music and dance. Mayoumba Folkloric Theater is composed of talented volunteers who act out Anguilla's story in a unique musical. Every Monday, Caribbean steel band music is featured at the hotel.

The island's most unusual hangout is **DUNE PRESERVE**, a project of reggae recording star Bankie Banx. Perched high on a dune overlooking beach and sea, it's a series of decks artfully made from driftwood and shipwrecks. Taxis don't like to come here because it's on a long, rough, sand road. If you're driving, look for the Dune Preserve sign on the road to Rendezvous Bay, then follow signs. If you're staying at the Sonesta Beach Resort, you can walk here on the beach. Bring a good flashlight (not the tiny one that comes with your room key) and wear sturdy shoes because it's rocky and wet. The complex is open daily from noon until the last guest leaves. Live music plays on Friday nights and sometimes other times, usually starting at 9pm. Drinks are always available and a simple menu of soup, bread, salads, chicken, ribs and fish is served for lunch or dinner.

SPORTS & RECREATION

Beaches

Beaches for swimming and snorkeling are at **Barnes Bay, Blowing Point, Crocus Bay, Junk's Hole Bay, Little Bay, Little Harbour, Maunday's Bay, Merrywing Bay, Mimi Bay, and Rendezvous Bay**. Also swim the **Prickly Pear Cays/Sandy Beach**, which is seven miles north of Road Bay and reached only by boat. For beachcombing and picnicking try **Cove Bay, Captain's Bay, Long Bay, Limestone Bay** in settled weather, and **Little Bay**.

Standout beaches are **Scilly Cay** for its swimming, dining, and music on a separate island. Go to **Mead Bay** for a mile of good beach plus hotels and restaurants, and **Shoal Bay** for jolly crowds, people watching, food, and beach rentals.

Observe special cautions at **Captain's Bay** for rough seas, **Katouche Bay** for currents and manchineel trees, **Little Bay** for a difficult climb down to the beach, and **Long Bay** for difficult access. For shelling, try **Shoal Bay East, Shoal Bay West, Captain's Bay, Long Pond Bay, Rowdy Bay, Savannah Bay**, and **West End Bay**. Good shelling varies greatly depending on sea conditions and the life cycles of various mollusks.

Bird Watching

Birders are well rewarded with sightings of common seabirds and song birds. Brown boobies nest on the offshore islands and the cliffs at Little Bay are a nesting ground for the red-billed tropicbird. Sandpipers and terns are commonly seen on the beaches. For a variety of wading birds, go to the salt ponds around the island. In the garden it's common to see hummingbirds, bananaquits, the king bird known locally as chinchary, and kestrels known here as killy killy.

Anguilla's national bird is the turtledove, identified by its brown body, pointed black tail, and pink breast. Look for it in the wild and on souvenir tee shirts.

Boating, Sailing, & Snorkeling

Take a snorkeling charter with **Hoo Haa Charters** out of Island Harbour and Sandy Ground, *Tel. 264/497-4040*. Fishing charters and sunset cruises are available through **Sandy Island Enterprises**, Tel. *264/497-6359*. Explore aboard a glass bottom boat from **Mike's**, *Tel. 264/497-5641 or 5058*. Sightseeing, fishing, and exploration trips are priced $15 to $50. *Chocolat* is the 35-foot catamaran owned by island-born **Rollins Ruan**, who offers luncheon cruises and sunset sails. *Tel. 264/497-3394*. Sail to offshore cays aboard *Bing!*, which can be booked through your concierge or call **Neville Connor**, *Tel. 264/497-5643*.

Anguillans are superb boat builders, and sailboat racing is a local passion. If you're on the island the first week in August, don't miss the races. Things can get frantic because of the local "hard lee" rule that requires both boats to tack away if they are on a collision course. The result is a seagoing version of chicken that becomes heart-stopping. Other races are scheduled on major holidays, usually including New Years Day, Easter Monday, Anguilla Day in May, and Whit Monday.

It is illegal to take any coral, sponge, starfish or shells from the seas around Anguilla. If you rent a boat, get local advice about where anchoring is permitted. In the marine parks, moorings are available by permit.

Diving

Dive operators include Anguillan Divers Ltd., Island Harbour, Tel. *264/497-4750* and **The Dive Shop**, Sandy *Ground, Tel. 264/497-2020*. See a submarine show of coral, sponges, rays, turtles, and a variety of wrecks ranging from ancient accidents to modern ships that were purposely scuttled to provide fish habitats. The wrecks of two 18th-century Spanish ships can be dived at **Junk's Hole Bay**. At a depth of 70 feet off Sandy Island a brilliant sea garden is formed by corals, sea fans, and reef fish; **Little Bay** is a popular site for night diving.

Horseback Riding

One- and two-hour trail rides on English or Western saddles are booked through **El Rancho Del Blues**, *Tel. 264/497-6164.*

Tennis

Tennis lessons are available from John Miller, tennis professional at **Cap Juluca Hotel**, *Tel. 264/497-6666 or 6317.* For information on public courts on Anguilla, *Tel. 264/497-2317.*

SHOPPING

With its scattered villages and sometime shops, Anguilla is not the island for power shoppers because there is no single spot where you can park once and browse from shop to shop. Nor is there much in the way of local crafts or unique, local shopping. An exception is the studio of **Cheddie Richardson**, a talented and self-taught local whose studio at The Cove is a world class shopping discovery. Don't be misled when you hear that he uses driftwood. He forms, stains, oils and burnishes woods until they emerge shining and unflawed. His work is museum quality and the best part is that he's usually on hand in person to chat with you. *Tel. 497-6027* for an appointment.

Island artists include **Lucia Butler**, who specializes in wooden house plaques, artist and potter **Marj Morani**, fabric designer **Jo-anne Saunders**, painter **Susan Fraff**, woodblock print maker **Tanya Clark**, watercolorist **Lynne Bernbaum**, and **Courtney Devonish**, a sculptor and potter whose works can be seen in his own gallery by the traffic light at George Hill Landing. The other artists may be found in their studios, but the best bet is to look for their works in local galleries.

Shop **Savannah Gallery** in the Lower Valley, just up from Koal Keel Restaurant, for contemporary arts from Anguilla and other Caribbean islands. **Michele R. Lavalette's** atelier at North Hill has original oils and pastels. It's closed May through October. Works by Lucia Butler, the "Grandma Moses of the Caribbean," are shown at Chinchary, Sandy Hill, Seafeather's Turnoff, East End. Call for an appointment, *Tel. 597-4259.* Susan Graff's impressionist paintings are at **La Petite Galerie** in Skiffles Villas in South Hill and can also be seen at her studio in Cul de Sac; *Tel. 497-6110* for an appointment November through April.

For souvenirs, including colorful Anguilla flags, a big selection of mobiles, and imported pottery, try **Alecia's Place** on George Hill next to Vision Center. For cottons in bright prints, shop **Beach Stuff** at Picture Point, South Hill. **La Petite Boutique** at South Hill is open weekdays only, offering Caribbean silk screen prints.

ANGUILLA'S COLORFUL STAMPS

Philately is a passion throughout most of the Caribbean, but on Anguilla it's especially fruitful, perhaps because of the explosion of island pride after the Revolution. With independence came an outpouring of Anguilla's exquisitely colorful postage stamps. Today stamp sales provide a major portion of the island's revenue. Visit the post office in the Valley to buy commemoratives and first day covers for collectors and a spectrum of everyday stamps, which are exquisite, to use on your post cards and as souvenirs and gifts. Prices start at only a few cents.

EXCURSIONS & DAY TRIPS

If you take a day trip to **St. Martin/St. Maarten** for sightseeing or shopping, don't forget to take your passport and immigration card for re-entry. Ferries leave Blowing Point every half hour from 7:30am to 10pm or later. Departure tax is $2. Immediately on arrival at the port, write your name on the manifest and pay the tax, then wait for the announcement to board. Tyden Air offers one-way and round-trip service including a golf package to **St.Thomas**, and day tours to **Nevis** and **St. Barts**. Book from the U.S. at *Tel. 800/842-0261*, or locally at *Tel. 264/497-2719*.

Make a day of it at **Sandy Island**, a white sand stretch rising out of the azure sea. Show up at the office, *Tel. 264-5643, Fax 497-6234*, in Sandy Ground next to the police station any day between 10am and 3pm and a ferry will whisk you to the island, where there's a glass bottom-boat, speedboat rental, water skiing, deep sea fishing, sailing, a bar, and a grill offering lobster, fish, chicken, and ribs.

Sombrero Island looks like nothing more than a rock on which a lighthouse was built, but it has a fascinating history dating to 1811. It has no water, no trees, and no harbor, but the rocky cliffs surrounded a rich deposit of guano, which was mined out to the last ton by 1890. After a shipwreck just off Sombrero in 1859, a lighthouse was completed in 1868. Today the rock has a small crew of keepers and a weirdly barren landscape alight with sea birds. Ask your hotel host about chartering a boat and guide to take you there. For a personalized tour, horseback ride, fishing trip, historic haunt or charter boat, call **Wildcat Services**, *Tel. 2655*. Tours are also available from **Malliouhana Travel &Tours**, *Tel. 264/497-2431*.

PRACTICAL INFORMATION

Area Code: 264

Banking hours: Monday through Thursday 8am to 3pm and Friday 8am to 5pm.

Communications: rental cell phones are available from the local office of

Cable & Wireless for $10 a day

Currency: official currency is the E.C. dollar, valued at about $2.68 to the US dollar, but all rates and menus quote U.S. dollars, which are accepted everywhere. Change in U.S. dollars may, however, not be available.

Current: North American-style, 110-volt power and fixtures are used.

Customs: Visitors can bring in personal effects, a quart of spirits, a half pound of tobacco, foods, and used clothing to a value of EC$50. There are severe penalties for smuggling illegal drugs or other goods in excess of the foregoing allowance.

Departure tax: $10.

Driving: on the left, British style. You'll need a valid driver's license and a local driving permit, which is available from the rental company.

Emergencies: Dial 911.

Holidays: Banks and most businesses close on New Year's Day, Good Friday, Easter Monday, Labour Day in May, Anguilla Day on May 30, Whit Monday, the Queen's Birthday in June, August Monday, August Thursday, Constitution Day in August, Separation Day on December 19, Christmas Day, and Boxing Day.

Government: Anguilla is a dependency of the United Kingdom. The nearest U.S. Embassy with consular jurisdiction is St. John's, Antigua, *Tel. 462-3505.*

Hazards: the poisonous manchineel tree is sometimes found along beaches.

Immigration: Citizens of the United States and Canada need photo identification, preferably a passport. British citizens must have a passport. All visitors must have a return ticket.

Medical matters: Anguilla has clinics in major settlements and a 36-bed hospital with inpatient and outpatient care. Ambulance and emergency room service are available around the clock.

Mail: addresses should end in "Anguilla, British West Indies."

Pharmacy: Paramount Pharmacy at Water Swamp, *Tel. 2366,* is open Monday through Saturday, 8:30am to 8pm, but emergency service is available 24 hours a day.

Time zone: Anguilla is on Atlantic Standard Time all year. During Daylight Savings Time, it's the same as New York time; October through April, it's one hour ahead of New York time.

Tourist Information: write Joan Medhurst and Associates, *775 Park Avenue, New York NY 11743, Tel. 800/533-4939.* On the island, visit the Tourist Board in the *Old Factory Plaza, The Valley, Tel. 497-2759. From elsewhere, Tel. 264/497-2759.*

Weddings: require 48 hours to process the license at the Judicial Department, which is open weekdays 8:30am to 4pm.

19. ANTIGUA & BARBUDA

Siboney tribes were the first known inhabitants of the Leewards as early as 1775 B.C. Christopher Columbus spotted the islands in 1493 and named Antigua for Santa Maria de la Antigua, whose namesake church was where he had prayed before making his second voyage to the New World.

Antigua was claimed for England in 1632 by a landing party from neighboring St. Kitts. British it remained until 1981, when it became independent. Its natural harbor was an important naval center for England and it remains one of the Caribbean's most popular harbors for yachts and cruise ships.

With France, Spain, and Holland roaming the Caribbean in search of war prizes, Britain established a naval base at Antigua in 1755. **English Harbour** is one of the most secure in the world and from the Dockyard, Admiral Horatio Nelson directed campaigns that still resound through naval history. On the southern side of the harbor, the remains of Fort Berkeley with its eight big cannons can still be seen. Above it are the romantic ruins of Shirley Heights where the 18th-century Governor Shirley lived in grand style.

Barbuda, established as a stud farm for slaves, has one of the seamiest stories in the islands. After the importation of slaves was outlawed, slavery itself lived on for decades with fresh manpower supplied by slaves giving birth to new slaves. Today slavery is simply an ugly chapter in the Caribbean's history book, but the descendants of the strong, handsome, smart people that were selectively bred here are now strong, handsome, smart, and proud Barbudans.

Barbuda was first colonized from St. Kitts but was given by King William III in 1690 to a General Codrington, governor of the Leeward Islands. In addition to breeding slaves, he introduced deer and other game and turned the island into a hunting preserve. Small deer, it is said, still survive in the thick underbrush deep in the island.

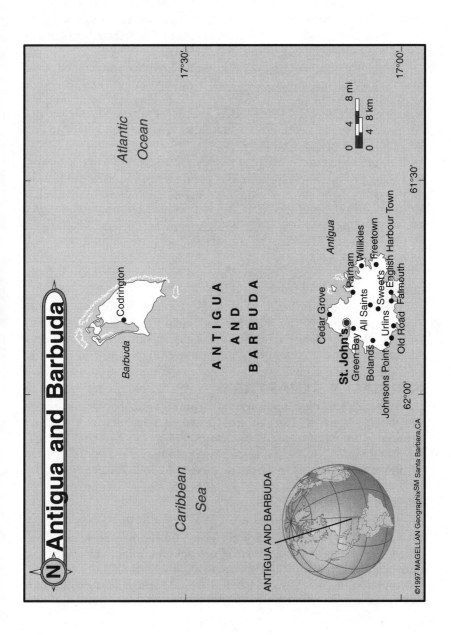

Antigua and Barbuda

N

Caribbean Sea

Atlantic Ocean

Barbuda

Codrington

ANTIGUA
AND
BARBUDA

Antigua

Cedar Grove

St. John's

Green Bay
All Saints
Bolands
Johnsons Point
Urlins
Old Road
Falmouth
English Harbour Town
Sweet's
Freetown
Willikies
Parham

17°30'
17°00'
61°30'
62°00'

0   4   8 mi
0   4   8 km

ANTIGUA AND BARBUDA

©1997 MAGELLAN GeographixSM Santa Barbara,CA

A paradise of long, pink sand beaches, Barbuda is little more than a sandspit surrounded by a reef. It's an idyllic Bali Hai for divers, snorkelers, beachcombers, and boaters, who feel like kids in the candy store with so many choices of good, beach-rimed anchorages. The **frigate bird sanctuary** here is one of the largest in the Caribbean.

Thirty-five miles northeast of Antigua lies the uninhabited rock **Redonda**. Its guano mines exhausted, it was abandoned and its equipment left to rust but it lives on as the private kingdom of an English eccentric who claimed it in 1865. Somewhere in Sussex, the heir to the throne of Redonda will hand over the title to his own son someday in a harmless bit of British fun.

Antigua went from crushing poverty after the abolition of slavery and the collapse of the world sugar market to an exclusive vacation hideaway for jet-setters. Now it is expanding its tourism base to appeal to middle-income tourists from North America and Europe, particularly the United Kingdom. Come to discover appealing resorts, ancient cobblestone streets, tradewind-swept highlands and beaches, and friendly people who make your visit memorable.

Climate

Breeze-cooled sunshine is the weather forecast on Antigua all year, with temperatures in the high 80s and nightly lows in the 70s. June through October is the rainy season, with periods of hazy heat and occasional showers. Occasionally, hurricanes bring tropical downpours.

ARRIVALS & DEPARTURES

Antigua's **V.C. Bird International Airport** is a hub that can accommodate large jets on its runways and process passengers in a modern terminal. It is served by **American Airlines**, *Tel. 800/433-7300* and **BWIA**, *Tel. 800/538-2942* or, for BWIA vacation packages, *Tel. 800/780-5501*.

Barbuda's **Codrington Airport** is served by **LIAT**, *Tel. 246/495-1187*.

ORIENTATION

Antigua covers 108 square miles, the largest of the Leeward Island chain. It and its sister island **Barbuda** (plus a scattering of rocks and cays) lie east of St. Kitts/Nevis and north of Guadeloupe. Flight time from New York is about three and a half hours; from Montreal or Toronto, about four and a half hours. You can get here from Miami in a little more than two hours.

GETTING AROUND

Taxis meet every flight and lines of cabs wait outside the larger hotels. There are no meters, but set rates are about $25 from the airport to English Harbour, $12 to St. John's, and $25 an hour. Many visitors find a driver they like and stick with him throughout the trip. Cabbies are pretty dependable about showing up as needed, so if you like the driver who brings you to your hotel from the airport, arrange with him for future transportation. Jeeps meet flights at Barbuda or call George Jeffry, *Tel. 460-0143*.

Renting a car on Antigua isn't recommended because roads are bad-to-worse, road signs are too few and too unclear, and driving is on the left, British style. Visitors are held up for a $12 local driver's license, which is little more than another tourist tax because no test nor other qualification is involved. Treat yourself to a designated (taxi) driver, and have a gin and tonic with lunch.

If you're determined to have a car, rentals are available from chains including **Budget Rent-a-Car**, *Tel. 800/472-3325;* **Hertz**, *Tel. 800/654-3131;* **Avis**, *Tel. 800/331-1212;* and **Dollar Rent-a-Car**, *Tel. 800/421-6868.* Antigua also has buses, but service is infrequent and, as far as we can tell, not according to any predictable schedule. Bus terminals are near the botanical gardens and near the marketplace.

WHERE TO STAY

There is an additional 8.5 per cent government tax over and above room rates. A service charge of 10 per cent is added to most hotel bills. When booking, ask if tax and service are included. At most all-inclusives it is. Note that many hotels and restaurants close in summer, which is just as well because air conditioning has been slow in becoming a hotel staple.

Antigua was heavily damaged by hurricanes in 1995 and some long-popular resorts are not ready for the 1997-1998 season. We have listed those that we know to be up and running.

ANTIGUA
Expensive

CURTAIN BLUFF, *P.O. Box 288. Tel. 268/462-8400, Fax 462-8409, U.S. and Canada 800/672-5833 or 212/289-8888. The 63-room resort hotel is on Old Road, 35-minute taxi ride from the airport. Rates start at $655 double and $555 single including gourmet meals. The hotel closes in October. American Express is the only credit card accepted.*

Snowy cottages blend against the bluff like a nun's wimple, a sight as arresting as the first view of the Sydney Opera House. It is all part of a plan hatched by Howard Hulford who fell in love with Antigua as a young pilot and came back to stake his claim. Before building, he camped on the property until he knew every nuance of the breezes and night sounds. Today as resident owner, he is the hotel's most enthusiastic guest, inviting other guests to his home for cocktails at least once a week. Rooms are done in warm beiges and blues, with wicker furniture and straw mats on the floors. Raised ceilings are a mellow pine.

Included in the rate are sailing, waterskiing, dive trips, snorkeling, tennis, deep sea fishing, squash, a putting green and equipment, croquet, fitness facilities and aerobics classes. In 1998, a 75-foot by 42-foot swimming pool was added.

You'll also get three meals chosen from extensive menus, afternoon tea, cocktails and canapes, and entertainment every evening. The dress code requires beach coverups at lunch and breakfast and jackets (but not ties) for gentlemen after 7pm from December 19 through April 14, except on Sunday and Wednesday. Hulford prefers that guests wear a collared shirt and enclosed shoes in the evening.

Selected as one of my Best Places to Stay; see Chapter 13 for more details.

INN AT ENGLISH HARBOUR, *English Harbour, mailing address Box 187, St. John's. Tel. 268/460-1014, Fax 460-1603; toll-free 800/223-6510. Rates at this 28-room hotel start at $290. It's 16 miles from the airport on Freeman's Bay.*

Nelson's Dockyard is only five minutes away from this hotel, which is in the national park high on a hill overlooking the famous harbor. Ask to be housed lower and close to the beach or up the hillside. Rooms have hair dryer, safe, refrigerator, and telephone. Use of non-motorized watersports equipment is complimentary; tennis courts are nearby; a water taxi zips guests to the Dockyard. Dine on the beach or in the restaurant; cocktails are served in the woody English-style bar.

JUMBY BAY ISLAND, *Long Island, mailing address Box 243, St. John's. Tel. 462-6000, Fax 462-6020; toll-free 800/421-9016. Rates at this 38-room, 12-villa resort start at $990 including airport transfers and all meals, sports, drinks, entertainment, and activities. Ask the taxi driver to take you to the Beachcomber dock northeast of the airport, where you will be met by the resort's launch.*

Whipsawed by hurricanes Luis and Marilyn, this grand old Moorish-style showplace was re-roofed with cedar shingles and given new soft furnishings featuring custom fabrics. The look for the 1997-98 season is all new. Have dinner with an appropriate wine in the estate house built in the 1700s, play tennis, fish, sail, water ski, roam the nature trails of this 300-acre preserve, bicycle, use the putting green, or play croquet. The rooms are what North Americans call junior suites, with separate sitting area and private terrace. Most have ocean views. The villas have one, two, or three bedrooms. The beach is a dream, the food gourmet, the tradewinds faithful (although at times you might wish for air conditioning.) This is one of the luxury resorts that helped put Antigua on the jet-set map.

LONG BAY HOTEL, *Long Bay, mailing address Box 442, St. John's. Tel. 268/463-2005, Fax 463-2439; toll-free 800/223-6510. Rates at this 20-room hotel start at $375 including breakfast and dinner. It's 12 miles from the airport.* With a serene bay on one side and a sandy beach on the other, this typically Antillean hotel offers rooms and six cottages. Sail, windsurf, fish, play tennis, snorkel or scuba dive. Dining is in your choice of two restaurants. Have a drink in your choice of two bars. Manager Chris LaFaurie is one of the family that has operated this friendly hotel since the 1960s. When you're not on the beach, hang out in the homey clubhouse, which has a game room and library.

PINEAPPLE BEACH CLUB, *Long Bay. Tel. 268/463-2006, Fax 463-2452; toll-free 800/345-0356. Rates at this 135-room resort start at $390 including meals, drinks, airport transfers and activities. Children under age six can't be accommodated.*

Completely refurbished in 1996 after the 1995 hurricanes, this resort promises a "no hassles" approach to vacationing. You'll be picked up at the airport, which is 25 minutes away, and wined and dined to a fare-thee-well. Most meals are served at a private table with a menu to choose from, unlike some all-inclusives that offer only buffets. Beverages including name-brand liquors, beer, wines by the glass and soft drinks are included. Also on the house are water sports with instruction, tennis play on four championship courts, use of the fitness center, and live entertainment nightly. Air conditioned guest rooms have a private patio or balcony (except for a few that do not), but no telephone or television. It's a popular spot for weddings and honeymoons, which are cheerfully booked and arranged.

ROYAL ANTIGUAN, *P.O. Box 1322, Deep Bay, St. John's, Antigua. Tel. 268/462-3733, Fax 462-3732. Rates are in the $200 range at this 282-room resort. A wide range of plans, from European Plan (no meals) to all-inclusive are available.*

Sprawled across 150 beachfront acres, this is a resort with everything for everyone: watersports, parasailing, fishing, aerobics, tennis, and swimming in the sea or the big, free-form pool. Dine in the resort's own restaurants (there are three) and lounges, or venture out on the island. From the outdoor restaurant you can see the markers indicating the wreck site of the freighter *Andes*, which was loaded with tar that caught fire in 1905 and sank the ship in a sizzle of steam. It's now a popular dive site. Spread a beach towel on the white sands of the resort's beach, gamble in the casino, or use the fitness equipment. All rooms have air conditioning, telephone, and television; ocean-view rooms, which are higher priced, have a mini-refrigerator and VCR. The resort, which has conference facilities, is also a popular meetings site.

ST. JAMES'S CLUB, *Mamora Bay, Antigua. Tel. 268/460-5000; in the U.S., Canada, Puerto Rico and U.S. Virgin Islands, 800/223-6800. Rates start at $210; villas from $560. Mamora Bay is a 25-minute cab ride from the airport. European and all-inclusive plans are available.*

The regal St. James's Club is one of those special places that loyal guests return to year after year. One hundred acres in one of Antigua's most secluded areas, a private peninsula, hold a meticulously groomed resort overlooking a storybook beach. Offering 85 rooms, 20 suites, and 72 two-bedroom villas, the resort stays small enough to offer personal services yet is large enough to offer a selection of restaurants, three swimming pools, a fleet of watersports fun, seven tennis courts, a putting green, a gymnasium, and a proper croquet court. The hotel can also arrange scuba dives or horseback riding for you.

On property are a beauty salon, gift shops, art gallery, nightclub and casino. Supervised children's programs offer a play center but caretakers don't provide beach play. Some parents have also complained that the children's menu is too limited (peanut butter sandwiches, hot dogs) and dinner too late for kids who are accustomed to eating before 7pm.

Traditional French cuisine is served overlooking the bay in the elegant Pascal's. For pasta, light California cuisine, grilled specialties, and Caribbean standards, eat at The Docksider. The Rainbow Garden is open for breakfast and gourmet dinners. Each week, the resort offers two festive buffets, one Caribbean and one international.

Moderate

COLONNA BEACH RESORT, *Hodges Bay. Tel. 268/462-6263, Fax 462-6430. Rates at this 124-unit resort are from $153. Children under ae 11 stay free. It's 10 minutes from the airport and St. John's. Suites and villas are available.*

Manger Vincenzo Amore takes you to the shores of Sardinia in this "little Italy" village resort with its red slate roofs, colonnaded facades, and lavish greenery. The swimming pool is a lollapalooza 600 square meters in size. Built into an old sugar plantation, the resort put its reception area in the cupola of the old mill. All rooms have television, telephone, private balcony or patio, and a view of the beach or pool. Dine poolside with an ocean view or at Sottovento with its emphasis on gourmet Italian dining.

COPPER AND LUMBER STORE HOTEL, *Nelson's Dockyard, mailing address Box 184, St. John's. Tel. 268/460-1058, Fax 460-1529; toll-free 800/633-7411. Rates at this 14-suite hotel start at $195.*

Children are welcome but they'll be bored, warns manager Andrew Gallagher. However, older children and their parents will be charmed by this historic (1783) complex in the heart of the yachtiest setting in the islands. Don't even think about booking during Antigua Sailing Week in April. International press and yachting bigwigs have all the best places booked for years ahead.

Rooms are individually decorated with four-poster beds, mahogany and brass everywhere including the baths, Oriental rugs, and dormer windows overlooking the harbor. You can play tennis or squash at the Dockyard, dine in the Ward Room or English Pub, and take the ferry to Galleon Beach for swimming and diving.

CLUB ANTIGUA, *Box 744, St. John's. Tel. 268/462-0061; Fax 462-1827; U.S. and Canada 800/223-6510. Rates start at $230 all inclusive. For singles, the rate is half the double room rate.*

Singles will love the solo pricing policy and parents will love the kids-stay-free program for children under age 12, yet this clubby resort is also so romantic that it offers a wedding package complete with a wedding chapel. The pool is so big and rambling that it needs a bridge and the beach is a stretch of satin sand studded with bright little day sailers that guests may sail free. There are few extras here. Meals, drinks, watersports including water skiing, and nightly entertainment and disco are included. Daily activities range from theme parties to beach bonfires and nightly movies; the supervised children's program plays all day every day except Sunday. The only extras are shopping, excursions, golfing the 18-hole championship course and gambling in a mini-casino.

The resort has 472 units ranging from standard rooms with ceiling fan, standards with air conditioning, junior suites, and beachfront cottages. Take breakfast at the Palm Restaurant. For lunch or dinner, the beachside Coconut Wharf serves pasta and pizza; the Crab Hole offers West Indian fare for lunch; the Palm grill serves burgers and dogs all afternoon plus late night snacks. Pub crawl among the six bars if you like. Guests may dine twice weekly at the more formal Flamboyant, serving a table d'hote menu.

HAWKSBILL BEACH RESORT, *Five Islands, mailing address Box 108, St. John's, Antigua. Tel. 268/462-0301, Fax 462-1515; toll-free 800/223-6510. Rates at this 99-room resort are from $360 including breakfast and dinner. It's eight miles from the airport and 15 minutes from St. John's.*

Take a room or the three-bedroom villa and swim on your choice of four beaches, one of them clothing-optional. It's charmingly called the Fourth Beach by staff who are too shy to utter the word nude. Topless sunning is seen at the other three. The meal plan lets you dine in the Beach Bay and Grill or in two open-air restaurants. The one on the beach has nightly entertainment. Room service is also available. Play tennis, sail, snorkel, or sign up for an excursion or activity at the social desk. Water skiing is available at extra cost. This is nature in the raw without air conditioning, television, or room phones to hamper the out-island ambience.

JOLLY HARBOUR MARINA CLUB, *Box 1793, Jolly Harbour, St. John's. Tel. 268/462-7771, Fax 462-7772; U.S. 800/223-6510. The resort is 20 minutes from St. John's. Winter rates start at $120 plus tax and service fee for a two-bedroom, one-bath condo.*

Take a one -or two-bath, two-bedroom apartment for what the British call a self-catering holiday, all at a club member price. Swim off Jolly Beach or in a big, freshwater pool. For a little extra you can play the indoor squash court, the floodlit tennis courts, or the neighboring 18-hole golf course. Your unit will have a private balcony or patio, fully equipped kitchen, air conditioning, ceiling fans, twin beds in one room and a queen-size bed in the other. Furnishings are basic blond, accented by fabrics in rich Caribbean blues.

For an added $50 per person daily, you can join the all-inclusive Club Antigua next door to enjoy live music and cabaret nightly, a children's club, bicycles, and planned activities plus all meals and drinks. A half day membership costs $40 and a late night pass is $20. If you're doing your own cooking, you can provision at a big shopping center that is only a short ride away on the free shuttle.

SANDALS ANTIGUA, *Dickinson Bay, mailing address Box 147, St. Johns, Antigua. Tel. 268/462-0267, Fax 462-4135; U.S. 800/SANDALS. Rates start at $2090 per couple for a minimum three-night stay. Included are all drinks, meals, facilites, activities, entertainment, taxes, and tips. The resort is 15 minutes from V.C. Bird International Airport.*

Romance reigns in this couples-only resort on one of Antigua's most perfect beaches. Choose among eight room categories ranging from a garden view to a grande luxe beachfront suite with its own balcony or patio. All rooms have air conditioning, king-size bed, hair dryer, safe, ceiling fan, coffeemaker, clock radio, telephone, and color satellite television. If you book a suite you'll have a special sitting area, fresh flowers, four-poster bed, upgraded amenities, terry robes, daily New York Times fax, and a full-stocked bar. All rooms are handsomely furnished with dark or pickled mahogany and pleasing prints, but the Honeymoon Seaside Rondovals are especially interesting because they are circular and have cone roofs.

Dine in El Palio for regional Italian dishes from an open show kitchen, Kimonos for Japanese dishes and entertainment, the O.K. Corral for Western-style grilled steaks, or the Courtyard Grill for grilled and deli items. Sail a Hobie Cat, canoe, kayak, water ski, swim in the five pools, soak in the whirlpools, or focus on the spa, which has conventional equipment plus Oriental hot and cold plunge pools and Chinese massage and facials (at added cost.). The tennis courts are lit for night play and there's outdoor chess, croquet, volleyball, and much more. If you want to island-hop to other Sandals in the Caribbean, all you pay is inter-island airfare, so some couples like to spend three or four nights here and the rest of the week on Jamaica or St. Lucia.

YEPTON BEACH RESORT, *Hog John Bay, mailing address Box 1427, St. John's, Antigua, West Indies. Tel. 268/462-2520, Fax 462-3240; U.S. 800/ 361-4621, Canada 514/284-0688. Rates at this 38-unit resort start at $185 plus $48 daily for breakfast and dinner. Studios, suites, and apartments with one or two bedrooms are priced to $560. Ask about packages and meal plans including an all-inclusive program that starts at $200 per person daily, double occupancy.*

This stately, three-story hotel is a bright patch of white, topped with red roofs and backed by green hills. Your room's balcony overlooks the wide white beach fading into an incredibly clear sea. The decor focuses on florals and rattan, with tile floors. Studios and apartments have kitchens, but don't miss the meals here with weekly specials including barbecue and reggae and a West Indies buffet with calypso. Swim in the freshwater pool, play tennis, try shuffleboard or volleyball, and use the resort's complimentary watersports equipment.

Cruises, car rental, horseback riding, sailing and scuba can be arranged. If you like some aspects of the all-inclusive life but not the constant cheerleading, this is the place.

Budget
ADMIRAL'S INN, *English Harbour, mailing address Box 713, St. John's. Tel. 268/460-1027, Fax 460-1534, toll-free 800/223-5695. Rates at this 14-room inn are from $116. Meal plans are available. It's a $25 taxi ride from the airport. A free shuttle takes guest to the beach.*

Even if you don't stay in this ancient inn, stop by for a meal in the restaurant, a favorite with yachties whose holy grail is English Harbour. Once a sailmaker's shop serving the English fleet here, it still has the hand-hewn beams and wrought iron chandeliers put here in the 1700s. Open the shutters and you're overlooking the harbor where yachts now congregate for the Caribbean's most important regatta, Antigua Sailing Week. It's an amusing nuisance that a curious bananaquit or blackbird may fly into your room looking for a handout, so you have to leave the shutters open until it flies out again. The best view is from the Joiner's Loft, a two-bedroom apartment with kitchen and living room overlooking the water; the best rooms are at ground level. Rooms have air conditioning or a ceiling fan. We prefer to go with the AC.

CORTSLAND HOTEL, *St. John's. Tel. 268/462-1395 or 800/223-9815. Rates at this inn start at $90. It's a half mile west of the city.*

The perfect perch for the business traveler is this small hotel in the lush gardens of the 'burbs of the capital. Rooms have two double beds, private bath and patio, television, telephone, and air conditioning. A shuttle runs to the beach at Dickinson Bay, ten minutes away.

BARBUDA
Expensive
K CLUB, *Barbuda, Antigua, West Indies. Tel. 268/460-0300, Fax 460-0305; in the U.S., Canada, Puerto Rico, and U.S. Virgin Islands, 800/223-6800. Rates at this 36-room, nine-suite resort start at $500 including all meals (but not drinks). From Antigua airport, take a 12-minute flight to Barbuda aboard the Club's own airplane and transfer to ground transportation for a 15-minute ride.*

Fashion designer Krizia owns and oversees this elegantly European resort. Set in a 230-acre shorefront park, it is a community of white bungalows, each nestled in a privacy screen of greenery and facing an incredibly white sand beach. The cuisine is Mediterranean; the wine list comprehensive. Dress in your most chic resort wear; your fellow guests are likely to be pace-setters from the worlds of fashion, industry, and entertainment.

Swim in the sea or pool, water ski, snorkel, play tennis day or night, play the nine-hole golf course, or enjoy the cozy game room, video room, and library. Massage is available and deep sea fishing can be arranged.

Selected as one of my Best Places to Stay. See Chapter 13 for more details.

GUIANA ISLAND'S COMING TOURIST BOOM!

*At press time, **Guiana Island**, which lies off the northeast side of Antigua, is being developed with a $220 million resort. It eventually will have 1,000 hotel rooms, retail shops, a casino, residences, and a 36-hole golf course. Prices are said to be in the moderate-to-luxury range, and opening is planned for 1999. For information, write: **Antigua and Barbuda Department of Tourism**, 610 Fifth Avenue, Suite 311, New York NY 10020. Tel. 212/541-4117, Fax 757-1607.*

WHERE TO EAT
Antigua's specialties include the unique black pineapple that is grown here, green figs (bananas are called figs in this part of the Caribbean), breadfruit, christophene (called chayote in Latin lands), conch, cockles, spiny lobster, and the whole range of ocean fish.

Pepperpot here is made with beef, pork and vegetables and it's usually served with fungi, the local name for cornmeal pudding with okra.

Ducana is a sweet pudding made from sweet potato, coconut, sugar, and spices, and boiled in a banana leaf.

Expensive

CHEZ PASCAL, *in the St. James's Club, Mamora Bay. Tel. 460-4491. It's open nightly except Sunday for dinner. Reservations are recommended. Main dishes are priced $20 to $36.*

Pascal and Florence Milliat from Lyon run a devoutly French kitchen here. Dine in the open air on a terrace overlooking the bay with candlelight, background jazz, and fresh flowers to kindle a romance. Start with a snail croissant, vichyssoise made with breadfruit instead of the more traditional potatoes, or a seviche made with freshly squeezed island limes and fresh conch or grouper. Order steamed fresh fish in tarragon sauce, snapper in a lime sauce and capers, mixed seafood in puff pastry, roast lamb or a perfectly-cooked filet mignon with a bordelaise sauce. For dessert there are tarts, cream puffs, or chocolate mousse. The wine list has some expensive vintages, which can double or triple the price of a meal.

COLOMBO'S RESTAURANT, *in the Galleon Beach Club, English Harbour. Tel. 460-1452. Main dishes are priced $22 to $32. Reservations are urged. It's open for lunch and dinner daily except September through the first week in October.*

Like most places in English Harbour, this one has a salty air and lots of nautical decor under a South Seas tiki roof. For lunch have spaghetti, a sandwich, hamburger or salad. At dinner, start with razor-thin slices of raw grouper marinated in lime juice and herbs or one of the soups. The veal dishes are unfailingly good – veal with mushrooms, veal scallops, veal Parmesan – or have lobster, shrimp flamed with rum, or a steak with a side dish of pasta. Italian and French wines are available. Live music plays, usually on Wednesday nights.

THE HOME, *Gambles Terrace, St. John's. Tel. 461-7651. Plan to spend $25 to $30 for dinner. It's open for dinner Monday through Saturday. Call for hours and reservations, which are essential.*

When CNN television went to Antigua for material for their "On the Menu" show, they sought out chef Carl Thomas, who grew up in Antigua and went to New York to hone his culinary skills before returning home to open his own restaurant. He bought a simple house in the suburbs outside St. John's, creating one big room out of several smaller ones and planting edible gardens. He finished the old wood floors, brought in raw pine furniture, rounded up accent pieces from island artists and crafters, and added a few imports to contribute an Afro-Haitian note. He smokes his own fish, a specialty here, and uses his own herbs to create such dishes as grouper in herb sauce. Try the pepper steak, which carries a hint of island molasses, and his signature bread pudding, which is scented with Caribbean nutmeg.

JULIAN'S, *Corn Alley at Church Lane, St. John's. Tel. 462-4766. It's open for lunch and dinner daily except Monday. Only dinner is served Sunday. Plan to spend $35-$40 for dinner. Reservations are essential.*

The room is cozy, with only eight tables and an air of elegance created by crisp linens and rattan chairs. Have broiled brie surrounded by spears of asparagus and wedges of grapefruit, roast duckling, a saucy snapper, pastry filled with wild mushrooms and feta cheese, or lamb roasted to pink perfection. Start with one of the soups and order wine by the glass or bottle. Chef Julian Waterer has a restlessly creative bent, so the menu changes often and guests are rarely disappointed.

LE BISTRO, *Hodges Bay on the north shore. Tel. 462-3881. Reservations are essential. It's open for dinner daily except Monday. Main dishes are priced $25 to $30.*

Linger over a superbly presented French gourmet dinner in a romantic bistro setting that is a favorite of North American food critics. Start with one of the soups, a marinated fish or lobster, or sea scallops in a cheese sauce splashed with cognac. The ziti in cream and Parmesan cheese sauce with mushrooms will remind you of a heavenly fettuccine Alfredo. Red snapper is served simply, swimming in a sublime blend of white wine and herbs. For a celebration meal, order the rack of lamb or a roast beef that is carved at the table, ladled with wine or tarragon sauce, and surrounded by a portrait of island vegetables.

Moderate

ADMIRAL'S INN, *Nelson's Dockyard, English Harbour. Tel. 460-1027. It's open daily for breakfast, lunch, and dinner except for September and the first two weeks in October. Reservations are suggested. Main dishes are priced $12 to $25.*

Quiet and romantic, with a pretty garden off the waterfront and a bar carved with the names of tars who visited here generations ago, this inn was built for use by the English navy in the 1700s. It still celebrates its old rafters and ancient stones. Look on the blackboard for today's choices, which usually center around whatever fish was brought in, steaks, and a native soup or stew. Ask for the Yachtsman's Special, which is always a nice plate at a nice price. Happy Hour, which is 6-7pm and sometimes 8-11pm, offers discounted drink prices. A steel band entertains on Saturday nights and on Mondays there may be a string band.

LOBSTER POT, *Runaway Bay, 10 minutes from St. John's. Tel. 462-2856. Plan to spend $35 for dinner. Call for hours and reservations. Ask for a table on the water.*

Choose from a lengthy menu and wine list, a veritable catalog of mouth-watering seafood, pasta, and Creole dishes. For openers, have one of the soups, phyllo stuffed with lobster, or grilled vegetables served with goat cheese and crustades. Shrimp is cooked in coconut milk and flavored with pungent curry; fish in pastry is ladled lightly with a fragrant tomato sauce; boneless chicken breast is stuffed with broccoli, sun-dried tomatoes, and chèvre. Lobster is served with lime butter. For native choices try one of the fungis or the pepperpot. For dessert have crepes filled with cinnamon- and nutmeg-spiced apples and topped with vanilla ice cream.

REDCLIFFE TAVERN, *at Redcliff Quay, St. John's. Tel. 41-4557. Call for hours and reservations. It's open daily except Sunday for lunch and dinner.*

A quiet place for a lunch or dinner in this bustling shopping and dining center in an old warehouse setting studded with antique machinery. Dine on the terrace or in the second-floor restaurant and bar. At lunch have a refreshing lobster salad, a grilled chicken sandwich, or a hearty soup. Choose from a dinner menu of Italian and Caribbean specialties such as the piquant crab fritters, smoked salmon and seafood in a fresh lime mousse, grilled lobster, pastas, steaks, and chops.

SHIRLEY HEIGHTS LOOKOUT, *Shirley Heights. Tel. 460-1785. Main dishes are priced $16 to $28. It's open every day 9am to 10pm. Reservations are recommended, especially when cruise ships are in port.*

The heights were a lookout point where British pickets watched for intrusions by rascally Dutch and French, so you can imagine the panoramic view the spot provides. If you want a break in your routine, come here for breakfast in the moist cool of the morning when English Harbour below is abuzz with yacht departures and dinghies bringing galley cooks to shore for the morning provisioning. For lunch have the pumpkin soup and a salad, sandwich or hamburger. Dining upstairs is fancier; the downstairs section is more pubby. Dinner specialties include lobster in lime butter, grilled fish or steak, and chicken. The big day here is Sunday, when locals and visitors (sometimes too many visitors) flock in for inexpensive barbecue and hours of music. Steel bands start at 3pm and reggae starts at 6pm.

THE WARDROOM, *in the Copper and Lumber Store, Nelson's Dockyard. Tel. 460-1058. Plan to spend $25-$35 for dinner.*

One of the two good places to eat in this historic complex (the other is the Mainbrace Pub), this is the quieter, fancier choice. Don't miss Happy Hour prices in the pub, then retreat to this brick courtyard for a view of the ramparts of the harbour while you dine on lamb chops, steak, fresh fish, lobster in puff pastry, or one of the Africa-inspired dishes such as couscous, chicken in phyllo with a touch of cinnamon or the peanut soup. For dessert try the bread pudding.

Budget

BIG BANANA/PIZZAS ON THE QUAY, *in the Redcliffe Quai, St. John's. Tel. 462-2621. Eat for under $20. It's open Monday to Saturday 8:30am to midnight and Saturday 4-10pm.*

The beautiful stone arches of an old warehouse set the scene for informal dining amidst crowds and happy din. Have one of the pizzas, baked potatoes ladled with your choice of filling, marinated conch, a sandwich or a salad. The specialty drinks, so thick you could eat them with a spoon, make better desserts than aperitifs. Live music plays on some nights.

FAMOUS MAURO *at Cobbs Corner, Falmouth Harbour, call VHF Channel 68, offers meals and snacks for $6 to $20. It's open for breakfast, lunch, and dinner daily except Sunday.*

Roberta and Mauro are Italians who serve continental, English or American breakfasts and then they start the pizza oven and put water on to boil for pasta. Choose one of the infallible pastas, divine pizza, salads, and Italian ice cream, or just stop by this popular yachters' hangout for an espresso and a pastry.

HEMINGWAY'S, *St. Mary's Street, St. John's. Tel. 462-2763. Main dishes are priced $8 to $16. Hours are daily except Sunday, 8:30am to 11pm.*

Look out over the busy streets of St. John's while you have a drink, a coffee, lunch or dinner at this popular upstairs restaurant. The setting is a typical Creole house, suitably bright with pastels and fretwork trim. The drinks are fruity, tropical, and potentially deadly; meals are pretty basic: sandwiches, burgers with fries, fried fish, pie with ice cream, and salads. This is a place to visit for the ambience and relaxing view.

Quick Takes

North American fast foodies who need a KFC fix will find **Kentucky Fried Chicken** on High Street and on Fort Road, where there's also a **Pizza Hut.**

M&M's Swiss & Sweet in Jolly Harbour, 20 minutes from St. John's, offers pastries, snacks, and coffee. **Pari's Pizza** is in Dickinson Bay. **Jackie's Kwik Stop** near English Harbour Village on the east side of Falmouth Harbour is a mini-mart with a small restaurant that serves local foods. For newspaper-wrapped fish and chips, stop by the **Mainbrace Pub** in the Copper and Lumber Store on Friday night 7-10pm. Since this is also Happy Hour, which runs 6-10pm on Friday, it's a good time to have a half-price drink and leave with a fish dinner picnic.

SEEING THE SIGHTS
ANTIGUA

History hunting is the chief sport for Antigua visitors, who can easily amble around St. John's major sites in a morning. **St. John's Cathedral** on Church Lane, *Tel. 461-0082*, dates to 1683 but the building has been replaced many times after earthquake and hurricane damage. The statues of St. John the Baptist and St. John the Divine at the entry are said to have been taken from a French ship that lost out to a British warship. **The Museum of Antigua and Barbuda**, *Tel. 462-1469*, in the old courthouse has some interesting displays from English and Amerindian history. It's open Monday to Friday 8:30am to 4:30pm and Saturday 10am to 2pm for a donation of EC$5 or more.

The **Antigua Rum Distillery** at Deep Water Harbour offers tours by arrangement. **Heritage Quay** and **Redcliffe Quay** are upscale shopping and dining complexes. Cruise ship terminals are at Heritage Quay and Deep Water.

If you're in St. John's on Saturday morning, don't miss the **farmer's market**. It's the island's favorite get-together, a time-honored way of buying and selling produce and catching up on the news. Although the **Botanical Gardens** on Temple Street at Nevis Street have been whip-sawed by hurricanes as recently as 1995, and some older trees have been lost, they're always worth a visit. The gardens were established in Queen Victoria's reign, a haven of lawns and blooms. The site is open every day 9am to 6pm for a donation of EC$5 or more.

The island's other sightseeing is at **Nelson's Dockyard National Park** at English Harbour, where the ruins of Shirley Heights tower grandly over the dockyard. Magnificent stone columns, arches, and foundations are left from the days when Governor Shirley was the Queen's representative in the Leewards. On Sundays, local families gather here to listen to reggae and steel bands, have a barbecue, and watch the sun set over the dockyard area.

At the **Dow's Hill Interpretive Centre** in the park, visitors view a multi-media show that depicts Antigua history from prehistory to the present. The old **Copper & Lumber Store**, which was just that for Nelson's navy, is now a resort where you can have a drink in the **Mainbrace Pub**. The resort also embraces the old **Capstan House and Canvas Store**. Other buildings in the national park include the **Shipwright's House**, the **Saw Pit**, the **Paint Store and Cells**, and a **blacksmith's shop**. The old **Officer's Quarters** now house a gift shop, restaurant, art gallery, and crafts workshop. For information on the historic sites of English Harbour, *Tel. 460-1053*.

Overlooking the Dockyard is the **governor's residence**, which was built for the Duke of Clarence, who later became King William IV. If you tip the caretaker, he may give you a tour when the governor is not in residence. Antique furnishings, which belong to the National Trust, are regal. The caretaker is proud to show them off and to tell you that Princess Margaret and Lord Snowden honeymooned here.

A drive through the center of the island brings you to **Betty's Hope Estate**, a sugar plantation founded in the 1650s. Continuing to innovate as agricultural methods modernized, it was in the Codrington family until 1920. The windmills have been restored, and further conservation and restoration continue. Drive the overland Fig Drive through rain forest and banana plantations. **Boggy Peak**, at 1,319 feet, is the highest point on the island. In the northeast corner of Antigua, **Indian Town** on the pounding Atlantic shore is a theme park of blow holes, boiling surf, and a wave-worn rock known as **Devil's Bridge**.

BARBUDA

On Barbuda, you'll see the ruins of **Highland House**, which was Christopher Codrington's estate, and remains of the old lookout, **Martello Tower and Fort**. Barbudians are on hand with small boats to offer 45-minute tours of the **mangrove swamps** and **frigate bird rookeries**. Don't miss them. Have one of the jeep-taxi drivers take you to the **Caves at Two Foot Bay**, where you can climb down a hole in the roof to see Arawak drawings.

FREGATA MAGNIFICANS

You'll never forget the magnificent frigate bird, known by scientists as **Fregata Magnificans**, *once you have seen him inflate his big, red balloon throat. It's a mating ploy, designed to attract female frigates who are so wowed by the spectacle that they gladly play the dating game. Eggs appear from September through February and by December through March chicks begin appearing. Hatchlings stay in the nest for up to eight months before they're able to get airborne on wings that look big enough to support a Piper Cub. Also known as the man-o-war bird or the hurricane bird, the frigate has an eight-foot wing span that can flap it to altitudes of 2,000 feet or more.*

The **Frigate Bird Sanctuary** *on the north end of Codrington Lagoon on Barbuda can be seen only by small boat. Locals will take you on a 45-minute spin in their small outboard-powered skiffs through shallow mangrove forests. With luck you may also spot pelicans, warblers, snipes, ibis, herons, kingfishers, mockingbirds, oyster catchers, and cormorants, the birds that perch on a tree or post with their wings outspread to dry.*

NIGHTLIFE & ENTERTAINMENT

Most resorts have evening programs that could range from quiet moon-watching around the bar to live music and dancing. Free-lance limbo troupes and other entertainers make the rounds of the resorts, so there's something playing somewhere almost every night. Yachties tend to hang out in bars handiest to marinas, such as the **ADMIRAL'S INN**, the **YACHT CLUB**, and the **MAINBRACE PUB** at the Copper & Lumber Store. Casinos at the Royal Antiguan, St. James's Club, in Heritage Quay and at the French Quarter Restaurant on Runaway Bay stay open to the wee hours. No admission is charged.

SPORTS & RECREATION

Bicycling

Rent an 18-speed bicycle for about $85 a week from **Sun Cycles**, Tel. *461-0324.* Five-speeds are also available. For an extra $10, Errol Hodge will drop off and pick up the bicycle outside St. John's. Deliveries in the city are free.

Camping

Close-up nature is the focus of **Katy-K Island Camp Excursions**, which overnight in tents on **Bird Island**. One-and two-night escorted tours start with a look at mangroves and coral reefs en route to the island where participants can aim their binoculars at whistling ducks, wild canaries, frigate birds, and five kinds of lizards. All meals and pick-up at your hotel are included at $160 per night, *Tel. 462-4802.*

Diving

The waters around Barbuda are strewn with wrecks, many of them unexplored. **The Chimney**, off southwest Antigua, is a cave dive in a depth of 60 feet with sponge-filled gullies down to 80 feet. It's filled with parrot fish, moray eels, nurse sharks, and lobsters. **Thunderhead**, just off the west coast, is a boat dive in 35 feet of water where wrecks and artifacts are strewn around the reefs. **Sunken Rock**, a 120-foot dive, is a coral canyon with a steep drop-off roamed be pelagic fish.

Dive operators include **Dockyard Divers**, *Tel. 460-1178 or 464-8591* and **Dive Antigua**, *Tel. 462-3483.*

Fishing

Go deep-sea fishing with *Legend*, *Tel. 462-0256.* a 35-foot Hatteras, *Lobster King*, *Tel. 462-4364*, a 38-foot Bertram, or *Overdraft*, *Tel. 462-0649*, a 40-footer.

Golf

The 18-hole course at the **Cedar Valley Golf Club** is three miles from St. John's, near the airport, *Tel. 462-0161*. The late Ralph Aldridge designed the course to follow the hilly contours of this part of the island. In places, the views of the northern coast are superb. A nine-hole course is at the **Half Moon Bay Hotel**, *Tel. 460-4300*.

Horseback Riding

Stables are at the **St. James's Club**, *Tel. 460-5000* and **Spring Hill Riding Club**, *Tel. 460-2700*.

Sailing

Sail on a picnic, snorkel, or sunset cruise aboard *Jolly Roger Pirate Cruise*, a two-masted schooner, *Tel. 462-2064*. Sailing catamarans offering day sails are **Wadadli Cats**, *Tel. 462-2980* and *Kokomo Cat*, *Tel. 462-7245*.

Tennis & Squash

If your hotel doesn't have tennis courts, **Temo Sports**, *Tel. 460-1781* has floodlit synthetic grass tennis courts and two glass-back squash courts. Squash is also played at the **Bucket Club**, *Tel. 462-3060*. **Curtain Bluff** (see above, *Where to Stay*) has a full-time tennis pro and four championship courts.

Windsurfing

Windsurf Antigua offers equipment and instructions for board sailers novice through expert, *Tel. 462-9463 or 462-0256*.

SHOPPING

Locals selling bead necklaces or offering to plait your hair roam the most popular beaches, and some crafters also sell their wares at the Saturday market. Handy for cruise ship passengers are the shops at **Heritage Quay**, which has such Caribbean stalwarts as **Little Switzerland** and **Columbian Emeralds**. **Islands Arts** is upstairs with a good selection of local and imported art in all genres, *Tel. 462-2787*.

Redcliff Quay, which has restaurants, jewelry, and clothing, is the home of **A Thousand Flowers**, *Tel. 462-4264*, which sells Indonesian sarongs and jewelry and **Base**, where the distinctive resort wear of English designer Steven Giles is sold, *Tel. 462-0920*. **Harmony Hall** at Freetown, Nonsuch Bay, is an art gallery, craft shop, bar and restaurant, *Tel. 460-4120*. It's open daily 10am to 6pm

The Women's Desk Workshop at the corner of High Street at Corn Alley in St. John's sells handmade fashions, crafts, and homespun preserves. Items will be packed and sent for you by **Seaview Pottery** in the village of Seaview, **Cockleshell Pottery** on the west side of St. John's, or **New Antigua Pottery** near the naval base.

EXCURSIONS & DAY TRIPS

Day trips from Antigua to **Barbuda** can be booked through your hotel host. Cost is about $125 to $139 per person including round-trip airfare, a sightseeing tour, a visit to the Frigate Bird Sanctuary, lunch, and pickup at your hotel..

Katy-K Island Camp Excursions, *Tel. 462-4802,* participants spend the night in tents on **Bird Island.** One-and two-night escorted tours start with a look at mangroves and coral reefs en route to the island where visitors can aim their binoculars at whistling ducks, wild canaries, frigate birds, and five kinds of lizards. All meals and pick-up at your hotel are included at $160 per night.

PRACTICAL INFORMATION

Area code: 268

ATM: a 24-hour ATM is in the Royal Bank of Canada, Market and High Streets, St. John's, Antigua.

Currency: the Eastern Caribbean dollar, commonly known as "E.C." is still sometimes referred to here as BeeWee, the old term for British West Indian money. The exchange rate is about EC$2.70 for US$1.

Current: the island uses 220-volt current but some hotels also have 110-volt, 60-cycle outlets. Ask in advance whether the hotel has built-in hair dryers (many do) and what sort of converters you'll need for any appliances you choose to bring.

Government: Antigua and Barbuda are an independent country. U.S. consular service is available through St. John's, Antigua, *Tel. 462-3505.*

Holidays include New Year's Day, Good Friday, Easter and Easter Monday, Labor Day in early May, Whit Monday, Caricom Day in early July, Independence Day on November 1, Christmas, and Boxing Day.

Hours: tourist shops are generally open 9am to 5pm Monday through Saturday, and sometimes longer depending on cruise ship arrivals and departures. Shops frequented by islanders are likely to close early on Thursday.

Immigration: visitors from the United States, Canada, and United Kingdom need a passport or birth certificate plus photo ID. Other visitors must have a passport. Everyone must have a return ticket. You can bring in a quart of liquor and 200 cigarettes.

Language: English is the official language and the everyday tongue as well.

Taxes: departing visitors are charged $12, which can also be paid in EC dollars. A government tax of 8.5 percent is added to hotel bills and seven percent is added to restaurant bills.

Tourist Information: contact Antigua and Barbuda Department of Tourism, *610 Fifth Avenue, Suite 311, New York NY 10020. Tel. 212/541-4117, Fax 757-1607; toll-free (888) 268-4227*, Monday through Friday 9am to 5pm Eastern time.

Weddings: only one (week)day is required to complete formalities through the Department of Legal Affairs, Redcliffe Street, St. John's. Arrive at least one day in advance and be sure to schedule the wedding during the week when offices are open. If you are divorced or widowed, bring original or court-certified divorce or death papers. Fees for the legalities total about $240.

20. MONTSERRAT

They call it the "Caribbean the way it used to be," a gentle world of bright seas and black beaches, gaily painted houses with cockeyed shutters, old stones forming barely-identifiable ruins, and friendly people eager not just for tourism but for settlers, especially retirees, who want to live here.

It is believed that Amerindians settled **Montserrat** about 500 B.C. and lived here until 2500 A.D. Christopher Columbus sighted the island in 1493 but it wasn't colonized until almost 200 years later when Irish settlers, fleeing persecution for their Roman Catholic faith, settled here from St. Kitts. Today, Irish names fill the telephone directory and the shamrock is woven into the fabric of life. Although most of the population is black, they speak English with a brogue. A council is elected locally but the island is a dependency of Britain with a British governor.

It is the hills, forests, rivers and waterfalls that are Montserrat's tourism forte. Lush and verdant, it's said to remind visitors of a tropical Ireland. Temperatures average 86.5 F by day and 73.5 by night winter and summer.

Visitors don't come here for the beaches. Most of them were volcanic black sand even before the 1997 blowup; lighter sand beaches are few and scattered. Come instead for the hiking, climbing, nature watching, history hunting, a bit of shopping, and sunshine days around the hotel swimming pool.

ARRIVALS & DEPARTURES

Connections into Montserrat's **W.H. Bramble Airport** are from such international hubs as San Juan, St. Maarten, and Antigua.. The flight from Antigua is 15 minutes. Service to Montserrat is provided by **LIAT**, *Tel. 664/491-2533*, **Montserrat Airways, Ltd**, *Tel. 664/491-6494* at the airport or, for 24-hour service, *Tel. 491-5342*; and **Winair**, *Tel. 664/491-2713*.

ORIENTATION

Not quite 40 square miles in size and shaped like a dollop of green on a turquoise sea, Montserrat is 167 miles southeast of Puerto Rico and 27 miles southwest of Antigua. Its capital is **Plymouth** on the southwest coast; its airport is on the north coast, eight miles away. It is divided into three parishes: **St. George's, St. Anthony's**, and **St. Peter's**.

GETTING AROUND MONTSERRAT

Distances are short but roads are steep and tortuous, so think twice about renting a car. Taxis meet every flight, and fare to Plymouth is about $12. For sightseeing you'll pay about $12 an hour, which is well worth it. Always agree in advance on a fare and specify whether you're talking American of Eastern Caribbean dollars, which trade at about 2.60 to the dollar. Buses charging EC$2.50 to EC$3 serve almost every settlement.

If you rent a car, your home driver's license won't do here so you'll have to pay EC$30 for a temporary local license at the airport or police station. No international car rental chains are found here; local car hire agencies include:

- **Bennette Roach Realty**, *Tel. 491-3844*
- **Edith's Car Rental**, *Tel. 491-6352*
- **Equipment & Supplies, Ltd.**, *Tel. 491-6602*
- **Ethelyne's Car Rental**, *Tel. 491-2855*
- **Fenco Rentals**, *Tel. 491-2169*
- **Jefferson Car Rental**, *Tel. 491-2126*
- **Montserrat Enterprises Ltd.**, *Tel. 491-2431*

• **Neville Bradshaw Agencies,** *Tel. 491-5270*
• **Pauline's Car Rentals,** *Tel. 491-2345*
• **Reliable Car Rental,** *Tel. 491-6990.*

Rentals cost about $40 daily with air conditioning or $30 without. Jeeps rent for about $45 a day. Gasoline costs about$2.50 a gallon. Bicycles, which are a good way to explore the island, are available from **Island Bikes** in Plymouth, *Tel. 491-4696* or, after hours, *Tel. 491-5552.* Rentals cost about $25 a day or $150 weekly. The company also conducts bicycle tours, races, and overnight tours that include lodgings.

WHERE TO STAY

Contact **Montserrat Tourism,** *Tel. 800/646-2002* for post-volcano hotel information. Because getting here involves at least one secondary flight, most visitors stay for a week or more, usually renting a villa or condo.

International booking agencies for homes, villas, and condos include:
• **Caribbean Villas & Condos,** *Tel. 800/321-3134*
• **Condo Villa World,** *Tel. 800/521-2980*
• **Hideaways,** *Tel. 800/843-4433*
• **McLaughlin Anderson Vacations,** 800/537-6246
• **Villa and Apartments Abroad,** *Tel. 800/433-0444*
• **Villa Holidays,** *Tel. 800/457-4244*
• **VHR Worldwide,** *Tel. 800/633-3284.*

WHERE TO EAT

Again, it will be necessary to get all new information when the current emergency clears. Favorite restaurants in the past have included the **BELHAM VALLEY RESTAURANT** in Old Towne, the **BLUE DOLPHIN** in Parsons, the **EMERALD CAFE** in Wapping, the **EVERGREEN** in downtown Plymouth; **MRS. MORGAN'S** on Airport Road, St. John's, **NIGGY'S BISTRO** in Kinsale, Plymouth, **OASIS** in Wapping, **SPREADEAGLE** on German's Bay, the **VUE POINTE** in the Vue Pointe Hotel in Old Towne and **ZIGGY'S** in Belham Valley.

SPORTS & RECREATION

Dive with **Aquatic Discoveries** at the Vue Pointe Hotel, Box 65, Plymouth, Montserrat, West Indies, *Tel. 664/491-3474, Fax 491-4813* or the **Sea Wolf Diving School**, Strand Street, Box 289, Plymouth, *Tel. 664/491-7807, Fax 491-3599.* Play golf at the **Montserrat Golf Club**, *Tel. 491-5220.* For watersports rentals, contact **Danny's Watersports**, *Tel. 491-5645.*

SHOPPING

Souvenirs of special interest include colorful postage stamps, arts and crafts sold by the Red Cross in the Tourist Information Centre in Plymouth, locally made marine jewelry, batiks, pottery, and works by local artists. The narrow streets of downtown Plymouth, filled with buildings built from ballast stones that came over with settlers centuries ago, are the perfect place to browse from shop to cafe, boutique to gallery.

PRACTICAL INFORMATION

Area Code: 664

ATM: look for Royal Touch machines in the Royal Bank of Canada to accept your MasterCard/Cirrus card.

Banking: banks are generally open 8am to 3pm Monday, Tuesday and Thursday, Wednesday 8am to 2pm and Friday 8am to 5pm. Represented on the island are the Bank of Montserrat, Barclays Bank, the Montserrat Building Society, and the Royal Bank of Canada.

Government: Montserrat is a British Crown Colony. U.S. consular duties are through St. John's, Antigua, Tel. 462-3505. Government offices on the island are generally open Monday through Friday 8am to noon and 1-4pm.

Holidays: bank holidays include New Years Day, Easter and Easter Monday, Whitmonday, the Queen's birthday celebrated the second Saturday in June, August Monday, Christmas, Boxing Day, and New Year's Eve.

Telephones: To arrange a local calling card using your Visa, MasterCard, Discover or American Express cards, call Cable & Wireless, *Tel. 800/877-8000.*

Tourist information: write Medhurst & Associates, Inc., *775 Park Avenue, Huntington NY 11743, Tel. 516/425-0900, Fax 425-0903; toll-free 800/646-2002.* In Canada, write New Concepts Canada, *2455 Cawthra Road, Suite 70, Mississauga, Ontario L5A 3PL, Tel. 905/803-0131, Fax 803-0132, toll-free 800/224-4749.*

Weddings: you'll need three working days (not counting holidays and weekends) to qualify, a birth certificate or passport, and divorce or death certificate if applicable to a previous marriage. The documents must be original and presented with the application form, which can be obtained ahead of time from the Department of Administration, Government Headquarters, Plymouth, Montserrat, West Indies. Applicants under age 18 need parental consent. No medical test is required. If you want to be married in a place other than in the registrar's office or on a yacht one mile or less offshore, permission must be granted by the governor. Local churches require that the bride and groom have three months of religious counseling before the ceremony. It can be coordinated with your home pastor. For a Roman Catholic ceremony, communication must be from your home bishop to the local bishop. Registration costs EC$20 plus EC$200 for a license without the publication of banns; clergy charge no fee but a donation should be offered. If the registrar performs the ceremony, the charge is EC$50 and he'll come aboard a cruise ships for EC$200.

21. NEVIS & ST. KITTS

Today, the tiny twin islands of the **Federation of St. Kitts and Nevis** (combined population 44,000) are a tourism backwater, treasured by travelers who are willing to go the extra mile. Although they were settled in 1623 to become the mother colony for all future English settlement in the Caribbean, the little islands let bulldozers and developers focus elsewhere while they enacted rigid environmental laws to protect their unique beauty.

By law, no structure on these islands can be taller than the palm trees, and that's just the beginning of their tough conservation laws. Vervet monkeys, which were introduced by French colonists centuries ago, outnumber humans by more than two to one. Unexplored shipwrecks number in the hundreds; white-tail deer roam in protected refuges. Even though tourism brings 100,000 people each year to the two islands, they remain sweetly remote, with a minimum of glitz.

Brimstone Hill, fortified with the biggest and best guns in the known world, was known as the Gibraltar of the Caribbean. In the islands, only Haiti's Citadel is larger. Alexander Hamilton was born here and Lord Admiral Horatio Nelson was married in the Federation, so almost every structure claims some real or supposed historic hook. In early records, St. Kitts was identified as St. Christopher but its nickname is now official.

By the time the **Bath Hotel** on Nevis was completed in 1778, it was heralded as the most ambitious structure yet built in the Indies. European and North American health seekers flocked to its 108-degree thermal sulphur springs, which remain today even though the old casino and brothel long ago succumbed. The hotel is being restored.

The first telephone came to the islands in 1890. Mail service to the islands began in 1929, when a young airmail pilot named Charles Lindbergh landed his seaplane parallel to Pinney's Beach.

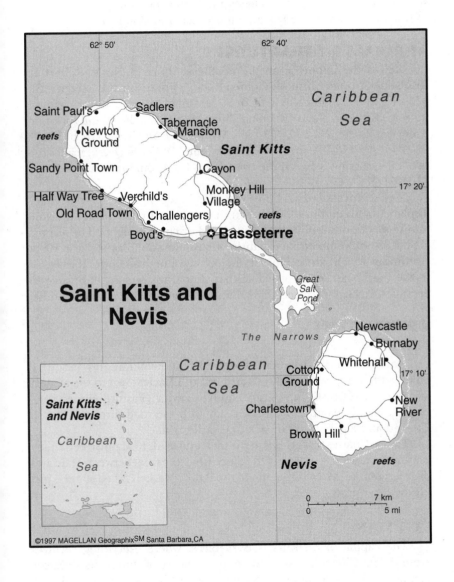

62° 50'   62° 40'

Caribbean
Sea

Saint Paul's•   Sadlers•
reefs   •Newton   •Tabernacle
         Ground   •Mansion
                        Saint Kitts
Sandy Point Town   •Cayon
                              17° 20'
Half Way Tree•   •Verchild's   •Monkey Hill
Old Road Town   •Village
         •Challengers   reefs
    Boyd's•   ✪ Basseterre

**Saint Kitts and
Nevis**
                    Great
                    Salt
                    Pond

         The Narrows   •Newcastle
                         •Burnaby
Caribbean   Cotton•   Whitehall•
Sea   Ground   17° 10'
         Charlestown•   •New
                          River
         Brown Hill•

                    Nevis   reefs

**Saint Kitts
and Nevis**

Caribbean

Sea

0   7 km
0   5 mi

©1997 MAGELLAN GeographixSM Santa Barbara,CA

Climate

Bring your coolest cottons for days in the sunny 90s and nights in the breeze-cooled 60s. The islands do lie in the hurricane belt, where rare storms could bring tropical deluges and high winds, but the usual effect of hurricane season is only a little more rain and cloud cover.

ARRIVALS & DEPARTURES

Newcastle Airport is on the northeast shore of Nevis. Robert L. Bradshaw Airport (formerly Golden Rock) is just north of Basseterre, St. Kitts. Fly into Antigua, San Juan, or St. Martin to catch a connecting flight into St. Kitts or Nevis. Regional lines that serve the islands include American Eagle, *Tel. 800/433-7300*, Winair, *Tel. 869/465-0810;* or LIAT, *Tel. 246/495-1187*. A government ferry, the *MV Caribe Queen*, makes the two-mile crossing between the two islands for a roundtrip fare of about $10, *Tel. 869/469-9373*.

Nevis Express Ltd., *Tel. 869/469-9755/6*, flies nine- and 18-passenger airplanes between Nevis and St. Kitts half a dozen times daily. The airline also serves 32 other islands on scheduled or charter flights. The airport at St. Kitts will complete an expansion that almost doubles its size in 1998. Its runway, which can land the largest jets day or night, is one of the largest in the Caribbean so it's probable that your travel agent will be able to arrange a much more direct flight than has been announced at press time.

ORIENTATION
NEVIS

Nevis, which rises to a 3,232-foot peak at its center, is only 36 square miles, with a ring road leading north out of **Charlestown** to the airport and around Newcastle Bay to turn south to Taylor's Pasture where a road cuts off to the sea at Red Cliff. Or stay with the road through Church Ground and Fig Tree, then back to Charlestown.

Prince Charles Street ends at the pier, and leads to Main Street, which is the chief downtown street. Off Prince Charles Street between Main and the pier, Market Street is the site of the Public Market. A taxi stand is just off the ferry pier.

ST. KITTS

The capital of St. Kitts is **Basseterre**, where everything revolves around The Circus, a traffic circle in the heart of things. Its Berkeley Memorial Clock is a popular meeting spot and landmark, surrounded by shops and restaurants. Just south of The Circus, Independence Square anchors the city layout, bounded on one side by the Cathedral. The airport lies just north of Basseterre.

Old-timers may be saddened to learn that the Southeast Peninsula on St. Kitts is no longer unreachable by road. Sir Timothy Hill has been tamed and the Dr. Kennedy Simmonds Highway opened. It's now possible to drive the edge of the island from Basseterre on a circular route, or take Simmonds Highway to the southeast coast, then backtrack. On the plus side, the peninsula remains a windswept wilderness. At this writing, none of the announced resorts has been built. The island has one basic, ring road (except for the spur to the peninsula), so just stick with it and you'll end up back in the capital.

FEDERATION ETIQUETTE

Short-shorts, swim wear and bare chests are not acceptable in public places. Wear beach clothes only on the beach. Men in business usually wear shirt and tie. Slangy "hi" or even "hello" aren't used as commonly here as the more formal "Good morning (afternoon, evening)", especially when you are addressing older people.

GETTING AROUND NEVIS & ST. KITTS

The two islands are separated by a two mile strait, which can be traversed with a six-minute air taxi ride or a 45-minute ride aboard *M.V. Caribe Queen.* Schedules vary, with two to four round trips a day except Thursday and Saturday, when the ferry does not run.

Taxi and tour fares are set and straightforward, published in the free tourist paper *St. Kitts and Nevis Visitor.* Within Basseterre, taxi fares at press time are $3, with $1 additional for each 15 minutes of wait time. Luggage in excess of two bags costs 50 cents per piece. Between 11pm and 6am, cabs add a surcharge of 25 percent. From Basseterre's Bradshaw International Airport, cab fares range from $5 to the closest points to $22 to Mount Pleasant and $48 to South Friars Bay. Confirm the charges before you start out.

Car rentals are available from **Sunshine Car Rental**, *Tel. 465-8651, extension 707;* in the U.S. and Canada, *Tel. 800/621-1270.* Free airport pickup and delivery is included, and clients will also be given a free city tour. Sunshine also books guided tours, horseback riding, air charter, and diving. Car rentals are also available from **Avis**, *Tel. 465-6507,* **Delisle Walwyn**, *Tel. 465-8449,* and **TDC Rentals**, *Tel. 465-2991* or use the courtesy phone at the St. Kitts airport. Ask about splitting your rental, with some days on St. Kitts and others on Nevis, and you can still get a weekly or monthly rate. A local driver's license costs $12; your hometown license won't do. Rentals cost $35-$50 a day.

WHERE TO STAY

Hotel tax on Nevis is seven percent; service charges of 10 percent are usually added to bills in lieu of tipping. Credit cards are accepted at hotels except where noted. Rates quoted are for a double room in high season. Summer rates are far less.

NEVIS

Expensive

FOUR SEASONS RESORT NEVIS, Box 565, Charlestown, Nevis. Tel. 869/469-1111; Fax 469-1111; U.S. 800/332-3442; Canada 800/268-6282. Rates for the 196 rooms and suites start at $575 for a double; suites to $3150 nightly for a three-bedroom luxury suite. For $60 additional per person, your flight into St. Kitts will be met by an air conditioned van. You'll then be spirited by launch to the resort's private pier on Nevis. If you fly into Nevis' small airport, it is 15 minutes, or about $12 by taxi, to the resort. For breakfast and dinner daily, add $80 per person or $40 for children ages 4-11. Rates and meals are plus 17 percent tax and service charge.

The esteemed AAA Five Diamond rating has consistently been bestowed on this regal resort, one of the most elegant in the islands. Designers have focused on modern musts: room safes, 24-hour room service, marble baths with separate showers, a washer-dryer in every bungalow, television sets with remote control, mini-bar refrigerators, extra-spacious rooms, screened porches, and direct-dial telephones. Then they surrounded the units with tropical plantings and let a seasoned, caring staff of 450 do the rest.

Robert Trent Jones, Jr., designed the championship golf course. You can bring your own clubs but don't bother – Callaways are available for rent. Bring a dozen balls; the ones you lost will be sold back to you at the end of the tenth hole by local children. The Tennis Centre has ten floodlit courts but play is so popular here that in-the-know tourists call well ahead to reserve court time. Swim in the ocean (no lifeguards) or in two seaside swimming pools. The beach is a lollapalooza that goes on for 2,000 feet. It's filled with a fun fleet of sail and pedal boats and board sailers; snorkel gear is available. Water skiing and scuba diving can be scheduled. The fitness center has sauna and whirlpool plus the latest workout equipment. Use of the exercise equipment and non-motorized watersports gear is complimentary.

Drink in the pubby ambience of the Tap Room. Dining is in the Cabana, Clubhouse, or Grill or Dining rooms, which offer the same dinner menus. Try the duck breast with mushrooms and spinach. Room service is always available too.

Children ages 3-9 have their own dining and games at any time of year, with nannies on hand at no added charge. The resort has a nice mix of ages, genders, and nationalities. Dress is informal, but tees and sandals aren't appropriate after sundown. At dinner, gentlemen should wear long trousers and closed shoes, but forget jackets and ties. Dining areas have ceiling fans, but not air conditioning.

THE HERMITAGE, *St. John Figtree Parish, Nevis. Tel. 869/469-3477, Fax 469-2481; U.S. and Canada 800/223-9832. Room rates in this 14-room resort start at $235. From the airport, it's a half-hour cab ride costing about $20. A meal supplement costs $45 per person daily for breakfast and dinner.*

Yet another hilltop plantation has been preserved and turned into an intimate inn favored by international jet setters and Hollywood elite. The key word is home-like, with books everywhere and a wealth of Victorian touches. Rooms have been individually decorated and are all different, but all have shower, ceiling fan, a private balcony or terrace, four-poster canopy bed, and an electric kettle for brewing morning coffee or tea. Some of the units have kitchenettes.

Meals are served under a trellis on the veranda. Swim in the pool or find entertainments in the TV room and bookshelves. A van shuttles guests to the beach. Horseback riding can be arranged, or take a romantic carriage ride. One evening a week, a local group comes in to serenade a buffet of traditional West Indies dishes.

HURRICANE COVE BUNGALOWS, *Oualie Beach, Nevis. Tel. 465-9462. Rates range from $145 nightly for a one-bedroom bungalow to $395 for a three-bedroom unit with private pool. A cab ride from the airport takes less than 10 minutes.*

Built for privacy and grand views of the beach, these cottages cluster around freshwater pools. Every maid-serviced unit has a fully furnished kitchen, which can be provisioned from nearby shops. Natural woods and Caribbean artwork decorate pleasant, airy rooms. Golf, tennis, restaurants, and shops are also nearby. For stays longer than two weeks, a discount applies.

GOLDEN ROCK ESTATE, *Box 493, Gingerland, Nevis. Tel. 869/469-3346; Fax 469-2113; U.S. and Canada 800/223-9832. Rates at this 15-room inn start at under $200 double, with a meal plan available. A taxi from the airport costs about $20 for the 30-minute ride.*

Getting here is half the fun – Not. However, *being* here is well worth the long climb up a rutted hillside to break out into this aloof aerie 1,000 feet above the ocean. The estate was founded in the 1700s to plant sugar cane, but today its outbuildings are transformed into quaint bungalows swathed in mango trees and bowers of flowers. The original cut-stone sugar windmill is now the honeymoon suite, ideal for newlyweds or for families of up to four. Ask about family packages, which include a learning vacation.

Hike high into the rain forest if you like, send your post cards home from the tiny, bright blue post office at Dieppe Bay, or just lounge in the gazebo catching up on your reading. Rambling English gardens grace the grounds, which are alight with flowering shrubs roamed by chattering monkeys. Swim in the pool, or take the bus shuttle to town, beach and restaurants. Have a drink in the bar, then have dinner on the garden porch of the old mansion. The cuisine is continental, usually starring local lobster (try the homemade bread stuffed with lobster), mango, bananas, "pumpkin" or fish. Meals are extra, except for tea, which features homemade banana bread and is included in the rates.

MONTPELIER PLANTATION INN, *Box 474, Nevis. Tel. 869/469-3462; Fax 469-2932; U.S. and Canada 800/223-9832. Rates at this 16-unit hotel start at $330 including breakfast. A taxi from the airport costs about $20 for the 30-minute ride.*

Once a Great House for one of the island's estates, this fine little hotel in the green foothills has 100 acres of grounds and 16 acres of lovingly groomed gardens. As comfortable as an old house slipper, it blends the prim comforts of an English country house with the rich history of an old sugar plantation.

You'll be accommodated in a cozy bungalow furnished with coffee maker and ceiling fan, your own patio, and either a shower or tub and shower. Take breakfast, luncheon, tea and your 8pm candlelight dinner in the breezy covered patio. In season there's dancing after dinner. The hotel doesn't accept children under age 8, and it closes in late summer.

A tennis coach is on property to help you make the best of the resort's courts. There's a swimming pool at the base of a centuries-old windmill; transportation to a private, picture-postcard beach is free.

MOUNT NEVIS HOTEL & BEACH CLUB, *Shaws Road, Newcastle, P.O. Box 494, Charlestown. Tel. 469-9373, Fax 469-9375; U.S. and Canada 800/742-4276 or 800/756-3847. Rates at this 32-unit resort start at $190 for a deluxe twin with patio; two-bedroom suites with kitchen start at $460. All rates include continental breakfast. The hotel is a 20-minute ride from Charlestown and five minutes from Newcastle Airport.*

From this perch on Round Hill Estate, you can see forever. Rooms are air conditioned and have cathedral ceilings, telephone, and cable television. Breakfast, lunch, and romantic dinners are served in the hotels' restaurant, known for its Caribbean and continental recipes including a pizza that has locals calling this Pizza Beach. The restaurant is open for lunch and dinner daily except Wednesday.

Swim in the 60-foot freshwater pool, ride horseback, fly a kite (they're provided), take a nature hike, or book golf or tennis nearby. The hotel's beach club is a five-minute ride down the hill on the free shuttle.

Watersports equipment is at hand; scuba diving, snorkeling, and deep sea fishing excursions can be arranged. The ruins of 200-year-old Cottle Church are on the family-owned resort, so be sure to do some exploring on your own.

NISBET PLANTATION BEACH CLUB, *St. James Parish, Nevis, West Indies. Tel. 869/469-9325, Fax 469-8964, U.S. and Canada 800/842-6008. Rates at this 38-unit resort start at $365 per couple in high season, including breakfast and dinner.*

An 18th century sugar plantation sets the scene for this unpretentious but elegant cluster of cottages plus the original Great House, now the restaurant. It was here that Fanny Nisbet, who married Horatio Nelson after William Nisbet died, ruled as mistress of the house. Spacious rooms are bathed in light with cool, white walls, fabrics in island colors, and straw mats over tile flooring.

Open-handed hospitality here includes a weekly rum punch party, afternoon tea daily, laundry service, postage for your postcards, and local telephone calls. Play croquet on the lawn, claim one of the hammocks hanging under the majestic palm trees, or snorkel off the wide, white sand beach. There's also a pool and tennis courts on property, and an 18-hole Robert Trent Jones, Jr. golf course a few minutes away. The hotel can also arrange scuba diving, horseback riding, sailing or sport fishing for you.

Breakfasts and dinners, which are included, favor British tastes for porridge, kippers and crumpets, with lots of selections for those who prefer omelets, yogurt with cereal, or a continental plate of cheeses and cold cuts. A Plantation Beach specialty is Nevisian banana pancakes, and there's Nevis honey for your pancakes or toast. Each day also brings a new breakfast specialty such as saltfish with johnny cakes, beans on toast, or waffles with strawberries.

OLD MANOR ESTATE & HOTEL, *P.O. Box 70, Charlestown. Tel. 469-3445, Fax 469-3388; U.S. 800/892-7093. Rates start at $195 including continental breakfast. A taxi from the airport costs about $20 for the 30-minute ride.*

Dating to 1690, this old sugar plantation has been newly refurbished to provide charming lodgings in the foothills of Mount Nevis. Have cocktails on the veranda overlooking neighboring islands, then dine in the legendary Cooperage. The hotel has a freshwater pool, a boutique selling original jewelry and art, and tennis courts. Horseback rides, tours, and other adventures can be arranged. A shuttle takes guests to the beach and town.

Moderate

OUALIE BEACH HOTEL, *Oualie Beach, Nevis. Tel. 800/682-5431, Fax 869/469-9176. Rates at this 22-room resort start at $135. The resort is only ten minutes from the airport. Deluxe and studio rooms with kitchen rate to $255.*

Big game fishing is the focus here during the annual Nevis Fishing Tournament each October and the energy lasts all year. Snorkel, fish for wahoo and mahi-mahi, scuba dive with the hotel's custom dive boat, sail a Sunfish or sail board, or work out on a Skimmer rowing machine.

More than half the rooms are in the Deluxe category with marble vanities, air conditioning, cable television, direct dial telephone, electronic safe, hair dryer, mini-bar refrigerator, four-poster canopy beds and a screened veranda facing the sunset. It's charmingly Caribbean, housed in colorful gingerbread cottages right on the beach. Children under age 12 sleep free in their parents' room; cribs are cheerfully supplied, and kids can order from their own menu in the dining room. The restaurant is especially popular on Saturday nights, when a Nevisian string band accompanies a thumping carnival masquerade.

ST. KITTS
Expensive

OTTLEY'S PLANTATION INN, *P.O. Box 345, St. Kitts. Tel. 869/465-7234, Fax 869/465-4760, U.S. 800/772-3039. Rates start at $250 including breakfast and dinner.*

Designated a AAA Four-Diamond property, this hillside resort on the site of an 18th century sugar plantation claims 35 verdant acres set with lawns and tropical gardens. The freshwater pool is spring fed; the restaurant is in what was once the sugar boiling house. Oversize, air conditioned guest rooms have a South Seas look: wicker furniture accented with antiques, ceiling fans, and muted fabrics bathed in light. A shuttle runs to the black sand beach. From here, venture out to shop or to hike the rain forest with its Green Vervet monkeys.

SUN 'N SAND BEACH RESORT, *P.O. Box 341, Basseterre, St. Kitts. Tel. 465-8037; Fax 465-6745; U.S. 800/621-1270; Canada 800/424-5500. Rates start at $160 for a studio apartment. Add $35 per person and $25 per child under age 12 for Modified American Plan (breakfast and dinner).*

Five acres of Atlantic beachfront are filled with gardens set with cottages, which have two bedrooms, and studio apartments, which can sleep one to three people. The resort has two tennis courts, a children's pool, beach-side restaurant, and an ice cream parlor. In the mini-mart are provisions, banking, and gift shopping; an 18-hole golf course is next door. Because this resort is on the Atlantic side, there's more surf and spume than on the Caribbean side, a plus to some visitors and a minus for those who prefer a quieter beach.

Moderate

BIRD ROCK BEACH HOTEL, *P.O. Box 227, Basseterre, St. Kitts. Tel. 465-8914 or 800/621-1270. Rates start at $140. Cab fare from the airport to the hotel, which is about two miles southeast of Basseterre, is about $7.*

"We didn't develop Bird Rock with diving as our goal" admits owner-manager Larkland Richards, "but from the outset of scuba diving, clients have raved about a fabulous rock and coral reef teeming with marine life just off our beach." So the hotel became a base of operations to St. Kitts Scuba, Ltd, a PADI and NAUI certified dive and watersports company.

The hotel is high above its own, 200-foot, half-moon beach near the deepwater port where cruise ships dock. Each suite has two bedrooms, one with a king-size bed and the other with two beds. Units also have two baths and a full kitchen. Each room has views to the southeast and northwest. When you're not cooking in your own kitchen, eat in the hotel's three restaurants. Swim in the freshwater pool, play tennis, book a tour through the front office, or outfit in the resort's own dive shop.

FORT THOMAS HOTEL & RESORT, *P.O. Box 407, Basseterre, St. Kitts. Tel. 465-2695, Fax 465-7518; 800/851-7818. Located within walking distance of Barreterre, the hotel is a $7 taxi ride from the airport. Room tariffs start at $110.*

Air-conditioned rooms gaze out over a commanding view of the sea and mountains, with Nevis in the distance. A shuttle takes you to the beach, or just stay in the hills to enjoy the swimming pool, lawn and table tennis, poolside bar, pizza and ice cream parlor, and steak and seafood grill. The mood is lively, with early Happy Hour on Fridays and frequent events such as beauty pageants and trade shows. As a result, the hotel is as popular with locals as with tourists, creating a nice blend of both.

FRIGATE BAY RESORT, *P.O. Box 137, Basseterre, St. Kitts. Tel. 465-8935, Fax 465-7050; U.S. 800/266-2185. Rooms start at $123; a meal plan that covers breakfast and lunch costs $35 per person and $27 per child daily. Taxi fare from the airport is about $10.*

Guests at this resort play free at the nearby Royal St. Kitts golf course. Air conditioned rooms overlook Frigate Bay, where most of the big, new hotels are found. Here, at the waist of the island, it's not more than a half mile walk from the Atlantic to the Caribbean. Suites are available with kitchen and one or two bedrooms. All have color television and a private balcony or patio. The decor, understated and mellow with its tiles and happy prints, whispers West Indian.

Dine in the resort's locally popular Garden Room, swim in the pool with its swim-up bar, browse the shop, or have the hotel arrange a baby sitter while you plan an adults-only outing in Basseterre, five minutes away by car. The beach is a short stroll away, and there's a big pool.

JACK TAR VILLAGE, *P.O. Box 406, Frigate Bay, St. Kitts. Tel. 465-8651; Fax 465-1031; U.S. 800/999-9182. All-inclusive rates at this 244-unit resort start at $210 single. Add $160 for a couple and another $150 for a triple. A taxi ride from the airport costs about $10.*

Unless you splurge on telephone calls and shopping, or drop a bundle in the casino, this resort will spring few budget surprises. Everything is included in one rate – your air conditioned room, meals, cocktails, drinks, sports, entertainment, tennis, bicycles, and a beach shuttle are all paid in one rate. Because it's on a narrow strip of seagirt land, you're a five-minute walk from the Atlantic and a 10-minute bicycle ride from the Caribbean. The resort also overlooks Lake Zuiliani.

Meals are served in a choice of restaurants, with food available at one or more places from 6:30am to 1am. Choose between two swimming pools, put the children in the kiddy club for ages 4-12, or go fishing from shore in the lagoon. This all-inclusive resort has the only casino in the Federation. Baby sitting or island excursions can be arranged at added cost.

As long-time Jack Tar fans, we've seen them in both up and down periods, so we recommend getting current recommendations before you book. When layoffs and other labor problems occur, service slips.

OCEAN TERRACE INN, *Box 65, Basseterre, St. Kitts. Tel. 465-2754; Fax 465-1057; U.S. 800/524-0512. From the airport it is a $6 cab ride to this resort near the city center across from the Fort Thomas Hotel. Rates start at $93.*

Air conditioned rooms at what locals call OTI have 13-channel color television. One-and two-bedroom apartments have complete kitchens. Take a seaview room with a private patio then walk to Basseterre's shops and sites. Enjoy the two pools and Jacuzzi or sign up for trips down to the ocean for dinghy sailing, deep sea fishing, scuba diving or snorkeling. A shuttle is also run to Turtle Beach on the peninsula. Return to one of the two bars for a sundowner before dinner in the inn's own West Indian restaurant. The steel band that plays here on Friday nights is one of the best in the islands.

SUN'N'SAND BEACH RESORT, *Box 341, Basseterre, St. Kitts. Worldwide Toll-free Tel. 800/223-6510 or 800/582-6208, Fax 869/465-6745. Rates start at $270 for a two-bedroom cottage or $160 for two in a studio apartment. Located in the Frigate Bay area, the 68-unit resort is about 15 minutes from the airport.*

Sprawled over five sun-drenched beach acres on a picturesque bay, the resort offers air conditioning, kitchenettes, cable television, and telephones. Its two tennis courts are lit for night play; an 18-hole golf course is within walking distance.

Budget
> **CENTRAL GUESTHOUSE & APARTMENTS**, *Central Market Street, Basseterre, St. Kitts. Tel. 465-2278 days or 465-4062 evenings.* In the heart of town, the guesthouse is a $5 taxi ride from the airport. Rates start at $25. If you want only a simple room within walking distance of the town's restaurants, shops, and sights, this is an affordable address.

WHERE TO EAT
> Most hotel and tourist shops list their prices in U.S. dollars, but restaurant menus are more likely to show prices in E.C. dollars. Restaurants that cater to tourists list both.

NEVIS
Expensive
> **CLIFFDWELLERS**, *Tamarind Bay. Tel. 469-0262 or 5195. Reservations are requested; entrees range from EC $45 to $70. The restaurant is open only during the winter season.*

Ride the hillside tram to the heights where this restaurant has one of the most spectacular settings in the Caribbean, with panoramic views and breathtaking sunsets. Plan your arrival to coincide with cocktails at sundown.

> **FOUR SEASONS RESORT**, *Pinney's Beach. Tel. 469-1111. Entrees range from EC $75 to $110. Both restaurants in the resort are open daily. It is just north of Charlestown. Reservations are recommended, especially in winter.*

You don't have to be a guest at this five-start resort to dine here in the rich, mahogany-accented dining room or in the sunny, informal Grill Room. Much praised are such dishes as grilled swordfish and crispy fried onion and tomato jam or the conch fritters with spicy mango relish. Order a freshly grilled burger or steak, the catch of the day, or homemade baked goods then stroll the grounds for awesome view of Pinney's Beach.

> **THE HERMITAGE INN**, *Gingerland. Tel. 469-3477. The inn is open for breakfast lunch and dinner every day. Reservations are urged, especially in winter. Breakfast and lunch prices start at EC $13; dinner is a fixed price of EC $94.*

Richard and Maureen Lupinacci came to Nevis from Pennsylvania to open an inn surrounded by gardens and known for its hospitality. Their West Indian specialties have a knowing touch but they haven't forgotten how to turn out a great steak.

> **MISS JUNE'S CUISINE**, *Jones Bay. Tel. 469-5330. Reservations are essential at this private home, where diners are welcomed three times a week. Jones Bay is north of Charlestown just south of Oualie Beach. Figure EC$60-70.*

Put yourself in a private house party where you'll assemble at 7:15-7:30 for cocktails hosted by Miss June's son, Darrell. She'll then beckon you to her dining room where linen-clad tables have been set for eight or ten. You'll drink wine from crystal glasses and sample delicious cuisine from fine china plates. Miss June might decide on an Asian, Caribbean, or Continental evening or a deft blending of cuisines from her extensive repertoire. The evening ends with coffee, liqueurs, brandy and port, all included in the price.

MOUNT NEVIS RESTAURANT, *in the Mount Nevis Hotel, Shaws Road, Newcastle. Tel. 469-9373. The hotel is 20 minutes from Charlestown and five minutes from the airport. Plan to spend $40 per person for dinner. The restaurant is open daily 8am to 10pm but is closed Sunday evenings. Reservations are essential.*

Caribbean haute cuisine describes the West Indian-continental creations of chef Jeff DeBarbieri, who trained at New York's Tavern on the Green and served as sous-chef at Fiorello's at Lincoln Center. The dining room is a breezy patio furnished with white wicker and overlooking the pool. Tables are clothed in peach linen; servings arrive on fine china. Start with a goat cheese appetizer fragrant with a slab of freshly grilled portabello mushroom or the lobster wontons with ginger-soy dipping sauce followed by fresh snapper in herbs, pork tenderloin with tamarind-mango chutney and mashed breadfruit, or a delicate pasta tossed with smoked chicken and roasted vegetables. For dessert have the creme brulée, which is spiced with cinnamon, allspice, nutmeg, and spice liqueur. The dress code is island formal, which means a shirt with sleeves and collar, long trousers, and closed shoes. Arrive before sunset so you can have a drink overlooking the sea and neighboring St. Kitts.

NISBET PLANTATION BEACH CLUB, *Newcastle. Tel. 469-9325. Reservations are essential; main courses start at EC $120. Meals including afternoon tea are served every day.*

The Great House of a legendary plantation offers dinner in a room that echoes with history. Fanny Nisbet, you'll remember, is the Nevis widow who won the heart of British naval hero Admiral Horatio Nelson. There's almost always some special entertainment or other event going on here, so call to ask what's happening. The menu will be a mixture of Creole and continental, elegantly presented.

Moderate

GOLDEN ROCK ESTATE BEACH BAR & RESTAURANT, *Pinney's Beach. Tel. 469-0549. Located halfway between Charlestown and the Four Seasons, the restaurant is open daily except Sunday, 11:30am to 3:30pm Prices range from EC $13.50 to $50.*

A favorite lunch spot after a day of shopping or touring, this informal restaurant offers charcoal grilled seafood and burgers, cold salads, and

hearty sandwiches. It's also locally popular for cocktails and sunset viewing.
OUALIE BEACH RESTAURANT, *Oualie Beach. Tel. 469-9735. The restaurant is open daily for breakfast, lunch and dinner, 7am to 10pm Reservations are recommended for dinner.*
You'll be seated right at the beach in this friendly hotel. Saturday is Caribbean Night with a Nevisian string band and a masked carnival troupe dancing to traditional cadences.

Budget
MOUNT NEVIS BEACH CLUB, *Newcastle. Tel. 469-9395. The restaurant, which is on the northern end of the island, is open for lunch and dinner daily except Wednesday.*
This beachy hangout overlooking Newcastle Bay prides itself on its pizza, which is available with a big selection of toppings..
MURIEL'S, *Upper Happy Hill Drive, Charlestown. Tel. 469-5920. It's open daily except Sunday for lunch and supper.*
Just one street back from the main street, this is the place for fried bananas, rice and beans with spicy jerk chicken, sweet potatoes, and other native fare served in a comfortably plain eatery.
EDDY'S BAR AND RESTAURANT, *Main Street, Charlestown. Tel. 469-5958. Eat for under $15. Hours vary seasonally, so call ahead.*
Happy Hour drinks are half price, usually on Wednesday when you also get free conch fritters and other nibbles with your daily ration of rum. You'll dine outside on a breeze porch overlooking the city. Try the cream of cauliflower soup, seafood curry, snapper with tomatoes and capers, stir-fried chicken and vegetables, or one of the grilled meats or fish. The decor is splashy with island colors. If you like the hot sauce, which is on the table for use on almost everything, buy it at the local supermarket. It's made by Eddy's mother.

ST. KITTS
Expensive
THE BALLYHOO, *The Circus, Basseterre. Tel. 465-4197. Reservations are advised. Plan to spend EC$16 to $55 for a dinner main course. The restaurant serves breakfast, lunch and dinner daily except Sunday, 8am to 10pm.*
Overlooking The Circus, which is the historic center of town and indeed of the island, this restaurant is the place to see and be seen. It's best known for its fresh, locally netted seafood, but you'll find a good selection of other West Indian and international favorites including American steaks and vegetarian dishes.

BIRD ROCK BEACH RESORT, *Bird Rock. Tel. 465-8914. The restaurant is open daily 7am to 10pm and is about a $7 taxi ride from Basseterre. Main dishes are in the EC $30-$45 price range.*

Continental specialties are served in an open air setting. Have a steak, chop, chicken in wine, or one of the daily specials depending on what the fishing boats brought in.

FISHERMAN'S WHARF, *Fortlands. Tel. 465-2754. Open daily from 7pm, the restaurant charges in the EC $45 range for Main dishes. Find it just west of Basseterre.*

The sea is the decor, surf sounds the music in this uncomplicated outdoor eatery on the harbor. The grill is always going for burgers and fresh fish, and the side dishes are on a small buffet. Views of the town and foothills are eyecatching, and there's live entertainment from time to time.

LEMON GRASS, *in the Fort Thomas Hotel & Resort, Fortlands. Tel. 465-2695. Located just west of Basseterre, the restaurant is open daily 7am to 10pm. Main dishes are priced EC $20 to $68 but light fare costs much less.*

If you're not staying at the Fort Thomas Hotel, here's an excuse to ramble the majestic site with its lush gardens and old cannons. Sit in a private gazebo to order fresh local seafood or take a light lunch in the pizza and ice cream parlor.

FRIGATE BAY RESORT, *on Frigate Bay. Tel. 465-8935. Dinner entrees are priced EC $35 to $55. The restaurant is a $10 cab ride from the airport and is open daily from 7:30am to 9:30pm.*

Enjoy anything from a West Indian breakfast to a light lunch or sumptuous dinner in a cool and pleasant resort. Have a drink first in the poolside bar, then one of the theme night buffets with matching entertainment. Themes could range from Carnival to Italian, but you can count on having a whale of a good time and plenty of good food..

OCEAN TERRACE INN, *Fortlands. Tel. 465-2754. The inn is open daily 7am to 9:30pm, serving entrees from EC $48, a table d'hote menu from EC $40, and lobster dinners at EC $53. Dinner reservations are recommended.*

Dine in a quiet room on a balcony overlooking the bay or on the breezy patio with its panoramic view. On Wednesdays there's an à la carte menu, fashion show, and steel band. Every other Friday night, there's a West Indian buffet with barbecued game hens on alternate Fridays. The poolside brunch on Sunday starts at noon. OTI, as some people call the inn, also operates Turtle Beach on the southeast peninsula where lunches are served seaside.

ROYAL PALM RESTAURANT *in Ottley's Plantation Inn, Ottley's. Tel. 465-7234. Ottley's is an a $9 cab ride from the airport. Entrees are priced EC $22 to $48. The restaurant is open daily; reservations are essential for dinner and brunch and are recommended for lunch.*

It's always an adventure to dine here because Chef Pamela Yahn has an a new culinary specialty every day in a style she calls New Island. While you dine, look out through ancient stone archwork to the sea on one side and Mount Liamigua and the Great House on the other. **STONEWALLS**, *Princes Street, Basseterre. Tel. 465-5248. The restaurant is open Monday through Saturday, 5pm to 11pm but is closed Saturday and Sunday June through October. Dinner reservations are recommended. Cross the street from Ballyhoos and find it on the left, about 2/3 of the way down the block.*

Succulent lobster in season, creative Creole and Cajun, fabulous ribs, and steadfastly Caribbean foods star in this popular garden. Seek out the stone walls in an a hidden corner of the historic zone only an a few footsteps from The Circus. It's a popular gathering place for locals as well as tourists, casual yet chic with its bar, innovative food, and live music. **TRINITY POOLSIDE BAR & RESTAURANT**, *Palmetto Point. Tel. 465-3226. The restaurant is about an a $5 taxi ride from the city. Hours vary seasonally, so call ahead.*

Bring your swim suit because diners are welcome to take a dip in the pool before ordering from an array of soups, salads, and sandwiches. Lobster and prawns are house specialties.

Moderate

COCONUT CAFE, *in the Timothy Beach Resort. Tel. 465-3020. Entrees can go as high as EC $50 but snacks, salads and burgers are in the EC $8 to $16 range. The cafe is open every day 7am to 11pm. A cab from the airport or Basseterre costs about $7 for up to four people.*

Splurge on grilled lobster or charcoal-broiled red snapper, or just get an a big, juicy fishburger and a salad. The spot is especially popular on Sunday nights for its Calypso buffet and its Sea Island B.B.Q. on Wednesdays but frequent visitors complain that sometimes both the food and the bands aren't up to snuff, especially on Sundays. Take an a waterfront table with a drink or a cup of coffee, and scope it out.

THE COOPERAGE, *in the Old Manor Estate & Hotel, Gingerland. Tel. 469-3445. Entrees start at EC $40. Reservations are recommended; the restaurant is open daily for breakfast, lunch, and dinner from 8am until the last order is taken at 9:30pm.*

There's a wonderful view of the Gingerland hills and surrounding sea from the terrace of this old sugar plantation. Favorites include steaks, grilled lobster, veal and lamb and the fresh catches of the day. Old Manor also operates the Beachcomber on Pinney's Beach, with shuttles running between the beach and the Manor. Grilled lobster and chicken are the order of the day. The covered porch here is popular for sundowners, lunch, and al fresco dining.

JACK TAR VILLAGE BEACH RESORT & CASINO, *Frigate Bay. Tel. 465-8651. The resort is a $10 cab ride from the airport.*

Call ahead to buy a day or evening pass to the resort with its all-inclusive meals and bar and its fast casino action.

THE LIGHTHOUSE RESTAURANT, *Deep Water Port Road. Tel. 465-0739 is open daily for lunch and dinner, and on Sunday for brunch. Entrees are in the EC$25 range and the hotel is an $8 cab ride from the airport.*

International dishes are served in a stunning, cliffside setting overlooking the city and harbor. This is the place for late and "lite" on weekends, lunch or dinner any time, and a pleasant Sunday brunch.

PJ'S BAR & RESTAURANT, *Frigate Bay. Tel. 465-8373. Entrees range from EC $15 to $50. The restaurant is closed Monday and is open other days from 10am.*

The whole wheat and French breads are homemade. So are the meat and cheese raviolis and made-to-order pizzas. For the vegetarian there are meatless pizzas and pastas. Mile-high sandwiches are made with the homemade bread.The eatery also has a bar that is popular with ex-pats and yachties, who gather here to watch big sporting events on television. Call ahead, and your pizza will be ready for take-out.

VILLAGE RESTAURANT *in the Sun 'n Sand Beach Resort, North Frigate Bay. Tel. 465-8037. Lunch prices start at EC $9; dinner prices are EC $20 to $50. Cab fare from the airport is $10; the restaurant is open daily 8am to 10pm.*

If you're due for a great burger, this is the place. Salads are as fresh as the seafood. The Mexican pizza is internationally famous.

MAMMOTH PINEAPPLES

Sugary pineapples weighing up to eight pounds have been introduced to St. Kitts and Nevis from the Republic of China and they are catching on as a crop. Make sure you get a taste of two varieties, Tainung No. 4 and Kain.

SEEING THE SIGHTS
NEVIS

Sightseeing in Nevis begins at the Department of Tourism Office on Main Street in **Charlestown**. Native crafts are sold in the area, so stock up on honey, hot sauces, and homemade chutneys. An ancient synagogue, the oldest in the Caribbean, is being worked by archaeologists who will usually show visitors around.

Just up Government Road, the old **Jewish Cemetery** is mostly just lawns and whitewashed fence. Most of the grave stones are gone.

One of the most exciting things about the 17th century synagogue that is still undergoing archaeological study here is that is was discovered only recently when David Robinson, curator of the **Nevis Historical and Conversation Society**, found the door of an old tool shed ajar, and stepped in. When he saw the stone columns and balanced arches inside, he knew he had discovered the "lost temple." It predates Curacao's temple, long touted as the Caribbeans' oldest, by almost 100 years. Nothing is formalized for tourists, but ask about it at the museums. If a dig is going on, you'll be welcome to have a look.

From town, head north and you'll pass **Pinney's Beach** with the fabulous Four Seasons Resort, then Nelson's Spring where Horatio Nelson came from Antigua for his water supplies. Continuing north you'll pass **Oualie Beach** and **Newcastle Bay** – all beaches are public here, even those at swank resorts – before the road turns south towards Brick Kiln. **St. James Anglican Church** near the village dates to the 1600s and has one of the few black crucifixes in the Caribbean.

The collection in the **Horatio Nelson Museum** at Bellevue is one of the finest reserves of Nelson memorabilia and naval artifacts in the world. Take time to study the scale model of his last ship, *Victory*, the most advanced ship of its time. While based in Antigua, the admiral came to Nevis to get water at what is now known as Nelson Spring. The museum is open Monday through Friday 9am to 4pm and Saturday 10am to 1pm, *Tel. 469-0408.* Admission is only a few dollars.

The **Museum of Nevis History** at Charlestown is housed in the birthplace of Alexander Hamilton, the United States' first Secretary of the Treasury. Its collections include pre-Columbian artifacts as well as everyday household articles used during colonial times. It's open the same hours as the Nelson Museum; visit both and get a discount. Hours and telephone are the same as the Nelson Museum above.

The wedding license of Horatio Nelson and Fanny Nesbit, a widow he married while on Nevis, can be seen at **Fig Tree Church**. Ask about it at the museums. Right next to Memorial Square, the courthouse and library were built in 1825 in a superb example of colonial stone work. When the shutters are closed, they serve as the local town crier. Check for posters advertising anything from concerts to bake sales.

ST. KITTS

Even if you have a rental car, take an island tour with a savvy guide to get you oriented before you strike out on your own. Let's start with St. Kitts, where **The Circus** in Basseterre is the center of city life. Amble around Independence Square and Liverpool Row to see colonial buildings that were burned time and again but always rebuilt to their original styles. Overlooking the **Berkeley clock tower** are a couple of popular, second-story restaurants where you can lurk for hours over a drink, watching the world go by. The **St. Christopher Heritage Society** at the corner of Bank and West Independence Square Street has a fine collection of historic photos depicting early St. Kitts life.

At the top of Church Street, see **St. George's Anglican Church**, which was first built in 1670 as a Catholic church, was burned, and was rebuilt in 1704 as Anglican. It burned twice more, and was damaged by an earthquake in 1974, but its imposing black stone fabric remains as part of a vital church. On Central Street, just off Fort Street, Mr. Vincent Grant, cobbler, will make an outline of your feet and make sandals with a perfect fit.

Driving west out of town, stop at **Romney Manor** to see petroglyphs left by the Caribs. Not far away, Bloody Point is where French and English soldiers massacred hundreds of Caribs in 1626. From **Challengers Village** surrounding the gorge, get a good view of **Mount Liamuiga**, a dormant volcano with its head in the clouds at 3,792 feet.

If you think you see a train, don't blame it on the rum punches. Many railroads were abandoned in the Caribbean, but St. Kitts' sugar train still runs on its narrow-gauge tracks, carrying cut cane from the plantations to the sugar plant at Needsmust. From there, sugar goes by rail to the deep water harbor.

Always keep one eye out for African green vervet monkeys, which came to the island as pets of French settlers and stayed on to breed in the wild. You may even see some at **Brimstone Hill**, a massive fort that covers 38 acres, 800 feet above the sea. Many of the ramparts have been restored. Climb them for superb views far out to sea. Inside, tour exhibits depicting the days when this fort was the Gibraltar of the Caribbean. It's open daily 9:30am to 5:30pm for an admission of EC$10.

Save a day for climbing **Mount Liamuiga**, lushly blanketed with mango trees. Above elevations where they can grow, hardwood forest takes over. A hike to the dormant volcano crater, which is found at 2,800 feet, takes five to seven hours roundtrip. Or, just stay at lower altitudes and hike the rain forest hoping to spot an African green vervet monkey or mongoose.

NIGHTLIFE & ENTERTAINMENT

Special events on St. Kitts and Nevis include an Alexander Hamilton Birthday Tea Party in January, Independence Week in September, and the highlight of the year, National Carnival from Christmas Eve through New Year's Day.

NEVIS

On **Nevis**, Saturday night at the **OUALIE BEACH RESTAURANT**, *Tel. 469-9735,* is Caribbean Night complete with native string band and a carnival masquerade with dancing and drumbeats. Dinner reservations are recommended.

ST. KITTS

Tucked away in a tropical garden off Princes Street in Basseterre, **STONEWALLS** is a popular conversation bar and noshery. The late crowd tends to gather at the cliffside bar of the **LIGHTHOUSE RESTAURANT** at the deepwater harbor. The best place to watch the passing scene day or night is the second floor of **BALLYHOO RESTAURANT** overlooking the Circus in Basseterre. **TOTT'S**, across from the post office, is the watering hole where a lot of students from the veterinary school on the island go after hours. Outsiders are welcome to visit the **casino** at Jack Tar Village all-inclusive resort, *Tel. 465-8651.*

Most locals gather at the **MONKEY BAR** on Frigate Bay beach by the **Timothy Beach Hotel**. On Friday nights, the music starts at 9pm and continues until the wee hours when all the tourists have gone to bed and only the locals remain.

At Carnival and other special events, look for St. Kitts' **clown troupes**, an island staple since 1740 and an organized group since the 1940s. They are said to "dance clown" in a riotous, gaudy performance filled with noise and swirling costumes.

MUSIC, MUSIC, MUSIC

The St. Kitts Music Festival held each year in mid-to-late June is one of the Caribbean's major music fests. The festival, which stars major artists in jazz, calypso, reggae, gospel and even Chinese folk music, lasts four days.

SPORTS & RECREATION

Beaches & Diving – Nevis

Sometimes white and sometimes a rich, volcanic black, the beaches of St. Kitts and Nevis are fun to explore for their variety. On Nevis, **Pinney's Beach**, a six-mile ribbon of white, is a favorite for its soft sands and fringe of palm trees. **Newcastle Beach** at the island's northern tip is also shaded by stately palms. **Hurricane Beach** just south of the airport has good view of St. Kitts and it's usually deserted.

Surfers flock to **Pizza Beach** and **Windward Beach**. Watersports rentals are available at pretty **Oualie Beach**, where some visitors complain about the lack of shade. Others love the constant sun. Dive operators include **Scuba Safaris**, *Tel. 469-9518* and **Nevis Water Sports**, *Tel. 469-9690*, on Nevis.

Beaches & Diving – St. Kitts

On St. Kitts, **Banana Bay** on the south shore has gently lapping waves and salt-white sands. **Turtle Beach** at the south tip of the southeast peninsular, **Frigate Bay Beach**, and **Friar's Bay Beach** have protected waters for family swimming, as well as refreshment stands. Annie, a fixture at **Frigate Bay**, can arrange anything from island tours to boat trips from her little stand on the beach. The beaches along here have rocky stretches; in-the-know visitors wear beach shoes. **White House Bay** has a sunken ship that makes interesting snorkeling; **Major Bay** is deserted except when cruise ships are in and bring hordes of day-trippers here.

The best dive sites include **Black Coral Reef**, where you can see rare black coral at depths from 40 to 70 feet. It's protected, so don't even touch it let alone take a piece. **Bloody Bay Reef** is pocked with small caves that are home to brilliant sea fans and lavender anemones. One of the largest reefs, Coconut Tree Reef, starts at 40 feet and goes as deep as 200 feet.

Booby Island, in the channel between the islands, hosts a variety of marine life. The Caves off the west coast of Nevis are a labyrinth of form and color.

Monkey Reef off the west coast of St. Kitts' southeastern peninsula, is 50 feet under water and is alive with fish, rays, and lobster. Grid Iron rises to within 25 feet of the surface, a favorite hangout for angel fish. **Nags Head** is for experienced divers who can deal with the strong currents at the southern tip of St. Kitts, where the Atlantic and Caribbean seas join. It's a superb spot to see pelagic fish as well as reef dwellers. **Redonda Bank** and **Sandy Point** are also popular with dive outfitters.

Although the area teems with unexplored wrecks, only a handful of sunken ships are on divers' checklists. The *River Taw* went down in only 50 feet of water and is now crusted with coral. The *M.V. Talata* sank in 70 feet of water in 1985 and is best explored by seasoned divers. The *Tug Boat*, which lies only 20 feet down, is popular with snorkelers and beginning divers. So is the sunken *Brassball*, which is only 25 feet under.

Dive operators on St. Kitts: **Kenneth's Dive Centre**, *Tel. 465-7043*, and **Pro Divers**, *Tel. 465-3223*.

Hiking

The islands offer three types of forest terrain: rain forest, dry forest, and mangrove swamp. In dry country look for house-high pipe organ cactus, spiky agave, gumbo limbo, and acacia trees that were introduced to Nevis in the 18th century to feed camels. Hear that bleating chirp? It's the West Indian tree frog, a tiny, 3/4-inch creature who is calling to attract females.

In higher, wetter forests, look for wild orchids, butterflies in every hue, and burr trees with roots large enough to house a family. Watch for fluttering hummingbirds and brightly plumed birds feeding on red and yellow flowers and find termite nests the size of sedans.

Eco-Tours Nevis offers a two and a half-hour Eco-Ramble on the uninhabited east coast of Nevis, a two and a half-hour Mountravers Hike to see the ruins of an old Great House, and a one and one-half-hour Historic Charleston tour. Book through your hotel.

Greg's Safaris, *Tel. 465-4121*, on St. Kitts leads off-road island safaris, rainforest and volcano hikes, and a sunset ramble on the southeast peninsula.

Golf

Play golf at the 18-hole Robert Tent Jones-designed course at the **Four Seasons** on Nevis, *Tel. 469-1111*. Resort guests pay $25 for nine holes and $40 for 18 holes; non-guests pay $75 and $125.

Kayaking

Turtle Tours offers a three and a half hour kayaking and snorkeling adventure along the south coast of St. Kitts. All equipment and a guide are provided. You'll paddle into remote bays, snorkel on virgin reefs, and gaze up at cliffs alive with monkeys, goats, and nesting birds. Book through your hotel.

SHOPPING

Batik, the dye technique perfected in Indonesia, is used to create wonderful Caribbean motifs for clothing and accessories sold in St. Kitts and Nevis at Island Hopper in The Circus, Barreterre, and T.D.C. Mall on Main Street in Charlestown. A trip to **Caribelle Batik** at the Gardens of Romney Manor is a double treat because it's at Old Road Town on the south coast, west of Basseterre and the site of a 350-year-old African Saman tree that covers half an acre. On the gorgeous grounds of a British earl's estate, the batik studio offers unique dresses, wraps, and scarves. Whipsawed by hurricane and fire, it has been rebuilt and improved. A telephone number wasn't available at press time, when rebuilding was being completed.

Along Rosemary Lane, look for an old Creole-style house at number seven. It's filled with antiques, not the least of them the home's wonderful woodwork. Saturday morning along the Bay Road in Basseterre is **market day**, where locals are seriously selling produce and spices. It's a colorful, truly native happening and a good place to buy spices and little nutmeg graters, but don't go merely to take photographs. Some locals will be offended. If in doubt, ask.

Happy Hour at the **Fort Thomas Hotel** on Friday evenings in season is devoted to fashion shows of local designers and shops. For local cookbooks, guides, and post cards, shop **Creole Graphics** on Liverpool Row and College Street. Along the same street find **Creole Publishing**, which sells bags of brown sugar to take home, and **Ashburry's Duty Free Shop** with its cargoes of Christian Dior, Baume & Mercier, Gucci, Givenchy and other greats. A **Slice of the Lemon** on the Circus is an exclusive agent for Portmeirion tableware, and also sells Christian Dior, Calvin Klein, Chanel and Ralph Lauren.

Pelican Mall at the cruise ship docks at Basseterre houses dozens of shops plus the national philatelic bureau where you can get art in the form of stamps for pennies. **Ram's** sells imported watches, leather, and crystal duty free and also sells tee shirts and souvenirs. **Little Switzerland**, part of a chain found throughout the Caribbean, sells fine crystals, watches, porcelain, Mont Blanc pens, and Japanese pearls.

By appointment you can view the collections of clothing designed and sewn on St. Kitts by **John Warden**, who has boutiques on both islands. For a private viewing, call *465-1713*. Between Rawlins Plantation and the Golden Lemon on St. Kitts, **Kate Design** is the home gallery and studio but Kate's silk scarves, watercolors, jewelry, placemats and prints are also sold at shops in Basseterre and Charlestown.

Most local shops, including pharmacies, carry a selection of hot sauces in all colors and heats as well as Nevis honey. Other local condiments include mango chutney, soursop jelly, and guava cheese. They make meaningful, inexpensive souvenirs and so do bottles of CSR (Cane Spirit Rothschild), the unique local spirit first developed by the Rothschilds. Many years ago, the Baron de Rothschild's chemists decided that the only place in the world they could distill their Cane Spirit Rothschild was on St. Kitts and Nevis where the waters and soil were ideal for growing the juiciest, tastiest cane. Thus began the production of Rum St. Kitts, which is said to "give you a tan from the inside." Try CSR, which is not a white rum but is unique. It has all the punch without the molasses taste.

The **Nevis Handicraft Co-op** at Dr. Walwyn's Plaza, Charlestown, is a picturesque place to find local crafts, homemade jellies, hot sauces, and coconut oil.

EXCURSIONS & DAY TRIPS

Day sails and moonlight cruises are offered aboard 47-and 70-foot catamarans by **Leeward Island Charters** on both islands, *Tel. 465-7474.*

Tropical Tours in Basseterre has car rentals, sightseeing tours, and scuba dives, *Tel. 465-4167*. **All Seasons Streamline Tours** at Bath Estate, Nevis, *Tel. 469-1139*, has 14-seater, air conditioned buses with PA systems for island tours. Also available are taxis tours. St. Kitts tours that can be arranged through your hotel include:

Island Tour, from $15 per person, includes such highlights as Brimstone Hill, Romney Manor, and Black Rocks.

Catamaran Party Cruise from $30 per person is a day sail to Nevis for swimming and snorkeling. Included is a barbecue lunch and open bar. Limbo to live music.

Rain Forest Tour for $35 is a hike to the top of Mount Liamuiga including a picnic lunch.

From St. Kitts, a day trip to Nevis costs $8 roundtrip. Take the ferry to Nevis for a day of shopping, departing at 7am and returning at 6pm.

PRACTICAL INFORMATION

Area Code: 869

Bank Holidays: January 2, Good Friday, Easter Monday, Labour Day in early May, Whitmonday, the first Monday of August, the last day of Culturama in early August, Independence Day on September 19, Christmas Day on December 25 and the following day, Boxing Day.

Banking hours: Monday through Thursday 8am to 3pm, Friday 8am to 5pm and Saturday 8:30am to 11am. ATMs are available at Royal Bank of Canada outlets, where most international bank cards will work.

Business hours: are generally 8am to noon and 1pm to 4pm. Monday through Friday. Thursday is early closing, with most shops closing at noon. The post office is open daily 8am to 3pm, except Thursday when it closes at 11am.

Cruise passengers: a new port in the heart of Basseterre, St. Kitts opened in 1996 to berth the largest cruise ships. Adjoining it is the 26-shop Pelican Mall, a marina, and a crafts shopping area featuring traditional Kittitian work.

Consul: the islands are served by U.S. consulates in Bridgetown, Barbados or in English Harbour, Antigua.

Currency: the EC dollar is exchanged at the rate of about $2.65 per U.S. dollar, but U.S. funds are accepted almost everywhere. The EC$ trades with the Canadian dollar at about two for one.

Driving: a local driving license is required at a cost of $12. Driving is on the left, British style.

Electricity: although 220-volt, 60-cycle service is used throughout St. Kitts and Nevis, most tourist hotels supply standard 110-volt power. Transformers and adapters may be needed at older or smaller hotels, so check with your hotel host ahead of time.

Government: The Federation of St. Kitts and Nevis has been independent since 1983. U.S. consular services are provided through St. John's, Antigua, *Tel. 462-3505.*

Immigration: Citizens of the United States and Canada need proof of citizenship in the form of a voter's registration, passport, naturalization papers, or a birth certificate. All others should bring a passport.

Medical matters: medical care on the islands is limited, and it's expected that doctor visits will be paid for on the spot.

Security: there is some petty street crime, although armed robbery is rare. Don't leave valuables unattended on the beach.

Taxes: departure tax is EC$27 or $10.

Tourist information: In Basseterre, St. Kitts, *Tel. 869/465-2620, Fax, 465-4040.* A tourist information office is located in Pelican Mall. On Nevis, *Tel. 869/469-1042, Fax 469-1066.* A tourist office is on Main Street in Charlestown. In the U.S., *Tel. 800/582-6208, Fax 212/734-6511*; in Canada, *Tel. 416/368-6707, Fax, 368-3934.* In the United Kingdom, *Tel. 071-376-0881, Fax 071-937-3611,* or write St. Kitts and Nevis Tourism, 10 Kensington Court, London W8 5DL.

Weddings: you can get married on the third day that one or both of you have been in St. Kitts or Nevis. You'll need a passport or birth certificate, a decree absolute if either is divorced or a death certificate if either party is widowed. If the ceremony is to be performed by a priest or pastor, a letter must be received from the couple's home clergyman. Catholic ceremonies must be performed in a Catholic church. The license costs $80 for three-day residents; $20 for residents who have been in the islands 15 days or more.

22. BARBADOS

If good things come in small packages, **Barbados** is indeed gifted. The easternmost island of the entire Caribbean necklace, this dewdrop-shaped island is 21 miles long and 14 miles at its widest point. It's been independent since 1966 but remains primly British in all the right ways: afternoon tea is a hospitality staple, croquet and polo are favored games, and a statue of Admiral Nelson gazes out over Trafalgar Square in Bridgetown. It's even referred to by some as "little England."

By the time first Europeans arrived, the Caribs had been ruling the island for centuries after wiping out the peaceful Arawaks who preceded them. Evidence of the Arawaks shows that they lived here as early as 400 B.C. The name Barbados, bestowed by Portuguese explorer Pedro a Campo in 1536, is thought to refer to beards on the banyan trees.

By the early 17th century, the British had armies of slaves planting the island to sugar, a boom crop at the time. The sugar bubble crashed, slaves were freed in 1834, and tourism emerged as the new cash crop. One of its first tourists was George Washington, who brought his brother here in 1751 for the warm, clean air in hopes it would cure his tuberculosis. It's said that pirate Sam Lord put out false lights on the reefs to lure ships to their death so he could loot their cargoes. Today his mansion is part of a Marriott resort, **Sam Lord's Castle**. It's filled with antiques that were obtained, some say, in less than honest ways.

Although the island was settled early in the 17th century, **Bridgetown** was destroyed repeatedly over the centuries by fire and hurricanes. Most of its historic buildings date from 1860, the year of the last great fire.

Today, Barbados produces 60 percent of its own oil, plus livestock, tropical flowers for export, and Sea Island cotton. Its chief products are tourism and offshore finance, but agriculture remains important.

Climate
Cooled by Atlantic breezes, Barbados basks in year-round sunshine dulled only by periodic depressions that spin up off Africa. Temperatures are usually in the high 80s by day and low 70s by night.

BACKRA JOHNNIES & OTHER RIFFRAFF

After the English Civil War, many prisoners from the losing side were "barbadosed" or sent to Barbados as bonded or indentured servants. Known as Red Legs, Ecky Beckys, or Backra Johnnies, those who survived their five-year sentence sometimes stayed on the island, where families might still today carry these labels.

ARRIVALS & DEPARTURES

Barbados is three hours, 40 minutes from Miami and four hours, 20 minutes from New York. Grantley Adams International Airport is a 30-minute drive from Bridgetown, the capital. It's served from the United States and Canada by **American Airlines**, *Tel. 800/433-7300;* **BWIA**, *Tel. 800/538-2942;* **Air Jamaica**, *Tel. 800/523-5585;* and **Air Canada**, *Tel. 800/ 776-3000.*

It's also served from Britain by **British Airways**, **BWIA**, and **Caledonian**; from Germany by **BWIA**, **LTU and Condor**; from Switzerland by **BWIA**, and from Holland by **Martin Air**. Inter-island flights are with **BWIA**, **LIAT**, and **Air Martinique**, *Tel. 784/458-4528.* A charter service flies nonstop to Barbados from Halifax, Nova Scotia. Call **Conquest Tours** at *Tel. 800/268-1205.* Flight time is 4-1/2 hours from New York, 3-1/2 hours from Miami, and 8 hours from London.

ORIENTATION

Barbados is only 21 miles long and 14 miles wide, with most visits starting either at Grantley Adams International Airport on the south coast or at the waterfront in **Bridgetown** on the island's southeast corner. The island is divided into parishes, which are usually included in any addresses.

A major highway runs from the airport west to the outskirts of Bridgetown before turning north to end at the **Parish of St. Peter**. Secondary roads thread the island. For visitors who arrive by cruise ship, Bridgetown Harbour has a shopping center, tourist information, and a handicrafts center within easy walking distance.

Life in Bridgetown centers around the marketplace, post office and Trafalgar Square with its parliament buildings. Parking areas are found in the market area, near the old synagogue, on Spring Garden Highway just east of Shallow Draught, and on the south side of the Careenage on at the end of Fairchild Street.

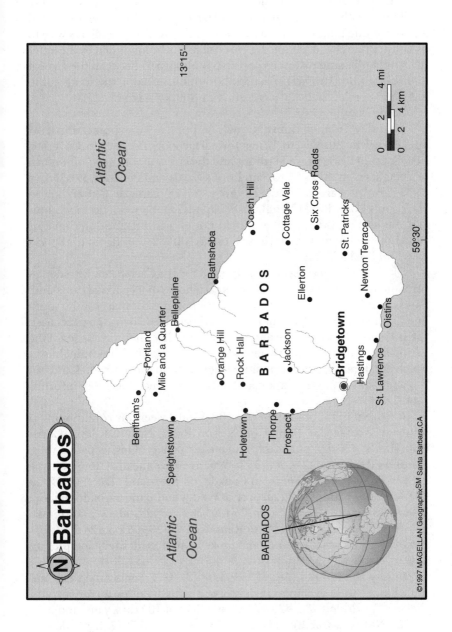

GETTING AROUND BARBADOS

Barbados has one of the most advanced infrastructures in the Caribbean, with more than 800 miles of paved roads. Taxi fares are posted and this is one island where drivers seldom try to gouge. Still, it's wise to establish a rate ahead of time. Licensed taxis can be identified by the letter "Z" on their license plates. Expect to pay about $25 between the airport and hotels along the west coast and $15 to hotels along the south coast. **A A Taxi Service**, *Tel. 426-3212*, runs 24 hours a day.

Some sample fares:

Grantley Adams International Airport to any point north of Speightstown, Bds$55, to Bridgetown Harbour, Bds$30, to Coverley, Bds$8. From Bridgetown Harbour and the city center to any point north of Speightstown, Bds$40, to Sam Lord's Castle and Pollands, Bds$38, to the Hilton or Paradise, Bds$12. From Sandy Lane or Glitter Bay to Harrison's Cove, Bds$12, to Bathsheba, Bds$45. Between the city center and the harbor, Bds$6. Rates should not exceed Bds$2.50 per mile or Bds$1.50 per kilometer. The hourly rate is Bds$32; waiting time is BDs$7 days and Bds$8 nights.

The bus system is exceptionally good for the Caribbean, with departures out of Bridgetown several times each hour for all parts of the island. Fares are Bds$1.50 and exact change is required. To depart for the south or east, catch a bus on Fairchild Street; to head north along the west coast, catch a bus on Lower Green and the Princess Alice Highway. Buses of the nationally owned system are blue with yellow stripes. Yellow mini-buses, which are the same price, run more frequently on shorter routes and can be caught at the public market and at Probyn Street. For more information, *Tel. 436-6820.*

Cars rent for about Bds$425 to Bds$700 a week; air conditioning is optional. **Access Car Rental** on Nelson Road, Navy Gardens, Christ Church, *Tel. 427-0215*, has cars, mini mokes, convertibles, jeeps and vans. **Courtesy Rent-a-Car**, *Tel. 800/303-3806* to reserve ahead of time from the U.S. *or Tel. 800/563-2886* from Canada; on the island, *Tel. 420-7153 or 431-4160*, has stations at the airport, at Wildey and at the Barbados Hilton. **Johnson Stables & Garage**, *Tel. 426-4205 or 429-3528*, offers car hire, taxi, guides, and airport pickup. **Auto Rentals**, *Tel. 428-9085 or 428-9830*, has vans with sun roofs, cars, and mini mokes, with free delivery and pick up at your hotel.

Sunny Isle Motors, *Tel. 435-7979 or 435-9277*, rents cars, vans, and mini mokes with pickup and delivery at your hotel or at the airport. *Corbin's Car Rentals, Tel. 426-8336*, has a fleet of 100 cars, vans, and mini mokes. **National Car Rentals**, *Tel. 426-0603 or 436-7572*, has a fleet of cars, mokes, and vans with hotel pickup and delivery. For 24-hour service at the airport, your hotel or the port call **P&S Car Rentals**, *Tel. 424-2052;* available are cars and four-wheel-drive Jeeps. **L.E. Williams Car Hire** offers convertibles, station wagons, and other cars including air conditioned automatics, for a minimum of three days. For drop-off at the airport, add $7.50. All the companies listed above take major credit cards. Motor scooters rent for $25 a day and bicycles for $20 daily. A deposit of $100 is required for the scooters and $50 for bicycles. A license is required to drive a motor scooter.

Driving is on the left, British style, and the top speed limit is 80 kilometers per hour.

Beware of friendly locals in Bridgetown who offer to "find you a park" for a small fee. You may return to find the car ticketed for illegal parking. The largest parking lots in Bridgetown are at Independence Square, Wharfside, and City Centre. Parking is also offered by many large stores and shopping complexes.

WHERE TO STAY

Be prepared for an additional 17.5 percent VAT on rooms, and a service charge, usually 10 percent. Red alert: this represents a stiff tax increase for Barbados so, when you're planning your trip, make sure you know whether room, package, or meal plan rates include these charges. Unless stated otherwise, all hotels listed here accept credit cards. Rates are quoted in U.S. dollars except where indicated. The Barbados dollar is worth about 50¢. Always ask about packages.

Key to locations: Parishes of St. Peter, St. James, and St. Michael are along Barbados' lee, or western, shore. Hotels in Parish of St. Joseph are on the wildly scenic Atlantic coast. Parish of St. Philip is on the island's southeast corner; Parish of Christ Church spreads along its southern shoreline and is the site of the airport.

Fair Warning: before using (and perhaps losing) the key for your hotel safe, make sure you know the penalty for losing it. At some resorts it is as much as $100.

Expensive

ALMOND BEACH CLUB, *Parish of St. James. Tel. 246/432-7840, Fax 432-2115; U.S. and Canada 800/425-6663. Mail address, 3301 Bartlett Boulevard, Orlando FL 32811. Winter rates at this 151-unit resort start at $450 per couple nightly, including meals, drinks, activities, airport transfer, and tips. It's about 25 minutes from the airport and 20 minutes from Bridgetown.*

Romance reigns at this premier, all-inclusive resort on a stretch of wave-washed beach. Your air conditioned room or suite will have its own patio or terrace, television, direct dial telephone, coffee maker, safe, and hair dryer. Choose a bedroom with walk-in closet, a junior suite, or the commodious one-bedroom suite with separate living room. Creamy beiges are the base color for accents in gentle pastels seen in the bedspreads, draperies, and framed watercolors.

Meals, drinks, and snacks are included, so indulge yourself in any of the four bars (including a piano bar) then dine in Enid's for Bajan fare, the open-air continental dining area, or in local restaurants participating in the dine-around plan. Afternoon tea is served in the best British tradition; room service can be used for lunch and dinner only.

Shop in the boutiques, sign up for a beach party, work out in the fitness center, play tennis, or just roam the grounds and gardens taking time to smell the flowers. This resort is best for adults; for a family resort, the company operates Almond Beach Village (see below). The only sour notes are the deposits required to get beach towels and a key to your room safe. Lose either, and you'll pay too much for them. Take reef runners for swimming. Just off the beach are some nasty coral patches.

ALMOND BEACH VILLAGE, *Heywoods, Parish of St. Peter. Tel. 246/ 422-4900, Fax 422-0617; U.S. and Canada 800/425-6663. Winter rates at this 290-room resort start at $450 nightly per couple, all inclusive. A child under age 16 traveling with two adults stays free in suites; additional children pay $50 nightly. The hotel is 22 miles from the airport and 12 miles from Bridgetown.*

The same laidback luxury that presides at the Almond Beach Club in St. James reigns here except that the all-inclusive concept has been expanded to include facilities for children. The 64-room family section also has meeting facilities. Choose among four restaurants. The Reef has children's menus and seafood; The Horizon is a grand, 250-seat dining room serving continental fare. Dine in La Smarrita for fine Italian cuisine kindled by candlelight. Through the dine-around plan, you can also sample local restaurants outside the resort.

Play nine holes of golf, squash, or tennis. Take your pick of nine swimming pools and a day-long riot of beach sports from banana boating to sailing, snorkeling and water skiing. Have your hair braided, go shopping in Bridgetown, and don't miss the weekly Bajan picnic.

COBBLER'S COVE, *Speightstown, Parish of St. Peter. Tel. 246/422-2291, Fax 422-1460; U.S. 800/890-6060. Rates at this 40-unit resort start at $390. It's ten miles from Bridgetown and 21 miles from the airport.*

All units here are luxury suites, surrounded by tropical gardens and edged by a brown sugar beach. Each has a separate living room, private lanai or balcony, and a kitchen. Features include hair dryer, air conditioning in the bedroom, safe, telephone, and wet bar. Meals from the award-winning restaurant can be delivered to your suite for an evening of dining in romantic privacy. Or, venture out to the breeze-swept bar and the open air dining room with its view of the ocean. Sun, swim, snorkel, sail, water

WHAT'S ALL-INCLUSIVE?

A step beyond Full American Plan, which means all meals are included, "all-inclusive" at most resorts means all meals, bar drinks, wine or beer with meals, and use of all the resort's bicycles, boats, and sports facilities. However, there are gray areas that could result in nasty surprises unless you settle them first. Among them are taxes, gratuities, tennis or golf lessons, spa services, children's programs, airport transfers, name-brand wines and liquors, and premium watersports such as water skiing, scuba diving, or deep sea fishing. To differentiate between barebones all-inclusive and truly all-inclusive, some resorts use such terms as Platinum Plan or All-Inclusive PLUS. When in doubt, ask.

ski, or play tennis, all on the house. Baby sitters are extra, and your hosts can also arrange tours or a guaranteed starting time at the Royal Westmoreland Golf Club. The suites most in demand are the Camelot and the Colleton, both part of the original mansion and among the most posh suites on the island.

COCONUT CREEK CLUB, *Derricks, Parish of St. James. Tel. 246/432-0803, Fax 0272. The 53-room resort is 4 miles from Bridgetown and about 15 miles from the airport on the west coast. Rates start at $323, which includes breakfast and dinner.*

Show business elite who escape to this clubby resort come for the privacy of small but cozy rooms and baths, private beaches protected by cliffs, and meals served on balconies with views that seem painted for each guest alone. Ask for a cliffside room overlooking the sea or a garden view filled with shrubbery and florals. Dine in the club's pubby restaurant, or take advantage of meal and tennis privileges at other hotels nearby. Use of the sailing cats, sunfish, wind surfers, or snorkel equipment is complimentary. Room service is available; breakfast on the balcony is a must. After dinner, local bands play for listening and dancing. Television sets are available for rent.

COLONY CLUB, *Porters, Parish of St. James. Tel. 246/422-2335, Fax 422-0667. Rates at this 98-room resort start at $428, which includes breakfast and dinner for two. It's about seven miles from Bridgetown and 16 from the airport.*

Take a beach-view room overlooking the sandy shoreline or ask for one of the garden rooms that are flecked throughout seven acres of grandly manicured gardens filled with feathery "singing" pines. Listen for their song when the wind blows. Swim in the sea or three freshwater pools, sign up for a speedboat ride or a sail, work out in the air conditioned fitness center, or play tennis day or night. The resort has been here since the 1950s, but most accommodations are kept up to snuff. Air conditioned rooms have a radio, telephone, bathtub and shower. Dine in your choice of two restaurants, then walk across the bridge to the island in the swimming pool, and dance to live music. The resort has its own tour desk and beauty shop; room service is available breakfast through dinner.

CORAL REEF CLUB, *Holetown, Parish of St. James. Tel. 246/422-2372, Fax 422-1776; U.S. 800/5-ELEGANT. Doubles in season start at $435 including breakfast and dinner. The club offers 67 units, of which some are hotel rooms and others private cottages. It's seven miles from Bridgetown and 18 from the airport.*

A member of Small Luxury Hotels of the World, this 12-acre hideaway provides Deluxe and Superior cottages on lanes that thread through flowering shrubs and end at a bright beach. Suites have luxury baths with marble vanities, double sinks, oversized bathtub, separate shower, and traditional English plumbing. Family owned and managed, the club offers a homey lounge with reading room, dining area and bar. Cottages, each done differently, have their own lanais.

GLITTER BAY, *Porters, Parish of St. James. Tel. 246/442-4111, Fax 246/422-1367. U.S. Tel. 800/223-1818; Canada except Toronto, 800/268-7176; Toronto Tel. (416) 964-6641. Rates at this 83-room resort start at $445. Suites and penthouse suites with one, two, and three bedrooms are available. Beach House suites start at $480.*

Sir Edward Cunard, the cruise ship magnate, chose this site along the Platinum Coast to build his mansion, designing it after the family palazzo in Venice. In its day, the greathouse and its guest houses entertained the rich and famous of the international jet set. A new day dawned in 1981 when the home became an exclusive hotel. A Princess International property, as is its sister hotel next door, the Royal Pavilion, this one rises four stories into the sunshine, with most rooms offering garden and pool views and some overlooking the ocean. Just footsteps from the sea, the Beach House has five suites that can be rented separately. Play tennis, swim in the pool, use any of the sailboats or snorkel gear, or go water skiing, all at no added charge. Golf, deep sea fishing, and scuba diving can be arranged for a fee.

Use the fitness center, visit the beauty/barber shop, or shop in the boutiques. Dining is in Piperade, which has a weekly floor show, or in either of the two restaurants at the Royal Pavilion. Afternoon tea and a manager's weekly cocktail party are on the house; room service can be brought 24 hours a day. Together, Glitter Bay and the Royal Pavilion are known as Pemberton Princess Hotels under management by Princess International (of Bermuda Princess fame).

Selected as one of my Best Places to Stay; see Chapter 13 for more details.

GRAND BARBADOS BEACH RESORT, *Carlisle Bay, Parish of St. Michael. Tel. 246/426-0890, Fax 436-9823; U.S 800/742-4276. Rates at this 133-unit hotel start at $250. It's a mile from Bridgetown and ten from the airport* Active business and leisure travelers treasure this hotel for its closeness to town and the horse track, and on-site windsurfing school, health club, diving, and sailing, snorkeling. They're all included. Relax on one of the beach chairs lined up on a long pier built out over the clear, aquamarine water, burrow into the sun-warmed beach sands, or soak in the whirlpool to lose the winter blues. Golf and horseback riding are nearby. The hotel has its own bars and two restaurants with nightly entertainment. Rooms have mini-bar, satellite television, air conditioning, radio, and telephone.

CRYSTAL COVE, *Appleby, Parish of St. James. Tel. 246/432-2683; fax 432-8290. Rates at this 88-room resort start at $390 including breakfast and dinner. It is about four miles from Bridgetown and 14 from the airport. Take Route 1 to the village of Fitts. Kitchenette suites are available.*

The beach can be rocky and some sunken pilings offshore are a nuisance, but this older resort with a newer name is worth a look because it's a member of the St. James Beach Hotel group whose member hotels exchange restaurant privileges and other perks.

ROYAL PAVILION, *Porters, Parish of St. James. Tel. 246/422-4444, Fax 246/422-0118, U.S. 800/223-1818; Canada except Toronto, 800/268-7176; Toronto Tel. 416/964-6641. Rates at this 75-unit resort start at $565. Suites and villas that sleep up to six persons are available. Add $60 per person daily for breakfast and dinner. During some periods, children under age 12 can't be accommodated. During low season, children stay free in a parents' room. The resort is about eight miles from Bridgetown and 19 from the airport.*

Drive up an avenue of royal palms to a grand sweep of greenery and blooms to what looks like a Mediterranean mansion. Moorish arches open onto endless sea views in this cool, three-story white building on a brown sugar beach that is lined with palm trees and flowering shrubs. All 72 supersize bedrooms have a sitting area, ocean views from a private balcony or patio, two twins or one king-size bed, clock radio, safe, telephone, air conditioning, hair dryer, and mini-bar with refrigerator. Next to the tennis courts, a three-bedroom villa makes a spacious home for three couples or a large family.

Play tennis on Astroturf courts, swim in the pools and through the waterfall, or use any of the non-motorized watersports equipment at no added charge. Play golf at the Royal Westmoreland nearby or let the concierge book your scuba or deep sea fishing trip. The air conditioned fitness center has all the latest Life Cycle equipment and a masseuse on call. Dine in the two restaurants here or in the sister property, Glitter Bay, next door. Afternoon tea and the weekly manager's cocktail party are the best way to meet interesting people from all over the world. Or, if you prefer a private hideaway, order from room service around the clock. Selected as one of my Best Places to Stay; see Chapter 13 for more details.

SAM LORD'S CASTLE, *Parish of St. Philip. Tel. 246/423-7350, Fax 423-5918. In Canada and the U.S. including the Virgin Islands and Puerto Rico. Tel. 800/765-6737. Rates at the 234-unit hotel start at $240.*

Formerly a Marriott but now managed by Carnival Hotels and Resorts, this 72-acre property underwent a massive renovation in 1996. Rooms open onto balconies overlooking the 3/4-mile white sand beach and azure waters topped with creamy wavelets. The beach alone covers 11 awesome acres but it's better seen and heard than swimmed. This is Barbados' east coast at its most crashingly beautiful, with nothing between here and Africa to tame the huge rollers. The site is a favorite with poets and dreamers but swimming can be dangerous.

Furnishings are in warm beiges and pastels, offering a basic layout in terracotta and rattan, or a more upscale unit with stately mahogany four-poster bed. Play tennis on the seven floodlit courts, enjoy the pools or beach, relax in the hydrotherapy pool, choose among three restaurants and two snack bars, have a drink in one of two lounges, or work out in the exercise room. Rooms have electronic locks, color television, and air conditioning. Get a room on one of the higher floors and upgrade as much as the bankroll will allow. Rooms in the main house have canopied beds fit for royalty.

It's the history of this haunted palace that makes its magic. Pirate Sam Lord built the Castle in 1820 with profits, it is said, gained by hanging false lights on Cobblers Reef to lure unwary captains. When their ships foundered, Lord helped himself to rich cargoes, some of them now antiques seen in the hotel. Artisans were brought in from England to create a real palace worthy of Lord's wealth.

SANDPIPER, *Holetown, Parish of St. James. Tel. 246/422-2251, Fax 422-1776; toll-free Tel. 800/5-ELEGANT. Doubles at this 23-suite inn start at $310. Meal plans are available. Children are welcome in some seasons.*

Formerly known as the Sandpiper Inn, this intimate little paradise snuggles in fragrant tropical gardens and towering palms. Your driver will deposit you under the porte cochère at the front entrance. Between the bar and the restaurant, which has popular Bajan buffets on special evenings, a charming gazebo bandstand seats musicians who play at least once a week in high season. Rooms are air conditioned and have a telephone and small refrigerator. There's a swimming pool, floodlit tennis courts, room service, and a beach bar. Few places do a better job of combining the feel of both British and Bajan ambience. Guests can share dining privileges with the Crystal Cove, Colony Club, Tamarind Cove, and Coconut Creek, making the meal plan a definite plus. **SANDY LANE**, *St. James. Tel. 246/432-1311, Fax 432-2954; in the U.S., Canada, Puerto Rico and U.S. Virgin Islands, 800/223-6800. This 120-unit resort is on Grenada's west coast six miles from Bridgetown and 17 miles from the airport. Rates start at $545 including breakfast and dinner daily and pickup at the airport in a Rolls-Royce.*

A member of Leading Hotels of the World, Sandy Lane has long set luxury standards in the Caribbean, pampering guests in an aloof, 380-acre estate rimmed with 1,000 feet of private beach. You'll be greeted personally at the airport and whisked to the hotel, where you'll be greeted with cold champagne and fresh fruit. Recently, the staff has been energized and motivated and the accommodations upgraded. All rooms and suites have air conditioning, wall safe, ceiling fan, mini-bar, and private patio. Play tennis day or night. Shape up in the health club. Water ski. Windsurf. Golf on the resort's own, 18-hole, championship course. Greens fees and all watersports are included in the rates. Swim in the sea or pool.

Sandy Bay serves gourmet meals with an exciting new menu every day. Seashell is a less formal restaurant. At the Oasis Pool Bar, one of five around the resort, you can lunch in your swimsuit. Musicians provide nightly entertainment. If you're not on a meal plan, dinner for two costs about $100. On special nights there are barbecues or folkloric musicales. Room service is available around the clock at no added charge. Shop the boutiques or have your hair done in the salon. Laundry is available and so is dry cleaning, a service rarely offered in Caribbean hotels.

SETTLERS BEACH, *Parish of St. James. Tel. 246/422-3052, Fax 422-1937; U.S. 800/223-6510. Rates at this 45-unit resort start at $225; two-bedroom cottages at $600. It's 7 miles from Bridgetown and 16 from the airport. Meal plans are available.*

This golden oldie has a loyal following of repeat guests who like the price for a cottage that has two bedrooms, two baths, and a full kitchen. There is a swimming pool and it's on the sandy beach, which is lined by taller, newer hotels that charge far more. The hotel has room service during limited hours, air conditioning, tennis courts, and a light and lemony decor that sets off the sunshine and surrounding lawns. Children under age 17 stay free in their parents' room.

TAMARIND COVE, *Paynes Bay, Parish of St. James. Tel. 246/432-1332, Fax 432-6317. Rates at this 166-room hotel start at $446. Meal plans are available. The hotel is about five miles north of Bridgetown and 15 miles from the airport.*

Because it's a member of the St. James Beach Hotel group, guests here can eat and play at sister hotels, so it makes sense to take the meal plan and dine your way from one end of the beach to the other. Swim from the pristine beach or take one of the luxury suites and skinny-dip in your own, private plunge pool.

The resort will remind you of Spain or the Algarve with its ombre tile roofs and blush colored walls. Your air conditioned room will have a telephone and a private patio or balcony where you can have breakfast delivered from room service. The hotel has two formal restaurants, nightly entertainment, a beachfront snack bar, freshwater swimming pools, and complimentary use of wind surfers, snorkel gear, and small sailboats. The concierge will also arrange for you to play golf, tennis or polo, or take a horseback ride.

TREASURE BEACH, *Paynes Bay, Parish of St. James. Tel. 246/432-1346, Fax 432-1094. Rates start at $350. Suites and a two-bedroom penthouse are available. The hotel is four miles from Bridgetown and 14 miles from the airport. Ask about meal plans. Children can't always be accommodated.*

A little jewel of exclusivity and caring service is this cluster of buildings that surround a small swimming pool and look out over the sandy beach to clear seas beyond. Rooms open onto a private balcony or patio, and have telephone and air conditioning. Furnishings are South Seas style; baths are small by current standards. Dine in the hotel restaurant where you'll meet a mixed group of Americans, Canadians, and Brits. Golf, watersports, and tennis can be arranged.

Moderate

BARBADOS HILTON, *Needhams Point, Box 510, Bridgetown. Tel. 246/426-0200, Fax 436-8946; U.S. 800/HILTONS. Rates at this 184-unit hotel start at $194. It's less than a mile from Bridgetown and ten miles from the airport.*

A pretty setting on a point of land edged with a wide, white sand beach greets visitors to a resort that's convenient for business or pleasure. Rooms overlook the ocean or garden from private balconies. Each has a telephone, satellite television, air conditioning, mini-bar and radio. A golf course isn't far away. Dine in the Verandah Restaurant or walk into Bridgetown and take your pick of places to eat.

BOUGAINVILLEA BEACH RESORT, *Maxwell Coast Road, Parish of Christ Church, tel.246/428-7141, Fax 428-2524; U.S. 800/8-BARBADOS. Rates at this all-suite, 97-unit resort start at $190 for a studio, $238 for a one-bedroom unit. It's four miles, or a $20 taxi ride, from the airport and five miles from Bridgetown.*

Swim off the white sand beach or in the big pool with its swim-up bar. Private balconies and patios in this four-story hotel overlook towers of flowers and greenery. Entertainment and shopping are nearby and a car rental agency, laundry, and tennis courts are on site. Units have television, fan, complete kitchen with microwave oven, air conditioning, and telephone. Enjoy the busy beach, where you can rent a boat or kayak, get up a game of volleyball, snorkel, or sail.

CASUARINA BEACH CLUB, *St. Lawrence Gap, Christ Church. Tel. 246/428-3600, Fax 428-1970; U.S. and Canada 800/742-4276 or 800/223-9815. Rates at this 158-unit resort start at $165 double. Studios and one-bedroom suites are also available. It's four miles from Bridgetown and less than six miles from the airport. The resort is wheelchair accessible. Children under age 11 stay free in their parents' room.*

The supersize lap pool at this handy, beachfront resort, is a must for power swimmers. Power sunbathers find plenty of room along its long, long length to line up their beach chairs. Put the children into the kiddy program, then spend your days playing tennis, beachcombing, sightseeing, shopping, and strolling the lush tropical grounds. By night, play the floodlit tennis courts or stroll to nearby restaurants and nightlife. All units in the four-story, family-friendly building have air conditioning and fan, kitchen, radio, telephone and a private balcony. Have a drink in one of the two bars, then dine in the resort's own restaurant. Family operated, this is one of island's best values, lovingly known as The Cas to its loyal repeaters.

CRANE BEACH HOTEL, *Crane Bay, Parish of St. Philip. Tel. 246/423-6220 fax 423-5343. Rates start at $180. Suites are available with one or two bedrooms. Meal plans are available. The hotel is on the far east shore, 14 miles from Bridgetown and five from the airport.*

The resort is abuzz with day-trippers who come for the Sunday brunch and the fabulous view of the unbroken Atlantic and of Prince Andrew's hilltop home on a nearby cliff. If you're not staying here, you can use the pool for a fee, (which means that if you are staying here, you're paying for exclusivity that you're not getting). Still, the views are so spectacular and the neighborhood so grand (Sam Lord's Castle) that this is a popular choice with romantics who love the crash of a seacoast more than the quiet of a sheltered cove. Spend your days around the windswept swimming pool, one of the most photogenic in the islands, or take the stone staircase down the cliff to a wildly roiling ocean beach. Typical of Barbados' east coast, it's often too rough for swimming here, but don't miss the view. Rooms, many of them with air conditioning and an antique four-poster bed, have a telephone. Some suites have a kitchenette. The hotel has its own restaurant and bar.

DISCOVERY BAY HOTEL, *St. James Beach, Holetown, Parish of St. James. Tel. 246/432-1301, Fax 432-2553; U.S. 800/742-4276 or 800/223-6510. Rates at this 88-unit hotel start at $245. It's seven miles from Bridgetown and 18 miles from the airport.*

Relax on this grand plantation among seas of shrubs and flowers right on St. James beach just a few miles north of Bridgetown. It's handy to shops and restaurants, or just stay "home" to enjoy the hotel's own restaurant and bar with live entertainers. Swim in the oversize pool, play tennis, or rent a sailboat. Rooms have mini-bar, telephone, private balcony or patio, radio, and air conditioning.

DIVI SOUTHWINDS, *St. Lawrence Gap, St. Lawrence, Parish of Christ Church. Tel. 246/428-7181; U.S. and Canada 800/367-3484. The 150-unit resort is four miles from Bridgetown and six from the airport. Rates start at $200.*

Handily located between Bridgetown and the airport, this resort sprawls over 20 acres on the beach. Play the slot machines, swim in the two freshwater pools, shop the boutique and mini-market, and have your hair done. The tennis courts are lighted for night play. Guests also play volleyball and basketball, and there are daily aquasize sessions. Rooms are air conditioned and have a private lanai or balcony. Kitchenettes are available.

SANDY BEACH HOTEL, *Worthing, Parish of Christ Church. Tel. 9246) 435-8000, Fax 435-8053. Doubles start at $205. The hotel is on the south coast, four miles from Bridgetown and six from the airport.*

Air conditioned, beachfront, and equipped with its own pool and restaurant, this is a modestly priced alternative to staying at a cottage or condo where you have to cook and clean. The hotel was built as a Best Western, so you can imagine a fairly standard bedroom and bath layout.

SILVER SANDS RESORT, *Silver Sands Beach, Parish of Christ Church. Tel. 246/428-6001. Rates start at $155. The 106-room hotel is on the south coast, about eight miles from Bridgetown and four from the airport.*

This seaside resort has rooms, studios, and one-bedroom apartments, all air conditioned. Play tennis, try the restaurants and pools, or rent watersports equipment from the concession. The beach is a lively one that is popular with board sailors.

Budget

ATLANTIS HOTEL, *Bathsheba. Tel. 246/433-9445. Rates at this eight-room hotel start at $55. Credit cards aren't accepted. It's on the east coast, nine miles from Bridgetown and about 18 from the airport.*

The beaches along this wave-whipped coast are not the best for swimming except during rare periods of prolonged calm, but they're popular with surfers and with people who love the roar and spume. Rooms, which have private baths, are pleasant and the food and hospitality are heartily Bajan.

BAGSHOT HOUSE, *St. Lawrence, Parish of Christ Church. Tel. 246/435-6956. It's about four miles from Bridgetown and five from the airport. Rates at this hotel start at $110. Credit cards aren't accepted.*

Stay in a small, family-run beachfront hotel at rates that are, for Barbados, a real buy. Mature vines and flowering shrubs form an enchanting garden on a serene lagoon. Share the sun deck with other guests and have a drink in the deck-side bar, which is hung with works by local artists. Not all rooms are air conditioned, and television is provided only on a rental basis, but rooms are furnished home-style and are kept fresh.

BROOME'S VACATION HOMES, *Pine Gardens, Bridgetown. Tel. 246/426-4955, Fax 437-3139. Rates at this 15-room guest house start at $50. Meal plans are available. It's less than two miles from downtown and about seven miles from the airport.*

Fourteen bathrooms are available to 15 rooms containing 25 beds, so it's a fairly safe bet that you can get a twin or double with private bath in most seasons. Children can be accommodated, and the Broomes will be glad to quote you a rate for breakfast, breakfast and dinner, or all three meals.

COCONUT COURT BEACH HOTEL, *Hastings Beach, Parish of Christ Church. Tel. 246/427-1655, Fax 429-8198. Rates at this 91-room hotel start at $95. It's not quite two miles from Bridgetown and nine from the airport.*

View the deep, blue sea from your room or apartment in this family-owned and family-operated, three-story apartment hotel. Your accommodations come complete with refrigerator, toaster, electric teakettle, ceiling fan, radio, and telephone. Apartments also have a stove. Sunbathe on the sandy pool terrace, seek shade under one of the many chickee huts, or step out onto the white sand beach. Diving, fishing, boat rentals, sailing, snorkeling, yoga, and a spa are nearby. The hotel has its own shops, restaurant, bar, dive shop, and live entertainment three nights a week. For thrifty travelers there are nightly Happy Hour and dinner specials.

CRYSTAL WATERS, *Worthing, Parish of Christ Church. Tel. 246/435-7514. This five-room guest house is three miles from Bridgetown and seven from the airport. Rates are from $35; no credit cards.*

Not all rooms have a private bath, but this is an affordable beach perch for the family who are used to sharing a bathroom. The hotel is on the beach, with simple lodgings that do not include telephone or air conditioning.

FAIRHOLME, *Maxwell, Parish of Christ Church. Tel. 246/428-9425. This 31-room inn is about 3.5 miles both from Bridgetown and the airport. Rates start at $28 for a double room with bath. Credit cards aren't accepted.*

The original greathouse has been added to with all manner of rambling ells, but the gardens and fruit trees date back to earlier times and have matured magnificently. At this price, don't expect furnishings featured in Architectural Digest. You may even like them better, however, for their patina and comfort. Studio apartments (from $35) each have a balcony or balcony, high ceilings, and exposed beams. The beach is a short walk away, and the inn has its own pool. A sister hotel across the street has a waterfront bistro and bar. The air conditioning works on coins, which is a nostalgic plus for those who remember using brass tokens for a few hours of heat in London hotels.

KINGSLEY CLUB, *Cattlewash, Parish of St. Joseph. Tel. 246/433-9422, fax 433-9226. Rates at this eight-room inn start at $92. It's about 12 miles from Bridgetown and 20 from the airport in eastern Barbados.*

This time-honored local inn where Bridgetown city folk like to take a holiday is handy to Andromeda Gardens and Bathsheba Beach, the popular surfing beach. Beaches on the Atlantic coast are exceedingly scrappy, so you'll need a car to go beaching elsewhere except in unusually settled weather. Meals are down-home Bajan, hearty and good, and are available in meal plans for one, two, or three meals a day. Children can be accommodated. Rooms are plainly and comfortably furnished and each has a private bath.

Villa Rentals

In addition to the listings here, private villas with maid service and other staff can be booked through **WIMCO**, *Tel. 800/932-3222; in the U.K., Tel. 800/89-8318.* VAT on home rentals is 7.5%, half that charged on hotel rooms.

WHERE TO EAT

The check for your meals will usually include a 15 percent VAT, and a 10 percent service charge is also usually added. Read the fine print on menus or your bill to note whether a VAT or other service charges are included in the prices. There is no need to tip twice. Menus usually list prices in U.S. dollars, Barbados dollars, or both. We list them in U.S. currency here. Note that Barbados is an exceedingly expensive island; if your hotel offers a meal plan, consider it carefully.

FOODS OF BARBADOS

There is still a lot of British heritage in the foods of Barbados, but today it's a unique blend of native ingredients, fruits of the sea, and memories of the Mother Country. Be brave and try:
- *Conkies (meat and cornmeal pies)*
- *Flying Fish*
- *Jug Jug (cornmeal pudding)*
- *Pudding and Souse (head cheese and blood pudding)*
- *Sea Moss Jelly*
- *Sea Urchin Eggs*
- *Turtle Steak*

WEST COAST

Expensive

COBBLERS COVE, *in the Cobblers Cove Resort, Road View, Parish of St. Peter. Tel. 422-2291. Reservations are recommended. Restaurants in the resort are open daily for breakfast, lunch, and dinner. Plan to spend $100 or more for dinner with wine.*

Chef Leslie Alexander won't settle for anything but the best for guests in this ultra-expensive resort, so expect a memorable meal in a romantic setting overlooking the sea. Starters include a simple orange and grapefruit salad topped with toasted coconut and citrus sorbet, or more complex tastes such as the cornmeal and black olive crepe with panfried shrimp on a bed of garlic, ginger, and tomato sauce. Choose the hot or cold soup, a crisp salad, and a main dish from a long list of fish, meat, and vegetarian choices. Try the barracuda in phyllo pastry and a confit of vegetables or the sauteed pork tenderloin with apple in Calvados sauce. Choose from a list of wines from Australia, California, New Zealand, and South Africa.

RAFFLES, *First Street, Holetown, St. James. Tel. 432-6557. Open only for dinner daily, Raffles features starters $5 to $9, main dishes $20 to $30 and wines $20 to $110. Reservations are essential.*

The decor is a whimsical safari complete with life-size zebra. Dine in air conditioned comfort on spicy Bajan, Jamaican, African, and international favorites. For the non-adventurous, good steaks are always available. Try the grilled fresh catch of the day, ribs, or shrimp.

THE REEF, *in the Coral Reef Club, Holetown, Parish of St. James. Tel. 246/422-2372. It's seven miles from Bridgetown and 18 from the airport.*

Dinner main courses are priced $27 to $30. Reservations are suggested. The restaurant is open for breakfast, lunch, and dinner daily. Dine in an airy restaurant closed on only one side, on an appetizer of smoked fish or homemade linguini followed by a hot or cold soup, a sorbet intermezzo, and blackened mahi-mahi, tournedos of beef with with a potato cake and pearl onions, or roast rack of lamb with a pine nut crust and minted couscous. A full English breakfast at the resort costs $15 for a big choice of eggs, pancakes, toast, cereals, fruit, and smoked fish. Luncheons range from English favorites (bangers and mash, rarebit) to international classics like the club sandwich, grilled chicken breast, or juicy beef burgers.

SANDPIPER, *in the Sandpiper Resort, Holetown, Parish of St. James. Tel. 246/422-2251. Open daily for breakfast, lunch, and dinner the restaurant offers main courses $42 to $60. Reservations are advised.*

Start with the Sandpiper Coupe, which is jumbo shrimp, muskmelon, and banana tossed in a ginger yogurt dressing, or the chilled celery and walnut soup. Main courses offer a couple of catches from local seas, or duckling, braised shin of veal in tomato sauce, rack of lamb, or medallions of beef sauteed with mushrooms and shallots. When flying fish, the national dish, is on the menu it's served marinated, grilled, then surrounded by creamed yam, glazed pearl onions, and tomatoes in herbs. Swordfish steaks are pan fried and served on a bed of spinach with shrimp sauce. If you're here for the breakfast (about $15 for the full English spread; $10 for the continental) there are all the usual breakfast treats plus a choice of smoked fish, rafts of fresh fruit, and a very nice selection of teas. For lunch, have the Sandpiper Caesar at $25. It's romaine tossed with jumbo shrimp. There's always a soup or two, open and closed sandwiches, burgers, and a specialty such as vegetarian pizza, fish of the day, or the egg dish of the day. The room is breezy and bright under a West Indian wood ceiling. Try one of the weekly buffets, followed by live entertainment.

SEASHELL, *in the Sandy Lane Resort, Parish of St. James. Tel. 432-1311. The resort is about a mile south of Holetown. Reservations are essential; ask about tonight's dress code. Plan to spend $100 for dinner for two. Main dishes are priced $23 to $27.*

Dine in colonial splendor in the last of the old resorts, where black tie is still worn at least once a week. Homemade pasta is served in a creamy wild mushroom sauce, spaghetti is sauced with fresh tomatoes and basil, carpaccio of beef is served with freshly shaved Parmesan. And that is only the starters. Try the steamed fresh fish with aromatic oil and angel hair or the barracuda in a crust of potato, zucchini and black olives. Choose anything from the dessert buffet for $10 and end the meal with a cappucino. Once a week, the hotel hosts a floor show.

SETTLERS' BEACH, *in the Settlers Beach hotel between Folkstone and Sunset Crest, St. James. Tel. 422-3052. Lunch prices are $10 to $45; a four-course dinner is $60 to $120; wines are $26 to $289. Call for reservations.*

Dine right on the beach under rustling palms. Luncheon is a la carte, daily. Try the Tuesday evening Bajan buffet featuring suckling pig, cou cou, flying fish and other native specialties.

Moderate

2ND STREET CAFE, *Second Street, Holetown. Tel. 432-5398.*

Owner-chef Lindry Lavine loves to create unique dishes such as his signature Caribbean Fantasy. It's a filet mignon coated with a tangy sauce, topped with prawns, and glazed with cheese. Dinner is served from 6:30 to 10pm.

WATERFRONT CAFE, *facing the careenage, Bridgetown. Tel. 427-0093. Entrees are under $20; the Caribbean buffet on Tuesday night is a super value.*

Surrounded by old stones and waterfront bustle is this popular hangout where the day's specials are shown on a blackboard. Tuck into such classics as lamb stew, pepperpot, gumbo, cou cou, fresh fish and johnny cake.

Budget
MUSTARS, *find the alley entrance in the back of the Scotia Bank. Across from it, a flight of stairs leads to Mustars.* A big plate of freshly fried fish plus a mound of macaroni pie or a heap of beans and rice costs about $5.

GRAPEFRUIT GREAT FRUIT
It's thought that grapefruit originated in Barbados, when a large citrus fruit called shaddock was brought from Polynesia and crossed with an orange.

EAST COAST
Expensive
PIPERADE, *in the Glitter Bay Hotel, about 10 miles north of Bridgetown at Porters, St. James. Tel. 422-4111.*

Chef Clayton Shipps came to Barbados from California to preside over a glowing, oceanfront terrace restaurant surrounded by gardens. On Monday, a buffet is followed by a music and dance program; on Fridays, a barbecue is followed by dancing. Other nights, choose from an ever-changing a la carte selection of Caribbean and Bajan foods with a California accent. Dinner is served from 7:30pm.

SOUTH COAST
Expensive
MERVUE HOUSE, *Marine Gardens, Christ Church. Tel. 435-2888. Reservations are recommended. Appetizers start at $6; main courses are $28-$60.*

Swedish chef Bertil presents inspired international dishes in an elegant, private home once occupied by a French merchant. Tables, which range from a romantic table for two overlooking the fountain to a banquet board set for thirty, are set up around the house. The wine list is massive, representing vintages from all over the world. Lunch and dinner are served Monday through Friday, dinner nightly, and a buffet lunch is served on Sundays.

PISCES RESTAURANT, *St. Lawrence Gap. Christ Church, tel 435-6564. Appetizers are priced $6 to $16 and main courses $28 to $60. Reservations are essential.*

The restaurants lights dance on the water, luring visitors to dine outdoors in a fragrant garden. The chef's own gardens surround herbs and fruit to be served with native seafood, The wine list is impressively arrayed with California and European selections.

REGENCY ROOM, *in Marriotts Sam Lord's Castle, St. Philip. Tel. 423-7350. Reservations are required.*

The weekend Castle Dinner held here each Wednesday is a regal experience once presented to Queen Elizabeth II during her Jubilee tour. Start the evening with cocktails outdoors overlooking the lawn, then take your place with no more than 30 lucky guests at a long banquet table straight out of Camelot. Dine by candlelight on poached mahi-mahi, beef Wellington, white chocolate mousse, Petits-fours, and other delectables fit for a queen.

LUIGI'S, *Dover Woods, St. Lawrence Gap, Christ Church. Tel. 428-9218. Reservations are preferred. Entrees are priced $22-$44.*

Miles and Lisa Needham preside over a cozy restaurant where pasta is king. First, check out the chalk board to see the specials for the day. They could include lobster tail in vodka tomato cream sauce, or a white clam and garlic pizza. Italian classics such as spaghetti with pesto and shrimp aglio & olio anchor the regular menu. Italian and California wines start at $19. Luigi's is open nightly from 6pm.

SECRETS, *Bagshot House, St. Lawrence, Christ Church. Tel. 435-9000. Reservations are requested.*

Mark and Amada Evelyn have created an outstanding seafood house in a charming little hotel smothered in flowering vines. Look out over a shining sea, sip a fine wine, and consider the menu while an impeccably-trained server hovers nearby, ready but unobtrusive. Select from a long list of seafood cooked in a variety of ways.

Moderate

CARIB BEACH BAR, *Second Avenue, Worthing, Christ Church. Tel. 435-8540. Reservations are accepted.*

Choose a sunny table with a beach umbrella or a table in the shade of a spreading palm tree. You'll overlook a natural lagoon where placid waters are perfect for a pre-lunch swim. Local seafood, Caribbean, and international specialties are popular with families.

CASUARINA BEACH CLUB, *St. Lawrence Gap, Christ Church. Tel. 428-3600. Reservations are accepted.*

There's something here for every price range, from hot dogs and burgers on the barbie between noon and 2pm to the West Indian floorshow and buffet on Saturday nights. Classic French cuisine is offered a la carte, and a snack menu is served from noon to 10pm. Take afternoon tea in the plush Piano Lounge, or come late for the Piano Bar. It's open until 2am.

TAPPS TAVERN & GRILL, *St. Lawrence Gap, Christ Church. Tel. 435-6549.*
Bar snacks start at $2; a 22-ounce Poterhouse steak is $30. Reservations are recommended. A trendy watering hole and meet market, Tapps offers entertainment six nights a week, good food and good booze in a relaxed water-view setting.

Budget
BEACHFRONT BAR & RESTAURANT, *Worthing, Christ Church. Tel. 435-8000. Enjoy two Happy Hours daily, one from noon to 1pm and the second between 5 and 6pm. when house drinks are served two for one.*
Overlook a lagoon while you rip into barbecue (they call it barbeque) all day, any day. A Bajan buffet is featured on Tuesday and Saturday evenings with live calypso and steelpan music. Come to watch the sunset, play beach volleyball, kayak, and rub elbows with a mix of visitors, cruise ship passengers, and locals.

BARBADOS' BUDGET FAST FOOD

*Even if you're an island purist who shuns American fast food while in the islands, give **KFC** a try. Five air conditioned KFC's are found around the island at Hastings, Trident House, Black Rock, Speightstown, and Collymore Rock. For under $10 you'll get a rock-ribbed Bajan meal consisting of the colonel's famous fried chicken plus rice, macaroni pie, vegetables, and local salads. **Shakey's Pizza** restaurants are found at Hastings and St. Lawrence Gap. In addition to pizza, specialties include Mojo potatoes, golden chicken, and gourmet sandwiches. For delivery call 435-7777 or 420-7777.*

*Barbados' leading fast foot chain is **Chefette**, found in three locations in Bridgetown and also in Rocklye, Holetown, and Oistins. Low-priced dining can also be found at **Barbecue Barn**, which features ribs, chicken, steak or fish with salad bar, baked potato or price, and hot bread. They're found in Rockley, Holetown, and on Broad Street. In the wee hours, no-frills local hangouts serving budget menus include **Enid's**, **Livy's**, and **Collins** in Baxterson Road in Bridgetown, the **Bird's Best** in Bay Street, and **Holmes Bar** in Holders Hill, St. James. Try such native specialties as roast pork cutters, beef stew and rice, calf liver cutters, soused pig's feet, black pudding and pig tail stew.*

SILVER ROCK, *Silver Sands Beach, Christ Church. Tel. 428-2866 or 420-6983.*

This is a surfer's hangout on one of the island's most gnarly beaches. For a small fee, you can leave your rigged windsurfer here. Visitors can also use the deck chairs and swimming pool. Come for breakfast, lunch, dinner or the Wednesday night live music party. A reggae party is held on some Sundays; Happy Hour between 5:30 and 6:30 daily is a local tradition.

SEEING THE SIGHTS

Historic Bridgetown combines the sun-drenched charm of the Caribbean with the busy, crowd-crammed commerce of a European waterfront. Since the earliest days, ships were careened (or laid down on their sides so their hulls could be cleaned) in the inner harbor known as The Careenage. An old screw-dock dry dock, an historic rarity that was in use until 1973, can still be see wharfside.

Rubberneck your way around Trafalgar Square, which probably dates to 1805 when the famous Battle of Trafalgar was fought. The Nelson monument built here predates the one in London by 38 years! See the Parliament buildings, circa 1870, with their stained glass windows. The fountain dates to 1865, when piped water first came to the capital. Still today around the island, stand pipes can sometimes be seen in settlements, spewing water for villagers' use. Even though most homes now have indoor plumbing, these vestiges are reminders of the days when plumbing was a modern addition. We're told that the water is safe to drink, so help yourself.

The city's churches include **St. Michaels Cathedral** just east of Trafalgar Square. It was built between 1784 and 1786 and has been repaired and rebuilt many times, but George Washington is said to have attended services in the original church on this site. The **synagogue** on Synagogue Lane dates to 1654 and was rebuilt in 1833 and 1983. Now a National Trust property, it's open 9am to 4pm, Tel. *432-0840.* You'll also see **St. Patrick's Roman Catholic Cathedral,** which dates to 1848 and was rebuilt in 1899.

Military history at **The Garrison** began in 1780 when 2,000 British troops were dispatched here to defend the eastern English islands against the French. Tour the entire complex including the military cemetery, the superb cannon collection, the **Barbados Gallery of Art,** and the museum. It's open Monday to Saturday 9am to 5pm and Sunday 2-6pm, Tel. *427-0201.* Admission is Bds$10 adults and half that for children. Heritage Passport holders pay half price. **The Barbados Museum** is one of the Caribbean's best, with galleries displaying artifacts from the pre-Columbian era to the present. In its research library, scholars can find a wealth of

---

SIGHTSEE BARBADOS AT A DISCOUNT

*Purchase the **Heritage Passport** from the Barbados National Trust for $35 and gain entrance to 16 attractions usually priced at $2.50 to $4 each. Or buy the mini-pass for $18. It is good for five National Trust sites. Among them are the must-see **Andromeda Botanic Gardens, Gun Hill Signal Station, Welchman Hall Gully, Tyrol Cot Heritage Village** and the **Sir Frank Hutson Sugar Museum**. Also available through the National Trust are home tours through modern mansions and old greathouses. Open House is held January through March only and offerings vary each time. Admission is charged.*

*For information, contact the **Barbados National Trust**, Ronald Tree House, 10th Avenue, Belleville, St. Michael, Barbados, West Indies, Tel. 246/426-2421, Fax 429-9055.*

---

genealogical material, photos, books, and old maps. The cafe is the perfect spot for a light lunch at moderate prices.

The **Mallalieu Motor Collection** at Pavilion Court, Hastings, includes a Vanden Plas Princess, a Bentley, a Citroen, a rare Lanchester and a Wolseley. Admission is Bds$5. *Tel. 426-4640* for an appointment.

Andromeda Gardens and Flower Forest, both in St. Joseph, are tropical showplaces that are kept beautifully groomed for the many weddings that are held in them. Both are open daily from 9am to 5pm Admission is Bds$12 for adults and Bds$6 for children ages 6-12. Plan to have lunch in the gardens' Hibiscus Cafe, *Tel. 433-9384*.

Banks Brewery in Wildey, St. Michael, charges Bds$6 for adults and $3 for children (ages 10-15) to tour the brewery, with proceeds going to charity. Call ahead, *Tel. 429-2113*, and make reservations for a tour on Tuesday or Thursday, 10am or 1pm. For tipplers, the **Mount Gay Visitors Centre** is a mecca. It's here that one of the most popular rums in the world is made in a distillery that was established in 1663. The tour starts with a 12-minute audio-visual presentation in an air conditioned room. You're then led through rooms where rum is refined, blended, aged, bottled and (this is the best part) tasted. Take Spring Garden Highway north out of Bridgetown just past the Bajan Queen and Jolly Roger. Tours lasting 30-40 minutes are held Monday through Friday 9am to 4pm and Saturday 10am to 1pm, *Tel. 425-9066*.

The Rum Factory & Heritage Park at Foursquare in St. Philip, is a new twist on the typical Caribbean rum factory tour. This one has an adjacent historical park with an art gallery, amphitheater, and shops filled with local crafts. It's open Monday through Thursday 10am to 6pm and

Sunday noon to 6pm. Admission is Bds$20. Children under age 12 are free when accompanied by an adult. For information, call the National Trust, *Tel. 426-2421.*

Sunbury Plantation House was reopened in 1996, lovingly restored after a fire. It's magnificently furnished with antiques and art objects and is open for daily tours between 9am and 5pm, *Tel. 423-6270.* Admission is Bds.$12. With advance planning you can also have dinner at the 200-year-old mahogany dining table set with Sam Lord's personal claret set and a pirate's ransom in silver and sparkle. Elegant Georgian surroundings re-create the mood of olden days.

Barbados' **greathouses** also include Villa Nova and Francia plantations, which at press time are closed for renovation. Villa Nova is slated to become a luxury hotel. Open to the public are:

St. Nicholas Abbey in St. Peter, *Tel. 422-8725,* built in 1650 and one of only three Jacobean houses still standing in the Western Hemisphere. It has Dutch gables and coral finials, with an herb garden in an ancient medieval layout. The estate, including its syrup plant, is open weekdays from 10am to 3:30pm. Admission is Bds$2.50.

Built in 1820, **Sam Lord's Castle** in St. Philip, *Tel. 423-7350,* was once the finest mansion in the English-speaking Caribbean. Its stunning plaster ceilings were created by Charles Rutter, who also did the ceilings at Windsor Castle in England. Much of the mahogany furniture is original. The castle is now part of a Marriott resort, and is open daily. Admission is Bds$2.50.

Tyrol Cot Heritage Village in St. Michael, *Tel. 429-0474,* was built in 1854 and was the home of Grantley Adams, Barbados "father of democracy." It's filled with the Adam's antiques and mementoes and is operated as a living history museum indoors and out. It's open Monday through Friday 9am to 5pm. Admission is Bds$10.

Brighton Great House, built in 1652 in St. George, has beams 20 feet wide and walls made from rubble and corn husks. **Drax Hall** in St. George, built in the mid-19th century, is a fine example of Jacobean architecture with steep gables, a curving staircase, and a carved hall archway.

The Northern Routing takes you to **Speightstown**, which was a busy port in the days when commerce was conducted by sailing ships, most of them from Bristol. Keep the ocean on your left, head north, pass Almond Beach Village, and turn right to Sugar Cane Club, stopping at the **Ross Gallery**. Keeping to your left you'll see a cluster of chattel houses, a typical schoolhouse, and a **Chapel of Ease**, which is typical of churches built in the 19th century Take a right at the tee, then right again to the wildlife reserve and **Grenade Hall Signal Forest**. The signal station here was used in the early 1800s to send messages by lights or flags between the north end of the island and Bridgetown. See the audio-visual presentation, then hike the coral path through a natural forest. It's open daily from 10am to 5pm, *Tel. 422-8826*. Drinks and snacks are available.

The Barbados Wildlife Reserve, *Tel. 422-8826*, is a place to look and listen for agouti, hare, hyrax, iguana, cayman, tortoises, mongoose, deer, otters and monkeys plus a symphony of birds. It's open daily 10am to 5pm.

If you set off in your rental car, allow at least three days for exploring, taking photos or a swim, picnicking, and stopping at roadside restaurants for a snack or a drink. The Central Routing starts at **Holetown**, where original settlers landed in May 1625, and claimed the island for King James. **St. James Church** here is one of the oldest in the Caribbean. Just before the bridge, head into the old town and check out any of the many good restaurants on First and Second streets. At the **Methodist Church**, drive up hill to the roundabout, go straight across, and continue up hill, turning right at the Y to the crossroads. Go straight again, continuing up hill and noting the geology of steps that were carved by wave action eons ago during the centuries that the island was rising out of the ocean.

Turning left at the junction, you're touring beautiful farm country patched with tiny fields growing flowers and fruits. Stop at **Challenor School** to shop for gifts made by handicapped children and sold for their benefit. Stop at **Highland Tours** for a drink, then turn left to enter **Welchman Hall Gully**, a mile-long wonderland of plants and flowers.

Leaving the gully, turn left and go back the way you came, turning left at Vault Road, then left at the junction, watching for the entrance to **Harrison's Cave**. Tour the cave, then the Flower Forest.

NIGHTLIFE & ENTERTAINMENT

Baxter's Road, known as the street that never sleeps, gets cranked up by 11pm and continues until dawn. Pub-crawl the area, dancing and drinking, but keep your wits about you. Barbados is relatively crime free but tiddley tourists in remote corners on dark nights are asking for trouble.

B4 BLUES, *St. Lawrence Gap. Tel. 435-6560*.

Closed on Saturday but it cooks on the other six nights of the week. Blues, rock, and jazz artists tune up after 7:30pm and carry on until the last guest leaves. Dinners are gargantuan. Try the Texas T-bone or the seafood platter for two.

THE HARBOUR LIGHTS, *Marine Villa, Bay Street, St., Michael. Tel. 436-7115*.

A hopping, happening, outdoor beach bar in Carlisle Bay. It's known for its live entertainment featuring the island's top names. On party

> ## NIP & TUK
> *Uniquely Barbadian, a **Tuk band** consists of a bass drum, snare drum, penny whistle, and triangle, accompanied by such characters as the Donkey Man, Shaggy Bear, and a masked man dressed as a woman with a great, wiggling "botsy" (bustle).*

nights, pay a set price and all drinks are free. Call ahead to see who's playing tonight.

PLANTATION TROPICAL SPECTACULAR, *St. Lawrence Road, Highway 7, Tel. 428-5048.*

A dinner show features fire eating, flaming limbo, and a steel band every Wednesday and Friday night Included are the show, full dinner with unlimited drinks, and transportation to and from your hotel for a tariff of $44. After 7:30pm you can also get show and drinks only for $20.

PIPERADE *in the Glitter Bay Hotel, Porters, St. James. Tel. 422-4111.*

A beachfront terrace surrounded by gardens, sets the scene for a Monday night buffet with live music and a dance troupe and a Friday evening barbecue followed by music and dancing. Dinner is served nightly from 7:30pm.

PALM TERRACE, *in the Royal Pavilion, Tel. 422-4444.*

Have a gala Wednesday evening buffet followed by a cabaret show featuring Carlyn Leacock, the TLC Dance Band, and the Palm Terrace Dancers.

REGGAE LOUNGE, *St. Lawrence Gap, Tel. 435-6462 .*

Pay $2.50 to $10 for an evening of night clubbing, usually with some drink special. Local bands give thundering reggae shows in the open air; when the live acts aren't on, there's a DJ.

1627 AND ALL THAT, *in Sherbourne Centre, Two Mile Hill, St. Michael. Tel. 428-1627.*

Enjoy a cultural dinner show extravaganza. Drinks, a Bajan buffet, the show, and transportation to and from your hotel are included.

39 STEPS *in the Chattel Plaza, Hastings, Christ Church.*

A superb wine bar offers a long list of international wines by the glass until midnight.

If your idea of nightlife involves the dark, undersea world, take a night dive aboard an **Atlantis submarine**, *Tel. 436-8929.* Huge spotlights play over the coral, sponges and fish to provide a show that you can't see during the day. The sub base is on McGregor Street, Bridgetown.

RUM SHOPS

Rum shops are to Barbados what pubs are to the British Isles – social institutions where people gather not just to drink but to thrash out politics, make plans, and talk over the day's problems. There are 1,600 rum shops on the island, ten for every square mile. Try one.

SPORTS & RECREATION

Beaches

On the west coast, try Mullins Beach and Holetown, which has calm water, handy restaurants, and clear water for snorkeling. Paynes Bay is also a good snorkeling trip. On the east, coast, which has the biggest coamers on the island, try Bathsheba/Cattlewash for sailing and sail boarding. Be forewarned that swimming here in the powerful Atlantic can be extremely dangerous.

South Coast beaches in **Christ Church** usually have small to medium wave action. They include **Accra**, which is busy and buzzing, and **Sandy Beach** on a pretty lagoon with a couple of beach bars and restaurants. **Casuarina Beach** is breezier and has more wave action for experienced wind surfers. Have lunch at the Casuarina Beach Hotel.

On the southeast coast, **Crane Beach** is a favorite for body surfing. Park at the hotel. North of Sam Lords, park at the top and go down the steps to **Bottom Bay** for pounding waves and dizzying scenery.

Cricket

A national passion, cricket is played at all levels through the island, reaching its zenith January through March when top teams come to Barbados from around the cricket-playing world.

Golf

The **Royal Westmoreland**, *near the Royal Pavilion hotel, Tel. 422-4653*, designed by Robert Trent Jones, Jr., offers 18 holes of championship golf. At Sandy Lane in St. James, *Tel. 432-1311*, play an 18-hole course set among flowering shrubs and million-dollar mansions, with spectacular views from its famous seventh hole.

Almond Beach Village, *Tel. 422-4900* and **Club Rockley**, *Tel. 435-7873*, both all-inclusive resorts, have nine-hole golf courses.

Hiking

The **Barbados Wildlife Reserve** is the home of the Barbados Green Monkey, as well as worlds of iguana, peacocks, mongoose, tortoise, and

---

GO FLY A KITE

Kite flying is an art form on Barbados, where you can often see bright and arty kites being flown on beaches and lawns. The national kite flying championship contest is held at the Garrison on Easter Sunday.

---

porcupine, and birds in walk-in aviaries. The reserve covers only about three acres so you can explore it easily in an hour, wandering through towering mahogany trees filled with monkeys.

You can hike the coasts for several stretches. From **Ragged Point** to **Consett Point** takes about two hours, then two hours more to **Martin's Bay** and, from there to **Bathsheba**, another one and a half hours. If you want to hike from Bathsheba to **The Choyce** or **Pico Tenerife**, plan on four hours of moderately arduous going.

Or, wander **Turner's Hall Woods** for an hour of two of easy, but steep, walking among silk cotton trees, cabbage palm, and trumpet trees. From above, approach the woods from the Gregg Farm-Turner's Hall Plantation Road. From below, the approach is near **Haggats**.

Hiking the 3/4-mile-long **Welchman Hall Gully** takes only about an hour of interesting rubbernecking through a moist valley crammed with greenery and nattering monkeys. There is an admission fee. Tourists are welcome to join weekly hikes offered by the National Trust, *Tel. 426-2421.* You'll be part of a lively crowd looking at the island's natural and historic highlights.

Polo

Polo is played at **Holders Hill** in St. James, usually between September and March, *Tel. 432-1802.*

Scuba Diving

Barbados has dozens of superb dive sites including walls, blue holes, caves, wrecks, and reef gardens. An artificial reef formed by the deliberate sinking of a 368-foot freighter lies in 125 feet of water where thousands of fish in dozens of species flash among ghostly masts and stacks. The dive operators listed here also offer snorkel expeditions.

Dive with:
- **Dive Boat Safari**, *Tel. 427-4350*
- **The Dive Shop**, *Tel. 426-9947*
- **Exploresub Barbados**, *Tel. 435-6542*
- **Willie's Watersports**, *Tel. 432-7090*

Squash
Play squash at the **Barbados Squash Club**, Christ Church, *Tel. 427-7913* or the **Rockley Resort**, Christ Church, *Tel. 435-7880.*

Tennis
If your hotel doesn't have tennis courts, play at the **Aquatic Centre**, Wildey, St. Michael, *Tel. 429-SWIM.*

SHOPPING

Unless you're a cruise passenger yourself, it's best to avoid shopping areas near the port when cruise ships are in. When 1,500 people come ashore at once, things get busy quickly, and some of us find Bridgetown prices far too ambitious. If all you want is bar or picnic supplies, stick to supermarkets.

Duty-free shopping in Barbados is handled much like that at airports in that you don't walk away with the goods, but find them waiting for you at the airport/ship when you depart. Among items sold this way are alcoholic beverages, tobacco products, and electronics; most others can be taken back to your hotel after purchase. Look for the special, duty-free shops, show your passport or airline ticket, and pay the duty-free price.

For Lladro, Hummel, Limoges and other collectibles plus fine linens and crochet work, shop at **Indian House** at Mall 34, Broad Street, Bridgetown. Just beyond Mall 34, **Columbia Jewel** has fine watches and a large selection of diamonds and emeralds. The store also has outlets in **Cave Shepherd** and at the port and airport. **The Royal Shop** at 32 Broad Street has all the top watches plus Italian gold.

HUCKSTERS & HAWKERS

A huckster is a vendor who carries around a tray of goodies, usually sweets, and sells them on the go. A hawker sets up a stall for sales, usually fruits and vegetables.

Cave Shepherd on Broad Street is one of the Caribbean's few real department stores, a three-story, air conditioned store dating to 1906. Shopping here is a nice change from the tourist places, especially if you need everyday items. It's a pleasant shock to buy a Tommy Hilfiger shirt or a pair of Levi's and not have to pay sales tax. The store runs a free shuttle to participating hotels.

Next door to Cave Shepherd on Broad Street, **Jewelers Warehouse** is a no-frills, off-price jewelry house with rock bottom prices in a decor fashioned after the old ice houses that once supplied ice to ships in the harbor. Ask about daily specials, which are an even better buy than everyday low prices. Each item is guaranteed by a certified appraisal. **Harrison's**, which are found all over the island including the airport and better hotels, has its main store at 1 Broad Street. It handles all the top name European cosmetics and perfumes, china, crystal, watches, leathers, pens, and liquors.

Find **Louis Bayley** stores on Broad Street in Bridgetown and in the Da Costas Mall selling cameras, jewelry, crystal, china, perfume, and collectibles. Their branch at Sunset Crest, St. James, also sells clothing. While you're waiting for your flight, shop their airport outlet. **Signatures** on Broad Street is an enormous skin care center, filled with lotions, fragrances, makeup and aftershaves from the world's best known manufacturers.

Also on Broad Street in the heart of town is the **Colonnade**, a frilly pink and white wedding cake designated as a building of historic interest by the National Trust. Inside, **Da Costa's Mall** has dozens of upscale shops. A clone, **Da Costa's West Mall** is in Holetown on Highway 1.

The Connoisseur at Paynes Bay, St. James is the answer for well-heeled tourists who like to picnic, or who are staying in a self-catering apartment. The shop is stacked with the finest foods from all over the planet: beers, American steaks, European cheeses, patés, good vinegars, sun-dried tomatoes, crab backs, smoked salmon, and much more. Stop in to stock up, then shop by phone in the future. They deliver. For everyday buys, however, supermarket prices are best.

Just off Broad Street on Prince William Henry Street, **Correia's Jewellery Store** has been family owned and managed since 1961. Shop for jewels or gold or, if you want a private consultation with gemologists Maurice or Marcelle Correia, *Tel. 436-6037.*

Take the turn opposite Sandpiper Inn and Settlers Beach to Greenwich Village, Trents Hill, St. James, and shop **Greenwich House** for antiques. A museum of Barbados' yesterdays, the pleasant shop is crammed with tea sets, Chinese export china, English porcelain, mahogany furniture including the classic Barbados rocking chair, and much more. It's open daily 10:30am to 5:30pm Tel. 432-1169.

Note on Visa Discounts: if you have a Visa credit card, ask for the **Barbados Welcomes Visa passport**, which entitles you to discounts and special deals at more than 100 establishments, *Tel. 437-3042.*

UNIQUE BARBADOS SHOPPING

*Our bias is towards shopping for locally made goods. Look for **Best of Barbados Shops** in the Sandpiper Inn, Southern Palms, Sam Lord's Castle, Flower Forest, Andromeda Gardens, Bridgetown Port, Quayside Centre, Mall 34, Caribbean World, Great Gifts, and the Mount Gay Visitor Centre. Since 1975, these unique shops have offered attractive, practical goods that are designed and manufactured in Barbados. Prices start at under $10 for a wide range of souvenirs from tee shirts to place mats, cookbooks, pottery, and writing paper.*

*   **Women's Self Help**, found next to Nelson's Statue at the end of Broad Street in Bridgetown, is the place to shop for crochet, embroidered goods, homemade sauces and jams, basketry, and handmade children's clothes. Proceeds go to a good cause.*

*   Local arts and pottery are also found at the **Barbados Museum** at The Garrison in St. Michael. Art galleries include the **Bagatelle Caribbean Art Gallery** in St. Thomas, **Mango Jam** at Pavilion Court in Hastings, Christ Church, **Queen's Park Gallery** at Barbarees Hill, St. Michael, **The Studio Art Gallery** at Independence Square, Bridgetown, and the **Verandah Art Gallery** in Bridgetown. **Talma Mill Art Gallery** in Enterprise, Christ Church, is open only by appointment, Tel. 428-9383. **Pelican Village** on Princess Alice Highway near Bridgetown Harbour, showcases working artisans and their wares. Native produce markets are found at Cheapside and Fairchild Street in Bridgetown; a fish market is in Oistins.*

*   Seashell art goes back centuries in Barbados, which is thought to be the port where whalers and sailors bought the elaborate seashell "Valentines" that are now seen in museums around the world. For seashells and things made from them, shop **The Shell Gallery** at Chattel Plaza, Hastings, Christ Church and at Carlton House in St. James, Tel. 422-2593. They're open daily 9am to 4:30pm and Saturday 9am to 2pm. Also Daphne's **Sea Shell Studio** on Congo Road, off Highway 5 from Six Roads in St. Philip, Tel. 432-6180. Getting married on Barbados? Some brides order a seashell bouquet.*

EXCURSIONS & DAY TRIPS

In St. Thomas parish, take a guided tour by electric tram into **Harrison's Cave**, a wonderland of waterfalls, pools, mist, stalactites, and stalagmites. It's at Welchman Hall, St. Thomas, *Tel. 438-6640.* Tours are presented daily except holidays 9am to 4pm; call ahead to reserve your space. Admission is $8 adults and $4 for children.

Aboard the submarine **Atlantis**, you can dive without getting your hair wet. It's a real submarine, with windows on the underwater world. The total trip takes an hour and a half, leaving from Bridgetown three or four times a day on a ferry that whisks you out to the sub, *Tel. 436-8929 or 800/253-0493*. You'll sink to depths of up to 130 feet to view the underwater world through your own porthole. Night dives are also available. Rates range from $69 to $94 per person. The ferry that takes passengers to the sub also offers Happy Hour cruises.

For an overview of the island or an aerial photo adventure, call **Bajan Helicopters**, *Tel. 246/431-0069*. Air conditioned Astar Jet Helicopters are kept at their own heliport in Bridgetown, where the company also operates a seaside bar. Day-long and overnight island excursions can be booked through **Chantours**, *Tel. 432-5591*.

Highland Outdoor Tours offers plantation and countryside tours by horseback, on foot or in tractor-pulled jitneys. The company also hosts mountain bicycle rides, *Tel. 246/438-8069 or 438-8070*. **L.E. Williams Your Company**, **Ltd.** is a longtime family business offering an 80-mile island tour in a comfortable coach. For $50 you'll see such sites as Animal Flower Cave, Cherry Tree Hill, Atlantis Hotel where a Bajan lunch is served, St. John's Church, Oughterson Zoo Park, and Sam Lord's Castle. Also included in the price is pick-up at your hotel and drinks on the coach. The Williamses also offer a nature and history tour stopping at Harrisons Cave, Flower Forest, and Sunbury Plantation Great House. The cost is $50 including lunch, hotel pickup, and drinks on the coach, *Tel. 246/427-1043 or 427-6006*.

Secret Treasures takes up to 30 people on tours of the island's rugged east coast for $40 per person, *Tel. 420-4488*. **Bajan Tours** offers six itineraries, each in a coach or mini-van, *Tel. 437-9389*. Mountain bike excursions for riders of all abilities are offered every day by **Mystic Mountain Bike Tours**, *Tel. 424-4730*. Rates start at Bds$95 per person.

Picnic sails, snorkeling expeditions and sunset sails are a perfect way to get in some tradewind sailing. *Why Not*, a sleek catamaran, serves a Bajan buffet with complimentary drinks after a morning of exploring waterwater parks or wrecks. Or, take a sunset sail from 4pm to 8pm, *Tel. 427-1043*. Canary-colored *Tiami* is another catamaran that sails for snorkeling, dinner, or sunset viewing out of Bridgetown, *Tel. 246/427-7245*. Expect to pay about $115 for a four-hour cruise that includes lunch, drinks, snorkeling equipment and return transportation to your hotel. A champagne sunset cruise is $85. Day sails are also available aboard the *Heat Wave*, *Tel. 423-7871*, and the *Irish Mist*, *Tel. 436-9201*. Party cruises are aboard sail and motor craft with **Jolly Roger Cruises**, **Inc.**, Shallow Draught Harbour, Bridgetown, *Tel. 246/436-6424*. Some include food, drinks, and/or a stop for snorkeling.

Harbour Master Cruises are four decks of flat-out fun including shows, dining, dancing, and three bars, one of them air conditioned. To book, *Tel. 430-0900.* **Butterfly Tours** offers three-hour tours in air conditioned vans for Bds$65 per person. Included are Deep Water Harbour, Bridgetown, Holetow, Speightstown, Cherry Tree Hill, the east coast, Bathsheba and St. John's Church. If you prefer a custom tour, call **Margaret Leacock**, *Tel. 246/425-0099.* She charges $30 per hour for a minimum of four hours and a maximum of four people. To book a deep sea fishing adventure call the *Blue Jay, Tel. 246/422-2098 or 422-2143.*

Book a one-day excursion to **Mustique and the Grenadines** through **Grenadine Tours**, *Tel. 435-8451*, or **St. James Travel and Tours**, *Tel. 432-2901.* The first stop on the all-day tour is Mustique where you'll have a full breakfast and a tour, then you'll fly to Union Island to board a catamaran that sails to Palm Island, Mayreau and the Tobago Cays. A buffet lunch is served on board; complimentary drinks are poured all day. Also available is the Union Island tour without the stop at Mustique.

CHATTEL HOUSES

Unique to Barbados, moveable wooden houses were named for chattel, which means "moveable possessions." Chattel houses are built atop blocks and can be moved when the owner moves. An instant shopping mall can be created when a group of chattel houses is set up.

PRACTICAL INFORMATION

Area Code: 246

ATM: Forty-one ATM machines are found on Barbados in Bridgetown, Collymore Rock, Hastings, Saint James, St. Lawrence Gap, and St. Michael.

Banking: Banks are open from 8am to 3pm Monday to Thursday and 8am to 5pm on Fridays. The Caribbean Commercial Banks at Broad Street, Hastings Plaza, Sunset Crest, and Six Cross Roads is open Saturday 9am to noon. They have a currency exchange and ATMs to provide cash advances on Visa and MasterCard. The Barbados National Bank at the airport opens at 8am and stays open until the last flight leaves or arrives every day including holidays, so you can change any leftover Bajan currency here.

Crime: Barbados is a pretty safe place but don't venture into poorer areas after dark.

Currency: the Barbados dollar is tied to the U.S. dollar at a rate of $2 Bds. to $1 U.S. You can use U.S. dollars almost everywhere and most restaurants and hotels quote prices in them. In shops and when dealing with cabbies or small merchants, establish which currency you're talking about.

Departure tax: $12.50 or Bds$25.

Driving: drive on the left, English style. In roundabouts, stay in the left lane if you are going to exit immediately. Otherwise stay in the right lane. The vehicle on the right has the right-of-way. When someone flashes a light at you at a junction, it usually means "go ahead; I'll wait." A local driver's license, which costs $5, must be purchased – a gouge, but easily available through any car hire company or police station. You must show a valid driver's license from your own country. Gasoline costs about 80¢ per liter.

Electricity: power is 110 volts at 50 cycles, which is adequate for most 60-cycle appliances (but not an electric clock).

Government: Barbados is an independent nation within the British Commonwealth. United States consular offices are in Bridgetown in the Canadian Imperial Bank of Commerce Building on Broad Street, *Tel. 436-4950.*

Holidays: National holidays include New Year's Day, Errol Barrow Day on January 20, Good Friday, Easter and Easter Monday, Labor Day on May 2, Whit Monday, United Nations Day in October, Independence Day on November 30, and Christmas Day and Boxing Day, December 25 and 26.

Immigration: Citizens of the United States and Canada don't need a passport. Photo identification, birth certificate, or other proof of citizenship and a return ticket are required.

Taxes are 15 percent on accommodations, food and beverage, and 20 percent on air line tickets.

Time zone: Barbados is on Atlantic time, an hour ahead of Eastern Standard Time. When the East goes on Daylight Savings Time, island time is the same.

Tourist information: write the Barbados Tourism Authority, *800 Second Avenue, Second Floor, New York NY 10017. Tel. 212/986-6516, Fax 573-9850; toll-free 800/221-9831.* In Canada, write Barbados Tourist Authority, *5160 Yonge Street, Suite 1800, North York, Ontario, M2N 6L9, Tel. 800/268-9122, Fax 416/512-6581. In* London, *Tel. 011/44-171-636-9448;* in Germany *Tel. 011/49-69-23-23-66.*

Weddings: Couples can be married on the day they arrive on Barbados if they make extensive preparations ahead. You'll need a marriage license, for which you'll need a valid passport or birth certificate, copies of applicable divorce or death certificates involving previous marriages, and a letter from the marriage officer or minister who will perform the ceremony. For a Catholic wedding, additional documents are needed. The license costs $62.50 if neither party is a resident of Barbados and $22.50 if one party is a resident. A revenue stamp must be purchased at any post office on the island. A $98 additional fee is required for use of a Catholic church, with $40.40 additional for an organist. For information, write the Barbados Tourist Authority, *800 Second Avenue, New York NY 10017.*

THE BRITISH WINDWARDS

23. DOMINICA

Thousands of years ago, the Kalinago people came by canoe from South America to settle the island we now call the **Commonwealth of Dominica**. Fleeing the Spanish, who were rounding up and enslaving Amerindians at each island they conquered, Caribs arrived, blended with the Kalinago, and dug in for a long siege. Their descendants inhabit Dominica to this day.

They called the island Waitu Kubuli, meaning "tall is her body." It's an apt term for an island whose 5,000-foot peak often has its head in the clouds.

When Christopher Columbus scouted the island on his second voyage he named it Dominica, (Dom in EE ca) because the day of discovery was a Sunday. Locals like to boast that it's the only island Columbus would recognize if he returned today. Aloof and alluring, it is dramatically beautiful, untamed, and probably untamable, an eco-tourist's nirvana.

 Only 29 miles long and 16 miles at its widest, the little island is poor in beaches but as rich in bold mountain scenery as it is in friendly, proud people. Here you'll find few pandhandlers and pushy vendors. What you will find are a nation of mostly black inhabitants with one of the largest concentrations of Carib Indians left in the islands. To visit them in their territory is a tourism must, an experience unavailable on any other island.

Exploring Dominica, you'll find cloud-crowned mountains riveled with 365 sparkling streams. You'll see rivers and creeks that suddenly drop, forming waterfalls. You'll find a boiling pool in the crater of a volcano, and forests scented with wild ginger and fragrant vanilla. From mile-high lakes to pebbled seashores, its vegetation is exciting in its range and diversity.

Offshore you'll spot whales and dolphin. Under the sea you'll float in sea gardens painted in brilliant reds, pinks, yellows and blues. In the rain forest you'll hear nattering birds – more than 170 species – and see rare butterflies.

Self-proclaimed as the Nature Island of the Caribbean, Dominica set aside almost 17,000 acres as **Morne Trois Pitons National Park** and 22,000 acres for the **Northern Forest Reserve. Cabrits National Park** protects the dry coastal forests and mangroves.

Typical of the volcanic islands of the Caribbean, Dominica has a number of volcanic hotspots, which in calm times are popular tourist attractions. It's also one of the wettest islands in the Caribbean with countless cooling showers almost every day, especially in the rain forests. The rainiest months are July through October. Portsmouth is said to be one of the drier settlements.

Because of the rain, heat, and range of altitudes, the variety of vegetation is a delight to botanists who find more than 1,000 species of flowering plants including 74 orchids and 200 ferns here. In addition to the many species of birds and bats, the island is home to 'possum, agouti, frogs, iguana, land crabs, and even the occasional boa constrictor.

Because Dominica lies between two French islands, Guadeloupe and Martinique, it is as much French as English. Roman Catholic churches predominate, although Roseau also has Anglican, Methodist, and other sects. The language is a Frenchy patois; some menus are in both English and French.

One of our favorite images of Dominica is a hike into the ruins of **Fort Shirley** where acres of old barracks and gun emplacements have been devoured by thick tangles of vines. Deep in the jungle, we met a group of fierce-looking locals carrying armloads of branches. When we smiled hopefully and greeted them, they began breaking off handsful of leaves and offering them to us. We'd seen sweet bay before, the leaf used for flavoring foods and bay rum, but never before had the scent been so pleasantly pungent as it was when these friendly islanders crushed a few in their hands and held them to our noses in wordless welcome.

Climate

Dominica is one of the wettest islands in the Caribbean. December and January are the driest months; June and July the wettest. Hot and humid best describes the rain forest, which can get chilly and even downright cold at high altitudes. Coastal areas of the island are unvaryingly hot and humid, relieved only by sea breezes.

DOMINICA'S NEW AREA CODE

*Dominica's new area code, **767**, is at press time scheduled to go into effect September 30, 1998. During changeovers, initiation periods and grace periods vary. If 767 doesn't get you through, try the old area code, 809.*

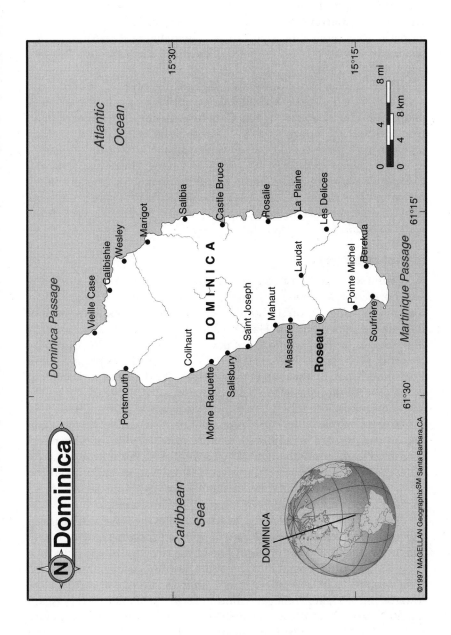

Dominica

N

Atlantic
Ocean

Dominica Passage

Caribbean
Sea

Martinique Passage

15°30'

15°15'

61°15'

61°30'

8 mi

8 km

4

4

0

0

Vieille Case

Calibishie

Wesley

Marigot

Salibia

Castle Bruce

Rosalie

La Plaine

Les Delices

Laudat

Pointe Michel

Berekua

Portsmouth

Colihaut

Morne Raquette

Salisbury

Saint Joseph

Mahaut

Massacre

Roseau

Soufrière

D O M I N I C A

DOMINICA

©1997 MAGELLAN GeographixSM Santa Barbara,CA

ARRIVALS & DEPARTURES

Connecting flights to Dominica fly from Antigua, Barbados, Guadeloupe, Martinique, Puerto Rico, St. Maarten, and St. Lucia. Regional air lines serving the island are **Air Guadeloupe**, *Tel. 767/448-2181;* **American Eagle**, *Tel. 767/445-7204;* **Cardinal Airlines**. *Tel. 767/449-0322;* and **LIAT**, *Tel. 767/448-2421.*

The island has two airports: **Melville Hall Airport** is a ride of one and a half hours, or $50, from Roseau. In a shared cab with at least four other people, the fare is about $16 each. **Canefield Airport** is 15 minutes, or $8 from the capital. Confirm a rate with the cabbie before you board, making sure you both understand whether you're talking U.S. or E.C. dollars.

Daily, high-speed ferry service runs among Guadeloupe, Marie-Galante, Les Saintes, Dominica, Martinique, and St. Lucia; contact **L'Express Des Iles**, *Tel. 767/448-2181, Fax 448-5787.* There's also a car ferry among these islands, stopping at Dominica four days a week. Book with the *Madikera* in Roseau, *Tel. 767/448-6977.*

ORIENTATION

Dominica is in the British Windward Islands, south of Guadeloupe and north of Martinique, an English rose between two French lilies. **Roseau**, the capital is on the southwest coast about 15 minutes south of Canefield Airport. Melville Hall Airfield is on the northeast coast near **Marigot**. Major thoroughfares are paved, two-lane roads. Roseau is the center of social and commercial life. Most business takes place here, in **Portsmouth**, and on the road between them. The drive is a pleasant, low-speed tour for those who like to linger in unspoiled villages to try snacks and souvenirs.

Roads don't serve the entire perimeter of the island but travelers can occupy endless days in rambling the more than 300 miles of (very poor) roads that lead up mountains and through villages. From Roseau, take a different road each day into Morne Trois Pitons National Park and other remote areas. Take your time. Distances are short but roads are so tortuous that it can take an hour to go ten or fifteen miles.

To orient yourself in Roseau, which straddles the **Roseau River** (also called the Queen's River), put the sea on your left and you're facing north. The town center lies on the south side of the river, a neat grid in which Queen Mary Street crosses the river at the East Bridge and Great George Street crosses at West Bridge. King George V Street is the chief road towards the east and Trafalgar. Almost every settlement on every island names its waterfront Bay Street and Roseau is no exception. Head south on Bath Road for a climb up **Morne Bruce**, where you can see the city and harbor for miles around.

GETTING AROUND DOMINICA

Taxis, which have set rates for trips between any two points, can also be hired for about $18 per hour and are an excellent value, especially for groups of two and more. For other trips, prices are regulated by the government but it's a good practice to verify the rate (and in what currency) before the trip begins. It can be hard to find a cab after dark, so make arrangements during the day. Taxis meet all flights at both airports but it's always wise to get the advice of your hotel host about the best way to get there when you arrive.

Taxi companies include **Mally's**, *Tel. 787/448-3114.* Custom tour companies offering guides, airport transfers, sightseeing, and hiking include **Antours**, *Tel. 787/448-6460*, and **Jon Vee Tours**, *Tel. 787/449-6463.*

Rental cars are available starting at about $50 a day plus EC$30 for a local driver's license. Gas costs about $2.50 per Imperial gallon, and it's hard to find on Sundays and holidays. Driving is on the left and the speed limit is 20 miles per hour in settlements and 10 miles per hour in school zones. Roads are steep or winding or both, with few stretches of straightaway longer than half a mile. When rounding a tight switchback, sound your horn. Relax and enjoy the experience. There are times when there isn't room to pass and somebody has to back up. It may as well be you.

Vehicles in a roundabout have the right-of-way; entering vehicles should yield. If you have an accident, call the police first and then the rental company. One more thing. Don't park closer than 15 feet to a corner or you'll get a ticket. If, after all this, you still want to drive a car rather than hire a taxi by the hour, here's a list of car rental agencies.

Budget Rent-a-Car, has cars at Canefield Airport, *Tel. 787/449-2080.* *To* reserve from the U.S., *Tel. 800/527-0700.* **Avis** has an agency in Roseau and will also pick up/ drop off at the airport, *Tel. 787/448-2481.* To reserve a car from the U.S., *Tel. 800/331-1212.* Car rentals are also available from **Auto Trade Ltd.**, *Tel. 767/448-2886;* **Ace Rentals**, *Tel. 767/448-4444;* **Bonus Rentals**, *Tel. 767/448-2650;* **Valley Rent-a-Car**, *Tel. 767/448-3233,* and **Wide Range Car Rentals**, *Tel. 767/448-2198.* Air conditioned sedans with automatic transmission are comfortable vehicles if you stay on the main roads; get a four-wheel drive vehicle to venture into the outback.

Crowded and hot but gaily authentic, 14-passenger minibuses ply the island and can eventually get you where you want to go. The fare from Woodford Hall (near Melville Hall Airport) to Roseau, for an example, is EC$3.50. Look for the designation H or HA on the license tag. Bus stops are marked by signs, and can always be found at the Old Market. Or, just wave down a bus if it has an "H" license. If you board at a bus terminus, try to find a bus that is almost full. They don't leave until they have a full load, and the wait can be long and hot if you're first aboard. Buses don't run on Sundays.

WHERE TO STAY

The government imposes a 10 percent hotel tax; meals including meal plans are plus three percent tax. Many hotels also add a service charge of 10 percent or more. Rates are quoted in and almost always paid in U.S. dollars. Ask whether your room rate includes room tax and service charge.

Unless otherwise noted, major credit cards are accepted. Your mailing address while in Dominica will end in Commonwealth of Dominica, West Indies. Write it all out, or your mail might go to the Dominican Republic.

A booking agency that can reserve your entire Dominica stay, diving or shore-bound, is **Caribbean Adventures**, *10500 Griffin Road, Suite 303, Fort Lauderdale FL 33328, Tel. 800/433-DIVE, Fax 954/434-4282.*

Expensive

ANCHORAGE HOTEL DIVE CENTER, *Castle Comfort a half mile from Roseau, mailing address P.O. Box 34, Roseau. Tel. 787/448-2638, Fax 448-5680. Rates at this 32-room hotel start at $125. Ask about dive packages and meal plans.*

Divers and yachties are among this hotel's biggest boosters, adding an undertow of international excitement because conversations overheard at dinner and the bar usually have a salty air. The hotel has its own dive shop, a rather pricey restaurant and bar (drink free on Thursday nights at the manager's cocktail party), a swimming pool and squash court. Excursions on land and sea including a whale watch cruise are offered. Rooms have air conditioning, television, and telephone.

Decor is fairly plain-jane but rooms are spacious and have basic essentials including two double beds and a private bathroom with tub or shower, television, air conditioning, and telephone. Each has a small, but private, balcony overlooking the pool. Room service, laundry, and babysitting can be arranged.

CASTLE COMFORT LODGE, *Castle Comfort, mailing address P.O. Box 2253, Roseau. Tel. 787/448-2188, Fax 448-6088; U.S. 800/544-7631, 800/729-7234 or 800/815-5019. Rates at this 16-room dive resort start at about $900 per person, double occupancy weekly including accommodations for two, breakfast and dinner daily, and dives. A non-diving person staying in the same room pays $605. The lodge is 1-1/2 miles south of Roseau.*

A neat white lodge stands out against the green lawns, where guests dive all day, then soak in the hot tub before dinner. At breakfast, feast on banana pancakes and then take another dive or leave for a whale watch, mountain bicycling tour, or a killer hike. If you're not certified, the hotel offers a resort course or full NAUI and PADI certification.

Dinners start with a local soup followed by a marinated salad, dasheen rolls, perhaps spaghetti africano and a choice of chicken or fish. Don't miss the coconut fudge. Rooms are air conditioned and some have cable television. Twins and doubles are available; tiled showers are supersize. Hosts provide a carafe of cold water in your room, a small touch that can mean a lot on a hot day.

CLUB DOMINIQUE HOTEL & VILLAS, *Calibishie. Tel. and Fax 787/445-7421. The hotel is 15 minutes from Melville Hall Airport. Rates at the new, 17-unit hotel had not been announced at press time.*

Perched on a 60-foot cliff overlooking the pounding Atlantic shore is one of Dominica's newest hotels (1998) and its cluster of villas. West Indian motifs mark the architecture: balconies, shutters, sharply peaked roofs, and window boxes overflowing with flowers. Views from the cliff top promise to be captivating; meals are American and Continental, combining local fruits and herbs with local and imported steaks and seafood. Two of the suites have full kitchens. Units have telephone, cable television, and VCR. Walk down to the white sand beach, swim in the pool, or practice your swing on the seaside driving range.

EVERGREEN HOTEL, *Castle Comfort, mailing address P.O. Box 309. Tel. 787/448-3288, Fax 448-6800. Doubles at this 16-room hotel start at $115 including full breakfast. It's on the west coast a mile from Roseau.*

A big gazebo overlooking the pool adds eye appeal to this tall, sunny, family-run hotel overlooking the seacoast. Rooms, which are elegantly floored in shining hardwoods to match louvered shutters, are air conditioned and have television and telephone. Some have balconies, with nightly views of the sun sinking into the sea. The pool and deck are ideal for sunning. If you prefer to swim in the sea, wear reef runners because the beach is rocky.

EXOTICA, *Box 109, Roseau. Tel. 787/448-8839, Fax 448-3855, Rates at this seven-unit lodge start at $146 double or $4102 for two for 28 nights. It's five miles from Roseau, a tortuous climb that requires cunning and a good transmission.*

Walk five minutes to the rushing river or just enjoy the nature show from your own chalet. You might spot a whale sounding in the sea, which lies 1,600 feet below (bring your biniculars), or a rare parrot in a tree so close you could touch it. The gardens surrounding the lodge are a seed catalog of dewy blooms and rich greenery. Cottages are made of wood and stone with solar hot water on their red tin roofs. You'll have your own kitchen and can do the cooking, hire a local cook, or dine in the lodge's own cafe. Units have fans, radio, telephone, and television.

FORT YOUNG HOTEL, *Victoria Street, P.O. Box 519, Roseau, Dominica, West Indies. Tel. 767/448-5000, Fax 448-5006; U.S. 800/223-6510 and Canada 800/424-5500. The hotel is 15 minutes or EC$8 by taxi from Canefield Airport and a five-minute walk from the city. Doubles at this 32-room hotel start at $125. Add $11 for continental breakfast and $36 per person daily for breakfast and dinner.*

The original 1770 fort forms the core of a handy, in-town hotel where rooms have high and woody ceilings, wood louvers at the windows, rattan furniture, fabrics in cool neutrals, and a cliffy, sea view from a small balcony or terrace. Popular with business travelers as well as fun seekers, the hotel has meeting rooms, direct overseas dialing in every room, and typing, telex, and fax services available. Day tours and car rentals are cheerfully arranged for you. The hotel has its own bar and restaurant, and a big swimming pool. Rooms are air conditioned and have cable television with 11 channels.

GARRAWAY HOTEL, *Place Heritage, 1 Bay Front, Box 789, Roseau. Tel. 767/449-8800, Fax 449-8807. Rates at this 31-unit hotel start at $125. From the airport it's an EC$8 taxi ride.*

A five-story hotel handy to the harbor and downtown Roseau, this family-operated hotel surrounds an open courtyard. Guests can find respite from city bustle on the rooftop terrace, but the sidewalk cafe and bar are a better place to watch the world go by. Rooms and suites are air conditioned and have satellite television, ceiling fans, and direct-dial telephones. Telex and fax are available.

LAURO CLUB, *Salisbury, mailing address Box 483, Roseau. Tel. 787/449-6602, Fax 449-6603. Rates at this 10-unit hotel start at $85 for a studio and $125 for a one-bedroom apartment. It's on the west coast halfway between Roseau and Portsmouth, a half mile from the village of Salisbury.*

Sidle up to the big, stone, outdoor grill early on Saturday night to gaze out to sea and keep an eye on the chef while he cranks up a gala feast. Musical entertainment comes later, after the chicken, steaks, and all the trimmings. Barracks-like "villas" are painted in pastels and starkly furnished with basics, but it's a lot of clean, comfortable living for the price. Cook in your own, fully equipped kitchen or dine in the club's very good Creole-Swiss restaurant. Climb down the long stone staircase to get to the beach, or enjoy the big swimming pool. Play ping pong, arrange an island tour, hike, or lounge under the palms and poinciana trees, enjoying the flowers.

PETIT COULIBRI GUEST COTTAGES, *Pointe Def, mailing address Box 331, Roseau. Tel. and Fax 787/446-3150. Rates at this five-unit property start at $200. It's a steep, winding, 10-minute drive from Soufriere.*

Back-to-nature purists will like this solar-powered resort at the back of beyond. A cluster of cottages in the cool hills where you won't miss air conditioning, these wood and stone dwellings let you do your own cooking and nothing much more except hike, explore, and swim in the pool. It's fairly isolated, so have provisions provided for your kitchen or arrange for a meal plan for about $20 per person for dinner; $10 more if you also want a full breakfast.

RED ROCK HAVEN HOLIDAY HOMES, *Pointe Baptiste, Calibishie, mailing address Box 71, Roseau. Tel. 787/448-2181, Fax 448-5787. Cottage rates start at $150 daily, falling to $110 daily on a monthly basis. It's on the north coast, four miles as the crow flies, or a 45-minute drive, from Melville Hall Airfield.*

Your cottage has a lofty view of the Atlantic, allowing you to laze away the days on your terrace watching the ocean. Or, walk down to one of Dominica's best beaches with good dive sites not far offshore. Cottages, which are furnished with colorful local fabrics and furniture, have cooling fans and radio. You can sleep four in the one-bedroom unit or up to six in the two-bedroom. For entertainment, delve into the library of books left by previous guests. There's a swimming pool, sauna and gift shop but you'll need a car to get to restaurants and attractions.

WESLEEANN APARTEL, *P.O. Box 1764, 8 Ninth Street, Canefield, Roseau, Dominica, West Indies. Tel. 767/449-0419, Fax 449-2473. Rates at this six-story hotel start at $110. The hotel is four miles from Roseau, near Canefield Airport.*

A home away from home for business travelers and long-term visitors, this hotel also makes a comfortable perch for leisure travelers who prefer a residential setting. Handy to the airport and capital, it has one-, two-, and three-bedroom apartments, and a penthouse apartment with private Jacuzzi. Suites are air conditioned and have ceiling fans, a fully-equipped kitchen with microwave oven, direct dial telephones, daily maid service, both 110-and 220-volt outlets in every room, cable television, and private balconies overlooking the water. Fax service and laundry are available. The hotel's tour desk can arrange pleasure sightseeing, a rental car, or meetings needs. The Penthouse lounge is a convivial place for a before-dinner drink with a nice mix of ex-pats and tourists.

Moderate
AMBASSADOR HOTEL, *Canefield. Tel. 787/449-1501, Fax 449-2304. Rates at this ten-room hotel start at $50 single and $68 double. It's at the Canefield airport.*

An ideal business address and an affordable place to stay in the Pringles Bay area, this small hotel has a restaurant, bar, air conditioning, balconies, parking, and room service. Rooms have telephone, television, and maid service.

CASTAWAYS BEACH HOTEL, *Mero, mailing address P.O. Box 5, Roseau. Tel. 787/449-6244, Fax 449-6246. The village lies just south of Salisbury, about 13 miles north of Roseau and eight miles from Canefield airport. Rates at the 26-room club start at $96. Ask about dive packages; add $30 per person daily for breakfast and dinner. The hotel is an EC$3 bus ride from Roseau. It closes in September and October.*

Spacious rooms with a ceiling fan, basic furnishings, private bath, and a couple of double beds are ideal for a couple or family, clean but in need of spiffing up. Air conditioning is available for a few dollars more. The beach is black volcanic sand. Dive with the hotel's own dive operation, or sit on your balcony and contemplate expanses of rustling coconut palms and colorful flowers. Hang out in the thatched-roof bar, where the rum punch is made from scratch – including cutting up a coconut. Then dine on hearty (but hardly gourmet) meals in the hotel's Almond Tree. (A recent traveler was offered a dinner choice of baked chicken, shepherd's pie, or macaroni and cheese; another warned against ordering anything called beef).

Breakfast, lunch, and afternoon tea are available from room service until 5pm. Pleasant touches include a dart board, tables made from enormous tree slices, volleyball, tennis, and an electric organ. Once a week, Windjammer Cruises guests pile ashore for a barbecue and mingle.

COCONUT BEACH HOTEL, *Picard, mailing address, Box 37, Roseau. Tel. 787/445-5393, Fax 445-5693. Rates at this 22-room hotel are $55 single, $65 double and $90 for a bungalow with kitchenette. Add $12 for continental breakfast and $40 for breakfast and dinner. It's equally handy to both airports, a ride of about $17 per person based on four passengers sharing one cab.*

Dominica doesn't have an abundance of beaches, but this sandy brown shoreline is one of the island's cleanest and best. Overlook Prince Rupert Bay and Fort Shirley from modest accommodations that can be discounted for stays of a week or more. Units have air conditioning or ceiling fan, private bath, kitchen, cable television, and telephone. The cooking is Creole, featuring fresh seafood and wildlife such as mountain chicken. Snorkeling, birdwatching, windsurfing, diving and volleyball are the activities.

FLORAL GARDENS, *Concord, mailing address Box 192, Roseau. Tel. and Fax 787/4445-7636. Rates at this 15-room hotel start at $70; suites at $80.*

You're in a flowery hillside overlooking the Saint Marine River and the forest preserves in a chalet where rooms are small but as charming as a yodel. Enjoy the lush grounds, hike the surrounding woodlands, shop the crafts boutiques and dine in one of Dominica's better restaurants. Entertainers often play the restaurant and bar. Rooms have air conditioning, porch or balcony, telephone, and room service.

Cottages with kitchen are available, as are car rental and a courtesy car. Your owner-host is O.J. Seraphin, who was once the prime minister. **HUMMINGBIRD INN**, *Morne Daniel, Rock-a-Way, P.O. Box 191, Roseau, Dominica, West Indies. Tel. and fax 767/449-1042. Rates at this 10-room inn are $55 single or $65 double with shared bath and $110 for a suite with private bath. It's between Canefield Airport and Roseau.* If you like the intimacy and affordability of a friendly inn, Jeane Finuacane's homey villa fills the bill. It's a short walk from Rock-a-Way beach and within 30 minutes by car from some of the island's most appealing natural attractions such as Middleham Falls. The best suite, the one with private bath, has a queen-size, four-poster bed, dining area, kitchenette and a veranda. Television is optional. Cooling is by night breezes and ceiling fans. Meals and drinks are available and are recommended, but must be arranged in advance.

PAPILLOTE WILDERNESS RETREAT, *Trafalgar Falls Road, mailing address P.O. Box 2287, Roseau. Tel. 787/448-2287, Fax 448-2285. Doubles start at $70. Add $30 daily for breakfast and dinner. The eight-room retreat is closed in September. Find it four miles northeast of Roseau on the road to Morne Macaque. By taxi it's a $20 ride from Roseau, and you can also get here by bus if you're willing to walk the last 15 minutes from Trafalgar.*

This retreat – tiny, secluded, and shrouded in the rain forest – is founded by marine biologist Anne Baptiste and her husband Cuthbert, who oversees the restaurant. This is, don't forget, the rain forest and that means endless rain but also a share of rainbows reigning over realms of mist-loving orchids, bromeliads, vines, and towering trees. It's perched at the apex of a valley that runs down to the sea, set in woodlands not far from an end-of-the-world waterfall where you can swim in a cool river.

Back at the retreat, a hot tub is fed by a natural hot spring. Your arrival is greeted by a peacock who might honor you with a spread of his magnificent plumage. Accommodations are cozily furnished with bold local artwork, woven straw mats on the floors, and handmade quilts much like those that are for sale in the boutique. The restaurant is locally renowned for its lusty, simple dishes featuring seafood, fresh fruit, and vegetables. The works of Haitian artist Louis Desire, who now lives on Dominica, are shown and sold in the resort. Most of the best hikes start in the next valley, near Laudat, a drive of less than a half hour.

REIGATE HALL HOTEL, *Mountain Road, Reigate, mailing address Box 200, Reigate. Tel. 787/448-4031, Fax 448-4034. Rates at this 17-room hotel start at $75 including breakfast. It's about two miles east of Roseau.*

Once a planter's greathouse overlooking Roseau from a lofty hilltop, this clubby, British-style hotel makes an ideal address for business and leisure travelers. Old stone walls can still be seen in places, setting a mood of mellow and time-proven hospitality. The floors are glowing wood, walls a cool white, furniture is planter style. Guest rooms are arranged around the swimming pool. Play tennis, dine in the hotel's own restaurant, or order from room service.

ROSEAU VALLEY HOTEL, *mailing address P.O. Box 1876, Roseau. The hotel is in the Roseau Valley 10 minutes from Roseau. Rates at this 11-unit lodge are in the $125 range for a self-contained unit.*

Your accommodations in this chalet have cooking facilities, so bring provisions with you from Roseau unless you want to take all meals in the hotel restaurant. You're perched on a steep mountainside, looking out over glorious scenery and handy to the best hiking areas.

SPRINGFIELD PLANTATION HOTEL, *Box 456, Roseau. Tel. 787/449-2401. Rates at this 15-unit hotel start at $70. Add $5 for continental breakfast, $25 for breakfast and dinner, and $35 for full American plan.*

It's scruffy but it's also the headquarters of an environmental group, so tree huggers will feel at home in the lush, green surroundings and furnishings from a bygone era. Take a room, suite, or cottage. Fans and a telephone are available. The restaurant and bar are pretty good but the accommodations are rustic, with emphasis on the rust.

SUTTON PLACE HOTEL, *25 Old Street, mailing address Box 2333, Roseau. Tel. 787/449-8700, Fax 448-3045. Rates at this eight-room hotel start at $100; suites at $105. It's in the heart of Roseau's business district.*

Although this is an ideal business address, it's also a sunny headquarters for the leisure traveler who wants to stay in the heart of the city in comfortable, upscale surroundings. The family-operated hotel has a swimming pool, good food, and a savvy, smiling staff that's eager to serve. Rooms and suites are richly furnished in antiques, reproductions, and charming collectibles that look right at home in a structure dating to before the turn of the century. Each unit has air conditioning, ceiling fan, direct-dial phone, hair dryer, radio, and cable television. Eat at the hotel's own restaurant and bar, or stroll the Bayfront promenade to find others.

Budget

CARIB TERRITORY GUEST HOUSE, *Crayfish River, Carib Territory. Tel. 787/445-7256. Rates at this eight-room guest house are $40-$50 double; add $6 for continental breakfast and $20 for breakfast and dinner. Land at Melville Hall Airfield and drive an hour south, or cross the island from Canefield all the way to the east coast.*

This primitive guest house is the only place to stay for miles around, but it's ideal for those who want to stay in the largest reservation of Carib Indians remaining in the Caribbean. There's a restaurant, bar, entertainment, telephone and television.

FALLSVIEW GUEST HOUSE, *Waterfall Road, Upper Trafalgar. Rates at this nine-room guest house start at $40. It's about four miles east of Roseau.*

Add $35 per person daily for breakfast and dinner. Cottages are available by the day or week. Arrange to have their courtesy car pick you up at the airport.

Natural accommodations in a natural setting overlooking Trafalgar Falls are a perfect home base for those who want to strike out on a new hiking path each day or just stay "home" to listen to birdsong, chuckling waters, and skittering wildlife deep in the bush. There's a good restaurant featuring local dishes and a bar, so this is the kind of place where guests sign on for a week or two of blissful relaxation. Open all year, the inn can arrange hiking, diving, and island tours. Rooms aren't air conditioned but there are fans, maid service, telephone, and television.

ITASSI COTTAGES, *Morne Bruce. Tel. 787/448-7247, Fax 448-3045. Rates are $40 to $110 daily. The cottages are 30 minutes from Roseau.*

You're high in the hills above Roseau overlooking the sea as far as Scotts Head in a comfortable lodge with a wrap-around veranda to catch the breezes. Cottages, which can can sleep up to six, are furnished with a homey mixture of hand-me-downs, handmade bed coverings, rustic calabash lamps, and plaited floor coverings. Cottages have a kitchen, ceiling fans, and cable television. The three units share a laundry.

GACHETTE'S SEASIDE LODGE, *Scott's Head. Tel. 787/448-4552, Fax 448-2308. Rates start at $70 daily. It's an hour's drive south from Roseau.*

The price is right for a basic cottage with kitchenette, fan, maid service, and television. Fishing, diving, and all the pleasures of the Soufriere area and the bay are nearby.

ROXY'S MOUNTAIN LODGE, *Laudat, mailing address Box 265, Roseau. Tel. 787/448-4845, Fax 448-4845. Doubles are $46; cottages $75.*

Perched at an altitude of 2,500 feet is this coolly forested hideaway with its own restaurant and a bar where hikers like to stop for a cold drink. Accommodations aren't the focus here. The scenery is. You'll have telephone, radio, television, and maid service; the cottages have a kitchen.

VENA'S GUEST HOUSE, *48 Cork Street near the corner of Queen Mary Street, Roseau. Tel. 787/448-3266. Rates at this 15-room guest house start at $20 single and $25 double including continental breakfast.*

If you like a local inn with rock-bottom rates and a city location, this one has a bar, restaurant, fans, and television but don't count on having a private bath. Out of town, **Vena's Paradise** at Pond Casse has doubles starting at $75 and an apartment at $95. Use the same address and telephone number for booking.

TWINS & DOUBLES FOR DIVERS

Resorts that cater to divers often have more twin rooms than doubles so, if you want a double bed, be sure to request one.

WHERE TO EAT

We have quoted prices in EC dollars because that's how they are listed on most menus on Dominica; the menu may also be in both English and French. Unless otherwise stated, credit cards are accepted but it's always wise to call ahead to check.

Dominica is one of the more unspoiled Caribbean islands, offering traditional West Indian foods, many of them locally grown, at reasonable prices. Smoked or stewed opossum (manicou) and agouti (a large rodent; think of it as squirrel, raccoon, or rabbit) are offered by local restaurants, especially in October and November when Dominica celebrates its own cultural heritage. Mountain chicken, which also appears on island menus, is a land frog. Crabs are netted in season, and are served in the shell. The dish is listed as crab backs.

The island is British, so cucumbers are in everything from salads to sandwiches. Inexplicably, rice and potatoes are often served on the same plate plus the starchy dasheen. Generically, the local go-withs are called "provisions," usually served with or as an alternative to rice. They include starches such as yucca or "pumpkin," which is akin to what North Americans call squash and Brits may call marrow.

Expensive

BALISIER, *in the Garraway Hotel, Place Heritage, One Bayfront, Roseau. Tel. 449-8800. Reservations are essential. The restaurant is open daily 7am to 10:30pm. Entrees are priced EC$30 to EC$62.*

A smart business address, the Garraway is also one of the best restaurants in the city where you'll dine overlooking the colorful bayfront or on the terrace overlooking the inner courtyard. The menu always offers a vegetarian choice plus steaks, chicken, mountain chicken, stuffed crab backs, curries, seafood, and pork. On Fridays, the buffet lunch is a good time to try a host of West Indian and Creole favorites. The Ole Jetty Bar is the place for drinks plain or fancy.

CASTLE COMFORT LODGE, *one mile south of Roseau. Tel. 787/448-2188. Three-course meals with coffee are priced $EC60 to $EC75. Call for hours and dinner reservations.*

Local fruits and vegetables create dishes that are served family style, using traditional family recipes for West Indian, American, and European classics. All dinners include a starter, main course, dessert, and coffee. This is a favorite dive hotel so you can expect hearty, farmhand servings of filling, no-fuss foods.

CLARKHALL RESTAURANT, *in the Layou River Resort, Layou (between Mahaut and Saint Joseph). Tel. 787/449-6081. Reservations are required; transportation is provided from some hotels. Hours are 7:15am to 9:30pm daily. Plan to spend EC$45 to $EC75.*

Chinese and Creole dishes complement each other nicely in this friendly restaurant a few miles inland from the east coast. Order a traditional Chinese meal or mix and match as you go from course to course. On Sundays from noon to 2:30pm the buffet brunch is a whale of a feed and an excellent sampler of a variety of dishes.

LA ROBE CREOLE, *3 Victoria Street, Roseau. Tel. 787/448-2896. Hours are daily except Sunday from noon to 9:30pm. Prices range EC$50 to EC$75. Reservations are essential. Find it between the Garraway and Fort Young hotels.*

The best callalou on the island starts a meal that could be anything from pizza to spicy crab backs, batter-fried chicken to shrimp sweetly wreathed in toasted coconut. To be more adventurous try the manicou, curried goat, or octopus stewed in red wine. End the meal with one of the homemade cakes. The setting alone is worth a meal here. A typical West Indian colonial stone house overlooks the sea; servers are dressed in traditional plaids with jaunty caps knotted to indicate their marital status.

MARQUIS DE BOUILLE RESTAURANT, *in the Fort Young Hotel, Victoria Street, Roseau. Tel. 448-5000. Entrees are priced EC$40 to EC$65. Reservations are suggested. The restaurant is open daily 7am to 10pm.*

Have a cocktail or a local Kabuli beer in the Balas Bar, one of the town's best meet markets, then order from a menu of savory, spicy Creole dishes accenting fresh seafood and rafts of fresh island fruits and vegetables. For lunch try roti, pumpkin soup, or flying fish with "bakes," a fried bread. Fish or chicken served the Creole way are smothered in a tasty sauce of tomatoes, onions, peppers and homegrown spices. End the meal with locally-grown coffee.

REIGATE HALL RESTAURANT, *Reigate Hall Hotel, Mountain Road, Reigate. Tel. 448-4031. Located a mile east of Roseau, it's open daily 1pm to 3pm and 7pm to 10:30pm. Entrees are priced EC$45 to EC$75. Reservations are recommended.*

Because of the long, slow, twisting climb into the green hills, this is a good place to come for a leisurely lunch and sightseeing ride. A splashy waterwheel serenades Creole foods rich in mysterious spices. Try the fish chowder, shrimp in a garlicky sauce, curries, chicken in red wine, and a host of seafood dishes, best done with a piquant Creole sauce. The setting is an old greathouse, rich in glowing hardwoods and old stones.

OCEAN TERRACE, *in the Anchorage Hotel, Castle Comfort. Tel. 448-2638. It's open breakfast through dinner, serving main courses priced EC$20 to EC$45.*

Dine on chicken or lobster with full Creole accompaniments, or order from the vegetarian menu. The scene is a busy hotel restaurant with a lively bar.

EAU ERTÉ

If you're an art fancier or a crossword puzzler, you've heard of Erté, one of the master artists of the early 20th century. He gave his name to a spring water that is bottled on Dominica as Eau Erté.

PAPILLOTE RESTAURANT, *in Papillote Wilderness Retreat on Trafalgar Falls Road, four miles east of Roseau. It's open 8am to 10pm every day. Unless you're a guest in the retreat, reservations are essential. Prices start at EC$53.*

Think of this as a day's excursion into the rain forest – with lunch. Bring hardy shoes, light rain gear, and a swimsuit and enjoy the hiking and swimming. Use the resort's mineral pool and garden path for EC$5. You'll overlook a wondrous green valley and hike through bowers of flowers and towering trees. Meals involve mountains of fresh fruit and vegetables as well as seafood, bouk (freshwater shrimp), mountain chicken (frog's legs), and banana leaf-wrapped mixtures steamed to perfection.

SUTTON PLACE GRILLE, *in the Sutton Place Hotel, 25 Old Street, Roseau. Tel. 449-8700. It's open daily 7am to 10pm Dinner dishes are priced EC$26 to EC$70.*

A courtyard inside century-old stone walls is for dining under the stars, or you can eat inside where it's air conditioned. For breakfast try buljow, a spicy blend of salt fish, vegetables, and boiled bananas. In season, crab backs are filled with flaked crab meat with heady seasonings and topped with buttery bread crumbs. For simpler fare, have grilled steak, chicken, or fish with a bit of fried bread and fresh local yams. There's a nice mix here of traditional and imported fare.

Moderate

CALLALOO RESTAURANT, *King George V Street 63, Roseau. Tel. 448-3386. Open for lunch and dinner, the restaurant accepts no credit cards. It's located downtown, just off Bay Street.*

The soup of the day is usually callaloo, and nobody does it better than Mrs. Peters, who runs this unadorned local favorite. She'll have mountain chicken, chicken, and lobster on the menu plus breadfruit puffs and a pile of "provisions" such as pumpkin, yucca, sweet potatoes and such. Try her soursop ice cream for dessert.

CASTAWAYS HOTEL, *Mero. Tel. 449-6244. Find the hotel 12 miles north of Roseau at Mero on the coast just north of St. Joseph. It's open every day breakfast through dinner. Plan to spend about EC$40 for dinner.*

Dine outdoors on the terrace on simple meals that focus on the catch of the day cooked in a Creole sauce, broiled lobster, or hearty chicken or chops served with local vegetables, dasheen puffs, and redbean rice. The mango chicken is stuffed with mango, ginger and lime. For dessert, the Rhum Cake is made with Macoucherie rum, which is distilled not far from here in an ages-old factory.

COCONUT BEACH RESTAURANT, *in the Coconut Beach Hotel, Picard, Portsmouth. Tel. 445-5393. It's open daily breakfast through dinner. Plan to spend EC$30 for dinner, less for breakfast and lunch.*

Yachties are among the regular guests here at a waterfront hotel that is also a dive and watersports center. Come for the beach barbecue on Sunday, or any day for fruit drinks with or without rum from the landmark Macoucheri rum factory nearby. Dine on affordable rotis and sandwiches or make a meal out of grilled fresh fish or lobster with provisions (trimmings).

CRYSTAL TERRACE, *in the Evergreen Hotel, Castle Comfort. Tel. 448-3288. It's open for breakfast, lunch, and dinner. Call for dinner reservations and hours and plan to spend about EC$50 for dinner.*

Named for the glittering crystal chandeliers that are its trademark, this terrace restaurant has a faithful breeze and good views of the sea. A specialty is the crab backs, but there are also fresh fish specials, chicken, and lobster served with plantains, kushkush, yucca, pumpkin, and other island produce. For dessert have fresh fruit or one of the sugary cakes.

FLORAL GARDENS RESTAURANT, *in the Floral Gardens Hotel, Concord. Tel. 445-7636. It's open daily for breakfast, lunch, and dinner; reservations are suggested for dinner. Plan to spend about EC$50 per person.*

Rustic best describes the woodwork and trestle tables of this homey restaurant deep in the interior up the Sainte Marie River at the edge of the forest reserve. The name says it all, describing the flowering trees and shrubs that make for an enchanting setting overlooking the river. Dine on one of the local specialties such as agouti, manicou, or crayfish or be less adventurous with chicken, fish, or vegetarian dishes that even meat eaters delight in. For dessert, have the homemade rum raisin ice cream.

GUIYAVE, *15 Cork Street. Tel. 448-2930. Hours are Monday through Friday, 8am to 3pm, Saturday 9am to 2:30pm. The patisserie is open Monday through Friday 9am to 6pm and Saturday 8am to 2pm. Meals are EC$25 to EC$55.*

Stop in for breakfast or lunch on the terrace of this popular hangout, where you can linger over coffee and watch Roseau's bustling life. The building is typically West Indian, with a second floor porch overlooking the street. For Creole cuisine, dine upstairs; for ice cream and patties, eat downstairs. For lunch choose from hearty West Indian standards featuring chicken, pork, conch (called by its French name lambi), crab, rabbit, and mountain chicken. Goat water, which is actually a thick, hearty, soupy stew, is a Saturday special. If you want only a cool drink, talk to the bartender about his famous juices made from exotic island fruits or the sea moss, which some people drink as a refreshing tonic. Buy baguettes, croissants, brioche, and French sweets at the patisserie to take out.

ORCHARD RESTAURANT, *King George V Street 31. Tel. 448-3051. Dinners average EC$35-50. Call about hours and reservations.*

An oasis in the heart of town is this shaded courtyard known for its black pudding, roti, meat pies, burgers and sandwiches. For dinner have the coconut shrimp, callalo thick with crabmeat, or lobster.

PEARL'S CUISINE, *Bay Street at Peebles Park. Tel. 448-8707. Plan to spend EC$35 for dinner. Hours vary, so call ahead.*

Dine on hearty portions of fresh fish, shrimp, or a tender stewed chicken that is guaranteed to cure the homesick blues. If you're on a budget, the three-course, fixed price menu is an excellent value. Ask about the daily specials.

RESTAURANT PAIHO, *10 Church Street. Tel. 448-8999. Dishes are priced EC$12 to EC$130. It's open Monday through Saturday 11am to 3pm and 5:30pm to 10:30pm; Sundays 6-10pm.*

Cantonese, Szechuan, and Hunan dishes are served indoors and out, and for take-out. The spring rolls are a knockout, and you can't go wrong with any of the pork, beef, chicken, duck, or vegetable stir-fries served with rice steamed to perfection. On weekends, lunch specials are an excellent buy.

SEABIRD CAFE, *Scotts Head Village, Soufriere. Tel. 448-7725. Dinner costs EC$20 to EC$40. Call for hours.*

Start with the soup of the day or the codfish accras, then have grilled fresh fish with provisions, herbed green beans, eggplant creole or christophene gratin, and a salad. The baked chicken breast comes with mango chutney, or dine more simply on a shrimp salad, pizza, or burger. For dessert have the homemade pineapple crisp or one of the tropical ice creams.

SYMES-ZEE EATERY, *34 King George Street. Tel. 787/448-2494. Plan to spend EC$45 to EC$50. Hours are Monday through Saturday 9am to midnight.*

A lively local spot in the heart of town and handy to hotels, this eatery specializes in local foods including mountain chicken, pork, seafood, and chicken with a Creole accent. Savor one of the exotic fruit juices such as paw paw or passion fruit. Live entertainers present Jazz Night on Thursdays.

WATERHALL RESTAURANT & BAR, *in the Roseau Valley Hotel, Copt Hall, Tel. 449-8176. Open daily 8am to 10pm, it requires reservations. Meals are $EC25 to $EC50.*

Located on the outskirts of Roseau, this intimate restaurant adds a personalized, family touch to Creole dishes made to order. Order steamed fish, rotis, curried chicken and daily specials, all served with organically grown vegetables.

Budget
BLUE MAX CAFE & DELI, *16 Hanover Street, Roseau. Tel. 449-8907. It's a block from the post office or courthouse downtown. Sandwiches are priced EC$10 to EC$17. Call for hours and to place a take-out order.*
This is as close as you'll come in Dominica to a New York deli. Order a piled-high pastrami or corned beef sandwich, mortadella on pita, provolone with jalapeño on a croissant, a Reuben, and so on. Sandwiches are tailored to your choice of filling, bread, toppings and dressings. Get a side of potato salad, pasta salad, or cole slaw. There's also soup, hummus, onion rings, salads and burgers. Try the flying fish sandwich with curly fries.

CARIBANA, *31 Cork Street. Tel. 448-7340. Menus items are in the EC$5-EC$10 range. It's open Monday through Friday 8am to 5pm and Saturday 8am to 2pm.*
Although Caribana is best known as a craft shop and art gallery, it's a delightful spot to have tea, fresh fruit juice, a sweet bun or other small snack, and the city's best cup of coffee, the robust Cafe Dominique. Once a month there are amateur nights and poetry nights in an arty, coffee-house setting.

MOUSE HOLE SNACKETTE, *3 Victoria Street downstairs under La Robe Creole. Takeouts start at EC$5; pay about EC$15 for a meal. It's open daily except Sunday 8am to 9:30pm They don't take credit cards.*
This little hole in the wall is famed for its roti, Indian flatbread rolled around a fragrant and spicy mixture of chicken, beef, pork and potato and spiced with curry. It's the perfect place to stop by for sandwiches, salads, juices, and sodas to take back to your lodgings or on a picnic.

MARGHERITA'S PIZZA, *6 Cork Street, Roseau. Tel. 448-6003. Hours are Monday through Saturday 7am to 11pm and Sunday 1pm to 10pm. Prices start at EC$20.*
On the dinner menu you'll find pizzas in three sizes and a variety of toppings plus Italian-American standbys such as lasagna, spaghetti and meatballs, ravioli, ziti, and calzones. Because it's so handy in the heart of town, it's also a good place to drop in for breakfast. At lunchtime, specials include sandwiches, Italian dishes, and salads.

FLORAL GARDENS HOTEL, *Concord Village, near the northeast coast. Main dishes are priced EC$15 to EC$50. The hotel's two restaurants, Chalot and Gallery, are open daily 7:30am to 10:30pm. Tel. 445-7636.*
Overlook Carib lands from the banks of the Pagua River while you sample hibiscus juice, crayfish cooked Creole style, agouti, and manicou or more conventional chicken, beef, and pork dishes with a Dominican

accent. Accompaniments usually include dasheen puffs and a cornucopia of vegetables such as carrots, beets and potatoes.

MANGO BAR & RESTAURANT, *Bay Street, Portsmouth. Tel. 445-3099. Dishes are priced EC$10 to EC$60 breakfast through dinner, 8am to 11pm.*

In a quaint West Indian wood cottage painted buttercup yellow and white and topped with a tin roof, discover Creole classics including mountain chicken, sea eggs, and lobster plus a wide variety of international dishes: spaghetti bolognaise, pork chops, baked chicken, lobster, lamb, and crayfish. Breakfasts are French or Creole style. At lunch, have a chicken sandwich and a freshly squeezed fruit punch. The location in the heart of Portsmouth makes it handy for in-town visitors.

OCEAN BREEZE RESTAURANT, *in the Lauro Club, Salisbury, on the coast halfway between Roseau and Portsmouth. Tel. 449-6602. Hours are 6pm to 9:30pm daily. Reservations are urged. Meals cost EC$45 to EC$75.*

On Wednesday and Saturday nights, dinner is grilled outdoors at the bar for an appreciative mix of locals, ex-pats, guests, and tourists who venture up from Roseau or down from Portsmouth. It's a gala evening with live music. Every night features menus of French and Creole favorites, usually with a splurge special such as lobster or steak.

SPRINGFIELD PLANTATION GUESTHOUSE, *Springfield. Tel. 787/449-1041. Located in Springfield, the guesthouse is east of Canefield. Prices are EC$40 to EC$75. Reservations are required. Hours are 7am to 10pm.*

Take a ride into the countryside for a true, Dominican dining experience featuring organically grown fruits and vegetables, locally raised poultry and goat and crabs, mountain chicken, and other beasts from the wild, all in saucy Creole style.

SUGAR APPLE CAFE, *in Exotica Cottages, Gommier, Giraudel, on the slopes of Morne Anglais southeast of Roseau. Tel. 448-8839. Reservations are required. Dinners are priced EC$60 to EC$110. Hours are 7:30am to 11:30pm every day.*

Drive up into the slope of Morne Anglais in Morne Trois Pitons National Park into an incredible garden busting with fruits, flowers, and fragrance. The Cafe sits surrounded by heliconias and Fae's Rock Garden. Sample johnny cake and saltfish seasoned with organically grown herbs or choose from a daily list of dishes depending on what came in fresh from the bush or butcher. Fresh produce abounds in almost every course from celebrated soups to cakes and ices. End the meal with freshly brewed local coffee.

> ## PEANUT PUNCH LIQUEUR
> *Found in liquor shops on Dominica, this sweet, nutty liqueur is delicious on crushed ice or over ice cream.*

SEEING THE SIGHTS

Dominica is one of the most rugged and inaccessible islands in the Caribbean, with cliffy coastlines and craggy mountains. It's graced with a wildness that on many other islands has been bulldozed and dynamited away. Sightseeing here is a matter of walking steep and twisted trails, diving on sea gardens, and driving narrow, steep roads that may lead only to a dead end in a village or seashore.

Tours and taxis are so inexpensive (about $20 per hour) that it pays to take at least a day or two with a professional driver, who will also turn out to be an excellent guide, advisor, and best pal.

At trailheads, "guides" clamor to be hired, but their offer to show you the way is more than mere kindness. They want a job, and terms need to be agreed upon in advance. It's best to get a professional guide from a reliable company, especially for the arduous hike to **Boiling Lake**. It's a three-hour walk each way, so don't go unless you're in good health. To connect with an experienced guide for any national park lands, *Tel. 448-2401*.

Middleham Falls is a strenuous, 90-minute hike through dense woodlands. If you're in shape, it makes a beautiful walk through flowers and fruit trees, ending at the falls and a natural pool where you can swim. Guides can also take you to sulphur springs in the **Valley of Desolation, Wotten Waven, and Grand Soufriere**, all of them a fascinating glimpse of a sulphurous hell.

Emerald Pool, just north of Roseau, is an easy walk handy to town, so it's likely to be more crowded than other waterfalls. Take your swim suit so you can swim in the natural pool. **Trafalgar Falls**, two spectacular cascades, are reached in a 15-minute walk from the road. The going can be slippery, but the chance to swim in the hot water (father) pool is worth an extra climb. The cold falls are known as the mother.

The Layou River, which flows out of the **Northern Forest Reserve**, is another spot where you can swim in cold river water after soaking in hot springs. Beware of strong river currents, especially during the rainy season. Take your camera to photograph the suspension bridge, which is something out of a Tarzan movie.

North of Portsmouth, visit **Cabrits National Park**, *Tel. 448-2401, extension 415*, which covers 1,300 acres. Its most accessible point of interest is **Fort Shirley**, which has ancient walls and wonderful ocean views. Tour the restored portion with its fine museum, then follow the trail through a steamy jungle that looks like the Temple of Doom. Around every bend in the path are more ruins, choked by vines and strangled by trees that have split old stone walls.

Once a powerful English outpost, it has now been reclaimed by nature but it has been tamed somewhat by the teamwork of local volunteers and by British sailors who come ashore to help out when they are in the area. A small, native gift shop is a good place to buy Carib baskets and local bay rum after-shave lotion. An audio-visual program shows in the visitor center. For all national park information, *Tel. 448-2401.*

Near Portsmouth, local guides take passengers through mangrove lagoons in small boats, stopping at a bamboo bar. Opt for a canoe trip, which will be quieter and allow you to see more of the wildlife. A powerboat trip is faster, but so noisy that you'll see less. Or, take the road that follows the Indian River up into the interior to tiny, colorful, shantytown villages such as **Bornes**, **Dos D'Ane**, **La Source**, and **Paix Bouche**.

Save a day for an expedition into **Carib Territory**, a 3,700-acre reserve filled with interesting, outgoing people whose basketry motifs have been passed down, generation by generation, since long before European settlement. Primarily they are farmers and fishermen today, much like any other Dominicans.

Morne Trois Pitons National Park is a treasure trove of sightseeing. Its best-known sites include **Boeri Lake**, a 3,000-foot-high crater filled with fresh water. Plan on a 45-minute hike each way. A trail to the top of the three-peaked mountain reaches an altitude of 4,550 feet.

The park's **Boiling Lake**, said to be the second-largest boiling lake in the world, is kept at temperatures up to almost 200 degrees by escaping gases burped by molten lava untold feet below the surface. The hike to the lake is seven grueling miles and should not be attempted without an experienced guide. One misstep on the slippery, muddy path, and your goose is cooked. Literally. The walk takes you through the eerie **Valley of Desolation**, a sulphurous purgatory devoid of plant or animal life.

Driving between **Portsmouth** and **Roseau** can occupy a day of stopping at villages, souvenir stands, restaurants, and overlooks. Between **Salisburg** and **Mahaut** stop at the **Macoucherie rum factory** with its old waterwheel, and the **Dominica Coconut Products factory** where coconut and aloe are used to make all-natural lotions and soaps.

Our favorite spot along this coast is **Rodney's Rock**, a large black headland between Layou and Mahaut. During one of England's many battles with the French, a desperately out-gunned Sir Admiral George

Rodney decorated the rock with lanterns that were placed as if in ships' rigging. The French, thinking the coast was protected by a mighty British fleet, were fooled into retreating.

Nearby, the village of **Massacre** is on the site of the Caribs' last stand. Survivors fled the island, or settled in what is now Carib Territory. Island artist Earl Etienne was born here in a village called a "kaleidoscope of color." His work is shown at **Gallery No. 4** in Roseau.

So overwhelming are Dominica's natural beauties, it's easy to overlook noisy and crowded **Roseau**. Still, it is the capital it and deserves tourist attention. Its **Botanical Gardens** contain examples of most of the trees, flowers and shrubs found on the island. In 1979, a bus was crushed here when an enormous boabob tree fell on it. It's still here as a reminder of nature's power. The gardens are the home of the **national park office**, a goldmine of information, maps, and guides, *Tel. 448-2401, extension 417*.

While in the city, visit the **Dominica Museum** in the old court house, a project of local historian Lennox Honeychurch, who was also responsible for the restoration of **Fort Shirley**. It's open Monday through Friday 9am to 5pm and Saturday 9am to 1pm. It has no telephone. Admission is $1. Wander into the **Anglican Cathedral** and have lunch in the **Fort Young Hotel** for a peek at an 18th century British fort. Ramble clean, narrow streets on 300-year-old cobblestones that came over as ship ballast with early planters and traders.

Slip into old churches, shop along Cork Street, browse the stalls along the **Roseau River** on market days. Keep in mind, however, that these market stalls provide a livelihood for these people. Chitchat and photography may be resented unless you are a serious buyer. Along the bay front, view historic displays in the small museum.

Soufriere, in the island's southern corner, has been settled since the 1600s when the French named it for the sulphur springs here. Note the historic **Catholic church**, then enjoy the beaches, diving, and snorkeling of **South Head** and **Soufriere Bay**. Scotts Head Village is a good place to have lunch.

NIGHTLIFE & ENTERTAINMENT

Dominica's visitors are most likely to be those with "lark" personalities, early to bed and up with the sun for diving, hiking, and mountain biking. As a result, nightlife choices are meager. In Roseau, try **SMILEY'S BAR** on the ground floor at Wykie's La Tropical Guest House. A 75-year-old colonial-style family house converted for guest use (five rooms; rates start at $20) it's a place to hang out, eat burgers or West Indian food, and sip rum until late hours.

There's live music almost every night.

Thursday is Jazz Night at **SYMES-ZEE EATERY**, *Tel. 448-2494*, or enjoy seaside barbecue and live music at the **ANCHORAGE HOTEL**, *Tel. 448-5680*. On Fridays, the gang goes to the disco at the **FORT YOUNG HOTEL**, *Tel. 448-5000*. On weekends, there's also the **WAREHOUSE DISCO** in Roseau.

In Portsmouth, enjoy a pub crawl along Bay Street, stopping at discos. Very popular with yachties is the waterfront **SHIPWRECK BAR** in the Canefield industrial area, *Tel. 449-1134*. It's also a popular restaurant owned by a local Yamaha outboard motor agent. Live or taped music plays nightly; on Sunday the revelry starts at noon and goes on half the night.

SPORTS & RECREATION

Diving

Exceptional dive sites are found around north and northeast coast of Dominica, and off the southeast shore. Reefs teem with colorful sponges and glowing crinoids, forming a home for rays, batfish, squid, and seahorses. Dive the dropoff known as The Wall, an underwater volcano, caverns filled with sea life, and crusty corals including stands of rare black coral.

Castle Comfort Lodge, *Tel. 800/544-7631, 800/729-7234, 800/815-5019 or 767/448-2188, Fax 448-6088*, offers one-stop shopping for accommodations with meals, diving, and scuba lessons. The lodge also offers tours, hikes, whale watching (whale season is November through March) and, at the end of the day, a hot spa.

Dive operators include:
• **Anchorage Dive Centre**, *Tel. 767/448-2638*
• **Dive Dominica, Ltd.**, *Tel. 767/448-2188*
• **East Carib Dive**. *Tel. 767/449-6575*
• **Nature Island Dive**. *Tel. 767/449-8181*

Hiking

For most hikes, it's a plus to have a hired guide and, to visit Boiling Lake, it's essential. Because guides charge a flat fee and are expensive, it's best to go with a group and share the cost. Bobby Frederick of **Ras Tours**, *Tel. 787/448-0412, is* a Dominica native who has lived in North America and knows how to give a meaningful tour. He charges about $100 for an all-day island tour including pick-up in his vehicle.

Easy hikes include a nature trail just off Pond Cassé-Castle Bruce Road, a quarter-mile stroll to **Emerald Pool**. It takes only about 20 easy minutes to hike to **Trafalgar Falls** on the west side of Morne Microtin. Other treks, including the eight-hour round trip to **Boiling Lake**, are both long and arduous. You'll scramble up and down boulders and slopes, sometimes using vines and roots to pull yourself up a muddy path. Prepare to be dirty, wet, and challenged to the fullest. If you're not in top physical shape, don't go. The fallen have to rely on their guides and companions to carry them out, which is almost as hard on the injured as it is on the rescuers.

TAKE A HIKE

Beware of free-lance "guides" who hover around most tourist areas offering their services. You may not be getting competent advice and some hikes can be strenuous, hazardous, or both. If you do choose such a guide, agree on a price ahead of time. Avoid the easier and better-known trails, such as Trafalgar Falls, when cruise ships are in port because of the crowds. Temperatures fall as you climb. No matter how steamy the day at sea level, take a light jacket when hiking into the mountains.

To reach **Middleham Falls**, get directions or a guide in Cochran. Near here, the **Stinking Hole** is a lava tube filled with bats. A 15-minute hike up the **White River** brings you to **Sari Sari Falls**, which drop like a silken sari into a cold pool where a quick plunge will make you forget the heat of the day. Take the road inland from Dublanc to the **Syndicate Nature Trail**, which runs 1,800-feet above sea level in the foothills of **Morne Diablotin**. It's the home of rare Sisserou and Jacquot parrots, which are easiest to find in early morning and late afternoon. The flowers and rainforest vegetation are magnificent and the hike takes only an hour.

Dominica established its first national Park, **Morne Trois Pitons**, in 1975, setting aside nearly 17,000 acres. Its two forest preserves were established in 1952 and 1977. **Cabrits National Park** was designated in 1986, further extending what appears to be a permanent commitment here to ecotourism.

Hikers will be well rewarded with sightings of agouti, bird life, iguana, frogs, and perhaps a boa constrictor, locally called tête chien (dog's head). No poisonous snakes live on the island. Natural history tours, hikes, birdwatching and photo safaris can be booked with **Ken's Hinterland Adventure Tours, Ltd.**, *Tel. 787/448-4850, Fax 787/448-8486.*

Sportfishing

Dominica has come into the world fishing arena with an annual sportfishing tournament that was first fished in 1996. Its winning marlin weighed 297 pounds. The waters also yield tuna, dolphin, barracuda, and reef fish such as grouper and snapper. **Rainbow Sportfishing** offers day cruising and charters aboard a 32-foot Sea Ray, *Tel. 767/448-8650* day or night. Spearfishing is prohibited; for other angling you'll need a permit from the Fisheries Development Division. The closed season for lobster is April 30 to September 1.

Sailing

Day sails, booze outings, picnic, dinner, and moonlight cruises are with **Carib Cruises**, *Tel. 787/448-2489, Fax 448-3500*, a 70-foot catamaran with a crew of five.

SHOPPING

Shops are generally open Monday through Friday, 8am to 5pm and Saturday 9am to 1pm.

Most islands have their own distinctive straw work, but Dominica's is exceptional. Collectable, even museum quality, these treasures are made from flowering larouma reeds that are prepared, dried, and dyed today much as they were centuries ago by pre-Carib settlers, the Kalinago people. Shop for one-of-a-kind baskets, bamboo items or items made from calabash or from fwije, a forest tree fern that is woven, sculpted and carved. Fern valises and knapsacks are especially desirable.

Bello syrups, hot sauces and jams make meaningful souvenirs. Take home gift baskets of Bello products including gourmet coffee. They're sold in many island shops. The best food shopping is in the IGA store on Old Street. In downtown Roseau, shop, **Artquake Caribana**, and **Gallery No. 4** for arts and crafts, **Cotton House Batik** in the Woodstone Mall on Kings Lake, Cork Street, and **Phia's Boutique** nearby for sportswear and wraps. **Tropicrafts** on Queen Mary Street in Roseau and Bay Street in Portsmouth carries dolls in native dress as well as woven grass mats, Carib baskets, pottery, and other crafts. The gift shop at **Papillote Wilderness Retreat**, four miles east of town on Trafalgar Falls Road, carries crafts made from bamboo and calabash, handmade quilts, sculpture by Haitian-born Louis Desire, and small paintings. It's open daily 8am to 8pm,

The island's most collectable artist, Earl Etienne, is shown at **Gallery No. 4** on Hanover Street, *Tel. 448-6900*. A native of the area known as Massacre, Etienne works in a variety of styles including one called "smoke on canvas" in which he uses carbon from a burned torch. Allow time for last-minute shopping at **Canefield Airport**, where you'll find good selections of arts, crafts, coconut soaps and cosmetics, and consumables including the famous local rum.

EXCURSIONS & DAY TRIPS

Unless you're staying on Dominica for an extended period, it's isn't practical to take excursions to other islands. On Dominica itself, many outings can occupy anywhere from an hour to a day depending on whether you want a power hike or prefer to dally over wildlife photography, birding, plant identification, and swimming in clear mountain pools. See listings under *Sports & Recreation* and *Seeing the Sights* for suggestions on outings that could be turned into all-day projects. The hike to **Boiling Lake**, for example, takes three or four hours each way and can certainly be considered a day trip.

Arrange a whale and dolphin watch cruise with **Anchorage Hotel & Dive Dominica, Ltd.**, *Tel. 767/448-2368, Fax 448-5680.* For about $50 per person you'll cruise for three or four hours in the waters where the skipper thinks he'll find today's sightings of spinner dolphins, sperm whales, blackfish, humpback whales, and bottlenose dolphins.

Along the north coast, stop at **Anse de Mai** to take pictures of the colorful fishing fleet. There is always the danger of an undertow, so be cautious if you swim here. Among this coast's better beaches are **Picard**, **Purple Turtle**, **Woodford Hill Bay**, **Pointe Baptiste**, **Turtle Bay**, and **Hampstead Beach**.

PRACTICAL INFORMATION

Area Code: **767** effective September 30, 1998; **809** until then.

ATM: a 24-hour ATM is found at the bayfront Royal Bank of Canada in Roseau.

Banking hours: generally, banks are open Monday through Thursday, 8am to 3pm and Friday 8am to 5pm.

Beer: Dominica's national beer is Kabuli

Camping is illegal in the forests.

Currency: U.S. dollars are accepted throughout the island and most prices, especially at hotels and tourist shops, are quoted only in them. The official currency is the EC dollar, which is worth about EC$2.67 to the $1, with a somewhat better exchange rate at banks than in hotels and shops. U.S. dollar travelers checks are readily accepted but, if you carry large denominations, shopkeepers may not be able to (or be willing to) make change in U.S. currency.

Dress: don't wear swim wear and immodest outfits in the streets. Take good hiking shoes and rain gear for the rain forests.

Drinking water: from public sources and in hotels is said to be safe to drink. Bottled spring water is sold throughout the island.

Driving: drive on the left, British style. The speed limit in Roseau is 20 miles per hour; no speed limits apply outside the capital.

Electrical current: Dominica uses a three-prong plug and 220-volt, 50-cycle power. For North American appliances, transformers and adapters are needed.

Emergencies: dial 999 for police, fire or ambulance.

Government: Dominica has independent status within the British Commonwealth. Send your mail to the Commonwealth of Dominica. If you write it all out, there's a better chance that your mail won't be misdirected to the Dominican Republic.

Holidays: banks and most businesses are likely to be closed on New Year's Day, Carnival Monday and Tuesday, Good Friday, Easter and Easter Monday, May Day (May 1), Whitmonday, August Monday the first Monday in August. Independence Day November 3, Community Day of Service on November 4, Christmas, and Boxing Day.

Immigration: U.S. and Canadian citizens need a return ticket and a valid passport or proof of citizenship with photo identification. French nationals may stay up to two weeks with an identity card.

Pets: animals require a valid veterinary health certificate and an importation permit from the Veterinary Officer, Ministry of Agriculture, Botanical Gardens, Roseau.

Taxes: Dominica imposes a three percent sales tax on food, drinks and merchandise and 10 percent room tax on accommodations. Each person under age 12 must pay $12 when leaving the island.

Telephones: as in much of the Caribbean, pay phones accept only prepaid cards. A Caribbean Phonecard is available from *800/877-8000* using a major credit card. Locally, see Telecommunications of Dominica on Hanover Street, Roseau, *Tel. 767/448-1000.*

Pharmacy: prescriptions, over-the-counter drugs, and the proprietor's own preparations are sold at Jolly's Pharmacy, Ltd., 37 Great George Street and 12 King George Street, Roseau, *Tel. 767/448-3388.*

Time zone: Dominica is in the Atlantic Time Zone, one hour ahead of Eastern Standard Time and the same as Eastern Daylight Time.

Tourism information: contact Dominica Tourist Office, *10 East 21st Street, Suite 600, New York NY 10010, Tel. (212) 475-7543, Fax 475-9278* or Dominica Division of Tourism, *Box 293, Roseau, Commonwealth of Dominica, West Indies. Tel. 767/448-2045, Fax 448-5840.* You'll find a Dominica Tourist Information Office in the Old Market Plaza, Roseau.

Weddings: either the bride or groom should arrive on the island 15 days before making the application. You'll need proof of citizenship such as birth certificate or passport plus divorce or death papers if applicable.

24. GRENADA

Simply said, we love **Grenada** and Grenada seems to love us. In years of island travel, we've found West Indians to be among the world's friendliest and most handsome people, but Grenadians are special. Alone among strangers here, we have been welcomed into their churches, work places, festivals and haunts. More than one Grenadian made it a point to thank us for the "intervention," in which U.S. and Caribbean troops landed on the island to quell unrest during the political turmoil of the early 1980s.

The islands of Grenada, Petite Martinique, and Carriacou comprise this island state in the **Lesser Antilles** between St. Vincent and Trinidad, a flight of a little more than an hour from San Juan. Confusingly, Grenada is not in the Grenadines, which belong to St. Vincent. Grenada wasn't sighted by Columbus until his third voyage, when he named it Concepción.

Peaceful Arawaks who lived here were a pushover for Spanish invaders but the more fierce, cannibalistic Caribs who moved in as they fled to Grenada from other islands weren't as easy for the Spanish to rout. Finally out-gunned by the French, the last Carib holdouts leapt off a cliff in 1651 to their death. The sad site, now the sleepy community of **Sauteurs** (Leapers) is today just a brief wave of the tour guide's hand, worthy only of a brief look and perhaps a stop for a cold drink.

Grenada's story is a familiar one in the Caribbean, where battling British and French traded islands like baseball cards. The British were chased off the island in 1609 and it stayed in French hands until 1783. Today it remains a pleasant blend of British language and customs, French place names, Carib basketry, African drumbeats, and language laced with French words and cadences. The predominant religion is Roman Catholic, a French heritage. Anglican and Presbyterian churches remain from the British era.

Grenada was a crown colony, then an associate state within the British Commonwealth and finally, in 1974, an independent nation. In 1979, radicals seized control and began to set up a socialist/communist government with ties to Cuba and the Soviet Union leading to, in 1983, a call from the governor general for help. Troops from the United States, Barbados, Jamaica, and the Eastern Caribbean States responded. Ostensibly their mission was to rescue stranded American students at the medical school here. Order was restored, democracy returned, and the "invaders" embraced as friends.

Carriacou, a yachting paradise where major portions of the film *White Squall* were shot, is a small, sister island with a population of about 8,000. **Petite Martinique**, smaller still, remains undeveloped except for a few holiday cottages and restaurants. Islets, rocks, and cays among the main islands provide stepping stones for yachties and lonely beaches for divers and day trippers.

Climate

Plan to swelter in high heat and humidity in summer along the coastlines, and bake in delicious sunshine all winter. Things change when you enter the rain forest, where temperatures quickly plunge and mists thicken into light rains. June through October, be alert for hurricane threats, which are rare but are possible.

ARRIVALS & DEPARTURES

Grenada's **Point Salines International Airport** is served from San Juan by **American Airlines**, *Tel. 473/444-2222*. **BWIA**, *Tel. 473/440-3818 and 444-4135* provides service from New York, Miami, Toronto, Zurich, Frankfurt, and London via other islands. **British Airways**, *Tel. 473/440-2796*, comes twice a week from London.

Other carriers connect via Barbados or Antigua. They include: • **Aerotuy**, *Tel. 473/444-4732*
• **Airlines of Carriacou**, *Tel. 473/444-3549 or 444-1475*
• **HelenAir**, *Tel. 444-4101, extension 2090* or, in Carriacou, *Tel. 473/443-8260*
• **LIAT**, *Tel. 473/440-2796 or 444-4121* or, in Carriacou, *Tel. 473/443-7362*
• **Region Air Caribbean**, *Tel. 473/444-1117 and 444-1118*

Ferries ply among Grenada, Carriacou and Petite Martinique several times a week and a cargo ferry sails to Trinidad once weekly. Fare for the three-four-hour journey is EC$20 one way and EC$30 round trip, with a $5 surcharge on weekends.

ORIENTATION

When you land at Point Salines International Airport you'll be at the southeast corner of Grenada, not far from the capital city, **St. George's**, where you'll arrive if you come by ferry or cruise ship. Grenada is divided

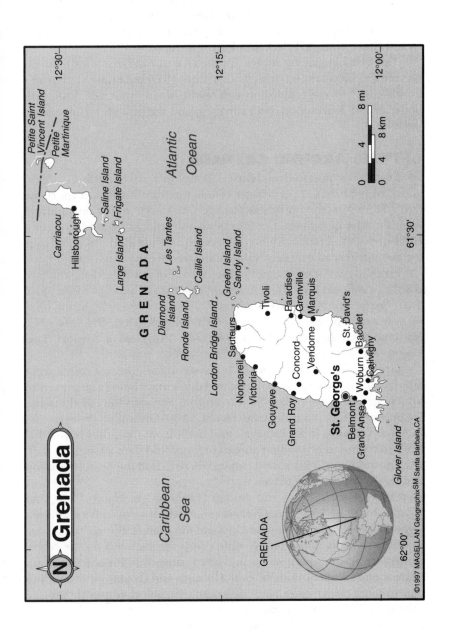

Grenada

N

Caribbean Sea

Petite Saint Vincent Island

Petite Martinique

Carriacou

Hillsborough

Saline Island

Frigate Island

Large Island

GRENADA

Diamond Island

Les Tantes

Ronde Island

Caille Island

London Bridge Island

Green Island

Sandy Island

Atlantic Ocean

Sauteurs

Tivoli

Paradise

Grenville

Marquis

Nonpareil

Concord

Vendome

St. David's

Victoria

Bacolet

Gouyave

Grand Roy

Calivigny

Woburn

St. George's

Belmont

Grand Anse

Glover Island

GRENADA

8 mi

8 km

4

0

4

0

12°30'

12°15'

12°00'

62°00'

61°30'

©1997 MAGELLAN GeographixSM Santa Barbara,CA

into parishes, with St. George being the business center and St. Andrew the most populous. Most hotels are found in **Grand Anse** between St. George's and the airport or in **L'Anse aux Epines,** which is southeast of the airport. The center of the island is mountainous and includes the **Grand Etang National Park and Forest Reserve.**

The best sightseeing routes are the coastal road that runs from **St. George's** to **Sauteurs** and roads that run through **Grand Etang.** Carriacou's capital and chief city is Hillsborough on the island's west side, just north of the airport. Fairly good roads rim the island and provide an interesting day tour.

GETTING AROUND GRENADA

From the airport to Grand Anse, L'Anse aux Epines, and St. George's, taxis charge $10 to $12 per person. Within a mile radius of the airport, the fare is $2.75. For trips outside St. George's, and any trip between 6pm and 6am, a surcharge is made. On Carriacou, cabs charge from $4 to go into Hillsborough to $10 for distant points such as Windward. An island tour for about $60 is an excellent value. Cab fares are daytime rates.

From the St. George's pier to the city or botanical gardens, cab fare is $3, to the resort area $7, L'Anse aux Epines, $12 and True Blue, $10. Taxis can be hired for $15 per half hour. Taxis meet every flight and ferry or you can call one from: **Raymond's Tour & Taxi,** *Tel. 444-1283;* **National Taxi Association,** *Tel. 440-5286;* **Progressive Airport Taxi Union,** *Tel. 444-1270.*

Grenada has a reliable public bus system that operates daily except Sundays. If you have plenty of time and don't mind being crammed into a hot mini-van on a wood bench, you can go almost anywhere on the island for between EC$1 (Grande Anse) and EC$4.50 (Grenville). Buses line up in **Market Square** in St. George's and don't leave until they have a full load, so try not to be the first aboard or you could have a long, hot wait. On your return, just ask a local person where to find the nearest bus stop and flag down the next driver.

On Carriacou, buses run among Hillsborough, Harvey Vale, and Windward for EC$2-$4. Boat rentals, either self-drive or with a guide, are a good way to get to remote beaches and out islands. Bicycle rentals are available at many hotels but we didn't seen any bicyclers on the roads, which are narrow, rough, steep, and often dangerous. Private and group tours are an excellent value on both Grenada and Carriacou. Even if you plan to rent a car, a tour will provide orientation before you tackle left-side driving on bad, poorly marked roads.

Rental cars are available from:
• **Avis/Spice Island Rentals,** *Tel. 440-3936* or *443-2384*
• **Budget Car Rental,** *Tel. 444-2277*

- **Sunshine Tours & Rentals**, *Tel. 444-4296*
- **Dollar Rent-a-Car**, *Tel. 444-4786*
- **C. Thomas and Sons Car Rentals**, *Tel. 444-4384*
- **Rent-A-Moke**, *Tel. 444-4431 or 440-6402*
- **Y&R Car Rentals, Ltd.**, *Tel. 444-4448*
- **McIntyre Brothers Ltd.**, *Tel. 444-3944*
- **MCR Car Rental**, *Tel. 440-2832/5398/5513*
- **Quality Rentals**, *Tel. 440-9789*.

Sedans, Jeeps, and Yamaha 175 bikes are available from **Maitland's Motor Rentals**, *Tel. 444-4022, 444-5762, 444-1807.*

On Carriacou, call **Barba's Auto Rentals**, *Tel. 443-7454* and **Martin Bullen**, *Tel. 443-7204.*

WHERE TO STAY

Rates are quoted and paid in U.S. dollars for a double room in high season; low season rates are 25-30 percent less. Usually rates are per room, but some hotels offer reduced rates for singles. There is an additional eight percent government tax and 10 percent service charge in lieu of tipping.

Your address in the islands will be Grenada, West Indies. Write it all out to avoid confusion with the Grenadines. Many Grenada hotels can be booked toll-free from the United States through the **Grenada Hotel Association**, *Tel. 800/322-1753* or **CHARMS**, *Tel. 800/223-9815.*

GRENADA

Expensive

CALABASH HOTEL, *L'Anse aux Pines, mailing address P.O. Box 382, St. George's. Tel. 473/444-4334, Fax 444-5050. Rates at this 30-suite hotel start at $350 including breakfast brought to your room and afternoon tea. Add $35 adults and $17.50 children for dinner. The hotel is on the south shore of the island, ten minutes or a $10 taxi ride from the airport.*

Lush lawns center a cluster of villas that turn their other face to the sea. The beach is baby powder dappled with the shade of coconut palms and sea grapes; the water clear as gin fizz. Rooms are a splendor of wicker and pastels, each with its own whirlpool or plunge pool in a very private garden. Mornings begin with breakfast served on your private balcony by your own maid.

Work out in the gym, play tennis day or night, swim in the sea or pool, use the complimentary watersports equipment, shop the boutique, then dine in one of the island's best restaurants. After dinner, go to the library to read or play snooker. The manager throws a cocktail party once a week;

live music plays often at the pool bar, grounds, or beach bar. The resort is dressy, with shorts and jeans not acceptable at dinner. Golf is ten minutes away. In high season, don't bring children under age 12 or, for the rest of the season, children under age three. Children of all ages are welcome in summer but children under age six should not be in the bar and restaurant after 6pm. Babysitters are available, and children can be served from room service.

Selected as one of my Best Places to Stay; see Chapter 13 for more details.

COYABA BEACH RESORT, *Grand Anse, mailing address P.O. Box 336, St. George's, Grenada, West Indies. Tel. 473/444-4129, Fax 444-4808. Rates at this 70-unit hotel start at $175. Up to two children may share the parents' room for $10 per child. Add $6 for continental breakfast, $12 for American breakfast, $35 for breakfast and dinner, and $45 for three meals daily.*

Famous Grand Anse beach spreads like a prayer rug in front of this sunbaked resort with its verdant grounds, big pool, and Arawak-theme decor (Coyoba means heaven in Arawak). Everything is open to the sea breezes – the lobby, restaurant and bar. Guest rooms, which feature two double beds, color television, and telephone, are decorated in earth tones that complement Arawak artwork and bouquets of brilliant heliconia or other exotic flowers. Play tennis, lounge by the pool with its swim-up bar, or sail off the beach. Have a drink before dinner, then dine in one of the resort's two restaurants.

GRENADA RENAISSANCE RESORT, *Grand Anse, mailing address P.O. Box 441, St. George's. Tel. 473/444-4371, Fax 444-4800. Rates at this 298-unit resort start at $193.*

One of the largest hotels in this part of the Caribbean, the Renaissance is an oversize version of a British inn with formal furnishings and formal gardens. Units have balcony or patio, air conditioning, and television. Use the air conditioned fitness center, enjoy the famous Grand Anse beach, use watersports equipment including jet skis, swim in the pool, play golf nearby, play tennis day or night, sign up for a scuba dive, and dine in the restaurants. Entertainers are on hand most nights. Seven two-story buildings make up the resort. Rooms are small but elegant with their carpeted floors and Regency furnishings. Each has a balcony or patio, radio, and room service.

LA SOURCE, *Pink Gin Beach, Point Salines, mailing address P.O. Box 852. Tel. 473/444-2556, Fax 444-2561. Rates at this 100-room spa start at $240 per person, double occupancy; suites at $275 per person. Rates are all-inclusive. Cab fare from the airport is $2.75.*

"Give us your body for a week and we'll give you back your mind," promise massage mavens here. You couldn't be handier to the airport or more pampered than you'll be at this exclusive spa with its everything-on-the house policy. Some of the spa treatments are extra but many are included. Enjoy calypso aerobics, wraps and rubs, weight training, yoga, saunas, water aerobics, stress management, massage for two, Tai Chi, yoga, sailing, swimming in the clear sea or two pools, "mashie" golf, tennis and even fencing.

Mahogany furniture includes four-poster beds complemented by expanses of marble, fresh flowers, white walls, and cathedral ceilings. Dine in the Great Room with its high, hardwood ceilings or more casually in the Garden Restaurant with its latticework and wrought-iron furnishings. For entertainment there may be a band or pianist. The beach is one of the Caribbean's loveliest.

REX GRENADIAN, *Point Salines, mailing address P.O. Box 893, St. George's, Grenada, West Indies. Tel. 473/444-3333, Fax 444-1111. Rates at this 212-unit hotel start at $215. Fare from the airport is $2.75.*

Grenada's answer to Palm Beach is this ambitious resort in a rocky forest that slopes down to a white sand beach. Units, most of which overlook the sea, are done in South Seas blues and greens, rich in wicker and rattan. Walk or paddleboat around the resort's own lake, swim in the island's most spectacular pool, have a drink in one of the bars, then dine in the International restaurant, with a different country featured every night, or in the Oriental, which features Eastern and Indian cuisine.

There's entertainment almost every night. Rooms are air conditioned and have ceiling fans, television, telephones, and balcony or patio. Car rental can be arranged on site, and the concierge can set up a tour or dive or find a babysitter. Room service is available.

SECRET HARBOUR RESORT, *L'Anse aux Epines, mailing address P.O. Box 11, St. George's. Tel. 473/444-4439, Fax 444-4819. Doubles at this 20-room are $230. Meal plans are available. Cab fare from the airport is $12; the resort is 15 minutes from St. George's.*

Arches are a Grenadian architectural passion, and they're especially attractive in this setting overlooking Mount Harmon Bay. Because it's owned by The Moorings, one of the leading yacht charter companies in the Caribbean, it's a favorite of yachties. Suites have sunken tubs, air conditioning, ceiling fan, telephone, and radio and authentic antique furnishings that were collected here and on other islands. Play tennis, snorkel, take a sailing lesson, swim in the sea or pool, and dine in the Mariner Restaurant overlooking the bay.

SPICE ISLAND BEACH RESORT, *Grand Anse, mailing address P.O. Box 6, St. George's, Grenada, West Indies. Tel. 473/444-4258. Rates at this 56-suite resort are $375 to $900 including breakfast and dinner. It's ten minutes or $10 from the airport.*

The luxury suites at the Royal Private Pool Suites at this resort are beyond superlatives. Imagine opening a garden gate that enters your own, very private garden with a 16 x 12-foot swimming pool, sauna, exercise bicycle, patio with lounges and dining table, and flowering vines twining down varnished hardwood fences. Stepping into your suite, you find a sitting area with television and full sound system, a bedroom richly hung with brocades and furnished in handmade mahogany pieces, and marble bath with double whirlpool and bidet.

Outside your door is one of Grenada's best beaches, thick with sugary dunes and awash in incandescent blue waters. Order breakfast from room service at no added charge. Dining is in the hotel's locally popular, open air, beachfront restaurant where the chef melds local produce, spices and seafood with continental presentations. Manager's cocktail parties, offered several times a month, feature full bar service and scrumptious canapes.

Included in tariffs are use of the air conditioned fitness center, tennis courts day or night, bicycles, watersports equipment, and greens fees at a nearby course. There's no pool here, but guests who don't have private pool suites can use the big freshwater pool at the resort's sister property, Blue Horizons. Laundry, dry cleaning, babysitting and tours can be arranged.

Selected as one of my Best Places to Stay; see Chapter 13 for more details.

TWELVE DEGREES NORTH, L'Anse aux Epines, mailing address *P.O. Box 241, St. George's. Tel. 444-4580, Fax 444-4580. Rates at this eight-unit apartment hotel start at $195 for two people in a one-bedroom unit. A maid/cook is included. Children under age 14 and credit cards aren't accepted; preference is given to guests who book for at least a week.*

Your day begins with the arrival of your personal maid, who takes care of everything from breakfast through dinner (which you can heat up after she leaves if you prefer late dining) and housekeeping. Unless you want to have a drink in the beach bar, your romantic idyll doesn't have to involve anyone but the two of you and your maid. Use of watersports equipment and tennis courts is complimentary.

Moderate

BLUE HORIZONS COTTAGE HOTEL, *Grand Anse, mailing address P.O. Box 41, St. George's, Grenada, West Indies. Tel. 473/444-4316, Fax 444-2815. Rates at this 32-suite hotel start at $160. Add $45 per adult and $35 per child for breakfast and dinner; $10 and $8 for continental breakfast. It's a $10 taxi ride from the airport.*

Neat cottages, each with a private porch, cluster prettily around a wide green lawn just 300 yards from the famous Grand Anse beach. The hotel has a pool and, because its owned by the same people who own Spice Island Beach Resort, guests have beach privileges including the use of beach chaises, watersports equipment, tennis court, and the fitness room. Each suite has a completely equipped kitchen, air conditioning, ceiling fan in the bedroom, daily maid service (including dishwashing), telephone, television, and mahogany furnishings crafted on the island. On the grounds are a chickee bar, breakfast room, library/lounge, and swimming pool. Tours and watersports can be arranged. When you check in, ask for a leaflet describing birds seen on the grounds. At least 21 species have been spotted here and it's fun to learn local names for them. La Belle Creole, the hotel's restaurant, is one of the best on the island.

FLAMBOUYANT HOTEL, *Grand Anse, mailing address P.O. Box 214, St. George's, Grenada, West Indies. Tel. 473/444-4247, Fax 444-1234. Rates at this 41-unit hotel start at $130. Cab fare from the airport is $10. Meal plans are available.*

The resort clings to a steep cliff in a stunning setting between Grand Anse and Morne Rouge bays. The walk to the beach is a steep one, but the trade-off is the view from your sky-high suite and, halfway down the walk, a freshwater swimming pool, bar, and restaurant. Rooms have mini-bars, color television, private balcony, hair dryer, air conditioning, direct-dial telephone, and maid service. Children are welcome all year; cribs are free. Room service is available.

LA SAGESSE NATURE CENTRE, *St. David's, mailing address P.O. Box 44, St. George's, Grenada, West Indies. Tel. 473/444-6458, Fax 444-6458. Rates at this eight-room inn start at $60. Taxi fare from the airport is $20.*

Your room in this pleasant pink bungalow will have a private bath, fan, and telephone. It's on a half-mile beach on the island's wild Atlantic coast just southeast of the rain forest. It's isolated, but the meals are great and the bar chummy, so there's need to venture out in search of food and friends.

Budget

CAMERHOGNE PARK HOTEL, *Grand Anse, mailing address P.O. Box 378, St. George's, Grenada, West Indies. Tel. 473/444-4110, Fax 444-3111. Rates at this 21-unit hotel start at $65. Meal plans and two-bedroom, self-catering apartments are available. It's three miles from St. George's and a $10 taxi ride from the airport.*

Popular with Europeans, families and groups, this attractively priced hotel is a short climb from the beach to a breezy hillside. Rooms and suites have air conditioning, ceiling fan, cable television, telephone, maid service, and veranda. It has its own bar and dining room; room service is available.

LAKESIDE GUEST HOUSE, *Lagoon Road, Belmont, St. George's, Grenada, West Indies. Tel. 473/440-2365. Rates at this eight-room inn start at*

$30. Taxi fare from the airport is $10. The hotel is between Grand Anse and St. George's on the Lagoon.

Overlook anchored yachts from all over the world from this cozy, family-operated guest house. It's within walking distance of a grocery store, where you can buy provisions to cook in the shared kitchen. Baths too are shared. St. George's, the beaches and restaurants are all a short drive away.

SIMEON'S INN, *Green Street, St. George's. Tel. 473/440-2717. Doubles at this nine-room inn are $45.*

Baths are shared and the inn has seen better days, but the elderly owner is pleasant and the location is in the center of town overlooking the harbor. It's the ideal headquarters for exploring the city, shopping the market, touring in-town museums and forts, and relaxing on the porch. A cooked breakfast and bedside fans are available.

CARRIACOU

Expensive

CARIBBEE INN, *Prospect. Tel. 473/443-7380, Fax 443-8142. Rates at this 10-room hotel start at $100; suites at $170. Cab fare from the airport is $8.*

Rooms at this worlds-end resort aren't anything special, but they're clean and spacious and the seascape views provide a million dollar decor. The suites, however, are special with their Italian tile floors, four-poster bed, and step-up shower overlooking the sea. Each is different; the one called Sparrow Bay has its own beach, West Indian tower, and double shower. Units have ceiling fan and telephone. Room service is available and the hotel's restaurant is one of Carriacou's best. Snorkel, swim off the beach, or take a boat to one of the nearby cays.

Budget

ADE'S DREAM GUEST HOUSE, *Main Street, Hillsborough. Tel. 473/ 7317, Fax 443-8435. Rates at this 23-room guest house start at $24, apartments at $34. Add $5 for air conditioning.*

Located right on the main drag in downtown Hillsborough, this is the place to see city life, Carriacou style. It's scrupulously clean and simply furnished. Watersports, restaurants and bars are nearby and you can get room service from Ade's own restaurant. Rooms have ceiling fan, private bath, telephone, and a balcony overlooking the teeming street. Kitchenette units are available.

BOGLES ROUND HOUSE COTTAGES, *Bogles. Tel. 473/443-7841, Fax 443-7841. Five cottages rent for $45-$57 a day. Cab fare from the airport is $8.*

Your quaint round cottage is only a few footsteps from a sandy beach; your hosts are sailors whose 50-foot yacht *Posh-Ratz* offers you sailing and diving. Cottages have wall fans, private bath with shower, a balcony overlooking the sea, and a galley-style kitchen.

GRAMMAS LUXURY APARTMENTS, *Main Street at Patterson, Hillsborough. Tel. 473/443-7256, Fax 440-7168. Rates at this seven-room hotel start at $45. Taxi fare for the ten-minute drive from the airport is EC$10.*

The family named it for Grandmother, who had just died, and they continue to honor her memory with the friendly, small-town hospitality she was known for. Because it overlooks the main street and rooms have balconies, this is the place to be during Carnival, the regatta, and other events. Book early. Rooms are airy and spacious, with basic bedroom, a furnished kitchen, and private baths, but they have only fans, no air conditioning. Television is available. There's a restaurant, bar and bakery downstairs with other restaurants only footsteps away. The town is so small, you're also handy to beaches and the ferry dock.

PEACE HAVEN, *on the main street in Hillsborough. Tel. 473/443-7475 or 443-8365. Rates at this six-room guest house are $45 double. The cab ride from the airport is $4.*

A handy address for business travelers on a budget, this guest house offers a clean room with private bath and ceiling fan. Some units have a kitchenette, and you can also have meals delivered.

SILVER BEACH RESORT, *Beausejour Bay, Carriacou, Grenada, West Indies. Tel. 473/443-7337, Fax 443-7165; U.S. and Canada toll-free 800/742-4276. Rates at this 16-room hotel start at $80. Self-catering cottages and meal plans are also available.*

Walk up the road to the Anglican Church for the May Day fete or down the road to Hillsborough with its restaurants. Or, just sit on your private patio or balcony to gaze at the shimmering sea. The beach is soft and sandy; the open-air restaurant and bar a favorite hangout; the food authentic and delicious. Don't miss the menagerie at the entrance, where turtles are kept. Rooms are plain, but they do have private bath, shower with built-in water heater, ceiling fan, desk/makeup table and chair, telephone, and clock radio. Diving, island tours, and boating can be arranged. The hotel also offers packages as a side trip from Grenada.

WHERE TO EAT

Menus in Grenada's tourist areas display prices in U.S. dollars. Add a 10 percent service charge in lieu of tipping, and an eight percent government tax. Unless stated otherwise, major credit cards are accepted.

Grenada is blessed with rich soil and enough rainfall to produce some of the Caribbean's most tasty vegetables and herbs. Goats, cattle, and sheep roam freely, fattening for the stew pot. Except for dairy and wheat products, it's possible to eat an almost totally Grenadian diet even at the most touristy hotels. Even the best foreign chefs proudly showcase island products. In hole-in-the-wall local places, try such dishes as oil down (vegetables cooked in coconut milk), coocoo (cornmeal cooked in coconut milk) and cow heel soup.

And don't forget to wash it down with Carib, the local beer.

GRENADA
Expensive
AQUARIUM BEACH CLUB, *Point Salines. Tel. 444-1410. Reservations are recommended. Plan to send $35 for dinner not counting drinks. Just past the airport, watch for the sign on the right; the restaurant is between La Source and the Rex Grenadian. Cab fare from Grand Anse hotels is $10. The restaurant is open daily except Monday, 10am to 11pm.*

The lights of St. George's are fireflies across the water as you dine surrounded by sea and spectacular rock cliffs. Start with minestrone or callaloo soup, then try the shrimp, lobster thermidor, chicken, or wienerschnitzel. For dessert there's carrot cake, chocolate mousse, or a banana split made with local bananas and exotic ice creams.

CICELY'S, *in the Calabash Hotel, L'Anse aux Pines. Tel. Tel. 473/444-4334. Reservations are essential. Dinner is served from 7pm, with the last order taken at 10pm. Plan to spend $55 for a three-course meal not counting drinks. The hotel is on the south shore just east of the airport.*

Dine in an elegant, old-island setting where service is impeccable, silver and crystal gleaming, and linens crisply starched. The chefs are an award-winning team including Graham Newbould, who was once private chef to Prince Charles and Princess Diana. Start with a chicken liver parfait or lobster ravioli, followed by grilled kingfish with gazpacho salsa, garlic perfumed shrimp, the vegetarian dish of the day, or a meat choice such as chicken kebob with tandoori chutney or honey roasted breast of duckling in a sauce of local citrus. For dessert there's sticky toffee pudding, pineapple icebox pudding with rum, crepe suzette, fresh fruit, or creme brulee.

We found the food flawless except for a shortage of salads. Plenty of vegetables arrive as side dishes with the main course, though. Although jackets aren't required, the restaurant is dressy. Shorts, jeans, and bare midriffs are not permitted in the bar or restaurant.

CANBOULAY RESTAURANT, *Morne Rouge. Tel. 444-4401. Dinner will cost $35-$55. Walk from many Grand Anse area hotels. Cab fare from the airport is $10. Hours are Monday through Saturday 6:30 to 11pm with the last reservation at 9:30. Lunch is served Monday through Friday, 11:30am to 2:30pm. The restaurant is closed Sundays and bank holidays. Reservations are urged. Wednesday is seafood night and Thursday is cabaret night during high season mid-December through the end of March.*

In a brightly painted wood house on a hilltop overlooking Grand Anse and St. George's, drink in the view and breezes while dining on Caribbean foods with African and Asian influences, all pleasingly presented in a carnival theme. Coocoo, a national dish, is polenta made with coconut milk, a delicious accompaniment to crisp flying fish or succulent lobster tail. The chef's specialties include *parang poulet*, which is boned chicken breasts filled with sweet potato stuffing, baked with a belt of bacon, and sauced with citrus caramel. In season, a fixed price meal is served. If you're a picky eater or allergic, ask what is on the menu when booking your table.

COCONUT BEACH, *on Grand Anse Beach. Tel. 444-4644. Reservations are suggested. Hours are 12:30 to 10pm daily except Tuesday. Dinner will cost $25-$50 and lunch about half that. Walk from area hotels; cab fare from the airport is $10.*

Sand in your shoes and gentle waves at your doorstep describe this relaxed restaurant set in an old beach cottage. Have a drink in the chickee bar if you like, then choose from appetizers that include callaloo soup, lobster cocktail, lambi salad, or juicy, local tomatoes. Lobster is served steamed, sauced, thermidor or in crepes and, for landlubbers, there's a long list of chicken dishes and a steak or two. For dessert, have the coconut pie.

LA BELLE CREOLE, *in the Blue Horizons Cottage Hotel complex, Grand Anse, beyond Pizza Hut. Reservations are required. Tel. 444-4316. Hours are 7:30-10am and 7pm to 9pm. Lunch is available at the pool 11am to 2pm The hotel is a $10 taxi ride from the airport and is within walking distance from most of the hotels along Grand Anse Beach. The fixed price dinner is $35.*

Glowing varnished wood archways frame a scene of greenery and flowers as you dine on an airy, hillside porch. Romance is kindled by candlelight as servers time your meal perfectly: chilled lobster mousse or flaked chicken garnished with eggs, followed by crisp salad, then cream of tannia soup or christophene vichyssoise. Entrees may include veal Creole served on a bed of callaloo, stuffed and baked rainbow runner, dorado in white wine sauce, or saffron lamb. A halfmoon plate is placed next to your dinner plate to hold a parade of island vegetables. For dessert there's farina pudding or ice creams made from tropical fruit.

MOUNT HELICON RESTAURANT & BAR, *Upper Lucas Street, St. George's. Tel. 440-2444. Plan to spend $35-$40 for dinner. Located in the heart of the capital, the restaurant is a $10 taxi ride from Grand Anse hotels. Hours are Tuesday to Saturday 11am to 11pm and Sunday 3pm to 11pm. Happy Hour is Friday, 5:30 to 8:30pm.*

Climb to one of the city's highest points to dine graciously in a one-time greathouse with a panoramic view of the city and harbor. White linen-covered tables are accented with pink napkins that pick up the pinks in the upholstery of white chairs. Live the life of a grand planter with a drink at the bar, then a grand feast. For starters you're offered crab backs, smoked herring balls, or one of the island's famous soups. Lobster is served with root vegetables and rice; stewed lambi (conch) comes with rice and peas. If you want to order anything special, call ahead.

RED CRAB, *L'Anse aux Epines. Tel. 444-4424. Not more than five minutes from most hotels along the southwest coast, the restaurant is open Monday to Saturday from 11am to 2pm and 6 to 11pm. It's closed Sunday. Plan to spend $45-$50 for dinner.*

Ask a taxi driver where he would take a woman on the night he planned to propose, and he'll probably mention this topnotch restaurant with its happy ambience and great steaks and veal. There's also a wide selection of seafood including lambi, shrimp, lobster, mahi-mahi, snapper, and grouper.

SPICE ISLAND BEACH RESORT, *Grand Anse. Tel. 444-4258. Reservations are strongly suggested. The restaurant, which is on the Grand Anse beach, is open daily for dinner 7 to 9:30pm. Dinner is $40 including drinks.*

The food here is so varied and good that most hotel guests opt for the meal plan and dine here nightly. Head chef Bernadette Checkley began cooking at home in Grenada at age 16, attended the Culinary Institute of America, and honed her skills as a cook for Canadian and French ambassadors. Her popular tannia cakes are somewhat like potato pancakes. The hotel features buffet one night, sit-down dining the next, dancing and music on Grenadian night, and a steel band on barbecue night. Saturdays are for seafood and nostalgic music. Start with green banana soup, a terrine of local vegetables, or fish cakes remoulade. A special entree is es*calope* of mahi-mahi infused with local ginger. If you're vegetarian, call ahead to order from a lengthy menu worthy of the best vegetarian restaurants: baked red beans with cheese, vegetable pancakes, lentil loaf, eggplant and tomato bake, and much more. The children's menu offers macaroni and cheese, fish and chips, or hot dogs with chips.

Moderate

BEACH SIDE TERRACE, *in the Flambouyant Hotel, Grand Anse. Tel. 444-4247. Reservations are recommended. Hours are 7:30am to 10:30pm. Lunch specials are in the $12 range. Plan to spend $20-$25 for dinner, more if you have lobster.*

Dining is on a hillside balcony looking out over almond trees to the seascape beyond. Lunch is casual; at dinnertime, white tablecloths come out for dining on Gouyave fish stew, lambi stroganoff, lemon ginger chicken, or seafood crepes. On Monday evenings there are crab races and Caribbean buffet; Wednesdays feature steel bands in season, and on Friday a full-course barbecue feast is served before the calypso and limbo show. On Sundays, a barbecue brunch is served 11am to 3pm; calypso and reggae are played 1:30-3:30pm.

BROWN SUGAR RESTAURANT, *Grand Anse, above South Winds Cottages. Tel. 444-2374. Hours are 6 to 11pm daily except Monday. Dinners are $25 to $35 including complimentary rum punch and transfer from your hotel. Reservations are essential.*

Linger over your rum punch while you watch the sun set into Grand Anse Bay and St. George's Harbour. Then have lambi fritters while you wait for the stuffed red snapper, coconut shrimp, or chicken with passion fruit. A steel pan group plays Friday evenings.

GREEN FLASH, *in the Siesta Hotel, Grand Anse. Tel. 444-4646. Hours are 7:30 to 11am and 6 to 9:30pm. Dinners are in the $18-$20 range. Walk from other Grand Anse hotels or take a cab ($10 from the airport).*

Because this is BYOB you'll save substantially on the cost of cocktails and wine. Spend the savings on steak or lobster, or dine economically on moussaka, curries, fish grilled to order, or enchiladas. A specialty is Caribbean lime beef, strips of sirloin marinated in local spices and cooked with christophene, yam, sweet peppers and other local vegetables. End' the meal with Turkish coffee, homemade mango sorbet, nutmeg cheesecake, chocolate creme brulée, or an ice cream sundae crowned with crushed tropical fruits. For breakfast, order omelettes, *huevos rancheros*, banana crepes, or homemade muffins. The setting is poolside under a cabana.

JOE'S STEAK HOUSE, SEAFOOD RESTAURANT AND BAR, *in the Le Marquis Complex, Grand Anse. Tel. 444-4020. Walk from most Grand Anse hotels. Hours are 5 to 11pm Tuesday through Sunday. Reservations are urged.*

"Eat at Joe's" seemed to us to be the "See Rock City" of Grenada's signage, until we couldn't resist giving it a try. Joe charcoal grills his steak and lobster, offers a children's menu, and knows how to bake a potato all fluffy and steamy. For meat and potato diners, let Joe serve chops, U.S. prime steak or chicken, plus French fries and cole slaw. He can just as readily steam vegetables with a light touch, bring out a crispy salad, or ladle a mean soup. If you're in the area during lunch hours, 11am to 5pm, try the Bad Ass Café next door for salad bar, burgers, and Mexican food.

LA DOLCE VITA, *in the Cinnamon Hill Hotel, Morne Rouge, Grand Anse. Tel. 444-3456. Plan to spend $25-$35 for dinner. Hours are Tuesday through Sunday 7 to 11pm. The bar opens at 6pm. The restaurant is closed on Monday. Walk from many Grand Anse hotels, or take a cab from the airport for $10.*

Sophisticated Italian dishes are served in a hillside setting overlooking Grand Anse and St. George's. The chef makes his own pastas, gnocchi and a nice list of red and white sauces. The lobster spaghetti is rich with delicate seafood; the lasagna is piquant with fresh herbs. Start with hot or cold antipasti; end the meal with a tangy ice.

MARINER RESTAURANT, *in the Moorings Secret Harbour Resort, Mount Hartman Bay, L'Anse aux Epines. Tel. 444-4549. The restaurant, which is 20 minutes from the airport and 15 minutes from St. George's, is open every day from 7am to 11pm. Reservations are urged. Dinners are $25-$35.*

Locals and many guests call this The Moorings, so ask for that or Secret Harbour if your driver draws a blank when you ask for the Mariner. The resort is owned by the yacht charter company, so it's a yachtsman's hangout favored by charterers for pre-and post-charter stays. Your fellow diners will be hotel guests and people from visiting yachts. Vegetables and herbs come from the garden, pastries from the restaurant's own oven, and seafood comes fresh from surrounding seas. Lobster thermidor and veal calypso are some of the specials on the dinner menu; bananas flambé provide a sweet finish to the meal. Call ahead to ask about theme nights, which include fun-filled barbecues, Grenadian Night, and the Sunday night carvery, often with local entertainers.

MORNE FENDUE, *south of Sauteurs, St. Patricks. Tel. 442-9330. Credit cards aren't accepted for the fixed-price lunch, which is $17 and is served Monday through Saturday, 12:30 to 3pm. Reservations are essential. The restaurant is about 25 miles from St. George's.*

Make a memorable day of your island tour by stopping for lunch at this 1912 greathouse built of river rock cemented together with a mixture of lime and molasses. Dine family style on authentic old family recipes for pork roast, yam balls, fried zucchini, pepperpot stew, garlic bread, callaloo, chicken, salads and rum punch. Dessert is local cherries over ice cream. To be welcomed into this private home is a privilege, so dress conservatively and mind your manners.

MOUNT RODNEY ESTATE, *Sauteurs. Tel. 442-9420. Lunch is served Monday through Friday by reservation only for $17. Credit cards are not accepted.*

Overlooking the tiny islets off the north shore of the island is this 1890s planter's house, whose British-born owners welcome visitors with a fruit drink or rum punch followed by a West Indian buffet. On the menu are breadfruit salad, tomatoes and cucumbers, coocoo, flying fish, honey nutmeg chicken and other local treats, with exotic ice creams for dessert. It's an ideal stop if you're on an island tour. Get an early start, plan to be here mid-day, and you can be back in the Grand Anse area by cocktail hour.

SUR LA MER RESTAURANT, *in the Gem Holiday Beach Resort, Morne Route, Grand Anse. Tel. 444-2288. Hours are 7:30 to 10am, noon to 3pm and 7:30 to 10:30pm. The bar stays open later. Happy Hour daily is 5 to 7pm. Free transportation is offered groups of four or more; all diners get free entry to the night club.*

Order from the menu of local and Creole specialties or come for the buffets. On Friday the West Indian buffet serves fresh fish, salads and Grenadian classics to the beat of local calypso musicians. Saturday night's barbecued fish, chops and chicken are followed by fire eating and limbo. The restaurant is dressy at dinner. Don't wear cut-offs and tees.

Budget

CHEF'S CASTLE, *Gore and at Halifax streets, St. George's. Meals are $6-$12. Hours are Monday through Saturday 9am to 10pm and Sunday 4pm to 10pm. No credit cards.*

If your children have a yen for American-style fast food, stop in here for beef or fish burgers, hot dogs, fried chicken or pizza. Ask what local dishes are on the stove today too.

LA BOULANGERIE, *in the Le Marquis Complex, Grand Anse. Tel. 444-4316. Hours are Monday through Saturday 8am to 8pm, Sunday 9am to 2pm. Eat for less than $10.*

An ideal spot for a sandwich, pizza or roast chicken, this is best known as a bakery specializing in *pain chocolat,* croissants and special breads including baguettes to eat in or take out.

PIRATES COVE, *in the Grand View Inn, Morne Rouge, Grand Anse. Tel. 444-2342. Dine for under $20. Walk from nearby hotels; cab fare from the airport is $10. Hours are 7 to 11pm daily; the bar opens at 5pm.*

Make a meal out of conch fritters or plantain fritters, or order the fish, lobster thermidor, or shrimp flamed with rum. For dessert, have the bananas Creole. The setting is a hillside overlooking the bay; servers are in buccaneer costume.

PORTOFINO, *on the Carenage, St. George's. Tel. 440-3986. Reservations are recommended. Dine for under $20. Cab fare from Grand Anse hotels is $10. The restaurant is open Monday through Saturday 11am to 11pm and Sunday 6 to 11pm.*

Cargo ships, cruise ships, yacht tenders, ferries, and water taxis provide the passing floorshow in this waterfront hangout where the pizza is world class. Also on the menu: steak, fresh seafood, lobster in season, vegetarian lasagna, clams in cream sauce, and a tangy key lime pie. End the meal with a Caribbean cappuccino. Call about jazz and Caribbean music nights, when you're welcome to bring your instrument and join in.

RED ROOSTER, *Grand Anse. Tel. 444-5400. Prices start at $5. Orders of $20 or more will be delivered for an additional $2.50. Hours are Sunday to Thursday 11am to 10pm, Friday and Saturday 11am to 11pm.*

Stop by for takeout or have a meal brought to your lodgings in L'Anse aux Epines, Grand Anse, or True Blue. Choose a combination plate, grilled chicken, rotis, salads, sandwiches, and sweets for individuals, children or families.

Quick Takes

Kentucky Fried Chicken, Pizza Hut, and Columbo's Yogurt form a fast food compound at Grand Anse. Liftoff, the restaurant at Point Salines Airport, is open daily 6:30am to 10:30pm. It's located upstairs, away from the travel rush, and is a good place for a pre-flight meal at modest prices. While some hotels, such as Spice Island Resort, will leave a snack in your room if you have an early flight, others don't serve until 7am or later. If you are flying dawn patrol, eat at the airport, *Tel. 444-4101.*

CARRIACOU

Moderate

CARRIBEE INN, *Prospect. Tel. 443-7380. On the north shore of the island, the inn is a $20 taxi ride from Hillsborough or the airport. Plan to spend $25 for dinner; more if you order lobster. Reservations are essential.*

The view from this hilltop inn is of Anse La Roche and gilded sunsets. Come in time for cocktails, then dine on conch fritters, curried conch, sweet and sour chicken or the chef's daily Creole special such as the pumpkin soup that he serves in a small pumpkin. On special evenings there may be a fashion show, live music, or an all-American feast of fried chicken, mashed potatoes, and corn on the cob. Lunch is in the $10-$15 range and features platters, sandwiches, and salads.

SILVER BEACH RESORT, *Beausejour Bay. Tel. 443-7337. Plan to spend under $20 for lunch, $30 or less for dinner. Call to ask about hours, reservations, and a package that includes transportation from Grenada. The resort is a five-minute walk from Hillsborough.*

Dine in sea breezes along the beach in end-of-the-world serenity broken only by the black greckles, locally called kling-kling, who pounce on any dropped crumbs. Many scenes from the film *White Squall* were shot here and a ship's figurehead left over from the movie stares out to sea from the tree that supports it. Order a Silver Bitch cocktail, then local dishes such as stew beef with "dumplin," curry vegetables, breaded and baked lamb chops, or fish in Creole sauce. Wines are available by the glass. At lunch time, the pizzas and rotis are delicious and cheap. For breakfast try the saltfish souse and bakes, an authentic West Indian breakfast of shredded salt cod salad and fried bread. French toast is served with baked beans and corned beef.

Quick Takes

Several small, moderately priced restaurants and boutiques edge Tyrrel Bay and cater to the yachting crowd who dinghy ashore here. Take the beach road west from Lauriston, then south along the shore from L'Estere. It's a good place to stop for lunch or a drink on a shaded porch overlooking the bay.

SEEING THE SIGHTS
GRENADA
St. George's

Allow at least one day for poking around **St. George's**, one or more days for hiking the rain forest, **Grand Etang**, and one or two days for touring the island. Even if you prefer to rent a car, it's best to spend the first day with a driver and guide. You'll be better fortified to find your way around, drive on the left, and make sense out of maps and road markers, which are not good. Tours are an excellent value starting at $10 per person for a three-hour tour of the city and market and costing as little as $50 for an all-day tour with lunch. Sailing tours are $25 and up.

Tour operators include **Sunshine Tours & Rentals**, *Tel. 444-4295*; **Sunsation Tours**, *Tel. 444-1594;* **Trendy Touring & New Trends Tours**, *Tel. 444-5757 or 444-4836,* **Spiceland Tours**, *Tel. 440-5127*; **Happy Island Tours**, *Tel. 440-9096* does island tours, deep sea fishing, diving, and overnight trips to Carriacou and Petite Martinique. **Henry's Safari Tours**, *Tel. 444-5313,* has a 28-passenger minibus for touring the island.

Jolly Tours, *Tel. 440-9822* provides sightseeing tours in English and many other languages. **K&J Tours**, *Tel. 440-4227*, specializes in historic, hiking, herbal, and cultural tours. Or, tell them your special likes and dislikes and let them organize a mystery tour for you. For a custom tour in an air conditioned minibus or cab, call the **National Taxi Association**, *Tel. 400-5286*.

A walking tour of St. George's should begin at **Fort George**, advises Carol Cruickshank, concierge at Spice Island Beach Resort. "From there you can look out over the entire area and get your bearings," she says. Take your camera. You'll see the horseshoe-shaped **Carenage** with its "Christ of the Deep" statue. It commemorates the burning and sinking of the Italian cruise liner B*ianca C* in Grenada harbor in 1961 and the help given to the passengers by the Grenadian people. Also on the Carenage are the cruise ship terminal and a ring of restaurants and shops including the spice vendors' market, not to be confused with **Market Square** in the heart of downtown. Beyond it, the larger Lagoon is filled with anchored yachts. The fort is now the headquarters of the Royal Grenada Police Force but you're welcome to tour its dark passages and dungeons. At the foot of the fort lies the library and financial complex and a rabbit warren of steep, narrow streets lined with shops and homes.

Nearby between Young and Monkton streets, the **Grenada National Museum** houses a pleasant hodgepodge of interesting oddments from throughout island history. It's open weekdays 9am to 4:30pm and Saturday 10am to 1pm, *Tel. 440-3725*. Admission is EC$2.50.

If forts are your forte, you'll also want to tour **Fort Frederick**, up Richmond Hill. The view of St. George's is majestic and the site is of interest for its oldness (1791) and its involvement in the 1983 intervention, when it was the headquarters of the Peoples Revolutionary Army. Also near St. George's is **Fort Matthew**, a classic siege fort built by the French in 1779.

Points of interest in town include the **traffic policeman** high on a platform where Scott Street meets Lucas Street, snappily directing traffic with his white-gloved hands. While other Grenadian traffic cops have gradually been replaced by lights, popular demand keeps this post manned. **Marryshow House** at Herbert Blaize Street and Park Lane is part of the University of the West Indies now but was one the home of the "Father of the Federation," T.A. Marryshow. It's a fine example of West Indian architecture.

The **Anglican Church** on Church Street was built by the British in 1825 on the site of a French church built in 1690. Stop by to hear Westminster chimes like Big Ben's, and to look at plaques and monuments commemorating important Grenadian events including a slave rebellion in the 1700s. Also on Church Street is the **Scots' Kirk, St. Andrew's Presbytery**, built in 1830. Further up Upper Church Street, the **Roman Catholic Cathedral** dates to 1818.

Amble the crowded, steep streets to enjoy fine Georgian buildings that survived the island's last severe hurricane, Janet in 1955. Don't miss **Market Square**, where farmers come to sell everything from fresh eggs to dasheen, tannia, oranges, coconuts and bananas as well as handcrafts, spices, and souvenirs. Along the **Esplanade**, which connects to the Carenage with a funny little tunnel 12 feet high and 340 feet long, waves crash against the wall while locals shop the meat and fish market.

End your city tour at the **Botanical Gardens** just beyond the roundabout where Lowthers Lane, Tantee Road, and Paddock Road meet. Founded in 1887, the gardens are a national treasury of blossoms, shrubs and trees and the bird life attracted by them. Not far beyond, in the suburb of St. Paul's, **Bay Gardens** are a tamed tropical tangle, threaded with paths where you can marvel at the lush growths and flashing birdlife.

St. George's seems packed with people all the time, but everyday visits are nothing compared to Carnival when parades and "jump-ups" fill the streets nonstop from Friday through Tuesday.

Elsewhere on Grenada

Annandale Falls, 15 minutes northeast of St. George's, is one of the more popular tourist attractions, so schedule your visit there when cruise ships aren't in port. It's a South Seas paradise with a 50-foot waterfall and a pool where you can take a dip. Also here is a souvenir shop and booths where visitors can change clothes. Admission is free; the Centre is open daily 8am to 4pm , *Tel. 440-2452*. **Concord Falls** nearby is a series of three falls, just the spot for a half-day hike and a swim. Admission to the privately-owned paths is $1. At **Woodlands** in St. George, take a guided tour of a sugar factory and buy local rum.

Other waterfalls include **Royal Mount Carmel Waterfall** in St. Andrews, a 70-foot-high cascade that crashes into a crystal pool. Admission is $1. **Seven Sisters Falls**, about an hour from St. George's, is easy to walk to. **Victoria Falls**, in the foothills of **Mount St. Catherine** on the west coast, is accessible only by a fairly rough footpath.

Two good driving tours both begin from St. George's. The first follows the coast road; the second heads east into the rain forest. Driving along the shore you'll pass picturebook villages at the edge of the Caribbean. When you reach **Gouyave**, there's a fishing museum that was closed and seemed inactive during our visit, but it might be livelier in June during the village's Fisherman's Birthday celebration. The fete features the blessing of the fleet, contests, food, crafts, exhibits, and music.

Outside town, visit **Dougladston** (DOO-gal-stun) **Spice Estate**. It's a living history museum where workers demonstrate how nutmeg, cocoa, coconut, and other island products are dried, sorted, and prepared for market using ages-old equipment left from the time when this was a more active warehouse. An active spice processing plant can be toured in downtown **Go**uyave, where tons of nutmeg are dried, cracked and graded. It is open weekdays 10am to 1pm and 2-4pm for admission of $1. It has no telephone.

Another spice processing plant can be found in **St. Paul's**, a St. George's suburb (take Lowthers Lane). Open to tours, it's the place to buy nutmeg products such as syrup, jam, jelly and liqueur.

Continuing north from Gouyave brings you to Sauteurs, or **Leapers' Hill**, where the Carib Indians committed suicide rather than submit to the French in 1651. Just to the east, where the Atlantic and Caribbean meet, **Levera National Park**, *Tel. 442-1018.* has hiking paths, fabulous beaches and snorkeling (although the surf can be savage) and a mangrove swamp where you might spot a brilliant tropical parrot. The park's interpretive center is open daily. Just south of **Levera Pond**, throw coins into the fountain at **River Sallee Boiling Springs**. The hot springs are thought by locals to have strong spiritual powers.

Turning south now, you'll pass through the parish of **St. Patrick** where, along the **St. Patrick's River valley** in the community of **Mount Rich**, find petroglyphs done by Amerindians. Now enter St. Andrew where **Grenville** is Grenada's largest population center. Come here on a Saturday morning when it's a colorful beehive of vendors, fishmongers, spice sellers, and fruit and vegetable stands. About six miles north of the city, **Lake Antoine** is a 16-acre pool in an extinct volcano. Just southeast of the lake, stop at **River Antoine Rum Distillery**, the oldest in the

Caribbean. Unlike any other rum factory you've toured in the islands, this one uses equipment that hasn't changed since the 19th century. In the gift shop, you can buy the resulting firewater. Free tours are offered daily 9am to 4pm. A more modern distillery, home of mellow **Westerhall Rum**, can be toured on the south coast.

From **Grenville**, it's possible to follow the coast back to **Point Salines** and **Grand Anse**, although deep fjords cut into the headlands and don't allow roads to get very close to the sea. In **St. David**, stop at **La Sagesse Nature Center**, *Tel. 444-6458*, to view bird life in a mangrove estuary lined with beaches, cactus scrub, and woodlands. An eight-room inn is also found here (see *Where to Stay*).

An alterative route from Grenville takes you back to St. George's across the mountains through **Grand Etang Forest Reserve**, which deserves an entire day or more for hiking, picnicking, and bird watching. Within minutes after leaving the coast, you have climbed more than one thousand feet where the air is at least ten degrees cooler. In **Grand Etang Forest Centre**, *Tel. 440-6160*, view interpretive exhibits covering the Forest's vegetation, forestry and wildlife. Grand Etang Lake, cradled in a volcano crater more than 1,700 feet above sea level, is a favorite spot for hiking. The park is open daily 8:30am to 4pm.

Woburn, a small conching village in the south near Grand Anse, makes a pleasant side trip from the resort area. Known as Conch Village, it has an enormous mound of discarded conch shells that grew over the years as fishermen discarded the pearly shells.

CARRIACOU

Carriacou Museum, *Tel. 443-8288*, bills itself as "the only museum in the Eastern Caribbean owned by the people, not the government." Located in an old cotton gin at Patterson and Main streets in **Hillsborough**, it displays a variety of arts and artifacts from Arawak times through European settlement.

Of special interest are the paintings of Canute Caliste, the island's Grandma Moses, which are displayed and sold here. He says simply, "I has a gift. I has a plan. I grows it," in describing his colorful, charmingly child-like paintings of island scenes and events. One display explains the Big Drum, Carriacou's famous ceremonial dance. The museum is open daily except Saturday, 9:30am to 3:45pm Admission is $2.

NIGHTLIFE & ENTERTAINMENT

Although most resorts bring in musicians several nights a week, Grenadians are early to bed and guests are glad to follow. One hotelier told us, "I have the live music because guests expect it, but by 10pm only a handful of people are still out here listening." Still, Grenada has nightlife to be found, especially on weekends and during festivals.

CASABLANCA PIANO BAR AND BILLIARD CAFE, *above the banks in the shopping strip at Grand Anse, Tel. 444-1631.*

Open until 3am serving snacks and drinks. Play pool and other games, or groove to live music or a DJ depending on the night,

FANTAZIA 2001 *is a disco at Morne Rouge, Grand Anse, Tel. 444-4224.*

People start drifting at 9pm but it takes until 11pm for things to get hopping. Wednesday is oldies night, Thursday is for rum punch and contemporary sounds, and Fridays feature local bands. On Saturdays the disco goes on all night. Secure parking is available.

ISLAND VIEW NIGHT CLUB in the fishing village of Woburn, *Tel. 443-2054.*

Plays oldies and goodies. Friday is ladies' night and Saturday is disco.

LE SUCRIER at Grand Anse, *Tel. 444-1068.*

Party on Friday and Saturday nights to the sounds of soca, reggae, soul, house, dub, and slows.

BIG DRUM

*Carriacou's **Big Drum** celebrations are unique, and it's the lucky traveler who happens to be here when one is scheduled. Women in bright costumes with many petticoats do the dancing, a holdover from the days when they danced for food and rum. It's called Big Drum because of the size of the gathering, not the drums, which are only about 20 inches high and 12 inches around. Three drums are beaten, accompanied by chac-chac, or maracas. Traditionally a Big Drum is held two years after a death to please the dead. It may also accompany a feast or be scheduled during a drought to call for rain.*

SPORTS & RECREATION

Bicycling

Ride Grenada, *Tel. 444-1157*, will arrange a bike and tour.

Deep Sea Fishing

Bezo Charters offer a 32-foot boat with IGFA equipment, fighting chair, bait, tackle, and beverages for no more than four anglers. Billfish are tagged and released. Call Graham or Ian at *Tel. 443-5477.*

Nice Vice, Tel. 444-4649 is a 30-foot cuddy cabin cruiser that can take up to 12 passengers fishing or cruising. A half-day fishing grip costs $300 for up to four, including snacks and equipment. A full-day outing is $450.

Xiphias Seeker is an air conditioned 35-foot Bertram sportfisherman, *Tel. 444-4422. Havadu, Tel. 440-4386* is a 32-foot deep sea fishing boat. **Kontiki Expeditions**, *Tel. 443-7404*, offers fishing trips out of Windward, Carriacou.

Diving

Grenada and its sister islands are a scuba diver's Toys 'R Us, with no end of reefs, bays, and islands. Renowned dive sites include **Boss Reef**, which runs all the way from the harbor to Point Saline and Grand Mal Bay (it was named "great sickness" because of an epidemic that struck here many generations ago), which has a wall dive.

A few wreck dives are possible including the 600-foot cruise ship *Bianca C.* After the tragedy, the statue Christ of the Deep on the Carenage was sent by the shipping line in thanks to Grenadians who worked valiantly to save lives when the ship burned. Today she's home to schools of jack, barracuda, and rays. **Kick 'em Jenny**, the cone of an extinct volcano, provides good visibility and plenty of bright coral. Other dive sites are found off **Sandy Island**, **Sister Rocks**, **Frigate Island**, **Twin Sisters**, and other off-island rocks and islets.

Dive operators include:

• **Carriacou Silver Diving Ltd**, Hillsborough, *Tel. 443-7882*. PADI and SSI courses are given in English and German.

• **Sanvics Scuba & Watersports**, at Renaissance Grenada Resort, has a dive boat, equipment, instructors, and free pickup at other hotels, *Tel. 444-4271*.

• **Dive Grenada** at Cot Bam, *Tel. 444-1092* offers free transportation and seven years experience on the *Bianca C.*

• **Scuba Express** is a dive boat that operates out of the True Blue Inn, True Blue, *Tel. 444-2133*.

• **Scuba World** works with both the Rex Grenadian Resort and Secret Harbor Hotel, *Tel. 444-1111*. It has its own dive boat and offers equipment, instruction, and dives.

• **Tanki's Watersport Paradise Ltd.**. *Tel. 443-8406*, is on Carriacou. Ask about packages that include a stay at Tanki's Hotel, which is one of the best values on Carriacou.

Hiking

Telfor Bedeau, *Tel. 442-6200*, has walked every mountain, cliff and river on the island and is one of the most knowledgeable guides in the Caribbean. A tireless outdoorsman, he has also rowed around the island in an 18-foot boat he built himself. Bedeau, who was born here in 1939, can design any type or length hike you want, tough or tenderfoot, including a 12-hour trek coast to coast across the island.

Arnold's Tours, *Tel. 440-0531, Fax 440-4118*, offers guide service for hikes described as "ironman", average, and gentle. Bedeau and other guides can take you on hikes of **Grand Etang National Park** and **Forest Reserve**, or you can walk some of the well-marked paths on your own. Still, it's useful to have a guide to hack away the razor grass, explain the diverse habitat, and to find the driest routes through frequent muddy spots. Wear hiking shoes with a good tread; abundant rainfall keeps the paths slippery and many hikers end up on a muddy belly pulling themselves along with the help of a vine.

Among the most interesting paths is a circle around **Grand Etang** itself, the big pond in an extinct volcano. Thought to have magical powers, it's sometimes the scene of immersion baptisms by Christian groups and of Shango "sacrifices" in which foods are floated out onto the lake. Locals sometimes come here with special requests such as healing or enlisting the water's magical powers in finding a spouse. If you're lucky, you'll spot a monkey along the way. The trip takes about 1-1/2 hours. An easy 15-minute jog from the Park Centre brings you to **Morne LaBaye**, the lookout tower atop a rounded hill with benches for rest and bird watching.

A three-hour hike to **Mount Qua Qua** takes you into cool cloud forest. The going can be slick and dirty, requiring grabs for roots and vines and plenty of mud on the clothes, but the views of wild orchids, wind-sculpted trees, and dramatic plunges are unforgettable. Tim O'Keefe, author of *Caribbean Afoot* (Menasha Ridge Press) reports meeting several people who turned back because they found the going too rough. Take a guide.

If you're game for a longer walk, take the Mount Qua Qua trail all the way to **Concord Falls** on a route that Arnold saves for his "ironmen" hikers. The trail leads through **Fedon's Camp**, where the view is stunning and the story grisly. Planter Julien Fedon, a mulatto, led a slave revolt in the 18th century and murdered 50 hostages here including the British governor. Fedon's cohorts were captured but his own fate was never known. Some say he lived out his life on another island; others believe he drowned while trying to escape. When you reach the falls, which are usually crowded with tourists, call a taxi or, if nobody is around, walk another half hour into Concord and flag a bus (any day save Sunday.)

Sailing & Powerboating

A 47-foot catamaran takes you on an all-day sail along the southern coast, with a stop at **Calivigny Island** for a buffet lunch. Half-day and sunset sails, and private charters can be arranged Call **Carib CATS**, *Tel. 444-3222.*

Carriacou Islander has a glass observation panel that lets you see the underwater world while you sail. Arrange an all-day excursions include lunch, air transfer, and a bus tour through **Sunsation Tours**, *Tel. 444-1656*, **Carriacou Tours**, *Tel. 443-8238* or **Down Island Ltd.**, *Tel. 443-8182*. **Catch the Spirit**, *Tel. 444-4371 or 444-5227*, is a 32-foot, twin engine pirogue that does fishing, snorkeling, diving, and barbecue tours.

The Moorings, *Tel. 444-4891*, offers day and half-day sails to Hog Island and Calivigny Island under power or sail, including soft drinks and snorkeling gear. Lunch is available.

Nice Vice, *Tel. 444-4649* is a 30-foot cuddy cabin cruiser that can take up to 12 passengers fishing or cruising. A nine-hour day cruise to Carriacou includes an island four, barbecue lunch, and snorkeling.

Starwind Enterprise, *Tel. 440-3678*, sails to nearby islands on picnic, scuba, and whale watching cruises. Mornings and evenings

SHOPPING

Grenada is the Spice Island, second only to Indonesia in the production of **nutmeg** and its byproduct **mace** (the spice, not the pepper spray), so the most meaningful souvenirs to take home include spices for your kitchen, whole spices strung as necklaces, and a realm of cosmetics, foods, flavorings and hot sauces made from spices and spice oils. Art lovers will find the works of talented local artists in galleries, and the island also has locally-made batik, pottery, and basketry. Grenada also has its own liquors including the sublime local Westerhall Plantation Rum, and tourist shops selling luxury goods from around the world.

Caution: the "saffron" sold here seems too good to be true at $10 a pint and it is. It's really tumeric. Also, when bargaining for anything, be constantly aware too that dollars are easily confused. To avoid paying just over 2-1/2 times the real price, always use the terms U.S. or E.C. as in, "You say this is 12 EC?"

Downtown **Market Square** in downtown St. George's is a swirl of color and commerce, one of the best native markets in the Indies. Tourists mingle with local housewives, bargaining for bananas and spices, baskets and vegetables. Although vendors are as spirited as any others in the Caribbean, and they will haggle up to a point, they'll also take no for an answer. Don't go if you're not willing to buy something. These vendors have toiled down from the hillsides bringing their produce by bus or donkey back. They are here to sell it, not just pose for your camera. This is the island's nerve center, the place to catch a bus or the latest rumors.

For local arts and sculpture as well as antique lithographs of Caribbean scenes, try **Yellow Poui Art Gallery** on Cross Street. **Frangipani** on the Carenage has local handcrafts and batiks. Stop in at **White Cane**

Industries on the Carenage, where gift items benefit the blind. Credit cards aren't accepted here. A similar industry, when you're out on the island, is NEWLOW in Palmiste, St. John. Goods are made by youths who are in vocational training.

Arawak Islands on Upper Belmont Road in St. George's sells things made from island spices: perfumes, body oils, potpourris, soaps, and teas. It's open Monday through Friday only. **Imagine**, which specializes in locally made dolls, ceramics, batiks, and straw work, is in the Grand Anse Shopping Centre and the Rex Grenadian Hotel.

Resort Row

Janissa's Boutique in Spice Island Resort has pricey designer clothing and swimwear, with large selections of Gottex and La Perla. **Spice Tea Grenada** in the Camerhogne Park Hotel at Grand Anse sells beach wraps, interesting foods such as banana ketchup, and their own tea blends.

United Artists gallery in the Le Marquis Complex, Grand Anse, features the works of local artists including Susan Mains, Canute Caliste, and Doris Williams, who sews heirloom Big Drum dolls and Big Mama dolls that come complete with locally made baskets. Jewelry sold in the shop is made from glass shards polished in nature's tumbler, the sea, and fastened with silver threads. For international newspapers, magazines, toiletries and sundries, visit **The Store** in the Rex Grenadian Resort at Point Salines.

Herreras Furniture, also called **Town and Country**, at L'Anse aux Epines sells local grass work, pottery, baskets, and lamps. Mahogany furniture made on the island is well made and a fabulous buy. If you're willing to tangle with the vagaries of international shipping, you can furnish a home for a song with hefty pieces that will last forever.

Airport

While waiting for your flight at Point Salines, shop at **airport stores** that include Columbian Emeralds and two liquor stores, all selling duty free.

EXCURSIONS & DAY TRIPS

Caribbean Horizons Tours & Services, *Tel. 473/444-1555, Fax 444-2899*, can set up an island tour, which is recommended before you start exploring on your own. In a tour of five to seven hours, they'll show you the rain forest, Grand Etang crater lake, the rum distillery, a stop at the beach, then Carib's Leap, Concord Falls, and a spice factory. Also available are a pirogue picnic, sailing, or a sunset dinner cruise. Popular excursions off-island include Carriacou and Sandy Island, snorkeling expeditions to islets and bays, and deep sea fishing.

Take a day or sunset cruise aboard *Rhum Runner* or *Rhum Runner II*, which dock in the harbor and sail on a variety of excursions – most of them featuring all the rum punch you can drink. Book through your hotel's concierge or *Tel. 440-4386*. **Fun Tours**. *Tel. 444-3167*, offers dive packages and day trips to neighboring islands including Carriacou, Tobago Cays, Bequia, Mustique, and Barbados. **Gren Cab**, *Tel. 444-4444* offers 24-hour service to any island destination.

Albin Fletcher, *Tel. 444-0912*, will take you on an island tour by bus (unless you have a car; he doesn't have one) on a hike, or in his boat for snorkeling. Call after 6pm.

CARRIACOU

If you'd like to see the island, any taxi driver can give you an island tour.

Based at Tyrrel Bay is the 76-foot yacht *Suvetar*, which does overnight trips to the Grenadines, whale and dolphin watch cruises, sunset sails, snorkel and scuba expeditions, and day trips to uninhabited island and bays.

A couple of half-day tours are enough to see this little island, with stops for snorkeling and swimming. In the north of the island you'll spot ruins including a massive sugar mill and the **Dover Ruins**, the remains of first church on the island. On the southeast end of the island at La Pointe are the remains of an old French greathouse.

Tyrrel Bay makes a nice stop for picture taking, snacking and boutique shopping in a tiny fishing community. If you're lucky, someone will be building a boat along the coast. The old methods are still used here, resulting in seakindly vessels that last for years.

One of the best side trips here is a short sail to **Sandy Island**, so perfect that it could serve as a poster for paradise. A long spit of white sand rises from clear turquoise waters. At one end the islet is crowned with palm trees. It's a must-see stop for every tour as well as visiting yachts so it can be crowded. There is talk of limiting access to prevent damage from overuse.

If you're in Carriacou for **Carnival** (just before Lent) it has a twist different from any other in the islands. In one event, players do a send-up of a Shakespeare's *Julius Caesar* complete with crowns, capes, comedy and mock beatings. An island of boatbuilders, Carriacou is also the site of a rousing regatta in August, when boats race and people party hearty.

PETITE MARTINIQUE

Hike to the top of the volcano for a panoramic view of the surrounding islands.

OTHER ISLANDS

A popular stop for excursion boats is **Calivigny Island** with its nice beaches, and **Glover Island**, where you can see the ruins of a Norwegian whaling station that was in use until 1925. A sprinkling of other islands is used by tour operators for snorkeling, picnics, swimming and by yachts for anchorages.

PRACTICAL INFORMATION

American Express: on Church Street, St. George's, *Tel. 440-2945.*

Area Code: **473** will be Granada's area code, but at press time **809** is still in use and the effective day for the new area code has not been announced.

Bank holidays: include Christmas, Boxing Day, New Year's Day, February 7 (Independence Day), Good Friday, Easter and Easter Monday, May 1 (Labour Day), Whit Monday and Corpus Christi (vary with the church calendar), August 4 and 5, Carnival Monday and Tuesday (August), and Thanksgiving (late October).

Bank hours: banks are found in major settlements and are generally open Monday through Thursday 8am to 3pm and Friday 8am to 5pm.

Business hours: generally, shops are open Monday to Friday 8am to 4pm and Saturday 8am to 1pm. Some shops close from noon to 1pm. Government offices including post offices are open 8am to 3pm.

Consulate: The U.S. Embassy is at Pointe Salines, St. George's, *Tel. 444-1173/8.*

Currency: the EC dollar, which trades at about EC$2.70 to the U.S. dollar. Bank exchange rates are slightly better that those allowed by hotels and shops. Prices in major shops and restaurants are in U.S. dollars, but don't carry large bills because change in U.S. funds is rarely available.

Current: 220 volts/50 Hertz. Most hotels have built-in hair dryers and special plugs that can be used for electric shavers, but you'll need adapters and transformers for computers, your curling iron, and other appliances.

Customs: visitors may bring in a quart of spirits, 200 cigarettes, or 50 cigars. To protect local agriculture from pests that have not yet invaded the island, there's a ban on bringing fruits, vegetables, meat and soil. Drugs, firearms, and ammunition are prohibited.

Driving: on the left. Most rental agencies can sell you the required local driver's license, which is EC$30. Gasoline costs about EC$6.50 per imperial gallon.

Emergencies: in St. George's dial 434 for an ambulance; in St. Andrew's dial 724; in Carriacou call 774.

Immigration: a valid passport and return ticket are required for entry, although citizens of the United States, Canada, and the United Kingdom need only two documents showing proof of citizenship, one of them with photo. Acceptable documents include a birth certificate, expired passport or voter registration card plus a driver's license. with photo.

Pharmacies: in Grenville, St. George's, Hillsborough (Carriacou), Petit Esperance, and Sauteurs. Gittens Drug Mart and Mitchell's Pharmacy in Grand Anse are open seven days a week.

Tax: a government tax of eight percent is charged on hotel bills and meals. Exit tax is $14 or EC$35 when leaving Grenada for other countries and $4 or EC$10 when leaving Carriacou for other Grenadian islands. For children ages 5 to 10, charges are half; children under age 5 are exempt.

Water: from local taps is said to be safe to drink.

Weddings: couples must reside in Grenada for at least three working days, have valid passports and birth certificates, and bring and a notarized letter from an attorney affirming that both have single status. If applicable, divorce papers, a deed poll to prove any name change, and/or a previous partner's death certificate must be shown. Both bride and groom must be at least 18 years old. Magistrates are available after 4:30pm to perform weddings; Protestant ministers are easily found. For a Catholic wedding, have your home priest liaise with a priest in Grenada, allowing six to eight months for the planning.

25. ST. LUCIA

Called the "Helen" of the Caribbean because of the beauty of a face that launched 1,000 ships, **St. Lucia** has been a beacon to sailors since well before recorded history. Her twin volcanic peaks, Petit Piton and Gros Piton, are recognizable landmarks from far out to sea. Most of the island is cloaked in thick greenery, from wild tangles of forest filled with wild orchids to lush banana plantations heavy with fruit.

Of the island's 238 square miles, 19,000 acres are national forest. Seen here on a lucky day is the rare Jacquot, or St. Lucia parrot, as well as 15 of the world's 27 orders of birds.

Like many of the islands, St. Lucia was yanked between European powers time and again. It was handed back and forth between the British and French at least 14 times. What remains is a beguiling pastiche of French words and place names, Anglicans and Roman Catholics living in harmony with newcomer religions, and memorable cuisine that blends the best of French cooking and island fish and produce.

In 1992, St. Lucia's Derek Wolcott won the Nobel Prize for Literature and in 1979, the Nobel Prize in Economics went to a St. Lucian, Sir W. Arthur Lewis. When it comes to best-of surveys, St. Lucia always scores with its anchorages, dive sites, natural attractions, romantic places to stay, snorkeling, honeymoons, and so on. Joan Devaux, owner of Diamond Botanical Gardens, won an eco-tourism award for her efforts.

Eco-tourism is, in fact, the island's new mantra. There's a new campground, miles of outstanding hiking trails, stellar scuba diving over pristine reefs, miles of good beaches, and superb nature watching at the offshore **Fregate Islands** and **Maria Island**. Only with a licensed guide can you reach many of the protected sites. Spearfishing and the collecting of live marine specimens is forbidden.

You'll see a lot of poverty and overpopulation, and will be pursued by pushy vendors. Roads are awful and in general the infrastructure is only beginning to emerge from Third World status. Some locals show too much of what is popularly known as attitude, but most folks are fun-loving, easygoing, and eager to welcome tourists. St. Lucia has a long way to go economically, but she's on her way and we cheer her progress. All in all, we give the island an enthusiastic thumbs-up.

Climate

May and June are the hottest months. Plan on lots of sunny days here, with cooler temperatures in the mountains and rain forests. July through November are the wettest months; February and March have the least rain.

ARRIVALS & DEPARTURES

St. Lucia has two airports, **Vigie Field** in the north part of the island outside Castries, and **Hewannora International Airport** at Vieux Fort on the southern tip of the island. Because the latter may be referred to by locals as Vieux Fort rather than its name, Hewannora, it's easy to be confused. Most international flights arrive here; inter-island connectors are more likely to serve Vigie. In any case, they are separated by 45 miles of bad roads, so factor that in when you are comparing prices and schedules. The drive from Vieux Fort to Castries on a rainy night, on dark roads filled with people, goats, and broken-down vehicles, is an experience we hope never to repeat.

St. Lucia is served from North America by **Air Canada**, *Tel. 800/776-3000* in the U.S. or *Tel. 800/268-7240* in Canada; **American Airlines** and **American Eagle**, *Tel. 800/433-7300.* **British Airways** serves the island from London, *Tel. 800/247-9297;* **LIAT**, *Tel. (246) 495-1187,* includes St. Lucia among its island-hopping itineraries. Inter-island service is also by **Helen Air**, *Tel. (758)-452-7196.*

You can also get here by ferries that ply among St. Lucia and many other islands. Service is infrequent and the passage long. Sail the *Windward, Tel. 758/452-1364, Fax 453-1654,* from Barbados, St. Vincent, Trinidad & Tobago, or Venezuela; or *L'Expres Des Iles, Tel. 758/452-2211* from Guadeloupe, Martinique, or Dominica.

INSIDER TIP FOR HONEYMOONERS

*BWIA, Tel. 800/780-5501, will upgrade you to First Class for $99 if you let **BWIA Vacations** book your entire honeymoon package in St. Lucia. Departures from Miami or JFK are available, and the deal also carries 2,500 extra Frequent Flyer miles. Rates start at under $700. There's some fine print involved, so call for full details. While it's a honeymoon deal, smart couples who are not actually honeymooning often ask for the Honeymoon Package everywhere because it's often the best deal.*

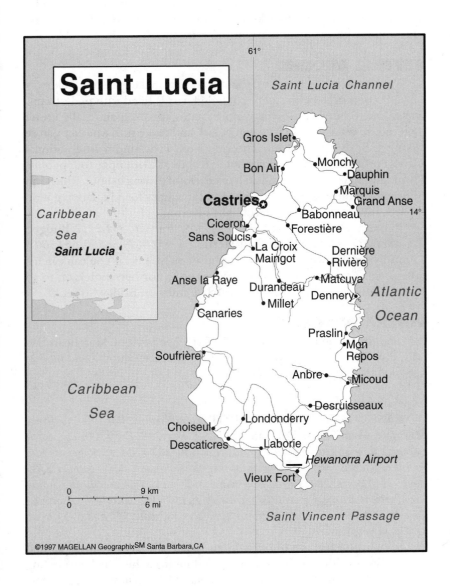

Saint Lucia

61°

Saint Lucia Channel

Gros Islet

Monchy
Bon Air
Dauphin

Marquis
Castries
Grand Anse

Caribbean
Babonneau
14°
Ciceron
Sans Soucis
Forestière

Saint Lucia
La Croix
Maingot
Dernière
Rivière

Anse la Raye
Matcuya
Durandeau
Dennery
Atlantic
Millet

Canaries
Ocean

Praslin
Mon
Repos

Soufrière
Anbre
Micoud

Caribbean
Desruisseaux

Sea
Londonderry

Choiseul
Descaticres
Laborie

Hewanorra Airport

Vieux Fort

Saint Vincent Passage

0   9 km
0   6 mi

©1997 MAGELLAN GeographixSM Santa Barbara,CA

ORIENTATION

St. Lucia is south of Martinique and north of St. Vincent & the Grenadines. It is extremely rugged, with mountains that scrape the clouds. Its capital, **Castries**, is in the north. The island is 238 square miles but, with the many switchbacks, it is possible to cover twice in road miles what you are covering in miles "as the crow flies."

GETTING AROUND

Taxis meet every ferry and flight, and they make excellent guides as well as expert drivers on steep, pot-holed, roads filled with pedestrians, goats, and other vehicles in various states of disrepair. Cabs aren't metered, so get a price before you board, and make sure whether you're talking U.S. or E.C. dollars. The ride from Hewannora International Airport to Castries and northern hotels is about $75 for up to four people. If you must have a rental car, you'll need a local driving license, which can be bought at the airport or at the rental car agency for $12. Driving is on the left, but most cars have right-hand steering.

Rental agencies include **Avis**, *Tel. 454-2046 or 800/331-2112*; **Budget**, *Tel. 452-0233 or 800/527-0700;* or **Hertz**, *Tel. 452-0679 or 800/654-3001.*

Individually-owned vans serve as buses on St. Lucia. You can catch a jitney near the marketplace in Castries to go to northern hotels or, to go to the southern end of the island, catch a jitney on Bridge Street.

WHERE TO STAY

The government hotel tax in St. Lucia is eight percent. Most hosts also add service charges or 10 percent or more. Rates are quoted and paid in U.S. dollars unless otherwise stated.

Expensive

ANSE CHASTENET BEACH HOTEL, *mail address Box 7000, Soufriere, St. Lucia, West Indies. Tel. 758/454-7000, Fax 758/454-7700; ask about packages through Ralph Locke Islands. Tel. 800/223-1108. Packages are also sold through 800/465-8242. Rates at this 49-room resort start at under $385 double; MAP at $55 per person is recommended because few other dining choices are available nearby. From Hewanorra airport, it's 1-1/2 hours to the resort and from Vigie Airport. airport, two hours. Cab fares are about $45 and $75 (for up to four persons).*

Looking back at the resort from the sea, it seems to float suspended in a jungle, one villa almost atop another climbing a sheer incline. Getting here is not half the fun, so this isn't the place for a quick overnight. The taxi ride from either airport is jouncy and hot; after dark in the rain it's downright suicidal. Arrive as early in the day as possible and settle down to unwind for a week or two.

The reefs off the resort, an underwater national preserve, are among the best in the Caribbean. Snorkel or scuba into a collage of color in which brilliant reef flirt with coral in incredible hues. Many people come here solely for the diving; resort guests share the reefs with day-trippers who come in by the boat load. The advantage in staying here is that you can time your dives to avoid the dive boats that throng to this popular dive site.

Aside from the incomparable diving, guests can also swim from two natural beaches, hike the Pitons, take a history tour of this old plantation region, play tennis on a concrete court, take a snorkel cruise, windsurf, kayak, shop the boutiques or have spa treatments. Entertainers are on hand six nights a week; a shopping trip into Castries is offered five times a week. Children under age 4 cannot be accommodated and the steep, rugged steps aren't suitable for the elderly or infirm.

Rooms are South Seas tropical, with oversize showers open to views of forest and sky. They don't have television, radio, or telephone so you're alone with the rustling palms (and any noises from neighboring units; there is no glass in louvered wood windows). All rooms are supersize and have hair dryer, refrigerator, coffee machine, and ceiling fan (which we wished, at times, was an air conditioner). Furnishings make good use of straw, wicker, and the charming madras prints that are an island trademark. Premium rooms have an ironing board and iron.

Choose between two restaurants and a couple of bars. The food, supervised by award-winning chef Jacky Rioux, is a definite plus, especially at these attractive, meal-plan rates. Sample the chilled red pepper soup, roast honey-glazed duck in red wine, and the oven-baked gratinée of christophene on black-eye peas with curry cream.

LADERA RESORT, *Soufriere. Tel. 758/459-7323 or 800/738-4752. Rates at this 19-unit resort start at $330. Ask about week-long honeymoon packages. Add $45 per person daily for breakfast and dinner. The resort is 40 minutes from Hewanorra Airport or an hour from Vigie on St. Lucia's southwest coast.*

Tropical hardwoods and earthy stone and tile provide the setting for 19th century French furnishings, wicker, and locally handcrafted pieces. You'll have your own, private villa or suite, perhaps with a private pool or plunge pool, and a view of mountains and sea that will take your breath away. Your neighbors, whom you may never see, may be movie stars or famous authors who come here for the romantic seclusion. Have high tea in the garden and cocktails in the bar, then dine in the resort's own Dasheene Restaurant where local produce and fish create what the chefs call Island Cuisine Courant.

LE SPORT, *Cariblue Beach. Tel. 758/450-8551, Fax 452-0368; toll-free Tel. 800/544-2883. Rates start at $225 per person per night, all inclusive. The hotel is 20 minutes from Vigie Airport.*

The price seems high but you're getting everything from airport transfers to food and drink plus two spa treatments every day. This resort and its sister La Source on Grenada combine all the best of an all-inclusive with the pampering of a health spa including delicious meals that aren't crammed with calories. It's a unique concept that is perfect for a honeymoon or a healing getaway. Oversize rooms have a big, marble bathroom, queen-size bed, telephone, private balcony, and mini-bar. Premium units have an ocean view and four-poster bed. A suite is available at $1,095. There's a nonstop list of activities including dancersize, or just lounge by one of the three swimming pools. Play tennis, use one of the bicycles to explore the countryside, or use any of the watersports equipment. Then soak in the hot tub or sauna before or after your complimentary massage.

ROYAL ST. LUCIAN, *Reduit Beach. Tel. 758/452-9999, Fax 452-6939, toll-free 800/255-5859. It's a $12 taxi ride from Vigie Airport. Rates at the 96-suite resort start at $365 nightly plus $60 per person for breakfast and dinner. Four-and seven-night packages are far less.*

This exclusive, all-suite hotel has one of the Caribbean's finest spas, a serene sanctuary where you can get a fitness analysis, take a wide range of exercise and workout regiments, and choose from a menu of scrubs, wraps, massages, and herbal treatments. You can take your treatments in the Royal Spa, in your suite, or on the beach. This is St. Lucia's only AAA four-diamond rated property. Swim in the four, interconnected pools with a waterfall, dine in en elegant beach setting in L'Epicure or in the more casual La Nautique, tan on the woody sun deck. Suites have a spacious bedroom and bath and a separate sitting area than opens onto a private patio or balcony. Rooms have color television, dial telephone, safe, and mini-bar.

WINDJAMMER LANDING VILLA BEACH RESORT, *P.O. Box 1504, Castries, St. Lucia, West Indies. Tel. 758/452-0913 or, in the U.S., 800/346-5358. Rates at this 114-unit resort start at $270 double and range to $670 nightly for a three-bedroom villa with private plunge pool. The resort is 15 minutes from Castries on Labrelette Bay.*

Sun-baked adobe villas with red tile roofs have a Mediterrean-Moorish look with lots of intricate tile work, with lots of louvers and lattices to invite tropic breezes. Fabrics tend to airy whites and pale beiges with brash accents in parakeet colors: yellow, turquoise, red. Villas have air conditioned bedrooms, cable television, microwave ovens, ceiling fan, and a private plunge pool. Guests get a welcome cocktail and a weekly invitation to the manager's cocktail party. Complimentary with some packages are provisions of fruit and champagne, day or night tennis, non-motorized watersports, and an introductory scuba lesson. Dine in your choice of five venues or have dinner served on your private terrace. Swim in the four pools or off the secluded, white sand beach in a serene, cerulean blue bay. Horseback riding, golf, and land or sea tours can be arranged. Each villa comes with a housekeeper-maid and, for families, a nanny can be provided. The resort is kid-friendly, with supervised children's activities and their own "cocktail" party.

Moderate

GREEN PARROT, *on the Morne, mailing address Box 648, Castries. Tel. 758/452-3399, Fax 453-2272. Doubles are $110. This 55-room hotel is 15 minutes from Castries.*

The home of the well-known Green Parrot Restaurant, this hotel has a big swimming pool with a side deck overlooking smoky mountains in the far distance and Castries below. Air conditioned rooms have telephone and cable television. On weekdays, a free shuttle is run to the beach. Car rental is on site, and there is live entertainment in the restaurant.

HARMONY MARINA SUITES, *Rodney Bay, mailing address Box 155, Castries. Tel. 758/452-8756, Fax 452-8677. Rates at this 30-suite resort are from $120. It's five miles north of Castries.*

This all-suite resort where you get a one-bedroom suite with or without a kitchen is a favorite with the boating crowd. Put two units together and you can sleep four or six with complete cooking facilities. Units have air conditioning, cable television, safe, private balcony or patio, and hair dryer. VIP suites have a double Jacuzzi and four-poster bed. The beach is 200 yards away. Nearby is a deli and convenience store where you can provision your yacht or apartment. The fun centers around waterports; if you're not boating, let them arrange a canoe trip or a dive. Babysitting can be arranged.

HUMMINGBIRD BEACH RESORT, *Soufriere. Tel. 758/459-7232, Fax 459-7003. Rates at this nine-room resort start at $145.*

Fly into Hewanorra, which is about 45 minutes from this hotel overlooking Soufriere Bay. For such a small place it gives you a big choice of accommodations, ranging from standard rooms with shared bath to a cottage with breakfast and dinner in the highly-rated restaurant for $300 a night. Shop the studio here for batiks or just sit around the big pool on the pool deck, gazing at the Pitons.

ISLANDER, *Rodney Bay, mailing address Box 907, Castries. Tel. 758/452-8757, Fax 492-0958. Rates at this 60-unit resort start at $120; apartments are from $130. It's at the north end of the island; fly into Vigie Airport.*

Choose an apartment with separate sleeping and living areas and a kitchen, or a room with a breakfast bar and refrigerator. King bedrooms have only the refrigerator. Dine on international cuisine in the restaurant, have a sundowner in the beach bar, and swim in the big, freshwater pool. Then take a chair under one of the umbrellas and read in the cool breeze. A shuttle runs to the beach, which is 300 yards away.

LA DAUPHINE, *La Dauphine Estate. Tel. 758/452-2691, Fax 452-5416. Rates for a house with housekeeping are from $155 for two and $275 for up to eight. The estate is four miles from Soufriere.*

High on a green mountainside, you're staying on a 200-acre plantation either in the four-bedroom guesthouse or the remodeled overseer's house. The two-bedroom cottage, built in 1890, is a picture of West Indian quaint, with its wide veranda and fretwork trim. Hike nature trails through the estate, or let the estate manager show you how crops are grown. The housekeeper takes care of the cooking and babysitting. You take care of the provisioning. You'll need a car to get to shopping and the beach.

MARLIN QUAY, *Gros Islet. Tel. 758/452-0393, Fax 452-0383. Rates at this 43-unit inn are from $127. It's at Rodney Bay, just north of Castries and Vigie Airport.*

Another result of the building boom around Rodney Bay is this two-story, Mediterranean-style villa hotel where you can get a double room; a villa with one, two, or three bedrooms; or an apartment with one or two bedrooms. Book one of the apartments that has a private, roof-top sun terrace with a plunge pool and whirlpool overlooking the marina. They're air conditioned and have a full kitchen, ceiling fan, daily maid service, and cable television.

The quay complex includes a 65-foot swimming pool, a playground for children, a restaurant and cocktail bar, and the area's other restaurants are not far away. Children under age 12 can have a roll-away bed or cot for $50 a week.

MARIGOT BEACH CLUB, *Marigot Bay, mailing address Box 101, Castries. Tel. 758/451-4974, Fax 451-4973. Rates start at $95 for a studio apartment. The hotel is 40 minutes from Vigie Airport and an hour from Hewanorra.*

An enchanted bay surrounded by palm trees, is the setting for red-roofed club right on the water. Units are brightly furnished with light, pickled woods, tropical-toned prints, and a fully-equipped kitchen. The hotel has a pool, sundeck, and beach; watersports and sailing are part of the scene. Cocktails and meals are available, and there's a well-stocked commissary for provisioning your apartment or boat.

SANDALS ST. LUCIA, *La Toc Road, Castries. Tel. 758/452-3081, Fax 453-7089, toll-free 800/SANDALS. Rates at this 273-room resort start at $880 per person, double occupancy, for a minimum three-night stay. Included are all meals, drinks, facilities, taxes, tips, and transfers from either airport. The resort* *is 1.5 miles from Castries, two miles from Vigie Airport, and 35 miles from Hewanorra Airport.*

Sandals wrote the book on all-inclusives and now it has almost a dozen of these romantic, couples-only resorts. Choose among ten accommodations ranging from a standard room in the main hotel to an ocean suite with its own, private plunge pool. Dining is in the Pavilion, which serves international dishes at dinner, Kimono's for Japanese food, the Pitons for Creole cuisine, and Restaurant La Toc for white glove service. Play tennis or golf, swim in the pools or off the beach, use the fully-equipped fitness center, and choose from a long menu of activities from karaoke and pool to volleyball land lawn chess. Sandals has two resorts on St. Lucia, with a free shuttle plying the 15-minute ride between them. Guests can dine and play at either.

SANDALS HALCYON, *Box GM 910, Castries. Tel. 758/453-0222, Fax 451-8435, toll-free 800/SANDALS. Rates at this 170-room resort start at $1,800 per week per person, double occupancy. Included are all meals, activities, drinks, entertainment, airport transfers, watersports including lessons, and taxes. The resort is 1-1/2 hours from Hewanorra Airport, five minutes from Vigie, and 15 minutes from the other Sandals.*

Prices are less at this Sandals, which is smaller than the sister resort above and has fewer facilities. Still, many couples prefer the more European ambience here, knowing they can board a free shuttle bus and enjoy all the features of the other Sandals too. Room have private balcony or patio, hair dryer, king-size bed, air conditioning, color television, telephone, coffeemaker, safe, and clock radio. Dining is in Mario's for gourmet continental food, The Pier with its ocean views, or Bayside, offering breakfast and lunch buffets and international cuisine at dinner. Choose among several bars and lounges and enjoy live entertainers nightly. Use any of the watersports equipment, with instruction from a qualified expert if you like. Swim in one of the pools, use the fitness center, or soak in the whirlpools. Play golf at the other Sandals.

CLUB ST. LUCIA, *P.O. Box 915, Castries. Tel. 758/450-0551, Fax 450-0281; U.S. 800/777-1250. Rates at this 372-room resort start at $230 per couple; half that per single, all inclusive. It's about eight miles north of Vigie Airport.*

Minimum rate rooms here aren't air conditioned, so they are a nice savings (about $26 difference daily) for people who prefer a ceiling fan. High-ceiling rooms are pleasant hideaways with rattan furnishings, plaited grass area rugs, private patio, and filmy window coverings to tame the tropic sun. This is a switched-on resort with happenings everywhere all the time, yet silence seekers can always find a secluded hammock or chaise on the beach or grounds.

One child stays free in a standard room; two in a family room with two paying adults. Included in the rates are meals, snacks, drinks including alcohol, all sports and recreation including access to the famous St. Lucia Racquet Club, and nightly entertainment. The only extras are play in the mini-casino and golf at the nine-hole Cap Estate where greens fees are $25 for nine holes and $30 for 18. A week-or two-week pass is available.

A supervised children's program operates daily for ages 4-12, and teens have their own evening activities. The complex has its own shopping area including clothing and a pharmacy. The excursions desk can arrange island tours, baby sitting, dry cleaning or laundry. Dine in the main restaurant,, the pizza parlor, or the beachside barbecue. Guests can also dine at a discount at the acclaimed Great House Restaurant nearby. With a week-long stay, one dinner here is free.

Swim in two big pools, one with a children's area and a volleyball area, explore two beaches on the resort's 50 acres, take a windsurfing lesson, use the health club alone or join an aerobics group, or bike, hike, and even take a lesson in patois!

WYNDHAM MORGAN BAY RESORT, *Choc Bay, Gros Islet. Tel. 758/ 450-2511 or 800/WYNDHAM, Fax 758/450-1050. All-inclusive rates at this 238-room resort start at $420 including meals and some drinks. It is just north of Vigie Airport, Castries.*

Snuggled into 22 sweetly forested acres is this luxury resort where every guest room has a balcony or terrace overlooking sparkling Choc Bay. Your room's cool amber tones and melon colors coordinate with wicker furniture, tile floors, and marble baths. Swim from the private beach or in the supersize pool, play tennis, or work out in the fitness center. The resort has its own restaurant, grill, and lounge and a day-long choice of watersports all included in the rates. Ask about Windham's kids-free program, and packages that include airport transfer, extra adventures, spa treatments or scuba diving.

Moderate

CARRIBBEES HOTEL, *La Pansee, mailing address Box 1720, Castries. Tel. 758/452-4767, Fax 453-1999. An oceanview double costs $115; garden-view rooms are $75. It's ten minutes from Virgie Airport.*

At these prices it's hard to belive you have an ocean view in the hilltop village of La Pansee looking down on Castries and the Caribbean. All rooms have air conditioning, shower, cable television, telephone, and a private patio. Swim in the pool, dine in the restaurant, soak in the hot tub, and enjoy evening entertainment. The hotel has tennis courts and a fitness center.

MOORINGS MARIGOT BAY RESORT, *Marigot Bay, P.O. Box 101, Castries. Tel. 758/452-4357 or Fax 758/452-4357. High season rates start at* *under $200 double for a rustic cottage with its own screened veranda. MAP (breakfast and dinner) is available at $50 per person.*

Marigot Bay is so secluded that the British fleet, masts and all, once hid here from the pursuing French navy. It's a longtime favorite hideaway for yachties who like the relaxed, South Seas feel of a rambling complex that seems, like Topsy, just to have "growed." If you want a swimming pool, opt for the Hurricane Hole section of the resort. In any case you won't be far from a lagoon where you can sail a dinghy, board sail, or move into a chartered yacht for a voyage of a week or more. (Moorings is a worldwide specialist in bareboating and captained or crewed charters.)

The resort has its own restaurants and bar, a good store where you can provision with anything needed for a voyage or cooking meals in your own cottage, a laundry, and babysitting services. PADI-approved scuba services are on the premises. The complex, like many in St. Lucia, is built on a steep hill. If you're not good with stairs, ask for one of the lower units.

RENDEZVOUS, *P.O. Box 190, Malabar Beach, Castries, St. Lucia, West Indies, 758/452-4211, Fax 452-7419; U.S. and Canada 800/544-2883. Doubles at this all-inclusive resort on Malabar Beach start at $380 per couple in high season. Tipping is not permitted. Airport transfers are included from either airport. Vigie, at 20 minutes away, is closest; Hewannorra is one hour and 20 minutes.*

Envision Adam and Eve under blue skies, barefoot on brown sugar sands, and you get the idea. Best of all, you don't have to open your wallet during your entire stay. All meals, wine with lunch and dinner, bar drinks, snacks, live entertainment, exercise classes, and a long list of activities are all paid by one price – even the golf clinic, tennis lessons, waterskiing, sailing, and airport transfers.

No singles, triplets, or children are accommodated at this romantic, couples-only hideaway. Rooms have four-poster beds, marble floors, ceiling fans, and private terraces. If you upgrade to a Sea Side Suite you'll have a sitting room, bedroom, and a marble bath with double sinks.

Have a drink at any of three bars, one of them a piano bar, and dine on the beach or in the air conditioned restaurant. Stroll the grounds hand in hand to marvel at the orchids, hibiscus, erotic anthurium, and brilliant hibiscus, then float around the meandering pool complete with its own palm tree island. Firm up with dancing and exercise, then relax in the whirlpool. A SunSwept resort, this is a sister property of LeSport in St. Lucia and LaSource on Grenada.

TUXEDO VILLAS, *Rodney Bay. Tel. 758/452-8553, Fax 452-8577. Rates start at $135 for a one-bedroom villa. Two-bedroom units are also available. It's just north of Castries and Vigie Airport.*

A two-story inn wraps around a courtyard and swimming pool. Air conditioned accommodations have cable television and telephone. The complex has its own restaurant and bar and it's within walking distance of the beach and other restaurants.

Budget

ALEXANDER'S, *Marie Therese Street, Gros Islet. Tel. 758/450-8610. Rates at this ten-room guest house are $30 double and $45 for two people in an apartment. Baths are shared.*

A typical West Indian house, with a porch over the street, is the perfect place to be for Gros Islet's street parties on Friday nights. It's only 300 feet from a bus stop where you can catch public transportation into Castries or around the island. Walk to Pigeon Island Beach. The restaurant downstairs serves hearty, inexpensive St. Lucian meals.

AUBERGE SERAPHINE, *Vigie Cove, mailing address Box 390, Castries. Tel. 758/453-2073. Doubles at this 22-room hotel start at $70; suites at $95. Vigie Airport and Pointe Seraphine are about ten minutes away.*

Each air conditioned bedroom has paned French doors that open onto a private balcony or patio overlooking the swimming pool and marina. Rooms have cable television and direct-dial telephone. The hotel has a gift shop, restaurant, and a complimentary shuttle to the beach.

BAY GARDENS, *Rodney Bay, mailing address Box 1892 Castries. Tel. 758/452-8060, Fax 452-8059. Rates at this 53-room hotel are from $75. It's 25 minutes north of Vigie Airport.*

This two-story hotel is a limey yellow trimmed with white fencework that sets off your private balcony. It's within easy walking distance of Rodney Bay's restaurants, nightclubs, and shops and to swimming at Reduit Beach. The atrium lobby and tinkling fountain give a rich look to the entry. Air conditioned rooms are done in sunny colors and cool tiles, with accents in straw and ceramics. Rooms have complimentary coffee and tea service, mini-bar, cable television, telephone, radio and a bathroom with tub and shower. Dining is in Spices international restaurant, or Sugars Ice Cream Parlour for forbidden treats. In the lounge and library there's table tennis and board games for guest use. If you don't feel like going to the beach, use the freshwater pool or the heated whirlpool.

BEACH HAVEN, *Vide Boutielle, mailing address Box 460, Castries. Tel. 758/453-0065, Fax 453-6891. Rates at this ten-room inn start at $65. It's ten minutes from Castries and five miles for Vigie Airport.*

Sunbathe on the football field-size sun deck with its lawn-like green carpet and good views of the palm-lined shoreline. Dine in the hotel's restaurant or take a short walk to the beach, shops, and restaurants. Rooms are air conditioned and have a private bath and color television.

CANDYO INN, *Rodney Bay, mailing address Box 386, Castries. Tel. 758/ 452-0712, Fax 452-0774. Rates at this four-room, eight-suite inn are from $75 double and $90 for a suite with full kitchen.*

The location in the heart of Rodney Bay's tourism hotspots is ideal. Air conditioned rooms in this cotton candy-pink inn have a private bath, television with remote control, and dial telephone. Many units have a balcony. For only a few dollars more you can get a suite with seating area and a kitchenette. The inn has a swimming pool and snack bar; you can walk to restaurants, the marina, beaches, and nightclubs.

COUNTRY INN, *Moulin-a-Vent. Tel. 758/452-8301, Fax 452-8301. Rates are from $55. It's 15 minutes from Castries and five minutes from Rodney Bay beaches.*

The owner of this six-room inn knows gardening, The grounds glow with greenery, flowers and a little lily pond. Air conditioned rooms have a private bath, king-or queen-size bed, a private patio, and a dining area.

DUBOIS, *Morne Fortune, mailing address Box 1380, Castries. Tel. and fax 758/452-2201. A double room is $35. The four-room inn is 20 minutes from Vigie Airport.*

Look down over Castries and the Vigie Peninsula from the family home where you'll share a bath and balcony with other guests. Television is available in the common room. Nearby is a local restaurant, but you'll need a car here.

GOLDEN ARROW INN, *John Compton Highway, mailing address Box 2037, Castries. Tel. 758/450-1832, Fax 450-2459. Doubles are $35. The 15-room inn is on the highway two miles north of Vigie Airport.*

Picture a roadside inn in Arizona or rural California, nothing fancy but pittance priced. All rooms have a private bath and most have a ceiling fan and television. Watch the sunset from the common porches; walk to restaurants, shopping and the beach. The hotel has a bar, dining room, and television lounge.

HARBOUR LIGHT INN, *Vide Boutielle. Tel. 758/452-3506. A double room with air conditioning is $60. This 16-room inn is two minutes from Vigie Airport and three minutes from Castries.*

The inn is pretty ordinary but it offers a lot for the price, including a million-dollar view of the sea. Walk to shopping and the beach. Rooms have television and shower and, if you want one without air conditioning, you'll pay even less. There's a choice of twin, double, or queen-size beds. Guests are welcome to use the common kitchen. There's a little restaurant and bar.

SKYWAY INN, *Vieux Fort. Tel. 758/454-7111, Fax 454-7116. Rates at this 40-room inn start at $85; a studio is $100. It's five minutes from Vieux Fort and Hewanorra Airport. Meal plans are available.*

The Vieux Fort area doesn't have as many hotels as the northern end of the island, so this two-story white stucco inn is a find if you want to stay near the airport and handy to the Maria Islands. Rooms here have telephone, television, private bath, ceiling fan, and air conditioning. The inn has a decent-size swimming pool suitable for swimming laps, a roof-top deck with majestic views of the mountains, sky, and arriving aircraft, and a shuttle to take you to town or the beach.

STILL PLANTATION AND BEACH RESORT, *Soufriere. Tel. 758/ 459-7060, Fax 459-7301. Studios are from $50. One-and two-bedroom apartments are from $60. It's two properties, one on the beach and one on the 400-acre plantation inland. They're about 40 minutes from Hewanorra Airport and an hour south of Vigie Airport.*

Fruits and vegetables served in the well-regarded restaurant at the Plantation are grown here on the estate. Two-bedroom apartments have a sitting room and kitchen; one-bedroom units have a kitchen. There's a swimming pool and a boutique that is popular with day-trippers. Most of the beach units, located on the north end of Soufriere Bay, have a full kitchen.

Club Med

The island also has an all-inclusive **CLUB MED** and memberships are available through *Tel. 800/CLUB MED.*

WHERE TO EAT

At lunch, shorts are acceptable at most places but at dinner gentlemen wear long trousers and a shirt with a collar. Beach wear isn't acceptable anywhere but the beach and, in beach restaurants, cover-ups should be worn. Check your bill to see if a service charge has been added. If so, you don't have to tip additionally. Prices on St. Lucia menus are usually quoted in both U.S. and E.C. dollars. These prices are in U.S. currency.

Note that almost every bar and restaurant has Happy Hour, but often at different times or only on certain days. With luck and a little planning, you'll never have to pay full price for cocktails.

Expensive

CAPONE'S, *Reduit Beach just north of the beach, Rodney Bay. Tel. 452-0284. Hours are daily except Monday 6:30 to 10:30pm Reservations are essential. Main dishes are priced $12 to $24. Pizza and pita sandwiches are served out front 11am to 1pm.*

Think speakeasy. Think the 1920s when Al Capone and his cronies spent winters in the chic, art deco hotels of Miami's South Beach. The gangster theme is played out here in the glitzy pink-and-black decor and in the names of dishes and drinks served by bartenders in 1920s hoodlum suits and shoulder holsters. If you order the Prohibition Punch, you get to keep the mug. The check is served in a violin case, and you'll pay up or else. The pizza, they promise unsmilingly, is "to die for." Start with a Little

Caesar salad, then charcoal-grilled steak or fresh fish or one of the pastas. Boneless chicken breast is stuffed with ham and cheese, then grilled over the coals. Dinner is serenaded by oldies played on the piano. Have a robust red wine with your meal and a bracing espresso after.

CHARTHOUSE, *Reduit Beach, Rodney Bay. Tel. 452-8115. Main dishes are priced $12 to $32. Hours are Monday through Saturday 6 to 10:30pm except September, when it is closed.*

One of the oldest and best liked tourist restaurants in the Rodney Bay area, the Charthouse stakes its reputation on its tender meats, most notably charcoal-grilled steaks, roast prime rib, and barbecued baby back ribs. There's also fish and lobster fresh from the fleet, which docks here every afternoon to bring the bounty into the kitchen. When you can get them in season, freshwater crayfish burst with juicy goodness. The restaurant overlooks the water and is open to the breezes and harbor sounds. Usually Nick himself is here to greet you. Ask him about his rum collection, then order from a list of more than 100 brands.

DASHEENE, *in the Ladera Resort, Soufriere. Tel. 459-7323. Reservations are essential. The restaurant is open nightly for dinner. Plan to spend $40 to $60.*

Guests at this swank resort are paying more than $300 a night, so you know you're among people who demand the best. The view is a spectacle, so arrive in time to enjoy the sunset. Dine in a romantic South Seas setting on such specialties as a spicy cold seafood soup, chicken breast piled with pecans, or grilled fresh fish with an interesting sauce made from an island ingredient such as coconut cream or tomatoes, peppers, and herbs. Smoked fish is a specialty, usually served in an appetizer crepe or spread. Plan ahead by ordering the creme brulée when you order your main course. It will be baked and sugar-sizzled by the time you're ready for dessert and coffee.

GREEN PARROT, *Red Tape Lane on the Morne, mailing address Box 648, Castries. Tel. 758/452-3399, 15 minutes from Castries. Plan to spend $35 to $45 for dinner. Hours are daily noon to 3pm and 7pm to midnight. Reservations are required.*

Everyone including locals comes here for the view from a terrace that seems suspended in space high above Castries. The hotel is dressy, requiring jackets on most nights, so ask about the dress code when you make reservations. On Monday, ladies who wear a flower in their hair and are accompanied by a gentleman in jacket and tie get a free dinner. Dine on West Indian foods including plenty of fresh fish and lobster and a choice of five curries while you're entertained by Princess Tina the belly dancer, local music and dance, or a limbo show. At lunch, order the omelet of the day or a sandwich with one of the soups such as pumpkin or callaloo. After dinner, order a Green Parrot from the bar. It's made with creme de mint, rum, cream of coconut and banana.

THE LIME, *Rodney Bay. Tel. 452-0761. It's open daily except Tuesday 11am to 2pm and 6:30-11pm. The staff vacations for three weeks between the middle of June and mid-July. Reservations are recommended. Main dishes are priced $12 to $26.*

Start with one of the lime drink specials (limin' is West Indian for hanging out and taking it easy) then stuffed crab, shrimp, roti, or charcoal-grilled fresh fish, lamb chops, or steak. At lunch, the rotis or chicken 'n chips are a heap of food for the price. The open-air restaurant sits among a jungle of plants that complement the lime green decor. Late Lime's, the nightclub next door, hums until the wee hours.

RESTAURANT LA TOC, *in Sandals, La Toc Road, Castries. Tel. 452-3081. Plan to spend $60 for dinner. Call for reservations, which are essential. The restaurant is open nightly 6:30-10:30pm.*

This utterly elegant French restaurant is part of a switched-on, all-inclusive resort where dishes are flamed, waiters wear white gloves, and desserts will spoil you forever. The setting, in a posh resort once operated by Cunard, is in a Bermuda pink villa surrounded by lavish pools and lush lawns and trees. Even though the restaurant is in the open air, smoking is not permitted. If you like the experience, explore the possibility or trying the resort's four other restaurants serving Southwest, Japanese, international and Creole cuisine.

SAN ANTOINE, *Old Morne Road, south of Castries. Tel. 452-4660. It's open for dinner daily except Sunday (December through March, dinner is served on Sunday). Plan to spend $50-$60. If you are a party of four or more, ask about free pick-up at your hotel.*

Choose from the menu or have the festive, five-course, fixed-priced dinner. The site was once a hotel built at the turn of the century and restored in the 1970s after a fire. Only the great stone walls, with their magnificent arches, remained. It still carries out the look of a stately, Victorian-area, West Indian greathouse. Dine in elegant surroundings overlooking the lights of Castries far below. The cuisine is unfailingly good, especially the fresh seafood surrounded by fresh local vegetables. Start with pumpkin soup, then have grilled mahi-mahi or snapper, roast rack of lamb, a steak, lobster, or chicken.

TROU AU DIABLE *and* **PITON,** *in the Anse Chastenet resort near Soufriere. Tel. 459-7000. Plan to spend $35 to $40 for dinner. The restaurants, one on the beach and the other hillside, are open daily, Piton for breakfast 7:30am to 10am and dinner 7-9:30pm and Trou au Diable for lunch and snacks 11:30am to 3 and 3:30 to 5:30pm, and for 7pm beach dining Tuesday and Friday. Reservations are essential.*

Chef Jacky Rioux from the Loire Valley was head chef at The Swan in Norfolk, once voted Britain's best restaurant, and his travels as chef aboard the *Sea Goddess* gave him a look at foods from the Mediterranean and Alaska to the Pacific Rim. Now he brings his skill to this prestigious beach resort where he uses imported foods as well as local seafood and vegetables and herbs grown nearby. Once a week there's a Creole buffet on the beach; another night there's a barbecue, so call ahead for information. At lunch on the beach, have a roti or a salad surrounded by the diving and yachting crowd, who are usually discussing the day's run.

The meaty pepperpot is a soupy-stew filled with vegetables and spices, a good choice if you plan a nap after lunch. When dining isn't beachfront under the palms and seagrapes, it's in a treehouse on a steep hill overlooking the beach and sea in the shadow of the Pitons. Start with the chilled red sweet pepper soup followed by honey-glazed duck breast in red wine jus, or king prawns in a sweet ginger vinaigrette. Jacky bakes local christophene in a gratin with black-eye peas and curry cream. For dessert, try his coconut gateau in rum sauce.

WINDJAMMER LANDING, *just south of Rodney Bay on Labrelotte Bay. Tel. 452-1311. Plan to spend $35 to $40 for dinner. Restaurants here are open for breakfast, lunch, and dinner.*

Find your way here on Sunday for the Jazz Brunch or on Thursday night for a Caribbean buffet, fire dancing, limbo, and rousing reggae.

Moderate

"A" PUB, *Rodney Bay. Tel. 452-8725. It's open daily for lunch and dinner. Plan to spend $25 to $35 for dinner. It's open every day 11am to midnight.*

One of the many good eateries in this touristy part of the island, this waterside pub attracts more visitors from sea than from the land. It's a project of Chris and Jenny, whose popular A-Frame marina and restaurant is now under new management across the lagoon and is called Georgio's. (Try it for great Italian food). Join in the salty pub atmosphere for sandwiches and burgers at lunch or steak or fresh fish for dinner. On Wednesday and Saturday, there's karaoke. Play darts or backgammon and make a night of it. It's within walking distance of hundreds of Rodney Bay hotel rooms.

CAMILLA'S, *7 Bridge Street, Soufrière. Tel. 459-5379. Hours are 8am to 10pm daily. Main dishes are priced $10 to $30. Reservations are suggested.*

Sit on the balcony (no air conditioning indoors) overlooking the teeming streets just a block back from the busy Soufriere waterfront. Start with a drink from a drink menu as long as your arm. Have a sandwich, hamburger, lobster salad or omelet for lunch or dine on fresh fish and French fries, lobster thermidor, crab, shrimp or the zesty chicken curry.

CHESTERFIELD INN, *at the lower end of Bridge Street, Castries. Tel. 452-1295. Plan to spend $20 for dinner. Call for hours and reservations.*

Traditional St. Lucian meals are served in a hospitable room furnished with antiques. Start with the fruity rum punch, then grilled fish or chicken, a native soup, or a curry. The Inn also has rooms and apartments for rent, making it an ideal choice for anyone who needs to stay in the city. The inn overlooks the city and harbor.

EUDOVIC'S, *Goodlands, Morne Fortune. Tel. 452-2747. Call for hours. Plan to spend $25 for dinner.*

Dine on St. Lucian fare among wood carvings done by master craftsman Vincent Joseph Eudovic, whose works are carved from rare woods and local tree roots. Have pumpkin or callaloo soup, one of the curries, fresh seafood, or goat stew.

FOX GROVE INN, *Mon Repos, Bicoud. Tel. and fax 454-0271. The inn is 20 minutes from Hewannora Airport. Plan to spend $20-$25 for dinner without wine. Reservations are required. The restaurant is open daily for breakfast, lunch, and dinner.*

Combine Swiss hospitality with fresh St. Lucia seafood, fruits, and vegetables and the combination can't miss. Arrive well before dinner for a horseback ride or nature walk, then have a drink overlooking Praslin Bay and Fregate Island Nature Reserve before dining on a Creole or continental meal. The inn also has ten bedrooms to rent at $55-$65 including a full breakfast.

HUMMINGBIRD *in the Hummingbird Beach Resort, on the beach north of the Soufriere River. Tel. 459-7232 or 454-7232. Call for hours and reservations. Plan to spend $25 to $30.*

Operated by Joyce, whose batik studio is also here, this open air restaurant looks out through a fringe of coconut palms over a harbor filled with sailboats and to the Pitons beyond. One wall is made entirely of the coal pots that are the mainstay of St. Lucian cottage cooking. The food is faithfully St. Lucian, always featuring one or two fresh fish dishes, island vegetables, salads, and chicken or chops.

HURRICANE HOLE, *in The Moorings, Marigot Bay. Tel. 451-4357. Main dishes are priced $8 to $15. It's open daily for breakfast, lunch, and dinner.*

Most guests in this resort are about to leave on a Moorings charter boat or have just returned, so there's a pleasant buzz about anchorages, beam reaches, and the sail down from Martinique or up from St. Vincent. Start with a sweet and deadly Hurricane rum punch to adjust your attitude, then have grilled fish with peas and rice, one of the curries, stuffed crab or the thick, crabby callaloo.

JIMMIE'S, *at the marina, Vigie Cove. Tel. 452-5142. Reservations aren't accepted. It's open daily for lunch and dinner. Main dishes are priced $14 to $28. Lunch dishes are $6 to $8. Jimmie's closes the last two weeks in July.*

Mingle with the boating crowd in this breezy, outdoor restaurant overlooking a seascape of sailboats and shining sea. Seafood is the star here, served in many forms plain and fancy. Try the seafood risotto, grilled snapper, conch, and St. Lucian calamari. In the Harbor Catch seafood platter you'll get a taste of everything the fishing boats brought in today. For dessert it's banana cake, banana ice cream, banana fritters, or banana split.

MORTAR & PESTLE, *in the Harmony Marina Suites Resort, Rodney Bay on the lagoon. Tel. 452-8756. Main dishes are priced $18 to $32. Reservations are essential for dinner. It's open daily 7am to 3pm and 7-10:30pm.*

Overlook the marina while you dine on stuffed land crab, New England-style conch chowder, salt cod, callaloo, or pork souse. It's fun to read the menu and discuss it with your server, who is proud of the Caribbean variety represented here. Here's your chance to try national dishes from many islands, from Jamaican jerk to Guyanan pepperpot.

STILL PLANTATION, *near Soufriere. Tel. 459-7224. Main dishes are priced $12 to $30. Reservations are suggested. It's open every day 8am to 11pm.*

Part of a working plantation, this is a popular stop on bus tours and gets crowded when cruise ships are in. The restaurant is set among what's left of an old still. Dine outdoors on slabs of giant trees or indoors. Most of the fruits and vegetables come from this family-run plantation, where the cash crops are cocoa and citrus fruit and the kitchen gardens yield pumpkin, avocado, breadfruit, yams, yucca, and much more.

Budget

CHACK CHACK, *Vieux Fort. Tel. 454-6260. Eat for $10 to $12.*

This simple cafe known for its pumpkin soup and fresh seafood is handy to the airport. It's named for a tree that produces large pods that, when dry, rattle hollowly to make a sound like chack-chack.

GINGER LILY, *Rodney Bay. Tel. 452-8303. Plan to spend $15 for dinner. It's open daily except Monday 11:30am to 2:30pm and 6:30-11:30pm. Happy Hour is Friday 6-7pm.*

Dine on the tropical terrace or call ahead for take-out. Ask about daily specials. The stir-fries and steamed rice are hard to beat. Cooking is mainly Cantonese style, but the chef can also crank up the spices if you like more heat. Order from a long list of chicken, beef, pork, seafood, and vegetarian dishes.

KEY LARGO, *Rodney Bay Marina, tel. 452-0282. Plan to spend $10-$12 for dinner. At Happy Hour, served nightly 6-7pm, you can drink at special prices.*

Check the signs as you come in for news of daily specials. Tables are set around a wood-fired brick pizza oven where Carlo from Rome turns out pizzas with your choice of ten million toppings including a sumptuous shrimp and artichoke combination.

MISS SAIGON, *Rodney Bay. Tel. 451-7309. Call for hours. Main dishes are priced $12 to $25.*

More than just a good Chinese restaurant, this one also serves Thai, Malay, Indonesian, and Indian food. Discuss with your server what's hot, what's not, and what can be toned down for those with less-than-asbestos taste buds.

SEEING THE SIGHTS

Castries is a squalid downtown that has little to show the visitor except for the deliciously primitive, century-old **marketplace** on Jeremy Street. Come here to shop for spices, hand-woven whisk brooms, and pottery charcoal pots that are used in most households for cooking. If you're doing your own cooking, this is also the place to stock up on fresh fruits and vegetables.

A cathedral stands on Derek Wolcott Square (formerly Columbus Square), but the town had a couple of fires that destroyed most of the colonial-era buildings. Rebuilding was done in a hodgepodge of whatever styles were quick and affordable at the time. Beyond Government House, which dates to the turn of the century, rises **Morne Fortune**, which has a grand view and some old military installations to poke through.

Pigeon Island National Landmark was just emerging from the jungle when we first saw it, an island that once held a mighty miliary complex filled with falling-down barracks, stone walls, mess halls, officer quarters, and much more. On the beach, a caretaker lived in a 1950s-style home and, the story went, sometimes served cold drinks to passing mariners. Then a causeway was built to the island, which can now be reached without a boat. A museum was opened, the ruins stabilized, and the show was ready for prime time. At the park's Interpretation Centre, watch the stirring multi-media presentation on St. Lucia history, then spend the afternoon roaming the grounds to picnic, watch the nature show, or eat in the Captain's Cellar Olde English Pub. It's administered by the St. Lucia National Trust, *Tel. 452-5005* and is open daily 9am to 5pm Admission is EC$10.

St. Lucia National Rain Forest covers 19,000 acres with exotic ferns, wild orchids, and towering hardwoods filled with bird life. To get a guide and information, contact the National Trust as listed above. Highest point in the jungle is **Mount Gimie** (pronounced Jimmy), which rises to 3,145 feet. There's a seven-mile nature walk, or get a guide and do some serious hiking.

Driving around the island you might stop at the fishing village of **Soufrière**, the island's second city, and at the "**drive-in**" volcano. Local guides are usually on hand to show you around for a fee. At the volcano's **Sulphur Springs**, steam shoots 50 feet high from bubbling mud. Don't miss the **Diamond Falls and Mineral Baths**, which were built under one of the French occupations in the late 1700s. For a small fee you can take a dip in waters warm as soup. The waterfall changes color, shading from yellow to blue to purple, because of its sulphur content.

Through the National Trust you can also arrange visits to **Maria Islands Nature Reserve** off the south coast. It's home to a couple of species found nowhere else. One of them is the Maria Island Ground Lizard. Off the southeast coast, the **Fregate Islands** are the home of colonies of the majestic frigate bird. Natural sights are closed to visitors during nesting seasons, usually mid-May through July, so contact the National Trust above about permissions, a licensed guide, and dates.

Marigot Bay, eight miles south of Castries, is a natural movie set, actually used in a couple of movies, including *Dr. Doolittle* starring Rex Harrison, but its better claim to fame is its role in battle. Because its entrance can't be seen by ships passing at sea, Admiral Rodney hid his fleet in here and camouflaged the masts by lashing palm fronds to them. The French fleet sailed right on by, thinking that the English had outrun them. It's now the home of **The Moorings** (see *Where to Stay*), boat rentals, restaurants, a beach, and good board sailing. There are changing rooms, so bring your swimsuit.

NIGHTLIFE & ENTERTAINMENT

If you're staying at a resort of any size, it's likely that live music plays at least some nights for dancing and listening. In the Rodney Bay area the hotspot is **INDIES**, *Tel. 452-0727*, a dance club with bars, DJs, stages, bands, and action. The cover charge is EC$20. Other good bets also listed above, under *Where to Eat*, include **CAPONE'S**, *Tel. 452-0284*, **GREEN PARROT**, *Tel. 452-3167*, and **THE LATE NIGHT LIME CLUB** at The Lime, *Tel. 452-0761*. The cover charge here is EC$20.

Every Friday night, the entire village of **Gros Islet** (pronounced "grossly") takes to the streets, cranks up the volume and holds a Jump Up until the wee hours. Vendors sell grilled chicken, beer, and rum drinks. The music is free. You might also watch local posters and tip sheets to see if anything is going on at **Pigeon Island**. It's the scene of most of St. Lucia's big festivals, including a big-name jazz festival in May, a comedy festival in April, and the Christmas Folk Fiesta in December.

SPORTS & RECREATION

Bird Watching

Because so much of the best birdwatching is in protected lands that can't be visited without a licensed guide, it's best to connect through the National Trust or through the **Caribbean National Resources Institute**, *Tel. 454-6060*.

Camping

Anse La Liberté Campground is found at Canaries. For information contact **St. Lucia Tourism**, *Tel. 800/456-3984* or *212/867-2950, Fax 212/*

867-2795. Information is also available from the **National Trust**, *Tel. 452-5005.* The campground has tent huts, cottages, trails, bare campsites, and a cooking center.

During **turtle nesting season**, mid-March through July, watchers are permitted to camp on the beach 4pm to 6:30am. Tents are provided. The cost is EC$15 per person; reservations are essential, *Tel. 452-8100 or 452-9951.*

Diving

Anse Chastenet Reef on the southwest shore of the island is one of the Caribbean's grand dives, and is also shallow enough in most areas for snorkelers. Other grand dive sites include the four seamounts called the **Key Hole Pinnacles**, a drift dive that drops to 1,600 feet called **Superman's Flight** and the **Coral Gardens** at the base of Gros Piton. On the point of Anse Chastenet, a plateau known as **Fairy Land** is filled with coral and sponges. Midway up the west coast, dive the wall off Anse La Raye. It's strewn with huge boulders that create a wonderland of underwater architecture.

Wreck dives off the island include the *Waiwinette*, a freighter in 990 feet of water off southern St. Lucia. It's recommended for expert divers who can deal with the street currents. Near Castries, the wreck of the *Volga* lies in only 20 feet so it's ideal for snorkeling and diving. The *Leslee M* lies upright in 60 feet of water near Anse Cochon on the west coast. It was purposely sunk to become an artificial reef. It's an eerie world of decks and hatches.

Dive operators include:
• **Scuba St. Lucia**, *Tel. 800/223-1108*
• **Buddies Scuba**, *Tel. 758/452-5288*
• **Dolphin Divers**, *Tel. 758/451-1476*

Most of the hotels offer dive packages including dives, instruction, certification, refills, and gear.

Fitness

If your hotel doesn't have a health club, call **Gonard "La Borde's" Gym** on Hospital Road, *Tel. 452-2788.* It has the most modern Weider equipment. **Caribbean Fitness Expression**, *Tel. 451-6853* offers toning, jazzercize and aerobics. Bodybuilders Rick Wayne and Mae Sabbagh operate **Body Inc.**, *Tel. 451-9744.*

Golf

Temporary memberships are available in the **Cap Estate Golf Club**, *Tel. 450-8523.* The nine-hole course can be played as 18 holes. The clubhouse has a bar and pro shop, and the course is known for its fabulous views.

Hiking

Through the St. Lucia National Trust, hire a licensed guide for visits to the **Union Nature Trail**, **Morne Le Blanc-Laborie** with its panoramic view of the southern plain of St. Lucia, **Fregate Island** for rare birds and boa constrictors, the **rain forest**, and **Hardy Point Cactus Valley**.

Horseback Riding

International Riding Stables in Gros Islet, *Tel. 452-8139,* offers rides for all levels including a tour and picnic, with time out for swimming at Cas en Bas. **Trims Riding School** is at Cas en Bas, *Tel. 452-8273.*

Squash

The **St. Lucia Racquet Club** at Club St. Lucia, *Tel. 450-0551,* has a square court and squash instruction,.

Tennis

Most major hotels have tennis courts but, if yours doesn't, the courts at the St. Lucian Hotel are available to the public for a fee, *Tel. 452-8351.* The **St. Lucia Racquet Club**, *Tel. 450-5441,* has nine floodlit courts.

SHOPPING

Pointe Seraphine was built especially for cruise ship passengers, a modern shopping center offering air conditioning shops and places to rest, people-watch, and snack. The center has arts and crafts galleries and such chain "duty-free" shops as Benneton, Columbian Emeralds, and Little Switzerland. Hours vary depending on ship dockings and the season, but the complex is generally open Monday through Saturday 8am to 5pm and Sunday until 2pm. To purchase goods here you must show your airline ticket or ship boarding pass. You can take away most of your purchases if you like, but liquor and cigarette purchases must be delivered to the ship or airport.

The other big shopping center on the island is **Gableswood Mall** north of Castries on the road to Gros Islet. Here you'll find shops and dining, somewhat like your mall at home. The island's own artists include **Alice Bagshaw** whose shop at La Toc features brilliant batiks and beachwear, *Tel. 452-2139.* Her works also are sold at Pointe Seraphine, Hewannora, Marigot Bay, and Rodney Bay. Regular St. Lucia visitors never leave without adding a Bagshaw to their wardrobes.

Masterful batik is also available from **Caribelle Batik** in Howelton House, Old Victoria Road, The Morne, *Tel. 452-3785.* Island clothing, some hand painted and other pieces mass-produced is sold at **Sea Island Cotton Shops**, which are found around the island.

Local master artist and carver **Vincent Joseph Eudovic** has a restaurant and studio at Goodlands, Morne Fortune, *Tel. 452-2747.*

EXCURSIONS & DAY TRIPS

Caribbean Horizons Tours & Services, *Tel. 444-1555, 3499 or 3945*, offers car rentals and a variety of tours by land or sea. Three plantations are open for yours. **Errard Plantation** near Dennery grows fruit and cocoa beans, and you'll be shown the crops and the traditional "dance" used to polish the beans. The tour ends with lunch, *Tel. 453-1260.* At **La Sikwe** you'll see a historic sugar mill with a 40-foot water wheel. Tours must be arranged through your hotel or through a tour operator.

At **Marquis Estate** on the northeast coast, *Tel. 452-3762*, you'll see how copra, bananas, coffee, and cocoa are grown. The tour includes a boat ride on the Marquis River and lunch, Reservations are essential. At **Morne Coubaril Estate**, *Tel. 459-7340*, you'll walk the original "street" used by mule carriages, visit a workers' village, see a sugar mill, and learn how manioc is grown.

PRACTICAL INFORMATION

Area Code: 758

Banks: open Monday through Thursday from 8am to 1pm; Friday 8am to noon and 3pm to 5pm. Bank holidays include New Year's Day, Easter Monday, National Day on December 13, Christmas Day, Boxing Day (December 26).

Camping: St. Lucia opened its first campground in 1997. For information, *Tel. 888/4-ST.LUCIA or 212/867-2950, Fax 867-2795.*

Currency: is the Eastern Caribbean Dollar, expressed on price tags as EC$. For $1 you can get about EC$2.70. Price tags in tourist shops, hotels and restaurants are usually in U.S. dollars, which are accepted almost everywhere. When negotiating, always know whether you're talking EC or U.S. because tradespeople aren't likely to point out your mistake when you fork over $10 for an EC$10 item.

Customs & Immigration: The more hip you look and act, the more likely that your luggage will be examined carefully for drugs. U.S. and Canadian citizens need a return ticket plus proof of citizenship such as a passport or a voter registration card plus photo identification. A driver's license alone won't do.

Electricity: St. Lucia uses 50-cycle, 220/230-volt power. If you have North American appliances, bring an adapter.

Government: St. Lucia is independent. U.S. consular representation is through Bridgetown, Barbados, *Tel. 246/436-4950.*

Hazards: the poisonous fer-de-lance is found along St. Lucia coasts. Schistosomes, parasites that can enter through body openings including wounds, inhabit the rivers. Don't drink river water, which can contain giardia.

Post Office: the General Post office where General Delivery is sent unless other instructions are given is on Bridge Street in Castries. It is open week days, 8:30am to 4:30pm.

Security: keep your valuables locked up and don't flash a bankroll. Lock your car or boat before leaving it for even a brief period, and don't leave valuables in plain sight.

Taxes: eight percent on hotels and $8 on departure, or $4 if you're leaving St. Lucia for another Caribbean island.

Time Zone: St. Lucia is on Atlantic Standard Time, one hour ahead of Eastern Standard Time. When the east is on Daylight Savings Time, St. Lucia's time is the same.

Tipping: at most hotels a service charge of 10-12% is automatically added to your bill.

Tourist information: write the St. Lucia Tourist Board, *820 Second Avenue, 9th Floor, New York NY 10017, Tel. 212/867-2950; Fax 370-7867, toll-free 800/456-3984.*

Weddings: can be arranged in seven working days. Couples must reside on St. Lucia for two working days before application for marriage is made. Then up to five days are needed for processing. Weddings are performed by the Registrar Monday through Friday; religious ceremonies can also be arranged.

26. THE CAYMAN ISLANDS

A royal land grant brought settlers to this low-lying, windswept Nowhere in 1734 and today it's an affluent Somewhere that can offer a Caribbean vacation different from any other. Geography sets the **Caymans** apart. They're tucked under Cuba and west of Jamaica, the tiniest of knots on the tapestry of Caribbean islands.

They were discovered by accident only because Christopher Columbus was blown off course in 1503 on his way from Panama to Hispaniola. He called them Las Tortugas for the sea turtles that are still an important part of island life. Their remoteness kept the Caymans from being a target for early plunderers. Settlers drifted in from England, Scotland, and Wales but, until radio communication opened the islands to the outside world in the 1930s, time stood still. The first airport wasn't built until 1953.

The name derives from *caymanas*, or crocodiles, that early explorers described in their journals. Nobody believed that these long-extinct crocs existed until 1993, when fossilized evidence was found on Grand Cayman. Subsequent findings were made on Cayman Brac in 1996.

The islands belonged to Jamaica until the English civil wars, when Jamaica was captured by Oliver Cromwell's forces and Britain hung onto the Caymans. The first settlers are thought to be escaped slaves and deserters from Cromwell's army. Britons drifted in, and in 1677, a fleet of French and their 500 slaves, fleeing from the Dutch, settled here. With the royal land grant in 1734, settlement began in earnest and, by 1776 when the American Revolution broke out, the islands became a battleground for American privateers and international pirates. Still uninhabited, **Cayman Brac** and **Little Cayman** provided just the haven they needed. Peace finally came in 1782 but tales of buried treasures, looted from nearby Jamaica and Cuba, linger on.

Tourism has grown hand in hand with financial services. An offshore haven and the world's fifth largest financial center, the islands have one of the highest standards of living in the world. The average household

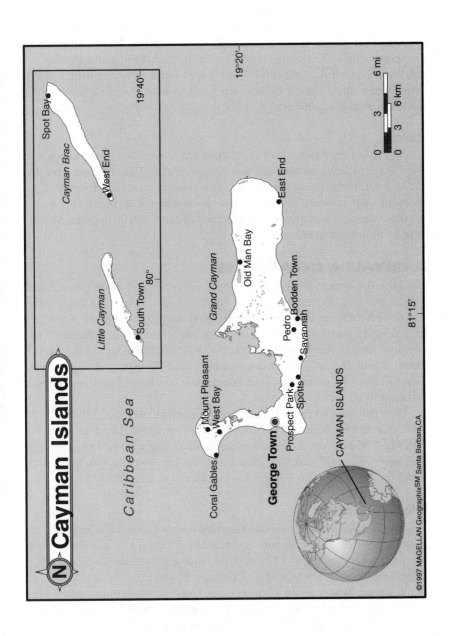

Cayman Islands

N

Caribbean Sea

Spot Bay
Cayman Brac
West End
19°40'

Little Cayman
South Town
80°

Coral Gables
Mount Pleasant
West Bay
Prospect Park
George Town
Spotts
Savannah
Pedro
Bodden Town
Old Man Bay
Grand Cayman
East End
19°20'

81°15'

CAYMAN ISLANDS

0   3   6 km
0   3   6 mi

©1997 MAGELLAN GeographixSM Santa Barbara,CA

income in 1997 was $68,000. Here you won't see homeless street children or encounter wheedling vendors on the beach. The average Caymanian is wealthier than the average visitor.

Bring your brokerage and bank accounts if you like, but this book assumes that you're coming primarily for a vacation. Here's where the Caymans shine. The diving is spectacular, the beaches blindingly beautiful, the accommodations and dining pricey but classy. The little islands now attract more than a million visitors a year, accounting for half its domestic national product.

Climate

Lying between latitudes 19 and 20 north and cooled by ocean winds, the Caymans have an average low temperature of 64 degrees and an average high of 86 degrees all year. The rainy season lasts from May to October, when there is always the possibility of a hurricane alert. Summers are hot and muggy, with highs that can reach 90 degrees. March and April are the driest months.

ARRIVALS & DEPARTURES

Grand Cayman is a flight of about an hour and 20 minutes from Miami and a little more than that from Tampa. More than 60 weekly flights serve **Owen Roberts International Airport** on Grand Cayman, including 49 nonstops from Miami and two weekly from Orlando. The national carrier, **Cayman Airways**, *Tel. 800/422-9626*, serves the island from Miami, Tampa, Orlando, Atlantic, and Houston. It also serves Cayman Brac. Its commuter line, **Island Air**, flies into Little Cayman and Cayman Brac.

You can also get to the Caymans on **American Airlines**, *Tel. 800/433-7300;* **Northwest Airlines**, *Tel. 800/447-4747;* and **U.S. Airways**, *Tel. 800/428-4322.* Watch your local newspaper's travel pages for news of charters from the U.S. and Canada. The Caymans can also be reached from Kingston and Montego Bay on **Air Jamaica**, *Tel. 800/523-5585.*

ORIENTATION

Shaped like a large L, **Grand Cayman** is about nine miles long and 12 miles at its widest. The airport is at the crook of the L, centrally located for points east and west. "Hotel Row" is along the famous Seven Mile Beach on the west shore north of George Town.

Cayman Brac is about 12 miles long, and little more than a mile wide. Its airport is at the far west end. **Little Cayman** is about 11 miles long and a mile wide, with an air strip on the southeast end.

GETTING AROUND THE CAYMANS

Taxis meet every flight and the fare from the airport to most hotels along West Bay Road (the Seven Mile Beach area) is $14 to $20.

Kemwel rental cars are available at the airport on Grand Cayman at high season rates of $259 for a two-door Suzuki to $324 for a Suzuki Jeep, both plus $12 daily Collision Damage Waiver. To reserve from the U.S., *Tel. 800/678-0678;* locally, *Tel. 949-4037.* Cars can also be delivered to resorts or homes.

Other chain rentals on Grand Cayman include:
- **Ace Hertz**, *Tel. 800/654-3131 or locally Tel. 949-2280*
- **Avis Cico**, *Tel. 800/228-0668 or 949-2468*
- **Budget Rent-a-Car**, *Tel. 800/527-0700 or 949-5605*
- **Thrifty Car Rental.**, *Tel. 800/367-2277*
- **Dollar Rent-a-Car**, *Tel. 345/949-4790*

On Cayman Brac, cars are available from:
- **Brac Hertz Rent-a-Car**, *Tel. 345/948-1515.* Reservations are required.
- **Four D's Car Rental**, *Tel. 345/948-1599*
- **T&D's Avis Auto Rentals, Ltd.**, *Tel. 345/948-2847.*

On Little Cayman, **McLaughlin Rentals**, *Tel. 345/948-1000*, has cars by the day, week, or month.

If you don't want to rent a car just yet but need provisions on the way to your condo, have **McCurley's Tours**, *Tel. 345/947-9626*, meet you at the airport. They'll make a grocery stop on your way to your lodgings.

Throughout the Caymans, driving is on the left, which can be a safety problem both for drivers and for pedestrians, who sometimes forget to look both ways. Note that **George Town** has a lot of one-way streets, indicated by international road signs. Yellow lines on roads mean "no parking." If you're behind a bus and it stops, stop behind it. Passenger doors open onto the road side.

WHERE TO STAY

Rates are quoted in U.S. dollars for a double room in high season. Summer rates are usually about 40 percent less. Add government room tax of 10 percent and most hotels add a service charge of 10-15 percent in lieu of tipping. Your mailing address while in the islands is Hotel, Box Number, Grand Cayman (or Little Cayman or Cayman Brac), British West Indies.

The famous **Seven Mile Beach** is Grand Cayman's hotel "strip," a solid line of hotels and condominiums that runs from just north of

Georgetown to the northwest point of the island. Major credit cards are accepted at all the lodgings listed here.

GRAND CAYMAN

Expensive

THE ANCHORAGE, *Seven Mile Beach, mailing address Box 30986. Tel. 345/945-4088, Fax 945-5001. Rates at this 15-villa condominium are from $265 for a two-bedroom apartment with full kitchen. It's five miles from George Town and a $10 cab ride from the airport.*

Settle into a spacious suite with big sliding doors opening onto the balcony overlooking the sea. Rooms are done in pastels and rattan with a cool, tropical appeal. Swim in the beach or pool. Accommodations have television, VCR, daily maid service, telephone, air conditioning and ceiling fans but the complex doesn't have a restaurant or bar. Cook in, use the community barbecue, or choose any of the many restaurants along West Bay Road.

CARIBBEAN CLUB, *Seven Mile Beach, mailing address Box 30499, Grand Cayman. Tel. 345/945-4099, Fax 945-4443. Children under age 11 aren't accepted in winter. Rates at this 18-room club start at $275 for a one-bedroom villa. Two-bedroom villas are also available. It's three miles from George Town and a $14 taxi ride from the airport.*

This villa resort is more homey than tony. It's made up of individually-owned villas that are decorated differently according to each owner's own whim. The club is on the beach and has no swimming pool but it does have tennis courts, a restaurant, room service except for breakfast, telephones, and television. All villas are air conditioned and have a fully-equipped kitchen. It's a home away from home, very popular with regulars who book year after year.

CLARION GRAND PAVILION, *mailing address Box 30117, Grand Cayman. Tel. 345/945-5656, Fax 945-5353, toll-free U.S. and Canada, 800/ HERITAGE. Rates at this 88-unit resort start at $350 for a double room. Two- and three-bedroom suites are also available. It's on Seven Mile Beach, 2.5 miles from the airport and a $14 taxi ride from the airport.*

When Queen Elizabeth II made her first visit to the Caymans, this is where she chose to stay. A luxurious hotel that looks like a grand plantation house, it has a the lobby of a mansion, all teak and leather with marble floors and a crystal chandelier. The grand theme plays out in the courtyard with its greenery and fountains. The hotel is across the street from famous Seven Mile Beach, a small inconvenience that is more than compensated by the caring, personal service.

Rooms are done in fruity pastels and have a coffee maker, mini-bar, bathrobes, a big selection of toiletries, and a trouser hanger/press. Work out in the fitness center then relax in the sauna or hot tub. Play golf nearby, get a boat from the hotel's watersports center, then have a cold drink at the pool bar. The hotel has its own restaurant and lounge. After dinner, find that your room has been freshened and the bed turned down.

HOLIDAY INN, *Seven Mile Beach, mailing address Box 904. Tel. 345/ 945-4444, Fax 945-4213, U.S. and Canada 800/421-9999. Rates at this 213-room hotel start at $228. It's three miles from George Town and a $15 taxi ride from the airport.*

One of the first hotels on Seven Mile Beach and still one of the most popular is this full-blown resort. Most rooms have two double beds and children sleep free, so it's a popular choice for families and group tours. It's the home of Coconuts Comedy Club and the Ten Sails Pub, where you can get a beer with good, English pub grub. Or, dine buffet style in the Verandah on some of the best meal values on the strip. The all-you-you-eat breakfast here will last until dinner time. Rooms are done in sunny tropical prints and florals, with a small seating area and a balcony overlooking the grounds or the ocean. There's a big pool and a Jacuzzi plus all the watersports.

HYATT REGENCY GRAND CAYMAN, *Seven Mile Beach. Tel. U.S. and Canada 800/233-1234, local 345/949-1234, Fax 949-8528. Rates at this 236-room hotel, which is three miles from Georgetown and a $14 taxi ride from the airport, start at $300. Meal plans are available.*

One of the most grand resorts along this stretch of the beach, this pastel and white British Colonial palace is the centerpiece of a resort complex that includes the Britannia Golf and Beach Resort. The hotel itself is across the street from the beach, but the crossing is not difficult and the pools on the hotel side are so attractive you may choose to go to the beach only to use the watersports equipment and beach bar.

The hotel opened in the 1980s, the first *grande luxe* hotel on the beach, but it was built before the craze for larger rooms and baths hit with full force. Still, we found the standard double to be airy and comfortable for two; a couple with children might prefer a suite or villa. If you stay in the Regency Club, rates include a continental breakfast, 24-hour concierge service, and complimentary canapes at cocktail time. Along the golf course, villas have one to four bedrooms and full kitchens, yet they're handy to the resort's other pleasures including three restaurants, four bars, four swimming polls, four tennis courts, boutiques, a beauty shop, a marine, dive shop, and a super kids program called Camp Hyatt. It's for children ages 3-12 and costs about $50 per day including lunch, treats, and craft supplies.

INDIES SUITES, *Seven Mile Beach, mailing address Box 2070. Tel. 345/ 945-5025, Fax 945-5024; toll-free 800/654-3130. Rates at this 41-suite resort start at $255 for a suite with full kitchen. Breakfast is included. It's five miles from George Town and a $19 taxi ride from the airport.*

This smart, blue-and-white resort just across the road from the white sand beach is family operated and family friendly. The complimentary buffet breakfast is a good chance to mingle with other guests, and it's nice to have your own kitchen, complete with microwave oven, to whip up meals when you don't feel like having lunch or dinner in a restaurant. One-bedroom suites can sleep four by using the sofa bed; two-bedrooms can accommodate up to six. The hotel has a dive operation, a swimming pool with a poolside bar, Jacuzzi, and weekly events such as a barbecue or a cruise. There's a coin laundry for guest use. A good choice of restaurants and bars is within walking distance along West Bay Road.

RADISSON RESORT GRAND CAYMAN, *Seven Mile Beach. Tel. 345/ 949-0088, Fax 949-0288, U.S. and Canada, 800/333-3333. It's on Seven Mile Beach, two miles from Georgetown and a $13 taxi ride from the airport. Mailing address is Box 30371, Grand Cayman, British West Indies. Rates at this 315-room hotel are from $215.*

This gaily red-roofed hotel was built to take optimum advantage of its frontage on famous Seven Mile Beach. Dine seaside or in the grill. The hotel has its own full-service dive shop and tour desk, an exercise center, freshwater pool, gift shops, a beachside bar, lounge with music and dancing, and fine dining. Rooms, done in soothing pastels and whites, are air conditioned and have telephone and television. Wheelchair accessible rooms are available.

WESTIN CASUARINA RESORT, *Seven Mile Beach, mailing address Box 30620, Grand Cayman. Tel. 345/945-3800, Fax 949-5825; U.S. and Canada 800/228-3000. Rates at this 351-room resort start at $180; suites are priced to $425. It's four miles from George Town and $16 by taxi from the airport.*

A white complex with sky-blue roofs rises right at the edge of a 700-foot expanse of Seven Mile Beach, this splendid resort offers all the luxuries of a Westin. The outside is landscaped with flowering shrubs and waterfalls, leading to dazzling swimming pools flanked by bleached decks and rustling date palms. One pool has a swim-up bar. Rooms are done in soothing neutrals accented in jewel colors, marble, and white wicker, with mini-bar and safe.

Watersports top the list of pastimes. Rent a boat or arrange a dive or snorkel adventure. The resort also offers massage, a children's program in season, an 18-hole championship golf course across the street, beauty salon, 24-hour room service, and on-site car rental.

Moderate

BEACH CLUB COLONY, *Seven Mile Beach, mailing address Box 903. Tel. 345/949-8100, Fax 945-5167; toll-free 800/482-DIVE. Rates at this 41-room resort are from $178. It's three miles north of George Town and a $14 taxi ride from the airport. Ask about dive packages and meal plans.*

Mostly a laidback dive hotel, the club has plenty to offer non-diving spouses who can lie on the beach, bubble in the whirlpool, wind surf, play tennis, or check out neighboring hotels for shopping and dining. The hotel is between the Grand Pavilion and the Hyatt Regency and a mile west of the golf course. Rooms are air conditioned and have telephone and television. Deluxe rooms have an ocean view and four-poster bed. Beach-front villas are also available.

BEST WESTERN SAMMY'S AIRPORT INN, *Owen Roberts Drive, mailing address Box 30746. Tel. 345/945-2100, Fax 945-2330. Rates at this 53-room hotel start at $110. It's three miles from George Town on the airport.*

An ideal business address or a place to stay if you're overnighting on Grand Cayman on your way to the out islands, this inn has air conditioning, a restaurant, swimming pool, lounge, telephone and television.

CAYMAN DIVING LODGE, *East End, mailing address Box 11. Tel. 345/947-7555, Fax 947-7560; U.S. 800/TLC-DIVE. Rates at this 14-room lodge start at $150 per person including three meals and a two-tank boat dive daily. It's 20 miles from George Town and a $49 taxi ride from the airport.*

This is about as far from Seven Mile Beach as you can get, a remote end of the island where you can jump off every day for a new diving adventure. Accent is on the diving, not the decor, but the value is good and you'll like the scuba-happy ambience. The lodge is beachfront and has air conditioning, a whirlpool, restaurant, dive shop, and a bar where everyone hangs out at the end of the day.

CAYMAN KAI RESORT, *North Side, mailing address Box 201. Tel. 345/94709055, Fax 947-9102, U.S. 800/223-5427. Rates at this 20-room resort start at $180. It's 25 miles from George Town and a $59 cab ride from the airport.*

Just below Rum Point on Grand Cayman's eastern end, this resort is off the beaten path on its own, uncrowded beach. Rooms have a ceiling fan, kitchenette and television but no telephone and not all units are air conditioned. Every unit has a screened patio with an ocean view. Live the beachcomber idyll in this small place with its own restaurant, a popular bar, swimming pool, and gift shop. Use the windsurfers and snorkel gear, or arrange a dive.

COCONUT HARBOUR, *Box 2086, Georgetown. Tel. 345/949-7468, Fax 949-7117; U.S. 800/552-6281. Rates at this 35-room resort start at $152 for an oversize room with kitchenette. It's a half mile south of Georgetown and a $12 taxi ride from the airport.*

Walk to the shore and swim out 20 yards and you're on fabulous

Waldo Reef. Rooms have air conditioning, ceiling fan, telephone, and television, and they open on a common walkway where there's room for a couple of chairs. The hotel has a big swimming pool surrounded by sun deck, restaurant and bar, whirlpool, and its own dive shop.

MORRITT'S TORTUGA CLUB, *East End, mailing address Box 496. Tel. 345/947-7449, Fax 947-7669; U.S. and Canada 800/447-0309. Rates at this 121-room resort are from $175. It's 26 miles from Georgetown and a $58 taxi ride from the airport.*

Once here on the far eastern shore of Grand Cayman, you can live the South Seas life in a three-story white condominium complex with sky-blue roofs. It's a perfect match for the white sand beach and blue sky of this popular windsurfing, sailing, and diving area. Your suite has a kitchen, telephone, television, and air conditioning. A restaurant, bar, and full watersports services are right here in a remote getaway at the opposite end of the island from busy Seven Mile Beach.

SLEEP INN HOTEL, *Seven Mile Beach, mailing address Box 30111. Tel. 345/949-9111, Fax 949-6699; toll-free 800/SLEEP INN. Rates at this 115-room hotel start at $175. It's two miles from George Town and a $12 taxi ride from the airport. Suites with kitchenette are available.*

The first hotel on "hotel row" north of Georgetown, the inn is just north of Kirk Supermarket and five minutes south of the golf course. Swim in the big, free-form swimming pool or walk to the beach. Air conditioned rooms have telephone and television and many rooms are wheelchair accessible. There's a restaurant and bar in the hotel, or you can easily pop up the road to other resorts.

SUNSET HOUSE, *Box 479, South Church Street. Tel. 345/949-7111, Fax 949-7101; toll-free 800/854-4767. Rates at this 59-room hotel are from $135. It's a mile from George Town and a $12 cab ride from the airport.*

It's all about diving at a hotel run "for divers by divers." A full dive shop includes an underwater photo center. The beach is a five-minute walk away. The hotel's seafood restaurant is a local favorite. Rooms are ordinary motel layouts with air conditioning, telephone and television, and there's a swimming pool and whirlpool. Kitchenettes are available.

Budget

ADAM'S GUEST HOUSE, *George Town, mailing address Box 312. It's near the hospital, a mile from Georgetown and a $12 cab ride from the airport. Rates at this five-room guest house start at $75. An apartment is available at $170.*

Enjoy the comforts of a private home with your own entrance and bath. Rooms have telephone, maid service, television, VCR, air conditioning, and ceiling fan. The hosts will be glad to find a crib (or, as they would say here in Britspeak, a cot) for the baby.

AMBASSADORS INN, *Box 1789, George Town. Tel. 345/949-7577, Fax 949-7050. This 18-room inn, a mile south of George Town and a $13 taxi ride from the airport, charges $90 for a double room.*

Secluded Smith's Cove is not far from this small hotel between George Town and South West Point. Air conditioned rooms have television, telephone and ceiling fan, and there's a bar and restaurant on site. Snorkeling and scuba can be arranged.

ENTERPRISE BED & BREAKFAST, *South Church Street, mailing address Box 482. Tel. 345/949-5569, Fax 949-6987. Rates at this eight-room inn start at $69 including a full breakfast. A deluxe unit that sleeps six is $138. It's on Red Bay, 3.5 miles from George Town and a $15 cab ride from the airport.*

This non-smoking inn offers an inexpensive place to stay while you're diving the Caymans. Rooms have television, telephone VCR, air conditioning, and ceiling fan. You're welcome to use the barbecue on the patio. Ask about dive packages.

ERMA ELDEMIRE'S GUEST HOUSE, *South Church Street, mailing address Box 482, George Town. Tel. 345/949-5569. Tel. 949-6987. Rates at this 10-unit inn start at $65. It's a mile from George Town and a $12 taxi ride from the airport.*

The Eldemires have been hosting guests here since 1970 and many long-time Cayman visitors wouldn't stay anywhere else. Stay in a standard room, a studio or a one-bedroom apartment ($100) and walk to nearby Smith Cove for a swim. Rooms are air conditioned and have a ceiling fan.

WHITE HAVEN INN GUEST HOUSE, *Batabano Road, mailing address 30424. Tel. 345/949-1064, Fax 945-4980. Rates at this three-room inn start at $60 including full American breakfast and airport pick-up. It's eight miles from George Town.*

You're met at the airport and treated like family at this small guest house two miles east of Seven Mile Beach. Rooms are air conditioned and have ceiling fans, telephone, television, and VCR. You'll need a car to get around, but this is an ideal headquarters for travelers who like to spend all day out on the island beaching, diving, picnicking, and exploring.

CAYMAN BRAC

BRAC HAVEN VILLAS, *Stake Bay, mailing address Box 89, Cayman Brac. Tel. 345/948-2473, Fax 948-2329. Rates at this six-villa complex start at $180 for a one-bedroom apartment. It's about eight miles from the airport on the island's southeast shore.*

You'll have an villa with air conditioning, television, kitchen, and your own veranda. Laundry machines are available for guest use.

DIVI TIARA BEACH RESORT, *Stake Bay, mailing address Box 238, Cayman Brac. Tel. 345/948-1553, Fax 948-1316, toll-free 800/367-3484.*

Rates at this 59-room resort start at $125. Ask about meal plans and dive packages. It's just off the runway near the airport.

Lounge around the big, blue swimming pool or do what most guests do, which is to dive a different reef every day. Deluxe rooms have television and a sea view and some have a private Jacuzzi; every room has air conditioning, ceiling fan, a porch or patio, and telephone. Have lunch or a drink poolside under a garden of butter-yellow umbrellas, play tennis or beach volleyball, relax in the whirlpool, go fishing, stroll the grounds with their magnificent tropical blooms, and spend evenings looking at your underwater photos taken and developed with the help of the resort's photo center. Dining in the Poseidon restaurant features American and Caribbean dishes. A free shuttle takes guests to a good snorkeling reef on the island's south side.

LA ESPERANZA, *Box 28, Stake Bay. Tel. 345/948-0518, Fax 948-0518. Rates at this five-unit condo are from $110 for a two-bedroom apartment. It's on the northeast shore in the settlement near the post office and about eight miles from the airport.*

The decor features sand-colored tile floors, filmy beige draperies, prim prints, and dark hardwood furniture with wicker and rattan accents. Accommodations are air conditioned and have a ceiling fan, television, telephone, and kitchen. Walk to the beach or use the inn's own Jacuzzi. There's a restaurant on site.

LITTLE CAYMAN

SOUTHERN CROSS CLUB, *South Hole Sound, mailing address Box 44, Little Cayman. Tel. 345/948-1099, Fax 948-1098; toll-free 800/899-2582. Rates at this 10-room hotel are from $330 including meals and airport transfers.*

Stay in one of the small cottages that string along the beach much like mom-and-pop motels were strung along roadsides in the 1950s. The club is just northeast of the airport and just offshore is Owen Island, a popular sandspit for picnicking, sunning, and beach combing. The decor is out-island basic, all wicker and rattan relieved by a few hardwood pieces and accents in bold prints. There's no air conditioning, but the ceiling fans and ocean breezes make things comfortable most of the time. Most guests come for the diving, although deep-sea fishing and bonefishing the flats are both packed with action.

PIRATES POINT RESORT, *Preston Bay, Little Cayman. Tel. 345/948-1010, Fax 948-1011; toll-free 800/327-8777. Rates at this 10-unit hotel are from $300 all inclusive. It's just west of the small air strip.*

We first met owner-manager Gladys Howard in the 1980s, when we learned that this personable Texan is a cookbook author and a Cordon Bleu graduate. With her head in Paris and her feet on the sands of this paradise island, she produces meals that bring guests back year after year.

Cuisine, wines, cocktails, and dives are all included. The chief appeal here is the diving on such famous points as Bloody Bay Wall, but non-divers will be content to sit on a breezy veranda, enjoy the flowering vines, and read or sun. If you like, Gladys will take you on a nature hike; once a week she throws a wine and cheese tasting on the beach.

Choose from a variety of accommodations ranging from standard rooms to cottages with two bedrooms. They're a good value for two diving couples or a couple with older children, but kiddies under age four aren't accepted.

SAM MCCOY'S FISHING & DIVING LODGE, *North Side, Little Cayman. Tel. 345/948-0026; fax 948-0057; toll-free 800/626-0496. Rates at this eight-unit lodge start at $208 including meals. Dive packages are available. It's on the island's northwest shore.*

Like most fish camps, this one has immense appeal to raw-boned divers and anglers, who are welcomed into the family and regaled with fish tales. Meals are served family style after Sam and his son Chip take you out for the day's diving, deep-sea fishing, or bonefishing. Rooms are air conditioned and have ceiling fans. There's a swimming pool or swim off the sand beach, where Sam throws a beach barbecue from time to time.

STAY IN A CAYMANS HOME OR CONDO

As a popular offshore investment center, Grand Cayman is a likely choice for real estate investors who have built houses or bought condos here. Hundreds of studios and apartments vie for the tourist dollar, allowing travelers to stay in affordable lodgings if they're willing to do their own cooking, provisioning, and washing up. Before booking, ask if maid service is included and whether it is daily, as in a hotel. It's also wise to ask if there is on-site management. If something breaks or fails, know who will be there to fix it.

Booking agents for homes and condos in the Caymans include:
International Travel & Resorts, *300 East 40th Street, New York NY 10016, Tel. 800/223-9815 Tel. 212/476-9444, Fax 476-9467*
Reef Fanta-seas, *4127 Fifth Avenue North, St. Petersburg FL 33713, Tel. 800/327-3835 or 813/323-8727, Fax 323-8827*
Robert Reid Associates, *500 Plaza Drive, Secaucus NJ 07096, Tel. 800/223-6510 or 201/902-7878, Fax 902-7707*
Star Travel, Ltd., *5805 State Bridge Road, Suite V, Duluth GA, Tel. 770/493-1747, Fax 493-8494.*

WHERE TO EAT

Restaurant food in the Caymans is costly, which may be one reason why the island seems to have so many condos where travelers can do their own cooking. Menu prices are high and, when you realize that every CI dollar actually means $1.25, plus a 15 percent service charge, it's enough to send you to the supermarket for picnic fare.

Pick up the free tourist booklets that you'll see around hotels and shops. Often they have news of specials and Happy Hours, or contain discount coupons. It's not uncommon to pay $10 just for a cocktail. Still, the islands do have good chefs and good food, and this is one place where you can feast on seafood and turtle to your heart's content. Almost hunted to extinction at sea, the green turtle is farm-raised and abundant here.

Local dishes in addition to turtle include the pudding-like "heavy cake," pepperpot soup made with greens and potatoes, conch fritters, and rundown, which is fish stewed in coconut milk with breadfruit and cassava. Escovitch is pan-fried fish served hot or cold with a vinegar marinade. Saltfish and ackee, Jamaican favorites, are found here. So is jerk cooking. From Cornwall come the meat patties called pasties. Traditional foods you may have a chance to try also include bullrush pudding, fish tea with johnnycakes, crab backs, and whelk pie.

Menus often list foods as "meat kind," which includes meats including turtle, and "bread kind," which has to do with the starches served with the meal. Usually they include white potatoes, breadfruit (often served in a dish that looks and tastes like potato salad), peas and rice, plaintains, cassava, or yams (not to be confused with sweet potatoes.) Most such foods have little flavor, but take on the flavor of the sauce or meat and serve as filler.

We list prices in U.S. dollars, which are used on most menus. However, it can be confusing. If you're in doubt, ask, because it makes a difference of about $25 in every $100 spent.

Expensive

CHEF TELL'S GRAND OLD HOUSE, *Petra Plantation, South Church Street. Tel. 949-9333. Reservations are essential. Main dishes are priced $22 to $35. The restaurant is open for lunch and dinner Monday to Friday and for dinner on weekends except in summer, when it's closed on Sunday. It's a mile south of Georgetown.*

An old greathouse has been transformed into a stage for television chef Tell Erhardt, who combines tastes from his German homeland with Caribbean and American favorites. A rave appetizer is the coconut shrimp, an island standard that Tell makes special by serving it with a mustard-apricot dip. Or, start with a salmon carpaccio with dill or the popular (but heavy) conch fritters. Duckling and pork are finished with a darkly sweet coffee liqueur that complements them delectably. Tell's special lobster dish is battered and sauteed with white wine, shallots, and mushrooms. You'll dine under ceiling fans in a worlds-end setting on the water surrounded by rustling palms.

HEMINGWAY'S, *in the Hyatt Regency, West Bay Road. Tel. 949-1234. Reservations are recommended. Main dishes are priced $22 to $42.50. It's open for lunch and dinner daily.*

This restaurant on the beach side features the Hemingway theme that brings on thoughts of good rum, good company, and a passion for the island life. Dine by candlelight in the sea breezes on fresh grouper with crabmeat stuffing, grilled wahoo, pounded conch steak served with lime butter, fresh mahi-mahi, or roast pork with mango sauce. Service can be superb or so-so, and the best daiquiris on the island can almost make you happy to wait for slow response, but at these prices we get more demanding when we are being ignored. On most nights there's live background music.

LANTANAS, *in the Caribbean Club on West Bay Road three miles north of George Town. Tel. 945-4099. Main dishes are priced $16 to $37. Reservations are essential. It's open daily for dinner.*

Never mind that lantana, the flower, is poisonous. This American-Caribbean restaurant has one of the most exciting menus on the island, drawing on trendy California and Florida tastes such as roasted vegetables (have the roasted garlic soup), grilled salmon with cilantro, grilled lobster with a tangy guacamole, home-made sausage, lobster quesadillas, and fresh fish served in your choice of ways included blackened. Or, try the jerk pork with peas and rice, Jamaican style. Chef Alfred Schrock is Austrian, so you can't miss by ending up with his strudel for dessert but there are also four creme brulées on the menu.

LIGHTHOUSE RESTAURANT AT BREAKERS. *Tel. 947-2047. Follow the coastline east for 25 minutes and home in on the lighthouse. Plan to spend $50 for dinner. It's open every day 10am to 10pm. Reservations are recommended.*

Master chef David will be at work in the kitchen with veal Marsala, lamb chops, a seafood mixed grill, stuffed mushrooms with four-cheese sauce, Fettucini Marenero or Cannelloni Supreme while you savor a drink and an enchanting view of the sea and sunset. It's not really a lighthouse, but it has all the salty flavor of a real one. Dine outdoors on the patio or indoors with air conditioning. End the meal with white chocolate mousse or a tiramisu. The wine list is one of the most impressive on the island.

RISTORANTE PAPPAGALLO, *in the Villas Pappagallo, eight miles north of George Town on West Bay Road. Tel. 949-1119. Main dishes are priced $20 to $38. It's open for dinner daily.*

The finest northern Italian food served on the island wins honors at the annual Taste of Cayman food extravaganza. The decor is stunning in glass and marble, with South Seas touches of grass and thatch. The setting is on a lagoon, a 14-acre mangrove sanctuary filled with birds. Specialties include pastas such as black taglioni with seafood sauce, lobster-stuffed ravioli, linguine in spicy seafood sauce, veal Parmesan, and good steaks with a side of pasta. The pastas are cooked to order, al dente, so don't expect quick service provided by restaurants where the spaghetti sits for hours in a steam table. Choose from a list of more than 80 wines, some of them imported from Italy exclusively by Pappagallo. The meal ends with the chef's *dolce del giorno*, or sweet of the day, and one of the specialty coffees. Don't forget to look at the thatched roof, which took six months to make using 100,000 palm fronds.

SEAVIEW, *in the Seaview Hotel on South Church Street. Tel. 949-8804. Dine for $40. It's open 7am to 11pm every day.*

Dine outdoors on a deck overlooking the palms and seashore while sundown paints the sky red and pink. The setting is informal and tropical. Chefs Don Sannachan and Bettina Zwingli came to the island from Europe by way of Canada, and you'll note Austrian notes in their Caribbean symphony. Have a drink before or after dinner at the piano bar, then pace yourself for a whopping feast that centers around prime rib roasted just right, a loaf of homemade bread at every place setting, and an 18-foot salad bar offering everything possible to go with the meat or fish you choose for a main course.

TOP OF THE FALLS, *in the Treasure Island Resort. Tel. 949-5324. Plan to spend $40 for dinner. It's open daily for breakfast, Tuesday through Saturday for dinner 5-10pm and Sunday and Monday 6-10pm.*

The falls are artificial, but they add a pleasant murmur to this restaurant on the third floor of the resort. Chef Roland Schoefer suggests a drink first in the Rustic Bar (Happy Hour is 5:30-7pm), then a feast featuring dishes including shrimp mango, oysters, stuffed mushrooms, rack of lamb, veal schnitzel, and plenty of seafood choices.

THE WHARF, *West Bay Road. Tel. 949-2231. Call for reservations and hours, which vary seasonally. Plan your meal to coincide with the showy tarpon feedings, which are nightly at 9pm.*

Most visitors come here at some point just to see the spectacle of flashing tarpon in the dark water, swimming by for their nightly handout. See it from the Ports of Call bar, which is also a popular hangout for sunset watching. Meals feature fresh seafood, served simply or in lusciously complex combinations like the lobster and bay scallops in a creamy dill sauce. Ask about daily specials, which usually include at least one fresh fish and a meat choice such as steak bearnaise or veal Marsala. Live music entertains almost every night.

Moderate

BENJAMIN'S ROOF, *Coconut Place. Tel. 947-4080. About three miles north of George Town, this restaurant serves main dishes priced at $13 to $35. It's open daily 3-10:30pm. Reservations are essential.*
Come for an afternoon drink and a snack while you're shopping or stay on for dinner. The restaurant is upstairs in a shopping center where an oasis of green has been created dozens of potted plants and trees. Live piano serenades a meal of gator tail, grilled seafood, fettuccine tossed with medallions of lobster, grilled lamb or pork chops, or pan-fried battered veal cutlets.

CRACKED CONCH, *West Bay Road. Tel. 947-5217. Call for hours and reservations. The lunch buffet is a bargain at about $10; dinner dishes are priced $20 to $30.*
Bob and Suzy Soto have done it again, winning honors at the annual Taste of Cayman food fair. The restaurant is named for a classic Caribbean dish, cracked conch. It is conch that has been pounded tender, dredged in cracker crumbs, and pan fried to succulent tenderness. Conch also shows up in chowder and fritters here. There's also plenty of other seafood including turtle and whatever snapper, wahoo or grouper the fleet brought in today.

The plank floor is from an old pirate ship, fib the Sotos, who actually laid a cement floor and then scored and stained it to look like wood. Doors and shutters in the bathrooms are done by Miss Lassie, whom they describe as the Cayman's Grandma Moses. The dive helmets were Bob's back in his helmet-diving days. Desserts center around coconut cream or key lime pie or cheesecake. Popular with locals, the restaurant has Happy Hour specials and a lunch menu offering baked potato stuffed with tuna, shrimp, conch, or chili, and a bunch of sandwiches including jerk chicken or turtle. If you're a soup-and-salad luncher have the special vichyssoise and the Greek or Caesar salad.

DJ'S CAFE, *across from the Holiday Inn at Coconut Place. Tel. 947-4234. Plan to spend $25 to $35 for dinner. It's open daily 11:30am to 2:30pm and for dinner from 5pm. A late-night menu is available in the bar.*
This long-popular hangout welcomes smokers and non-smokers alike and it doesn't add a service charge as most Caymanian eateries do. Tip at your pleasure. Dine on lobster, steak, stone crab or fresh fish. If it isn't the freshest available, the chef takes it off the blackboard. For dessert, there's cheesecake. For lunch have sandwiches, burgers, salad or soup.

HOG STY CAFE & PUB, *on the waterfront in George Town. Tel. 949-6163. It's open every day for breakfast, lunch, and dinner, with the pub menu available all day. Dinner main dishes are priced $15 to $20.*

The cute name really reels in the tourists, but locals too come here for the fresh local food, traditional English pub food, good beer, and good company. Sit on the deck overlooking the water and dine from neutral tableware set on bright, tropical table coverings. U.S. Choice beef sizzles on the grill, or order fresh fish, lobster or one of the smoked meats or fish. Pub grub includes meat or seafood pasties, shepherd's pie, sausages, fish and chips, and cheese and tomato sandwiches with pickled onions.

Budget

BILLY'S, *North Church Street, George Town. Tel. 949-0470. Hours are 11am to 3pm and 5-10pm Monday through Saturday. Burgers are under $6; a pizza can run about $15; platters about $10. Only when you get into fresh seafood do prices edge higher to the $20 range. It's on the north side of town on the main road to Seven Mile Beach.*

Try the pizza with jerk chicken or pork, a cheeseburger, lobster Creole, jerk conch with peas and rice, or a good selection of spicy Indian dishes – curries, tandoori dishes, masala dishes, and vindaloos. This is budget island dining in a pretty garden set back from the road.

PIRATES DEN, *in the Galleria Plaza on West Bay Road. Tel. 949-7144. Hours are 11:30am to 1pm. Eat for $10-$15.*

Nothing ever gets too fancy here, and it's a fun place to bring the children for the pirate decor, juicy burgers, and nachos. For a more substantial meal have the steak or grilled fish. For snacking have quesadillas or nachos and the zestiest chicken wings on the island. Ask about daily specials.

STAR DINER, *downtown George Town. Tel. 947-5300. Eat for $10-$15. Hours are Monday to Friday 6:30am to 4pm and Saturday 8am to 2pm. No credit cards.*

An old-fashioned diner with a 1960s theme sells burgers, sandwiches, frozen yogurt, and a different special every day. It's one of the few places where you can get a very early breakfast.

Quick Takes

You'll pass the occasional jerk shack but the favorite roadside sell here is cauldrons of fish tea, a spicy fish stock that is served with johnnycakes, which are fried bread. Fish tea may also be found at local festivals but it's a folk dish rarely seen on restaurant menus.

For a filling pasty, try the **Wholesome Bakery** in George Town facing the harbor. To have a meal catered to your condo, call **Burton Ebanks**, *Tel. 345/949-7222,* and place your order well in advance. He'll prepare a traditional Caymanian feast for you. **Subway** (the North American chain) sandwich shops are in the West Shore Centre and at Anderson Square. The island also has a **Wendy's, I Can't Believe It's Yogurt**, and two **Burger Kings**.

SEEING THE SIGHTS

Nature is the biggest attraction in the Caymans, where you'll find few of the stony ruins and old mansions seen on other islands. **George Town** is a neat and pleasant place to browse but its points of interest are few, except for the library and courthouse, which date to the 1930s, and the museum, which was built 1833. It's a good example of the "upstairs house" that prosperous Caymanians were building by then.

The **Cayman Islands National Museum** on Harbour Drive in George Town, *Tel. 949-8368*, is well worth a visit to see the theater, have a snack in the cafe, and view oddments and artifacts having to do with history and nature. Admission is CI$4 adults and CI$2 for children. Hours are Monday to Friday 9am to 5pm and Saturday 10am to 2pm. Tickets are sold until half an hour before closing.

Queen Elizabeth II Botanic Park, *Tel. 947-9462*, was opened by Her Majesty herself in 1994 and today is a treasury of birds and blooms. Covering 65 acres, the park has a two-acre lake with three island rookeries and a Heritage Garden of plants that were popular in the 19th century. All the flowers and vegetables are labeled for tourists. It's open during daylight hours.

The only turtle farm of its kind in the world, **Cayman Turtle Farm** at Northwest Point, is a heartening look at what can be done to save the world's dwindling turtle population. You can eat turtle soup and turtle steak on the island, knowing it is a renewable resource that also produces turtle shell combs and jewelry (that is still considered endangered and cannot be brought into the United States). Guides explain the life cycle of the turtle, and you'll watch in fascination as hundreds of the creatures, from fingerlings to meaty, eating-size turtles tumble over each other in healthy profusion. The farm is open daily 9:30am to 5pm and admission is CI$4 for adults and CI$2 for children. There is a restaurant and a souvenir shop where you can get allowable souvenirs such as the turtle in a pirate suit that is the symbol of the Caymans.

In the north of **Grand Cayman**, not far from the Turtle Farm, is an area known as **Hell** because it is a moonscape of black lava devoid of any life. Its main appeal is a post office where you can send postcards from Hell. It's a good place to pick up extra stamps, which are beautiful and make nice gifts to collectors. While you're wandering around the islands, stop at any of the 13 **Tortuga Rum Company** stores for Tortuga Rum Cake and Hell sauce, which make good souvenirs and gifts.

ABOUT ATLANTIS

*A group of investors pooled their $250,000 in 1983 with the goal of creating a **sightseeing submarine** that would appeal to tourists. Although the successful company now operates submarines in Aruba, the Bahamas, Barbados, Mexico, St. Thomas, Hawaii and Guam, is was Grand Cayman that they chose for their first passenger rides. That says something about the quality of the reefs and wall here. In a futuristic cylinder with a seat and porthole for each person, the electric submarine can take 48 people 150 feel into the deep.*

"It's the ultimate field trip," grinned the captain of our sub, pleased to see a number of school-age children on board. The entire adventure lasts about an hour and a half, including the ride out from shore in a ferry, transfer to the submarine, and about 50 minutes under water. Because every trip is different depending on what sea life shows up, the crew shares the excitement of the passengers. One trip isn't enough.

*Connect with the Atlantis experience in George Town Harbour for the trip aboard the ferry, Yukon II, to the dive site a mouth south of George Town in **Cayman National Marine Park**. Dives are made Monday through Saturday. Reservations are essential and should be made 24 hours or more in advance, Tel. 949-7700, or from the U.S. and Canada, Tel. 800/887-8571. The ride costs $90 for adults and $45 for children. Children under age 4 are not admitted. Note that the submarine does not have a bathroom on board.*

*Atlantis Grand Cayman also operates the world's only **deep-diving research submersible**. It can carry two passengers and a pilot to depths of 800-1,000 feet down the Cayman Wall. Along the way, passengers can see the wreck of the Kirk Pride, which lies on a ledge 800 feet down the wall. The experience, which includes a one-hour dive, costs $300.*

Along the island's northwest coast the **West Bay** area is filled with 200-year-old lanes and footpaths where you'll see a catalog of island architecture from gingerbread cottages to wattle-and-daub cabins. They were built early in the 18th century using ironwood woven with green wood twigs (wattles) that were then plastered with "daub." The two-room cottages with their separate butteries were closed with wooden shutters, and raised on 18-inch stilts to allow storm water to float past. Originally thatched with silver palm, which had to be replaced often, the homes were later shingled with cedar shakes. A brochure is available from the National Trust, *Tel. 494-8469.*

Float through underwater sea gardens aboard the world's only research submersible for tourists. The vessel carries only two passengers and a pilot and can explore 1,000 feet down the famous **Cayman Wall**, Or take an air conditioned, 64-, 48-, or 24-passenger **Atlantis submarine** to see shipwrecks, sponges, and coral gardens; *Tel. 800/887-8571* from the U.S. or book through your hotel or cruise ship.

On **Little Cayman Island**, **Booby Pond Nature Reserve** hosts one of the largest colonies of red-footed boobies in the western hemisphere and the only breeding colony of frigate birds in the Caymans.

Aerial Sightseeing

Fly with **Seaborne Flightseeing Adventures** aboard a 19-passenger Twin Otter or sightsee aboard a six-passenger helicopter with **Cayman Helicopters Ltd.**, *Tel. 949-4000.*

NIGHTLIFE & ENTERTAINMENT

COCONUTS COMEDY CLUB in the Holiday Inn, *Tel. 947-4444,* features top stand-up comics from the United States and Canada five nights a week. Also playing the **HOLIDAY INN** is the ageless Barefoot Man, George Nowak, who has been a fixture here for 20 years. Order a Banana Mudslide and listen to him do a set of calypso, reggae, and soca hits.

HARQUAIL THEATER and the **PROSPECT PLAYHOUSE** are worth a visit if they're playing a West Indian satire or British farce. Schedules are listed in give-away booklets found in all hotels. These publications include *Key to Cayman*, *What's Hot*, *Destination Cayman*, and *Caymanian Compass*. They're also the best source of information about who is playing at local dance clubs and hotels.

SPORTS & RECREATION

Bicycling

Bicycle rentals are $10 to $15 a day and scooter rentals about $25. On Grand Cayman get two wheels from:
• **Cayman Cycle Rentals**, *Tel. 945-4021*
• **Eagle Nest Cycles**, *Tel. 949-4866*
• **Soto Scooter & Car Rentals**, *Tel. 945-4652.*

On Little Cayman, rent a a bicycle from **McLaughlin Rentals**, *Tel. 948-1000.*

Diving

Because these islands lie far out to sea and have no rivers to carry silt into the waters, visibility is unbelievably good. Divers can sometimes see as far as 120 feet. All three islands are ringed by living coral reefs, and dramatic walls and drop-offs aren't far from shore. Most of these operators offer packages that include accommodations. Their boats accommodate ten to 20 people. Be sure to book a scuba or snorkel trip to the area known as **Stingray City**, where you'll be part of a ballet of graceful rays soaring above, under, and around you.

Little Cayman Diver II offers live-aboard diving by the week at an all-inclusive price. Prices range from $300 to $450 for certification, $85 to $150 for a resort course, and $50 to $70 for a two-tank dive. All are PADI facilities and most are also NAUI, SSI, NADS, and/or YMCA.

Dive operators on Grand Cayman include:
- **Soto's Cruises**, *Tel. 345/945-4576, Fax 945-1527*
- **Sunset Divers**, *Tel. 800/854-4767 or 345/949-7111, Fax 949-7101*
- **Tortuga Divers, Ltd.**, *Tel. 345/947-2097, Fax 947-9486*
- **Treasure Island Divers**, *Tel. 800/872-7552, 345/949-4456, Fax 949-7125*

On **Cayman Brac**, dive with:
- **Brac Aquatics, Ltd**, *Tel. 800/544-BRAC or 813/962-2236, Fax 813/264-2742*
- **Peter Hughes Dive Tiara**, *Tel. 800/367-3484, Fax 948-1563*
- **Reef Divers Brac**, *Tel. 800/327-3835 or 813/323-8727*

Dive on **Little Cayman** with:
- **Reef Divers**, *Tel. 800/327-3835 or 813/323-8727*
- **Little Cayman Diver II**, *Tel. 800/458-2722 or 813/932-1993*
- **Paradise Divers**, *Tel. 800/450-2084 or 345/948-0004*
- **Pirates Point Resort**, *Tel. 800/327-8777 or 345/948-1010, Fax 948-1011*
- **Sam McCoy's Fishing & Diving Lodge**, *Tel. 800/727-0496 or 345/949-2891, 948-0026, Fax 948-0057 or fax 949-6821*
- **Southern Cross Club**, *Tel. 800/899-2582 or 345/948-1099, Fax 948-1098*

Fishing

Half-day reef and tarpon fishing charters cost about $250 for three or four anglers. Deep-sea fishing is $550 to $1,000 per day or $375 to $650 per half day. Charter Boat Headquarters can also supply a fly-fishing guide for $135 a half day. Boats, and the number they can accommodate, vary.

Go fishing off Grand Cayman with:
- **Oh Boy Charters**, *Tel. 949-6341*
- **Bayside Watersports**, *Tel. 949-3200*
- **Black Princess Charters**, *Tel. 949-0400*
- **Captain Marvin's Aquatics**, *Tel. 945-4590*
- **Cayman Sunset**, *Tel. 949-3666*
- **Charter Boat Headquarters**, *Tel. 945-4340*

- **Crosby Ebanks**, *Tel. 945-4049*
- **Deep Sea Fox**, *Tel. 945-4340*
- **One Day at a Time**,*Tel. 947-2244*
- **Peacemaker Charters**, *Tel. 916-2478*
- **Sunlight Charters**, *Tel. 945-4340*
- **Temptress**, *Tel. 949-0400*
- **Island Girl Charters**, *Tel. 947-3029*

On **Cayman Brac**, fish with:
- **Edmund "Munny" Bodden**, *Tel. 948-1228*
- **Shelby Charters**, *Tel. 948-0535*
- **Southern Comfort**, *Tel. 948-1314*
- **Frank Bodden**, *Tel. 948-1537 or 948-1428*

On **Little Cayman**, charter with:
- **Sam McCoy**, *Tel. 800/626-0495 or 345/949-2891*
- **Southern Cross Club**, *Tel. 948-1099*

Golf

Britannia Golf Club in the Hyatt Regency Grand Cayman, *Tel. 949-8020*, is an 18-hole Scottish-style "links" layout designed by Jack Nicklaus. Play a round for $80 in winter and $50 in summer. **The Links at SafeHaven**, *Tel. 949-5988*, is a par-71, 18-hole championship course designed by Roy Case in the style of Scottish seaside courses. Play is $95 in winter and $80 in summer, both including cart rental.

Horseback Riding

Take a guided trail ride with **Blazing Trails**, *Tel. 949-7360* or **Nicki's Beach Rides**, *Tel. 949-4729*. Both are on Grand Cayman.

Houseboating

Live and cruise aboard a 57-foot houseboat from **Cayman Delight Cruises**, Box 277, West Bay, Grand Cayman, British West Indies, *Tel. 345/949-8111, Fax 949-8385*.

Parasailing

Cayman Skyriders at the Holiday Inn and Hyatt Regency, Seven Mile Beach, *Tel. 949-8745*, offers parasailing.

Sailing

Sail to snorkeling, beaches and reefs aboard a 44-foot yacht with **Wet 'n Wild Watersports**, *Tel. 949-9180*. The boat specializes in North Sound, Steven Mile Beach, and Stingray City.

Windsurfing

Rent a board from the **Bic Center**, *Tel. 947-7492* or **Don Foster's Watersports**, *Tel. 800/83-DIVER or 345/945-5132.*

Watersports

Kayak, sail, parasail, or rent a reef runner or glass-bottom boat from **Aqua Delights**, *Tel. 945-4786.*

SHOPPING

There is no duty or sales tax here, and shops spill over with luxury imports from all over the world. West Bay Road along Seven Mile Beach is lined with hotels, most of which have boutiques, and shops. It's pretty much the same merchandise found everywhere in Caribbean duty-frees – Lladro, Waterford, Gucci, Italian leathers and Swiss watches – but these islands are on some cruise ship itineraries that don't provide other chances to get such items.

Our bias, of course, is towards local products that are unique to each island. Caymanian artists have a passion for black coral and in some studios we have seen museum-quality works the size of a hat rack. The beauty and workmanship is unequaled, but with today's environmental concerns about coral, especially black coral, it can be awkward for a travel writer to promote buying them. We like shops such as **Pure Art** on South Church Street, *Tel. 949-9133,* and at the Hyatt Regency; the **Island Art Gallery** in the Anchorage Shopping Center, *Tel. 949-8077*; the **Kennedy Gallery** on Fort Street, *Tel. 949-7093,* featuring watercolors by local artist Robert E. Kennedy; and **Artifacts, Ltd.**, *Tel. 949-2442,* and the **Heritage Craft Shop**, *Tel. 949-7093,* both on the waterfront at George Town.

The **English Shoppe** at the cruise ship landing, *Tel. 949-2457,* has jewelry and watches. On the water, **Sunflower Boutique**, *Tel. 949-4090,* has bouquets of colorful, hand-painted clothing. Also in George Town on Fort Street is the department store-size **Jewelry Centre**, *Tel. 949-0070,* which sells everything from gemstones to caymanite, a brownish pink stone found only in the Caymans. It's tumbled and made into glowing jewelry pieces that make a nice remembrance of this special island.

EXCURSIONS & DAY TRIPS

Aboard the *Rum Point Ferry* you'll go to one of Grand Cayman's best beaches. On the north shore, it is shown on maps as early as 1773. Have a drink in the **Wreck Bay**, an island landmark, or just hang in a hammock and read. The fare is $15; children under age 12 go free. The beach can also be reached by road.

Little Cayman Island has one of the largest breeding colonies of red-footed boobies in the hemisphere and the only breeding colony of frigate birds. The mile-long **Salt Rock Nature Trail** can be walked on Sunday morning with a volunteer naturalist. The **Booby Pond Nature Reserve** is administered by the National Trust, *Tel. 494-8469*. The island's small air field can be reached on **Island Air**, a division of Cayman Airways, *Tel. 345/ 949-2311*.

For less than $100 you can fly to **Cayman Brac** and back with Cayman Airways, *Tel. 345/949-2311*. The island is best known for its bonefishing, deep-sea fishing, and diving on riotously colorful reefs and on a 330-foot freighter that was sunk as an artificial reef. However there's also good land exploring on the 140-foot bluffs with its lighthouse, caves, exotic plants, and bird life including frigate birds, brown boobies, and peregrine falcons. With luck, you'll spot the rare Cayman Brac parrot.

There's a little **museum**, *Tel. 948-2622*, at Stake Bay that has bits and pieces from island history. Let the curator tell you about the hurricane in the 1930s that wiped the island clean of landmarks. "There wasn't a tree, a fence – anything to tell us where our home and land had been," an old-timer told us, still able to remember the surreal shock of it all. Islanders had taken shelter in the caves near the bluff, not realizing that hurricanes come in two parts. When calm returned during the passing of the eye of the storm, many thought it was over, left the safety of the caves, and were killed. The museum has small reminders of the tragedy. Admission is free. It's open Monday to Friday 9am to noon and 1-4pm and on Saturday 9am to noon.

PRACTICAL INFORMATION

Area Code: 345

ATM: at least five ATMs are found in the islands. In Georgetown, an ATM is in the Cayman National Bank, Fort Street and Harbour Drive. Others are found in Industrial Park and on West Bay Road.

Beer: the favored local beer is Stingray.

Business hours: shops are usually open daily except Sunday 9am to 5pm Banks are open 9am to 2:30pm Monday to Thursday and on Friday 9am to 1pm and 2:30-4:30pm

Currency: the Cayman Islands dollar (CI$) breaks down to one hundred cents. It's worth about $1.25 and, while U.S. dollars are accepted almost everywhere, you'll make out better if you use credit cards or CI dollars.

Current: North American-style 110-volt, 60-cycle appliances and plugs are used here.

Dress Code: topless and nude bathing are prohibited by law. The Caymans are dressy; long trousers are worn to dinner and beach wear isn't suitable for shopping or dining rooms. Think "resort chic."

Emergencies: call 911 for police help and 555 for an ambulance. A Learjet on Grand Cayman is available for med-evac service. The hospital on Grand Cayman has a two-person decompression chamber. Medical and dental services in the islands are good; 24-hour prescriptions are available at the hospital and in private pharmacies.

Government: The Caymans are a British crown colony. U.S. consulate services are available on Grand Cayman.

Holidays: banks and most shops are closed New Year's Day, Ash Wednesday, Good Friday, Easter Monday, Discovery Day on May 19, the Queen's Birthday (varies), Constitution Day on July 7, Remembrance Day on November 10, Christmas, and Boxing Day.

Immigration: citizens of the United States and Canada don't need passports to enter the Caymans but a return ticket and proof of citizenship are needed. For proof if you don't have a passport, take a notarized birth certificate plus some government-issue photo identification. A driver's license alone won't do, and voter registration is no longer accepted as proof of citizenship.

Telephones: to access AT&T USA Direct, *Tel. 800/872-2888;* to dial MCI Direct, *Tel. 800/624-1000*; to access U.S. Sprint, *Tel. 800/366-4663*.

Time zone: the Caymans are the same as Eastern Standard time all year.

Tourist information: write Cayman Islands Tourism, *420 Lexington Avenue, Suite 2733, New York NY 10170. Tel. 212/682-5582.* In Canada, write Cayman Islands Tourism, *234 Eglinton Avenue East, Suite 306, Toronto, Ontario M4P 1K5, Tel. (416) 485-1550.* Tourist information desks are found at Owen Roberts International Airport and at the North Terminal cruise ship dock in George Town. The office is at The Pavilion, *Cricket Square, Elgin Avenue, George Town, Tel. 345/949-0623.* Reservations for flights and hotels and requests for information can be made at *Tel. 800/346-3313.*

Weddings: you'll need a non-resident marriage license and a letter from the marriage officer who will officiate. You can get married on the day you arrive. Application for the license, which costs $200, can be obtained from the Chief Secretary's Office, *Room 406, Government Administration Building, George Town, Grand Cayman, British West Indies, Tel. 345/949-8092, Fax 949-5936.* You'll also receive a brochure listing companies that make wedding arrangements. Also required are two witnesses for the ceremony, proof of citizenship, parental approval if under age 18, proof of single status, and either the pink immigration slips you received on entry or proof that you're on a cruise ship.

27. CUBA

Since 1990, tourism has surpassed sugar production as **Cuba's** chief source of income. As of this writing, however, it remains a difficult destination for Americans for many reasons. One is the fear of action by anti-Castro groups in South Florida. Security concerns result in delays of up to six hours in flights from Miami. While legal flights do serve Havana from the United States, most visitors enter from another gateway such as Jamaica and other islands, Toronto or Montreal, or Mexico and other Latin American countries.

Second are the restrictions on American travel by the U.S. government, and the fact that Americans have no consular representation in Cuba. In the event of any difficulties, such as a lost or stolen passport, things get complicated. The U.S. is represented in Havana by the **Swiss Embassy** and by a **Special Interest Section**, Avenida Calzada, *Tel. 33-3551/9.*

Third are human rights concerns over whether one should be patronizing government-owned hotels and restaurants that, only a generation ago, were confiscated from private owners much as Jewish funds and factories were expropriated by the Nazis in the 1930s and '40s. Many tourist hotels, restaurants, and companies once belonged to families who may have been jailed or executed, or who fled with little more than their lives.

Fourth is a controlled press that keeps people in other countries from hearing about travel-related problems (among many other, more widespread problems) that include tourist murders and hotel bombings. They do occur, according to returning travelers.

Lastly are fears over nuclear safety. According to *The Wall Street Journal*, the Juagua Nuclear Power Plant near Cienfuegos does not even meet Chenobyl standards. One of the first steps taken after the reunification of Germany was the dismantling of similar plants in East Germany. Juagua is a problem even for nuclear power proponents. For anti-nuclear forces, it's a nightmare.

Nevertheless, Cuba is one of the Caribbean's most beautiful islands. Tourists are welcome and prices are cheap. It's just a matter of time before it once again becomes a premier playground and a major cruise ship stop. To book a hotel in **Varadero**, Cuba's premier beach resort, try **Havanatur Tour & Travel**, *Tel. 53/66-7154, Fax 66-7026*, or find it in Varadero on the Avenida de la Playa between Calles 36 and 37.

For now, one way that Americans can visit the island with minimum hassle is with a group such as:

• **Center for Cuban Studies**, *124 West 23rd Street, New York NY 10011, Tel. 212/242-0559, fax 242-1937*. The center arranges custom tours for teachers, journalists, and those doing professional research.

• **Conference of North American and Cuban Philosophers and Social Scientists**, *1443 Gorsuch Avenue, Baltimore MD 21218, Tel. 410/243-3118, Fax 235-5325*.

• **Global Exchange**, *2017 Mission Street, Suite 303, San Francisco CA 94110, Tel. 415/255-7296, Fax 415/255-7498*.

• **Caribbean Music & Dance Programs**, *1611 Telegraph Avenue, Suite 808, Oakland CA 94612, Tel. 510/444-7173*.

• **CAMBAS Associations**, *25 W. 43rd Street, Suite 1603, New York NY 10036 and R. Compagna or O. Perez-Medina, Box 5265, Coralville IA 51141, Fax (no Tel.) 319/337-2045*.

• **U.S./Cuba Labor Exchange**, *P.O. Box 39188, Redford MI 48239, Tel. 313/561-8330*. Week-long labor seminar packages for union members depart from Cancun, Mexico.

• **Venceremos Brigade**, *Box 7071, Oakland CA 94601, Tel. 415/267-0606*.

For more information:

A **Cuban Tourist Office** is at *55 Queen Street East, Suite 705, Toronto, Canada M5C 1R6, Tel. 416/362-0700, Fax 362-6799*. In Mexico, contact the **Cuban Tourist Board**, *Insurgentes Sur Numero 421, Complejo Aristos, Edificio B, Local 310, Mexico City 06100 DF, Mexico, Tel. 525/574-9454*.

Cubanacan, a hotel corporation that can provide information but not reservations, is at *372 Bay Street, Suite 1902, Toronto, Ontario, Canada M5H 2W9, Tel. 416/601-0343, Fax 601-0346*. In Mexico, Cubanacan is at *Sonora Number 149-301, Colonia Hipodromo Condes, DF 06140, Mexico*.

Cubana de Aviacion, the national airline, has offices at *4 Place Ville Marie, Suite 405, Montreal, Canada H3B 2E7, Tel. 514/871-1222, Fax 871-1227*. In Mexico, contact *Cubana de Aviacion, Temistocles 246, Colonia Polanco 11550, Mexico DF, Mexico, Tel. 525/255-3776, Fax 525/255-0835*.

Cubana Airlines in Jamaica is at *22 Trafalgar Road, Kingston, Tel. 876/927-7355*.

RUM & COCA COLA

One thing that hasn't changed since the heydays of the Andrews Sisters is Cuba's penchant for "working for the Yankee dollah." Dollars, or **divisas,** *circulate freely. Even if you're coming here from another country, bring U.S. dollars including a good supply of small bills. Credit cards and travelers checks issued by American companies can't be used but U.S. dollar travelers checks issued by non-American banks are accepted. Getting a refund for any checks lost or refused in Cuba can be difficult, so keep good records.*

FOODS OF CUBA

Cuban food has become one of the ethnic staples of the American diet thanks to the talented chefs and restaurateurs who settled in South Florida, so many of the foods you'll encounter in Cuba will need no introduction.

• Ajiaco (meat stew)
• Black Bean Soup
• Green Plantain Soup
• Langosta Enchilada
• Moros y Christianos (Moors and Christians; i.e. black beans and white rice)
• Picadillo (ground beef with raisins and olives)
• Ropa Vieja (beef that is falling-apart tender)

28. THE DOMINICAN REPUBLIC

Christopher Columbus called the land now known as **The Domincan Republic** "the most beautiful island that man has ever seen" when he landed at Hispaniola in 1492. Indigenous people, the Taino Indians who were descended from the Arawaks, had called it Haiti (land of mountains) or Quisqueya, meaning the mother of islands.

Within less than 13 years, the 600,000 Tainos were exterminated in one of the New World's most shameful genocides. In 1997, a site discovered in East National Park is thought with "strong possibility" according to the Associated Press to have been the site of a mass Taino slaughter in 1503 known as the Jaragua Massacre. Exploration of the 150-foot cenote, or sinkhole, continues. Still today, the Spanish of the islanders is studded with Taino words: barbacoa for barbecue, batoa meaning a trough or small tub, coa for a sharp wood rod, iguana, tabaco, yuca, maiz, and conuco, which is a plot of land for cultivations.

Spain settled the large, fertile island early in its explorations, establishing a community at Isabella on 1494. Christopher's brother, Bartholomew Columbus, founded **Santo Domingo** two years later and by 1509, Christopher's son Diego was ruling the island from his uncle's capital city. Sir Francis Drake sacked the city in 1596; France moved in very early and won the island in a treaty in 1697 only to lose it again to Spain in 1861.

The second republic was declared in 1865 after Spain lost the island once again, but its affairs were so turbulent that the United States occupied the Dominican Republic from 1916-1924. Dictator Rafael Trujillo ruled with an iron hand from 1924 until he was assassinated in 1961. His successor, Juan Bosch, was rousted in 1963 and a civil war in 1965 was broken up by another American intervention and brief occupation. Still today, visitors worry about civil strife, and crime can be a

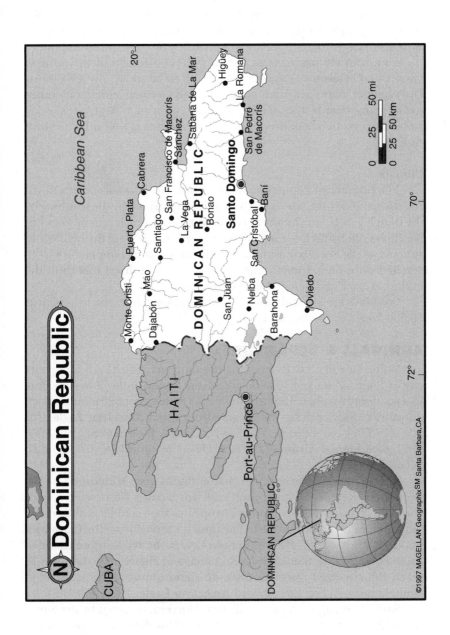

N

Dominican Republic

CUBA

Caribbean Sea

HAITI

Port-au-Prince

DOMINICAN REPUBLIC

20°

Monte Cristi
Dajabón
Mao
Puerto Plata
Cabrera
Santiago
San Francisco de Macoris
Sánchez
Sabana de La Mar
Higüey
La Romana
San Pedro de Macoris

DOMINICAN REPUBLIC

La Vega
Bonao
Santo Domingo
San Juan
San Cristóbal
Baní
Neiba
Barahona
Oviedo

70°
72°

0   25   50 mi
0   25   50 km

©1997 MAGELLAN GeographixSM Santa Barbara,CA

problem anywhere, but tourist hotels have their own security forces and can be considered safe.

The shouting and gesturing seen on the streets sometimes may make visitors edgy, yet it's part of the national culture, so don't panic. What appears to be a violent uprising will probably be over within an hour.

American visitors account for only about a fourth of the tourism impact here. German is as likely as English to be spoken by a waiter or housekeeper. Signs are often in Spanish and German and, in deference to Germans, beer is available from breakfast through bedtime. Weekly arrivals stream in from Europe and South America as well as from North America.

Climate

The Dominican Republic may occasionally feel the tail end of a North American cold front, which will be windy but warmed by the sunshine by the time it gets here. The north coast has twice as much rain in winter as the capital. In Santo Domingo, daytime highs range from the high 90s in summer to the low 90s in winter. The lowest recorded temperature is 59, reached once on a January night. February is the driest month in the capital, August and September the wettest.

Lowlands are hot and humid; the mountains, which rise to as high as 10,000 feet, can be wet and cold.

ARRIVALS & DEPARTURES

Visitors are likely to fly into **La Union Airport**, which is 13 kilometers east of Puerta Plata and 10 kilometers from Sosua, or into **Las Americas International Airport** in Santo Domingo, which is about 20 minutes from downtown. Service is by **American Airlines** and **American Eagle**, *Tel. 800/433-7300;* **Air Canada**, *Tel. 776-3000;* **APA International**, *800/693-0007;* **Continental Airlines**, *Tel. 800/231-0856;* and **TWA**, *Tel. 800/221-2000.*

TransGlobal Tours operates charter flights from Minneapolis to the Dominican Republic. Watch your local travel pages for news of special charters. A major destination for Europeans, the republic is also served by a number of major European lines and it's served from the Caribbean by **ALM**, *Tel. 809/687-4569.* Other airports in the republic are found at Samana, Barahona, Santiago, La Romana, and Higüey. The best way to reach the city-sized resort at **Casa de Campo** near La Romana is to connect through San Juan aboard **American Eagle**, *Tel. 800/443-7300.*

Santo Domingo's domestic airport, **Herrera**, is served by **Air Santo Domingo**, *Tel. 809/683-8020,* which flies to all the domestic airports listed above.

Try to take only as much luggage that you can manage yourself. Thievery is a problem, so try to keep your possessions out of the hands of baggage handlers and porters.

Avoid inter-island flights on domestic airlines. According to the U.S. State Department, civil aviation in the Dominican Republic doesn't meet international safety standards and its air services are barred from American airports. See sidebar below.

FLYING CAN BE HAZARDOUS TO YOUR HEALTH

*At press time, the United States State Department is still standing by its report of January 1993, in which the Federal Aviation Administration found the **Dominican Republic Civil Aviation Authority** not in compliance with international aviation safety standards. Operations to the United States by Dominican air carriers are not permitted unless they arrange to have their flights conducted by a carrier from a country that meets these standards. American military personnel are not permitted to use carriers from the D.R. for official business except in extenuating circumstances. Travelers can contact the U.S. Department of Transportation, Tel. 800/322-7873, for more information.*

ORIENTATION

The eastern side of the island of **Hispaniola**, whose western third is the Republic of Haiti, The Dominican Republic is bordered on the north by the Atlantic Ocean and on the south by the Caribbean Sea. Its chief city is **Santo Domingo**; other major settlements include **Santiago** in the center of the island north of the spine of mountains, **La Romana** and the sprawling Casa de Campo resort in the southeast, **Puerta Plata** with its fabulous beach resorts on the Atlantic, **Punta Cana** and the **Playa Bravaro** in the east, and **Samana**, a peninsula that juts grandly into the Atlantic on the northeast coast.

Chief routes in the Dominican Republic include:

From Santo Domingo, the **Carretera Duarte** heads north to Santiago then through the Cibao Valley and towards Puerto Plata. It continues northeast via Esperanza, Laguna Salada, and Villa Vasquez to Monte Cristi. Leaving Santo Domingo, it's a toll road; coming back, it's not. Running west from the city, the **Carretera Sanchez** goes to San Cristobál, Bani, and Azua to Barahona and ends at Lago Enriquillo. Going east from the city is the **Carretera Las Americas**, where you'll hit a toll booth just before reaching the airport. The road then goes to Boca Chica to Juan Dolion, San Pedro de Macoris, La Romana, and Altos de Chavón. "Roads" continue east, but they are heavy going.

Driving in Santo Domingo is no fun. There is no "ring road" bypass and traffic is heavy. However, the Colonial Zone is infinitely walkable. You can wander from square to square, old street to old church, plaza to park. Basically, the zone is the southeasternmost square of streets on the west side of the Ozama River where it meets the Caribbean Sea.

SPEAKING DOMINICAN-ESE

Like most Spanish-speaking countries, the Dominican Republic has its own slang. If you ask the distance to any point and are told "alli mismo," which means "just over there," you could be talking eight kilometers or more. A little bit is "un chin" and even less is "un chin chin." A large amount is a "rhumba." Locals rarely call Santo Domingo by name. It is "the capital."

GETTING AROUND THE DOMINICAN REPUBLIC

Except for the highways between major cities, roads in the Dominican Republic are so awful that you can't count on getting above about 25 miles per hour. If you rent a car, check it over carefully to make sure everything works, and that the spare tire is sound and fully inflated. You'll probably need it. Report any damage and have it noted on your receipt or you could be charged for it when returning the car.

The advantage to hiring a car from one of the well-known North American chains is that you can make reservations from home via a toll-free number and, when you're rushing to turn it in at the airport before you leave, you're less likely to be given a fast shuffle if there are any disputes. To get a car, you must be at least 25 years old and have a credit card. Driving is on the right. Road blocks are common, so don't over-react. Sometimes police will just wave you through but at other times you'll have to show your papers and make a contribution (a dollar or two) to the cop's favorite charity. It's just part of the local scene, so take it in stride.

Reservations for **Hertz** can be made in the U.S. through *Tel. 800/654-3030;* in Santo Domingo, *Tel. 221-5333.* **Thrifty's** reservations center is *Tel. 800/367-2277* in the U.S. and Canada, or locally *Tel. 686-0133.* **Budget Car and Truck Rental** can be reached at *Tel. 567-0173* or toll-free in the U.S. and Canada, *Tel. 800/527-0700.*

Bus service runs throughout the republic, ranging from utilitarian buses and cramped vans known as *guaguas,* to air conditioned coaches with attendants and bar service. Guaguas that make fewer stops are called ex*presos* and cost a bit more. Both are a trip, literally and figuratively, for visitors who want a taste of the real Dominicana. Publicos are taxies that take several passengers, stopping where each wants to get out. They're best hailed at a hotel or in the public squares or, if you can find a working telephone, they can be called. One company with 24-hour service island-wide is **Taxi Anacaona**, *Tel. 530-4800* or *Tel. 534-1298.*

Negotiate taxi fares in advance and ask to see the driver's ID. Meters aren't used here and heaven help the tourist who trusts to luck at the end of the ride. Private drivers also offer taxi service; these cars don't carry the word publico and are best avoided. The minimum rate for a taxi is RD$45, with an hourly rate of RD$100 but a recent traveler told me he paid a driver $100 for an entire day, during which he also took the driver to lunch. The driver indicated he would have done it for $60 (US).

One 24-hour taxi service, **Taxi Anacoana**, publishes its taxi rates as RD$45 minimum plus RD$5 per kilometer or RD$100 per hour. Its minibus rates are RD$65 minimum plus $7 per kilometer or RD$155 per hour.

Agree on a price in advance too if you're hopping on a motorcycle taxi. These *motoconchos* take passengers and are fast and agile in heavy traffic and bad roads, but they often take gringos for a ride in more ways than one. Picture yourself without a helmet, astraddle a speeding scooter behind a stranger, and you get the picture.

Scheduled **Caribe Tours** buses run from the terminal at Avenida 27 de Febrero at the corner of Calle Leopoldo Navarro to Barahana, Bonao, Cabrera, Jarabacoa, La Vega, Monte Cristi, Nagua, Puerto Plata, Samana, Sanchez, San Francisco de Macoris, Santiago, and Sosua. Fares range from 10-40 pesos. Small, privately owned guaguas can also be found around the republic; fares are only a few pesos.

WHERE TO STAY

You'll have to pay a government tax of 11 percent and a 10 percent service charge in lieu of gratuities. Rates shown are for a double room in high season. Summer rates may be less. If these rates look like a bargain, you're right. Few places in the Caribbean offer so much value for the money.

Unless stated otherwise, rates are quoted in U.S. dollars and credit cards are accepted. Note that hotels usually quote for two people in a double room, but all-inclusives often quote per person.

SANTO DOMINGO & VICINITY
Expensive

CASA DE CAMPO, *La Romana. Tel. 800/877-3643 or 305/856-5405. Casa de Campo (La Romana) airport is two miles from the 450-unit resort. Rates start at $125. Ask about the Kids Free program in summer. Hotel rooms and villas and homes up to four bedrooms are available. Ask about meal plans and packages.*

Picture a gated, 7,000-acre city that has been set aside as a playground exclusively for tourists. Its golf courses including "Teeth of the Dog" and the shorter "Links" are internationally famous, one of the resort's chief drawing cards. The many gates and guards are reassuring to travelers who have had doubts about staying in the Dominican Republic. On the down side they may discourage you from venturing outside the compound, which would rob you of a chance to discover one of the Caribbean's richest and most colorful cultures. If all you want, however, is a kick-back golf vacation in the sunshine, this place has splash and class at about half what the same luxuries would cost on St. Thomas or Mustique.

Accommodations are luxuriously furnished by Oscar de la Renta, a former tenant. If you book a house or villa, it comes with a maid/cook and perhaps other staff. Eat in, or venture out to the resort's French, Italian, Mexican, and pizza restaurants. Dance the merengue in the disco, play tennis or polo, dare the golf courses, take a tour to Santo Domingo (about $50), take a snorkeling trip to Catalina Island, or hire a driver for the day to explore the island. Children's activities provide a pleasant way for kids of all nationalities to play together. Planned activities for adults include tennis matches, donkey polo, weekly theme parties, and talent shows.

Part of the resort is Altos de Chavón in the heights overlooking the Chavon river. It's a fairytale town with cobblestone "streets," tiled roofs, an archaeological museum, a 5,000-seat amphitheater featuring internationally known stars, plus shops, restaurants, and galleries galore, all created in modern times to look like a village that is centuries old.

EL EMBAJADOR HOTEL, *Avenue Sarasota 65, Santo Domingo. Tel. 809/221-2131 or, in the U.S. Tel. 800/463-6902. Rates at this 198-room hotel start at $115 and, on the executive floor, at $130 including continental breakfast. It's about 20 minutes from Las Americas Airport, three miles from the city center.*

Your air conditioned room will be grandly furnished in French provincial pieces, setting a note of elegance that remembers the days when the military head of state, Trujillo, had his own penthouse here. Rooms have television, telephone, and mini-bar. Dine in the hotel's fine restaurants, one Asian and the other a supper club. Drink and dance in the lounge, play tennis, swim in the pool, or soak in the whirlpool before or after your massage. If you like a city high-rise hotel with a big casino, this one has it all.

HOTEL V CENTENARIO INTER-CONTINENTAL SANTO DOMINGO, *Avenue George Washington 218, mailing address Box 2890, Santo Domingo. Tel. 809/221-0000, toll-free 800/327-0200. Rates at this 200-room, 29-suite hotel start at $230. It's a ride of about 25 minutes from the Santo Domingo airport.*

Overlooking the Caribbean in the heart of Santo Domingo, this is one of the finest hotels in the Caribbean. Amenities include 24-hour room service, laundry and valet service, a casino, and a choice of restaurants and bars. Rooms have color cable television with 35 channels, marble bathroom with hair dryer, dual-line dial telephone, mini-bar, safe, radio, and a connection for your modem. Parking is underground. The complex offers underground parking, a swimming pool with outdoor whirlpool, shops, a floodlit tennis court, air conditioned square courts, massage and workout facilities, and a paddle tennis court.

Selected as one of my Best Places to Stay; see Chapter 13 for more details.

HOTEL SANTO DOMINGO, Independencia Avenue at Abraham Lincoln, Santo Domingo. *Tel. 809/221-1511, Fax 535-4050. Rates at this 215-room hotel start at $120. On the executive floor, continental breakfast is included. Meal plans that include dinner are available. It's two miles from the Colonial Zone.*

This swank, quietly elegant hotel set among acres of manicured greenbelt is well located downtown near University City, shopping and restaurants. Rooms have mini-bar, television, and telephone. Rooms on the executive floor have balconies overlooking the sea; standard rooms may overlook the Caribbean or the gardens with their palms, and Valencia orange trees. Choose between the hotel's two gourmet restaurants, or eat poolside at Las Brisas. Have a drink before or after in the popular piano bar. The hotel also has tennis courts, a big swimming pool, room service, and a sauna. Parking is free for guests.

SHERATON SANTO DOMINGO HOTEL & CASINO, *365 George Washington Avenue, Santo Domingo, mail address P.O. Box 8326. Tel. 809/221-6666, Fax 687-8150. Rates start at $100. The hotel is about 30 minutes from Las Americas International Airport and five minutes from the historic zone.*

Combine business with pleasure at a first class business hotel, or just come for the fun of staying in the heart of town near the Colonial Zone, entertainment, and shopping. The hotel, which overlooks the sea, has a swimming pool, lighted tennis courts, health club and sauna, three restaurants, 24-hour room service, and a disco. Commodious rooms with balconies have individual temperature control, coffee maker, hair dryer, television, cable television, and a mini-bar.

RENAISSANCE JARAGUA HOTEL & CASINO, *Avenue George Washington 367, Santo Domingo. Tel. 809/221-2222, Fax 686-0528, toll-free* *in the U.S. and Canada Tel. 800/228-9898. Rates at this 300-room hotel start at $180; suites are from $420. Meal plans are available. It's downtown, about 20 minutes from Las Americas Airport.*

Atlantic City-on-the-Caribbean describes this glitzy casino hotel with its big 1,000-seat cabaret and flashy casino. All you need is right here in a 14-acre, waterfront hotel: shops, restaurants ranging from gourmet to deli, 24-hour room service, bars indoors and out, entertainment, a beauty salon, disco, gaming, a swimming pool with a dozen private cabanas, a good fitness center, floodlit tennis courts, swimming pool, and a whirlpool. Rooms are air conditioned and have telephone, mini-bar, and cable television. Suites are downright palatial. The deluxe floors have 24-hour food and butler room service. Parking is free.

Moderate

BARCELONA GRAN HOTEL LINA & CASINO, *Avenue Maximo Gómez at Avenue 29 de Febrero, Santo Domingo. Tel. 809/563-5000, Fax 686-5521, toll-free 800/942-2461. Rates at this 217-room hotel start at $85. On the Executive Floor, breakfast is included. Located in the heart of city shopping and entertainments, it's 20 minutes from Las Americas Airport.*

The hotel is an attractive high-rise but its best feature is that it's the home of the renowned Lina Restaurant, one of the city's dining icons. Rooms have telephone, television, room service, and a small refrigerator. The decor reminds us of the 1930s, sober and overstuffed for maximum comfort and hominess. Sea-view rooms are available. The hotel has a swimming pool, whirlpool, modern workout facilities, shops, and a coffee shop in addition to the Lina. It has tennis courts and a casino; golf can be arranged. Parking is free.

CONTINENTAL, *Avenue Maximo Gómez 16, Santo Domingo. Tel. 809/688-1840, Fax 687-8397. Rates at this 100-room hotel start at $75. It's a mile from the Colonial Zone.*

Catering to business travelers is this air conditioned hotel with a coffee shop, swimming pool, free parking, and a bar with live entertainment. Rooms have telephone, television, and room service. If you're here on business, make use of the (mostly Spanish language) secretarial services.

ESTRELLA DEL MAR, *Cabarete. Tel. 809/571-0808, Fax 571-0904, U.S. 800/472-3985. Toll-free in the Republic. Tel. 1-200-2672. Rates at this 75-room resort start at $85 per person, double occupancy. Children pay $40. The resort is 20 minutes from the airport, where you'll be met.*

Every room has its own balcony with a view of the gardens or the beach and sea. Guest rooms, which are decorated in soft plaids and solids to complement them, have two double beds, telephone, television, a bathroom with shower, air conditioning, and a ceiling fan. This coast is famous for its windsurfing tournaments, so come here to hone your skills on boards provided by the resort, which can also provide lessons in windsurfing, sailing, or scuba. There's a big pool in the center of the cluster of buildings that form the resort; dining is buffet style. Activities go on all day from morning jogs and aerobics to bonfires on the beach. **RENAISSANCE CAPELLA BEACH RESORT**, *San Pedro de Macoris, mailing address P.O. Box 4750, Santa Domingo. Tel. 809/526-1080 or 800/ HOTELS-1, Fax 809/686-0503. Rooms at this 283-unit resort start at $150. Ask about meal plans, which are a good value. The resort is 45 miles east of Santo Domingo and 25 miles, or a $25 taxi ride, from Las Americas airport. Bus service is $1.*

Swim off the beach or in one of the two pools with their swim-up bars and waterfalls. Play tennis day or night, billiards, or board games in the game room. Rent a bicycle or motor bike, use the fitness center, sail or snorkel, and take your pick of three restaurants. The children's program operates all year. Beautifully furnished rooms reflect the upscale tone of this popular vacation spa for outsiders and Dominicans alike. Air conditioned rooms have telephone, television, and room service. Dine in the restaurant or coffee shop, swim in the pool or beach, plan tennis or golf, have a sauna, and enjoy live music with dancing in the lounge. Parking is free.

Budget

CASA BONITA, *Kilometer 16, Carretera de la costa, Barahona. Tel. 809/ 696-0215, Fax 223-4805. Domestic airlines and charters go into Barahona, or rent a car in Santo Domingo for the 104-kilometer drive to this small city in southwest Dominican Republic. Rates at the 12-room hotel are from $60 including breakfast and dinner.*

The female chief of the Tainos, Anacoana, ruled this humid coastal area of the island where shallow waters teem with reef fish. Pirate treasures have been found along these shores, but today's coin is the area's remoteness from the back-to-back resorts that have been built along Boca Chica in the south, Playa Bavaro in the east, Samana, and the north coast at Puerto Plata. The little Casa offers air conditioned rooms, a pool, free parking, and occasional musical entertainments plus hearty, healthful, very Dominican meals morning and evening. Your fellow guests are likely to be Dominicans.

HISPANIOLA HOTEL CASINO, *165 Independencia, Santo Domingo. Tel. 221-1511, Fax 535-4050. Rates at this 265-room hotel start at $65 double including meals. It's across the street from the Hotel Santo Domingo (see above), where guests can use the facilities.*

The address is prestigious yet the price is a pittance for an air conditioned room with telephone and television. Young travelers like the hotel for its lively disco, Italian gourmet dining, the swimming pool and sauna, tennis courts, and live entertainment. The romantic Hispaniola Bar is a popular rendezvous. Tennis and a casino are at the hotel across the street.

HOTEL & CASINO NACO, *Tiradentes 22, Santo Domingo. Tel. 809/ 562-3100, Fax 544-0957. Rates at this 107-room hotel start at $45. It's a 25-minute ride from Las Americas Airport.*

A good budget choice situated between the waterfront and the botanical gardens, this medium-size hotel has the feel of a small, European city hotel. It is gritty and plain-jane, but it's handy for business appointments, dining, shopping and sightseeing. Air conditioned rooms have telephone and television. The hotel has a swimming pool, coffee shop, restaurant, room service, a casino, sauna, a lounge with live entertainment, and free parking. Secretarial services are available.

NAPOLITANO HOTEL & CASINO, *George Washington 101, Santo Domingo. Tel. 809/687-1131m fax 687-6814. Rates at this 72-room hotel start at $55. It overlooks the Caribbean, just footsteps from the Colonial Zone.*

All rooms overlook the sea so, if you want to stay in the city, you can't get a much better deal. Rooms are air conditioned and have room service, telephone, and television. The hotel has a restaurant, coffee shop, disco, casino, swimming pool and free parking.

PUERTO PLATA AREA
Expensive

JACK TAR VILLAGE BEACH RESORT & CASINO, *Carretera Luperón Kilometer 5.5, Playa Dorada, mailing address Box 268, Puerto Plata. Tel. U.S. 214/987-4909 or 800/999-9182. Locally, dial 809/320-3800. Rates at this 300-room, all-inclusive resort start at $200. Suites have up to four bedrooms.*

The Jack Tar people are old pros at the all-inclusive resort business and they have fine-tuned this one until it hums. Swim in an adults-only pool or play with the family in the activities pool. The resort caters equally to couples, singles, honeymooners and families with children ages 3-12, with activities for all ages. For children younger than age 3, babysitting is available at $5 an hour. Ride horseback, take scuba lessons, play tennis or an 18-hole round of golf, then dine and disco the evening away or take your chances in the large, action-packed casino.

Accommodations are in pleasant villas clustered around the tennis courts, restaurants, and bars. Rooms, which have maid service twice a day, are done in whites and terracottas, fortified with fruity, tropical colors. Each unit has a private balcony or patio, bath with shower and tub, and air conditioning. Deluxe rooms have coffee maker, hair dryer, shoe shine service, and remote control television. For a few dollars extra, rent the key that allows you to use the room safe. Lounge on your secluded patio and read, or plug into an activities schedule that lists tennis including group lessons, snorkeling, scuba lessons, shuffleboard, volleyball, water aerobics, water sports, and play on an 18-golf Robert Trent Jones-design golf course. Greens fees are free, but a caddy is mandatory at a charge of about $16. The hotel can arrange an all-day tour of the Cibao Valley, Samana, or Santo Domingo, or half-day tours of Puerta Plata or Sosua Beach, with glass-bottom boats and snorkeling.

PARADISE BEACH CLUB & CASINO, *Playa Dorada. Tel. 809/562-7475, Fax 566-2436, U.S. 800/472-3985. Rates at this 436-room resort start at $130 per person all-inclusive. It's ten miles from the Puerto Plata airport.*

There isn't another cent to be paid after you reach the airport because you'll be transferred to the resort and wined and dined until you're put back on the plane. Two- and three-story white buildings with steeply peaked roofs cluster around the seaside and a huge pool three miles from Puerto Plata village. Choose a standard room, super room or a suite with balcony overlooking the water. Rooms are air conditioned and have telephone, safe, cable television, telephone, and full bath. We like the top floors, where rooms have peaked ceilings and look out through white shutters to trees and gardens. The bed is skirted in white and spread with a pink and blue floral to match the draperies. Join in the non-stop activities, or find a place to yourself.

The hotel offers buffet dining in Hibiscus, grilled specialties in Eden's, or Italian gourmet dining in Michelangelo. Swim at the beach club or in the pool. Have your hair done, play tennis, ride horseback, use the bicycles, join in an aerobics class, rent a scooter, shop, or walk to the 18-hole championship golf course. All activities, drinks, meals, taxes, and tips are included, although you'll pay the caddy at golf. Then spend the evening in the casino or dancing in the Crazy Moon disco.

Moderate

CLUB TROPICANA, *Sosua. Tel. (718) 726-5482, Fax 726-7528. Doubles are $120 all inclusive for stays of five nights or more. Airport transfers are included.*

In the heart of Sosua's "millionaire row" you'll find this suites hotel with king or queen-size beds, air conditioning, and cable television. Swim off the resort's private beach or take the free hourly shuttle to Sosua for the main beach or shopping. Scuba lessons are offered in the resort's pool; snorkel equipment is provided. Children ages 2-11 pay half price; younger children are free. Use of the hotel safe and airport transfers are extra for shorter stays.

The resort offers a waterfall and mountain tour that includes jeep, bus, and horseback transpiration, lunch, and drinks for $160 per person.

Or, take the paddling excursion on the Rio Yaque dell Norte. It's $170 per person including transportation, lunch, and drinks. Combine all three packages listed above and make a week-long trip and you'll get an additional two days in the mountain town of Jarabacoa with ranch accommodations, horseback rides, a paddling lesson, river running, meals, and unlimited drinks.

Budget

CLUB SPA LA MANSION, *San Juan de las Matas, Santiago. Tel. 809/688-3390, Fax 524-5798. Rates at this 270-room resort start at $68 all-inclusive. Three-room cottages are also available. The hotel is an hour south of Puerto Plata or a 100-mile drive from Las Americas International Airport..*

You're in the heart of the country's tobacco-growing region and the island's largest concentration of cigarette and cigar factories. It's far from the beach, so you are more likely to be a part of the real Dominican Republic, vacationing with locals. business travelers, and with outsiders who shun the beaten path. Air conditioned rooms have telephone and television. The hotel has a coffee shop, restaurant, swimming pool, tennis courts, and a sauna. Babysitting is available; parking is free.

HEAVENS, *Playa Dorada, Puerto Plata. Tel. 809/320-5250, Fax 320-4733; U.S. 800/835-7697. Rates at this 150-room resort start at $115 per person, double occupancy, all-inclusive. Airport transfers are included.*

A cluster of three-story white stucco buildings with red roofs are saved from looking boxy by a sort of cut-out in the top floor that brings sunshine into interior rooms. All rooms have air conditioning, safe, cable television, telephone and a full bath; suites have two double beds, balcony and a separate living area. Parking is outside your unit, motel-style. Popular with a nice mix of Europeans, Canadians, and Americans, the resort is on a sand beach shaded with chickee huts and dotted with sunfish sailboats. They and all the other watersports equipment are yours to use free.

Dine in a choice of restaurants, drink in the Sunset or the Sunrise, then dance the night away in the disco. Rent a scooter to go shopping, or walk to the 18-hole championship golf course. Work out in the well-equipped gym, then have a sauna or massage. Babysitting can be arranged.

PUERTO PLATA BEACH RESORT & CASINO, *Playa Dorado. Tel. 809/562-7475, Fax 566-2436, U.S. and Canada 800/472-3985. Rates at this 216-room resort start at $105 all inclusive. Fly into Puerto Plata.*

Another of the string of resorts that line this gorgeous Atlantic beach, this popular spot offers so much for the money that guests can overlook a few scratches and dents in the decor. Rooms are pleasant enough, opening onto sea or garden views; buildings have touches of Victorian trim. Doubles have one double bed; suites have two double beds, a balcony and a separate sitting area. Rooms are air conditioned and have a full bath with tub and shower, safe, cable television, and telephone.

Activities buzz day and night, so you can join in the games, aerobics, and group fun or just go off on your own to kayak, sail, ride horseback, play golf on Playa Dorada's 18-hole Robert Trent Jones course, or shop the boutiques. Dining is from the menu in Michelangelo or buffet style in La Chichigua. Hang out around the pool to meet people from all over the world, or sit in the breezes in the beachside gazebo to catch up on your reading. The resort has tennis courts, massage, a beauty shop, scooter rental, a bank, babysitters on call, a casino, and lots of great entertainment with live music and dancing.

PUERTO PLATA VILLAGE, *Playa Dorada. Tel. 809/320-4012, Fax 320-5113. Rates at this 282-room resort start at $95 per person, all-inclusive. Fly into Puerto Plata, where you'll be met and transferred to the resort.*

Walk up the grand front steps of what looks like a grand plantation mansion and onto the veranda of this Creole village along the famous sands of northern Dominicana. You'll be met at the airport, served a cocktail on check-in, and hosted to every meal and activity including drinking and cigarettes, all on the house. Ride horseback, play tennis, sail, windsurf, snorkel, take a scuba clinic, swim in the pool with its own bar or splash with the children in the kiddy pool. The resort adjoins the region's 18-hole golf course; a free shuttle runs to the Playa Dorado Beach for casino play. Shows, good times, dancing to live tunes, and much more make this one of the Caribbean's best buys.

SOSUA BY THE SEA, *Sosua. Tel. 800/531-7043 or write Sosua by the Sea, Box 02-5548, Miami FL 33102. Rates at this 81-room hotel are $75 including breakfast and dinner. The hotel is 20 minutes, or an $8 taxi ride, from the airport at Puerto Plata.*

Accommodations are in a studio or one-bedroom apartment in a modern, beachfront hotel with air conditioning, satellite television, wet bar, telephone, and in-room safe. The four-story hotel curves around the pool in jaunty angles that avoid a boxy look and give each balcony or patio more privacy than if they were all in a row. The resort has its own dining room with French cuisine, a casual restaurant serving barbecue and a breakfast buffet, a lounge with live music for dancing. It also has a beauty salon, massage, gift shops, and a big, curvy pool with a separate whirlpool.

WHERE TO EAT

The national dish of the Dominican Republic is la bandera (the ensign or flag), a plate of white rice, red beans, stewed meat, salad, and fried plantains. When in doubt about other foods, order la bandera and you can usually be sure it's a good meal at a good price. The traditional

Spanish stew, *sancocho*, is made in many different ways here, depending on the region. *Sancocho prieto*, for example, is made with seven meats. *Locrio* is the local paella, made with rice, saffron, and whatever else the cook has on hand.

Try fish in coconut milk, goat dishes such as *azua* or *Montecristi*, crab dishes, Johnny cakes (*yaniqueques*), and *mangu*, a puree of green plaintain that's recommended for traveler's diarrhea. It's on the breakfast menu at most hotels. *Casabe* (casava bread) and *catabias* (manioc fitters stuffed with meat) are Taino traditions still enjoyed to this day.

SANTO DOMINGO
Expensive
ANTOINE, *in the Hotel Santo Dominto, Avenida George Washington 361. Tel. 221-6666. Dishes are priced $8 to $25. It's open for lunch and dinner weekdays and for dinner only Saturday and Sunday. Reservations are urged.*

Dressy and swank, this hotel restaurant is also a favorite celebration spot for local birthdays and anniversaries. The food ranges from local favorites such as the fresh fish and lobster to Swiss-French classics and international tastes from Spain, the Mediterranean, and steaks that would please any British Beefeater. Have the snapper in a tomato and herb sauce, tournedos you can cut with a fork, or calamari in an assertive garlic sauce. Before or after dinner, have a leisurely drink at Yarey's Lounge, the piano bar.

CHEZ PIERRE, *in the Hotel V Centenario, Avenue George Washington 218. Tel. 221-0000. Plan to spend $40 to $50 for dinner. The restaurant is open 6pm to midnight; reservations are suggested.*

Have a drink first in the Piazza bar, a popular meeting place for business persons after work. Go easy on the tapas, though, to save yourself for perfectly prepared French classics such as beef burgundy, coq au vin, rack of lamb with fresh herbs, or filet mignon accompanied by just the right wine, music, and attentive, unrushed service.

FIGARO, *in the Jaragua Renaissance Hotel, Avenue George Washington 367, Santo Domingo. Tel. 809/221-2222. It's open daily except Monday 6:30pm to midnight. Dishes are priced $6 to $29. Reservations are recommended.*

Relax in an Italian bistro hung with trussed cheeses and sausages and fragrant with tempting smells. Watch chefs at work in the shining, open kitchen while they work magic with steaks, pastas, prosciutto with fresh mozzarella, lobster Fra Diavolo, fresh fish tossed with pasta al dente, and veal Parmigiana. End the meal with espresso and tiramisu or one of the tangy ices.

VESUVIO, *Avenida George Washington 521. Tel. 689-2141. Main dishes are priced $8 to $25. Hours are daily 11am to midnight. Reservations aren't accepted. Gentlemen wear jackets.*

The Italian family who have operated Vesuvio since the 1950s have entrenched themselves in local culinary history. The restaurant is now serving its second and third generations of grateful Santo Dominicans and its appeal hasn't faded. Start with one of the homemade soups and take your time because every dish is made from scratch and to order.

The seafood, with its Mediterranean savors and sauces, is always a safe bet. Order the sampler platter to get a taste of everything that came in on today's boats. There's also squid, veal scaloppini, pasta in vodka sauce, freshwater crayfish afloat in garlic butter, seviche, or a carpaccio. The dessert menu stars rum cake soaked in local rum or the popular classic Tres Leches, a cake in cream.

Moderate

LA CANASTA, *in the Hotel Santo Dominto, Avenida George Washington 361. Tel. 221-6666. Dishes are priced $6 to $18. It's open for breakfast, lunch, and dinner. Dinner reservations are suggested.*

Dive into an authentic Dominican meal here, which might be the la bandera classic with its attraction arrangement of rice, red beans, plantain, salad, and meat stewed until it's falling apart. Locrio, the local paella may be on the menu, or have the sancocho, a native stew. Fresh fish is a favorite, and at lunch there's a nice choice of sandwiches, soups, stews, and salads. The hotel is convenient for tourists but you'll see everyone here from greenhorn touristas to Dominicans who are in the city on a shopping trip. After dinner, check out the casino or the Omni Disco.

LAS CARAS, *in the Hotel V Centenario, Avenue George Washington 218. Tel. 221-0000. Plan to spend $25 for dinner. Underground parking is available. The restaurant is open 7pm to 11pm; reservations aren't necessary.*

Stop at the lobby bar in this magnificent hotel for a drink, then feast on a real Dominican buffet in this informal restaurant. Eat all you care to from tables loaded with salads, seafood dishes hot and cold, vegetables, breads, meats and desserts.

LINA, *in the Barcelo Gran Hotel Lina, Avenue Maximo Gómez at 27 de Febrero. Tel. 563-5000. Main dishes are priced $8 to $28. It's open daily for lunch and dinner. Reservations are essential; gentlemen wear jackets.*

The restaurant carries the legacy of Lina Aguado, who was the personal chef of the dictator Trujillo. She later opened a restaurant (not this one), but her cooks did learn her methods and recipes. That brings us to today's succulent paella Valenciana and fresh snapper in a secret sauce of tomatoes and herbs. Wonderful snips of herbs and such exotic ingredients as Pernod, Roquefort, almonds, and lime zest blend seamlessly into meats, poultry, casseroles, and fresh seafood dishes. The setting is regal, with fine china, original art works, mirrors and a pianist playing semi-classics. Your fellow diners are likely to be wealthy locals, so the night calls for dressy outfits and your best bangles.

PAPPALA PASTA, *Doctor Baez 23. Tel. 682-4397. Dishes are priced $8 to $25. Jackets are required. It's open daily except Monday for dinner. Reservations are suggested.*

It's not far from government offices so this Italian restaurant attracts top politicos as well as in-the-know travelers. Dining rooms are small, giving a cozy feeling to your table or booth while you talk serious business or romance. Typical of a good business restaurant, the service is unhurried, giving you plenty of time to savor each course and the right wines to go with it. Leaded glass lamp shades, glowing woods, and beveled glass give a rich look to rooms that are decorated with modern art.

An Italian feast starts with a choice of appetizers followed by home-made pastas including an outstanding seafood pasta and pestos like Mama used to make. Fresh fish is dusted with flour, fried briefly in butter, and spritzed with lemon juice, or have the fish sauced in a tomato and pepper sauce flavored with garlic, olives, and capers. Carnivores will like the veal dishes or the filet mignon in mushroom sauce with a splash of brandy.

Budget

Two million Santo Dominicans, much like New Yorkers who like to grab a meal on the run, often stop at a street-side cart or hole in the wall for a hot sandwich or a shot glass-size cup of hot, strong Dominican espresso. You can get a lot for the equivalent of $2. As long as it's cooked and hot, we'll go for it but we'd hold the chopped tomatoes, raw onions, or fruit.

THE DELI, in the Jaragua Renaissance Hotel, Avenue George Washington 367, Santo Domingo. *Tel. 809/221-2222, is open 24 hours a day. Selections are priced $3 to $10.*

Eat in, or order something to take out for a beach picnic, a long drive, or just to eat in your room after a hard day. Order the usual deli fare from a menu of generous sandwiches and salads, a grilled burger, or a local meat patty with a bottled drink or a coffee to go. At breakfast time there's a choice of sweet buns.

PIZZA HUT, *Tel. 221-0088 for delivery to your hotel room.*

All the usual favorites are here and, if you can speak Spanish, try for some local specialties that aren't seen on North American menus.

PLAZA CRIOLLA, *Avenida 27 de Febrero at Anacoana facing the Olympic Center.*

A modern shopping complex with plenty of places to browse, window shop, snack, dine, or have a coffee, this air conditioned shopping complex offers budget eats.

PUERTO PLATA

Since this is an area of all-inclusive resorts, it's unlikely you will be eating outside your own hotel. However, **PIZZA HUT**, in the Playa Dorada Plaza, *Tel. 320-2000,* will deliver to your hotel room. All the usual favorites are here and, if you can speak Spanish, ask about the local specialities that aren't seen on North American Pizza Hut menus.

CASO DE CAMPO, LA ROMANA

Take the Modified American Plan at an added $49 per person per day and you can eat breakfast and dinner anywhere in the complex. **TROPICANA**, *Tel. 523-3333,* which is open only for dinner and requires reservations, is one of the classiest restaurants in the resort, offering fresh fish and local classics made with fresh island produce.

In **LA CANA**, which is upstairs over the open, thatched lounge, dine on steaks, seafood and chicken. Often there's a beach barbecue and buffet with ribs, steaks, fish, chicken or roast suckling pig. Go for it.

SEEING THE SIGHTS

More than 90 percent of Dominicans are Roman Catholic, which means that much of the best sightseeing and celebrating have to do with churches and feast days. Every city and hamlet has a patron saint whose feast day is always a colorful, all-day festival, the best of the year. Churches from the grandest to the most humble are cool, hospitable havens where you can take a quiet moment – usually seeing a historic highlight or local vignette (candle lighting, veiled women at prayer) at the same time.

Just before leaving the Carretera Mella at the airport, find **La Caleta** park and museum. Nearby on the bay, boats take passengers to **La Caleta National Park**, an underwater park where you can snorkel. Tours can be arranged through **Ecotourisa**, *Tel. 221-4104.*

In Santo Domingo, take half a day to visit the **Jardin Botanica** and the **Parque Zoologico Nacional** on the north side of town at Avenue Republica de Columbia, *Tel. 687-6211.* Admission is RD$15; hours are daily except Monday, 9am to 5pm. The **Philatelic and Numismatic Museum** is in the Central Bank on Pedro Henriquez Urena Street, Tel. 686-0677. It's open Monday through Friday from 9am to 4pm displaying one of the most complete collections of coins and stamps in the Caribbean. Most are available for purchase.

The **Colonial Zone** on the west side of the Rio Ozama beckons travelers away from the beaches and into a time warp of sliver-size streets, noise, grit, architectural beauty, and exuberance. The **Calle Las Damas** is the oldest street in the new world, lined with relics such as the **Cathedral of Santa Maria de Menor**, the oldest cathedral in the New World. It was built between 1514-1523. The sanctuary is a wondrous sight and, if you're a worshiper, well worth a mass any Sunday starting at 6am.

Even older is the **Capilla de los Remedios** nearby. It was built as a temporary chapel for the city while the cathedral was building built. See it Monday through Saturday 9am to 6pm or attend a Sunday mass starting at 6am.

Many of the 16h- and 17-century homes in this area were restored in the 1970s. Note the Gothic-Elizabethan portal on the Nicolas de Orlando Hostelry. It's an architectural gem. **The National Pantheon** was built between 1714 and 1745 and serves as the burial ground for Dominican heroes. It's on the Calle Las Damas and has no telephone. Admission is free daily except Sunday, 10am to 5pm. The **House of the Jesuits** nearby is one of the city's oldest structures, dating to the early sixteenth century. In the Museo de las Casas Reales, **The Museum of Royal Houses**, see everything from pre-Columbian artifacts to royal carriages. It's also on the Calle Las Damas, *Tel. 682-4202*. Admission is RD$15 Tuesday through Saturday 9am to 4:45pm and Sunday 10am to 1pm. Pop into every church you pass; they're ancient and awe-inspiring.

The zone is split by El Conde, a wide pedestrian walk lined with shops. It leads west to the **Parque Independencia**, a good spot to observe Dominican families parading their babies and meeting their friends. **Parque Colón** in the zone honors Christopher Columbus with a big statue that was sent from Paris in 1897.

Another of the city's great squares is the Plaza de la Cultura, home of the **Museum of Dominican Man**, *Tel. 687-3623*, the **Museum of Natural History**, *Tel. 689-0106*, and the **Gallery of Modern Art**, *Tel. 682-8260*. Admission to each is RD$15; all are open daily except Monday 10am to 5pm. The plaza is also the home of the **national theater**. Watch local posters for information about any current productions. If you're a scholar and are here to do serious research, the plaza is also the home of the **National Library**, *Tel. 688-4086*.

At the sharp bend in the Ozama River and seen from blocks around it is the **Torre del Homenaje**, or Tower of Homage, on Paseo Presidente Bellini. It was built in 1502-1507 and rivals the Tower of London for its cruel history in housing the condemned. Above it have flown the flags of seven nations that have ruled here. Imagine how impressive it looked in 1509 when it towered over the city on the day when Don Diego Columbus, the new viceroy, took office. Admission is RD$15 and it's open daily except Monday 8am to 7pm.

On the other side of the Ozama on the Avenue of the Americas, **Acuario Nacional**, the national aquarium, *Tel. 592-1509*, is the largest in the Caribbean. It's open free on weekdays 8am to 5pm, Saturday 8am to 4pm and Sunday 9am to 12:30pm. Across the way, a splashy water park gives the family a place to cool off on thrilling water slides. Sometimes water shows are scheduled in the evening, *Tel. 591-5927.* Admission is RD$60 on weekdays and RD$80 on Saturday and Sunday. Hours are daily except Monday 10am to 7pm.

Nearby on the Avenue España, **El Faro a Colón** (Columbus Lighthouse) is a monument to the discoverer of the Americas. It's filled with memorabilia, including his tomb (although nobody is sure if he's inside). It's open daily except Monday, 10am to 5pm. Admission is RD$15.

OUT ON THE ISLAND

Once you leave the resort areas of the D.R., you'll need a good Spanish phrase book and a good map. Restaurants and sightseeing are not yet geared to yanqui tourists as much as they would like to be, although you'll find the people warm and wonderful.

East of Santo Domingo, the city of **San Pedro de Macoris** is a place to capture the flavor of small-town life after the madness of the capital. The steeple of the **Iglesia San Pedro Apostol** dominates the city, so keep to the right after crossing the bridge and you'll find it and the old city. Wander around the **Parque Duarte** and have a cold drink at one of the cafes or vendors.

Northwest of Santo Domingo 155 kilometers is **Santiago** (de los Caballeros). It's an industrial city but a good headquarters for exploring the rum and tobacco-growing **Cibao Valley**. The city was founded in 1504 by Christopher Columbus' younger brother, Bartholomew. It's the home of rousing carnivals in February and August, the gothic **Cathedral of Santiago the Apostle** with its carved mahogany alter, and museums devoted to folkloric music and dance and to tobacco. The inner city's center is another **Parque Duarte** (Juan Pablo Duarte founded the Republic, so a lot of things are named after him). This and the Calle del Sol, the main drag, are the places to hang out, shop, and find something to eat.

Because of the many beach resorts in the area, **Sosua** is more tourist-savvy than most cities. Calle Pedro Clisante is closed to motor traffic, and everyone turns out to stroll, eat, drink, shop for (simply awful) paintings from sidewalk vendors, and hang out. Puerta Plata's main street is solidly touristy but in the side streets you can still find the old Caribbean and some well-preserved Victorian houses.

The **Amber Museum** at the corner of Calle Emilion Prudhomme and Calle Duarte, *Tel. 586-2848,* is open most days 9am to 6pm for a token admission. The collections are upstairs in a lovely old house. The downstairs is a shop selling souvenirs and jewelry. The area's **Malencón** (promenade) runs for about four kilometers from the Fortaleza San Felipe to Long Beach. The fort, built by the Spanish in the mid-1500s, is open daily from 9am to noon and 3-5pm for a token admission. Tours are also offered Monday through Friday 9am to noon and 2-5pm at the **Brugal Rum Distillery** on the Avenida Colón. A cable car runs to the top of the 2,400-foot **Pico Isabel de Torres**, where a botanical garden and a statue of Christ are the attractions. When the cable car isn't running, the road to the top makes a challenging hike.

The **Samana peninsula** sticks out into the Atlantic like a beckoning finger. It's the home of several beach resorts but the city itself burned in the 1940s and most of its ancient buildings, including the church, were lost. If your island wanderings bring you this way, the Malecón is across from the harbor and it's lined with restaurants and bars. It's a popular boating area (although the Atlantic can be rough), where you can sometimes find a whale watching excursion or rent a boat with guide for deep sea fishing.

ROAD FOOD

Fruit stands found along roadsides spill over with colorful fruits and vegetables and vendors usually have bottled drinks to offer as well. Your best bet for finding anything from canned foods to motor oil are small grocery stores of the Colmados chain. They're found everywhere and are, in small villages, the local hangout and communications grapevine as well as the place to provision.

NIGHTLIFE & ENTERTAINMENT

The world's largest discotheque is the **Malecón**, Santo Domingo's famous seaside boulevard. Simply stroll with the crowds, stopping here for a drink and there for a coffee, and you're part of an exciting nightly spectacle.

For live jam sessions, look to the following places in Santo Domingo. Call ahead to find out who is playing and when.

EL CONUCA, *Calle Asimiro de Moya 152, Tel. 686-0129/*
EL YREY BAY in the Sheraton Santo Domingo. *Tel. 221-6666/*
GUACARA TAINA, Avenida Mirador in Parque Mirador del Sur, *Tel. 533-1051/*
MERENGUE BAY in the Jaragua Renaissance Resort, *Tel. 332-2222.*

"Casinos" are found all over the place, but some are simple affairs with a few slot machines. Among the most chic casinos in Santo Domingo are those at the **Renaissance Jaragua Resort & Casino**, *Tel. 332-2222* and the **Omni Casino** in the Sheraton, *Tel. 692-2102.*

COCKFIGHTS

*Every city, neighborhood, and hamlet in the Dominican Republic has a **gallera** for cockfights, an ancient sport where hapless roosters fight to a bloody death to the delight of screaming audiences who have bet on the outcome. Even if women were not barred from attending (although this old rule is relaxed in the cities now), we'd prefer to ignore this cruel sport, but cock fighting is an important part of the local culture and it may as well be mentioned here. In tourist areas, the fights are even offered as a tour and admission is charged. The "sport" dates to ancient China and Persia and is a passion in many Caribbean islands still today.*

Game-cocks are specially bred and raised for their moment in the gallera, when they are weighed, fitted with razor-sharp spurs, put into the ring with an opponent of the same weight class, and begin slashing away at each other. Things get so spirited that fist fights can break out among the bettors. Take a flash photograph that is blamed for altering the results of the fight, and you might find yourself part of the bloody entertainment.

SPORTS & RECREATION

Most visitors are likely to be at a resort where all sports are available. However, you can also make your own arrangements for the following sports:

Billiards: can be played at the Sebelen Bowling Center. *Tel. 540-0101.*

Golf: for information about public courses, *Tel. 563-7228.* Country clubs that allow public play are found in major cities. Golf resorts include Casa de Campo and all the Puerto Plata area resorts.

Jogging: in Santo Domingo, popular green spaces for city joggers include the Miardor Sur, the Paseo de los Indios, and the Olympic Center. Runners use the Malecón in early morning.

Polo: play or train at **Sierra Prieta** and **Casa de Campo**, *Tel. 523-3333.*

Sportfishing: contact **the Nautical Club Andres** in Boca Chica, *Tel. 685-4940.*

SHOPPING

Fifty million years ago when thick forests covered the island, sap dripped from trees and became fossilized as amber. Today this jewel-like stone is one of the most sought-after souvenirs in the republic. To tell the real thing from imitations requires ultraviolet light or fire (which, unfortunately, melts it), but one test is to rub it vigorously to see if it becomes mildly magnetic. Better still, buy amber only from a reliable merchant and not from a street vendor. Don't buy rough amber; its export is restricted and it could be confiscated from you at the airport.

Black coral is harvested off Samana and is made into souvenirs, but it is a rare and endangered product. It is illegal to bring it into the United States or Europe. While it's not illegal to take mahogany, these magnificent old trees too are disappearing in the name of progress so some tourists prefer to buy paintings rather than mahogany carvings.

For investment-quality works of art, shop El **Pincel Galeria**, Gustavo Mejia Ricard 24, Santo Domingo, *Tel. 544-8019.* The covered **Mercado Modelo** in the Colonial Zone along Calle Mella is a lively market where you're not only invited to bargain, it's expected. The better your Spanish, the better the deal – although a good poker player can manage pretty well without speaking a word.

In **Puerto Plata**, shop the **Tourist Bazaar** along Calle Duarte, the **Plaza Shopping Center**, and the boutiques along **Calle Beller. Altos de Chavón** at La Romana is an art buyer's heaven with its galleries and artists-in-residence. Vendors also ply most of the popular tourist beaches.

EXCURSIONS & DAY TRIPS

Your best bet for a reliable tour is through your hotel. Or you can book with:
• **Cafemba Tours**, *Tel. 586-2177, 320-3969, or 571-2536*
• **Domitur**. *Tel. 530-7313, Fax 530-6500; in the U.S., Tel. 305/541-1476*
• **Emely Tours**. *Tel. 687-7114 or toll-free in the Dominican Republic, Tel. 1-200-3262.*

Tours of the national parks, wildlife centers and historic sites can be arranged by **Ecotourisa**, *Tel. 221-4104.* Also offering tours is **Omni Tours**, *Tel. 565-6591.*

Los Haitises National Park in southern Bahia de Samana and west of Sabana de Mar can be reached only by boat. Your hotel host can book a day tour out of Sabana de la Mar, Samana, or Sanchez. Whale watching in these waters can be awesome, especially in Samana where whales congregate. Charter flights fly into Samana from Puerto Plata and Playa Dorado, or you can drive to Samana or Sanchez to catch a boat. Tours last about three hours.

At least 15 percent of the republic has been set aside as **national parks**. Many areas are closed to visitors, or are open only to guided groups, so it's best to take a tour. To venture into the outback alone, you'll need a permit. Call the office of the director of national parks, *Tel. 685-1315* or write the Director, National Park Service, Calle las Damas 6, Santo Domingo. Since the highest mountains in the Caribbean are here, climbing **Pico Duarte** (10,417 feet) is a challenge for experienced climbers; a permit is required.

PRACTICAL INFORMATION

Area Code: 809

ATM: to use your MasterCard/Cirrus card, look for ATH Dominicana, Banco Popular Dominicana, and Red Cash. Cash advances through MasterCard are available through CrediProgreso in major cities, *Tel. toll-free 1-200-3233*, for information. Any Banco Popular will also advance cash against your Visa, MasterCard, Diners Club or Carte Blanche.

Business hours: generally banks and offices are open Monday through Friday from 8:30am to 5pm. Post offices keep longer hours. Almost everything closes for two hours at noon and the ministry of tourism recommends that tourists take a siesta like everyone else.

Credit cards: major credit cards are a must for hotels, some meals, and rental cars, but cannot be used to get cash in anything but pesos.

Crime: black marketing in currencies is prohibited but it seems rife, especially in the Parque de Colón, but it could be a sting set up by the police. Everyone you talk to does it, or claims to, but we're not willing to take a chance. Speed traps along the highway between Santo Domingo and Boca Chica are common, with tourists the most usual "culprits." Keep your cool; the fine could be 10,000 pesos if you can't sweet-talk your way out of it. Street crime is a problem, and U.S. passports are one of the most popular heists. Safeguard your cash, credit cards, return air tickets, passport, and driver's license.

Currency: the official currency is the Dominican peso (RD$), which is divided into 100 centavos and is worth about 8¢. At one point a law was passed requiring all visitors to change at least $100 into pesos, but it is largely ignored. Still, it could be enforced without notice so be prepared to go with the flow. Dollars circulate freely and are especially popular for tips, so carry a good supply of one-dollar bills. U.S. dollar travelers checks are easily exchanged in banks and elsewhere, but travelers checks from other countries are usually accepted only in banks or in hotels that regularly host people from those countries. Commercial banks such as Banco Popular and Banco de Reservas can also exchange yen, Swiss francs, Canadian dollars, Spanish pesetas, German marks and British pounds. If you use traveler's checks to pay bills, smaller merchants and restaurateurs may not be able to make change in dollars, so carry checks in modest denominations to avoid getting stuck with a pocketful of pesos. Contrarily, you could get dollars for change at the airport even if you pay in pesos. The best bet is to use credit cards wherever possible for both safety and for the optimum exchange rate. When making a currency exchange, ask for a receipt. You may need it to prove that you exchanged the funds legally; it must also be shown if you want to change pesos back into dollars, pounds, marks, or francs. Any amount of cash can be brought into the country but not more than $5,000 or the equivalent can be taken out.

Divorce: See a lawyer who specializes in divorce, present a notarized statement in which both parties agree to the split, and it can all be over within 24 hours. Local tourist publications are filled with ads for attorneys who specialize in these quickies.

Dress: Religion, especially Roman Catholicism, is a very strong influence on everyday life. Don't visit churches in shorts. Women should wear head covering; men should uncover their heads as a sign of respect. When attending services, many local women wear long sleeves and veils.

Driving: your home driver's license will suffice here.

Drugs: for simple possession of narcotics or anything in the cannabis family, you'll pay a fine of RD$300 to RD$1,000 or spend six months to a year in prison, or both. For distributors and traffickers things get even worse. There is no bail in drug offenses.

Electricity: American-style plugs are used; power is 110-120 volts, 60 cycles. Power failures are common, although most hotels have back-up generators.

Emergencies: dial 911 for any medical, fire, or police emergency. All-night pharmacies in Santo Domingo include Los Hildalgos, 27 de Febrero 241, *Tel. 565-4848* and San Judas Tadeo, Independencia 57, *Tel. 689-6664*. If you'll be traveling into the interior near the Haitian border, ask your doctor about malaria prophylaxis.

Film and photos: bring plenty of film, but don't photograph natives at work without permission or payment or both. In tourist areas, paid posing is the norm. It is forbidden to take any military photos, including shots of personnel in uniform.

Government: The Dominican Republic is independent. The U.S. Embassy is on Calle Cesar Nicolas Penson at Calle Leopoldo Navarro, Santo Domingo, *Tel. 541-2171*.

Hazards: except in modern tourist hotels and restaurants, don't drink the water or ice cubes. Use bottled water for drinking and brushing your teeth. According to the official Dominican Republic *National Tourism Guide*, only 80% of the urban population has potable water.

Holidays: include January 1, January 6, January 26, February 27, May 1, August 16, and December 25. Carnival takes place throughout

February. In addition to the major holidays a number of patron saints' days are celebrated in individual communities.

Immigration: citizens of the United States, Canada, and most other nations can stay up to 60 days with a passport and the purchase of a Tourist Card costing $10 at consulates worldwide or on arrival at one of the international airports.

Measures: the Dominican Republic is officially on the metric system, but foods are sold by the pound and ounce, fabrics by the yard, cooking oil by the pound, gasoline and motor oil by the Imperial gallon, and drinks in bottles containing .0756 liter.

Pets: while it's usually safer and more comfortable for a pet to stay home than to endure the heat and confusion of the islands and the stress of a long flight, it is possible to bring a dog or cat to the Dominican Republic. Dogs must have proof of rabies and Parvo vaccination within the last 30 days and a health certificate no older than 15 days. Cats require the same, minus the Parvo shot. Don't try to enter without the certificates or the pet will be quarantined for 8-30 days.

Post offices are generally open Monday through Friday 7:30am to 5pm and Saturday 7:30am to noon. For express mail service, contact EMS Express Service, *Tel. 809/532-2432.*

Taxes: you'll need a $10 tourist card on entry and will pay a $10 departure tax on leaving. To avoid standing in long lines, get a package that pre-pays the tourist card. The departure tax is paid to the air line. Usually dollars are accepted but this could vary with the line so check ahead a few days before your departure.

Telephone: rent a cellular telephone for RD$20 per day plus RD$16 per minute of air time. Included are a battery and charger. Reserve in advance at *Tel. 800/353-8271 or 809/220-1111. Ph*ones can be picked up at Las Americas International Airport or at the Codetel communications center at Triadentes Avenue 1169, Santo Domingo.

Water supplies: like electrical current, can be undependable. Some hotels have been known to turn off the water after a certain hour; some don't always have hot water. It's always wise to fill a sink with water before soaping up. Drink bottled water.

29. HAITI

Haiti does not have a tourism promotion agency in North America, nor is this a good time to go there. Here is the U.S. State Department's report on Haiti as of press time:

Country description: Haiti is one of the least developed countries in the Western Hemisphere. There are shortages of goods and services throughout the country.

Entry requirements: Haitian law requires a passport to enter. In practice, officials frequently waive this requirement if travelers have other documentation, such as a birth certificate, indicating they are American citizens. Due to fraud concerns, however, air lines will not board passengers for return to the U.S. unless they are in possession of a valid passport. For additional information contact the **Haitian Embassy**, *2311 Massachusetts Avenue N.W. Washington D.C. 20008, Tel. 202/332-4090.*

Medical facilities: Medical care in Port-au-Prince is limited and the level of community sanitation is low. Medical facilities outside the capital are almost always below U.S. standards. Life-threatening emergencies may require evacuation by air ambulance at the patient's expense. Doctors and hospitals often expect immediate cash payment for health services. U.S. medical insurance is not always valid outside the U.S. Travelers may wish to consider supplemental medical insurance with specific overseas coverage, including medical evacuation. In mid-1996, Haitian-made pharmaceuticals were ordered off U.S. shelves following the suspicious deaths of Haitian children from renal failure.

Community sanitation levels are low and medical care is limited. For further information about diseases that are endemic in Haiti, and other health concerns, contact the Centers for Disease Control and Prevention's international traveler hotline at *Tel. 404/332-4559.* The Internet address is: *http://www.cdc.gov/.*

Crime: the advisory contains a long list of crime concerns including the chilling information that "neighborhoods formerly considered safe have recently attracted criminal activity as well." Robbery, carjacking, and murder are common, and local enforcement agencies seem to be unable to stem the tide, find and punish the culprits, or help travelers who are hurt or stranded. If your driver's license or passport are stolen they can't be replaced until you get back to the States. Car jacking and holdups along the Route Nationale 1, the port area, the airport road and the Cité Soleil are a problem.

Civil unrest is rife, and often United States citizens are the targets, warns the State Department. "Avoid large crowds, which have been known to turn violent," says Washington. The state department's advice is to keep car doors and windows locked and, if you're held up, comply without resistance.

Roads are poor; traffic laws are not enforced. Too, the U.S. Federal Aviation Administration has found the Haitian Civil Aviation Authority not in compliance with international safety standards. For further information, contact the U. S. Department of Transportation, *Tel. 800/322-7873.*

Drug penalties are severe, and have nothing to do with the "due process" you expect in the U.S. and Canada. If convicted, offenders may face long jail sentences and substantial fines.

If you do go to Haiti, the state department recommends that you register with the **Consular Section of the U.S. Embassy**. The embassy is on Harry Truman Boulevard in Port-au-Prince, *Tel. 509/22-0200, 22-0354, 22-0368, or 22-0612, Fax 509/23-1641. The* **consular section** is on Rue Oswald Durand, *Tel. 509/23-7011 or 23-8971, Fax 23-9665.*

Our advice: wait until things are more settled before visiting this beautiful country.

THE THREE "S" ISLANDS

30. SABA

The Dutch West Indies are usually thought about in two groups, the ABC islands of Aruba, Bonaire and Curacao, and the "S" islands of St. Maarten, **Saba**, and St. Eustatius, which everyone calls Statia.

The top of a huge, inactive volcano, Saba sticks up out of the water like a 3,000-foot-high sugar cone. It's so steep that for centuries its settlements were connected only by steps carved into the stone. It took 20 years to build by hand, but a road runs from the air strip to the other end of the island, **Fort Bay**. So steep are the cliffs surrounding the island that early settlers were able to keep pirates away by rolling big boulders down on them. Stalwart people, still living in fairytale cottages trimmed in gingerbread, make their living in tourism and appreciate your visit.

Windwardside is all whitewash, green shutters and red roofs, clinging to a hillside 1,200 feet above the sea. The island's other settlements are **Hell's Gate**, **The Bottom** (from the Dutch word for bowl), and **St. John's**. The entire island is a Brigadoon of yesterday's niceties, so take time to walk its lanes and pause at overlooks to gaze down on seascapes and farm fields.

Surrounding the island like a sparkling necklace is the **Saba Marine Park**, an unbroken marine preserve that offers some of the most dazzling dives in the Caribbean. Activities are strictly controlled everywhere in the park to a depth of 200 feet. User fees are charged. Pick up a waterproof map in the park office at **Fort Bay**, which will lead you through 11 sites along a snorkel trail. Because of its steep sides, Saba has no beaches, so visitors either swim off a boat or in hotel swimming pools.

Climate

Year-round perfection best describes sunny days in the high 80s and seabreeze-cooled nights in the mid-70s. Except during the rare tropical depression, rainfall is regular and welcome. Precipitation averages from 7.7 inches in October to as low as 3.4 inches in February.

ARRIVALS & DEPARTURES

Saba's **Juancho Yrausquin Airport** is 15 minutes from St. Maarten on **Winair**, with connections to St. Kitts and Statia, *Tel. 800/634-4907 or 203/ 261-8603.* By ferry, the trip to Saba takes about an hour from St. Maarten. *Voyager 1* departs Philipsburg daily at 8:30am and leaves Saba at 4pm. Roundtrip fare is $60; one-way fare is $40. Children under age 12 travel for half price. If you're day-tripping, add lunch and a tour for $30. *The Edge* high-speed ferry makes a round trip from Simpson's Bay, St. Maarten, on Wednesday, Friday, and Sunday for $60 plus $30 for lunch and a tour. To get harbor and ferry information, *Tel. 5993/82205* in Statia or *Tel. 5995/24096* in St. Maarten.

ORIENTATION

Saba covers only five square miles, but distances can be deceptive because everything is straight up and straight down, with lots of windings and switchbacks. From the airport on the northeast corner of the island, a road rises up through Hell's Gate, forking to go up **Mount Scenery** or to Windwardside and continuing on to the capital at The Bottom.

A post office and tourist information office are at Windwardside, about halfway between the airport and Fort Bay. The island villages are **Hell's Gate**, **Windwardside**, **St. Johns**, and **The Bottom**. The highest point on the island is Mount Scenery, which is about 2,800 feet high. Saba is 150 miles east of Puerto Rico and 28 miles south of St. Maarten.

GETTING AROUND SABA

Taxis meet every flight and ferry, offering a two-hour tour for about $40. Once your luggage is parked, walking is one of the best ways to get around and hitchhiking is socially acceptable. Scooters and rental cars are available, but driving on these narrow, steep roads with their numerous cliffs is not for the faint of heart. The island has ten miles of concrete roads, but most visitors prefer not to drive them.

If you must have a car, rentals are available from **Doc's Car Rentals** in Windwardside, *Tel. 5994/62271,* and **Johnson's Rental**, Windwardside, *Tel. 5994/62269.*

WHERE TO STAY

A government room tax of eight percent is added automatically to hotel bills. Most hotels also add a 10-15 percent service charge. Although most of the hotels don't offer toll-free reservations from North America, **Dive Saba**, *Tel. 800/883-SABA,* offers reservation service with and without dives. Ask about optional meal plans and grocery packages.

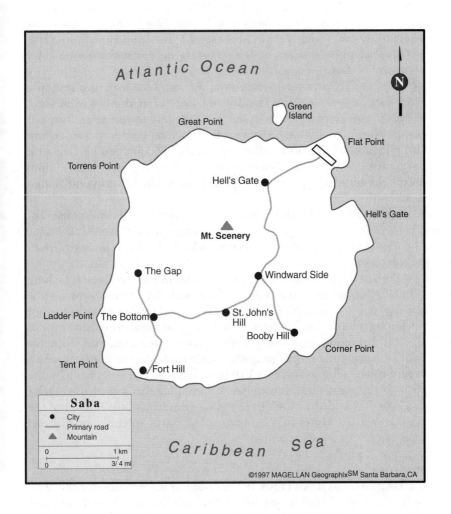

Atlantic Ocean

Green Island

Great Point

Flat Point

Torrens Point

Hell's Gate

Hell's Gate

Mt. Scenery

The Gap

Windward Side

Ladder Point

The Bottom

St. John's Hill

Booby Hill

Corner Point

Tent Point

Fort Hill

Caribbean Sea

Saba
- City
— Primary road
▲ Mountain

| 0 | 1 km |
| 0 | 3/4 mi |

©1997 MAGELLAN Geographix^SM Santa Barbara,CA

For mail purposes, your address while here will end in Saba, Netherlands Antilles.

Expensive

QUEEN'S GARDENS RESORT, *P.O. Box 21, Troy Hill, Saba. Tel. 5994/63494, Fax 63495; U.S. 800/599-9407. Rates at the 12-suite hotel start at $150 for two people in a studio with kitchenette; $200 for a one-bedroom suite with kitchen. Don't bring children under age 12. Two-bedroom units are $300. Rates include airport transfers, daily maid service, and continental breakfast. Ask about dive packages, weekly rates, and weekend specials.*

Looking like an oversize mansion, the hotel sits majestically atop a 1,200-foot hill over looking The Bottom. Rooms are done in whites and pastels to complement views of sky and greenery including century-old mango trees. You'll have a spacious living room, bedroom with ceiling fan, telephone, television, bathroom, and a full-equipped kitchen with microwave, coffee maker, electric stove, and refrigerator. Dive, climb Mount Scenery, or just bake by the pool. Dining is in the very good Mango Royale.

WILLARD'S OF SABA, *Booby Hill, P.O. Box 515, Windwardside. Tel. 5994/62498, Fax 62482. Rates at this seven-room hotel start at $250 double. Children under age 14 cannot be accommodated. Ask about packages, which include airport transfers.*

Dive packages include dive transfers and five to ten dives. It's a long climb up Booby Hill to reach this cliffside aerie 2,000 feet above the sea, but the view is well worth it. Swim in the heated pool or relax in the hot tub gazing out over red roof-dotted hillsides and the azure ocean beyond. Uncluttered rooms are furnished in wickers and weavings, with accents of bold aquamarine and orange against white walls and tile floors. Stay in a luxury room, a bungalow, or a VIP suite at $400. The hotel has a locally popular restaurant and its own bar. A meal plan that includes breakfast and dinner is available. Built by the great-grandson of the builder of the famous Willard Hotel in Washington D.C., this splendid small hotel accepts only 14 guests at a time.

Moderate

CAPTAIN'S QUARTERS, *Windwardside. Tel. 5994/62486, Fax 62377. In the U.S. write Captain's Quarters, 401 East 118th Street, Suite 3, New York NY 10035. Tel. 212/289-6031, Fax 289-1931. Rates at this 12-room hotel start at $85 per person double occupancy including full American breakfast, taxes, service charge, welcome drink, and airport transfers. Children under age seven stay free in parents' room.*

Two old houses, one of them dating to 1850, team up to create a lovely inn with four-poster beds, airy and spacious rooms, and charming touches of antiques and brickabrack. Each room has a wet bar, cable television, safe and private balcony. The hillside setting is perfect for views of Mount Scenery from the balconies. The hotel has a stunning cliffside pool, library, a locally acclaimed restaurant, and an outdoor bar where everyone congregates. Saturday is barbecue night at the pool.

COTTAGE CLUB, *Windwardside. Tel. 5994/62386 or 62346, Fax 62476. Rates at this 10-room hotel start at $137 for two people in a cottage. Discount packages are offered divers, business travelers, deep sea fishers, and honeymooners. There is no service charge. Tip at your discretion.*

Ten gingerbread cottages with brick walkways and bowers of frangipani and night jasmine cluster around the pool in this divers' hangout. You'll have a complete little home with full kitchen, bathroom, telephone and fax, and cable television. Private balconies look out over Saba's incredible Mount Scenery, the village of English Quarter, and the endless Caribbean. Walk into Windwardside for shopping and dining, or hang out in the marble-floored lobby to read, listen to classical music, or enjoy the breezes and views. The pool is surrounded by spacious decks, which are ideal for copping rays. Ask about the grocery package that stocks your kitchen before you arrive.

JULIANA'S *Windwardside. Tel. 62269, Fax 62389. Rates start at $115 double including breakfast. Ask about dive packages.*

Rooms, an apartment, and a cottage make up a small inn set in a tropical garden with its own pool atop a 1,500-foot hill. Rooms have private bath and balcony with superb sea views. A communal room offers games, videos, television, and classes and slide shows for divers. Breakfast and lunch are served in the café. Juliana Johnson has done the little complex with a sweet Saban touch—a little gingerbread, wood paneling, mellow pastels, and lots of hibiscus outside your windows. Have breakfast, lunch and dinner in Tropics Cafe, where Juliana offers homemade bread, fresh salads, daily specials and a full bar.

THE GATE HOUSE, *Hell's Gate. Tel. 5994/62416, Fax 62250. U.S. address The Gate House, P.O. Box 903, LaGrange IL 60525. Tel. (708) 354-9641, Fax 352-1390. Rates at the six-room hotel start at $95 double and $85 single. Ask about packages, which include breakfast and transfers. Meal plans and dive packages are available.*

Combine a quiet village setting with typical Saban architecture trimmed in just enough gingerbread. Wake up in a room bright with splashy Caribbean colors and catch the sunrise from your balcony. The hotel added a pool in 1997. Its restaurant is open for breakfast and dinner.

MIDTOWN APARTMENTS, *The Bottom. Tel. and Fax 5994/63263. Rates at this nine-unit hotel are $75 for a one-bedroom apartment and $100 for two bedrooms.*

Move into a cozy *pied-a-terre* with fully-equipped kitchen, dining and living area, cable television, and air conditioning. Typically Saban in gingerbread-trimmed white with a red roof, the unpretentious hotel is comfortably furnished in blond woods and deep-tone fabrics. Each unit has a balcony overlooking the capital. Walk to the supermarket, government offices, post office, and the library.

SCOUT'S PLACE, *Windwardside. Tel. 62269, Fax 62388. Rates at this 15-room inn start at $85 double including continental breakfast.*

Red roofs and plenty of porches give a Saban look to a self-admitted "cheap and cheerful" boarding house where you'll share a bath and may not have hot water. For a few dollars more, you can get a private bath, balcony, and a four-poster bed. The hotel's chief appeal is its location in the center of Windwardside within walking distance of the dive center. A full breakfast is available at the hotel's restaurant.

Budget

CRANSTON ANTIQUE INN, *The Bottom. Tel. 5994/63203, Fax 63469. Rates at the six-room inn start at $58 double including breakfast. The inn is about a mile from the ferry dock at Fort Bay. No credit cards.*

Simple hospitality is the hallmark in the inn where Queen Julianna once stayed. The rooms have magnificent four-poster beds plus a hodge-podge of styles. Walk to Ladder Bay to gaze out over waters that were once prime hunting for whales. Swim in the pool. The hotel has its own restaurant specializing in fresh fish and roast island pig, all enhanced with locally grown herbs.

EL MOMO COTTAGES, *P.O. Box 519, Booby Hill, five minutes from Windwardside. Tel. and Fax 5994/62265. Rates at this four-cottage complex are $30 single and $35 double.*

If you like camping, you'll like roughing it in these cute gingerbread cottages, each with private porch and daily maid service. Guests share a communal bath building with toilet, shower, and sinks and a communal living room. There's also a pool, extra porches, and a studio where local crafts are produced. Breakfast is available.

Private Housing

Cottages are available for rent on Saba at very modest rates, usually less than $100 nightly for one or two bedrooms and a fully-equipped kitchen. Real estate agents include **Johnson's Real Estate**, *Windwardside,* Tel. 5994/62209 and **Saba Real Estate**, *Windwardside, Tel. 5994/62203.*

WHERE TO EAT

Unless noted otherwise, these restaurants take at least some credit cards, usually MasterCard and Visa. Discover and American Express are found in the larger islands, but are less widely used in smaller places.

Expensive

MANGO ROYALE, *in the Queens' Gardens Resort, Troy Hill. Tel. 63494. Hours are Tuesday through Saturday 6:30-9pm and Wednesday through Saturday, 11:30am to 2pm Sunday brunch is served noon to 3pm. Reservations are suggested. Plan to spend $22 to $35 for dinner.*

Arrive in time for cocktails at sunset, then try the roast saddle of goat with essence of mint, Saba spiced shrimp, or Peking dumplings. On Friday evening there's a barbecue with live music and a steel pan band plays with the Sunday brunch.

WILLARD'S OF SABA, *Booby Hill. Tel. 62498. Reservations are essential. Plan to spend $22 to $35 for dinner. Hours are 11:30am to 3pm and 6pm to 9pm daily.*

Part of a smart little hotel, (the family is related to the Washington, DC Willard Hotel people) this poolside dining room has breathtaking views of the island and sea from atop a 2,000-foot hill. Arrive early enough to have before-dinner drinks at the bar. Cook your own meal on a hot lava stone, or let the chef rustle up a rainbow fish, broiled lobster, roast beef or pork in an interesting Asian, French, or Creole sauce, and a fruit dessert or ice cream. Hotel manager Corazon de Johnson, who is from the Philippines, is also the chef. Try her *maruya*, which is banana and jackfruit wrapped in a crepe or her breaded chicken *couzon* with red hot sauce. The wine list features Italian vintages from the Bava vineyards. Linger over your meal to enjoy the fireplace, which is lit when the temperature goes below 65 degrees.

Moderate

BRIGADOON RESTAURANT, *Windwardside. Tel. 62380. Open daily from noon to 2pm and 6pm to 9:30pm, the restaurant offers entrees for $9 to $20. Reservations aren't required except for groups.*

Choose a lobster from the tank, or order fresh fish with a Creole, Caribbean, or continental touch. The steaks are always good, and chicken is served with fresh island vegetables. Located in a 19th century Saban home, Brigadoon offers homemade desserts and locally popular theme buffets such as a fish fry, Italian Night, or Mexican Night. Try the fish pot, a melange of fresh fish in a savory tomato base.

CAPTAIN'S QUARTERS, *Windwardside. Tel. 4-62377. Reservations are recommended but not essential except for parties of eight or more. Open for lunch and dinner every day with the last seating at 8:30pm, the restaurant has prix fixe luncheons in the $20 range. Dinner main dishes are $14 to $22.*

Start with a homemade soup, then begin an adventure in Creole, Indonesian, French, or Dutch favorites except on Saturday nights when everyone turns out for barbecue featuring grilled chicken, ribs, and steaks. Unhurried service on a veranda surrounded by native fruit trees means an extended, pleasurable evening of dining, good wine, and good company. The 19th century home of a sea captain, this restaurant-hotel complex has a salty, New England look. Dress is informal but gentlemen usually wear a jacket or long-sleeve shirt. The hotel's formal dining room is The Captain's Table; its garden dining pavilion is The Orchard Café. Beware the CQ Special served at the CQ Bar. One of its ingredients is 150-proof cask rum.

LOLLIPOP'S BAR & RESTAURANT, *between St. John's and The Bottom. Tel. 63330. Plan to spend $20-$25 for dinner. The restaurant is open breakfast through dinner and offers free transportation to and from your hotel. Reservations aren't required except for large groups.*

Look out over the ocean and surrounding hills while you sample stuffed land crab, locally caught fish, grilled lobster, piquant fish cakes, or stewed goat. Ask about free pickup at your hotel.

SABA CHINESE BAR & RESTAURANT, *Windwardside. Tel. 62268 or 62353. One is in town and the other is a five-minute walk up the hill. Closed Mondays, the restaurants don't accept credit cards. They're open for lunch and dinner until midnight. Dishes are priced $5-$18.*

In addition to the usual Cantonese favorites, these restaurants offer steak, fries, and salads all day. Take-outs are available.

SCOUT'S PLACE, *Windwardside. Tel. 62205. Reservations are required for lunch and dinner. Breakfast is served 7:30am to 10:30am; lunch at 12:30 and dinner at 7:30. Plan to spend $12 for lunch and $18 to $26 for dinner.*

Every table in this locally popular, open-air restaurant overlooks the sea, so arrive early enough for a sundowner cocktail while you watch for the green flash. Try such local specialties as curried goat, or traditional fare such as fresh seafood, chicken, and steak. Salads and sandwiches are served all day.

QUEENIE'S SERVING SPOON, *The Bottom. Tel. 63225. Call for hours. Plan to spend $10 to $20 for dinner. Credit cards aren't accepted.*

If you want to try truly native Saban cuisine, come here for the salt fish, stewed goat, goat curry, stuffed crabs, and lots of fresh, local vegetables served family style. The homemade Saba Spice liqueur here is one of the best.

Budget
CARIBAKE BAKERY AND DELI, *in Windwardside at Lambees Place next to the post office. Tel. 62539. Lunch specials are under $6. It's open 7am to 3pm Credit cards aren't accepted.*

Here's the place to get a Hebrew National hot dog, a deli sandwich on homemade bread, soup, pizza, sodas, and a variety of baked breads and sweets to eat in or take out.

IN TWO DEEP, *Fort Bay. Tel. 63438. Eat for less than $10. The restaurant is open daily 8am to 6pm.*

New England style chowders and fish dishes mean good eating in an air-conditioned room overlooking the harbor. Divers like this spot for hearty omelettes and eggs Benedict in the morning, sandwiches and salads for lunch, and the pubby ambience for Happy Hour.

TROPICS CAFE, *Windwardside across from Juliana's. Tel. 62469. Open for breakfast, lunch and dinner, the cafe offers dining for under $10.*

Eat in this poolside cafe overlooking the Caribbean, or order from the take-out menu. Food is simple and inexpensive: burgers, sandwiches on homemade bread, salads and fresh fish. Tropics has long been the island's favorite breakfast nook, so try the home-style cooking some morning.

Snack Attack

For snacks, cold drinks, and burgers, try **Glendie's** on the Range Road behind the police station in The Bottom, and **Pop's** on the harbor at Fort Bay.

SEEING THE SIGHTS

The **Harry L. Johnson Memorial Museum** at Windwardside is open Monday through Friday, 10am to noon and 1pm to 4pm. Admission is $2. Once the home of a Saban seaman who lived here in the mid-19th century, the house is furnished in the style of the times. Collections of old island artifacts and family mementoes are tended by devoted volunteers.

The island's chief point of interest is **Mount Scenery** with its giant ferns, wild orchids, and nodding wildflowers. From Windwardside, climb the 1,064 steps to the mountaintop.

NIGHTLIFE & ENTERTAINMENT

Each village has bulletin boards and posters announcing special events, which could include performances by local or imported calypso or reggae stars. On weekends, **GUIDO'S PIZZERIA** dims the lights, cranks up the disco, and dances until 2am, Te*l. 62330.* Come any time after 6pm for pizza, spaghetti and burgers.

SPORTS & RECREATION

Bicycling

Island Trails, P.O. Box 869, Springfield OR 97477, *Tel. 800/233-4366, Fax 541/747-7781* offers hike-bike packages including island hoppers on Saba, Statia, Montserrat, and Dominica.

Diving

Although Saba's steep sides offer no beaches, its diving is so stunning that scuba divers come here from all over the world. The island, which is actually the peak of an enormous cone, continues to drop steeply at the water's edge into a wonderland of reefs, dropoffs, and caves. The Marine Park has a guided snorkeling trail.

Dive tours are available through:

- **Dive Saba**, *Tel. 800/883-SABA* or *713467-8835*, is a Houston-based travel agency that can handle any Saba booking including cottages, hotels with and without a dive package, and combination packages with stays on Saba plus Statia or St. Maarten.
- **Unique Destinations, 307 Peaceable S**treet, Ridgefield CT 06877, *Tel. 203/431-1571*
- **Scuba Voyage**, *595 Fairbanks Street, Corona CA 91719, Tel. 800/544-7631, 909/371-1831, Fax 371-0478*
- **Go-Diving**, *5610 Rowland Road, Suite 100, Minnetonka MN 55343, Tel. 613/931-9101 or 800/328-5285.*

Island Trails, *P.O. Box 869, Springfield OR 97477, Tel. 800/233-4366, Fax 541/747-7781* offers packages including island hoppers on Saba/ Statia, Montserrat, and Dominica.

Local Saba dive operators offering dives, lessons, and equipment include:

- **Saba Deep Sea Diving Center**, *P.O. Box 22, Fort Bay, Saba, Tel. 5994/ 63347, Fax 63397*
- **Saba Reef Divers**, *Windwardside, Saba, Tel. 5994/62541, Fax 62653*
- **Sea Saba Dive Center**, *P.O. Box 530, Windwardside, Saba, Tel. 5994/ 62246, Fax 62362*

Based in St. Maarten is the liveaboard dive boat **Caribbean Explorer**, *Tel. 800/322-3577*. During a week-long cruise you'll dive as many as five dives a day on Saba and St. Kitts.

Hiking

Island Trails, *P.O. Box 869, Springfield OR 97477, Tel. 800/233-4366, Fax 541/747-7781,* offers hike-kayak, hike-bike, and hike-whale watching packages including island hoppers on Saba/Statia, Montserrat, and Dominica. Included are accommodations, guide, equipment, and most meals.

WALKING MOUNT SCENERY

*Imagine yourself climbing **Mount Scenery**, starting with passage through a secondary rainforest with trees 15-30 feet high and glades of tree ferns and Mountain Palms. When you get to about 2,700 feet, the air chills and you're in the cloud forest known here as the "elfin" forest, where you can almost reach out and touch forest spirits that seem to swirl all around you in the silent mist. The dominant tree here is the Mountain Mahogany, soaring to a hundred feet or more.*

Keep an eye peeled for the aole lizard, the cute and harmless raver snake, tree frogs with their cheerful chirp, and iguanas seeking out patches of sun.

*On steep cliffs over the ocean, you may spot a bridled tern, sooty tern or brown noddy. They nest on Green Island off Saba's north shore in April and May. As you return to lower slopes you may see a redtail hawk or American kestrel. In the rain forest, you may be lucky enough to spot the rare bridled quail dove, which locals call wood hen. Two birds, the trembler and the purple-throated hummingbird are found almost exclusively in the forests here. A number of hikes is offered, ranging from a 90-minute loop to hero hikes that take all day. Contact the **Saba Conservation Foundation** in the Bottom or Friends of Saba Conservation Foundation Inc., 506 Tiffany Trails, Richardson TX 75081.*

Snorkeling

Ask at the **Saba Marine Park** office in Fort Bay, *Tel. 63295* for the waterproof trail guide to the **Edward S. Arnold Snorkel Trail**. The self-guided tour visits 11 underwater sites that you can easily find on your own. A fee of $2 is charged for use of the park.

Tennis

There's a no-frills tennis court at The Bottom, but this isn't the island for a tennis-intensive vacation.

SHOPPING

Don't miss this chance to buy authentic **Saba lace** as well as home-made, 150-proof **Saba Spice** liquor. It's exotically flavored with fennel, cinnamon, cloves, and nutmeg, each a little different according to the brewer's personal recipe. Shops sell the liquor, lace, and drawn-thread Spanish work, but it's likely you'll shop along the roadsides as your driver stops at private homes offering these goods for sale. The **Artisan Foundation** at The Bottom is a good place to buy the hand-screened fabrics made on the island. **Around the Bend** at Scout's Place, Windwardside, is one of the island's best boutiques, always offering smartly unique baubles and gewgaws as well as the ubiquitous tee shirts. The rest of the shopping is along the Main Road between the Square Nickel and the Post Office. Stroll the entire settlement, poking into each shop: **Peggy's Boutique** for Saban drawn work, **Hillside Boutique** for clothing and colognes, the **Little Shop** for fish and parrot mobiles and island-made jewelry, and **Saba Tropical Arts** for Mieke Van Schadewijk's silk-screen tee shirts. An old-fashioned fabrics and notions shop is up Cemetery Road so, if you are a seamstress, don't miss it.

EXCURSIONS & DAY TRIPS

Getting to Saba is difficult, so you won't want to make side trips from here. However, a stay on St. Maarten makes a good pre-or post-Saba visit. *Voyager, Tel. 5995/24096,* is a high-speed boat that links St. Maarten, St. Barts, and Saba.

PRACTICAL INFORMATION

Area Code: 5994

Banking: the Barclay bank is open Monday through Friday, 8:30am to 12:30pm.

Currency: the Netherlands Antilles Guilder (NAfl), which is pegged to the dollar at the rate of NAfl 1.80 to $1. However, menus, hotel rates, and shop prices are quoted in dollars. There is no need to convert U.S. dollars to guiders, but some shopkeepers may not be able to give you change for large bills or large denomination travelers checks. Bring plenty of ones, fives, tens, and twenties. Use your charge card where possible.

Dress code: casual chic. Don't wear swimwear on the street. Covered arms (jacket, sweater) are expected of gentlemen in the evening.

Electricity: U.S.-style 110 volts, 60 cycles.

Entry: U.S. and Canadian citizens require proof of citizenship such as voter registration or passport, not a driver's license. Other visitors need a passport or alien registration card. No customs formalities apply because there are no duties; this is a free port.

Government: The "S" islands are part of the Netherlands Antilles. U.S. consular representation is in Curacao, St. Anna Boulevard 19, *Tel. 5999/461-3066.*

Medical care: the island has a decompression chamber and a medical center with a resident doctor and nurses, *Tel. 63239, 63288, or 63289.* For a decompression emergency, call the Saba Marine Center at *Tel. 63295.* There's a drugstore, The Pharmacy at The Bottom, but it is open only on weekdays, *Tel. 63289.*

Pets: admitted temporarily with a health certificate no older than 10 days from the date of entry and a record of inoculations including rabies at least 30 days prior to entry.

Weddings: if you want to get married on Saba, you'll need to apply a month before you expect to get here and present a birth certificate and any divorce or death papers that apply. The fee is $16. Contact Saba Tourism, *Box 6322, Boca Raton FL 33427, Tel. 561/394-8580, Fax 488-4295; toll-free 800/722-2394.*

31. STATIA

Officially **St. Eustatius**, this island of 2,100 people is called **Statia** by almost everyone. It was so important as a shipping point for Americans fighting the Revolutionary War that Benjamin Franklin's mail from Europe was routed through here. When American independence was declared in 1776, Statia was the first foreign power to salute the stars and stripes. For its pains in aiding the infant republic, the island was sacked by the British in 1781. Snorkelers and divers can still explore old warehouses and pubs that fell into the sea after the sea wall was blown away by Admiral Rodney and his troops.

With the end of the slave trade, agriculture on the island was finished and, as steam ships replace sailing ships, it was no longer as important a port on the tradewind route. Left to slumber for a century, the little island stayed aloof and unspoiled. Still today it remains a hideaway for tourists who can take time to go the "extra mile." You'll find no slick, high-rise resorts here. This is the place to recharge your solar batteries at some of the most affordable prices in the Caribbean.

One of the "S" islands of the Netherlands Antilles, Statia is an autonomous part of the Kingdom of the Netherlands.

Climate
Plan on days in the high 80s and nights no chillier than the low 70s. Statia is hot and humid, but ocean breezes keep you comfortable. The wettest months are June through October, when there is also always the remote chance of a hurricane watch.

ARRIVALS & DEPARTURES
Statia's **Franklin Delano Roosevelt Airport** is a 17-minute flight from St. Maarten on **Winair**, *Tel. 5995/54237* or, on Statia, *Tel. 5443/82381*. Connections are made to St. Kitts and Saba. There is no ferry service.

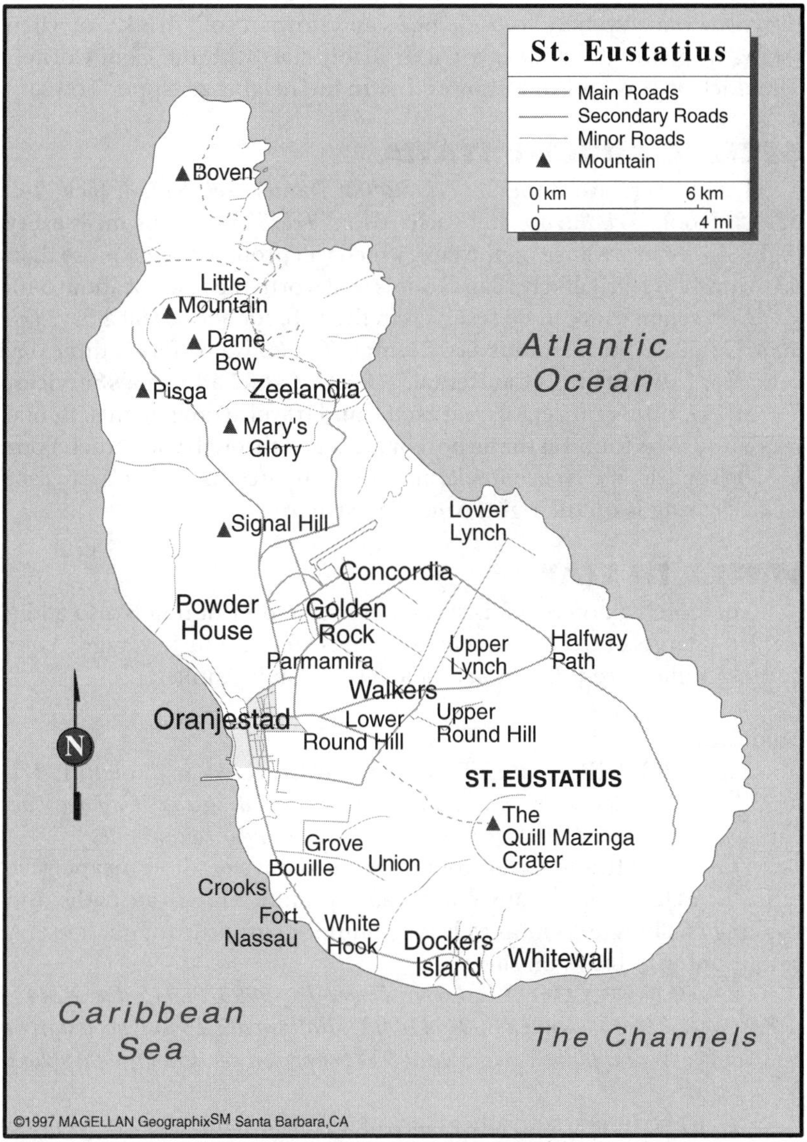
St. Eustatius
Main Roads
Secondary Roads
Minor Roads
Mountain
0 km
6 km
0
4 mi
Boven
Little Mountain
Dame Bow
Pisga
Zeelandia
Mary's Glory
Atlantic Ocean
Signal Hill
Lower Lynch
Concordia
Powder House
Golden Rock
Parmamira
Upper Lynch
Halfway Path
Walkers
Oranjestad
Lower Round Hill
Upper Round Hill
ST. EUSTATIUS
The Quill Mazinga Crater
Grove
Bouille
Union
Crooks
Fort Nassau
White Hook
Dockers Island
Whitewall
Caribbean Sea
The Channels
N
©1997 MAGELLAN GeographixSM Santa Barbara,CA

ORIENTATION

Shaped rather like a kidney bean, Statia is only about five miles long and two miles wide with its airport in the center. Its chief town is **Orajestad**, where the Cool Corner is the hangout center of downtown. Everyone ends up here to trade news and down a cold drink. So, when asking or giving directions, you'll probably start with the Cool Corner. The dock area is known as Lower Town; the heights as Upper Town.

GETTING AROUND STATIA

Taxi drivers are Bondell, *Tel. 82406*; Daniel, *Tel. 82358*; Jack, *Tel. 82275*; Hook, *Tel. 82780*; and Richardson, *Tel. 82378*. Cabs meet every flight. Agree in advance on the fare, which will probably be no more than $5 to any hotel. A half-day island tour is well worth the price of about $40.

Avis rental cars can be reserved in the U.S. for about $60 a day, *Tel. 800/331-1212*. **St. Eustatius Car Rental**, *Tel. 82572*, offers a three-day rental for $100. **Brown's Car Rental**, *Tel. 83366* and **Lady Ama's Services**, *Tel. 82451*, offers car rental, real estate, and travel arrangements. Rental cars can also be found at the airport or arranged through your hotel. Your U.S. driver's license is acceptable, and you'll also need a credit card to rent a car. Driving is on the right, American style.

WHERE TO STAY

The hotel tax on Statia is seven percent and most hotels also add a service charge of 10-15 percent to rooms, food, and beverage. Your address while here will end in Statia, Netherlands Antilles.

Moderate

AIRPORT VIEW APARTMENTS, *Golden Rock, St. Eustatius. Tel. 5993/82474. Rates at this nine-unit building start at $80 double for a one-bedroom apartment. Walk here from the airport in under five minutes.*

The perfect headquarters for the business traveler, these inexpensive efficiencies have ceiling fans, coffee maker, television, private baths, and cooking facilities indoors as well as an outdoor barbecue for guest use. A restaurant with bar is on site.

GOLDEN ERA HOTEL, *Lower Town. Tel. 5993/82345, Fax 82445, U.S. 800/223-9815; Canada 800/344-0023. Rates at this 20-unit hotel start at $88 double. A meal plan is available at $30 per person per day; breakfast alone is $7 daily.*

Clean and utilitarian, rather like a nice Amsterdam hotel, the Golden Era offers a comfortable, affordable room with air conditioning, cable television, telephone, and refrigerator. Swim the long lap pool, or walk to the museum. The PADI dive shop is next door, and some of the best diving on the sunken ruins of Lower Town is found right off the pier. The hotel has its own pool bar and a restaurant featuring local seafood and fruits.

LA MAISON SUR LA PLAGE, *Zeelandia Beach. Tel. 5993/82256, Fax 82256; toll-free 800/692-4106. Rates for the ten cottages start at $120 per couple including continental breakfast. The hotel is one mile from the airport.*

The French accent makes this spot popular with diners who come here for the views and classic continental cuisine. Swim in the seawater pool or just enjoy the views of the Atlantic and The Quill. Basic but comfortable, the hotel at press time was still rebuilding after losing five of its units in Hurricane Luis. There isn't air conditioning, and the Atlantic can make for risky swimming off the awesome, two-mile-long beach, but seekers of a remote getaway will like this remote location on Statia's northeast coast. Horseback rides can be arranged. Play checkers or backgammon in the comfortable TV room, where there are also books and a video library.

TALK OF THE TOWN, *L.E. Saddlerweg z/n. Tel. 5993/82236, Fax 82640; toll-free 800/223-9815 or 800/742-4276. Rates, which include breakfast, start at $86 for a double room and $98 for an efficiency. The 20-unit hotel is in Golden Rock, a five-minute walk from the airport.*

Most rooms face on the big pool, which is surrounded by tropical blooms. Rooms have air conditioning, cable television, radio and direct-dial telephone; efficiencies have a fully-equipped kitchenette. The hotel's restaurant serves breakfast, lunch, and dinner to a loyal following of guests, tourists, and locals.

Budget

COUNTRY INN, *Biesheuvelweg. Tel. 5993/82484. Located in Concordia just minutes from the airport, this six-room inn offers singles for $35 and doubles for $50 including breakfast. No credit cards are accepted.*

Mrs. Pompier welcomes you to her garden setting and makes you feel right at home in an air-conditioned room with radio, cable television, and alarm clock. Breakfast is included and, if you like, she'll also rustle up lunch and dinner.

DANIEL'S GUESTHOUSE *on Rose Mary Laan, tel.5993/82358. Efficiency rooms are $40.*

Baths are shared in this basic, diver-friendly inn.

KING'S WELL HOTEL, *Bay Road at Smoke Alley, between Upper Town and Lower Town. Tel. 5993/82538, Fax 82538; toll-free 800/692-4106. Rates at this eight-room hotel are from $55 including full breakfast.*

The home of one of Statia's favorite restaurants is this unpretentious inn with large rooms that have a balcony, small refrigerator, television and bath with shower but no tub. Rooms at the back of the hotel have the best views, ceiling fans, and waterbeds. Cruising sailors who came to rest here, hosts Win and Laura offer sailing lessons, a health spa, pool and a hot tub. They'll also be glad to set up your diving and sightseeing. Don't miss dinners in their restaurant.

Cottage Accommodations

A package that includes accommodations in a hotel or cottage, diving, ground transfers, and air transportation from St. Maarten is available from **Dive Statia**, *1220 Brittmore Road,, Houston TX 77043, Tel. 713/467-8835, Fax 461-6044; toll-free 800/883-7222.*

LINGER LONGER

When booking any Caribbean accommodations, but especially those in the more inaccessible islands, always ask about weekly rates. Both hosts and guests are more attuned to longer visits because getting here is so difficult that shorter stays are not practical.

WHERE TO EAT

Expensive

KING'S WELL, *in the King's Well Hotel on Bay Road in Lower Town by Smoke Alley, Oranjestad. Tel. 82538. Plan to spend $40 for dinner. It's open daily for breakfast, lunch, and dinner.*

Three spacious rooms including a breezy terrace are the home of a restaurant operated by an Irish-German couple, Laura and Wyn, whose cuisine marries great U.S. Prime steaks and roasts with good German recipes for schnitzel and roast beef. Of course, the menu also offers fresh lobster and seafood, which are served with fresh island vegetables. Try the home-smoked fish. At breakfast, have the fresh, hot donuts. Lunch features thick deli sandwiches including some made with Wyn's own, homemade sausage.

L'ETOILE, *Heilligerweg. Tel. 82299 or 82424. Main dishes are priced $8 to $22. Reservations and credit cards haven't been accepted but call to see if these policies are still in effect. Hours are Monday through Saturday noon to 10pm and Sunday noon to 6pm.*

This is the home of traditional Statia meals such as goat water (a thick stew made with goat mutton), pepperpot, curries, patties, whelk stew, stuffed land crab, pork ribs, and barbecue chicken. At lunch, dine economically on sandwiches, salads, hot dogs, and burgers.

MAISON SUR LA PLAGE, *Zeelandia Beach. Tel. 82256. Reservations aren't accepted but call about specific hours. It's open daily for breakfast, lunch, and dinner. Plan to spend $35-$40 for dinner.*

Look out through the trellis to a fabulous sea view while you dine on tasty French cuisine that starts with a pastry-wrapped terrine, a divine soup, or the escargot. Main dishes include roast lamb, chicken in wine, or a perfectly cooked filet mignon lightly splashed with a red wine sauce. For dessert have a pastry, fresh fruit, or a French cheese with biscuits.

OLD GIN HOUSE, *Lower Town. Tel. 82319. Main dishes are priced $12 to $22. It's open for breakfast, lunch and dinner Credit cards and reservations are not accepted.*

You'll want to dine on the terrace, but have a drink first in the wood-beamed pub. Lunch specials are offered every day, so you can dine economically on a fish sandwich or hamburger. At dinner, listen to the day's specials and take your pick. It could be lamb chops, a filet, lobster, or chicken served with plenty of fresh vegetables from Statia farms.

Moderate

B's GARDEN, *Fort Oranje. Tel. 82733. Dinner main dishes are in the $15-$20 range. It's open for lunch and dinner daily except Sunday and for lunch only on Monday. Credit cards aren't accepted.*

French and international dishes are served in this pretty patio near the tourist information office. Come for a sandwich or burger with a cold beer at lunch time or have dinner in a romantic courtyard framed by the old stone fort. The French influence shows in the fish baked in white wine and a scattering of shrimp, filet mignon with green peppercorn sauce, chicken cooked in wine until it falls off the bones, or grilled fish and chicken with a classic continental sauce.

BLUE BEAD BAR & RESTAURANT, *on the waterfront in Oranjestad. Tel. 3-82873. Plan to spend $10 to $25 for dinner. Credit cards aren't accepted.*

Popular for sunset watching with breathtaking views, this Indonesian, Dutch and West Indian restaurant overlooks Gallows Bay. Have the satay with spicy peanut sauce, one of the Indonesian rice dishes, Dutch pea soup, or a simply-grilled piece of chicken, fish, or beef with Creole sauce and fresh local vegetables. Have an after-dinner drink and listen to the steel band.

GOLDEN ERA HOTEL, *Lower Town. Tel. 82345. Plan to spend $18 for lunch and $25 for dinner without wine.*

This is the place to try authentic West Indian and Creole dishes, Statia style, in a restaurant that seems to hang out over the bay. There's stewed fish, curries, and tropical fruit-flavored ice creams. The buffets on Sunday night, accompanied by live music, are a favorite with locals and visitors alike.

TALK OF THE TOWN, *L.E. Saddlerweg, halfway between the airport and Oranjestad in Golden Rock. Tel. 82236. Plan to spend $20-$25 for dinner.*

Reservations aren't taken. It's open daily for breakfast and dinner; the bar stays open after the restaurant closes at 10pm.

The food here is honest and adequate, making equal appeals to the visiting North American, the Dutch business traveler, and European sunseekers. Have a steak, broiled fresh fish or breast of chicken, or a salad and the soup of the day. It's sure to be homemade and hearty – chicken with rice, fish soup, Dutch pea soup, pumpkin, or pepperpot. The chicken and pork satays are served Indonesian style with a fiery peanut sauce. Wash it down with a cold Heineken.

Budget

CHINESE RESTAURANT, *Prinsesweg 9, Upper Town. Tel. 82389. Dine for under $15. No credit cards are accepted. Dishes are priced $5 to $18. It's closed Sunday.*

Chinese dishes here have an Indonesian or West Indian accent, resulting in a nice choice of steaks, fish and chops with Creole sauce, chop suey, satays, gado-gado, sweet and sour pork, colorful stir-fried vegetables, and curries. The little dining room can be stuffy; consider ordering take-out and eating in your lodgings.

COOL CORNER BAR & RESTAURANT, *Fort Oranjestraat. Tel. 82523. It's open daily except Sunday for lunch and dinner. Dishes are priced $6 to $12.*

This is the Macy's clock of Oranjestad, the place where everyone meets, greets, and seats to watch the world go past. Order Chinese food to eat in or take out.

FRUIT TREE RESTAURANT AND CRAFT, *downtown on Prinsesweg. Tel. 82402. Dine for under $15. It's open daily including Sunday brunch.*

Stoke up on native specialties such as oxtail, peas and rice, pea soup, stewmeat, funchi and fish, johnnycake and saltfish, bush tea, "boilegg," fish soup, and much more.

STONE OVEN BAR & RESTAURANT, *15 Faeschweg. Tel. 82809. Main dishes are in the $8-$15 range. Reservations are essential but no credit cards are accepted. The restaurant is open for lunch and dinner, Tuesday through Sunday.*

Colorful Caribbean surroundings set the mood for Creole dishes such as fish and rice, goat water, fungi, curried goat or chicken, or fish in Creole sauce. Eat inside or on the patio.

Quick Takes

Superburger, *Graaffweg, Tel. 82412,* offers traditional burgers and shakes plus West Indian dishes such as peas and rice, curries, and goat water. Try one of the ice creams for dessert. Credit cards aren't accepted.

WITHOUT RESERVATIONS

It's always wise to phone early in the day when you want to eat in a small restaurant on a small island. Chefs are working with limited supplies, space, and refrigeration and need to know how many fresh fish and lobsters to order, how much soup to brew in the pot, or how many steaks to thaw. In smaller places it isn't uncommon to be asked what you'd like to have for dinner when you call for reservations.

SEEING THE SIGHTS

In the heart of **Upper Town Oranjestad**, the **St. Eustatius Historic Foundation Museum** is an ideal place to get a quick overview of the island's roistering history. Once the headquarters of Admiral Rodney, who sacked the island for aiding the rebellious Americans, the museum has some authentically-furnished rooms and exhibits on sugar refining, pre-Columbian finds, and needlework. Don't miss the gardens with their 400-year brickwork. The museum is open daily 9am to 5pm and on Saturday and Sunday mornings. A small admission is charged, *Tel. 82288.*

Two cemeteries, one Jewish and the other Dutch Reformed, tell an eloquent story from the 1700s. The old Jewish cemetery on the edge of town has the remains of a **mikvah**, one of the oldest ritual baths in the New World. The **synagogue** on Synagogpad off the square is in ruins, but it dates to 1740, two years before the date of the oldest gravestone that can be found in the Jewish Cemetery. The **Dutch Reformed Church** near the fort dates to 1775 but was so badly damaged in a hurricane a few years later that it stood in ruin until the 1980s when the tower was restored. Climb it for a view of town.

Fort Oranje was built in 1629 by the French and expanded in 1636 by Zeelanders. The cannon-studded fort is now government offices that are not a tourist attraction, but look for the plaque presented by Franklin D. Rooosevelt. It acknowledges the salute fired from here to the new United States in 1776, the first official recognition received by the new republic. In Upper Town, **St. Eustatius Historical Foundation Museum** is on Van Tonningenweg 12, *Tel. 82288.* It's open Monday through Friday 9am to 5pm and on weekends 9am to noon. The old Doncker **mansion** now houses the museum, which has exhibits depicting Statia history from the Amerindians through European discovery and settlement.

Fort Amsterdam on the northeast side of the island began as Battery Concordia. It's shown on a 1781 map but by 1874 was described as a ruin. The views from here of the surrounding seas are worth the trip.

Drive along the Bay Road to see the ruins of **Lower Town**, once the heart of the city. The sea wall and piers were destroyed by Admiral Rodney, but the 18th century ruins still tell an eloquent story above and beneath the water. Take the road to Lynch, where **Lynch Plantation** holds the only domestic museum in the Dutch Caribbean. Displays depict everyday life during the colonial era. A tour can be arranged through the **Statia Tourism Office**, *Tel. 82209* weekdays 9am to 5pm Admission is free, but donations are gladly accepted.

Driving south from Oranjestad through **Crooks** and **Hogsty**, you'll come to the site of **Fort Nassau** and then to the ruins of **Fort de Windt**, which has a grand view of St. Kitts nine miles across the sea. The fort is tucked under the towering **Mazinga**, a 1,968-foot mountain rising from Back Off Bay and the rocky White Wall.

Climb **The Quill**, a perfectly formed extinct volcano that cradles a tangled rain forest in its crater. Go with a group to make sure you don't miss the many rare and wonderful botanicals found here: tree ferns, mahogany trees, giant philodendron, ginger, surinam cherry, balsam trees, trumpet wood, and a world of orchids and bromeliads. If you're lucky, you'll get a glimpse of the rare blue pigeon. Your hotel host or the tourist office listed above can find you a competent guide.

Newly opened in the winter of 1997-98 in the Companie area in the southeast section of The Quill is the **Miriam C. Schmidt Botanical Gardens** with a picnic pavilion, barbecue areas, marked walking trails, a bee yard, and orchid gardens. In progress is **The Museum of the First Salute**, a living museum being created by the St. Eustatius Historic Foundation, Wilhelminaweg #3. It isn't expected to be fully operational until about 2006, but ask about its progress.

Jump-up Alert: Statians love jump-ups, or spontaneous street parties, so don't be surprised if your car is stopped at a blockade. Get down and party!

NIGHTLIFE & ENTERTAINMENT

Evenings here start with cocktails, then dinner, and quiet rounds of rum drinks at the **COOL CORNER**, Fort Oranjestraat, *Tel. 82523*, or **TALK OF THE TOWN**, L.E. Saddlerweg, halflway between the airport and Oranjestad in Golden Rock, *Tel. 82236*. Sometimes local bands play on weekends at local restaurants.

The liveliest nightspot is **STONE OVEN BAR & RESTAURANT**, 15 Faeschweg, *Tel. 82809*, where "Jolly Time" starts at 9pm and goes on until the cows come home.

SPORTS & RECREATION

Beaches

Some of Statia's beaches are beige sands and others black volcanic sand. Seek out **Oranje Baii** off Lower Town, **Zeelandia**, or **Lynch Beach**. The best surfing waves are at **Concordia Bay**. Keep in mind that lifeguards are seldom seen. Take all precautions.

Diving

Diving in Statia is natural history at its best, but it's also an archaeological adventure as you float over warehouses, taverns, and goods that slid into the sea during an earthquake. Dive the **Marine Park** to view 'cudas, rays, turtles, moray eels, sharks and several types of grouper. Dive spectacles include the **Grand Canyon**, **The Cliffs** covered in coral and sponge, the **Double Wreck** with two coralized ships in 60 feet of water, and **Hangover Reef** with its fabulous fish and coral.

Call **Dive Statia,** *Tel. 5993/82435;* **Golden Rock Dive Centre** at the tourist office, *Tel. 5993/82433;* **Dive Travel,** *Tel. 800/883-7222 or (713) 467-8835;* or **Blue Nature Water Sports,** *Tel. 5993/82725.*

Hiking

Climb **The Quill**, which is an extinct volcano, to look for rare hummingbirds found only here. The 12 trails are well marked but it's best to go with local guides who can tell you the names of birds and wildflowers seen along the way. There are no facilities of any kind, so get an early start and take water and food. Opened in 1998 was an easier, more shady trail with more rest stops. Participating hotels provide a voucher for guided walks or call the **tourist office**, *Tel. 82433.* Eco-tours can also be arranged through an Oregon company, **Island Trails**, Tel. *800/233-4366 or Fax 541/747-7781.*

Hiking **Gallows Bay**, look for unique blue trading beads brought by the Dutch to the islands. They're occasionally still found here but, if you don't find any, they're for sale in local shops. Guided hikes are available with **St. Eustatius Tourist Development**, *Tel. 82433.* Historic walking tours are offered by the **St. Eustatius Historical Foundation Museum,** *Tel. 82288.*

Snorkeling

Guided hiking and snorkel tours are offered by **Island Trails**, an Oregon-based company, Tel. *800/233-4366 or 541/747-7781.*

THE NATURE OF STATIA

Hiking The Quill is not just one adventure but many, depending on the birds and plants that are in sight or in season when you go. Statia regulars will tell you that once is not enough. A dramatic monolith that rises to 2,000 feet, the distinctive peak was called Kuil, meaning pit or hole, by early Dutch settlers.

You'll hike through a lush rainforest to the crater, then will descend into the crater of an extinct volcano. It's a garden of Eden filled with giant philodendron as large as elephant ears, giant tree ferns, waxy begonias laden with pink and white blooms, and many species of figs (bananas) and plantains. While you're in The Quill, look for the balsam tree, which has thick, tough leaves and a shiny, reddish-purple fruit related to the mammee apple.

Bromeliads are everywhere, sometimes in bloom. Related to the pineapple, they are plants that live on other plants without being parasitic. A popular house plant because of their spectacular blooms, bromeliads come in dozens of colors and configurations. Most types store their own water, blooming riotously when the mood hits them. Trumpet wood and towering mahogany trees are also found inside the crater.

Along your Statia rambles, you'll see breadfruit, which was brought to the New World by Captain Bligh in 1793, Surinam cherry with its delicious fruit, maiden apple, ginger, 17 kinds of orchids, iguanas, and big, scary land crabs that, properly prepared, are delicious on the dinner table. On Statia, 54 types of birds have been recorded, including 25 resident and breeding species, 12 species of sea birds, and 21 migratory species. Listen for the sound of the coqui tree frog, and watch for the harmless, but slithery, racer snake.

Tennis

Play the concrete-surfaced public tennis courts at the **Community Center** on Rosemary Lane day or night for a few dollars, *Tel. 82249.* Bring your own racket and balls.

SHOPPING

Generally, shops on St. Eustatius are open Monday through Friday 8am to noon and 1:30pm-5:30pm. Saturday hours are usually 10am to noon, 2:30-5:30pm.

St. Eustatius Art Gallery in Upper Town shows the works of local artists and crafters, *Tel. 82452.* Shop for paintings, steel drums, straw work, and embroidery. Another place to get local arts and crafts is **Hole**

in the Wall next to the Catholic churchyard in Upper Town, *Tel. 82265*. It really is a hole in a wall, charmingly filled with oddments such as slave beads, botanical jewelry, hand-painted fabrics, and earrings made from clay pipe stems.

Mazinga Giftshop on Fort Oranje Straat, Upper Town, *Tel. 82245* is a typical, small-island souvenir shop filled with treasures and trash. It's the place to get your postcards, tee shirts for the children back home, paperbacks, and jewelry.

EXCURSIONS & DAY TRIPS

Statia itself is a popular day trip from **St. Maarten**. The best excursions on the island involve picnicking, going to a beach, snorkeling, or hiking **The Quill**, all of them covered above under *Sports & Recreation*. You can get a taxi tour for about $40 a half day for up to four people and a hiking guide for about $20 and up, depending on the length and difficulty of the hike. Your hotel host or the tourist office can make the date.

PRACTICAL INFORMATION

Airport information: *Tel. 82620*

Area Code: 5993

Banking: Barclays Bank is open Monday-Thursday 8:30am to 3:30pm and Fridays 8:30am to 12:30, then 2-4:30pm. The Post Office bank opens Monday-Friday at 7:30am until 4pm. Windward Islands Bank is open Monday-Thursday 8am to noon and 1-2:30pm. On Fridays it's open 8am to noon and 2-4:30pm.

Business hours: generally 8am to 6pm, with supermarkets remaining open until 7pm.

Currency: The Antilles guider is tied to the U.S. dollar at a rate of NAfl1.80 to US$1. Dollars are accepted just about everywhere but you will probably get your change in guilders..

Electricity: North American-style 110 V.A.C., 60-cycle current is in use.

Government: The "S" islands are part of the Netherlands Antilles. U.S. consular representation is in Curacao, St. Anna Boulevard 19, *Tel. 5999/461-3066*.

Holidays: banks and shops are likely to be closed New Years, Good Friday, Easter Sunday and Monday, Whitsunday, Labour Day on May 1, Statia Day on November 16, Christmas, and Boxing Day.

Immigration: Americans and Canadians must have a passport, birth certificate or affidavit with picture, or a certificate of naturalization, re-entry permit, or green card.

Mail can be posted at the main post office on Cottage Road. It's open Monday through Friday, 7:30am to 4pm, *Tel.* 3-82207. Your address while here will be Statia, Netherlands Antilles.

Medical emergencies: Queen Beatrix Hospital has two doctors on call around the clock, *Tel.* 82211.

Pets: bring a health certificate no more than 10 days old and a record of inoculations including rabies.

Taxes include a seven percent hotel tax and a departure fee of $5 when leaving for another destination in the Dutch Caribbean. For other destinations, the fee is $10.

Telephones: To call Statia from North America, dial 011, then 599 (for Netherlands Antilles), then 3 (for Statia) then the five-digit number. To make a call within Statia, only the last five numbers are needed.

Time Zone: Statia is on Atlantic Standard time, which is the same as Eastern Daylight Savings Time. When New York is on Standard time, Statia's time is one hour later.

Tourist information: from the U.S, *Tel.* 800/722-2394. On the island, *Tel.* 82433 for phone or fax. The tourist office is opposite the Cool Corner restaurant at 3 Fort Oranjestraat, *Tel.* 5993/82433. It's open weekdays only, 8am to noon and 1pm until 4:30 or 5pm.

Weddings: two weeks before the marriage, residence must be established on the island. You'll need a birth certificate, two passport photos, and any applicable divorce or death certificates.

32. SINT MAARTEN/ ST. MARTIN

A charter boat skipper on the Dutch side best sums up the differences between the two ends of this island when he warns, "Our cruise takes us to the French side, therefore some nudity may be observed." It's one island and one people, but French tourists tend to go to the French side and everyone else goes to both sides.

The island is only 37 square miles, yet two nations divided it up with St. Maarten belonging to the Dutch and St. Martin to the French. To be precise, **St. Martin** is a commune of Guadeloupe, which is an overseas territory of France. **St. Maarten** is Dutch-governed by way of Curacao. About 32,000 people inhabit the Dutch side and 28,500 the French. It's the smallest land mass in the world to be shared by two governments.

Because they share the international airport, which is on the Dutch side, they're combined in this chapter. Still, St. Maarten is avidly marketed in North America while St. Martin, like the other French islands, has a ho-hum attitude towards English-speaking folks.

This isn't to say that Americans and non-French Canadians aren't welcome. Just don't expect them to provide as many toll-free numbers or English language brochures and other aids as you'll get from most other Caribbean islands. However, if you don't speak French and want to go to a French island, this one is the best choice because everyone is used to jumping from English and French to Dutch and patois.

Philipsburg on the south edge of the island is its main city and point of entry; **Marigot** and **Grand Case** are the major settlements in the French side, with a small airport at **Grand Case** for charter planes. The dividing line goes right through **Simpson Bay Lagoon**, which is surrounded by beach homes and resorts.

It was probably the Arawaks who first paddled canoes to this little island and named it Sualouiga, or Land of Salt. Although salt production is no longer the industry it once was, at least 12 salt ponds around the island continue their natural evaporative process. By the time Christopher Columbus landed on November 11, 1493, on the feast day of St. Martin of Tours, most of the Arawaks were already displaced by the cannibalistic Caribs. They in turn quickly succumbed to Spanish muskets, enslavement, and religious persecution.

Spain took little interest in the island until 1631, when the Dutch began eyeing it. The Spanish built a fort and dug in well enough to repel a three-week siege led by Peter Stuyvesant, later to become governor of New York. It was in this battle that the peg-leg governor lost his leg.

By 1648, no longer needing a Caribbean base, the Spanish simply sailed away and the Dutch moved in – only to find that the French had gotten there first! After some fevered diplomacy, an agreement was struck and the island was divided by the French and Dutch in 1648. For centuries St. Maarten languished, a poor country cousin to prosperous St. Eustatius, now called Statia.

In World War II, after both Holland and France fell to the Nazis, the Allies blockaded St. Martin to keep it from becoming a German base. A landing strip, later to become Princess Juliana International Airport, was built in 1943 for military reasons. When the war ended the island was a sleeping princess, ready to came awake to the sweet kiss of tourism dollars. The first hotel (as opposed to a guest house or boarding house) opened in 1974; the first resort in 1954. Its first guests were Queen Juliana and Prince Bernhard. Today the island has more than 4,000 rooms on the Dutch side alone, not counting the many condos and shopping areas that have made it one of the most cosmopolitan islands in the Caribbean. All casinos are on the Dutch side.

Only mildly hilly, with **Paradise Peak** rising to a modest 1,391 feet at the north end of the island, the island is rimmed with flawless beaches interrupted only by coves and bays cut into the coastline. In the clear waters, snorkelers can see fish and coral gardens twenty and thirty feet down.

St. Martin is the French spelling and refers to the French side; the Dutch side is Sint Maarten, which is usually now shortened to St. Maarten. By the spelling, you'll know which side we mean. It hardly matters because there are no borders to cross and, while school children are taught in French on one side and in Dutch on the other, the islanders speak a patois all their own. Most locals also speak some English.

The chief difference is in the telephone system, in which Dutch numbers have five digits and French have six (see *Practical Information* at the end of this chapter).

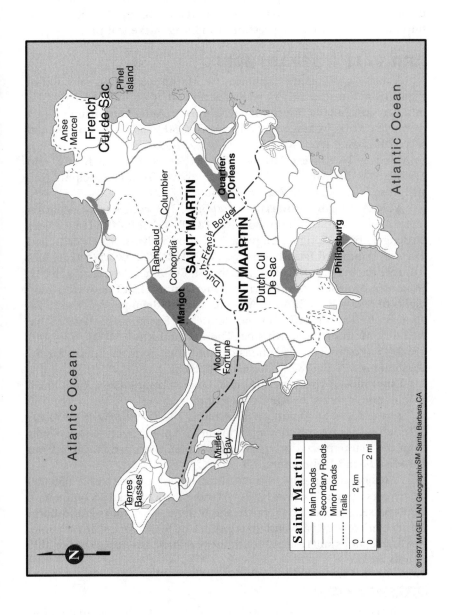

Saint Martin

Main Roads
Secondary Roads
Minor Roads
Trails

0   2 km
0   2 mi

©1997 MAGELLAN GeographixSM Santa Barbara,CA

Atlantic Ocean

Atlantic Ocean

Atlantic Ocean

Pinel Island

Anse Marcel

French Cul de Sac

Columbier

Rambaud

Concordia

Marigot

SAINT MARTIN

Quartier D'Orleans

Dutch-French Border

SINT MAARTEN

Dutch Cul De Sac

Philipsburg

Mount Fortune

Mullet Bay

Terres Basses

N

Climate

"Highs today in the mid-90s and lows tonight in the '70s," could be recorded and played daily as the weather forecast for this year-round paradise. Hazy cloudiness is more common June through October, when hurricanes and tropical depressions can bring buckets of rain.

ARRIVALS & DEPARTURES

A major hub for the Caribbean, St. Martin has a good selection of flights from Europe, the United States, and other Caribbean islands. Fly into **Princess Juliana International Airport** on **American Airlines** direct from New York, Miami, and San Juan, *Tel. 800/433-7300.* **Continental** serves the island from Newark, *Tel. 800/231-0856.* In season, service is provided by **Northwest Airlines**, *Tel. 800/447-4747* from Boston and Minneapolis. **US Air**, *Tel. 800/428-4322,* arrives from Philadelphia. Service from Paris is by **Air France**, *Tel. 800/237-2747.*

ALM Antillean Airlines, *Tel. 800/327-7230,* comes to St. Maarten from Aruba, Curacao, and Bonaire; **LIAT**, *Tel. 246/495-1187* brings passengers from Antigua, Anguilla, St. Croix, St. Kitts, St. Thomas, and Tortola; **Windward Islands Airways** (WINAIR), *Tel. 599/545-4230,* flies from St. Thomas, St. Kitts/Nevis, Saba, St. Eustatius, Anguilla, St. Barts, Dominica, Montserrat, and Tortola. **American** and **LIAT** have scheduled flights to Puerto Rico; **LIAT** to Anguilla; **Air Guadeloupe**, *Tel. 590/87-73-46* to St. Bart's, **WINAIR** to Guadeloupe, St. Eustatius, St. Barts, Saba, Anguilla, Montserrat, St. Kitts, St. Thomas, and Nevis. **BWIA**, *Tel. 800/ 538-2942* flies to Trinidad, Jamaica, Barbados, and St. Lucia. **Air St. Barthélemy**, *Tel. 590/87-73-46* serves St. Barts.

Esperance Airport near Grand Case accommodates only small airlines and is served by **Air Guadeloupe**.

Ferries travel St. Maarten and St. Barts, *Tel. 24096 or 87-10-68. White Octopus* departs from Bobby's Marina in Philipsburg and *Voyager I* sails from the marketplace dock in Marigot. Aerial tours are available from **Paradise Island Helicopters**, *Tel. 5995/54308.*

A major cruise ship port, St. Maarten welcomes about 650,000 passengers a year at its new (1997-98) tender dock that can accommodate 6,000 passengers per hour. It's in the heart of downtown Philipsburg. Under construction is a wharf that can dock up to six cruise ships at a time. It will have shops and restaurants; by the year 2000, passengers will be able to walk ashore.

ORIENTATION

The island is a sort of oval with a smaller oval sticking out to the west, surrounding **Simpson Bay Lagoon** with a necklace of beaches. The main highway heads east from the airport, then north to circle the island as far north as **Grand Case**, where there's a small airport, and around to head south through **Orleans**, past the **Great Salt Pond**, and west towards the airport again. There's said to be a marker at the border, but in our many "border" crossings, we've never noticed it. The northern end of the island is a botanical park.

Philipsburg, capital of the Dutch side, is on a narrow strip of land between **Great Bay** and **Great Salt Pond**. Its center is **Wathey Square** and the **Courthouse**, with shops lining Front Street, Back Street, and side streets for a mile or more in both directions. **Marigot** is the chief settlement on the French side, midway up the island's west coast, with piers on both **Simpson Bay** and the **Baie de La Potence**. There's parking at the south end of the Rue de La Liberté and just off the Place Du Marché. Almost all the streets are one-way so allow plenty of time for finding your way around. Continuing north brings you to **Grand Case**, a favorite for dining and browsing.

GETTING AROUND SINT MAARTEN/ST. MARTIN

Cabs operate on official, posted fares based on two passengers per trip and $1 for each addition person. Rates rise 25 percent after 10pm and 50 percent after midnight. If you don't rent a car, a taxi tour is the best way to get around. Taxi stands are found at Wathey Square in Philipsburg and near the tourist information bureau in Marigot.

To call a cab in Marigot, Tel. 87-56-54; in Philipsburg, *Tel. 22359;* in Grand Case, *Tel. 87-75-79.* Taxi fare from Juliana Airport to Marigot is $8, Grand Case $20, Esperance Airport $20. Cab fare from Marigot to Grand Case is $10. The highest fares on the list are to L'Habitation, which is $25 from Philipsburg and $30 from Maho. The minimum fare published is $4.

If you rent a car, it can be delivered to your hotel or picked up at the airport. Car rentals are available on presentation of a credit card imprint or a cash deposit of $350 to $1500 depending on the company, plus an additional collision damage waiter. Your home driver's license is accepted. Rentals cost $25 to $55 per day, usually with unlimited mileage. Driving is on the right, North American style.

Car rental agencies include **Avis**, *Tel. 87-50-60;* **Hertz**, *Tel. 87-73-01,* **Esperance**, *Tel. 87-51-09;* **Express Rent-a-Car**, *Tel. 87-87-59;* **Hibiscus Car Rental**, *Tel. 87-74-53;* and **Tropical Car Rental**, *Tel. 87-94-81.* Scooters rent for about $30 a day from **Eugene Motor**, *Tel. 87-13-74* or **Moto Caraïbes**, *Tel. 87-25-91.* Bicycles can be rented for about $12 daily from **Bike Power**, *Tel. 87-13-74.*

Buses travel about once every hour among Mullet Bay, Simpson Bay, Cole Bay, and Grand Case. Buses also shuttle regularly between Marigot and Philipsburg between 6am and midnight. Fares are $1 and $1.50.

WHERE TO STAY

The fallout of hurricanes Luis and Marilyn in 1995 is still taking a toll on St. Maarten/St. Martin hotels. By late 1997, some hotels including the swank Port de Plaisance had still not reopened. Some hotels have opened only certain sections or rooms. Even hotels that are listed on the Internet as re-opened did not open as planned. Here is a list of what is available now; we will offer more choices in future editions.

In Dutch St. Maarten, government tax is eight percent and service charges are 10-15 percent. In French St. Martin, government hotel tax is five percent and service charges are usually 10 percent. When booking, ask if tax and service charges are included in the tariffs you are quoted.

Your address when on the island will be St. Maarten, Netherland Antilles, or St. Martin, French West Indies. Area code 590 denotes the French side and 5995 the Dutch side.

Expensive

BELAIR BEACH HOTEL, *Little Bay, St. Maarten, mailing address Box 140, Philipsburg. Tel. 5995/25295. The 72-suite hotel is 10 minutes from Philipsburg and 10 minutes from Marigot. Rates start at $355 for two people in a one-bedroom suite; for six people in a two-bedroom suite, the rate is $589. A minimum stay of three nights is required except December 20-January 2, when a ten-night booking is required.*

You're right on the ocean in your own, cozy apartment with a fully equipped kitchen that has a microwave oven, toaster oven, refrigerator with icemaker. Accommodations have color cable television, VCR, two telephones, spacious balcony, and hair dryer. Furnishings are blond woods with peach and aqua pastels; floors are terracotta with straw rugs. Dine al fresco in the Sugar Bird Cafe, or rent a car on the premises and explore all the restaurants and nightlife of the Dutch and French sides. The wave-washed beach is wide and sandy, a cove that curls around a Windex-colored sea. Or, swim in the oceanfront swimming pool. Tennis is free; watersports are available. Children under age 18 sleep free when sharing a two-bedroom suite with two adults.

ESMERALDA RESORT, *Baie Orientale, 97150 St. Martin. Tel. 590/87-36-36, Fax 87-35-18. Rates at this 65-unit resort start at $300 for two in peak season, including continental breakfast. Children are age 12 sleep free in a room with two paying adults. Cab fare from the airport is about $20.*

The whites and buttery pastels of the rooms are complemented by the white sands of the beach and the azure sea and pools. Rooms and suites are in 15 villas, each with its own swimming pool (17 pools in all). Have breakfast and dinner poolside in L'Astrolabe, which features fresh fish with a continental touch. For lunch, choose among five restaurants including the oceanside Coco Beach Bar & Grill. Play tennis day or night (they have racquets and balls if you did not bring your own), snorkel off the mile-long beach, or arrange for added pleasures such as jet skiing, parasailing, water skiing, windsurfing, scuba diving, deep sea fishing, golf, horseback riding, and much more. Room service is available at extra cost and barbecue grills are available for rent. The resort has 24-hour front desk service, nightly turndown, satellite television, and a free library. Each room has a safe, direct dial telephone, kitchenette, air conditioning and private terrace.

LA SAMANNA, *Baie Longue, mail address P.O. Box 4077, 97064 St. Martin, French West Indies. Tel. 590/87-64-00, Fax 87-87-86; toll-free in the U.S. 800/854-2252. Rates at the 79-room resort start at $350 for a double room including breakfast in The Restaurant. Villas are available with up to three bedrooms. The hotel is 10 minutes, or a $10 cab ride, from the airport.*

Long known for its luxury touches, this hotel and villas complex is heavily booked by repeat guests, so make your plans early. Island arts and motifs decorate rooms that are designed for homey privacy. The property faces the Caribbean and backs up to Simpson Bay Lagoon with its bobbing boats and swooping waterfowl. Right on the French-Dutch border, it's handy to both the shopping of Philipsburg and the dining in Marigot, with plenty of sightseeing and nightlife between. The pampering begins when you register in your own room with its fresh flowers, stocked bar, air conditioned bedroom, and private terrace or patio overlooking the ocean.

Dine in The Restaurant or the Terrace Grill or order from the 24-hour room service menu. Watersports and tennis are complimentary; cruises and deep sea fishing can be arranged at additional cost. Use the fitness center privately or with a certified trainer, swim in one of the pools or off the long beach, check out a book from the library, make an appointment for spa services, or plan an island picnic.

L'ESPLANADE CARAÏBES, *Grand-Case. Tel. 590/87-06-55. The 24-suite hotel is a 30-minute drive from Queen Juliana airport or 15 minutes from Marigot. Rates start at $210. Meal plans are available.*

The first truly luxurious hotel on the French side of the island, this hotel won a Super Star Hotel designation from Star Service, and accolades from *Les Romantiques*, a newsletter devoted to romantic getaways. Ocean-view suites are surrounded by gardens alight with pink bougainvillea and yellow allamanda. Rattan furniture and tile floors are livened with bright island prints and accented with rich Brazilian woods. Have breakfast brought to your room, then dine out the rest of the day at the two dozen restaurants that line the road along Grand-Case. Or, shop the Superette for supplies and picnic in your suite. Although the hotel has no restaurants, its big pool has a swim-up bar.

The resort has its own boat for deep sea fishing. Along the beach, which is a five-minute walk away, you can snorkel, swim, windsurf, or parasail.

LE FLAMBOYANT HOTEL RESORT, *Route des Terres Basses, Baie Nettlé, 97150 St. Martin. Tel. 590/87-60-00, Fax 87-99-57; toll-free 800/221-5333. Rates at this 271-suite resort start at $195. It's just west of Marigot and on the opposite side of Simpson Bay from the airport. Taxi fare from Juliana Airport is $15.*

Your studio or suite has all you need for light cooking and a carefree, private vacation. Walk to the sea or lagoon or just hang out at the resort's own Jacuzzi. The pool is enormous; the nearby marina offers boat excursions.

LE MÉRIDIEN L'HABITATION/ LE DOMAINE, *Anse Marcel, B.P. 581, 97056 St. Martin. Tel. 590/87-67-00, Fax 87-30-38, 800/543-4300. Rates at the 396-room complex start at $256 at the older L'Habitation and $288 at Le Domaine, where rooms have an ocean view. It's 12 miles from the airport, six from Marigot, and three from Grand Case. Taxi fare from Juliana Airport is $30; from Marigot, $18.*

This member of the prestigious Meridien group is set in a 180-acre seaside garden edged by the bay and ocean, a sea of sunny yellow roofs. One resort, it's comprised of L'Habitation and Le Domaine de Lonvilliers, sharing a 1,600-foot beach, two freshwater swimming pools, two Jacuzzis, six tennis courts, squash courts, boutiques, archery, beauty salon, massage facilities, a major marina, and a car rental. A shuttle takes guests to the casinos, Marigot, and Philipsburg. Your room is done in bold colors and an African beat. It is air conditioned and has direct dial telephone, balcony or terrace, satellite television, safe, hair dryer, and mini-bar. Dining is in the casual Le Barbeque, La Belle France, or the open-air La Veranda featuring Italian fare. Breakfast is served in La Balaou.

MAHO BEACH HOTEL & CASINO, *Maho Bay. Tel. 52115 or, in the U.S. 800/223-0757. Rates start at $225. MAP is available, but has to be arranged at the desk on arrival. Taxi fare from the airport, which is five minutes away, is $5-$7. Parking in the three-level, 24-hour car park is $15 a week.*

On the plus side, this is a big complex containing everything needed for a great time – restaurants, a comely casino, (as well as a big bank of slot machines in the hotel lobby), some of the best night spots on the island, a brown sugar beach pounded by powerful coamers, and a street of shops selling everything from fine fashions and crafts to toothpaste and diamonds. The hotel's rooms are spacious and are tastefully but sparsely furnished with the bare basics. Balconies have a grand overview of the beach and we loved having a birds-eye view of a busy runway swarming with airplanes from all over the world. The Rhode Island-size pool, advertised as the largest on the island, has a swim-up bar.

On the minus side: the gaggles of group travelers who are processed like cheese. When we complained about the unreliable fulfillment of our breakfast vouchers, an uncaring desk manager shrugged that she had no control over food service, which is handled by concessionaires. However, we're told that attitudes have improved greatly since a recent staff-sensitivity training program was given. Bath amenities are sparing; the bath is dimly lit, and there are no extras such as clock radios, pad and pen by the phone, or hair dryers. Neither the satellite television nor direct-dial telephones worked much of the time.

One bright spot is Peter's Health Club on the second floor, (see *Where to Eat*). Rumboat Cafe and Cheri's Cafe, both part of the hotel complex, are among the most popular night spots on this end of the island. Opposite each other overlooking the street, they are popular meet markets and people-watching platforms for islanders as well as visitors. The hotel's activities desk is staffed most hours of the day to book anything from meals to excursions. Car rental and indoor parking are in the hotel; a taxi stand and bus stop are just outside.

PRIVILEGE RESORT & SPA, *Anse Marcel, St. Martin. Tel. 590/87-38-38, Fax 87-44-12; toll-free 800/525-4800 in the U.S. and Canada. Rates are from $210 including continental breakfast. It's in the northeast part of the island, 12 miles from the airport.*

A member of Small Luxury Hotels of the World, this seaside resort has one of the best spas on the island. Swim in the spacious pool with its breezy sun deck overlooking the ocean. Enjoy the sauna, tennis and squash courts, a second swimming pool, fitness center and a choice of restaurants and bars including a night club. Rooms and suites are airily done in powder puff neutrals and pastels with accents in deep tones; baths are marble.

Nearby there's horseback riding, diving, sailing, and deep-sea fishing. At the day's end put yourself in the hands of spa experts for a massage or a treatment from a long list of wraps and rubs.

Moderate

CAPTAIN OLIVER'S, *Oyster Pond. Tel. 590/87-30-00. Rooms at this 50-room inn start at $180. Ask about bungalows with kitchen and patio.*

The captain likes to advertise that you can park in France and dine in Holland. The setting on the border is a big marina with a great bar and restaurant, big swimming pool, boat rides, and sailing including overnights. Ask about packages that include some nights afloat and some on land.

CUPECOY BEACH CLUB, *Cupecoy Lowlands, Simpson Bay, mailing address Box 3007, Philipsburg. Tel. 5995/52243, Fax 52243. Rates at this 88-*

unit resort start at $175. Apartments with one, two or three bedrooms are available.

The resort's white buildings curve around a salt-white beach. Units are decorated differently because they're privately owned and rented out by a professional management team that operates it like a first class hotel (but without the planned activities). If you opt for a "double" it will be the bedroom of a full-size apartment, locked off from the other rooms. If you have a family or want to share an apartment with another couple, it's a real plus to have one of the two-or three-bedroom condos with extra baths and a full kitchen. Accommodations have air conditioning, telephone, and television. The club has a swimming pool and two bars and it's near the Mullet Bay Golf Club.

CLUB ORIENT NATURIST RESORT, *Orient Bay. Tel. 590/87-33-85, Fax 87-33-76. Rates start at $196. It's 10 miles from the airport.*

This naturist resort offers chalets and individual studios, and the option of wearing clothes or nothing at all. It's on the clothing-optional beach and has tennis courts. Accommodations have cooking facilities.

GRAND CASE BEACH RESORT, *Grand Case. Tel. 800/447-7462. Taxi fare from the airport is about $15. Rates at this 71-suite resort start at $220 for a studio with kitchenette; apartments are from $320. Rates include continental breakfast.*

Walk to the legendary restaurants of Grand Case from this waterfront resort. Or you can cook in your own kitchen or sidle up to the resort's own Panorama Beach for American-style burgers and hot dogs with a French bistro accent. Breakfasts are served on the patio in Sea Grapes. Play complimentary tennis, snorkel, dive, paddle boat, sail, or swim in the pool or ocean. Beach towels and beach chairs are also complimentary. Air conditioning is available in some units; views are of the sea or garden. For families, two-bedroom units are available, some with loft.

HOLLAND HOUSE BEACH HOTEL, *P.O. Box 393, Front Street 43, Phillipsburg. Tel. 5995/22572, Fax 5995-24673. Rates start at $130 single and $145 double. Parking is on Back Street.*

The downtown location of this European-style hotel is a plus for people who like to walk to restaurants, shops and casinos, but it also offers a sand beach as fine as any on the island. The hotel and its restaurant are much more Dutch than most of the island's resorts, making it a favorite with business and government travelers as well as with North Americans who want a taste of the old Sint Maarten. Dutch features include shining wood floors, solid wood doors, a tiny elevator, and a basic kitchenette in most units. Rooms also have cable television and a phone. Each unit has a balcony overlooking the beach or street, with just enough latticework to provide a little shade.

If you'll be here for Carnival, make reservations early and ask for a room on the street side so you'll have a million-dollar view of the parade.

HORNY TOAD GUESTHOUSE, *Simpson Bay, mailing address Box 3029 Philipsburg. Tel. 5995/55423, Fax 53316; toll-free 800/417-9361, extension 3013. Rates at this eight-unit guesthouse are from $180. It's ten minutes from the airport. Credit cards aren't accepted.*

Americans Erle and Betty Vaughn provide some of the Caribbean's warmest hospitality in this beachfront inn that started out as an ample mansion built in the 1950s by a former governor. The inn doesn't serve food but there's a barbecue you can use and units have kitchenettes. Several restaurants including the popular Lynette's and a Pizza Hut are within easy walking distance. Ask for the room in the round house with the sea view. Younger children under age seven don't find a lot to do here, but this homey hideaway makes a good choice for families that shun rah-rah resorts.

MARY'S BOON, *Simpson Bay, mailing address Box 2078. Tel. 5995/ 54235. Rates at this 14-studio inn start at $175. Meal plans are available. Children are welcome only in summer. It's five minutes from the airport.*

Mark and Carla Cleveland (who are from Houston) are the spark plugs who have taken over Mary Pomeroy's popular inn and restaurant on the beach near the airport. Your accommodations come with kitchenette, private bath and patio, television, telephone, and air conditioning. There's a small library and a great beach with watersports equipment but mostly this is a simple inn where you can sun, relax, and read. We didn't find airport noise to be a problem. In fact, it's fun to watch the big planes, freshly arrived from all over the world, as they come in for a landing. Meals in Pomeroy's, the inn's restaurant, are outstanding.

PASANGGRAHAN, *15 Front Street, mailing address Box 151, Philipsburg. Tel. 5995/23588, Fax 22885; toll-free 800/223-9815. Rates at this 24-room guesthouse start at $115. It is closed the month of September.*

This was the island's first government guest house and it shows its age in good and bad ways. Ask for one of the newer, renovated rooms with air conditioning. The restaurant (see *Where to Eat*) is a find, whether or not you are staying here. The perfect address for people who prefer city life to resorts, this one is in the center of town yet it's on a pretty sand beach so you have the best of both worlds.

Budget

CARL'S UNIQUE INN, *Cole Bay, mailing address Box 175. Tel. 5995/ 42812, Fax 45376. Rates at this 16-unit inn are from $75 including continental breakfast. Studios are available. It's a $7 taxi ride from the airport.*

Popular with business travelers, including a conference room with theater seating for up to 50, this tastefully appointed inn just east of the airport is a handy address for leisure travelers who like to stay near Philipsburg. Nearby, a grocery store and bakery can supply provisions if you get one of the studios with a kitchenette.

CHEZ MARTINE, *Grand Case. Tel. 590/87-51-59, Fax 87-87-30. Rates at this six-room inn start at $80 double and $60 single. It's 9.7 miles from the airport.*

If you want to be on the Grand Case beach, let Martine put you in a room or apartment in a home-like, unpretentious, no-frills guest house.

HEVEA, *163 boulevard de Grand Case. Tel. 590/87-56-85, Fax 87-83-88. Rates at this eight-room inn are from $55. Meal plans are available. It' 9.7 miles from Juliana Airport.*

Picture a romantic four-poster, carved mahogany bed shrouded in gauzy netting in a high-ceiling room with exposed beams. Known for its fine dining, Hevea offers dinner at a special price to its overnight guests. The beach is across the street. Studios and apartments are available in the look that its owners call "un *jolie petit hotel de style colonial.*"

JOSHUA ROSE GUESTHOUSE, *Back Street 17, Philipsburg. Tel. 5995/24317, Fax 30080. Rooms are from $50.*

You're in the heart of the Dutch capital only a short walk from the city beach and all of its restaurants including the Chinese restaurant located on the site. Twin and double rooms are available.

ROSELY'S HOTEL, *Marigot. Tel. 590/87-70-17, Fax 87-70-20 has 48 rooms starting at 280F including continental breakfast. It's 6.2 miles from the airport.*

Enjoy the busy port of Marigot while staying at this affordable hotel reminiscent of a well-worn hotel in a small French city. Apartments and studios are available.

SOL HOTEL AMBIANCE, *Oyster Pond, St. Martin. Tel. 590/87-38-10, Fax 87-32-23 or 800/476-5849. Doubles at this eight-unit hotel start at $125 including continental breakfast. Ask about no-frills weekly rates. It's 9.3 miles from Queen Juliana Airport just inside the French border.*

You're handy to the marina and restaurants in this hillside lodge. With the no-frills plan you get maid service only once a week. If you want only an inexpensive place to hang your hat, this is it.

SUNRISE, *Cul-de-Sac, tel.590/29-57-00, Fax 87-39-28; toll-free 800/476-5849. Rates at this 20-unit inn start at $130 for a studio, including continental breakfast. It's 10.3 miles from Queen Juliana Airport in the northeast part of the island.*

You're out of the mainstream on the far northeast corner of the island handy to the clothing-optional pleasures of Orient Beach. You'll need a car for restaurants, provisioning, beaching and sightseeing, but the hotel does have a swimming pool.

Villa Rentals

If you want to rent a home or villa on the French side by the week or month, try:

- **Carimo**, *Tel. 590/87-57-58, Fax 87-71-88*
- **Immobilier St. Martin Caraïbes**, *Tel. 590/87-55-21*
- **West Indies Immobilier**, *Tel. 590/87-56-48*
- **International Immobilier**. *Tel. 590/ 87-79-00*
- **Sprimtour**, *Tel. 590/87-58-65*
- **Interprom**. *Tel. 590/87-32-46*

On the Dutch side try **St. Martin Rentals**, *Tel. 5995/44330*. Private villas on the island can also be booked through **WIMCO**, *800/932-3222* or *401/849-8012*. Maid service and staff are available.

Caribbean Islands Travel Service, *7145 Deer Valley Road, Highland MD 20777, Tel. 800/476-5849 or 301/854-2027*, offers full booking service including the best airfares to St. Martin. The agency specializes in the naturist resorts of **Orient Beach**, but can also book other St. Martin accommodations with and without cooking facilities.

WHERE TO EAT

Note that traffic is atrocious, most streets are one-way, and parking is limited. Consider taking a taxi, especially when dining in Grand Case. Most areas also have good bus service. The franc circulates in St. Martin but not as universally as in other French islands. Menus list prices in dollars or in both francs and dollars. On the Dutch side, U.S. dollars are listed on all menus, which sometimes also express prices in guilders.

Try a **Guavaberry cocktail** made with the unique island liqueur. The botanical name for the popular local berry is Euginia Floribunda. It ripens in mid-December and is unrelated to the better-known guava.

Expensive

ANTOINE, *Front Street 49, Philipsburg. Tel. 22964. Main dishes are priced $18 to $36. Reservations are recommended. It's open Monday through Saturday for lunch and dinner.*

Dine by candlelight in a romantic setting overlooking Great Bay. The food is French with Creole touches. Classic French dishes include a perfect onion soup, steak au poivre, duckling with cherries, lobster thermidor, and filet mignon with bearnaise sauce. On the Creole side are fresh fish dishes with spicy sauces, curries, and tropical fruits and vegetables. Try the veal scallops in Dijon cream sauce. The wine list is long and comprehensive.

HEVEA, *Boulevard de Grand-Case. Tel. 87-56-85. Main dishes are priced $25 to $35. Call early to reserve a table between 6:30 and 11pm. The restaurant is small, so reservations may have to be made a day or more in advance.*

Dress up for a special evening at a white linen-draped table set with fine china and surrounded by French provincial armchairs upholstered in ruby red. The owners came from France so they offer authentic dishes including chicken in wine, duck breast, Caesar salad made to order, filet mignon with bordelaise sauce, and classic potages. Caribbean influences come into play in the fresh seafood, citrus sauces, and tropical fruits and vegetables.

L'AUBERGE GOURMANDE, *Boulevard de Grand Case. Tel. 87-73-37. Main dishes are priced $20 to $35. Seatings are at 7 and 9pm Reservations are essential.*

The setting is an old West Indian house, its pillars guarding the facade that has distinctive archways with matching arched shutters. The porches are intricate fretwork typical of Creole homes of the 1800s. Good wines can send the price of a Grand Case meal soaring, but hosts Christine and Phillipe Cassan offer a "wine service" in which you get a taste of a suitable wine with each course. Start with the mussel soup or cold potato soup with just the right hint of chives and parsley. Fresh fish and lobster can be grilled or sautéed and brandished with one of Phillipe's magical sauces. For dessert, have cream puffs, creme brulée or a chocolate gateau.

LE PERROQUET, *75 Airport Road, west of Philipsburg. Tel. 54339. Main dishes are priced $19 to $28. Reservations are essential. It is open for dinner daily 6-10pm except Monday. It's also closed the months of June and September.*

So close to the airport you could have dinner here during a layover or while waiting for a late flight, this gourmet French restaurant is created in a stately Creole house situated to catch breezes blowing across this narrow strip of land between the Caribbean and Simpson Bay. Choose something from the cart, or study the menu. It offers such exotics as ostrich (which is now being raised on the sister island of Curacao) and wild boar. Or, dine more conventionally on fresh red snapper in a garlicky butter sauce, duck with orange sauce laced with orange liqueur, filet mignon in a bordelaise sauce, or spicy seafood soups generously laden with mussels, bits of crab and lobster, and fish stock that is obviously homemade by a skilled hand.

LE POISSON D'OR, *on the waterfront in Marigot. Tel. 87-72-45. Reservations are essential. It's open daily for dinner. Plan to spend $50-$60.*

An old stone greathouse with a wrap-around veranda is the setting for a restaurant that seats less than 50, so reserve a day or two ahead. Goose liver is sautéed and served with poached pear, soups are simmered to perfection, lobster comes with simple garlic butter, and fresh snapper may be ordered pan-fried and splashed with white wine and a little parsley. Just reading the menu will transport you to France.

LE TASTEVIN, *Boulevard de Grand Case. Tel. 87-55-45. Reservations are essential. It's open daily for lunch and dinner but credit cards aren't accepted at lunch.*

Located on the ocean side of the boulevard is this Burgundian restaurant specializing in Franco-Caribbean delectables. Take a table on the deck overlooking the water, where the blue and white table linens are a match for the sea and sky beyond. Furnishings are bamboo and rattan, with candles centering the tables to create a romantic setting under a tropic moon. Tonight's menu might offer duckling in lime sauce, filet mignon with bearnaise sauce, a curry, chicken in white wine, or beef in red wine. For dessert have fruit and cheese or a creamy flan.

LA VIE EN ROSE, *Boulevard de France at rue de la République, Marigot. Tel. 87-54-42. Main courses are priced $30 to $40; plan to spend $80 per person for dinner. It's open for lunch and dinner daily except Sundays in summer. Reservations are required.*

Picture Paris in the days following World War 1, when Edith Piaf sang in smoky night clubs and couples strolled along the foggy Seine after dinner. In modern France, piaf is slang for a chanteuse; with luck, you may hear one here. Dine by candlelight or, if you can get a reservation on the veranda, outdoors overlooking the sea from the second-floor balcony. This is the spot for a special, romantic dinner. Order the fish soup, a chop in red wine sauce, chicken breast with capers, or fresh fish in a cloud of spinach souffle. Save room for a sweet made in house by a superb pastry chef.

LADY MARY, *docked at Bobby's Marina, Philipsburg. Tel. 53892. Reservations are essential; the boat sails at 7pm and returns at 10pm. Tickets are $65 including dinner and all drinks.*

The boat *Lady Mary* was built in Panama City, Florida, as a private vessel in 1972 (the original parlor stove and upright piano are still on board) and today she's a popular dinner boat. A liveaboard couple, Jean-Pierre (J.P.) and Lorna Gilbert, host guests personally, serving drinks and then dinner and wines while the boat sails the protected waters of Simpson Bay Lagoon. The waters are one of the world's most important mullet nurseries; around the lagoon are the twinkling lights of the hotels and private mansions built by European millionaires. Fill your plate at the buffet where coconut chicken, fish in tomato sauce, a couple of salads, French bread, and peas and rice have been set out. Then dine on the top deck while J.P., a French Canadian with an accent as thick as quiche Lorraine, keeps your wine glass filled. For dessert there's cake with fruit and rum sauce, followed by coffee and liqueurs.

LE BEC FIN, *119 Front Street in the Museum Arcade, Philipsburg. Tel. 22976. Reservations are essential for dinner. Plan to spend $10-$20 for lunch in the cafe; $30-40 for dinner in the dining room. The cafe opens at 8am for breakfast and lunch. Dinner is served nightly.*

Overlook Great Bay while you dine on flaming extravaganzas fired at your table. Equally dazzling are the cloud-like souffles or Baked Alaska for dessert. Fresh fish with imaginative sauces is always available and the grilled lobster is a consistent winner. For starters try the velvety lobster bisque or the snail-stuffed vol-au-vent with creamy fennel sauce. One of the island's most dependable gourmet restaurants, Le Bec Fin once hosted Queen Beatrix. Lunch specials are available for take-out.

L'ESCARGOT, *84 Front Street, Philipsburg. Tel. 5995-22483. Starters are $7.50-$12.50 and entrees $17.50 to $28.50. Plan to spend $40 for a three-course dinner without wine. Reservations are urged. Hours are 10:30am to 3pm and 6pm to 11pm.*

This French restaurant in the heart of the Dutch side is as Parisian as a baguette and as friendly as Mom's parlor. It's merrily painted in red, white, and blue, the colors of the Dutch and French flags as well as the Stars and Strips and Britain's Union Jack. Once a private home, the building is loaded with historic hominess overlaid with French posters and a-flutter with the attentions of the French owner-hosts, Joel and Sonya. The snails, prepared seven different ways, are a must. The meal then marches on through quiche Lorraine, a salad, and entrees such as swordfish in Creole sauce, yellowtail snapper in white wine sauce, crisp duck in pineapple and banana sauce, or steak au poivre vert.

Be here on Saturday nights for the hilarious dinner shows in which the host and his cronies dress up like celebrities and lip-sync to their records. There are no tables for two on Saturday nights. You'll be seated wherever there's room, which is part of the fun.

Moderate

CAPTAIN OLIVER'S RESTAURANT & MARINA, *in the Captain Oliver Resort, Oyster Pond. Tel. 87-30-00. It's open daily noon to 5pm and 7-10pm. Main dishes are priced $18 to $30. Reservations are suggested.*

Oliver Lange began in the restaurant business with his Le Mors aux Dents in Paris, and brought his skills to the sunny skies of St. Martin in the 1980s. Overlook a classy marina filled with yachts from all over the world while you dine on fish stew, conch, grilled lobster, tuna or wahoo steak, snapper, or the ever-popular fisherman's platter.

CHESTERFIELD'S, *Bobby's Marina, Great Bay, Philipsburg. Tel. 23484. It's open every day for breakfast, lunch, and dinner until 10pm and the bar stays open later. Credit cards aren't accepted. Plan to spend $10 for lunch and $16 for a dinner main dish or $25-$35 for a four-course meal.*

This nautical, open-air porch on the water is popular with the yachting crowd. Start with conch fritters or escargot baked in garlic butter, a salad and sautéed sea scallops, or beer-battered fried shrimp. The Scallops Madagascar is a creamy curry treatment for succulent scallops. The Duck Chesterfield is crispy roast duckling in a pineapple and banana sauce. The pepper steak is 12 ounces of strip sirloin served with a sauce of black peppercorns and cognac cream. For dessert have the mud pie or rum raisin ice cream with chocolate sauce. The Sunday Brunch with free champagne is a bonanza.

DA LIVIO, *189 Front Street, St. Maarten. Tel. 5995-22690. Hours are noon to 2pm Monday to Friday and 6 to 10pm Monday through Saturday. Plan to spend $25 for dinner.*

A jaunty green awning adds class to the entry to what is otherwise an unprepossessing, narrow storefront. Inside, however, you're in a fine Italian inn filled with scents of garlic, basil, good cheeses, and simmering sauces. The rich and famous (including Paul Newman, Eddie Murphy, and Harry Belafonte) have come here for more than 20 years for the homemade pastas and sauces. Choose from a menu of seafood, beef, veal, and chicken classics all prepared with an Italian spin. Daniel Jurczenko and his staff suggest a cappuccino after dinner and an Italian wine with your meal.

THE FRIGATE, *on Mullet Bay west of the airport. Tel. 52801. Plan to spend $25 to $35 for dinner. Call for hours and reservations.*

You'll feel like the overseer of a grand plantation when you sink into one of the big, wicker armchairs in this pleasantly tropical room. Steak, chicken, or lobster are cooked in the open kitchen while you help yourself from the salad bar. This is a must for the carnivore who wants nothing more than an uncomplicated steak, a choice of potato, and plenty of salad to go with them.

GRAND CAFE EUROPE, *in the Maho Plaza across from Casino Royale. Tel. 54455. Dine for under $20. Call for hours, which vary seasonally. It's closed Sunday.*

Europeans and North Americans mingle here for charcoal-grilled steaks and such imported seafood specialties as Dover sole, smoked eel, and herring, washed down with plenty of beer.

IL NETTUNO, *Boulevard de Grand-Case. Tel. 87-77-38. Reservations are recommended. Main dishes are priced $18 to $30; lunch platters are in the $10-$15 range. It's open daily noon to 3pm and 6-10:30pm. Reservations are recommended.*

Dine on the deck overlooking the water that only yesterday was the home of your dinner. The catches of the day can be grilled, fried, or blackened but pastas are the stars of this menu so don't miss the lobster ravioli or penne tossed with salmon. Traditional Italian favorites such as veal Parmesan, chicken in tomato sauce, and saltimbocca are above reproach. Ask what sauces are simmering on today's stove because the chef loves to wing it with the freshest and most interesting ingredients he can find.

LA ROSA TOO, *in the Maho Plaza Shopping Center. Tel. 53470. Reservations are urged. It's open for dinner daily except Tuesday, 6-11pm. Main dishes are priced $18 to $26.*

This Sicilian restaurant within walking distance of the hundreds of hotel rooms in a big resort and shopping complex is one of the more accessible restaurants. The locale also has frequent bus service. Italian classics include chicken Parmesan, veal Marsala, pastas tossed with tidbits of juicy seafood, or filet mignon that goes perfectly with a side order of pasta. Or, order the fresh fish or lobster unadorned, accompanied with a simple salad and lots of crusty bread. The splashy waterfall is a nice touch, providing a sound filter for the general bustle of a busy shopping center. Dine indoors with air conditioning, or on the terrace when there's a breeze.

MARY'S BOON, *off the airport road, Simpson Bay. Tel. 54235. Reservations are essential, especially for dinner, which is served at 8pm. Daily specials including appetizer, dessert, and coffee are under $35.*

Every day brings a new treat: veal Dijonais, roast duck, lobster Creole, shrimp Provençal, chicken cordon bleu. Meals are served family style, and you help yourself as dishes are passed. Arrive early enough to have a drink at the honor bar and enjoy the view over the water to Saba in the hazy distance.

LYNETTE'S, *Airport Road at the end of the runway of Queen Juliana Airport. Tel. 52865. Plan to spend $25 for dinner. Reservations are recommended.*

This is a good-times place where you overlook the lagoon while dining on grilled fish, curries, pumpkin soup, calalloo, crab backs, fried plantains, lobster Creole, steak, chicken or chops in Creole sauce, and Bananas Foster. The salads at lunch are a mouthful. On Tuesday and Friday evenings, the island's king of calypso performs.

OLD ROCK CAFE AND GRILL, *on Simpson's Bay opposite the Atrium Hotel. Tel. 42369. It's open daily for breakfast, lunch, and dinner. Plan to spend $25 for dinner.*

It's fun to cook your own chicken, seafood, beef or a combination on the hot rock that is set in front of you. The salad bar is free with meals. If you're not into rock cooking, order the fresh seafood combination platter or a steak that is delivered on a sizzling platter.

RANCHO ARGENTINA, *in the La Palapa Center, east of the airport on the Dutch side. Tel. 52495. Steaks are sized to your order in a price range of $8.50 to $15.50; salads are $4.95 to $6.95.*

A huge barn of a room with a sky-high thatched ceiling and a floor of rustic brick and terra cotta, this is the place to go for the best steak this side of Buenos Aires. Sit at a mahogany table the size of an aircraft carrier. It's set with thick, cowhide placemats and leather-covered menus. Live music filters down from the stage while you order a steak by the type, size and doneness you want. While it's cooking, have Argentine bean soup or a fish cream soup, followed by a Caesar salad, mixed greens with Gorgonzola, or a crisp and interesting corn salad. If you don't like steak, order the barbecued ribs or chicken, but vegetarians have rough sledding here. Meats come with grilled corn on the cob and fried potatoes.

WAYANG DOLL, *137 Front Street, Philipsburg. Tel. 22687. A 19-dish rijsttafel costs $24.90 per person; a 12-dish version is also available. It's open nightly for dinner 7-10pm; reservations are suggested.*

Dining in the Dutch West Indies calls for trying at least one rijsttafel, the feast brought by the Dutch from Indonesia. In ancient times, as many as 350 dishes were paraded to the table; today 19 seems like more than enough. Central to the meal is nasi putih, or steamed white rice. A group of hotplates is set up in the center of the table, and dishes flood in from the kitchen: beef in coconut, pork in soy sauce with ginger, Javanese chicken, chicken in kemiri nuts and coconut milk, meatballs in soy sauce with a hint of nutmeg, gado gado (salad), chili fried vegetables, marinated shrimp, and much more.

Everyone samples everything with plenty of steaming, flavorful rice. The chef is Indonesian-born Edu Joedhosowarno, who still prepares his family's recipes for spice blends in a time-worn stone mortar and pestle. The restaurant is housed in an old home and is decorated simply but exquisitely with Indonesian artifacts. When the breezes slow, it can be too warm. Ask to be seated near one of the (too few) fans.

Budget

GRILL & RIBS CO., *Front at Old Street, Philipsburg. Tel. 24723. All you can eat is $10.95. Located upstairs and next to Pizza Hut, it serves lunch and dinner daily.*

Chicken ribs, and all the trimmings provide a whale of a feed for little *dinero.*

HARBOR POINT, *Maho Beach Hotel, Tel. 52115, extension 4933. Salads and sandwiches start at $4.95; dinners average $20. The Wednesday night barbecue serves all you can eat and drink for $25. Hours are 7am to 11:30pm.*

Feel a buzz of international excitement here overlooking the airport runway with distant views of St. Kitts, Statia, and Saba stretching to the blue horizon. It's as good a place for a business lunch as for a family affair because the landings and takeoffs provide diversion while you munch on burgers, fresh fish, salads, or sandwiches. Arrive early enough for a drink at the bar, presided over by Motie the bartender and his two parrots. Live music performs Wednesday through Saturday evenings on the torchlit terrace.

HOLLAND HOUSE, *Front Street 43, Philipsburg. Tel. 22572. Dinner is $15 to $20. It opens for breakfast at 6am and serves dinner until 10pm.*

It's a little corner of Holland set in a garden filled with yellow allamanda vines and rustling palms in the rear of a downtown hotel. The menu is one of the few we saw that is written in English and Dutch and listed prices in both dollars and guilders. The food and setting will transport you to a small hotel in Amsterdam. Feast on such Dutch treats as pickled herring, boiled eggs, Dutch beers, good cheese, and hearty main dishes such as snapper in white wine, vegetarian pasta, or duck a l'orange.

KRISHNA INDIAN BAR, *Coliseum Alley #2, Philipsburg. Tel. 23796. Dine for $10-$15. The restaurant is open Monday through Saturday for lunch and dinner, and on Sundays too in high season. Reservations are accepted.*

A favorite for lunch on shopping days, as well as a good spot to end the day is this authentic Indian restaurant in downtown Philipsburg. Choose from a large menu that includes chicken vindaloo and classic Indian vegetarian dishes as well as such island favorites as curried goat, fried fish, and shrimp Masala.

LE BALAOU, *3 Rue du Crabe, Grand Case. Tel. 87-26-22. It's open for lunch and dinner. Dishes are priced $8-$12.*

Set right on the beach on a terrace built on stilts in the sand, this informal restaurant is a good place to have a cold drink or lunch, or dinner in the cool of the evening. Joel and Marie France are aptly named; they specialize in French dishes and in fresh seafood. Keep it simple with a crisp salad, grilled snapper, and sizzling *pommes frites*.

OLD CAPTAIN, *105 Front Street opposite Orange School. Tel. 26988. An all-you-can-eat lunch is $12.*

A wacky combination of sushi bar, salad bar, and Cantonese restaurant adds up to a lot of good eating from a heavily laden buffet.

PASANGGRAHAN, *Frontstreet 15. Tel. A fixed-price meal costs $15. The restaurant is open breakfast through dinner.*

One of the island's earliest government guest houses, this one was named the Indonesian word for resting place. Now wrapped in verandas and lattice, it is a classic of colonial architecture, delightfully shabby and reeking with musty charm. A blackboard announces the day's choices: shark in tomato sauce, old-fashioned meatloaf, Jamaican-style fish and chips, or broiled salmon. The breezy front porch is right on the street, a pleasant place to watch the world go by.

PETER'S HEALTH SPA, *in the Maho Beach Hotel. Tel. 52115, extension 4951 or 52540. Credit cards are accepted but hotel guests cannot charge to their rooms at the hotel. Enter from the street or the parking garage. From the hotel lobby, take the elevator to the second floor. Plan to spend $5-$6 for breakfast and $6-$10 for lunch or dinner. The spa is open Monday to Friday 7am to 8pm and Saturday 8am to 6pm.*

One of the best finds on the island, this holistic health center is where you can work out, get a massage, and enjoy a fabulously healthful meal while reading from Peter's library of health books. For breakfast get a toasted whole grain roll slathered with peanut butter and drizzled with honey. For lunch, order a veggie burger, a salad or stir-fry, a guiltless dessert, or a smoothie made fresh to your order from fruits and/or vegetables. The dining room is tiny, with a trio of tables and a couple of bar stools but take-out is as popular as eat-in, so there's rarely a seating problem.

PORTOFINO LE JARDIN, *Grand Case in front of the pharmacy. Tel. 29-08-28. Eat for under $20.*

Every Wednesday is Country & Western night at this busy meet market and combination ice cream parlor, saloon, ristorante, and pizzeria. Celebrate Happy Hour with the aprés-beach crowd from 5am to 7pm, then hoedown on attractively priced barbecue.

RIC'S PLACE, *69 Front Street. Tel. 26050, Philipsburg. Snack and nosh for $10. It's open 8am to 9pm Happy Hour specials are served daily 5-6:30pm.*

A sports bar where you can get a good burger, a Philly steak, burritos, fries, nachos, fritters and sandwiches, this is a pleasant gathering spot downtown for beers and the big game on the big screen. Ric and Kathy Hetzel are Texans who promise unlimited refills of iced tea with lunch or dinner.

SHIVSAGAR, *3 Front Street, Philipsburg. Tel. 31210. Plan to spend $12 for dinner. Call for hours. It's on the second floor opposite Barclay's Bank.*

Fiery Indian tandooris and curries give you a lot for your money here, especially if you order one of the vegetarian specialties. There's also fresh fish and chicken and kebobs, all served with mountains of artful vegetable garnishes and plenty of flat bread.

TURTLE PIER, *on the airport road, Simpson Bay. Tel. 52563. Dine native style for under $10 or splurge for the lobster. Open daily, it doesn't take credit cards.*

Bring the children to this living zoo overlooking Simpson Bay Lagoon and let them see the parrots, monkeys and turtles before or after a dinner of chicken or ribs. There's beer on tap; live music plays a couple of times a week.

Quick Takes

North American fast food has come to St. Maarten. A **Subway** sandwich shop is next to the movie building on Pondfill Road in Philipsburg and another is on Airport Road, Simpson Bay. The **Stop & Shop/Waterfront Terrace** at the Simpson Bay Yacht Club across from the airport is open every day 7:30am to 8:30pm, offering breakfast, lunch, salads, French bread sandwiches, chili, homemade soups, beer, wines, liquor, and soft drinks to eat in or take out. The **Burger King** at Simpson's Bay has an outdoor playground where the kids can riot while Mom and Dad finish their fries.

Chalks on Front Street, *Tel. 20873,* serves breakfast and lunch and will deliver in the Philipsburg area for a dollar extra. **L'Epicerie**, the French delicatessen, has outlets in Marigot at the Marina Port la Royale and in St. Maarten at the Sheraton Port de Plaisance.

WHEELCHAIR-ACCESSIBLE RESTAURANTS ON SINT MAARTEN/ST. MARTIN

Wheelchair-accessible restaurants (although some ramps are steep or narrow and may require extra help) on St. Martin/St. Maarten include: Antoine, Bavaria Bar & Restaurant, Cafe Toscana, Chez Martine, Cloud 10, Coconuts, Don Camillo, Good Fellows Bar & Restaurant, Grand Cafe Europe, Harbor Point, Kallalou Bar & Restaurant, Holland House, La Belle Epoque, La Chaloupe, Lagoonies Bar & Restaurant, La Riviera, La Rosa Too, Le Bar De La Mer, Le Perroquet, Mary's Boon, Old Captain, Pasanggrahan, Pizzamania, Ren & Stimpy, and Sandro's Hostaria.

SEEING THE SIGHTS

Start with a history tour because the old forts were built on the spots with the best views. Begin at the remains of **Fort Amsterdam** in Philisburg on Great Bay Harbor. Built in 1631, only ten years after the Pilgrims landed in America, it was the first Dutch military outpost in the Caribbean. It fell two years later to the Spanish, who turned it into the strongest bastion east of Puerto Rico. It was destroyed by retreating Spaniards in 1648 at the end of the bitter Eighty Years War and today only a few walls remain.

Around the island, you can also view the remains of **Fort Bel-Air**, **Sint Peter's Battery**, and **Fort Willem**, now the site of a television tower. Some stone walls and fragments are all that remain of a mighty fort that between 1801 and 1846 served the English, Dutch, French, English again, then the Dutch again, growing stronger with each new occupation. Its decline began after a hurricane in 1819 destroyed most of the buildings. The view from here is the best on the island. Walk. It's too treacherous to drive. It's up **Fort Hill**, just west of **Philipsburg**.

The **Sint Maarten Museum** on Front Street in Philipsburg, *Tel. 24927*, is one of the island's best gift shops, with an inventory of items that are somehow meaningful – either because they represent the island, the Ivory Coast where most of the island's slaves came from, or Holland, the mother country. Upstairs, where admission is only $1, view a small but nicely displayed collection of memorabilia and artifacts. Then view the hour-long video taken during Hurricane Luis, which devastated the island in September 1995. Most of the storm's physical scars are were gone in less than two years but its memories are fresh in the minds of islanders. For tourism information, *Tel. 22337* or call the museum directly.

To take a walking tour of historic downtown Philipsburg, start at the **museum** at Frontstreet 7 and pick up a brochure describing a self-guided tour. It will lead you past wonderful old homes and shops, most of them Caribbean classics distinguished by gingerbread trim, wrought iron railings, colorful shutters, and overhanging porches. The building at Frontstreet 95 was the slave market.

At Frontstreet 88, see the **Oranje School**, built as a church in 1738. It later became a house, and is now **L'Escargot**, a restaurant. **The Courthouse**, the most prominent landmark just off the pier at Wathey Square, was built in 1793 and restored in 1864, 1870, 1966, and 1995. Its simple, functional architecture makes a good backdrop for tourist photos.

At Frontstreet 15, the **Pasanggrahan Royal Guest House** was built as a government guest house in 1904. In the Dutch colonies, all government guest houses were called Pasanggrahan, the Indonesian word meaning resting place. Not far away on the opposite side of the street, the Guavaberry Shop used to be a tavern and before that a town house. It was built of cedar in the 1830s.

Take the children to the **Sint Maarten Zoo** on Arch Road in Madame Estate, Tel. 32030, and spend the day viewing 35 tropical species including a large reptile collection and a walk-through aviary. There's also a playground for children. The zoo is open weekdays 9am to 5pm and weekends 10am to 6pm. Admission is charged.

Don't miss **Market Day** at the port in Marigot on Wednesday, Friday and Saturday mornings. It's not a tourist event but a real market where you can shop for produce and local goods in an old West Indian building. Pay the prices asked for fish and produce; haggle for the rest.

On Sandy Ground Road next to the Marina Port La Royale, the **Saint-Martin Museum** features Arawak artifacts found by the Hope Estate Archaeological Society. Included is a reproduction of a burial site discovered in 1994 and dating to the 4th century A.D. Exhibits feature a wide range of finds from very old shell implements to photography. Take a tour with an English-or French-speaking guide, or browse on your own, ending up in the gift shop. The museum is open daily except Sunday, 9am to 1pm and 3pm to 7pm. For information, call the tourist office, Tel. 87-57-21.

Climb to the top of **Fort St. Louis** for a spectacular view of the harbor and, looking inland, of **Paradise Peak**. It's the highest point on the island, a 1,500-foot hill covered with greenery. The fort was built in 1786. It has its own parking lot, and the climb after that is steep but well worth it. If you choose also to climb Paradise Peak, you'll have a superb view of the island.

The northern part of the island, a **botanical park**, is best seen on foot. A sprinkling of islands, the **Grandes Cayes** just offshore, are a favorite with scuba divers. Just north of the area known as **Orient** (famous for its nude beach) along Le Galion Beach Road, the **Butterfly Farm**, , *Tel. 87-31-21*, is open daily from 9am to 5pm. You're welcome to walk the netting-covered gardens to see hundreds of butterflies flitting in the shrubbery weekdays 8am to noon and 1-5pm. Admission is $10. Continuing southwest on the main road you'll come to Orleans, an old French area still filled with Creole houses.

NIGHTLIFE & ENTERTAINMENT

The most dazzling after-dinner entertainments center around whatever bars have live music that night, and the casinos, where heavy hitters stream after dinner for blackjack, baccarat, Caribbean stud poker, roulette, crabs, and slots. All are open daily from noon to 3am.

They include:
- **ROUGE ET NOIR** *in the Seaview Hotel*
- **PELICAN CASINO** *in the Pelican Resort*
- **ATLANTIS CASINO** *in the Treasure Island Hotel in Cupecoy*
- **CASINO INTERNATIONAL** *in Divi Little Bay Resort*
- **GRAND CASINO** *in Mullet Bay Resort*
- **GOLDEN CASINO** *in the Great Bay Beach Resort*
- **CASINO ROYALE** *in the Maho Beach Hotel*
- **COLISEUM CASINO** *on Front Street in Philipsburg*
- **MOUNT FORTUNE CASINO** *in the Sheraton Port de Plaisance*
- **LIGHTNING BINGO CASINO** *on Welfare Road in Cole Bay*

For additional information on some of the casinos, see the sidebar below:

ST. MAARTEN'S CASINOS

Atlantis Casino at Cupecoy Beach has a private gaming room for higher-stakes baccarat, French roulette, chemin de fer and seven-card stud poker.

Casino Royale at the Maho Beach Hotel, is the largest on the island. It's open every day, 1pm to 4am. Table limits range from $5 to $2,000 for blackjack and $5 to $500 for craps.

Golden Casino at the Great Bay Beach Hotel is especially popular with hotel guests, who get a $10 match bet coupon. Slots pay as much as $2,500.

Coliseum Casino, in an ancient Roman motif, has three floors – one for slots, one for poker machines and a third for private gaming featuring blackjack, roulette, and Caribbean stud poker.

Lightning Casino in Simpson Bay is a Las Vegas-type casino with blackjack, roulette, craps, slot machines, horse racing, and bingo. The resort offers nightly dancing under the stars on the Pelican Reef Terrace.

Rouge et Noir in the heart of Front Street, Philipsburg, is a Las Vegas-style casino with future-fantasy decor, slot machines, a Sigma Derby horse machine, video Keno, and video poker.

Two popular nightclubs are **CHERI'S CAFE**, *Tel. 53361*, a showy sidewalk hangout at Maho, and **COCONUT'S**, above the Casino Royale at Maho, *Tel. 52833*. Dancing starts at 10:30pm nightly except Sunday. Cover charge is $5; drinks start at $3. The **NEWS CAFE** is at Simpson Bay, where 1960s nostalgia rocks until 4am, Tel. *42236*.

Other popular night spots include the **CAFE GRAND EUROPE** and the **RUMBOAT CAFE** at Maho, and **PUB 1950s**, where live music plays on Friday and Saturday nights. On the waterfront at Marigot, the Nicole Mouton Dancers can be seen Thursdays and Saturdays at the **FRENCH CAN-CAN**, *Tel. 87-56-16*. **LE PRIVILEGE DISCO** in Anse Marcel, *Tel. 87-38-38*, has a different theme every week (including a topless week) with dancing, video, pool and drinking until 5-6am.

The **SUALOUIGA FESTIVAL** starts every Friday at 4pm in the Open Market in Philipsburg. Shop and snack while you wait for the entertainment to start at 7pm. It goes on with food, drink, and dancing in the streets until midnight.

The **SUNSET BEACH BAR** on Maho Beach stays busy noon through the late hours. There's music every night, cheap shooters and $2 beers, and a 16-ounce Pain Killer. The mix ranges from Buddy Holly fans to Generation Xers, all of them scarfing down burgers, pizza, and whatever free stuff is being featured tonight. If you're inspired to dance, there's a little deck. This is a fair weather spot, with no indoor seating. When the fleet is in (U.S. ships sometimes come in here) every bar, shop, and restaurant on the island is packed. Cruise ship impact is mostly in downtown Philipsburg, which is always livelier when a ship or two are in port.

King Beau Beau is the island's calypso king, a 20-year veteran of hospitality who performs at resorts and casinos. See local advertising for news of his appearances. He is usually at **LYNETTE'S**, *Tel. 52865* on Fridays and at **PUB 1950s** on Wednesday, *Tel. 35482.* It's in the Amsterdam Shopping Center.

The legal age for drinking and gambling is 18.

SPORTS & RECREATION
Beaches
Cautions: few lifeguards are found on Caribbean beaches. Get local knowledge, be aware of changing sea conditions, and observe all precautions.

Dawn Beach, beloved for its fluorescent sunrises, is a favorite for sandcastle contests and crab races. **Guana Bay** is a favorite with boogie boarders, and it's uncrowded, but under some conditions the sea can have a strong undertow. **Little Bay Beach** is the place to snorkel. Visibility is best when the winds are not from the southeast. **Maho Beach** is a brown sugar cookie right under landing airplanes. Wet-bikes are available for rent and the beach bar offers bargain priced beers, water, and pizza. **Mullet Bay** is a mile of white sand plus facilities including showers, snacks and shops. **Simpson Bay Beach** has long stretches of sand and lots of elbow room.

Beaches on the Dutch side are more prim, with full bathing suits the custom. On the French side, topless and nude bathing are seen more often. **Bain Rouge** is strewn with boulders that provide privacy to nude bathers. **Grand Case** is lined with gourmet restaurants. **Baie Longue** can get rough and its sands are coarser than most. **Orient Beach** is the island's only official naturist beach where nudity is the norm rather than the exception. It's busy with dining, shops, and watersports.

Boating
Stardust Marine on Anse Marcel, *Tel. 87-40-30* offers bareboats or crewed yachts, sail or power. *Golden Eagle* sails from Great Bay Marina, Philipsburg, on full-and half-day trips to St. Barts, Prickley Pear and Tintamarre Island, *Tel. 30068, Fax 75828*. Snorkel gear is provided. *Sand*

Dollar is a sleek powerboat that takes groups of up to six people on sightseeing and snorkel outings, *Tel. 42640*.

Fishing

Deep sea fishing charters aboard *Black Fin* hunt for wahoo, tuna, marlin and dorado. *Tel. 42640*. Sightseeing and snorkel trips are also offered by this speedy sportfishing boat. Water ski, sail, dive, fish or snorkel with **Pelican Watersports**, *Tel. 42640*.

Golf

The only 18-hole golf course on the island is at **Mullet Bay Resort**, which was closed by the 1995 hurricane. At press time, there was talk of a reopening in 1998. To reserve a tee time when they re-open, *Tel. 52801*.

Horseback Riding

Caid and Isa, *Tel. 87-32-79*, near the Meridien has six paso fino horses that can be hired for a 2 1/2-hour trip over the hills of Anse Marcel to the Beach at Petites Cayes. Trips are daily except Sunday at 9am to 3pm. The **Bayside Riding Club**, *Tel. 87-36-64*, offers pony rides, two daily rides, and champagne beach rides under the full moon. It's next to Orient Bay on the road to Le Galion Beach.

Running

All runners are invited to join the **Road Runners Club** for a Fun Run every Wednesday and an early bird run of two to 15 kilometers on Sunday. For information, *Tel. 22467 or 22842*.

Sailing

One of the most unusual sailing stints in the islands is the **St. Maarten 12-Metre Challenge** at Great Bay in Philipsburg. America's Cup yachts, including Dennis Conner's 1987 entry *Stars and Stripes* and Canadian contender *Canada II*, sail in regattas lasting about two and a half hours. You can sign on as crew, even if you have no previous sailing experience. Everyone has a ball.

Sightseeing, snorkel, picnic, and sunset sails aboard the *Lambada*, *Tel. 42640*. Picnic and sunset sail with *Gabrielle* out of Bobby's Marina, *Tel. 23170 or 24096*.

For day or liveaboard charters, book with:
• **The Moorings**, *Tel. 800/535-7289*
• **Sun Yacht Charters**, *Tel. 800/772-3500*
• **Stardust Marine**, *Tel. 800/634-8822*
• **Nautor's Swan Charters**, *Tel. 800/356-7926*
• **Marine Time** in Marigot, *Tel. 87-20-88, Fax 87-20-78*

Scuba Diving

Superb reef and wreck dives surround St. Martin, but you'll need a boat because not much can be found close to shore. Dive operators include:
- **Lou Scuba Club** *at Nettlé Bay, Tel. 87-16-61, Fax 87-92-22*
- **Blue Ocean**, *Nettlé Bay, Tel. 87-66-89*
- **Octopus** *in Grand Case, Tel. 87-20-62*
- **S.M.C. Dive Center**, *Tel. 87-48-61*
- **Orient Beach Watersports**. *Tel. 87-40-75*
- **Mary's Boon** (see *Where to Stay* above) offers dive packages

Sky Diving

Take a tandem jump with **Skydive St. Maarten**, *Tel. 75634 or 52206*. No experience is needed. You and your instructor, strapped together, will jump from a Cessna 206 at an altitude of 9,000 feet and will reach 120 miles per hour in free fall before the chute opens. You'll make a soft landing on the beach, have a congratulatory rum punch, and go home with a tee shirt. Cost is about $245. Photos and video are available.

Snorkeling

Virtually every hotel and marina offers snorkel tours to the region's breathtaking reefs, many of them in only ten or 15 feet of water. Good spots include the waters around Orient Bay, Green Key, and Flat Island (Tintamarre). Spear fishing in the underwater marine parks is illegal.

Windsurfing

If your hotel doesn't have board sailers for rent, try **Orient Watersports**, *Tel. 87-40-75*, or **Blue Ocean** at Nettlé Bay, *Tel. 87-66-00*. For information about local windsurfing events, contact the **St. Martin Windsurfing Association** in Marigot, *Tel. 87-93-24*.

SHOPPING

Shops are open daily, especially in cruise ship areas, except on Christmas and Good Friday. Long after Front Street's modern arcades have closed, **Maho** in the island's southwest corner stays open for the hundreds of tourists there. Between the duty free prices and fine imports from all over world, this is a nirvana for shoppers in search of high-priced jewelry, clothing and gewgaws.

Generally, shopping hours are 8am to noon and 2 or 2:30pm until 6pm, with longer hours when cruise ships are in port. On the French side, hours are generally 9am to noon or 12:20, then 2 or 3pm until 6pm. In Maho, most shops stay open until 10pm. **Front Street**, which runs almost the entire length of Philisburg, is filled with arcades where you can lose yourself in emeralds, cigars, embroideries, leathers, crystal, and fine watches but we don't get excited about such imports. Instead, we like the Guavaberry Shop on Front Street, which sells liqueurs made from this piquant island fruit.

For swimwear and coverups look for **Java Wraps** on Front Street's "shopper's row," which runs the length of the bay. **Trident Jewelers** features imports from Belgium and Israel. **Little Switzerland** is a Caribbean evergreen, found on most islands. Here, it's in both Philipsburg and Marigot. **Columbian Emeralds International** has shops at Maho, downtown, and Marigot. **The Shipwreck Shop** on Front Street features Caribbean crafts, straws, reeds, batiks, hammocks and herbs.

In **Marigot**, shop for international luxuries and such French products as tableware, silver, china, Daum glassware, Cartier-inspired jewelry, and Givenchy toiletries along the harbor front at the **Marina Port la Royale** and along the **Rue du Général de Gaulle**. Diesel jeans and workwear are found at Life, on the Rue de la Liberté.

Local artists **Gloria**, **Peter**, **and Robert Lynn** have a studio at 83 Boulevard de Grand Case, *Tel. 87-77-24*, which is open "by chance or appointment." Their work is also found at galleries around the island.

Haitian art and furniture, Tiffany lamps, and original paintings are featured at the **Gingerbread Gallery** at the main entrance to the marina. It's open seven days a week. For wines in Marigot, shop Le **Gout De Vin**. At Howell center, **Supermarché Match** sells French gourmet foods. It's open daily, and on Sunday mornings, and it accepts credit cards. Market days in Marigot's **Market Square** are a confusion of colorful goods and staccato languages. Don't miss the market, which is open Wednesday, Friday, and Saturday mornings. Duty-free shopping is also at Marigot's **Marina Port la Royale**.

EXCURSIONS & DAY TRIPS

It's quick and easy to make side trips by boat or airplane to neighboring islands including Anguilla, Saba, St. Kitts, and St. Barts.

Ferries leave every half hour between 8am and 5:30pm for Anguilla, and again at 7pm and 10:30pm One-way tickets, which can be bought at the boat, cost $10 for the 15-minute day trip, $11 at night. Departure tax is $2.

Catamarans leave for **St. Barts** from Bobby's Marina, Philipsburg, at 9am daily except Sunday. Round trip fare for the 1 1/2-hour trip is $55, which includes free drinks. For reservations, *Tel. 22366*. An all-day ferry trip to St. Barts costs $80 including lunch and a tour; an all-day excursion to Saba with lunch and tour costs $90. Service aboard a high-speed ferry is provided by **Pelican Watersports**, *Tel. 42640.* Ferries sail from Marigot to St. Barts at a cost of $62 found trip. For reservations and schedules, *Tel. 87-20-28.* For service from Marigot to St. Barts, *Tel. 87-99-03.*

Voyager I and *Voyager II* invite you to make a day trip to **Saba** or **St. Barts** aboard a sleek, high-speed catamaran, *Tel. 24096 or 87-10-68.*

To book an expedition to the island's best archaeological sites with the **Association Archeologique Hope Estate**, call *Tel. 590/29-22-84.* Members well versed in island history can also arrange walking tours of communities rich in architectural history.

PRACTICAL INFORMATION

Area Code: **590** for French St. Martin; **5995** to reach the Dutch side.

ATM: MasterCard and Cirrus holders can look for signs indicating these member groups: ABN-AMRO, Bankomatiko, and Geldautomaat.

Banking hours: on the Dutch side, banks are usually open Monday through Friday 8:30am to 3pm. Some banks are open Saturday mornings. On the French side, banks are usually open on weekdays, 8am to 3pm.

Beer: the locally brewed beer is Soca.

Currency: officially, the Dutch florin or guilder (written N.A. F. or NAfl) and French franc are used but U.S. dollars are used freely and nearly all prices are quoted in them. There's no need to calculate exchange rates or to exchange funds.

Customs: There are none. This is the only completely duty-free port in the Caribbean. U.S. citizens can bring back up to $600 each and families can pool their allowance. Citizens over age 21 can bring in a quart of liquor. Canadians are permitted up to C$500 in goods. Adults who meet the minimum drinking age in their province can bring back 40 ounces of liquor or two dozen 12-ounce cans of beer.

Driving: drive on the right, North American style. Your home driver's license is valid here. If you're involved in an accident, don't move the car. Immediately *Tel. 22222* on the Dutch side or *Tel. 87-50-04* on the French side. Remember that road signs and speedometers are in kilometers.

Electrical current: bring adapters for 220 volts if you're staying on the French side. On the Dutch side, standard U.S., 110-volt power is used.

Emergencies: on the Dutch side, *Tel. 22222* for police and fire emergencies, and *Tel. 22111* for an ambulance. On the French side, *Tel. 87-50-04* for police, *Tel. 87-50-08* for fires, and *Tel. 87-74-14* for an ambulance.

Gambling: the island has ten casinos, all on the Dutch side.

Government: U.S. consular matters concerning the Dutch side are handled through Curacao, St. Anna Boulevard 19, *Tel. 5999/461-3066;* for the French side, through Bridgetown, Barbados, *Tel. 246/436-4950.*

Immigration: U.S. and Canadian citizens need a passport that is not more than five years out of date. Naturalized citizens must show an original naturalization certificate with photo identification. For stays or more than two weeks on the Dutch side or three weeks on the French side, a valid passport is needed.

Medical emergencies: medical help is available in Philipsburg and Marigot. In emergencies, airlift is available to Puerto Rico or the United States. The island also has six dentists. For an ambulance, *Tel. 87-86-25*; for a pharmacy, *Tel. 87-50-79.*

Pets: animals more than three months old can visit the island temporarily on presentation of a health certificate no more than ten days old, and a record of inoculations including a rabies shot no more than 30 days old.

Shopping hours: on the Dutch side, shops are generally open Monday through Saturday 9am to noon and 2pm to 6pm. On the French side, Monday through Saturday 9am to 12:30pm and 3pm to 7pm. Hours may vary with holidays and seasons.

Taxes: Leaving the islands for other international destinations, everyone over the age of two pays $12. Leaving for other islands in the Netherlands Antilles, the tax is $5. If you fly out of Esperance Airport, departure tax is 15F, but is usually included in ticket prices. Government room tax is five percent on hotels. There is no tax on purchases.

Taxi: on the Dutch side, call the dispatch office at *Tel. 22359*; airport taxis are at *Tel. 54317.* On the French side, *Tel. 87-56-20.*

Telephones: To call the Dutch side from the French side, dial 19-5995 plus the five numbers. To call the French side from the Dutch side, dial 06 plus the six numbers. To call St. Martin from North America, dial 011-590 plus the local number, station to station. If you're calling person to person, dial 01-590.

Time zone: St. Maarten is on Atlantic Standard Time all year, which places it an hour later than New York except when New York is on Daylight Savings Time, when both hours are the same.

Tipping: airport porters expect $1 a bag; taxi drivers usually receive 50 cents to a dollar depending on the run, and more for a long, narrated tour.

Tourism Information: from the U.S., *Tel. 800/786-2278* or write St. Maarten Tourism, *Walter Nisbeth Road, 23 Philipsburg, St. Maarten, Tel. 5995/22337, Fax 5995/22734.* The tourist office on the French side is in Marigot, *Boulevard de France 97150, Tel. 590/87-57-23.* For further information on St. Martin from the U.S., *Tel. 900/990-0040*. The call costs 95 cents a minute. Or, write the French Government Tourist Office, *444 Madison Avenue, New York NY 10022*. In Canada, write the French Government Tourist Office, *1981 Avenue McGill College 490, Montreal, Quebec, H3A 2W9, Tel. 514/288-4264, Fax 844-8901; or 30 St. Patrick Street, Suite 700, Toronto, Ontario M5T 3A3, Tel. 416593-6427, Fax 979-7587.*

Weddings: to be married in St. Maarten, couples must be at least 21 years old and must make written application to the lieutenant governor for a temporary tourist permit not to exceed three months. Birth certificates, divorce or death papers (if applicable) and valid return tickets must also be presented. After all this is translated into Dutch by an official, it's notarized and approved. Couples then have a 10-day waiting period and pay a 90-guilder fee (about $50) before a local clergyman can perform the wedding at the Wedding Hall in Philipsburg. To be married on the French side, one partner must have resided in the French West Indies for at least 30 days before applying for a license. No fee is involved but papers have to be presented in French.

THE
FRENCH
WEST
INDIES

33. GUADELOUPE

A scattering of islands between Montserrat and Antigua, **Guadeloupe** was discovered in 1493 by Christopher Columbus, who found it inhabited by fierce Caribs. They called it Karukera, Island of Beautiful Waters, but Columbus named it for Santa Maria de Guadalupe de Estremadura before beating a hasty retreat in the face of Carib hostility.

France claimed the island in 1635, drove out the Caribs, imported slaves, and established sugar plantations that are still a major industry here. For a century, the islands were a battleground between the French and British. In 1763, the French got Guadeloupe and other French islands in exchange for French claims to Canada. Finally it became French once and for all with the Treaty of Paris in 1815, a tiny pawn in a complicated European peace.

The music is African, the head scarves are Madras from India, the food and wine are French. The land is a lush green tangle astir with clouds of yellow butterflies, rising into hills with their heads in gauzy clouds. When its hills fall to the sea, they meet sands fringed with brilliant *flambouyant* (say flahm-boy-yahn) trees. In the interior, glistening fields of sugar cane are destined for the distilleries.

The main island, Guadeloupe, is made up of **Basse-Terre**, the capital, and **Grande-Terre**, home of **Pointe-à-Pitre**, which is the main population center and commercial hub. It isn't whimsy that made settlers call the highest island "basse" and the flatter one "grande." The terms refer to the high and low winds that blow over them.

Total land area is 530 square miles, not including Guadeloupe's other islands, principally **Marie-Galante**, **La Désirade**, and **Les Saintes**. The population is about 500,000, most of them black and half of them under age 20.

Although tourism is a force here, and that mostly from blue collar French tourists on package tours, Guadeloupe has a long way to go before it is too touristy. Like the other French islands, this is a playground for

Francophones who smoke like fiends, drive like maniacs, and expect everyone to speak their language. Take a French phrase book and try to be a good sport about it. Even the French have problems with the native patois, which is riddled with English, Spanish, Carib, Portuguese and African words.

As a reward you'll meet wonderful French and West Indian people, experience an exotic island with some of the best food on earth, and leave with a feeling of insider discovery. Best of all, there is no exit tax except for charter flights.

Climate

The highest temperature ever recorded on Guadeloupe was 92 on an October day, the lowest 54 on a February night. Sound like heaven? You're right! Temperatures vary only about five degrees winter and summer, reaching about 82 degrees by day and falling to 66-72 degrees at night.

July through September are the wettest months, averaging16.4-17.6 inches per month. You can expect showers of a millimeter or more of rain 18-27 days out of every month.

ARRIVALS & DEPARTURES

Guadeloupe's **La Raizet International Airport**, which is 2.5 miles from Pointe-à-Pitre, is served by **American Airlines/American Eagle**, *Tel. 800/433-7300*, **Air Canada**, *Tel. 800/776-3000, an*d **Air France**, *Tel. 800/ 237-2747*. Connections through **Air Guadeloupe**, **Caraïbes Air Tourisme**, and **Air Caraïbes** can be booked through trunk airlines.

To charter with **Air St. Martin** and **Air St. Barthélemy**: *Tel. 590/87-73-46*. By ferry, Guadeloupe connects to Martinique, Dominica, and St. Lucia via *Express des Iles*, *Tel. 590/83-12-45*. Round trip fare to Martinique is about $110. The island is also a popular cruise ship port.

ORIENTATION

Picture a butterfly with its right wing known as **Grande-Terre**, its left as **Basse-Terre**, and its body in the middle as **Pointe-à-Pitre** on the **Rivière Salée**. Basse-Terre is the island's scenic, sightseeing half and the home of the **National Park** covering a fifth of the island's total land mass. The capital and second city, also called Basse-Terre, is centered by the cathedral and edged by a busy waterfront, where taxis wait just off the tourist dock. Most of the shops and restaurants are within a short walking distance of the pier.

The island's first city, **Pointe-à-Pitre** is, like most Caribbean port cities, defined by its harbor and quais. Its restaurants and shops are on

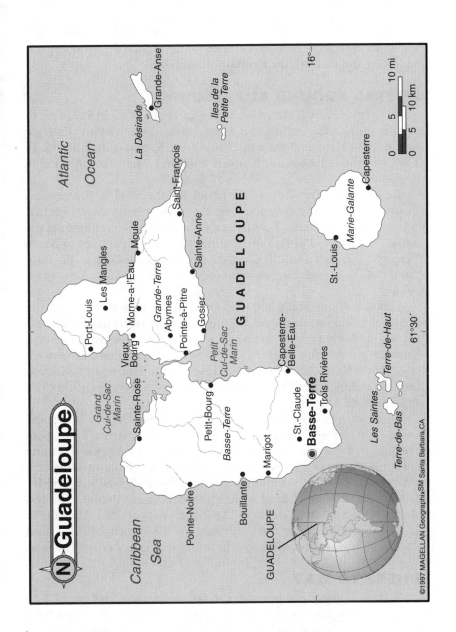

Guadeloupe

Atlantic Ocean

Caribbean Sea

Grand Cul-de-Sac Marin

Port-Louis
Les Mangles
Sainte-Rose
Vieux Bourg
Morne-à-l'Eau
Moule
Grande-Terre
Abymes
Pointe-à-Pitre
Gosier
Sainte-Anne
Saint-François
La Désirade
Grande-Anse

Petit Cul-de-Sac Marin

Pointe-Noire
Bouillante
Petit-Bourg
Basse-Terre
Marigot
St.-Claude
Basse-Terre
Trois Rivières
Capesterre-Belle-Eau

GUADELOUPE

Iles de la Petite Terre

Marie-Galante
St. Louis
Capesterre

Les Saintes
Terre-de-Bas
Terre-de-Haut

GUADELOUPE

16°

61°30'

0   5   10 mi
0   5   10 km

©1997 MAGELLAN GeographixSM Santa Barbara,CA

streets on and leading from the waterfront. The tourist office is just off the ferry dock; bus stops and the post office are along Boulevard Chanzy/ Boulevard Honne, a few blocks north of the waterfront.

One of the most beautiful drives is the **Route de la Traversée**, which cuts across the middle of Basse-Terre and runs through the national park, rain forest and through the **Crayfish Waterfalls**.

GETTING AROUND GUADELOUPE

Taxis meet every flight and you can expect to pay about $22 to get to hotels in the Gosier area or about $13 to get into Pointe-à-Pitre. Cab fare from Pointe-à-Pitre or Deshaies to Basse-Terre is about $70. A surcharge of 40 percent is tacked on between 9pm and 7am. To call a radio-dispatched cab: *Tel. 20-74-74, 82-96-69, or 83-09-55.*

Buses serve every village on the island, but they are best for travelers who speak French. If you want to have a go, simply stand at an *"arret-bus"* and wave down a driver. Fare from the airport to the terminal on rue Peynier in Pointe-à-Pitre is only about $1.25. To catch a jitney to Basse-Terre, go to the Gâre Routière de Bergevin or, to Grand-Terre, the Gâre Routière de Mortenol. They serve the local work day, usually running 5am to 6pm.

Rental cars are available but recent travelers have reported hassles with mechanical problems and disputes over repairs—an unpleasantness that you don't want to face, in French, when you're at the airport rushing to turn in the car before catching a flight. So, stick to a rental car chain that has offices in North America. You can reserve a car from home and, if you need to challenge a bill later, you can continue negotiations after you return home.

Agencies include **Avis**, *Tel. 82-33-47;* **Budget**, *Tel. 90-26-37;* and **Hertz**, *Tel. 91-00-63*. Depending on current promotions, you'll pay about $350 per week for a car plus the island's 9.5 percent VAT. Keep in mind that age limits for rental cars are at least 21 and, at some companies, 23. Driving is on the right; your home country's driver's license will serve for 20 days. After that, you'll need an International Driver's Permit. Wordless international road signs are used. The island's network of 1,225 miles of roads is one of the best in the Caribbean and the French make the most of them. This is heads-up driving at its most exciting this side of Le Mans.

WHERE TO STAY

Add a 5-10 percent government tax and service charges of 5-15 percent to your room rate. Rates are quoted in dollars or francs for a double room in high season, according to how they were quoted to us by the hotel. Low season rates are less, but many hotels and restaurants close for at least a month sometime between May and October.

Your address in the island will be address or box number, town and postal code, Guadeloupe, French West Indies. Guadeloupe markets itself mostly in France and in French Canada. Most servers and hotel staff speak little or no English and see no need to learn it.

The exchange rate is roughly five francs to the U.S. dollar.

Expensive

L'ANSE DES ROCHERS ANCHORAGE, *St.François 97118. Tel. 590/93-90-00, Fax 93-91-00. Rates at this 356-room hotel start at $200 European plan; meal plans are available. It is 24 miles from the airport.*

Sprawled over 27 acres is a resort so large that it's almost too long a walk from some of the farthest villas to the restaurants. Choose a room with bath or one of the hillside villas with bedroom, bath, and kitchenette. Floors are familiar terracotta tile, complemented by autumn and earth tones with bright accents including reproduction "cathedral" radios that were popular in the 1930s. Dining is in a formal restaurant with menu service or at the Black Mangé where buffet meals are themed every night to a different decor and type of food. After dinner there may be a folkloric dance show or a music program. Or, go dancing in the disco. If you don't feel like dining in the restaurant, get something quick at the snack bar. Swim in the dazzling pool, which has its own waterfall, or off the beach. Play tennis, shop the mini-mall, or rent a car on site to explore the island.

AUBERGE DE LA VIELLE TOUR, *Gosier 97190. Tel. 590/84-23-23, Fax 84-33-43. Rates at this 180-unit hotel start at $264 including full breakfast. It's 5.6 miles from the airport, a cab ride of about 58F.*

One of the most splendid resorts on the island, The Auberge is finished with rich antique reproductions and every suite has an ocean view. Its lobby is in the remains of an old sugar mill dating to the 1700s and the theme throughout is one of timelessness. Its beaches are small, but the hotel will send a boat to whisk you to someplace more private. Dine informally in the poolside terrace, in the gourmet restaurant, or in another restaurant that specializes in Creole cuisine. Just often enough, managers call for a blowout barbecue and limbo dancing. Kitchenettes are available in some of the town houses but with food this good, why cook? The tennis court is lit for night play and the hotel has a swimming pool and watersports equipment, including wind surfers.

FLEUR D'EPÉE NOVOTEL, *Bas-du-Fort, 97190 Gosier. Tel. 590/90-40-00, Fax 90-99-07; U.S. 800/221-4542. Rates at this 190-room hotel start at $221 including full American breakfast. The hotel and its twin the Marissol are 4.5 miles from the airport, a ride of about 58F.*

This French counterpart of a good North American chain hotel stands on a crescent of beach that can get crowded when plane-loads of package tourists arrive from France. Rooms have all the necessities including air conditioning, mini-bars and terraces, most with a sea view. Choose among four restaurants. The hotels also offer pool swimming and watersports.

FORT ROYAL TOURING CLUB, *Point du Petit Bas-Vent, Deshaies 97126. Tel. 590/25050-00, Fax 25-50-01. Rates at this 198-room hotel start at 1,200F including continental breakfast. The hotel is 22 miles from the airport on the island's northwest coast.*

Clubby elegance describes this hotel, which overlooks two superb beaches and is handy to the national park. Every room has a balcony or patio with majestic ocean views. Furnishings are typical of the wicker-rattan-tile school of upscale tropical design; beds are glowing mahogany. Sleep in a hotel room or a bungalow. The hotel has its own dive shop and watersports center, always buzzing with activities. Play miniature golf, swim in your choice of pools, or play tennis. Deshaies, by the way, is pronounced roughly day-hay.

GOLF MARINE CLUB HOTEL, *Avenue de L'Europe, St. François 97118. Tel. 590/88-60-60, Fax 88-68-98. Rates at this 74-room hotel start at 900F including continental breakfast. Meal plans are available. Cottages and suites are available. The hotel is 24 miles from the airport.*

The beach is two blocks away, but some travelers prefer a private pool to a public beach any day. This hotel is handy to town and shopping but the street side can be noisy, so request a room overlooking the garden. A public golf course is across the street; the hotel has its own tennis courts and restaurant. Rooms are a standard, livable size, but the suites with a roll-away bed can be a tight fit for more than two or three adults or a couple with more than two kids.

HAMAK, *St. François 97118. Tel. 590/88-59-99, Fax 88-41-92. Rates at this 54-unit hotel start at $230 including full breakfast. It's 24 miles from the airport or a 167F taxi ride.*

Chic best describes the one-bedroom bungalow where you'll be surrounded by flowering shrubs. Off your front patio is a hammock where you can dream the days away; off the back patio there's a fresh water shower where you can rinse off the sand before entering your smartly decorated home. Light-colored furniture and accents of original island art make for comfortable living, although the bathrooms are small by modern American standards and the beach is skimpy compared to those of, say, Anguilla. Rooms are air conditioned and have telephone, mini-bar, twin beds, hair dryer, telephone and room service. The golf course is just footsteps away.

The hotel also offers tennis, a dining room with a view of the beach, and watersports except for a swimming pool. Television and kitchenettes are available.

HOTEL LA TOUBANA, *Chateaubrun, Ste. Anne 97180. Tel. 590/88-25-78, Fax 88-38-90. Rates at this 32-room hotel start at $192 including continental breakfast. It's 14.5 miles from the airport.*

Your charming, red-roofed bungalow will have a kitchenette, telephone, and air conditioning as well as a spectacular view down the hillside and across the water to outlying islands. Dine indoors or outside overlooking the swimming pool at the hotel's restaurant, Le Boabab. Walk down the cliffside path to the beach, or swim in the pool. The hotel has tennis courts and can arrange any water activities from sportfishing to day sailing.

LA CREOLE BEACH HOTEL, *Pointe de la Verdure, Gosier 97190. Tel. 590/90-46-46, Fax 90-46-66. Rates at this 156-room hotel start at $202 with continental breakfast. The hotel is 5.6 miles from the airport.*

Swim off the two beaches or in the swimming pool, play tennis, dive, sail, snorkel, take a cruise to Islet du Gosier, or book a deep sea fishing trip. This is resort living in an air conditioned room or apartment with its own balcony and view of the sea. The decor is French colonial with rich looking natural woods, vibrant fabrics and carpeted floors. Choose between the hotel's two restaurants, one of them a splendid seafood restaurant right on the seaside and the other poolside. Car rental is available on site.

LE COCOTERAIE, *St. François 97118. Tel. 590/88-79-81, Fax 88-78-33. Rates at this 50-room hotel start at $400 including continental breakfast. Located on the easternmost point of Grande-Terre, it is 24 miles from the airport. The cab ride costs about 167F.*

A swank annex to Le Meridien, this all-suite hotel will be mostly occupied by Francophones, so you're on your own when it comes to getting an extra pillow or information from the front desk. Still, it's one of the French islands' most plush hotels with its big, round bathtubs and spacious balconies overlooking the marina or the swimming pool. There's a stretch of beach reserved just for Cocoteraie patrons; otherwise you share the Meridien's beach and very full menu of activities, dining, tennis, and much more. Your room, furnished in rich mahogany with madras prints complemented by jewel tones, has a mini-bar and safe.

LE MÉRIDIEN ST.-FRANÇOIS, *St. François 97118. Tel. 590/88-51-00, Fax 88-40-71, U.S. 800/543-4300. Rates at this 265-room hotel start at 1,995F including continental breakfast. A MAP meal plan is available. The hotel is 24 miles from the airport and a 20-minute walk from the community of St. François on the island's easternmost point.*

The largest, tallest hotel in this popular tourist conclave in eastern Guadeloupe, the Méridien overlooks a golf course designed by Robert Trent Jones. Four-star quality adds up to a switched-on hotel abuzz with activities almost around the clock. If you can't keep up with the schedule, tune it in on the closed circuit television. Rooms have air conditioning, television, telephone, room service at breakfast only, and balconies, most of them with a sea view. Play tennis or boule, swim in the pool, have a massage, or shop the boutiques. Golf and watersports can be arranged.

Dining is in the Balaou for buffet dinners, the Casa Zomar for lunch, and the Bambou for sandwiches and snacks. After dinner, have a quiet drink in one of the bars or dance the night away in the disco. If you have your own airplane or want to charter a flight to visit any other islands, a small airport is nearby. Car rental is available on site.

LE RELAIS DU MOULIN, *Chateaubrun 97980, Ste.-Anne. Tel. 590/88-23-96, Fax 88-03-92. Rates at this 40-unit complex start at $145 including continental breakfast. It's 18 miles from the airport.*

A landmark since its tower was built as part of a sugar plantation, this picturesque resort offers bungalows and apartments with bath, kitchen, sleeping area, and a private patio or balcony. Each has air conditioning, a mini-bar and telephone. Rent a bicycle on site for exploring the village and countrywide, or use your rental car to reach the beach. Most guests prefer to stay on the grounds, enjoying non-beach rates while they swim in the pool or read in a hammock. Meals are available in Le Restaurant near the pool or Le Courcelle indoors.

PLANTATION STE.-MARTHE, *97118 St. François. Tel. 590/93-11-11, Fax 88-72-47. Rates at this 120-unit hotel start at 980F including continental breakfast. It's 24 miles from the airport, a cab ride of about 167F.*

Built around the ruins of an 18th century sugar plantation but only faintly resembling the greathouse that might once have graced these grounds, this hotel has sea views from some of the rooms. It isn't beachfront, but a free shuttle bus to the shore is provided. Prepare to be wowed by the lobby with its marble floors, shining woodwork and double staircase. Your spacious room or duplex suite will have air conditioning, telephone, television, safe, and a mini-bar. If you get one of the duplexes, sleeping is in a loft over the sitting room.

Although the hotel was built in the 1990s, its design is reminiscent of New Orleans in the 1890s, with balconies that provide open-air living right off your room or suite. Swim in the enormous pool, play tennis, or work out in the health club. A pianist usually plays evenings in one of the two bars; dining is in the faithfully French restaurant, La Vallée D'Or.

Moderate

AUBERGE DE LA DISTILLERIE, *Tabanon 97170. Tel. 590/94-25-91, Fax 94-11-93. Rates at this 15-room inn start at $130 including continental breakfast. Modified American Plan, with breakfast and dinner, is also available. It's 12.4 miles from the airport.*

This cozy Creole inn, handy to the Lezarde River and the national park, is located in the cool uplands above the northeast coast. Stay in a cottage or one of the rooms in the main house. Almost all accommodations have a balcony or terrace and there are a pool, one of the best Creole restaurants on the island, a bakery, and bar. Some units are air conditioned. The decor is country West Indian with open wood beams, wicker furniture, and lavish use of island arts.

CALLINAGO BEACH AND CALLINAGO VILLAGE, *Pointe de la Verdure 35, Gosier. Tel. 590/84-25-25, Fax 84-24-90. Rates at the 40-room Callinago Beach start at 634F for a double room with continental breakfast and at the 150-unit Village at 506F for a studio or apartment with kitchenette. The hotel is about two miles east of Pointe-à-Pitre.*

Choose a hotel room, studio, or two-bedroom apartment in a beachfront complex that looks like a little pink and white village. Your picture window overlooks the bay and, if you're in an apartment, a spiral staircase leads to the upstairs sleeping loft. Dine in the resort's own French-Creole restaurant, or in the poolside cafe. Room service is available for breakfast in the rooms (not the apartments). Play tennis, swim off the beach or in the freshwater pool, water ski, sail, snorkel, or windsurf.

CANELLA BEACH RESIDENCE, *Pointe de la Verdure, Gosier 97190. Tel. 590/90-44-00, Fax 90-44-44. Rates at this 150-room hotel start at $163 without meals. Meal plans are available. The hotel is 5.6 miles from the airport.*

A cluster of buildings is built to resemble a colorful West Indian village furnished with bright primary colors to set off crisp white floors and rattan furniture. Each unit has a kitchenette and a private terrace or balcony. Swim off the beach in a pretty cove or in the swimming pool. Play tennis, snorkel, water ski, sail, fish, windsurf, or have the hotel arrange an excursion to another island. Most water sports are complimentary. Have a sundowner at the beach bar before dinner.

Le Verandah restaurant is one of the hotel's best features. You'll find Canella somewhat more English-friendly than most Guadeloupean resorts.

CAP SUD CARAÏBES, *Petit Havre 97190. Tel. 590/85-96-02, Fax 85-80-39. Rates at this 12-room inn start at 550F including continental breakfast. It's between Ste.-Anne and Gosier, nine miles from the airport.*

This is one of the island's Relais Creole, simple inns that might be compared to Puerto Rico's paradors. Personal service, air conditioned rooms, a swimming pool, and an airport shuttle add up to a pleasant experience at modest prices. Rooms are all decorated differently; each has a balcony. They have either shower or bath, so specify your preference.

DOMAINE DE PETITE ANSE, *Plage de Petite Anse, Bouillante 97125. Tel. 590/98-78-78, Fax 98-80-28. Rates at this 135-room hotel are from $130 including continental breakfast. It's 30 miles from the airport.*

It's a long ride from the airport but the drive brings you to the coast of Basse-Terre, handy to the diving pleasures of Pigeon Island and the hiking pleasures of the national park. Stay in a hotel room with a balcony and a view of the sea or in your own bungalow with terrace, bath, and kitchenette. Accommodations are air conditioned and have a safe and refrigerator. A dive shop is on site and the hotel, one of the Relais Creole inns, is popular with active young Europeans who come for hiking, scuba diving, watersports, and volleyball. On site is a restaurant, bar, and swimming pool.

ECOTEL GUADELOUPE, *Route de Gosier, Gosier 97190. Tel. 590/90-60-00, Fax 90-60-60. The hotel is 5.6 miles from the airport. Rates at this 44-room hotel start at $110 including continental breakfast.*

Choose a poolside or garden view in this blandly middle-class hotel, which was built as a hotel school and still looks a bit dorm-like. Still, the value is good because it's upland; you're not paying beach-front prices. "Eco" is too grand a term, but the property does have nice gardens and trees. Furnishings can be described as ordinary and the air conditioning is cranky. Breakfast is served in the open air and there's a snack bar, but this is the heart of hotel country, where a large choice of restaurants awaits nearby.

GRANDE ANSE HOTEL, *Trois Rivières 97114. Tel. 590/02-90-47, Fax 92-93-69. Rates at this 24-room hotel start at $120 including continental breakfast. It's 33.7 miles from the airport. Meal plans are available.*

Located on the southern tip of Basse-Terre, this hotel is handy to the national park, black sand beaches, Soufrière, and the ferries to Les Saintes. Come here for the mountain views from a private balcony in your own bungalow. The hotel, which is a Relais Creole, has a restaurant, bar, and swimming pool. Rooms, plainly furnished in hardy hardwoods and neutral fabrics, have air conditioning and a refrigerator. Your fellow guests will probably be French; the staff speaks only limited English.

HOTEL ST.-JOHN ANCHORAGE, *rue Frebault at the harbor, Pointe-à-Pitre 97110. Tel. 590/82-51-57; fax 82-52-61. Rates at this 44-room hotel start at 512F including continental breakfast. It's in town at the waterfront, two miles from the airport.*

Part of the exciting new waterfront complex with its ships and shops is this four-story, modern hotel. It's an ideal choice for business travel but has little to recommend it to the vacationer. There's a coffee shop on the main floor.

L'ORCHIDÉE, *32 Boulevard Général de Gaulle, Gosier. Tel. 590/84-54-20, Fax 84-54-90. It's 5.6 miles from the airport. Doubles at this 18-suite hotel are from $140.*

If you're a city person who likes an in-town restaurant with a balcony overlooking the hustle and bustle, this hotel is English-friendly, convenient, and air conditioned. Studios accommodations, which are ideal for the business traveler, have a kitchenette. Furnishings are dark hardwoods that contrast with the crisp, white tile floors and set off the pleasing, blue-green color scheme. The hotel has a dining room, and guests may also use the local recreation center's swimming pool.

LA SUCERIE DU COMPTÉ, *Comté de Loheac, Ste.-Rose 97115. Tel. 590/28-60-17, Fax 28-65-63. Rates at this 50-room hotel start at F470; meal plans are available. It's 15 miles from the airport.*

An old sugar mill once covered these wooded acres and its wreckage, including an old train, sprawls charmingly around the landscape. Cottages have two small units, each with small bedroom and bath and a bow window that expands your view of the ocean or landscape. Ask for a sea view and air conditioning; not all rooms have them. Rooms don't have telephone or television but the hotel has its own restaurant and swimming pool. Fishing, diving and other watersports are cordially arranged.

TROPICAL CLUB, *Moule 97160. Tel. 93-97-97, Fax 93-97-00. Rates at this 72-unit hotel start at $179 for a room that sleeps one to four people. Children sleep free. Continental breakfast is included. It's 16 miles from the airport on the east coast of Grande-Terre.*

The high coamers of the eastern shore draw the surfing crowd to this high-energy hotel, which offers a double bed and two bunks in each room. Appeal is mostly to young couples and families who want to enjoy the brown sand beach, swimming pool, surfing, and a lot of planned activities including tennis, aerobics and boule. Every suite has a kitchenette and a private balcony. For the best sea view, ask for a room on the top floor. Bathrooms have only a shower, no tub, and the decorator used a rubber stamp, but the value is excellent and everything you need is right here. The hotel has a restaurant that serves a good variety of French and Creole food, and a popular bar.

Budget

LA SUCERIE DU COMPTÉ, *Comté de Loheac, Ste. Rose 97115. Tel. 28-60-17, Fax 28-65-63. Rates at this 50-room hotel start at $85. It's 15 miles from the airport. Meal plans are available.*

Tourists come here just to see the ancient grounds, which are littered with rusted remnants of an old sugar factory. Plantation life is re-created in charming, but small, air conditioned rooms. The beach, which is on Basse-Terre's north coast, is a ten-minute walk away but the stroll is made pleasant by the shade of flowering shrubs. Rooms have a rich, woody look and lace trims. The hotel has a swimming pool, tennis court, and a locally popular restaurant and bar.

RELAIS DES SOURCES, *Ravine Chaude 97139. Tel. 25-31-04, Fax 25-30-63. Rates at this 15-room inn start at $90. It's 11 miles from the airport in northern Basse-Terre. Meal plans are available.*

Visitors come here for the nearby thermal springs and a wooded hillside setting filled with flowers and birdsong. There's a miniscule swimming pool, but beaches are miles away. Stay in a bungalow, which will be more pleasant than the main building. You'll have a kitchenette, telephone, air conditioning and television. The restaurant serves wholesome, natural foods and there's a bar. Ask the friendly staff about hiking and tours of the nearby countryside.

Club Med

Guadeloupe has a **Club Med** all-inclusive resort, *Tel. 800/CLUB MED.* Memberships are available.

Accommodations Alternatives

For information about renting an apartment, villa or a house with up to five bedrooms, contact the **Association des Villas et Meubles de Tourism**, *Box 1297, 97186 Pointe-à-Pitre, Guadeloupe, Tel. 590/82-02-62, Fax 83-89-22.* Prices range from 1,500F to 16,200F weekly.

Accommodations in private homes, ranging in price from 1,200F to 5,500F weekly, are booked through **Gîtes de France**, *Guadeloupe Tourism Office, Box 759, 97171 Pointe-à-Pitre, Guadeloupe, French West Indies, Tel. 590/91-64-33, Fax 91-45-40.* Villas with up to three bedrooms with private pool, ocean view and maid service can be booked through Chris and Josie Dock, **Dock Villas**, *St. Felix, 97190 Gosier, Guadeloupe, French West Indies, Tel. 590/84-34-77, Fax 90-22-32.* Prices are $600 to $2,000 weekly.

WHERE TO EAT

When you arrive, pick up a copy of Ti Gourmet at the airport or downtown tourist offices. It's a handy booklet listing restaurants all over Guadeloupe that offer something extra, usually a free drink, to visitors who show this guide. Don't forget to take it with you every time you eat out.

Expensive

AJOUPA RESTAURANT *in the Auberge de la Vielle Tour hotel, Montauban, Gosier 97190. Tel. 84-23-23. It's a 5.6-mile ride from the airport and a short walk from many other Gosier hotels. Main courses are priced $23 to*

$45. Reservations are urged. It's open for dinner nightly except April through October, when it closes.

Gaze out over the sea and Ilet du Gosier as your meal arrives in the hands of servers in traditional island dress. Choose an appetizer from the rolling cart, and end the meal with a memorable Brie or Camembert. Dine on tender-pink lamb, fish soup redolent with fresh herbs, fresh snapper, and French bread slathered with mango butter.

CHEZ DEUX GROS, *on the road between Gosier and Ste. Anne. Tel. 84-16-20. Plan to spend $50 for dinner. Reservations are recommended. Ask for a table as far from the street as possible.*

Because this restaurant is also an antique shop, you can buy the decor including, presumably, the table you eat from. Waitresses, wearing skirts that match the tablecloths, will bring you a filet, duckling, shrimp-stuffed pasta, salmon in a satiny sweet sauce, or one of the raw meat and fish specialties so popular with the French. If you order one of the ten-minute desserts, be prepared to wait half an hour. If you're less patient, ask for an ice or gateau that is already prepared. The restaurant is built on a steep hill that rises from the edge of the road so you'll get a quieter table and a better view from the higher terraces.

CHEZ VIOLETTA, *Perinette Gosier, just east of Gosier. Tel. 84-10-34. Reservations are suggested, especially if cruise ships are in. Dinner will cost about $50.*

Violetta herself is gone now, but she was the queen of Creole among French West Indian chefs. Her memory lingers on in the kitchens here, known for a spicy Creole doudou sauce that's delicious on fresh-caught vivaneau (red snapper). Violetta's flair for blaff hasn't been lost, and there's also boudin, conch stew, shark, and a timeless banana cake. Still trading on Violetta's reputation, the restaurant is popular with tourists, especially Americans, who feel at home here even if they don't speak French. The trappings are more colonial than Creole, giving the room a regal, formal look.

LA CANNE A SUCRE, *Quai 1, Port Autonome, Pointe-à-Pitre. Tel. 82-10-19. Reservations are urged. Main courses in the brasserie range from F50-F120; in the upstairs dining room they are F90-F200. Open Monday through Friday for lunch and dinner and Saturday for dinner only, it's closed Sunday.*

The restaurant overlooks the cruise ship docks, which can be crowded, but cruisers soon move on to the shops and aren't likely to overwhelm this eatery, which is a sensational mixture of Creole with nouvelle French. Take your time as the French do, starting with a leisurely rum punch made with the local white lightning and plenty of fruit juices. Watch it. It packs an unexpected wallop.

Dine downstairs on fish in lobster sauce or lobster in puff pastry, a duck breast salad, or a fragrant chicken in herbs and wine. Upstairs dining is a little more formal (although both rooms call for your best bib and tucker) more expensive.

Chefs make excellent use of chicken, duckling, fresh fish, langouste and crab plus delicate sauces whispering with island citrus, passion fruit, mango, papaya, and spices. Try paté de foie gras laced with old rum, succulent skate (a ray-like sea creature that tastes like scallops) or the chicken stuffed with ground conch and herbs. The signature dessert is an ice cream coupe layered with rum, banana, butterscotch, and a few secrets.

LA PLANTATION, *Galerie Commerciale de la Marina, Bas du Fort. Tel. 90-84-83. The shopping-marina complex is two miles east of Pointe-à-Pitre. Main dishes are priced F125 to F235. Hours are lunch and dinner Monday through Friday and Saturday dinner 7-10:30pm It's closed Sunday. Reservations are essential.*

Dine upstairs in an air conditioned room overlooking yachts from all over the world, translating the menu with help from the pleasant staff. The food is French; the chef is an Italian, Gianni Ferraris, whose crawfish and foie gras salad is a local legend. Dine lightly on steamed fish or chicken with rafts of steamed vegetables, Creole conch and fish dishes, or a hearty steak sauced in tarragon butter.

PLANTATION STE.-MARTHE, *St. François. Tel. 93-11-11. It's open daily breakfast through dinner. Reservations are essential. Plan to spend 200-300F for dinner.*

Choose your meal and wines carefully from a comprehensive menu and wine list worthy of this upscale resort. Featured are the tartares and carpaccios favored by the French, razor-thin slices of raw meat or fish sprinkled with fresh herbs and bursting with flavor. The seafood stews are always a good choice, or splurge on the lobster, rack of lamb redolent of fresh rosemary, or a filet mignon in peppercorn or red wine sauce. For dessert have the creamy mousse made with white, milk, and dark chocolate.

Moderate

LA CHAUBETTE, *Route de Ste.-Anne. Tel. 84-14-29. reservations are recommended and are essential on Sunday. It opens Monday through Saturday at noon and takes the last order at 8pm It's open Sunday only by appointment. Main dishes are priced F50 to F75. The restaurant is 10 minutes east of Pointe-à-Pitre on the road to Ste. Anne.*

Sit on the front porch of an old Creole house where you're cradled in hospitality while dining on fresh fish, lobster, or chicken followed by a sweet banana flambé. This roadside stalwart has been a classic since the early 1970s.

THE FESTIVAL OF FEMALE COOKS!

It's as hot as the hinges of hell on Guadeloupe in early August when Point-à-Pitre celebrates one of its most important feast days. Savvy travelers come anyway for one of the best feeds in the islands.

*Honoring St. Laurent, patron saint of cooks, the **Fête des Cuisinieres** (note the feminine usage; this is a festival of female cooks) began in 1916 and has turned into a folk festival fantastique. The day begins with a solemn mass, a reminder that this is a saint's day in a Roman Catholic city. Then it's joie de vivre to the max as five hours of feasting, dancing, and rum guzzling begin.*

Women dress in traditional Creole head scarves with gold jewelry and silk foulards and form a procession carrying baskets and trays filled with flowers, kitchen utensils, and tons of food to the open schoolyard where guests are served. To the tune of the beguine, which is said to have been born on Guadeloupe, they sing about the agony and ecstasy of cooking.

To lucky travelers who get a seat, it's a chance to try the best dishes of the island's best cooks including chefs from more than 200 restaurants. Tel. 888/4-GUADELOUPE for the date of this year's festival and for hotel reservations.

LA COURCELLE, *in the Relais du Moulin resort, Chateaubrun, Ste. Anne. Tel. 88-23-96. Plan to spend $35-$50 for dinner. Hours vary seasonally so call for reservations.*

The landmark stone tower of this inn and its cluster of cottages beckons the traveler to sample the inn's two dining areas (the other is Le Restaurant, out by the swimming pool). Depending on the season, either or both might be open, but you can always count on an unhurried meal of French and West Indian dishes, with a bottle of wine, at a moderate price. La Courcelle, which is air conditioned, resembles an Elizabethan lodge. Dine on a hearty fish soup, crusty French bread, a simply dressed green salad, croque monsieur (hot ham and cheese sandwiches), raw tartares and carpaccios, or steak and *pomme frites*. Planters probably chose this location for its view centuries ago and the hilly countryside still provides an unbeatable scene.

LA VERANDAH, *in the Hotel Canella Beach, Pointe de la Verduce, Gosier. Tel. 90-44-00. It's a drive of 5.6 miles from the airport, southeast of Bas-du-Fort. Reservations are suggested. Hours are noon to 2pm and 7 to 10pm every day. Dinner main dishes are priced $16 to $25.*

The beach is nearby and you can dine indoors in an air-cooled pink-and-white dining room or outdoors on the patio with its potted palms and ocean breezes. Try typical French Caribbean classics such as the *oursin* (sea urchin caviar, pronounced oor-san), salt fish, and a realm of seafood choices ranging from simple grilled fish and lobster to saucy seafood soups and stews.

Budget

LA GRANDE PIZZERIA, *Bas-du-Fort, two miles east of Pointe-à-Pitre. Tel. 90-82-64. Snack for F50 or less or spend more for a full dinner. Open nightly, it serves until the wee hours.*

Dine simply outdoors on plastic tables and chairs spiffed up with bright linens in a seaside setting that is popular with locals and visiting yachties. Nosh on pizza, salad and basic pasta dishes or splurge on more grand pastas and risottos lavished with shrimp, lobster, chicken, or beef.

SEEING THE SIGHTS

Take one day for driving the coastal roads of Basse-Terre, stopping at the Compagnie Fermiere de Grosse Montagne to see a working sugar factory with a paint job that will knock your socks off. Just before Ste. Rose, stop at the **Musée de Rhum** where a tour and tasting costs about $5. Along the south coast, it's one fabulous beach after another, including **Malendure Beach** where glass-bottom boat tours leave for Pigeon Island. South of here, **Vieux-Habitants** is one of the island's oldest churches.

Continuing south, you'll come to the capital, the city of **Basse-Terre**, with its old fort dating to 1643. Originally Fort Charles, it was renamed **Fort Delgrés** in 1990 for abolitionist Louis Delgrés, who died in 1802. Stroll the little capital to see the monuments, outdoor markets, and prim colonial buildings straight out of Fantasy Island. Drive through Saint Claude and to the top of **La Soufrière**, the dormant volcano with a peak reaching to 4,813 feet. From the parking area at **Savane à Mulets**, sulphurous vapors can still be seen. The museum there explains this volcano's place in the Caribbean's ring of fire, *Tel. 80-33-43*. If you feel like a hike, climb the 4,813-foot mountain, which takes two rigorous hours.

Continue south to **Vieux Fort** where the **Centre de Broderie** displays laces that mave been made on the island for centuries. Hundreds of patterns are on display and make meaningful souvenirs. Continue now to **Trois Rivières**, where Indian drawings in the **Parc des Roches Gravees**, *Tel. 92-91-88*, date to 400 A.D. It's one of the best concentrations of Arawak drawings in the Caribbean. The park is open daily 9am to 5pm. Admission is 5F.

From Bannier, you have a good view of **Les Saintes**. Or, head inland to **Carbet Falls** (Chutes du Carbet) and **Grand Etang**, the Great Pond. Just outside **Petit-Bourg**, stretch your legs at a six-acre **botanical garden** when you can see at least 100 varieties of trees, shrubs, and flowers, *Tel. 95-50-50.* The gardens are open daily 9am to 5pm. Admission is 40F. Budget an entire day or more for discovering the national park's rainforest paths, its zoo and botanical gardens, and waterfalls including the breathtaking **Cascade aux Ecrévisses**, *Tel. 80-24-25.*

The chief focus in the town of **Point-à-Pitre** is the waterfront, which can easily be toured in half a day. Orient yourself at the **Place de la Victoire**, a central park, and the impressive **Centre St.-John Perse**, a dock and shopping complex that can accommodate four cruise ships at once. It's a pleasant hangout for browsing, dining, and watching the tourist world go by.

Sightseeing highlights in town include the **Musée Schoelcher**, 24 rue Paynier, *Tel. 82-08-04,* which contains memorabilia left by Victor Schoelcher. He is considered the father of the emancipation movement that led to the freeing of French West Indian slaves in 1848. The building itself dates to 1887. It's open weekdays 8:30am-11:30am and 2-5pm. Admission is 10F. Housed in a classic gothic-style mansion at the corner of rue Noisiere and Achie Rene-Boisneuf is a museum devoted to Alexis Leger, the Guadeloupean known as St.-John Perse who won the Nobel prize for literature in 1960. The museum is open Thursday through Tuesday 8:30am-11:30am and 2:30-5:30pm. Admission is 10F.

Grand Terre

This island is flatter but it too is worth a day's sightseeing. Take the "Riviera" road leading to the tourist hotels and stop at **Bas-du-Fort** to look over the marina and old **Fort Fleur d'Epée**. Just off the main highway, stop at the **Aquarium de la Guadeloupe** at Place Creole, Marina Bas-du-Fort, 97190 Gosier, *Tel. 90-92-38.* It is open every day 9am to 7pm. It's considered to have the fourth largest collection of marine life in all France. Continuing east past Ste. Anne and St. Francois, stop at Pointe des Chateaux, where massive boulders resemble huge castles. Across the water, you can see the island of **La Désirade**. Staying on the coast you'll pass a colonial mansion, **Maison Zevcallos** and will go through **La Moule**, once the capital. Destroyed in a hurricane in the 1920s, it never regained its former grandeur, but its good beaches still draw a lot of tourists.

Stop at the **Musée Edgar Clerc** on Parc de la Rosette, three miles past La Moule towards Campeche, *Tel. 23-57-43,* to see one of the most comprehensive collections of Arawak and Carib artifacts in the world. It's housed in a historic building that is itself worth seeing. Admission is 10F and hours are Monday to Friday 9am-12:30pm, and 2-5:30pm; Saturday and Sunday it stays open until 6:30pm.

Continuing north brings you to the Gate of Hell, Porte d'Enfer, a rugged coastline with spectacular views and **La Pointe de la Vigie** with its stark white cliffs. The road back to Pointa-à-Pitre takes you through **Morne-a-l'Eau**, where a huge cemetery is lit with thousands of candles on All Saints Day, November 1.

NIGHTLIFE & ENTERTAINMENT

To listen to live Caribbean music jam sessions in Gosier, try the **ELYSÉES MATIGNON**, Bas-du-Fort. *Tel. 90-89-05;* **LE ZENITH** Bas-du-Fort, *Tel. 90-72-04;* or **NEW LAND**, Route de la Riviera, *Tel. 84-34-91.* The legal drinking age in Guadeloupe is 18.

Casinos at Gosier and St. François are open 9pm to 3am nightly for slots, blackjack, chemin-de-fer, and American roulette. Admission charge is 70F and drinks are astronomically priced at 45F. You must be at least 21 years old and present photo identification. Although dress is informal, shorts aren't permitted.

Try to catch a performance of the **Ballets Guadeloupeans**, who often appear at hotels. Like other folkloric troupes that have become popular in the islands, the group keeps ancient dances and music alive through joyous performance. Islanders claim that the beguine was invented here, so ask a local to teach you.

SPORTS & RECREATION

Beaches

Beaches around Guadeloupe range from the dark sands of western **Basse-Terre** to the long, powdery sands of **Grand-Terre**. Public beaches are free except for parking, which costs a few dollars at some. Most hotels allow non-guests to use their beach chairs, changing rooms and towels for a fee.

Topless bathing is common everywhere; **Pointe Tarare** is the best-known nude beach. **Place Crawen** on Terre-de-Haut and **Ilet du Gosier** also see a lot of nude swimmers.

Bicycling

Bicycling here is a popular sport as well as a good way to get around. The 10-day **Tour de la Guadeloupe** held each August is a major world bicycling event. To rent a bicycle in Pointe-à-Pitre, contact **Dingo Location**, *Tel. 83-81-19.* In St. François, rent from:
• **MM**, *Tel. 88-59-12*
• **Easy Rent**, *Tel. 88-76-27*
• **Karucycle**, *Tel. 82-21-39*
• **Rent-a-Bike**, *Tel. 88-51-00*

For mountain biking or the 18-speed VTT, contact the **Association Guadeloupéenne de VTT**, *Tel. 82-17-50.*

For motorbike rental, contact **Vespa Sun**, *Tel. 91-30-36* or **Motor Guadeloupe**, *Tel. 82-17-50.* Rentals cost about 170F daily with insurance, plus a F1,000 deposit.

Camping

To rent a "camping car" with its own beds and waterworks, contact **Camping Cars Vert Bleu** in Deshaies, *Tel. 28-51-25;* **Vacances** in La Moule, *Tel. 23-17-52;* or **Local' Soleil** in Gosier, *Tel. 84-56-51.* For information about camping the national park, contact the Tourist Information sources listed below under Practical Information. Most campsites have no facilities.

The best campground is **Les Sables d'Or** on Grande Anse Beach near Deshaies. It has bathrooms and showers, and offers tents for rent, *Tel. 28-44-60.* Good camping facilities are also found at **La Traversée**, Pointe Noire, *Tel. 98-21-23.*

FRENCH BOCCIE

*The French have a passion for a game called **Petanque**, or merely **boule**. It resembles the Italian game boccie in that a ball is thrown, but these are heavier. If you want to "go native," check out a Petanque set from your hotel's activities center and ask how to play it. It's a sure way to make friends even if you don't speak the same language.*

Diving

Jacques Cousteau called Pigeon Island, which lies off Guadeloupe's west coast, one of the world's 10 best dives. Unfortunately, his endorsement has increased the crowds to dismaying proportions but the brilliant, abundant fish life puts on a satisfying show.

Dive operators that also offering lodging include:
- **Les Heures Saintes**, *Tel. 98-86-63*
- **Chez Guy et Christian**, *Tel. 98-82-43*
- **Aux Aquanautes**, *Tel. 98-87-30*

Other scuba schools and operations based in hotels include:
- **Aqua-Fari** in Gosier at Callinago, *Tel. 84-26-26*
- **Caraines Plongée** at Canella Beach, *Tel. 90-44-90*
- **La Captainaire** at Marissol, *Tel. 90-84-44*
- **Caribmer Scuba** at the Meridien. *Tel. 88-51-00*
- **Plongée Club de l'Autre Bord** at the Tropical Club, *Tel. 93-97-10*

Dive trips can also be booked at **Terre de Haut**, a small island off Basse Terre, with **Centre Nautique des Saintes**. Single dives usually cost F150 to F320 depending on the distance to the dive site. For information, contact the Office of Tourism, *Tel. 82-09-30*.

Fishing

Go deep sea fishing with **Caraïbe Pêche**, *Tel. 990-97-51;* **Evasion Exotic**, *Tel. 90-94-17;* **Fishing Club Antilles**. *Tel. 90-70-10;* or with Franck Nouy at Le Rocher de Malendure, *Tel. 98-70-84*. The season for barracuda and kingfish is January to May. From December through March, fish for tuna, dolphin, and bonito.

Fitness

You'll find a modern thermal spa with a full range of treatments at **Espace Santé de Ravine Chaude** near Lamentin on Basse-Terre, *Tel. 25-75-92*. **Espace Tonic** in **Pointe-à-Pitre**, *Tel. 83-88-34* offers fitness, muscle development, and aerobics.

Flying

Take flying lessons or, if you are a licensed pilot, rent a Cessna from **Les Ailes Guadeloupéennes** at Raizet Airport, *Tel. 83-24-44*. To fly ultralight seaplanes from Gosier and St.-Francois beaches, *Tel. 90-83-98*.

Golf

Play the 18-hole **Golf de St. François**, *Tel. 88-41-87*, a 6,755-yard, par-71 course designed by Robert Trent Jones, Sr. It has a clubhouse, restaurant, bar, and English-speaking pro. Greens fees are $50 daily.

Hiking

Hike the **Parc National**, *Tel. 81-24-83*, offering 200 miles of marked trails with a guide from the Bureau des Guides de Moyenne Montagne. Guides work by the hour on a sliding scale; a four-hour hike of **La Soufrière** costs about $60. For English language maps and brochures, contact the National Park Office, Habitation Beausoleil, Monteran, St.-Claude 97120, Guadeloupe, French West Indies, *Tel. 80-24-25, Fax 80-05-46*.

Horseback Riding

Get a horse, riding lessons, or a horseback picnic excursion from **Le Criolo** in St. Felix, *Tel. 83-38-90*. Horseback riding is also available from:
• **Poney Club** in La Loule, *Tel. 24-03-74*
• **La Ferme de Campeche**, *Tel. 82-11-54*
• **La Martingale in Baie-Mahault**, *Tel. 26-28-39*

Sailing

Charter a bareboat or crewed sailboat for day or overnight sailing, or for one-say sails to Martinique or St. Martin. Agencies include:

- **ATM Yachts**, *Tel. 90-92-02*
- **Cap Sud**, *Tel. 26-68-32*
- **Jet Sea Yachting**, *Tel. 90-82-95 or U.S. 800/262-JETC*
- **Massif Marine Antilles**, *Tel. 90-82-80*
- **The Moorings**, *Tel. 90-81-81 or U.S. 800/535-7289*
- **Star Voyages Antilles**, *Tel. 90-86-26.*

Also available are packages that include some nights aboard a sailboat and others in hotels.

Snorkeling

The best snorkel spots include the **St. François reef** and **Ilet du Gosier** off the Gosier hotels.

Squash

Two squash courts are found at **Viva Forme** in the Village Viva, Bas-du-Fort, *Tel. 90-98-74.*

Tennis

If your hotel doesn't have tennis courts, try the **Marina Club in Pointe-à-Pitre**, *Tel. 90-84-08* or the **Centre Lamby-Lambert** in Gosier. *Tel. 09-90-97.*

Windsurfing & Surfing

International board sailing events, including the Funworld World Cup, are held on Guadeloupe's surfer-friendly waters. If your hotel doesn't offer lessons and rentals, contact the **Union des Centres de Plein Air** in St. François, *Tel. 88-64-80.* Surfboards, which rent for about F100 a day or F500 weekly, are available from Philip Gazé, **Comité Guadeloupéen de Surf**, *Tel. 91-77-64.* The best surfing waters are considered to be **Moule Port Louise** and **Anse Bertrand** from October through April and, in summer, **Ste. Anne**, **St. François**, and **Petit-Havre**.

SHOPPING

The best buys on the island are French perfumes, china, crystal and local rums. The most meaningful souvenirs include handmade laces, pottery, straw and wicker work, and batik fabrics. Among the significant collectibles are salacos, which are split bamboo hats made in **Les Saintes**, and handmade doudou dolls.

Shops are generally open 9am-1pm and 3-6pm daily and on Saturday morning. Find most of the tourist shops along rue Frebault in Pointe-à-Pitre. At the corner of rue Frebault and rue Thiers, the Marché Couvert (covered market) is crammed with colorful displays of spices, fruits, vegetables and surging crowds shopping for tonight's dinner. For local antiques and whimsies, shop Tim-Tim at 15 Rue Henri 1V, *Tel. 83-48-71.* For a taste of the local popskull, visit the **Distillerie Bellevue** on rue Bellevue-Damoiseau. *Tel. 23-55-55.* Made here is a pure and powerful rum brewed from fermented sugarcane juice, not from molasses.

EXCURSIONS & DAY TRIPS

Inter-island waters can be rough, so you may want to consider visiting Guadeloupe's out islands by air. However, there is ferry service to **Marie-Galante**, **Les Saintes**, and **La Désirade**, all of them picturesque, end-of-the-world islands that are well worth a visit. You can get to any of them and back in a day. Round trip fares range from $20 to La Désirade to $32 for Marie-Galante and Les Saintes.

Call the **Express des Iles**, *Tel. 83-12-45*; the **Brudey Freres**, *Tel. 90-04-48*, **Socimade Boats**, *Tel. 83-32-67*; **Le Mistral**, *Tel. 88-48-63 or 20-04-43;* the **Princess Caroline**, *Tel. 86-95-83;* or the **Amanda Galante**, *Tel. 83-12-45.*

LES ILES DES SAINTES

Think of it as a movie set, a cluster of colorful buildings around a sunbaked waterfront that is too prim, too pretty, too perfect to be believed. Believe it. **Terre-de-Haut** has just enough visitors, most of them day-trippers from yachts, smaller cruise ships, and other islands, to sustain a tourism industry that is big enough to be appealing but too small to overwhelm the island. Columbus named them Los Santos, a sprinkling of saintly sentinels just six miles off Guadeloupe.

Unlike the mother island with its largely black population, Terre-de-Haut was settled by white descendants of early French privateers. One story is that the island was settled by prisoners who were set free, so they brought in women from France and set up housekeeping. Still seagoing folk, they're known for their salaco hats, made from split bamboo and resembling coolie headgear. If you can find one for sale, grab it. Their Breton-style boats are unique, known throughout the islands as *santois*. Some of the best beaches and bays in the entire Caribbean are found on the miles of shoreline in the Saintes. It's obvious why they're so popular with nature lovers who prefer to bathe in the buff.

Shops are generally open 8am to noon and 2-5:30pm. A few stay open through lunch. The island has no customs and immigration, so your return trip should be through Guadeloupe. The only bank is open only two days a week, so have credit cards, cash, and travelers checks to use in restaurants and hotels (where accepted). If you need wheels, rent a scooter.

You can walk to just about everything, including **Fort Napoleon** overlooking the harbor. Built in 1867, it is open 9am to noon for an admission charge of about F20. If you're in top form, climb **Le Chameau**, an old lookout tower that provides a panoramic view for miles around.

Arrivals & Departures

The scattering of islands that make up the Iles des Saintes has one major islet, **Terre-de-Haut**, which has an air strip that can accommodate 20-passenger airplanes. From Guadeloupe, it's a 15-minute flight costing about $35 round trip on **Air Guadeloupe**, *Tel. 590/82-47-00*.

By ferry, it's a trip of about an hour from the quai in Poite-a-Pitre or from Basse Terre, for a round trip fare of about $36. Hours vary according to the day of the week, so check ahead with Freres Brudey, *Tel. 90-04-48*, or **Expres des Iles**, *Tel. 82-15-62*. Ferries and flights are met by taxis. Once settled you can travel by shank's mare, or rent a scooter, which requires a deposit of F1,500.

Where to Stay

KANAOA, *Pointe Coquelet, Terre-de-Haut 97137, Iles des Saintes. Tel. 590/99-51-36, Fax 99-55-04. Rates at this 19-room inn start at F650 including continental breakfast. Meal plans are available. It's 1.2 miles from the Iles des Saintes airport.*

Canoe is one of the Carib words that survives today in English and its name is ideal for this uncomplicated, functional hotel on a small beach on Anse Mire on the northwest coast of Iles des Saintes. Rooms have showers but no tubs or other extravagant features but the hotel has its own restaurant and pool. Bring your French dictionary. Little *Anglais* is spoken *ici*.

BOIS-JOLI, *Anse a Cointe, Iles des Saintes. Tel. 590/99-50-38, Fax 99-55-05. Rates at this 30-unit inn start at $118 for a studio and $268 for a cottage. Rates include breakfast and dinner. It's two miles from the Iles des Saintes airport.*

We would rate this a budget hotel because you get a lot for the money: accommodations in a cottage or the main house plus a good Creole breakfast and dinner. Reserve months in advance; regulars here make next year's reservation as they leave. Some units have a shower, some a tub. Not all have air conditioning or a telephone. State your preferences when you book. The beach is grand and the settlement is a long walk or short drive (two miles) away.

Friendly hosts can arrange watersports, diving, boating to outlying islets, and fishing. The name means "pretty woodland" and the flowering shrubs are gorgeous, but a rain forest it isn't.

VILLAGE CREOLE, *Pointe Coquelet, 97137 Terre-de-Haut, Les Saintes. Tel. 590/99-53-83, Fax 99-55-55. Rates at this 22-room inn start at $150 without meals. It's on the north edge of town, 1.2 miles from the airport.*

Although it's on the water, it's more a country garden than a beachfront resort. Your cottage is typically West Indian, practical and comfortable, with separate sleeping and living areas, a private patio, and use of a washer and dryer. Most guests come for a week or more, which is a good idea considering that getting here involves an extra airplane or ferry ride. There is no restaurant, but you'll have a kitchen and can walk or bicycle to a couple of dozen good eateries. The management practices benign neglect, respecting your privacy to the point of being invisible much of the time, so this isn't the spot for the tourist who needs a 24-hour front desk on call. Units have air conditioning, mini-bar and telephone.

LA SANTOISE, *Bourg, Terre-de-Haut 97137, Iles des Saintes. Tel. 99-52-50. Rates at this 10-room inn start at 350F including continental breakfast. It's just over half a mile from the airport on the island of Iles des Saintes.*

Combine the crowded living of a French village and West Indian sunshine and you have this sunbaked, streetside hotel where you can watch the tourists go by. Sometimes meals are offered for about 80F but otherwise you won't have a problem finding good food around town. Rooms, which are upstairs over the unassuming lobby, are bland and basic but they do have air conditioning and a tile bath.

MARIE-GALANTE

The round top of a long-extinct volcano, this little island has a population of more than 8,000, most of them making a living from fishing, sugar, and rum. Some of the beaches go on for five pristine miles, but the waters can be scrappy, so swim only with care.

The main settlement is **Grand-Bourg**, where visitors can see a church dating to the 1840s, relax in a sidewalk cafe, or shop for souvenirs including some of the Caribbean's best rum. It's made here at **Vieux Fort**, where the factory offers tours and tastings. Tour **Chateau Murat**, *Tel. 97-03-79, open daily 9:15am-5pm. Admission is 10F.*

Where to Eat

L'AUBERGE DE L'ARBRE A PAIN, *Rue Jeanne d'Arc 32, Grand Bourg. Tel. 97-73-69. It's a half mile from the airport. Marie Galante is a 20-minute flight from Guadeloupe. Meals cost $15 to $23. Call for reservations before leaving Guadeloupe.*

Named for the breadfruit trees that are harvested for the table, this restaurant was so popular with day-trippers that the owners opened a handful of hotel rooms. Meals will be simple and superb: blaff, fresh fish sauteed in butter, cassoulet of lamb, chicken in wine, island vegetables, and a nice choice of sweets.

LE MOUILLAGE, *on the dock at Deshaies. Tel. 28-41-12. It's open daily for lunch and dinner. Dine for under 40F.*

The bar here is a popular meeting spot for cruising boaters from all over the world. Start the day with croissants or *pain au chocolat* from the nearby boulangerie, which in the morning smells intoxicatingly of fresh bread and woodsmoke. For lunch and dinner there are fish stews, wonderful peasant soups, fresh fish, salads, and more of that crusty bread.

LE MADRAS, *on the beach just north of the dock, Deshaies. Tel. 28-40-87. It's open daily for lunch and dinner. Dine for less than 40F.*

Dine indoors or on the beach. Call ahead if you want something special. Otherwise just take pot luck, which is sure to be good.

LA DÉSIRADE

Come here for the beaches. Small buses meet every flight and ferry. The settlement, Grand-Anse, has a small guesthouse, restaurant, and church.

PRACTICAL INFORMATION

Area Code: 590

ATM: find a MasterCard/Cirrus ATM at LeRaizet Airport. Also look for ATMs in Credit Agricole banks in major settlements.

Banking: banks in Pointe-à-Pitre are usually open Monday through Friday 8am to noon and 2-4pm. Some are open Saturday mornings.

Crime: keep valuables including your air ticket and passport in the hotel safe, and don't leave valuables in sight in a locked car. Beware of quick, agile thieves on motorbikes, who can lift a purse from your shoulder and be gone before you know what hit you.

Currency: the French franc, which consists of 100 centimes, is the official coin. U.S. dollars are accepted everywhere and major credit cards are accepted at most tourist hotels, restaurants, and shops but you'll need francs for small restaurants and shops.

Current: voltage is 220 volts, 50 cycles. You'll need a converter and plug adapter to use North American appliances.

Dress Code: bikinis or just bottoms are worn on most beaches, but don't wear swimwear in town. By night, gentlemen wear sports shirts and slacks; women wear chic resort wear. Don't forget coverups for protection from the sun. For hiking the national park, take a windbreaker and hiking shoes. Dress in the casinos is informal; jackets and ties are not required.

Government: Guadeloupe is a *département* of France. U.S. consular matters are handled through Bridgetown, Barbados, *Tel. 246/436-4950*.

Immigration: unless you're staying longer than three weeks, you'll need only a valid passport or one that expired not more than five years ago. Other acceptable identification for U.S. and Canadian citizens is a voter registration card accompanied by government-issued photo identification such as a driver's license. A driver's license alone, however, is not proof of citizenship. You'll also need a return ticket.

Holidays: when banks and some shops are closed include New Year's Day, Easter, Labor Day on May 1, VE Day, Ascension Day, Pentecost Monday, Slavery Abolition Day in late May; Bastille Day July 14, Schoelcher Day in late July, Assumption Day (dates relate to the church calendar and Easter), All Saints Day on November 1, and Christmas.

Medical matters: Guadeloupe has five hospitals and more than two dozen clinics. To call an ambulance, *Tel. 90-22-95*.

Pets: are admitted if they are over three months old and have recent health certificates from a licensed veterinarian in your home country. That doesn't mean that your hotel allows pets, but some do. Check ahead. It is also common on the French islands for pets to be allowed in restaurants.

Telephone: to call Guadeloupe from North America, dial 011-590 plus the number for station calls, and 01-590 for person-to-person. When calling from Guadeloupe, dial 19+1 for North America or 1+area code for other Caribbean islands except French islands. For them, just dial the number. A Telecarte is a prepaid phone card sold in post offices and by other vendors who display the sign "Telecarte en Vente Ici." If you don't have one, dial 10 and wait for an operator, then call collect or use a credit card.

Time: Guadeloupe time is one hour earlier than Eastern Standard Time. It is expressed in the 24-hour clock, e.g. 11pm is 23:00 hours.

Tourist information: The Guadeloupe Tourist Office at *5, Square de la Banque, Pointe-à-Pitre, Tel. 82-09-30* is a goldmine of information and maps for the visitor. For further information from the United States, call the French Tourist Information, *Tel. 900/990-0040*. The call costs 95 cents a minute. Or, write the French Government Tourist Office, *444 Madison Avenue, New York NY 10022*. In Canada, write the French Government Tourist Office, *1981 Avenue McGill College 490, Montreal, Quebec, H3A 2W9, Tel. 514/288-4264, Fax 844-8901; or 30 St. Patrick Street, Suite 700, Toronto, Ontario M5T 3A3. Tel. 416/593-6427, Fax 979-7587*.

Weddings: one member of the couple must have resided on Guadeloupe for at least a month. You'll need certification of single status, a birth certificate with a raised seal, a medical certificate including a blood test no more than three months old, and French translation for all documents in English. There is no charge for the *Bulletin de Mariage* and the *Livret de Famille* that are delivered at the ceremony.

34. MARTINIQUE

"Bonjour, Madame," the old woman smiled, holding out a hideously ossified pufferfish in hopes I would buy it. It's still one of the ugliest accessories in our home, but that charming woman in her faded head scarf won my heart on that blowtorch day in Fort-de-France. We chatted within the limits of my French, and I felt I had connected with **Martinique** – the island known as the Paris of the Antilles.

Sandwiched between the English islands of Dominica and St. Lucia, almost 2,000 miles from New York and 4,261 miles from Paris, visitors find a *region* of France, a step above *département*, as much a part of the mother country as Paris itself – rather like a state in the U.S. or a province in Canada. It's about twelve miles wide and 30-odd miles long, a total of 425 square miles. Polished and well positioned in commerce as well as tourism, the island has one of the highest standards of living in the Caribbean.

The Carib Indians called this the Isle of Flowers, and floral it remains. Rich harvests of fruits and vegetables roll from its soil while untilled lands are smothered in frangipani, wild orchids, hibiscus and neon-bright bougainvillea.

Discovered by Christopher Columbus in 1502, ten years after he first reached the Americas, Martinique was annexed by France in 1674 and it remains French to this day despite attacks from the English who, among other adventures, mounted cannon on a rock off the island and turned it into a battleship. They held for 18 months, so tenaciously that the French dislodged them only after floating some barrels of rum to the defenders and getting them smashed. The rock easily fell back into French hands that night, but the victors were so impressed with the mayhem the British had caused for all those months, they paraded their prisoners through the streets as heroes. In an equally passionate burst of patriotism, Britain commissioned the rock into the Royal Navy. Today it's a major tourist attraction.

Once Martinique's largest city, St. Pierre thrived until 1902, when it was buried in a violent volcanic eruption. Within three minutes, 30,000

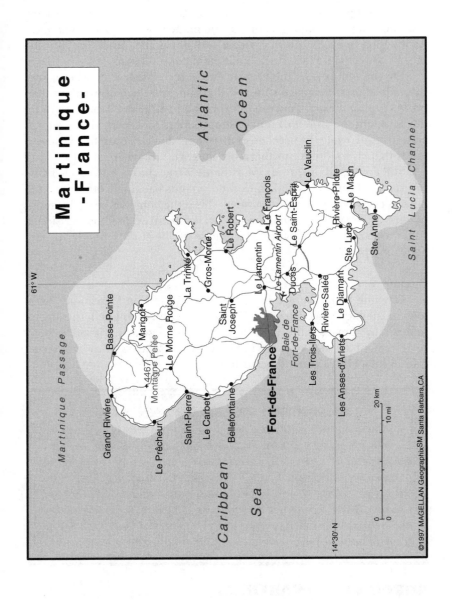

Martinique
-France-

Atlantic
Ocean

Martinique Passage

Caribbean
Sea

Saint Lucia Channel

61° W
14°30' N

Grand' Riviére
Le Prêcheur
Saint-Pierre
Le Carbet
Bellefontaine
Fort-de-France
Basse-Pointe
Marigot
Le Morne Rouge
▲4467
Montagne Pelée
Saint
Joseph
La Trinité
Gros-Morne
Le Robert
Le Lamentin
Le Lamentin Airport
Ducos
Le François
Le Saint-Esprit
Baie de
Fort-de-France
Les Trois-Îlets
Rivière-Salée
Le Diamant
Les Anses-d'Arlets
Le Vauclin
Rivière-Pilote
Le Marin
Ste. Luce
Ste. Anne

0   10 mi
0   20 km

©1997 MAGELLAN GeographixSM Santa Barbara,CA

people died in fast-moving lava spewing from **Mont Pelée**. Today the capital is **Fort-de-France**, a sophisticated city of more than 100,000 people.

All the flourish and panache of good things French is here: smart fashion, beautiful language, and cuisine made magic with *je ne sais quoi*. Africa adds an exotic touch, a wiggle, a rhythm. The Caribbean contributes its towering forests, rugged hills, and constant sun.

On the minus side, the French smoke ferociously everywhere, and they adore their language so much that they're reluctant to admit that other languages exist. Tourism information in English is scanty; signs in the museum are only in French; shopkeepers look pained at visitors' accents. And, while the beaches south of Fort-de-France are the bleached sands that visitors seek, northern beaches are a dingy grey.

Still the Island of Flowers, Martinique is trees heavy with exotic fruit, forests filled with ferns and vines, wild orchids hanging from trees, and bowers of blooms beyond imagining. This is the home of the tradewinds, *les alizes*, where summer simmers all year. If you can get past the occasional gallic arrogance, you'll find Martinique to be a rich, modern, and appealing paradise.

Climate

Daytime highs average in the mid-to-high 80s on Martinique, with lows in the high 50s or low 60s. Humidity at 7am averages in the low to mid-80s; by 5pm it's in the high 70s. Rain comes regularly, with an average of 18 days of .04 inch or more in February and 27 days of at least some rain in July. Hurricanes do occur in this area.

JOSEPHINE'S ISLAND BEGINNINGS

Marie Josephe Rose Tascher de la Pagerie, who would later become the Empress Josephine, was born on Martinique in 1763. In an arranged marriage, the teenager was wed to the Viscomte Alexandre de Beauharnais. As a member of the despised aristocracy, he was guillotined in Paris in 1794 but his attractive, 31-year-old widow was more fortunate. She charmed Parisian society, managed to get back some of the Beauharnais lands that had been confiscated, and caught the eye of Napoleon himself. It was he who renamed her Josephine.

ARRIVALS & DEPARTURES

Martinique's **International Fort-de-France Lamentin International Airport** has direct flights from New York's JFK and from San Juan and

Miami. It's served by:
- **North American Airlines**, *Tel. 212/333-8680*
- **American Airlines** and **America Eagle**, *Tel. 800/433-7300*
- **Air Martinique**, *Tel. 60-00-23*
- **Reseau Aerien Francais des Caraïbes**, *Tel. 55-33-00*
- **LIAT**, *Tel. 51-10-00*

Air France, *Tel. 800/237-2747,* serves the island from Paris and Miami. It is a major hub with good connections to many other islands including Guadeloupe, Antigua, St. Martin, Dominica, St. Lucia, Barbados, St. Vincent, Mustique, Union Island, and Canouan.

Emeraude Express, a high-speed catamaran, runs among Martinique, Dominica, and Guadeloupe, *Tel. 596/63-12-11, Fax 63-34-47.*

ORIENTATION

Martinique is a favorite cruise ship port, attracting almost half a million visitors a year. If you come by ship you'll be in the heart of Fort-de-France, which has excellent passenger terminal facilities. **Lamentin International Airport** is also handy to the capital, a 15-minute ride southeast of the city and 40 minutes by car from most of the hotels.

Fort-de-France is a city not unlike a settlement on the French Riviera, clogged with traffic and crowded with shoppers and sightseers. Its park is **La Savane**, which is bounded by the waterfront, Fort Saint Lo, Avenue des Caraïbes, and the Rue de la Liberté. It's possible to drive almost around the entire island to explore settlements at **St. Pierre**, **Trinité**, **Lorrain**, the tiny fishing village of **Case Pilote**, and touristy **Anse Mitan**.

GETTING AROUND MARTINIQUE

Taxi stands are found at the airport, at major hotels, and in downtown Fort-de-France. For a radio taxi, call *Tel. 63-63-62.* From the airport to the hotels at Pointe du Bout, the fare is 149F; from the airport to the city center costs about 63F. Between 8pm and 6am you'll pay a 40 percent surcharge. About 80 percent of the island's taxis are Mercedes, a real plus compared to some of the rattletraps found on some islands.

Collective taxis, which bear the sign TC, are eight-passenger limousines that are an affordable alternative to busses. About 400 TCs roam the island 6am to 6pm; a typical fare is Fort-de-France to Ste. Anne, 25.55F, one way. In Fort-de-France the main terminal is at **Pointe Simon**. Another quick way to get to Fort-de-France from Pointe de Bout, Anse Mitan, and Anse a l'Ane is aboard ferries known as vedettes. By road it's a long way 'round; by sea, it's a straight shot for a one-way fare of 24F adults and 10F children.

To rent a car, you need only a driver's license issued in your home country. Rental companies include **Avis**, *Tel. 70-11-60;* **Budget**, *Tel. 63-69-00* or *70-22-75;* **Hertz**, *Tel. 66-06-64 or 51-01-01;* and **Thrifty**, *Tel. 66-09-59.* Cars are available at the airport and most major hotels. Except at the airport, where hours depend on international arrivals, most car rental agencies are open 8am to noon and 2:30 to 5pm.

The island also has bus service, but it can be a battle unless you speak French. Even so, rides can be hot and waits long. To catch a minivan, which charges fares of 5-25F, go to Pointe Simon on the waterfront.

WHERE TO STAY

Martinique offers almost 5,000 rooms in more than 80 hotels and guest houses. Modestly priced **Relais Creoles** are family-run guest houses; **gîtes** are rooms or studios in private homes, Te*l. 596/73-67-92.* When you book, ask about hotel tax, which is levied on some properties, and about service charges, which can add 5-20 percent to your bill. Unless stated otherwise, these hotels accept major credit cards. Take a French phrase book. English is not the first language here and locals consider that your problem, not theirs.

When a hotel has an FAB plan, for Full American Breakfast, that means the kind of cooked breakfast preferred by Americans and Britons rather than the light breakfast of croissant and coffee or chocolate that are a continental (CP) breakfast.

Your address while in the islands will be Hotel, Street or Box, Five-Digit Code and City, Island, French West Indies.

Expensive

ANSE CARITAN, *97227 Ste. Anne. Tel. 596/76-74-12, Fax 76-72-59. Rates at this 96-room hotel start at $203 including continental breakfast. It's 26.6 miles from the airport in the island's southernmost point.*

A ginger beach takes over where the flower-filled gardens stop at the seaside. The restaurant here is popular with tourists from all over the area, who come here for the native Creole cuisine. After dinner, there's almost always live music. Swim in the pool, go diving, sail, or schedule a deep sea fishing expedition. Helpful staff will do their best in whatever language you speak.

LE MÉRIDIEN TROIS-ISLETS, *Pointe de Bout, Martinique 97229, French West Indies. Tel. 596/66-00-00, Fax 66-00-74, toll-free 800/543-4300. Rates at this 295-unit hotel start at US$232 including continental breakfast. The hotel is 16 miles from the airport.*

It's owned by Air France, so this hotel is known more for its tour groups and package deals than for the charm sought by individual travelers. Yet it soldiers on, always crowded with a loyal clientele. Every room overlooks the water and, after dark, the views are of the twinkle of Fort-de-France across the bay. Food is served in the signature restaurant La Capitaine or beside the beach in Le Cocoterais. Once a week, Ballets Martiniquais stages a dance show after dinner. The marine and watersports center are on site so you can swim in the pools or hire a boat to find your own, private island or beach. Book a scuba outing or a snorkel sail, hire a board sailer, or arrange to go water skiing. The hotel also offers tennis, shops, a tour desk, car rental, and gambling machines.

HABITATION LAGRANGE, Le Marigot *97225. Tel. 596/53-60-60, Fax 53-60-58. Rates at this 17-unit hotel start at $350 including full breakfast. The hotel is 23 miles from the airport, on the island's northeast coast. By cab it's about $40. If you're driving, it's just past the shrimp farm north of Le Marigot.*

A greathouse dating to the turn of the century has been added to, creating a homey and unpretentious inn surrounded by gardens and banana trees. Take a room or the junior suite in the greathouse, or stay in one of the gardenside units. Rooms are air conditioned and have ceiling fan, direct-dial telephone, private porch, mini-bar, and bathrooms supplied with elegant toiletries, bathrobes, and antique shaving mirrors. On site are a small pool, miles of walking paths, bar and restaurant, pool table, and a lighted tennis court. Come here for pampering from a family of owner-hosts, superb native food, and the sense of elegant yesterdays, not for beaches. It's a long, rough ride to the shore, which is dingy, volcanic sand. Room service is available for breakfast.

HOTEL LA BATELIÈRE, *09200 Schoelcher, Route 32. Tel. 596/61-49-49, Fax 61-70-57. Rates at this 197-unit hotel start at $150 per person including full breakfast. Suites are available to sleep four to six. It is north of Fort-de-France, 5.4 miles from the airport.*

One entire window wall of your room opens to your private balcony or terrace, where you can look out to sea or enjoy a garden view of flowering shrubs and trees a-twit with birdlife. The beach is wide and sandy, and the social schedule is a busy one (albeit mostly in French). Dine in the Bleu Marine or on the beach near the swimming pool. Play tennis on floodlit courts (there's a small surcharge to pay for lights after dark), try your luck in the casino, and dance after dinner in the lively disco.

HOTEL PLANTATION LEYRITZ, *Basse-Pointe 97218, French West Indies. Tel. 596/73-53-92, Fax 78-92-44. Rates at this 68-unit hotel start at $330 double including continental breakfast. The hotel is at the north end of the island, 38 miles from the airport. The taxi ride is about $55 but most people rent a car.*

Built as a banana plantation more than 300 years ago, this gracious old greathouse survives untouched by time among flowering gardens and oceans of green lawn. Sleep in a slave cottage (with indoor plumbing now, of course), the guardhouse (we like the gunnery slits that serve as windows), the carriage house with its private decks, or the old kitchen.

Sleep in the shadow of Mont Pelée, in an air conditioned room decorated in mellow plaids.

By day there's always the chance that crowds of day-trippers will swarm in from cruise ships. To avoid them, lunch early or late and ask to be seated in the small dining room rather than the main room. Usually, though, this is a quiet alternative to the yeh-yeh bustle of Pointe du Bout. The beach is a half hour away by free shuttle. Or, just stay by the pool and tennis courts and enjoy the mountain views. Informal, elegant meals are served three times a day; entertainment or dancing to live music play a couple of times weekend.

NOVOTEL CARAYOU, *Pointe du Bout, 97229 Trois Islets. Tel. 596/66-04-04, Fax 66-00-57. Rates at this 201-room hotel are from $225 including full breakfast. It's 15.6 miles from the airport on Fort-de-France Bay.*

You're not far from golfing in this busy chain hotel, and there's a beach where you can swim, windsurf, or sail. A blue and white color scheme gives the rooms a spiffy look. Up to two children under age 16 can sleep free in their parents' room and the children's program allows kids from all nations to play together in a happy hodgepodge of languages. Dine on the terrace overlooking Fort-de-France or on the beach. The hotel has a swimming pool, bars, a tennis court, and a boutique selling sundries and smart resort wear.

NOVOTEL DIAMANT, *Pointe de la Chery, Diamant 97223. Rates at this 181-room hotel start at $225 with full breakfast. It's 16.4 miles from the airport and 30 kilometers from Fort-de-France on the southwest corner of the island near Diamond Rock. Meal plans are available.*

The beaches that rim the resort aren't supersize (this is a big hotel for only five acres), but the chief appeal here is the windsurfing, for which the French have a passion. Watch the experts, or give it a whirl. Scuba too is hot, or you can play tennis, swim in the pool, or rent a car to go exploring. Like most of the large hotels here, this one tends to fill up with groups, but the staff cheerfully switch from French to English, German, and patois as the need arises. Rooms are air conditioned and children under age 16 sleep free with their parents. Even the family dog is welcome here.

SOFITEL BAKOUA, *Point Du Bout. Tel. 596/66-02-02, Fax 66-00-41. Rates at this 139-hotel start at $274 including full breakfast. One-bedroom suites are available. It's 15.6 miles from the airport.*

One of the most swank beach hotels in Martinique and adjoining the equally posh Méridien is this hillside complex with one of the new, optical-illusion swimming pools with an edge that allows water to flow into seeming nothingness. It's easy to imagine that you're swimming in the ocean. Part of an international chain of hotels, this one is somewhat more English-speaking than most. Rooms have cool white tile floors, and the matching tile bath is hand painted in colors to complement the floral prints of the draperies, spread, and upholstery. The air conditioning and mini-bar refrigerator are welcome additions.

The resort has tennis courts, two restaurants, a bar, boutiques, a beauty shop, and a watersports center where you can get a windsurfer, snorkel equipment, or a sunfish sailboat. If this is a special day, order a bouquet for your sweetie from the hotel's florist shop.

Moderate

BEST WESTERN VALMENIÈRE, *Avenue des Arawaks, Fort-de-France. Tel. 596/75-75-75, Fax 75-69-70; toll-free 800/528-1234. Rates at this 120-room hotel start at $109 including continental breakfast. It's 4.4 miles from the airport.*

The best business address in the city is this newish chain hotel on the main road into the city from the airport. It's not the place for beaches and woodlands, but business travelers will enjoy the special business rooms that have a bed that disappears during the day allowing the room to be used as an office. Suites are especially roomy, with two doors from the hall so a business visitor can be admitted into the living room. The hotel has a restaurant and bar, air conditioning, a swimming pool, workout facilities, and a full range of (mostly French-speaking) secretarial services.

BEST WESTERN BAIE DU GALION, *Anse Tartane 97220. Tel. 596/ 56-65-30, Fax 58-25-76; toll-free 800/528-1234. Rates at this 150-room hotel start at $164 including continental breakfast. It's 15.6 miles from the airport on a peninsula midway up the east coast of the island. Meal plans are available.*

This is the Atlantic side of the island and waters can be rough, but it is swimmable on many days and, when it's not, there is always the pool. It's a lollapalooza – big, blue, and a favorite gathering spot for guests from all nations. Best Western does a fine job of keeping these rooms attractive and clean. Each has a telephone, television, refrigerator, safe, and air conditioning. The hotel has a good restaurant and bar, and tennis courts. Much of the Caravelle Peninsula is a nature reserve, so it's a good choice for hikers and bird watchers.

LA DUNETTE, *97227 Ste. Anne. Tel. 596/76-73-90, Fax 76-76-05. Rates at this 18-room hotel start at $134 including continental breakfast. It's 26.6 miles from the airport on the southern end of the island in the village of Ste. Anne.*

If you like rah-rah activities and free meals, this isn't the place. Small and laid back, this is everything that the nearby Club Med is not. Enjoy the shining white sands of the famous Saline beach while you stay in a an unassuming, three-story hotel with cheery tropical furnishings, television, telephone, and air conditioning. Kitchenettes are available. Join your fellow guests for sundowners on the garden terrace every day, then have dinner in the hotel's modestly-priced restaurant.

LA PAGERIE MERCURE INN, *Pointe du Bout 97229. Tel. 596/66-05-30, Fax 66-00-99. Rates at this 98-room hotel start at $161 including full breakfast. Meal plans are available.*

Think of it as a small, Mediterranean hotel transplanted here to the waterside near the marina (but not on a beach). The bar attracts yachties from the marina, so you can count on an interesting crowd here and during meals outdoors by the pool. Rooms are air conditioned and have a small balcony; studios with kitchenette are available. For the beach and beach sports you'll have to walk to nearby beach hotels.

SAINT AUBIN, *Trinité 97220. Tel. 596/69-34-14, Fax 69-41-14; toll-free 800/223-9816. Rates at this 15-room inn are from $100 including continental breakfast. It's on the the northeast coast, 15 miles from the airport. Dinner is available to guests.*

Picture a pink greathouse with Victorian gables and fretwork. Rooms are air conditioned and have television, private bath, and telephone. Book the top floor (no elevator) for a larger room or the second floor to share the deck with others on this floor. The setting is hilly countryside, with a public beach and a pool. You're only a couple of miles from the beaches and nature walks on the Caravella Peninsula. Dinners for guests are served at a fixed price of about $30.

Budget

AUBERGE L'ANSE MITAN, *97229 Anse Mitan. Tel. 596/66-01-12, Fax 63-11-64. Rates at this 26-room inn start at $95. Breakfast is available. It's 16.4 miles from the airport across the bay from Fort-de-France.*

The drive is a long way around, but ferries from Pointe du Bout cross to Fort-de-France. This is one of the island's older hotels, but it's family-operated and kept in fairly decent shape. Rooms are air conditioned and have a telephone and private bath with shower. Studios with kitchen are available.

HOTEL DIAMANT LES BAINS, *97223 Diamant. Tel. 596/76-40-14, Fax 76-27-00. Rates at this 24-unit hotel are from $90 including continental breakfast. Meal plans are available. The hotel closes seasonally. It's 16.4 miles from the airport in the southwest part of the island.*

Picture the roadside cottage motels that were popular in North America a generation ago. This family-run complex offers accommodations on the beach or in a garden setting, or bedrooms in the main building where you can share the deck-like porch with others in the same row of rooms. Fixed-price meals served in the inn are affordable and authentically Creole. Rooms are air conditioned and have television, telephone, a small refrigerator, and hand-made furniture. Swim off the beach or in the hotel's pool.

HOTEL L'IMÉRATRICE, *Rue de la Liberté, 972000 Fort-de-France. Tel. (596)63-06-83, Fax 72-66-30; U.S. 800/223-9815. Rates at this 24-room hotel are from $95. It's 4.4 miles from the airport. A continental breakfast is available. Small children stay free with their parents; children ages 8-15 stay at half price.*

City bustle and noise are an inevitable part of the scene here, so get a room away from the street if you want quiet and a room with a balcony overlooking the Savane if you want to watch the world go by. Quieter rooms are on the third-fifth floors; a bar is on the second floor. Favored mostly by businesspeople, this is typical of a moderately-priced, small, inner-city hotel with bars, lounges, and a popular restaurant, and easy access to city restaurants and sightseeing. Your air conditioned room can have a television if you like.

LE LAFAYETTE, *Rue de la Liberté 5, Fort-de-France. Tel. 596/73-80-50, Fax 60-97-75. Rates at this 24-room hotel start at $65 including continental breakfast. It's 4.4 miles from the airport in town on La Savane.*

This simple inn, catering to the business and budget traveler, offers rooms with twin beds, mini-bar, private bath, telephone, television, and dark rooms that are clean, basic, and handy to everything in town including restaurants. The hotel itself doesn't have one. Rooms on the street side can be noisy but during festivals and parades they are the best choice to view the fun.

LA MALMAISON, *Rue de la Liberté 7, Fort-de-France. Tel. 596/73-90-85, Fax 60-03-93. Rates at this 20-room hotel start at $65. It's 4.4 miles from the airport.*

Like its neighbor hotel mentioned above, this one is not the resort of your dreams, but it is a safe, clean, affordable place to stay in the heart of the capital. Le Planteur restaurant and bar is just footsteps away.

Villa Rentals

Vacation home rentals can be arranged by the **Martinique Tourist Office**, *Tel. 596/63-79-60*. The island has more than 200 *Gîtes de France*, which are apartments or rooms in private homes. Contact **Logis Vacances Antilles**, *Tel. 63-12-91*.

Les Islets de l'Imperatrice are two small islands off Le François on the Atlantic coast. Each has a 19th century cottage with a beach and a full-time maid and cook. One has five bedrooms, one has six. Rates are $200 per person per day including airport transfers, lodgings, food, drink, and use of watersports equipment. Contact Jean-Louis de Lucy, *Tel. 596/65-82-30, Fax 63-18-22*.

Martinique also has a **Club Med**, and memberships are available for all-inclusive vacations here, *Tel. 800/CLUB MED*.

WHERE TO EAT

The dining alone is reason enough to go to Martinique. Chefs create a wondrous blend of continental tastes and techniques with Caribbean exotics such as sea urchin, breadfruit, soursop, and christophene. Seafood, which reigns on every menu, may be cradled in a zesty Creole sauce or dusted with flour and sautéed, light as a veil, in butter. Dessert is likely to be fresh fruit followed by an incredible French cheese. Breakfasts are the typical French *petit dejeuner* of croissants, fruit, butter, jam, and coffee liberally laced with hot milk.

Prices are in francs (at about five francs to the U.S. dollar) and menus are in French. However, a little translation is in order even if you already know your *fromage* from your *pain*. On Martinique menus you'll see fresh water crayfish known as *z'habitants* or *cribiches*; conch, known as *lambi*; sea urchin eggs are called *oursin*; *soudons*, which are little clams; and *langouste*, or Caribbean lobster. *Blaff* is named for the sound made by the fish as it hits boiling water to make a soup that contains fish, lime juice, garlic, onions, herbs, bay rum berries, and peppers. *Boudin* is a spicy blood sausage, which tastes better than it sounds.

Pistache are peanuts; a *planteur* is a planter's punch. *Colombo* is curry on other islands but here it could mean a somewhat different spice mixture. *Feroce* is a salad made with avocado, salt codfish, and ferociously hot peppers. *Accras* are fritters made with fish or vegetables; beignets are sweet fritters often served for breakfast. Draft beers are *bieres pression*.

Conversely, some hosts cheerfully provide translated menus with such items as "rooster with sauce," which the whole world knows as *coq au vin*, and an "at will" buffet, meaning all you can eat. We pictured the snapper with green pepper as fish stir-fried with bell peppers, Asian-style. It turned out to be a green peppercorn sauce, which was also good but not what we expected. *Quiche*, a familiar term to Anglophones, is translated as a tart.

Visit the Tourist Office to pick up a copy of *Ti Gourmet* (Ti is the island way of saying "le petit", as in "ti punch"). It has the latest restaurant news in both English and French, and it contains many coupons that entitle diners to a special bonus such as a free cocktail or a discount. You can also save by looking for the *prix fixe* (fixed price) dinner or the *table d'hote* meal. It means table of the host, which is to stay the chef chooses what you'll get.

Unless mentioned otherwise, the restaurants listed take credit cards and have a bar and wine list. Warning: most Martinique restaurants except hotel restaurants close on Sunday and some close on Saturdays as well. Make your Sunday reservations on Friday or Saturday or lay in a supply of picnic foods. Note that the French often travel with their dogs, which are welcome at many restaurants. If you're allergic, stick to restaurants that bar pets.

Expensive

DIAMANT LES BAINS, *in the Hotel Diamant Des Baines, Diamant, in the southeast part of the island. Tel. 76-40-14. Meals are priced 100-200F. Hours are daily except Wednesday noon to 2:30pm and 6:30-10:45pm. The restaurant closes seasonally, so call for reservations.*

This award-winning restaurant is done in deep green, which mirrors the lush fringe of green that shades your view of the pool and palms beyond. Dine on local pumpkin stuffed with crab au gratin, grilled lobster, curried red snapper, swordfish with green peppercorns, and the coconut custard dessert. There's a children's menu, and take-out is available.

LA CASE CREOLE, *Place de l'Église, Diamant. Tel. 76-10-14. Meals cost 100-250F. It's open for lunch and dinner daily. Free transportation from Diamant area hotels is available.*

Ask for a room in the back room, not the one overlooking the road. The decor, with its plastic furniture, isn't going to melt your butter but we like the hospitality and food. Have the fricassee of local freshwater crayfish, the big seafood platter with lobster, shrimp and fish, conch salad marinated in lime juice, or stuffed crab. The ubiquitous coconut pudding is the favored dessert.

LA FONTANE, *Kilometer 4, Route de Balata, Fort-de-France. Tel. 64-28-70. Plan to spend 300F for dinner. Reservations are required. The restaurant is open for dinner daily except Sunday and Monday.*

Madame Berthe Zami presides over tables where the menu lists fricassee of freshwater crawfish, poached sea urchins, veal chop Roquefort, or breast of duckling with mango sauce. A dessert specialty is a sampling of almost a dozen homemade ice creams. The decor is one of the island's most elegant, featuring antiques and fresh flowers.

LA MOUINA, *Route de Redoute 127, just above Fort-de-France. Tel. 79-34-57. Reservations are recommended. It's open for lunch and dinner Monday to Friday and for dinner on Saturday. Plan to spend 100F to 200F for dinner.*

Old timers will remember this as a Lamentin restaurant but it has moved into an old colonial villa in Redoute, about 1.5 miles north of Fort-de-France next to the police station. Operated by the Karschesz family, it specializes in French classics such as soufflé aux ecrévisses, grilled kidney, tournedos Rossini, duck a l'orange, escargot, and raspberry charlotte. A specialty is snapper en papillote, fresh fish that pops steaming and fragrant from the parchment in which it is baked.

LA MURAILLE, *rue Martin Luther King 46, Fort-de-France. Tel. 63-47-96. Meals are priced 95-200F. Hours are noon to 2:15pm and 7:30-10:15pm. It's closed Sundays and holidays.*

Look down over the lights of the city from this richly woody room set with mahogany furniture, deep red linens, and white china with a red pattern. Specialties include the many raviolis – steamed ravioli, ravioli soup, fried lobster ravioli, and the like. Shrimp or beef will be flash-cooked at the table, Asian-style, or have the duckling with oriental noodles. The coconut custard is a dessert favorite. Take-out is available. The restaurant is air conditioned, and offers free parking.

LA PETITE AUBERGE, *Plage de Gros Raisins, Sainte-Luce. Tel. 62-59-05 or 62-28-84. Prices range from 99F at lunch to 270F at dinner. It's on the south coast between Le Diamant and Le Marin. Hours are daily noon to 2:30pm and 7-9:30pm.*

Dine on a light, bright veranda furnished with molded white plastic tables and chairs, pastel draperies, leaded glass lampshades, and lots of potted greenery. Choose a lobster from the tank, or have the chef's special clams. T-bone steak is lavished with morel mushrooms and the farfalle is tossed with fresh salmon. Highchairs and a special menu are available for children. The restaurant faces the sea and swimming pool. Live music plays some nights.

LA VILLA CREOLE, *Anse Mitan, Trois-Islets. Tel. 66-05-53. Hours are noon to 2pm and 7-10pm except Sunday. No lunch is served on Mondays. Meals are priced 150-205F.*

Guy Bruere Dawson has managed this jungly indoor-outdoor place since the early 1980s and in 1994 he was awarded the Medal of Tourism for his outgoing hospitality. Guy himself provides the entertainment with his voice and guitar, so plan on staying on after dinner to dance in the romantic, lamp-lit garden. Island seafood is served plain or in sauces; the tender filet mignon can be ordered with a buttery tarragon sauce.

LE DEUX GROS, *Fond Bellemare, Case Pilote. Tel. 61-60-34. Meals cost 120-280F. It's open daily except Monday for lunch and dinner. Reservations are recommended.*

Picture yourself in Nice or St. Tropez, dining outdoors overlooking the sea. Add in some tropical seagrape trees and two friendly chefs and you have it. The grilled chops, steaks, lobster and fish are always popular or there's carpaccio of autumn duck. For something different have the salmon steamed in a cabbage leaf, sliced sea bass in coconut milk, or the chateaubriand of white fish. For dessert have the goat cheese with port wine sauce or the cantaloupe with three sherbets. A children's menu is available, and parking is no problem.

LE FOULARD, *Bord de Mere, Schoelcher. Tel. 61-15-72. Hours are daily except Sunday and holidays noon to 1:30 and 7:30-9:30pm. Reservations are recommended. Meals are priced 180-300F.*

Catherine and Marcel gladly welcome you in French, English, or German to their stately, air conditioned, white-tablecloth restaurant in the marketplace next to the sea. The restaurant is one of Martinique's oldest and is pretty much an infallible choice. Have the saffron shrimp, lobster crepes, fish en papillote, or filet mignon with sauce bordelaise.

You can also get oysters in season, and a homemade cassoulet, one of those French comfort foods that combines meat and white beans in a fragrant, filling stew. Save room for the cream puffs.

LE TROU CRABE, *Le Coin, Le Carbet, (south of St. Pierre). Tel. 78-04-34. Meals cost 95-200F. It's open daily for breakfast, lunch, and dinner, except for Sunday dinner and the entire month of September.*

Take a pastel-clothed table under a palm tree just off the beach and let Corinne and Frederic serve you fresh lobster from the live tank, stewed crayfish, grilled meats or fresh fish, or fish "cooked" in lime juice. A specialty is the quenelles with a classic nantua sauce made with white wine, crayfish butter, cognac, and other flavorings in a bechamel or velouté base.

LE VERGER, *Place d'Armes, Lamentin. Tel. 51-43-02. It's open daily for dinner. Reservations are suggested. Dinner will cost 200F to 250F. Follow the signs to La Trinité and look for the turn-off after the Esso gas station.*

A gaily painted country cottage sets the mood for pheasant, duckling, rabbit, herbed chicken dishes, and the chef's signature sea urchin blaff. Choose from a good French wine list and finish with a French cheese and crisp biscuits.

LEYRITZ PLANTATION, *Basse-Pointe. Tel. 78-53-92. Reservations are required. Plan to spend 250F for dinner.*

Because this plantation, which dates to the 1700s, is such a popular shore excursion with cruise passengers on a package that includes a meal and a plantation tour, it's best to avoid this hotel on days when the fleet is in. Come for the sweeping views of the volcano and the surrounding countryside and to dine on country Creole curries, chicken in coconut milk, sausages, and fresh, local vegetables. Steaks and seafood are also on the menu and the soups are *formidable*.

Moderate

AUX FRUITS DE MER CHEZ FOFOR, *Boulevard Henry Auzé, Le Robert. Tel. 65-10-33. It's at the Atlantic side between Le François and La Trinité. Meals are priced 80-250F. The bar opens at 10am; lunch is served noon to 3pm and dinner 7-10pm. It's closed Sunday dinner and all day Monday.*

Look for this restaurant in the marketplace next to the sea, about 200 yards from the church. Dine on the terrace or indoors where mahogany chairs are arranged around tables spread with white, cutwork tablecloths. The clams are served cold, or order a clam blaff. Red snapper is fried with green peppercorns; the fish stew is flavored with a mystery of wonderful spices and herbs. The seafood platter is a good sampling for hearty appetites. For dessert, there's coconut flan.

CABANA PLAGE, *Pointe Faula, Le Vauclin. Tel. 74-32-08. Find it on the Atlantic shore south of Le François and north of Le Marin. It's closed Wednesdays* *and is open noon to 3:30pm and 7-9:30pm, or until 10:30pm on Friday and Saturday. The bar opens at 11am*

Your kids and pets are welcome to join you in this open-air, seaside sidewalk restaurant. Have lobster grilled or fricasseed, prime rib with bordelaise sauce, fruit salad, or, with advance notice, tuna or swordfish fondue. Hosts Gisele and Beatrice specialize in shrimp flamed with rum and pizzas from the wood-fire oven to eat here or take out.

CANNELLE, *in the Hotel Alamanda 11, Anse Mitan, Trois-Islets. Tel. 66-03-66. Hours are noon to 2:30pm and 7:30-9:30pm daily.*

This terrace restaurant overlooks the bay, sort of, but the parking lot is in the way. Focus instead on the food: conch crepes with shellfish sauce, shrimp flamed with rum, blanquette of fish with cucumber, chicken breast stuffed with seasoned crab, or flaming bananas for dessert.

CELESTE'S, *Place de la Mairie, Case Pilote. Tel. 78-72-78. Meals are priced 80-180F. Hours are 8am to 9:30pm daily except Monday. It's also closed Sunday for dinner.*

It's right off the busy street, but what a haven of quiet and good smells! Black lacquer furniture contrasts smartly with crisp white table linens. The cuisine is a blend of nouvelle, French, and Creole. Choose one of the draft beers (which aren't that common here), then dine on kingfish with a vaguely vanilla sauce, duckling with passion fruit, or dorado tartare. There's a children's menu and free parking, and pets can come too.

CHEZ GRACIEUSE, *Cap Chevalier, Sainte-Anne, on the south coast. Tel. 76-93-10. Hours are noon to 4pm and evenings by reservation except all day Monday, Saturday and Sunday evenings, and the month of June, when the restaurant is closed. Meals are priced 90-200F.*

Overlook a fringe of garden and then out to sea and Chavalier Islet, where a water taxi will take you for a swim after lunch. Have chicken or goat curry, fricasseed conch, or the Gracieuse Platter filled with a sample of everything the fleet brought in today. For dessert, there's coconut blanc mange or bananas flamed with rum. There's a children's menu, and your well-behaved pet is also welcome.

FLAMBOUYANT DES ILES, *Anses d'Arlet. Tel. 68-67-75. It's on the way out of the town towards Petite Anse. Meals are priced 75-150F. It's open daily except Tuesday for lunch and dinner. On Sunday, it's closed for dinner.*

Flambouyant (flahm-boy-yahn) is another name for poinciana trees, the brilliant red-orange trees seen throughout the Caribbean. Overlook the sea and the flambouyant trees from a porch where Sunday brunch features a Creole buffet. Have curried fish, grilled octopus, freshwater crayfish in coconut milk, and beignets *grand-mere* for dessert.

L'HIPPOCAMPE, *Grand Anse, Anses d'Arlet. Tel. 68-65-80 or 68-69-78. Find it leaving Grande Anse heading towards the market. Meals cost 60-250F. Hours are noon to 10pm daily. The bars opens at 9pm.*

Saturday night is the big night here with lobster and entertainment. Have one of the seafood quiches, shrimp, freshwater crayfish with passion fruit, shark in green peppercorn sauce, or a vegetarian gratin. For dessert have the fresh fruit tart. The setting is an open-air terrace surrounded by a tangle of blooming vines and fragrant greens. Take-out and a children's menu are available.

INDIGO, *Port de Plaisance, Quai Stardust, Le Marin. Tel. 774-76-74. Dishes are priced 78-230F. Breakfast, lunch and dinner are served daily from 7:30am. Le Marin is on the south side of the island north of Ste. Anne and east of Ste. Luce.*

Yachties from nearby anchorages and marinas love this floating restaurant with its big bar, nautical decor, and wood deck flooring. Have one of the mountainous seafood platters, then hang around to enjoy the crowd and the live music that plays just about every night.

LA DUNETTE, *Le Bourg, Sainte-Anne. Tel. 76-73-90. Meals are priced 90-200F. Hours are daily noon to 3pm and 7-10pm except June, when it closes for the month. Reservations are suggested.*

The big noise here is Lobster Night on Wednesdays, but any time is a good time for dining here in the heart of town overlooking the bay. Owner-chef Gerard suggests the fish tandoori, fresh lobster from the tank, red snapper stuffed with sea urchin caviar, and his homemade chocolate cake for dessert. After lunch, go hiking or water skiing. At night, have a drink before and after at the piano bar.

LA PLANTATION, *in Martinique Cottages, Pays Mele; Jeanne-d'Arc, Lamentin. Tel. 50-16-08. Reservations are essential. It's open Monday through Friday for lunch and dinner and Saturday for dinner only. Plan to spend 150F to 175F for dinner. It's 20 minutes from Fort-de-France, handy to the airport.*

Jean-Marc and Peggy Arnaud, who are brother and sister, run this stylish dining room as a country retreat for locals who enjoy driving out of the city to dine on roast pigeon with guava sauce or a Brazilian lobster served in a sauce of butter, brandy, tomatoes, and wine.

LA CARAVELLE, *in the Caravelle Studio Hotel, Route du Chateau Dubuc, Anse l'Etang-Tartane, Trinité. Tel. 58-07-32. It's open nightly 7-9:30pm. The salad bar on the terrace is open 11am to 4pm daily. Prices are 100-180F.*

Sit at an outdoor table under a jaunty blue and white umbrella and look far out over the Atlantic while you fill up at the salad bar. At dinner have the freshwater crayfish called z'habitants, grilled lobster, coquilles St. Jacques, or escargot in pastry with Chartreuse Verte liqueur.

LA QUENETTE, *Mare Poirier, Diamant. Tel. 96-76-47 or 76-27-90. It's open daily except Monday noon to 2pm and 7-10pm. Meals are priced 70-150F.*

Capture the real feel of the islands in this plant-filled restaurant with its straw-covered posts, grass ceiling, and a mural that shows an early sailing ship. Madame Eustache has been here for 20 years, serving the best and freshest local fish and produce. Try her grandmother's fish soup, conch-stuffed breadfruit, fish broth with shrimp, or filet mignon with green peppercorn sauce. For dessert, have the bananas flamed with orange liqueur. At lunch, quick meals feature salads and grilled fish or meat.

LA VAGUE DU SUD, *Boulevard Kenny at rue Schoelcher, Sainte Luce on the south coast. Tel. 62-59-46. Meals are priced 70-220F. Reservations are suggested.*

Dine on the water's edge in this fishing village where the restaurants owners keep their boat. They bring in the fish, lobster and conch that are sent to the kitchen to make fish stew, blaff, conch seviche, lobster avocado cocktail, or shark etoufée. Shaded by perky red and white-striped awnings and surrounded by a picket rail, the outdoor dining room has white tablecloths overlaid with pink, and birch chairs with rush seats. On Sunday, have the lobster fricassee dinner for 130F.

LE CHATEAUBRIAND, *in the Bahoua Hotel, Pointe de Bout. Tel. 66-02-02, Fax 66-00-41. Plan to spend 180-280F. It's open nightly 7-10pm. Reservations are recommended.*

Overlook the bay of Fort-de-France from a chic hotel. Choose a lobster from the tank or order the chateaubriand for two. The accordion music seems too Parisian for the tropics, but most nights there's a steel band and dancing on the danceable tile floor. On Fridays, the Grand Ballet of Martinique entertains while diners enjoy a Creole buffet.

LE COC HARDI, *rue Martin-Luther-King. Tel. 71-59-64. A two-minute taxi ride from La Savane, it's open Thursday through Tuesday for lunch and dinner and Wednesday for dinner. Dishes are priced 100-200F. Reservations are advised.*

When you tire of seafood, come here for supersize cuts of steak and chicken grilled over a wood fire. Owner Alphonse Sintive brings in regular shipments of the best meats from his contacts in France, where he was a master butcher before going to Indochina and Algiers with the French Foreign Legion. The friendly, rakish proprietor seems to pervade the place. You're invited to pick your own steak. It will be cooked to perfection and served with a suitable sauce and island vegetables.

LE DIAM'S, *Place de L'Église, Le Diamant. Tel. 76-23-28. A set menu is 99F; meals are priced to 200F. A children's meal is 40F. Reservations are essential. The restaurant is open for lunch and dinner except Tuesday. Lunch is not served on Wednesday. It closes for two months in early summer and a month in late summer.*

This prize-winning restaurant is a hot ticket these days, so reserve well ahead. Try the prawns diablo, the filet mignon, or the mahi-mahi with sugarcane vinaigrette.

LE FACTORIE, *Quartier Fort, Saint-Pierre. Tel. 78-12-53. Prices are 100-175F. Hours are 11:30am to 2:30pm and evenings by reservation.*

High over the bay near Le Prêcheur, order freshly grilled lobster, stuffed turtle, a seafood quiche, shrimp fritters, chicken with crayfish (chicken fresh from the butcher is a specialty), and a fresh fruit coupe for dessert. Madras-covered tables and a breezy porch setting make this spot a cool respite when you're sightseeing the old ruins.

LE JOSEPHINE, *in the Hotel L'Impératrice, rue de la Liberté 15, on the Savane in Fort-de-France. Meals are priced 75-200F. Hours are 7am to 10pm except Sunday.*

The hotel name means "empress" and the restaurant is named for Martinique's most famous daughter, the Josephine who married Napoleon. The air conditioned dining room is on the second floor where soft green furniture and plaids in golds and beiges create a romantic softness. Around the room, display cases show island antiques and memorabilia, making it a favorite with locals. Start with the accras (fritters), then have the crayfish stew or a filet mignon. For dessert choose one of the ice creams.

LE MELODIE, *Les Abymes, Le Prêcheur. Tel. 52-90-31. Dishes are priced 60-180F. Hours are 11:40am to 3:30pm and 7-9pm except for Sunday and Tuesday evenings, when it's closed.*

This makes an ideal resting place when you're exploring the island north of St. Pierre. Visit Habitation Ceron, an old planation near the Anse Ceron to see an old sugar factory and water mill, *Tel. 52-94-53,* then settle down at a madras-covered table in this restaurant overlooking the beach. Dine on lobster you choose from the tank, octopus cooked in a clay pot, or shrimp or conch fritters. Specialties include pineapple dorado (mahi-mahi) and curried shark. Children and pets are welcome.

LE SYPARIS STATION, *Route de la Galère, Sainte-Pierre, on the beach near Le Prêcheur. Tel. 78-36-73. Hours are noon to 3:30pm and 7-10pm. Items are priced 75-180F.*

You're almost at the water's edge in this open-air restaurant with its molded white plastic chairs (which can feel sticky on bodies that are too bare). Tables are spread with gay blue and yellow prints accented by bright napkins fanned in your wine glass. Chef Jocylyne suggests a fishing trip before lunch, then lobster from the tank or sizzling beef tournedos surrounded by local vegetables. Music plays at the Friday night barbecues. Jocelyn also offers take-out or delivery to your villa.

LE PLANTEUR, *1 rue de la Liberté, Fort-de-France. Tel. 63-17-45. It's open daily except Sunday for lunch and dinner, and Sunday for dinner only. Reservations are suggested. Plan to spend 150F for dinner.*

Upstairs overlooking La Savane and the harbor with its boat traffic is this pleasantly rosy room created by owner-chef André-Charles Donatien.

He is a Martinican who learned to cook in the family kitchen in Carbet, then went to Burgundy to learn from the masters. Start with his pumpkin soup followed by fresh fish stewed in a cream tomato sauce.

LE REGAL DE LA MER, *rue de l'Embarquadere, Anse Mitan, Trois-Islets. Tel. 66-11-44 or 66-11-46. Prices are 90-250F. Hours are noon to 2pm and 7-11:30pm except Sunday.*

Michele, Jacques, and their children come from a Breton family of restaurateurs; they carry the family flag high in this bushy, garden setting with patches of sun and shade. Choose a fresh lobster from the tank, or have a salmon or cod carpaccio. If you're not a seafood lover, have the filet mignon with morel mushrooms. For dessert there's local fruit or ice cream. In season, a Creole group plays nightly.

MANOIR DE BEAUREGARD, *Chemin des Salines, Sainte-Anne on the south coast. Tel. 76-73-40. Meals are priced 110-160F. Hours are daily noon to 2pm and 7:15-10pm.*

An old manor house has been turned into an inn and restaurant with all the charm created by antique furnishings and old stone walls. Have the lobster and prawn salad, conch stew, pork filet in orange mango sauce, or cracked conch with green peppercorn sauce, with the coconut creme brulée for dessert. There's a wine list, a children's menus and live music most nights.

POI ET VIRGINIE, *rue de Bord de Mer, Sainte Anne. Tel. 76-72-22. It's open for lunch and dinner Sunday through Saturday and for lunch only on Tuesday. Plan to spend 100F.*

Look down over the sea from this airy dining room with its ceiling fan and fresh flowers. The award-winning menu features fresh tuna with bell peppers, chicken baked in coconut milk, saffron crayfish, crab salad, and, of course, langouste.

SOUS DES COCOTIERS, *Pointe Faula, Le Vauclin. Tel. 74-35-62. Meals are priced 50-180F. It's open daily except Monday for lunch and for dinner Thursday through Saturday. It closes mid-September to mid-October. Reservations are requested, especially for the Friday night soirée.*

Dine outdoors in this beach-side restaurant with nothing above but the sun or moon, a few palms, and perhaps a table umbrella. Dine on clams, grilled or fricassee lobster, crab au gratin, or the refreshingly cold avocado mousse with shrimp. For dessert there's breadfruit gratin or coconut custard. On Fridays, there's live music and dancing on the terrace.

YVA CHES VAVA, *Avenue du Général de Gaulle, Grande Rivière. Tel. 55-72-72. It's on the northwest coast. Dishes are priced 80-180F. It's open daily noon to 5pm and evenings by reservation.*

You're well out of the tourism mainstream in this corner of the island, where Yva has been getting raves for her lobster with spicy sauce, poached z'habitants, seafood soups and stews, coq au vin, and breadfruit souffle. For dessert there's a cobbler-like *bananas gratin*. Pets and kids are welcome, and Yva will also provide a take-out picnic if you like.

Budget

AU POISSON D'OR, *Anse Mitan, Trois Ilets. Tel. 66-01-80. Plan to spend 80-195F for dinner. Hours are noon to 2:30pm and 7-10pm daily except Monday and during July.*

Plastic tables and chairs have a cheesy look, but they're relieved by colorful red and green cloths overlaid with madras plaid that matches the servers' costumes . Have the conch marinated in lime juice, grilled lobster in Creole sauce, or shark, and Banana Surprise for dessert. The setting is relaxed and welcoming; bamboo walls and lots of potted plants give the room a tropical look. It isn't air conditioned so go late and ask for a table where the breezes are best.

CLUB NAUTIQUE, *Le Francois. Tel. 54-31-00. It's open daily for lunch and dinner daily and for lunch only on Sunday. Dine for about 75F to 100F.*

Take a boat trip to the coral reefs just offshore, then return in time for a ti punch or a *décollage*, a rum drink turned green with herbs. Watch yourself because it packs quite a punch. For something less deadly, order a *planteur*, a rum and fruit punch. Dine on turtle steak, broiled langouste, fresh fish or grilled chicken in pleasantly inelegant comfort overlooking the water.

LA PIZZERIA DU MUSÉE, *rue Victor Hugo, St. Pierre. Tel. 78-31-13. Prices start at 70F; pizzas at 40F. Hours vary, and it is closed Saturday and Sunday.*

Just 50 yards from the museum is this air conditioned restaurant where pizzas are pulled out of a wood oven and where Italian, French, and Creole classics are also on the menu.

LE BLENAC, *rue Blenac 3, Fort-de-France. Tel. 70-18-41. Every day there's a special menu costing 45-50F; and a special involving a little lobster at 145F. Dishes are priced to 190F. Hours are 11:30am to 10pm daily except Sunday, when it closes after lunch.*

Dine in air conditioned comfort near La Savane on chef salad, fish soup, stuffed clams or clam (soudons) blaff, grilled scallops with herb butter, lobster salad, or meltingly tender tournedos. For dessert, have the coconut custard. On Mondays the special is always a couscous made with fresh fish.

LE CARGO BLEU, *75 rue Victor Hugo, Saint-Pierre. Tel. 78-26-60. It's next to the ruins of the theater. Hours are Monday through Thursday 9am to 6pm and Friday and Saturday 9am to midnight. Meals are priced 79-150F. It's closed Sundays and the month of September.*

Dining is on a veranda furnished with ice cream parlor-style chairs and tables for four. Every day, a 79F special Creole Plate is offered. On weekends, order beef fondue for the whole table. Specialties include chicken liver salad, shellfish pineapple, and ice creams for dessert.

LE DON DE LA MER, *Tartane, Trinité. Tel. 58-26-85. Hours are daily noon to 4pm and 7-10pm. Meals are priced 80-190F.*

The white plastic tables and chairs so popular on the island are covered with perky madras or matching solid colors on this upstairs terrace with a view of Marigot Point. The Louison family catches the seafood, then prepares it. Select sea urchin, soudons with hot and spicy sauce, shrimp in broth, or grilled fish or lobster. For dessert, let Madame serve bananas flambé.

L'OASIS, *Tartane, Trinité. Tel. 58-21-58 or 58-40-19. Hours are daily 11:30am to 4pm and 7-10pm. It's closed mid-October through mid-November. The restaurant is next to the Hardy Distillery. Meals are priced 70-180F.*

Home-style Creole cookery looks right at home on tables covered with red and white checked tablecloths in a porch-like terrace overlooking the Atlantic. Specialties of the chef, Jean-Marc, include stuffed crabs, shrimp and sea urchin fritters, seafood kebobs, stewed crayfish, curries, squash gratin, or grilled steaks, chops, or lobster, which you can pick out from the live tank. For dessert, there's homemade ice cream or coconut flan.

MARIE-SAINTE, *160 Victor Hugo, Fort-de-France. Tel. 70-00-30. It's open for lunch daily except Sunday. Reservations aren't accepted, so come early or late to avoid waiting in line. Plan to spend 50F to 60F.*

Cheery and inexpensive is this family-style restaurant where you'll eat from a brightly tiled table. Specialties include fish stew, with banana beignets for dessert.

SECOND SOUFFLÉ, *27 rue Blenac. Tel. 63-44-11. Open daily except weekends for lunch and supper, the restaurant accepts no credit cards.*

Stop in this handy downtown spot for vegetarian dishes such as okra quiche, eggplant stew, fresh fruit juices, eggplant with plantains, eggplant souffleé or a light-as-a-feather yam soufflé.

Quick Takes

Delifrance delis are found all over the island, offering take-out breads, sandwiches, meat-filled patties and individual quiches at fast-food prices. **American Pizza** in Fort-de-France is just that, *Tel. 75-45-75.* A food court typical of those found in malls in the United States is **Food Circus** in the Centre Commercial Galeria in Lamentin. It's open daily except Sunday 9am to 9pm, with seven food stalls to choose from. Dishes are priced 20-80F.

For a real Creole breakfast, have the banana beignets at **Le Marie Sainte** at 160 rue Victor Hugo in Fort-de-France, *Tel. 63-82-24.*

MARTINIQUE DRESS CODE

While the dress code on the French islands is pretty loose, we recommend wearing long shorts, long trousers, a skirt or a knee-length sarong because so many restaurants are furnished with molded plastic chairs, which may be practical but are hot, sticky, and uncomfortable. While some have cushions, many do not. For dinner, resort chic for women and collared shirts for men are de rigeur.

SEEING THE SIGHTS

Start your explorations at the **Martinique Tourist Office** next to the waterfront on the Boulevard Alfassa, *Tel. 63-79-60*. It's open weekdays from 7:30am to 12:30pm and 2:30 to 5:30pm. On Saturday it's open 8am to noon. The tourist desk at the airport stays open until the last flight comes in. Pick up free maps and brochures and a free copy of *Choubouloute*, which will bring you up to speed on today's happenings on the island.

From the tourist office downtown, you can arrange a tour by taxi or motor coach or pick up instructions for a half dozen self-guided tours. Tours also pick up at hotels.

A walking tour of the capital begins with its narrow, balconied streets straight out of yesteryear. Orient yourself at **La Savane**, the largest greenspace and the only place to find a shady spot away from the murderous traffic. Along its edges, vendors sell cold drinks and snacks. It's here that you'll catch the ferries to Pointe du Bout and the beaches. Along the park's east side, **Fort St. Louis** is the home of government offices so it's not open for tours, but do have a look at its ancient face as you imagine it as a sentinel against the invading British, the Savane filled with troops going through their daily drills.

The **Schoelcher Library**, *Tel. 70-26-67*, an architectural show-off that was built in Romaneque-Byzantine style for the Paris Exposition of 1889, is named for Victor Schoelcher, who led the fight for the abolition of slavery in the mid-19th century. You'll see his statue in the **Palais de Justice**. The library, or **Bibliothèque** as it is known in French, is on the Rue le la Liberté on the Savane. It's open Monday, Tuesday and Thursday 8:30am to 12:30pm and 2-6pm; on Wednesday and Friday 8 a.m to 1pm and Saturday 8:30am to noon.

Spend an hour in the **Musée Departemental de Martinique**, which is also on the Rue de la Liberté, *Tel. 71-57-05*. Although few descriptions are in English, you'll get the gist of artifacts dating to pre-Columbian eras. Hours are weekdays 8:30am to 5pm; Saturday 8am to noon. Admission is 20F.

The centerpiece of the city is **St. Louis Roman Catholic Cathedral**, an iron structure built in 1875 on Rue Victor-Schoelcher. Congregations have sat on this site since the 1600s. Overlooking the city, **Sacré-Coeur de Balata Cathedral** is a copy of a church by the same name in Montmartre. It's found on Route N3, six miles north of town. While you're in Balata, stroll the superb **botanical garden**, Jardin de Balata, *Tel. 64-48-73*. Also in the garden is a restored Creole house that is open daily 9am to 5pm Admission is 35F adults and 15F for children.

Driving north on the coast you'll pass the fishing villages of **Case-Pilote**, home of the island's oldest church, and **Bellefontaine**. The road brings you to **Carbet**, where Columbus landed in 1502. More than three hundred years after Columbus commented, "My eyes would never tire of seeing such vegetation," Paul Gauguin arrived to be mesmerized by the island's bright foliage and swirling life. He lived and painted here in 1887. A small museum, *Tel. 78-22-66*, is devoted to him including a complete collection of reproductions of all of his Martinique paintings. Also shown is memorabilia connected with writer Lafcadio Hearn, whose book *Two Years in the West Indies,* provides a hauntingly realistic look at the city of St. Pierre. Hearn had no way of knowing that time would stop in 1902 for the people and places he brought to life in his pages. Admission is 20F; it's open daily 9am to 5pm.

The area also offers a small **zoo**, *Tel. 78-00-64.* **Carbet Botanical Garden**, *Tel. 78-18-07,* has **Valley of the Butterflies** and a peppy little refreshment stand, Le Poids du Roy.

The drive north from **Fort-de-France** on Route N2 brings you to the site of **St. Pierre**, which was known as the Paris of the West Indies before its destruction in the 1902 volcanic eruption. Everyone died including a governor who tried to quell a growing panic by persuading everyone to remain in the city. The only survivor was a prisoner in the local jail. A **museum** on the spot captures the horror and heartbreak of an event that obliterated a city and its 30,000 inhabitants.

Take a one-hour tour aboard the **Cyparis Express**, a small train that costs about 40F adults and 20F for children. Narration is only in French. The train is named, by the way, for Cyparis, that lone survivor mentioned above. You'll see ruins including those of the jail, the church, which was built in 1640, and the theater. They poke up here and there, sometimes as part of newer buildings, like plaintive gravestones for people deep below today's St. Pierre.

The **Musée Vulcanologique**, *Tel. 78-15-16,* is a painful look at relics that were dug out of the rubble: twisted toys, half-melted household goods, clocks that stopped at the fateful hour. This wasn't Pompeii, destroyed in the dim mists of forgotten history. This was a city that was alive when the Aswan Dam opened, when Enrico Caruso made his first phonograph recording, and when the silent film *Salome* was being made. Admission is 20F.

If you're a diver, book a dive off **St. Pierre** where 12 sunken wrecks in the anchorage date to the 1902 eruption. Even the sea was no refuge for the sudden fury of **Mont Pelée**. Only one ship escaped, a freighter that had just started to get underway when the eruption hit. His crew suffocated, the captain managed all alone to get the ship out of the harbor to spread word to the outside world that the city of St. Pierre was no more.

Morne Rouge, which was also buried by the volcano, is a cool, upland village where you can pick up **La Trace** for a drive across the island to the Atlantic side. It has been the main route across the northern part of the island since early porters made the 15-hour trip on foot, carrying 40 kilograms of goods on their heads. An area of banana and pineapple plantations, it's also a place to find old island inns and a guide if you want to hike 4,600-foot **Mount Pelée**. Loose stones and volcanic rubble make it a hazardous climb; don't try it alone.

The last village along the northern Caribbean coast is **Le Prêcheur**, which has hot springs that are probably fed by the same deep inferno that burst out at St. Pierre. Hike flower-lined nature trails, small canyons, and waterfalls along the **Falaise River**.

Although the gentle seas turn to crashing coamers as you near the Atlantic on the coast road, and swimming can be hazardous, continue the drive through quaint hamlets and scenic overlooks. **Grand Rivière** is a picture-postcard village on the Martinique Passage. **Basse-Pointe** on the northeast coast is the home of **Leyritz Plantation**, a sugar factory and gardens where you can tour the quirky **Musée de Poupées Végétales**, *Tel. 78-53-92*, dolls made from local plants to resemble famous French women. It's open daily 9am to 5pm; admission is 20F, *Tel. 78-53-92*. The plantation, now a hotel, is a good place to have lunch or dinner. Reservations are a must, *Tel. 78-53-92*.

Heading inland from Basse-Pointe brings you through pineapple fields to Ajoupa-Bouillon, which was founded in the 1600s. Tour **Les Ombrages** botanical gardens, which are open daily 8am to 4pm, on marked pathways through thick jungle growth filled with flowers. From the village, take a 30-minute walk to **Saut Babin**, a 40-foot-high waterfall and to the **Gorges de la Falaise** to take a cooling swim before hiking back to your car. Because of the fear of rock slides, the gorge is sometimes closed, usually October to mid-December.

On the **Caravelle Peninsula**, which probes out into the Atlantic midway down the east coast, find the ruins of **Chateau Dubuc**, the family home of Louis-François Duboc who is credited with keeping the French Revolution from spreading to the islands. It was also the ancestral home of Aimée Duboc de Rivery who was captured by pirates, sold to the Sultan of Constantinople as a slave, and became the mother of Sultan Mahmoud II. The peninsula is a popular hiking and watersports center, home of **Anse-Spoutourne**, *Tel. 73-19-30*, where sailboards, boats, and other gear can be rented.

At **Sainte-Marie** north of the capital, **St. James Distillery** operates the **Musée de Rhum**, *Tel. 69-30-02*, in a pleasantly galleried Creole house. The tour includes samplings. Admission is free; hours are weekdays 9am to 6pm and weekends 9am to 1pm.

Morne des Esses nearby is a straw plaiting center; stop at roadside displays to bargain for straw souvenirs. At **Fonds Saint-Jacques**, a 17th century sugar plantation, visitors are welcome to the **Musée de Père Labat** with its relics from bygone plantation days.

Just outside **Les Trois-Ilets**, which lies across the harbor from Fort-de-France, is **La Pagerie**, *Tel. 68-38-34*, where the woman who would become Empress Josephine of France was born in 1763. She was christened Marie-Joseph Tascher de la Pagerie in the little church that still stands on the village square. Sixteen years later, she married Alexandre de Beauharnais in the same chapel. Although the family home, La Pagerie, was destroyed in a hurricane only three years after her birth, part of the estate serves as a museum filled with family memorabilia including a love letter written to Josephine by Napoleon in 1796. Admission is 20F. Hours are daily except Monday, 9am to 5pm.

As you leave Les Trois-Islets, stop at **Pointe Vatable** where **La Maison de la Canne** is a museum, *Tel. 68-32-04*, devoted to 300 years of sugar cane production. Admission is 20F. It's open daily except Monday, 9am to 5pm. Parc de Floralies here is a botanical garden and the area also has a pottery center.

NIGHTLIFE & ENTERTAINMENT

Gamble in the casinos at the **Méridien** and **La Batelière** hotels. They're open every night from 9am to 3am. The entry fee is 70F and photo identification is required. You must be age 18 or older. Games include slots, blackjack, and American or French roulette.

Try to catch a performance by **Les Grands Ballets de la Martinique** and **Les Balisiers**. Both troupes perform the unique music and dance of the island.

Discos in Fort-de-France include **BLUE NIGHT** at Boulevard Allegre 20, *Tel. 71-58-43* and **LE NEW HIPPO** next door, *Tel. 76-423-42*. **LE SWEETY** is at Rue Capitaine Pierre Rose, *Tel. 71-83-41*. Zouk, the Caribbean sound, might be playing at **PETTUNE** in the Diamant Novotel, *Tel. 76-25-47*. **LAS TAPAS**, Rue Garnier Pages 7, *Tel. 63-71-23*, has Caribbean music and dancing. **LA VILLE CRÉOLE** has a Parisian bistro ambience, with singers doing Edith Piaf or Jacques Brel. It's at Anse-Mitan, *Tel. 66-05-53.*

For live local music in Fort-de-France, try **L'ALIBI**, Morne Tartenson, *Tel. 63-45-15*; **LE BITACO** in Ravine Village, *Tel. 79-66-26*; **LE CARGO**, Boulevard Allegre. *Tel. 71-59-50;* **LE MANIKOU**, Zac de Riviere Roche, *Tel. 50-96-99;* or **LE MANOIR**, 1.5 route des Religeuses. *Tel. 70-26-23.*

In early December, Martinique hosts one of the Caribbean's best jazz festivals, starring big-name stars from throughout the jazz world. For information about this year's blow-out, write Martinique Tourism, listed below under *Practical Information.*

SPORTS & RECREATION
Beaches
The best and whitest beaches are those in the south of the island. Volcanic activity created black sand beaches in the north. Although there are no official nude beaches on Martinique, most hotels cater to Europeans who sunbathe topless. The best beaches around the south of the island include **Cap Chevalier** on the Atlantic in the southeast, **Place de Salines** near Ste. Anne with its fringe of palm trees, and **Le Diamant**, overlooking Diamond Rock.

Bicycling
Mountain biking with an 18-speed VTT all-terrain bike is available through **J. Vartel**, VT Tilt, Pointe du Boute, *Tel. 66-01-01* or **Basalt**, Bellefontaine, *Tel. 55-01-84*. Bicycle and motorbike rentals are available from **Discount** in Pointe du Boute, *Tel. 66-54-37*; **Funny**, *Tel. 63-33-05*; and **T.S. Autos**, *Tel. 63-42-82*, both in Fort-de-France. In Le Diamant contact **Scootonnerre**, *Tel. 76-41-12;* in Lamentin, **Centrale du Cycle**, *Tel. 50-28-54.*

For information about bike itineraries, contact the **Parc Naturel Regional**, 9 Boulevard Général de Gaulle, Fort-de-France, *Tel. 64-42-59.*

Camping
Martinique is one of the Caribbean's most enlightened islands when it comes to tenting, backpacking, and even RVing! You can pitch a tent darned near anywhere you like in the summer months between June and September. For information, contact the **Office National des Fôrets**, 3.5 kilometer, route de Moutte, Fort-de-France, Martinique, French West Indies, *Tel. 596/71-34-50.*

Campgrounds with showers and toilets include **Tropicamp**, 6 rue Schoelcher, Ste. Luce, *Tel. 62-49-66*; **Nid Tropical** in Anse-a-l'Ane, *Tel. 68-31-30*; a camp at Pointe Marine near the beach of Ste. Anne, *Tel. 76-72-79*;

and a camp at Vauclin on the southeast Atlantic coast, *Tel. 74-45-88.* Camping "cars" with four berths, dining table, stove, refrigerator, shower, sink, and radio-cassette player are available from **West Indies Tours**, *Tel. 596/54-50-10 or 62-44-50.*

Canoeing & Kayaking

Contact **Basalt** in Bellefontaine, *Tel. 55-01-84.*

Fishing

Go deep sea fishing for tuna, barracuda, dorado, kingfish, and bonito aboard the *Auberge du Care* in Case-Pilote north of Fort-de-France, *Tel. 596/78-80-56.* Sportfishing adventures are also booked through **Caribtours**, *Tel. 66-02-56.*

Fitness

If your hotel doesn't have a fitness center, try **Espace Loisirs**, *Tel. 66-03-16.* Found at Pointe du Boute, it has squash, tennis, gymnastics, weight training, aerobics, and spa treatments. A local gym in Ste.-Luce is **Ti Baume Village**, *Tel. 68-06-33.*

Flying

Flying lessons and aerial photography can be arranged through **Antilles Air Service**, *Tel. 51-66-88.* Cost is about 8000F per hour including the pilot. Planes are also available for rent to qualified pilots through the **Aero-Club de la Martinique**. Ask at the **Lamentin Airport**. Ultralight flight instructions are available from **Thierry Voyer**, *Tel. 64-50-61* or through **Passeport Pour La Mer**, *Tel. 64-04-48.*

Golf

An 18-hole Robert Trent Jones, Sr. golf course is at **Trois Islets**, about a mile from the Pointe du Bout resort area and 20 miles from Fort-de-France. The pro speaks English. Contact **Golf de l'Impératrice Josephine**, *Tel. 596/68-32-81.* Hotel guests and cruise passengers get a discount on greens fees. The complex also has tennis and a pro shop.

Hiking

Hike the **Parc Naturel Regionale** with a guide for about $12 per person. Difficult trails include a climb of **Mont Pelée**; easier trails follow gorges, the nature trail at **Ajoupa Bouillon**, and the path to the ruins of **Chateau Dubuc**, *Tel. 64-42-59.* **Cariballad**, *Tel. 54-51-88*, offers offbeat hiking tours that start by bus to the trailhead. Included are the guide, lunch, and insurance for prices of $65-$70 depending on the itinerary.

Village des Z'Amendines at St. Laurent, *Tel. 69-89-49,* offers one-week packages that include four hiking days, accommodations, and meals. Some of the best views of the island can be seen from the top of **Mount Vauclin**, which is almost 1,700 feet high. Try to be in village of **Le Vauclin** every morning about 11am when fishermen begin returning with their catches. Tour the 18th century **Chapel of the Holy Virgin** and have fresh fish for lunch, then tackle the hike.

Horseback Riding

Ride through spectacular scenery in the beaches and hillsides with **La Gourmette** in Didier, *Tel. 64-20-16;* **Ranch de Galochat** near Anses d'Arlets, *Tel. 68-63-97;* **Black Horse Ranch** near La Pagerie in Trois Islets, *Tel. 68-37-80;* **Centre Equestre de Thoraille** in Rivière Salée, *Tel. 68-18-66;* **La Cavale** near Diamant Novote, *Tel. 76-22-94;* and **L'Hippicampe** at Lamentin, *Tel. 57-06-71.* A one-hour ride with a guide costs about $16; lessons are about $55 per hour.

Sailing

Boat rentals by the hour can be found at most large resort hotels and boats and by the day can be found at larger marinas. Try Albert Mongin at **Le François**, *Tel. 54-70-23;* **La Creole Cata** at the Pointe du Bout Marina, *Tel. 68-30-32;* the **Hotel Riviera** at Le Francois, *Tel. 54-68-54.*

Take the vedette *Evasion* from Petite France in Le François for a boat picnic to Islet Thièrry and the Baignoire de Josephine, *Tel. 54-96-87.* Sailing outings are also available through **Aquadiam** at Le Diamant, *Tel. 776-49-39;* **Nautica Antilles** at Lareinty in Lamentin, *Tel. 51-69-72* and **Planete Bleue** at the Pointe du Bout Marine, *Tel. 66-06-79.*

Charter yachts are available from **Moorings Antilles**, at Le Marin, *Tel. 74-75-39, Fax 74-76-55;* **Sun Sail**, Le Marin, *Tel. 74-77-61, Fax 74-77-80;* or **France Caribe Charter** at Pointe du Bout, *Tel. 66-15-52, Fax 66-15-46.*

Scuba Diving

Martinique has awesome reef and wreck diving. Ask for packages; solo dives are about $40.

Licensed dive operators include:
- **Lychee Plongée** at the Pointe du Bout Marina, *Tel. 66-05-26*
- **Coral Club Caraïbes** at the Hotel Frantour, Anse-a-l'Ane, *Tel. 68-31-67*
- **Atout Plongee** at Schoelcher, just north of Fort-de-France. *Tel. 70-29-33*
- **Tropicasub** near St. Pierre at LaGuingette. *Tel. 78-38-03*
- **Ti Bleu** at Buccaneer's Creek in Ste. Anne, *Tel. 76-76-74*
- **Mondia Sub SARL**, Pointe la Chery, Le Diamant. *Tel. 76-25-80*

Tennis

Two lighted tennis courts are available for rent at the golf course in **Trois Islets**, 20 miles from Fort-de-France. Contact **Golf de l'Impératrice Josephine**, *Tel. 596/68-32-81*. Private clubs welcome non-members as guests when space is available. For information, contact **La Lique Regionale de Tennis** in Lamentin, *Tel. 51-08-00*.

Windsurfing

Drive the coast, where you'll find many shacks offering boardsail rentals for about 100F per hour. One of the best spots for windsurfing is **Cap Michel** near Cap Chevalier, but you'll have to rent a board elsewhere.

SHOPPING

The most popular finds here are French perfumes and other luxury items as well as native straw work, patchwork, dolls, and shell items. Island rums and spices are also a good deal. If you pay for luxury items with travelers' checks or a credit card, ask for a discount. Many stores knock off 20 percent . There's also a good duty-free shop at the airport and it's usually open before major departures. On the way, stop at **La Galleria**, which is a modern shopping center with shops and restaurants.

In the city, shop **Au Gommier** at Rue Victor-Hugo 22 for handmade dresses and linens, *Tel. 67-23-54*. **Cadet-Daniel** at Rue Antoine-Siger, *Tel. 71-41-48* specializes in French china and crystal. Shop here for one the beaded necklaces worn with a traditional Creole costume. For arts and crafts, shop the **Centre des Metiers d'Art** on Rue Ernest Deproges, *Tel. 70-25-01*. Department stores include **Roger Albert** on Rue Victor-Hugo, *Tel. 71-71-71*, **Nouvelles Galeries** at Rue Lamartine 87, *Tel. 63-04-60*, and **Galeries Lafayette** at Rue Victor-Schoelcher 10, *Tel. 71-89-50*.

For gifts and games, shop **Phileas Fogg** at the marina in Pointe du Bout, *Tel. 66-07-17*. The theme is nautical. If you're a boater, check out the **nautical flea market** downtown at 23 Rue Bolivar, *Tel. 60-58-48*. On sale are used equipment and bankrupt stocks.

EXCURSIONS & DAY TRIPS

See Martinique's underwater wonderland aboard *Aquascope*, semi-submersible vessels based at Le Marin, *Tel. 74-87-41;* and **Marine Pointe du Bout**, *Tel. 68-36-09*. Cost for the hour-long voyages is about 100F for adults, 50F for children.

To make an excursion to Antigua, Dominica, Barbados, St. Lucia, St. Vincent or Mustique, call **Air Martinique**, *Tel. 51-09-90*, or **Caribbean Express**, *Tel. 63-12-11*.

PRACTICAL INFORMATION

Area Code: 596

ATM: find an ATM at Le Lamentin International Airport. On the island look for Credit Mutuel and Minibanque 24, both of which accept MasterCard/Cirrus cards.

Current: Martinique uses French-style, 220-volt current.

Currency is the French franc, which is worth about U.S.20¢. Although most hotel prices are quoted in U.S. dollars to U.S. inquiries, meals and shops operate in francs. Change your money at the airport or in Fort-de-France, where a B*ureau de Change* is across from the tourist information office.

Driving: you must be at least 21 years old and have a driver's license from your home country.

Emergencies: Dial 17 for police, 18 for fire, and 70-36-48 for an ambulance. Fort-de-France has a hospital and pharmacies.

Government: Martinique is a *region* of France; U.S. consular matters are handled through Bridgetown, Barbados, *Tel. 246/436-4950*.

Language: French is the language of government and business but the everyday tongue is a patois well larded with Spanish words. Because most menus are in French, it is useful to have a dictionary.

Tourist Information: For further information from the United States, *Tel. 800/391-4909*. Or, write the French Government Tourist Office, *444 Madison Avenue, New York NY 10022*. In Canada, write the French Government Tourist Office, *1981 Avenue McFill College 490, Montreal, Quebec, H3A 2W9, Tel. 514/288-4264, Fax 844-8901; or 30 St. Patrick Street, Suite 700, Toronto, Ontario M5T 3A3. Tel. 416/593-6427, Fax 979-7587*. In Fort-de-France, the tourist office is on the Boulevard Alfassa, *Tel. 63-79-60*. It is open weekdays 8am to 5pm and Saturdays until noon. Pick up free, English language guides that often contain discount coupons for restaurants.

Weddings: One of the couple must have resided on the island for at least a month before applying for the free license. You'll need a birth certificate, a certificate of good conduct including certification of single status, a residency card, a medical certificate including a blood test no older than three months, and a French translation of any English language documents.

35. ST. BARTS

Sometimes written St. Barth and originally named for Christopher Columbus' brother Bartolomeo, this tiny paradise is **St. Barts** to the English-speaking world and St. Barthélemy (bar-tella-ME) to the French. Geographically it is just east of St. Martin, but politically it is as much a part of France as is Lyon or Dijon. Its people vote in French elections; its immigration is seamless for the French, who are required to have only a national identity card.

St. Barts doesn't market as heavily in North America as many of the other islands, so you may have to call hotels directly if they don't have toll-free numbers. When you do, it's likely that the clerk will speak little English or may not understand your French. The French spoken here is a quaint, old Norman dialect.

Even worse, the island has no direct flights so visitors have to make the last leg by ferry or STOL airplane. Still, the motivated, persistent traveler will find the vacation of a lifetime in this eight-square-mile tropical French fairytale between Guadeloupe and St. Martin.

Throughout history St. Barts was, like most of the islands, yanked back and forth among conquering nations. In an interesting twist of history in 1784, Louis XVI of France traded it for a warehouse in Gothenberg, Sweden. And so the capital was named **Gustavia** for the Swedish king. Streets were paved, duty-free trading began, and blond babies began appearing in what today is still a very pale-skinned populace. In time, France bought the island back and French it has remained.

Slavery existed here to a small extent, but under the Swedish governor slaves were freed earlier than on neighboring islands. With little means of earning a living from impoverished white landowners, free blacks left the island in the mid-1800s. As a result, St. Barts has fewer blacks than almost any other island in the Caribbean.

During the buccaneer years, St. Barts grew rich on booty. The notorious Montbars the Exterminator, filled with hatred for the way the Spaniards had exterminated island aborigines, cut a wide swath through

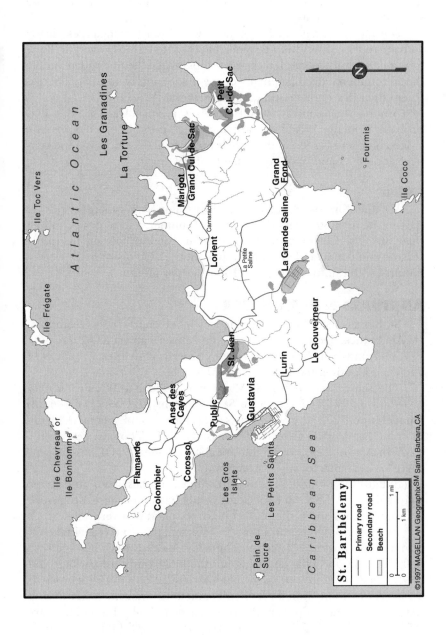

St. Barthélemy

Primary road
Secondary road
Beach

1 mi
1 km

©1997 MAGELLAN Geographix℠ Santa Barbara,CA

Atlantic Ocean

Caribbean Sea

Ile Toc Vers
Ile Frégate
Ile Chevreau or
Ile Bonhomme

Les Granadines
La Torture

Fourmis
Ile Coco

Marigot
Grand Cul-de-Sac
Petit Cul-de-Sac
Grand Fond
Camarache
Lorient
La Petite Saline
La Grande Saline
Le Gouverneur
St. Jean
Lurin
Gustavia
Anse des Cayes
Public
Flamands
Colombier
Corossol
Les Gros Islets
Les Petits Saints
Pain de Sucre

the area. During one hurricane, he disappeared at sea. Hopeful treasure hunters still dream of finding the riches he is thought to have buried somewhere on St. Barts.

During the American Revolution, with French sympathies clearly with the rebels, American privateers that operated from friendly St. Barts took a heavy toll on British merchant ships. When the war ended and St. Barts' commerce declined, many of the inhabitants went to St. Thomas where their descendants still speak a medieval French.

Among the island's natural riches is a small tree called Gaiac, probably from the Arawak or Carib meaning Tree of Life. It blooms with a deep blue and is seen in dooryards around the island. It's found only here and on a handful of other islands. Look for it.

Climate

Weather forecasters can use a rubber stamp here, calling for perfect days in the high 80s every day winter or summer, and nights no cooler than the 60s. Except during low pressure periods during hurricane season, rain is light and infrequent. July through October are the wettest months, with rainful averaging 9-10 inches per month.

ARRIVALS & DEPARTURES

St. Barts is served via St. Martin, which in turn has flights from Paris via **Air France**, *Tel. 800/237-2747*; from Amsterdam via **KLM**, *Tel. 800/374-7747*; and from the United States by **American Airlines**, *Tel. 800/443-7300* and **Continental Airlines**, *Tel. 231-0856*.

The island is served from St. Maarten or San Juan by **Winair**, *Tel. 800/634-4907 or 590/27-61-01* and **Air St. Barthelemy**, *Tel. 590/87-73-46*. **Air Guadeloupe**, *Tel. 590/87-53-74* flies to St. Barts from Esperance Airport in French St. Martin. From St. Thomas, fly **Air St. Thomas**, *Tel. 590/27-71-76* or Air Guadeloupe. Flights are aboard 20-seat STOL aircraft, and there are no lights for night landings.

Still, this is a plucky little airport with car rentals, a bar, and shops. Across the road, La Savane shopping center has a food store, drug store, and more shops and is the perfect place to spend leftover francs.

By ferry from Simpson's Bay, St. Maarten, the sea crossing takes 40 minutes. *The Edge* sails Tuesday, Thursday, and Saturday. Passage costs $50 plus a $5 port charge. Ask about the lunch and tour package, *Tel. 5995/42640 or 42503, extension 1553 or 1092*. Book a day or more in advance. In season, Monday service is sometimes available. *White Octopus* makes a 90-minute trip from Bobby's Marine in Philipsburg to St. Barts twice a week. *Tel. 5995/23170*. The ferry *Gustavia Express* plies between St. Martin and Gustavia or Marigot, *Tel. 590/27-77-24, Fax 27-77-23*. Cost for the 1 1/2-hour trip is about $40 plus $6 port tax, one way. Ferries also include *Voyageur I* and *Voyageur II*, which cross between Gustavia and Marigot for $62 including port taxes, *Tel. 590/87-20-78.*

The ferry *Bateau Dakar* serves St. Barts, Guadeloupe, and St. Martin, *Tel. 590/27-70-05.* Luxury resorts sometimes arrange private pickup at St. Martin for about $80 per person. Ask.

ORIENTATION

Although the island of St. Barts is only about nine miles long and a mile wide, its neighborhoods have distinct flavors. Everything centers on the capital and port, **Gustavia**, with the village of **Public** just above it to the northwest. Keep traveling northwest to find the villages of **Corossol**, **Columbier**, and **Flamands**.

To the northeast of Gustavia on the opposite shore is **Saint Jean**, site of the airport. Continuing east from Saint Jean brings you to **Lorient**, a corruption of the original name, Quartier d'Orleans, where you'll find a post office and gas station. Continuing east, the road leads to **Marigot** or, with a southern turn, to **Vitet**. **Salines** is the old salt panning area.

Around **Gustavia harbor** city streets form pincers around the water. Chief among them are Rue Jeanne d'Arc, Rue de Centenaire, and the Rue de la République.

GETTING AROUND

Taxis meet every ferry and flight or can be hailed at the quai in Gustavia or at the airport; to call one, dial *27-66-31.* Taxis charge a flat 25F for runs up to five minutes and 20F for each additional three minutes. Fares are higher at night and on Sunday and holidays. Cabs at night are available from Jean-Paul Janin, *Tel. 27-61-86;* Raymond Greaux, *Tel. 27-66-32,* Mathilde Laplace, *Tel. 27-60-59;* Robert Magras, *Tel. 27-63-12* or Lina Bernier, *Tel. 27-60-54.*

Car rental agencies are found downtown and at the airport where there is one gas station, which is credit card-operated around the clock. The minimum purchase is 50F. The other gas station is in Lorient but it's closed Thursday, Saturday afternoon, and Sunday.

Cars are available at the airport from:
• **Hertz**, *Tel. 27-71-14*
• **Avis**, *Tel. 27-71-43*
• **Budget**, *Tel. 27-67-43*
• **Edmond Gumbs**, *Tel. 27-75-32*
• **Europcar**, *Tel. 27-73-33*
• **Soleil Caraibes**, *Tel. 27-70-01*
• **Chez Beranger**, *Tel. 27-89-00*

The land is hilly, roads are steep and potted, and most cars are manual shift. Your home driver's license is accepted here.

Motorcycles, scooters, and motorbikes can be rented from **Rent Some Fun,** which also has 18-speed mountain bikes, *Tel. 27-70-59.*

WHERE TO STAY

The hotels themselves have given us their prices in dollars or francs, or both, so we report them as they were quoted to us. Prices are for a double room in high season. In some cases, singles are less. Summer and shoulder season rates may be lower.

Ask if service charges are added to the bill in lieu of tipping. There is no point in tipping twice.

Expensive

CHRISTOPHER HOTEL, *Point Milou. Tel. 590/27-63-63, Fax 27-92-92; toll-free 800/221-4542. Rates at this 40-room hotel are from $360 including buffet breakfast. Ask about packages, which are offered year 'round and result in substantial savings. The hotel is 3.5 miles from the airport.*

This Sofitel hotel, which can be booked through a toll-free number in the U.S. if you're willing to stay on Hold for long periods, welcomes you with a bottle of rum and fresh fruit and you immediately feel at home. Accommodations are air conditioned and roomy, with private sitting areas overlooking the sea. Furniture is crafted from local hardwoods and accessorized in sunny colors. Tile baths have indoor gardens. Swim in the sea or the big, free-form pool; a fitness center has classes and workout equipment. Dine on French specialties in the hotel's own restaurant, L'Orchidée, or on the teak pool deck at Le Mango.

FRANÇOIS PLANTATION, *Columbier, 97133 St. Bartelemy. Tel. 590/27-78-82, Fax 27-61-26. Rates at this 12-bungalow resort start at $315 including full breakfast. It is two miles northwest of Gustavia and ten minutes from the airport.*

Famed for its restaurant, views of the Bay of Flamands, and comfortable cottages nestled in a tropical garden, François is warmly hosted by owner-managers named François and Françoise. Cottages have a kitchenette, private veranda, mahogany furnishings with pastel fabrics, and white marble baths.

LE TOINY, *Anse de Toiny. Tel. 590/27-88-88, Fax 590/27-89-30. In the U.S. and Canada call 800/932-3222 or 401/849-8012, Fax 401/847-6290. Rates at this 12-suite hotel start at $820.*

Tiny, personal, and plantation style, this island jewel is built in the hills overlooking a sapphire sea edged in foamy surf. The beach is a short walk down the hill. Gourmet French food is served in Le Gaiac, or order from room service. Lavender, peach and mint pastels decorate the 12 private villas, each furnished with handmade mahogany furniture fashioned after French West Indian planter styles. Baths are done in Italian tiles; each villa has a private pool, air conditioning, telephone, television with video, and a full kitchen.

HOTEL GUANAHANI, *Anse de Grand Cul de Sac, St. Barthelemy 97098, French West Indies. Tel. 590/27-66-60, Fax 27-70-70; toll-free in U.S., Canada, Puerto Rico, and U.S. Virgin Islands, 800/223-6800. Rates at this 80-room resort start at $205, suites at $505. Included is continental breakfast.*

Cupped around the beaches of the Grand Cul de Sac and gently edged with green hills, the Guanahani combines such European creature comforts as satellite television, air conditioning, and hair dryer with the relaxed West Indian comforts of traditional Gustavia furniture and pastel tones or rich, dark woods accented with bold tones.

Best remembered for its eye-popping pool and Jacuzzi, the resort also has two, coral reef-sheltered sand beaches. Some units have private pools. Shop the boutique, dance after dinner to live music after having your hair done in the beauty parlor. The tennis courts are lit for night play; try all the watersports from sailing to snorkeling. Dining is in L'Indigo beachfront overlooking the pool or in Bartolomeo, known for its Mediterranean food. Continental breakfast and light suppers are also available from room service.

HOTEL MANAPANY, *Anse de Cayes, St. Barts, French West Indies. Tel. 590/27-75-26. In the U.S. Tel. 212/719-5750 or 800/847-4249. Rates for the 32 fully-equipped cottages start at $500.*

Crimson-roofed cottages march gaily down a steep, lushly forested hill that ends at a private beach and sparkling cove. Play tennis, soak in the Jacuzzi, have a massage, work out in a fully-equipped fitness center, or ride horseback. Have a sundowner at the piano bar, then dine by candlelight on the terrace that is transformed by night into a trattoria. Le Ballahou is romantic and French; The Ouanalao is an appealing Italian café. Meals here have received the Diploma of European Excellence. The decor is rosy, glowing with tile floors and understated tones to accent the stark white of cool wicker and gauzy bed coverings. Accommodations have direct dial telephone, television with closed circuit videos in 13 languages, and air conditioning.

HOTEL ST. BARTH-ISLE DE FRANCE, *Anse de Flamands. Tel. 590/ 27-61-81, Fax 27-86-83, U.S. 800/932-3222. Rates start at $420. It's two miles from the airport.*

The only squash court on the island is just one of the pluses of this splendid beachside lodge with its clustered cottages. Rooms are furnished in mahogany antiques, with ceiling fans, mosquito netting, Caribbean artworks, air conditioning, telephone, television, and mini-bar. Swim in the sea or in the pool. Order from 24-hour room service and eat on your private terrace.

HOTEL YAUNA, *Anse des Cayes. Tel. 590/27-80-84, Fax 27-78-45. Rates at this 12-unit hotel start at $300. It's 1.3 miles from the airport.*

Each suite has a king or queen-size bed, a sofabed that will sleep two children, a fully-equipped kitchenette, television with VCR, safe, air conditioning, and ceiling fans. Furnishings are restful blues and corals; from your terrace or balcony, you'll have a view of the Anse des Cayes. Breakfast is available from the hotel. Prepare your own lunches and dinners or dine in nearby St. Jean.

Moderate

EL SERENO BEACH, *Grand Cul-de-Sac. Tel. 27-64-80, Fax 27-75-47. Rates at this 34-unit hotel, which is not quite four miles from the airport, start at $200 including continental breakfast.*

This young-at-heart beachfront resort has a fitness center, wind surfing and lessons, and a popular, poolside restaurant, the West Indies Cafe.

LA BANANE, *Flamands. Tel. 27-68-25, Fax 27-68-44. Rates at this nine-unit inn, which is a mile from the airport, start at $150.*

The hotel's owner, Jean Marie Riviere, makes you feel at home in this intimate little resort where every suite has telephone, television, safe, mini-bar, and hair dryer. The beds are antique mahogany four-posters romantically draped with netting. Walk to Lorient Beach or swim in one of the two pools. The hotel's restaurant serves breakfast and dinner and does cabaret two or three nights a week.

SEA HORSE HOTEL, *Domaine le Levant, Petit Cul-de-Sac. Tel. 590/27-75-36, Fax 27-85-33. Or, book with E&M Associates, 212/599-8280 or 800/223-9832. The 10-unit resort is 10 minutes from the airport. Rates start at $175 for a junior suite; villas are from $295 including tax and service charge.*

Marigot Bay Club restaurant is on the resort's beach, but the hotel itself doesn't have a restaurant. It's a pleasant walk through the pretty blue gaiacs, flowering trees found only on this and a handful of other islands. The hotel's charm as a hideaway is enhanced by its affordable (for this island) tariffs, so ask about packages. All units have an air conditioned bedroom, living room, kitchenette and covered terrace. There's also a two-bedroom villa, a lap pool and a barbecue for guest use. The view is of gorgeous Marigot Bay.

Budget

HOTEL NORMANDIE, *Lorient. Tel. 27-61-66, Fax 27-98-83. Rates at this eight-room hotel start at $70. The hotel is three miles east of the airport. No credit cards are accepted.*

A simple, out-island inn favored by business travelers and budget vacationers, this one is not on the beach but it has a swimming pool, air conditioned rooms or ceiling fans, and friendly, family management. Continental breakfast is available at added cost.

HOSTELLERIE DES TROIS FORCES, *Vitet. Tel. 27-61-25, Fax 27-81-38. Rates at this eight-room hotel, which is three miles east of Gustavia, start at $75.*

Unpack in your own pleasant, gingerbread bungalow high in the hills of Morne du Vitet. Your cottage has a kitchenette for cooking up breakfasts and lunches; make reservations for dinner in the hotel's famous restaurant. If you want air conditioning or a private terrace, request them when you book. The hotel has its own pool, and a hillside location that gives a nice view of surrounding hills.

Villa Rentals

Rental agencies specializing in beach houses and villas by the week or month include **Ici & La**, *Tel. 590/27-78-78* and **Sibarth Real Estate**, *Tel. 590/27-62-38*. A four-bedroom villa with pool costs $4,500 to $10,000 per week in high season; one-bedroom bungalows are $1,200 to $1,800 in winter. Meals and a cook are available at extra cost.

Private villas on St. Barts can also be booked through **WIMCO**, *Tel. 800/932-3222 or 401/849-8012*. Maid service and staff are available.

WHERE TO EAT

It's likely on St. Barts that your menu will be priced in francs or in dollars and francs, but not in dollars alone. Unless specified otherwise, these restaurants take major credit cards. St. Barts is an expensive island, reflecting the French love of uncompromisingly good food and wine. Plan to spend $60 or more in an expensive restaurant, $35 to $45 at a moderately priced place, and up to $35 even in some spots that are rated by local tip sheets as inexpensive!

St. Barts and the French islands are dressier than many of the other Caribbean islands. Long trousers or designer jeans should be worn for dinner, never shorts. Jackets are rarely worn but, when making reservations at the toniest restaurants, ask about the dress code.

It isn't usual in French restaurants to drink water with meals, so it won't be served unless you ask for it. Even so, it's likely you'll be served a bottled water for which you will be charged. Like many islands, St. Barts gets its water from cisterns that catch rain water and from desalinization, an expensive process. Don't waste this precious resource.

GUSTAVIA

Expensive

AU PORT, *Face à la Poste. Tel. 27-62-36. Entrees are in the $25-$50 range. A set menu is offered at 180 francs or about $36. Reservations are recommended. The restaurant is open only for dinner and is closed seasonally.*

Right in the heart of town at the harbor, this longtime favorite features French and Creole cooking such as filet of sole in champagne sauce with rice and wild mushrooms, or lobster cassoulet with baby vegetables. For a starter try the conch and lobster sausage with avocado cream sauce. The decor is richly nautical, with blue and white table linens and a big, mahogany ships wheel.

COTE' JARDIN, *Rue Corbet just below the Swedish bell tower. Tel. 27-70-47. Plan to spend $50-$80 for dinner. Reservations are recommended.*

Wicker and white linen give a cool, breezy look to this crisply elegant dining room. Or, dine on the terrace surrounded by rustling greenery. The rack of lamb is flavored with fresh thyme; the salmon is served sensuously rare, seared only on one side. Whatever the chef's whim each day, it is sure to be sensational.

CARL GUSTAF, *700 Rue des Normands. Tel. 27-82-83. Breakfast, lunch, and dinner are served daily. Reservations are recommended for dinner. Plan to spend $60 for dinner with wine.*

Overlook the harbor on the lattice-covered terrace, where tables are set with snappy white linen and the French cuisine is perfectly complemented by your choice of wines from an extensive cellar, which you are invited to visit. "Chef de brigade" Patrick Gateau, late of the Crillon in Paris, suggests a tartare of fresh red tuna with cream cheese and chives, Sevruga caviar served on ice, steamed monkfish with mixed new vegetables and a touch of lime, or veal with paprika and basil fettucini. At lunch, tomatoes stuffed with velvety chicken mousse are sublime. Dessert is warm chocolate praline cake topped with melting chocolate. Come early for a sundowner at the piano bar.

LE SAPOTILLIER, *rue Du Centenaire. Tel. 27-60-28. Open for dinner only, the restaurant closes seasonally. Main courses are in the 180F range. Make reservations, please.*

Traditional French cuisine with a delicious focus on seafood is served indoors or in the romantic garden under an old sappodilla tree. Specialties include lasagna escargot, frog's legs, and seafood such as turbot and sea bass. Or try the foie gras of duck with juniper berry sauce, veal ragout with Roquefort and vegetables, or one of couscous dishes. For dessert, have the baked grapefruit and oranges or the black and white chocolate mousse.

WALL HOUSE, *La Pointe. Tel. 27-71-83. Plan to spend 150 to 185 francs; more if you order lobster. Lunch and dinner are served. Reservations are urged.*

The perfect place to have lunch after seeing the museum, this restaurant is just opposite the Wall house, one of the oldest buildings on the island. For lunch have a salad, grilled fish, or one of the carpaccios or toasted sandwiches. At dinner, classic French cuisine rules. Choices include mussel soup, roast lamb with fresh herbs, roast turbot with fennel and tomato sauce, and shrimp ragout with fresh mint.

Moderate

CHEZ DOMI, *due du General de Gaulle. Tel. 29-84-11. Open for lunch and dinner daily; prices are $35 to $45.*

Chef Dominique presides over a small, locally popular restaurant where diners dote on his curries as well as octopus with dumplings, lobster stew, or crayfish.

EDDY'S, *rue du Centenaire, across from Le Sapotillier. Eddy's has no telephone, but it's wise to stop by in person to reserve a table. It's open for dinner, and the garden is open for light lunches. Plan to spend $35 to $45.*

Enter the setting of Balinese teak and bamboo through a garden filled with souvenirs from Bali, where Eddy and his wife Brigitte have vacationed for years. Chef Philou Burlot offers Thai shrimp in green curry, conch baked in phyllo pastry, pork tenderloin breaded with coconut and served with pineapple sauce, or fresh fish en papillote.

L'ENTREPONT, *on the far side of the harbor. Tel. 27-90-60. Open for dinner only, the same spot at lunch is called Chez Francine. Plan to spend $35 for dinner.*

Old St. Barts hands may remember that a French restaurant with this name once operated on this same spot, but today's version serves Italian specialties including a spectrum of tempting pizzas. Dine in a tropical garden under coconut palms, serenaded by sea breezes and the sounds of the harbor.

Budget

L'IGUANE, *Le Carré D'Or. Tel. 27-88-46. Open for lunch and dinner until 11pm daily except Sunday, it offers meals in the $10 to $15 range. Credit cards aren't accepted.*

The only sushi restaurant on the island, this one features raw, cooked, and vegetarian sushi prepared by Chef Paul Ming Po So, formerly of Sushi Hana in Miami Beach. Also served are sandwiches and salads. During the day it's mostly a coffee and ice cream shop; entertainers at night bring in the sushi crowd.

LA MANDALA, *rue Thiers. Tel. 27 96 96. Hours vary seasonally, but it's generally open daily noon to 3pm and 5pm to 11pm and on weekends for brunch. Tapas platters are priced $7 to $10; a prix fixe dinner is $34.*

Take a furlough from the French food and try this hip tapas bar with a new menu every evening. High above the port, La Mandala promises a beautiful view, streaky sunsets, and some of the best live music on the island with plenty of banter from barman Boubou. You might nibble on a basket of raw vegetables with sour cream and herbs, followed by a breast of chicken in coconut milk. Have a chocolate sweet for dessert.

LE RÉPAIRE, *Quai de la République. Tel. 27-72-48. The restaurant is open from noon to 10:30pm daily. Main dishes average about $15.*

Sit at a yachty teak grate table on the quai and order an ice cream sundae, an American or French breakfast, lunch, cocktails or dinner. Yacht crews come ashore to hang out here from early morning through dinner, enjoying good wines from a moderately priced wine list and dining on chicken bouillabaisse, grilled langouste, steak and French fries, or raw fish favorites such as the carpaccio of dorado or the tuna tartare.

COLUMBIER

FRANÇOIS PLANTATION, *Columbier. Tel. 27-78-82. Open daily for dinner, the restaurant is closed Sundays in low seasons. Entrees are in the 100F to 250F range. It's two miles northwest of Gustavia.*

Once part of a plantation and furnished in glowing mahogany pieces, François (the owners are named François and Françoise) has a cellar packed with more than 250 wines, some of them rare or esoteric. The menu is traditional French featuring flavorful soups, delicate cream sauces, and deftly drifted herbs. A house specialty is the rib steak with creamy potatoes gratin dauphinoise. For dessert try the exotic rosemary, basil, and strawberry mousse or the creme brulée with a hint of ginger and lime. After dinner, have a cigar in the fumoir.

PUBLIC

MAYA'S RESTAURANT, *on the beach, Public. Tel. 27-75-73. The bar opens at 4:30pm. Main courses are in the 140F-180F range, or about $28 to $36. Reservations are required. Maya's is open for dinner except Sunday and is closed in low season.*

Dine on Creole and Caribbean specialties created by Maya Gurley, who is from Martinique, and her American husband, Randy. Start with a rum *planteur* (planter's punch) then have the christophene gratin, grilled lobster, squid sautéed in ginger and garlic, or wahoo *en brochette*. Ask about daily specials, which change with the catch, the market, and the chef's inspiration. Watch the hot sauces and don't miss the coconut tart for dessert.

ANSE DES CAYES

LE OUANALAO, *in the Hotel Manapany. Tel. 27-66-55. Entrees are in the 100F-400F range, The restaurant is open daily in season for lunch and dinner; reservations are required.*

The food, the welcome, and the warmth add up to a special evening of Italian cuisine from the wand of Gilles Najac. Or, dine by the pool bar where Marion the barman dishes out a mean planteur, ti punch, or any mixed drink you can suggest. Some nights, there's a lobster barbecue by the pool.

NEW BORN, *on the beach, Anse des Cayes. Tel. 27-67-07. Find it on the road to the Hotel Manapany. Dishes are priced $18 to $25. Call for hours and reservations.*

It's just a beach shack, but the Greaux family has had a loyal following since 1990 for its unfailingly good, traditional St. Barts food. Feast on Creole staples such as accras (codfish cakes), curried goat or shrimp, calalloo, turtle steak, salt cod salad, chops in Creole sauce, and desserts such as coconut flan or flaming bananas.

SAINT-JEAN BAY

Expensive

ADAM, *on the Carenage. Tel. 27-93-22. Reservations are recommended. A three-course, fixed price menu is 190F, about $38.*

In a charmingly unpretentious Creole house with a wide deck surrounded by deep pink bougainvillaea, choose from light, traditional, and vegetarian dishes. Owner-chef Vincent Adam may suggest tenderloin of beef, tabouli with lobster, sweetbreads, or the imported salmon garnished with caviar and oyster.

CUP'S, *across from Filao Beach, St. Jean Bay. Tel. 27-70-92. Fixed priced menus are 140 and 200 francs. Call for reservations and hours.*

Brothers Arnaud and Mathias named their restaurant after the America's Cup, and decorated their restaurant in blue and white. Bring your bathing suit for a swim in the pool, then enjoy a drink while you look over the model sailboats and antique sailing photographs before tucking into a three-or four-course menu dreamed up just for today.

EDEN ROCK, *St. Jean Bay. Tel. 27-72-94. Open for lunch and dinner, this hotel restaurant serves meals in the moderate category in the downstairs brasserie or more expensive menus upstairs on the terrace. Reservations are recommended.*

The builders of St. Bart's first hotel just after World War 11 chose this beauty spot on dramatic cliffs overlooking the two beach crescents that make up St. Jean Bay. Now owned by British imports Jane and David Matthews, the hotel serves French-Creole foods.

LE COLONIAL, *in the Centre Commercial, St. Jean Bay. Tel. 27-53-00. Reservations are urged. The restaurant is open daily for dinner. Plan to spend $30 to $45.*

A long staircase brings you into a gracious old home and garden where Cambodian-influenced menus feature sautée of beef with lemongrass, fresh fish flavored with ginger wrapped in a banana leaf, and peppery garlic shrimp with coriander. For dessert have the cold mango soup.

Moderate

LE PATIO, on*e mile from the airport towards Saint-Jean in the Village St. Jean Hotel. Tel. 27-70-67. Open daily except Wednesday from 6:30pm, the restaurant is eat-in or take-out. Reservations are essential. Dinner is in the 100F-300F range. A fixed-price dinner is about 180F.*

Take a table on the tile terrace where white linen cloths are topped gaily in red spreads. You're high above Saint-Jean Bay in the breezes, dining on cold and hot antipasto, fish couscous, lamb chops with artichokes, Cornish game hen marinated in lemon and herbs, and homemade pastas with a French-Italian accent. Pizzas are available in more than a dozen exotic flavors including lobster. Or, splurge on the prime rib for two. In season, jazz sometimes plays.

LE PELICAN, *on the Plage de Saint-Jean one mile east of the airport. Tel. 27-64-64. Reservations are urged, especially for dinner. Open daily for lunch and dinner, the restaurant is closed Sundays in summer. Main courses are in the 100-300F range. Credit cards aren't accepted.*

Classic French cuisine and seafood star at this indoor-outdoor spot where lunches are sunny and surfside while dinners are intimate, candlelit affairs in one of three dining rooms. Sample Creole specialties such as accras, blood pudding, or crab, or a simple grilled catch of the day, done to perfection. Everything is accompanied by French wine, of course.

LE TROPICAL, *300 feet up the hill from the beach, St. Jean Bay. Tel. 27-64-87. Plan to spend $25 to $35. Call for hours and reservations.*

Chef Wendy Henderson oversees this hotel restaurant, set in a garden filled with flowers. Dine poolside from the buffet on pasta with fresh basil, seafood salad with pineapple and coconut, sweet pepper salad with goat cheese, chicken fragrant with fresh herbs, and much more.

Budget

BRASSERIE CREOLE, *St. Jean Bay. Tel. 27-68-09. Meals are priced 30F to 60F. It's open daily for lunch and dinner. American Express cards are accepted.*

Ask for the menu du jour, which will list such treats for today as frog's legs, beef Burgundy, blanquette de veau, or curried chicken. Or dine indoors or out on salads, sandwiches, or an omelet.

LE TOM BEACH, *in the Tom Beach Hotel. Tel. 27-53-13. Open only for lunch, the restaurant offers parking in an underground garage. Lunch costs $10 to $20.*

Dine right on the beach on grilled chicken or fish, lobster, sandwiches and salads.

GRAND CUL-DE-SAC

Expensive

BARTOLOMÉO, *in the Hotel Guanahani. Tel. 27-66-60. Main dishes are in the 200-250F range. Reservations are recommended, especially if you are not a guest at the hotel. Open daily for lunch and dinner, the restaurant is closed seasonally.*

Only the best cuisine will pass muster in this classy hotel. Order from a lengthy wine list of French, Italian, and California vintages, then listen to the piano while making a choice from a menu of Mediterranean dishes. Every Monday, Tuscan foods are featured. In a less formal setting, the hotel's poolside restaurant, Indigo, is open for breakfast and lunch. On Saturday nights, L'Indigo serves a barbecue buffet followed by a colorful cabaret show.

LA GLORIETTE, *Grande Cul-de-Sac. Tel. 27-75-66. Open for lunch and dinner daily, the restaurant offers a Creole meal at 140F and a French menu at 170F. Reservations are suggested.*

You're right on the beach overlooking swimmers and sailors while you dine on barbecued chicken or lobster, stuffed crab, cassoulet of lobster, conch stew, and other French-Creole specialties from a menu that changes often.

LE LAFAYETTE, *at Grande Cul-de-Sac, east of Marigot. Tel. 27-62-51. Open for lunch daily, the restaurant is closed from late spring through fall. Reservations are recommended. Plan to spend $25-$60.*

It looks and feels like a beach burger joint until you taste the food, which is sophisticated, expensive, continental, and sublime. Chèvre, Roquefort, and other specialty cheeses add an exotic touch to ordinary salads. Fresh herbs bless the grilled fish. Have barbecued lobster, crisp roast duckling, or grilled snapper with hot pepper sauce. For dessert have the very chocolate cake, fruity sherbet, or a tart. On weekends, models circulate to show fashions from the club's boutique. Come early enough for a swim and a rum punch before lunch.

WEST INDIES CAFE, *in the Hotel El Sereno Beach. Tel. 27-64-80. Reservations are recommended. Plan to spend $60 or more for dinner.*

The "in" spot in town is the wildly successful project of Christian Hegg. Have a leisurely drink, then a late dinner from a choice of carpaccios, salads, fish, lobster, pastas, chicken and beef, followed by a ringing cabaret show.

CHEZ POMPI, *Grand Cul-de-Sac. Tel. 27-75-67. Prices are in the $10 to $15 range. It's open for lunch daily except Sunday.*

Pompi loves food and art, so he sells them both in this charmingly unaffected ("naif" is the French way of describing it) restaurant. Have lobster salad, stuffed crab, chicken stew, or goat stew.

LE RIVAGE, *on the beach near the St. Barth Beach Hotel. Tel. 27-82-42. Dine for 40-60F. It's closed late August through early October.*

Dine on raw marinated salmon, hot goat cheese salad, pasta with langouste, plum flan, and the house specialty after-dinner drink, vanilla rum.

MARIGOT

MARIGOT BAY CLUB, *Marigot. Tel. 27-75-45. Lunch is served in season; dinner is served nightly. Plan to spend $60 for dinner. Reservations are essential.*

Chef Florant Demangeon presents a nice selection of fresh fish including snapper, wahoo, shark, and grouper. Try the lobster tart served with lightly steamed vegetables, the lobster ravioli, or broiled lobster. Intimate and romantic, with unhurried service, there are only 16 tables.

POINTE MILOU

L'ORCHIDÉE, *in the Christopher Hotel at Pointe Milou northeast of Gustavia. Tel. 27-63-63. Reservations are essential, especially if you are not a guest at the hotel. Prices range from under $20 for lunch or snacks to $100 or more for a fine dinner with wine. A fixed price menu is priced at about $50.*

Classic French cuisine is served in this elegant Sofitel hotel overlooking beach and sea. Dine by candlelight on chef Bruno Benedetti's mahi-mahi in a pastry braid, or sea bass in a sauce that has a faint whiff of vanilla. In the hotel's poolside bar, light and low-calorie salads and snacks are featured.

GRANDE SALINE

LE TAMARIN, *in Grande Saline east of Gustavia. Tel. 27-72-12. Hours vary seasonally and the restaurant closes Mondays in summer. Entrees are in the 100F-150F range. Reservations are essential and you still may have to wait.*

This popular country restaurant is just off the Grande Saline beach with its parade of bikini-clad beauties. Dine in a Haitian atmosphere of flowers and deep pastels, wicker and dark woods. This is a spot for lingering over a drink in one of the hammocks slung under a century-old tamardind tree. Feast on honeyed chicken, grilled chops or fish, fresh carpaccios (paper-thin slices of raw meat or fish), steak tartare, and chocolate desserts. Corky, the resident parrot, presides.

VITET

LES TROIS FORCES, *in Vitet, two miles east of the airport. Tel. 27-61-25. Open daily for lunch and dinner, the restaurant is closed for a month in late summer. Reservations are essential. Dinner will cost about $50.*

French, Creole, and Japanese cuisine is featured in this hotel restaurant operated by a family from Brittany, who brought a sense of that province into the decor and ambience. Don't rush your meal because everything is made to order, from the freshly grilled lobster to the dessert crepes. Owner-chef Hubert Delamotte swizzles up locally famous rum drinks and his award-winning cuisine centers around the wood oven where potatoes are baked in the ashes and where shrimp, lobster, fish, and meats are grilled. Or, have a fish soufflé. Save room for one of Hubert's wicked, swan-shaped cream puffs. Lunch is casual, but dinners are more dressy.

LORIENT

CHEZ JOJO, *Lorient, Tel. 27-63-53. It's open for lunch and does not take credit cards. Eat for under $10.*

It's part supermarket, part snack bar, where you can get fried chicken or a burger with fries and all the trimmings for about $8.

ANSE LE TOINY

LE GAIAC, *in the Hotel Le Toiny, Anse Le Toiny. Tel. 27-88-88. Reservations are essential. Plan to spend $60 for dinner. Hours vary seasonally.*

It's worth a trip out to Toiny Point to dine in this chic, 30-seat restaurant in the main house of the swank Hotel Le Toiny. Laurie Smith and David Henderson welcome you to their dining room overlooking the main pool and a long, long view from the hillside out to sea. It's named for flowering gaiac trees, a rare tree found only in a handful of places in the French islands. Chef Maxime des Champs trained at a series of Michelin-starred restaurants before coming here to fuse island foods with classic French cuisine.

His specialties include cold caviar soup with anise and beets, roast boneless pigeon layered with red cabbage and sweet potato, yellowtail snapper with curried lentils, and medallions of lobster with passion fruit vinaigrette and candied sweet peppers. At lunch, have stuffed land crab with christophene salad, minced chicken sautéed with almonds, or an awesome club sandwich made with chicken, lobster, or smoked salmon.

SNACK ATTACK

For sandwiches, pizzas, hot dogs, nachos, and cotton candy, go to the far side of the harbor and look for **La Sandwicherie**. *It's squeezed in next to the Bistro des Arts.*

SEEING THE SIGHTS

Greater downtown Gustavia consists of a handful of boutiques, duty free shops, some good restaurants, and the colorful open-air market near the Mairie, or town hall. You could explore it on foot in a few hours, marveling at fine old structures dating back to early Swedish and French settlers. Start your visit at the blue and white tourist office on the pier, where maps and brochures are available. It's open Monday through Friday 8:30am to 6pm and Saturdays 9am to noon.

On the water at the end of the Rue Schoelcher, find the **Museum of Saint-Barthélemy**, *Tel. 27-87-27*, filled with arts and artifacts dating back to pre-Columbian days when the island was called Ouanalao. The story continues through the arrival of the Spanish, French, Swedes, and Dominican Fathers. The museum is open Monday through Thursday 8:30am to 12:30pm and 2:30pm to 6pm; Friday 3pm to 6pm and Saturday 9am to 11am. Admission is 10F or about $2.

Driving north west from Gustavia, find the little (population about 300) villages of **Colombier** and **Corossol**, where the **Inter Oceans Museum**, *Tel. 27-62-97*, is filled with glowing seashells. Admission is 20F. It's open every day 9am to 5pm. This is also one of the best villages to see women in traditional sunbonnets, starchy white wimples called quichenottes. They hope you'll buy their palm and straw weavings. Your purchase is the best hope of taking a photograph. Otherwise, your camera won't be welcome.

Go west and south from the capital to Grande Saline, once a mighty salt flat. Salt is no longer raked here, but the beach at Grande Saline is a find. Northwest of Gustavia on the Atlantic, **Lorient's beach** is popular for its coamers and good surfing. East of Lorient at Pointe Milou, which is peppered with villas, lies the more tranquil **Bay of Marigot**, then the resort area of **Grand Cul de Sac**.

NIGHTLIFE & ENTERTAINMENT

The evening starts at sundown, when cocktails and watching for the green flash are a nightly ritual. On weekends, **LA BANANE**, Lorient, *Tel. 27-68-25,* offers French dining around the pool. Cabaret shows play at the

WEST INDIES CAFE in El Sereno Hotel, *Tel. 27-64-80*. **LE PELICAN** in Saint-Jean, *Tel. 27-64-64*, has a piano bar overlooking the bay, with live music and dancing nightly except Sunday. **FEELING** in Lurin, *Tel. 27-88-67*, has a cabaret show every Thursday. On Wednesday, the club offers billiards competition. Drink cocktails, wine or espresso with toasted sandwiches and snacks until the wee hours.

L'INDIGO in the Hotel Guanahani, Grand Cul-de-Sac, *Tel. 27-66-60* has a dinner show just off the beach, around the pool. **BAR DE L'ESCALE** in Gustavia is a dressy American bar open nightly on a terrace on the waterfront, always hopping before and after dinner. It's open every night from 6pm, For reservations, T*el. 27-86-07*.

SPORTS & RECREATION
Beaches

Topless and nude bathing are common at St. Barts beaches and swimming pools. Don't be embarrassed to ask your hotel host for guidance in finding (or avoiding) a beach that is topless, clothing optional, or heavily homosexual. Take all precautions for your own swimming safety; beaches don't have lifeguards.

On the windward side, **Baie de Saint-Jean** is a family beach with restaurants and watersport rentals. **Anse de Lorient** is popular with surfers and swimmers and is said to be the most homosexual-friendly beach on the island. **Anse de Marigot** has a calm, sheltered beach for swimming, sunning, and mooring a boat. **Anse Marechal** is liked for its palm forest and fine, white sand. **Grand Cul-de-Sac** is a shallow lagoon with a seaside restaurant and good windsurfing. **Anse de Petit Cul-de-Sac** is an anchorage for the local fishing fleet. **Anse Toiny** is usually washed by breakers, so it isn't recommended for swimming but it's a wildly beautiful beach for walking. **Anse de Grand Fond** and **Washing Machine** are, like Anse Toiny, on the windward side of the island and are not recommended for swimming except in settled weather. Crashing waves, diving pelicans and windblown spume make these areas superb for walking. **Anse de Grande Saline** on the south side of the island has a wide stretch of sand and very gradual descent. **Anse de Chauvette** is an emerald pool reached only by boat. It's a wonderful find for skin diving.

On the leeward side, **Anse de Gouveneur** is accessed via Lurin. **Anse de Grand Galet** in the heart of Gustavia is good for shelling, swimming, and watching sunsets. Also in town, **Anse de Public** is good for sunset viewing. **Anse de Corossol** is a little beach frequented by families; the bay is used by fishermen. **Anse de Reine** and **Anse de Gascon** on the northwest shore are reached only by boat, and have good diving and snorkeling.

Anse de Columbier, with its pristine sands, is a 20-minute walk from Flamands. **La Petite Anse**, found just around the northern point of the island, is a sea garden popular with scuba divers. Just beyond it is **Anse des Flamands** with a rim of white sand. **Anse a Galets** and **Anse des Cayes** on the north coast are popular spearfishing spots.

Boating

Boat rentals are available from **Marine Service** at the Yacht Club in Gustavia, *Tel. 27-70-34*. Waterskiing, deep sea fishing, snorkel and scuba trips, and day sails can be arranged.

Fishing

Book a sportfishing trip with **Ocean Must**, *Tel. 27-62-25*, **Marine Service**, *Tel. 27-70-34*, or **Capitaine Jerome Leford**, *Tel. 27-62-65*. Half-day charters are about 2,500F with drinks; full-day charters are about 4,000F with meals and drinks. Both prices are for four people and include gear and bait.

Hiking

Walk the old path left when a bulldozer blazed a way between **Gouverneur** and **Saline** to find the secluded cove known as **Chauvette**. Clouds of butterflies flit among wildflowers and blizzards of pear blossoms, while cattle browse in the golden grasses beyond. Along the way you'll see ruins of old wells.

Horseback Riding

To arrange lessons or a ride call **Ranch Des Flamands**, *Tel. 27-80-72*. Daily two-hour trail rides cost about $35.

Parasailing

Book with **Wind Wave Power**, *Tel. 27-62-73*.

Sailing & Yachting

For yachties, the best place for news, networking and supplies is **Loulou's Marine** in Gustavia, *Tel. 27-62-74*. For day sails, snorkeling, sunset sails and picnic cruising try **Marine Service**, *Tel. 27-70-34* and **Ocean Must**, *Tel. 27-62-25*. A full day's sail with meals and drinks costs about 480F per person.

Scuba Diving

St. Barts has its own underwater fireworks spelled out in sponges, coral, and brilliant reef fish off beaches on the main island and a sprinkling of islets nearby. Wreck divers can explore the *Lutece*, a 1965 fishing trawler that was sunk as an artificial reef in 1994, and a once-fabulous yacht, the *Non-Stop*.

Trips cost about 250F, gear included. Night dives are available. Dive operators include:
- **Marine Service**. *Tel. 27-70-34*
- **St. Barth Plongée**. *Tel. 27-54-44*
- **Ocean Must**. *Tel. 27-62-25*
- **Rainbow Dive Boat**. *Tel. 27-91-79*
- **Scuba Club la Bulle**. *Tel. 27-68-93*

Squash

An air conditioned squash court is in the deluxe hotel **Isle de France** on Anse des Flamands beach, *Tel. 27-61-81.*

Tennis

If your hotel doesn't have tennis courts, try **Le Flambouyant Tennis Club**, *Tel. 27-69-82;* the **Youth Association of Lorient** and the **Sports Center of Columbier**, *Tel. 27-61-07 or 27-62-38.* Lessons are available through Yves Lacoste at **SB Sports Agency**, *Tel. 27-68-06.*

Water Skiing

Skiers of any level of proficiency can book with **Marine Service**, *Tel. 27-70-34.* Also try **Ocean Must**, *Tel. 27-62-25.*

Windsurfing

The best board sailing is at St. Jean, Grand Cul de Sac, Washing Machine, Flamands, and Lorient. Rentals and lessons are available from **St. Barth Wind School**, *Tel. 27-62-73.*

SHOPPING

As a duty-free port, St. Barts spreads a wonderful bazaar of imports in stores familiar to Caribbean shoppers such as Little Switzerland, Diamond Genesis, Samaly, Versace, Le Colobri and Oro de Sol, all found in Gustavia. Those in search of uniquely St. Bartian souvenirs can try **La Quichenotte**, a store named for the starchy bonnet that is still worn by local women on feast days. The **St. Barths Line Laboratory** in Lorient makes and sells natural cosmetics, the island's only export. Advertised in the most tony fashion magazines in Europe and the United States, they're available here at hometown prices.

Shop for locally-made straw hats and baskets, which are exceptionally delicate. **Les Artisans** in Les Hauts Du Carré D'Or in Gustavia has handmade jewelry, local arts and crafts, and old and new maps. Original jewelry is made by young goldsmith **Fabienne Miot**, whose studio is on the Quai de la Republique.

Two dozen or more talented painters hark to their muses in St. Barts, where they work in media and metiers to suit every taste. See their work at such galleries as **Marigot Bay Art Gallery**, across from the Marigot Bay Club; **The Painter's Gallery** on the Carenage in Saint Jean, **Le Bistrot Des Artes** on the Rue Jeanne d'Arc; **J. Fabas Atelier** on the Rue de la Paix, **Martine Cotten Pastels** at the Rue du port and **Angle**, quai de la République.

Among unique souvenirs are the 50-franc/50-ecu coins that were minted in 1988 to commemorate the enduring friendship between Sweden and St. Barts. The coins are legal tender in both Sweden and St. Barts but most of them end up in collections. The island also has a tee shirt factory just past L'Escale in Gustavia. Note that most shops close for two hours at noon but may stay open until 7pm.

EXCURSIONS & DAY TRIPS

Although most travels on St. Barts center around getting to restaurants and beaches, three sightseeing routes are recommended. From **Gustavia**, go northwest to **Public** to see the old Swedish cemetery. Stop in **Corossol**, a photo-op fishing village with a world class seashell museum. **Columbier** is the home of straw work and white bonnets. **Flamands**, population 250, offers hotels and beaches.

On an eastern loop from Gustavia, go to **Saint Jean** with its flashy shopping and restaurants, **Lorient** with its boutiques and a post office, then to **Marigot**, **Grand Cul-de-Sac**, and westward through the **Grand Fond Valley** with a side trip to **Salines** for the salt ponds and birdwatching. Return to Gustavia on the Royal Road.

Three tours are offered by the **Office of Tourism**, *Tel. 27-87-27*, all leaving by mini-bus from the pier in front of the office on the Quai Général de Gaulle in Gustavia, The 45-minute trip through **Colombier**, **Flamands**, **Corossol**, **Public**, and back to **Gustavia** makes one stop and costs 150F for three people and 200F for four or more. A one-hour excursion from Gustavia through **St. Jean**, **Salines**, **Grand Fond**, **Cul de Sac**, **Marigot**, and **Lorient**, returning to Gustavia, has two stops and costs 200F for up to three people and 250F for four or more. A 1 1/2-hour trip adds the villages of **Colombier** and **Corossol** to the previously described one-hour trip. Cost is 250F for up to three and 300F for four or more.

Excursions on St. Barts and to neighboring islands can be booked with **Saint-Barth Voyages** in the rue Duquesne on the far side of the harbor, *Tel. 27-79-79*.

PRACTICAL INFORMATION

Area Code: 590

Banking: Gustavia has a number of banks. Bank holidays include Good Friday, Armistice Day on May 8, Bastille Day on July 14, All Saints Day on November 1, Christmas, New Years Day. Banking hours are generally Monday to Friday, 8am to noon and 2pm to 3:30pm

Currency: although the French franc is the official currency, many prices are quoted in U.S. dollars, which circulate freely. Also legal tender, but purchased mostly as souvenirs, are coins minted in 50-franc and 50-Swedish ecu denominations. Sold here and in Sweden, they're symbolic of the bond that still exists among Sweden, France, and St. Barts. The franc trades at roughly five to the dollar.

Electricity: service is 220 volts. North American appliances needed adapters and converters. Your hotel may have them, but call ahead, especially if you need a computer hook-up.

Emergencies: a doctor is on call, *Tel. 27-76-03*. To call the police, *Tel. 27-66-66 or 27-60-12*; for fire, *Tel. 27-62-31*.

Government: St. Barts is part of Guadeloupe. U.S. consular matters are handled through Bridgetown, Barbados, *Tel. 246/436-4950*.

Immigration: Americans and Canadians need a valid passport or one that expired not more than five years ago, or a birth certificate or voter registration accompanied by a government-issued photo identification (such as a driver's license). Visitors also must have a return ticket. For stays of more than three months, a passport is needed.

Language: French is the official language and, while English is commonly spoken more than on some other of the French islands, knowledge of French is helpful.

Mail: post offices are found in Gustavia and Lorient. Both are small and have limited hours. The one at St. Jean Commercial Center across from the airport is open weekdays 9am to noon and 3pm to 5:30 and Saturday mornings until noon.

Medical matters: Gustavia has a hospital, *Tel. 27-60-35*, as well as doctors, dentists, and specialists. Pharmacies are at La Savane Commercial Center in St. Jean, *Tel. 27-66-61*, and in Gustavia, *Tel. 27-61-82*.

Pets: dogs and cats older than three months are allowed in temporarily with certificates of rabies inoculation and health from a licensed veterinarian. Check with your hotel, however, before bringing a pet.

Tax: departure tax at the airport is 30F. There is no hotel tax, but service charges add 5% to 15% to the bill.

Telephones: buy a prepaid telephone card at the post offices, book store and gas station. To call St. Barts from the United States dial 011-590. To call the United States from St. Barts dial 19-1. Phone booths are found Gustavia, at the airport, and at several other spots on the island.

Tourist Information: The tourist office on the Quai de Général de Gaulle in Gustavia is open weekdays. *Tel. 27-60-08.* For further information from the United States, *Tel. 900/990-0040.* The call costs 95 cents a minute. Or, write the French Government Tourist Office, *444 Madison Avenue, New York NY 10022.* In Canada, write the French Government Tourist Office, *1981 Avenue McGill College 490, Montreal, Quebec, H3A 2W9, Tel. 514/288-4264, Fax 844-8901; or 30 St. Patrick Street, Suite 700, Toronto, Ontario M5T 3A3, Tel. 416/593-6427, Fax 979-7587.*

OUT ISLAND SURVIVAL

Getting to small islands often involves riding two or more airplanes or a combination of airplanes and ferries, so it's best to keep control of your luggage rather than checking it all the way through from your home airport to the destination. If you can't manage with carry-ons, check bags to your intermediate stop such as St. Thomas or St. Martin, claim them there, then check them for the next leg. It's also essential to reconfirm your return trip with the carrier that brought you to the destination.

JAMAICA

APPENDIX

36. JAMAICA

Jamaica has its tourism ups and downs but, despite the occasional bad press, it is one of the savviest of tourist destinations with excellent resources for pre-trip planning and on-island support. Every major community has an office of tourism and Jamaica is also represented throughout North America and in such far-flung cities as London, Tokyo, Paris, and Frankfurt.

Today's attitude towards tourism is summed up by a step-on guide who joined a small group of us who were touring in a mini-bus. She began by defining the word you'll hear constantly in the island, *"Irie,"* meaning "All right." Remember the children's song, "If you're happy and you know it, clap your hands"? She soon had us caroling like kids, "If you're happy and you know it, say Irie!" for verse after hilarious verse.

Another guide solemnly thanked us for coming. "You are important to us," he said to a cluster of tourists at an agriculture park. "You feed our families." It's true that Jamaica has drugs and crime, the occasional sullen face, and service that can be as slow as frozen butter on cold toast. Still, Jamaica gets a hearty Irie from us.

Jamaica is also cashing in on its growing importance as a financial crossroads. **Kingston**, the largest English-speaking city south of Miami, boasts world class business hotels, upscale shopping, top entertainment and dining, and an increasingly powerful banking center.

It's said that, in describing Jamaica to Queen Isabella, Christopher Columbus crumpled a piece of paper in his hand to show how dramatic mountains crumple up into the clouds and careen down forested hillsides to flawless beaches. He named the island for St. Jago, but it soon reverted to Xaymaca, the Arawak word for "wooded and watered."

The island has a roistering history filled with pirates, earthquakes, endless battles between English and French, sugar and slaves, and screaming hurricanes. So remote are the mountains that escaped slaves, organized as the Maroons, fought the government to a standstill. To this day, they are independent and free in the remote hills of Cockpit Country.

PARLEZ-VOUS ARAWAK?

When the Spanish arrived in Jamaica, it was peopled by peaceful Arawaks who soon died of disease, slavery, and massacre. Today, nothing remains of the tribe but scraps of language. Jamaica (xaymaca means land of woods and water), hammock, canoe, tobacco, potato, hurricane, maize, barbecue, cannibal, and canoe are all Arawak words.

Jamaica's history began with the Arawaks, who migrated to the island from the Orinocco area of South America. Their history here has been traced to as early as 1000 A.D. European conquest began on May 4, 1494 with the coming of Christopher Columbus, who landed at what we now call Discovery Bay. Later, he was to call Montego Bay the "Bay of Good Weather."

Columbus was stranded for a year at St. Ann's Bay on the north coast where he founded Seville Nueva. By 1538, it was abandoned and the capital became Spanish Town on the south coast. The island was captured by the English in 1655 after the Spanish, discouraged at finding no gold or silver here, gave up without a fight. A century of lawlessness followed, fueled by piracy and skulduggery. Notorious pirate Henry Morgan was headquartered in Port Royal, where his unusual business practices were overlooked by his pal, the governor. Port Royal thrived as a cesspool of prostitution, rum swoggling, and thievery until an earthquake struck without warning in 1692. In a cataclysm of Old Testament proportions, Port Royal slid into the sea.

The slave trade continued to flourish. Sugar cane, and its byproducts rum and molasses, ruled the island while black backs, glistening in the sun, gradually stiffened in resentment. Rebellion finally boiled over, lives were lost on both sides, and eventually the slaves were freed. Many of the island's grandest greathouses were burned in the turmoil. Those that survived were mostly those of masters who had been kind, a pleasant thought to hold when you are touring or staying in a manor that is now an inn.

Planters too were rebels. During the American Revolution, they voted to join the colonies. The thought was quickly suppressed by the king's men but still today, Americans feel a kinship with the free-thinking Jamaican people.

At one point Jamaica was thought to be in danger of falling into the Cuban orbit, but the socialist government was thrown out and the country began a recovery program based on industry, banking, and a hearty welcome for people willing to invest in its tourism industry. In terms of

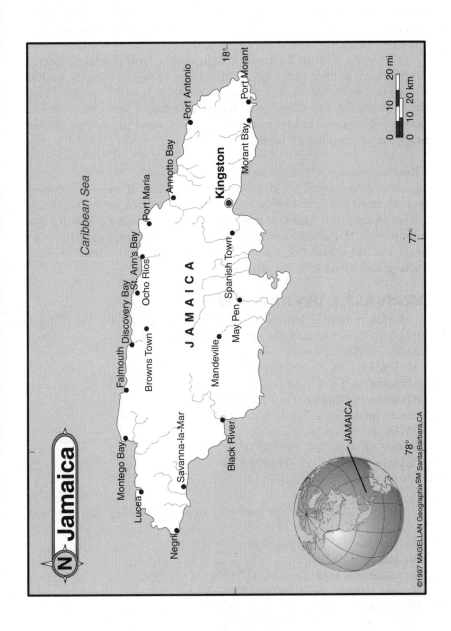

human justice, it has a long way to go. Drugs and crime are as rampant here as they are in major North American cities. Homeless children can be seen on Kingston streets. Education is not compulsory; unemployment and poverty are sad to see but the turn-around is in motion. It's exciting to watch.

Today's cash crops are bauxite, rum, spices, farm products, coffee, international finance and, most of all, tourism fueled by friendly, funny, sometimes exasperating, but always interesting, Jamaican people. The third largest of the Caribbean islands covering 4,400 square miles, Jamaica offers more beauty and more variety in more places than almost any vacation paradise on earth.

Climate
Mountainous and huge, Jamaica has a variety of weather ranging from the chill and drizzle of the high mountains to the steamy heat of the coasts. During hurricanes, as much as 10 inches of rain can fall in a 24-hour period. Highs in Kingston are in the mid-90s most days and lows are in the low 60s or high 50s. January through March are the driest months in Kingston; October is the rainiest.

ARRIVALS & DEPARTURES
Norman Manley International Airport lies on a long spit of land tucked under Kingston right in the harbor. It is served by:
• **ALM**, *Tel. 876/924-8092*
• **Air Canada**, *Tel. 876/924-8211*
• **Air Jamaica**, *Tel. 876/922-4661*
• **Air Jamaica Express**, *Tel. 876/922-4661*
• **American Airlines**, *Tel. 876/924-8305*
• **BWIA**, *Tel. 876/929-3770*
• **British Airways**, *Tel. 876/929-9020*
• **Cayman Airways**, *Tel. 876/926-1762*
• **US Airways**, *Tel. 800/622-1015*

Sir Donald Sangster International Airport at Montego Bay is served by:
• **Air Canada**, *Tel. 876/952-5160*
• **Air Jamaica**, *952-4300*
• **American Airlines**, *Tel. 876/952-5950*
• **British Airways**, *Tel. 876/940-0890*
• **Continental Airlines**, *Tel. 876/952-4495*
• **Northwest Airlines**, *Tel. 876/952-4033*

Air Jamaica also flies into **Negril**, *Tel. 876/957-4210,* and **Ocho Rios**, *Tel. 876/974-2566.* Jamaica Express also serves **Ken Jones Aerodrome**, 45 minutes west of the main resort area of Port Antonio. However, at this writing flights do not coordinate well with international arrivals, and they require transfer to a satellite airport near Kingston. Except for those who come in corporate jets, most visitors prefer to make the three-hour trip from Kingston by car.

ORIENTATION

The third largest of the Caribbean islands, Jamaica is 146 miles long and 22 to 51 miles wide. It is divided into three counties and 14 parishes. Thanks to its sophistication as a tourist destination, it provides one of the best road maps (but not the best roads) in the Caribbean. Request one in your information packet from the Jamaica Tourist Board (see *Practical Information*).

Highways are numbered but can be difficult to follow because signs are infrequent, often leaving you at a fork with no clue to which one to take. Usually, signs just point to the next village, so it's more important to know the names of the communities along your route than to know the route numbers. Keep track of the compass and stop to ask the friendly locals any time you're in doubt about a direction.

Numbered highways include the A4, which runs southeast from Kingston and around the coast, turning north and following the coast to where it becomes the A3 at Annotto Bay. The A3 then turns south back to Kingston or turns west to continue following the north coast to St. Ann's Bay, where it becomes the A1. It stays with the coast, turning south to end at Negril, 55 miles southwest of Montego Bay.

The route from Kingston to Ocho Rios is the A1, going west out of Kingston to Spanish Town, then north. After crossing Mount Diablo, it forks. Take the A1 to St. Ann's Bay and Montego Bay or the A3 to Ocho Rios. A2 starts at Savanna-La-Mar and goes southeast to Black River, then winds wildly north and east to bring you to Mandeville, May Pen, and back to Spanish Town. One more suggestion: don't drive at night, especially on unfamiliar roads. We have been lost while alone but also with drivers and guides who were lost too.

Jamaica's six main tourism areas are: **Montego Bay** on the northwest coast with its grand beaches; **Negril** on the west coast with its low-rise buildings and high-rise palm trees; **Ocho Rios** with its hills and waterfalls; **Port Antonio**, land of hills and hideaways; and **Mandeville** inland in mountains 2,000 feet above sea level; and **Kingston** with its culture, commerce, and cuisine.

GETTING AROUND JAMAICA

Hard-surfaced principal highways are bad; hard-surface secondary roads are worse; and other so-called roads are a commando course of narrow tracks, potholes, soft shoulders, and other terrors. Although the speed limit on the open road is 50 miles per hour, we can't remember ever being able to reach it or the 30 miles-per-hour limit in towns. A change for the better, however, is taking place on the north coast highway linking Negril, Montego Bay, Runaway Bay, Ocho Rios, and Port Antonio. In 1997, a $60 million improvement program was started, which will probably completed by 2000. An additional $200 million is being spent island-wide to upgrade traffic signals and road surfaces.

Still, roads are so hazardous that one major credit card company just withdrew its automatic collision damage waiver insurance for cars rented on Jamaica. Hill driving is especially snaky and steep, with single lanes in places. If you meet someone coming the other way, one of you has to back up. Allow twice as much time to get anywhere as you think it will take and drive twice as carefully as you would at home. As long as you adjust your attitude to accept delays, it's part of the charm of the place.

Taxis, some of which are metered, charge according to rates set by the Jamaica Union of Travellers Association, but be sure to agree on a rate, and in what currency, before you load your bags aboard. Ride only taxis that have a red license plate and a "PP" designation and in mini-vans with a red "PPV" plate. Buses are hot, slow, and crowded and are not recommended even as a cross-cultural experience.

The lack of reliable public transportation in Jamaica makes a rental car a necessity unless you can arrange transfers to a big resort and are content to stay there. Considering the fine quality of Jamaican resorts and the wide choice of excursions they offer, this is not a bad option.

Rental car rates and insurances are high and a deposit of hundreds of dollars may be required. If you must have a car, it's best to stick with cars that can be booked from the United States. **Kemwel's rental cars** are available in Kingston or Montego Bay at about $299 to $439 per week plus $6 collision damage waiver. To reserve from the U.S., *Tel. 800/678-0678.* **Avis** has agencies in Kingston and Montego Bay, *Tel. 800/331-1212;* **Budget** has agents in Kingston, Montego Bay and Ocho Rios, *Tel. 800/ 527-0700;* and **United Car Rentals** has agents in Kingston and Montego Bay, *Tel. 800/815-5019,* in the U.S. and Canada.

The Discover Jamaica road map, which is a must, has detail maps of Spanish Town, Port Antonio, Mandeville, Montego Bay, Negril, Ocho Rios, and Kingston, plus a map of downtown Kingston.

Kingston

Cruise passengers debark along Ocean Boulevard, which is within walking distance of the crafts market, National Gallery, post office, St. William Grant Park, and other points of interest. If you're in a rental car, you'll come in from the airport on Windward Road, which becomes Spanish Town Road or the A1, a major thoroughfare from Grant Park to the northwest and Spanish Town. Parallel to it a few blocks south, Marcus Garvey Drive is the highway that follows the waterline of Kingston Bay.

Kingston will remind you of London in the way roads simply change names for no apparent reason. Chief east-west roads include Dunrobin Avenue/Washington Boulevard and Old Hope Road/Hope Road/Hagley Park Road running west from Hope Botanical Gardens to Spanish Town Road. If you stick with Old Hope Road and veer south, it becomes Slipe Road into the heart of downtown. To find a residential address in the surrounding mountains after dark in the rain requires not just a good map, but luck and extrasensory perception.

Mandeville

The A2, also known as Winston Jones Parkway, skirts the west edge of Mandeville. The city's chief north-south road is New Green Road/ Caledonia Road/Perth Road. Main roads to the west are Calendonia Road or Villa Road. Main Street is the main drag, running south from Caledonia to Villa and Park Circle, where the police station is located.

Montego Bay

The A1, also known as the Queen's Drive, brings you into Montego Bay from the east along the north coast. It jogs south of the airport and will take you into the city and out the other side. As it does, it assumes such names as Port Street, Humber Avenue and Cottage Street (one way east and south) or St. James Street and Barnett Street (one-way to the north).

Negril

Stick with Norman Manley Boulevard, which is also the A1, along the coast. To one side is the ocean, which can hardly be seen from the road because the beach is filled with shoulder-to-shoulder hotels. To the other lies a wilderness known as the Great Morass. The A1 ends at the crafts market, where there's also an office of the Jamaica Tourist Board and a post office. It's at West End Road, which goes west and Sheffield Road, which heads east.

Ocho Rios

The A3 brings you into Ocho Rios from the south, then it is also known as Dacosta Drive as it turns west towards St. Ann's Bay. Running parallel to the highway just north of it, Main Street has a Jamaica Tourist Board office, shopping, and crafts.

Port Antonio

The A4, also called Allan Avenue and West Palm Avenue, is the main route through Port Antonio following East Harbour, then West Harbour. To find the heart of the old city, leave the A4 by turning right on Gideon Avenue across from the parish church, and drive to the end at historic Titchfield School, then back via Fort George.

Spanish Town

The A2 goes through Spanish Town east and west on Bourkes Road/Oxford Road/Wellington Street. Approaching from the east, take Barrett Street northeast at the Prison Oval cricket ground, then north on White Church Street to the park, which is the center of the city. From the west, leave the A2 on Manchester Street, which will take you to King Street and the center of town.

WHERE TO STAY

Rates are given in U.S. dollars for two people in a double room in high season. Rates will be lower in summer and shoulder seasons. Always ask about packages. There is an additional 15 percent tax on rooms. Service charges, which are usually added in lieu of gratuities, usually add another 10 to 15 percent.

Note that many of Jamaican resorts are all-inclusive and the tariff quoted includes all meals, drinks, airport transfers, sports, free stays, programs for children and much more, including those whopping taxes and tips. While a nightly rate of $400 or more may seem high, take another look at what you're getting for the money.

Your mailing address here will be c/o Hotel, Post Office Box Number, City, Jamaica, West Indies.

KINGSTON
Expensive

CROWNE PLAZA KINGSTON, *211 Constant Spring Road, Kingston 8. Tel. 876/925-7676, Fax 925-5757; U.S. and Canada 800/618-6534. Four miles from New Kingston, the financial center of Jamaica, the hotel is 14 miles north of Norman Manley International Airport; airport shuttles run regularly. Rooms in this 135-room hotel start at $199. Taxi fare from the airport is about $20.*

The best in business amenities has come to the edge of town in a modern, high-rise hotel. Each room has a "smart desk" with two-line telephone, direct dial service, voice mail, and dataport for your computer modem. In the Club floor, which has private key access and its own registration and checkout, rooms, also have fax machines. Live in comfort with individual climate control, cable television with remote control, safe, coffee maker, and mini-bar. Each room is permanently designated smoking or non-smoking.

After hours, enjoy the hotel's swimming pool, tennis, squash, and fitness center with sauna and whirlpool. The 18-hole Constant Spring Golf course and one of the city's swankiest shopping malls are just a few minutes away.

Dine on international gourmet food or spicy Jamaican dishes in the hotel's flagship restaurant, Isabella. Fort Belle Bistro is informal and poolside. Some suites, kitchenettes, and a two-bedroom Presidential Suite are available at rates up to $550.

MAYFAIR HOTEL, *4 West Kings House Close, Kingston 10. Tel. 876/ 926-1610. Rates at this 40-unit hotel, which adjoins the governor's residence, start at $150. Taxi fare from the airport is about $20.*

The address couldn't be better. For elegance and privacy you can't beat the eight houses, each in its own garden, that are available in addition to the hotel rooms and suites. It's city living, convenient to everything, with friendly poolside barbecues twice a week, and a long pool for swimming laps.

STRAWBERRY HILL, *Irishtown. Tel. 944-8400, Fax 994-8203; U.S. and Canada 800/OUTPOST. Guests are picked up and transported free from Kingston's airport. The drive is 40-50 minutes; a seven-minute helicopter transfer is available at added cost. Rates are $175 to $625, double or single occupancy, including continental breakfast.*

You're cradled in the Blue Mountains 3,100 feet above sea level when you stay in this little heaven with its 360-degree view of green hills. Chris Blackwell of Island Records fame bought the hideaway for entertaining artists including Bob Marley and the Rolling Stones. After it was destroyed by a hurricane in 1988, it was rebuilt as a complex of 12 villas with studio suites or suites with one to four bedrooms, some with kitchen.

Rich mahogany and rattan furniture, built by gifted local craftsmen, contrasts with lots of whites and neutrals. Wrap-around porches are inspired by colonial times, when a breeze could always be found on one side of the house or other. Take dinner on the terrace, then relax in the library. A fireplace and electric mattress pads take the chill off cold mountain nights. Telephones, VCRs, television, CD players and fax machines are available on request. "New Jamaica" cuisine is the order of the day, combining traditional ingredients with international touches. Try the curried cho-cho soup with grilled shrimp and fresh cilantro, dasheen gnocchi, grilled snapper with mango and sweet pepper salsa, and

Blue Mountain creme brulée. High tea is served on weekends, and on Sundays, a special Jamaican brunch. Massage and yoga, excursions, tours, and guided hikes can be arranged.

WYNDHAM KINGSTON HOTEL, *77 Knutsford Boulevard, Kingston 10, Jamaica. Tel. 876/926-5430, Fax 876/929-7439. U.S. and Canada toll-free 800/WYNDHAM. Taxi fare from the airport is about $20.*

If you need a first class business hotel for all or part of your stay, the Wyndham is equal to the best anywhere. On the four Presidential Club floors, rooms have two-line phones with computer port access. The Business Centre is open 24 hours a day, Four Presidential Club floors have complimentary breakfast, cocktails, and hors d'oeuvres in a gracious Club Lounge with its own concierge. All rooms are oversize and have direct dial phones, individual thermostatic control, satellite television with remote control, and a hair dryer, safe, and coffeemaker in each room.

There is plenty here for the leisure traveler who wants to stay in the heart of downtown Kingston: an Olympic-size swimming pool, health club, duty-free shopping, lighted tennis courts, and a gaming room with 50 slot machines. The hotel's Jonkanoo Lounge is one of the city's most upscale nightspots, featuring live jazz. For more casual dining and drinking, try the pool bar where there's a poolside barbecue once a week. The Terrace Cafe serves informally breakfast through dinner; the Palm Court with its pasta bar is the hotel's destination restaurant, serving international cuisine.

Selected as one of my Best Places to Stay; see Chapter 13 for more details.

JAMAICA PEGASUS, *81 Knutsford Boulevard, P.O. Box 335, Kingston 5, Jamaica. Tel. 876/926-3690/9, Fax 876/929-3833.*

Like the Wyndham and within walking distance of it, this goliath hotel is a snappy, business-savvy gathering spot for diplomats and local and visiting businesspeople. Both hotels are in the heart of what is developing as a major Caribbean financial, cultural, and business center. The art gallery in the Pegasus shows some of the island's best artists and the hotel is also home to one of Kingston's two Bijoux jewelry stores, famed for their fine watches, crystals and gems sold duty free. The casual restaurant serves a breakfast buffet laden with traditional fare plus native specialties including ackee, tropical fruits, and liver with boiled bananas. High tea is served daily at the Promenade. Choose between two restaurants and two bars plus those at the Wyndham next door within walking distance.

HOTEL FOUR SEASONS, *18 Ruthven road, Kingston 10, Jamaica. Tel. 876/929-7655, Fax 876/929-5964, U.S. and Canada toll-free, 800/74-CHARMS. Rates at this 80-room hotel start at $125.*

Not to be confused with the elegant, international Four Seasons chain, this European-style hotel has its own elegance in an intimate,

---

ABOUT SUPERCLUBS

*Among Jamaica's famous all-inclusive resorts are SuperClubs that call themselves super-inclusive because there are no extras at all, not even tipping (it isn't permitted). They include the **Grand Lido** and **Hedonism II** in Negril and **Breezes Runaway Bay** and **Montego Bay**. All of them are on white sand beaches. All offer gourmet dining, a wide range of motorized and non-motorized watersports, premium brand drinks, all-night entertainment, and non-stop brouhaha. Even weddings are free. Of them all, Hedonism II is the swingingest, with one section where clothes are required only at meals. The favorite hangout is a huge hot tub known as the sperm bank. If you want to go as a single, couple, or family, ask which resort is best for kind of the vacation you have in mind. Call 800/859-SUPER and ask about packages that include accommodations, air fare, and much more.*

---

garden setting. The hotel has only 39 rooms and is as well known for its cuisine as for its modern facilities: telephones, air conditioning, and satellite television.

Holder of two AAA diamonds and a member of The Best Hotels and Resorts in the Caribbean, it's an excellent choice for visitors who want to stay in the heart of town but prefer a smaller and more personal hotel.

Moderate

MORGAN'S HARBOUR HOTEL, *Port Royal. Tel. 876/924-8464, Fax 876/924-8562 or 8146. U.S. and Canada 800/526-2422; Miami, Tel. 305/666-0447. Rates start at $169.*

Only a dubloon's throw across the harbor from downtown Kingston, this lands-end resort is typical of marina resorts that are common in the Caribbean yet are rare in Jamaica, which is off the beaten path for the round-the-world sailing crowd. This 45-room hotel is a nice blend of yachties, beach bums, and chic visitors from all over the world. Best of all for the tourist who can spare only a few days for a Jamaican getaway, it's a short jump from the airport, which lies on the long strip of land that ends at Port Royal.

Rooms are air conditioned and have satellite television. Through the marina you can sign on for sailing, deep sea fishing, and all the watersports. Then have a gourmet dinner, a moonlight cruise, and disco until dawn. Start the day with a swim off the resort's private beach and you can still make an early flight with little worry about traffic tieups.

TERRA NOVA HOTEL, *17 Waterloo Road. Tel. 876/926-9334, Fax 876/960-0281. Rates at this 35-room, 14-suite hotel start at $165. Cab fare from the airport is about $20. It's a five-minute drive from the business district.*

A grand mansion built in the 1920s as a wedding present for a young couple, this plantation greathouse and its newer wings offer double rooms and junior suites with air conditioning, telephone, and television. Junior suites are designed for the businessperson, offering a work desk, direct dial telephone, seating area, and satellite television linked to international news and movie networks. The restaurant is liked locally for its Jamaican food, especially its soups and fresh seafood.

Budget

IVOR GUEST HOUSE, *Jacks Hill, Kingston 6. Tel. 876/977-0033 or 927-1460. Rates at this three-room guest house start at $80 including continental breakfast. It's 20 minutes northeast of the city in the hills.*

Escape the city in this mountainside inn, known for its views and its popular restaurant and bar that look out over a sea of city lights far below. Cottages, which are richly furnished in Jamaican mahogany, have private bath, fans, and telephone, and children are welcome. Television is available in the lounge.

MAYA LODGE, *Jacks Hill. Tel. 876/927-2097 or 800/532-2271. Rates at this nine-room lodge start at $50 for two in a twin room and communal bath. Campsites and hostel accommodations are also available. The lodge is three miles northeast of Kingston in the Blue Mountains. Credit cards aren't accepted.*

This is rough, outback living surrounded by the natural beauty of the craggy mountains. The hostel is a cabin that can sleep five to ten people who pay $20 per person and share the campground bath facilities. Tent sites are $5 per person, with an extra $10 to rent the use of a two-person tent. It's the ideal base camp for exploring nearby streams and forests; from your doorstep you can hike the historic Vinegar Hill Trail. The lodge is at an altitude of 1,750 feet on 16 wilderness acres. Traditional Jamaican meals including Blue Mountain coffee are served in the Maya Garden Cafe.

OCHO RIOS

Taxi fare from Kingston to Ocho Rios is about $120 each way. From Montego Bay, its about $70 each way.

Expensive

CIBONEY OCHO RIOS, *Main Street, P.O. Box 728, St. Ann, Jamaica. Tel. 876/974-1027, Fax 974-5838; U.S. and Canada 800/333-3333. Rooms at this 300-unit, 45-acre resort start at $300 per person per night all-inclusive. Transfer from Montego Bay's airport, 67 miles away, is complimentary.*

A AAA Four-Diamond Radisson resort, Ciboney (pronounced SIB-bonnee) provides meals, all beverages, some spa services, tennis, squash, lawn and beach games, entertainments and activities, and a host of watersports all at one price. Packages that include transfers from Montego Bay, tips, and taxes are the best value. In the low season, room upgrades may also be offered. Centered around the Great House, which is fashioned after the grand manors of the plantation era, are villas with one, two, or three bedrooms. Every suite has its own private pool; honeymoon villas have a privacy fence, swimming pool in an enclosed courtyard, and a Jacuzzi with Roman tub in the master bedroom. Each villa has a fully-stocked bar, satellite television, and VCR.

The Elysium Spa here is one of the island's finest European-type spas and fitness centers, with separate facilities for men and women and a long menu of fitness equipment and professional services such as reflexology, skin care and body tone treatments, massage, facials, paraffin treatments, and a full-service beauty salon. Swim-up bars are found at the Greathouse and Beach Club pools.

Take your meals in Orchids, which specializes in haute cuisine developed in concert with the Culinary Institute of America, in the The Manor Restaurant and Bar for piano-accompanied Jamaican classics indoors or out, the Casa Nina for Italian specialties, or the Ciboney Grill & Market Place with its trendy, contemporary menu and colorful market decor. After dinner, dance the night away at Nicole, featuring live music and entertainment.

JAMAICA INN, *Main Street, two miles east of Ocho Rios. Tel. 876/974-2514; U.S. 800/837-4608 or fax 800/404-1841. Rates at this 45-unit inn start at $475 including all meals. The hotel is a two-hour drive from Montego Bay and 10 minutes from Ocho Rios.*

Since the 1950s this refined, family-operated, Wedgewood blue hotel has been the choice of movie stars and political bigwigs, including Winston Churchill, who came to Jamaica to capture its brilliant color with his oil paints. Rooms are furnished in Jamaican antiques. Each room opens onto a furnished private veranda with views of the Caribbean. Amenities include special colognes and shampoos, cotton robes, fresh flowers, and cotton robes. Meals from chef Wilbert Matheson's kitchen were praised in a cover story in *Gourmet* magazine; dining is *al fresco* on a romantic terrace. Planter's Punch is served afternoons on the beach. Rates include use of the hotel's watersports equipment, croquet, unlimited tennis, and the exercise room.

It's all slightly prim, old Jamaica, and comfortable as an old house slipper yet formal enough to make guests feel privileged. The rule requiring gentlemen to wear jackets after 7pm has been relaxed in summer but, in high season, jackets and ties are required and it's not uncommon for men to dine in black tie just as they did in the days when Winston Churchill came here, stayed in the White Suite, and painted the ocean view from his balcony.

Now on its second and third generations of families who come back year after year, the property spreads over six acres of oceanfront with its own cove and a private, 700-foot brown sugar beach. Every room – actually they're more like junior suites – has a balcony furnished almost like a living room with rocking chair, writing desk, breakfast table, wing chair with ottoman, and louvered doors that open up a sleeping space furnished with antiques. It's a dazzling surprise to step into your room here and see the turquoise ocean so close and clear.

The staff ratio is high, 130 people to 45 rooms, and most of them have been here so long they anticipate guest needs as if they were old family retainers. Rooms are serviced three times a day with fresh towels, flowers and fuss. The owners are often in residence; longtime manager Rudi Schoenbein sits in an open office where guests can drift in and out to make comments, ask questions, or just pass the time of day. It's rather like staying at a Jamaican home in the 1940s, your hosts ever-attentive.

Although outings and tours of all kinds can be arranged, Jamaica Inn attracts successful, high-voltage guests who come here for what the Inn calls "relentless relaxation." There are no activities, group meetings, or spas, although you can play tennis free at a neighboring hotel or borrow the inn's snorkeling gear. Horseback riding and golf can be arranged. Sailing and sea kayaking off the inn's beach are free. Massage in your room is by appointment.

PLANTATION INN, *P.O. Box 2, Ocho Rios. Tel. 974-5899, Fax 974-5912; U.S. 800/752-6824. Rates start at $215 for a superior double room and range to $534 nightly for two in a one-bedroom penthouse suite. The resort is on Main Street at Coconut Grove, Ocho Rios, 90 minutes by car from the airport at Montego Bay and 15 minutes from Boscobel Airport, which accommodates private and charter aircraft.*

Even if you take the European Plan (no meals), you'll be greeted with a fruit basket and welcomed to a weekly cocktail party, afternoon tea, and the Inn's watersports. Or take a meal plan for $60 per person daily for breakfast and dinner or the $90 per person per day all-inclusive plan that provides airport transfers, three meals daily, open bar, and hotel taxes and service charges. Children pay half the adult rate. For $130, the Platinum Plan offers all other features plus daily golf (15 minutes away) and scuba diving, a horseback riding session, and a tour of Ocho Rios.

Mahogany furniture and delicate creams and pastels give a rich look to ocean-view rooms overlooking a splendid sand beach backed by a fringe of palms. In addition to its 63 rooms, the resort has 17 luxury suites with mini-bars and two villas with private pools. Play tennis, get a massage at the spa, have breakfast on your balcony, or hang out at the pool overlooking the ocean. For dinner, have grilled shrimp on the Bougain-villea Terrace, then dance to the Inn's own band or retreat to the quiet intimacy of the piano bar.

JAMAICA GRANDE RENAISSANCE RESORT, *Main Street, St. Ann, mailing address Box 100, Ocho Rios, Jamaica. Tel. 876/974-2201; U.S. 800/ 228-9898. The resort is 67 miles, or 1 3/4 hours from the airport at Montego Bay. Fare on the resort's shuttle is $25 round trip. Doubles start at $360 including meals, drinks and watersports. Stays of four days or more also include free airport transfers.*

This 720-room Renaissance resort has a James Bondian glamor thanks to its night club, casino with 80 slots and electronic blackjack, and movie-set surroundings. Night life here is hot, hot, hot. Any disco named Jamaican Me Crazy is worth an evening after a day spent in one of the pools or hot tubs. The "fantasy" pool is a city in itself, with a swim-up bar, waterfalls, and hanging bridge. Choose among five restaurants including the casual L'Allegro, the elegant Dragons, and the beach grill. Then spend a wild evening at the famous "Jump-Up" Carnival, a frenzied native tradition turned high-tech and trotted out nightly during busiest seasons.

Rooms feature balconies overlooking the sea and hills. Colors tend to the sun-burnished tones of beiges and melons, complementing furnish-ings of bentwood and bamboo. Take your pick of beach toys from colorful sailing prams to speedy jet-skis or just stake your claim to a quiet spot in sun or shade on the 1,300-foot white sand beach. Play tennis day or night, enroll the children in a year-round activities program, use the exercise center with its supervised aerobics, or have a massage or a hairdo.

ABOUT SANDALS

The name is perfect for this chain of romantic, barefoot, all-inclusive resorts for couples. Six of them are found on Jamaica – in **Negril, Dunn's River, Ocho Rios,** *and three in* **Montego Bay.** *When you stay at one you have dining and playing privileges at all six including golf at the Sandals in Ocho Rios. It's a culture shock at first to find that you won't have to open your wallet while you're at any Sandals. Premium brand bar drinks, wines with lunch and dinner, three scrumptious meals a day, and all sports and watersports are part of the deal. Dinner will be served by a white-gloved waiter at a table for two. Romance reigns.*

For an even more regal and romantic stay, book one of the suites with exclusive Suite Concierge Service. Your rooms will have a fully stocked bar, robes for him and her, four-poster bed, V.I.P check-in, and other perks. The toll-free number is Tel. 800/SANDALS.

Budget

SANDCASTLES APARTHOTEL, *Main Street, Ocho Rios. Tel. 800/ 562-7273, 876/974-5877, Fax 876/974-5362. The nearest airport is Montego Bay, 1 1/2 hours away. Rates start at $150.*

Turreted, castle-like apartment buildings are nestled among palms and greenery edged by a buttercream-white beach and the brilliant Caribbean. Stay in a studio, one-, or two-bedroom apartment or penthouse, each with a fully-equipped kitchen. Shop for provisions at the adjacent Ocean Village Shopping Centre. Swim in a freshwater pool, or off the beach, where you'll also find water scooters, day sailers, and wind sailers for rent. You're surrounded by other resorts, each with their own nightclubs and restaurants, so you can dine out for a month without running out of new places to sample. The resort has its own restaurant and bar too.

MONTEGO BAY

A taxi to most Montego hotels from the airport and among local hotels and restaurants costs about $10 each way.

Expensive

HALF MOON CLUB, *Rose Hall, mailing address Box 80, Montego Bay. Tel. 876/953-2211, Fax 953-1731. Rates at this 220-unit resort start at $300. Ask about meal and all-inclusive plans.*

Manager Heinz Simonitsch is a legend not just on Jamaica but throughout the Caribbean for his success in maintaining a high level of service and repeat guests. He has also won environmental awards for his eco-sensitive operation. The resort's 12-acre nature reserve is a mangrove wetland filled with bird life. So large is the resort that you'll have to take the shuttle to the golf course and shopping. Old-line guests prefer staying closer to the main buildings but for those who prefer privacy, there more remote cottages and villas. Even units that are right on the beach, however, are designed for maximum privacy indoors or out. Furnishings show their age here and there, but like those in a genteel mansion, it means a deeper glow on the mahogany here and a richer red in the oriental rug there.

Play tennis, golf, table tennis, or squash. The beach is picture-perfect, and watersports equipment is available for guest use. The resort has three restaurants, three bars, a dive center, and shops. Horseback riding can be arranged. Bicycles are available for guests.

TRYALL GOLF, TENNIS & BEACH RESORT, *Sandy Bay, mailing address Box 1206, Montego Bay. Tel. 876/956-5660, Fax 876/956-5673; U.S. and Canada, 800/742-0498 or 800/238-5290. Rates at this 47-room resort start at $270; the 49 villas at $375. It's 13 miles west of Montego Bay.*

Known for its 18-hole, 6,920-yard, seaside championship golf course, Tryall offers villas up to five bedrooms, each staffed with cook, butler, and maids. Or, stay in the Great House, which houses 52 deluxe hotel rooms, two restaurants, and three lounges. Guests can play the famous Plummer-designed golf course, swim laps in a supersize pool, sun and swim on the private beach, play tennis or explore the resort's 2,200 acres.

ROUND HILL HOTEL & VILLAS, *Hopewell, mailing address Box 84, Montego Bay. Tel. 876/952-5150, Fax 876/972-2159. Rates at this 36-room, 28-villa resort start at $300 double without meals. Villas are from $470. Meal plans are available. The hotel is eight miles west of Montego Bay.*

Opt for the Platinum Plan and you'll get all meals, cocktails, a half hour massage, a tour of Barnett Estate, a one-day scuba dive and a raft trip on the Great River. Ranked in the top 10 percent of the world's finest hotels by readers of *Condé Nast Traveler* magazine, this splendid property views the Caribbean from high above a coral rock peninsula. Luxury villas with up to four bedrooms are individually owned and decorated. They come with maid service that includes the preparation of your breakfast and nanny care for the children. Each villa has a private pool. Explore the resort's 100 acres, play tennis, work out in the fitness center, and dine in the hotel's elegant restaurant. Watersports and tours can be arranged.

WYNDHAM ROSE HALL, *mailing address Box 999, Montego Bay. Tel. 876/953-2650, Fax 876/953-2617; toll-free 800/WYNDHAM. Rates for the 489 rooms and 19 suites start at $175 for room only and from $355 for two, all inclusive.*

From the moment you arrive at the open-air entryway and enter a lobby as big as Rhode Island, awe is the key word at this busy, buzzy resort along 1,000 feet of wave-lapped beach. Once a 400-acre sugar plantation, the grounds are now sweetly planted to tropical blooms and flowering trees. Each of the 489 rooms and 19 suites has a private balcony looking out over the mountains or sea. The decor is crisp and clean with tile floors, neutral accents, and expanses of color in draperies and spreads. Play tennis by day or after dark under the floodlights. Go scuba diving, fishing, hiking in the Blue Mountains, or snorkeling off the beach. The hotel has three big, interconnecting swimming pools and its own, 18-hole championship golf course rambling from the shore to the hills.

Moderate

DOCTORS CAVE BEACH HOTEL, *Post Office Box 94, Montego Bay. At Doctors Cave, off Route A1. Tel. 876/952-4355, Fax 876/952-5204. Rates at this 80-room hotel start at $130.*

You'd pay more for this much comfort if you were right on the beach, but it's just across the street. Right in town and handy to colorful shops and thronging streets, the hotel offers air conditioned rooms with telephone, kitchenettes in the suites, dining and a piano bar, swimming pool, whirlpool, and a fitness room. Rooms are typical of the islands, furnished in rattan and deep pastels against neutral backgrounds. Television is available in the lounge.

COYOBA BEACH RESORT & CLUB, *Mahoe Bay, Little River. Tel. 876/953-9150 or 800/237-3237. The 50-room resort is five miles from the Montego Bay airport. Rates start at $180 for accommodations but ask about the all-inclusive and platinum plans, which are an excellent value.*

A member of Elegant Resorts of Jamaica is this intimate, red-roofed, three-story inn with private balcony or terrace in each room, air conditioning, satellite television, a private beach, watersports, tennis courts, two restaurants and access to three nearby golf courses. Rooms overlook the ocean or garden and have a dining area.

HOLIDAY INN SUNPREE RESORT, *Rose Hall, P.O. Box 480, Montego Bay. Tel. 876/953-2485, Fax 876/953-2840; U.S. and Canada 800/ HOLIDAY. The hotel is eight miles east of the Montego Bay airport. Rates at this 516-room resort start at $165 per person, double occupancy. Included are food, drinks, taxes, tips, and airport transfers. Children under age 12 stay and eat free when sharing a room and existing bedding with parents. Children ages 13-19 pay $50. The resort is five miles east of Montego Bay International Airport.*

Picture a big, zesty Holiday Inn anywhere in the world, then add a casino, extra large rooms, a great beach lapped by warm waves of neon-bright azure water, childs play, and everything you want to eat, drink, and do. Once you arrive you can put your wallet away. Included are dining in a choice of fancy or informal restaurants, drinking and entertainment at bars and lounges, watersports, theme night buffets with music and dancing, watersports, tennis, beach games, and activities.

One of the most family-friendly resorts in the islands, this one offers separate check-in for children, who are greeted by Smiley the Happy Clown. There's also a nursery for babies aged six months to two years and activities for every age group including a disco for teens. Children's programs end at 9pm, after which babysitting is available at $3.50 per hour; after midnight, $5 per hour. Rooms range from standard doubles with two double beds to suites with private Jacuzzis. It's all spread among eight separate buildings. Rooms have direct dial telephone, color cable television, hair dryer, and a private balcony or terrace.

JACK TAR VILLAGE MONTEGO BAY, *Gloucester Avenue, mailing address P.O. Box 144, Montego Bay. Tel. 876/952-4340, Fax 876/952-6633; U.S. Tel. 800/999-9182 or 214/891-9003. Located on the north coast between the airport and downtown, the resort is less than five minutes from the airport. Rates start at $150 per person daily, including taxes, gratuities, airport transfer, meals, drinks, and most activities.*

Rates at this hassle-free resort include nonstop meals from 6:30am to

1am, drinks from 10am until the wee hours, snacks, non-motorized watersports, nightly entertainment, a Kids Club for children ages 3-12, air conditioned accommodations, tennis, and discounted golf five minutes away. Children under age six stay and eat free in season; in summer, that's ditto for children under age 12. The hotel underwent an extensive renovation in 1996 and service, which has had its ups and downs over the years is at this writing in an up mode. All rooms overlook the beach, but superior rooms, at $30 more than standard, are closer to the beach and restaurants.

SEACASTLES, *Rose Hall. Tel. 876/953-3250, Fax 876/953-3062; U.S. 800/752-6824. Rates at this 198-suite resort start at $168 per person including meals, drinks, sports, and transfers to and from the airport at Montego Bay. The resort is on the north coast at Rose Hall, ten minutes from the airport.*

Studio, one-, two-, and three-bedroom suites in this cutely turreted "castle" are air conditioned and have satellite television and a private balcony overlooking the ocean or mountains. Rooms are airy and pleasant, done in island pastels, wicket and whites, with plenty of storage room for a stay of a week or two. Enroll the children in a program suitable to their age group, with their own nanny, then relax and enjoy a cashless paradise where meals are served in three restaurants. Three bars stand ready to pour premium liquors or your choice of fresh fruit drinks. Swim in the freshwater pool, play tennis or beach volleyball, and stay up late to enjoy live music and entertainment. A doctor is on call and a nurse on duty 24 hours a day.

THE WEXFORD INN, *Gloucester Avenue. Tel. 876/952-2854 or 800/ 237-3421. Rates at this 61-unit, in-town inn start at $120. It's two miles from the airport.*

Take a room or apartment in this pink and white inn, in a style that might be found at any American interstate interchange. It's halfway between two of the area's best beaches, Walter Fletcher and Doctor's Cave. Units are air conditioned and have ceiling fan, telephone and television. Kitchenette units are available. There's a swimming pool, room service, and a restaurant on the premises.

Budget

ATRIUM AT IRONSHORE, *mailing address Box 604, Montegeo Bay 2. Tel. 876/953-2605, Fax 876/952-5641. Thirty-three apartments with one, two, or three bedrooms are priced from $90. It's on the seaside road just east of the airport on the land side of the street.*

This homey apartment complex has its own, very British pub where you can play dominoes, darts, or skittles between sets. Live entertainers play nightly. The one-, two-and three-bedroom suites come with a house-keeper-cook who will prepare your menu or hers. Or, dine in the resort's own restaurant. The free-form pool with its waterfalls pouring from under the gazebo is the heart of the resort.

NEGRIL

Only a few years ago, Negril was a sleepy fishing village with miles of white sand beach that were thought to be of little use because they back up to a vast swamp known as The Great Morass. Now the beach is lined with resorts and the swamp is being developed, to the delight of some and the dismay of others. Chances are newcomers will like the choice of many modern resorts on some of the world's most beautiful waters, but if you loved the Negril of the 1980s, be prepared to see many changes. If you loved the Negril of the 1960s, you won't even recognize the place. One saving grace is that, by law, no hotel can be taller than the highest palm tree.

Many of Negril's resorts are along the famous sand beach, but others take advantage of the dramatic scenery and greenery of a five-mile stretch of coastal cliffs. Taxi fare from Montego Bay to Negril is about $70 each way. Alternatives including renting a car or taking a commuter flight into Negril's airstrip.

Expensive
POINCIANA BEACH RESORT, *Box 44, Negril. Tel. 876/957-4100; U.S. 800/468-6728. Winter rates at this 130-room resort start at $380 per couple daily, all inclusive. Suites are from $487. You will be picked up at the airport in Montego Bay for the 90-minute drive to Negril. At additional cost, you can fly into Negril aboard 18-seat Air Jamaica Express commuter planes.*

The beach is seven miles of turbinado sugar edging incredibly clear water. A clubby, come-back place with high acceptance from repeat visitors, Poinciana has a year-round children's camp, a five-star PADI scuba facility, a beauty salon, a commissary, three restaurants including gourmet dinners, great cheeseburgers at the Beach Grill, and a spa with a gym outfitted for working out or serious body building. Rooms are done in neutrals with accents of blush and green. Book a room with two double beds, a one-bedroom suite, or a two-bedroom villa with kitchenette. The all-inclusive price means, say your hosts, that you need arrive only with the clothes on your back, a little sunscreen and some dancing shoes.

SWEPT AWAY, *Norman Manley Boulevard, Negril. Tel. 876/957-4061, Fax 957-4060, U.S. and Canada 800/545-7937. Rates at this 134-room resort start at $425 per couple including meals, drinks, sports, tax, tips, and transfers from the airport at Montego Bay.*

A village of red-roofed white cottages nestles in lush gardens set back from a long strip of white sand beach. Its big swimming pool, surrounded by a big deck, looks like a giant footprint from the air. A bonanza for active couples, the resort offers golf, tennis, fitness, and activities as well as food and drink for the romantic beach vacation of a lifetime. Rooms, which have light colored tile floors and lots of dark wood shutters to close against the bright sun, have balconies overlooking the garden or sea.

Moderate

BEACHCOMBER CLUB, *Norman Manley Boulevard, mailing address Box 98, Negril. Tel. 876/957-4171, Fax 876/957-4097. Rates at this 45-unit resort start at $130. It's 90 minutes from the airport at Montego Bay.*

Sleep in a four-poster bed, discover afternoon tea as it should be, and swim from a talcum beach along Negril's famous "resort row." Chickee huts along the beach provide shade, or lounge on your big, private, covered veranda to gaze out over gardens or the sea. Dine on Italian classics in Gambino's. Air conditioned suites have a kitchen, a big bathroom with soaker tub, and a spacious living room. Shop the resort's own Benetton or Tajmahal.

CHARELA INN, *Norman Manley Boulevard, Negril Beach, mailing address Box 33. Tel. 876/957-4277, Fax 876/957-4414. Rates at this 39-room resort start at $140. It's 50 miles from the airport at Montego Bay and a mile south of the Negril airport.*

Family-owned and operated by the Grizzle family, this resort is renowned for its La Vendome Restaurant with its nightly, five-course table d'hote meal, and folkloric shows two nights a week. Settle into a room with ten-foot ceilings and a four-poster bed and spend days on the flawless, white sand beach edged by a windex sea. Use of kayaks, sunfish, and sailboards is free. Once a week, the Grizzles offer a sunset cruise along the coast. Rooms are screened from the beach by thick plantings of palms and poinciana, so their balconies provide a shady place to read or snooze after you've had your daily sunbath. Rooms have air conditioning, ceiling fan, and room service. Children are welcome; planned activities are offered just for them.

NEGRIL GARDENS, *P.O. Box 58, Negril. Tel. 876/957-4408, Fax 876/957-4374; U.S. 800/652-7824. Rates at the 65-room resort start at $125 for a double room. Add $40 per person daily for breakfast and dinner daily. All-inclusive plans start at $304 per couple plus $40 child under age 12 for one or two children sharing their parents' room. The resort is 54 miles west of the airport at Montego Bay.*

Stay in the Beachside building or Gardenside, which is across the road in lush woodlands filled with birdsong. Sun and stroll on seven miles of private beach or swim in the freshwater pool. There's tennis or volleyball, dining in the Orchid Terrace on the beach side, and bars on both the beach and garden sides. Meal plans include breakfast only, breakfast and dinner, or an all-inclusive plan that covers all meals and non-motorized watersports. Air conditioned rooms have two doubles or one queen-size bed. All have ceiling fan, satellite television, and a safe.

NEGRIL TREE HOUSE. *Norman Manley Boulevard. Tel. 876/957-4287, Fax 876/957-4386. In the U.S. and Canada. Tel. 800/NEGRIL-1. Rates at this 55-room, 12-suite resort start at 145. Ask about packages that include transfers from the airport at Montego Bay.*

Beach and sea add up to the perfect vacation in two-story cottages with balconies that overlook the beach or gardens. Sun and swim on the beach, take laps in the big, teardrop-shaped pool, soak in the whirlpool, parasail, sail, snorkel, or join in the games. Rooms are air conditioned or have ceiling fans; suites have kitchens and some have television. The hotel has two bars and a restaurant.

POINT VILLAGE, *Rutland Point, Box 105. Tel. 876/957-9570, Fax 876/957-4351, U.S. Tel. 800/752-6824. Rates at this 256-suite resort start at $168 per person per day all inclusive; up to two children under age 16 sharing with two adults are free. Transfers to and from the airport at Montego Bay, which is 90 minutes away, are included.*

Families, couples, and singles make for a nice mix in this all-suites resort where you can have a studio or one-, two -or three-bedroom apartment and all the trimmings for one price. Three bars and three restaurants give you a choice of venues for meals and cocktails. Theme nights (Port Royal Night, Jamaica Night) are especially lively with music, entertainment, and food galore. Children's programs are also included, so let the kiddies build sand castles or go on supervised treasure hunts while you swim in the freshwater pool, play tennis or beach volleyball, sail, work out, or snorkel. Suites are conditioned and have satellite television. Settle into an ocean or garden view suite, then put your wallet away until you leave. From the moment you're picked up at Montego Bay's airport until you're taken back to catch your plane, everything is included.

Budget

CHUCKLES, *mailing address Box 101, Westmoreland, Negril. Tel. 876/957-4250, Fax 876/957-9150. It's just south of the crafts market where Norman Manley Boulevard turns into West End Road. Rates at this 73-room resort start at $90 for a double room. Two-bedroom villas are available. It's two miles from the Negril airport, two hours from Montego Bay.*

This is a price-appeal resort offering a great many deals, so ask about packages that include meals and airport transfers. Air conditioned rooms have two double beds, safe, television, telephone, and essential furnishings in busy prints and basic beige. The activities calendar is head-spinning, so families and couples can be kept busy and singles can mingle.

A shuttle runs to the beach, but most guests can't drag themselves away from the big pool, pool bar, and whirlpool. The hotel has a restaurant, a bar, tennis courts, a fitness room, volleyball, and table tennis. Tours and watersports can be arranged.

NEGRIL BEACH CLUB, *Norman Manley Boulevard. Tel. 876/957-4220, Fax 876/957-4364. Rates at this 72-room resort start at $94.50.*

Smack on the white sand, seven-mile beach is this air conditioned resort offering rooms, suites, and apartments with full kitchens. The hotel has a tour desk and swimming pool, a restaurant, room service, and child-friendly activities.

RONDEL VILLAGE, *Norman Manley Boulevard. Tel. 876/957-4413, Fax 876/957-4915, U.S. Tel. 800/544-5979. Rates at this 16-unit resort start at $95; villas at $170.*

Accommodations are set among tropical gardens along an ivory scarf of sand or across the street from it. Villas all have private whirlpool spa, balcony, living and dining room, and kitchenette. Air conditioned bedrooms have satellite television, telephone, and balcony. Enjoy the swimming pool, dining in Cecile's, and discover the British tradition of elevenses (drinks at 11am) in the bar. Sail, snorkel or dive with the on-site watersports concession.

XTABI, *West End, mailing address Box 19. Negril. Tel. 876/957-4336, Fax 876/957-0121. Rates start at $80. It's 90 minutes from the airport at Montego Bay and five miles south of Negril.*

This resort doesn't share the sands of Negril Beach but it's even more beautiful in many ways because dramatic stone cliffs edge the sea. Jump right in to snorkel and explore sea and caves, or swim in the pool. Dine in the clifftop restaurant, and sunbathe on the rocks. Accommodations are in air conditioned bungalows.

FALMOUTH & RUNAWAY BAY

This area between Montego Bay and Port Antonio is best accessed from the Montego Bay airport, which is about an hour west of here. Most hotels, especially all-inclusives, include airport transfers in their quoted rates.

Expensive

LIDO SUPERCLUB, *Rio Buena, Trelawny. Tel. 876/954-0000 through 0019, Fax 876/954-0020; U.S and Canada 800/654-1337. Rates at this 180-room, adults-only, all-inclusive resort start at $300 all-inclusive.*

Swim and sun on the 2,000-foot beach or the Olympic-size pool, dine in your choice of four restaurants, sit in on a show, try the three bars, or play the nine-hole, par 28, executive golf course. The only extras are tours off property, greens fees at $10 per person per round, cart rental and club rental.

FRANKLYN D. RESORT, *Box 201 Runaway Bay, St. Ann, Jamaica. Tel. 876/973-3067, Fax 876/973-3071, U.S. 888/FDR-KIDS. Rates at this 76-suite resort start at $1,700 per person per week including accommodations, airport transfers, meals, drinks, entertainment, activities, and your own Girl Friday. Children under age 16 stay, play, and eat free. The hotel is 30 minutes west of Ocho Rios and an hour east of Montego Bay.*

One of the most family-friendly resorts in the world, this one has seals of approval from the Family Channel and the National Parenting Center. Your own nanny, cook, housekeeper, and friend joins you daily to cater to your every whim. (Or, if you are honeymooning and want to be alone, she can also make herself scarce.) She'll do the dishes, prepare meals, or take the children to the Learning Center where they can play video games, learn French, collect shells, or do arts and crafts.

Moderate

GOOD HOPE GREAT HOUSE, *P.O. Box 50, Falmouth, Trelawny. Tel. 876/954-3289, Fax 876/954-3289; U.S. and Canada, 800/OUTPOST; London 0-800-614-790. Rates start at $80. Round trip transfer from Montego Bay, which is 40 minutes away, is $60 additional.*

Grandly built in Georgian style in 1755, the ten-bedroom greathouse was home to owners of a 2,000-acre plantation. Lost in the Cockpit Country, the house overlooks Queen of Spain Valley and the Martha Brae River. Think of it as an elegant dude ranch where there's nothing to do but rock calmingly on the porches while gazing out over a working plantation known for its ugli fruit and anthurium exports. Seek out a private spot under a great tree on the green lawn, ride horseback through unspoiled trails, play tennis or swim in the pool, or bring your binoculars and check off your bird sightings.

Rooms are coolly decorated in gauzy whites and pastels, accented with dark mahogany floors. The old counting house sits alone beyond the Great House, a honeymoon suite with striking black and white tile floors, filmy hangings on the four-poster bed, chintz-covered furniture, and a bathtub behind a decorated screen. The Coach House has five bedrooms, which are available separately or a family can rent the entire house.

A project of Chris Blackwell, who was raised in Jamaica and founded Island Records (Bob Marley, U2, Steve Winwood, Grace Jones), the plantation is the essence of relaxed elegance. It shows its age, sometimes in awkward ways such as the placement of plumbing, but more often in sweetly charming ways – mellow old woodwork, worn wood floors, stone construction that reveals where an ancient hot water system once worked, and the "dungeon" under the counting house. Breakfast, lunch, and dinner are available in the same dining room where planters gathered centuries ago. Unless you want to spend all your time here on the grounds, you'll need a car, but romantics will like the idea of settling in here for several days and pretending that this ancient plantation is their own.

EATON HALL BEACH HOTEL, *Runaway Bay, mailing address Jamaica Reservation service, 1320 South Dixie Highway, Suite 1102, Coral Gables FL 33146. In Jamaica. Tel. 876/973-3404; in the U.S. Tel. 800/JAMAICA. Rates at this 50-unit resort start at $107 per person, all inclusive.*

Sleep in a four-poster bed in a cliffside resort built around a 19th century guesthouse. One price includes an air conditioned room or suite, meals, nightly entertainment, tennis, a private beach, and drinks at the pool bar. Most rooms overlook the water.

Budget

RUNAWAY HEART COUNTRY CLUB, *Ricketts Avenue, Runaway Bay, St. Ann. Tel. 876/973-1671, Fax 876/973-2693. Rates at this 20-room resort start at $50 per person without meals. Ask about packages that include breakfast and dinner.*

Because it operates as a training facility for future hospitality professionals, the service here is exemplary. Rooms, which have private balconies, have twin, double or king beds, television, air conditioning, and a telephone. After a drink in the piano bar, have dinner in the restaurant where students and their talented teachers create sumptuous meals with only the occasional slip. The country club has a swimming pool and golf course. At the price, it's an extraordinary find.

SOUTH COAST & TREASURE BEACH

The last place in Jamaica to escape the crowds and cruise ship day-trippers, this area doesn't offer the island's best beaches, but its nature watching is unequaled and its mountain towns are frozen in a pleasantly distant past.

Budget

ASTRA COUNTRY INN, *Ward Avenue, mailing address Box 69, Mandeville. Tel. 876/962-3265, Fax 876/962-1461. Rates at this 20-room inn start at $60.*

High in 2,000-foot mountains is this breezy family inn that takes pride in its personal service and providing a community experience including countryside tours. Rooms and food are pretty basic, as could be expected for this price. There isn't air conditioning, but nights are so cool you'll need a light blanket. Rooms have refrigerator and satellite television. The restaurant is open breakfast through dinner and there's a bar, children's playground, nature park, swimming pool, and sauna.

JAKE'S VILLAGE, *Treasure Beach, Calabash Post Office, Saint Elizabeth. Tel. 876/965-0552, Fax 876/965-0552; U.S. and Canada, 800/OUTPOST. Rates start at $75 per room. Treasure Beach is on the south coast, about two hours south of Montego Bay and three hours west of Kingston.*

Old island hands sometimes liken Treasure Beach to Negril before it was developed. Stopping just short of garish, this cluster of five cottages is brightly Jamaican with overtones of the gaudy Art Deco hotels that are also owned by Chris Blackwell of Island Records fame. Furnishings are wildly eclectic, ranging from Jamaican primitives to cast iron beds. There are no phones, television, or air conditioning, but ceiling fans stir up sufficient comfort after the sun goes down. Dine on spicy Jamaican fare in the open air. Swim off the small, private beach or in the fresh-water pool. Fish with local fishermen, or arrange a horseback, bicycle, or scuba outing.

MANDEVILLE HOTEL, *Box 78, Mandeville. Tel. 876/962-2460 or 962-9764, Fax 876/962-0700. Rates at this 60-room hotel start at $75. Ask about packages and senior citizen discounts.*

You're 2,000 feet up in the highlands in a room, suite or apartment with up to three bedrooms in a full-service hotel with two restaurants, a swimming pool, and a locally popular pub. Beds are four-poster mahogany, lending a classic look to comfortable, homey rooms. Golf can be arranged. You'll need a rental car to get here and get around.

PORT ANTONIO

Taxi fare from Kingston to Port Antonio is about $120 each way, a grueling ride of three hours. Alternatives include renting a car or taking a commuter flight into Port Antonio's small air strip.

Expensive

TRIDENT VILLAS & HOTEL, *Route 4, Port Antonio, Jamaica, West Indies. Tel. 876/993-2602, Fax 876/993-2590, toll-free 800/237-3237. The 27-unit resort is about two miles from of the local airport, which is served by commuter planes. The drive from Kingston is about three hours. Rates start at $350 double; meal plans include MAP at $65 per person daily; all-inclusive plans are also available.*

Peacocks strut and preen for guests as they breakfast on the patio of one of Jamaica's most elegant resorts. The hosts pamper ordinary guests as if they were all as rich and famous as the big-name elite of politics, show business, and fashion who vacation here. Some reserve the entire Castle, a movie set in itself with a grand dining room and massive chandelier, and suites with plantation furniture, Laura Ashley-look fabrics, and 1930s cathedral radios. The beach is small, but there's always the big pool for swimming. Play tennis, hike the nature trails, have a massage, or play croquet. Rooms have mini-bars, safes, room service, and air conditioning, but not TV. Dining here is old-Jamaica elegance at its finest and most dressy.

Selected as one of my Best Places to Stay; see Chapter 13 for more details.

Moderate

DRAGON BAY, *next to Blue Lagoon, mailing address Box 176, Port Antonio. Tel. 876/993-8514, Fax 876/993-3284, U.S. 800/633-3284. Rates at this 90-unit hotel start at $110.*

It was swashbuckling, 1950s-era movie star Errol Flynn who first brought tourism to this corner of Jamaica, and now Dragon Bay best captures the glamor of the bay, the flower-filled forest, and the lagoon. Air conditioned villas with up to three bedrooms and three baths gaze out over waters that were filmed in such movies as "Club Paradise" and "Cocktail." Swim in the sea or the freshwater pool, snorkel, sail, dive, play tennis or beach volleyball, or charter a deep sea fishing expedition. Your villa has a kitchen, telephone, television, maid service and a cook on request. The hotel has dining and bars, taxis on site, and 50 acres for you to roam when you're not in or on the water. Children are welcome to enroll in the children's program.

FERN HILL CLUB, *San San, mailing address Box 100, Port Antonio. Tel. 876/993-3222, Fax 876/993-7373. Rates at this 31-room resort start at $150, spa suites at $190.*

Although this is a club, it also accepts guests. Our room in the original building was small, dark and shabby, so be sure to ask for something newer or a room that is recently refurnished. Loyal regulars assure that improvements continue year in and year out. The road is a long, twisty climb that takes you far above the beach, but the trade-off is the sensational views and hilltop breezes. There's a pool, restaurants, a friendly bar, a swimming pool, and a beauty shop. Golf and horseback riding are available. Rooms are air conditioned and television is available on request. A free shuttle takes guests to the beach.

GOBLIN HILL VILLAS, *San San, mailing address Box 26, Port Antonio. Tel. 876/633-3284 or 800/472-1148. One-bedroom villas are $1,550 weekly including cook/maid. Food is additional. Two-bedroom units for four are also available.*

Let the cook work her own magic in the market and kitchen. All you have to do is settle into a fully-furnished villa with a view of a grassy hillside leading down to the beach that belongs to San San Estate. Guests have the use of the beach, swimming pool tennis courts, a library and game room and beach sports. Units have a safe and kitchen but no telephone or television. Furnishings are wicker and bamboo, with straw mats on shiny floors and light-colored print upholsteries. The two-bedroom villas have a big living room with seating for six and a staircase leading to the second floor sleeping area. For kiddies, there is a zesty play program daily. Eat in the Birdwatchers Terrace restaurant on the cook's day off and enjoy nightly cocktails in the treehouse bar that is straight out of Swiss Family Robinson. It's created in a giant ficus tree.

HOTEL MOCKING BIRD HILL, *Box 254, Port Antonio, Jamaica. Tel. 876/993-3307, Fax 876/993-7133. Rates at this 10-room hotel start at $100. Meal plans are available.*

The intimacy of a bed and breakfast inn greets visitors to this blue and white perch high in the hills east of Port Antonio, handy to (but you probably won't want to walk down) beaches at Frenchman's Cove, San San, and Boston Bay. Rooms have balconies with soul-stirring views of the distant sea and nearby vegetation thick with flowering vines. The only dark note is the din that often steals up the slopes from nearby settlements where radios blare constantly. Owner-hosts Shireen Aga and Barbara Walker sell locally made products in their Gallery Carriacou. They put fresh flowers in sun-bright bedrooms, and offer eco-tours of the surrounding countryside. There's no air conditioning, television, or room phones, but the parlor-library is the perfect place to settle down with a glass of wine and a book on Jamaican birds or wildflowers. The inn's restaurant, Mille Fleurs, is one of the region's best.

JAMAICA PALACE HOTEL, *Box 277, Port Antonio. Tel. 876/993-2020 or 800/472-1149. Rates at this 60-unit hotel start at $160; suites sleep up to four. Ask about meal plans.*

Ambitiously styled in black and white marble to look like a Venetian palace, this hotel has a big swimming pool shaped like Jamaica, three restaurants and two bars, and a life-size chess game in the garden. Rooms, which are popular with German and Italian tourists but which some North Americans find a bit over the top, are lavishly furnished with Persian rugs, ornate artwork, and round beds. The formal restaurant, with its mottled red walls, is a an unappealing place to have an otherwise-elegant meal. Television is available at extra cost. The resort isn't on the beach, but it offers a free beach shuttle. Golf privileges and packages are available.

Budget

BONNIE VIEW PLANTATION HOTEL, *Box 82, Port Antonio. Tel. 876/993-2752. Rates at this in start at $75.*

You're perched high above the nearest beach after climbing a commando course of a road, but longtime visitors come back time again to the shabby gentility of this hideaway for the cool mountain air and panoramic views of the green countryside.

DEMONTEVIN LODGE, *Port Antonio. Tel. 876/993-2604. Rates at this 13-room inn start at $52 with private bath and $39 without.*

An in-town location is the home of proper British hospitality in a truly lovely old mansion that has seen better days. The furnishings can be best described as eclectic but the food is outstanding, the folks are nice, the location is great, and the prices can't be beat.

DRAGON BAY BEACH RESORT, *Box 176, Port Antonio. Tel. 876/993-8514 or 800/633-3284. Rates at this 29-unit resort start at $96 for a double room; suites are from $135. Add $46 per person daily for breakfast and dinner. An all-inclusive rate is available.*

Recent managers seem to have let standards slip in the wake of waves of European group tourists who are wowed by the fact that this resort was seen in the movie *Cocktail* starring Tom Cruise. On the plus side, the beach in its quiet cove is picture-perfect and the resort has everything you need to make a stay of it: lush floral surroundings, two restaurants, three bars, tennis courts, swimming pool (plus a private pool in one villa), room service, volleyball and boccie courts, massage, and watersprorts rentals. Rooms are done in typical rattan and cotton furnishings and have refrigerators. Suites have sofabeds in their living rooms.

Villas

Villas throughout Jamaica can be booked with **Villas by Linda Smith**, *Tel. 301/229-4300.*

WEDDINGS ON THE HOUSE

*Some resorts, including the **Plantation Inn** in Ocho Rios, **Point Village** and **Negril Gardens** in Negril, and **SeaCastles** in Montego Bay, provide a free wedding package with the booking of at least five nights. Included are the services of a marriage officer, the license, a floral tiara and bouquet for the bride, a boutonniere for the room, wedding cake, and a bottle of chilled champagne.*

WHERE TO EAT

Everyone's favorite Jamaican eateries are flamboyantly-named roadside shanties where jerk meats and seafood are cooking over pimento wood fires. It's impossible to list them or to predict who will be where during your visit, but a lunch of jerk chicken or pork, washed down with a cold Red Stripe beer, is as warming as a hug and as Jamaican as an anancy web. Every jerk artist has his or her own recipes for the secret blend of spices that are rubbed into the meat, the way the meat is cut, and the kind of wood used to cook it. They love telling you about it, always implying that only they know the real secret.

In restaurants, a 15 percent tax will be added to your bill, which should be checked to see if a service fee was also added in lieu of a tip. There's no need to tip twice or to tip a percentage of the total bill including tax. Don't let your dining decision be influenced by taxi drivers, who are often on the take from restaurateurs to steer customers their way. When making reservations, ask whether free transportation is provided (sometimes it is) and what you should expect to pay in cab fare from your hotel.

If it's far different from what the cabbie quotes you (ask before you get in), you know your driver may be trying to gouge you.

Prices quoted below are in U.S. dollars, which is how they are listed on most tourist menus. When dining in smaller places, Jamaican dollars will also be shown. Unless stated otherwise, credit cards are accepted. The dress code is resort chic, with dressy pants outfits or frocks for women and long trousers and closed shoes for men. The oldest and most elegant resorts may ask gentlemen to wear jackets for dinner, but ties are rarely required any more.

KINGSTON
Expensive
BLUE MOUNTAIN INN, *Gordon Town Road. Tel. 927-1700. Open Monday through Saturday for dinner and Monday through Friday for lunch, the inn offers main dishes priced $18 to $40. The inn is 30 minutes from downtown Kingston. Gentlemen wear jackets at dinner; because of the chill of the altitude, women are also advised to bring a wrap.*

In this rustic 18th century coffee plantation, a local accent is put on continental classics. Shrimp is crusted in cashews; the smoked marlin is stuffed with crab and crowned with papaya salsa; the rack of lamb is an English feast. Fresh local vegetables accompany lobster, chicken, fresh fish, or a steak. Complete the meal with a fruity sorbet or a creamy cheesecake. The scene overlooks the Mammee River, high on slopes covered in trees and flowering shrubs. Come at lunchtime for the view and again at dinner for the unbridled elegance.

HOTEL FOUR SEASONS, *18 Ruthven Road. Tel. 926-8805. It's open daily breakfast through dinner. Plan to spend $25 to $35 for dinner.*

Don't confuse this small hotel with the Four Seasons chain. It's an intimate, 39-room "boutique" hotel with German management, lots of continental dishes on the menu, and a pleasant European charm in the heart of New Kingston. Dine on festive red linen spread over white wrought iron furniture on an open-air plantation porch lined with columns. The luncheon buffet is one of the city's best buys.

ISABELLA'S, *in the Crowne Plaza Hotel, 211 Constant Spring Road. Tel. 925-7676. It's open daily for lunch and dinner. Reservations are essential. Plan to spend $40 for dinner.*

Stop in the lobby bar first for cocktails set to piano music, then dine on red snapper in a bed of freshly frazzled mushrooms, freshly made pastas, or roast chicken with a hint of the island's famous jerk seasonings. This is a dressy, business location, the first choice for a romantic dinner for two or for discreet service and good dining while discussing a business deal.

IVOR GUEST HOUSE, *Jack's Hill. Tel. 977-0033 or 917-1460. Reservations are essential. The inn is 20 minutes from downtown out Jack's Hill Road. A five-course meal with wine costs $35 to $50. It's open for lunch, tea, and dinner daily until 9:30pm.*

A 19th century greathouse overlooks the lights of the city from high on a 2,000-foot mountain. The imaginative, but limited, menu changes daily but there is always a choice of three main dishes plus a starter, soup, salad, and dessert. Furnished traditionally in rich woods, it's a favorite with local businesspeople as well as with in-the-know visitors.

LA BRASSERIE, *in the Jamaica Pegasus Hotel, 81 Knutsford Boulevard. Tel. 926-3690. Reservations are accepted. Plan to spend $20-$30 for dinner. It's open daily 7am to 11pm.*

Relaxed elegance poolside gives the traveler a choice of healthful selections at the salad bar and pasta bar or a menu offering Jamaican and American favorites. It's a good choice for the newly arrived visitor who wants a buffet meal with plenty of choices. Try a little of everything to see which of the Jamaican dishes you like.

MAYFAIR HOTEL, *4 West King's House Close. Tel. 926-1610. Main dishes are priced $12 to $20. It's open nightly for dinner, 7-9:30pm. Reservations are suggested.*

A Jamaican colonial room with tall, mahogany columns gazes through big, glass doors onto a shaded veranda. The restaurant, which serves a small hotel, offers international and local cuisine. The fish dishes, chicken, and soups are always good.

PALM COURT, *in the Wyndham Kingston Hotel, 77 Knutsford Boulevard, yrl. 926-5430. Main dishes are priced $15 to $50. Reservations are suggested. It's open daily for lunch and dinner until 10pm.*

The hush of an elegant hotel setting is broken only by piano music and the murmur of business and leisure visitors. Dine on the mezzanine from a menu that is mainly northern Italian with emphasis on local seafood and deftly sauced pastas.

PORT ROYAL, *in the Jamaica Pegasus Hotel, 81 Knutsford Boulevard. Tel. 926-3690. Reservations are accepted. Open Monday through Friday for lunch and dinner and Monday through Saturday for dinner, this is the hotel's* *signature seafood restaurant. Reservations are recommended. Plan to spend $35 for dinner.*

One of the city's premier seafood restaurants, Port Royal trades on the old world charm of this big, downtown hotel, a member of the Forte Grande chain. The Friday evening seafood buffet is a budget-stretcher, a way to get your fill of fish, shrimp and the like and all the trimmings in a premier restaurant at a buffet price.

STRAWBERRY HILL, *Irish Town, St. Andrew. Tel. 944-8400. Reservations are required. The restaurant is open for lunch and dinner daily, serving dishes in the $19 to $27 range. Find it a half hour northeast of Kingston.*

The drive is a long, winding one, but it brings you to a charming village of villas often frequented by music and film stars in search of a hideaway. Dine on curried shrimp with roasted ginger chips, jerk loin of lamb glazed with guava and roasted garlic, or smoked marlin.

Moderate

BAMBOO VILLAGE, *Village Plaza, 24 Constant Spring Road, downtown Kingston. Tel. 926-8839 or 929-2389. Plan to spend $10 to $25 for dinner. Hours are noon to 10pm daily. Reservations are suggested. Take-out orders are welcomed.*

Chinese food is almost always a good choice anywhere in the world. In this upscale Chinese restaurant, order Peking duck, seafood Warbar, or Cantonese classics made with beef, chicken, pork, seafood, or all vegetarian.

JADE GARDEN, *in the Sovereign Center, 106 Hope Road. Tel. 978-3476. Hours are noon to 10pm daily; on the last Sunday of the month, dim-sum are served 10am to 9pm Reservations are essential; take-out orders are welcome.*

Chefs from Hong Kong have turned this storefront restaurant into an Oriental garden including two enormous, saltwater aquariums. The menu lists more than 100 items to mix and mingle. Ask about daily lunch specials.

TERRACE CAFE, *in the Wyndham Kingston Hotel. Tel. 926-5430. Hours are 6:30am to 11:30pm daily. Dishes are priced $8.50 to $15.*

You're in the heart of a city but the patio provides resort atmosphere for a meal of sandwiches, salads, poolside barbecue, and a bounteous breakfast buffet featuring the usual favorites plus Jamaican breakfast dishes such as salt fish and ackee.

Budget

COUNTRYSIDE CLUB, *19-21 Eastwood Park Road. Tel. 929-9403. It's in the Eastwood Park section two miles from New Kingston. Menu items are priced $5.25 to $16. Hours are Monday through Friday 11:30am to 1am.*

This clubby restaurant is popular with locals who come here for the

Jamaican cooking, fresh seafood selections, and steel band music. Live entertainers play three or four nights a week, so call ahead to see what's going down.

DRAGON COURT, *in Dragon Centre, 6 South Avenue. Tel. 920-8477. Hours are noon to 10pm daily. Take-order orders are welcomed. Reservations are suggested for eating in. Meals are priced $5 to $20.*

When you tire of Jamaican food, here's a place to fill up on dim-sum, barbecue, and a long list of Sino-American dishes combining beef, tofu, chicken or pork with crisp-tender vegetables.

HOT POT, *2 Altamont Terrace. Tel. 929-3906. Call for hours. Reservations and credit cards are not accepted. Plan to spend $10 to $15 for dinner; less for lunch.*

Start with a freshly squeezed fruit juice, then have something strictly Jamaican such as salt fish and ackee, a goat stew, one of the soups, fricasseed chicken, or patties.

NEGRIL
Expensive

FEATHERS, *in the Swept Away Resort, Norman Manley Boulevard. Tel. 957-4061. Reservations must be made 24 hours in advance unless you're staying at the resort. It's closed Mondays. Plan to spend $25-$35 for dinner.*

The most elegant of the restaurants in a high quality, all-inclusive resort, Feathers has earned an international reputation for its healthful cuisine, veggie bar, pizzas with exotic toppings, pastas, and seafood lightly prepared without breading and deep frying. The hotel is on the beach; the restaurant is across the street where it is the social center for pampered resort guests.

LA VENDÔME, *in the Charela Inn, Westmoreland, Negril Beach, 3 1/2 miles from the town center. Tel. 957-4277. Reservations are suggested. Dinner is served nightly 6 to 10pm, costing $25 to $35 without wine.*

Lush tropical gardens form a scented scene for outdoor dining under the stars on a cool terra cotta terrace overlooking a beach lined with palm trees. Or, choose an indoor table in the air conditioning. The cuisine is French with Jamaican touches done with fresh fruits, vegetables, and herbs, accompanied by a fine choice of French wines and champagnes personally selected by your hosts Daniel and Sylvia Grizzle. Choose from the menu or the fixed-price, five-course, gourmet meal.

Start, for example, with a homemade paté followed by duck in orange sauce, a seafood sampler, or fresh snapper. Live entertainers play Thursday and Saturday nights.

Moderate

CHUCKLES, *in the Chuckles Negril Resort. Tel. 957-4250. Open 7:30am to 10:30pm, the restaurant offers dishes priced $9 to $18.*

Johnny Chuck is the general manager at this 70-odd room hotel on a private beach, hence the name of a relaxed, upstairs-downstairs restaurant where you can sit near the buffet or ask for a distant, candlelit table and have a romantic dinner from the menu.

GAMBINO'S, *in the Beachcomber Club Resort. Tel. 957-4170. Call for reservations and free transportation. The restaurant is open breakfast through dinner every day. Plan to spend $20 to $30 for dinner.*

Located on a seven-mile stretch of beach, this resort completes the hospitality picture with a homey Italian restaurant featuring homemade pastas ladled with a choice of savory sauces. Order from the menu or have the buffet, which offers Jamaican classics alongside southern Italian standards.

NEGRIL TREE HOUSE, *Norman Manley Boulevard. Tel. 957-4287. Open daily 7am to 11pm, it offers meals in the $7 to $26 range.*

Pizza is the specialty here and it is served any time, any way, with any topping. Come in time for a sundowner at the beachfront bar, then have a look at the tree that grows in the main building. Dine indoors or out, on pepperpot or red bean soup followed by a callaloo quiche or an escovitched fish smothered in sliced onions and sweet peppers. For dinner, the lobster spaghetti and oven-roasted chicken are among host Gail Jackson's signature dishes. Her Tia Maria parfait is a boffo dessert.

RONDEL VILLAGE, *Norman Manley Boulevard, Westmoreland. Tel. 957-4413. Dishes are priced $8 to $22. Call for hours and reservations.*

Lobster or fresh fish are favored most nights in this seaside restaurant but it's special on Sunday night when a barbecue features lobster, chicken, and suckling pig.

SEETHING CAULDRON, *in the Negril Beach Club, just above the crafts market on Norman Manley Boulevard. Tel. 957-4220. Hours are 8 to 10:30am and 6-10pm daily. Meals are in the $20 range.*

Have the roast pig, fresh lobster from Jamaican reefs, a chop or chicken, accompanied by a heap of salad, peas and rice, and a fresh fruit drink. Negril, Budget

CALICO JACK'S, *in the Sea Splash Resort, Norman Manley Boulevard. Tel. 957-4041. Main dishes are priced $7 to $25.*

Choose from two dining venues (the other is Tan-Ya's) in this family-run, 15-suite beach resort. Have snapper or lobster from the beach grill or, from the kitchen, smoked lobster, shrimp in lemon pepper, Jamaican crab backs, or roast chicken with fruit salsa.

OCEAN EDGE RESORT, *West End Road west of Negril. Tel. 957-4362. Open daily 7:30am to 11:30pm, it offers meals in the $8.50 to $15 range. Call about pick-up at your hotel.*

Breathtaking sea views set the mood for the Captain's Plate, a grilled lobster in garlic butter. Most people don't get beyond this daily special, which is one of the best lobster values in town, but there's also a choice of Jamaican and American soups, salads, chicken, sandwiches, and curries.

ROBINSON CRUSOE, *in Foote Prints on the Sands, Norman Manley Boulevard, Westmoreland. Tel. 957-4300. Meals are priced $10 to $15. Hours are 8am to 10pm daily. Reservations are essential.*

Play beach bum in style in this cozy beachfront nightspot. Specialties of the house include stuffed fish and fish cutlets stewed in Robinson's secret sauce.

XTABI, *Lighthouse Road, West End. Tel. 957-4336. Dishes are priced $4 to $25. Hours are 8am to 11pm daily.*

Sundown on the cliffs is a spectacular sight. Visitors are welcome to come to sunbathe and explore the five caves before dining on lobster, prime steaks, fresh seafood, chicken, or pork, all prepared to order on the charcoal grill. Good choices at lunch include the conch burger and the lobster Benedict.

OCHO RIOS
Expensive

ALMOND TREE, *in the Hibiscus Lodge Hotel, 83 East Main Street. Tel. 974-2813. It's open daily 7am to 10pm. Dinners are in the $25-$30 range. Reservations are recommended.*

Have a drink overlooking the Caribbean before the light fades and the candles are lit. Then choose from a menu featuring fresh seafood, prime steaks, or one of the veal dishes. Start with red bean or callaloo soup, and end the meal with an exotic fruit dessert. For something different, have the beef fondue served for two. The bar swings, literally, in rope chairs. Live music plays three nights a week.

JAMAICA INN, *Main Street, two miles east of Ocho Rios. Tel. 876/974-2514. Reservations are essential. Call to ask about hours and prices because the inn's guests, most of whom are on a meal plan, come first. There isn't always room for outsiders. Plan to spend about $60 for dinner.*

One of Jamaica's most charming and sophisticated inns and the chosen vacation hotel for the likes of actor Albert Finney and author Alistair McLean, it's the home of Chef Wilbert Matheson who trained in England with the Roux brothers of three-star Michelin fame. Feast on his poached fillet of snapper with tomato and basil coulis, Jamaican grilled chicken with ginger sauce, or the jerked chicken with hearts of palm. A simple specialty of the house is salted coconut chips, shaved from fresh coconuts and slow-baked until they are golden.

A typical dinner might start with smoked chicken and papaya vinaigrette or jerk pork with pineapple and ginger. Then comes a choice of three soups and a Caesar salad, followed by your choice of grilled grey snapper, sirloin steak with asparagus and oyster sauce, native curried goat, or seafood pasta, all served with vegetables of the day and followed by selections from the dessert table. With coffee comes homemade fudge. The open-air restaurant is on a grand terrace rimmed with a white balustrade. Dine under cover or under the stars at a candlelit table. Before dinner, relax in the woody bar. After dinner, play croquet in the moonlight or dance on the terrace. In season, a coat and tie are worn after 7pm; in summer gentlemen wear long trousers and a shirt with collar. Since vacationers find it hard to tell winter from summer here, inquire about the dress code when you make reservations.

THE LITTLE PUB, *59 Main Street. Tel. 974-2324. Reservations are suggested for dinner. It's open daily 7am to midnight. Dinner dishes are priced $14 to $25. Lunches are in the Budget category.*

Set in a Georgian-style complex in the heart of town, it's a popular hangout for breakfast and lunch. Order something from the outdoor grill or from the kitchen. The lobster lunch is a lollapalooza. At dinner, the room becomes a nightclub offering dinner-theater with cabaret-style entertainment. Until the show starts at 10pm on Wednesday, Friday and Saturday, enjoy the slots.

THE MANOR, *in the Ciboney Ocho Rios Resort, Main Street. Tel. 974-1027. It's 1.5 miles southeast of town. Plan to spend $50 to $60 for dinner with wine. Reservations are essential.*

Looking like a mahogany-furnished dining salon in a colonial Jamaican greathouse, this cozy room has a cluster of tables, a grand staircase, and stone walls. Tables are covered in pink linen, complimented by the green and pink print of the chair seats. Equally desirable dining rooms in the resort are Orchids, furnished in mellow pastels with softly muraled walls, and the Market Place painted in gaudy Creole colors and trimmed in white fretwork. Whatever your choice of dining at this plush Radisson resort, you'll have a memorable meal.

Starters might include smoked marlin with cucumber cream or bacon-wrapped banana, followed by breast of chicken and shrimp Creole, smoked pork chops with roasted onion sauce, or grilled kingfish and fried plantains. There may even be a freshwater fish specialty tonight, such as Black River perch stuffed with breadfruit and fresh herbs. The desserts may include rum cake, sweet potato pone, breadfruit and pineapple pie, or bread pudding with whiskey sauce.

JAMAICAN JERK CHICKEN

Here, from the Jamaican Tourist Board, is the "official" recipe for jerk chicken. It gets its name from the way it is jerked quickly back and forth over a fierce pimento wood fire to keep it from burning. The proportions are up to you to figure out.

Marinate 12 hot peppers overnight in a broth of soy sauce, beef bouillon, allspice, and cinnamon. Quarter a chicken and let it swim in the broth for four hours in the refrigerator. Grill over a pimento wood fire for at least six minutes on each side or until it's done through. The recipe concludes with this advice, "Grab a leg, take a bite, and hang on."

THE RUINS, *Da Costa Drive, a five-minute walk from the pier. Tel. 974-2442. Hours are Monday through Saturday for lunch and dinner and Sunday for dinner only. Reservations are suggested. Dinner costs $25-$35.*

One of the most spectacular settings in Jamaica is this open air restaurant built right on the edge of a natural, 40-foot waterfall. Dine under cover or under the palms and starlight on eastern dishes such as lotus lily lobster or chicken that has been flavor-enhanced with a low-calorie mixture of soy, garlic, and spices. Jamaican classics are always on the menu, and there's a good choice of vegetarian dishes. On weekends, there's live entertainment.

SEA PALM, *in the Golden Seas Beach Resort, Oracabessa, east of Ocho Rios on the A3. Tel. 975-3251. Dinner dishes are priced $10 to $25. Hours are daily 7:30 to 10am and 7-10pm.*

A visit here makes a nice drive, especially if you combine it with a visit to Firefly. The seaside restaurant serves American and Jamaican breakfasts and, for dinner, international and Jamaican cuisine including fresh fish, peas and rice, piquant soups, and desserts made with exotic, tropical fruit.

Moderate

L'ALLEGRO, *in the Jamaica Grande Hotel, St. Ann, Tel. 974-2201. Main dishes average $14. It's open daily from noon to midnight. Reservations are suggested.*

This upscale pink-and-white hotel's Italian restaurant, L'Allegro, is as faithful to its theme as its other restaurant, Dragons, is to the oriental look. Dine on delicate pasta favorites, especially the seafood sauces, the minestrone, and a Caesar salad. If you want a late-night snack, pizzas are served 11pm to midnight.

EVITA'S ITALIAN RESTAURANT, *in the Mantalent Inn overlooking Ocho Rios. Tel. 974-2333. Menu items are priced $5.75 to $21.95. Reservations are suggested. It's open daily for lunch and dinner. Find it west of town on the road to Dunn's River Falls, off to the left going up the mountain.*

Eva Myers likes to regale her guests with lists of the Hollywood stars, prime ministers, ambassadors, and musicians who continue to dote on her homemade pastas. And she can regale you in English, French, German or Spanish. The house dates to the 1860s, an early Victorian gingerbread confection. It's high over the city, cooled by mountain air and blessed with views of the city and bay. Dine indoors or out.

Choose among 30 innovative pasta dishes including jerk spaghetti, crab rotelle, and a vegetarian "Rasta" lasagna. Or depart from the pasta menu and have a sauté of fresh fish, lobster in creamy herb sauce, grilled steak with mushrooms, or stuffed fish. Children under age 12 dine for half price for half portions. Show proof of your birthday or anniversary, give a day's notice, and Eva will provide a free cake. The birthday child dines free.

CAFE MANGO, *52 Main Street. Tel. 974-2716. Hours are daily 7am to 11:30pm. Dishes are priced $5 to $15.*

Start with a cocktail in the Gazebo Bar, then sample pizza with a Caribbean accent, pasta, Mexican taco and tortilla dishes, or Jamaican soups, stews, jerks, and curries.

DRAGONS, *in the Jamaica Grande Hotel, St. Ann. Tel. 974-2201. Dishes average $18. Call for reservations, which are accepted for Tuesday through Sunday 6pm to 11pm.*

Cantonese and spicy Szechwan classics are served in this elegantly ornate room in one of the area's best hotels. Dress up for a swank night out and a feast of Peking duck, stir-fry beef with vegetables, crisply roasted chicken in sweet sauce, or crusty, deep-fried pork in a sweet and sour sauce.

TRADEWINDS, *47 Main Street. Tel. 974-2433. Plan to spend $15 to $18 for dinner. It's open breakfast through supper.*

Dine indoors on tropical wicker furniture or outdoors under the stars. Eat barbecue chicken, lobster, or a humdinger of a seafood platter with a selection from the day's net and all the trimmings including fries and salad.

Budget

BIBIBIPS. *Main Street. Tel. 974-1287. Near the Carib Ocho Rio's beach, it serves meals in the $6-$10 range. No credit cards are accepted. Call for hours.*

This is the place to get authentic Jamaican foods including peas and rice, curries, patties, snacks and sweets.

BLUE CANTINA, *81 Main Street. Tel. 974-2430. Eat for about $10. Call for hours.*

This is the place for the best tacos on the island, regular visitor Marty Bush tells us. For a great box lunch to take to the beach, suggests Bush, get the goat curry or chicken.

DOUBLE V JERK CENTRE, *109 Main Street. Tel. 974-0174. No credit cards are accepted. Plan to spend $10-$12.*

Because it's not too handy to the docks, this jerk center is not as likely to be filled with tourists as those that attract cruise ship passengers. It's best to come here for lunch because, as the afternoon goes on, some of the jerks tend to get over-cooked.

OCHO RIOS JERK CENTRE, *Da Costa Drive, no telephone. Hours vary.*

Almost everyone stops here eventually to try a different jerk every day – not just the usual chicken and pork, but jerked conch or snapper.

PARKWAY INN, *60 Main Street. Tel. 974-2667. Dine for $10 to $15. It's open breakfast through dinner.*

Request the "local" menu at this locally popular place and you'll have more native food choices and discounted prices compared to what is offered on the tourist menu. On weekdays, there's a fashion show with dinner.

TASTE OF THE CARIBBEAN, *Main Street at the entrance to the Jamaica Grande Hotel. Tel. 974-2716. Items are priced $3 and up. Breakfast through dinner is served daily; happy hour is celebrated Monday through Friday 5-7pm with snacks and discounted drinks.*

This gaily painted, indoor-outdoor hotspot is truly the place to have a taste of the Caribbean. Breakfast on ackee and scrambled eggs, lunch on a patty, and have a jerk specialty for dinner. Pizza, pasta, tacos, nachos and salads are fresh and good. Call ahead for take-out.

MANDEVILLE & CHRISTIANA
Moderate

ASTRA COUNTY INN, *62 Ward Avenue, Mandeville. Tel. 962-3265. Open daily breakfast through dinner, the inn serves dinners in the $15 to $20 range.*

The Wednesday night poolside barbecue with live music is a good place to spend a midweek evening. This is a health resort, so fruits, vegetables and juices get first billing.

BAMBOO VILLAGE, *in the Ward Plaza, Mandeville. Tel. 926-4515. Dishes are priced $10 to $15. Reservations are recommended.*

Dine on seafood Warbar, filet of beef Bamboo, and all the chop sueys and foo yongs that North Americans love about Cantonese cuisine.

MANCHESTER ARMS PUB & RESTAURANT, *in the Mandeville Hotel, 4 Hotel Street. Tel. 962-9764. Dishes are priced $8 to $20. Hours are 6:30am to 10pm. Transportation from nearby lodgings is available.*

Start your evening in the very British pub for the special rum punch, then dine on homestyle meals: pepperpot soup, lobster thermidor, jerk chicken, jerk pork, perhaps a roast. Dining is inside in elegance or more casually outdoors by the pool. Because this is a popular business hotel catering to international visitors, you can have ackee and saltfish for breakfast, an English breakfast with kippers, or American bacon and eggs. Luncheons are simpler, featuring soups, salads, sandwiches or patties, and cold drinks including milkshakes.

NASTURTIUM, *in the Villa Bella Hotel, Christiana, Manchester. Tel. 964-2243. Menu items are priced $5 to $15. Hours are 7:30am to 10pm daily.*

Jamaican and Japanese dishes give you a new choice of terayakis and jerks including the Taste of Jamaica sampler of traditional West Indian meats and vegetables. It's fun to ask about each, try them, and decide which favorites you'll order more often during your island visit.

MONTEGO BAY

Expensive

AMBROSIA, *in the Wyndham Rose Hall. Tel. 953-2650. Reservations are essential. Hours are Tuesday through Sunday, 6pm to 10:30pm. Main dishes are priced $15 to $29.*

Dine outdoors in a Mediterranean setting on Caesar salad, skewered lamb, pastas, seafood, sumptuous soups made with island vegetables, and fruity desserts.

CRUSOE'S *in the Wyndham Rose Hall. Tel. 953-2650. Dishes are priced $14 to $32. Reservations are suggested.*

Robinson Crusoe himself could have painted the vibrant decor of this brightly imaginative restaurant, drenched in island colors. Have the swordfish with cucumber salsa, shrimp clothed in toasted coconut, or the piquantly spiced crab cakes.

DAY-O PLANTATION RESTAURANT AND BAR, *Lot 1 Fairfield. Tel. 952-1825. Reservations are urged; free pick-up at area hotels is provided. Dishes are priced $14 to $26. Hours are Tuesday through Sunday 6-11pm.*

Jamaican musician Paul Hurlock and his wife Jennifer personally host this faithfully Jamaican restaurant in the old-world setting of a plantation house. Have fresh seafood, then spend the evening dancing or listening to live music.

ROUND HILL HOTEL AND VILLAS, *eight miles west of Montego Bay. Tel. 952-5150. Plan to spend $40-$60 for dinner. Reservations are required. Hours are daily 7:30am to 10pm.*

Come on Monday and Friday to dine under magical stars on dazzling buffets filled with dozens of salads, meats, scrumptious seafood, and eye-popping desserts. Or, if you prefer table service, come on other evenings for callaloo or pepperpot soup, a salad dressed in fresh herbs, and one of the seafood or chicken dishes prepared with local produce and continental flair. Ask about the dress code. It's informal on some nights for barbecue but is formal and even black tie on special Saturdays. This is one of Jamaica's most cherished old resorts, once frequented by Cole Porter and Oscar Hammerstein and now a haunt of rich and royal regulars.

SEAGRAPE TERRACE, *in the Half Moon Club, two miles east of Montego Bay on the water at Rose Hall. Tel. 953-2211. Open daily 7:30am to midnight, the restaurant recommends reservations. Plan to spend $40 for dinner, not counting wine.*

One of the most romantic settings in the islands is this stony terrace just off a sugar beach under bowers of seagrape trees skittering with birds. At lunch, you'll dine in the cool shade overlooking bright sails flapping on Sunfish that are lined up along the beach. At dinner, the moonlight can be achingly beautiful. Many of your fellow guests will be Half Moon repeaters who come here year after year for the luxurious surroundings, meticulous service, and remarkable food. They take the food plan and rarely leave the resort unless it is to play golf or dine or the Sugar Mill across the road. Have the pumpkin soup, a curry or a steak, and finish up with rum raisin ice cream.

SUGAR MILL, *on the Half Moon Golf Course. Tel. 953-2314. Dishes are priced $15 to $30. Hours are noon to 3pm and 7:30-10:30pm daily. Reservations are urged. Free transportation is available from Sandals, the Holiday Inn, Wyndham, Sea Castles, and the Half Moon Club.*

The Half Moon Club, a favored winter spa for the rich and famous, fashions an old sugar mill setting into understated elegance in this terrace restaurant on its golf course, a short shuttle ride away from the hotel and villas. It's overseen by legendary Swiss chef Hans Schenk, a member of the Confrèrie de la Chaine des Rôtisseurs. Have today's curry, or steak or lobster with one of the chef's famous sauces made with fresh herbs plus a hint of Dijon or a dollop of island hot sauce. The restaurant is best known for its bouillabaisse and for its tableside flambé specialties such as steak in brandy or fruit flamed with rum. Ask to see the wine list, which is comprehensive. Entertainers are usually on hand with a song.

VERANDAH RESTAURANT & BAR, *in the Coral Cliff Hotel, just east of Gloucester Avenue, Miranda Hill. Tel. 952-4130. Plan to spend $20 for dinner.*

A favorite gathering spot overlooking the seafront since the 1920s is this relic of the gracious Old Jamaica. The big, breezy dining room is furnished in white wicker, with a wrought iron chandelier overhead and jaunty striped awnings keeping out the mid-day sun. Let the server suggest a seafood special such as lobster thermidor or the pan-fried snapper. Or, or try one of the fiery curries, a steak, or chicken. Meals are prettily presented with garnishes of fresh fruit or a fillip of finely chopped herbs.

THE VINEYARD AT COYOBA, *in the Coyoba Beach Resort, Mahoe Bay, Little River, two miles east of Montego Bay. Tel. 953-9150. Open daily 7pm to 10pm, the restaurant serves in the $15-$35 range. Reservations are suggested.*

Have a drink in the Polo Grounds Lounge, then dine on Caribbean tastes with a French flair. The ambience and service is that of an old greathouse where you're cared for by friendly family retainers.

Moderate

THE PELICAN, *Gloucester Avenue. Tel. 952-3171. Open daily 7am to 11pm, it offers free pickup for dinner. Dishes are priced $5 to $20.*

This is a popular gathering spot for a Jamaican or American breakfast and has been since the 1960s. Dinners focus on home-town standards such as juicy burgers, barbecued chicken, grilled steaks, fish, pepperpot, and curries as well as a wide choice of vegetarian foods. Save room for dessert at the old-fashioned soda fountain, where the hot fudge sundae with whipped cream is a huge hit.

TOP OF THE BAY, *in the Montego Bay Club Resort, Gloucester Avenue, White Sands Beach. Tel. 952-4310. Open daily 7am to midnight, the restaurant serves meals in the $12 to $23 bracket.*

Overlook busy, happily touristy Doctor's Cave Beach while you dine on seafood, curries, jerk chicken, or a steak. Four nights a week, live entertainers are on hand, so you can dance after dinner.

Budget

GREENHOUSE, *on Gloucester Avenue adjoining the Doctors Cave Beach Hotel. Tel. 952-7838. Hours are 7am to 11pm daily.Meals are priced $8 to $15.*

Ask about daily Jamaican specials such as rundown, salt fish and ackee, or curry goat. Or grab a burger or pizza and be on your way back to the beach. Call ahead for take-out.

TASTE JAMAICA, *in the Half Moon Plaza, on the beach road eight miles east of Montego Bay. Tel. 953-9688. Snack for $5 to $10; means are priced in the $20 range. It's open daily 9am to 10pm.*

Stop in to pick up a fancy picnic from a feast of foods designed to cater to wealthy tourists who stay in villas belonging to the swank Half Moon Club. Sandwiches and cold drinks are available for take-out but the best selections here are the homemade pastries and breads. Gather up a beach picnic: a bottle of wine, a baguette, and a chunk of good cheese.

PORT ANTONIO
Expensive

BLUE LAGOON, *Fairy Hill. Tel. 993-8491. Go east from Port Antonio about two miles on the A4. Plan to spend $20-$25 for dinner. Reservations are accepted. It's open Monday through Wednesday 11am to 5 pm. and Thursday through Sunday until 10pm.*

The Blue Hole, as it is noted on Jamaican maps made before the film *Blue Lagoon* came out, has become almost too popular since the movie, but it's still hard to resist the allure of this ink-blue water and its mineral bath. Use the changing rooms and make a day or evening of it by dining in this spectacular terrace restaurant at the edge of the water. The $3 admission is waived for diners. Specialties include jerk chicken or pork, spicy sausage, fresh lobster, lamb chops, or crayfish surrounded by fresh, local vegetables. Before dinner, try the Blue Lagoon cocktail, made with a mystery ingredient that we guess is blue Curacao liqueur. Entertainers play on weekends.

LE GAUCHO, *in the Jamaica Palace Hotel. Tel. 993-2020. Call for hours and reservations and plan to spend $40 to $50 for dinner.*

Olé! In this Argentine-theme restaurant, fork into a top sirloin steak, a tender filet mignon or a T-bone steak, all served sizzling hot from the grill with a foil-wrapped baked potato and your choice of salad. There's also chicken and seafood but steak-starved carnivores will love this place.

THE FALCON, *in the Jamaica Crest Resort, Fairy Hill. Tel. 993-8400. Dinner dishes are priced $15 to $30. Reservations are essential; transportation is available.*

Commanding views of the Blue Mountains and the Caribbean bless a resort whose signature restaurant perches like a falcon over the view. The menu offers traditional American and Jamaica dishes and, after dinner, there is dancing in the disco.

TRIDENT VILLAS & HOTEL, *just east of Port Antonio off the A4. Tel. 993-2602. Plan to spend $50-$75 for dinner. Reservations are essential. Dinner is served 7-10pm.*

One of the most upscale resorts on Jamaica offers air conditioned dining in an elegant, woody room reminiscent of Jamaica's rich, colonial past. Tables are set with starchy linens, crystal, silver, and pewter stemware. You may see a movie star or famous model at the next table while you dine on continental cuisine prepared by European chefs and served by white-gloved waiters who come and go, silent as ghosts except for the whispered report of what dishes is being put in front of you. It may be coconut soup, mahi-mahi with a delicate Dijon sauce, or a fork-tender steak served with crisp-tender vegetables and creamy Irish potatoes.

This is one of the few restaurants that serves the very expensive 100 percent Blue Mountain coffee. Service is impeccable, the wine list impressive, the candlelight incredibly romantic, and the dress code fancy. Jackets are required for gentlemen.

Moderate

FERN HILL CLUB, *San San. Tel. 993-3222. Dishes are priced $12 to $20. Hours are 8am to 9:30pm daily; the bar stays open until midnight. Reservations are essential.*

The best bets here are special occasions when a local dance troupe performs or a barbecue is set up. Arrive early enough for a sundowner overlooking one of the best sunset views in the Caribbean. Lunch is simple, with choices of refreshing sandwiches, jerks, and cold drinks.

MILLE FLEURS, *in the Hotel Mocking Bird Hill. Tel. 998-7134. Hours are 8:30am to 9:30pm. Reservations are essential. Plan to spend $40 for dinner.*

Have a drink first in the homey living room of this small hotel while you page through one of the coffee table books describing Jamaican history or nature. Then dine on the porch, which seems afloat in a forest of flowering shrubs overlooking the sea far in the distance. Local fruits and organically grown vegetables are woven into wonderful fish, chicken, and vegetarian dishes. Try the sweet potato soup.

Budget

JERK PORK CENTER, *Boston Bay, no telephone. Have a meal for $10-$15 including a beer.*

Drive east from Port Antonio to Boston Beach, a popular beach with locals and tourists, where jerk cooks have set up shop to offer some of the best and most authentic jerked chicken, beef, and pork on the island.

RAFTER'S REST, *at the Rio Grande Rafting Center. Tel. 993-2778. Open daily 8am to 7pm, it offers snacks and meals in the $5 to $15 range.*

Relax on a deck overlooking the river where rafting trips end and passengers debark. The scene is fun to watch as rafters stop their craft with uncanny ability and somehow get their (often elderly and/or portly) passengers to the dock without a hitch. Dining during the day is on simple sandwiches, sweets, and cold drinks. At dinner, the grill is fired up to cook burgers, chicken, lobster, and fresh fish, which are served with rafts of fresh local vegetables.

WOODY'S LOW BRIDGE PLACE, *Tel. 993-3888. in Drapers, across from the school, east of Trident. No credit cards are accepted. Meals are priced in the $10 range.*

Reggae plays while you savor the fish or lobster that Woody himself caught this morning and grills with herbs from his own garden. The place is tiny, with only three tables and a few bar stools, but stop in anyway in hopes there will be room for you.

YACHTSMAN'S WHARF, *16 West Street at the end of the commercial dock. Tel. 993-3053. Dishes are priced $7 to $15. Credit cards aren't accepted. Hours are 7:30am to 10pm.*

Ferries for Navy Island shuttle back and forth from this busy dock, so this eatery and Errol Flynn-esque bar is a popular hangout for tourists as well as for yachties anchored in the harbor. You can always get a filling meal of burgers, sandwiches, curry, or seafood and chicken platters with the trimmings. If you're not hungry, just stop in for a drink to see the souvenirs left here by visiting sailors.

TREASURE BEACH ON THE SOUTH COAST

YABBA, *in the Treasure Beach Hotel, Treasure Beach, 10 miles south of Black River on the South Coast, on Great Pedro Bay. Tel. 965-0110. It's open daily, 7am to 10pm Dishes are priced $6 to $25.*

If explorations bring you to the south coast, try this beachfront hotel restaurant for local or international cuisine prepared with fresh vegetables from the owner's farm.

SEEING THE SIGHTS

Few islands offer the variety that Jamaica does in both natural wonders and cultural sightseeing. Its city life is among the Caribbean's most sophisticated; its country life varies from aloof greathouses to squalid villages, from mountainside aeries to seasides and riverfronts. Its underwater world is a showplace of aquatic life forms.

Jamaica is the home of a nature preserve filled with crocodiles and of rain forests where lucky visitors might spot a rare parrot. It has museums and historic shrines, including the homes of Noel Coward and Bob Marley. It's an island you can travel for years without seeing it all. Admissions rates are listed in Jamaican dollars, which are worth about three U.S. cents.

KINGSTON

Driving and parking in the city are difficult, so take a guided tour, at least at first to acquaint you with the lay of the land. The tourism essential here for reggae fans is the **Bob Marley Museum** at 56 Hope Road, *Tel. 927-9152.* Once his home and the site of the Tuff Gong recording studio, it is filled with memorabilia of the star's life and work. It's open 9am to 5pm Monday-Thursday and Friday, and 12:30 to 5:30pm Wednesday and Saturday. Admission is J$180 adults and J$25 children.

Devon House, 26 Hope Road, *Tel. 929-7029,* is an 1881 mansion built by George Stiebel, a black Jamaican who became a millionaire through his mines in Latin America. Plan to spend at least half a day touring the splendor of the home and enjoying the grounds, which have restaurants, sweets shops, boutiques, and crafts shops. Admission is J$110. Hours are daily except Sunday 10am to 5pm. While you're here, note the prime minister's residence next door, a stately mansion with a Tara-like columned facade. Continuing along Hope Road, you'll also pass the governor's mansion, called King's House.

For insight into Jamaica's cultural heritage, spend half a day in the **National Gallery of Art** in the Kingston Mall at 12 Ocean Boulevard, *Tel. 922-1563*. Sculpture and paintings show the development of Jamaica's most famous artists. Hours are Monday through Friday 11am to 4:30pm Admission is J$40. Then spend half a day at the Craft Market on Port Royal Street to see Jamaica's arts translated into everyday souvenirs in wood, straw, and batik.

Northwest of the city, **Castleton Botanical Gardens** are a wonderland of flowers and shrubs. They're open every day except Sunday and are free. **Hope Botanical Gardens** are also open daily free, but a small admission is charged for the zoo. On the grounds are 50 acres of labeled trees and shrubs, shops, a restaurant, and rides. West of the city, **Caymanas Park** has horse racing, a passion with Jamaicans, on Wednesday, Saturday, and holidays.

If you're into mineral baths, it's interesting to see and soak in the **Rockford Mineral Bath**, *Tel. 938-5055*. It's a natural spring that appeared during an earthquake in 1907 and soon became a fashionable spa. It's still popular for picnicking, massage, swimming, and whirlpool treatments. Admission to the public bath is J$60 and to the private baths J$380 to J$1200. A cafeteria and juice bar are on the premises.

Take the ferry from West Beach Dock on the 30-minute ride to **Port Royal**, which was destroyed by an earthquake in 1692. A lawless pit of pirates and prostitutes, it was swallowed in a cataclysm that many saw as divine punishment for its sins. More than a third of the city slid into the sea.

Today's historic highlights include **Fort Charles**, one of the six forts that guarded the entrance to Kingston Harbour during the centuries when Spain and English were duking it out over the island. It was built before the earthquake, strengthened and re-strengthened until it became a major fortress commanded by Horatio Lord Nelson himself. Jamaica was captured by the British in 1655 and it was so well fortified that it never fell again.

Parts of the complex still show the effects of the day the earth moved. Called **Giddy House**, one structure is tilted 45 degrees. The fort and its fine maritime museum are open 10am to 5pm Monday through Thursday, and Friday 10am to 4pm. Admission is J$30, *Tel. 924-8782* for the museum or *Tel. 922-0620* for the fort. While you're in town, note **St.**

Peter's Church along the Palisades. In its overgrown but interesting churchyard you can see the grave of Lewis Galdy, a victim of the 1692 quake. It is said that the earth swallowed him, then spat him out again.

Lime Cay is open all day free. Take a cruise to enjoy its white sand beaches in the heart of a busy harbor. Driving to Spanish Town on Washington Boulevard, which is the A1, takes you to the village of White Marl where the **Arawak Museum**, *Tel. 922-0620*, is on the site of one of the largest Arawak communities on the island before the arrival of Christopher Columbus. It's open Monday to Thursday 9:30am to 5pm and Friday until 4pm. Admission is J$5 but history buffs will want to give more to help preserve the place. The **People's Museum** in Spanish Town's Constitution Square shares the same hours and telephone. Enjoy the square itself, with its rim of fine old homes, a colorful marketplace, and rustic shacks. Note the remains of **King's House**, once the residence of governors, where famous guests included Lord Nelson, King William 1V, and Captain Bligh who gained fame aboard the mutinous *Bounty*. It has been a ruin since it burned in the 1920s. Then spend an hour in the museum to see how Jamaicans lived in the 18th and 19th century.

Fort Clarence Beach southwest of Kingston is the site of Twin Sisters Cave, a prehistoric cave that formed below sea level. It's open daily except Wednesday and Thursday 10am to 6pm. Admission is J$80.

FALMOUTH & MONTEGO BAY

Take a late afternoon cruise out of Rose's by the Sea, found east of Falmouth, aboard *Glistening Waters, Tel. 954-3427*. The coast is bathed in luminous colors as the sun goes down, toasted by drinks provided by your host.

Rafting the **Martha Brae** is one of Jamaica's tourism cliches, but don't miss it because every trip down the river is a fresh meeting with its wildlife and a personable Jamaican who poles the rakish bamboo raft. Tours, which cost about $20, include transportation from your hotel, a drink, entertainment by a mento band, and a river trip that lasts about an hour and a half, *Tel. 952-0889*. Ten miles west of Montego Bay, experience **Evening on the Great River**, *Tel. 952-5047*, which includes a boat ride up the torchlit river, a folkloric show, dinner, open bar, and music.

Choose from several tours to old plantations and greathouses. They include **Barnett Estates** on Fairfield Road, an 18th century mansion and plantation that is toured by jitney, *Tel. 952-2382*. It's open Monday to Friday 9am to 4pm. The tour costs $15. **Belvedere Estate** near Chester castle gives you a look at a working plantation, a historic village, and the ruins of the greathouse and sugar factory, *Tel. 952-6001*. A day-long tour costs $25 including lunch, daily except Sunday.

Greenwood Great House is east of Montego Bay, , Tel. 953-1077, a home that was furnished by poet Elizabeth Barrett Browning with antiques and rare musical instruments. It's open daily 9am to 6pm Admission is $10. **Rose Hall Great House** east of Montego Bay was built for a sugar planter in 1760. Magnificently restored, it's roamed by the ghost of its evil mistress, Annie Palmer. Tours are given daily 9am to 6pm, *Tel. 953-2323.* Admission is $15 for adults and half price for children.

The remains of **Fort Montego** can still be seen on a hill overlooking the harbor. Come for the craft market that is found here now. Tour the **Marine Park** in a glass-bottom boat, *Tel. 979-2281.* Cost is $30; boats operate daily except Sunday. At the **Rockland Bird Feeding Station** near Anchovy, *Tel. 952-2009,* visitors can watch every afternoon, 2-5pm as injured birds, which know they can get a kind handout here, are hand fed. Admission is J$300.

South of Falmouth, **Good Hope Plantation** once grew coconut and raised cattle. It's a popular spot for horseback riding on marked trails, *Tel. 954-3289.*

MANDEVILLE & CHRISTIANA

Located west of Kingston about two hours, **Mandeville** is a popular vacation point for senior citizens who want to escape the sweaty, switched-on youth scene on the beaches. Still as British as beans and toast, it was built on a flatland 2,000 above sea level in 1816. It is named for Lord Mandeville, eldest son of the Duke of Manchster for whom this parish was named. Many of the original Georgian buildings are still here, moldering grandly among modern shops and shanties. Stroll around the city center to view the courthouse, built in 1816, the limestone parish church dating to 1820, and the 18th century **Marshall's Pen Greathouse**. The grounds of the mansion are home to many rare birds, so see how many you can spot. It's open by appointment for a group, for an admission of $10.

Mrs. Stephenson will let you tour her garden, a showplace of rare orchids, fruit trees, and anthuriums, for $5, daily except Sunday. Ask your hotel host to make the appointment. Your hotel can also arrange for your to play the Manchester Club, a nine-hole golf course that is the Caribbean's oldest. Near the city, stop at the SWA Craft Centre where Jamaican dolls, made by women of St. Mark's Anglican Church, are sold.

Up Shooter's Hill, take a free, 40-minute tour of the **Pickapeppa Company**, home of the hot sauce that is a Jamaican religion. It's open Monday through Friday, *Tel. 962-2928.* North of Black River, the **Appleton Estate Distillery** tour welcomes visitors with a free bottle of Jamaica's most famous rum. Admission is $12, Tel. *963-9215.* Hours are Monday to Friday 9am to 4pm. Another factory tour at Walderston near Christiana visits the **Magic Toy Factory** where wood toys and souvenirs are made. It's a good site for picnicking and nature walks. Tours are by appointment, *Tel. 990-6030.*

NEGRIL

Anancy Park is Negril's answer to Disneyland, a little playland of rides, miniature golf, go karts, nature trails, fishing, boating, and snacking. Its name means spider; Anancy is a favorite character in Jamaican fairytales. Prices are per attraction, J$30 to J$160 each. The park is open Tuesday through Sunday, 1pm to 8pm.

The Craft Market on Lighthouse Road sells local jewelry, clothing and woodwork in a two-story, open-air mall. It's open every day 8am to 6pm and sometimes later although individual stall operators may close on some days. Drive to **Negril Lighthouse**, a 100-year-old landmark that has a limitless view. Admission is free and it's open daily 9am to 6:15pm. Take a picnic sail to **Booby Cay Coral Island** to snorkel and explore, *Tel. 957-4323.* If you want to see what life is like at Hedonism II, the all-inclusive resort that is heralded as a hotbed of hanky-panky, buy a day pass or night pass, *Tel. 800/859-SUPER* to get the details. For about $70 you can get a taste of the lavish, all-inclusive life. The resort is mainstream on one side, and nude on the other side, where clothing is required only at meals.

OCHO RIOS

When the English conquered Jamaica they misunderstood the Spanish name Las Chorreras, meaning "the waterfalls," which they took as Ocho Rios, meaning "eight rivers." You won't find eight rivers at Ocho Rios.

Ride with **Calypso Rafting**, *Tel. 974-5199,* down the **White River** on a bamboo float like those used on other Jamaican rivers. At night, the way is lit by torches and a serenade is provided by jungle drums. The ride is priced at $35.

Coyoba River Garden and Museum at Shaw Park Estate, *Tel. 974-4568,* lies high above the city on the river that once supplied Ocho Rios' water. Winding paths thread through lush gardens filled with ponds and waterfalls; the museum is filled with artifacts from Jamaican history. On Wednesday nights, the Moonshine Festival for $45 buys park admission, a Jamaican dinner, transportation from your hotel, entertainment, and moonshine. Reservations are essential. At other times, admission to the park and museum are $4.50. It's open daily 8:30am to 5pm.

One of the most popular tourist attractions in the area is **Dunn's River Falls**, *Tel. 974-2857,* partly because cruise ships tout it widely and partly because everyone loves the guides who are on hand to help visitors climb the terraced, 600-foot, slippery waterfall. Guides go barefoot, but we recommend wearing good, gripper-sole, canvas or plastic shoes. You'll undoubtedly get dunked, if not bruised, so don't take a camera. Long chains of hand-holding tourists and cheerful local guides make the climb, which is cooling and beautiful as well as a jolly sharing among peoples from all over the world. Admission is $6, but most people tip the guides extra. Plenty of hucksters are on hand to take your money in exchange for sleazy goods or taking a photograph, but keep your hand in your pocket. More authentic souvenirs are sold elsewhere. The wierdos who pose here have nothing in common with the real Jamaica.

Driving the A3 south from Ocho Rios takes you through **Fern Gully**, a moist and shaded Oz of ferns of all sizes. More than 600 ferns are found in a valley so perfect it could have been drawn by Disney artists.

One of the area's prettiest spots also has a nostalgic tug for those who love Noel Coward's plays. His drawing room comedies could have been lived here at **Firefly**, his name for the hilltop overlook at Grants Pen in the hills above Port Maria. Here he lived, wrote, and entertained a long list of Hollywood and Broadway notables as well as, one day for lunch, Her Majesty, Queen Elizabeth II. The menu, guides will tell you, was canned pea soup because the lobster mousse he had planned to serve had melted.

It's as though he still lives here, with some of his clothes hanging in the bathroom and his glasses next to his portable typewriter. Little has been changed since he died here in this bedroom, with its hauntingly beautiful views, in 1973. Tour the home and linger on the grounds with their lawns, the view, and the stone marker placed at the overlook that Coward loved so much. Refreshments are sold in the old stone building where lookouts for pirates and enemy ships are said to have been posted three hundred years ago. Admission is $10; hours are 8:30am to 5pm daily, *Tel. 997-7201*. Find Firefly 20 miles east of Ocho Rios above Oracabessa.

During the same excursion, tour **Goldeneye** which has been open off and on. When we last checked, it was open Tuesday through Sunday 9am to 7pm. The house was built by Ian Fleming, creator of James Bond, in 1946. He wrote all of the 13 original 007 books here in a home where visitors included Truman Capote, Graham Greene, and his neighbor, Noel Coward. Much of the original memorabilia has been removed, but Fleming's writing desk remains. It's 13 miles east of Ocho Rios in Oracabessa, *Tel. 974-5833*. Admission is $5.

Have lunch at **Harmony Hall**, which is on the A3 four miles east of Ocho Rios. It's primarily an art gallery in a Victorian mansion that once served as a minister's manse, but the food is varied, fresh, moderately priced, and caringly presented. Admission to the galleries, which are open daily 10am to 6pm, is free.

Even though we've been several times to **Prospect Plantation**, which is just west of downtown Ocho Rios, *Tel. 974-2058,* it is always an interesting view of a working plantation that is part of a school. Jitney drivers know their hospitality well, always providing plenty of patter and information about coconuts, cacao, pimento, and coffee. They'll stop often to grab a handful of spicy leaves for guests to sniff or to point out a mongoose skittering across the road, and as a grand finale will climb a coconut tree using only bare hands and feet.

One area of the plantation contains trees that were planted by famous visitors including Noel Coward, Sir Winston Churchill, Charlie Chaplin, and Henry Kissinger. Admission is $10 plus the tips you'll want to give the driver and various helpers and hangers-on. Included are the tour and a sticky-sweet rum punch. It's three miles east of Ocho Rios, on the A3. If you want to ride the Plantation on horseback, call ahead.

Historic sites near Montego Bay include **Rio Neuvo Battle Site** and **Great House**, where the final battle was fought between the British and Spanish, *Tel. 975-5441.* It is east of Ocho Rios, past Prospect Plantation. **Seville Great House** and **Heritage Park** near St. Ann's Bay is the ruins of a Spanish stronghold that once contained a church, sugar mill, and a castle, *Tel. 972-2191.* Admission is $4; hours are daily 8am to 5pm. If you want to see the area by helicopter, and it is a breath-catching sight, *Tel. 974-2265.* Or, drive up **Murphy Hill** for the view of Ocho Rios from an old farm 2,000 feet high.

PORT ANTONIO

Swashbuckling movie star Errol Flynn can be credited with putting Port Antonio on the tourism map. Jamaica's northeast coast has a reputation for non-stop rain, which is undeserved because most of the rain comes quickly and then it is over, leaving dewy greenery and brilliant flowers behind. Flynn settled in the area and his widow, Patrice Wymore, still lives and ranches here.

They were among the many Hollywood stars who came here in the 1930s and '40s when this was a busy banana port, easily reached by ship or railroad. Now the railroad has rusted away and the few cruise ships that tried stopping here have gone elsewhere.

Despite the difficulty of getting here from the nearest jet airports at Kingston and Montego Bay, Port Antonio continues to grow. Many of its visitors come because of its remoteness. Luminaries including Eddie Murphy, Tommy Tune, Whoopi Goldberg, Peter O'Toole, and Mr. and Mrs. John F. Kennedy, Jr., enjoy the privacy they can find here.

The town itself has little to offer except a ramshackle waterfront and a seedy downtown with only a few notable sites. One of them is **DeMontevin**

Lodge, a Victorian relic that served as an admiral's home and is now a very good restaurant, *Tel. 993-2604*. The fort at the tip of Titchfield Peninsula is now a school that isn't open to the public, but it's interesting to look at from the street.

Folly, east of Port Antonio on the A-4, was built in 1905 by American millionaire Arthur Mitchell as a gift to his wife, who was the daughter of New York jeweler Charles Tiffany. Today cracks, chunks, clutter and vines spill from the broken spine of what was an extravagant mansion. The story is a sad one. Long before 1905, builders knew that mortar should be mixed with fresh water, not sea water, but someone here didn't get the memo.

Signs of trouble began to show soon after the Mitchells moved in. Eleven years later, knowing that the house was suffering from an incurable cancer, they had to abandon it. It's said that Mrs. Mitchell was too heartbroken ever to return. Now Folly's grounds and romantic ruins are sometimes used for concerts but otherwise it's not a safe place to venture after dark. Admission is free; there is no telephone nor, as far as we could tell, any caretaker.

The **Blue Lagoon**, one mile east of San San Beach, *Tel. 993-8491*, is an inky well of clear water 200 feet deep, fading to faint aquamarine around its wooded edges. The best way to see it is to dine at the restaurant that overlooks it. If you are a mountain biker, ride the Blue Mountains with experienced guides, *Tel. 974-7075*. For the less hardy they offer an all-downhill, 15-minute thrill ride.

Spend a day fishing, hiking, swimming, and picnicking at **Crystal Springs Resort** where orchids cling to trees and tropical birds soar overhead. If you catch a fish, it can be cooked for you in the resort's restaurant. Located near Buff Bay, the resort charges J$100 admission. It's open daily 9am to 5pm.

Just a short boat ride from Port Antonio is **Navy Island**, Errol Flynn's old haunt and now the site of villas, cottages, a beach, a busy bar, and a good restaurant. Make the most of it, exploring grounds filled with bright hibiscus, bougainvillea and palms planted by the swashbuckling movie star himself. Take your swim suit or, if you forget it, swim the nude beach called **Trembly Knee Cove**. A day on the island costs J$100. Take the ferry any time from 7am to 10pm.

Southeast of Port Antonio, explore the rare formations and tropical caverns at **Nonsuch Caves** and the **Gardens of Athenry**, *Tel. 993-3740*. They're in the village of Nonsuch. Admission is $5 adults and $2.50 for children. Hours are 9am to 5pm The last tour starts at 4:30pm. The cave was formed more than a million years ago and, long before European discovery, were a shelter for Arawak Indians whose artifacts were found here. Enjoy the shaded gardens with their regal coconut palms and views of the sea. Then tour the caves with their stalactites, stalagmites, and fascinating geological history.

Drive west from Port Antonio eight miles where, just past Hope Bay on the A4, you'll come upon **Somerset Falls**, *Tel. 926-2952*. Admission is $3. Swim in the deep pool, take a gondola ride to the hidden waterfall, and have a cold drink and a sandwich at the snack bar. Another popular waterfall is found near Manchioneal, 25 miles south east on the coast road from Port Antonio. From Long Bay, take the road south through Eccelstown and watch for **Reach** (also called Reich) **Falls** on your right. The road emerges back on the A4 at Manchioneal, and you can take it back north along the coast.

The area's crowning tourist attraction is its rafting trips on the **Rio Grande**, where Jamaica's rafting mania began. Crude bamboo rafts had been used for years to bring bananas downriver but here we meet Errol Flynn again. It's said that the fun-loving star, ever the consummate host, popularized rafting by getting his friends to bet on who could make it first to the finish line.

Book with **Rio Grande Attractions**, Rafter's Rest, Margaret's Bay, *Tel. 993-2778*. Trips costing $45 can accommodate two people, and they run daily 8:30am to 4:30pm. The trip glides eight glorious miles through thick growth and neat plantations past banks where vendors have spread their wares in hopes that rafters will stop for a cold drink or a souvenir. It's all so pleasant, we went back by car to drive the road that follows the river. The trip ends at **Rafter's Rest** where you can sit on a deck overlooking the docks as rafters debark. Plan your 2 1/2-hour raft trip so you'll land here at lunch time, then linger over a sandwich and a couple of Red Stripes. If you have a rental car, it can be transferred for a small fee from the put-in point to where you debark. Runaway Bay

Overlooking **Discovery Bay**, where Christopher Columbus first set foot on Jamaica, is **Columbus Park**, an outdoor museum filled with relics from the island's past. It's open daily 9am to 5pm Admission is free. Along the bay, Puerto Seco Beach has changing facilities, a restaurant, bar, and watersports rentals.

THE SOUTH COAST TO BLACK RIVER

Historic **Black River** was the first city in Jamaica to have electricity, telephones, and automobiles. Take a boat ride up the Black River, where crocodiles eye tourists hungrily from the banks with **Black River Safari**, *Tel. 965-2513* or **Jacana Aqua Tours**, *Tel. 965-2466*. From Black River, a drive north on the A2 brings you to Middle Quarters. Continue north to Y.S., also called **Wyess Falls**, for a challenging hike that brings you to a crashing waterfall.

East of **Treasure Beach** near a place called Yardley Chase, a 1,600-foot cliff is known as Lover's Leap. The story of the two slaves who jumped off the cliff is probably only that, but it is a breathtaking overlook well worth a stop. Admission is $3 and it's open daily 10am to 6pm. **Mayfield Ranch** nearby offers horseback riding for $20 per hour.

APPLETON RUM

*When you think Jamaican rum, think **Appleton**, an estate that has been producing rum since the 1700s. The plantation was founded, the story goes, by Francis Dickinson, who helped Oliver Cromwell wrest Jamaica away from the Spanish in 1655. Today the distillery in the Black River Valley, in the shadow of the Nassau Mountains, still uses old copper stills and then puts the rum in charred oak barrels where it ages for as long as 12 years.*

NIGHTLIFE & ENTERTAINMENT

Hundreds of thousands of overseas visitors flock to Jamaica for Reggae SunSplash in late July and Reggae Sunfest in August, both at the Bob Marley Centre in Montego Bay. The first event features top names in reggae; Sunfest is a nine-day Carnival blowout. Jamaica has its own National Dance Theatre Company, performing mid-July to mid-August with mini-seasons in November and December and special performances at sunrise on Easter.

Jamaicans love music and partying long into the cool of the night. It's likely that your hotel or resort will have bars and a lounge with live music and dancing. Even in the most remote hills, guest houses either have live entertainers on site or nearby.

See individual sections under *Where to Eat* for additional after-dark suggestions. If you like gambling, try the **Hot Slots** at the Wyndham Rose Hall, Montego Bay, Jamaica Grand in Ocho Rios or the Windham Kingston among others. **Electronic blackjack** is offered at the Jamaica Grande, Ocho Rios.

KINGSTON

COUNTRYSIDE CLUB, *19-21 Eastwood Park Road. Tel. 929-9403. In the Eastwood Park section two miles from New Kingston.*

Live music plays several nights a week until 1am.

THE LITTLE PUB, *59 Main Street. Tel. 974-2324.*

Make reservations for dinner and enjoy a cabaret show. It's open until midnight.

GLENN'S RESTAURANT AND PUB, *in the Towers Cloister Tower. Tel. 975-4360.*

Glenn's has a jazz club where Jamaican jazz star Sonny Bradshaw often plays. Call for free pickup for dinner, then stay for the music.

COYOBA GARDENS, Shaw Park Road. *Tel. 974-6235.*

Showcases a river and gardens but on most Wednesday evenings it holds Moonshine Festivals featuring Jamaican music and dance.

JAMAICAN ME CRAZY, *in the Jamaica Grande Renaissance Resort, Main Street, St. Ann. Tel. 974-2201.*

This nightclub is a frenzied favorite for after-dinner music and dancing.

For live jam sessions in Kingston, try **CARLOS CAFE**, 22 Belmont Road, *Tel. 926-4186*; the **COUNTRYSIDE CLUB**, *Tel. 929-9403*; **JONKANOO LOUNGE** in the Wyndham Kingston, *Tel. 926-9403*; **PEPPERS** at 31 Upper Waterloo Road, *Tel. 925-2219.*

MIRAGE CLUB & DISCO, in the Sovereign Centre at 108 Hope Road, is a three-level bedlam of music, bars and entertainment, each night with a different theme; *Tel. 978-8557* or the 24-hour information line at *Tel. 978-9233.*

MONTEGO BAY

One of the island's great after-dark experiences is **Evening on the Great River**, which includes a boat ride up the torchlit river, a folkloric show, dinner, open bar, and music, *Tel. 952-5047.* Wear bug spray, not perfume.

NEGRIL

RICK'S CAFE, *West End. Tel. 957-0380.*

Rick's Cafe is to Negril sunsets what Mallory Docks are to Key West Sunsets, except this is better because there's a full bar.

Elsewhere, pub crawl among any number of nightspots and discos along **West End Road**, Negril's version of a Las Vegas "strip."

PORT ANTONIO

FOLLY GREAT HOUSE, *east of town on the A4.*

An abandoned ruin that is often the scene of concerts featuring internationally famous musicians. Ask at your hotel and watch local newspapers and posters. When an event is held, food vendors are on hand or you can bring a picnic. Otherwise, don't go here after dark.

Elsewhere, the "in" spot is **THE ROOF**, 7 James Avenue, *Tel. 974-1042.* For jazz it's **BLUE LAGOON**. For an unusual nightclub experience,

---

JAMAICA'S HOLLYWOOD CONNECTION

During the 1950s, "Twenty Thousand Leagues Under the Sea" and "Island in the Sun" were filmed in Jamaica and the island caught on with cameramen. "Dr. No" with Sean Connery was shot here in the 1960s followed by "A High Wind in Jamaica" with Anthony Quinn and "In Like Flint" starring James Coburn. "Papillon" starring Steve McQueen and Dustin Hoffman was shot here, followed by "Live and Let Die" with Roger Moore. The list goes on: "Club Paradise" starring Peter O'Toole, "Cocktail" starring Tom Cruise, the British television series "Goldeneye" and ABC's "Going to Extremes." "Cool Runnings" starring John Candy told the story of the Jamaican bobsled team. Today the island is a favorite of cinema, fashion photographers, and videographers as well as a favored vacation spot for movie stars. Take a closer look at the person behind the shades. It could be a celebrity!

---

dance in the **GREEN GROTTO CAVES** on weekends at Runaway Bay. A Broadway-style Jamaican musical, *Caribbean Dream*, plays at **THE LITTLE PUB COMPLEX**, 59 Main Street, Ocho Rios, *Tel. 974-2324.*

SPORTS & RECREATION

Jamaica's two blockbuster sporting events are the **Johnnie Walker World Champion of Golf**, played in December in Montego Bay and paying the richest purse in professional golf, and the **International Marlin Tournament** in Port Antonio in October. It's one of the Caribbean's oldest and most prestigious sportfishing tournaments. Jamaica also has sportfish tournaments on the North Coast, Ocho Rios, Falmouth, Montego Bay, and on the South Coast.

Beaches – Montego Bay Area

If you're not staying at a beach resort, discover one of Jamaica's beach clubs that offer watersport rentals, meals, entertainment, change facilities and showers. One of the best is the Rose Hall Beach Club, White Sands, near Montego Bay, Tel. 952-5164. The all-inclusive price of $55 pays for everything including pickup from your Montego Bay area hotel and the use of boats. It's open daily 10am to 5:30pm. Admission to Walter Fletcher Beach or **Cornwall Beach** is $1.

Beaches – Ocho Rios Area

James Bond Beach Club charges $5 for beach admission and $10 to $40 for use of boats, wave runners, and other watersports equipment, *Tel.*

975-3663. Admission to Puerto Seco Beach is $5. At Irie Beach, St. Ann, you'll swim in the river 700 feet above sea level. Swing on a jungle rope and plop into the water, play water volleyball, and shop the pottery, *Tel. 974-5044.* Admission is J$150.

Bicycling

In Montego Bay, rent a bike from **Montego Bike Rentals**, *Tel. 952-4984* or **Tropic Ride Car & Bike Rental**, *Tel. 952-7096.*

In Negril, contact:
• **Banmark Bike Rental**, *Tel. 957-0196*
• **D.T. Bike Rental**, *Tel. 957-0014*
• **Holiday Bike Rental**, *Tel. 957-4968*
• **Nortigo Bike Rental**, *Tel. 957-4627*
• **Rambo Bike Rental**, *Tel. 957-471*
• **Salmon's Bike Rental**, *Tel. 957-4671*
• **Wright's Bike Rental**, *Tel. 957-4908*

In Ocho Rios, try **Abe Rental & Sales Ltd.**, *Tel. 974-1008* or **Jakes Bike Rental**, *Tel. 973-4403.* In Port Antonio, rent from **D&L Rentals**, *Tel. 993-3282* or **Rainbow Rentals**, *Tel. 993-2248.* Caution: Jamaica's roads are narrow and rough and bicyclists must share them with careening traffic.

Bird Watching

Contact the **Touring Society of Jamaica**, *Tel. 954-2383,* for information on island-wide birding tours. The island hosts 25 species and 21 subspecies that are found nowhere else on earth. The total number of species found here is more than 250.

Fishing

Sportfishing boats cost about $400 the half day including captain, crew, and tackle for four to six guests. In Montego Bay, call the **Yacht Club**, *Tel. 979-8038* or **Rhapsody**, *Tel. 979-0104.* Aboard the **No Problem**, *Tel. 995-2912* you'll have a day or half day of fishing with drinks and tackle for $350 to $650. In Negril, call:
• **Best Boat Reef Tour**, *Tel. 995-3357*
• **Blue Whale Divers**, *Tel. 957-4438*
• **Dolphin Divers**, *Tel. 957-4944*
• **Sea Raider**, *Tel. 957-4244*
• **Wild Thing**, *Tel. 957-5392.*

In Ocho Rios, fish with **King Fisher**, *Tel. 974-2726;* **Mitzy**, *Tel. 974-2527;* **Sunfisher**, *Tel. 994-2294;* or **Triple B**, *Tel. 975-3273.* In Port Antonio, charter with **Bonita II**, *Tel. 993-3086.*

Golf

Where else would your caddy carry your golf bag on his head? Be sure to get a caddy, because he'll know the course and its quirks. Even if you have a cart, the caddy will walk. Greens fees range from $13 to $140; clubs, including graphite models, rent for $12 to $35 per round. Carts cost about $35 per round; caddies charge $6 to $15.

- **Mandeville**: the Caribbean's oldest golf club opened in Mandeville not long after the game was invented in Scotland. It's is a nine-hole course with 18 separate tee positions, allowing players to complete an 18-hole round. Also offered are tennis and squash, *Tel. 962-2403.*
- **Kingston**: the **Constant Springs Golf Course** is 6,198 yards, par 70, built on the site of a sugar plantation where bits of old mills can still be seen on the fairways, *Tel. 924-1610.* **Cayamas Golf Course**, dating to the 1930s, was the island's first 18-hole course, *Tel. 922-3386.*
- **Montego Bay**: **The Half Moon Club's** famous 7,130-yard course was designed by Robert Trent Jones, *Tel. 953-2650.* Canadian Robert Moote designed the links-style course at the **Ironshore Golf and Country Club**, *Tel. 953-2800.* It's famed for its frustrating blind shots. The internationally famous **Tryall Golf Club**, *Tel. 956-5681,* is a 6,407-yard challenger 12 miles west of Montego Bay surrounded by sea and hillsides that produce winds that can make shots go wild. **Wyndham Rose Hall Country Club**, 15 minutes east of Mo'bay, is a 6,598-yard course known for its devious doglegs, *Tel. 953-2650.*
- **Ocho Rios**: play the **Sandals Golf and Country Club** course, high up in the hills, *Tel. 975-0181.*
- **Runaway Bay**: courses are round at the **SuperClubs** Runaway Bay resort, *Tel. 973-2561* and the **Village Green Golf Club**, east of Duncans at the Braco Lido Resort. The latter is a par-28, nine-hole layout with putting green and pro shop, *Tel. 925-2325.*

Hiking

Some of the most beautiful mountains in the Caribbean are the Blue Maintains of Jamaica, rising to as high as 7,402 feet above the sea. The highest peaks of the Grand Ridge or John Crow at 5,750 feet, St. John's Peak at 6,332 feet, Mossman's Peak at 6,703 feet, High Peak at 6,812, and Blue Mountain Peak, towering above the island at 7,402 feet. You almost have to be in their lofty tops, which are often lost in sweetly moist clouds, to see them.

Even before the word eco-tourism became trendy, Peter Bentley was housing hikers in rustic hostels and tents and supplying guides who cook meals before taking hikers into the outback. Book with **MAYA LODGE**, Jacks Hill, *Tel. 876/927-2097 or 800/532-2271,* where you can sleep in a tent or share a big room with up to 20 other hikers. Or, let Bentley suggest classier lodgings. The important thing is the hiking, high in coffee country and into the clouds, then deep into valleys wet with rushing streams and crashing cataracts.

The trek to **Blue Mountain Peak** is 21 miles, usually tackled in two days because you'll bed down for half the night then start at 2am to reach the peak in time for the sunrise. Other hiking trails take two to three days, although guides can find just the right length and difficulty for almost any hiking need.

Among the island's most interesting trips is the grueling, 14-hour trek across Cockpit Country; among the easiest is the pilgrimage to Bob Marley's grave in the village where he was born. Take the B-3 south from Brown's Town, which is south of Discovery Bay. Then, at Alexandria, go east to the village of Nine Mile. Guides can also be found through **Sense Adventures**, which is also a project of eco-tourism pioneer Peter Bentley, *Tel. 927-2097*, and through **Valley Hikes** in Port Antonio, *Tel. 993-3881.* The latter offers hiking and horseback expeditions of a half day to several days, overnighting at local farms.

Horseback Riding

Most areas of Jamaica are not far from stables where horses can be provided for riding the beach or rain forest. Arrange a ride through your hotel. Rides are usually priced at $12 to $130. At **Chukka Cove** near Runaway Bay, polo is played weekly. Trail rides and lessons are available, *Tel. 972-2506.*

Also in Ocho Rios is **Hooves Limited**, *Tel. 974-6245.* In Black River, rides are available by appointment with **Ashton Great House and Hotel**, *Tel. 965-2036.* In Montego Bay, ride at **Barnett Estate**, *Tel. 952-2382* or **Rocky Point Riding Stables** at Half Moon, *Tel. 953-2286.*

Scuba Diving

Dive operators include **Gimmicky**, *Tel. 800/815-5019.* A PADI five-star facility, it puts together dive packages that include accommodations, dives, meals, and airport transfers.

In Ocho Rios, **Resort Divers** is a PADI five-star operation offering dining, parasailing, and watersports, *Tel. 973-5750.* Other operators are found at many of the resorts and at **Island Dive Shop**, *Tel. 972-2529* and **Reef Divers**, *Tel. 973-4400.*

In Negril, dive operators are found at many of the resorts, or contact:
- **Island Charter Company Ltd.**, *Tel. 957-6163*
- **Marine Life Venture**, *Tel. 957-4834*
- **Resort Drivers**, *Tel. 957-4061*
- **Scuba World**, *Tel. 957-5100*

At Montego Bay, try:
- **Reef Keepers**, *Tel. 979-0102*
- **Rest Drivers**, *Tel. 974-5338*
- **Sea World**, *Tel. 953-2250*

In Kingston, contact the **Buccaneer Scuba Club**, *Tel. 967-8061*. In Montego Bay, call **North Coast Marine Sports**, *Tel. 953-2211;* **Poseidon Divers**, *Tel. 952-3624*; or **Sea World**, *Tel. 953-3250*.

Snorkeling & Sailing

In Montego Bay, take a snorkeling cruise aboard **Calico**, *Tel. 952-5860*. Sailing Tuesday through Sunday 10am to 3pm, the skipper offers transportation, snorkel gear, drinks and lunch for $50. Aboard **Freestyle**, *Tel. 995-3912*, you'll have a two-hour sail and snorkel stop with drinks and equipment for $25 to $35. The party boat **Jamaica Queen V** takes two half-day cruises a day featuring an open bar, massage, and snorkeling. A sunset cruise aboard **CHICO**, *Tel. 952-5860*, costs $25 for a two-hour cruise Wednesday through Saturday at 5pm for transportation, drinks, and light snacks.

In Ocho Rios, party and sail with **Heave Ho Charters**, *Tel. 974-5367*. Two cruises are offered by **Red Stripe**, *Tel. 974-2446*. Lengths vary; rates are $25 to $50. Sailing are Monday through Saturday.

Surfing

Among the best wind and waves for surfers is **Boston Beach** east of Port Antonio.

SHOPPING

Jamaica loves its reputation as a duty-free nirvana but, for ordinary folks who aren't looking for diamonds, French scents, and designer watches, $10 off on a $50 teardrop of perfume isn't all that exciting. If you're in the market for an addition to your Limoges collection or a very special piece of jewelry, shop at home first to get an idea of what you would pay at traditional, discount, and mail order sources for the same item, then comparison-shop in the Caribbean. However, if you're only in the market for a meaningful souvenir of a vacation in Jamaica, look instead for the works of local artists and potters, for local hot sauces, Jamaican rum, dolls, batiks, wood carvings, and the other homespun crafts that come from the soul of the people whose works you'll find along roadsides, in small galleries, and in native markets.

By law, purchases made in duty-free stores must be made in foreign (not Jamaican) currency. Credit cards are accepted in stores. Only in the local markets will you need cash and, even there, U.S. dollars will do. City shops keep banker's hours; cruise terminal and airport shops open depending on when cruise ships or flights are in; hotel shops have varying hours.

Caribbean art is catching on in international art markets but it's not too late for collectors to get in on the ground floor. Although much of its art is rooted in the African and European homelands of its settlers, and in patterns first laid down by the Arawaks, Jamaica's art really began in 1922 with the arrival of Edna Manley who is considered the mother of modern Jamaican artistic expression. Names to watch for include artists Barry Watson, Carl Abrahams, Susan Alexander, Hope Brooks, Everald Brown, Margaret Chen, Alfred Chong, Karl "Jerry" Craig, Lawrence Edwards, Colin Garland, Milton George, Christopher Gonzales, Amy Laskin, Kenneth Martin, Petrona Morrison, Seya Parboosingh, George Rodney, Lois Sherwood, Tina Spiro, Robert Stoddard, Barry Watson, Osmond Watson, and David Boxer, who is a talented artist as well as curator and director of the National Gallery of Jamaica.

The nation's best-known ceramicists include Cecil Baugh, Norma Rodney Harrack, Jag Mahta and Gene Pearson. Late artists whose works have already grown in value include Edna Manley, Karl Parboosingh, John Dunkley, and Eric Cadien.

Kingston has more than 20 art galleries, among them the **Gallery Pegasus** in the Jamaica Pegasus Hotel, *Tel. 926-3690*; **Mutual Life Gallery** at 2 Oxford Road, *Tel. 926-9024*; the **National Gallery of Art** in the Ray West Building, 12 Ocean Boulevard, *Tel. 922-1561*; and **Things Jamaican** in Devon House, 26 Hope Road, Tel. 926-6867. The latter is also represented at the airport and downtown in Montego Bay.

In Ocho Rios, browse the **Harmony Hall Art Gallery** at Tower Isle, *Tel. 975-4222*; the **galleries** in the Taj Mahal Shopping Centre, *Tel. 974-6507*; or **Sun Art Gallery** in the Half Moon Shopping Centre, *Tel. 953-3455*. Port Antonio's up-and-coming gallery is the **Gallery Carriacou** in the Hotel Mockingbird Inn, *Tel. 993-7267*. In Rio Bueno, stop at **the Gallery Joe James**, *Tel. 954-0046*. In Negril, several galleries are found along West End Road. In Montego Bay, the **Gallery of West Indian Art** is at 1 Orange Lane, *Tel. 952-4547* and the **Heaven's Art Gallery** is at 2 Church Lane, *Tel. 952-2852*.

KINGSTON

Large shopping malls such as Sovereign Shopping Center house many of the big-name, duty-free shops found in resort areas. Shop **Chelsea Galleries**, 12 Chelsea Avenue, Tel. 929-0045, for Jamaican and other Caribbean art works. It's open Monday through Friday, 9:30am to 5pm. **Swiss Stores**, famous for their Rolex watches and fine jewelry, were

COFFEE: THE ULTIMATE SOUVENIR

Driving up and up into the Blue Mountains, you're in the coffee-growing region after about 3,400 feet. James Bond, Ian Fleming's master spy who was born in Jamaica in Fleming's typewriter, wouldn't drink anything but Blue Mountain coffee. To that, many coffee drinkers say amen. Most South American coffee is the robusta bean, not the more fragile, more aromatic arabica bean grown in this thin, clear air. Low in caffeine and high in flavor, the coffee takes a year or more to germinate and many more years to produce a cash crop. The cherries must be ripened to perfection, then hand picked one at a time. Crops are only now recovering from a hurricane in 1989 that all but destroyed the coffee plantations.

When you're buying coffee, which is one of the best souvenirs to take home, read labels. Only certain coffees can be certified as Blue Mountain. Others are called Blended Blue Mountain (80 percent Blue Mountain), High Mountain Blend (not necessarily from the Blue Mountains), or Low-Land Coffee. The real thing is too expensive to be served in any but the best resorts. Still, it's sold here at less than you'd pay at home so now is the time to stock up.

founded in Jamaica in 1935 by a Swiss family. In Kingston they're found in the **Jamaica Pegasus Hotel**, at 107 Harbour Street, and in the **Mall Plaza** on Constant Spring Road.

NEGRIL

Tajmahal's Duty Free Shops found throughout the island are located here at the Beachcomber Club and the Grand Lido, *Tel. 957-4911*. Shop for gold and gems. **Chelsea Galleries** in the Grand Lido, *Tel. 957-4011*, sells high quality Caribbean arts.

OCHO RIOS

Have lunch at **Harmony Hall**, then shop the two-story art gallery for practical or decorative local paintings, pottery, and woodwork, *Tel. 975-4222*. Downtown, **Jewels & Time** sells jewelry including an interesting line made from antique coins, *Tel. 974-6493*. Shop **Something Jamaican** in Soni's Plaza on Main Street, *Tel. 974-6428*.

For local crafts, recordings, spices, sauces, coffees and carvings. Also at Soni's is a **Bollomongo** selling tee shirts, coffee, swimwear and souvenirs, *Tel. 974-0161*. **Chulani** at Soni's sells imported perfumes, jewelry, crystal, and watches, *Tel. 974-2421*. **Colors**, with three locations including Soni's and the Ruins, sells Cuban cigars, electronics, and cultured pearls, *Tel. 974-9271*. Find **Irie Beach** at Bonham Spring Farm, *Tel. 974-5044* to shop the **Red Ginger Boutique** for hand-thrown local pottery and arty summer wear. Wassi Art pottery is also sold at **Wassi Art, Ltd.**, Great Pond, *Tel. 974-5044*. Tour the factory here to see free-wheeling designs reflecting Caribbean and African color and motifs.

MONTEGO BAY

For cruisers, shopping here centers around the cruise ship terminal with its **Royal Shop** where you can pick up Mont Blanc pens at duty-free prices, **Jewels & Time** for gems and antique jewelry, and **Presita** for tanzanite, the latest gem fad in the islands. Downtown, the **City Centre Building** is filled with lavish shops selling jewelry, watches, china, crystal, and diamonds. The complex covers an entire block. **Bijoux Jewelers** are at the airport and at 57 St. James Street in the Casa Montego Arcade, *Tel. 952-2630*. They carry Lagos gold and silver jewelry, Hummel, Baccarat, Lalique, and their own famous Waterfall diamond ring.

Casa de Oro is in the cruise terminal, the Half Moon Shopping Village, and the City Centre Building. Shop there for famous-name watches, Mikmoto pearls, and leather goods, *Tel. 952-3502*. For perfumes, shop **Chulano** in the City Centre or at the airport, *Tel. 952-2377*. The stores also sell famous watches and has a big selection of tennis bracelets.

The French Shop in the Casa Montego Arcade has jewelry, watches, Lladro, and Capodimonte, *Tel. 952-2991*. **Copasetic** in the Half Moon Shopping Village is a chic place to pick out sterling silver and other jewelry, leather jewelry, island perfumes and dolls, Jamaican pottery, and a wide choice of crafts, *Tel. 953-3838*. **Swiss Stores** in the same shopping center is the place to buy your Rolex, or drop in at Tropicana to get Mikmoto pearls or a Patek Philippe watch.

EXCURSIONS & DAY TRIPS

Take a side trip to Cuba for $197 plus $15 for a visa. Round trip from Montego Bay to Havana is aboard **Caribic Air Services**, Tel. 876/953-2600. For a weekend flight and hotel package in Havana or Varadero, the cost is $310. Packages include breakfast and a tour of Havana. Take plenty of U.S. dollars with you; Jamaican dollars or credit cards won't do.

To book a truly Jamaican vacation, book with **Countrystyle Community Tours** in Mandeville, *Tel. 876/962-3725, Fax 962-1461, toll-free 800/ JAMAICA*. The group specializes in small guest houses, homestays and villas, meals in community restaurants, and tours to historic sites, farms, local discos, gardens and entertainments.

With **Island Car Rentals, Ltd.**, take a choice of seven tours include the Blue Mountains, Port Antonio, Ocho Rios, Black River, Port Royal, and

Kingston cultural or historic. Offices in Kingston, *Tel. 926-8861*; Montego Bay, *Tel. 952-5771;* or Ocho Rios, *Tel. 974-2334* will arrange the outing. From the U.S., *Tel. 800/892-4581*; from Canada, *Tel. 800/526-2422*. Or, take off in your own rental car to see Blue Mountain coffee country. The best route is the B-1, which travels between Kingston and Buff Bay via Newcastle.

Take an overnight cruise with **Heave-Ho Charters**, *Tel. 974-5367*. A multi-hull sailboat, skipper and crew, and itinerary will be customized to your pleasures. From North America, Fax *876/974-5461*.

MONTEGO BAY AREA

To tour **Cockpit Country**, the wild hills where escaped slaves known as Maroons live independent lives, travel with **Maroon Attraction Tours**, *Tel. 979-0308*. An all-day tour costs $50 including lunch and drinks.

Take the **Hilton High Day Tour**, which spends the day on a private plantation and includes a sumptuous lunch of suckling pig with 12 Jamaican vegetables, cold drinks, and a typical native dessert, *Tel. 952-3343*. Cost is $55 to $65 all inslusive from 8am Tuesday, Wednesday, Friday, and Sunday.

PRACTICAL INFORMATION

Area Code: 876

ATM: in major centers look for ATMs at National Commercial Bank branches to accept your MasterCard/Cirrus card. There's also an ATM at Montego Bay's airport.

Bank holidays: New Year's Day, Ash Wednesday, Good Friday, Easter Monday, Labor Day (late May), Independence Day (first Monday in August), National Heroes Day (mid-October), Christmas Day, and Boxing Day.

Banking hours: generally, banks are open 9am to 2pm Monday to Thursday and on Friday 9am to noon to 2:30 to 5pm. Most businesses are open Monday through Friday 8:30am to 4:30pm. Offices are seldom open on Saturday.

Beer: the local beer is Red Stripe.

Crime: including violent crime is a big problem on Jamaica. Use your room safe. Don't take valuables to the beach, even if you lock them in the trunk of a car. Get local advice about where to venture after dark, and check the spy glass before opening your hotel room door. Keep in mind that a vendor you met on the beach, even though you felt you made a friend, should not be calling at your hotel room.

Currency: the Jamaican dollar floats according to international markets but it is worth roughly three U.S. cents. A Jamaican $100 bill is worth about US$3. The best exchange rates are for purchases made by credit card, so charge as many expenses as possible. The best exchange rates are at banks; a less favorable exchange rate is given by hotels, merchants, and exchange bureaus. Except for liquor, purchases made at in-bond, duty-free shops must be made in American dollars. Note that credit cards are accepted at major hotels and restaurants but not at gas stations.

Customs: visitors from the United States may leave Jamaica with US$400 in goods after staying 48 hours. Two liters of liquor per person are allowed duty-free if at least one liter is manufactured in Jamaica. Canadian residents may claim $300 in goods each year based on a seven-day trip and $100 based on a 48-hour stay. Alcohol and tobacco products are not eligible. Residents of the United Kingdom are allowed 200 cigarettes, 50 cigars, one liter of spirits, and other goods to 36 Pounds Sterling.

Departure Tax: save at least $15 to pay this tax, which is subject to change without prior notice.

Driving: is on the left, British style. Your home driver's license is accepted. The speed limit is 30 miles per hour in urban areas and 50 miles per hour on highways, but roads are so poor you'll be lucky to make half that.

Government: Jamaica is an independent country, with a U.S. consul in Montego Bay. The capital is Kingston. The U.S. Embassy for Jamaica is in the Jamaica Mutual Life Center, 2 Oxford Road, Kingston, *Tel. 929-4805/9.*

Hazards: ackee is the national food, served everywhere and truly delicious, but it must be harvested and prepared correctly or it is poisonous. It's illegal to take it back to the U.S. even if it is canned or frozen.

Hospitals: are found in Kingston, Montego Bay, Mandeville, Ocho Rios and Port Antonio. Most resorts and hotels have a list of doctors and dentists on call.

Immigration: visitors from the U.S. and Canada need proof of citizenship such as a passport (which can have expired no more than a year ago) or birth certificate photo I.D. Others, including visitors from the U.K. need a passport.

Pets: are not permitted to enter Jamaica. There are no rabies here and officials hope to keep the island rabies-free.

Tax-free status: Americans can deduct the cost of meetings and conventions in Jamaica as just as if the meeting had been held in the U.S.

Taxes: a 15 percent tax is charged on purchases, accommodations, and meals. Departure tax at the airport at this writing is J$400, but it's subject to change without prior notice.

Time Zone: Jamaica observes Eastern Standard Time all year. It does not observe Daylight Savings time.

Tipping: it is common in Jamaica for hotels and restaurants to add 10-15 percent of the bill as a tip. If in doubt, ask if a service charge or trip has been added.

Tourist Board: offices of the Jamaica Tourist Board are found in Black River, in Kingston at the airport and downtown, in Montego Bay at the airport and on Cornwall Beach, and in city centers in Negril, Ocho Rios, and Port Antonio. In the U.S. offices are in Atlanta, Boston, Chicago, Dallas, Detroit, Los Angeles, Miami, New York, and Philadelphia. In these cities, check the local telephone book. In other cities, *Tel. 800/233-4582*. In Canada, *Tel. 416/482-7850, Fax 482-1730*. Overseas, Jamaica Tourist Board has offices in Barcelona, Frankfurt, London, Paris, Rome, and Tokyo.

Tourist Help Line: *Tel. 0888-991-9999 or 0888-991-4400* for tourism information and help.

MORE SOUTHERN WINDWARDS

37. ST. VINCENT & THE GRENADINES

St. Vincent, at 18 miles long and 11 miles wide, is the largest of a string of slipper-size islands that include Bequia (say BECK wee), Mustique, Canouan, Palm Island, Petit St. Vincent, Union Island, and Mayreau as well as a sprinkling of rocks and islets including the famous Tobago Cays. Tradewind sailing and the proximity of the islands makes **St. Vincent & the Grenadines**, known familiarly as SVG, a favorite with yachties.

To the north is St. Lucia and Grenada is to the south. Topped by a 4,000-foot volcano, La Soufriere, St. Vincent has a ruggedly cliffy east shore and a west coast rising sharply into the hills from black and brown beaches. Its steep inland is lushly forested, filled with deep valleys and rushing waterfalls. Its volcanic soil sprouts rich harvests of tropic fruits, vegetables, spices and arrowroot, the starch used to thicken baby food.

St. Vincent is as British as cricket and crumpets, but because the islands were at times under the French flag, charming French touches also remain. Its darker side is what many returning tourists are calling an "attitude" as well as allegations of government corruption in an ABC *Nightline* television feature that aired in 1997. An American couple were held for many months in a squalid jail before the "case" against them was thrown out. We followed the case closely via our sailing friends, and we recommend getting current reports from recent visitors before booking your trip here.

Before European settlement, the Ciboneys inhabited the islands and they were displaced by the Caribs. They in turn broke into two groups, the original "yellow" Caribs and "black" Caribs that resulted from the union of Caribs and escaped slaves. It's said that during one of their uprisings, English planters were fed through their own cane grinding machines by vengeful slaves. It's another of the delicious legends that bring history alive when you crawl around old forts and windmill ruins.

This is one of a handful of places where Carib Indians can still be found. After a final defeat by the British, the black Caribs were rounded up and sent to lands now known as Honduras and Belize; the yellow Caribs withdrew to a remote area near Sandy Bay, where their descendants remain.

Bequia, nine miles south of St. Vincent, is another world, an old whaling station known for its shipbuilding. The *Gloria Colita*, a 131-foot schooner was launched here in 1940 and found later in the Bermuda Triangle, abandoned and drifting. The mystery of what happened aboard has never been solved. Sailors from around the world have hung up their oars on this little paradise and they continue to pass on their boatbuilding skills from one generation to the next.

Mustique wasn't developed until the 1970s, when an international company moved in to build homes for the rich and famous (Mick Jagger, David Bowie, Elton John). **Canouan** has a small settlement and great beaches. **Mayreau**, with its population of 200, is a Robinson Crusoe island with spectacular sands. **Union Island**, with its 1,000-foot Mount Toboi, is popular with day trippers and the **Tobago Cays** are a must-see for day visitors.

Palm Island was called Prune Island until John and Mary Caldwell moved in and planted hundreds of coconut palms. Its Casuarina Beach rims the entire west side of the island. **Petit St. Vincent**, locally called PSV, is about the size of Palm Island. Beaches surround almost the entire coastline, and its nearby sandbars, **Punaise** and **Mopion** offer outstanding snorkeling and swimming.

Climate

Temperatures can hit three digits in Boston and Minneapolis in summer while St. Vincent and the Grenadines are basking in breeze-cooled 90s. Look for calmer winds, stickier humidity, and more rain June through October and keep alert for hurricane watches. Only rarely does a hurricane hit any one island, but they do occur.

ARRIVALS & DEPARTURES

St. Vincent's **E.T. Joshua International Airport** has same-day connections from Barbados, Grenada, Martinique, St. Lucia, and Trinidad. It is served from San Juan by **American Eagle**, *Tel. 458-4586*. **LIAT**, *Tel. 457-1821*, offers an "explorer" fare that buys stops at three Grenadine islands. **Air Martinique** serves St. Vincent and the Grenadines, *Tel. 458-4187*.

Airlines of Carriacou serve Union Island, *Tel. 444-2898, extension 2005 or 2035*. **Mustique Airways**, *Tel. 458-4380*, serves Mustique. **St. Vincent Grenadines Air**, *Tel. 456-5610*, also serves the area.

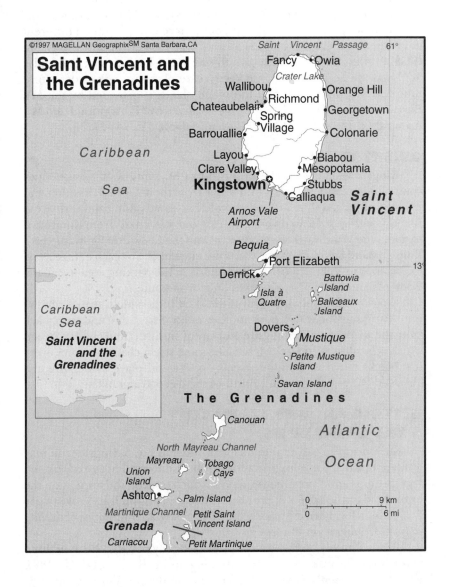

©1997 MAGELLAN GeographixSM Santa Barbara,CA

Saint Vincent and the Grenadines

Saint   Vincent   Passage   61°

Fancy   •Owia
Wallibou   *Crater Lake*
Richmond   •Orange Hill
Chateaubelair•
Spring   •Georgetown
Village
Barrouallie•   •Colonarie

Caribbean   Layou•   •Biabou
Clare Valley•   •Mesopotamia
Sea   **Kingstown**✪   •Stubbs
Galliaqua   **S a i n t**
Arnos Vale   **V i n c e n t**
Airport

Bequia
•Port Elizabeth   13°
Derrick•
Battowia
Island
Isla à
Quatre   *Baliceaux*
Island

Dovers•
•*Mustique*

Petite Mustique
Island

Savan Island

T h e   G r e n a d i n e s

Canouan

Atlantic

North Mayreau Channel
Mayreau   Tobago   *Ocean*
Union   Cays
Island
Ashton•   •Palm Island

Martinique Channel   Petit Saint
Grenada   Vincent Island

Carriacou   •Petit Martinique

Caribbean
Sea
Saint Vincent
and the
Grenadines

0   9 km
0   6 mi

Bequia is ten minutes by air from St. Vincent or Union Island. Both scheduled flights and charters are available. Mustique, which is privately owned, has plane connections from St. Vincent and Barbados.

Scheduled ferries go from St. Vincent to Bequia several times daily except Sunday for a fare of EC$10, but different boats run on different days. Service to Canouan (EC$13), Mayreau (EC$15), and Union Island (EC$20) is less frequent, perhaps only one or two boats a week. Schedules are always subject to change, so keep a careful check on your departure times. Service to Bequia and the other islands is provided by the **MV Barracuda**, *Tel. 456-5180.* Bequia is also served by **MV Admiral I** and **MV Admiral II**, *Tel. 458-3348* and **MV Sand Island**, *Tel. 458-3472.*

ORIENTATION

Kingstown, the capital and seaport of St. Vincent, is on the south coast of this oval island and is only a mile from the airport. At its other end is **La Soufriere**, a 4,000-foot-high volcano. Roads don't quite ring the island, but they do head up both the east and west coasts from Kingstown forming the Windward Highway (east) and the Leeward Highway (west). **Young Island** lies only 200 yards off the mainland. To reach it, take a taxi to the dock in Villa and use the telephone in the parking area to call the Young Island ferry. The trip takes only two minutes.

Kingstown's layout is typical of the West Indies. Main streets rim the waterfront starting with Upper and Lower Bay Street first and then, back from the water, the shopping areas of Grenville Street and Halifax Street, which is locally called Back Street. The same street changes names every few blocks much as London streets do. A good place to begin is the Tourism Office, which is just north of the Deep Water Wharf.

GETTING AROUND ST. VINCENT & THE GRENADINES

St. Vincent's road system includes 300 miles of paving, so you may want to rent a car for at least a day or two, but be aware that roads are steep and tortuous and Vincentians spend as much time on the horn as on the brakes and gas pedal. Rates are about $40 daily and you'll also have to pay EC$40 for a local drivers license unless you have an international driving permit. Driving is on the left, British style.

Kim's Rentals on St. Vincent offers a variety of cars with or without automatic transmission or air conditioning, and 4WD jeeps, T*el. 456-1884, Fax 456-1681.* **Sam's Taxi Tours** is at Cane Garden, St. Vincent, and Port Elizabeth,, Bequia, *Tel. 456-4338.* Bicycle rentals are available on St. Vincent at **Sailors Cycle Centre**, *Tel. 457-1712,* and at Bequia from the **Lighthouse**, *Tel. 458-3084.* Dennis Murray, *Tel. 457-2776 or 457-9113* rents motor bikes.

Public mini-buses serve all of St. Vincent at fares ranging from EC$1 to EC$5. To flag one down, wave your hand or point a finger to the ground, indicating "stop here." The main bus terminal is at the **New Kingstown Fish Market**. Fares range from EC2 to EC8.

Taxi fares are published, but should be confirmed with the driver before boarding. Be sure you understand whether you're talking EC$ or US$ to avoid (1) an honest mistake on the part of you or the driver or (2) a bait and switch.

A typical fare from the airport to Kingstown is EC$15; fare to the furthest point, Sandy Bay, is EC$90. Taxis can be hired by the hour at EC$40. Tips are welcome, usually at 10-15 percent.

Taxis and mini-buses are available on Bequia, meeting the ferries and small plane flights from St. Vincent and Barbados. Union Island also has taxis and small buses.

WHERE TO STAY

Unless listed otherwise, all these hotels accept at least some major credit cards. There's a seven percent government tax and, at most hotels, a service charge of 10-15 percent.

Rates, which are payable in U.S. dollars, are for a double room in high season. Low season rates may be discounted 40 percent or more, and singles are often available at a discount over double rates. Your address while in the islands will be address, island, St. Vincent & the Grenadines, West Indies. Don't abbreviate, or there is a chance your mail will be sent to Grenada.

BEQUIA
Expensive

PLANTATION HOUSE HOTEL, *P.O. Box 16, Bequia, St. Vincent & the Grenadines, West Indies. Tel. 784/458-3425, Fax 458-3612. Rates at this 25-room hotel are from $300. Unless you have a lot of baggage, walk to the hotel from the dock. It's a 15-minute stroll. The airport is two miles away.*

Porches around this pleasant, beachside, pink bungalow are situated to catches breezes from all directions. Dine on Italian classics on the terrace or snack in the beach bar and grill. Tuesday nights are lively with the weekly Jump-Up, and Happy Hour is celebrated daily from 5 to 6pm, but otherwise this is a place to soak up silence and sweet tropic scents in the shade of the coconut palms. Accommodations are in the main lodge and in cottages, vividly decorated and lightened by bed netting, or in a three-bedroom bungalow. There's a dive shop, freshwater swimming pool, restaurant, and tennis court on site. Walk into Port Elizabeth, sail aboard a crewed yacht, or take the water taxi to Lower Bay for the day.

Moderate

OLD FORT COUNTRY INN, *Mount Pleasant, Bequia, St. Vincent & the Grenadines, West Indies. Tel. 784/458-3440, Fax 457-3340. Rates at this six-apartment inn start at $160. Add $10 for continental breakfast and $40 for breakfast and dinner.*

Stony and historic, dating to the mid-1750s, this romantic inn has been furnished with medieval touches by Austrian hosts Sonja and Otmar Schaedle. Each unit has a kitchenette and private bath. The beach is a six-minute walk down from the breezy, mosquito-free hilltop with its commanding view of the sea and surrounding islands. Do take the meal plan. The creole cookery here ranks among the Grenadines' best. The inn covers 32 acres, so take time to explore their tropical splendor.

SPRING ON BEQUIA, *Bequia, St. Vincent & the Grenadines, West Indies. Tel. 784/458-3414. Rates at this 10-unit inn, which is three miles from the airport, start at $120. The resort is a mile from Port Elizabeth and hosts will pick you up. Meal plans are available.*

Built on a 200-year-old plantation overlooking Spring Bay, this friendly little inn has its own, 500-foot beach with a beach bar. They are a five-minute walk away, down a palm-fringed path from the main building. There's a freshwater pool, a tennis court with rackets to borrow, nearby hiking trails, watersports, and sailing trips to neighbor islands.

Meals are served at an added cost of about $60 daily. Most rooms have balconies, and all have private bathrooms with showers but no tubs. Rooms are not air conditioned.

Budget

FRANGIPANI HOTEL, *Bequia, St. Vincent & the Grenadines, West Indies. Tel. 784/458-3255, Fax 258-3244. Rates at this 15-room hotel start at $55 double. It's two miles from the airport and walking distance from the dock. Ask about meal plans.*

Not all rooms have a private bath, but most have a sundeck, ceiling fan, dressing room and bathroom. Thursday is Jump-Up night here with a barbecue and on Mondays a steel band plays, but on other evenings it's dining, reading, and early to bed.

Bequia has long been a shipbuilding island, and its flavor is captured well here in what was once a chandlery. Accommodations are pretty basic, but they have a pleasantly yacht-like flavor: wicker, hardwoods, woven sweetgrass floor coverings, and louvered doors to let the breezes through. The hotel has a restaurant, bar and gift shop and offers snorkeling, tennis, and windsurfing.

CANOUAN

TAMARIND BEACH HOTEL AND YACHT CLUB, *Canouan, St. Vincent & the Grenadines, West Indies. Tel. 784/458-8044, dZ 458-8851; in the U.S. 800/961-5006. Doubles in this 42-room hotel are from $300 including breakfast and dinner. A full meal plan is available.*

Your room is only footsteps from a white sand beach that meets a blue-green sea, with a view of restful green hills rising behind the hotel. Sun on the beach or read in the breezy shade of thatched lounges. Watersports are provided. The hotel has an airline desk, two restaurants, babysitters on call, laundry service, a shop, and telephone service. Menus offer plenty of variety, with focus on Mediterranean flavors and West Indian classics. Dine on freshly grilled meat or fish or choose from a list of pizzas and pastas.

MAYREAU

SALTWHISTLE CLUB, *Mayreau Island, St. Vincent and the Grenadines, West Indies or One University Avenue, Suite 502, Toronto, Ontario Canada M5J 2P1. In Toronto, Tel. 416/366-8559, Fax 416/366-0358. Rates at this 17-unit resort start at $490 for a double room. No credit cards are accepted.*

The only hotel on this tiny island gives you a *pied-a-terre* amidst 23 tropical acres and beaches on both the Caribbean and Atlantic. Play tennis, volleyball, or shuffleboard. Sail, windsurf, or scuba dive. Accommodations include double bungalows, double rooms and suites, all with private baths. All rooms have ceiling fans and a private porch or patio, and most have a king-size bed. Dining is in the open air to the serenade of gentle waves and rustling palms.

MUSTIQUE

Mustique is an extremely private, exclusive, expensive island. Many of its best lodgings are in private homes and villas that rent by the week for rates starting at $3,500 for two bedrooms. Some villas go for as much as $15,000 weekly. Usually maid and staff, car and perhaps some watersports equipment are included, but you'll have to arrange your own provisions (easily done, with advance planning and plenty of cash).

One villa, **Les Jolies Eaux**, was built by Princess Margaret and is now owned by her son and his wife, who rent it out for $9,000 weekly. **Obsidian**, a six-bedroom villa that rents for $10,000 weekly, is owned by the Earl of Litchfield.

A booking agent that specializes in islands including Mustique, where more than a dozen private villas are offered, is **WIMCO**, *Tel. 800/932-3222*. **Resorts Management** can also provide reservations at Mustique's private homes, *Tel. 800/225-4255*, and so can **Mustique Company Ltd.**,

P.O. Box 349, Kingstown, St. Vincent & the Grenadines, West Indies, *Tel. 784/458-4621, Fax 456-4565.*

Expensive

THE COTTON HOUSE, *Mustique. Tel. 784/456-4777, Fax 456-5887, U.S. and Canada, 800/447-7462. Rates at this 24-unit resort start at $890 including meals, transportation and an island tour. Fly out of St. Vincent aboard Air Mustique. You'll be met at the airport.*

Once a private club and now open to the public, Cotton House retains its former air of lofty exclusivity. Houses and cottages are strung together to form a resort anchored by a coral and stone mansion built in the 1700s. Play tennis, sail, arrange to go deep sea fishing, or just relax on the grounds to read, sun, and get acquainted with fellow guests over cocktails. Lunches are served poolside; the restaurant is renowned for its continental dining with an Indian accent; there are three bars. Transportation to island beaches is provided free.

FIREFLY HOTEL, *Mustique, mail address P.O. Box 340, Kingstown, St. Vincent & the Grenadines, West Indies. Tel. 784/456-3514 or 458-4621. Rates at this five-room hotel are from $250 nightly.*

Intimate and exclusive, this tiny jewel is known for the grand piano (imagine how they got it here!) in its lounge and for breathtaking sunset views. Dine by candlelight on pastas with a Caribbean lilt. By day, ride a thoroughbred from a nearby stable, play tennis, or just lounge in a hammock under the palms, catching up on your reading. The two swimming pools, joined by a waterfall, are surrounded by flowering tropicals.

PALM ISLAND

PALM ISLAND BEACH CLUB, *Palm Island, St. Vincent & the Grenadines, West Indies. Tel. 784/458-8824, Fax 458-8804 or 212/242-4700, Fax 242-4768; toll-free 800/999-7256. Rates at this 24-unit resort start at $295. It's a mile from the private air strip.*

Have the run of an entire, 110-acre, paradise island surrounded by five sandy, white beaches. To old-timers, it's still Prune Island but all that changed when hundreds of coconuts were planted and they sprouted into a fairyland of trees. Snorkel, scuba, play tennis, and take the daily yacht cruise to picnic on surrounding islands. The dining is creole, with lobster featured once a week. The book *Desperate Voyage* was written by the resort's founder, John Caldwell, who was shipwrecked in the Pacific while trying to sail to America from Australia. When he got under sail again, he arrived on Prune Island and never left.

PETIT ST. VINCENT

PETIT ST. VINCENT RESORT, *mail address P.O. Box 12506, Cincinnati OH 45212. Tel. 515/242-6951; reservations in the U.S., Canada, Puerto Rico and U.S. Virgin Islands, 800/223-6800. Rates at the 22 cottages start at $600 per couple including three meals and afternoon tea daily. Take a charter plane from Barbados to Union Island, where you'll be picked up by the resort. No credit cards are accepted.*

The *ne plus ultra* of island hideaways and a member of Leading Hotels of the World, this is a private, 113-acre island rimmed with salt-white sand beaches and afloat in a jade green sea. You'll have your own cottage with two queen-size beds, living room, bedroom, dressing room, bath and a private patio where your breakfast is delivered every morning.

If you choose to leave your cottage (room service is included if you prefer it), dine in the breeze-cooled restaurant overlooking the harbor. Luncheon is always a buffet and once a week there's a barbecue get-together. Activities include sailing trips to nearby islets, snorkeling, scuba diving, deep sea fishing, sailing a Sunfish or Hobie Cat, or playing tennis day or night. The boutique sells exotic clothes from all over the world.

ST. VINCENT

Expensive

CAMELOT INN, *P.O. Box 787, St. Vincent & the Grenadines, West Indies. Tel. 784/456-2100, Fax 456-2233; in the U.S. 800/593-6510. Doubles at this 22-room inn start at $275 including breakfast and dinner. It's a two-mile ride from the airport.*

High overlooking Kingstown is this modern hotel with such old-world touches as wide verandas, perky white gingerbread trim, and piano music played through dinner. King Arthur's Dining and Knights Room is open for breakfast and dinner; Gueneviere Terrace is open for three meals. Modern touches abound: queen-size bed, remote control television, air conditioning, ceiling fan, direct dial phone, a state-of-the art gym, a tennis court, and a beauty salon.

GRAND VIEW BEACH HOTEL, *Villa Point, St. Vincent & the Grenadines, West Indies. Tel. 784/458-4822, Fax 457-4174; in the U.S. 800/223-6510 or 800/633-7411 in the U.S. and 800/424-5500 in Canada. Rates at this 19-room hotel start at $210. For breakfast and dinner daily, add $38 per adult and $22 per child. It's at Villa Point, an EC$15 cab ride from the airport.*

A modern, first-class resort rose from a plantation house that dates to the turn of the century. Its site on Villa Point looks out over a sprinkling of green cays and endless blue seas. The eight acres of grounds are lush with blooms and greenery, dropping steeply to the beach. Play tennis or squash, swim up to the pool bar, swim off the beach, work out in the fitness center, relax in the sauna, or sail one of the hotel's watercraft. Your room will have air conditioning, satellite television, and telephone. Order from room service or dine in the ocean-view dining room.

Moderate

EMERALD VALLEY RESORT & CASINO, *P.O. Box 951, St. Vincent & the Grenadines, West Indies. Tel. 784/456-7824, Fax 456-2622. Rates at this 12-cottage resort start at $100. It's six miles or an EC$40 taxi ride from the airport.*

This is the home of St. Vincent's only casino, so it's the place for you if you want to play blackjack, craps, roulette, slot machines, and Caribbean stud poker. Your air conditioned cottage will have a kitchenette, a terrace facing the river, and a view of flowering gardens filled with birdsong and sweet scents. Swim in the two pools, play tennis, or go hiking in the surrounding nature trails. Dine in the casino or on the poolside terrace overlooking the floodlit gardens.

LAGOON MARINA & HOTEL, *P.O. Box 133, St. Vincent & the Grenadines, West Indies. Tel. 784/458-4308 or 800/743-4276. Rates at this 19-room hotel start at $100. It's at Ratho Mill on the southern end of the island, an EC$20 taxi ride from the airport.*

This snappy, upscale hotel is popular with the yacht set, where each room has a balcony overlooking the water. Use it as your base for boating the islands, or as a pre-or post-charter hotel. There's a restaurant, bar, swimming pool, and always a whirl of yachties coming in for supplies, drinks, chitchat, meals, showers and fuel.

PETIT BYAHAUT, *St. Vincent & the Grenadines, West Indies. Tel. 784/ 457-7008. Rates at this seven-tent eco-resort (limit 14 guests) start at $250 double and $160 single including meals. Accessible only by sea, it offers free water taxi service with stays of three or more nights.*

Popular with active travelers who dive, snorkel, and hike, this is a buoyantly free, self-sustaining environment in a 50-acre valley on the leeward side of St. Vincent. Every day the Things to Do menu bursts at the seams: hike to La Soufriere or the Vermont Nature Trails, go to Trinity Falls or the Falls of Baleine, snorkel, or take a dive on the dramatic leeward coast with its sheer walls and underwater caves. Accommodations are in room-sized tents on roofed decks against the hillside overlooking the sea and beach. Each has a queen-size bed, hammock, solar-powered electric lights, and showers.

Meals are picnics by day and, by night, wholesome gourmet fare by candlelight. Note: a group of 14 can rent the entire resort for $1,500 per day plus diving.

Budget

BEACHCOMBERS HOTEL, *P.O. Box 126, St. Vincent & the Grenadines, West Indies. Tel. 784/458-4283, Fax 458-4385. Rates at this 14-room hotel start at $80 including continental breakfast. It's two miles from the airport, or EC$15 by taxi.*

A small, family-operated hotel on Villa Beach, rimmed by sheltering palms and flowering shrubs, this affordable place has a health spa with steam room, sauna, gym, massage, facials, and a plunge pool. Every room has a private bath, telephone, and patio.

COBBLESTONE INN, *P.O. Box 867, St. Vincent & the Grenadines, West Indies. Tel. 784/456-1937, Fax 456-1938. Rates at this 19-room inn start at $72 double. The inn is three miles from the beach and ten minutes from the airport.*

Housed in an 1814 cobblestone landmark, this popular business hotel has affordable rates, two restaurants including one on the rooftop, two bars, and a shopping arcade at street level. Rooms are air conditioned and all have private bath and telephone.

HERON HOTEL, *P.O. Box 226, St. Vincent & the Grenadines, West Indies. Tel. 784/457-1631, Fax 457-1189. Rates at this nine-room hotel start at $57. It's an EC$15 taxi ride from the airport. Credit cards aren't accepted.*

Nothing fancy, and that's just fine with the leisure and commercial travelers who come back time and again to this comfy, breeze-cooled, West Indian guest house in the heart of Kingstown. It overlooks the harbor and, even though it's three miles from the beach, guests like its handy location at the waterfront on Bay Street, a five-minute walk from the main shopping district. Rooms are air conditioned and have private bath and telephone.

KINGSTOWN PARK INN, *P.O. Box 1594, St. Vincent & the Grenadines, West Indies. Tel. 784/457-2964, Fax 457-2505. Rates at this seven-room inn start at $55 double including breakfast. It's in Kingstown Park, five minutes from downtown Kingstown and an EC$20 taxi ride from the airport.*

A wrap-around veranda embraces this stately bed-and-breakfast inn with its mahogany furnishings. Relax on the sun deck, which has umbrellas for shade, or use the inn as a headquarters while you enjoy island tours, shopping, and watersports. There's a restaurant, bar, on-site car rental, and maid service. If you want air conditioning, ask for the one room that has it; the only television is in the lounge.

OCEAN VIEW INN, *P.O. Box 176, St. Vincent & the Grenadines, West Indies. Tel. 784/457-4332. A double room with continental breakfast is $45. It's five minutes from the airport and two miles from Kingstown.*

The modest, five-bedroom villa is set amidst tropic gardens, a two-minute walk from the white sands of Indian Bay. It's an ideal hideway just far enough from town for quiet days and fine views from the veranda where breakfast is served. Other meals are available, and the innkeeper will also be glad to book your tours, boat trips, dives, and watersports.

UNION ISLAND

Expensive

YOUNG ISLAND RESORT, *P.O. Box 211, St. Vincent, St. Vincent & the Grenadines, West Indies. Tel. 784/458-4826, Fax 457-4567; U.S. and Canada 800/223-1108. Winter rates start at $430 for two including breakfast and dinner. You'll be met at the airport and taken to the dock, where a launch transports guests to the island.*

Escape to a Caribbean garden of eden, once the private domain of a hotel executive and now a 35-acre island haven just off St. Vincent. Thirty smart cottages march up a leafy hillside from the beach and pool area to a hilltop that looks out towards Bequia and Mustique. Two of the cottages have private plunge pools; some have wet bars and wooden decks with hammocks. All have the island's famous indoor/outdoor showers, buoyant tropical decor, and views of a jungle where you might see a parrot, agouti, or iguana. Scuba diving, sailing, and tours to St. Vincent can be arranged. On the island, enjoy the beach with its floating bar, tennis, steel band serenades, a weekly cocktail party hosted by the manager, and tasty selections from a menu of continental or West Indian fare. Breakfast will be served in your room at no extra charge.

Moderate

ANCHORAGE YACHT CLUB, *Union Island, St. Vincent & the Grenadines, West Indies. Tel. 784/458-8221, Fax 458-8365. Rates at this 12-unit club start at $150 including continental breakfast. Charter a plane, fly in on Air Martinique, or take the four-hour ferry ride. The hotel is at the air strip.*

Choose an air conditioned room, bungalow, or cabana, all with hot water, telephone, and balcony overlooking the beach or bay. Although it has only a dozen rooms, the hotel has pace and pizzazz thanks to a stream of visiting yachts and air passengers who stop here for drinks and the French/West Indian cuisine. A sportfishing excursion can be arranged. The hotel has a boutique, full-service travel agency, sailing or motorboat outings, and a laundry.

Budget

CLIFTON BEACH HOTEL, *Union Island, St. Vincent & the Grenadines, West Indies. Tel. 784/458-8235. Rates at this 25-room complex start at $33 without meals, $50 double with continental breakfast, and $70 with breakfast and dinner.*

A complex comprised of hotel, guest house, apartment and cottage accommodations gives you a choice to cook in or dine out. Order from the hotel's West Indian menu in the oceanfront dining room, or snack on the terrace overlooking the small dock. Drinks are served in a breezy, carousel-shaped, outdoor bar. Watersports, jeep rentals, and sails to neighboring islands can be arranged. Rooms are air conditioned and have private baths and television.

LAMBI'S GUEST HOUSE, *Front Street, Clifton, Union Island, St. Vincent & the Grenadines, West Indies. Tel. or fax 784/458-8395. Doubles at this 14-room guest house in the settlement start at $30. At the new* **Lambi's Hilltop Hotel** *(same telephone) rates also start at $30 including pickup at the airport and dock.*

Business and leisure travelers alike find good value in these good-enough digs, one high on a hill and the other at the busy waterfront. The hilltop facility is new, with panoramic views of the islands, a restaurant, and a bar. The guest house has room service, steel band entertainment, a shop, and a restaurant. Provision at Lambi's "supermarkets," which are loaded with things needed by passing yachts: food, ice, baked goods, film, hardware and the like.

SUNNY GRENADINES HOTEL, *Clifton, Union Island, St. Vincent & the Grenadines, West Indies. Tel. 784/458-8327, Fax 458-8398. Rates at this 18-room hotel, which is just outside the airport, start at $85 double.*

Walk to the hotel and unpack in a room overlooking the harbor. Each room has a private porch and view. The hotel has its own restaurant and bar, and offers boat rental, snorkeling, and scuba gear.

TAKE A DIVE

If you're a diver, always ask about dive packages, which include accommodations in a mid-range hotel, tank refills, and other features. Packages in the $650 range, per person, double occupancy, include accommodations for seven nights, breakfast, a welcome drink, ten boat dives, and equipment. Contact **Dive St. Vincent**, *Tel. 784/457-4928.*

WHERE TO EAT

It's possible to eat well in St. Vincent & the Grenadines for under $50 a day but, since most menu prices here are in EC, that is how we list them. Top prices are usually for lobster, with many cheaper choices in fresh fish and other native dishes. Credit cards are accepted unless otherwise noted. If you're in doubt, call and inquire. Prices are for dinner; luncheons are almost always lighter and less costly. The exchange rate is about EC$2.70 to US$1.

BEQUIA
Moderate

COCO'S PLACE, *Lower Bay. Tel. 458-3463. Dinner is about EC$50. Open daily for breakfast, lunch and dinner, Coco's has Happy Hour daily 6-7pm.*

Surf and turf describes the menu as well as the guest list, which includes the yachting crowd and landlubbers. Have a burger and a beer, grilled fish, and the usual West Indies accompaniments. Live music plays Tuesday nights for a barbecue dinner.

CRESCENT BEACH INN, *Industry, Bequia. Tel. 458-3400. Hours are 8:30am daily until the last dinner guest finishes. Reservations are recommended. Plan to spend $EC50 for dinner.*

If you're lucky enough to be on the island during the full moon there's always a barbecue here. Otherwise, try West Indian fish, lobster, whelk, and turtle dishes or the beef or chicken, all served with fresh island fruits and vegetables.

FERNANDO'S HIDEAWAY, *Lower Bay. Tel. 458-3758. Reservations are essential. The restaurant is open for dinner only Monday to Saturday. Prices are in the $EC50 range.*

Monday is barbecue night. The rest of the week, enjoy curries, fresh fish, plantains, pumpkin and callaloo soup, peas and rice, and other traditional Grenadines fare.

FRANGIPANI HOTEL RESTAURANT, *Port Elizabeth. Tel. 458-3255. Reservations are essential. The barbecue buffet is EC$65; dinner entrees are priced EC$40 to EC$80. The restaurant is open for breakfast, lunch, and dinner every day.*

Overlook the waterfront and Admiralty Bay from an open-air dining room specializing in West Indian foods and fine imported wines. Locally known as Frangi's, the spot offers buffet, steel bands, and jump-up on Thursday nights.

GINGERBREAD RESTAURANT & BAR, *Port Elizabeth. Tel. 458-3800. Hours are 8am to 9:30pm; the Cafe and shop opens at 7am Entrees are priced EC$30 to EC$50. Reservations are recommended.*

Overlook Admiralty Bay from the upper floor of the Gingerbread Complex while you dine on fresh seafood to the accompaniment of a live band three nights a week. Gingerbread also operates an outdoor barbecue at the bayfront daily, where they grill chicken between noon and 3pm. This complex also houses two boutiques, a travel agency, telephones, sailboard and bicycle rents, and a dive operator.

GREEN FLASH, *in the Plantation House Hotel, Admiralty Bay. Tel. 458-3425. Open daily for lunch and dinner, the restaurant charges EC$30 to EC$80 for dinner. Reservations are urged.*

When you tire of the West Indian touch, come here for Italian food including pizza. Grilled meat and fish are always on the menu too. The hotel's Verandah Restaurant is one of the island's finest, a colonial villa serving alluring luncheons and dinners featuring fresh island seafood and produce. Try the chicken in green sauce, the lobster, or succulent fresh fish smothered in spicy Creole sauce.

KEEGAN'S, *Lower Bay Beach. Tel. 458-3530. The restaurant serves breakfast, lunch, and dinner, and snacks all day in the bar. Prices are EC$10 to EC$60. Credit cards aren't accepted.*

Have the catch of the day, conch, chicken or lobster accompanied by fresh tropical fruits and vegetables in this peachy, beachy spot.

LE PETIT JARDIN, *Back Street, Port Elizabeth. Tel. 458-3318. Hours are 11:30am to 2pm and 6:30 to 9:30pm daily. Reservations are essential. Plan to spend EC$50 to $EC75 for dinner.*

Choose from the daily menu or order a la carte. Bequia native Owen Belman went to sea as a chef on private mega-yachts and honed his cooking talents at the Culinary Institute of America before coming home and founding a primly comfortable restaurant in a garden of herb and fruit trees. The house, built of native stone and wood, makes a homey place to dine.

MAC'S PIZZERIA & BAKE SHOP, *Admiralty Bay between Frangipani and the Plantation House. Prices are EC$10 to EC$50. Winter hours are 11am to 10pm daily; in summer Mac's closes at 9pm and is closed Mondays. Credit cards aren't used. Reservations are advised. Mac's is closed September and October.*

Stop in for fresh bread, muffins, cinnamon buns to take to your boat or lodgings or dine in on quiche, salads, conch, pita bread sandwiches made with fresh sprouts, or a sensational lobster pizza.

OLD FORT RESTAURANT, *Mount Pleasant. Tel. 458-3440. Open daily, the restaurant serves breakfast, lunch, and dinner. Reservations are required. Fixed price three-and four-course dinners are EC$50 to EC$85.*

The feel of an old castle, a fireplace, and a menu fit for princelings adds up to a unique dining experience. The German owners spent 11 years rebuilding this treasure from the ruins of a greathouse. Try the spring lamb, the langouste in Creole sauce, or a grilled whole fish while gazing out on grounds where plum trees bloom and peacocks preen. Beyond them , the Grenadines spread below.

SPRING ON BEQUIA, *Spring Bay. Tel. 458-3414. Open daily for lunch and dinner, the restaurant serves meals in the EC$60 range. Call for reservations.*

A specialty here is the Sunday curry lunch, a time to try a variety of West Indian adaptations of curries fiery and mild. At breakfast have the banana pancakes with guava syrup. For dessert, don't miss the frozen key lime pie. Relax in the open air dining room and soak up the farmhouse comforts of a working plantation built overlooking a sea of coconut palms 200 years ago.

WHALEBONER INN, *Port Elizabeth. Tel. 784/458-3233. Reservations are essential for dinner. Plan to spend EC$50-$70 for dinner. The Inn is open daily, 8am to 10:30pm. Find it on the waterfront next door to the Frangipani.*

Judge its success by the number of dinghies at the dock. In a vacation spot where yachties outnumber fly-in visitors, look for the places where they hang out. The seafood is fresh and it's served with homegrown vegetables and Creole sauce; the beef curry is legendary. In season, lobster is on the menu. Less expensive fare includes rotis, fish 'n chips, pizza, burgers, and sandwiches. Shop in the boutique for silk screen prints and handmade resort outfits.

MAYREAU

DENNIS' HIDEAWAY, *Saline Bay, Mayreau. Tel. 458-8594. Prices are EC$10 to EC$50. Call for hours and reservations.*

Dennis himself, a former charter skipper, will probably be on hand to introduce you to dishes made from locally fattened chickens and goats, fish and lambi from local reefs, and fish from surrounding waters. A local scratch band plays for tips on Wednesdays and Saturdays when a belt-busting seafood special is served.

MUSTIQUE

BASIL'S BAR & RESTAURANT, *downstairs at the Cobblestone Inn on Bay Street. Tel. 457-2713. Reservations are essential. Entrees are priced EC$10 to EC$75. The restaurant is open daily from 8am through dinner.*

Lunch buffet style or dine by candlelight in a room where you might spot a movie star or a British royal, or lose yourself in a fantasy involving Bergman and Bogie or Crosby and Lamour. The seafood is always a good choice; the bar with its burly bouncer, Basil Charles, is the island's favorite hangout. Live music plays a couple of nights a week, but be prepared to pay modest a cover charge when it does.

FIREFLY HOTEL, *Mustique. Tel. 458-4621. Reservations are required. Plan to spend about EC$60 for dinner.*

Informal and filled with islanders as well as visiting celebrities, Firefly serves Caribbean classics plus pizza and pastas. Show up just before sundown for a drink at the bar, where you might see the green flash when the sun sinks into the ocean.

ST. VINCENT
Expensive

FRENCH RESTAURANT, *Villa Beach. Tel. 458-4972. Open daily 9am to 9:30pm, it serves dinner main courses in the EC$40 to EC$75 range. Reservations are recommended.*

Gourmet French cuisine takes on a West Indian accent in a distinctive restaurant where you'll dine in the open air on curries and crepes while overlooking yachts anchored in the bay. Choose your lobster fresh from the tank and end your meal with an airy mousse. At lunch time, order a delicate fresh fish or salad, quiche, or an omelet.

THE LAGOON & GREEN FLASH BAR, *Blue Lagoon, Ratho Mill, on the south shore of St. Vincent. Tel. 458-4308. Entrees are priced EC$35 to $55. Reservations are advised. It's open daily from 7:30am.*

Have a drink with a view in the Green Flash bar, then dine on lamb chops, steak, smoked fish, chicken, freshly caught seafood, and daily specials with a choice from a comprehensive wine list. At lunch try the homemade soups, a sandwich, the famous coconut shrimp or conch fritters. At breakfast, the menu lists omelettes, pancakes, and French toast.

SUNSET SHORES RESTAURANT, *Villa Beach. Tel. 458-4411. Entrees are priced EC$35 to $EC75. Hours are 7:30am to 9:30pm. Reservations are advised.*

Stop in any time before 9:30am for an English or West Indian breakfast. Continental breakfast is also available. Overlook Young Island while you dine on fresh fish, lobster, steak, or the day's chef's special, all offered with fresh vegetables and tossed green salad. Eat in the main restaurant, with its linen covered tables and rattan chairs, or by the pool.

YOUNG ISLAND RESORT, *Tel. 458-4826 for reservations, which are required, and ferry arrangements for the 200-yard ride to the island from Villa Beach. Dinner without wine costs EC$120. The restaurant serves breakfast, lunch, and dinner.*

Revel in the luxury of this posh, 32-acre resort while you dine in the finest seafood and imported meats and birds. Dress in smart, informal wear and hope for native music, which is often played. Three full-course, fixed-price dinner menus are offered. Ask about the Saturday night barbecues with steel band music.

Moderate

A LA MER, *in the Indian Bay Beach Club, Indian Bay. Tel. 458-4001. It's ten minutes from Kingstown and five minutes from the airport. Main dishes are in the EC$30 to $55 range. Reservations are suggested. It's open daily from 7:30am to 10pm.*

Dress chic and casual for an evening of seafood specialties, fresh bread, and homemade pastries at a mid-price resort on the sea. A beach barbecue is offered every Friday night in season.

LIME RESTAURANT & PUB, *Villa Harbour. Tel. 458-4227. Both pub and restaurant open at 10am and serve all day, with Happy Hour 9 to 10pm. Main dishes start at EC$25.*

Clubby and informal, this indoor-outdoor hangout is popular with locals and visiting yachties. Light meals are served all day; in the evening food ranges from snacks to full, candlelight dinners. Main dishes focus on seafood; after dinner choose a coffee from the espresso bar.

SURFSIDE BEACHBAR AND RESTAURANT, *Indian Bay Beach. Tel. 457-5362. Meals are $EC10 to $EC50 and are served 10am until 10pm. The bar stays open until the last customer leaves.*

The view of Young Island and the coast serves as an appetizer for pizza, rotis, curries, charcoal broiled steaks, and fresh island seafood.

VEE JAY'S ROOFTOP DINER, *on Upper Bay Street. Tel. 457-2845. Main dishes are priced EC$12 to EC$45. Reservations are required for dinner. Hours are Monday through Saturday from 9am.*

This is the place to "go native." Enjoy the view from the open air deck. Try a fruit juice such as mauby, linseed, peanut punch sorrel, or passion fruit, followed by rotis, liver, conch, burgers and fries, fish and chips, or a low-calorie salad. Every Wednesday and Friday night there's Karaoke for Creole Evening.

VILLA LODGE, *Breezeville overlooking Indian Bay. Tel. 458-4641. Prices range from EC$25 to EC$55. Hours are from 7:30am every day.*

This is a hotel restaurant, which means long hours and great breakfasts, luncheons, and dinners in a pretty setting with lots of interesting people coming and going. Try the fixed price breakfast, which offers a variety of foods including saltfish, pancakes and fresh fruit. Later there's barbecued steak, seafood and chicken with plenty of vegetables and fruit in eye-popping portions.

Budget

AGGIE'S, *Grenville Street. Tel. 456-2110. Plan to spend EC$15 to $30 for a main dish. Credit cards aren't accepted. Open Monday through Saturday from 9am and Sunday 5pm to midnight, Aggie serves Happy Hour Fridays 4pm to 6pm.*

This is the place to sample West Indian dishes the way things ought to be: souse, whelks, peas and rice, and piquant soups. Fresh fish leads the menu and lobster is served in season.

BASIL'S BAR & RESTAURANT, *in the Cobblestone Inn on Bay Street. Tel. 457-2713. Main dishes are priced EC$8 to EC$45. Hours are 10am until late hours, every day.*

Candlelight dinners and buffet lunches bring everyone to this downtown classic eventually. On Fridays there's a Chinese buffet, with take-out available. The eclectic menu features grilled fresh fish, tender steaks, burgers, sandwiches, lobster salad, escargot and much more.

BOUNTY RESTAURANT & ART GALLERY, *Halifax Street, Kingstown. Tel. 456-1996. Hours are Monday to Friday 8am to 5pm and Saturday 8am to 1:30pm. Most dishes are under EC$10.*

Sample West Indian roti, British fish and chips, Italian pizza, or American hot dogs and burgers washed down with iced tea or iced coffee or an exotic fruit punch. The gallery shows and sells works by island artists.

CHERYL'S COALPOT, at *Gibson Corner above the Botanic Gardens. Tel. 457-0197, is open from 10am until the last guest leaves. Dinner including dessert costs about $EC20.*

Eat Creole specialties al fresco in a lush garden setting. Let Cheryl make you a bowl of fish stew or pepperpot soup, a curry, pan-fried fresh fish, or a simple, butter-sautéed chicken breast drifted with island spices.

PIZZA PARTY, *Arnos Vale across from the airport. Tel. 456-4932. Dishes start at EC$15. No credit cards.*

Have a pizza delivered to your dock or hotel, eat in, or call ahead for a takeout order. Pizza is the chief food here, but there's also barbecued chicken, local West Indian specialties, and ice cream.

UNION ISLAND

ANCHORAGE YACHT CLUB RESTAURANT, *in the yacht club, Clifton. Tel. 458-8221. Reservations are recommended. The restaurant is open from 7am until the last dinner guest finishes. Prices are EC$20 to EC$60.*

Start the day here with fresh croissants and French bread. Snacks are available after 9:30am and the barbecue is fired up every day in time for dinner. Come on Monday, Thursday, Friday or Saturday night for reggae and steel band music. On Tuesday and Wednesdays enjoy easy listening at the piano bar, where you can order a great mango daiquiri. Order the fish or chicken with creole sauce, which is always saucy and spiced just right.

LAMBI'S, *on the waterfront in Clifton. Tel. 458-8549. Prices are EC$15 to EC$25. Credit cards aren't accepted. Breakfast is served 8am to 10pm, lunch noon to 3pm; dinner 7 to 10pm.*

Popular with the dinghy set, this is the place for quietly casual dining upstairs or even less formal snacking downstairs.

SYDNEY'S, *Clifton (towards the airport). Tel. 458-8320. Dishes are priced EC$10 to EC$25. Reservations for dinner are suggested. The restaurant is open daily breakfast through dinner.*

Come to meet the crowd during Happy Hour, 6 to 7pm or any time for seafood, crepes, pasta, and rotis. A pleasant little shack with a fenced deck, Sydney's offers dining in sun or shade.

Quick Takes

Good news for fast foodies. There's a **Kentucky Fried Chicken** in Kingstown at the corner of Melville and Grenville streets. You can eat for about EC$15. It doesn't take credit cards.

SEEING THE SIGHTS
ST. VINCENT

Kingstown, St. Vincent's capital, surrounds Kingstown Bay and the surrounding hills with a crowding of life and motion. The center of island life is the docks on Upper Bay Street; shopping is just west of the deep-water wharf in an area outlined by Upper Bay, Hillsboro and Halifax streets and South River Road. Just west of the deep-water wharf at the corner of Bay and Bedford streets, Market Square is a carnival of local color on Fridays and Saturdays when locals converge to shop, sell, and gossip. Get there before noon, and don't take photos without asking. These are working folks, trying to sell their wares, so a tip in exchange for a photo is a welcome courtesy.

Go west on Grenville Street to look at three of the town's best churches, all built in the early 19th century. **St. George's Anglican Cathedral** is brightly painted in Georgian style, with a red-robed stained glass angel overlooking the street. It was commissioned by Queen Victoria for St. Paul's Cathedral in London, but she refused it because she believed angels should be white. It ended up here.

Across the street, find **St. Mary's Catholic Cathedral**, built in 1823 and restored in the 1930s in a hodgepodge of styles, and **Kingstown Methodist Church** with interesting headstones in its cemetery.

On Berkshire Hill west of town, find **Fort Charlotte**, *Tel. 456-1165*, and a museum that depicts the history of the Black Caribs. The fort, built in 1806, once held 600 troops and 34 cannon. It stays active today as a Coast Guard lookout post. On a clear day you can see Grenada, 66 miles to the south. To the north lie views of the west coast and mountains. Take your binoculars. The fort is open daily during daylight hours until 6pm.

Head north out of Kingstown on the Leeward Highway. **The Botanical Gardens**, *Tel. 457-1003*, dating to 1765, are among the oldest in the New World. Among its treasures is a breadfruit tree said to be a descendent of the first trees introduced to the Caribbean by Captain Bligh of *Bounty* fame, who visited here in 1793. The Soufrière tree found here is the national flower, and is so rare that it hasn't been found in the wild since 1812. In the aviary are a dozen rare parrots that, with luck, you might spot around the island. These were confiscated from poachers and given safe haven in the gardens. If you're approached by a "guide" be aware that he's a free agent and expects a fee. Settle on a price before starting the tour. The gardens are open all day until 6pm and no admission is charged.

At the garden is the **National Archaeological Museum** and a remarkable collection of Carib stone and pottery dating to the time of the Ciboney, who were believed to inhabit the islands before the Caribs came, perhaps as early as 4000 B.C. The museum is open Wednesday 9am to noon and Saturday 2pm to 6pm.

Drive about five miles northwest up the **Buccament River Valley** to Table Rock for a dip and picnic, then continue to the **Vermont Nature Trails** and walk one of the well-marked loops. If you're a serious hiker, do them all to see a variety of forest and mountain terrain. With luck, you'll spot the rare St. Vincent parrot, which is best found in late afternoon.

Continuing on the Leeward Highway, you'll find ancient **petroglyphs** just north of the village of Layou on land owned by Mr. and Mrs. Victor Hendrickson, who usually welcome visitors for a small fee of about EC$5. Stay with the Leeward Highway for another half hour to see **Barrouallie**, once a whaling settlement. Today its boats are used to catch blackfish, a small whale. Continuing north you'll come to **Wallilabou**. It's on an inviting bay where you can swim and picnic. The road continues north to Chateaubelair and Richmond, where hikers pick up one of the trails to La Soufrière.

A mile north of **Georgetown**, just above **Rabacca Dry River**, another trailhead starts the long route to the volcano. Don't tackle either without a local guide and advice.

To reach the **Falls of Baleine**, a dashing 60-foot cascade that drops into a rock-lined pool, you'll need a boat trip. Most tour operators offer lunch and snorkeling equipment on the Falls trip. See *Excursions & Day Trips* below, or call the tourist office, *Tel. 457-1502*.

Back in Kingstown, drive the **Queens Drive** in the hills east of town. It begins between town and the airport, at Sion Hill, winding up Dorsetshire Hill, where you can see a marker at the place where the Carib chief Chatoyer was killed in one of the bitter battles between Europeans and aborigines.

Heading north from the runway, Vigie Highway takes you to the **Mesopotamia Valley**, locally called Mespo, with its verdant farms. Where three rivers join to form the Yambou River, look for petroglyphs on the banks where the road runs alongside the river. Just north of Mespo, tour **Montreal Gardens**, which aren't as busy as Kingstown's more famous Botanical Gardens but are just as fragrant and exotic. Another route from the airport follows the east coast from Villa Point through Indian Bay to Calliaqua Bay. This is the island's hotel "strip" with lots of good beaches, restaurants, and bustle.

It's from here that ferries leave for **Young Island** and **Fort Duvernette**, a must-visit site for those Caribbean travelers who can't miss one more rock fortress. Continuing up the coast, you're in banana and coconut country with colorful settlements named Biabou (buy-a-boo), Colonarie (kahn-a-ree), Georgetown, and Orange Hill Estate, once one of the largest coconut plantations in the islands. It covers 3,200 acres and is being resettled by small farmers in a government development project.

Continue across the **Dry River** north to Sandy Bay, Owia and Fancy, the northernmost settlement on the island. From the Owia Salt Ponds there's a good view of St. Lucia, 20 miles to the northwest.

BEQUIA

Sightseeing on little Bequia is a simple matter of working your way around the island, clockwise or counter-clockwise, out of **Port Elizabeth**. It's just one superb beach after another: **Princess Margaret Beach**, **Lower Bay**, **Industry Bay** for snorkeling, **Hope Bay** for advanced windsurfers, and **Friendship Bay** on the south side of the island.

In the golden age of whaling, Bequia was one of the Caribbean's leading whaling stations, settled by Scots whose ancestors had been mariners for centuries. Boatbuilding, including model boats, is still an island industry. For a climb to the best vantage point on Bequia, climb **The Mountain**, which is a 900-foot hill.

MUSTIQUE

Surrounded by a beaches in a glowing aura of international wealth, Mustique is a beachcomber's heaven. Visit **L'Ansecoy Bay** on the north end of the island for the beach and for views of the French ship Antilles, which grounded here in the early 1970s. Its hulk can be seen above water. On the east coast, try **Macaroni Bay** and for swimming and snorkeling, **Geliceaux Bay**, **Lagoon Bay**, **Britannia Bay**, and **Endeavour Bay**.

Charlestown, the main settlement in Canouan, is on a grand beach on the west coast of this island of farmers and fishermen. Or, swim at **Mahault Bay** on the north, **Carenage Bay** on the east, and **Friendship Bay** and **Glossy Bay** on the south coast. For hiking, Mount Royal is 900 feet high. In the north of the island, ramble the remains of a village that was destroyed in a 1921 hurricane and abandoned.

MAYREAU

Station Hill is the settlement on Mayreau; the best beaches are in **Saline Bay** and **Salt Whistle Bay**. All the Togabo Cays are a wildlife reserve, offering a fantasia of sea gardens for snorkeling.

UNION ISLAND

On Union Island, which has the second largest population in the country, **Mount Toboi** is the highest peak in the Grenadines, visible from most of the other islands. **Clifton** is the settlement, where you'll find a branch office of St. Vincent Tourism.

Snorkel on **Lagoon Reef** and **Frigate Island** just off Ashton Harbour, and try the beaches at **Chatham Bay** on the west coast, **Bloody Bay** on the northwest coast, and **Richmond Bay** on the north shore.

NIGHTLIFE & ENTERTAINMENT

In Mustique, **BASIL'S** beach bar is the place to cluster. There's barbecue and jump-up on Wednesdays, jazz on Fridays and, in late January or early February, a blues festival. At Canouan, try the **TAMARIND BAY RESORT** for drinks and pizzas. At Union Island find the **BOLL HEAD BAR** on the main street and little **SYDNEY'S BAR** on the airport road. Yachties come ashore at the **GRENADINES PUB** between the Sunny Grenadines Hotel and Grenadines Dive, and make for a lively evening.

In Bequia, walk the winding waterfront path and listen for the music. Most nights of the week, the best spot is **GINGERBREAD** where local groups play without loud speakers. A gingerbread-trimmed, Caribbean style, high-roofed building it's a popular hangout for boaters. During regatta time, around Easter, it's packed. Generally, Gingerbread has local bands on Monday, Tuesday, Friday, Saturday and Sunday. Wednesday is the night to howl at **PLANTATION HOUSE** and the **BEQUIA BEACH CLUB**; Thursday are the hot dates at **FRANGIPANI**. Watch for posters, which are the local grapevine.

SPORTS & RECREATION

Beaches

You're never far from a truly terrific beach in these islands, but if you'd like to combine a ride in a power or sailboat with snorkeling, swimming off deserted beaches, and dolphin watching, book with **Sea Breeze Nature Tours**, *Tel. 458-4969*. Most of the boats listed under the *Yachting* section below also visit remote beaches and the best reefs for snorkeling.

The toasty beige beaches are mostly along the south shore of St. Vincent; northern beaches aren't as pretty because they're covered with soft, but dingy grey, lava sand spewed by La Soufriere. Eastern beaches can have high and dangerous surf; generally the western shore is calmer and the black sands of **Buccament Bay** or **Questelle's Bay** have an exotic, ebon shine. **Villa Beach** on the west coast has white sands. Also see *Seeing the Sights* for beach information on other islands.

Bicycling

Sailor's Cycling Tours in Kingstown, *Tel. 456-1712, Fax 456-2821,* take you into the wilderness to see the volcano, the falls, rain forests, and historic sites. If you travel with your own bike and need parts, Sailor's has a good inventory and will ship parts throughout the Caribbean.

Fishing

Charter with **Crystal Blue Sportfishing** out of Indian Bay, Kingstown, St. Vincent, *Tel. 457-4532, Fax 456-2232.* Spear guns are prohibited in some areas so, if you go fishing on your own, get information from the **Fisheries Department**, *Tel. 456-2738.*

Hiking

Mountain hiking to **La Soufriere** is an all-day adventure, so consider hiring a guide at $25 to $35. If your hotel can't recommend one, try the **Department of Tourism**, *Tel. 457-1502.* The active volcano, which erupted as recently as 1979, rises 4,049 feet on St. Vincent's north coast.

Closer to Kingstown, the **Vermont Nature Trails** are winding threads through a valley and dense rain forest. Strike out on your own or book with **Petit Byahaut**, *Tel. 457-7008,* which also offers tours to Trinity Falls, La Soufriere, and Falls of Baleine.

Tennis & Squash

On St. Vincent, play tennis at:
• **Kingstown Tennis Club**
• **Grand View Beach Hotel**
• **Prospect Racquet Club**
• **Emerald Valley Resort & Casino**
• **Young Island Resort**

On Bequia, tennis courts are found at Spring on Bequia, the Friendship Bay Hotel and Plantation House. The Gingerbread Complex in Port Elizabeth also has courts or call **Sunsports**, *Tel. 458-3577.*

In the southern Grenadines, tennis courts are found at the **Cotton House Hotel** on Mustique, **Petit St. Vincent Resort**, **Palm Island Beach Club**, and **Canouan Beach Hotel**.

Squash courts are found on **St. James Place** in Kingstown. A fee is charged. For reservations, *Tel. 456-1805.* Squash courts are also available at the **Grand View Beach Hotel** and the **Prospect Beach Racquet Club**.

Scuba

• **St. Vincent: Dive St. Vincent**, *Tel. 457-4948,* offers dives, resort courses, or full certification as well as underwater camera rental. **Petit Byahaut** does reef and wreck dives. Equipment is available for rent, *Tel. 457-7008.* **St. Vincent Dive Experience**, *Tel. 457-5130 or 456-9006*, offers one-and two-tank dives, night dives, dive packages, courses, and equipment. An introductory dive in their pool is free.

- **Bequia**: Bequia Dive Resort is on the beach at the **Bequia Beach Club**, *Tel. 458-3248*, at Friendship Bay, offering one-and two-tank dives, instruction, equipment rental and snorkeling. **Dive Bequia**, *Tel. 458-3886*, offers day and night dives, equipment, and certification courses. **Dive Paradise** at the Friendship Bay Hotel, Tel. 458-3563, has two dive boats serving divers from beginners to advanced **Sunsports** in Port Elizabeth, Tel. 458-3577, is a full-service PADI facility.
- **Other Islands**: diving is available on many islands through Union Island-based **Grenadines Dive**, *Tel. 459-8138 or 458-8122.* **Dive Canouan**, *Tel. 458-8044* offers snorkel and dive tours on Canouan, Tobago Cays, Mayreau, and Palm Island.

Windsurfing

Equipment and instruction are available through **Paradise Windsurfing**, Bequia, *Tel. 458-3222*. Many resorts also have windsurfers for guest use.

Yachting

Crewed yachts are available from **Anchorage Yacht Club**. *Tel. 458-8647* or *458-8221;* **Beachcomber Hotel**, *Tel. 458-4283;* **Blue Water Charters**. *Tel. 456-1232;* **Escape**, *Tel. 458-3072;* and the schooner **Friendship Rose**, which offers day sails with lunch and drinks, *Tel. 458-3202.*

Day sails with picnicking and snorkeling are available from **Nirvana**, *Fax 456-9238;* **OK Baby**, *Tel. 457-9147;* **Passion**, which has two professional fighting chairs for sportfishing, *Tel. 458-3884;* **Pelangi**, a 44-foot sailboat that is available by the day or longer. *Tel. 458-3255;* **The Quest**, a 44-foot CSY skippered yacht by the day or longer. *Tel. 458-3425;* **Touch of Time**, a 54-footer, *Tel. 458-3084;* and **Wind & Sea**, a 65-foot catamaran, *Tel. 458-8647.*

Charter by the week or more from **Lagoon Marina Yacht Charters**, *Tel. 458-4308*, **Barefoot Yacht Charters**, *Tel. 456-9526*, and **Nicholson Yacht Charters**, *Tel. 617/225-0555* or locally *Tel. 460-1530.*

SHOPPING

The game plan here is to stock up on splashy local batiks and screened prints, which are as unique as they are exquisite. Local crafts including wood carving, straw work, bamboo items, coconut art, and leather are also meaningful souvenirs. On Bequia, model boats are the prized souvenirs.

ST. VINCENT

Stechers Jewellers & Gift Shop in the Cobblestone Arcade, **Voyager** on Halifax Street, and **Y. De Lima** on Bay Street, Kingstown have duty-free gifts and big-name collectibles such as Lladro, French perfumes, and English china. Shop **Noah's Arcade** and **Sprotties** on Bay Street, and **Visions by Dawn** on Granby Street for screen print fabrics and native crafts. Local crafts, including the famous Bequia model boats, are found in the **Artisans Craft Shop** in the Bonadie's Building on Bay Street.

Patrice Fashions at E.T. Joshua Airport is a good place to get last-minute gifts and accessories. The island's department store is **Sprott Brothers** on Bay Street, selling everything from clothing and linens to books and paint.

THE GRENADINES

Just opposite the main dock in Bequia, **Bayshore Mall** is the place to bank, provision, make phone calls, and shop for Windjammer clothing. Around the island you'll find a book store, art galleries, crafts shops, and, on the grounds of the Anglican Church, **Carib Wear**. For model boats try **Mauvin's** or **Sargeant's** on Front Street. **Sprottie's Silk Screens** is in Port Elizabeth, and the **Whaleboner Boutique** on Belmont Beach also sells handmade silk screen clothing and batiks. For hardwood souvenirs, tee shirts, teas and herbs, shop Noah's Arcade in the **Frangipani Hotel**.

Mustique and Union Island each have a handful of classy, ultra-pricy boutiques. Palm Island has a **Yacht Club Boutique**.

EXCURSIONS & DAY TRIPS

Only ten minutes from Kingstown you're in **Fenton Valley**, an unspoiled gully filled with thick, cool shrubs and flowering vines. One waterfall, the **Falls of Baleine**, is 63 feet high. The **Fenton** and **Mesopotamia valleys** are a popular substitute tour when **La Soufriere**, the island's blockbuster attraction, is lost in the clouds. If time allows, of course, you can see the volcano, valleys, and much more.

The volcano itself is a moonscape of lava outpourings, frozen in the place where they cooled from liquid to solid. **Rabacca Dry River** was carved by lava in the 1902 eruption that took more than 2,000 lives here. The volcano last blew in 1979 but today's intrepid visitors hike to its crater and look down into the steamy hell inside. Needless to say, local advice should be followed and all precautions should be taken. Your hotel can arrange a guide, or book with one of the tour operators listed below.

To reach the crater, which is sometimes buried in cloud cover, you'll hike a winding trail through tangled rain forest and steep hillsides. The adventure takes about three hours to cover about 3,000 feet, and longer if you stop for rests, views, photography, and bandaging blisters.

Whale watching is increasing popular, and **dolphin watch** trips ply the area between Indian Bay and the Falls of Baleine. Tour operators include **Baleine Tours**, *Tel. 457-4089.* **HazEOC Tours** offers excursions to the volcano, nature trails and waterfalls, *Tel. 457-8634.* **Sea Breeze Nature Tours** go by boat to the leeward coast to see the coastal beaches, snorkeling hotspots, and **Falls of Baleine**, *Tel. 458-4969.* With **Sam Taxi Tours, Ltd.**, take your choice of sightseeing or shopping trips, *Tel. 456-4338 or 458-4475* on St. Vincent and *Tel. 458-3686* on Bequia. **Fantasea Tours**, *Tel. 457-4477* makes boat tours to the Falls of Baleine, outlying islands, nature trails and good reefs for snorkeling.

PRACTICAL INFORMATION
Area code: 784

Banking: Kingstown has almost a dozen banks. Branches of the National Commercial Bank of St. Vincent are also found in Canouan, Union Island, Bequia, and at E.T. Joshua airport where hours are extended to accommodate most flights. Barclays Bank in Kingstown has a branch in Bequia. Banks are usually open Monday through Friday, 8am to 1 or 3pm with Friday hours including 3pm to 5pm.

Business hours: Government offices are generally open 8am to noon and 1pm to 4pm and Saturday mornings. Shops are open 8am to noon and 1pm to 4pm Monday through Friday and Saturdays 8am to noon.

Camping: The islands have no campgrounds and camping is not encouraged except by organized groups such as Boy Scouts and Girl Guides. A camping-like experience is offered by Petit Byahaut (see *Where to Stay*).

Currency: The EC dollar is linked to the U.S. dollar at about EC$2.67 to US$1 depending on what currency exchange you use. Hotels, shops, and restaurants give the least advantageous rates; banks come closer to the official exchange.

Dress: is casual, but beachwear should not be worn in shops or restaurants.

Driving: is on the left. If you don't have a valid international driving license, you'll have to pay EC$40 for a local license at the airport, the police station on Bay Street or the Licensing Authority on Halifax Street.

Electricity: Current here is 220 volts, 50 cycles. U.S. standard 110-volt appliances need a transformer. Most hotels provide dual shaver points.

Emergencies: call the Kingstown police at *Tel. 457-1211* and the Kingstown General Hospital at *Tel. 456-1185*.

Government: St. Vincent and the Grenadines gained independence from Great Britain in 1979 but still have a governor general who is appointed by and represents the Crown. U.S. consular matters are handled through Bridgetown, Barbados, *Tel. 246/436-4950*.

Holidays: banks, government offices, and most businesses are closed on January 1, January 22, Good Friday, Easter Monday, Labour Day (early May), Whit Monday, Carnival Monday and Tuesday (early July), August Monday (first Monday of the month), October 28, Christmas, and Boxing Day.

Immigration: all visitors must have a passport except nationals of the United Kingdom, U.S., and Canada, who need only proof of citizenship such as birth certificate or voter's registration. All visitors must have a return or ongoing ticket.

Locals: may be known as Vincentians or West Indians.

Mail: if you need to receive mail in care of General Delivery, have it sent to the General Post Office, Kingstown, St. Vincent & the Grenadines, West Indies. It's open weekdays 8:30am to 3pm and Saturday 8:30am to 11:30am. Towns and most villages have postal sub-stations.

Medical: a general hospital is found in Kingstown, with smaller hospitals in Georgetown, Chateaubelair and on Bequia. St. Vincent also has three private hospitals and clinics. Half a dozen pharmacies are found in Kingstown and Bequia has one. Try the People's Pharmacy on George's Plaza, Kingstown, *Tel. 457-0225*. It's open Monday through Saturday 8am to 8pm, fills prescriptions, and has a good selection of over-the-counter medications.

Pets: cannot enter St. Vincent and the Grenadines without a six-month quarantine. Pets from the United Kingdom, Australia and New Zealand are admitted on presentation of a health certificate.

Taxes: include a seven percent tax on accommodations and a departure tax of EC$20.

Telephones: Purchase prepaid credit cards from Cable & Wireless offices and from phonecard vendors near Cardphones, which are located at major population centers.

Time Zone: St. Vincent and the Grenadines are on Atlantic Standard Time, which is one hour ahead of Eastern Standard Time.

Tourism Information: Write the Department of Tourism, *P.O. Box 834, Kingstown, St. Vincent & Grenadines, West Indies* or visit the office on Bay Street. Other offices include St. Vincent & the Grenadines Tourism, *801 Second Avenue, New York NY 10017. Tel. 212/687-4981 and 800/729-1726 or 6505 Cove Creek Place, Dallas TX 75240, Tel. 800/235-3029*. Also St. Vincent & the Grenadines Tourism, *Suite 504, 1000*

University Avenue, Toronto, Ontario M5J 1V 6, Canada. Tel. 416/924-5796, Fax 924-5844.

Weddings. a three-day residence is required in the islands before a marriage can take place. Two licenses can be used. The Governor General's license is available from the Ministry of Justice and it's good for three months. An ordinary license can be obtained from the Registrar, after which notice of the ceremony must be published in the Registry for at least seven days.

38. TRINIDAD & TOBAGO

Barely able to lay claim to the Caribbean, the nation of **Trinidad & Tobago** lies at the end of the chain of islands, just off the coast of Venezuela. Trinidad is one of the most business-oriented islands, the most polyglot, the most sophisticated, with a lot to offer the leisure visitor too.

Christopher Columbus didn't discover "Trinibago" until his third voyage, in 1498. By 1592, Spain was actively colonizing the islands. The British captured it from Spain in 1797 and it became officially British in 1814. After slavery was abolished in 1834, indentured servants streamed in, mostly from India, a program that did not end until 1917. As a result of its waves of newcomers over the centuries, today's population is 30 percent Catholic, 24 percent Hindu, 11 percent Anglican, and five percent Muslim.

Tobago was founded by the French, whose capital at Port Louis was described in 1767 as a single row of buildings with warehouses on the beach, shops, inns, and a *jolie* tavern. It was all burned to the ground in 1790 by mutinous French troops, who were fighting their own version of the French Revolution. When the island became British, the capital was renamed **Scarborough**.

A busy base for the Allies during World War II, Trinidad formed its own government in 1956 and gained independence from Britain in 1962. A republic in the Commonwealth, it has a president, prime minister, house of representatives and senate. Tobago has a separate House of Assembly.

The Caribbean stewpot is at its most flavorful here. The old French patois is fading in favor of English, although you'll still hear Hindi spoken in Indian neighborhoods. The islands have a flavor, a look, a language, and even parties all their own. Everyone wants to be here for Carnival, which ends on Ash Wednesday, but if you miss that there is Eid-ul-Fir, the beginning of the Islamic New York. In March, Phagwah marks the beginning of the Indian springtime. April is the time for Tobago's hilarious goat and crab races, and the gamefishing tournament. Ramajar,

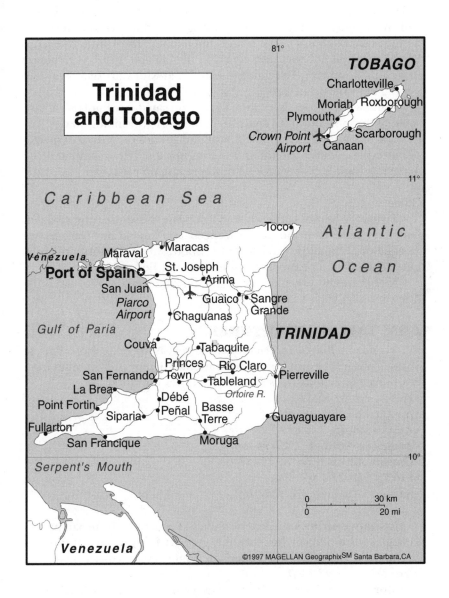

Trinidad and Tobago

TOBAGO

Charlotteville
Moriah Roxborough
Plymouth
Crown Point Airport Scarborough
Canaan

Caribbean Sea

Toco *Atlantic*

Maracas *Ocean*

Venezuela Maraval
Port of Spain St. Joseph
San Juan Arima
Piarco Airport Guaico Sangre Grande
Chaguanas

Gulf of Paria *TRINIDAD*

Couva Tabaquite
Princes Town Rio Claro
San Fernando Pierreville
La Brea Tableland
Point Fortin Débé *Ortoire R.*
Siparia Peñal Basse Terre Guayaguayare
Fullarton
San Francique Moruga

Serpent's Mouth

0 30 km
0 20 mi

Venezuela

©1997 MAGELLAN GeographixSM Santa Barbara,CA

81°
11°
10°

a steel band festival, is held in May, which is also the time of the big regatta in Tobago. In Trinidad in June, you'll hear tassa drums announcing the start of Hosay, an Islamic festival similar to Carnival. Tobago celebrates its Heritage Festival in July with folk dancing and calypso. Emancipation and Independence are celebrated in August and the World Steelband Festival usually comes to the islands in October. The Hindu festival of Divali, a festival of lights, also comes in the fall and there's a great jazz festival in November. December is consumed with Christmas, with the singing of Venezuelan carols.

Trinidad & Tobago is a nation where you can dance until dawn, dive some of the most beautiful dive sites in the world (including oil rigs!), or go back to nature in a land that boasts 430 species of birds, 620 species of butterflies, 2,300 varieties of flowering shrubs, 700 orchids, and 100 mammals – some of them found nowhere else on earth.

Climate
This is the hottest corner of the Caribbean, the southernmost island. Only a few miles from the coast of Venezuela, Trinidad and Tobago have an equatorial climate much like that of South America's northern coast. One September, a record 101 degrees was reached.

Nights are always cool, rarely higher than the low 70s. February is the driest month; August the wettest.

ARRIVALS & DEPARTURES
Trinidad's **Piarco International Airport** is 16 miles from Port of Spain; Tobago's **Crown Point International Airport** is eight miles from Scarborough. Trinidad is served from all over the world by:
• **BWIA**, *Tel. 627-BWIA*
• **Air Canada**, *Tel. 664-4065*
• **Air Caribbean**, *Tel. 623-2500*
• **American Airlines**, *Tel. 664-4661*
• **Guyana Airways**, *Tel. 627-2753*
• **LIAT**, *Tel. 627-1942*
• **Surinam Airways**, *Tel. 625-0102*.

Executive Airlines, an American Eagle carrier flies from San Juan to Tobago's Crown Point International Airport using 64-seat turboprop aircraft, *Tel. 800/433-7300*. **American Eagle** serves Tobago from San Juan, *Tel. 800/443-7300*.

More than a dozen flights go between Trinidad and Tobago daily. Ferries run between the two islands but the trip can be very rough, *Tel. 627-8473* for the high-speed **Condor Express**, or *Tel. 625-3055* for the ferry.

BWIA INSIDER TIP

BWIA, Tel. 800/780-5501, will upgrade you to First Class for $99 if you let BWIA Vacations book your entire honeymoon package in Trinidad or Tobago. Departures from Miami or JFK are available, and the deal also carries 2,500 extra Frequent Flyer miles. Rates start at under $1,000. There's some fine print involved, so call for full details.

ORIENTATION

Trinidad covers 1,864 miles and lies only five miles off the coast of Venezuela. The mountains of its **Northern Range** rise as high as 3,085 feet. Its capital is **Port of Spain**. Twenty-one miles northeast of Trinidad is **Tobago**, which is 28 miles long. Its central spine of mountains rises to 1,860 feet; the capital is **Scarborough**.

TRINIBAGO'S OWN LANGUAGE

*Get yourself a **beat pan** (steel drum) and turn out for the **Bacchanal** or **fete**, which indicate any big party. Don't drink too much, though, or **crapaud smoke you pipe**. In other words, you're in trouble. Whether you're a **dougla** (mixed Indian and African) or a **freshwater yankee** who picked up foreign ways while staying abroad, you'll enjoy the **ol' talk** with your friends and perhaps a bit of **hip wine** as your middle grinds to the beat of the **mas**. If you're **obzokee** (awkward), don't feel no **boderation**. Fitting in with the friendly locals should be **sockeye**, which means easy as pie.*

GETTING AROUND TRINIDAD

Taxis meet all flights and charge fixed fares. The fare from Piarco International into Port of Spain is $20; to Maraval $24, to Diego Martin $27 and to San Fernando $31. A 50 percent surcharge is made between 10pm and 6am Fares from Crown Point International to Scarborough are $5 to Crown Point, $6 to Pigeon Point, $12 to Scarborough, $11 to Grafton or Turtle Beach, $10 to Mount Irvine, $30 to Roxborough, $36 to Speyside, and $40 to Charlotteville.

Trinidad

Kemwel rental cars are available at the airport at high season rates ranging from $229 to $319, all plus $12 daily Collision Damage Waiver. Reserve from the U.S., *Tel. 800/678-0678*; locally, *Tel. 639-8507*.

Other rentals at Piarco include **Auto Rentals**, *Tel. 669-2277*; **Econo-Car Rentals**, *Tel. 669-2342;* **Singh's Auto Rentals**, *Tel. 664-5417*; and **Thrifty Car Rentals**, *Tel. 669-0602.*

Tobago

Kemwel rental cars are available at the airport and at the Turtle Beach Hotel at high season rates ranging from $169 to $299 weekly, all plus $12 daily Collision Damage Waiver. Reserve from the U.S. at *Tel. 800/678-0678;* locally, *Tel. 639-8507.*

Other rental cars on Tobago include:
- **Auto Rentals**, *Tel. 639-0644*
- **Carlton James Car Rental**, *Tel. 639-8084*
- **Econo-Car Rentals**, *Tel. 639-8378*
- **Hill Crest Car Rental**, *Tel. 639-5208*
- **Paradise Rentals**, *Tel. 660-5195*
- **Peter Gremli Car Rentals**, *Tel. 639-8400*
- **Quashie's Car Rental and Taxi Services**, *Tel. 639-8427*

Driving is on the left and major roads are paved and fairly good. Back roads, however, can be very rough going, especially in the rainy season. Keep your tank full. Outside urban areas, gas stations are far apart and, on Tobago, they close early and all day Sunday. If you'll be staying in Port of Spain, make do with taxis. Traffic is bad and parking difficult.

Mini-buses serve most corners of Trinidad. A yellow band indicates a city bus operating around Port of Spain; red bands indicated buses going to eastern Trinidad; green-banded buses are heading south and a black-banded bus is headed for Princes Sound. A brown band indicates that the van operates between San Fernando and the southwest (Eric Point, Point Fortin).

In Tobago, mini-buses are identified by a blue band. In Port of Spain, the best place to catch a mini-bus is on South Quay, where anyone will be glad to steer you to the best van for your destination. From South Quay, you can also get an airport transit. For **bus information**, *Tel. 623-7872.*

WHERE TO STAY

Prices are quoted in U.S. dollars. There is a 15 percent VAT (government Value Added Tax) on rooms, and a service charge, usually 10-15 percent. Some hotels add a utilities surcharge.

Your mailing address while here will be Trinidad or Tobago, West Indies.

TRINIDAD

Expensive

TRINIDAD HILTON, *Lady Young Road, mailing address Box 442, Port of Spain, Trinidad, West Indies. Tel. 868/624-3211, Fax 624-4485; toll-free 800/HILTONS. Rates at this 394-room hotel start at $225.*

Everything the traveler could want in a big-city business hotel is found here in a snazzy, high-rise hotel just east of Queen's Park Savannah. Dine in La Boucan or poolside in the Terrace Garden. Have a drink in the lobby bar, poolside or in the Carnival Bay where easy listening reigns until 1pm. Room service is available 6am to midnight. If you stay on the Clubroom floor, continental breakfast and evening refreshments are available. On these floors you can also request a non-smoking room. Swim, play table tennis, play the chevron tennis courts day or night, shop the hotel's shops, and park free in the hotel's lot.

Every room has a balcony with a panoramic view, direct-dial telephone with message light, voice mail, and satellite television. Some rooms are wheelchair accessible. One-and two-bedroom suites are available.

Moderate

ASA WRIGHT NATURE CENTRE AND LODGE, *Spring Hill Estate, Arima, Trinidad. Tel. 868/667-4655, Fax 914/273-6370; toll-free in the U.S. except New York, Tel. 800/426-7781. Rates start at $90 per person, double occupancy, including all meals. Credit cards aren't accepted.*

Eco-tourism lodges like this one are catching on in the Caribbean, but this was one of the first, a rustic lodge and cottages that are air conditioned and have private baths but are otherwise as close to nature as you can get. Live in a natural paradise on a 200-acre conservation and study center used by professional and amateur naturalists. This is the home of one of the world's most accessible colonies of oilbirds and a Sears catalog of other birds and wildlife including unique and South American species that are found nowhere else in the Caribbean.

HOLIDAY INN, *Wrightson Road at London Road, mailing address Box 10171, Port of Spain. Tel. 868/625-3361, Fax 625-4166; toll-free 800/465-4329. Rates at this 235-unit hotel start at $99; ask about the breakfast plan that comes with two $6 breakfast vouchers daily for a room tariff of $104. The hotel is in downtown Port of Spain.*

You are in the heart of a howling downtown madhouse, which will suit many travelers just fine. From the top floors, look out over the city and bay. Rooms come with one king or two double beds, predictable Holiday Inn furnishings, air conditioning and a hair dryer in each bathroom. La Ronde, the rooftop, revolving restaurant is one of the city's hotspots for dinner and later. The hotel has a swimming pool with pool bar, secretarial services, shops, room service, and ever-ready taxi service outside the door.

The address is a good one for the business traveler or for the vacationer who needs a comfortable city lair for a few days before or after a rugged outdoor expedition. Suites are available.

HOTEL NORMANDIE, *10 Nook Avenue, St. Ann's, mailing address Box 851, Port of Spain. Tel. 868/624-1181, Fax 624-1181. Rates at this 51-unit hotel start at $75. It's 3.5 miles from downtown Port of Spain.*

A golden oldie that dates to the 1920s and still has a loyal following among regular business and leisure travelers, this hotel is close enough to the city to be a good headquarters but far enough from the din that you can enjoy your balcony or patio and the swimming pool in a garden-filled courtyard. Some writers are reminded of Tennessee Williams, others of Somerset Maugham. We think it's more like a Swiss chalet with a few Spanish mission motifs. It's attractive, even swank, and has its own, very good art gallery. It's handy to a shopping mall, restaurants, arts and crafts. Ask for one of the loft rooms if you have children. They'll sleep free in the loft. Rooms are air conditioned. Studios are available.

KAPOK HOTEL, *16-18 Cotton Hill, St. Clair. Tel. 868/622-6441, Fax 622-9677. Rates at this 94-room hotel start at $75.*

You're only a few minute's drive from the Savannah in an air conditioned room or kitchenette suite comfortably furnished in rattan and tropical fabrics. The hotel has a swimming pool and is the home of a rooftop restaurant serving food from the Pacific Rim. There's a coin-operated laundry for guest use, a beauty shop, and secretarial services.

ROYAL PALM HOTEL, *7 Saddle Road, Maraval. Tel. 868/628-6042, Fax 628-5086. Rates at this 68-unit hotel start at $80. The hotel is about three miles from Port of Spain.*

Accommodations in this hotel, which is patronized mostly by Caribbean and South American travelers, range from a tiny double room with private path to spacious suites with kitchenette, living area, dining area, and a bedroom ell. Dine in Buccaneer's Cove Restaurant & Bar for Caribbean food, Ali Baba for Arabic cuisine, Maharani's for Indian dishes, and A. Pang for Chinese food.

Handily located in downtown Maraval, it's within walking distance of four banks, four fast food outlets, a supermarket, a bus stop, and three shopping malls. It's a handy perch for quick trips into town or for leaving town to go to the beaches. Tennis, horseback riding, golf, and use of a gym can be arranged. The hotel has cable television, air conditioning, direct-dial telephones, and an on-site pharmacy, coin laundry, dry cleaner, disco, and book shop. If you stay three days or more and pay regular rates, the hotel will rebate 20 percent of your cab fare from the airport.

Budget

CARIBBEAN CONDO VILLAS, *140 Majuba Cross Road, Petit Valley. Tel. 868/632-0113, Fax 625-6980. Rates start at $38 per person including breakfast. The villas are 15 minutes from downtown Port of Spain and 30 minutes from beaches and golf. The inn is about three miles from Port of Spain, between Maraval and Diego Martin.*

Nestled in the foothills of a pleasant residential area is this complex of two-bedroom condos, each with one twin bedroom and one double bedroom. Modern baths have Kohler fixtures with hot and cold running water, shower, and tub. Units have television, a balcony overlooking landscaped groups and the surrounding hills, a fully-equipped kitchen, and ceiling fans.

MONIQUE'S GUESTHOUSE, *114/116 Saddle Road, Maraval. Tel. 868/628-3334 or fax 622-3232. Rates at this 20-room inn start at $40 plus $3 for continental breakfast. Kitchenette units are available.*

Monique's is large enough to offer a selection of singles, doubles and triples, airport transfer, rental cars, a restaurant and bar but it's small enough to have caring, personalized service. One room is handicap accessible. Most of the others have two double beds. Guests enjoy the common room for television and reading; swimming pool privileges are available nearby.

PAX GUEST HOUSE, *Mt.St. Benedict, Tunapuna. Tel. 868/662-4084. Rates at this guest house start at $60 per person including three meals and high tea daily. Credit cards are not accepted; baths are shared. It's halfway between Port of Spain and the airport.*

The name Pax, the Latin word for peace, suits this place well because it was once a religious retreat for Dutch priests. Now it's a pleasant, homespun hideaway for the traveler in search of the old Caribbean. Just sit on the veranda and enjoy the birds and bees. Your room will have a sink with a cold water tap, but for essential bathroom facilities you'll use communal facilities down the hall. The food is served family style, with accent on Trinidadian dishes. It's best if you have a rental car, although buses pass nearby.

ZOLLNA HOUSE, *12 Ramlogan Terrace, La Seiva, Maraval. Tel. 868/628-3731, Fax 628-3737. Rates at this seven-room inn start at $55 with private bath and $50 with shared bath. It's two miles from Port of Spain. Take Saddle Road to La Seiva Road, then turn uphill for less than half a mile.*

Overlook the capital and the Gulf from this hillside porch in the beautiful Maraval Valley. The setting is so lush that visitors have trouble finding it, so this is just the hideaway for the world-weary traveler who wants just to sit in the garden, read, and enjoy the trees and flowers. Room aren't air conditioned, but have ceiling fans.

TOBAGO
Expensive
GRAFTON BEACH RESORT, *Black Rock, Tobago. Tel. 868/639-0191, Fax 639-0030. Rates at this 110-unit resort start at $215. It's on the northwest coast, four miles south of Scarborough.*

Most of the rooms have twin beds, so reserve early if you want a king-size bedroom or a suite with a king-size bed and its own Jacuzzi. Rooms have air conditioning, ceiling fan, a stocked mini-bar, full bathroom with tub and shower, satellite television, and private balcony or patio. Swim in the big pool with its swim-up bar, lounge on the beach with its fringe of rustling palm trees, play squash on an air-conditioned court, sail, canoe, windsurf, or scuba dive. The hotel has a game room with table tennis, darts, and billiards, and guests can play the Mount Irvine Golf Course. Live entertainers are on hand nightly and on weekends, the discotheque hums until the wee hours. Dining is in Neptune's, but light snacks are also available at the beach bar and at the pool.

MOUNT IRVINE HOTEL & GOLF CENTRE, *Mount Irvine, mailing address Box 222, Scarborough. Tel. 639-8871, Fax 639-8800. Rates at this 105-unit hotel start at $195; suites are from $510. It's a five-minute ride from the airport.*

One of the most grand old hotels (1972) in the Caribbean is this golf resort sprawling over 150 acres that were once a sugarcane plantation. The ruins of the old sugar mill form a romantic setting for the swimming pool. The resort has an 18-hole championship golf course with its own restaurant and bar, or dine at the Sugar Mill on international cuisine and dance the night away on the patio, where live music plays nightly. The beach, the lawns, the flowering shrubs are all part of the pleasing scene. Stay in the main building or in a cottage that has two units, each with its own bathroom. Accommodations are air conditioned and have telephone and television. Children can stay free in their parents' room.

Moderate
KARIWAK VILLAGE, *Store Bay, Box 27, Scarborough. Tel. 868/639-8442, Fax 639-8441. The village is two minutes from the airport. Rates at the 18-unit complex start at $90.*

The name evokes visions of Arawak planters, peacefully tending a village of thatched huts. Today's huts are comfortable rondettes with lots of sliding doors into the outdoors, porthole-like round windows, and tropical furnishings. The restaurant here is one of Tobago's best. Rooms are air conditioned and have a telephone. The beach is just a five-minute walk away.

RICHMOND GREAT HOUSE, *Belle Garden, Tobago. Tel. 868/660-4467. It's 18 miles from the airport. Rates at this six-unit inn start at $75 including continental breakfast.*

The original greathouse was built here in the late 18th century to take advantage of majestic views. Today it's owned by Dr. Hollis Lynch, a professor of African history and self-admitted eccentric. He's a lively host, as is the manager, Brother George, whose fund of stories and folklore never runs dry. Enjoy the house antiques and African art, dine on home-grown foods and homemade bread, and enjoy nearby hiking and birding. Lodging is in a double room with four-poster bed and hand-pieced quilt or a suite. The hotel has a swimming pool and is within walking distance of uncrowded beaches.

Budget

ARTHUR'S BY THE SEA, *Crown Point. Tel. 868/639-0196; fax 639-4122; toll-free 800/223-9815. It's near the airport, a four-minute walk from Store Bay. After leaving Crown Point, find it on the Milford Road. It's a 15-minute drive to Scarborough. Rates at this 15-room hotel start at $55.*

A crisply white two-story hotel surrounds a pool and plenty of greenery. The front desk cheerfully arranges snorkeling, sailing, golf, bird watching, nature tours, dives, and car rentals. Dine in the hotel's own open-air restaurant. Watch television in the lounge or rent a set for your room. High-ceiling rooms have air conditioning, a choice of carpeted or wood floors, a private patio, private bath with shower, and two double beds.

Bed, Breakfast, & Bookings

To book bed and breakfast in a private home, contact:
• **Trinidad and Tobago Bed and Breakfast Society**, *1 Wrightson Road, Port of Spain, Trinidad, West Indies, Tel. 868/627-BEDS, Fax 868/663-4913*
• **Tobago Bed and Breakfast Association**, *c/o Federal Villa, 1-3 Crooks River, Scarborough, Tobago, West Indies, Tel. 868/639-3926, Fax 868/639-3566*
• **Accommodations Unlimited**, *Ariapita Avenue at Luis Street, Woodbrook, Trinidad, Tel. 868/628-3731, Fax 868/628-3737*

WHERE TO EAT

The Indian influence, sometimes by way of Mother England, is stronger here than anywhere else in the islands, but its fiery curries and economical rotis have spread northward to become staples as far away as St. John. Trinidad's unique cuisine is a blend of Indian, Chinese, European, and Caribbean flavors. You can eat here more economically than at home. Even at the Hilton, one of the priciest places in town, a dinner buffet costs only about $20.

TRINIDAD
Expensive

LA BOUCAN, *in the Trinidad Hilton, Lady Young Road. Tel. 624-3211. Main dishes are priced under $22; appetizers are $3.50 to $11. Reservations are essential. It's open Monday through Saturday noon to 2:30pm and 7-11:30p.m Wednesday through Friday, high tea is served 4-6pm.*

Ask for a seat with a good view of the Geoffrey Holder mural, a colorful depiction of a Sunday afternoon on the Savannah. It is hard to resist the buffets, which are offered at both lunch and dinner. They are as colorful, generous, and varied as those on the best cruise ships. If you order from the menu, try traditional foods such as callaloo, pumpkin soup, pepperpot and curries spiced to order from mild to four-alarm fire. Steaks and seafood are always on the bill of fare. The fish platter, which features several different catches cooked to order, is always good. On weekends a dance band plays, but we like the piano serenades that play during the week. The table settings, linens and surroundings are upscale and charmingly old-Trinidad.

LA FANTASIE, *in the Normandie Hotel, 10 Nook Avenue, St. Ann's. Tel. 624-1181, Hours are noon to 2pm and 7-10pm every day. Main courses are priced $12 to $30.*

Many years ago, a plantation covered this site off the Savannah and this restaurant takes its name. The decor is delightfully Deco, a carry-over from the 1920s origins of this well-preserved hotel. Dine indoors with the air conditioning if you feel like dressing up with a jacket, or outdoors on the terrace. The food is French-influenced, with island touches such as the tamarind sauce served over a steak or chop, or a banana and wine sauce for fish freshly pulled from Trinidad's seas. End the meal with a moist fruit cake sauced with rum custard. The ambience, service, and decor are regal.

SOLIMAR, *6 Nook Avenue, St. Ann's. Tel. 624-6267. Dine for under $20, near the Hotel Normandie and 3.5 miles from the city center. Call for reservations. It's open for dinner daily except Sunday and for six weeks each summer. Hours vary seasonally.*

If you want to try all the international dishes of Trinidad, you might get them here in one meal – vegetables tempura, sweet and sour pork, Greek salad, a pasta dish, or a crisp veal schnitzel, all accompanied by a fine wine. Ask about daily chef specials, especially the catch of the day and soup of the day. Chef Joe Brown was born in England, and worked in hotels before opening his own place here. For dessert, have his double chocolate mousse laced with Kahlua. Dine in a romantic setting of cozy rooms, low lighting, and plenty of potted plants. Popular with visitors from all over the world, Solimar tends to attract North Americans and Brits as well as Caribbean tourists.

Moderate

RAFTERS, *6 Warner Street on the corner of Woodford Street, Newtown, Port of Spain. Tel. 628-9258. Main dishes are priced $6 to $23. Hours are Monday to Friday 11:30am to 3pm and Monday through Saturday 6:30-11pm.*

Locals and visitors alike love the good-times atmosphere in this crowded, family place. On Wednesday, Friday and Saturday nights there's a big seafood buffet for under $20, followed by disco (no cover) or live music (TT$10 cover charge). At lunch there's a good choice of specialty sandwiches, burgers, barbecue, burritos, and snack platters. At dinner the scene shifts to another section of this old market, candles are lit, and everything centers around fresh fish, lobster, shrimp, escargot, conch, or whatever else the net brought in.

LE CHATEAU DE POISSON, *Cornelia Street at 38 Ariapita Avenue, Woodbrook. Tel. 622-6087. Reservations are recommended. Dine for $20-$22. Dinner is served Monday through Saturday from 7pm.*

This is a good place to go for dinner any time, especially after a drink and rendezvous at Veni Mangé (see below) where dinner is not served. A charming old Trinidadian home has been transformed into a seafood restaurant where the catch is fresh and cooked to order.

TIKI VILLAGE, *in the Kapok Hotel, 16-18 Cotton Hill, St. Clair. Tel. 622-6441. It's open for breakfast, lunch and dinner daily. Dine for under $20. Reservations aren't necessary.*

Everyone will have fun at this Polynesian restaurant where you can start with crisp lumpia (egg rolls) or the pu-pu platter and work your way through a long menu of fish, chicken, pork, and beef specialties, some of them brought to the table in flames. The authentic luau fish is served whole, floured and fried to crusty perfection and then sauced. Chicken breast is served in black bean sauce, shrimp or pork come in a tangy sweet and sour sauce; tofu is stuffed with fish; squid is stir-fried with sweet peppers.

If you're a dim sum addict, this is the place to come for the traditional Chinese dim sum brunch, which is served 11am to 3pm only on weekends and holidays. At lunch, the buffet is a terrific buy. It's served on weekdays except holidays. The restaurant is on the top floor of this popular hotel overlooking Queen's Park Savannah and the views alone are reason to eat here.

VENI MANGÉ, *67 Ariapita Avenue, Woodbrook. Tel. 624-4597. It's northwest of the city center. Dine for under $20. Call for hours, which vary* *seasonally, and reservations. Only lunch is served, although the bar stays open on Friday until 9pm.*

Allyson (the locally famous TV cook) and Roses (her sister Rosemary) run this delightful eatery in a stucco bungalow decorated with the works of local artists. The name of the place means "come, eat." The sisters may offer pumpkin or callaloo soup, a curry, Creole hotpot, and always a vegetarian dish such as lentil stew or an eggplant casserole. The home-made desserts and exotic tropical ice creams are divine.

Budget

ADAM'S, *15 Saddle Road, Maraval. Tel. 62-BAGEL or 22435. Foods are priced $2 to $5. It's open Monday though Saturday 7am to 7pm. Credit cards aren't accepted.*

Stop by for a loaf of bread or bagels for tomorrow's breakfast, or eat in. The menu is light, featuring specialty breads, sandwiches, and pastries. This is always a good place to have a proper afternoon tea with biscuits.

HONG KONG CITY, *at Piarco International Airport. Tel. 669-8888. It's open 24 hours. It also has a location at the corner of Tragarete Road and Maraval Road, Newtown. Tel. 622-3949 and at St. Helena Junction, Piarco. Tel. 669-4461. Dishes are priced from about $4.*

Everything you love about your hometown Chinese restaurant can be found here, and then some. Order stir fries, vegetarian dishes, savory soups, and crisply fried bits of seafood or pork. The 24-hour airport location is a godsend for travelers who come and go at odd hours. The other locations are elegantly decorated with lots of red and gold.

PEKING PALACE, *44 Independence Square, Port of Spain. Tel. 627-3546. Hours are Monday to Saturday 11pm to 10pm. Free, secure parking is available. Prices start at about $5. Credit cards are accepted.*

Start with a flavorful soup, then have chicken with Chinese noodles, a beef stir-fry, pork or chicken in a sweet pineapple sauce, or a simple rice dish rich with flavorful bits of meat and vegetables. The egg rolls are crisp, hot, and crammed with crisp-tender vegetables.

PELICAN PUB, *2-4 Coblentz Avenue, Cascade, Port of Spain. Tel. 624-7486. Dishes are priced $6 to $10. It is open daily from 11am.*

A traditional English pub offers draft beer and pub-grub favorites including meat-filled pastries, hearty sandwiches and sizzling burgers.

WOODFORD CAFE, *62 Tragarete Road. Tel. 622-2233. Hours are Monday to Saturday 11am to 10pm. Credit cards are accepted. Dine for $10 to $15.*

Actually two restaurants, the Woodford serves traditional local cuisine and its sister restaurant Monsoon serves local East Indian dishes. Have a roti, goat stew, a vegetarian curry, spicy chicken, seafood stew, funchi, coo-coo, flying fish, lentil stew, conch, and other truly local dishes.

TOBAGO

Expensive

LE BEAU RIVAGE, *in the Mount Irvine Hotel & Golf Centre, Buccoo Bay. Tel. 639-8871. Reservations are essential. Main dishes are priced $24 to $30. It's open only for dinner daily except Monday and Tuesday. It's a five-minute drive northwest of the airport.*

Dine in a splendid setting overlooking the 18-hole golf course and Mount Irvine Bay at this upscale hotel. (also see Sugar Mill). The food is French with Caribbean touches such as the grilled snapper in a snappy Creole sauce, grilled lobster with a side dish of the local polenta, breast of chicken pound thin and cooked with a filling of ham and cheese, roast duck served with mango sauce instead of the cherries that might be used in France, or a roast of lamb with a drift of rosemary and surrounded by local vegetables. Desserts too center around exotic tropical fruits.

OCEAN VIEW RESTAURANT, *in the Grafton Beach Resort, Black Rock. Tel. 639-0191. Main dishes are priced $10 to $29. Call for hours and reservations.*

Well, you can see the ocean, but the name of this airy restaurant is a stretch. However, the views of the grounds and the pool are restful if you want to take your eyes off the food, which is touristy and good. The buffet offers all you can eat, a cruise ship-type "groaning board" filled with charcoal grilled chicken or mahi-mahi, vegetables, salads, pastas, rice pilafs, and a salad bar. Live music plays most nights. Come to enjoy a friendly crowd of locals, divers, and tourists from all over the world.

SUGAR MILL, *in the Mount Irvine Hotel & Golf Centre, Buccoo Bay. Tel. 639-8871. Reservations are essential unless you are staying at the hotel. Main dishes are priced $10 to $28. It's open for lunch and dinner daily and is a five-minute drive northwest of the airport.*

Dine in an open-air restaurant wrought from the ruins of a sugar mill built in the 1600s. A web of wood rafters provides shelter from any showers but otherwise you're in a breezy outdoors filled with birdsong and the scent of flowering shrubs. At lunch, dine simply on sandwiches, salads and soups. If you prefer, there are grilled chicken and chops to make a full meal, but save yourself for dinner when you can start with a satiny seafood bisque or lobster in puff pastry, followed by lobster Newburg, grilled mahi-mahi, a steak, roast beef, or chicken in a sauce of bananas and mangoes. Live music plays most nights. The wine list is comprehensive, offering a good choice of international vintages.

Moderate

BLUE CRAB, *Robinson Street at Main Street, Scarborough. Tel. 639-2737. Main dishes are priced $6 to $20. Reservations are essential for dinner and* *are recommended for lunch. It's open every day for lunch 11am to 3pm and evenings by reservation.*

The full flavor of a sunny out-island permeates this friendly hangout next to the Methodist Church, a family-run restaurant in a 1920's bungalow with a wrap-around porch. If you order lobster, you can spend a lot but otherwise offerings are home style, moderately priced cuisine such as cracked conch, seafood stew, flying fish, stuffed crab backs, vegetarian rice dishes, suckling pig, and imported steaks or local fish grilled over a coconut husk fire. When mom makes a "cook-up" it's a rice pilaf filled with whatever bits of meat and vegetables the day's market provided. Hosts Alison and Ken Sardinha lived in New York, saving to return to their homeland and open their own restaurant. You'll find them to be accommodating hosts who like North American visitors. If you fall in love with the place, ask about the rooms that the Sardinhas offer for rent.

DILLON'S, *on Airport Road near Crown Point. Tel. 639-8765. Main dishes are priced $6 to $25. It's open daily for lunch and dinner.*

The succulent seafood here packs 'em in and, since reservations aren't taken, you may have a long wait if you arrive at peak hours. Stan Dillon is a longtime fishing guide and charter operator, so he knows fresh fish when he sees it. Have a seafood stew, stuffed snapper, the steak and lobster combo, lobster thermidor, or grilled chicken or steak, served with salads and fresh island vegetables.

ROUSELLE'S, *Old Windward Road, Bacolet. Tel. 639-4738. Main dishes are priced $8 to $15, more only if lobster is available. Hours are Monday to Saturday 3-11pm. Reservations are essential.*

Come here to dine or just to lime with the locals and dive crowd. The bar is an old favorite. The menu features mostly seafood, done with Tobagonian touches and served with side dish that might include peas and rice, coocoo, French fries, salads, garlic bread, and really good vegetables including bok choy, carrots, green beans, and good ol' Irish potatoes. For dessert there's pineapple pie.

Budget

D CARAT SHED, *Milford Road, Hampden in the Lowlands. Tel. 639-7522. Meals are priced $6 to $15. Call for hours.*

It's an unassuming local place serving seafood and Tobagonian specialties such as meat or chickpea rotis, patties, coocoo, fish stew, curry goat and rice and peas.

Quick Takes

Roadside vendors everywhere offer doubles, which are curried chickpeas in fried dough, roti (various fillings rolled in a griddle-fried bread), and dhalpuri (chickpea-filled roti). Pastelles, which are more likely to be served during the Christmas season or Carnival, are patties that are filled with minced meat seasoned with olives, capers, and raisins and steamed in a banana leaf. Black cake is made with dried fruit and is soaked in rum and cherry brandy. It's traditionally served for weddings, but watch for it on menus too.

SEEING THE SIGHTS
TRINIDAD

Port of Spain is a mad, mad world but its sightseeing attractions merit a visit. The "lungs" of the city is **Queen's Park Savannah**, a big greenbelt that is still a favorite park and home of the race track and botanic gardens. Founded in 1820, the gardens have specimens from all over the world. On Upper Frederick Street just south of the Savannah, the **National Museum and Art Gallery**, *Tel. 623-5941*, is a treasury of works including the paintings of Trinidad's own 19th-century master, Cazabon. It's open daily except Monday 10am to 6pm and admission is free.

Note the colonial mansions along Queen's Park West. They're known as the **Magnificent Seven**. On Art Street, **Trinity Cathedral** was completed in 1818; the **Cathedral of the Immaculate Conception** on Independence Square, a few blocks southeast of Trinity, was built on the waterfront in 1832. So much fill has been added that it now stands half a kilometer inland.

In a swing around the northern part of Trinidad, you'll find **Maracas Bay** 35 minutes from the city. Miraculously, it has escaped becoming just another hotel city. Changing rooms, snacks, cold drinks and vendors are on hand here and at **Las Cuevas Beach** just beyond Maracas. Beware the undertow. At an altitude of 360 meters up in the Northern Range, stop at **Asa Wright Nature Centre**, *Tel. 667-4655*. Hike the eight trails or take a guided tour at 10am or 1:30pm. The Centre is open daily 9am to 5pm. The site can be reached from Port of Spain for about $35 by taxi. Admission is $6 for adults and $4 for children under age 12.

Five miles up the Lupinot Valley, off the Eastern Main Road, find the restored **greathouse** of Charles de Lopinot, a French planter who came to Trinidad in 1800 and is said to haunt the house still. It's open 6am to 6pm daily and is of special interest at Christmas, when Venezuelan carols known as parang are sung here. Admission is free. There's no phone.

Trinidad's highest waterfall, **Maracas Falls**, is north of St. Joseph. It's an impressive, 270-foot cascade a little more than a mile back from the road. Take a picnic lunch and your binoculars for birdwatching.

Climb high above Port of Spain to **Fort George**, which is open daily until 6pm Admission is free. From **Chaguaramas**, you can get a boat to

---

ABOUT CARNIVAL

Throughout the Caribbean, **Carnival** *is the biggest event of the year, but in Trinidad it's a way of life that goes on around the calendar. Locals barely recover from one year's blowout before they are making feverish plans for an even better, flashier costume next year. It's all put together by troupes called* **mas,** *some of them numbering hundreds of people who organize their own costumes and take to the streets together.*

If you're here during Carnival, watch newspapers for the addresses of these mas because outsiders are welcome to join in for a fee of $50 to $100. This buys the costume, which you get to take home with you. The whole thing lasts from sunrise on Monday to midnight on Tuesday but you'll have to arrive several days ahead of time to get the full flavor of it all. By Wednesday morning, it's off to church for the start of Lent.

---

the area locals call "down the islands," where you'll find ruins, several caves, and picnic facilities. Admission to the caves is about $2. They're open daily 9am to 2:30pm on weekdays and to 3pm on weekends. For information, call the Chaguaramas Development Authority, *Tel. 634-4364.* Don't miss **Galera Point** with its lighthouse overlooking crashing rocks and the confusion of Caribbean meeting Atlantic. Sheltered water can be found at **Salybia Beach**.

Along Trinidad's east coast, seek out the beaches at **Manzanilla** and **Mayaro** for palm-lined sands and rough, Atlantic wave action. The Narvia Swamp is the freshwater home of the **Bush Bush Wildlife Sanctuary**. A permit is required to visit here, *Tel. 662-5114.*

In a southern loop from Port of Spain, you'll go through busy and industrial **Chaguanas**, where you can buy traditional pottery. From Chaguanas, head west and go left on the old Southern Main Road. The potters mentioned under Shopping are found a mile south of here. Visit the **Caroni Bird Sanctuary**, *Tel. 645-1305,* home of the scarlet ibis. Admission is $10 adults and $5 children. At **La Vega Garden Centre** near Gran Couva, , *Tel. 653-6120,* picnic in the bamboo forest. Admission to the nursery sales area is free; group tours sometimes schedule more extensive visits, which aren't available to individual travelers.

At Waterloo, note the **Sewdass Sadhu Chiv Mandir temple**, built in the 1930s by a single Hindu. Pilgrims continue to visit the site. At Pointe-a-Pierre, the **Wild Fowl Trust**, *Tel. 662-4040,* is on the grounds of the oil refinery but it is visited by group tours. Individuals can visit Monday to Friday 10am to 5pm. Saturday noon to 4pm and Sunday 10:30am to 6pm. A token fee is charged. **San Fernando** is the island's second city, a commercial center.

At **Princes Town**, bubbling mud indicates volcanic activity which can also be seen at **Pitch Lake**, *Tel. 648-7697*. Near La Brea, oozing pitch swirls and boils, sometimes spewing up things that have been buried for years in the churning tar. The museum is open daily 10am to 6pm Admission is TT$15 adults and TT$10 for children.

TOBAGO

If you come ashore from a ferry or cruise ship you'll land in the heart of Scarborough, handy to the bus terminus, post office, shopping and banks. Don't miss the colorful **marketplace**, which is best in the mornings and the **Botanic Station**, which is reached through the Scarborough Mall. It's a botanic garden and plant nursery. Along Piggott Street, note the **Cenotaph** that honors the many Tobagonians who served in the two world wars.

Along Fort Street, note the **Methodist Church**, which dates to 1824; **Scarborough Hospital**, which has been here since 1819, and the **Old Prison**, which is now the warden's residence. Once a jail for condemned prisoners, it once put on a show of repeatedly raising and lowering the dead body of the leader of a slave revolt. Onlookers thought that all the rebels were being hanged, and the revolt was quickly put down.

The view from **Fort King George**, which dates to 1777-1779, is a good one. Britain garrisoned 600 soldiers and 20 officers here between 1802 and 1820, although many of the original buildings were destroyed in a hurricane in 1847. The **Tobago Museum**, *Tel. 639-3970,* has a nice collection of pre-Columbian artifacts and displays depicting Tobago's long French and English history. It's open weekdays 9am to 5pm. Admission is $1.

Along Bacolet Street, which leads from Scarborough to the Windward area, note some public buildings, schools, a cemetery, and **Gun Bridge**, near the firehouse. It's made from the rifle barrels of the French soldiers who once manned Fort King George.

From the airport, a tour of the **Lowlands** region will take you to **Fort Milford**, built by the British in the 1770s, **Crusoe's Cave**, the beach at **Pigeon Point**, and the historic sites at **Bon Accord**. Climb **Signal Hill** for the view. Northwestern Tobago is known as the Leeward region where you'll find some historic sites including **Fort Bennett**, built by the Dutch in the 1620s, and **Fort James** in Plymouth, built by the British in the mid-1700s. Travelers like to ponder the **mystery grave** of Betty Stevens, who died in 1783. Her stone is inscribed, "She was a mother without knowing it." Did she die in childbirth? Act as a surrogate mother without knowing how much her kindness was appreciated? Passers-by continue to wonder.

Lovers' Retreat at Back Bay is an Arawak site where many artifacts have been uncovered. **St. David Anglican Church**, built in 1825, was once the site of a treadmill used to punish slaves. At **Great Courtland Bay**, a monument remembers settlers from Latvia who tried colonizing this area between 1639 and 1693. Their colony failed, but their descendants return once a year. On this site, the Dutch had a fort in the 1600s.

For a memorable nature walk filled with bird sightings, hike from Arnos Vale to Culloden along the coast. Locals call it the **Warden's Road**. This area is strewn with ruins of sugar plantations. The Amos Vale Hotel sits in the groves of what was once a fine plantation. At Golden Lane, note the **slave cemetery** with gravestones for such names as Gang Gang Sarah, Quashie, Quaccoo, Kwasi, and Kwamina. Entering Culloden, note the huge **silk cotton tree**. Its "cotton" was used by Africans to wrap the dead and the tree still has a strong spiritual value to people who live here. Many of the artifacts displayed at museums in Trinidad and Tobago were found at Culloden Bay.

The southeastern side of Tobago, known as the **Windward** region, is the home of Mount St. George, the original capital of the island. The area is dotted with historic sites, plantation ruins, beaches, and natural treasures including **Lure Estate Waterfalls** in Goldsborough. The ruins of **Richmond Estate** can be seen in Glamorgan; Richmond Great House is how a guest house in Belle Garden. It's filled with African artifacts. At **King's Bay**, stop to see the waterfall; **Speyside** is a tourist center known for its fishing and diving. Its rusting cane grinders still bear the date of their manufacture in Glasgow, 1871.

The region known as **Northside** is bounded by Scarborough, Les Coteaux, and the sea. It's a residential area filled with small inns, nature trails, pretty bays, and the **natural bird sanctuary** at Brothers Rock and Sisters Rock.

Sightseeing tours are available from **Sun Fun Tours** in Canaan, Tobago, *Tel. 639-7461.*

NIGHTLIFE & ENTERTAINMENT

For live jam sessions, try **MASCAMP PUB**, Ariapita Avenue at French Street, Port of Spain, *Tel. 623-3745.* It's like Carnival all year long.

In Tobago, try **BOBSTER'S** champagne bar at Coco Reef Resort, *Tel. 639-8571;* **BONKERS** at Store Bay Local Road in Crown Pointe, *Tel. 639-8718* or **KARIWAK VILLAGE**, which has weekend entertainment at Crown Point, *Tel. 639-8442.* **LE GRAND COURLAN RESORT & SPA**, Black Rock, *Tel. 639-9667* has live entertainment nightly.

The most exciting nightlife isn't in the clubs but on the most remote beaches during leatherback turtle nesting season, March through June. See the list of nature tour operators below to connect with a turtle watch.

SPORTS & RECREATION

Diving

Diving Tobago is to drift with the strong currents known as **Bocas** as you glide silkily through majestic coral forests, fleets of rays, armies of eels, and seascapes that slide by like a kaleidoscope. Rising from the outer edge of the continental shelf off South America, the islands are located at the junction of the North Equatorial Current from the Atlantic and the Guyana Current from the mighty Orinoco River in South America. The abundance and variety of sea life continues to surprise and delight even the most jaded divers.

Your dive master will carry a marker to help identify for you the corals, sponges, and the Superdome, the largest known brain coral in the Caribbean. You'll see mantas, shark, tuna, barracuda, mackerel and thousands of brilliant reef fish that flash blue or yellow as the sun hits them. Tobago has one of the largest nesting sites for **leatherneck turtles** in the Caribbean, and both divers and non-divers are welcome to join a turtle watch during egg-laying season March through June.

On Tobago, dive with:
- **Tobago Marine Sports at Crown** Point, *Tel. 639-0291*
- **Aquamarine Dive**, *Tel. 660-4341*
- **Dive Tobago**, *Tel. 639-0202*
- **Man Friday Diving**, *Tel. 660-4676*
- **Ron's Watersports**, *Tel. 622-0459*
- **Tobago Dive Experience**, *Tel. 639-0791*
- **Viking Dive**, *Tel. 639-9209*

Tobago dive operators, in cooperation with the Department of Tourism, offer a framable parchment certificate certifying your dives on eight of Tobago's drifts.

On Trinidad, try **Ron's Watersports and Dive Centre**, *Tel. 673-0549*. Or, call **Winston's Supermarket**, *Tel. 648-3411*, in Point Fortin and ask for Vonan. He lives behind the store and is a local fisherman and free-diver who might be available to take you out with him. Call one or two days ahead.

Sailing

Day cruises, sunset cruises and island charters are available with **Kalina Cats** in Scarborough, *Tel. 639-6304*.

Squash

Play the squash courts at the **Grafton Beach Resort**, Black, Rock, Tobago, for $56.50 for 45 minutes, *Tel. 639-0191*.

SHOPPING

At last, here's a place where you're not constantly exhorted to buy overpriced "duty free" baubles and knick-knacks. Port of Spain offers everything from luxurious department stores to street vendors selling leather shoes from Venezuela. And, if you want those high-priced collectibles, Trinidad has them too.

The best souvenirs include locally-made pottery, recorded Caribbean music, local batiks, and crafts. If you want a real steel pan, this is the place to get one that is perfectly tuned. The toy pans sold to tourists are just for noise and show.

Karie's has shops at the airport departure lounges and in the Town Center Mall, selling souvenir T-shirts, towels, caps, and bags. It's a good place to load up on soft goods that travel well; *Tel. 669-1655* for the mall location, *Tel. 669-2356* at Piarco Airport, *Tel. 639-0154* and at Crown Point, Tobago.

For local crafts, shop **Craft Creators** on the second level in West Mall, Westmoorings, *Tel. 637-6488*; **Glitter Wood** in the Long Circular Mall and in the Hilton and Normandie hotels, *Tel. 637-7421*. Glitter Wood's Signature Collection features expensive, one-of-a-kind jewelry. **"Fo Carib Heritage"** on the ground floor of the Gulf City Shopping Complex in San Fernando sells Trinidadian crafts. Crafts are also carried by **Olayinka** on Level Three in the Circular Mall, St. James, *Tel. 628-2276*; **Poui Batik** and **Ajoupa Pottery** in the Ellerslie Plaza in Maraval, *Tel. 622-5597*; **Paper Based** in the Market at the Normandie, *Tel. 625-3197, extension 4343*; and **The Card Loft** on the first floor in the Excellent City Centre on Frederick Street, Port of Spain.

For batik shop Althea Bastien's **The Batique**, 43 Sydenham Avenue in St. Ann's, *Tel. 624-3274,* or **Pamela Marshall** at Loui Designs, *Tel. 622-2645*. For straw and cane work shop the **Blind Welfare Association** at Duke and Edward streets, *Tel. 624-1613*. Ceramics and pottery are also sold at **The Clay Den**, in the West Mall, Westmoorings, *Tel. 624-2425*.

EXCURSIONS & DAY TRIPS
TRINIDAD

Island tours, nature tours, and golf or scuba packages can be booked with **The Travel Centre**, Uptown Mall, Edward Street, Port of Spain, *Tel. 868/623-5098, Fax 868/623-5101*.

Nature tours can also be arranged with:
- **Avifauna Tours**, *Tel. 633-5614*
- **Caroni Bird Sanctuary Tours**, *Tel. 645-1305*
- **KPE Nature Tours**, *Tel. 637-9664*
- **Nature Tours Unlimited**, *Tel. 665-2683*

- **South East Eco-Tours**, *Tel. 644-1072*
- **Caribbean Discovery Tours**, *Tel. 624-7281*
- **Pax Nature Tours**, *Tel. 662-4084*

TOBAGO

Nature tours of Tobago can be scheduled with:
- **David Rooks Nature Tours** in Scarborough, *Tel. 639-4276*
- **Tobago Buccoo Reef Tours**, *Tel. 639-9058*
- **Buccoo Reef Cooperative**, *Tel. 639-8582*
- **Educators**, *Tel. 639-7422*
- **Pioneer Tours**, *Tel. 660-4327*
- **William Trim**, a tour guide and forester in Speyside, *Tel. 660-5529*

Glass-bottom boat tours are offered by **Calypso Empress** out of Pigeon Point, *Tel. 639-9058*. Sailings are at 11:30am daily.

PRACTICAL INFORMATION

Area Code: 868

ATM: more than 73 ATMs are found in Trinidad and Tobago in major settlements and shopping centers. Look for Republic Banks' Blue Machine, which accepts Linx, Visa, Plus MasterCard and Cirrus.

Crime: according to a consular information sheet, crime is on the rise, more on Trinidad that Tobago. Don't roam beaches after dark, and take precautions against theft anywhere, any time. If your passport is stolen, report it to the local police or American Embassy, 15 Queen's Park West, Port of Spain, *Tel. 622-6372*. If your birth certificate or driver's license is stolen, it probably cannot be replaced until you get home. Drug laws are stiff; offenders can expect a lengthy jail sentence and a fine. Even a small amount of marijuana can land you in deep trouble.

Currency: the TT dollar exchanges at about TT$6.24 to US$1. If you prefer, think of each TT$1 as about 16 U.S. cents. U.S. dollars are accepted everywhere, but locals may not have change in U.S. so, for local shopping, it's best to have local funds. If you charge restaurant and hotel bills to a credit card, you get the optimum exchange rate for each day of your stay.

Customs & Immigration: a passport is required but not a visa if your visit will be three months or less.

Dress: Trinidad is a business center and people tend to dress up except at the beach. Church dress is conservative, so don't wear shorts or sleeveless tops. Tobago is much more casual.

Electricity: North American-style, 110-volt electrical plugs are used.

Emergencies: for a police emergency, dial 999; for a fire dial 990.

Government: Trinidad and Tobago form an independent nation and has a U.S. embassy at Port of Spain.

Health Care: it's a good idea to purchase supplementary health insurance that is good for overseas travel. Doctors and hospitals here usually expect cash on the barrelhead. Hospitals are found in Port of Spain, Scarborough and San Fernando. Clinics are found throughout the islands. Pharmacies that keep late hours include, in Trinidad, Bhaggan's on Independence Square, *Tel. 627-5541*. It's open until 11pm most nights and until 9pm on Sundays and holidays. The Hilton also has a pharmacy. Scarborough Drugs on Tobago, *Tel. 639-4161* is at the corner of Carrington Street and Wilson Road. It's open daily until 8pm and Sunday and holidays until noon.

Hours: most business are open Monday through Friday 8am to 4:30pm and Saturday 8am to noon. Malls are open all day Saturday and later during the week. Banks are usually open 8am to 2pm Monday to Thursday and 8am to noon and 3-5pm on Friday. Government offices are open weekdays 8am to noon and 1-4:30pm.

Pets: are quarantined for six months before admission.

Tourism information: write TIDCO, *Cheryl Andrews Marketing, 1500 San Remo, Suite 145, Coral Gables FL 33146, Tel. 305/663-1660 or toll-free 888/595-4868*. A tourist information booth is at the Scarborough Mall.

Weddings: since 1996, the waiting period for weddings of non-citizens has been reduced to three days. Work with your hotel's wedding consultant, or call tourism officials toll-free at *Tel. 888/595-4868* for information on the required documents and procedures. Weddings can be performed on both Trinidad and Tobago.

THE
U.S.
CARIBBEAN

39. PUERTO RICO

Puerto Rico – America's "Shining Star of the Caribbean" – lies between St. Thomas and the Dominican Republic, its north shore on the Atlantic Ocean and its south on the Caribbean Sea. The island is 100 miles long and 32 miles wide. Among its many treasures is El Yunque, the only tropical rain forest in the eastern United States. Only 3 1/2 jet hours from New York and two from Miami, Puerto Rico offers all the spicy Latin flavor of a foreign country, yet you're still at home where U.S. dollars and postage stamps are in use.

Christopher Columbus carried the Spanish flag to island after island but eventually Spain lost most of her Caribbean holdings to the English, French, Dutch, and Danes. Puerto Rico is the only Caribbean island under the U.S. flag where you can still capture the Latino legacy left by the original Conquistadores. For adventurous vacationers, it means a chance to taste mofongo, mavi, juicy tropical fruits, dizzying rum drinks, and lush seafood harvests fresh from the sea. Yet for those who like a touch of home, it also means McDonald's, Pizza Hut, Kentucky Fried Chicken, Sears, Radio Shack, Ma Bell coin telephones that take only a dime, and driving on the right side of the road.

Let's start with the beaches because they rim the island like a necklace of sugar cookies – sandy, sweet, fragrant and warm. The beach resort areas nearest **San Juan** include **Condado**, **Miramar**, **Ocean Park**, and **Isla Verde**. Drive the coast roads around the big island, stopping at every pretty beach you see. For a real getaway, take a ferry to the islands of **Culebra** or **Vieques** in the east or Mona off the west coast.

Puerto Rico's spine of mountains is a magnet for hikers and nature lovers. It is here in lofty coffee plantations that a special harvest is made each year of rare coffees to be presented to the Vatican. Plan at least three days if you want to explore inland Puerto Rico along the mountain road. You'll probably get lost a few times, meet a lot of friendly natives, stop at a pineapple stand, and eat wonderful food at rundown shacks.

No matter when you go, there's likely to be a fiesta somewhere on the island. It may be a religious or folk festival, a tournament in any sport from auto racing to baseball, or a seasonal harvest celebration. Other festivals such as the Casals Festival each June are cultural events that attract world class artists and musicians. Most of the smaller towns are a fiesta in themselves on Friday nights when people dress up and take to the streets. The best blowout in each town is the feast day of its patron saint, when parties go on for a week or more. The largest are those in San Juan (June 23-24), Loiza (June 25), and Ponce (December 6-15).

Waves of settlers arrived on Puerto Rico starting around 3,000 B.C. including Arawaks, followed by the Tainos, whose culture was one of the most advanced in the Americas. Within 50 years of Columbus' first call here in 1493, they had almost disappeared, victims of enslavement and disease.

A Spanish stronghold almost from the beginning of Spanish exploration in the Americas, San Juan was fortified in the early 1500s by **Juan Ponce de León**, who is buried in the San Juan Cathedral. By the 1630s it was a walled city sprawled under the imposing **El Morro**, a 200-acre fort that repelled the most savage English attacks. Only in 1598 was it taken by the English, and then only briefly. Its stones seemingly indestructible through the ages, it's still one of the Caribbean's most majestic forts.

The Spanish quest for gold had some success in Puerto Rico, with meager findings along the rivers, but soon the cash crop became sugar cane harvested on fields tended by slaves brought in from Africa. Their language and lore, and to some extent the color of their skin, melted seamlessly into local culture.

When the world sugar market collapsed, Puerto Rico slumbered through the ages, eking out an income from exporting coffee and tobacco. Running for office in 1929, Luis Muñoz Marin described it as a "land of beggars and millionaires." In 1940, per capita income was only $120. Then came the end of World War II, the building of a Hilton hotel, and the island was transformed forever. The natural hospitality of the people, sunny winters, clear waters, and a continuing building boom in hotels has turned Puerto Rico into a world-class player in leisure and business travel.

When you first hear the ear-piercing cry of the coqui tree frog, which is found only on Puerto Rico, it's a shock. Then this nightly chorus gets into your blood until it's a lullaby. Soon, you can't imagine nights without the coqui's chirp echoing through flower-scented breezes. "*Soy tan puertoriqueño como el coqui*" means "I'm as Puerto Rican as a coqui." The little fellow is pictured everywhere as a symbol of the island.

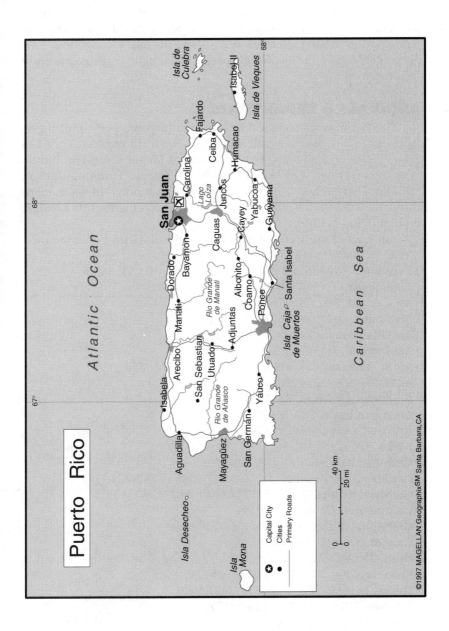

Puerto Rico

Isla Mona

Isla Desecheo

Atlantic Ocean

Isla de Culebra

Isabel II

Isla de Vieques

Fajardo

Ceiba

Humacao

Carolina

San Juan

Lago Loíza

Juncos

Yabucoa

Cayey

Guayama

Aguadilla

Isabela

Arecibo

Dorado

Manatí

Bayamón

Caguas

Aibonito

Coamo

Ponce

Santa Isabel

Isla Caja de Muertos

San Sebastián

Utuado

Adjuntas

Río Grande de Manatí

Mayagüez

San Germán

Yauco

Río Grande de Añasco

Caribbean Sea

Capital City
Cities
Primary Roads

40 km
20 mi

©1997 MAGELLAN GeographixSM Santa Barbara,CA

Climate

The northern coast of Puerto Rico, exposed to the northeast tradewinds, is wetter than the south coast. There is no dry season, just a pleasant spread of sunshine and showers throughout the year. Daytime temperatures in San Juan rarely reach above the low 90s; nighttime lows get no cooler than the low 60s. Be prepared for light, cooling showers in the mountains.

ARRIVALS & DEPARTURES

The Caribbean's main airline hub, San Juan is a beehive of flights from more than a dozen North American cities including New York, Los Angeles, Boston, Baltimore, Detroit, Hartford, Miami, Dallas-Fort Worth, Washington Dulles, Orlando, Philadelphia, Tampa, Toronto, Chicago, and Dallas. From here American Eagle flies to another 40 destinations throughout the Caribbean. San Juan also has direct flights from London, Frankfurt and Madrid.

San Juan's **Luis Munoz Marin International Airport** is served by:
- **ACES**, *Tel. 800/846-2237 or 787/791-5840*
- **Aerolineas Argentinas**, *Tel. 787/791-8181 or 800/333-0276*
- **Air Calypso**, *Tel. 787/253-0020*
- **Air Canada**, *Tel. 800/776-3000*
- **Air France**, *Tel. 800/237-2747*
- **Air Guadeloupe**, *Tel. 787/253-0933*
- **Air Jamaica**, *Tel. 800/523-5585*
- **Air St. Thomas**, *Tel. 800/522-3084 or 787/791-4898*
- **ALM**, *Tel. 800/327-7230*
- **American Air Lines**, *Tel. 787/749-1747*
- **American Eagle**, *787/749-1747*
- **British Airways**, *800/247-9297*
- **BWIA**, *Tel. 800/538-2942*
- **Canadian Airlines**, *Tel. 787/791-0404*
- **Caribbean Air Express**, *Tel. 800/981-9045 or 787/721-5345*
- **Carnival Airlines**, *Tel. 800/274-6140 or 800/824-7386*
- **Continental**, *Tel. 800/525-0280*
- **COPA**, *Tel. 800/9981-8284 or 787/722-6969*
- **Condor**, *Tel. 800/645-3880*
- **Delta**, *Tel. 800/221-1212*
- **Flamenco**, *Tel. 787/723-8110 or 725-7707*
- **Iberia**, *Tel. 800/772-4642 or 787/721-5630*
- **Isla Nena**, *Tel. 741-6362 or 741-1577*
- **KLM**, *Tel. 800/826-7976*
- **LACSA**, *Tel. 800/225-2272 or 787/724-3330*
- **LIAT**, *Tel. 787/791-3838*

- **Martin Air**, *Tel. 800/627-8462*
- **Northwest Airlines**, *Tel. 800/225-2525 or 800/447-4747*
- **Pan Am**, *Tel. 800/359-7262*
- **Towers Air**, *Tel. 800/221-2500*
- **TWA**, *Tel. 800/221-2000 or 800/892-8466*
- **United**, *Tel. 800/241-6522 or 800/538-2929*
- **USAir**, *Tel. 800/842-5374*
- **Vieques Air Link**, *Tel. 787/722-3736*

Frequent air service is also available from San Juan to Vieques, from Vieques to Fajardo, from Fajardo to Culebra, and from Vieques to St. Croix. Among the island's private airports is one at the **Hyatt Dorado Beach Hotel**. Mayagüez has an airport served by **American Eagle**. **Carnival Air** flies from New York to Aguadilla and Ponce.

Ferries depart every half hour from Pier Two in Old San Juan for Cataño and Hato Rey, *Tel. 788-1155*. For schedules, rate information, and reservations for passenger ferry service among Fajardo, Vieques, and Culebra, *Tel. 863-0852*. Transportation for cars is available on the cargo ferry, *Tel. 863-0852*. Allow at least a week for planning and reservations.

SMALL CHANGE

Porters always seem to be in short supply at San Juan's airport, so have quarters on hand for the rental luggage cart machines. Even if you're only changing planes here, you have to handle your own bags in and out of customs. It can be a long haul without the rental cart. For the telephones, you'll need dimes.

ORIENTATION

Metropolitan San Juan has spread like a giant amoeba that has gobbled up Toa Baja, Cataño, Bayamon, Trujillo Alto, Carolina, and Guayanabo almost as far as Caguas, which will probably soon be part of the megalopolis. **Old San Juan**, an island that forms half the rim of San Juan Bay, is a time machine frozen in the 16th century. It's a place to roam and sightsee, and rest in shaded plazas paved with centuries-old stones. East of Old (or Viejo) San Juan are the high-rise tourist hotels of Condado and Miramar. Hato Rey is the city's financial and commercial hub. Eastward into Carolina, you're in the 'burbs with their real estate developments and American-style shopping malls and supermarkets.

From San Juan, Route 3 goes east past **Luquillo** with its famous beach to **Fajardo**, where ferries leave for offshore islands. South of Route 3 spreads **El Yunque,** the magnificent rain forest covering the **Sierra Luquillo.**

Driving south from San Juan takes you through **Caguas, Cayvey** and on to the colonial city of **Ponce.** Or, head east from Caguas to the resort area of **Humacao.**

It's possible to drive around almost the entire perimeter of the island, going west from Ponce, skirting inland through **San Germán**, and back to the coast at busy **Mayagüez.** Then north to **Aquadilla** and east along the coast to the attractions of **Arecibo** with its radio telescope and the caves of **Rio Camuy**, through the resorts of **Dorado** and back to San Juan. An alternative route, if you have plenty of time, is to drive the spine of the **Cordillera**, the mountain range through the middle of the island.

GETTING AROUND PUERTO RICO

White-painted taxis participating in the **Tourism Taxi Program** operate on a zone system. Fare from the airport to nearby districts including Isla Verde and Puntas las Marias is $8. In Zone 2, from the airport to Condado, Ocean Park, and Miramar, the fare is $12. Zone 3 from the airport to Old San Juan, tourism piers, and Puerta de Tierra is a $16 fare. A Zone 5 fare of $6 applies from the piers to Puerta de Tierra. Fare for the Zone 6 ride from the piers to Condado, Ocean Park and Miramar is $10. Zone 7 is from the piers to Isla Verde, costing $16.

Metered cabs have a $1 initial charge, then charge 10 cents for each additional 1/13 mile plus additional fees for baggage, waiting time, reserved rides, and night travel. Charter taxis charge $20 per hour. If you have complaints about taxis, call the Public Service Commission, *Tel. 756-1919,* or the airport police, *Tel. 791-4155.*

Free trolleys shuttle every 15 minutes from 6am to 2am around the Isla Verde district so it's easy to enjoy all the hotels, clubs and shops of this upscale tourist area without having a car. City buses in the San Juan area are frequent and good. Bus stops are marked by orange, white and magenta signs reading Parada, with yellow and white lines marking bus stops on main highways. Bus terminals are in the Covadonga parking lot in Old San Juan (long-distance buses) and on Plaza de Colon for short routes. For information, Tel. 763-4141.

Public transportation by *publicos* (vans) covers the island at rates ranging from, for example, $10 to $25 for the trip from San Juan to Mayagüez, depending on the route taken and how many stops are made. Catch a publico at the airport, Rio Piedras Plaza, or in the town plaza in any community. For information about routes to Mayagüez, call **Lineas Sultana,** *Tel. 765-9377. For* information about publicos to Ponce, *Tel. 764-0540.*

Parking space is at a premium almost everywhere, so consider carefully whether you really need a rental car. Hotels may charge $12 a day or more for parking if it's available at all. Restaurants have valet parking, if any. If you do rent, avoid cut-rate rental agencies that don't have satellite offices island-wide because you could be stranded if you break down out on the island. Major car rental companies also offer transportation from hotels or the airport to their lots, and their cars are equipped with anti-theft devices.

Rental car agencies include:
· **Avis**, *Tel. 800/874-3556*
· **Budget**, *Tel. 787/791-3685 or 800/468-5822*
· **Hertz**, *Tel. 787/791-0840 or 800/654-3131*
· **National**, *Tel. 787/791-1805 or 800/568-3019*
· **Thrifty**, *Tel. 787/253-2525 or 800/367-2277*

Kemwel Rental Cars can be reserved in the U.S. at *800/678-0678.* For **Wheelchair Getaways Rent-a-Car**, *Tel. 787/726-4023 or 800/868-8028.* In Mayagüez or Ponce, try **Popular Leasing**, *Tel. 787/265-4848 or 800/981-9282.*

WHERE TO STAY

There is a nine percent hotel tax. Some hotels often add a service charge of 15 percent or more in lieu of tipping. Rates given are for a double room in high season. Unless stated otherwise, major credit cards are accepted.

OLD SAN JUAN

GRAN HOTEL EL CONVENTO, *100 Cristo. Tel. 787/723-9020. Rates at this 59-room hotel start at $220. It's a $16 taxi ride from the airport and $6 by cab from the pier.*

You're not just in the heart of history, you are part of history when you stay in a building that is almost 400 years old. Built as a convent and lavishly restored in 1996, it is one of the old city's most talked-about showplaces. Two levels are stores, restaurants and cafes. The hotel covers three floors. Its facilities include a plunge pool, fitness center, small casino, and a full-service business center. The hotel has a restaurant, swimming pool and gaming, and it is wheelchair accessible.

GALLERY INN AT GALERÍA SAN JUAN, *Calle Norzagaray #204-206, Old San Juan PR 00901. Tel. 787/722-1808, Fax 787/724-7360. Rates at this 22-room inn start at $95, suites at $200, Rates include continental breakfast. Cab fare from the airport is $16 and from the pier $6.*

Everything you've ever dreamed of in a bed and breakfast inn is found here in a romantic, 300-year-old building that rambles from the north wall of the old city through a warren of stony courtyards, balconies filled with flowers, and hidden rooms. It's so private, there isn't even a sign outside, so don't arrive without a reservation and directions. Most rooms have private bath and some have air conditioning, but each is so different, so eclectic, that most guests choose a favorite and book it year after year.

Built for a Spanish artillery captain, the home is now the studio of talented artists Jan D'Esopo and Manuco Gandia whose works are part of the decor and are also for sale in the gallery. Visitors can look on as a frenzy of creative activity produces paintings, sculptures, silkscreening, mold making, and bronze castings. In her spare time, Jan plays her Steinway concert grand or brings in talented conservatory students to play for her guests. This is the ideal *pied-a-terre* for exploring the old city on foot. Parking is very limited, so skip the rental car until you're ready to leave for the countryside.

WYNDHAM OLD SAN JUAN, *101 Marina, Old San Juan. Tel. 787/ 721-5100 or 800/822-4200 U.S. and 800/631-4200 Canada. Rates at this 240-room hotel start at $240; stay on the Concierge level and pay a rate of $275, which includes continental breakfast. It's a $16 taxi ride from the airport.*

Stay in the old city in style and comfort worthy of the fussiest business traveler or vacationer. The hotel has a swimming pool, a casino, and is wheelchair accessible.

GREATER SAN JUAN
Expensive

CARIBE HILTON, *Fort San Geronimo, Puerto de Tierra, San Juan. Tel. 787/721-0303 or 800/HILTONS in the U.S. and Canada. Rates at this 733-room hotel start at $330, suites at $660. Valet parking is $14 daily, self parking is $5 a day. On the concierge level, breakfast is included. Taxi fare from the airport is $12; from the pier, $6. The hotel can also be reached by the A7 bus.*

The beach is a tiny jewel rarely found in the heart of the city, and the hotel offers classy accommodations for business or pleasure plus a 400-year-old fort to explore and photograph. Oceanview rooms gaze out over crashing surf and the ramparts of Fort San Jeronimo. Work out in the health club or book one of the rooms or suites that has its own Action Stepper fitness machine. There's a full spa, two freshwater pools, six tennis courts lit for night play, a playground for the children, a massive casino, and four excellent restaurants as well as lounges and bars. Accommodations are spacious and posh, offering luxury touches for the leisure traveler plus the desk, telephones, and business center that a working visitor requires.

CONDADO BEACH TRIO, *1061 Ashford Avenue, Condado, San Juan PR 00907. Tel. 787/721-6090, Fax 787/468-2822, U.S. 800/468-2775. Rates at two hotels that operate as one start at $195; suites at $275. The trio comprises* *the Condado Beach Hotel, La Concha Hotel, and El Centro, the convention center. The 20-minute cab ride from the airport costs $12. An all-inclusive plan is available.*

It's a handy business address in the heart of crowded Condado's "hotel row," popular with gamblers and with nostalgia seekers who enjoy staying in the grand old Condado Beach, which was built just after World War I. The beaches (there are two) are a knockout and this is also the home of some of the island's best folk music and dance presentations. The casino is small but swank, and guests can choose from a variety of restaurants, bars, and night clubs with dance floors. The hotels have freshwater pools, room service, watersports, tennis courts, and a tour/activities desk. This is the largest convention center in the Caribbean, so it's not for the traveler who likes an intimate hotel out of the mainstream.

CONDADO PLAZA HOTEL & CASINO, *999 Ashford Avenue, Condado PR 00907. Tel. 787/721-1000 or 800/468-8588. Rates at this 587-room hotel start at $220, suites at $320. The hotel is a $12 cab ride from the airport.*

First-class service and accommodations mean a private balcony for every room, a choice of three swimming pools, a sandy beach, black tie gaming and dancing, and a spectrum of restaurants including Mandalay Oriental, Las Palmas poolside grill, elegant Capriccio's, the award-winning La Posada for Puerto Rican food, or Tony Roma's for its famous ribs. Room service and La Posada operate around the clock. It is managed by the same company as El San Juan Hotel & Casino, so guests in either can charge meals to one account.

CROWNE PLAZA BEACH RESORT & CASINO, *Highway 187, Kilometer 1.5, Isla Verde, San Juan PR 00979. Tel. 787/253-2929 or 800/2 CROWNE. Room rates start at $169 plus $6 for parking or $10 for valet parking. From the airport, exit right on Route 26 towards San Juan, then exit right on Highway 187. Just past the traffic light, the hotel is on your left. Drive time is five minutes; cab fare is $8.*

Play blackjack, Baccarat, roulette, craps and the slots by night and bake the days away on renowned Isla Verde Beach. The 254-room, high-rise hotel brings the tropics indoors in its airy rooms and suites. For special perks including nightly turn-down, continental breakfast, newspaper, and nightly hors d'oeuvres and honor bar, stay on the Crowne Plaza Club Floor. Dining is in Windows on the Sea, known for its traditional Puerto Rican dishes. Old San Juan is 15 minutes away, and the concierge can arrange a golf game for you 30 minutes from the hotel.

Although Crowne Plaza Hotels and Resorts can be reserved through Holiday Inn, they have dropped the Holiday Inn name and are distancing themselves from the price-appeal chain.

EL SAN JUAN HOTEL & CASINO, *Avenue Isla Verde, Isla Verde PR 00979. Tel. 787/791-0390; in the U.S., Canada, and U.S. Virgin Islands, call 800/223-6800. Rates in this 389-room, 20-suite hotel start at $320 double. The hotel is a five-minute taxi ride from the airport.*

For luxury leisure travelers and business travelers too, this hotel offers the best of both: 15 acres on the beach, grounds landscaped with palms and flowering shrubs, as well as meeting rooms and a business center. Rooms are air conditioned; some have a Jacuzzi or sunken tub; many have a private terrace or balcony. Lose yourself in the gardens, or savor all the bustle of a big hotel: five restaurants, 24-hour room service, tennis courts that are lit for night play, a state-of-the-art fitness center, and an extensive watersports center with board sailing, deep sea fishing, and parasailing. Ask about the optional meal plan.

RADISSON AMBASSADOR PLAZA HOTEL & CASINO, *1369 Ashford Avenue, Condado, San Juan PR 00907. Tel. 721-7300, U.S. 800/333-3333 . Rates at this 233-room hotel start at $169. It's a $12 taxi ride, or 15 minutes, from the airport.*

You're in Condado's action-packed tourist strip, only ten minutes from Old San Juan, half a block from the beach, and surrounded by shops, restaurants, and bars. The hotel rises in two towers, one of 146 rooms and the other with two-room suites. Stay on the Ambassador Club floor with its own lounge, concierge, and prestige perks. Swim in the rooftop pool, which has its own whirlpool, work on in the fitness center, shop the boutique, choose from three restaurants, and stay late in the Cabaret Lounge to listen to live music. The hotel has its own beauty shop, game room, and travel desk and the casino is said to be one of the island's most user-friendly.

RITZ-CARLTON SAN JUAN HOTEL AND CASINO, *6961 State Road 187, Isla Verde, Carolina PR 00979. Tel. 800/241-3333. At press time, the new, 419-room, 45-suite hotel has not announced its 1998 rates. It will also have a 45-room club floor. It's five minutes from the international airport and 15 minutes from Old San Juan.*

We know Ritz-Carltons, Isla Verde, and this stretch of beach, so we don't hesitate to recommend a hotel that is not open at press time but is surely destined for all-star status. New in 1998, the resort sits on almost eight acres including its own, 450-foot beach. Views are of the sea or of El Yunque rain forest. Public areas and guest rooms have been decorated by local artists.

A bustling business hotel with a ballroom, meeting rooms and a business center, the Ritz is also ideal for the leisure traveler who wants unabashed luxury, the beach, a full-service spa, and a city location handy to the airport, financial district, Old San Juan, and shopping at Plaza Las Americas. Nightlife and dining at Condado are ten minutes away. Dine in the Vineyard Room, the hotel's signature restaurant serving California and continental cuisine or in more information restaurants indoors and out. Room service answers 24 hours a day.

Swim in the supersize, 7,200-square foot pool, soak in the whirlpools, play tennis on the hotel's courts, and gamble late and luxuriously in the 17,000 square foot Monte Carlo by the Sea Casino. Hotel guests have golf privileges at nearby courses. The Fitness Center offers aerobics, exercise equipment and free weights. Three fishing clubs are nearby; horse racing is 20 minutes away.

SANDS HOTEL & CASINO BEACH RESORT, *187 Avenida Isla Verde, Isla Verde PR 00913. Tel. 787/791-6100, Fax 791-8525; U.S. 800/443-2009. Rates at this 417-unit hotel start at $220; suites at $270. It's an $8 cab ride from the airport. Parking is $5 per day; valet parking, $10.*

The gambling glitter of the Sands Hotel in Atlantic City is cloned here. On the beach and surrounded by lush, flowery tropical plants, the hotel does a brisk tour and group business. Dine in Ruth's Chris Steak House, Giuseppe for northern Italian cuisine, or the informal cafe. Legends Live at the Copa is one of the island's most exciting night clubs. For the ultimate luxury, stay in the Plaza Club, the resort's five-star prestige section.

Moderate

COLONY SAN JUAN BEACH HOTEL, *José M. Tartak #2, Isla Verde PR 00979. Tel. 787/253-0100, extension 2007, Fax 787/253-0220. Rates at the 71-room, 11-suite hotel start at $100. It's an $8 cab ride from the airport.*

When a beachfront hotel is built this close to the airport it is tailor-made for today's shorter vacations. Swim off the beach or in the roof-top pool with its swim-up bar and outdoor whirlpool. The European-style boutique hotel has gourmet dining as well as a terrace bar and grill, a children's center, business center, and valet parking. San Juan's business district and nightlife are all nearby.

EMBASSY SUITES, *8000 Tartak, Isla Verde PR 00902. Tel. 787/791-0505; U.S. 800/362-2779. Rates at this 300-suite hotel start at $175 including breakfast cooked to order and evening cocktails. The hotel is an $8 cab ride, five minutes from the airport.*

Any time we can get a homey, one-bedroom suite with two televisions, microwave, refrigerator, and coffee maker for this price, with a full breakfast on the house, we are sold. The hotel has an Outback Steakhouse, casual dining in the Atrium Cafe, a swimming pool with pool bar, and a casino. It's handy to Old San Juan, the beach, shopping, restaurants, and expressways, and it's wheelchair accessible. Don't confuse this address with the Embassy guest house in Condado.

RADISSON NORMANDIE, *Avenida Muñoz Rivera, Puerto de Tierra, San Juan PR 00902. Tel. 787/729-2929, Fax 787/729-3083; U.S. 800/333-3333. Rates at this 177-room hotel start at $117, suites at $205. Rates include breakfast.*

A nostalgic favorite, this ship-shaped hotel was built before World War II and named for the French cruise liner *Normandie.* Long a choice for honeymoons in the sunshine and still a great location for vacationing and business, the hotel is refurbished time and again to its original, art deco splendor. The hotel has an excellent restaurant, a lounge, a swimming pool with pool bar, a casino, room service and a beauty salon.

SAN JUAN MARRIOTT RESORT, *1309 Ashford Avenue, San Juan 00907. Tel. 787/722-7000 or 800/981-8546. Rates at this 525-room resort start at $180, suites at $210. Located on the beach in Condado it's a $12 taxi ride from the airport.*

High-rise hotels along San Juan's hotel "strip" can be seen from miles out to sea, and this 21-story beauty tops them all. Entering the lobby, you immediately grasp the sense of luxury and ease that marks a first class, modern hotel with advanced voice mail systems, 24-hour room service, in-room VCRs, and a full range of services including concierge, car rental, tour desk, a shopping arcade, and beauty shop. Live music plays in the lobby during cocktail hour, so it's a good place to meet friends. Dine in Ristorante Tuscany for northern Italian cuisine, the poolside grill, or La Vista which features a theme buffet every evening and, at breakfast and lunch, menu or buffet service. Calypso music plays on Saturday and Sunday afternoons poolside and there's merengue dancing in the lounge Thursday through Sunday from 9pm until almost dawn. The massive pool is a stunner.

Budget

CASA CARIBE, *57 Calle Caribe, Condado, San Juan PR 00907. Tel. 787/722-7139. Rates at this 7-room guest house start at $55 including continental breakfast. Cab fare from the airport is $12.*

You're near the beach in a delightful little inn favored by Puerto Ricans and savvy visitors who like the garden setting, breezy porch, and comfortable, clean rooms that have air conditioning and a ceiling fan.

CASA DE PLAYA, *86 Isla Verde, Isla Verde PR 00979. Tel. 787/728-9779. Rates at this 22-room hotel start at $75. From the airport it's an $8 taxi ride.*

Handy to town, the airport, and near the beach is this unassuming hotel with its own restaurant.

DAYS INN CONDADO LAGOON, *6 Clemenceau Avenue, Condado PR 00907. Tel. 787/721-0170 or 800/325-2525. Rates at this 44-room hotel start at $89. Cab fare from the airport is $12.*

The location is ideal for business travel or as a home port while you're exploring Old San Juan, the shopping and dining of "hotel row" and the attractions of the north side of the island. The hotel is a typical, price-appeal Days Inn with a restaurant and a swimming pool.

EL CANARIO BY THE LAGOON, *4 Clemenceau Street, Condado, San Juan PR 00907. Tel. 787/722-8640. Rates at this 40-room hotel start at $65 including breakfast.*

Back from the beach one block and on a quiet street, this small hotel has the homey look and feel of a European inn. Most of the rooms have a balcony and there is a laundry for guest use. The hosts will be glad to arrange tours and to steer you to nearby restaurants and entertainment.

OLIMPO COURT HOTEL, *603 Avenida Miramar, Miramar. Tel. 787/724-0600. Rates at this 45-room hotel start at $57. Cab fare from the airport is $8.*

Don't expect mints on your pillow at this price, but it's hard to beat the location for the traveler who wants to sleep near the airport. The hotel has its own restaurant.

TRAVEL LODGE, *Route 37, Isla Verde, mail address Box 6007, Loiza, PR 00914; Tel. 787/728-1300 or 800/468-2028. Rates at this 88-room hotel start at $93. From the airport it's an $8 cab ride.*

Just like its sister hotels in the U.S., this chain hotel is a good, solid value without frills and it is handily located on the busy main street. You'll have a comfortable room with bath. The beach is just a short walk away. The hotel has a swimming pool, restaurant, and bar, and it's within walking distance of dozens more good eateries.

WIND CHIMES INN, *53 Taft Street, Condado PR 00911. Tel. 787/727-4153. Rates at this 10-room guest house start at $55 including continental breakfast. Taxi fare from the airport is $12 and it's on the A7 bus route.*

The price is right for a room near the beach and handy to Condado's dazzling convention center, restaurants, hotels, and boutiques. Rooms are air conditioned and have a ceiling fan. Kitchens are available. Walk a block to the beach or just relax on the patio in the shade of palms and flowering vines, listening to the wind chimes. Yes, credit cards are accepted.

SOUTHEAST PUERTO RICO

PALMAS DEL MAR, *mail address: Box 2020, Humacoa, Puerto Rico 00792-2020. Tel. 787/852-6000 or U.S. 800/725-6273. Found at Kilometer 84.6 on Road #3, Route 906, Humacao. A 45-minute drive from the San Juan airport, the resort has 250 rooms and suites. Rates start at $138 nightly for a double room in low season and range to $710 nightly for a three-bedroom villa in high season. Ask about packages. Included in the resort are the **Candelero***

Hotel and *Palmas Inn, which are reserved through the telephone numbers above, and the* **Wyndham Hotel & Villas***, Tel. 787/852-6000 or 800/468-3331.*

Your domain includes a Gary Player-designed, 18-hole golf course said to have more scenic holes than any other course in the world, and a tennis center managed by Peter Burwash International. Snorkel right off the beach; take a horse from the Equestrian Center and cantor off through the surf. Scuba dive with the resort's own dive masters, the only on-site dive operation on the island.

Put yourself in a spacious hotel room with a private balcony or in a villa to house the entire family. Furnishings are tropical and bright; accessories are drawn from Puerto Rican folk art. The Adventure Club gives children, ages 3 to 13, the time of their lives while adults sun, read, or play golf or tennis.

Developed in the 1960s by Charles Fraser, known for his ecologically-sensitive developments, the resort is a complete community with branch banks, churches, school, shops, casino, beauty services, restaurants, lounges, and permanent residents living in homes costing $225,000 to $1 million. Once registered, you can charge everything in "town" to your account.

Choose from an ever-changing list of planned activities, a dozen restaurants, workout facilities, scuba, deep sea fishing, sailing, swimming pools galore, bicycling, and camaraderie without crowding. The grounds, graced with 3,000 coconut palms, cover 2,750 acres.

The **Candelero Resort** reopened in 1998 as a Wyndham after a $4.5 million renovation. Rooms are done in tropical greens and blues. Each has a mini-refrigerator, electronic door lock, in-room safe, and a private balcony or patio. The hotel, which now faces the golf course, has 6,000 square feet of retail shopping.

If you like a big resort with all the bells and whistles and enough to do for weeks without having to traipse all over the island, this is the place.

Selected as one of my Best Places to Stay; see Chapter 13.

EAST OF SAN JUAN
Expensive

EL CONQUISTADOR RESORT & COUNTRY CLUB, *Carretera 987, kilometer 3.4, Las Croabas; Tel. 787/863-1000, Fax 787/863-3280; in the U.S., Canada, and U.S. Virgin Islands, call 800/223-6800 or 800/468-5228. Room rates start at $345; suites at $770. From the San Juan airport, it is 31 miles east to the hotel, which is northeast of Fajardo.*

Splayed around and carved into an imposing bluff overlooking the ocean, this dazzling resort sprawls on for 500 lush acres in the colorful fishing hamlet of Las Croabas. In addition to the hotel there are clusters of accommodations, each a village itself with its own style. Stay in Las Casinas village for away-from-it-all privacy or Las Olas for panoramic views of the Caribbean. La Marina is harborside and has a salty ambience. The Grand Hotel is the heart of the resort, for guests who prefer a hotel setting. You're surrounded by shops, swimming pools, jacuzzis, tennis courts and restaurants. Watersports center around private Palomino Island. There's also a marina, 18-hole championship golf course, and fitness center. For the children, Camp Coqui promises all-day, supervised fun.

For added luxury and service, stay on the hotel's Club Conquistador VIP floor, which has its own lounge serving complimentary breakfast, cocktails and afternoon coffee.

HOSTAL BAHIA MAR, *Fulladosa Cove, Culebra, mailing address P.O. Box 41292, Minillas Station, Santurce PR. Tel. 787/717-1855 or 763-5289, Fax 787/754-8409. Rates are $325 nightly for two and $550 nightly for four including meals and taxes.*

The opening of this 16-unit, European style inn on the island of Culebra is exciting news for locals as well as for visitors in search of a fantasy island. High above the cove overlooking Great Harbor, you can see St. Thomas on most days. Fully-equipped units have air conditioning and kitchen with microwave oven. Watersports equipment is available in the cove; swimming and snorkeling are behind the barrier reef in Dakity Cove. The hostel operates a high-speed catamaran to Culebrita Island and whale watching outings. A minimum three-night booking is required.

WESTIN RIO MAR BEACH & COUNTRY CLUB, *6000 Rio Mar Boulevard, Rio Grande PR 00745. Tel. 787/888-6000, Fax 787/888-6600. U.S. and Canada call 800/WESTIN-1 or 800/4 RIO-MAR. Rates start at $325 double; MAP and FAP are available. Children under age 18 sleep free in their parents' room. It's between Rio Grande and Fajardo off Route 3 on Highway 968, Kilometer 1.4, 19 miles east of San Juan and about $65 by taxi from the airport. Parking is $12 daily.*

This 481-acre playground is bordered by the Atlantic, the Mamayes River, and El Yunque Caribbean National Forest. The tennis complex boasts 13 courts and there are two championship golf courses, one a 6,800-yard course designed by George and Tom Fazio and the other a 7,000-yard course created by Greg Norman. The hotel has a complete dive shop offering dives, gear, certification, snorkel trips, and scuba "discovery" courses.

The hotel is done in Mediterranean modern, with classic pieces accented by whimsical shapes and colors. Rooms have balconies overlooking the garden or beach, hair dryer, telephones at desk and bedside, signature toiletries, and a safe with key.

Work out in the fitness center and health studio, then choose from a long menu of spa services and treatments including body toning, anti-stress treatment, body wraps, salt glo, deep tissue massage, and jet-leg massage. If you like gambling, seek out the Las Vegas-style casino. It has its own concierge, a player's lounge with drinks and appetizers (under Puerto Rican Law, drinks cannot be served at the gaming tables) five ATM machines including three in the pit area, and free limousine pick-up at the airport for high rollers. Play Caribbean Stud Poker, Let It Ride, Pai Gaw Poker and a Big Six wheel. In addition you can play blackjack (classes for resort guests are free) and 224 slot machines.

Choose among 10 places to drink and dine, including the outstanding Palio, the hotel's signature restaurant and a clone of the original in the Swan at Walt Disney World. Nightly theme buffets at Marbella (mar BAY ya) are a buy; for Puerto Rican food try Cafe Carnival or La Estancia. The Grille at the golf club is known for its steaks; Bolero in the hotel is for tapas before dinner and cigars and brandy after.

The children's center is staffed all year; day care costs $35 including lunch, craft supplies and a tee shirt. Babysitting is available at $5 an hour. The hotel has three pools: a quiet pool for adults, a wading pool with sandy play area for tots, and a busier pool with waterfall and water slide for all ages. The hotel has shops and a beauty salon, valet parking, and a free shuttle serving the hotel, tennis center, and golf club.

Selected as one of my Best Places to Stay; see Chapter 13.

Budget

ANCHOR'S INN, *Route 987, Kilometer 2.7, Fajardo. Tel. 787/863-7200. Rates at this seven-room guest house start at $55 including breakfast.*

Share the same dazzling cape as the exclusive El Conquistador at less than half the price. This inn is near the beach, it is wheelchair accessible, and credit cards are accepted. The inn's restaurant is popular for its local seafood and prime meats. Try its coffee pub too.

CEIBA COUNTRY INN, *Route 977, Kilometer 1.2, Ceiba. Tel. 787/885-0471. Rooms at this nine-room guest house start at $70.*

Wheelchair accessible and handy to the U.S. Naval Station, this is an affordable address for travelers who have a car for sightseeing and restaurants.

NORTHWEST PUERTO RICO

Expensive

HYATT DORADO BEACH HOTEL, *Dorado PR 00646. Tel. 787/796-1234 or 800/233-1234. Rates start at $450 for a deluxe double room; casitas at $750. For MAP add $70 daily. The hotel is 22 miles west of San Juan; airport shuttles for the 45-minute ride charge $15.*

The two Hyatts in Dorado are hard to choose between except that this is the one with the two 18-hole golf courses. And what courses they are! Designed by Robert Trent Jones and kept in bandbox condition, they're among the best in the world. Add in a shining crescent of toasty beaches, plenty of tennis courts (some lit for night play), and 1,000 acres of gardened grounds.

Rooms, which have marble baths and terracotta tile floors, are furnished South Seas style in wicker, rattan and bamboo, accented in ice cream pastels. Your room will have a mini-safe, patio or balcony, air conditioning and ceiling fan, hair dryer, direct dial telephone, mini-bar refrigerator, and cable television. Casita rooms, which are the premium, split-level suites, have skylights. Bathrobes are provided for guest use. Su Casa, the original estate house, serves as the signature restaurant offering gourmet dining in a candlelit, open-air room shrouded in fragrant foliage. Meals are also available in the equally dressy Surf Room and in the more informal Ocean Terrace.

Shuttle buses run between the two Hyatts, giving guests twice the choice of beaches, dining, shops, and other facilities. Camp Hyatt for the kids is one of the best children's programs on the island and it operates year 'round. Miles of pathways make the resort perfect for bicycling.

HYATT REGENCY CERROMAR, *Highway 693 Dorado PR 00646. Tel. 787/796-8903; U.S. 800/233-1234. Rates at this 506-room resort start at $310; suites at $750. Add $65 daily for breakfast and dinner (MAP). The hotel is 22 miles west of San Juan; airport shuttles for the 45-minute ride charge $15.*

One of a Hyatt double play that offers all the restaurants and facilities of two luxury landmark Hyatt Regency resorts, the venerable Cerromar has one of the most eye-popping swimming pools in the world. A 1,776-foot river flows on past waterfalls and grottos from one pool to another. Going with the flow, it takes a delicious half hour just to float the course. The hotel has a full spa, workout facilities, a year-round children's program, 24-hour room service, and 21 tennis courts. Dine indoors or out in a choice of restaurants here and at the neighboring Hyatt.

Room features include a mini-bar, air conditioning, hair dryer, private safe, and tropical decor rich in sea and earth tones. Most have a private balcony.

Moderate

COSTA DORADO BEACH, *Route 466, Kilometer 0.1, Isabella. Tel. 787/872-7255. Rates at this 53-room hotel start at $95. It's a two-hour drive from San Juan, between Arecibo and Aguadilla.*

Don't confuse this with the Hyatt Dorado Beach, which is a far grander, most expensive resort an hour east of here. There is a beach, though, and the hotel has a restaurant, swimming pool, and tennis courts.

It's wheelchair accessible, and is a good stopping point on the Atlantic north of the main highway from Arecibo to Aguadilla.

WEST & SOUTHWEST PUERTO RICO
Moderate
BEST WESTERN MAYAGÜEZ RESORT & CASINO, *Route 104, Kilometer 0.3, Mayagüez PR 00680. Tel. 787/832-3030, Fax 787/265-3020. Rates at this 141-room hotel start at $125. Ask about packages.*

A booming business hotel as well as a family resort, this affordable chain hotel has a restaurant, lounge, swimming pool, a casino, and tennis courts and it is wheelchair accessible. Expect good, no-frills value.

HOLIDAY INN AND TROPICAL CASINO MAYAGÜEZ, *Route 2, Kilometer 149.9. Tel. 787/833-1100 or 800/HOLIDAY. Rates at this 154-room hotel start at $121. The hotel is two miles north of the city, ten minutes south of the airport.*

Although it's not on the beach, this impressively modern hotel is set on steeply dramatic grounds filled with forestry and flowers. There's a big swimming pool, a casino, a restaurant and a lounge.

Budget
GUTIERREZ GUEST HOUSE, *Route 229, Kilometer 16.1, Las Marias. Tel. 827-2087 or 827-3453. Rates at this 13-room guest house start at $47. Credit cards aren't accepted. It's an hour east of Mayagüez in the mountains.*

If all you want is a humble mountain getaway in a pleasant inn with a swimming pool, this is the overnight for you.

RINCÓN
HORNED DORSET PRIMAVERA HOTEL, *Route 429, Kilometer 3.0, Rincón. Tel. 787/823-4030. Rates at this 30-room hotel start at $280. The hotel is 15 minutes north of the airport at Mayagüez or 2 1/2 hours from San Juan via the northern route through Arecibo then south through Aguadilla.*

Rincón, known as a world capital of surfing, is on a windswept cape overlooking the Mona Passage on Puerto Rico's west coat. Known familiarly as the Primavera, the hotel is a sprawling collection of dashing suites and villas obviously designed for discerning travelers who shun the beaten path. Handmade mahogany furniture, including the stately four-poster beds, was made on the island. Marble and red clay tiles are set off by louvered wood doors that open to balconies overlooking the sea, and rich tapestry-type draperies and upholstery. Bathrooms are lavishly furnished with bidet, footed bathtub, and glowing brass trim.

The main building houses the restaurants. The hotel has a freshwater pool, library, and bar. Rooms have ceiling fan but no radio or television, room service (except breakfast) and no accommodations for children under age 12. Dining is in the open air for breakfast and lunch; dinner in the main dining room offers a choice of open air or air conditioning.

SOUTH COAST

PONCE HILTON, *Avenida Santiago Caballeros 14, Ponce. Tel. 787/ 259-7676, Fax 787/259-7674, or 800/HILTONS. Rates at this 156-room hotel start at $190 plus $10 daily for valet parking and $4.50 daily for self parking. Ask about packages. The hotel is seven minutes from the city.*

Ponce is coming into the spotlight as a tourism center and this exclusive Hilton meets the challenge by offering luxury surroundings, three restaurants, and a casino that jingles from noon to 4am. The cove-shaped swimming pool with its splashy waterfalls is surrounded by tropical landscaping that sets off the striking turquoise and white of the hotel. For children there's a playground and a kids' camp in summer; for working travelers there's a well-equipped business center. Rent a boat or watersports equipment, ride a bicycle, swim off the beach, and let the concierge arrange sightseeing excursions to nearby attractions. The hotel is wheelchair accessible.

DAYS INN PONCE, *Route 1 at Exit 52. Tel. 787/841-1000 or 800/325-2525. Rates at this 121-room hotel start at $90.*

Located in the heart of the city's commercial area, this is a budget-wise choice for the traveler who wants a basic room and bath with a moderately priced restaurant, children's pool, swimming pool, and whirlpool. The hotel is wheelchair accessible and has free cable television with movie channels.

Country Inns (Paradores) Throughout Puerto Rico

The *parador* network of country inns is sponsored by the Puerto Rican Tourism Company to provide budget lodgings in less-traveled parts of the island. Most sites are chosen for their outstanding natural beauty. Unless stated otherwise, all paradores listed below offer double rooms for less than $76 nightly. All are booked in the U.S. through *Tel. 800/981-7575* or, outside San Juan in Puerto Rico, *Tel. 800/443-0266.* Note that some paradores also have their own toll-free numbers. Accommodations are basic and not all have room telephones, but all take credit cards.

PARADOR BANOS DE COAMO, *end of Route 546, mailing address Box 540, Coamo PR 00769. Tel. 787/825-2239, Fax 787/825-2186.*

Bathe in two swimming pools fed by natural hot springs. All 48 rooms have private balconies, are air conditioned, and have a telephone and cable television. The dining room offers local and international dishes and there's a bar.

PARADOR BOQUEMAR, *Box 133, Boquerón PR 00622. Tel. 787/851-2158, Fax 787/851-7600. Overlook Boquerón Bay near Cabo Rojo.*

A nature refuge and other attractions of southwestern Puerto Rico are nearby. The 63 rooms have refrigerators and air conditioning and some overlook the bay. The hotel has a bar, restaurant, and swimming pool.

PARADOR CASA GRANDE, *Route 612, Kilometer 0.3, Utuado PR 00600. Tel. 787/894-3939, Fax 787/894-3939, toll-free 800/866-8644.*

Once a coffee plantation, this 20-room parador is near two reservoirs stocked with bass. It's a short, scenic drive from Coguana Indian Ceremonial Park. You'll stay in a rustic cottage with a balcony; walk to the main house and pool. There's a restaurant and bar but no air conditioning, room phone or television.

HOTEL PARADOR EL FARO, *Route 107, Kilometer 2.1, mailing address Box 5148, Aguadilla PR 00605. Tel. 787/882-8000, Fax 787/882-1030.*

This 32-room parador has air conditioning, telephone, television, a restaurant and bar, tennis courts, and water sports and it's wheelchair accessible.

HOTEL PARADOR HACIENDA GRIPINAS, *Route 527, Kilometer 2.5, mailing address Box 387, Jayuya PR 00664. Tel. 787/828-1717, Fax 787/828-1719.*

Near the village of Jayuya, known for its crafts and Taino Indian history, this 19-room parador is near one of the island's highest peaks. The old estate house once anchored a coffee plantation and it's surrounded by flowers and shrubbery. Its restaurant specializes in traditional foods.

PARADOR J.B. HIDDEN VILLAGE, *Box 937, Aguada PR 00602. Tel. 787/868-8686, Fax 787/868-3442.*

On a country road near the historic hamlet of Aguada, this 24-room parador has a restaurant that has been named a Méson Gastronimico, indicating exceptional value in good, local cuisine. Your balcony will overlook the swimming pool; nearby are ocean sports, bowling, and roller skating. Rooms are air conditioned, wheelchair accessible, and have cable television and telephone.

PARADOR EL GUAJATACA, *Route 2, Kilometer 103.8, mailing address Box 1538, Quebradillas PR 00678. Tel. 787/895-3070, Fax 787/895-3589; toll-free 800/964-3065.*

A dramatic seashore where the Guajataca River pours into the sea is the setting for this 38-room parador. Rates here are in the $76-$125 category, more than the other paradores, but you'll have a souvenir shop, tennis courts, swimming pool, restaurant and bar, air conditioning, telephone, cable television, and a million dollar location.

HOTEL Y PARADOR EL SOL, *9 East Santiago R. Palmer, mailing address Box 1194, Mayaguez PR 00680. Tel. 787/834-0303, Fax 787/265-7567.*

Lower floors of this 52-room parador, which is in downtown Mayagüez, wrap around a tiled swimming pool. Rates include a continental breakfast and the staff are glad to help you find your way around the attractions of the west coast. Rooms have refrigerator, hair dryer, air conditioning, telephone and cable television. The parador has a restaurant and bar.

HOTEL PARADOR JOYUDA BEACH, *Route 102, Kilometer 11.7, mailing address Box 1660, Cabo Rojo PR 00681. Tel. 787/851-5650, Fax 787/265-6940.*

This 43-room hotel is on a beach famous for its seafood restaurants, sunsets, and fishing charters. Play volleyball on the beach and swim in the sea. Rooms have air conditioning, television, and telephone, and there's a restaurant and bar.

HOTEL PARADOR LA FAMILIA, *Route 987, Kilometer 4.1, mailing address Box 21399, Fajardo PR 00738. Tel. 787/863-1193, Fax 787/860-5345.*

Close to El Faro lighthouse, the beaches, and waters of a beautiful resort area, and handy to the ferry terminal where boats leave for Culebra and Vieques, this 28-room parador has air conditioning, a restaurant and bar, and cable television but no room phones.

PARADOR LA HACIENDA JUANITA, *Route 105, Kilometer 23,5, mailing address Box 777, Maricao PR 00606. Tel. 787/838-2550, Fax 787/838-2551, toll-free 800/443-0266.*

Once the greathouse of a 19th century coffee plantation, this 21-room parador is family operated and has a restaurant and bar. Swim or play tennis, then explore the surrounding mountains and rain forest. Rooms have four-poster beds; the lobby is decorated with antique coffee-making equipment.

PARADOR MARTORELL, *6A Ocean Drive, mailing address Box 384, Luquillo PR 00773. Tel. 787/889-2710, Fax 787/889-4520.*

This 10-room, family-run parador is next to famous Luquillo Beach with its colorful vendors, shapely palm trees, and acres of pristine sand. Rooms are air conditioned and have cable television; restaurants are nearby. Rates include a full breakfast.

HOTEL PARADOR OASIS, *64 Luna Street, mailing address Box 144, San Germán PR 00683. Tel. 787/892-1175.*

A historic building makes up part of this 50-room parador in a charming old, inland town. Rooms have air conditioning, telephone, and cable television. The courtyard has a small pool and poolside dining. The parador is wheelchair accessible and it has a small gym.

PARADOR POSADA PORLAMAR, *Box 405 La Parguera, Lajas PR 00667. Tel. 787/899-4015.*

Right on the water in a resort village, this 18-room parador is wheelchair accessible and air conditioned. All around are places to dine and have fun. Boats leave from its dock for the area's outstanding dive sites.

PARADOR VILLA ANTONIO, *Route 115, Kilometer 12.3, Rincón PR. Tel. 787/823-2645, Fax 787/823-3380.*

Cottages and apartments on the beachfront are handy to Rincon and west coast attractions. Enjoy the swimming pool, playground, and tennis courts and use the barbecue. Rates at this 55-room parador are in the $76-$125 range. Rooms are air conditioned and have color television.

PARADOR VILLA PARGUERA, *La Parguera, mailing address Box 273, Lajas PR 00667. Tel. 787/899-7777, Fax 787/899-4435, toll-free 800/ 288-3975. Rates at this 62-room parador are in the $76 to $125 range.*

Rooms have two double beds, a balcony, air conditioning and telephone and there's a restaurant and bar. Take a night cruise to Phosphorescent Bay, swim in the saltwater pool, and enjoy the Saturday night dancing and show.

PARADOR VISTAMAR, *6205 Route 113, Kilometer 7.9, Quebradillas PR 00678. Tel. 787/895-2065, Fax 787/895-2294.*

When you stay in this 55-room parador you're in the heart of one of Puerto Ricans' favorite vacation regions on a hilltop overlooking the rugged Guajataca coast. There are swimming pools, a basketball court, tennis courts, a laundry, garden pathways, dancing and live music on weekends, and a gift shop. Nearby are the Rio Camuy caves and other points of interest. Rooms have air conditioning, telephone, and cable television and are wheelchair accessible.

PARADOR PERICHI'S, *Route 102, Kilometer 14.3, Cabo Rojo PR 00623. Tel. 787/851-3131, Fax 787/851-0560.*

Many people know this 30-room parador for its steak-and-seafood restaurant but it's also an ideal place to stay while you're exploring southwest Puerto Rico. The design is modern Mediterranean with an open air terrace and landscaped grounds surrounding the basketball and tennis courts and the big swimming pool. Rooms, many of them overlooking Joyuda Beach, have air conditioning, telephone, and cable television and are wheelchair accessible.

WHERE TO EAT

Here is great news for less-than-adventurous foodies! Throughout Puerto Rico, you'll see familiar mainland fast food outlets – not just McDonald's, Subway, Taco Bell, Pizza Hut, and KFC, but more upscale chains such as Chili's, Shooter's, and Pizzeria Uno and specialty chains such as Baskin Robbins and Orange Julius. Even Condado's landmark Chart House is one of the California chain, and Palio at the Westin Rio Mar is a clone of the one at the Swan in Walt Disney World.

The locally popular **Pollo Tropical** chain features fruity roast chicken, rice, beans, and plantains. Fast food or gourmet fare, Puerto Rico offers the widest range of Caribbean, Latin, and American foods in the islands. Unless stated otherwise, these restaurants accept credit cards.

OLD SAN JUAN
Expensive
CHEF MARISOLL CONTEMPORARY CUISINE, *202 Cristo Street. Tel. 725-7454. Park free for two hours at La Cochera. Hours are Tuesday to Friday noon to 2:30pm and Tuesday to Sunday, 7-10pm. Main dishes are priced $20 and higher. Reservations are essential.*

Dine in a romantic courtyard on the creations of Marisoll Hernandez who learned her art at Hilton hotels abroad. Only eight tables are available, so make reservations well ahead and prepare yourself for an unusual feast according to the best of today's marketplace. There will be a couple of wonderful soups and perhaps pheasant, a curry, a roast, and always the catch of the day.

LA CHAUMIÈRE, *367 Tetuan Street, Old San Juan behind the Tapia Theater. Tel. 722-3330. Reservations are urged. Main dishes are priced $20 to $40. Hours are 6pm to midnight nightly except Sunday.*

Dine on classic French cuisine in a rustic, heavily beamed room that takes you to the French countryside. Start with one of the patés, oysters Rockefeller, or a soup followed by roast lamb, the chateaubriand with vegetables served for two, veal Oscar, bouillabaisse, or *coq au vin*.

IL PERUGINO, *105 Cristo Street. Tel. 722-5481. Open for dinner nightly 6:30 to 11pm, the restaurant requires reservations after 4pm. Main dishes are priced $20 to $30.*

It calls itself San Juan's best Italian restaurant and displays the awards that seem to prove it. Owner-chef Franco Seccarelli is on hand nightly to make sure guests receive the kindest welcome, superb dining, and one of the most comprehensive wine lists in the city. Try the pastas, polenta with shrimp, carpaccios, rack of lamb, or marinated salmon. The building, a restored, 200-year-old townhouse, is named for Perugia, Franco's home town.

RESTAURANT GALERIA, *205 San Justo, Old San Juan. Tel. 725-0478. Reservations are urged. Open daily except Monday noon to 10pm, the restaurant offers main dishes for $12.95 to $21.95.*

Choose from Cuban and Puerto Rican dishes with international style. Start with the cream soup of the day, escargot in garlic butter, or octopus salad, then try the seafood risotto or the halibut. Live piano music plays Wednesday through Saturday. An area is set aside for smokers. **YUKIYU,** *311 Recinto Sur, Old San Juan. Tel. 721-0653. Main courses are priced $10 to $20. Hours are noon to 2:30pm and 5-11pm. Reservations are suggested; parking is by valet.*

You may not get beyond the sushi bar, a rare find in Puerto Rico. Choose from a long list of sushis then move on to the grilled lamb with polenta, fresh salmon with udon noodles, lobster tail in a creamy sauce, fresh cod in basil butter, or hibachi chicken. If you prefer, your favorite stir-fry combinations will be made for you tableside in a frenzy of fiery theatrics.

Moderate

AL DENTE, 309 *Recinto Sur, Old San Juan. Tel. 723-7303. Reservations are recommended. The restaurant is open Monday through Saturday 11:30am to 10:30pm. Main dishes are in the $15-$20 range.*

The style is casual Italian and the food a fusion of continental flavors and fresh Puerto Rican harvests. Start with the spinach stuffed with rice and cheese, then try the specialty of the house, fettuccine with shrimp and red and green sweet peppers. Veal is served in a variety of ways including a delectable, veal-stuffed tortellini; chicken comes in a sassy sauce of white wine, black olives, mushrooms, capers and tomatoes.

AMADEUS, *Calle San Sebastian 4601, Plaza San Jose. Tel. 722-8635 for reservations. Hours are Tuesday through Sunday noon to 2am but last orders are taken at midnight. Entrees are $14-$20.*

Set in an old stone building built for a wealthy trader in the 1700s, Amadeus features a refreshingly different combination of nouvelle cuisine (try the caviar pizza with smoked salmon) and Caribbean flair, such as the christophene salad with crabmeat. Have a vegetable tart before choosing a meat or seafood main dish.

EL PATIO DE SAM, *Calle San Sebastian 102, Plaza San Jose, Old San Juan Tel. 723-1149 or 723-8802. The kitchen is open Sunday through Thursday 11am to midnight and Friday and Saturday until 1am. Main dishes are $10 to $35. Reservations aren't required. Park at Ballaja and your ticket will be validated.*

Lavish use of plants and potted trees turns this air conditioned indoor restaurant into an outdoor patio known among Americans for its juicy burgers. For something different try the seafood-stuffed sole, breaded cheese stuffed shrimp, or rabbit in garlic sauce. Standards such as homemade lasagna, barbecued ribs, and beef *en brochette* are popular with homesick Americans. For dessert there's flan or Hungarian chocolate torte.

LA MALLORQUINA, *207 San Justo Street, Old San Juan. Tel. 722-3261. Hours are Monday through Saturday, 11:30am to 10pm. Main dishes are priced $14 to $30. Reservations are recommended for dinner but are not accepted for lunch.*

Opened in 1848 and set among the arches and courtyards of a colonial-era building filled with antiques, this is a local icon packed at lunch time with visitors. If you want to try traditional Puerto Rican dishes in an old-island setting, this is the place to order asopao (gumbo), arroz con pollo (chicken with rice), garlic soup, corn sticks, and homemade flan.

ROYAL THAI, *Recinto Sur #135, Old San Juan. Tel. 725-8424. Reservations are accepted. Main dishes are priced $16 to $22.*

The only Thai restaurant in town welcomes diners to bright surroundings surrounded by "swimming" fish on the walls and pink and white linen cloths topped with glass. Start with a spring roll or satay, then choose shrimp sautéed in red curry with coconut milk or half a Long Island duckling boned and served flambé in a sauce of choo chee curry paste and coconut milk. Put out the fire with a fruity dessert.

Budget

BUTTERFLY PEOPLE CAFE, *Calle Fortaleza 152, Old San Juan. Tel. 723-2432. Light dishes are priced $5 to $10 but steaks are also available.*

This is a witty, whimsical operation that we were delighted to find still thriving under the care of the "butterfly people" we met a few years back. They're a real family who love butterflies and have a real sense of what has lasting appeal to travelers and locals alike. Shop the gallery for butterflies in a variety of art forms. Then lunch on a cold soup, a creamy fruit drink, a steak, or quiche.

HARD ROCK CAFE, *253 Recinto Sur, Old San Juan. Tel. 724-7625. Prices are $4.50 to $17. Reservations aren't required but call for news of special events involving live music or happy hours. Hours are 11am to 2am daily; merchandise is sold 9am to midnight.*

If you "collect" Hard Rock Cafes, this busy, din-filled cafe is one to add to your list. Chicken or beef is served with pico de gallo, guacamole and sour cream. Eat inexpensively on red-hot chili or a sandwich, or splurge on a steak. The sizzling fajitas are a favorite and the classic H.R.C. hamburger is a juicy treat. Rock memorabilia on display includes items that belonged to John Lennon, Pink Floyd, and Phil Collins.

GREATER SAN JUAN

Expensive

CASA ITALIA, *275 Avenida Domenech, Hato Rey. Tel. 250-7388. Reservations are recommended; valet parking is available. Owner-chef Massimo*

Manscuso welcomes dinner guests daily except Mondays. Main dishes are from $20.

Antipasto, pasta, risotto, meat dishes and seafood come from the kitchen freshly made to order. This warmly elegant living room setting is the place to dine unhurriedly on a traditional succession of appetizers such as the carpaccio of beef, pastas or gnocchi, a porcini risotto, then a main dish of saltimbocca or tournedos Rossini.

CAPRICCIO, *in the Condado Plaze Hotel & Casino, 999 Ashford Avenida, Condado. Tel. 725-9236. Entrees are priced $17 to $25. Diners are offered two hours free parking at the hotel. Reservations are recommended.*

Gaze out over the Atlantic from a relaxed, romantic setting while dining on northern Italian specialties such as chicken Scarpariello or scallopini in marsala sauce with porcini mushrooms.

COMPOSTELA, *106 Avenida Condado, Santurce. Tel. 724-6088. Dinner for two without wine costs about $80. Reservations are suggested. The restaurant is open for dinner daily except Sunday.*

Owner-chef José Manuel Rey prizes himself on adapting peasant dishes for modern tastes. He sprinkles fresh halibut with the juice of freshly roasted pepper and olive oil infused with coriander. His scallops are done with caramelized sweet onions and sautéed foie gras; his duck is roasted with an exotic coffee glaze. The wine cellar boasts 300 labels. White-clothed tables sit among chrome columns and lots of greenery, creating an ambience that is popular with up-market locals as well as visitors.

EL ZIPPERLE, *352 Roosevelt Avenue, Hato Rey. Tel. 763-1636 or 751-4335. Call for hours and reservations. Main dishes start at $20.*

Dine in a darkly splendid room surrounded by wine vaults filled with one of the finest wine lists in Puerto Rico. The paella Valenciana is a specialty. The family who have operated the restaurant since 1953 also offer such continental choices as wiener schnitzel, roasts, and fresh seafood in delicate sauces. Save room for a Viennese dessert.

GIUSEPPE RISTORANTE, *in the Sands Hotel & Casino, Isla Verde. Tel. 791-1111. Reservations are recommended by owner-chef Giuseppe Acosa. Pastas start at $15; entrees at $20.*

Tables are clustered around a banquette that forms a gazebo for a mountain of flowers. A pink and white decor is anchored by a garnet carpet; paintings ring the room. Giuseppe recommends his trio of three pastas in different sauces. Italian classics on the menu include veal scaloppini in white wine, a meltingly tender osso bucco, steaks, filet, jumbo shrimp in garlic butter and a memorable linguine fruita d'mare.

MIRO MARISQUERIA CATALANA, *76 Condado Avenue, Condado. Tel. 723-9593. Main courses are priced $10 to $25. Use the valet parking. Hours are Tuesday through Sunday, lunch and dinner from 11:30am.*

Pungent Catalonian dishes prepared with the freshest seafood make for a special evening hosted by owner-chef José Lavilla. Start with marinated salt cod with onions and peppers or the calamari, then the superb paella cooked for two or more. Other choices include cod in cream sauce, grilled tuna with peppercorns and roast peppers, baked halibut with fresh herbs or, for parties of six or more, roast suckling pig. If you love to make a meal out of tapas alone, this is the place to choose from a long list that includes salads, fried cheese with tomato marmalade, and homemade Catalan style tomato bread.

NORMANDIE RESTAURANT *in the Radisson Normandie, Avenida Munoz Rivera, Puerto de Tierra at the corner of Calle Los Rosales. Tel. 729-2929. Hours are 6-10pm daily. Plan to spend $80 for dinner for two. Parking is $3.*

Located in a showy atrium in a distinctive art deco-era hotel, this restaurant is worth the trip just to see the architecture. Order from the menu of specialties that are cooked tableside, or let the waiter suggest something from tonight's specials. Ask to see the extensive wine list.

PIKAYO, *in the Tanama Princess Hotel, 1 Calle Joffre, Condado. Tel. 721-6194. Dinner for two costs about $80 without wine. Reservations are suggested. It's open Monday through Friday for lunch and dinner and Saturday for dinner only.*

Cajun has come to Puerto Rico with owner-chef Wilo Benet and his wife Lorraine. Order blackened fish or popcorn shrimp, or wonderfully doctored Puerto Rican dishes such as plantain fritters stuffed with bleu cheese or bacalao. He serves his escargot with wild mushrooms and balsamic vinegar and his Louisiana crab cakes with tostones and a buerre blanc made with chipotle peppers.

PORTOBELLO RISTORANTE, *Avenida F.D. Roosevelt 1144, Puerto Nuevo. Tel. 277-0911. Reservations are recommended; valet parking is available. Closed Monday. Entrees start at $17.95; pastas at $12.95.*

The gnocchi in pesto is superb, but for something meatier try the filet mignon, pork chops, salmon, or veal scallops.

RAMIRO'S RESTAURANT, *1106 Magdalena Avenue, Condado. Tel. 721-9056. Main dishes are priced $10 to $35; a multi-course, fixed price dinner is about $60. Reservations and valet parking are essential. Hours are daily noon to 3pm and 6:30 to 11pm.*

You'll remember an evening at Luis Ramiro's as a culinary highlight of a lifetime. Original, deftly created dishes include steamed cuttlefish with herbs, smoked lobster in light lemon sauce, cold avocado cream with smoked salmon, lamb pie with port wine and raisins, lentil and chickpea soup, and artichoke hearts foie gras – and that's just the starters. Main courses include a succulent roast duckling with guava and an unforgettable venison with pear in a sauce of wine, blackberries, and Armagnac or fish mousse served in sweet peppers shaped like flowers. The wine cellar boasts 25,000 bottles bearing 400 labels from wineries around the world. Dress for an upscale neighborhood.

RUTH'S CHRIS STEAK HOUSE, *in the Sands Hotel, 187 Isla Verde Road, Isla Verde. Tel. 253-1717. It's open nightly for dinner; valet parking is complimentary. Plan to spend $80 for dinner for two.*

Revered for its butter-tender, corn-fed prime beef, Ruth's blasts its steaks to seared perfection in an 1800-degree broiler designed by Ruth Fortel herself. After dinner, take in a show at the hotel's own night club.

SWEENEY'S ORIGINAL SCOTCH 'N SIRLOIN, *in the Ambassador Plaza Hotel, 1369 Ashford Avenue, Condado. Tel. 721-9315. Reservations are requested. Plan to spend $80-$100 for dinner for two.*

Make an evening of it at the Ambassador, where you can have a drink at the Sports Bar before dinner at Sweeney's. Then dance after dinner in the Cabaret Lounge or try your luck in the casino. This is a time-honored meat and potatoes place, so order a dry-aged steak, prime rib, or rack of lamb. There's also lobster, fresh fish, a salad bar, and an impressive wine list.

Moderate

AJILI MOJILI, *Calle Joffre at Calle Clemenceau, Condado. Tel. 725-9195. Make reservations and use the valet parking. Hours are Monday through Thursday, 6 to 10pm Friday and Saturday to 11pm. Main courses are priced $9.95 to $24.95.*

Pronounce it "ah-HILL-ee moh-HILL-ee." Dining here is like going home to Mom, if your mother happens to be Puerto Rican. The air conditioning adds to the comfort of an unpretentious room where the focus is on good food and fellowship. Regional dishes from around the island are featured on a menu that changes twice a month, but there's always arroz con pollo plus pumpkin fritters, a guinea hen of the day, and a selection of mofongos and inexpensive rice dishes. Most of the meats, seafood and produce come from local farms. Desserts come on a trolley. Take your pick.

BACK STREET HONG KONG, *in the El San Juan Hotel & Casino, Route 187, Isla Verde. Tel. 791-1224. Reservations are recommended. Hours are 6pm to midnight nightly except Sunday, when hours are 1pm to midnight. Entrees are priced $18 to about $30.*

The illusion is that of a gracious private home owned by people who have traveled and collected in the Far East. Built for the 1964 World's Fair, the restaurant was shipped here and re-assembled. Entering, it's easy to forget you're in a hotel as you are transported to a Hong Kong street. With attentive service and crisp pink table linens, the restaurant features its orange sauce served with your choice of sautéed lobster, jumbo scallops, diced chicken sliced beef, or jumbo shrimp. Live Maine lobster is almost always on the menu at today's market price. The menu has an impressive selection of Chinese poultry, seafood, and beef specialties, all expertly sauced and presented.

CASA DANTE, *Avenida Isla Verde 39, Isla Verde. Tel. 726-7310. Open every day. Main dishes are $7.95 to $28.95 for a 12-24-ounce lobster tail.*

Dante and Milly personally welcome guests to this relaxed, family, Puerto Rican restaurant. The house specialty is crushed plantain with your choice of pork, steak, shrimp, lobster, chicken, veal, or fish in a variety of presentations.

CHART HOUSE, *1214 Avenida Ashford. Tel. 724-0110. Reservations are suggested and are a must on weekends; valet parking is available. Hours are daily, 5pm to midnight. Main dishes start at $16.95.*

For those who like a classic steak and seafood house with pasta in place of the ubiquitous French fries, this is the place to start with shrimp cocktail and then launch into a New York strip, extra-thick prime rib, or a charbroiled teriyaki tuna. Try the native dorado (mahi-mahi) in Creole sauce. Vegetarians will like the fettuccine with portobello "steak." House specialties include artichokes in season, served with aioli, and "mud" pie for dessert.

The dress code is resort casual to go with the yachty elegance. The building alone is worth the trip. Once the home of the German consul, the grand villa was built a decade before World War I began.

EL CAIRO RESTAURANT, *Avenida Roosevelt (Route 23) Ensenada #352, Caparra Heights Tel. 273-7140. Valet parking is available; it's open daily for dinner. Main dishes start at $11.75.*

It's fun and different to try this Arabian-Lebanese restaurant and to shop its gift counter for Arabian items and take-out pastries. Belly dancers perform Friday and Saturdays, yet it's all G-rated and families are invited. Start with hummus or falafel, then choose from a host of Middle Eastern classics: shish kebob, steak tartare, curried chicken with Arabian rice, curried lamb, or a plentiful sampler platter filled with all the above and then some.

EL CHOTIS, *Calle O'Neill #187, Hato Rey, about six miles south of Condado off Route 1. Tel. 758-3086. A valet will park your car. Plan to spend about $20-$40 per person for dinner. Call for hours and reservations.*

Relax in what looks like an old Spanish tavern to enjoy paella, a good red wine, and a rousing flamenco (Friday and Saturday). Lobster is served grilled or in Spanish sauce; the tuna and potato salad makes a delicious appetizer or light meal. Many people come here to make a meal out of tapas alone.

EL TAPATIO RESTAURANTES MEXICANOS, *Avenida Jesus T. Piñero 1025, Puerto Nuevo. Tel. 781-2006 or 781-3126. Main dishes start at $11; tacos at $8.95. Reservations are recommended; valet parking is available.*

Show up on a Friday, Saturday, or Sunday for live mariachi music while you dine on traditional Mexican favorites prepared with or without hot, hot peppers. The chicken with mole pablano is a classic – chicken prepared with a hint of chocolate and served with green rice, refried beans, and guacamole. The fajitas platter for two is a feast.

HAVANA'S CAFE, *409 Calle del Parque, Stop 23, Santurce. Tel. 725-0888. Main dishes are priced $5 to $20. Hours are 7am to 10pm Monday through Friday and 11:30am to 10pm Saturday and Sunday.*

Enjoy authentic Cuban dishes in a casually elegant room reminiscent of Havana in the 1950s. Try mofongo stuffed with shredded beef or shrimp, fresh codfish, or lobster timbales. Tuesday is cigar night.

HUNAN HOUSE, *141 Avenida F.D. Roosevelt, Hato Rey. Tel. 250-8039. Reservations are accepted. Main dishes range from $10.50 for rice or noodle dishes to $36 for the Peking Duck.*

Comfortably family-oriented, this Chinese restaurant has the usual favorites such as butterfly shrimp and vegetarian dishes plus such inventions as chicken with mango, pearl shrimp, Singapore curried chicken, and beef Mongolian style.

IL CAPO, *Calle Loisa 2478, Puenta Las Marias. Tel. 268-5319. Closed Mondays, the restaurant accepts major credit cards and offers live music on Fridays. Main dishes start at $12.95; pastas at $9.*

Good Italian flavors accompanied by wines from a well-stocked cellar, plus a cozy and comforting ambience for all the family add up to a pleasant evening. Start with melon and prosciutto or carpaccio of beef topped with Parmesan cheese and olive oil dressing. On the pasta list are a memorable ravioli with lobster in champagne cream and a simple, classic lasagnes, or penne with vodka sauce. Main dishes, which include veal Marsala, boneless breast of chicken, sirloin steak, shrimp and salmon, are all served with homemade fettucini marinara.

ICHE'S INTERNATIONAL CUISINE, *Calle Parkside 4, C-2, Guyanabo. Tel. (7887) 782-6910. Main dishes are in the $18-$22 range. Reservations are recommended. Valet parking is available; the restaurant is open daily except Monday for lunch and dinner. On Monday, only lunch is served.*

Richard Kleiman hopes you'll stop by to sample the relaxed elegance of his eclectic restaurant where risotto and tempura share the same page on the menu. Main dishes range from New Zealand lamb to fresh cod.

KIMPO GARDEN, *Avenida Jesus T. Pinero 264, Hato Rey. Tel. 767-0810. Credit cards are accepted; main dishes start at $11.*

David Chang is your host as you relax in a casual restaurant where Szechuan is featured but the lobster is served Cantonese style. Start with the cold noodles in sesame sauce or the crab lau-lau. The chef's specialties include shrimp or lobster in black bean sauce. For the meat eater in your party there's a sizzling steak platter with fresh vegetables. Typical Chinese chicken dishes are made with orange sauce, broccoli or scallion, and ginger.

LA FONDA DE CERVANTES, *in the Hotel Iberia, 1464 Wilson Avenue, Condado. Tel. 722-6433. Main dishes are $10 to $20. Call for hours and reservations.*

Dine indoors or out in a Mediterranean ambience with music drifting in from the piano bar. Start with grilled shrimp or an octopus appetizer, then sample a seafood zarzuela, the planked fish, or the paella a la Valenciana for two.

LOS CHAVALES RESTAURANT, *Avenida F.D. Roosevelt #253, Hato Rey. Tel. 767-5017. Valet parking is available; major credit cards are honored noon to midnight, Monday through Saturday. Main dishes start at $20; chateaubriand for two is just under $50.*

Relaxed enough for family dining, but elegant enough for business or romance, this white tablecloth restaurant with its scenic, trompe l'oiel murals has a fine selection of California, French, Spanish and Portuguese wines to complement Spanish and international dishes. Among five menu offerings that serve two or more is a grilled seafood platter, rack of lamb, double sirloin, and a paella like mamacita used to make. Desserts for two include crepes Suzette at $13.95 and baked Alaska at $12.95.

LUPI'S MEXICAN GRILL & SPORTS CANTINA, *Isla Verde Road, Kilometer 1.3, Isla Verde. Tel. 253-2198 or 253-1664. Open daily 11am to 5am. Lupi's doesn't require reservations. Main dishes are $10 to $20.*

A rollicking sports bar with live music nightly after 11pm, this is the place to tank up on zesty Tex-Mex dishes such as fajitas and nachos before an evening of cheering the team and line dancing into a wee hours. Lupi's is also found at 313 Recinto Sur in Old San Juan, *Tel. 722-1874*, with the same hours and live jazz.

MEDITERRANEO RISTORANTE ITALIANO, *Avenida Ashford 1021, Condado. Tel. 723-7006. Parking is in back of the restaurant, which is open daily except Monday. Reservations are recommended. Main dishes are priced $10 to $22.*

Giancarlo and Anna Bonegatti are on hand with a personal invitation to try their homemade pastas, which include ravioli with fresh asparagus, vermicelli served country style with bacon, mushrooms, Italian sausage and green peas, and spaghetti smothered in a succulent seafood mixture. There's also gnocchi and osso bucco, then tiramisu for dessert.

MIRO, *Avenida Condado 76 next to the Hotel El Portal. Tel. 723-9593. Valet parking is available; the restaurant is closed Mondays. Paella for two is $14.95. Other dishes start at $13.25.*

Owner-chef José Lavilla will welcome you to his warmly Catalonian marisqueria and may suggest one of his many inspired specialties such as cod with roasted peppers, tomatoes, garlic, and cinnamon, or the cod with garlic cream. The menu also offers lobster, tuna, chicken, pork medallions and a classic New York strip with onions and mushrooms. For a truly special event, call ahead and arrange to have the suckling pig, a feast that is prepared for six or more.

RESTAURANTE FELIX, *Carretera #1, Kilometer 25, Caguas, 20 miles south of San Juan. Tel. 720-1625. Closed Mondays, the restaurant is open for lunch and dinner. Call for reservations. Plan to spend $50 per couple for dinner.*

Celebrate with lobster or the chateaubriand for two, and don't miss the cream of yautia soup and the Caesar salad.

ST. MORITZ, *Avenida Ashford 1005 in the Hotel Regency, Condado. Tel. 721-0999. Reservations are recommended; all major credit cards are honored. Main dishes start at under $16; the lamb provençale for two is $49.*

The name promises a Swiss touch in this ocean-view dining room. Start with Swiss cheese croquettes and, if you're still in a yodeling mood, have the minced veal with roesti potatoes, or the veal schnitzel cordon bleu. The rack of lamb provençale for two is served with English mustard, a feast of vegetables, and baked potatoes. The dessert cart is laden with choices from flan to fruit tarts.

ZABO, *14 Candina Street, Condado. Tel. 725-9494. The parking entrance is on Ashford across from Citibank. It's open for lunch and dinner, Tuesday through Saturday. Main dishes are $18 to $25.*

Have a drink in the cozy bar, then relax in this restored, 1910 country house while dining on conch fritters in mango and sesame sauce, rack of lamb in tamarind and ginger sauce, or salmon in parchment with black bean sauce. Eat indoors in air conditioning or on the balcony outdoors. This is a popular grazing bar. Many guests come only for tapas or only for dessert.

Budget

BIG APPLE, *1407 Ashford Avenue, Condado. Tel. 725-6345. Hours are 7am to 10pm. Prices are $5 to $10.*

Dine in or take out the best in New York deli treats, from mile-high corned beef on rye and bagels with cream cheese to Hebrew National hot dogs and cold meats.

CARUSO ITALIAN RISTORANTE, *1104 Ashford Avenida, Condado. Tel. 723-6876 for hours. Main dishes start at $6.75.*

Like the best little neighborhood Italian restaurant in your home town, Caruso serves up classic southern Italian cuisine in an unpretentious room filled with good smells. The spaghetti in meat sauce is a budget favorite, but there are also veal and chicken dishes, and lobster Fra Diablo at splurge prices depending on size. Flaming desserts and homemade tiramisu are house dessert specialties.

DENNY'S, *in the Isla Verde Mall, Isla Verde. Tel. 253-3080, is open 24 hours. Most main dishes are $10 or less.*

Although this is a member of the popular chain known for its inexpensive meals and Grand Slam breakfasts, it also offers local foods through its Sabroso Criollo menu. Other Denny's are around the city and in major cities island-wide.

FRIDAYS, *Calle Ortegon, in the San Patricio Shopping Center, Guayanabo. From Old San Juan, take Route 18 south, then southwest on Route 1. Tel. 781-4310. Open daily for lunch and dinner and for Sunday brunch 11am to 3pm, the restaurant serves meals for $10 to $20.*

Build your own burger from a choice of a dozen toppings, or splurge on the New York strip steak. This is a big-screen sports bar where you can watch the main event while scarfing down fajitas or loaded potato skins. Or, have a real meal featuring lemon chicken topped with fettucine and spinach. Sunday brunch is a special event.

JERUSALEM RESTAURANT, *Calle O'Neill G-1, Hato Rey. Tel. 764-3265. Nothing on the menu is more than $15; valet parking is available.*

Light eaters can make a feast from one or two appetizers, all of them under $5. They include Middle Eastern musts: baba ganoush, hummus, falafel, or taboulleh. Main dishes focus on fish or lamb, cooked and served in the Arabic manner. The sampler platter is the best buy; for dessert there's baklava. When you call for reservations, ask the best time to arrive for the belly dancer show. It's family oriented, exotic, and straight out of a 1950s movie.

RESTAURANT EL MUELLE 13 RESTAURANT, *Calle O'Neill 177, tel 787/767-7825. Main dishes start at $12. It's open daily; offering valet parking.*

A friendly, family restaurant specializing in seafood offers such local staples as rice with bacalao (cod) or paella Valenciana for two, a superb buy at $25.90. Steaks and chicken are served in a variety of cuts. Try the mofongo with lobster or the lobster salad.

EAST OF SAN JUAN TO FAJARDO
Expensive

PALIO, *in the Westin Rio Mar Beach Resort, 6000 Rio Mar Boulevard, Rio Grande, 19 miles west of San Juan. Tel. 888-6200. Reservations are essential. The restaurant is open nightly for dinner; take a taxi ($20 from*

Fajardo) or drive in and valet park for $6. No self-parking is available. Plan to spend $50-$60 for a three-course dinner without wine.

A woody, Mediterranean room welcomes diners who are first served a tiny pitcher of red wine in a 2,000-year-old tradition of Roman welcome. The food here is northern Italian in a grand sweep of choices. Start with the grilled vegetable terrine, roasted portabello mushrooms with sun-dried tomato dressing, or fried calamari rings served with spicy tomato sauce and roasted pepper aioli. Tuscan white bean soup or Caesar salad precede a meal of inspired pastas or meltingly tender meats such as the 12-ounce filet of Black Angus beef with flamed morels or the rosemary chicken with braised savoy cabbage. Many dishes are accompanied by satiny risottos, which aren't to be missed. Let the sommelier suggest a wine from more than 200 selections; let the server suggest a dessert from tonight's list of sweets.

Moderate

MARBELLA, *in the Westin Rio Mar Beach Resort, 6000 Rio Mar Boulevard, Rio Grande, 19 miles west of San Juan. Tel. 888-6200. Reservations are recommended. Buffet breakfast is $13.50; lunch $15.95 and dinner $23.95. Only valet parking is available.*

The dramatic decor in a bright, three-story-high room overlooking the sea sets the mood for a riot of great eating from buffets laden with fresh fruits, hot and cold dishes, bushels of breadrolls, and some of the best pastries on the island. Each night celebrates a different theme such as Italian, Caribbean, Puerto Rican, Asian, or Greek, so call ahead to see what's on for tonight. Menu service is also available for those who can resist the buffet.

The hotel's other moderately priced restaurant, **La Estancia**, is in the tennis club and is open for lunch and dinner. Valet park, then take the free shuttle. Pan-seared red snapper is served in orange ginger sauce, Cornish game hem is stuffed with yuca and topped with Spanish sofrito sauce, and there's a mofongo of on the day.

Budget

LOLITA'S, *Carretera 65 de Infanteria, Kilometer 41.8 between Fajardo and Luquillo. Tel. 889-5770. Prices are $2.25 to $12.95. Credit cards and reservations aren't accepted.*

With 24 hours notice you can have mole pablano, but mostly this is an impulse place when you have a yen for Mexican food. A big selection of burritos, tacos, and nachos is budget priced; combination platters are a hearty meal for little *dinero*. Round out the meal with beer, fresh juices, or a cocktail with or without alcohol, ending with the flan.

SOUTH COAST

RESTAURANT EL ANCLA, *Avenida Hostos Final 9, Playa Ponce, Ponce. Tel. 840-2450. Reservations are accepted but not required. Main dishes are priced $15 to $35. It's open for lunch and dinner daily.*
You'll be at sea, literally, in a family-run restaurant built on a pier over the water. Start with a half dozen crispy tostones, followed by a paella prepared for two, filet mignon with French fries, or the red snapper in lobster and shrimp sauce.

LA CAVA DE LA HACIENDA, *in the Ponce Hilton, Avenida Santiago Caballeros 14, Ponce. Tel. 787/259-7676. Reservations are urged. Hours are 7am to 10:30pm daily. Plan to spend $35 per person for dinner.*
As the name suggests, La Cava looks like a wine cellar, intimate and darkly cool. It's part of a brighter restaurant, La Hacienda. The two, rambling from one room to the next, offer elegant dining on an inspired menu that changes often. Always excellent are the fish and lobster dishes, fresh vegetables, toothsome breads and rolls, and luscious desserts.

LA TERRAZA, *in the Ponce Hilton, Avenida Santiago Caballeros 14, Ponce. Tel. 787/259-7676. Call ahead for hours and reservations. Plan to spend $25 for dinner.*
Dine outdoors for breakfast, lunch, and dinner, especially at dinner time when such themes as Steak Night or Lobster Night are held. Before dinner, have a margarita at Los Balcones in the hotel and have an after-dinner drink while listening to live Latin sounds in La Bohemia lounge.

PITO'S SEA FOOD CAFE, *Route 2, Kilometer 252, Las Cucharas, a mile southwest of Ponce. Tel. 841-4977. Main courses are $10 to $20. Hours are 11am to midnight daily. Reservations aren't required.*
Sit outdoors overlooking Cucharas Point or indoors in the air conditioning while you dine on chicken steak or fresh fish from the seas off Ponce.

TANAMA RESTAURANT, *in the Holiday Inn & Tropical Casino, Route 2, El Tuque, Ponce. Tel. 844-1200. Two can dine for about $50. Hours are 6am to 10pm Sunday through Thursday, and Friday and Saturday until midnight. Reservations aren't required.*
It's always a nice surprise to find fine local cuisine in a chain hotel. We also like the family-friendly ambience and the sea views. After dinner, there's gaming in the casino or listening in the lounge.

WEST & SOUTHWEST
Expensive
HORNED DORSET PRIMAVERA, *Route 429, Kilometer 3, south of Rincó. Tel. 823-4030. Reservations are essential for dinner and recommended for lunch. Hours are noon to 2:30 daily and dinner seatings at 7pm, 8pm, and 9pm.*

Main dishes are priced $25 to $30 and a fixed price meal is available for $50 without wine.

Worth a special trip, this devotedly French restaurant keeps its standards to that of its parent, the Horned Dorset in upstate New York. Accustomed to a sophisticated, international clientele, the chef always has fresh seafood ready for the broiler to serve with an inspired sauce. Also on the menu are Long Island duckling, the finest meats, and delicately steamed vegetables.

Moderate

BLACK EAGLE RESTAURANT, *Route 413, Kilometer 1.0, Ensenada, Rincón, tel.823-3510. Main courses are $10 to $20. Hours are 11am to 11pm daily. Reservations aren't required.*

Enjoy the laid back, seaside ambience of this pleasantly touristy restaurant west of Rincón on a breezy point of land. Seafood is caught just offshore and is served flopping-fresh; steaks are flown in the from the United States.

GALLOWAY'S, *Poblado Boquerón, Cabo Rojo (south of Mayaguez). Tel. 254-3302. Main dishes are priced $8.95 to $17.95. Call for hours and reservations.*

Known for its seaviews and sunsets, this restaurant specializes in mofongos in a variety of flavors including chicken, lobster, or shrimp and in asopaos, or gumbos. For openers, try the crusty cheese balls.

HOLLY'S RESTAURANT, *in the Holiday Inn, Highway 2, Kilometer 149.9, Mayaguez. Tel. 833-1100. Plan to spend $50 for dinner for two.*

Sample Puerto Rican food, fresh fish, an abundance of island vegetables, and a nice choice of sweets in this quietly elegant spot before an evening of gaming in the casino or listening to salsa sounds in Holly's Lounge.

THE DINE AROUND PROGRAM

*One of the most exciting dining options in the Caribbean is Puerto Rico's **Dine Around Program**. Pay one set price of $49 per day, which buys breakfast at your hotel and dinner at any of 12 other restaurants in the San Juan area. Ask your travel agent, or inquire when you arrive at your hotel whether it's available. The program does not apply in peak seasons.*

SEEING THE SIGHTS
SAN JUAN

If you love old stones, it's a thrill just to stroll the slit-sized lanes of **Old San Juan** to soak up the delicious oldness of it all. Many streets have changed so little, you can imagine yourself in the days of swaggering Conquistadores, shy señoritas batting eyelashes behind their fans, and good friars gliding through the crowds. Then suddenly you see a Sony sign or a carelessly dropped gum wrapper and the 20th century comes rushing back.

Don't drive into the old city, where on-street parking is next to impossible. Instead, ride the two **free trolley tours** that cover two routes in the heart of Old San Juan. They operate every day, 16 hours a day plus evenings during Gallery Nights (Noches de Gallerias) and they are all wheelchair accessible. If you have a car, park it at the Covadonga lot, where trolley service begins and ends. It's one of a handful of parking areas in the old city. Others are below El Morro, at La Puntilla near El Arsenal, and Felisa Rincón near the Marina.

Get off and on as you please, spending a few minutes here and a few hours there. To "do" the city right, with enough time at museums and the forts plus time out for the many shops and fine restaurants, will take several days of trolleying.

El Morro Castle, *Tel. 729-6960,* is a must, the oldest fortress still extant in the Americas. It was begun early in the 1500s and fell only once, and that briefly, to the English enemy. It saw service as late as World War II. Now managed by the U.S. Park Service, it has a souvenir shop, museums, and book stores, and miles of dungeons and ramparts to explore. Guided tours are given in English at 10am and 2pm and in Spanish at 11am and 3pm.

Also managed by the U.S. Park Service is **San Cristóbal** on Norzagaray Street, *Tel. 729-6960.* Connected by moats and tunnels, this fort defended the city against attacks from the land side while El Morro stood sentinel against sea raiders.

Early Spanish planners built the city around grand plazas. A new one is **Quincentennial Plaza** on the city's highest point. It adjoins San José Plaza where you'll find **San José Church**, *Tel. 725-7501,* the second oldest in the Americas, and the ancient Dominican Convent. The church is open daily from 7am to 3pm and offers services on Sundays at noon and 1pm. The convent is the home of a book shop that sells Puerto Rican literature, posters, and folk art.

Casa Blanca, *Tel. 724-4102,* was, the trolley guide will explain, the home of Juan Ponce de León. Tour its fountain-filled gardens and its superb museum of artifacts from the 1500s and 1600s. It's open Tuesday through Saturday, 9am to noon and 1pm to 4:30pm. At the end of Cristo Street, **Casa del Libro**, *Tel. 723-0354,* is a printing museum housing one of the most important collections of pre-1500s volumes in the New World. It's open Thursday through Saturday, 11am to 4:30pm. Next door, the **National Crafts Center** displays local arts and crafts and nearby, the Banco Popular has a gallery featuring local arts.

In the **Plaza de la Rogativa**, see a sculpture of women bearing torches, commemorating an event during a British siege in which the women, who were merely staging a religious procession, fooled the English into thinking that reinforcements had arrived.

San Juan Cathedral is a Gothic masterpiece built in 1540 on the ruins of an early cathedral that was destroyed in a hurricane. It's here that the body of Ponce de León, seeker of the Fountain of Youth and Puerto Rico's first governor, lies in a marble vault. Next comes the **Capilla del Cristo** with its silver altar. It was built in gratitude to the Christ of Miracles by a man who had lost control of his horse and would have plunged over the edge of the cliff if a miracle hadn't brought the horse to a stop. The tiny chapel can be seen through the gate but if you want to go inside, it's open Tuesdays 10am to 3:30pm. A **Children's Museum** at 150 Cristo is entered through the legs of a wood giant. Inside, children can frolic through a village of playhouses, play dentist, and learn about cars and airplanes. Hours are Tuesday to Thursday, 9:30am to 3:30pm and weekends 11am to 4pm.

La Fortaleza, *Tel. 721-7000, extension 2211,* a grand ramble of archways and courtyards, is the oldest executive mansion in continuous use in the New World, dating to 1533. Guided tours are offered Monday through Friday, 9am to 4pm.

Seen from the trolley at Fortaleza and San Jose streets is the **Plaza de Armas**, surrounded by Spanish Colonial buildings as ornate as wedding cakes. On the Plaza Colon is the **Tapia Theater**, which is being renovated, and the 18th century Government Reception Center. Walk the Paseo de la Princessa, a boulevard that surrounds the old city walls, to San Juan Gate, the last survivor of the gates that were once the only passages through the mighty city wall.

South of the Plaza de Hostos is the **Arsenal de la Marina**, built in 1800 as a marina for small boats that patrolled the shallow waters around the city. At **La Casita**, home of a tourism information office, stop for information on the following museums, a cold drink and a rest on a park bench.

The **San Juan Museum of Art and History** was once the city's marketplace. Now it's filled with fine arts and changing displays. **The Museum of the Americas**, which opened in 1992, displays folk art of the region. It's open Wednesday through Sunday, 9am to 4:30pm. On the

Plaza San Jose, small museums include one devoted to Pablo Casals, the renowned cellist who moved from Spain to Puerto Rico in 1956 to protest the Franco government. The **Casa de los Contrafuentes**, an 18th century home, now houses a **Pharmacy Museum** and the **Latin American Graphic Arts Museum and Gallery**.

Walk or take a cab to the top of the hill east of the city wall to see the **Carnegie Library**, which dates to 1916 and was restored after a hurricane in 1989.

SIDE TRIPS IN & NEAR SAN JUAN

At the **University of Puerto Rico** on the Avenida Ponce de León in Rio Piedras, *Tel. 764-0000,* browse the museum with its collection of artifacts from the pre-Columbian Taino Indians, and botanical gardens filled with tropical trees, flowering shrubs, bamboo, ponds, palms, and shaded pathways. Hours vary, so call for information.

El Yunque, whose official name is the **Caribbean National Forest**, is found 16 miles east of San Juan. The only tropical rain forest in the U.S. National Forest System, it is laced with roads and hiking paths that take you through sun-dappled trees and flowers deep into gullies wet with waterfalls. It's the home of the rare Puerto Rican parrot, which one ranger who has been here 20 years says he has heard but never seen.

It is a chilly climb to its fog-shrouded peaks and a long, hot walk to depths where waterfalls dash into clear, cold pools. The walk to **El Yunque Peak**, with its awesome view, takes about 45 minutes from the Mount Britton Lookout Tower and two hours each way on the path that leads from the Palo Colorado Visitor Information Center.

The 30-minute hike to **La Mina Falls** takes you through a fern gully filled with shy wildflowers and towering trees, ending at a wispy waterfall. Climb **Yokahu Tower** for panoramic view and stop at the many observation points, visitor information points, and picnic areas for a closer look. The visitor center at **El Portal** has a gift shop with a good selection of nature guides, maps for camping and hiking the 28,000-acre forest, cold drinks, and rest rooms.

Whatever your route, it's either hot and wet or cold and wet, so it's wise to take a sun hat and poncho. There are no predatory animals, we were told, and we saw few mosquitoes.

Free tours of the **Bacardi Rum Plant**, *Tel. 788-1500,* with its small museum and pleasant grounds, are offered Monday through Saturday. It's in Cantaño (the point of land on the opposite side from the bay from the airport) at Kilometer 2.6 on Route 888.

Take half a day to seek put the colorful marketplaces in **Rio Piedras** near the plaza and off Canal Street in **Santurce**. Open daily, the outdoor vendors display fresh island produce by locals for locals.

OUT ON THE ISLAND SOUTH

Heading south from San Juan across the mountains, you'll pass the **Carite Forest Reserve** north of Guayama along Route 184. Stop at **Lake Carite**, stopping for snacks at a long line of folksy food stands selling pit-roasted pork, blood sausage, tripe, tropical fruits, and queso blanco (white cheese). In Guayama, the **Casa Cautino Museum** is housed in an 1887 mansion furnished with the belongings of the original family that lived here a century ago. Take the trolley tour of historic **Arroyo**, *Tel. 866-1609*.

Ponce is Puerto Rico's second city, known as the Pearl of the South. Its gas-lit streets are a movie set of neo-colonial buildings in the style known as Ponce Creole, built with riches gained from sugar and shipping. Stop at the tourist office in the Citibank on the Plaza de las Delicias, or *Tel. 841-8160* for information on any Ponce sightseeing. **La Perla Theater** has been a cultural center since 1864, when it opened with a dramatic Catalonian production.

Other must-see sites in Ponce include the **Ponce History Museum**, housed in two buildings dating to 1911 and the Plaza Las Delicias with its **Cathedral of Our Lady of Guadeloupe**. She's the city's patron saint and her feast day in February prompts one of the island's most colorful fiestas. The plaza is a place for musing and people watching, and its side streets lead past more restored 19th century treasures.

The **Parque de Bombas** (firehouse) was built in 1883 as an exhibition hall and now it is a general museum with Fire Brigade memorabilia. Two restored historic homes are the **Castillo Serralles**, the mansion built by the Don Q rum fortune, and **Casa Paoli**, now a folk center, built as a home for opera star Antonio Paoli at the turn of the century. North of town on the Canas River, **Hacienda Buena Vista** was built in 1883 as the greathouse for a coffee plantation. Tour the house, slave quarters, and the still-functional coffee machinery including the only surviving coffee husker known to exist. Reservations are essential, *Tel. 722-5882*.

Crown jewel of Ponce's sightseeing is the **Ponce Museum of Art**, *Tel. 848-7309*, housing more than 1,000 paintings and 400 sculptures. Its contemporary collections, Italian Baroque pieces, and 19th century pre-Raphaelite paintings are outstanding.

Tibes Indian Ceremonial Center is built on the site of the oldest burial site yet found in the Antilles. A Taino village has been re-created complete with ceremonial ball court, homes, and dance ground. The complex has a museum, exhibits, an orientation movie, and a cafeteria. It's on Route 503, Kilometer 2.7. *Tel. 840-2255*. Hours are 9am to noon and 1 to 4pm daily except Wednesdays and holidays.

If you continue west from Ponce along a route known for its fine seafood restaurants, you'll reach Guanica and the **Dry Forest Reserve** off

Route 333. One of the finest examples of tropical dry forest in the world, it's the home of more than 700 varieties of plants, 1,000 types of insects, and more than 100 bird species both migratory and resident. Walk its trails under lignum vitae trees, stopping at picnic areas and Spanish ruins. Between Guanica and La Parquera is the famous **Phosphorescent Bay**, (Bahia de Fosforescente). Cruises in the area sail at night to view the natural luminescence in the water. Offshore, dive the continental shelf.

If you follow an inland route west from Ponce towards Mayagüez, it rewards you with a visit to San Germán, the second city founded by the Spanish. Its **Porta Coeli Church** dates to 1606 and it streets and plazas still retain the sleepy, sun-baked look of a 17th century colonial village. Leaving on the road to Lajas, you'll pass the **Alfred Ramirez de Arellano y Rosell Art Museum**, *Tel. 892-8870*. Shown are 19th century furniture and a small art collection. It's open Wednesday through Sunday, 10am to noon and 1 to 3pm.

NORTHEAST OF SAN JUAN

Route 3 leading east from San Juan is filled with commuters and commerce as well as tourists rushing to **El Yunque** and the famous beach at **Luquillo**. Almost anywhere along the highway you'll find simple restaurants serving authentic local food at modest prices, as well as roadside stands selling fried foods, fresh produce, and a native drink called mavi. Made from tree bark, it's mildly fermented.

Fajardo and the surrounding area are one of the island's seagoing centers, with massive marinas offering watersports of all kinds. At the island's eastern corner, **Las Cabezas de San Juan Nature Reserve**, locally called El Faro after its 1882 lighthouse, has hiking trails and boardwalks ending at the lighthouse with a spectacular view. From Puerto Real, catch a ferry to **Vieques** where the tiny fishing village of Esperanza has end-of-the-world restaurants and inns. **Mosquito Bay** here is phosphorescent (another bioluminous cove is on the southeast coast). The island offers three museums including a lighthouse, a fort and an old sugar mill. Farther out to sea lies **Culebra**, largely a wildlife refuge, with some first class beaches.

Continuing south from **Fajardo** brings you to Palmas de Mar Resort, a city in itself. In downtown Humacao, see **Casa Roig**, *Tel. 852-8380,* a home built in the 1920s by architect Antonin Nechodoma and now a museum devoted to contemporary art and architecture.

NORTHWEST

Beaches along the Atlantic coast can be rough, but for surfers that means great waves at such places as **Jobos Beach** near Quebradillas. For calmer waters try the area near Isabela known as **The Shacks.** South of Quebradillas, **Lake Guajataca Wildlife Refuge** has miles of hiking paths through lush forests filled with sinkholes.

One of the island's blockbuster attractions is the **Arecibo Observatory,** *Tel. 878-2612,* which holds endless fascination for space groupies. Cornell University has erected mammoth equipment over a giant sinkhole to listen for radio signals from distance galaxies. The visitor center is open to the public Wednesday through Friday noon to 4pm and on Saturday, Sunday and holidays, 9am to 4pm Admission is charged.

South of Arecibo on Route 111 west of Utuado, **Gaguana Indian Ceremonial Park,** *Tel. 894-7325,* was built 800 years ago by the Taino Indians as a ceremonial and religious site. Its stone walkways and ball courts have been unearthed, and a small museum built. The park is open Wednesday through Sunday 9am to 4:30pm.

East of Arecibo on Punta Morillo, a 19th century **lighthouse** has been restored and outfitted as a museum. It is open Wednesday through Sunday 8am to 5pm, *Tel. 879-1625.* Just south of Arecibo on Route 10, **Rio Abajo Forest,** *Tel. 724-3724,* offers boat rides on a verdant valley lake. Just as in many national forests, camping is allowed by permit.

Rio Camuy Cave Park, *Tel. 898-3100,* with its caverns and underwater rivers is as ancient and wildly natural as Arecibo is modern and manmade. Near the town of Lares, the Camuy River disappears into a giant labyrinth of caves carved out by the water. Trams carry passengers deep into a sinkhole and cave where impatiens bloom in tiny patches of light admitted by holes in the limestone high above. Truly one of the National Park Service's most exciting rides, the tram can accommodate only limited crowds. Arrive early. The park has picnic areas, rest rooms, a gift shop, and food service.

THE WEST & SOUTHWEST

Cabo Rojo and the picture-postcard fishing village of **Boquerón** surround a long bay that probes three miles inland, spreading one of the island's largest and finest balnearios, or public beaches. **Buyé Beach** north of Boquerón is another beaut; so is **Joyuda Beach** with its long string of seafood restaurants. **Cabo Rojo Wildlife Refuge,** Route 301, Kilometer 5.1, *Tel. 851-7258,* has information displays and nature trails. The bird watching is particularly good.

Although it's a commercial city known for its tuna processing plans, Mayagüez has some appealing attractions. At the city center, the plaza has an imposing statute of **Christopher Columbus** and is surrounded by historic buildings including the **Yaguez Theater,** a National Historic Monument that has been caringly restored. It is used to stage Spanish language plays and concerts. There's a small zoo with a children's playground, and the U.S. Department of Agriculture's Tropical Agricultural Research Station has rambling gardens that invite self-guided tours through acres of exotic plants.

Mona Island, *Tel. 723-1616*, which lies 50 miles off Mayagüez, is managed by the U.S. Department of Natural Resources and can be reached only by chartered boats. The passage can be a frisky one, so consult your doctor about seasick medication. The island is the perfect place for primitive camping at the edge of the world. The best place to find a boat and skipper is in Puerta Real, Cabo Rojo.

Driving north from Mayagüez brings you to **Rincón**, a surf-washed shore in the foothills of La Cadena Mountains. A favorite of eco-tourists, it's a place to catch a whale watching cruise or to hole up in a small country hotel. The **Rincón Maritime Museum** is on Route 413, Kilometer 2.5 and it's open weekdays noon to 4pm.

It's thought that Columbus' exploration of Puerto Rico began somewhere along the northwest coast in 1493. The **Aguadilla** area is locally renowned for its and crafters' shops and for its coconut palm-fringed beaches. One of the best and calmest is **Crash Boat Beach** north of Aguadilla. **Ramey Air Force Base** is now a civilian area gradually turning to tourism.

NIGHTLIFE & ENTERTAINMENT

Puerto Rico is sufficiently Americanized that most shops stay open through the siesta hours, but also Latin enough to love music, dancing, and socializing long after midnight. Casinos, which usually have adjacent bars, often have live music and dancing and are always a good bet for night owls because they stay open until as late as 4am.

Dancing

THE CLUB IBIZA, *in the La Concha Hotel in Condado. Tel. 722-5430.*

Attracts the young crowd for dancing Thursday through Sunday nights.

CIGAR MANIA

Smoke stogies with fellow smokers at the Cigar Bar at the El San Juan Hotel & Casino in Isla Verde, Bolero's in Westin Rio Mar Beach in Palmer, Ruth's Chris Steak House in the Sands Hotel, Tuscany Restaurant in the Marriott Hotel (1309 Ashford Avenue, Condado), the smoking balcony at the Hard Rock Cafe, Havana's Cafe, the cigar bar at Egipto, the cigar room at Red, and Cafe Europe. It's important to call ahead for hours of cigar evenings because not all cigar-friendly places allow smoking all the time.

RED, *at the San Juan Convention Center. Tel. 722-5430.* Dancing, a cigar room, and a sports bar for ages 21 and over. On Fridays, admission is for ages 23 and over.

LAZER, *on Calle Cruz, Old San Juan. Tel. 725-7581.* Open every night, offering different themes and age limits.

EGIPTO, *Robert H. Todd Avenue #1, Santurce. Tel. 725-4664.* Different themes including a sports night, and elegant Friday and Saturday affairs for ages 23 and over.

Dance the merengue at the **COPA ROOM**, *Tel. 791-6100*, or the **PLAYERS LOUNGE** until 3am in the Sands Hotel. Admission is for ages 25 and older; Orchestra music at the **TERRACE BAR** in the Caribe Hilton starts at 8pm on Thursday, 10pm Friday and Saturday, and 2pm Sunday afternoon for dancers of all ages. For a very dressy night out, dance at the **CHICO BAR** in the El San Juan Hotel & Casino, *Tel. 791-1000*, until 1am week nights and 3am Friday and Saturday.

Dance music plays live in the **LOBBY LOUNGE** at the Marriott Hotel, *Tel. 722-7000*, from 7pm to 1am Sunday through Wednesday and 6pm to 3:30am Thursday through Sunday. If you need dance lessons, ask the concierge or front desk. If you're over 40 and love Latin dancing, try **LA FIESTA LOUNGE** in the Condado Plaza, *Tel. 721-1000*. Dancing is 5pm to 2am Monday through Thursday, until 3am Friday and Saturday, and until 1am Sunday.

In the Palmas Del Mar resort at Humacao, drink and dance at the **PALM TERRACE RESTAURANT & LOUNGE**, *Tel. 852-6000*, until 2am.

Good Listening

Listen to live jazz at **CAFE MATISSE** in Condado, *Tel. 723-7910*, on Wednesdays and blues on Fridays, both until 1am In Punta las Marias, jazz starts Fridays at 10pm at **MANGO'S CAFE**, *Tel. 268-4629*. Jazz and Latin rhythms play Friday and Saturday nights from 9:30pm at **VIVAS** in the Condado Beach Hotel & Casino, *Tel. 721-6090*. At the junction of Roosevelt and De Diego Avenues, jazz plays nightly. Order dinner before 10:30 to enjoy the music, which begins after the kitchen closes.

Live Jam Sessions

Live Caribbean music such as salsa is usually (but call ahead to be sure) played at the **CHICO LOUNGE** in the El San Juan Hotel & Casino, San Juan, *Tel. 791-1000*; **EGIPTO**, Robert H. Todd Avenue #1, Santurce, *Tel. 725-4664*; **EL ESCAMBRON BEACH CLUB**, Puerta y Tierra, *Tel. 722-4785*; **PALADIUM**, 65 Infanteria Avenue, Trujillo Alto, *Tel. 760-9069*; and **VICTORIA'S**, 57 Delcafe Street, Condado, *Tel. 724-0975*.

Casinos

Casinos, which are open to hotel guests and non-guests alike, open at noon and close as late as 4am. Dress is casual. Puerto Rican law doesn't permit the serving of drinks at gaming tables, so casinos have lively bars where drinks and snacks are served. If gaming is an important ingredient in your vacation, it's more convenient to stay at a casino hotel.

Hotels with casinos include:
· **Condado Plaza Hotel & Casino**, *Tel. 787/721-1000*
· **El San Juan Hotel & Casino**, *Tel. 787/791-1000*
· **El Conquistador**, *Tel. 787/863-1000*
· **Crowne Plaza Hotel & Casino**, *Tel. 787/253-2929*
· **Wyndham Hotel & Casino**, *Tel. 787/721-5100*
· **Diamond Palace**, *Tel. 787/721-0810*
· **Radisson Ambassador**, *Tel. 787/721-7300*
· **Embassy Suites**, *Tel. 787/791-0505*
· **Sands Hotel**, *Tel. 787/791-6100*

Out on the island, casinos are found at:
· **Holiday Inn Tropical Casinos** in Ponce, *Tel. 800/981-2398*
· **Holiday In Mayagüez**, *Tel. 800/981-8984*
· **Hyatt Regency Cerromar Beach & Hyatt Dorado**, *Tel. 787/796-1234 or 800/981-9066*
· **Best Western Mayagüez**, *Tel. 787/831-7575 or 724-0161*
· **Ponce Hilton**, *Tel. 787/259-7676*
· **Westin Rio Mar Beach**, *Tel. 787/888-6000*

PUERTO RICO'S FOLKLORE & FLAMENCO

*LeLoLai is a program that gives visitors a week-long choice of cultural shows, music and dancing, museum and dining discounts, and tours. For information on the $10 LeLoLei card, Tel. 787/723-3135 weekdays or Tel. 791-1014 weekends and evenings. Hotels that participate by offering folkloric music and dance programs include the **Caribe Hilton** and **Sands Hotel**. Programs are also held at the **Condado Convention Center**.*

SPORTS & RECREATION
Beaches

Luquillo, off Route 3 an hour east of San Juan, is one of the most beautiful beaches in the world and has many quiet areas but, if you prefer a more festive beach, it also has vendors and food stands. It's impossible to list all the beaches of Puerto Rico and its satellite islands because they go on for mile after glorious mile. Simply drive any coast road, and drop off the highway when you see a likely spot (taking all precautions, of course, in areas where there is no lifeguard).

Balnearios, or government-run public beaches have dressing rooms, lifeguards, and parking, and are open daily except Monday. For information, *Tel. 722-1551 or 724-2500.* They include **Luquillo** listed above and **Seven Seas** in Fajardo. West of San Juan, try **Punta Salinas Beach**. Also handy to the city are **Carolina Beach** in Isla Verde and **Escambron** in Puerta de Tierra.

East of Humacao is the public beach at **Punta Santiago**. Swim on the south coast at **Punta Guilarte** east of Guayana, **Cana Gorda** west of Ponce, at **Boquerón** south of Mayagüez or at **Anasco** north of Mayagüez. Along the north coast between Arecibo and San Juan are **Cerro Gordo** and the beach at **Dorado**. **Vieques** has a public beach, **Sombé**, along its southwest shore.

TAKEN ABACK

In San Juan, it is tradition to go to the beaches at midnight on June 23 and walk three times into the sea backwards to insure good luck in the coming year. It's the feast day of San Juan Bautista, patron saint of the city.

Bicycling & Horseback Riding

Ride with **AdvenTours**, *Tel. 832-2016 or 831-4023.*

Fishing

Deep sea and sport fishing trips can be booked through your hotel or through **Club Nautico de San Juan**, Miramar. *Tel. 723-2292 or 724-6265.* Club Nautico is also found in Fajardo, *Tel. 860-2400* or reserve from the U.S., *Tel. 800/628-8426.*

Caving

Explore rivers and caves with **Attabeira Educative Travel**, *Tel. 767-4023,* or **Aventuras Tierra Adentro**, *Tel. 766-0470.*

Golf

Often the scene of internationally televised golf tournaments, Puerto Rico is one of the Caribbean's best choices for a golf vacation. At the **Westin Rio Mar Beach Resort**, *Tel. 888-8811,* Greg Norman designed the River Course, which is surrounded by wetlands filled with bird life, and George Fazio designed the Ocean Course. Both are between the ocean and El Yunque rain forest. The twin **Hyatts** at Dorado have four golf courses designed by Robert Trent Jones, Sr., *Tel. 796-8961 or 796-8916*. **El Conquistador Resort and Country Club**, *Tel. 863-6784*, has a par-72, 6,700-yard course designed by Arthur Hills. It's in Fajardo, 31 miles east of San Juan. Gary Player designed the par-72, 6,690-yard course at **Palmas Del Mar** in Humacao, *Tel. 852-6000*. The resort's second course opened in December of 1997.

The closest public golf course to San Juan hotels is **Bahia Beach Plantation**, Tel. 256-5600, which covers 75 acres of beach and lakes. **Berwind Country Club** in Rio Grande, Tel. 876-3056, is a private club that is open to the public four days a week. At **Aguirre**, *Tel. 853-4052*, the nine-hole golf course is set in an old sugar plantation. The nine-hole **Club Deportivo De Oeste** course runs up and down hills near Mayagüez, *Tel. 851-8880*. In western Puerto Rico near Ramey, the **Punta Borinquen Golf Club**, *Tel. 890-2987*, is a par-72, 18-hole course known for its windy fairways.

At Ceiba on the east coast, play two courses at Roosevelt Road**s Club**, *Tel. 865-4851*. Military personnel and their guests can play the **Fort Buchanan Golf Club** in San Juan, *Tel. 273-3852*. New courses without telephone numbers at press time are the **Dorado Del Mar** northwest of San Juan, and an 18-hole course at **Coamo**. The first tee time is usually 7am. Greens fees with a cart start at $20.

Kayaking

Ismael Ortego, *Tel. 720-7711 or 759-1255*, offers night kayaking excursions that begin at 6:30pm at the Condado lagoon and caravan to Cabezas de San Juan near the Fajardo lighthouse. You'll paddle the bay for three hours at a cost of $30 per person, minimum six people. Shorter explorations of the Condado lagoon are also offered for singles or couples.

Scuba

Dive with:
- **Black Beard West Indies Charters**, *Tel. 887-4818*
- **Caribe Aquatic Adventures**, *Tel. 729-2929*
- **Caribbean Divers**, *Tel. 722-7393*
- **Caribbean School of Aquatics**, *Tel. 72806606*
- **Castillo Watersports**, *Tel. 791-6195 or 728-1068*
- **Coral Head Divers** *in Palmas del May Resort, Tel. 850-7208*
- **Dive Copmarina** *in Guanica, Tel. 821-6009*
- **Dorado Marine Center**, *Tel. 796-4645*

Tennis

The best bet is to stay at a hotel that has tennis courts. Public play can be found at the **Isla Verde Tennis Club**, which has four lighted courts in Villamar, *Tel. 727-6490.* **San Juan Central Park** at the Cerra Street exit on Route 2, Santurce, has 17 courts with lights, *Tel. 722-1646.*

Whale Watching

January through April, whale watch with **Vikings of Puerto Rico**, *Tel. 823-7010.*

SHOPPING

Puerto Rico has a special program that arranges your visits to the shops and studios of local artisans. You'll follow a network of roads called the Rutas Artesanales to meet crafters in person and see their works in progress. For information on the **Fomento Arts Program**, *Tel. 787/758-4747, extension 2291;* the **Puerto Rico Tourism Company artisan office**, *Tel. 787/721-2400,* or the **Institute of Puerto Rican Culture Popular Arts Center**, *Tel. 787/722-0621.*

Of special interest to shoppers in search of local crafts are:
• **Aguadilla** de San Juan, 205 Old San Juan, *Tel. 722-0578*
• **Artesanias**, Castor Ayala, Rote 187, Kilometer 6.6, Loiza, *Tel. 876-1130*
• **Artesanos La Casita** at the La Casita Information Center, Old San Juan. *Tel. 722-1709*
• **Centro de Artes Populares**, 253 Cristo, Old San Juan, *Tel. 722-0621*
• **Hacienda Juanita**, Route 105, Kilometer 23.5, Maricao, *Tel. 838-2550*
• **Kiosko Cultural**, El Area de la Feria, Plaza Las Americas, Hato Rey, *Tel. 396-5230*
• **Mercado de Artesanias**, Plaza de Hostas, Recinto Sur, Old San Juan (no telephone; it's open Friday evenings and weekends)
• **Plaza las Delicias**, Ponce (no telephone, open weekends only)
• **Puerto Rican Arts and Crafts**, 204 Fortaleza, Old San Juan, *Tel. 725-5596.* It's open daily 9am to 6pm, 5pm on Sunday.

The first Tuesday of the month is **Gallery Night** (Noches de Galerías) in Old San Juan, where more than 30 art galleries stay open from 7 to 10pm. Browse from shop to shop.

If you're looking for native crafts, s*antos* (hand-carved religious figures) are a popular collectable. Puerto Ricans also do basketry, leather work, papier-maché sculpture, and fine arts. Shop for antiques in buildings that are as old or older than the treasures themselves along Calle del Cristo. **Butterfly People**, Calle Fortaleza 152 in Old San Juan, is a wonderland of butterflies from all over the world, framed and frozen in time to display in your home in every size from miniature to mural. Purchases will be packed and shipped to your home if you like.

Barrachina Center at 104 Fortaleza Street, Old San Juan, claims to be the largest jewelry shop in the Caribbean and offers free samples of pina colada, which they say was invented here. Shop for custom jewelry, liquor, leather goods and sunglasses. It's open Monday through Saturday 9am to 6pm

Casa Papyrus, upstairs at 357 Tetuan Street in Old San Juan sells music and books and is also a coffee shop hangout for artists and writers. It is open daily 10:30am to 8pm. For handmade leather goods from a famous maker, shop **Dooney & Bourke's Factory Store** at 200 Cristo Street. **La Gran Discoteca** at 203 San Justo Street, is the largest record store in the Caribbean. At **Malula**, at 152 Fortaleza Street, shop for antiques and treasures from around the world. **Joseph Machini**, whose custom jewelry is also sold in Ketchikan, Alaska, has a shop at 101 Fortaleza Street. In the patio here is the **Frank Meisler Gallery** featuring whimsical sculptures and Judaica.

Puerto Rico's divinely aromatic **coffee** makes a meaningful souvenir and it is seen in gift shops and supermarkets throughout the island. One brand, Alto Grande, has been produced at the same hacienda since 1939. It's available in a variety of attractive gift packagings. Locally-distilled rum is an excellent buy except at the airport where it is priced higher than in supermarkets.

EXCURSIONS & DAY TRIPS

A hydrofoil makes a 2 1/2-hour trip from Old San Juan to **St. Thomas** on Saturday, returning on Sunday. Relax in an airplane-style seat and watch the movie in air conditioned comfort, *Tel. 787/776-7417.* Round trip fare is $100.

For adventure and nature tours, **Copladet Nature and Adventure Travel**, *Tel. 765-8595,* will plan your trip on foot, horseback or vehicle to the rain forest, Luquillo Beach, the caves, Caja de Muertos Island, or San Cristobal Canyon. Sign up with **Colonial Adventure** for walking tours of Old San Juan, *Tel. 729-0114.*

Book an outdoor adventure with **Encanto Ecotours**, *Tel. 272-0005.* They'll take you to one of the islands or find a hiking, kayaking, or rafting adventure to your liking. Relaxation and wellness tours to the island's best nature spots are arranged by **Tropix Wellness Tours**, *Tel. 268-2173.* Nightlife and dining tours are offered by **Rico Suntours**, *Tel. 722-2080 or 800/844-2080.*

Fun Cat, *Tel. 728-6606,* is a 49-passenger sailing catamaran sailing out of Fajardo on two-and three-hour sunset cruises that include snacks and rum drinks for $55 per person. The same skipper also has a six-passenger sailboat that sails the bay for three or four hours for $495, including a sailing lesson if you like.

Anticipation III Harbor Cruises make two-hour voyages to El Morro on Wednesday from 6pm to 8pm and Friday, Saturday, and Sundays 7pm to 9pm. The $29.95 fare includes unlimited soft drinks or wine, hot and cold appetizers, disco and dancing. A cash bar serves other drinks.

Plan an entire day for **Rio Camuy Cave National Park**, *Tel. 898-3100,* a 300-acre network of sink holes, caves, and gullies formed by the Camuy River. Trams take visitors deep into the underground, visiting a couple of sinkholes including one so large it could hold El Morro. You can easily find the park on your own, 1 1/2-hours west of San Juan on Route 129, Kilometer 18.9, but most hotels also offer day trips by bus. The visitor center has a cafeteria and theater.

El Yunque National Forest deserves at least one entire day, and longer if you're a serious hiker or wildlife buff. If you drive in, it's difficult to find parking spaces but if you come on a group tour, there won't be enough time for anything more than brief hikes. The park is threaded with rest stops and kiosks where you can get souvenirs, drinks, and souvenirs. Find it 45 minutes east of San Juan on Route 3, then Route 191. Tours are offered by most hotels, or call *Tel. 888-1880.*

Leaving from La Parduera docks in Lajas are boats that sail **Phosphorescent Bay** by night, *Tel. 899-5891 or 899-2972.*

PRACTICAL INFORMATION:

Area code: 787

ATM: more than 250 ATMs around the island accept MasterCard/Cirrus cards. They're found in settlements from Aguada to Yauco.

Crime: crime is a problem in Puerto Rico, so keep your wits about you and always lock your room and car. Put values in your room safe or the hotel safe.

Customs & Immigration: an agricultural inspection looks for plants and products that are prohibited entry to the United States. Many fruits are allowed to be taken to the States including basketball-size pineapple that are packed and sold at the airport to take home in season. If you're unsure about agricultural products you want to take home, call the United States Department of Agriculture, *Tel. 787/153-4505 or 253-4506.* Entry for citizens of other countries is the same as entering the United States.

Driving: holds few mysteries for the North American driver. Your driver's license is good here and most cars, equipment, and highway signs are familiar. An exception is the stop sign, which is red and six-sided but contains the word PARE. Also new to many Americans is use of kilometers in road markers. Speed limits are, however, posted in miles. Car theft is a problem; lock up and, if the rental agency provides a security device, use it.

Emergencies: much of Puerto Rico is on the 911 system, but check the telephone book in your hotel room so you will know for sure. For medical emergencies in San Juan, *Tel. 754-2222;* on the island, *Tel. 754-2550.* Travelers Aid at the airport is open weekdays 8am to 4pm, *Tel. 791-1034 or 791-1054.*

Government: Puerto Rico is a commonwealth of the United States.

Hazards: crime, including rampant car theft, is a problem in Puerto Rico. Take the same precautions you would take in the United States.

Holidays: bank holidays include January 1, January 6, January 16, George Washington's Birthday (usually celebrated February 22), Palm Sunday, Good Friday, Easter, Memorial Day (around May 26), July 4, July 15, July 27, Labor Day (early September), October 12, November 11, November 19, Thanksgiving day (third Thursday of November), December 25, December 31.

Tourist information: Puerto Rico Tourism Company, *575 Fifth Avenue, 23rd Floor, New York NY 10017, Tel. 212/599-6262 or 800/223-6530.* In Miami, *901 Ponce de Leon Boulevard, Suite 604, Coral Gables FL 33134. Tel. 305/445-9112 or 800/815-7391.* In Los Angeles, *3575 W. Cahuenga Boulevard, Suite 560, Los Angeles CA 90068. Tel. 213/874-5991 or 800/ 874-1230.* In Canada, *Tel. 416/368-2680.* On the island, information centers are maintained at the Luis Muñoz Marin Airport, *Tel. 791-1014;* near Pier One in Old San Juan, *Tel. 722-1709;* at the airport in Aguadilla, *Tel. 890-3315;* on Route 100, Kilometer 13.7 in Cabo Rojo. *Tel. 851-7070;* and in the Fox Delicias Mall in Ponce, *Tel. 840-5695.* Towns that have their own tourism offices, usually open weekdays only, are Adjuntas, *Tel. 829-2590;* Anasco, *Tel. 826-3100, extension 272;* Bayamón, *Tel. 798-8191;* Cabo Rojo, *Tel. 851-1025;* Camuy, *Tel. 898-2240* (this one, at Kilometer 4.8 on Route 119 is open daily); Culébra, *Tel. 742-3291;* Dorado, *Tel. 7965-5740;* Fajardo, *Tel. 863-4013;* Guanica, *Tel. 821-2777;* Jayuya, *Tel. 828-5010;* Luquillo, *Tel. 889-2851;* Naguabo, *Tel. 874-0389;* Rincón, *Tel. 823-5024;* San Juan, *Tel. 724-7171;* and Vieques, *Tel. 741-5000.*

Weddings: at least ten days before you're going to be married, have a VDRL blood test from a federally certified laboratory, either in the U.S. or Puerto Rico. Have a doctor sign and certify the marriage certificate and blood test; take them to a Registro Demografico for a marriage license. A passport or other photo ID, plus copies of applicable divorce papers must be presented. Officials keep limited hours and only on weekdays, so plan well in advance. The marriage license is prepared by the minister who performs the ceremony.

40. THE U.S. VIRGIN ISLANDS

On his second voyage to the New World, Christopher Columbus dropped anchor off the Salt River, St. Croix, on November 14, 1493, and sent a boat ashore in search of fresh water. He named the island Santa Cruz before being driven off by hostile Caribs. Sailing on to St. Thomas, St. John, and Tortola, he named the group Las Virgenes in honor of the 11,000 virgins of St. Ursula who died at the hands of marauding Huns.

The first settlers on St. Croix were a motley group of Dutch, English, and French who could never quite get along and soon sailed on. By 1649, the English had a settlement near what is now Frederiksted, but they were driven out by Spaniards based at Puerto Rico. Finally, the island became St. Croix in 1639 when the governor of the French islands took it over as his private game park. When he died, he left it to the Knights of Malta, a group of French aristocrats who took possession of the island and planted sugar. Their debt-ridden effort ended in 1695 and France abandoned the island.

The Danish West India and Guinea Company surveyed St. Croix in 1733, sold plantations, and soared into a golden age of sugar riches. Planned on a grand scale equal to the city that is now Oslo, Christiansted emerged at a time when neo-classical architecture, with its graceful arches, was in vogue. Spurred by strict building codes and inspections, and built by exacting artisans, the city became a showplace.

Fearing German expansion during World War I, the United States bought the Danish West Indies in 1917, giving them territorial status and granting U.S. citizenship to their inhabitants. They were administered by the U.S. Navy, then by the Department of Interior until 1952 when a governor was appointed. Islanders vote on their own government as well as their member of congress.

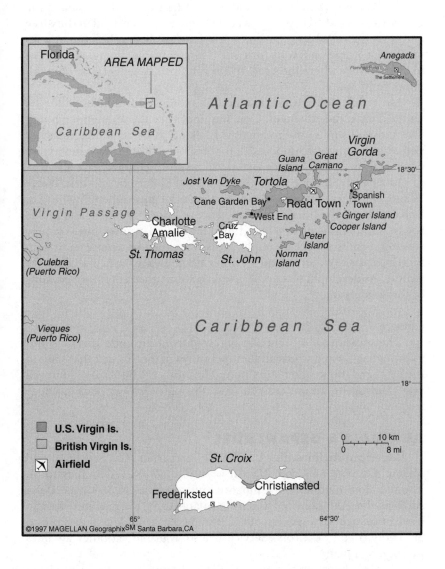

Florida

AREA MAPPED

Caribbean Sea

Atlantic Ocean

Anegada

Flamingo Pond

The Settlement

Virgin Gorda

Guana Island

Great Camano

18°30'

Jost Van Dyke

Tortola

Spanish Town

Cane Garden Bay

Road Town

West End

Ginger Island

Cooper Island

Virgin Passage

Charlotte Amalie

Cruz Bay

St. Thomas

St. John

Peter Island

Norman Island

Culebra (Puerto Rico)

Vieques (Puerto Rico)

Caribbean Sea

18°

■ U.S. Virgin Is.

☐ British Virgin Is.

☒ Airfield

0   10 km
0   8 mi

St. Croix

Christiansted

Frederiksted

65°

64°30'

©1997 MAGELLAN GeographixSM Santa Barbara,CA

St. Croix is 28 miles long and seven miles wide, the boyhood home of Alexander Hamilton and once dotted with more than 100 sugar plantations. Its terrain ranges from rain forest to dry desert.

St. Thomas, 13 miles long and three miles wide, is the capital of the U.S. Virgin Islands. Today known to cruisers as a disneyland of duty-free and to yachties as a happy haven, St. Thomas has alluring beaches, resorts in all price ranges, a few historic sites, some notable dining, and lots of hidden pockets where the savvy visitor can find a quiet getaway only two hours from Miami.

Most of **St. John**, which is nine miles long and five miles wide, is a national park. Its settlement, **Cruz Bay**, looks like the setting for a South Seas movie. Its hills are threaded with hiking paths; its shining beaches and windex waters are unbeatable for unspoiled beauty. As leases expire on resorts, even more of the island will revert to national park status.

In 1996, the three U.S. Virgin Islands were joined by a fourth, **Water Island**, which was turned over to the territorial government by the U.S. Department of the Interior. Included are two docks, a beach, and public roads. A resort is being developed and $3.3 million in government money is being spent to spruce up public areas. Take the five-minute ferry from St. Thomas to Water Island's Honeymoon Beach, which is open to visitors. As developments occur, they'll be announced in future editions of this guidebook.

Climate

The occasional "Alberta Clipper" cold front can come this far south to bring flag-fraying winds and temperatures in the 70s, but that's about the extent of the weather story here. Most days are 80-ish and sunny all year. During hurricane season, June through October, rain is more frequent and heavier and humidity can be cloying.

ARRIVALS & DEPARTURES

American Airlines flies into St. Thomas from JFK, San Juan, and Miami, *Tel. 800/433-7300*. **US Airways**, *Tel. 800/428*-4322 flies to St. Thomas from Baltimore-Washington and continues to St. Croix. **Delta Airlines**, *Tel. 800/221-1212* flies from Atlanta to St. Thomas and on to St. Croix. **Prestige Airways**, *Tel. 800/299-8784* flies from Miami and JFK to St. Thomas and St. Croix. Service is also available via other air lines through San Juan.

Local air lines serving the U.S. Virgin Islands and other Caribbean points include:
• **Air Anguilla**, *Tel. 264/497-2643*
• **Air St. Thomas**, *Tel. 590/277-7176*
• **American Eagle**, *Tel. 800/433-7300*

• **Bohlke International Airways**, *Tel. 340/778-9177*
• **Dolphin Airlines**, *Tel. 800/497-7030*
• **LIAT**, *Tel. 246/495-1187*

Fly among the islands by **Virgin Islands Seaplane**. One-way fare from St. Croix to St. Thomas is $50. A 1 1/2-hour tour that includes 35 minutes of flight time is also available from St. Thomas for $55 per person, *toll-free Tel. 888/FLY-TOUR* or locally, *Tel. 777-4491*. **Carib Air** flies from St. Thomas or Fajardo to St. Croix, *Tel. 778-5044*.

Scheduled daily service between Christiansted and Charlotte Amalie aboard a high-speed boat is from **Fast Ferries**, *Tel. 773-FAST*.

A ferry operates every two weeks from St. Thomas and St. John to San Juan, Puerto Rico. The trip takes about two hours and the cost is $60 one way or $80 round trip, both including ground transportation to the San Juan Airport or Condado, *Tel. 340/776-6282*. A hydrofoil makes a 2 1/2-hour trip from Old San Juan to St. Thomas every Saturday, returning Sunday. Relax in an airplane-style seat and watch the movie in air conditioned comfort, *Tel. 787/776-7417*. Round trip fare is $100.

Ferries run between St. Thomas and St. John and from both islands to the British Virgin Islands of Tortola, Virgin Gorda, and Jost Van Dyke. Schedules vary according to time of year and day of the week, and can be curtailed by weather.

ORIENTATION

St. Croix is only 28 miles long and seven miles wide, but it takes as long as an hour to get from **Christiansted** to **Frederiksted**. It's an impractical distance just for dinner, but a lovely drive for a day-long excursion with stops for shopping, swimming, and lunch. For such a small island it offers great diversity, from dry and cactus-rich landscape of the east to the craggy rain forest and the cliffy north coast.

St. Thomas is anchored by **Charlotte Amalie**, where ferries depart and cruise ships dock. **Red Hook** is at the east extreme of the island, and **Cyril E. King Airport** is just west of Charlotte Amalie. The island is 13 by three miles.

St. John is nine by five miles, with most activity centering around **Cruz Bay**, where ferries arrive from St. Thomas. Centerline Road goes from one end of the island to the other, allowing you to get from Cruz Bay to **Coral Bay** in about half an hour. Locals refer to the stretch of Centerline after Coral Bay as East End Road. Most of the best beaches and ruins are on North Shore Road; South Shore Road leads to Gift Hill Road, which connects to Centerline. The road is inland, but plenty of roads lead down to such beaches as **Great Cruz Bay**, **Chocolate Hole**, and **Hart Bay**.

RIGHT WAY, WRONG WAY

For reasons we can't fathom, the U.S. Virgin Islands continue to drive on the left, English style, even though almost all vehicles have their steering wheels on the left, American style. It can be immensely confusing to visitors, especially in traffic circles, so highway injuries take a high toll among tourists. Be especially cautious, not just when driving, but when crossing the street.

GETTING AROUND THE U.S. VIRGIN ISLANDS

Taxi fares are published by the Virgin Islands Taxi Association, and range from $4.50 for one person traveling from the airport into town to as high as $10 for transport from the airport to the Red Hook area. The rate for each additional passenger is about 50 cents less than the primary fare. Additional charges are 50 cents per suitcase or box, $1.50 for trips between midnight and 6am and a 33 per cent surcharge for radio dispatch. A two-hour tour for two costs $30 with $12 each for additional passengers.

Taxi companies include:
· **East End Taxi Service**, *Tel. 775-6974*
· **Independent Taxi**, *Tel. 775-1006*
· **Island Taxi**, *Tel. 774-4077*
· **Sunshine Taxi**, *Tel. 775-1145*
· **V.I. Taxi Association**, *Tel. 774-4550*
· **24 Hr. Radio Dispatch**, *Tel. 774-7457*
· **Wheatley Taxi Service**, *Tel. 775-1959*

If you have a problem or complaint, take it to the V.I. Taxi Commission, *Tel. 776-8294*. Note the driver's name and license number, which should begin with the letters TP.

Arrange an **Avis** rental car from the U.S. at *Tel. 800/331-1084,* or in St. Thomas at *Tel. 774-1468*. **ABC Auto Rentals** have cars and jeeps; *Tel. 776-1222 or 800/524-2080*. **Budget Rent-a-Car** has seven locations around St. Thomas, *Tel. 776-5774 or 800/626-4516*.

Buses on St. Thomas are roomy and comfortable, but are not the fastest way to get around the island. Fares are 75 cents in town and $1 for other points on the island. Not all communities can be reached by bus. Catch a bus at Emancipation Garden.

Getting Around St. Croix

The airport is on the southeast shore of the island, about halfway between Frederiksted, which is on the west coast and Christiansted, the island's main city located mid-island on the north coast. Routes are numbered and are easy to follow if you keep track of your location on the map that comes with your rental car.

Kemwel rental cars are available at the airport on St. Croix, or can be delivered to a hotel or home. Prices in high season range from $199 to $319 weekly, plus $8 daily Collision Damage Waiver. From the U.S. *Tel. 800/678-0678;* locally *Tel. 773-7200.* For an **Avis** car, *Tel. 800/331-1084* from the U.S. or locally *Tel. 778-9355.*

Taxi companies include:
- **St. Croix Taxi Association** *at the airport, Tel. 778-1088*
- **Antilles Tax Service,** *Christiansted, Tel. 773-5020*
- **Caribbean Taxi & Tours,** *Christiansted, Tel. 773-9799*
- **Cruzan Taxi Association,** *Christiansted, Tel. 773-6388*
- **Territorial Taxi Umbrella,** *Tel. 692-9744*
- **Combine Taxi & Tours,** *Frederiksted, Tel. 772-2828.*

Taxi fares are posted and should be confirmed in advance. Round trip fare is double the one-way charge plus a charge for waiting time of more than 10 minutes. Between midnight and 6am, there is a $1.50 surcharge for rides out of town and $1 in town. Bags are 50 cents each; trunks are more. Minimum fare is $2. Lone passengers pay four times the rate charged per-person for two, e.g. the posted charged from the airport to Christiansted is $10 per person for two plus $5 each additional person. One person would pay $20; three people $25; four people $30.

Buses, *Tel. 773-7746,* go between Christiansted and Frederiksted every 40 minutes between 5:30am and 9:30pm every day. The route starts at Tide Village east of Christiansted and ends at Fort Frederik. By transferring at La Reine terminal, you can also get to and from the airport. Look for VITRAN bus stops. Fare is $1 for adults, 55 cents for seniors aged 55 and older. Transfers are 25 cents. Exact change is required.

Getting Around St. John

If you are on a day trip and just want a tour of St. John, hop aboard one of the open air jitneys that meets every ferry. A tour is recommended, even if you're going to explore later on your own, because drivers have their own patter and style. There are no public buses on St. John.

St. John Car Rental, *Tel. 776-6103* offers Vitaras, Sidekicks, Cherokees, Wranglers, and vans that hold up to eight people. Jeep rentals are available from **O'Connor Car Rental** at the Texaco Station, *Tel. 776-6343.* Water taxis are available from **Inter-Island Services,** *Tel. 776-6282.* Rental cars are available from **Conrad Sutton Car Rental,** *Tel. 776-6479;* **Courtesy Car Jeep Rental,** *Tel. 776-6650;* and **St. John Car Rental,** *Tel. 776-6103.*

WHERE TO STAY

Add eight per cent government tax to all hotel tariffs in the U.S. Virgin Islands. In addition, a service charge is sometimes, but not always, applied in lieu of tipping. Rates quoted are for a double room in high season. Summer rates are lower.

Private villas can be booked through **WIMCO**, *Tel. 800/932-3222 or 401/849-8012*. Maid service and staff are available. Private pool villas and condos can be booked by the week through **Calypso Realty**, *Box 12178, St. Thomas 00801, Tel. 340/774-1620, Fax 340/774-1634; toll-free 800/747-4858*.

A variety of studios and apartments with up to three bedrooms are booked through **Ocean Property Management**, *Box 8529, St. Thomas VI 00801, Tel. 340/775-2600, Fax 340/775-5901; toll-free 800/874-7897*. On St. John book through **Vacation Homes**, *Box 272 Cruz Bay, St. John VI 00831, Tel. 340/776-6094, Fax 340/693-8455*.

Virgin Islands packages that include airfare, accommodations, and other features are offered by **American Airlines**, *Tel. 800/433-7300*, in four categories: moderate, superior, deluxe, and all-inclusive at savings of about 25 percent over piecemeal rates.

APPLES TO APPLES – COMPARING ROOM AMENITIES

When booking a hotel or motel room, it's safe to assume that you're getting daily maid service with fresh linens, soap, shampoo, and the like. If your room has a coffee maker, it probably is provided with coffee and makings. The mini-bar is stocked with drinks and snacks.

However, in self-catering accommodations such as cottages, villas, apartments, townhouses, bareboats, and homes, services and facilities vary widely. Probably not a crumb of food, soap, tissues, shampoo or other hotel-type amenities will be provided. Know before you go. Do you get fresh linens daily? Once a week? Do you do all the cleaning, cooking, dishwashing and bed making? Must you bring your own bedding and towels? What about beach towels? Is there a cleanup fee when you leave? How far is the nearest market where you can provision? Beach? Golf course? Tennis court? Restaurant? Must you have a rental car?

Only by comparing apples to apples can you find the best value.

ST. JOHN

Expensive

CANEEL BAY, *P.O. Box 720, Cruz Bay, St. John, U.S.V.I. 00831. Tel. 340/776-6111, U.S. and Canada, 800/928-8889. Rates at this 171-room resort start at $350 double in high season. Full American Plan is an additional $95; breakfast and lunch plan, $75. Children pay $47.50 and $37.50.*

This is a resort that you'll either love or hate. Those who love it are so loyal that some rooms are booked years in advance; to stay in some areas, you have to wait for someone to die. Guests are met at the ferry dock in St. Thomas and brought to this legendary Rosewood resort and former Rockefeller hideaway. It was restored and reopened in the fall of 1996 without, by demand of its loyal clientele, the addition of air conditioning, television, room phones, and other intrusions.

On arrival you're welcomed with a chilled face cloth, then are taken by tram to your room, which will have its own patio, a mini-bar with refrigerator, coffee makings, and a wall safe. Two color schemes were chosen, one in coral and teal and another in sunny yellows and raspberry to set off new, handmade furniture from the Pacific Rim.

Trams make the rounds every 20 minutes and are the only way, except for more walking than is practical, around the far-flung grounds. For people whose workaday lives involve waiting for buses and trains, it can be less than amusing, especially in a tropical downpour. Picture yourself padding out to find the nearest phone to order room service or call home, and having no air conditioning in August, and you see why some people are puzzled at this resort's mystique.

Cuisine here ranks with the best in the region. Eat at the Beach Terrace overlooking St. Thomas, Turtle Bay Estate House serving gourmet cuisine and fine wines, or in the Equator in the former Sugar Mill restaurant, where the brilliant menu is based on foods found around the equator from Brazil to Indonesia. The Caneel Bay Bar has live music nightly, and drinks are also served at the popular Breezeway/Starlight Terrace. After dinner at Turtle Bay, dance to live music.

For sloths, Caneel Bay offers sunning, seven grand beaches, shaded reading nooks under rustling palms, and sunset sails aboard a private yacht. Hikers can explore the 170-acre resort's own nature trails or seek out advanced trails in the Virgin Islands National Park, which surrounds the resort, to see more than 500 species of plant life. Take an excursion to St. Thomas or to a sister resort, Little Dix Bay, on Virgin Gorda in the British Virgin Islands. Explore sugar mill ruins, snorkel the underwater trail, windsail, dive, or kayak. The Tennis Park has 11 all-weather courts, complimentary tennis clinics, private lessons, weekly tournaments, and an outstanding Pro Shop.

Children, once barred, are now welcome to Caneel Bay with an optional children's activities program for $50 daily including lunch. Half days are $35. Caneel Bay isn't for everyone. While loyalists love its open-air environment, we found that the same windows that let in surf sounds and breezes also let in the howling Christmas winds and the conversations of other guests as they pass by, chat on a neighboring patio, or yell at each other to be heard in the shower. Louvered windows and doors cannot be closed. So privacy, which is one of the resort's proudest features, can also be elusive. For these prices, we want air conditioning that can be turned on if need be.

THE WESTIN ST. JOHN, *Great Cruz Bay. The island's most elegant hotel was a Hyatt until the 1997-8 season when it reopened as a Westin after a multi-million-dollar refit. Rates at this 285-room resort start at $425, tel 340/693-8000 or 800/WESTINS.*

Covering 34 acres of magnificently landscaped grounds, this resort has an enormous 1/4-acre swimming pool, restaurants, bars, entertainments, and plenty of bells and whistles. Rooms and suites are spread among ten low-rise buildings connected by gardens lined with flowers and palms and threaded with red brick walks. Play tennis on floodlit courts, dine in the restaurants, the deli or the pool bar and grill, shop the boutique for smart resort wear, and enroll the children in the Westin Kids Club. Work out in the fitness center or arrange fishing, kayaking, snorkeling, windsurfing, diving, sailing, or a golf game on St. Thomas' Mahogany Run course.

Moderate

GALLOWS POINT SUITE RESORT, *P.O. Box 58, St. John 00831. Tel. 340/776-6434 or toll-free 800/323-7229. Rates at this 60-unit resort start at $190 for a one-bedroom, one-bath unit with full kitchen, living room, and balcony. Don't bring children under age 5. You'll be met at the ferry dock and transported to the resort, which is a five-minute walk from "downtown."*

A cluster of two-story, plantation style buildings surround a cliffy coast and short strength of sandy beach on the outskirts of Cruz Bay. Units are privately owned and all different, but you can count on comfortable surroundings with everything you need to cook some or all of your meals. Sleep two in the bedroom, two more on the sofabed. Loft units, which sleep one or two more, have an additional half bath. The suites are air conditioned and have ceiling fans; some have cable television, and telephone. The resort has a pool and gift/gourmet food shop and is the home of Ellington's, one of the best restaurants on St. John.

ESTATE CONCORDIA, *mail address 17 East 73rd Street, New York NY 10021. Tel. 800/392-9004 or 212/472-9453, Fax 212/861-6210; locally, Tel. 340/776-6240, Fax 776-6504. Rates start at $135 double, plus $25 each* *additional person. A rental car is needed to get here from Cruz Bay, 40 minutes away.*

The views of Ram Head and the Salt Pond are breathtaking as you rough it easy in a hillside aerie with 20-foot ceilings, ceiling fan, and a full kitchen with dishwasher and microwave. Furnishings are spare but comfortable, with efficiencies and studios accommodating up to three and the duplex sleeping up to six in two twin beds, a queen-size sofabed, and roll-aways. This is the most remote corner of St. John, with superb shelling, snorkeling, and hiking. The nearest restaurants and shopping are in Coral Bay.

Budget

CINNAMON BAY CAMPGROUND, *P.O. Box 720, Cruz Bay 00831. Tel. 340/30 or 539-9998. The park's 126 tent sites and cottages are $15 to $95 depending on how much equipment is provided. Ride the campground shuttle from the ferry for about $5.*

One of the most popular campgrounds in the world, this one is booked months in advance. Choose a plain campsite for your own tent and gear, a platform with tents, cots, cooker, ice chest and tableware, or a spartan cottage furnished camping style. This is roughing it in paradise, with the sea at your doorstep. There's a restaurant and a camp store where basic supplies can be purchased. The bathroom is communal, campground style.

CONCORDIA ECO-TENTS, *mailing address 17 East 73rd Street, New York NY 10021. Tel. 800/392-9004 or 212/472-9453, Fax 861-6210; locally, Tel. 340/776-6240. Doubles are $95; additional persons are $25. Rent a car at the ferry dock for the 40-minute drive to Coral Bay.*

Perched high in isolated hills just outside the national park boundary on the southeast corner of the island near Coral Bay, Estate Concordia is one of the Maho Bay Camps but is 25 minutes by car from the other camps and 40 minutes from Cruz Bay. A rental car is a must. Permanent tents are made of fabric supported by a wood frame, with such high-tech features as solar and wind energy and composting toilet. This is living next to nature overlooking the sea and intruding as little as possible on the hills. Furnished are a refrigerator, cooking equipment, linens, and an ice chest you can supply from the office's ice machine. While the tents are built to catch the breezes, they can be warm when winds die. There's a big pool, or hike to the beach.

CRUZ INN, *Box 797, Cruz Bay, St. John 00830. Tel. 340/693-8688 or 800/666-7688. Studios are priced from $75 plus a $5 surcharge for a one-night stay.*

Just a short walk from the dock, tennis courts, shopping, restaurants and the bus stop is a modestly furnished crash pad that gives you the bare essentials for about the lowest price on the island. Units have private bath, refrigerator and air conditioning. Apartments, which require a stay of three nights or more, sleep three to six people on beds, sofabeds and futons. All have a bathroom and kitchenette.

HARMONY RESORT *at Maho Bay, mailing address 17 East 73rd Street, New York NY 10021. Tel. 800/392-9004 or 212/472-9453, Fax 861-6210. Doubles are $95-$150 nightly plus $15 each additional person. A shuttle from the ferry costs about $5 per person.*

A step up from the same management's Maho Bay Campground, these tent-cottages are made from recycled materials and are sparsely but adequately furnished. Solar panels provide energy to heat bath water and operate the microwave. The design scoops in any trade winds, but on a calm day we wished for some high-voltage air conditioning. Furnished are kitchen gear and all linens. Your camp will have its own bathroom and deck. Use the same transportation, restaurant, cultural events and water sports as Maho Bay Campground.

THE INN AT TAMARIND COURT, *Box 350 Cruz Bay, St. John 00831. Tel. (430) 776-6378 or 800/221-1637. Single rooms with shared bath are $48; doubles with private bath start at $88. Continental breakfast is included. The Inn is in town within walking distance of the ferry dock.*

The flagstone courtyard of this unpretentious inn is one of Cruz Bay's most popular hangouts, with big shade trees, lively music, cheap food, and good booze. The location in the center of things makes it popular with business travelers and a good headquarters for island excursions. It's not on the beach and doesn't have a pool, but room rates were the best we could find on St. John for amply furnished, air conditioned accommodations with daily maid service. Walk to tennis, beach shuttles, shopping, and a bunch of restaurants.

MAHO BAY CAMPS, *Tel. 340/776-6240 or 800/392-9004. Rates are $60 nightly for two plus $10 additional per child and $12 more per adult. Visa and MasterCard are accepted. A shuttle from the ferry costs about $5 per person.*

Permanently pitched tents on wood platforms are surrounded by thick, glossy, tropical foliage. They sleep up to four people in three rooms furnished with two twin beds and a sleep sofa. Bed linens, a propane stove, cooler, towels, and cooking and eating utensils are supplied. Each area shares a barbecue and water faucet. Toilets and pull-chain showers are communal.

Eat breakfast and dinner in the outdoor restaurant if you like, or shop in the camp store for frozen foods, produce, canned goods, bread, milk, juices, beer, wine, and basic paper products. Leave your leftovers in the "help yourself" center for arriving guests to use. Take an art or education workshop, snorkel and swim, hike, and enjoy the sunsets from your own deck.

RAINTREE INN, *downtown Cruz Bay. Tel. 340/693-8590 or 800/666-7449. Rates at this 11-room inn are from $75; weekly rates are available.*

Efficiencies at this non-smoking property have everything you need for cooking plus private bath, air conditioning, telephone, and proximity to the socko Fish Trap restaurant. A three-night minimum stay is required. A popular choice for business travelers, the inn is your basic, budget beige, but it offers laundry service and is in a good Cruz Bay location. Children under age 3 stay free.

ST. THOMAS
Expensive

BOLONGO BAY BEACH CLUB INCLUSIVE BEACH RESORT, *7150 Bolongo, St. Thomas VI 00802. Tel. 800/524-4746. Rates at this 75-room resort start at $270 per day single occupancy or $440 per couple including room, food, drink, activities, tax, gratuities, watersports, scuba, and airport transfers.*

The all-inclusive concept has immense appeal to travelers who weary of being charged every time they pick up a beach towel or book a tour. Everything here is exceptionally good quality from food and drink to snorkel cruises, tennis, fitness and aerobics, volleyball, basketball courts, an all-day sail, and nightly entertainment. It's a total vacation without having to open your wallet.

A semi-inclusive rate without meals and drinks is available for those who want to spend more time out on the island. All of the large, air conditioned bedrooms overlook the sea and were refurbished in 1997. They have television, ceiling fan, safe, private balcony with a view of the blue and telephone. Some have a kitchenette. Babysitters and cribs are available. Children under age 12 stay free with parents who are on the Continental (semi-inclusive) Plan.

DOUBLETREE SAPPHIRE BEACH RESORT & MARINA, *P.O. Box 08088, St. Thomas 00801. Tel. 340/775-6100 or 800/524-2090. Rates at the 171-unit resort start at $310 for a suite with full kitchen. Suites sleep four; villas sleep up to six. The optional meal plan is $70. Children under age 13 stay, eat, and play free with their parents. The resort is 35 minutes from the airport, 25 minutes from Charlotte Amalie and five minutes from the Red Hook ferry.*

You're welcomed with the big, sweet cookies that are a Doubletree trademark. Check into a spacious suite decorated in cool whites and pastels. Each has a private balcony with ocean view, air conditioning, microwave, coffee maker, full-size refrigerator, satellite television, telephone, ceiling fans, air conditioning, and a living-dining area where a bottle of rum welcomes you. Maid service includes fresh flowers daily. The beach is a picture postcard of white sand and turquoise water.

Children can play all day, 8:30am to 5:30pm with other children in a supervised program filled with learning and fun. For an additional charge of $15, parents can put children in the Nite Klub until 10pm.

The resort is 15 minutes from the famous Mahogany Run golf course but, unless you're an ardent golfer, you won't want to leave the resort. It has its own marina and dive center including scuba lessons, sea kayaking, and deep sea fishing; free use of non-motorized watercraft, tennis, volleyball, a gift shop. Shuttle service into Charlotte Amalie is $7 round trip or $4 each way; into Red Hook, it's $2 each way.

Have a drink in the Seagrape Beach Bar, then dine in the Sailfish Cafe with its Mexican favorites, the Seagrape Restaurant on the beach or the Steak House at The Point. Then have an after-dinner drink at the bar, which is open until 2am. Live entertainers play five nights a week, with Calypso and steel drums three nights a week. On Sunday afternoons, the reggae beach party is not to be missed.

MARRIOTT'S FRENCHMAN'S REEF RESORT, *Flamboyant Point, mailing address P.O. Box 7100, St. Thomas 00801. Tel. 340/776-8500 or 800/524-2000 for Frenchman's Reef, 800/232-2425 for Morning Star. Rates at this 501-unit resort start at $275, suites at $375. A MAP meal plan is available. The resort is three miles east of Charlotte Amalie.*

Still only half open at press time but promised to be back on line by 1998, after a $40 million renovation, this classic resort faces both the harbor and the Caribbean. Choose Frenchman's Reef for a cliffy high-rise with a view or Morningstar for more upscale accommodations on the beach. Together the hotels have shops, restaurants, room service, in-room ironing boards and mini-bars, tennis courts, and a full range of watersports. The main swimming pool with its waterfalls and swim-up bar is a humdinger. Be sure to tell your driver where you're staying; the resorts' check-in desks are separate.

RENAISSANCE GRAND BEACH RESORT, *Smith Bay Road, mailing address P.O. Box 8267, St. Thomas VI 00801. Tel. 340/775-1519 or 800/322-2976. Rates at the 297-unit resort start at $285. A cab ride from the airport is $15 per person.*

This AAA Four Diamond resort on St. Thomas just keeps getting better, consistently boasting one of the highest Guest Satisfaction Index scores in the Renaissance chain. The 34 acres of grounds are groomed and gardened, providing restful views of sea and landscape. Units are spread over hill and dale but call a shuttle if you don't feel like walking. And if you can't walk at all, the resort's six wheelchair accessible units are a rare find in the Caribbean.

The beach is just off a huge pool area, so you can float the day away in the ocean, pool, sailboat or raft. The resort's Smuggler's Restaurant, where you can mix your own Bloody Mary on Sunday mornings, is an island favorite. The children's program is free, providing up to 12 hours a day of supervised fun and care.

One-bedroom suites have a balcony, coffee machine, refrigerator, wet bar, and a queen-size sofabed. High-tech equipment is furnished in the fitness center, which also has men's and women's steam, sauna, and extensive spa services. A plus is a comfortable lounge with rest rooms where travelers can hang out between checkout and a late departure.

If you prefer to stay in self-catering accommodations on the resort property, book with **Pineapple Village Villas**, *Tel. 340/777-3985, Fax 775-5516; toll-free 800/992-9232*; privately-owned villas start at $150 nightly.

RITZ-CARLTON, *699 Great Bay, St. Thomas 00802. Tel. Tel. 340/241-3333, Fax 775-4444; toll-free 800/241-3333. U.S. and Canada 800/241-3333. High season rates start at $400 per room. Ask about packages. The 148-room, four-suite hotel is 30 minutes from the airport or about $10 per person by taxi. Airport transfer by limousine can be arranged by the hotel, which is found on the island's eastern tip.*

Surely the *ne plus ultra* of St. Thomas resorts and the first Ritz-Carlton in the Caribbean, this one has all the five-star features of other Ritz-Carltons around the globe. From the moment you're welcomed at the portico and ushered across gleaming marble floors to the check-in desk, the coddling from perkily-uniformed staff is complete.

Built in the fashion of a grand palazzo, the property rims a fine beach and overlooks a brimming pool with an "infinity" edge that makes you think you're swimming on the horizon. From the main building, which houses some guest rooms, the lobby, meeting rooms, and The Cafe for fine dining, buildings cluster around a salt pond nature preserve filled with waterfowl. The rooms are spacious and come with all amenities; specify sun or shade when you book. Plan your days around swimming, the beach, sailing excursions aboard the resort's own catamaran, tennis, the fitness center,, diving, snorkeling, golf and more. The hotel has its own beauty salon, and shops selling designer clothing and accessories. Jackets are not required, but this resort calls for your very best resort wear.

Selected as one of my Best Places to Stay; see Chapter 13 for more details.

Moderate

BEST WESTERN CARIB BEACH, *70 Lindberg Bay, St. Thomas 00802. Tel. 340/774-2525, Fax 777-4131; toll-free 800/792-2742. Rates at this 69-room hotel start at $109 plus 13 per cent tax.*

The perfect place for an affordable, weekend getaway in the sunshine, this hillside inn isn't fancy but it overlooks a flawless beach, serves modestly priced buffets nightly, and brings in entertainers often. Typical of this price-appeal chain, the hotel has television and telephones in the

VIRGIN ISLANDS HOTEL WEDDINGS

If you want to get married in paradise, a number of companies provide complete wedding planning including accommodations for the couple and their families, the ceremony, flowers, reception, photographer, and a honeymoon hideaway. Contact:

FANTASIA WEDDINGS AND HONEYMOONS, *Suite 310, 168 Crown Bay, St. Thomas VI 00802, Tel. 340/777-6588, Fax 776-0020; toll-free 800/326-8272*

RENAISSANCE WEDDINGS, *Box 8267, St. Thomas VI 00801, Tel. 800/322-2976*

WEDDINGS BY IPS, *9719 Estate Thomas, Suite 1, St. Thomas VI 00801, Tel. 340/774-4598, Fax 776-3433; toll-free 800/937-1346*

WEDDINGS ISLAND WAY, *10-1-29 Peterborg, mailing address Box 11694, St. Thomas VI 00801, Tel. 340/775-6505, Fax 777-6550; toll-free 800/582-4784 or 800/755-5004*

SAPPHIRE PRECIOUS WEDDINGS, *Box 8088, St. Thomas VI 00801, Tel. 340/775-6100, extension 8117; toll-free 800/524-2090.*

rooms, a swimming pool, air conditioning, tennis, and watersports rentals. A sister **Best Western** nearby has 90 rooms and is right on the beach, so rates are higher, starting at $189; *Tel. 340/777-8800.*

L'HOTEL BOYNES, *Blackbeard's Hill, Charlotte Amalie. Tel. 340/774-5511 or 800/377-2905. Rates at this eight-room inn start at $115, single or double occupancy, including continental breakfast. Taxi fare from the airport is about $5 per person.*

Sam Boynes, owner and host of this hillside retreat is part of the hospitality magic. A great-great grandson of the French secretary of the navy under Louis XV, he named the hotel after the Paris original of the same name where Napoleon was married. Old island hands may remember the inn as The Mark St. Thomas, a dinner restaurant long revered for its fabulous city views and cozy setting in a mansion built in 1785.

Boynes has refurbished the house, adding a wealth of antiques and collectibles from his travels. He's a black innkeeper who speaks Japanese, regales his guests with island history and his genealogy, and hosts one of the most interesting inns in the Caribbean. Rooms are all different, each with private bath, ceilings that seem 20 feet high, and original, two-century-old stonework, woodwork and floors. They have cable television and direct dial telephone. Most have air conditioning.

The grounds are steep and small, but landscaped with such artistry that guests will be happy here reading and looking out over the island's best view of Charlotte Amalie. There's a tiny pool and a hot tub. Walks are steep but it's not far to the shopping and dining district downhill or Blackbeard's tower up the hill.

POINT PLEASANT RESORT, *Estate Smith Bay, St. Thomas, VI 00802. Tel. toll-free 800/777-1700 or locally 340/775-7200. Rates at the 134 suites, which range in size from studios to two-bedroom units, start at $255 nightly. Cab fare from the airport is $15.*

Spread atop a steep, cone-shaped hill like color on a snow cone, this all-suites resort has it all for the vacationing couple or family: three swimming pools, two restaurants including the renowned Agavé, a marina with motorized and non-motorized watersports, nature trails, and a tennis court. If you don't care to navigate the resort on foot, use the free shuttle service. In an unusual program, the resort allows each villa four hours use of a car daily at no cost except for a mandatory $12.50 fee for insurance and fuel.

The villas are individually owned so each is furnished differently but those we saw were fresh and attractive, with a cliffy overlook from the balcony, tile floors with jute area rugs, a welcome bottle of rum on the table, and a fully equipped tile kitchen. Suites are air conditioned and have ceiling fans.

WYNDHAM SUGAR BAY BEACH CLUB, *on Route 30, East End, mailing ing address 6500 Estate Smith Bay, St. Thomas VI 00802. Tel. 800/ WYNDHAM. Doubles at the resort start at $270 per couple all inclusive. Ask about packages and, in summer, the kids-free program. The resort is a $10 cab ride from the airport.*

Once part of a sugar plantation, this 32-acre site has alternating strips of sugar beach and rocky headland, with views from your balcony of tireless surf. Every room has a television and refrigerator; furnishings have a mellow, colonial look accented with floral motifs. Dine outdoors and waterside at the Mangrove Cafe. Snorkel, play tennis, golf the Mahogany Run Golf Course, take a Jeep adventure, scuba dive, and swim in the interconnecting, freshwater pools where you can swim your way to from whirlpool to waterfall. Every evening, take in a boisterous revue in a cruise ship-like lounge, then dance afterwards until 1am. The hospitality is total from the moment you step off the airplane until you're taken back to the airport. Everything from food to drinks and non-motorized watersports is included in one fee.

Budget

DANISH CHALET, *Charlotte Amalie. Mailing address Box 4319, St. Thomas 00803. Tel. 340/774-5764, Fax 777-4886; toll-free 800/635-1531. Rates at this ten-room inn start at $75. It's ten minutes from the airport.*

It's like going home to the folks when you stay with Frank and Mary Davis, former yachties who settled down here and opened an inn where drinks at the honor bar are only $1. Rooms are homey, with air conditiioning or ceiling fan and telephone. The restaurants and shops of town are a five-minute walk away and it's 15 minutes to some of the island's best beaches. A continental breakfast is included and it is served in a pleasant setting where you'll meet other guests. You can also share the Jacuzzi and library with a nice mix of other guests.

HOTEL 1829, *Box 1576, St. Thomas 00801,. Tel. 340/777-7100, Fax 777-7200; toll-free 800/524-2002. Rates at this 15-room inn start at $75; larger rooms are priced to $170.*

This charming inn was built as a home by a French sea captain for his bride. It took ten years and was completed in 1829, hence the name. Now a National Historic Site, the house has air conditioning, private baths with each room, cable television, and balconies in some rooms. A continental breakfast is included. The restaurant here is popular and the dark little bar is straight out of the 1950s. There is a tiny swimming pool, just large enough for a cooling splash. There's no elevator, so this isn't a good choice if you have a problem with stairs.

ISLAND VIEW GUEST HOUSE, *Box 1903, St. Thomas. Tel. 340/774-4270, Fax 774-6167; toll-free 800/524-2023. Rates at this 15-room guesthouse start at $60.*

Located halfway between town and the airport, this is a good headquarters for island exploring if you have a car. Parking is provided. Rooms are air conditioned and have television and telephone. The relaxed little inn has an arresting view of the sea far below from its own pleasant pool and breezy deck. In the foreground are acres of bright shrubs.

MAFOLIE, *Box 1506, St. Thomas 00804. Tel. 340/774-2790, Fax 774-4091; toll-free 800/524-2023. Rates at this 23-room inn start at $81 including continental breakfast. It's 10 minutes from the airport.*

The view of the harbor 800 feet below is one of the great pleasures of this delightful small hotel. A free shuttle takes guests to famous Magen's Bay beach, or you can spend your days in the freshwater pool with its big, sunny deck. Drink service is available at the pool all day. Rooms and suites (some with kitchenette) have air conditioning, ceiling fan, cable television, and all the comforts of a small, homey bedroom. The same nice family have been in charge for 25 years and they keep things running smoothly.

ST. CROIX

During peak seasons when bookings are hard to get, the **Small Inns Association of St. Croix** will help you find a room in a member inn. Call toll-free: *Tel. 888/INN-USVI.*

Expensive

BUCCANEER HOTEL, *Gallows Bay, mailing address P.O. Box 25200, Christiansted 00824. Tel. 340/773-2100 or 800/255-3881. Rates in this 150-unit resort start at $210 for a double room in season. Take East End Road east out of Christiansted for two miles. The resort is a $12 taxi ride from the airport.*

A historic treasure founded in 1653 by a French settler, this charming property is on ground that was once planted to sugar. Its lobby is in the remains of an old mill. The resort has been in the same family since 1947. Our deluxe beachfront room was as big as a ballroom, with cavernous closets, a big bathroom with double sinks, refrigerator and ceiling fans as well as air conditioning and remote control cable television. Butter yellow and Danish blue fabrics complement the blue and white tiles, vaulted pine ceiling, mellow rattan furniture, and mahogany woodwork. The window seat overlooking the beach is a bookworm's delight.

Swim in the pool, which has its own bar, or choose one of three surrounding beaches. Play the 18-hole golf course or eight tennis courts, choose from four restaurants, use the fitness center, or make an appointment in the spa. In addition to the beachfront units, other rooms, suites and a guesthouse are high on the hill with soaring views. Take a hike, or call for the shuttles that are always available.

WESTIN CARAMBOLA BEACH RESORT & GOLF CLUB, *Estate Davis Bay, Kingshill, P.O. Box 3031, St. Croix 00851. Tel. 800/228-3000 or 340/778-3800. Rates at this 151-unit resort start at $245. Take Route 69 north from the airport and turn left when it ends at Route 80. Cab fare from the airport is $12 for one or two persons.*

Looking down from Parasol Hill, a killer hill used in the annual St. Croix International Triathlon, the hotel complex looks like a bouquet of red hibiscus, each building roofed in crimson. Rooms are as spacious as suites, most of them with a private screened porch and a dim, wood interior that provides respite from the brilliant sunshine. Luxury features abound: air conditioning, a fitness center and spa, hair dryers and coffeemakers in rooms, television, telephone, and room service. The Davis Bay Suite has two bedrooms and a private veranda that the Rockefellers once used to entertain groups of up to 100.

Robert Trent Jones, Sr. designed the golf course that is only a five-minute shuttle ride away. Tennis courts are lit for night play. The restaurants provide tony dining by candlelight or a lighter, deli experience. The beach was restored after the last hurricane and looks sandy and inviting despite a few rocky areas; just off shore, the 3000-foot wall is one of the island's best dive spots. Ask about the children's program, popcorn and movies, and activities for all ages. The site, aloof and scenic, is a popular one for weddings and the hotel has its own wedding planner who can make arrangements for everything from the cake and flowers to accommodations for the entire wedding party.

Moderate

CHENAY BEACH RESORT, *P.O. Box 24600, St. Crois 00824. Tel. 800/548-4457 or 340/773-2918. Rates start at $185 for a cottage with full-size refrigerator, cooktop, and microwave oven. On the northeast end of the island three miles east of Christiansted, it's a $13 taxi fare from the airport. Add $65 per person per day for a meal plan that includes breakfast, lunch, dinner, and drinks.*

This lively, 50-unit resort has a big lap pool, a rim of beach, a locally popular restaurant with theme nights and parties, tennis, and good snorkeling just off the beach. Rooms are done in sunny colors, with air conditioning, ceiling fan, radio, television, microwave, coffee maker, dial telephone, small dining area, and mini-bar. For families traveling together, connecting cottages are available at family rates. Children are catered to with their own games and menu.

SEAVIEW FARM INN, *180 Two Brothers, Frederiksted, 00840. Tel. 340/772-5367 or 800/792-3060. Rates at this eight-suite inn start at $130 including Happy Hour in the bar and a basket of breakfast makings delivered to your suite each morning. Cab fare from the airport is $10.*

The look from the road is that of a Virginia farm with its white farm fence, but the tropical nature of this sprawling mini-resort emerges when you check into a breezy cottage, take a dip in the pool, and hang out at the open air grill and bar complete with model sailboats you can race. Suites have four-poster beds, kitchenette, screened porch, and plenty of cross ventilation as well as air conditioning and ceiling fan. No TV or phones in the rooms, but there is a big screen TV at the bar, and telephones at the pool bar. The view is of a salt pond filled with waterfowl, a plus for birders who like to use the inn's telescope. Massage is available by appointment. For modem hookup, ask Dulcy and Roland Kushmore, your hosts.

THE WAVES ATCANE BAY, *P.O. Box 1749, Kingshill, 00851. Tel. 340/778-1805 or 800/545-0603. Rates start at $140 for a studio apartment with screened balcony and full kitchen. Cab fare from the airport is $13 for two.*

This 12-unit hideaway is a find for divers because hosts Kevin and Suzanne Ryan have their own dive shop here plus a natural pool where beginners can take their first scuba or snorkel lessons. The beach is small and very attractive. Balconies hang right over the waves. There's a restaurant, which is an inexpensive hangout popular with passers-by.

SPRAT HALL PLANTATION, *Route 63, Fredericksted, 00841. Tel. 340/772-4305 or 800/843-3584. Rates start at $100. Cab fare from the airport is $10 for two.*

Mr. and Mrs. Jim Hurd can't seem to keep up with the maintenance of this old pile, but the scruffy charm and the Hurd's priceless fund of island lore more than make up for the lack of spit and polish. Mrs. Hurd was born here, in a greathouse that goes back to the 1650s. In the main house are two big bedrooms. Nearby are a couple of two-bedroom cottages and a one-bedroom honeymoon cottage. Hike or ride the grounds on horseback. They go on for acres of winding paths and pillowy hills planted with 700 fruit trees Eat in the dining room or in the Hurd's rustic Beach Club restaurant just a short walk away.

Budget

BEST WESTERN HOLDER DANSKE, *1 King Cross Street, Christiansted, St. Croix 00840. Tel. 340/773-3600 or 800/528-1234. Rates at this 44-room hotel start at $89 single. Cab fare from the airport is $10 for one or two persons.*

Stay in the heart of downtown with its pace and pizzazz, handy to restaurants and shopping. The hotel has a pool and sundeck; each room has a balcony or patio overlooking the harbor, telephone, and cable television. Some kitchenettes are available.

CLUB COMANCHE, *1 Strand Street, Christiansted 00820. Tel. 800/524-2066 or 340/773-0210. Rates at this 24-room hotel start at $49.50. A cab from the airport costs $10 for one or two persons.*

Convenience, a great city location, full-featured suites with air conditioning and cable television, a superb South Seas-look restaurant, a harbor view from your balcony and low cost make up for the somewhat cheesy furnishings of this 250-year-old club. Diving instruction is available in the big, saltwater pool. Rooms have air conditioning, television and telephone. For $126 nightly you can stay in the old windmill right on the water.

DANISH MANOR HOTEL, *2 Company Street, Christiansted. Tel. 340/773-1377 or 800/773-1377. Rates at this 34-room inn start at $85 including continental breakfast.*

A busy, buzzy downtown location is ideal for shopping and dining Christiansted, but don't expect an ocean view unless you specify a room on the third floor. Courtyard views are of a swimming pool and plenty of greenery. It's a popular gathering spot for guests. Rooms have air conditioning and cable television. The beach is a five-minute ferry ride away.

FREDERICKSTED HOTEL, *442 Strand Street, Frederiksted, St. Croix 00840. Tel. 340/773-9150 or 800/524-2025. Rates at this 40-room hotel start at $85. Take a cab from the airport, which is about 10 minutes away, for $8 per couple.*

The charm of a small, European hotel and the convenience of a downtown location add up to a fine value within walking distance of beaches, shopping, , and restaurants. The hotel has its own restaurant and sun deck; each room has a small refrigerator and a microwave oven.

HILTY HOUSE INN, *Questa Verde Road, Gallows Bay, mailing address P.O. Box 26077, 00824. Tel. and fax 340/773-2594. Rates at this five-room inn start at $85 including continental breakfast. A one-bedroom cottage is also available. Credit cards aren't accepted. Cab fare from the airport is $10.*

Hugh and Jacqui Haore-Ward found this converted 1732 rum factory and have turned it into an enchanted inn. In a region where fireplaces are almost unknown, here is a huge one that is lit on Christmas Eve. Jacqui makes her own jams for breakfast from local fruits such as tamarind and mango. After a day of diving or exploring, relax in the old library with books and television. Or sign up for one of Jacqui's famous ethnic dinners held Monday nights, with authentic mood, music, and food. Rooms are all different, and all beguiling, with wonderful angles and crannies created by old walls that were built with another use in mind. There's no air conditioning, but ceiling fans augment the hilltop breezes.

ON THE BEACH RESORT, *P.O. Box 1908, Frederiksted, 00820. Tel. 340/772-1205 or 800/524-2018. Rates start at $85 per person including continental breakfast. Cab fare from the airport is $8.50 for two. The resort is a half mile south of town.*

Although this inn bills itself as "proudly serving serves the homosexual and Lesbian community," all lifestyles are welcomed and our impression was one of a happy, homogeneous group of people being hosted royally by owner-manager Bill Owens. Suites and villas overlook a seagrape-shaded sand beach, a warm cove with good snorkeling, and a seaside courtyard where breakfast is free and lunch and dinner are a delight.

Owens often throws a BYOB barbecue, with guests bringing the side dishes while he cooks a turkey or pig. On the beach side, units have bedroom, living room, screened porch with pass-through to the kitchen, and an ocean view. Seafoam green fabrics are accented with iridescent amethyst; floors are Italian tile. A second unit across the narrow street has its own pool and two-bedroom suites.

PINK FANCY, *27 Prince Street, Christiansted, 00820. Tel. 340/773-8460 or 800/524-2045. Doubles start at $75 including continental breakfast and Happy Hour drinks. Cab fare from the airport is $10 for two.*

George and Cindy Tyler are part of the magical mix of this sprawling old relic. Dating to 1780, the buildings have been refurbished with comfy wicker, shiny mahogany floors, air conditioning and ceiling fans. An old hangout for show business folks, it is decorated with old showbiz posters and memorabilia. It's still popular with business travelers who, if they want only to crash and burn, take one of the small, inexpensive rooms. The heart of the 13-room inn is the cobblestone courtyard around the pool, where breakfast and cocktails are served. There's a gazebo for small weddings, and learn-to-cook weekends are offered in summer. Parking is on the street, but you won't need a rental car if you want only to hang out around the pool and enjoy Christiansted's shopping and dining.

USVI VILLA RENTALS

This guide does not list privately-owned villas that are available on a one-to-one basis because we can't vouch for the condition of units that are under absentee management. However, professionally managed private homes and villas can be booked through the following places below:

ST. JOHN
Caribbean Villas & Resorts, *Wharfside Village, St. John 00830, Tel. 800/338-0987, Fax 207/871-1673*
Caribe Havens, *P.O. Box 455, St. John 00830, Tel. 340/776-6518*
Destination St. John, *Box 8306, St. John 00830, Tel. 800/776-6969 or 800/562-1901*
Holiday Homes of St. John, Inc., *Mongoose Junction, Cruz Bay, St. John, 00831, Tel. 340/776-6776 or 800/424-6641*
Island Getaways Vacation Villas, *Kathy McLaughlin, P.O. Box 1504, St. John 00831, toll-free Tel. 888/693-7676*
Katherine DeMar Vacation Homes, *P.O. Box 272, Cruz Bay, St. John 00831, Tel. 340/776-6094*
Marlene M. Carney, Star Villa Rentals, *P.O. Box 599, Cruz Bay, St. John USVI 00831, Tel. 340/776-6704*
Mary-Phyllis Moguieira, Mameyu Peak, *St. John 00830, Tel. 340/776-6876*
Park Isle Villas, *P.O. Box 1263, St. John 00831, Tel. 800/416-1205 or 693-8261*
Sea View Homes, *P.O. Box 644, Cruz Bay, St. John USVI 08831, Tel. 340/776-6805*
Serendip Vacation Apartments, *P.O. Box 273, Cruz Bay, St. John USVI 00831, Tel. 340/776-6646*
Villa Portfolio, *P.O. Box 618, Cruz Bay, St. John USVI 00831, Tel. 800/858-7989 or 340/693-9100*
Windspree Vacation Home Rentals, *6-2-1A Estate Carolina, St. John 00830, Tel. 693-5423.*

ST. THOMAS
Calypso Realty, *P.O. Box 12178, St. Thomas 00801, Tel. 340/774-1620, Fax 774-1634. In addition to a selection of other villas, this company has one that meets A.D.A. standards for the physically challenged.*
McLaughlin Anderson Vacations Inc., *100 Blackbeard's Hill, St. Thomas 00802, Tel. 340/776-0635, Fax 777-4737, toll-free 800/537-6246 or 800/666-6246.*

PRINCE STREET INN, *402 Prince Street, Frederiksted, 00840. Tel. 340/772-9550 or 800/771-9550. Rates at this four-room inn start at $42. No credit cards are accepted.*

Once a Lutheran parsonage, this inn finds privacy in the heart of town thanks to its attractive gates and courtyard. Wooden cottages have living room, bedroom, bath and kitchen, adding up to a whale of a deal for the price. Walk to beaches, shopping, and restaurants.

HURRICANE UPDATE

In all the years we have been traveling the tropics, one hurricane theme is repeated time and again. "Please tell them that we are open and operating," plead hoteliers whose guests have been scared away by over-dramatic press reports. Innkeepers are partly to blame because, when damage occurs, they invariably underestimate how long it will take to get things back in order. They don't re-open on time, or they claim to be running normally, and guests find themselves staying at Fawlty Towers. Even in the worst storms, some hotels don't close at all and others have only minor disruptions such as a brief or partial power failure. There's only one way to get the straight scoop and that's to call the airlines to see if you can get in and out. Then phone the hotel itself and ask, "Are you open and operating normally?" and then pin them down, "What services are unavailable or curtailed?" If the answer to #1 is "next week", call again and keep calling until you can be assured that the hotel is (not will be) operating fully. Better still, talk to someone who has just returned from the same hotel.

WHERE TO EAT

Dinner hours in the Virgin Islands seem awfully early when compared to French and Spanish islands but, even though kitchens close at 9 or 10pm, the drinking, dancing, music, and good times might go on for hours depending on the restaurant.

ST. THOMAS
Expensive

HERVÉ RESTAURANT & WINE BAR, *Kongens Gade. Tel. 777-9703. Hours are Monday through Saturday for lunch and dinner. Find the restaurant between Zorba's and Hotel 1829. Plan to spend $30-$40 for a three course dinner; $25 for a two-course lunch.*

It's the buzz of St. Thomas. Hervé and Paulette put together a welcoming ambience and great food in a relaxed, bistro setting on Government Hill, the perfect place to take a break from downtown shopping. For a hearty meal, take the lamb shank braised with vegetables with fresh herbs and red wine. Or dine more delicately on chilled shrimp with papaya cocktail sauce, spinach and vegetables en croute, or a poached artichoke stuffed with crab and served with cold ravigotte sauce.

Moderate

AGAVÉ TERRACE, *in the Point Pleasant Resort. Tel. 775-4142. The resort is found on the east end of the island between the Renaissance Grand Beach Resort and Red Hook. Plan to spend $10-$15 for breakfast and $20-$40 for lunch or dinner. Reservations are recommended. Dinner is served nightly from 6pm; brunch is served on Saturday and Sunday.*

The views from this all-villa resort overlooking Pillsbury Sound are awesome. Brunch starts with a morning Happy Hour drink and Eggs Florentine or a tropical fruit plate ringed with fresh, fragrant muffins. At dinner, appetizers in the $5-$9 range include a five-pepper dip with chips, conch chowder, or iced gazpacho. Choose a pasta specialty such as linguine with tenderloin medallions and Gorgonzola-walnut cream sauce, or one of the steaks. They come in two sizes.

Ask about the catch of the day, then fine-tune your order according to cooking method and sauce. If you've had fisherman's luck today, bring your own fish and let the chef serve it to you. Dinners came with a special salad tossed table side, fresh bread, and the house pasta. It takes an entire menu page to describe the desserts, after dinner drinks, coffees and teas; the wine list won an Award of Excellence from Wine Spectator magazine. Dress is resort-casual and kids are welcomed with their own menu.

BLUE MARLIN, *next to the ferry dock in Red Hook. Tel. 775-6350. The restaurant is open daily for dinner. Plan to spend about $30 for a meal.*

New owners have expanded the seafood menu to include French, Italian and Spanish touches but have retained the former owners' talents for creating chicken and beef dishes with subtle seasonings and a light touch. The ambience is nautical, with a nice mix of tourists and locals mingling in the seaside air.

THE CAFE IN THE RITZ-CARLTON, *Great Bay. Tel. 775-3333. Reservations are recommended. Dinner Main dishes are $24-$29; pizzas are $11.50-$17.50. The restaurant is open daily for breakfast, lunch and dinner.*

Even if you're not staying here, come for a dining experience that includes a walk through the palatial marble lobby, down the grand staircase, and into the pleasant, open-air Cafe. The pizzas are extravagantly topped with traditional pepperoni and trimmings, or try the guava barbecue chicken with shredded jack cheese. Have carmelized onion pizza or one topped with Thai shrimp, shiitake mushrooms, asparagus and cilantro. Choose from a menu that includes grilled basil shrimp in a banana leaf or Caribbean lobster and sweet potato stew. There's also a macrobiotic selection, and, for meat-and-potatoes eaters, a superb grilled sirloin with chunky whipped potatoes.

LA SCALA, *in Palm Passage between Waterfront Highway and Main Street, a five-minute walk east of the post office. Tel. 774-2206. Dine for $20-$30, less if you order pasta or a pizza.*

Secluded in a sliver-size alley lined with shops, this open-air restaurant spills into the passageway and is separated only by a fence from the passing throngs. Yet it's an oasis of peace and fragrant foods, with caring service and soothing flamenco music. The Basil Grilled Salmon is lavished with spinach and white beans and the Grilled Paillard of NY Strip comes with an interesting potato-mushroom risotto. Linguine with conch is a Caribbean touch. Grilled vegetable pizza with smoked mozzarella is good but skip the grilled salad pizza, which is difficult to eat either with utensils or the fingers.

Budget

FRIGATE RESTAURANT *in the Mafolie Hotel, Red Hook. Tel. 774-2790. Reservations are recommended. Complete dinners start at $14.50. The bar opens at 5:30 and dinner is served nightly from 6 to 10pm.*

Arrive before sunset to have a drink while drinking in the sensational view of water, sky, and islands. Add a salad bar, a slab of steak or seafood, and a fluffy baked potato or a bed of rice to make a substantial meal at a reasonable price.

PADDY O'FURNITURE'S IRISH BREW PUB, *Frydenhoj, East End. Tel. 779-1760. Lunch and dinner is served daily except Monday 11:30am to 10pm; the bar stays open until midnight. Dishes are priced $2.95 to $11.95.*

Paddy brews his own beers including Pitbull Irish Stout made with four different malts. This is the place to get the local skinny, scarf down a couple of cold ones, and fill up on burgers, sandwiches, fish and chips, salads, and light meals.

ST. CROIX

Expensive

DUGGAN'S AT THE REEF, *on Route 82, Teague Bay. Tel. 773-9800. The restaurant is open for dinner every day, lunch Monday through Saturday, and Sunday brunch 11am to 3pm. Main dishes start at $14.50; appetizers as $6. Reservations are suggested.*

This outdoor eatery overlooks the water and Buck Island. Order any of the superb pastas as appetizer or entree. Or choose from a galaxy of starters such as conch tempura or beef teriyaki, flying fish, then a choice of soups and salads, the catch of the day prepared in a variety of ways, filet mignon, rack of lamb, veal piccata, homemade desserts, and international coffees. A house specialty is Irish whiskey lobster served with a five-ounce filet.

THE GALLEON, *Green Cay Marina, Estate Southgate. Tel. 773-9949. The bar opens at 5pm and dinner is served nightly 6-10pm. Main dishes start at $17.50; pastas at $15; chateaubriand for two is $50. Reservations are recommended. Five minutes east of Christiansted, the restaurant is a $12 cab ride for one or two.*

Start with gravlox or the baked brie crusted with almond crumbs, then the tossed salad with the house herb dressing and a large or small pasta such as Beef Fedora – the house fettuccine tossed with wild mushroom cream sauce and skirted with thin strips of grilled sirloin in a bleu cheese demi glace. Salmon is served with dill butter; rack of lamb can be carved at your table. A house specialty is grilled filet mignon topped with lobster meat and bearnaise sauce. Everything is served with freshly baked bread, rice and vegetables. Check out the cognacs and after-dinner drinks too. Dress is resorty but elegant.

GINA'S, *in the Buccaneer Resort just east of Christiansted. Tel. 773-2100. Taxi fare from town is $6 for two. Main dishes are priced at $16 to $23. Open for dinner only; reservations are suggested.*

Italian gourmet cuisine is featured here in such dishes as Fettucine Caribbean with shrimp, scallops, black beans, and rum. Or, savor the Grilled Vegetable Napoleon with pesto and mascarpone. The raviolis are homemade.

THE GREATHOUSE AT VILLA MADELEINE, *19 A-4 Teague Bay. Tel. 778-7377. A meal featuring appetizer, salad and entree will cost $35-$40. Open nightly for dinner, the villa is a $11 cab ride from Christiansted and $24 from Frederiksted.*

Feel right at home in the main house of this cozy resort where a library and billiard room welcome dinner guests to make an evening of it. Start with chilled shrimp on cous cous or a lobster Napoleon followed by a romaine salad with raspberry vinaigrette and an entree such as the pork tenderloin filled with chèvre, sage, and prosciutto or the roast duck leg served with mango puree and fruited Armagnac. Salmon, lobster and catch of the day are the seafood selections, but there's also chicken, steaks and veal. On weekends, there's piano entertainment.

THE MAHOGANY ROOM *at the Westin Carambola Beach Resort. Tel. 778-3800. Plan to spend $50 for a three-course dinner.*

Dine in air conditioned splendor on polished mahogany furniture in a plush, greathouse setting. The mahi-mahi is prepared with hazelnuts; rack of lamb or classic chateaubriand are prepared to order; fresh yellowfin tuna is a specialty. Everyone raves about the black bean soup and rice first course, but pace yourself. It's filling. The Carambola is also renowned for its champagne Sunday brunch and a Friday night buffet with live music and entertainment.

Moderate

BANDANA'S, *in the Sea View Farm Inn, 180 Two Brothers, Frederiksted. Tel. 772-2950. Open for lunch and dinner daily, the restaurant features main dishes averaging $20.*

Watch the sunset over the salt pond from this open-air restaurant with its nautical theme, then order another round while you sail the miniature sailboats in the canals that surround the bar. The grill is hot, ready to cook your steak, chicken, or salmon to order. The menu is an uncomplicated one for meat-and-potatoes diners who enjoy a convivial atmosphere and casual eating.

BOMBAY CLUB, *5A King Street, Christiansted. Tel. 773-1838. Main dishes start at $13 after 5pm, but appetizers, salads, and fajitas at $6-$10 are good value. Open Monday through Friday for lunch and dinner, the restaurant is open for dinner only on Saturday and Sunday.*

A great place to escape from the bustle of Christiansted shops is this courtyard where you can hang out in the bar to see major sports events on television or take a table far from the bar and linger over a meal. Order a two-fisted burger, sandwich or salad, or end your day with a 10-ounce filet mignon with a salad. For a lighter dinner focus on appetizers such as conch cocktail, roasted garlic with brie, or cheese nachos.

CAFE DU SOLEIL, *Prince Passage, Strand Street, Frederiksted. Tel. 772-5400. Reservations are suggested. Dinner is served Wednesday through Sunday; Sunday brunch is 10am to 2pm Dine for $20-$40.*

Locally caught fish is prepared with a deft touch, or try the lamb kabobs, shrimp, or Caribbean lobster. Brunch centers around fluffy omelets or feathery pancakes. Because this open-air eatery overlooks the sea from the second story, it's a popular spot for cocktails and watching for the green flash. Downstairs, Turtles Deli offers quick sandwiches and take-out picnics.

COLUMBUS COVE, *at Salt River Marina, Salt River National Park. Tel. 778-5771. Open daily 8am to 11pm, the restaurant takes only American Express credit cards. Plan to spend about $15 for dinner; but luncheon fare is available all day in the $6-$10 range.*

The only restaurant within the national park, this wildly natural site is not far from the spot where Christopher Columbus first set foot on St. Croix. From the restaurant, catch a boat tour of the river and sea then stay on for a meal. For weekend brunch there are eggs Florentine or fresh fruit waffles. Lunch might be a chicken platter, fish plate, sandwich or burger. Dinners start at 6pm and feature steaks, pastas, shrimp, and fish. Home-made desserts are tempting: key lime pie, chocolate walnut pie, or raspberry Bailey's cheese cake. On Wednesdays there's a Caribbean barbecue of chicken or ribs with all the trimmings including corn on the cob.

DOWN BY THE BAY, *in the Chenay Beach Resort. Tel. 773-2918, ext. 316. Open for breakfast, lunch, and dinner daily; reservations are suggested. Plan to spend about $10 for lunch and $15-$22 for dinner.*

The location is a simple, outdoor terrace but the hospitality makes this a favorite for international dining and after-dinner dancing under the stars. Every night sees a new French, Spanish, Italian, or Cajun specialty; the weekly pig roast, with its West Indian buffet and live music, is a sellout. So are other buffet nights, such as the all-you-want pasta on Wednesdays. On Fridays, there's a belly dancer. Save room for one of the desserts, which vary nightly but might include Dutch cheesecake with toasted almonds or French meringues with fruit.

CAMILLE'S, *Queen Cross Street near the corner of Company Street, Christiansted. Tel. 773-2985 is open for breakfast and lunch from 7:30am and all day Saturday. It reopens at 5pm daily except Sunday as a Mediterranean bistro. The kitchen closes at 10pm. Dinner will cost $15-$20.*

This air conditioned restaurant is a popular gathering spot for breakfast and lunches featuring New York-style deli sandwiches, fresh salads, and inventive soups. In the evening, locals gather in this cozy converted greathouse to order wine by the bottle or glass to accompany hearty roasts, seafood, fish stew, lamb ragout, hot sandwiches, or light salads.

COMANCHE CLUB, *Strand Street, Christianstead. Tel. 773-2665. Main dishes are $12.50 to $19; daily specials are $12.50 to $15.50. Reservations are accepted. The restaurant is open for lunch and dinner Monday through Saturday. Lunch guests may use the pool for a small fee.*

An ancient war canoe hanging from the ceiling sets the scene in this locally popular, second story restaurant overlooking the waterfront. Portions are brobdignagian, so show up with a huge appetite and tear into the unforgettable Beef Curry Vindaloo with 10 Boys (a cart brings the "boys", which are accompaniments). The mixed grill brings together lamb, filet of beef and calves liver. The lobster, says the menu, is "Always scarce; always expensive." Chicken is served with oyster stuffing and, if you're in a splurge mode, have the caviar with blinis at $50. Save room for the Rum Raisin Bread Pudding with your choice of caramel or fudge sauce.

DINO'S *at the Buccaneer. Tel. 773-2100. Call for reservations and for hours, which vary seasonally. Plan to spend $25 for dinner.*

Overlook the lights of Christiansted from this hilltop perch while dining on fresh pastas that are made right here daily. Sit in the wine bar cafe or the dressy, elegant main dining room with its stargazer view of the green terraces of a fine, family owned resort.

HILTY HOUSE, *Questa Verde Road, Gallows Bay. Tel. 773-2594. Fixed price dinners are $25 plus gratuity and drinks. Taxi fare from Christiansted is*

$5. Dinners are held weekly by reservation. Call several days in advance. Only local and travelers' checks and cash are accepted; credit cards are not.

Although gourmet cook Jacquie Hoard-Ward offers her international gourmet dinners only on certain nights, they are worth the wait. You'll be welcomed into a private home in an 18th century rum factory and served a theme meal – Middle Eastern, Caribbean, French, and so on, with all the right music, tableware, and accessories.

HARVEY'S, *Company Street at King Cross Street, Christiansted. Tel. 773-3433. Open daily except Sunday from 11:30am to 9:30pm, Harvey's takes no credit cards. Eat for under $15.*

Goat stew, stewed fish, whelks, ribs and chicken, rice and beans, fungi, sweet potato and other West Indian specialties are dependable at this crowded, family style spot. The tropical drinks are dynamite, especially the Whammy. Homemade pies made with tropical fruits such as pineapple or coconut are complimentary with your meal.

KENDRICK'S, *Gallows Bay, Christiansted. Tel. 773-9199. Main dishes cost $18-$15; pastas $16-$21; appetizers $7 to $8.50. It's open daily for lunch and dinner. Reservations are advised. The restaurant is at Chandlers Wharf in Gallows Bay Marketplace just east of Christiansted.*

Dine upstairs with the fine dining menu in a yacht club setting or downstairs at the clubby bar where salads and burgers are in the $8-$10 range. Chef David and Jane Kendrick are enthusiastic hosts in this big, two-story restaurant with a fine view of the harbor and lights of the city. Start with homemade eggplant ravioli in tomato-basil butter, proceed to chilled champagne gazpacho, then try a Roquefort Caesar or spinach salad. Chef David offers four pastas including homemade pappardelle with sauteed shrimp. Or order rack of lamb, filet mignon, pecan crusted roast pork, breast of duck, or a seafood specialty. The menu is inspired and extensive.

LE ST. TROPEZ, *Limetree Court, Frederiksted. Tel. 772-3000. Reservations are suggested. The restaurant is open for lunch and dinner daily except Sunday. Main dishes start at $14.*

Daniele and Andre Ducrot are usually on hand with a personal welcome as guests are ushered into this crowded, fragrant bistro. On oilcloth-covered tables, blackboards tattle tonight's soups, salads, seafood and specialties, all of them with a French accent starting with the escargot. The wine list is extensive and cigars are available. Ask them to put Edith Piaf on the sound system and imagine yourself in a torchlit Parisian courtyard on a moist June evening. Before leaving, visit the gift shop with its European imports.

NO BONES CAFE, *Gallows Bay. Tel. 773-2128. Take a cab from Christiansted for $4. Dinners are in the $12-$15 range. Hours are Monday through Friday 11am to 9pm and Saturday 5-9pm.*

Wild and crazy guy Chef Tamas makes his chowder with 31 ingredients, serves his catfish Cajun style, and plays 1930s and '40s jazz while serving stingers and sidecars for Happy Hour. Try fish and chips English style, double dipped shrimp, po' boy sandwiches, marinated mussels with linguine, or tonight's stir-fry special. Tamas hopes you'll order Just Feed Me, which is each night's surprise. Don't forget to compliment Chile, the watch parrot. Takeouts are available.

ON THE BEACH, *a mile south of Frederiksted on the shoreline. Tel. 772-4242 or 772-1205. Lunch and dinner Main dishes are in the $10-$15 range. Take a cab from Frederiksted for $3.50 or from Christiansted for $20.*

Part of a small resort that fronts on a beach fringed with palms and sea grapes, this open-air favorite has a magical friendliness kindled by owner-host Bill Owens. On any excuse, he'll throw a pig roast or barbecue, inviting his hotel guests to bring the side dishes. Order a huge mahi-mahi sandwich with remoulade sauce, roast vegetable pizza, or a vegetarian sandwich made with sun-dried tomatoes and basil bread. Don't miss the tiny, but imaginatively stocked, gift shop.

PICNIC IN PARADISE *at the Carambola Beach Club. Tel. 778-1212. Sunday Brunch is $10-$25; lunch under $10; dinner Main dishes start at $16.50. Hours are 4pm to 9:30pm Wednesday through Sunday.*

In a setting where the rainforest meets the sea, use one of the changing rooms after an afternoon of snorkeling the North Star Wall, then have a sundowner overlooking the Ham's Bluff lighthouse. On cool nights take refuge indoors, where there's a fireplace. Luncheons star salads and classic sandwiches plus omelettes, and a couple of hearty main dishes. At dinner, the chef offers wings du jour and other appetizers followed by special soups and salads, and main dishes such as filet mignon in a three-peppercorn Madeira sauce, Cornish game hen crusted with ginger and roasted garlic, homemade manicotti, curried vegetable stew, and divine seafood concoctions.

SPRAT HALL PLANTATION, *one mile north of Frederiksted off Route 63. Tel. 772-0305. Fixed price meals are in the $25 range not including wines. Cab fare from Frederiksted is $6 each for two. Reservations are essential and should be made between 10am and noon. Seating is 7:30-8pm.*

When you phone for reservations, you'll be given a choice of two or three main dishes and the chef takes it from there, leading you through a West Indian culinary adventure of tannia soup, pork loin with wild orange sauce, local lobster, parrotfish cutlets, freshly baked bread, conch in wine and butter, and the like. The ambience is that of a 1650 greathouse that has seen better days but has not lost its warm hospitality.

STIXX, *in the Pan Am Pavilion between Strand Street and the harbor, Christiansted. Tel. 773-5157. Plan to spend $15-20 for dinner; under $10 for lunch. Open daily, Stixx serves breakfast from 7am and dinner to 10pm. Reservations are recommended for deck seating.*

Combine a memorable view *of* Christiansted Harbor with a jolly mix of divers, sightseers, vacationers, and local working folks in a place that's as perfect for a quick, early breakfast as it is for a leisurely dinner. The shrimp scampi pizza is a favorite or have a buffalo burger, steak, or fresh seafood. The champagne brunch on Sundays is served 10am to 2pm.

THE TERRACE, *in the Buccaneer Resort just east of Christiansted. Tel. 773-2100. Main dishes are priced at $10 to $25. Cab fare from Christiansted is $6 for two.*

The view is sublime, whether you're looking out to sea by day, watching the sunset, or looking out over the twinkling lights of the resort. Start with rock lobster cakes with Creole mayonnaise and grainy mustard, then rum-planked salmon or a simple, tomato-eggplant turnover in puff pastry.

THE WAVES AT CANE BAY, *on Route 80 near Cane Bay Beach. Tel. 778-1805. Reservations are suggested. Dinners are $14 to $16. Cab fare from Christiansted is $16; from Frederiksted, $20.*

Family run by Kevin and Suzanne Ryan and as friendly as a hometown pub, this open-air spot on the edge of the water offers frozen cocktails, fresh fish, steak, pasta, and vegetarian choices all served in generous portions suited to hungry scuba divers.

TIVOLI GARDENS, *Strand Street, Christiansted. Tel. 773-6782. Dinners are in the $20-$25 range. It's open for lunch Monday through Friday and dinner nightly until 9:30pm Reservations are suggested.*

The twinkling lights remind you of the other Tivoli overseas; the cool breezes are provided by its second floor porch location. At lunch have a sandwich or coquille St. Jacques. For dinner there are mushroom caps stuffed with lobster, broiled lobster tail, fresh fish and pastas. End the meal with homemade ice cream or their popular chocolate velvet dessert. The wine list offers more than 100 choices.

TUTTO BENE, *2 Company Street, Christiansted. Tel. 773-5229. Dinner costs in the $20-$25 range. Hours are Monday through Friday 11:30am to 2:30pm and daily 6pm to 10pm, with dessert, drinks and coffees available until closing. Reservations are taken only for parties or five or more.*

Oh, the pastas! When Italians vacation on St. Croix, this is where they eat. The name means "all good" and you can't go wrong with hearty, peasant pastas accompanied with good bread and good olive oil. The bistro offers cozy booths big enough to seat half a dozen. There's a small bar in the corner.

Budget

ALLEY GALLEY, *1100 Strand Street, Christiansted, under the Club Comanche bridge. Tel. 773-5353, or the* **EAST END DELI** *across from the Ball Park in Gallows Bay. Tel. 773-3232. Lunches are under $10. Both locales are open seven days a week from 8am with early closing on Sundays.*

These Caribbean versions of a classic New York deli have piña coladas on tap, duty-free spirits, supersize sandwiches made with Boar's Head lunch meats, and realms of gourmet cheeses, wines, breads, sweets, and salads. Call ahead to ask the specialties of the day, then order a picnic to take away.

JAVA MON, *King's Wharf, Christiansted. Tel. 773-2285, extension 119. Eat for $5-$10. Open Monday through Saturday 7am to 6pm and Sunday 7am to 1pm, the restaurant takes no credit cards.*

This is the place for coffee in an air conditioned oasis with a Happy Days-style soda fountain. Have a cappuccino or ice cream float, order black bean soup for lunch, or order a boxed lunch for your day at the beach. Dinner specials are offered nightly.

MORNING GLORY COFFEE & TEA, *in the Gallows Bay Market Place, Christiansted. Tel. 773-6620. It's open for breakfast and lunch, 7am to 5pm daily except Sundays, when hours are noon to 5pm. Fill up for $5-$10. Credit cards aren't accepted.*

Have coffee at a full espresso bar, or order waffles, New Orleans beignets, muffins and cookies, a zesty granita, or a deli sandwich. Morning Glory has the largest selection of freshly roasted coffees on the island.

SPRAT HALL BEACH RESTAURANT, *a mile north of Frederiksted on Route 63. Tel. 772-5855. Open daily from 9am to 4pm with lunch served 11:30am to 2:30pm, it accepts no credit cards.*

It's nothing fancy, but its location on one of the island's best beaches makes it a regular stop for locals and visitors like. For $2 you can use the changing rooms and showers, then have pumpkin fritters, conch chowder, tannia soup, fish salad, or some other old island specialty from the kitchen of island-born Joyce Hurd. Heartier fare includes ginger curried chicken, fresh fish steak, or a cooked vegetarian plate.

TONY'S STRAND STREET CAFE, *on Strand Street in Christianstead. Tel. 773-8484. Sample local specialties from $4 and up.*

Breakfast is served all day in this Virgin Islands version of a fast foods joint. Grab a sandwich and sixpack to take to the beach, or dine in on local soups, salads, and specialties.

ST. JOHN

Expensive

ASOLARE, *Cruz Bay. Tel. 779-4747. Closed Tuesdays, the restaurant is open daily 5:30pm to 9:30pm. Reservations are recommended.*

Chef Carlos Beccar Varela presides over a kitchen where the specialties are from the Pacific Rim and Asia. Closed for most of 1997 for renovations, it is once again one of the island's premier dining spots.

ELLINGTON'S, *Gallows Point. Tel. 693-8490. Reservations are recommended. Dine for about $40. Open daily, the restaurant serves breakfast, lunch and dinner until 10pm.*

Get here before sunset to enjoy the views of Pillsbury Sound. Linger over cocktails, then pace yourself for an elegant evening featuring one of the best wine cellars on the island. Choose lobster, steak, the catch of the day, or a pasta specialty. Try Beef Ellington, which is prepared for two, or the chicken with honey mustard sauce. Ask about the restaurant's name (it has nothing to do with Duke Ellington) and the Richard Ellington who was an island character in the 1950s.

EQUATOR, *in the Caneel Bay resort. Tel. 776-6111. Reservations are essential for dinner, which is served 7pm to 9pm. Cars aren't permitted past the outer parking lot. Plan to spend $40-$60 for dinner.*

Dressy, elegant, and the picture of attentive service, this restaurant is in the grand, round, stone building that once housed Caneel Bay's Sugar Mill restaurant. The design, with a roof that rises several stories, is a marvel of 18th century engineering. Every dish is a still life painting: plump shrimp in miso, handmade tortillas wrapping tender cabrito, salmon under a drift of fresh herbs, and chocolate mousse garnished with candied Anaheim pepper and composed on a palette of sauces. Choose from a well-stocked cellar of good American and European vintages.

ORDER IN ON ST. JOHN

*When you don't feel like dining out in St. John, call Seamus Mulcare, who operates **Room Service**, Tel. 693-7362. A talented cook and caring caterer, he'll deliver a memorable meal with all the trimmings.*

Moderate

FISH TRAP, *in the Raintree Inn, Cruz Bay. Tel. 693-9994. Have lunch for $10-$15 and dinner for $20-$25. It's open daily except Monday for lunch and dinner. Find it across from the Catholic Church.*

Outdoorsy and informal, this is a popular limin' spot for locals. It's an easy walk from the ferry dock, but just far enough that day-trippers miss it. Chef Aaron chops and steams away in his little galley, shoving out one fine chicken, fish, and pasta dish after another. Try the stir-fry shrimp and vegetables, the black bean tostada with three cheeses or the seafood sampler salad. Save room for one of the dessert specialties made by owner Laura Willis. Her Coconut Cake with Caramel-Rum sauce was featured in Bon Appetit magazine.

LIME INN, *Cruz Bay. Tel. 776-6425 or 779-4199. Two streets up from the ferry, turn right on the one-way street just past the Lutheran Church, walking against traffic. It's open Monday through Friday for lunch, daily except Sunday for dinner 5:30 to 10pm Dine for under $25.*

A latticed garden sets the scene for fish, steak or burgers grilled over an outdoor charcoal grill. Lobster is always a favorite when it's available, and the Wednesday night, all-you-can-eat shrimp is a bonanza for shrimp lovers. Try one of the homemade soups or choose from a long list of salads.

MONGOOSE RESTAURANT, *in Mongoose Junction. Tel. 693-8677. Dine for under $20. Open seven days a week, the restaurant serves breakfast, lunch, and dinner. Reservations are accepted.*

A short walk from the ferry dock is this touristy but convenient bistro. Have a fruity drink then a deli sandwich or a Mediterranean main dish.

SHIPWRECK LANDING, *34 Freeman's Ground, Route 107, Coral Bay. Tel. 693-5640. Main dishes are priced $12 to $16. Hours are 11am to 10pm daily; the bar stays open later. The restaurant is eight miles from Cruz Bay.*

Come here not just for the legendary kitchen overseen by Pat and Dennis Rizzo but for the ride to the east end of beautiful St. John. Start with a rum with lime and coconut milk and a bowl of conch fritters. Then try something Cajun such as blackened grouper or snapper, a burger or a taco salad, chicken tangy with ginger, fish and chips, or a juicy steak. Live entertainment plans several nights a week, with jazz on Sunday. The Rizzos have also taken over the old Don Carlos restaurant location and opened Sera Fina, featuring European cuisine.

SEEING THE SIGHTS
ST. THOMAS

The **Paradise Point Tramway** is not just the island's most spectacular view, its hilltop destination is a favorite hangout for photographing the harbor and watching the sunset. In seven smooth, pleasant minutes you're 700 feet above sea level with a panoramic view of the harbor. Board the tram, off Long Bay Road just above Wendy's, *Tel. 774-9809.* Fare for adults is $10, children $5. Once at the top you can shop for souvenirs, order a drink, or nosh on hot dogs, burgers or ribs.

Seven Arches Museum is up Government Hill at Freeway Alley and King Street, *Tel. 774-9295.* Once the home of a Danish craftsman, it's furnished in antiques that offer a glimpse of colonial times. The $5 donation includes a guided tour and a drink in the walled, flower-filled garden. Hours are daily except Sunday and Monday 10am to 3pm.

Dive 90 feet deep to see the fish and coral off St. Thomas aboard the **Atlantis submarine**. During the two-hour tour you'll leave from Havensight Mall next to Yacht Haven Marine, then board an air conditioned submarine for a one-hour voyage that covers more than 1 1/2-miles of sea bottom. The dive can also be combined with a flightseeing seaplane tour, *Tel. 777-4491 or 776-5650* or, from the U.S., *800/253-0493*. **Coral World**, an outstanding water attraction that was destroyed by Hurricane Marilyn, is being restored. While you're on the island, *call 774-2955* for an update.

Allow at least half a day at **Mountain Top**, *Tel. 774-2400*, elevation 1,500 feet, for a look at tropical birds, an aquarium filled with tropical fish, a Caribbean village, and a museum of artifacts from pre-Columbian days through the swashbuckling pirate era. From Charlotte Amalie, take Route 30 (Veteran's Drive), to Mafolie Road (30 North) and turn left onto Route 33. Bear left at the "Y" in front of Sib's and follow the road to Mountain Top, which is said to be the home of the original banana daiquiri.

Take a self-guided tour of **Estate St. Peter Greathouse** in the volcanic hills of St. Thomas, *Tel. 774-4999*. From the 1000-foot-high observation deck on a clear day you can see 20 other islands. Sip punch while exploring the lush botanical gardens. It's open daily 9am to 5pm. From Charlotte Amalie, take Route 40 (Solberg Road).

ST. CROIX

To take a walking tour of Christiansted start at the **Old Scalehouse**, built in 1856 and cross to **Fort Christiansvaern**, 1738, which has dungeons and cannons. It's open every day, 8am to 5pm Look across the water to Protestant Cay, called that because Protestants, barred from the Catholic cemetery, were buried here. Cross Hospital Street and look at the **Steeple Building**, built as a Lutheran Church in 1735 and now a must-see **museum** of local history, *Tel. 773-1460*. It's open Monday through Friday, 9:30am to 3pm, with a one-hour closing from noon to 1pm.

Across the way, note the West Indian & Guinea Company Warehouse, built 1749. It was the site of slave auctions. It's now a post office and has rest rooms if you need some by now.

Walk up Company Street to the 18th century **Apothecary Hall**, then onto the Market Square and to Prince Street where Holy Cross Catholic Church dates to 1828. Heading down Prince Street to King, turn right to see the **Pentheny Building**, built as a private mansion in the 18th century. Walking east on King Street you'll see the library and a Lutheran Church dating to 1740. Across the street, **Government House** is a superb example of Danish colonial style dating to 1747.

To take a walking tour of **Frederiksted**, start at **Fort Frederik**, *Tel. 772-2021*, which dates to 1750. Its museum is good but it overemphasizes hurricane history when most visitors, we'd guess, are more interested in swashbuckling, battles, and pirates. Across the street see the **Old Customs House**, built in the 1700s and added to in the 1800s. It was here that local sugar was weighed for shipment. Continuing east on Strand Street, enjoy a pretty promenade of neo-classical and Victorian buildings. Turn back to King Cross Street and go two blocks inland to Old Apothecary Hall, another in the time-warp buildings that the visitor can ponder while imagining this as a swirling center of 17th century trade.

HARBOR NIGHT

Every other Friday is Harbor Night at the pier in Frederiksted when the docking of a major cruise ship is celebrated with a street party attended by cruisers, locals, and land-based tourists galore. Stroll the blocked-off streets to sample homemade foods and buy local crafts. Explore the old fort, which is open and well lighted. Then dance to live music until midnight.

Asking as you go if necessary, move on to the Benjamin House on Queen Street. It's an elegant townhouse with a wrought iron balcony. Staying on King Cross to **St. Paul's Anglican Church**, built in 1812, you'll pass the old cemetery. Going west now to Market Street, you'll see **St. Patrick's Catholic Church** and rectory, with a cemetery dating to the 18th century.

Turn back towards the sea on Market Street, passing the old Market Square, once the heart of the city. On King Street you'll see more historic buildings. Note the **Flemming Building** on the corner of King and **Custom House**. It was built from dismantled sugar factory chimneys.

St. George Village Botanical Garden is not only a brilliant garden stuffed with greenery and good smells, it is a National Historic District. Built on the site of an Arawak village that became a Danish community, it once contained a rum factory, greathouse, lime kiln, cemetery, and aqueduct. Stroll through orchids, ferns, an orchard of tropical trees, a cactus garden, galleries, stony ruins, and a gift shop. It's just off Route 70, east of West Airport Road, Route 64; *Tel. 692-2874* for hours, which vary seasonally. Admission is $5.

Whim Plantation on Route 70 near Frederiksted is a complete plantation with a superbly restored greathouse that offers tours led by elderly docents, some of whom actually worked here years ago. Thelma Clarke, now in her 70s, showed us the grand piano dating to 1866, the chairs donated by island resident Victor Borge, 18th century furnishings, and the famous planter's chair that served as a combination chair and boot jack. Have a sugary piece of Johnny Cake, browse the gift shop, and allow an hour or two for roaming the grounds to get the true, tropical flavor of this ancient place. For information, *Tel. 772-0598*. Admission is $5 adults and $1 for children. In summer, Whim is closed on Sundays. Tours of the **Cruzan Rum Distillery** can be boring for little ones, but grownups like the samples. Admission is charged. For information, call the tourist bureau at *Tel. 772-0357*.

See the **St. Croix Aquarium** on the waterfront in Frederiksted, *Tel. 772-1345,* and try to link up with one of the educational snorkel trips offered. The aquarium is open Wednesday through Sunday, 11am to 4pm.

One of the island's best nature preserves is in **Salt River Bay National Historic Park and Ecological Preserve**, which you can find on Route 751 off Route 75. Once the site of Amerindian ceremonies and the spot where Christopher Columbus is said to have first landed, it is the home of one of the largest mangrove forests in the Virgins. The birdlife is abundant and varied but otherwise there are no facilities at present.

While you're out on the island, you may also want to try running up **The Beast**, also known as Mount Eagle. It's the island's highest point, at 1,650 feet, found on Route 69. When you see the words "The Beast" in the pavement you know you have arrived. Each year it's the scene of the grueling American Paradise Triathlon.

ST. JOHN

Since much of St. John is **national park** land, explorations should begin at the National Park Service Visitors Center on North Shore Road in Cruz Bay, *Tel. 776-6201*. Get maps and instructions for the many hiking trails and snorkeling sites including ranger-led hikes and swims. It's a real plus to go with guides or guidance not just because of the expert narration but because rangers often provide the necessary equipment or pick-up/drop-off at a remote site.

The whole island is peppered with ancient ruins, some barely identifiable and others as exciting as **Reef Bay Great House**, which was inhabited as late as the 1950s when the lady of the house was murdered. Various stabs have been made at restoring the house, so we don't know what condition it will be in when you get there, but the park service tends to it as funds are available.

Also administered by the park service is **Annaberg Plantation**, an 18th century sugar mill complex that has been partially restored. The views are spectacular, the ruins extensive, the nature watching excellent. Sometimes local artisans set up their shops in the plantation to enrich the scene. It's on Leinster Bay off the North Shore Road. For serious explorations, rent a four-wheel-drive and snoop into every road you see. Most will lead you either to a great beach or a great view.

NIGHTLIFE & ENTERTAINMENT
ST. CROIX

Friday nights at the **HIBISCUS BEACH HOTEL**, *Tel. 773-4042*, feature a complete dinner package with soup, salad, a choice of four entrees and all the trimmings plus music and dance performed by Rico and the All Stars and the Caribbean Dance Company. The evening costs $35, or pay $15 for the show alone.

BLUE MOON on the waterfront at Frederiksted, is the place for jazz, coffee, nursing a rum drink or noshing on bistro food. It's open Tuesday through Friday for lunch, Tuesday through Saturday for lunch and dinner until 10pm and Sunday for dinner until 9:30.

THE SALOON just off Strand Street on Market, a block south of the pier in Frederiksted is not only air conditioned but nearly smokeless thanks to special smoke extractors. Or, sit outdoors. Live entertainment starts at 9pm. Darts start at 7:30 on Tuesday and Wednesday. There's plenty of food, free popcorn, a big beer menu, and the usual margaritas and coladas.

At the **BUCCANEER HOTEL**, *Tel. 773-2100*, listen to a steel band on Sunday, calypso/reggae on Friday nights, and jazz on Saturday. **CHENAY BAY**, *Tel. 773-2918*, has a steel band from 7pm on Saturday; **HOTEL ON THE CAY** features a steel band Thursday through Monday 5pm to 9pm. Guitar and song start Thursday through Sunday at 7pm at **CHEESEBUR-GERS IN PARADISE** and nightly at **TIVOLI GARDENS**.

For crab races, an old wagering favorite since the days of the buccaneers, be at **KING'S LANDING YACHT CLUB** Monday at 5:30pm or **STIXX** on Fridays at 5:30pm. For darts, try **KING'S LANDING**

SUPPORT YOUR LOCAL BEER

*St. Croix' own beer, **Santa Cruz**, is brewed near Frederiksted and offered in draft or long necks. At press time, plans for the brewery include a museum, restaurant, gift shop and a theater where the Caribbean Dance Company will perform. Other brews on the Virgin Islands include: **Blackbeard's Ale** and **Captain Kidd's Golden Ale**; in the East End of St. Thomas, Paddy O'Furniture's Irish Brew Pub features four homebrews, including Pitbull Irish Stout made with four different malts.*

YACHT CLUB on Sunday evenings or **THE SALOON** on Tuesdays and Wednesdays from 7:30.

In 1997, laws were enacted that will result in the development of casinos on St. Croix. St. Croix also passed a special law that allows cruise ships to open their casinos while in port. Aboard most cruises you'll find shops and casinos closed in port.

ST. THOMAS

One of the best amphitheaters in the Caribbean for the presentation of concerts and broadway shows is the **REICHHOLD CENTER FOR THE ARTS** in St. Thomas. Check local newspapers while you're here to see if anything is playing. It could be a star or show of international importance. Also check your hotel's Dining/Nightlife Channel 4 for the latest buzz.

Other places include:

HARD ROCK CAFE, *on the waterfront at International Plaza in Charlotte Amalie, Tel. 777-5555.*

Open all day and half the night for noshing and listening among a fortune in rock memorabilia.

IGGIE'S, *in the Bolongo Lime Tree Resort, Tel. 776-4770.*

A good-times lounge for sing alongs and watching sports on the big screen. Dine informally, then plug into showtime at 9pm. On Wednesdays there's a Carnival buffet with steel band music and a limbo show. The resort also has restaurants and a disco.

TURTLE ROCK BAR, *in the Wyndham Sugar Bay Resort, Smith Bay, Tel. 777-7100.*

Not far from Red Hook, this resort bar has a different drawing card every night. It could be live performances, karaoke, dancing, or reggae, If you want to eat here, find a good selection of dishes in the resort's Mangrove Restaurant. There's no cover charge in the bar. The fun starts with Happy Hour 4 to 6pm and continues to closing, which could be any time depending on the crowd.

ST. JOHN

The best bet for dining and nightlife on St. John is to go to downtown Cruz Bay and follow the sound of music.

MOCKO JUMBIES

*A Virgin Islands traditional folk entertainment is **Mocko Jumbies**, stilt dancers in bright costumes who perform at every Carnival and parade. Mocko Jumbie dolls are catching on as collectible crafts.*

SPORTS & RECREATION
ALL VIRGIN ISLANDS

Yacht brokers who can find the right boat and crew for your sailing vacation include:
- **Admiralty Yacht Vacations**, *Tel. 800/544-0493*
- **Bajor Yacht Charters**, *Tel. 800/524-8292*
- **Easy Adventures**, *Tel. 800/524-2027*
- **Island Yachts**, *Tel. 800/524-2019*
- **Proper Yachts St. John**, *Tel. 776-6256*
- **Regency Yacht Vacations**, *Tel. 800/524-7676*
- **Stewart Yacht Charters**, *Tel. 800/432-6118*
- **Virgin Islands Charter YachtLeague**, *Tel. 800/524-2061*
- **Virgin Islands Power Yacht Charters**, *Tel. 800/524-2015*

Book anything from a brief sunset or snorkeling sail to a week-long charter on which you'll share the storybook life of a crew, usually husband and wife, who live aboard the boat. The variety of boats and their comforts is enormous, so allow plenty of time for choosing and booking. Power and sailboats accommodating two to 20 people charter for $1,200 to $1,500 per person for seven nights, including food, drinks, sightseeing, and watersports. Some of the larger boats even come with a helicopter and masseur! You can also book a package that combines yachting and hotel stays; for more information, *Tel. 776-5950 locally or, in the U.S., Tel. 800/ 524-7676 or 401/848-5599.*

ST. THOMAS
Beaches

Sailboarders and snorkelers who have their own equipment like **Bluebeard's Beach** at the end of Bluebeard's Road, Route 322, which branches off Route 30 near Red Hook. Bring your own gear; no rentals are available here. **Coki Beach** is favored for its view of Thatch Key and the Leeward Passage. The beach has bathrooms, a food stand, and snorkel gear for rent. It's on the northeast Coast. Also on the north shore, just west of Magens Bay, is **Hull Bay**, a popular anchorage for local fishermen. Waters along the western tip can be frisky, which makes it popular with surfers when the surf's up, but usually the waters are calm and clear. The bay has a restaurant.

East of downtown, next to Morningstar Beach, is **Limetree Beach**, a picture-perfect beach on a natural cove. Come to walk the sands and photograph iguanas. **Magens Bay**, which is a public park owned by the island, has been named in top-ten lists of beautiful beaches. Admission of $1 per car, $1 per adult, and 25 cents per child gains access to covered picnic tables, showers, dressing rooms, boutique, snack bar, sailboat rentals, and snorkel rental. It's on the north shore at the end of Route 35.

Morningstar Beach is a busy, commercial place with gear and lounge chair rentals, bars, boardsailer instruction, and a good view of boats saiing past the east point of the harbor. It's near town at Marriott's Frenchman's Reef Beach Resort. **Sapphire Beach** on the east end of the island is enjoyed by snorkelers and boardsailers. It has a marina, restaurants, and a dive shop that rents equipment.

Boating

Powerboat Rentals are available from **Nauti Nymph**, *Tel. 775-5066.* Power, sail, and sportfishing charters are available from **The Charterboat Center** at Piccola Marina in Red Hook, *Tel. 775-7990 or 800/866-5714.* Speedy Mako and Scarab powerboats for exploring or skiing are rented through **See and Ski** at American Yacht Harbor, Red Hook, *Tel. 775-6265.*

Ocean Runner Powerboat Rentals at Cruz Bay, *Tel. 693-8809*, offers Hydrasports boats from 22 to 25 feet.

Diving

The **St. Thomas Diving Club** on Bolongo Bay is your key to scuba diving St. Thomas. It's a five-star PADI facility, *Tel. 776-2381, Fax 777-3232; toll-free 800/LETS DIVE.*

Golf

Golfing is free at the nine-hole **University of the Virgin Islands** but, to most people, golf means **Mahogany Run**, *Tel. 775-5000 or 800/253-7103,* the fabulous Fazio-designed course overlooking the Atlantic. It's an 18-hole, championship, 6,033-yard, par 70 course feared and famous for its "devil's triangle" of devious holes.

Sea Kayaking

Paddle through unspoiled wetlands and mangrove swamps with **Virgin Island Ecotours**, *Tel. 340/773-2155 or 777-6200.*

Submarine Exploration

Atlantis Submarine operates out of Building VI, bay 1, in the Havensight Mall, *Tel. 776-5650 or 800/253-0493.* One-hour voyages explore the underwater mysteries of St. Thomas to a depth of 90 feet. Reservations are essential. The trip costs about $70.

ST. JOHN

Beaches

Caneel Bay can be reached through the famous resort of the same name, but it's also popular with boaters who anchor off its famous shores. If you arrive by land, stop at the front desk for a day visitor guide. If you arrive by boat, don't set so much as a toe above the high tide line or you are intruding on private, and very exclusive, property. The bay is on the north shore, close to Cruz Bay.

Hawksnest Bay on the north shore of the island near Cruz Bay is smaller and more quiet than Trunk Bay, so it's popular with locals. Changing facilities are available. The west side of the beach is part of Caneel Bay Resort. Again, don't trespass.

Trunk Bay is famed for its underwater snorkeling trail. The beach is picture-perfect with its talcum sands and luxuriant fringe of trees and shrubs. There's a place to change, and a small shop. If you'd like more advanced snorkeling, ask at the national park about a snorkel tour to Flanagan's Cay off the southeast coast.

Cinnamon Bay at the campground in the national park offers great snorkeling in clear waters, a store, restaurant, watersport rentals, and a fine sand beach.

Fishing

To find a fishing guide, charter boat rental, tackle, or other connections, call the island information center at *Tel. 776- 6922.*

Diving

Call **Water Sports of all Sorts**, *Tel. 776-6850,* for scuba dives. **Low Key**, *Tel. 800/835-8999 or Tel. 693-8999,* is located at Wharfside Village offering equipment, dives, parasailing, kayaking, and underwater photo services.

Hiking

Virgin Islands National Park is crisscrossed with miles of hiking trails, historic ruins, hills and dales, forests and flowers. When leaving the ferry dock, keep walking left and you'll come to a National Park Service information office.

Since most of St. John is part of the Park, its hiking trails are abundant and well mapped. You can go it alone or join one of the guided walks with an environmentalist who can point out natural features you might miss on your own. Notices of upcoming hikes are posted at the interpretive center of the National Park.

Horseback Riding
Ride a horse or donkey through the **Virgin Islands National Park**, which covers most of St. John, *Tel. 340/693-5161.*

Underwater Exploration
Atlantis Submarine, based in St. Thomas, operates out of Cruz Bay one day a week, *Tel. 776-5650.*

ST. CROIX
Beaches
Let your hotel host suggest a new beach every day according to winds and sea conditions, keeping in mind that you're on your own without lifeguards. West of Christiansted, **Salt River Bay**, where Columbus first landed, offers a beach with frisky winds and waves, and no facilities. Continue along the North Shore Road to **Cane Bay Beach** and **Davis Bay Beach**, which offer excellent snorkeling about 100 feet off out. From Christiansted, take the ferry to the Hotel on the Cay, which has a beach, restaurant, and bar.

West of town, **Estate Golden Rock** has a beach a fifth of a mile long; **The Buccaneer** on Route 82 charges admission and rents beach chairs on its beach, which has food and drinks. The beach at **Green Cay** is remote and lovely, reached by rental boat from Green Cay Marina. Also east of town watch for Reef Condominiums and the **Reef Beach** opposite them, which is popular with board sailors. Off Route 60, find **Grapetree Beach** where seagrapes offer shade and a concession offers snorkel and sailboard rentals, drinks, food, and rest rooms.

Boating & Snorkeling
A trip to **Buck Island Reef National Monument**, which lies six miles from Christiansted, is a must. Skippers provide snorkel gear. Call **Llewellyn's Charter**, *Tel. 773-9027* or **Terero II**, *Tel. 773-3161 or 773-4041.* Personal watercraft and kayaks can be rented at **St. Croix Water Sports Center**, *Tel. 773-7060.* Sails, trips to Buck Island, big game fishing, diving, windsurfing, parasailing and non-motorized watersports are available at Cutlass Cove Beach behind The Mermaid restaurant. It's open daily 9am to 5pm. *Call extension 741 at the Buccaneer, Tel. 773-2100.*

Bicycling
Ride mountain bikes over the rolling hills with **St. Croix Bike & Tours**, *Tel. 340/773-5004.* You'll climb Creque Dam Road if you're up to it, and explore the rain forest. Less hardy bikers can stay on flatter lands on a seashore tour to Hams Bluff.

Golf

All three golf courses offer instruction and equipment rental. The 18-hole course at **Carambola Golf Club**, *Tel. 778-5638*, was designed by Robert Trent Jones and has a Gold Medal Award from Golf Magazine. **Buccaneer Golf Course**, *Tel. 773-2100,* is a pretty 18-hole course on the seaside. A nine-hole course is on the east end of the island at **The Reef**, *Tel. 773-8844.*

Hiking

Link up with the **St. Croix Environmental Association**, *Tel. 773-1989,* for serious hiking or **Take-a-Hike**, *Tel. 778-6997,* for guided walks of historic areas. Hikers will enjoy Salt River National Park, Caledonia Valley, and Estates Mount Washington and Butler Bay. Both groups require reservations. It's always a plus to go with a guide who can point out unique plants or tell you local names for familiar tropicals.

Identify catch-and-keep, monkey-don't-climb, nothing-nut, clashie melashie, cock-a-locka, and other shrubs and flowers. If you have a chance, try wild fruits such as genip (also spelled gneep), soursop, and the milky, sweet sugar apple.

Horseback Riding

Ride horseback across strands of white sand through the surf with **Paul and Jill's Equestrian Stables**, *Tel. 340/772-2880.*

Scuba Diving

Hang around the **Aqua-Lounge Club** to learn about the underwater scene. Even the bartenders are divers, so everyone decompresses here from 5-7pm. Every night something new is sparking, such as bring-your-catch barbecue night, rap sessions, signups for dive buddies, and night dives. Located in an old Danish warehouse with easy access from King Street or the boardwalk, the air conditioned club offers free parking in the Anchor Inn lot. It's at 58A King Street, *Tel. 773-0163.*

Dive operators offering scuba trips, instruction, refills and gear include:
- **Dive Experience**, *Tel. 773-3307*
- **Cane Bay Dive Shop**, *Tel. 773-9913 or 772-0715 or toll-free 800/338-3843*
- **Cruzan Divers**, *Tel. 772-3701 or toll-free 800/352-0107*
- **Anchor Dive Center**, *Tel. 778-1522 or 800/532-DIVE*
- **V.I. Divers**, *Tel. 773-6045 or 800/544-5911*

Snorkeling

Guided snorkel trips are offered by the **St. Croix Aquarium and Marine Education Center**, *Tel. 772-1345.*

Tennis

In addition to the many courts at resorts, St. Croix has public courts at **D.C. Canegata Park** in Christiansted and **Fort Frederik Park** in Frederiksted.

SHOPPING

Even though Americans are still on American territory, customs limits must be observed and luggage is subject to search, either before leaving the islands or when changing planes in San Juan. Any purchases that total more than $1200 are subject to a five per cent tax and amounts over $2200 are subject to regular duty charges, even if you bought "duty free" in the islands. Island-made products in any amount are duty free, but be sure to get a receipt for any purchase of more than $25. In addition, you can ship home gifts of up to $100 per day.

Each U.S. resident over age 21 can bring back six bottles of liquor duty free as long as one of them is made in the U.S. Virgin Islands. Remember that plants and farm products can't be brought to the mainland, nor can protected products such as turtle shell and black coral. Customs questions? Locally, call *Tel. 773-5650.*

ST. THOMAS

A popular cruise ship stop, St. Thomas is famed for stores packed with crystal, china, watches, jewels, cameras, perfumes, and liquors sold tax free. Cruise passengers come ashore clutching the maps and discount coupons given to them on board and swarm into shops whose hours are determined by when ships are in port. When they are, you can shop on Sunday mornings. Otherwise, plan to shop the other six days of the week.

An open-air market along the waterfront sells mostly tee shirts, sleazy · rayon sarongs, and claptrap. Some booths are piled high with brand name leather goods, which may or may not be authentic, but nothing bears a price tag so you're on your own to make a deal. Even in the best shops we saw very few price tags, so St. Thomas is a place for shoppers who know exactly what model watch or camera, what carat jewel, or what brand perfume they want, and will recognize a good buy when they see it. If you're just browsing, you'll have to ask about prices one piece at a time.

In downtown Charlotte Amalie, most shops are along **Main Street** (Dronnigens Gade) and the waterfront, and on the narrow alleys that run between them. East of downtown nearer the cruise ships docks, **Havensight Mall** also has prestige shops such as Gucci, Little Switzerland, A.H. Riise, and Columbia Emeralds International as well as a pharmacy, beauty salon, and bank. **Ritalini Shoe Boutique** there, *Tel. 776-3313,* has thousands of pairs of Italian shoes in women's sizes 4 to 12, as well as Bruno Magli shoes for men. After you get home, they'll ship additional pairs at duty-free prices.

Look for such shopping meccas as:

Hibiscus Alley along Main Street has a **Coach**, **Cardow's Diamond Center**, **Local Color** for accessories, and the **West Indies Coffee Company** as well as a store selling memorabilia connected with the Virgin Island's America's Cup Challenge, which will be sailed in the year 2000. **Lover's Lane** carries everything from exotic erotica to bridal and bath boutique items. It's on the waterfront at the corner of Raadets Gade, upstairs. **Palm Passage** is, between Main Street and the waterfront. Its stores include **Fendi**, **Nicole Miller**, **Diesel Jeans**, **MCM**, and **Versace**. **Scandinavian Center** in the Havensight Mall has handmade products from Scandinavia including a complete line of Royal Copenhagen, Georg Jensen silver and precious gems. The center also has an art gallery filled with Caribbean and Danish scenes.

Cosmopolitan on the waterfront has Bally, Sperry Topsider, Sebago and other famous name shoes plus international sportswear brands. **Drake's Passage Mall** in the historic district is the only air conditioned mall downtown. Shops sell leather foods, clothing souvenirs, sweets, and clothing. If you're been inspired by the colonial mahogany furniture of the islands, you can buy greathouse furnishings at **Mahogany Island Style** in Al Cohen's Plaza on Route 38. Poster beds, armoires and planter's chairs are shown; international art works and accessories are also sold. On Raphune Hill, Route 38, look for **Mango Tango Art Gallery** for originals, limited edition prints, and gifts. It's open daily 9am to 5:30pm, Sundays 10am to 1pm.

Located downtown and around the island are such standout jewelry stores as **Amsterdam Sauer**, **Cardow**, **Little Switzerland**, **Diamonds in Paradise**, **Diamonds International**, and **Columbian Emeralds International**. For loose diamonds and jewelry at rock bottom prices, check out the **Diamonds International Liquidation Center** at the waterfront. At Red Hook, **Doucet Stanton Jewelers** is a family-owned business featuring handmade Scandinavian silver pieces as well as local art. It's in **American Yacht Harbor** Building C2-1.

If you need ordinary supplies at ordinary prices, St. Thomas has a **K-mart** in Tutu Park Mall, a ten-minute cab ride from the docks. Our favorite shopping haunt is a 25-stall arts and crafts mall opposite the **Renaissance Grand Beach Resort** in Smith Bay. Local vendors display their home-made wares.

Since every American over age 21 can take back five fifths of liquor or six fifths if the liquor is produced in the U.S.V.I., it's best to get island brews such as Cruzan Rum, Havensight Liqueur, Chococo, Clipper Spiced Rum, Old St. Croix, Estate Diamond, and Southern Comfort.

Exemptions apply only on purchases made in the U.S.V.I. and not to the same brands bought aboard ship.

ST. CROIX

King's Alley, the brightest diamond in **Christiansted's** shopping tiara, re-opened in 1996 more brilliant than ever before. In one spot downtown, find twelve luxury hotel suites furnished in Danish West Indian style, *Tel. 340/773-0103*, plus restaurants including a Thai and a chop house, and 20 upscale shops. Its smaller sister in Frederiksted runs from Strand Street to King Street, handy to the pier. The hotel here, by the way, is right next to the seaplane pier so it's the perfect place to stay if you're just making a quick overnight trip to St. Croix.

The shopping game in St. Croix is to choose a **Crucian bracelet**. The unique designs rely on a hook or button latch. Each jeweler has its own designs in gold or sterling and some people make a collection of as many different models as they can find. Also featured here is the Caribbean gemstone *larimar*, a blue stone found only in the islands. **Baci** on Company Street in Christiansted, specializes in jewelry made from ancient coins.

Also in Christiansted is **Charisma** in the Pan Am Pavilion, specializing in local sarong designs known as the Cruzan Wrap. For conventional clothing in cool, tropical linens and cottons, try **Strand Street Clothing** on Strand Street, Christiansted.

For local artwork, visit an **artists' cooperative** in the Pentheny Building (ask directions from King's Alley.) It's closed Sunday and Wednesday. Because the work is shown and sold by the artists themselves, prices are lower than those in galleries.

ST. JOHN

It's fun to shop in little St. John because few here try to compete with the glitzy stores of St. Thomas. Stores feature folk arts, resort wear, crafts, seashells, custom jewelry, unusual gifts, and locally made foods and spice blends. Look for books published by the **American Paradise Publishing Company**, which was founded by local mariner "Cap'n Fatty" Goodlander. His guides, cookbooks, and humor books are authentic and readable. Ask for them in local book and gift shops. Another St. John specialty is pottery featuring petroglyph motifs inspired by Arawak drawings.

It's worth a day trip to St. John on the ferry to shop **Wharfside Village**, **Mongoose Junction**, **Pink Papaya Gallery** in the Lemon Tree Mall behind the Chase Bank, and other shops, all of them a stone's throw from the ferry dock.

Columbian Emeralds, *Tel. 776-6007* has a shop in Mongoose Junction and so does Island Galleria, *Tel. 779-4644* with its crystals, perfumes, and collectibles.

EXCURSIONS & DAY TRIPS

ST. CROIX

Sweeny Toussaint, manager of **St. Croix Safari Tours**, *Tel. 773-9561 or 800/524-2026*, is a knowledgeable, attentive, and personable guide. He can arrange everything from airport transfer to sightseeing, car rental, and watersports. For a mystery trip out of St. Croix complete with lunch and champagne, let **Bohlke International Airways** set the pace, *Tel. 778-9177*. The line flies to St. Thomas, St. John, the British Virgins, St. Barts, or Puerto Rico.

Buck Island National Monument is St. Croix' most meaningful day trip. Sail, hike, snorkel, have a beach barbecue, or scuba dive. The uninhabited island is 6,000 feet long and half a mile wide, rising to 340 feel above sea level. It lies only one and a half miles off the northeast coast of St. Croix. Endangered species nesting here include the hawksbill turtle and brown pelican as well as leatherback and green sea turtles. On land, walk marked trails across the island through giant tamarind trees, hillsides covered with guinea grass, and lowland beaches. In the water, snorkel over a marine wonderland of elkhorn coral, brilliant sea gardens, and schools of darting fish. A marked underwater trail describes the sights.

Mile Mark Watersports offers dive expenditions, *Tel. 773-2628 or 773-3434*. Boats can be rented in Christiansted and half a dozen outfitters also offer half-and full-day excursions with time allowed in and out of the water. Snorkel gear is provided, *Tel. 773-1460*.

To take a self-guided driving tour, take Hospital Street out of Christiansted to East End road, Route 82 and note Gallows Bay on your left. Until recent years it was a busy port, now a good place for shopping and dining. Continuing on Route 82, pass the family-owned **Buccaneer** with its restaurants and 18-hole golf course and Green Cay Marina. Bear left, staying on Route 82 and keep a sharp eye for nesting blue heron. You'll pass **Chenay Bay, Coakley Bay**, the famous **Duggan's Reef Restaurant** and come to **the St. Croix Yacht Club**. Look up to your right to see a castle, which is privately owned. Ask locals about its story.

Point Udall is the easternmost point under the United States flag, but don't try to drive to the beach. Roads wash out regularly and, at press time, are impassable. From here, take Route 82 back to Christiansted or go south on Route 60 along the coast. Stay along the water and you won't get lost as you pass **Great Salt Pond** with its waterfowl. Turning left at the

Airport market, Route 624 and left on Route 62, you'll continue along the south shore past farm fields filled with big Senepol cattle. The breed was developed on St. Croix. To return to Christiansted, turn right on Route 70, locally called Centerline Road, where most of the shopping centers, banks and other everyday commercial centers are found.

To take a tour of the north and west of St. Croix through the radically different terrain of the rain forest, start early in the day because there are many stops you'll want to make along the way. Take Route 75 out of Christiansted and turn right on Route 80. At the Salt River Marina sign turn right to the **Salt River National Park and Ecological Preserve**. See the place where Columbus is said to landed in 1493. Take time to look for birds, then return ro Route 80 and head west on the scenic North Shore Road with its views of the other islands in the hazy distance. At LaValle village, turn right to **Cane Bay Beach** for a swim, then stay on Route 80 to Route 69. Turn left and climb a steep hill leading to a view of Carambola. Route 76, Mahogany Road, leads to a stone quarry. On your left, watch for **LEAP**, an environmental project where items made from local woods are sold.

At Route 63, turn right and follow the shore road to **Sprat Hall Plantation**, an ancient greathouse that is now a hotel. Call ahead if you want to arrange a hike, meal, or horseback ride. Continuing along Butler Bay you'll pass the Coast Guard station and continue to Frederiksted with its shopping and dining. Leave town on Route 70, stopping **at Whim Plantation**, the **botanical gardens**, and the **rum distillery** on Route 64. Return to Christiansted via Route 66.

ST. THOMAS

Sail the *Lady Lynsey* out of the Ritz-Carlton on half day, all day, and sunset sails, *Tel. 775-3333*. Aboard the all-day sail and snorkeling expedition, you'll visit St. John or Jost Van Dyke and will be served a continental breakfast and gourmet buffet luncheon for $135-$145. A half day sail including continental breakfast (on the morning sail) and lunch costs $85 per person. The Sunset Sail is out for two hours and includes fruit, fresh vegetables, and finger sandwiches for $45.

Excursions from St. Thomas to the British Virgin Islands including the famous **The Baths** on Virgin Gorda and the hiking trails of Jost Van Dyke are available through:
• **Limnos Charters**, *Tel. 775-3203*
• **Stormy Petrel and Pirate's Penny**, *Tel. 775-7990 or 800/866-5714*
• **High Performance Charters**, *Tel. 777-7545*

ST. JOHN

When you arrive at the ferry dock in **Cruz Bay** you'll be met by nattering crowds of drivers, all vying for your sightseeing business. Even if you plan later to take off on your own scooter or rental car, take at least a short tour with one of these guides if only for the theater alone. Each driver has his own "shtick," each jitney its own decorations.

One "must-see" is **Annaberg Sugar Mill**, administered by the National Park Service, *Tel. 776-6201*. More than 140 windmill ruins dot St. Croix, but St. John had only five, all of them built between 1740 and 1840. The site is a knockout, with views far out to sea. Although it was farmed well into the 20th century, its use as a sugar plantation died with the freeing of Danish West Indies slaves in 1848. Take a half-hour, self-guided walking tour of the slave quarters, village, windmill, and gardens. To reach the site, take the North Shore Road, about five miles east from Cruz Bay.

If possible, be on St. John the last Saturday of the month when "St. John Saturdays" feature kite flying, arts and crafts, local musicians, and booths selling island foods.

PRACTICAL INFORMATION

Area Code: 340

American Express: *Tel. 774-1855*

ATM: on St. Croix, an ATM is found in the Banco Popular in the Sunny Isles Shopping Center. At St. Thomas find an ATM at the airport and at banks downtown and in shopping centers. Banks on the island include Banco Popular, Chase Manhattan, Citibank, First Federal Savings, First Virgin Islands Federal Savings, and ScotiaBank. A Chase Manhattan branch is at Cruz Bay, St. John.

Crime: when you're going to the beach, leave valuables in the hotel safe and not in the car, not even in a locked trunk. Take the same precautions you would at home.

Current: electrical service is the same as on the United States mainland.

Currency is the United States dollar.

Emergencies:, dial 911 for police, fire, and ambulance. .

Holidays: banks and government offices are closed on most of the same holidays celebrated on the mainland including New Year's Day and Christmas plus, Boxing Day, Friendship Day on October 13, and Thanksgiving, which is in late October.

Immigration: you don't need proof of citizenship to get into the Virgin Islands, but may need it on returning to the United States. Canadians need proof of citizenship such as a birth certificate or passport. Britons need a passport.

Locals: are called Cruzans if from St. Croix.

Pharmacies: in St. Thomas include the Sunrise Pharmacy, Red Hook, *Tel. 775-6600*; K-Mart in the Tutu Park Mall, *Tel. 777-3854*. On St. Croix, People's Drug Store in Christiansted, *Tel. 778-7355* and the pharmacy in the Sunny Isles Shopping Center, *Tel. 778-5537*. In Frederiksted, D&D Apothecary,*Tel. 776-6353*. In Cruz Bay, St. John, St. John Drug Center, *Tel. 776-6353*. The hospital in St. Croix is in Christiansted, *Tel. 778-6311*. The hospital in St. Thomas is in Sugar Estate, *Tel. 776-8311* and it has a 24-hour emergency room. In St. John, an emergency medical technician is on call at *Tel. 776-6222*. For fastest help, ask at the hotel's front desk for the names of nearby doctors, clinics, and drug stores.

Postage: the familiar American eagle delivers the mail in the U.S. Virgin Islands and U.S. postage stamps are used. No additional postage is required to send letters and post cards to the mainland.

Taxes: there's a departure tax but it's added to your airplane ticket, so you don't have to stand in line and pay it separately as is common on other islands. Hotel bills are plus eight per cent tax. There is no sales tax.

Tourism information: *Tel. 800/372-8784 or 340/774-8784*. In Canada, *Tel. 416/233-1414*. Or write the U.S. Virgin Islands Department of Tourism, *Box 6400, St. Thomas VI 00804*. Visitor information offices are at the airports and in downtown Charlotte Amalie across from Emancipation Garden.

Weddings: to get married on St. Thomas or St. John, request a marriage license application from the Clerk of the Territorial Court, *P.O. Box 70, St. Thomas USVI 00804; Tel. 774-6680*. For a St. Croix wedding, contact the Family Division, Territorial Court of the Virgin Islands, *P.O. Box 929, Christiansted, St. Croix USVI 00821, Tel. 778-9750*. Allow plenty of time because you must both appear in person at the court to retrieve the paper work. After the application is received, filled out and notarized, it is sent back to the islands and an eight-day waiting period begins. Fees are $25 each for the application and license and $200 for a ceremony performed by a judge. (Courts are open Monday through Friday on St. Thomas and Monday through Thursday on St. Croix; if you want to get married on a weekend, arrive early enough to do the paperwork. Note holidays). Personal checks are not accepted. A number of professional wedding consultants plan weddings in the U.S. Virgin Islands. For a brochure listing them and the services they offer, *Tel. 800/372-USVI*. Also see our sidebar listing of wedding planners under *Where to Stay*.

Western Union: found at Pueblo Supermarkets on St. Thomas. For telegrams and money transfers on St. John, try Connections, *Tel. 776-4200*. Western Union is also available at St. Thomas Islander Services, *Tel. 774-8128*.

INDEX

THINGS CHANGE!

Phone numbers, prices, addresses, quality of food, etc, all change. If you come across any new information, we'd appreciate hearing from you. No item is too small! Drop us an e-mail note at: Jopenroad@aol.com, or write us at:

Caribbean Guide
Open Road Publishing, P.O. Box 284
Cold Spring Harbor, NY 11724

TRAVEL NOTES

TRAVEL NOTES

TRAVEL NOTES

TRAVEL NOTES

TRAVEL NOTES